Nineteenth-Century Literature Criticism

Topics Volume

Guide to Gale Literary Criticism Series

For criticism on	Consult these Gale series
Authors now living or who died after December 31, 1959	*CONTEMPORARY LITERARY CRITICISM (CLC)*
Authors who died between 1900 and 1959	*TWENTIETH-CENTURY LITERARY CRITICISM (TCLC)*
Authors who died between 1800 and 1899	*NINETEENTH-CENTURY LITERATURE CRITICISM (NCLC)*
Authors who died between 1400 and 1799	*LITERATURE CRITICISM FROM 1400 TO 1800 (LC)* *SHAKESPEAREAN CRITICISM (SC)*
Authors who died before 1400	*CLASSICAL AND MEDIEVAL LITERATURE CRITICISM (CMLC)*
Black writers of the past two hundred years	*BLACK LITERATURE CRITICISM (BLC)*
Authors of books for children and young adults	*CHILDREN'S LITERATURE REVIEW (CLR)*
Dramatists	*DRAMA CRITICISM (DC)*
Hispanic writers of the late nineteenth and twentieth centuries	*HISPANIC LITERATURE CRITICISM (HLC)*
Native North American writers and orators of the eighteenth, nineteenth, and twentieth centuries	*NATIVE NORTH AMERICAN LITERATURE (NNAL)*
Poets	*POETRY CRITICISM (PC)*
Short story writers	*SHORT STORY CRITICISM (SSC)*
Major authors from the Renaissance to the present	*WORLD LITERATURE CRITICISM, 1500 TO THE PRESENT (WLC)*

ISSN 0732-1864

Volume 60

Nineteenth-Century Literature Criticism

Topics Volume

Excerpts from Criticism of Various
Topics in Nineteenth-Century Literature,
including Literary and Critical Movements,
Prominent Themes and Genres, Anniversary
Celebrations, and Surveys of National Literatures

Denise Evans
Mary L. Onorato
Editors

GALE

DETROIT • NEW YORK • TORONTO • LONDON

STAFF

Denise Evans and Mary L. Onorato, *Editors*

Gerald R. Barterian, James E. Person, Jr., *Contributing Editors*
Amy K. Crook, *Assistant Editor*

Aarti D. Stephens, *Managing Editor*

Susan M. Trosky, *Permissions Manager*
Kimberly F. Smilay, *Permissions Specialist*
Sarah Chesney, *Permissions Associate*
Steve Cusack, Kelly A. Quinn, *Permissions Assistants*

Victoria B. Cariappa, *Research Manager*
Laura C. Bissey, Julia C. Daniel, Tamara C. Nott, Michele P. LeMeau,
Tracie A. Richardson, Cheryl Warnock, *Research Associates*
Alfred A. Gardner, *Research Assistant*

Mary Beth Trimper, *Production Director*
Deborah L. Milliken, *Production Assistant*

Mikal Ansari, *Macintosh Artist*
Randy Bassett, *Image Database Supervisor*
Mikal Ansari, Robert Duncan, *Imaging Specialists*
Pamela A. Reed, *Photography Coordinator*

This book is printed on acid-free paper that meets the minimum requirements of American National Standard for Information Sciences—Permanence Paper for Printed Library Materials, ANSI Z39.48-1984.

Library of Congress Catalog Card Number 84-643008
ISBN 0-7876-1128-x
ISSN 0732-1864
Printed in the United States of America

10 9 8 7 6 5 4 3 2 1

Contents

Preface vii

Acknowledgments xi

The Chartist Movement and Literature

Italian Romanticism

The Sentimental Novel

Victorian Fantasy Literature

Preface

Since its inception in 1981, *Nineteenth-Century Literature Criticism* has been a valuable resource for students and librarians seeking critical commentary on writers of this transitional period in world history. Designated an "Outstanding Reference Source" by the American Library Association with the publication of its first volume, *NCLC* has since been purchased by over 6,000 school, public, and university libraries. The series has covered more than 300 authors representing 29 nationalities and over 17,000 titles. No other reference source has surveyed the critical reaction to nineteenth-century authors and literature as thoroughly as *NCLC*.

Scope of the Series

NCLC is designed to introduce students and advanced readers to the authors of the nineteenth century, and to the most significant interpretations of these authors' works. The great poets, novelists, short story writers, playwrights, and philosophers of this period are frequently studied in high school and college literature courses. By organizing and reprinting commentary written on these authors, *NCLC* helps students develop valuable insight into literary history, promotes a better understanding of the texts, and sparks ideas for papers and assignments. Each entry in *NCLC* presents a comprehensive survey of an author's career or an individual work of literature and provides the user with a multiplicity of interpretations and assessments. Such variety allows students to pursue their own interests; furthermore, it fosters an awareness that literature is dynamic and responsive to many different opinions.

Every fourth volume of *NCLC* is devoted to literary topics that cannot be covered under the author approach used in the rest of the series. Such topics include literary movements, prominent themes in nineteenth-century literature, literary reaction to political and historical events, significant eras in literary history, prominent literary anniversaries, and the literatures of cultures that are often overlooked by English-speaking readers.

NCLC continues the survey of criticism of world literature begun by Gale's *Contemporary Literary Criticism (CLC)* and *Twentieth-Century Literary Criticism (TCLC),* both of which excerpt and reprint commentary on authors of the twentieth century. For additional information about *TCLC, CLC,* and Gale's other criticism series, users should consult the Guide to Gale Literary Criticism Series preceding the title page in this volume.

Coverage

Each volume of *NCLC* is carefully compiled to present:

- criticism of authors, or literary topics, representing a variety of genres and nationalities
- both major and lesser-known writers and literary works of the period
- 5-8 authors or 4-6 topics per volume
- individual entries that survey critical response to an author's work or a topic in literary history, including early criticism to reflect initial reactions, later criticism to represent any rise or decline in reputation, and current retrospective analyses.

Organization

An author entry consists of the following elements: author heading, biographical and critical introduction, list of principal works, excerpts of criticism (each preceded by a bibliographic citation and an annotation), and a bibliography of further reading.

- The **Author Heading** consists of the name under which the author most commonly wrote, followed by birth and death dates. If an author wrote consistently under a pseudonym, the pseudonym will be listed in the author heading and the real name given in parentheses on the first line of the biographical and critical introduction. Also located at the beginning of the introduction to the author entry are any name variations under which an author wrote, including transliterated forms for an author whose language uses a nonroman alphabet.

- The **Biographical and Critical Introduction** outlines the author's life and career, as well as the critical issues surrounding his or her work. References are provided to past volumes of *NCLC* in which further information about the author may be found.

- Most *NCLC* entries include a **Portrait** of the author. Many entries also contain reproductions of materials pertinent to an author's career, including manuscript pages, title pages, dust jackets, letters, and drawings, as well as photographs of important people, places, and events in an author's life.

- The list of **Principal Works** is chronological by date of first publication and identifies the genre of each work. In the case of foreign authors with both foreign-language publications and English translations, the English-language version is given in brackets. Unless otherwise indicated, dramas are dated by first performance, not first publication.

- **Criticism** in each author entry is arranged chronologically to provide a perspective on changes in critical evaluation over the years. All titles of works by the author featured in the entry are printed in boldface type to enable the user to easily locate discussion of particular works. Also for purposes of easier identification, the critic's name and the publication date of the essay are given at the beginning of each piece of criticism. Unsigned criticism is preceded by the title of the journal in which it appeared. Publication information (such as publisher names and book prices) and some parenthetical numerical references (such as page and line references to specific editions of works) have been deleted at the editors' discretion to provide smoother reading of the text. Footnotes that appear with previously published pieces of criticism are reprinted at the end of each essay or excerpt. In the case of excerpted criticism, only those footnotes that pertain to the excerpted text are included.

- A complete **Bibliographic Citation** provides original publication information for each piece of criticism.

- Critical excerpts are prefaced by **Annotations** providing the reader with a summary of the critical intent of the piece. Also included, when appropriate, is information about the critic's reputation, individual approach to literary criticism, and particular expertise in an author's works, as well as information about the relative importance of the critical excerpt. In some cases, the annotations cross-reference excerpts by critics who discuss each other's commentary.

- An annotated list of **Further Reading** appearing at the end of each entry suggests secondary sources on the author. In some cases it includes essays for which the editors could not obtain reprint rights.

Cumulative Indexes

- Each volume of *NCLC* contains a cumulative **Author Index** listing all authors who have appeared in Gale's Literary Criticism Series, along with cross-references to such biographical series as *Contemporary Authors* and *Dictionary of Literary Biography*. Useful for locating authors within the various series, this index is particularly valuable for those authors who are identified with a certain period but who, because of their death dates, are placed in another, or for those authors whose careers span two periods. For example, Fyodor Dostoevsky is found in *NCLC,* yet Leo Tolstoy, another major nineteenth-century Russian novelist, is found in *TCLC* because he died after 1899.

- Each *NCLC* volume includes a cumulative **Nationality Index** which lists all authors who have appeared in *NCLC*, arranged alphabetically under their respective nationalities.

- Each new volume in Gale's Literary Criticism Series includes a cumulative **Topic Index**, which lists all literary topics treated in *NCLC, TCLC, LC 1400-1800*, and the *CLC* Yearbook.

- Each new volume of *NCLC*, with the exception of the Topics volumes, contains a **Title Index** listing the titles of all literary works discussed in the volume. In response to numerous suggestions from librarians, Gale has also produced a **Special Paperbound Edition** of the *NCLC* title index. This annual cumulation lists all titles discussed in the series since its inception. Additional copies of the index are available on request. Librarians and patrons have welcomed this separate index: it saves shelf space, is easy to use, and is recyclable upon receipt of the following year's cumulation. Titles discussed in the Topics volume entries are not included in the *NCLC* cumulative index.

Citing *Nineteenth-Century Literature Criticism*

When writing papers, students who quote directly from any volume in Gale's Literary Criticism Series may use the following general forms to footnote reprinted criticism. The first example pertains to material drawn from periodicals, the second to material reprinted from books:

[1]T.S. Eliot, "John Donne," *The Nation and Athenaeum*, 33 (9 June 1923), 321-32; excerpted and reprinted in *Literature Criticism from 1400-1800,* Vol. 10, ed. James E. Person, Jr. (Detroit: Gale Research, 1989), pp. 28-9.

[2]Clara G. Stillman, *Samuel Butler: A Mid-Victorian Modern* (Viking Press, 1932); excerpted and reprinted in *Twentieth-Century Literary Criticism,* Vol. 33, ed. Paula Kepos (Detroit: Gale Research, 1989), pp. 43-5.

Suggestions Are Welcome

In response to suggestions, several features have been added to *NCLC* since the series began, including annotations to excerpted criticism, a cumulative index to authors in all Gale literary criticism series, entries devoted to criticism on a single work by a major author, more illustrations, and a title index listing all literary works discussed in the series.

Readers who wish to suggest authors, single works, or topics to appear in future volumes, or who have other suggestions, are cordially invited to write: The Editors, *Nineteenth-Century Literature Criticism*, 835 Penobscot Bldg., 645 Griswold St., Detroit, MI 48226-4094; call toll-free at 1-800-347-GALE; or fax to 1-313-961-6599.

Acknowledgments

The editors wish to thank the copyright holders of the excerpted criticism included in this volume and the permissions managers of many book and magazine publishing companies for assisting us in securing reproduction rights. We are also grateful to the staffs of the Detroit Public Library, the Library of Congress, the University of Detroit Mercy Library, Wayne State University Purdy/Kresge Library Complex, and the University of Michigan Libraries for making their resources available to us. Following is a list of the copyright holders who have granted us permission to reproduce material in this volume of *NCLC*. Every effort has been made to trace copyright, but if omissions have been made, please let us know.

COPYRIGHTED EXCERPTS IN *NCLC,* VOLUME 60, WERE REPRODUCED FROM THE FOLLOWING PERIODICALS:

Children's Literature Association Quarterly, v. 7, Summer, 1982; v. 8, Fall, 1983. Copyright © 1982, 1983 Children's Literature Association. Both reprinted by permission of the publisher.—*MLN,* v. 98, January, 1983. Copyright © 1983 by The Johns Hopkins University Press. All rights reserved. Reprinted by permission of the publisher.—*Nineteenth-Century Fiction,* v. 37, March, 1983. Copyright © 1983 by The Regents of the University of California. Reprinted by permission of the publisher and the author.—*Representations,* Winter, 1988. Copyright © 1988 by The Regents of the University of California. Reprinted by permission of the publisher and the author.—*Signs: Journal of Women in Culture and Society,* v. 4, Spring, 1979. Reproduced by permission.—*South Atlantic Quarterly,* v. XLI, October, 1942. Copyright 1942 by Duke University Press, Durham, NC. Reprinted with permission of the publisher.—*Studies in American Fiction,* v. 10, Spring, 1982. Reproduced by permission. —*Zeitschrift für Anglistik und Amerikanistik,* v. 11, 1963.

COPYRIGHTED EXCERPTS IN *NCLC,* VOLUME 60, WERE REPRODUCED FROM THE FOLLOWING BOOKS:

Avitabile, Grazia. "Conclusion: Manzoni and Nicolini—1820-1823." From *The Controversy on Romanticism in Italy: First Phase 1816-1823.* S. F. Vanni Publishers and Booksellers, 1959. Copyright © 1959 by Grazia Avitabile. Reproduced by permission.—Brown, Herbert Ross. From *The Sentimental Novel in America 1789-1860.* Duke University Press, 1940. Copyright © 1940 by Duke University Press, Durham, NC. Reproduced by permission.—Davidson, Cathy N. From *Revolution and the Word: The Rise of the Novel in America.* Copyright © 1986 by Oxford University Press, Inc. Reprinted by permission of Oxford University Press, Inc.—Douglas, Ann. "The Legacy of American Victorianism: The Meaning of Little Eva." From *The Feminization of American Culture.* Edited by Ann Douglas. Alfred A. Knopf, 1977. Copyright © 1977 by Ann Douglas. All rights reserved. Reprinted by permission of Alfred A. Knopf, Inc.—Hearder, Harry. From *Italy in the Age of the Risorgimento, 1790-1870.* Longman, 1983. Copyright © 1983 The Longman Group. Reproduced by permission.—Honig, Edith Lazaros. "Magical Women: The Positive Force of Woman Power." From *Breaking the Angelic Image: Woman Power in Victorian Children's Fantasy.* Greenwood Press, 1988. Copyright © 1988 by Edith Lazaros Honig. All rights

PHOTOGRAPHS AND ILLUSTRATIONS APPEARING IN *NCLC,* VOLUME 60, WERE RECEIVED FROM THE FOLLOWING SOURCES:

The Chartist Movement and Literature

INTRODUCTION

Chartist literature stands as an important source of historical and cultural information about working-class life in nineteenth-century Great Britain. The movement from which the literature arose flourished from about 1837 to 1854. Committed to improving the lives of working-class people and achieving democratic political reforms, Chartism was a powerful and influential response to the industrial revolution and the growth of an entrepreneurial middle class. The movement's Charter of 1838 advocated six points: universal suffrage, yearly elections, secret ballots, no property-owning qualifications for members of Parliament, equal electoral districts, and salaries for members of Parliament. While the six points of the Charter dealt specifically with voting and electoral reform, Chartism came to encompass much broader social, political and cultural goals. Notably a movement of a literate and often self-educated working class, Chartism from the start inspired a large body of literature, including speeches, essays, poetry and songs, stories, and novels—all of which appeared in the extensive Chartist press. In addition to producing its own literature, the movement was sometimes represented, usually critically, in the industrial novels of middle-class writers such as Elizabeth Gaskell and Charles Kingsley. The organized movement had dissolved by the mid 1850s, yet it left an important legacy for the later development of socialist literature and the Labour Movement in England.

Chartism emerged in the 1830s in response to difficult economic circumstances and numerous restrictions and laws which benefited the middle and upper classes at the expense of working-class people. Important precursors were the unstamped press, which priced newspapers out of the reach of the lower classes, and Ebenezer Elliot—the "Corn-Law Rhymer"—who set an example of political poetry in the 1830s. Virtually all Chartist writing was published in the *Northern Star* or in one of the dozens of other papers that made up the Chartist press. Along with essays and speeches, the early writing emphasized poetry and songs. These were intended to inspire and educate a popular audience, blending the folk language of protest with more complex ideas of class and social reform. After 1848, as the movement's impetus merged with larger political reforms sweeping Europe, there was more

fiction—stories that were moral fables, and serial novels that examined the movement and its leaders. Two of the most enduring of the latter are Ernest Jones's *De Brassier: A Democratic Romance* (1851-52) and Thomas Martin Wheeler's *Sunshine and Shadow: A Tale of the Nineteenth Century* (1849-50). After the demise of the movement, some of its leaders and participants turned to writing autobiographical and historical accounts.

Much of the literature produced by Chartists is considered weak and not especially memorable. As such it has greater historical than literary value. All of the leading Chartist writers were movement leaders as much as—or often more than—poets and novelists. Their verse typically aimed, like popular ballads or protest songs, for a wide and uncritical audience. Some of the poets, notably Thomas Cooper, aspired to the highest literary standards and used complex forms and meters, but such efforts were less than successful, and generally failed to reach the intended audience. Chartist novels borrowed plot structures and styles from popular romantic fiction and struggled with the tension between artistic aims and didactic purpose. Along with their own self-representations, Chartism and its concerns and leaders were portrayed by middle-class industrial and social reform novelists. Elizabeth Gaskell's *Mary Barton* (1848) and Benjamin Disraeli's *Sybil; or, the Two Nations* (1845) both deal with Chartist concerns, while Charles Kingsley's *Alton Locke, Tailor and Poet. An Autobiography* (1850) is generally considered to have been inspired by Thomas Cooper's works.

Chartism as a political and social movement had run its course by around 1854, though various writings by and about Chartists would continue to be published for the next few decades. While the movement as a whole failed to achieve any of its stated political goals, it had a lasting impact on the development of working-class culture. Most importantly, the movement is credited with shaping a working-class consciousness amenable to the new middle class as well as to the traditional aristocracy. It also marked the emergence of a working-class literary voice and the possibility of self-representation, which led to the first full and positive portraits of working-class lives. All of this ultimately helped shape the socialist novels of the later nineteenth and twentieth centuries.

1

REPRESENTATIVE WORKS

Ben Brierly
  Tales and Sketches of Lancashire Life. 5 vols. (stories) 1862-3

John Burland
  Poems on Various Subjects (poems) 1865

James Burnley
  Looking for the Dawn: A Tale of the West Riding (novel) 1874

Thomas Cooper
  The Demagogue: A Comedy in Five Acts (drama) 1841
  The Purgatory of Suicides, A Prison Rhyme (poem) 1845
  Wise Saws and Modern Instances (stories) 1845
  Alderman Ralph, or the History of the Borough and Corporation of Willowacre (novel) 1853
  The Family Feud (novel) 1856
  Old-fashioned Stories (stories) 1874
  Poetical Works (poems) 1886

Benjamin Disraeli
  Sybil; or, the Two Nations (novel) 1845

Thomas Doubleday
  Political Pilgrim's Progress (novel) 1839

John M. Fothergill
  Gaythorne Hall (novel) 1884

Thomas Frost
  The Secret (novel) 1850

Elizabeth Gaskell
  Mary Barton (novel) 1848
  North and South (novel) 1855

M. C. Halifax
  After Long Years (novel) 1874

Ernest Jones
  "A Factory Town" (poem) 1847
  "The Funeral of the Year and Its Epitaph" (poem) 1848
  De Brassier: A Democratic Romance (novel) 1851-2
  The Lass and the Lady; or, Love's Ladder [completed by Thomas Frost] (novel) 1853-5
  The Maid of Warsaw, or the Tyrant Czar; A Tale of the Last Polish Insurrection (novel) 1854
  Women's Wrongs: A Series of Tales (stories) 1855

William Jones
  Poems, Descriptive, Progressive, and Humourous (poems) 1853

Charles Kingsley
  Alton Locke, Tailor and Poet. An Autobiography (novel) 1850

W. J. Linton
  "Hymns to the Unenfranchised" (poems) 1839
  Records of the World's Justice (sketches) 1839

Harriet Martineau
  The Rioters, a Tale (novel) 1842

Gerald Massey
  Voices of Freedom and Lyrics of Love (poems) 1851
  Poems and Ballads (poems) 1854
  Poetical Works (poems) 1861

Henry Solly
  James Woodford, Carpenter and Chartist (novel) 1881

John Watkins
  What are your Politics? or, Judge for Yourself (drama) 1840
  *John Frost: A Chartist Play in Five Acts (drama) 1841

Thomas Martin Wheeler
  Sunshine and Shadow: A Tale of the Nineteenth Century (novel) 1849-50

*This play was published in a second edition in 1842 as *John Frost, a Political Drama in Five Acts*.

OVERVIEW: NINETEENTH-CENTURY WORKING-CLASS FICTION

Mark Hovell

SOURCE: "The Charter and its Origin," in *The Chartist Movement*, edited by T. F. Tout, Longmans, Green & Co., 1918, pp. 1-7.

[*In the following essay, Hovell outlines the evolution of the Chartist movement, from its "working class" origins to its "radical" end.*]

The Chartist Movement, which occupied so large a space in English public affairs during the ten years 1838 to 1848, was a movement whose immediate object was political reform and whose ultimate purpose was social regeneration. Its programme of political reform was laid down in the document known as the "People's Charter," issued in the spring of 1838. Its social aims were never defined, but they were sufficiently, though variously, described by leading men in the movement.

It was a purely working-class movement, originating exclusively and drawing its whole following from the industrialised and unpropertied working class which had but recently come into existence. For the most part it was a revolt of this body against intolerable conditions of existence. That is why its programme of social amelioration was vague and negative. It was an attempt on the part of the less educated portion of the community to legislate for a new and astounding condition of society whose evils the more enlightened portion had been either helpless or unwilling to remedy. The decisive character of the political aims of the Chartists bespeaks the strength of political tradition in England.

The "People's Charter" is a draft of an Act of Parliament, a Bill to be presented to the House of Commons.[1] It is drawn up in a clear and formal but not too technical style, with preamble, clauses, and penalties, all duly set forth. It is a lengthy document, occupying some nineteen octavo pages, but brevity itself in comparison with a fully-drawn Bill for the same purpose from the hands of a Parliamentary draughtsman. The preamble is as follows:

> Whereas to insure, in as far as it is possible by human forethought and wisdom, the just government of the people, it is necessary to subject those who have the power of making the laws to a wholesome and strict responsibility to those whose duty it is to obey them when made,

> And whereas this responsibility is best enforced through the instrumentality of a body which emanates directly from, and is immediately subject to, the whole people, and which completely represents their feelings and interests,

> And whereas the Commons' House of Parliament now *exercises* in the name and on the supposed behalf of the people the power of making the laws, it ought, in order to fulfill with wisdom and with honesty the great duties imposed on it, to be made the faithful and accurate representation of the people's wishes, feelings, and interests.

The definite provisions fall under six heads—the famous "Six Points" of the charter. First, every male adult is entitled to the franchise in his district after a residence of three months.[2] Second, voting is by ballot. Third, there will be three hundred constituencies divided as equally as possible on the basis of the last census, and rearranged after each census. Fourth, Parliament is to be summoned and elected annually. Fifth, there is to be no other qualification for election to Parliament beyond the approval of the electors—that is, no property qualification. Sixth, members of Parliament are to be paid for their services.—

Besides these fundamentals of a democratic parliamentary system, there are minor but highly important provisions. The Returning Officers are to be elected simultaneously with the members of Parliament, and they are to be paid officials. All elections are to be held on one and the same day, and plural voting is prohibited under severe penalties. There is no pauper disqualification.[3] All the expenses of elections are to be defrayed out of an equitable district-rate. Canvassing is illegal, and there are to be no public meetings on the day of election. A register of attendance of the members of Parliament is to be kept—a logical outcome of payment. For the infringement of the purity of elections, for plural voting, canvassing, and corrupt practices, imprisonment is the only penalty; for neglect, fines.[4]

As an arrangement for securing the purity of elections and the adequate representation of public opinion in the House of Commons, the "People's Charter" is as nearly perfect as could be desired, and if a sound democratic government could be achieved by the perfection of political machinery, the Chartist programme would accomplish this desirable end. The Chartists, like the men of 1789 in France, placed far too great a faith in the beneficent effects of logically devised democratic machinery. This is the inevitable symptom of political inexperience. We shall nevertheless see that there were Chartists, and those the best minds in the movement, who realised that there were other forces working against democracy which could not be removed by mechanical improvements, but must be combated by a patient education of the mind and a building up of the material welfare of the common people—the forces of ignorance, vice, feudal and aristocratic tradition.

The political Chartist programme is now largely incorporated into the British Constitution, though we have wisely rejected that multiplication of elections which would either exhaust public interest or put an end to the stability and continuity of administration and policy. In itself the Chartist Movement on its political side represents a phase of an agitation for Parliamentary Reform which dates in a manner from the reign of Elizabeth.[5] The agitation began therefore when Parliament itself began to play a decisive part in public affairs, and increased in vehemence and scope according as the importance of Parliament waxed.

The abuses of the representative system were already recognised and turned to advantage by politicians, royal and popular, during the latter half of the sixteenth and the first half of the seventeenth century; but beyond a single timid attempt at reform by James I, nothing was attempted until the great politico-religious struggle between 1640 and 1660. It is here that we must look for the origins of modern radical and democratic ideas. The fundamentals of the representative system came up for discussion, and in the Instrument of Government, the written constitution which established the Protectorate in 1653, a drastic scheme of reform, including the normalisation of the franchise and a sweeping redistribution of seats, was made. In the preliminaries to this the question whether true representation was of persons or of property, which goes to the root of the matter, was debated long and earnestly by the Army in 1647. In the debate on the Agreement of the People, the Radical and Whig standpoints are clearly exhibited.[6]

> *Mr. Pettus*—Wee judge that all inhabitants that have not lost their birthright should have an equal voice in Elections.

> *Rainborough*—I think its clear that every man that is to live under a Government, ought first by his own consent to putt himself under that Government.

> *Ireton*—. . . You must fly for refuge to an absolute naturall right. . . . For my parte I think itt is noe Right att all. I think that noe person hath a right to an interest or share in the disposing or determining of the affaires of the kingdome and in chusing those that shall determine what lawes wee shall bee ruled by heere, noe person hath a right to this, that hath not a permanent fixed interest in this kingdome.

Here obviously the question of manhood or property suffrage is the issue. Colonel Rich declared that manhood suffrage would be the end of property.

> Those that have noe interest in the kingdome will make itt their interest to choose those that have noe interest. Itt may happen that the majority may by law, not in a confusion, destroy properties: there may bee a law enacted that there shall bee an equality of goods and estate.[7]

There was at the same time a demand for short and regular Parliaments, and that elections should be made "according to some rule of equality or proportion" based upon "the respective rates they (the counties and boroughs) bear in the common charges and burdens of the kingdome . . . to render representing House of Commons as neere as may bee an equal representative of the whole body of the People that are to elect." Parliament was to be elected biennially and to sit not more than eight months or less than four.[8]

Here, therefore, is the nucleus of a Radical Programme: Manhood Suffrage, Short Parliaments, and Equal Representation. We have even a hint at the doctrine of "absolute naturall right," which lies at the base of modern democratic theory since the French Revolution, and which found an echo in the minds of all

Chartists two hundred years after the famous debates at Putney. With the downfall of the Commonwealth such conceptions of abstract political justice were snowed under by the Whig-Tory reaction. Henceforth both parties stoutly upheld the "stake in the kingdom" idea of representation. The height of this reaction came in the High Tory days of Queen Anne, when the legal foundations of the aristocratic regime were laid. The imposition of a property qualification upon would-be members of Parliament dates from 1710, when it was enacted that the candidate for a county must possess £600 a year and for a borough £300 a year, in both cases derived from landed property.[9] This act was passed in the face of some Whig opposition, as the Whigs would have made exceptions in favour of the wealthy merchants of their party. Two years later followed the first of the enactments throwing election expenses upon the candidate.[10] A further diminution of popular control resulted from the Septennial Act, though this was a Whig measure.

The Radical tradition, however, was not dead but sleeping. It lived on amongst the dissenting and nonconformist sections, whose ancestors had fought and debated in the days of Cromwell and had been evicted in 1662. The revival of Nonconformity under the stimulus of Methodism, the growth of political and historical criticism during the eighteenth century, and the growing estrangement between the House of Commons and the people at large, brought about a resurrection of Radicalism. In the second half of the century the Radical Programme appeared in full vigour.

The first plank of the Radical platform to be brought into public view was the shortening of the duration of Parliaments. In 1744 leave to bring in a Bill establishing Annual Parliaments was refused only by a small majority. In 1758 another Bill was refused leave by a much more decisive vote. In 1771 Alderman Sawbridge failed to obtain leave to introduce a similar measure, although he had the moral support of no less important persons than Chatham and Junius.[11] In the same year a Wilkite society recommended that Parliamentary candidates should pledge themselves to support a Bill to "shorten the duration of Parliaments and to reduce the number of Placemen and Pensioners in the House of Commons, and also to obtain a more fair and equal representation of the people."[12]

By this time the flood of controversy aroused by the Wilkes cases was in full flow, and the tide of Radical opinion was swelled by the revolt of the American Colonies. In 1774 Lord Stanhope, and in 1776 the famous Major John Cartwright, published more sweeping plans of Parliamentary Reform. Cartwright's scheme is set forth in the pamphlet, *Take your Choice.* Annual Parliaments and the payment of members are defended and advocated on the ground that they were "the antient practice of the Constitution," an argument which was a mainstay of the Chartist leaders. Payment of members was in force down to the seventeenth century, the oft-cited Andrew Marvell receiving wages from his Hull constituents as late as 1678. In claiming Annual Parliaments as a return to ancient ways Cartwright had the authority, such as it was, of Swift.[13] Universal suffrage, vote by ballot, and the abolition of plural voting also found a place in Cartwright's scheme, but he maintained the property qualification for members of Parliament.[14] Thus four of the six "points" of the Charter were already admitted into the Radical programme. It only required a few years to add equal electoral districts and the abolition of the property qualification.

These were added by a committee of reformers under the guidance of Fox in 1780. The whole programme figured in the interrupted speech of the Duke of Richmond in the House of Lords in the same year and in the programme of the Society of the Friends of the People (1792-95). The Chartists were not unaware of the long ancestry of their principles.[15] There was a prophetic succession of Radicals between 1791, when the first working men's Radical society—the London corresponding Society—was founded, and 1838, when the Charter was published. Down to the outbreak of the French Revolution the Radical faith in England, as in France, was mainly confessed in middle-class and some aristocratic circles. Wilkes, Fox, Sawbridge, and the Duke of Richmond are types of these early Radicals. With the opening of the States-General and the rapid increase of terrorism in France the respectable English Radicals began to shelve their beliefs. On the other hand, the lower classes rallied strongly to the cause of Radical reform, and the Radical programme fell into their keeping, remaining their exclusive property for the next forty years. When the middle class in the days after Waterloo returned to the pursuit of Parliamentary Reform, it was reform of a much less ambitious character. The working classes still held to the six points. During these forty years Radicalism became a living faith amongst the working class. It had had its heroes and its prophets and its martyrs, and when the salvation promised by the Whig reform of 1832 had proved illusory, it was perfectly natural to raise once more, in the shape of the "People's Charter," the ancient standard of popular reform.

By this time, however, the six points had acquired a wholly different significance. In the minds of the early Radicals they had represented the practical realisation of the vague notions of natural right. The programme was a purely political one, and was scarcely connected either with any specific projects of social or other reforms, or with any particular social theory. It represented an end in itself, the realisation of democratic theory. By 1838 the Radical programme was recognised no longer as an end in itself, but as the means to an end, and the end was the social and economic regeneration of society.

Notes

[1] The Charter is divided into thirteen sections:

I.	Preamble.
II.	Franchise.
III.	Equal Electoral Districts.
IV.	Registration Officer.
V.	Returning Officer
VI.	Deputy Returning Officer
VII.	Registration Clerk.
VIII.	Arrangement for Registration.
IX.	Arrangement for Nominations.
X.	Arrangement for Elections.
XI.	Annual Parliaments.
XII.	Payment of Members.
XIII.	Penalties.

[2] Residence of three months is only mentioned casually, in connection with registration.

[3] Added in 1842.

[4] For full text see [William Lovett, *Life and Struggles of William Lovett.* London, 1876], pp. 449 *et seq.* This is the revised edition of 1842, but is substantially the same as that of 1838.

[5] [E. and A. G. Porritt. *The Unreformed House of Commons. Parliamentary Representation before 1832.* Cambridge (University Press), 1903], i, 1.

[6] [W. Clarke. *The Clarke Papers*, 1647-49, 1651-60, edited by C. H. Firth. 3 vols.], i. 299-307.

[7] *Ibid.* p. 315.

[8] *Ibid.* pp. 363 *et seq.*, "Agreement of the People." Gardiner, *Select Documents of the Puritan Revolution*, "Heads of the Proposals."

[9] Porritt, i. 166.

[10] *Ibid.* i. 185-195.

[11] [G. S. Veitch. *The Genesis of Parliamentary Reform.* London, 1913], p. 34.

[12] *Ibid.* p. 32.

[13] *Life of Major John Cartwright*, by his niece F. D. Cartwright, London, 1826, i. 82.

[14] Veitch, p. 48.

[15] Lovett, *Life and Struggles*, p. 168. The preface to the first (1838) edition of the "People's Charter" contains a brief history of the "Six Points" from 1776 onwards.

P. J. Keating

SOURCE: "The Two Traditions, 1820-80," in *The Working Classes in Victorian Fiction,* Routledge and Kegan Paul, 1971, pp. 1-30.

[*In this excerpt from a book about the working classes in Victorian fiction, Keating provides an overview and analysis of mid-century industrial and urban fiction.*]

I

'If you look for the working classes in fiction,' wrote George Orwell in 1940, 'and especially English fiction, all you find is a hole.' He goes on to qualify this statement:

> For reasons that are easy enough to see, the agricultural labourer (in England a proletarian) gets a fairly good showing in fiction, and a great deal has been written about criminals, derelicts and, more recently, the working-class intelligentsia. But the ordinary town proletariat, the people who make the wheels go round, have always been ignored by novelists. When they do find their way between the covers of a book, it is nearly always as objects of pity or as comic relief.[1]

It is important to distinguish between the quantitative and qualitative judgements being made by Orwell. On the one hand, it is simply untrue that the urban working classes ('the people who make the wheels go round') have always been ignored by novelists. There is, in fact, a considerable body of English fiction which deals with, or purports to deal with, not merely the exceptions acknowledged by Orwell but 'the ordinary town proletariat'. In the Victorian period alone there were some hundreds of novels written on this very subject. On the other hand, Orwell's objection to the presentation of the working classes 'when they do find their way between the covers of a book', while a slight exaggeration, is more just. For there are few English novels which deal with working-class characters in a working-class environment in the same sense as there are novels about the middle or upper classes in their own recognizably real settings: in other words, novels which treat of the working class as being composed of ordinary human beings who experience the range of feelings and emotions, social aspirations and physical relationships, that it is the special province of the novelist to explore.

Most working-class novels are, in one way or another, propagandist. They are usually written by authors who are not working class, for an audience which is not working class, and character and environment are presented so as to contain, implicitly or explicitly, a class judgement. The author may wish to show, for instance, that the working classes are basically no different from other people, or that they are, in a spiritual sense at least, more fortunate than other social groups: or that they are not at heart violent and so long as their just complaints are listened to sympathetically the middle and upper classes have nothing to fear from them. Or even more directly, that they need help, that they shouldn't drink, that more schools, hospitals or workhouses—as the case may be—should be built for them. Put simply the most important single fact about the fictional working man is his class.

The historical reason for this is easy to see. During the nineteenth century there were two periods when a significant number of novelists seriously attempted to present the working classes in fiction. Both were times of social upheaval when real or imagined class fears compelled people to look afresh at the basic social, economic and political structure of society. In the 1840s and 50s the motivating force was the outcry over the condition of industrial workers, together with the middle-class panic engendered by Chartist politics: in the period 1880-1900 it was the problem of urban slum conditions and the widespread public debate on Socialism. The fictional response in both periods was almost entirely non-working class. For the novelist who wished to write about the working classes but was not himself from a working-class background, the publicity arising out of these moments of crisis enabled him to create a social framework for his fiction within which he could present a way of life in every respect alien to his own, and closed to him at moments of greater stability. In both periods the fictional response trails behind political and social reform movements. The industrial novel develops only after the Blue Books and Chartism have paved the way, and the urban novel of the 1890s has a similar dependence on reform agitation of the previous decade. This is one reason for the narrow range of working-class experience presented in fiction, and it also explains why the fiction of each period is dominated and restricted by the single image of a Victorian city. In the earlier period Manchester is used to symbolize both the greatness and shame of Industrial England;[2] in the later period the East End of London serves the same dual function for Imperial England. In both cases novelists were following rather than anticipating the forces making for change. When the crisis declined the interest of novelists declined also.

In so far as it is possible to talk at all of a genuine working-class literary tradition in the Victorian age, it is to be found in certain regional poets (both dialect and non-dialect), in a considerable mass of Chartist verse and doggerel, and most interestingly in the memoirs of working men who rose to positions of eminence in public life. Apart from a few Chartist novels imaginative prose is non-existent.[3] A critical search in Victorian literature for a working-class tradition leads inevitably to the pessimistic conclusion reached by William Empson: 'It is hard for an Englishman to talk definitely about proletarian art, because in England it has never been a genre with settled principles, and such as there is of it, that I have seen, is bad.'[4]

Theoretically, of course, it is not necessary to be of the working class to write an outstanding novel about the working class, as Émile Zola's great trilogy, *L'Assommoir* (1877), *Germinal* (1885) and *La Terre* (1887) indicates. Nor does it follow that a working-man turned novelist will be able to write a good novel about his own class. Thomas Wright and Robert Blatchford are perfect examples of working-class writers who produced important documentary studies of working-class life and very poor novels on the same subject. Nor again is it a matter of sympathy for or hostility towards the workers as a class. This is almost totally unimportant. The crucial point is whether the novelist is effectively committed to artistic principles or to an overt class viewpoint. Most Victorian novelists come into the second category, and their presentation of working-class characters can be seen to become more successful as they themselves retreat from a position of authorial didacticism. This was very much the point made by Engels in his famous letter to Margaret Harkness:

> I am far from finding fault with your not having written a purely socialist novel, a *Tendenzroman,* as we Germans call it, to glorify the social and political views of the author. That is not at all what I mean. The more the author's views are concealed the better for the work of art. The realism I allude to may creep out even in spite of the author's views. Let me refer to an example.

Engels's example is Balzac, whose sense of realism was so intense that it compelled him 'to go against his own class sympathies and political prejudices'.[5] What Engels is praising in Balzac is his analysis of social relationships, not his treatment of working-class characters—there are in fact no urban or industrial workers in the *Comédie humaine*. With the partial exception of Dickens, this sense of realism is not applicable to the English novelists, who usually present working-class characters in relation to a specific social issue, and are therefore pre-eminently concerned with a form of realism analogous to a sociological document or parliamentary report. In their work we do not feel the realism creeping through in spite of the author's personal views. Rather, the reverse is true—we are too often conscious that the author's concern with social antidotes has weakened the power of his documentary realism. The constant presence of social purpose in the working-class novel leads to a manipulation of the characters' actions, motives and speech, in order that they may be used finally to justify a class theory held by the author. However hard the novelist tries to suppress his sympathy, or hostility, his own class viewpoint becomes transparently clear, and the artistic value of the particular work suffers. This is obvious enough when applied, for instance, to a temperance reform tale, but it is also true, in varying degrees, of most working-class novels written in the nineteenth century. Too often individual working-class scenes in Victorian novels are praised for their historical accuracy, while the total pattern and effect of the novel is either ignored or excused. When we look more closely at how exactly working-class characters are treated in relation to characters of other classes, we find time and time again that the novelist has unconsciously set into motion a process of avoidance which prevents him from dealing with his professed subject— the working classes.

This central weakness is most apparent in the imposition of unnatural values and attitudes upon working-class characters, allowing them free expression and a full life only in so far as this fits in with the author's preconceived, socially desirable image of them. William Empson's observation that 'proletarian literature usually has a suggestion of pastoral, a puzzling form which looks proletarian but isn't',[6] is very relevant here. For although it is not my intention to use the phrase 'proletarian literature' in the sense that Empson uses it ('the propaganda of the factory-working class which feels its interests opposed to the factory owners'), his perceptive exploration of the ways that pastoral conventions may be subconsciously employed to hide latent radical or political ideas has a worth beyond the Marxist frame within which he places it. The technique, or to use Empson's terminology again, the 'trick' of pastoral, appears under many strange guises in Victorian working-class fiction, and just because a novelist will often vehemently defend his working-class scenes on the grounds of realism, this should not allow us to ignore the fact that what is carefully observed class reality to the author may well come over as pastoral to the reader.

Any attempt to show how the working classes are portrayed in Victorian fiction must return again and again to the apparent difficulties experienced by novelists in trying to establish a balance between commitment to a class viewpoint and artistic form. Prior to 1880 the problem is there but novelists seem barely conscious of it: after 1880 it becomes an issue of central importance and is most successfully resolved, I shall argue, in the short stories and ballads of Rudyard Kipling. Before looking in detail at the attempts by late-Victorian writers to solve this and other problems, it is necessary, if we are to be sure of what is new and what inherited in their work, to place them in a wider nineteenth-century setting.

II

The industrial novel of the 1840s and 50s is the only type of English working-class fiction to have received much attention from literary and social historians. In comparison the novel of non-industrial urban working-class life has been totally ignored. Ever since Orwell's common-sense rejection of Dickens as a 'proletarian writer' (a critical approach which differed little from that of Gissing forty years earlier), it has generally been accepted that the 'people who make the wheels go round' hardly exist in fiction, and certainly cannot be said to constitute a viable literary tradition. It is only in recent years that the work of George Gissing and Rudyard Kipling has been treated with the respect it deserves and so far this revaluation has produced little that is new on their contributions to working-class fiction. The slum novelists of the nineties have received even less favourable treatment, and are usually dismissed by literary historians as inferior imitators of either Zola or Dickens, according to the historian's point of view.

This prejudice in favour of the industrial novel is particularly surprising because not only were there far more novels written during the Victorian period which deal with the urban rather than the industrial working class, but in qualitative terms there is little to choose between the two. The industrial novels have retained a lasting interest largely because of their unusual subject matter, but hitherto the same critical allowance has not been given to the urban novel. Yet the fiction produced by writers such as Augustus Mayhew, Gissing, Kipling, Arthur Morrison, Henry Nevinson or Somerset Maugham is as successful as anything in the industrial tradition with the possible exception of *Hard Times,* the first half of *Mary Barton* and *North and South.* And if this fiction is considered for its presentation of the working classes then *Hard Times* also disappears and we are left with Mrs Gaskell as the sole representative. One major reason for this discrimination is the difficulty of defining what exactly is meant by the two words 'working' and 'class'. This can be clarified by examining how the meanings differ when applied to two separate literary traditions—the industrial and the urban.

To talk of the industrial tradition is to mean a handful of novels written primarily in the fourth and fifth decades of the nineteenth century. The earliest is Harriet Martineau's *A Manchester Strike* (1832). This is followed by Mrs Trollope's *Michael Armstrong* (1839-40); *Helen Fleetwood* (1839-40) by 'Charlotte Elizabeth' [Mrs Tonna]; Disraeli's *Coningsby* (1844) and *Sybil* (1845); Mrs Gaskell's *Mary Barton* (1848) and *North and South* (1855); and Dickens's *Hard Times* (1854). There the tradition virtually ends until the twentieth century. As has already been suggested, in-

Harriet Martineau, author of The Rioters, A Tale.

terest in industrialism as a subject for fiction was closely related to the rise and decline of Chartism, and once public concern with this particular form of conflict abated so did the novelist's ready-made frame of reference. In the 1860s and 70s the old framework was no longer valid, and novelists, lacking the kind of personal involvement that might have led them to write naturally of working-class life, simply waited until a new social framework was created for them. Then there was a resurgence of working-class fiction.

Of later industrial novels there is George Eliot's *Felix Holt* (1866), the only important novel written in response to the agitation for working-class enfranchisement in the sixties, and more concerned with this than industrialism; Charles Reade's attack on Trade Union villainy, *Put Yourself in His Place* (1870); Gissing's *Demos* (1886), in which the workers are urban rather than industrial; and William Morris's dream utopia *News From Nowhere* (1891), in which no recognizably real worker of any kind appears. The only late-Victorian industrial novel which deserves a place beside those of Mrs Gaskell and Disraeli is W. E. Tirebuck's now totally forgotten *Miss Grace of All Souls* (1895), certain passages of which Tolstoy was reported to have described as among 'the best examples of modern English fiction'.[7]

There is no difficulty about defining the worker in these novels. He is part of a composite portrait called Labour and is shown to be in bitter conflict with a further composite portrait called Capital. The Oxford English Dictionary gives as a definition of 'working class': 'The grade or grades of society comprising those who are employed to work for wages in manual or industrial occupations'; and defines 'class' as: 'A number of individuals . . . possessing common attributes, and grouped together under a general or "class" name.' The industrial worker fits perfectly into both of these definitions. In each novel the workers share in common skills, occupations, wage levels, and most important of all, interests and attitudes. Each worker is part of the same instantly recognizable whole. This is not to say that all workers are presented as identical or interchangeable types. Indeed, it is a constant pre-occupation of the industrial novelist to show that within the working-class world there exist social hierarchies almost as rigid as those in society as a whole. In *Mary Barton,* for instance, Job Legh, John Barton, Jem Wilson and Davenport are completely unlike each other so far as intelligence, wage-earning capacity, occupational skill and moral strength are concerned, but they all appreciate that these distinctions are nothing compared with the class attitudes that bind them together. In the industrial novel the difference between a respectable artisan and the poor is decided by such factors as unemployment, the relative size of the family to be supported or personal character weakness. However high one may rise, or however low another may fall, each recognizes the possibility of himself in the other. They do not represent two separate worlds.

This sense of class oneness is conveyed more than anything else by the stark hostility of the industrial-town landscape (varied only by areas of appalling slums), and by the uniform tone of seriousness adopted by the novelists. Just as the novels were written because of a social problem, so are the characters treated with a moral intensity that is always directed towards heightening the tragedy of the working-class situation. Where there are efforts to present a more inclusive view of working-class life, these take the form of lingering remnants of an older, more communally centred, rural culture which is rapidly being subverted by the mass regimentation of industrialism. Families are still shown helping each other in moments of distress; they may join together for conversation or supper; they may even be entertained by a song or have a drink in the pub, but the most striking thing about such gatherings is the atmosphere of solemnity that prevails.[8] Rarely do these characters exhibit any feeling of spontaneous joy or happiness. Nobody in an industrial novel laughs, makes jokes or dances, and nowhere is this negative characteristic more apparent than in Dickens. The difference in treatment can be clearly seen by comparing the presentation of Rachael, in *Hard Times,* with a woman who is her almost exact urban working-class equivalent, Mrs Plornish in *Little Dorrit.* In financial terms Rachael is probably better off than Mrs Plornish and the social positions they occupy in their respective communities are about the same, but it would be impossible to imagine Rachael, or indeed any industrial worker, being given the speech patterns and personal idiosyncrasies that belong to Mrs Plornish. These qualities are allotted by the novelist, and to be seen to manipulate such a serious subject as an industrial worker in order to make the reader laugh would have been considered an act of bad faith, or even taste. This is partly due to the acute awareness in both author and reader of social crisis, but also, and more fundamentally, to the entirely different kinds of convention and attitude that governed the literary treatment of the industrial and urban workers.

In real life the industrial labourer was the product of a new kind of environment. No one really comparable with him had existed before, and in writing about him novelists had no literary tradition to draw on. The urban working class, on the other hand, was the product of a radically changed environment, and, in however altered a form, had played a variety of parts in centuries of English literature. Unlike their industrial counterparts, the late-Victorian urban novelists can be seen in relation to several lines of tradition. Apart from the debate on French naturalism, in which they found themselves often unwillingly involved, they could look back to the attempts of earlier-Victorian writers, dominated by Dickens, to present the working classes in fiction, and beyond, to an age-old tradition of London low-life scenes in English literature. In literary forms as diverse as the picaresque novel, the literature of roguery, criminal biography, eighteenth-century poetry and drama, Elizabethan and Jacobean drama, and in the early fiction of writers such as Deloney and Nashe, there can be found many scenes in which lower-class town 'types' or 'characters' play parts of varying extent and importance. It is mainly the darker sides of town life that are examined—the tavern, brothel, criminal conclave, or the smart urban confidence trickster fleecing the innocent country bumpkin—but neither the poor nor the more respectable members of the lower classes are ignored.[9]

What has always fascinated the writer on London low life is the existence within the same basic environment of widely disparate social groups and individuals, seemingly independent of each other and yet, when compared with the middle and upper classes, seen to be bound together by their relative poverty. On 12 April 1783, Boswell records that Dr Johnson 'talked to-day a good deal of the wonderful extent and variety of London, and observed, that men of curious enquiry might see in it such modes of life as very few could even imagine. He in particular recommended us to *explore Wapping,* which we resolved to do'. Nine years later Boswell carried out this resolution but 'whether from that uniformity which has in modern times, in a great degree, spread through every part of the metropolis, or from our want of sufficient exertion, we were disappointed'.[10] Save for the absence of class terminology this exchange might well have been made exactly a century later. The different responses of the sympathetic and the sensation-seeking slummer is a very common late-Victorian experience, but it is by no means peculiar to that period, nor indeed to post-Industrial Revolution society. Both before and after Johnson, 'men of curious enquiry' writing about London have always noted the existence of 'such modes of life as very few could even imagine'.

This point is of some importance when we consider the presentation of the urban working classes in fiction. In historical terms the nineteenth century is cut off from earlier centuries by the whole complex of social changes connected with the Industrial Revolution—unprecedented urban development, the gradual transformation of the English economy from a rural to an industrial base, the breakdown of old types of relationship between employer and employee, and the rise of organized working-class politics. The class terminology we use today is a product of those changes:

> There was no dearth of social conflicts in pre-industrial society, but they were not conceived of at the time in straight class terms. The change in nomenclature in the late eighteenth and early nineteenth centuries reflected a basic change not only in men's ways of viewing society but in society itself.[11]

In the eighteenth century the words used to describe social divisions were 'rank', 'order', 'state', 'station' or 'degree'; and when referring to specific economic groups, 'interests'. The lower classes in this sense did not constitute an 'interest' but existed as separate, occupational groups, largely isolated from each other, both ideologically and geographically. As Diana Spearman has pointed out: 'There is no evidence that these groups considered themselves to belong to one class; indeed it is most unlikely that they did, for there was nothing to unite them: their interests were not identical and there was no theory to persuade them they were.'[12] The term 'working class' (as distinct from 'lower class' which had existed earlier) seems first to have appeared around 1815, and by 1824 the word 'class' was firmly established as a social label.[13]

The sense of social turmoil indicated by the changing nature of class terminology is most clearly seen in the vast growth of cities during the nineteenth century. In 1800 there was no town outside of London with a population of 100,000; by 1891 there were twenty-three. During the century the populations of towns such as Liverpool, Birmingham, Manchester and Sheffield multiplied tenfold. London increased phenom-

enally from under 1 m. in 1801 to 4½ m. a century later, when it contained approximately 14 per cent of England's population. By 1891 almost a third of the total population lived either in London or in cities containing more than 100,000 inhabitants.[14]

The great changes in the basic structure of working-class life brought about by the twin forces of urbanization and industrialism are reflected in entirely different ways in the two literary traditions. While the industrial novel adopts the idea of town life as comprising two large, economically interdependent, conflicting class groups, the urban novel stresses more than ever before the variety and mystery of the London streets. It highlights individual types, especially the bizarre and grotesque, and concentrates on what distinguishes lower-class groups from each other rather than what unifies them, on the idea of contrast rather than conflict.

The most important pre-nineteenth-century influence on the urban novelists is Hogarth. Keith Hollingsworth, referring to the 'Newgate' novel, has noted that 'in the twenties and thirties one finds his name constantly',[15] and the same is true of the Victorian age as a whole. The two most significant urban working-class novelists, Dickens and Gissing, both greatly admired Hogarth. In the 1841 Preface to *Oliver Twist,* Dickens allowed Hogarth to be his only predecessor in treating of the 'miserable reality' of lower-class criminal life; and in a remarkable conversation preserved by Forster, Dickens speaks at some length about Hogarth's work.[16] One of the details Dickens noted with special interest was the way Hogarth created slum environments which seemed as much alive as their wretched inhabitants, a technique Dickens himself was to use with wonderful effect. Just as Dickens looked back to Hogarth in order to find a parallel with his own 'realism', so Gissing, drawing comparisons from a time which gave a more specific definition to the term, stated his preference for the painter above the novelist because Hogarth 'gives us life—and we cannot bear it'. As a child Gissing had spent many hours poring over a book of Hogarth's plates, and in his first novel, when Mr Tollady takes Arthur Golding on a tour of the slums, he advises the painter to 'be a successor of Hogarth, and give us the true image of *our* social dress'.[17]

Yet even these acknowledgments give little indication of the extent of Hogarth's influence on Victorian literature. It is essential to distinguish between two aspects of his low-life scenes. First, the detailed portrayal of the suffering poor in urban slum environments, and secondly, the strong element of caricature he employs to heighten the meaning of his social message. The bodies of Hogarth's characters are bent and twisted, their faces distorted and grotesque. In the midst of appalling poverty there is a milling vigour, a sense of continual movement and life, however debased. Hogarth aimed to evoke sympathy by means of repulsion, a technique diametrically opposed to that of the industrial novelists who tried to evoke sympathy through pity.

Ready to learn from Hogarth were the great English engraver-caricaturists of the late-eighteenth and early-nineteenth centuries. In the work of Gillray, Rowlandson and the two Cruikshanks, Hogarth's detailed environments receive less attention and his sense of caricature more. The low-life figures swell to gigantic proportions filling the whole canvas; the obscenely bloated bodies with their bumpy, deformed heads, rubbery lips and protruding teeth, eclipse both metaphorically and literally the environments they inhabit. Furthermore, with Hogarth it was the narrative content of his paintings that eighteenth- and nineteenth-century novelists found so attractive; the paintings existed as works of fiction in their own right. The later caricaturists, however, concentrated on coloured prints rather than paintings and became increasingly involved in book illustration, using their talents to interpret someone else's words. In the literature of sport and travel that was so popular for the first forty years of the nineteenth century, the caricaturists combined with writers to produce imaginative guides to English country and town life. The various partnerships that were established proved unequal to say the least: the writers being, in the main, little better than hacks and the illustrators men of genius. In works such as the *Dr. Syntax* tours and *The Microcosm of London* (1808) the drawings completely dominate the written commentary; while Rowlandson's superb 'Characteristic Sketches of the Lower Orders', originally commissioned to accompany *The New Picture of London* (1820), take on a life of their own. Here the characters and types have little to do with changing social conditions. They are timeless street figures, selling their wares, berating passers-by, or scrounging a tip: in artistic terms they are a mixture of Hogarth's debased urban creatures and the traditional cartoon portrait of Hodge. Yet their power is undeniable. The distorted bodies coloured in pastel shades create at one and the same time a sense of suppressed humanity and colourful, vigorous life.

The imbalance between illustration and text was only corrected with the appearance of Pierce Egan, Surtees and Dickens, who rejected the feeble travelogue style in favour of an imaginative, humorous treatment of the traditional subjects. Like their illustrators, Egan, Surtees and Dickens possessed a taste for the farcical incident, mysterious urban character, and contrasting modes of London life, and it was these qualities they passed on to their successors throughout the middle years of the century. Dickens, of course, immediately surpassed the humble efforts of Egan and Surtees, and proceeded to develop themes and techniques which the lesser writers could hardly have imagined, but when

considering his presentation of working-class characters it is always important to remember the literary tradition to which *Sketches by Boz* and *The Pickwick Papers* belong.

The archetypal urban novel of the early-nineteenth century is Pierce Egan's *Life in London* (1821). This novel, which John Camden Hotten called 'the most popular work in British literature',[18] is a hymn of praise to the variety of life to be found in London, or as Egan himself describes it, 'a Camera Obscura View of the Metropolis':[19]

> POUSSIN never had a more luxuriant, variegated, and interesting subject for a landscape; nor had SIR JOSHUA REYNOLDS finer characters for his canvas than what have already had a sitting for their likeness to embellish LIFE IN LONDON.[20]

As befits its subject matter it is an extravagant and uneven work that moves swiftly from high to low society, from East to West London, from one social oddity to another. The simple narrative is interspersed with songs and ditties, poetic invocations and extensive footnotes, all directed to prove one single thought:

> LONDON! thou comprehensive word,
> What joy thy streets and squares afford!
> And think not thy admirer rallies
> If he should add your *lanes* and *alleys*.[21]

What fascinates the Corinthians on their rambles through the metropolis is the omnipresent urban culture. The traditional literary use of a journey (as used, for instance, by Fielding and Smollett), was to introduce various aspects of society by moving from town to town, or more customarily from country to town, thus contrasting rural and urban ways of life. In Egan the visitor from the country provides a starting point but no more, for life in London is all life, everywhere and of every kind. The diversity of manners, morals, colourful slang, speech patterns, and human types is to be found, Egan frequently stresses, in nowhere but London. If, however, the Corinthians are bewildered by the infinite variety of London life, they are quite sure where *real* life is to be found:

> 'Yes my dear Coz. It is a motley group,' replied Tom; 'but it is a view of real life; and it is from such meetings as these, not withstanding they are termed very *low*, that you have a fine opportunity of witnessing the difference of the human *character*. In the circles of fashion you will scarcely meet with any contrast whatever.'[22]

This is after they have been to watch a pit-fight between a monkey and a dog, and it takes several other encounters with lower-class London ('Chaffing Peter' the dustman, a costermonger and his donkey, a visit to the docks, a dance with the prostitutes and sailors in a 'sluicery', and an initiation into the methods of the 'Cadgers' in the 'back slums of the Holy Land'), before the class moral of the metropolitan rambles is stated: "It is," said LOGIC to TOM, "I am quite satisfied in my mind, the LOWER ORDERS of society who really ENJOY themselves."[23] This sense of enjoyment is graphically conveyed by the Cruikshanks' illustrations. While the slim, elegantly tailored figures of Tom and Jerry stroll through London, they are surrounded by leering, cavorting lowerclass characters dressed in picturesque rags.

Life in London represents a real starting point in the history of the urban novel. Egan looks back to the London low-life tradition and forward to the 'Newgate' novel, Mayhew's extensive gallery of street types, and also to Dickens's equally varied gallery of eccentric characters who, while they may be classified under the general heading 'lower class', often possess vague, undifferentiated social backgrounds. Yet if Egan does concentrate on the picturesque elements of lower-class life, there is to be found in his novel an awareness of poverty (which for Egan is no problem), and a line of distinction drawn between those who work for their living and those who beg or thieve. Most important of all, *Life in London* is the first novel in which we find directly stated the division of the London classes into two topographical blocks, with the lower classes living in the East and the upper classes in the West. Much later in the century it was the general realization of this fact which was to provide the urban equivalent of the industrial novel's Labour and Capital conflict. Egan still presents this contrast in picturesque terms (Almacks and ALL-MAX, 'the COVES in the *East*—and the SWELLS at the *West*'), but the class potential is strongly there.

Where the novelists who succeed Egan differ from him is in their return to an Hogarthian slum environment peopled mainly by the suffering poor; though an environment rendered more horrific and brought up to date by Carlyle's penetrating vision of the signs of the times, and humanized by Dickens. Egan's city had been constructed on a simple linear principle which allowed him to focus attention on Tom and Jerry moving leisurely from sight to sight. For both Carlyle and Dickens the city is organic, a total world of contrasting yet interdependent parts. This much their interpretations share, but differ entirely in mood and tone. Carlyle's city is symptomatic of a social malaise, a 'wasp-nest or bee-hive', in which all is confusion and turmoil, with human activity a revolting compound of 'wax-laying and honey-making, and poison-brewing and choking by sulphur'. Diogenes Teufels-dröckh has no need or desire to ramble through Weissnichtwo: he can sit at his attic window and from there 'see the whole life-circulation of that considerable City'. By removing, as it were, a communal roof, he can reveal the myriad, teeming, ironically independent cells of the modern city organism:

> Upwards of five-hundred-thousand two-legged animals without feathers lie around us, in horizontal positions; their heads all in nightcaps, and full of the foolishest dreams. Riot cries aloud, and staggers and swaggers in his rank dens of shame; and the Mother, with streaming hair, kneels over her pallid dying infant, whose cracked lips only her tears now moisten. All these heaped and huddled together, with nothing but a little carpentry and masonry between them;—crammed in, like salted fish in their barrel.[24]

This does not describe the city of Dickens's early sketches and novels. Like Egan he was concerned primarily with London, and like Carlyle he was fascinated by the turmoil and confusion of modern city life, but he transcended both Egan's view of London as a playground for the upper classes and Carlyle's tone of personal disgust. London is defined, almost exclusively, in terms of its streets, the veins of the city organism. It is not simply that many of the most memorable characters in *Sketches by Boz, Pickwick Papers* and *Oliver Twist* literally 'belong' to the streets, though contemporary reviews abounded with praise and criticism of Dickens for revealing so much of this side of London life. It is rather that street life is realized so vividly—its variety, activity and manners made so central to Dickens's view of society—that everything else seems pallid in comparison. Even the respectable middle-class characters are continually drawn to the streets; their homes are merely temporary stopping places or final havens of rest in which no one can really believe. The moral worth of such characters is determined by the amount of sympathy they are capable of feeling for those worse off than themselves; though they must also be willing to prove the genuineness of their feelings, for sympathy expressed but not acted upon Dickens always interprets as hypocrisy. The streets of London become their proving-ground where they make contact with other classes and act out their concern in the public gaze. Tom and Jerry's leisurely stroll gives way to a mood of urgency and rush. One contemporary reviewer wrote:

> Reading Boz's Sketches is like rattling through the streets of London in a cab: the prominent features of the town strike upon the eye in rapid succession, new objects perpetually effacing the impression of the last; all is bustle and movement, till the jerk of the stoppage announces that the 'fare' or the 'sketch' is ended.[25]

This captures very well the external nature of Dickens's London, though it neglects his special power of investing the ordinary and the mundane with an air of mystery and strangeness; employing the London streets to reveal a life with which everyone was familiar but which no one actually knew. Gissing fully appreciated this aspect of Dickens's early work: 'Never had been known,' he wrote of *Sketches by Boz,* 'such absorbing interest in the commonplace.'[26]

The enormous impact of Dickens largely accounts for the predominance of London in Victorian working-class fiction. Apart from Manchester (briefly in the late forties), and until the emergence of the East End in the 1880s, no other city established a distinctive enough image in fiction to challenge London's supremacy. But Dickens's influence extends far beyond this. He determines the very tone of the urban novel, and his influence on the presentation of working-class characters in fiction is felt even today, though it is difficult to see precisely why this should be so. Gissing decided that Dickens 'treats at once of the lower middle class, where he will be always at his best; with the class below it, with those who literally earn bread in the sweat of their brows, he was better acquainted than any other novelist of his time, but they figure much less prominently in his books.'[27] This observation is perfectly just. Excepting the shadowy Daniel Doyce, the intellectual working man and the superior artisan are entirely absent from his novels, and even if we place the widest interpretation on the 'respectable' working class the only representatives are the Plornishes, Toodles, Mrs Nubbles and Betty Higden. One group sharing many qualities in common can be defined as criminal or debased working class (Bill Sikes, the Artful Dodger, Nancy, Rogue Riderhood, Gaffer Hexam, Mrs Brown and Magwitch), but characters such as Mrs Gamp, Sam Weller, Silas Wegg, Venus, Bailey Junior, the 'Marchioness', Boffin, Rob the Grinder and Deputy, are almost impossible to define in meaningful class terms. Some of these can be described as working class on the strength of their occupations or slum backgrounds, but they are no more offered as working-class representatives than the criminals. On the other hand, the Toodles, Plornishes, Betty Higden and Jo, do play class roles in their respective novels, as do Stephen Blackpool and Rachael in *Hard Times.* The greater proportion of Dickens's lower-class characters belong to the Hogarth-Rowlandson-Egan line of tradition. Together with an even more extensive gallery of characters who can be classified rather uneasily as 'lower middle class', they are products of the labyrinthine streets of the modern city. They differ from the lower-class characters of Rowlandson and Egan because of Dickens's Carlylean awareness of rapidly changing social conditions, but the difference is still a matter of degree rather than kind; an impression which gains strength when we consider the great care Dickens took to pick the right illustrators for his novels. The best of these, Cruikshank and Phiz, possessed a sense of caricature that descended straight from Hogarth.

If, however, Dickens rarely deals extensively with the poor or working classes, an overwhelming sense of their existence is never absent for long. Even at moments when the novel is not dealing with a lower-class theme we are suddenly made aware of a horrifying backcloth of rickety houses, crowded alleys and filthy humanity-packed courts. No opportunity is missed to address the reader on the state of the poor; no effete aristocrat or pompous merchant is presented without a lower-class comparison being implied; no genuine social grievance is allowed to pass without Dickens championing its reform. Most prevalent of all is his loathing of all kinds of oppression or suffering. A vast number of minor characters are orphans or former workhouse inmates who appear briefly and then pass out of the novel, leaving behind them only the information that they were orphans or workhouse inmates and that their lives can never be clean because of it. The blackest mark against Bounderby is his imagined slum childhood, romantically embellished and employed to give himself strength of character. Dickens's own view of the effects of such a childhood is non-Smilesian and environmentalist. Magwitch, Bradley Headstone, even Uriah Heep can evoke sympathy when they talk of their past lives:

> Father and me was both brought up at a foundation school for boys; and mother, she was likewise brought up at a public, sort of charitable, establishment. They taught us all a deal of umbleness—not much else that I know of, from morning to night. We was to be umble to this person and umble to that; and to pull off our caps here, and to make bows there; and always to know our place, and abase ourselves before our betters. And we had such a lot of betters![28]

This sense of oppression, helplessness, suffering or unhappiness, permeates Dickens's novels, and not merely the working-class sections of them. The presentation of characters such as Florence Dombey, Caddy Jellyby, Little Dorrit, Little Nell, Tom Pinch, or Smike, plays a large part in making it seem as though Dickens's novels are concerned almost exclusively with the working classes.

More directly, Dickens reinforces this generalized humanitarian concern with a series of superb class confrontations in which representatives of the wealthy or oppressing classes are defeated by representatives of the poor or oppressed. In the early, exuberant *Pickwick Papers,* Sam Weller's victory over Serjeant Buzfuz is straightforward; the result of verbal dexterity and greater knowledge of life. But in the confrontations between Mr Dombey and Toodle or Captain Cuttle; Bounderby and Stephen; Mr Dorrit and John Chivery; Joe Gargery and Miss Havisham, the working-class representatives are largely inarticulate and the victory takes place only in the mind of the reader. It entails both a moral and a class judgement.

There is, of course, a further and occasionally contradictory side to Dickens's treatment of working-class life. A strong feeling for its humanity and vitality needs to be set against the suffering and oppression. A comparison of two slum descriptions, one by Charles Kingsley, the other by Dickens, can demonstrate this most clearly. Here, Sandy Mackaye takes the young, idealistic poet, Alton Locke, on a sight-seeing tour of working-class London:

> It was a foul, chilly, foggy Saturday night. From the butchers' and greengrocers' shops the gaslights flared and flickered, wild and ghastly, over haggard groups of slip-shod dirty women, bargaining for scraps of stale meat and frostbitten vegetables, wrangling about short weight and bad quality. Fish-stalls and fruit-stalls lined the edge of the greasy pavement, sending up odours as foul as the language of sellers and buyers. Blood and sewer-water crawled from under doors and out of spouts, and reeked down the gutters among offal, animal and vegetable, in every stage of putrefaction. Foul vapours rose from cow-sheds and slaughter-houses, and the doorways of undrained alleys, where the inhabitants carried the filth out on their shoes from the backyard into the court; and from the court up into the main street; while above, hanging like cliffs over the streets—those narrow, brawling torrents of filth, and poverty, and sin,—the houses with their teeming load of life were piled up into the dingy, choking night. A ghastly, deafening, sickening sight it was. Go, scented Belgravian! and see what London is![29]

Kingsley's sole intention is to describe to the reader the horrors of working-class life; to recreate the feeling of repulsion experienced by himself. Even allowing for our knowledge (drawn from other sources) that conditions in St Giles's were appalling, it is notable that Kingsley has deliberately chosen what would normally be a fairly gay scene—a street market at its busiest moment, Saturday evening—and that he makes no attempt whatsoever to present it from a working-class viewpoint. The gaslights are 'wild and ghastly', the shoppers are 'haggard groups of slip-shod dirty women', and odours from the food stalls are 'foul'; the food is all adulterated and everyone is swearing. The roads are obviously never cleaned as the 'blood and sewer water' mingles with 'offal, animal and vegetable, in every stage of putrefaction'. The streets are 'narrow, brawling torrents of filth, and poverty, and sin'.

There is no vitality, humour, banter or laughter, and there are no family shopping outings. The horror belongs entirely to Kingsley. And the final sentence makes it clear that this scene has been chosen as typical of working-class London as a whole: it is not simply an isolated plague spot. This kind of slum description is the most common in Victorian fiction before the eighties. They are not incidental but hold a central place in the novels, in that they are being used to grip the reader and stir his conscience. Almost everything else that happens in the novel depends upon such scenes for its validity. To show the shoppers laughing or joking, in this example, would defeat Kingsley's main purpose in writing the novel, as would any suggestion that the participants might express other opinions about it than his own. There is nothing indeed to be said in its favour. It is all foul and should be swept away by progressive legislation, and meanwhile if we wish to praise a working man, we can do so by showing him as someone fit for middle- and upper-class society; someone who has no kinship with the 'slip-shod dirty women' of St Giles's.

It is not difficult to find similar scenes in Dickens, though his awareness of their potency as class propaganda is much sharper than Kingsley's, and his sense of subtlety in discriminating between different kinds of working-class environment is infinitely greater. One technique peculiar to Dickens is to give a minimum of physical description, and instead merely suggest a slum environment by suddenly bringing before the reader a tumbling mass of inhabitants who are by no means squalid or lacking in humour. This example is from *Bleak House*; it follows on the discovery of Nemo's dead body:

> By this time the news has got into the court. Groups of its inhabitants assemble to discuss the thing, and the outposts of the army of observation (principally boys) are pushed forward to Mr. Krook's window, which they closely invest. A policeman has already walked up to the room, and walked down again to the door, where he stands like a tower, only condescending to see the boys at his base occasionally; but whenever he does see them, they quail and fall back. Mrs. Perkins, who has not been for some weeks on speaking terms with Mrs. Piper in consequence for an unpleasantness originating in young Perkins' having 'fetched' young Piper 'a crack,' renews her friendly intercourse on this auspicious occasion. The potboy at the corner, who is a privileged amateur, as possessing official knowledge of life and having to deal with drunken men occasionally, exchanges confidential communications with the policeman and has the appearance of an impregnable youth, unassailable by truncheons and unconfinable in station-houses. People talk across the court out of the window, and bare-headed scouts come hurrying in from Chancery Lane to know what's the matter. The general feeling seems to be that it's a blessing Mr. Krook warn't made away with first, mingled with a little natural disappointment that he was not. In the midst of this sensation, the beadle arrives.[30]

What is so striking about this passage is not that the working-class participants have become human beings—on the contrary, they still possess the two-dimensional qualities of cartoon figures—but that the slum itself has been humanized. It has not corrupted, deformed, degraded or in any significant way imposed itself upon the inhabitants; rather, this normal process has been reversed, and the vitality and vigour of the inhabitants have been used to create and define their environment. Variations of this technique are used to present some of Dickens's most memorable working-class settings—Bleeding Heart Yard, Mrs Gamp's Holborn and Staggs's Gardens. Where we do get physical descriptions of slums they are often of the 'filth, putrefaction and poverty' variety (in *Bleak House* alone there are Tom-All-Alone's and the brickmaker's house to set against and contrast with the above scene), but unlike Kingsley, Dickens refused to believe that this represented the whole of working-class life.

Indeed, it is more common to find criticisms of Dickens for painting working-class life in too glowing terms, than of Kingsley for painting it too bleakly. For just as Hogarth painted a 'Beer Street' to complement his 'Gin Lane', so Dickens, especially in his early novels, emphasized certain moral positives in working-class life which he shows as flourishing in even the foulest rookery. Today little attention is paid to this side of his work, but in the late-nineteenth century it was often considered the most characteristic and successful feature. The famous *philosophie de Noël* scenes usually involve the middle classes, but many of the qualities that characterize the Christmas attitude are permanently embedded in Dickens's respectable working men and women. All of the characters who can be classified in this way, and most of the suffering poor as well, are strongly endowed with honesty, moral strength and good-neighbourliness—virtues which are usually rewarded by individual philanthropy. And if death comes before earthly reward is possible, then there is the consolation that 'hearts may count in heaven as high as heads'.[31] So firm is Dickens's conviction that the poor are distinguished from other classes by their kindness to each other, that, in *David Copperfield,* as first Emily and then Mr Peggotty wander throughout Europe, there emerges a sense of this quality as providing the foundation stone for an International Brotherhood of the Poor.[32] Even in a novel as late as *Great Expectations* when Dickens's view of society had changed considerably, it is Joe Gargery and Biddy who represent the most pure moral values to be found in the book. And in his next, far more ambiguous novel, *Our Mutual Friend,* many of the same qualities are given, without qualification, to Betty Higden. This image of the 'good' working man, as a model either to copy or react against, was to prove Dickens's most influential legacy to late-Victorian working-class fiction.

Apart from Dickens, interest in street types and the suffering poor as the two representative aspects of urban working-class life was further kept alive during the mid-Victorian period by *Punch,* the vaguely reformist tone of which achieved its strongest expression in the drawings of John Leech: 'A Court for King Cholera' (1849) and 'St. James turning St. Giles out of his Parks' (1850). While Leech spoke for the poor, the cartoons of Charles Keene served to foster the idea of the urban workers as being individuals rather than a class. His drunken cabbies, street urchins and housemaids with their pert charm and ever-ready wit, did much to establish the image of the cheerful cockney. Keene's cockney characters look back to Sam Weller and forward to Phil May and E. J. Milliken's 'Arry—a line of tradition which attains some importance in the eighties and nineties. In addition to these pictorial images of the working classes made popular by *Punch,* mention should also be made of a similar kind of subject matter employed by mid-Victorian narrative painters. The idealized view of the working classes held by the Pre-Raphaelites is epitomized, at least in its non-medieval aspect, by Ford Madox Brown's 'Work' (1865), which glorifies working-class muscle in a manner that anticipates Socialist-Realism. More typical of Victorian genre painting are Frith's panoramic views of English society: 'Ramsgate Sands' (1851), 'Derby Day' (1858) and 'The Railway Station' (1862). Other similar paintings are Erskine Nicol's 'Waiting for the Train' (1864), George Elgar Hicks's 'Billingsgate' (1861) and Arthur Boyd Houghton's 'Holborn in 1861'. Like the mid-Victorian working-class novelists, these painters were fascinated by the interrelationship of different classes in English society, but by the time we come to Sir Luke Fildes's 'Applicants for Admission to a Casual Ward' (1874), the social compromise has fallen apart, the poor are now a separate group, isolated and outcast, and we move from Dickens's to Gissing's world.

As we have seen, it is extremely rare to find in early- or mid-Victorian literature a sense of the urban working classes as comprising people who 'work' or wish to work, or who, taken collectively, constitute a social class. The whole sweep of the urban tradition had acted against the establishment of a class image of the kind found in the industrial novel. The vastness of London; the many different grades of wealth and poverty to be found in close proximity, and the tradition of presenting colourful street types in sharp pictorial outline, or as literary props for romantic low-life scenes, all tended to encourage an awareness of what diversified the urban workers rather than what united them. Yet if we place together the inhabitants of Egan's 'back slums', Mayhew's street tradesmen and characters, Dickens's seething slum populations and Kingsley's craftsmen, then it is possible to reach a viable, if necessarily broad, definition of the urban working class. But first, in order to summarize the argument so far, as well as to make it more inclusive, it is worth attempting a classification of the different types of working-class novel written before 1880, and then a further classification of the different kinds of working-class characters who appear in them.

III

It is possible to distinguish between five distinct types of novel in which the working classes play more than a fleeting part:

1. The novel dealing with a cross section of English society in which the working classes appear as just one part of a total social pattern. The 'ramble through the metropolis' is the most traditional formula. In its nineteenth-century form this is established by Egan's *Life in London,* and Dickens's early novels belong to the same tradition; his later novels represent a more profound treatment of the same formula.

2. The romance. This differs from type 1 in that working-class life is presented as ugly and debased, and serves either as a starting point for the working out of a tortuous, often criminal, plot, or for the rise from rags to riches of a low-born, or supposedly low-born, hero. Once this purpose has been served the working-class theme is gradually faded out. The class structure of the romance is usually based on a direct relationship between the very rich or aristocracy and the poor. Apart from an occasional, sentimentally presented exemplary working man, the poor are shown to be morally and physically inferior to other classes, their way of life something to escape from as soon as possible. Examples in the 'Newgate' tradition are: Bulwer Lytton's *Paul Clifford* (1830), Harrison Ainsworth's *Jack Sheppard* (1839), Renton Nicholson's *Dombey and Daughter* (1850) and Douglas Jerrold's *St. Giles and St. James* (1851). Examples in the 'rags to riches' tradition: Maria Cummins's *The Lamplighter* (1854), F. W. Robinson's *Owen: A Waif* (1862) and *Mattie: A Stray* (1864).

3. The non-romantic novel of working-class life set entirely in a working-class environment. This type of novel hardly exists before the eighties, though it becomes much more common later. The earlier-Victorian equivalent is the novel of street life which is influenced by Dickens and Mayhew, and bound together with a dash of Newgate crime. While the plot is largely romantic there is a considerable feel for the complex structure of working-class life, and much detailed sociological observation. Good examples are: Augustus Mayhew's *Kitty Lamere* (1855) and *Paved with Gold* (1858); James Greenwood's *The True History of a Little Ragamuffin* (1866); Thomas Wright's *Johnny Robinson* (1868) and *The Bane of a Life* (1870).

4. The 'Condition of the People' novel. Social propaganda directed at a non-working-class audience with the intention of transforming middle- or upper-class attitudes. The working-class scenes are in the main realistic, though heavily weighted towards the more poverty-stricken aspects of industrial and urban life. As we have seen, the industrial novels come under this heading, as does *Alton Locke*. Other similar novels in the urban tradition are: William Gilbert's *Dives and Lazarus* (1858), a semi-fictional account of a slum doctor's experiences which contains slum descriptions of the Kingsley variety, and which is virtually unique in describing the work of the Medical Inspectors of Health; and J. E. Jenkins's *Ginx's Baby* (1870), a bitter satire on the workings of mid-Victorian philanthropy.

5. Novels directed at a working-class reading public with the intention of transforming manners or habits. These are mainly brief, exhortatory homilies published in great numbers by religious and Temperance Tract societies. They possess little literary interest, and here only temperance reform fiction will be discussed. Probably the most influential writer of temperance fiction was Mrs Clara L. Balfour, and two tracts by her, *Scrub: or the Workhouse Boy's First Start in Life* (1860), and *Toil and Trust: or The Life Story of Patty the Workhouse Girl* (1860), are characteristic of the genre. The full-length temperance novel was not directed exclusively, or perhaps even mainly, at the working classes, but was used to urge the middle and upper classes to change their intemperate ways and help reform the workers. A good example of a full-length temperance novel, middle class in setting but containing working-class scenes, is Mrs Henry Wood's *Danesbury House* (1860). The differences between fiction of this kind aimed at working- and non-working-class reading publics, were less a matter of content and style than of publishing price and format.

In these five types of novel we can distinguish between six kinds of working-class character:

1. Respectable. He is usually a skilled artisan who is shown to be devoted to his family, or, if unmarried, to his neighbours' welfare. He represents the highest social rank in working-class fiction, though very rarely does he quite correspond to the 'aristocrat of labour' or the 'educated working man' as described by Thomas Wright in his fascinating studies of the mid-Victorian urban working classes. In temperance fiction he is used as an idealized contrast to the drunkard; in the 'Condition of the People' novels he acts as a stabilizing force between revolutionary sentiment and middle-class orthodoxy, unless morally corrupted by unemployment or victimization. In Chartist fiction he is the idealized hope of revolutionaries. In romances he is the recipient of upper- or middle-class philanthropy which enables him to escape from his own class background.

2. Intellectual. The kind of working man who plays such a prominent part in histories of working-class movements, sociological studies of the reading public, or who presents himself in memoirs, is almost totally absent from pre-1880 fiction. The only two figures who can be called working-class intellectuals are Felix Holt and Alton Locke. Felix Holt is an interesting example as his personal attitudes (especially his determination to retain his connections with the workers rather than use his education to escape from them) foreshadow those of many later heroes, especially in twentieth-century literature. But the working-class theme of the novel is explored in a very shallow manner. George Eliot's attitude is similar to the 'Condition of the People' novelists, while the tortuous plot places *Felix Holt* firmly as a working-class romance. Alton Locke retains more interest as an intellectual working man because through him we see a side of London life which Dickens never touches. Kingsley's treatment of working-class characters is close to that of the industrial novelists (with whom he is usually categorized) in that he explores the physical and moral relationships between the respectable, politically conscious craftsmen and the debased creatures of an East End Sweater's Den and the Bermondsey slums. Crossthwaite and Jemmy Downes (like Higgins and Boucher in *North and South*) do not belong to different social groups. They epitomize contrasting degrees of moral strength in responding to what is essentially the same situation.

3. Poor. The most common type of Victorian working-class character. Unskilled, often illiterate, poor through no fault of his own, he is an object of social pity. He is usually shown to possess a high standard of morality and good-neighbourliness, and is helped over immediate material problems by individual philanthropy. He may be adopted, or have his life transformed, by wealthy patrons; but more often his death, or the death of his wife or child, is employed as a conscience-stirring moment of pathos.

4. Debased. The second most common type in pre-1880 novels. He is defined in terms of drunkenness, brutality or moral viciousness. These are really character traits and the debased working man is distinct from the criminal whose anti-social activities are to some extent rationalized. His debased qualities may sometimes be regarded as having been caused by his poverty, though more frequently he is criticized by the author for tarnishing the image of the more respectable sections of working-class life. In romances he is beyond help, a wife- and child-beater, taking their money to buy beer, and may be used as a device to drive the working-class child from home, the first step from rags to riches. He is the obvious target for temperance reformers.

5. Eccentric. He is working class by virtue of his environment, but is defined primarily in terms of personal idiosyncrasies; especially an out-of-the-way occupation, or a bizarre, humorous manner of speech.

6. Criminal. More properly termed 'low' than working class, he plays a minor role in 'Newgate' novels (the major criminals usually being upper-class changelings), and in novels of street life. The debased working man may become a criminal, by murdering his wife or child when drunk, for instance, but usually working-class criminals belong to the literature of roguery. They are petty robbers, pick-pockets, confidence-tricksters or fences, and are often presented as corruptors of children.

IV

However disparate the various kinds and groups of urban working-class characters discussed so far appear to be, they did share a common culture. Louis James has mentioned how surprised Thackeray was to discover, through reading some fiction aimed at a working-class audience in 1838, the extent and inclusiveness of this sense of shared urban values: 'Moreover, it was not just a continuation of the old popular cultures which expressed themselves in broadsheets, chapbooks, and popular drama—it was new, and had formed itself in the past decade. It was quite cut off from the middle and upper classes.'[33] James goes on to show that the authors and readers of this literature were very conscious of what it meant to belong to an urban working class:

> It is interesting to note how directly these periodicals were the expression of the new life of the towns. Their existence relies on interest in events and people in a particular urban society—the suffix 'in London,' 'in Liverpool,' and so on, is important. Most of these periodicals were neither scandal sheets, nor general gossip magazines drawing on the appeal of glamour in the fashion of modern 'society' columnists. They tried to reveal the organism of town life, claiming omniscience.[34]

If these workers were linked culturally by an awareness of the organism of town life, they also shared the economic insecurity inherent in servicing the consumer demands of a huge, non-industrial city. For Victorian novelists the urban working man is pre-eminently a Londoner, and the industrial worker is nearly always a northerner. London factory life is virtually ignored throughout the period, and, as has just been noted, the highly skilled, steadily employed urban artisan receives far less attention from novelists than the poor and the debased.

Gissing's workers 'who literally earn bread in the sweat of their brows', and Orwell's 'people who make the wheels go round', are obviously the same. They can be divided into two main occupation groups. First, those who follow a skilled or semi-skilled trade, or who provide a service for the benefit of the community as a whole (e.g. house painter, tailor, cab driver); and secondly, those who work at an unskilled, manual job (e.g. casual labourer, dock worker, road sweeper). To these must be added the large number of street traders in the nineteenth century (e.g. costermongers, fish sellers, flower girls, newsboys) who provided a service for both their own communities and those of the middle and upper classes. Furthermore, within a specifically working-class area the social distinction between, for instance, the small shopkeeper and his customers, is less sharp than in predominantly middle- or upper-class areas. The sense of class association resulting from this produces a separate category of people. They have been well described by Richard Hoggart: 'Some are self-employed; they may keep a small shop for members of the group to which, culturally, they belong or supply a service to the group, for example as a "cobbler," "barber," "grocer," "bike-mender," or "cast-off clothing dealer." '[35]

This point is important. For what largely determines whether or not we can call many urban characters working class depends not merely on the environment they inhabit (the sunken aristocrat living in the slums and so loved by romantic novelists is obviously not working class), nor does it necessarily depend upon how much money someone earns, for this may vary as much as their occupations. What does matter is how far that person associates himself, in terms of status, values and attitudes, with his working-class environment. Thus, depending upon their psychological or social presentation, a publican or a domestic servant may or may not be regarded as working class. Orwell's angry rejection of the 'criminal' and 'derelict' is a reaction against those writers who see such types as representative members of the working class, but he is really being over-sensitive. The criminal, derelict, fence or prostitute may, according to circumstances, be working class, just as they may, in other circumstances, be middle or upper class. In so far as it is possible to establish an upper dividing line, over which anyone who steps ceases to be regarded as working class, that line is represented by the office worker. Allowing for the obvious exceptions mentioned above, Gissing's social classification of *The Nether World* as comprising 'the two great sections of those who do, and those who do not, wear collars',[36] will be followed throughout this book.

What needs further emphasis about these different kinds of worker is the precariousness of their individual financial situations. Victorian philanthropists liked to distinguish between the respectable working man and the poor, but in many cases the distinction was more imagined than real. Mayhew subtitled his great work,

'Those that will work, those that cannot work, and those that will not work', thus clearly drawing several important distinctions. And his brother Augustus went to some pains to make the same point—that there is little sense in discriminating between the working class and the poor, for the transient nature of their employment quite easily leads to a reversal of their positions:

> Not to speak of the really destitute and the outcast, the well-to-do in London are surrounded by thousands whose labour lasts only for the summer—such as brickmakers, market gardeners, harvest men, and the like; besides multitudes of others, such as navigators and ground labourers, who can ply their trade only so long as the earth can be made to yield to the spade and the pick; and others again, as the dock labourers and 'longshore men, who depend upon the very winds for the food and fuel of themselves and families.[37]

The fact that many Victorian novelists show urban working-class characters as continually unemployed is not necessarily a bar to calling them workers. In such uncertain economic conditions, unemployment may be frequent and of varying duration. The important point is that when, or if, the working man does work it is at one of the kinds of job discussed here. His wife and children are subject to the same qualifications. In Victorian fiction the street urchin employing his strength or wits to earn a few coppers, and the long-suffering wife making matchboxes at home, are very common urban types. Almost all of the people considered here can be described, in Gissing's words, as 'that class of city population just raised above harsh necessity'.[38]

Notes

[1] 'Charles Dickens', *Inside the Whale* (1940), 11-12.

[2] Not all of the industrial novels are actually set in Manchester: *Sybil* is set in the Midlands, and Dickens's Coketown is deliberately generalized. But Manchester features in the novels by Harriet Martineau and Mrs Gaskell, it is eulogized in *Coningsby*, and Mrs Trollope made it the first stop on her fact-finding tour of the north. Whether specifically named or not, it is the image of Manchester more than any other city that dominates the industrial novel. For the symbolic importance of Manchester during the early-Victorian period, see Asa Briggs's *Victorian Cities* (1963), Ch. 3.

[3] Apart from several historical romances the principal Chartist novels are: Thomas Martin Wheeler, *Sunshine and Shadow: A Tale of the Nineteenth Century,* serialized in the *Northern Star,* 1849-50: Thomas Frost, *The Secret,* serialized in the *National Instructor,* 1850: and Ernest Jones, 'The Working-Man's Wife', *Woman's Wrongs* (1855). A late-Victorian novel which possesses many of the same characteristics as Char-

tist fiction is H. J. Bramsbury's *A Working Class Tragedy,* serialized in *Justice* from June 1888 to April 1889.

[4] 'Proletarian Literature', *Some Versions of Pastoral* (1935), 3.

[5] Letter dated April 1888. George J. Becker (ed.), *Documents of Modern Literary Realism* (Princeton, 1963), 484.

[6] *Some Versions of Pastoral,* 6.

[7] Hall Caine, 'Memoir of W. E. Tirebuck', preface to Tirebuck's posthumous novel *'Twixt God and Mammon* (1903).

[8] The most notable exception to this generalization is Disraeli's portrayal of 'The Temple of the Muses' in *Sybil,* Bk. III, Ch. X. In *Hard Times* Sleary's circus is employed deliberately to heighten the monotonous life of the Coketown workers.

[9] See Charles W. Camp, *The Artisan in Elizabethan Literature* (New York, 1924), and F. W. Chandler, *The Literature of Roguery* (2 vols., 1907).

[10] Boswell, *Life of Johnson,* ed. G. Birkbeck Hill, 1934, vol. IV, 201.

[11] Asa Briggs, 'The Language of "Class" in Early Nineteenth Century England', *Essays in Labour History,* ed. Asa Briggs and John Saville (1960), 41.

[12] *The Novel and Society* (1966), 41.

[13] Briggs, 'The Language of "Class" . . . ', 43. See also Raymond Williams, *Culture and Society* (1958), Introduction.

[14] Briggs, *Victorian Cities,* 57; G. D. H. Cole and Raymond Postgate, *The Common People 1746-1946* (University Paperbacks, 1964), Ch. XXXVII.

[15] *The Newgate Novel 1830-47* (Detroit, 1963), 33.

[16] *The Life of Charles Dickens* (1893), Bk. VI, Ch. 2.

[17] Gissing, *Charles Dickens* (1898), 90; *Workers in the Dawn* (3 vols., 1880), I, 247.

[18] Introduction to his edition of *Life in London* (1869). All page references are to this edition.

[19] *Life in London,* 46.

[20] *Ibid.,* 45.

[21] *Ibid.,* 47.

[22] *Ibid.,* 259.

[23] *Ibid.,* 320.

[24] *Sartor Resartus,* Bk. I, Ch. 3.

[25] *The Spectator,* 26 December 1836.

[26] *The Immortal Dickens* (1925), 20.

[27] *Charles Dickens,* 40.

[28] *David Copperfield,* Ch. XXXIX.

[29] *Alton Locke,* Ch. VIII.

[30] *Bleak House,* Ch. XI.

[31] *Our Mutual Friend,* Ch. XVI. The phrase refers specifically to Betty Higden.

[32] *David Copperfield,* Ch. XL.

[33] *Fiction for the Working Man 1830-1850* (1963), 1.

[34] *Ibid.,* 18.

[35] *The Uses of Literacy* (1957), 20.

[36] *The Nether World* (3 vols., 1889), I, 166.

[37] Augustus Mayhew, *Paved With Gold* (1858), Ch. 2.

[38] *Charles Dickens,* 15.

CHARTIST FICTION AND POETRY

Anonymous

SOURCE: "The Chartists and Their Laureate," in *English Review,* vol. XVI, No. XXXI, October, 1851, pp. 55-86.

[*In the following essay, the critic expounds upon the dangers posed to the British monarchy by democratic thinkers such as Lord John Russell, "the reforming Prime Minister," and Ernest Jones, "the chartist laureate."*]

CHARTISM? Is not chartism defunct? may many a reader cry. Where are the noisy meetings of two years ago? Where is the loud parade of forces physical and moral? Where are the million pikes with which we were then threatened? Where is the O'Connell of that formidable movement—the redoubtable Fergus O'Connor? Surely, politically and virtually, this movement is defunct. The hubbub of voices has ceased to rise, the clouds of dust have scattered, the waves have subsided into peace. The safety of Old England seems no longer endangered by our domestic foe. What has become of Carlyle's forebodings and awful mystic prophecies? Surely the event has disproved them all. Where are the turbulent leaders of sedition, and where are their besotted followers? Has not all passed like a fever-dream? Like the unsubstantial fabric of a vision, leaving not a wrack behind? And may we not eat and sleep in safety now, and hug ourselves upon our calm security? Such is the notion, probably, of many of our readers, or something not far from it: they are disposed to say of these late formidable dangers, and of their own anticipations of insurrectionary violence,

> The earth hath bubbles as the water hath,
> And these are of them!

But is our political horizon really so cloudless? Is there no handwriting on the wall? Is there no little cloud rising out of the sea that bodes a coming tempest? Is chartism or, in other words, is pure and unmixed democracy really defunct amongst us? It is our present duty to dispel this agreeable delusion. We believe, on the contrary, that it is making gigantic, though comparatively quiet and silent strides, and that our constitution is in the extremist danger, or will be at least, some few months hence. For chartism has made a most illustrious convert, well-nigh the most illustrious in this land, even the Prime Minister of the British Empire. Lord John Russell has now pledged himself, alas! to introduce a bill next session for a large increase of the suffrage, which must of necessity conduct, in our opinion, to universal suffrage, and so to unmitigated chartism and pure democracy; and we fear that little reasonable hope can be entertained of successful opposition to it.

We shall return to this all-important theme anon; to this engagement of the minister's, which sounds, we fear, the knell of ruin to our country: meanwhile, it may suffice to affirm, that within the last year democracy has made a number of converts. It has found a talented, an elegant, we might almost say an aristocratic exponent in the weekly paper called *The Leader,* which goes beyond chartism far, in its advocacy of communism and equality: its earlier demagogues have made way for men possessed of a more liberal education, and pertaining to a higher sphere of social life: it has ceased to talk of blood and wounds, and therefore it has become the more intensely dangerous. For we have nothing to fear from democracy, the pike in its hand; every thing from its gradual, and, if we may so say, "constitutional" demolition of our constitution in Church and State.

Before we enter further on this grave question, we purpose to introduce our readers to the chartist laureate, a gentleman by birth, by education, by social status, and an orator and poet, in our estimation of positively startling power. For the present, we propose to deal with him as a poet only; because we feel, that as such, he has real claims upon our attention: it is not just that he should be passed by whilst many possessed of far less brilliant genius are commended and applauded to the skies. In our estimation he is a great, though undoubtedly a faulty poet; and we believe that we shall have succeeded in conveying this impression to our readers long before we draw this article to a close in which it is our intention, first, to comment on several of the leading poems of Mr. Ernest Jones, as the exponent of chartism, and then, in conclusion, to consider the prospects and the dangers of democracy.

First, then, it deserves to be noted, as a fact of some literary importance, that Ernest Jones, though a poet of this Tennysonian era, has not the slightest affinities in thought, or style, or manner, with the famous Alfred Tennyson. This is, of course, enough to seal his condemnation with the majority of the critics of the day, and may serve to account, (not forgetting, however, the influence of that bitter envy which always *will* pique mediocrity against genius,) may serve to account, we say, for the tone of disparagement, and the almost comic airs of patronage, in which *The Leader,* and other journals, have indulged with reference to Mr. Jones's poetry. Here and there, indeed, his poems have found enthusiastic and most warm-hearted admirers, as we see from the advertisements on the cover of his last publication, *Notes to the People;* but he is too emphatically *"sui generis,"* has too marked a style of his own, and, above all, is too essentially distinct from the fashionable poets of the day,—in all respects, is too utterly devoid of Tennysonian mannerism, (with which all the secondary rhymesters, Mackay, Allingham, Westwood, &c. furnish us in such abundance—not forgetting the author of "Festus," and the rubbish of Sydney Yednys,)—he is too devoid of participles past, serving the purposes of nouns proper, and of adjectives figuring as capitals, and of that word-beauty, bordering on the finical, for which "In Memoriam" is so conspicuous, and further, of that vague indefiniteness of meaning which is happily so *"suggestive,"* and has such a potent charm for most lovers of poetry in this generation, not to be well-nigh certain to be disregarded! Not that he needs richness of colouring, for in this he may be rather said to excel his contemporaries; and single lines of great power he is rather too fond, in our opinion, of indulging in—so that he does, in a measure, possess certain Tennysonian characteristics: yet he lacks the principal of these. For, first, he assuredly has not, or has not yet displayed, that exquisite tenderness of feeling, and that deep internal passion, which are the glory of Tennyson's muse, as displayed in his "Love and Duty," "The Gardener's Daughter," "Locksley Hall," &c.; nor has he equalled the charming simplicity and pathetic grace of "The Lord of Burleigh," "Lady Clare," and "The

May Queen." But, on the other hand, Ernest Jones possesses a stern power and a majestic sweep of song which are emphatically his own. Lyrically he is more impulsive, though dramatically less so: at times he displays an almost barbaric splendour, so rich is his fancy, so brilliant is his imagery. In some respects his style may be said to approximate rather to that of Byron; but yet it differs essentially, being, we think, less passionate, but stronger and more sensible. Fancy of the most brilliant character is, perhaps, Ernest Jones's marked characteristic; but then this fancy is sustained by great powers of thought and vigour of language. Against all these qualities we have to set a certain love of splendour, which we might almost stigmatize as gaudiness, and the occasional preference of sound to sense, and we fear we must add, a general seeking for effect, which will scarcely escape the observation of the reader.

Let us now pass from these general eulogiums and censures to the more particular notice of his various productions, the earlier of which we can only afford space to name. "The Wood Spirit" is a prose romance of a very fantastic character, which will remind the reader strongly of "Fouquè"; it is fraught with grand materials, and possesses magnificent passages, and further, it contains some really very charming lyrics, which Mr. Jones never has surpassed; yet is there little art in the whole. There is nothing of the chartist element to be found in this work, nor in our author's finest poem, which, we believe, followed next, "Lord Lindsay," a composition which portrays the evils attendant on doubt, suspicion and uncertainty, with a force that has been rarely equalled. The sympathies of this work would rather seem to us eminently aristocratic than democratic, a proud and poor patrician being its hero. We would gladly dwell upon the beauties of "Lord Lindsay," but having resolved to confine our citations to his latest batch of poems, appearing in his *Notes to the People,* we shall only say, that it possesses very much of self-sustained grandeur and of descriptive power, combined with a high amount of lyric beauty. "My Life," which came next in order, was an attempt to pourtray the fortunes of a supposed aristocrat, who becomes a demagogue upon conviction; it is only fragmentary, but is marked with more of sweetness and pathos than we generally find in Mr. Jones's productions, whilst its satire is keen and biting, and reaches home.

Within the last few months this author has thought fit to institute a new organ of communication with his chartist friends; this is a weekly publication, entitled *Notes to the People,* almost exclusively edited by Mr. Jones himself, containing, essays, tales, histories, songs, and sundries, all designed to promote the progress of pure democracy, or of popular rights: the first four members of this year were devoted, for the most part, to the publication of poems, which, it seems, had been composed by the author during his late political imprisonment. It imports us little as critics how or where these works were written; whether with red ink or with blood, as Mr. Jones suggests to us; their artistic power and beauty is our theme, not excluding, however, their essential truth or falsity; and now we address ourselves seriously to the task of making our readers acquainted with the laureate of democracy.

The first of these poems, then, is entitled "The New World." We had better give the title, perhaps, in full:— "The New World; a Democratic Poem, dedicated to the People of the United Queendom, and of the United States"; and the preface thus commences—"Let no one accuse me of presumption in seeking so large an audience; the poorest tribute may be offered to the richest treasury. The poet is a citizen of the world and he is glad where the barrier of different languages no longer intercepts the travelling thought. Between the men of America and England should be eternal union, therefore I address them both. I write for the rising republic as well as for the decaying monarchy; but, alas! there is much of the Dead Sea apple on either shore of the Atlantic." Then follows an exposition of Mr. Jones's political creed: the decay of England's greatness is traced with only too much truth; as where he says, that though "it dazzles the world by its attitude of quiescent grandeur," yet "its commerce will die because it is unsound at the core: foreign competition has been met by home competition, and both have been founded on the fall of wages and the land's desertion for the loom; thus home trade has been destroyed," (seriously impaired at the least,) "for with the working class it flourishes or fades. Food is the staple wealth, and England has been made a pensioner on other lands for daily bread: we can command it still, but the hour of weakness may come; then, when we ask the nations for a loaf, they may remember that we gave them cannon-balls, and pay us back in kind." There is much more with which we generally concur upon the subject of unrestricted competition, but we would not seek to solve such a question here: pass we to the poem—indubitably a grand political manifesto, a species of prophecy of the years to come, in which the fate of England is shadowed forth under the name of Hindostan. The poet conceives for his purposes our Eastern empire to be destroyed, and a native monarchy to arise in its stead, resembling the Europe of the middle ages; of this monarchy he traces the gradual decay, till it takes the form of a virtual dogeship with a ruling aristocracy: of course, Mr. Jones wishes us to look on this as an equivalent to our English constitution; then succeeds the fall of the aristocracy, to which he conceives that we are fast approaching, and the absolute reign of the middle classes, the party of a Bright and Cobden, whom this author obviously holds in great abhorrence, though they are the "avant-garde" and pioneers of democracy. Finally, he paints the downfall of the system of competition and of middle-class government, and the access of the masses to power, when, after a short period of strife, every thing of course rights itself, and a flowery Utopia is the result. The poet commences by an energetic eulogy of America, or rather of the United States, thus:—

> From freedom born to time, transcendent
>   birth!
> Colossus destined to bestride the earth,—
> While heaved old empires with unwonted
>   woes,
> Man's sanctuary, America, arose.
> Dull Europe, startled by thy first wild tones,
> Propped up thy cradle with her crumbling
>   thrones;
> And France, sad nurse of thy rude infant
>   days,
> Lulled thy first slumber with her
>   'Marseillaise.'

Then follows a fine descriptive passage, in the course of which our author says,

> No common guards before thy borders
>   stand,
> The elements themselves defend thy land;
> Eternal frost thy northern frontiers meet;
> Around thy south is rolled eternal heat.

This oratoric burst of eloquence will no doubt tell upon our trans-atlantic friends; and still more may they admire the picture of their country's future, in which the democrat shines so conspicuous.

> Young nation-Hercules, whose infant grasp
> Kingcraft and churchcraft slew, the twin-
>   born asp,
> What glorious visions for thy manhood rise
> When thy full stature swells upon our eyes!
> A crown of northern light shall bind thy
>   head,
> The south pole at thy feet its billows
>   spread,
> With island gems thy flowing robe be
>   graced,
> And Tyrian cameos glitter at thy waist;
> Warm as its skies and spotless as its snow
> Thy mighty heart shall beat at Mexico;
> And on that mystic site of unknown eld
> Such city rise, as mortal ne'er beheld;
> Till Europe sees thy sovereign flag unfurl'd
> Where'er thy waters wash the western
>   world.

These are certainly splendid lines; a little of the prize-poem order possibly,—but where is the prize-poem to match them? The poet does not, however, paint the future of America as undisturbed by disasters; on the contrary, he forebodes civil strife, war of the poor

against the rich, of the many against the few, of the Black against the White; yet he concludes by prophesying a triumphant close to all, and the permanent reunion of the shattered states. Then, after this species of introduction, he enters on the main subject of his poem: the fortunes of Hindostan as emblematic as those of England and the world. He paints powerfully our sinking Eastern empire (such as he believes it will be) and the efforts of our ministers at home to obtain new subsidies from Parliament, to resist the gathering forces of rebellion. Ironically he places these words on the minister's lips:

> ' 'Twere selfishness,' he chides, ' 'twere
>   gross neglect
> Their suit, and duty's service to reject;
> To leave them lost in anarchy and night,
> And, worse, *without the blessed Gospel
>   light!'*
> Upbraided oft for India's conquering
>   scheme,
> You urged, 'We civilize, reform, redeem!'
> In proof whereof '—a smile escaped his
>   lips—'
> 'You sent out bishops in your battle ships!' &c.

> . . . . .

> 'Think of the souls entrusted to your care!
> Think of the earthly hell awaits them there!
> Of cursed Suttee—of Almeh's shameless
>   trade—
> And Venerable Heber's sainted shade!'—
> Rang down the senate hall responsive
>   cheers,—
> For senates judge too often by their ears.

Well, fresh succours are sent; and a great leader, one of course who has risen from the ranks (this being so usual in our service), is found to rally the scattered forces of our empire: he is forcibly described, but we cannot find space for the portraiture. However; his subordinate generals, being aristocratic tent-loungers, will not second his endeavours, and the Company and President counteract them also; so he is compelled, though most unwillingly, to retire before the Indian army, which waxes of course prodigiously from the presage of victory thus acquired. At last the struggle comes: it is long and bloody:—

> Here crashed the shot—there swept the
>   Indian spear,
> And death won grandeur from an English
>   cheer.
> Devotion vain! vain science' deadliest pride!
> God, hope, and history take the Hindoo's
>   side:
> Here but a host, in misused courage strong,—
> A nation there with centuries of wrong.

Then carnage closed beneath its cloudy
    screen;
Oft paused the guns—but terror shriek'd
    between;
And grimly smiled, the sulphury curtain
    through,
The gleaming form of chivalrous Tippoo!

We break off here, though all is fine: the English are
defeated. "Courageous died that white-haired general."
Now comes the hour of bloody retribution. The poet
assumes that our Indian authorities in Church and State
are the foulest of oppressors; the honest truth, that
they are upon the whole beneficent rulers, not suiting
his purposes. The final retreat of the English to the
shore is graphically described. Then, for the last time,
they rally "under some young chief," who has yet the
power and spirit to lead them on to victory. We must
again extract some noble lines:—

The crest-fallen armies, scatter'd and hewn
    down,
Give one last rally for their old renown;
And when the blue sea meets their longing
    eyes,
Turn yet again to face their enemies;
Once more the famous flags parading see,
'Sobraon,'—'Aliwal,'—and 'Meeanee,'—
Poor war-worn banners 'mid sulphureous
    gloom,
*Like ghosts of victories round an empire's
    tomb*'[1].

The thunder died to calm—the day was
    done—
And England conquer'd 'neath a setting
    sun!
At break of dawn the leader left his tent,
And walked the mountain's craggy
    battlement.
Far stretched the inland—not a foe seemed
    there—
Lorn lay the Ghaut beneath the untroubled
    air,
And, close in shore the strong obedient
    fleet
Attend, alike for succour or retreat.
The electric thought like lightning kindling
    came,
'Renew the war, and dare the glorious game!
Swoop on each straggling band, that singly
    hies
To hoped-for havoc of a host that flies!'
Hark! thrilling cheers from rock to harbour
    run:
Alas! they shout but for their safety won!

A mighty shadow, deep, and stern, and still,
Threw o'er the fleet and flood each Indian hill;

The encampment's flag just reached the
    rising light,
Like lingering glory of the evening's fight:
One hour, its last farewell majestic waved
Old England's pride, unchallenged and
    unbraved:—
*But a soft wind at sunrise, like God's hand,
Quietly bent it homeward from that land!*
Sad wound the weary numbers to the sea,
The signal's up, and Hindostan is free!

By this time we think our readers will be disposed to
concur with us, that Ernest Jones is a poet, and a very
eminent poet—one scarcely to be equalled indeed
among his contemporaries in his own peculiar do-
main.—We should pass rapidly perhaps over the period that follows, and yet the poetry is so grand that
we have not the heart to do so. We think our readers
will pardon us for presenting them with certain passages, which will assuredly take their place among the
standard "beauties" of out country's literature, and are
not unlikely, some of them at least to become "household words." The poet proceeds then to paint the era
of medieval chivalry and romance, under this Indian
parallel: he says:

Then chivalry his proudest flag outroll'd,
And superstition crown'd her kings with
    gold;
Then solemn priests through awful temples
    pass'd,
Whose new god excommunicates the last:
Then banner'd towers with wild romances
    rung,
And bards their harps to love and glory
    strung;
Like moonlight's magic upon sculptures rare,
They show'd the true, but made it seem too
    fair.

But now also comes the era of decline, which is very
forcibly portrayed. The following lines appear to us to
be singularly fine of their kind, applicable rather to the
ancient Roman empire than to any modern monarchy;
but thus fade the glories of this fabled Oriental realm:—

Spread east and west their vast dominion
    wide,
From broad Amoo to Tigris' arrowy tide:
But valour's early impulse dies away
In easy, loitering, somnolent Cathay.
Most empires have their Capua:—bold
    endeavour
Retrieves a Cannæ, but a Capua never.
Through that huge frame the times their
    signs impart,
Inert extremities and fevered heart;
Diluted laws with weaken'd pulses act,
Through province nominal, but realm in fact;

The sword of state escapes a feeble hand,
Nor dares to punish those who may
    withstand.
Powers, reft of substance, make amends in
    show;
Courts fear their generals, generals fear the
    foe:
Around the expiring realm the vultures wait,
The North knocks loudly at its Alpine gate,
Siberian tribes and Tahta nations come,
The Goths and Huns of Oriental Rome,
And westward rising, like the unruly Frank,
Impatient Persia presses at its flank,
While in the capital, with dangerous heat,
Sedition's flames against the palace beat,
And bold ambitious nobles, brooding ill,
Pass faction's mutiny as people's will.

From this point onward our poet seems to have kept France in his mind's eye throughout this portion of his poem, not that her nobles ever displayed such an excess of spirit, but certainly the fortunes of her royal line are narrated here. Four admirable lines express them—

With crime's hot ravage, time's more dull
    decay,
A great, old line, far lingering, droops away,
And leaves its race, more fallen from age to
    age,
Departed grandeur's mournful heritage.

However, royal blood makes a stand, so to speak, in the veins of one monarch, "Louis le Grand," we presume, whom Mr. Jones dismisses rather unceremoniously in the lines—

Till one long life exceeds in sin and years—
The palace laughs amid a land of tears,
As if that house, down hastening to the
    dust,
Took one last deepest draught of power and
    lust.

In what follows, Louis Quatorze, and Louis Quinze, "Louis le Désirè," seem blended in one, where we read,

A tearless funeral marks a regal death:
The chain is raised—the nations draw their
    breath,
As through the curious crowd's ungrieved
    array,
*That cold black pomp rolls its slow weight
    away.*

And now comes the unhappy Louis XVI on the stage, so good and so mild; but one who had yielded too much, who was too little a representative of any prin-

ciples, to be classed with our own martyr monarch; at least, in our estimation. Mr. Jones says very finely—we may say, beautifully:—

From sickly, studious seclusion led,
Ere time could dry the tears that duty
    shed,—
In saddened youth, from childhood without
    joy,
Stepp'd to the throne a gentle-hearted boy.
Nature denied him health and strength, but
    gave
A generous spirit, and a patience brave.
*Such is the mould of martyrs—and what
    more*
Must meet to make one, fortune had in
    store.
Alas! for him who's doomed to face her
    rage
With thoughts too large to fit a narrow age.

Such was certainly not precisely the character of Louis XVI; but the resemblance is near enough to show that the poet's prophecy has been suggested by the past. Louis, also, was a liberal, at least to the extent of wishing to bestow a constitution, similar to our own, upon his people. Our author makes his visionary king sigh over the woes of his nation, and at last resolve to rend their fetters by one decree. He does so:

Throughout the realm bids servile tenure
    cease,
In hope bestowing happiness and peace,
And as a rocket on a mine is hurl'd
Give's liberty's great watchword to the
    world.
Mistaken hope! for since the world began,
A law ne'er yet has made a slave a man.
No golden bridge expected freedom
    brings,
No Jordan flows along the lives of kings.
O earthly foretaste of celestial joy!
Kings cannot give thee—swords cannot
    destroy;
Gold cannot buy thee; prayers can never
    gain;
Cowards cannot win thee; sluggards not
    retain.

And so the people, being socially oppressed, continue to suffer, and think the king the cause; in which impression the nobles confirm them: the latter grasp more and more at all power as their lawful due: at last the monarch is constrained to take arms against them, if he would keep the very semblance of authority. Here follows one of the most beautiful passages in the poem, which seems to show that Ernest Jones's sympathies at the bottom may be aristocratic yet. In this distress

of the monarch we find he is not all deserted: some
faithful servants abide beside him:—

> Then forms are seen, unknown in happier
> hour,
> *Great-hearted courtiers of a sinking power:*
> Who saved the sire, neglected or undone,
> Stake all he left, their lives, to save the son.
> *Brave gentlemen, whose unavailing lance*
> *Throws round his fall their gallantry's*
> *romance;*
> *Uncoronetted peers, who own, and claim*
> *No title, but their old illustrious name,*
> *Through swarming foes devotedly draw*
> *nigh,*
> *And, highborn, come to claim a death as*
> *high.*

Nor less beautiful is what follows:—

> Then, touched with grandeur in his lowlier
> state,
> Rose the poor peasant to as proud a fate:
> Less polished, yet as precious, honour's
> gem,
> No history e'er shall set in gold for them!
> Toil's chivalry, they sink by myriads down,
> Victors unlaurell'd, martyrs without crown:
> *They craved no grandeur, and they hoped*
> *no fame;*
> *Wrong triumph'd, duty call'd them, and*
> *they came.*

Is not this nobly conceived and grandly spoken? Mr.
Jones teaches us how to write! We have the better
cause, but we may not possess, alas! as happy a
genius. All that follows here is singularly fine. The
monarch withdraws from the capital: after an interval
of truce he and his rebel nobles meet for a last peaceful interview, the royal-hearted sovereign having refused to risk the lives of his faithful followers on one
desperate cast. Myriads of the people witness this
interview. The king, unhappily, being weak and ill, is
brought in a litter to the field: a cry rises against him,
of "Base luxury!" the multitude imagine him a tyrant
wrapped in sloth: the doom of the monarchy is sealed.
The nobles mark the favorable moment: they avail
themselves of the popular feeling; they seize the king
as prisoner, and his farewell sign commands his faithful followers to forbear. All is over. Only his mock
trial and execution remain. Powerfully Mr. Jones
says:—

> Then Freedom pass'd her Jordan's parted
> flood:—
> The cruel scaffold drank a hero's blood,—
> While Justice' verdict, in the book of Time,
> That found him king, records no other
> crime;

> And eager crowds their joyous clamours
> send
> Above the ashes of their only friend.

Thus far we shall all sympathize: in what follows truth
and error are strangely intermingled.

> But blame the people not—blame those
> instead,
> Who rich and great, the poor and weak
> mislead[2];
> To selfish ends their ready passions use—
> Who, prompt the deed, and then the act
> accuse!
> The murderer might as well with pleading
> vain,
> His heart exculpate and his hand arraign.
> And, from the event be this great moral
> traced:
> Virtue on thrones is like a pearl misplaced.
> Break sceptres! break beneath the Almighty
> rod,
> For every king's a rebel to his God.
> Atonement for the sins of ages past,
> The tarrying stream ran purest at its last;
> Thus olden superstition's altars bring
> The lamb, and not the wolf, as offering.
> Still with the millions shall the right abide,
> The living interest on the victim's side,—
> Strange balance, that, 'twixt sympathy and
> fate,
> Atones in pity what it wronged in hate!
> The selfsame king, in different times of men,
> Had been, their martyr now, their idol then;
> And History, as the record sad she keeps,
> Traces the mournful truth, and writing
> weeps.

>   . . . . .

> Yet not in vain that gallant life has flown;
> A glorious seed that gentle hand has sown:
> Bread on those troubled waters, dark and
> dim,
> Fruit for long years—tho' not returned to
> him.

From this point onward the narrative interest of the
poem may be said to cease; the stream grows wider—
it may be, more practically useful in its author's eyes,
but indisputably less romantic: the rocks, the crags,
the castled heights, have flown afar; the river broadens and broadens, and sandy wastes spread out on
either shore; the individual gives way to the general.—
The new constitution is next described. Soon the
moneyocracy get a-head; the people's social state remains the same; nay, it rather grows worse and worse
under the influence of competition: here, of course,
the present state of England is shadowed forth. The

chartist leaders find their antitypes also, in certain bold speakers, who are placed on their trial for sedition. Here Mr. Jones positively revels in his poetical denunciations of the law officers of the crown, with whom, if we remember rightly, he maintained a wordy conflict—we think it was with the present Lord Chief Justice Jervis in particular. The portraiture is certainly not a flattering one; but we, who remember that gentleman's pertness in the Hampden case—(amongst other strange absurdities, he stated that he claimed a far more absolute supremacy for the Queen of England over the Church than had ever been exercised by the Pope of Rome)—we, who remember this pert audacity, are not inclined to feel as shocked as we otherwise might be, by Mr. Jones's violence.

> There brazen faction's never-blushing mask,
> The public prosecutor plies his task;
> For, when the pard has struck his
>   murderous blow,
> The jackal comes and tears his mangled foe.
> In him is centred all that perfects knaves—
> The heart of tyrants and the soul of slaves;
> A bishop's sophistry, a bigot's fire,
> A lawyer's conscience, and a brain for
>   hire.

"Bitter words, my masters!" but they break no bones, that is one comfort; and we can scarcely wonder at the wrath of him who was for months deprived of all commune with his friends, of almost all books, of paper and ink "in toto," and was treated, in fine, as a criminal of the very lowest order. Accordingly, the judge also does not escape. The ensuing lines seem to us not capable of being easily rivalled for their bitter and biting power: they are founded, it seems, on fact.

> Yet come their blows so hard, so home their
>   hits,
> On cushioned seat the judge uneasy sits;
> With ignorant glibness refutation tries,
> (Like sin, that reasons with its guilt—he
>   lies!)
> From shallow premise inference false would
>   wrench,
> And spouts 'Economy' from solemn bench;
> 'I drink champagne—that gives the poor
>   man bread,
> The grower takes our calico instead.
> I keep my hunter—why that brow of gloom?
> Does not my hunter also keep his groom?
> I roll my carriage—well! that's good for
>   trade!
> Look at the fortunes coachmakers have made.'
> Then his last argument, when others fail,
> 'To JAIL! TO JAIL! *you wicked man! to jail!*'

> Now bring your fine blood-hunters to the
>   plough,

> And o'er the spade your liveried lacqueys
>   bow!
> If they must eat, 'tis right they should
>   produce;
> And, if you covet pomp, repay in use.
> 'Twere almost vain to these dark knaves to
>   show,
> So many lands but so much food can grow;
> That so much land but so much produce
>   bears,
> *And that our wheat is better than their*
>   *tares!*
> That idle luxury turns, in evil hour,
> To unproductive toil productive power;
> And coachmaker and lacquey, horse and
>   groom,
> Impair production while they still consume.
> But deep the people drink the precious lore,
> And discontent speaks louder than before,
> While near and nearer yet, with every year,
> Claim the dread creditors their long arrear.

What political economists of ordinary stamp would answer to these arguments we know not; we suspect that they could only take refuge in a supposed *necessity;* but the real answer seems to us to be, that with wise care earth might be made to produce, first, enough for all, and then a superfluity for some. Beauty is, in a measure, a luxury certainly, though the highest works of art should be the property of the world, yet there are many rare and costly things which all cannot possess, but which some may and if I do, no other man is wronged, *ipso facto,* by my possession. Yet this rests on the assumption that such article of luxury is either not convertible into an article of utility for the use of all, or that it is not needed for that purpose. As long as our working classes are wretchedly underpaid, so paid as not to enable them to possess themselves and their families of the necessaries, of the ordinary comforts of life, so long wealth will appear an anomaly; so long it will be hard to justify unprofitable labour of any kind. This principle must not be pushed to an extreme—no principle can be without degenerating into wrong and error; but we cannot but conceive that the first necessity of every state is to provide for the good of its working classes, high or low. If the bees be once in good condition, there can be no possible objection to drones swilling any superfluous honey. And, as a matter of fact, the upper classes are not drones in England, but workers also in their sphere, and their luxuries, kept within due bounds, will react upon the working classes to their benefit, and tend to bind all men together by ties of mutual need and brotherhood. In Britain, however, under existing circumstances, we fear that the judge's argument scarcely holds good; under a wise system of mutual protection and association it certainly would do so. But let us return to the poem before us.

Our author next launches forth in a vigorous diatribe against emigration, as worse than needless, were a just policy resorted to; then he stigmatizes our system of pauperism; then, under the figure of "Ceylon's neighboring isle," he points attention to the woes of Ireland. Much of this he does, very mischievously and unjustifiably. Things are bad, but not so bad as it suits Mr. Jones to represent them, who is, we are compelled to say it, in our estimation, whether consciously or not, a thriver upon discontent and a trader in sedition.

We are not sorry, indeed, that such men should be found to represent the wrongs of the working classes, and we are ready to labour for the redress of these wrongs, fully as faithfully as they can, only not quite by their side. Mr. Jones, if he ever reads this, must pardon the frankness of our political criticism: let him know in us—an open, if not a worthy foe!

Now follows a grand section, describing the final outbreak of the people's wrath, and the overthrow of camps, courts, and councils. This is not what we dread most in this country, as we have already indicated, though after certain downward steps have once been taken, of which a large increase of the suffrage is by far the greatest, it is not impossible that the final downfall of the peerage and the throne may be accelerated by such an outbreak. But as yet, at all events, the country is not ripe for it: it would only reawaken and rally all the sound conservative thought and feeling of the nation. For further extracts from this poem we lack space. Two fine episodes succeed: one describing a future rising "en masse" of the black man against the white; another pourtraying the return of the Jews to Judea, but not, unhappily, in a Christian spirit. We must quote some few lines here.

> They leave, they leave, a God-collected
>   band,
> Their homeless houses in the stranger's
>   land.
> You scarce would deem that risen race the
>   same—
> Thus one great thought transfigurates the
>   frame:
> Greed spurns its gold, affliction dries her
>   tears,
> Youth scorns its follies, age forgets its
>   years.
> The faint old man uprising in his bed,
> Leans on his shrunken arms his silvery
>   head;
> Around him stand, half-sandall'd to depart,
> *His stalwart sons, the pillars of his heart.*
> What splendours kindle in that faded sight!
> He sees—he sees—Judea's far-off light:
> Why bends he as one listening? Hush! he
>   hears

> *The cedars whispering of their thousand*
>   *years:*
> A sudden ardour nerves his frame—he cries
> 'My cloak and staff!—Hosannah!, . . .' sinks
>   and dies.
> Low bend those mariners of life's fond wave
> Around the barque safe anchor'd in the
>   grave:
> Though young, and strong, and eager for
>   the way,
> That old man won the promised land ere
>   they.

Then follows a glowing description of a grand Australian empire, or rather republic, yet to rise; all manner of wonders of steam and electricity find their place; rain is drawn from the skies at will as lightning has been; heat is guided to distant and barren mountains; life is prolonged almost unmeasureably, pain and discord having finally disappeared; peace is perfect; one language is spoken over all the earth; there is no mine and thine, all property being in common; the very volcanoes expire; the very poles rebloom, since once, as geology tells us, they were inhabitable; in fine, our author sets the most glowing picture of the Millennium before our eyes, omitting the indispensable groundwork—that sense of reverence, that hatred of sin, that love of duty, that conquest of self-indulgence—without which the very earth he paints would be a hell. Then he concludes audaciously—we may say, blasphemously—but certainly with no little power and beauty:

> Then, as the waifs of sin are swept away—

The poet has not told us how; has not even attempted to suggest; but we resume,—

> Then as the waifs of sin are swept away,
> Mayhap the world may meet its destined
>   day;
> A day of change and consummation bright,
> After its long Aurora, and old night.
> No millions shrieking in a fiery flood
> No blasphemies of vengeance and of
>   blood—
> Making the end of God's great work of
>   joy,
> And of Almighty wisdom—to destroy
> No kindling comet, and no fading sun,
> But heaven and earth uniting melt in one.
>
>   . . . . .
>
> The voyage is o'er. The adventurous flag is
>   furl'd,
> The pilot, Thought, has won the fair New
>   World.
> The sailor's task is done. The end remains.

Must *he,* too, expiate his work in chains?
What though old prejudice the path
    opposed,
Though weeds corrupt around the vessel
    closed,
Though discord crept among the jealous
    crew,
His heart's his compass—and it told him
    true!

No, it told him not true: it painted him, if the heart was concerned at all, and not rather the fancy, an unreal and most delusive vision. The communism, the absolute equality, the absence of faith in a self-revealed and personal GOD here depicted, would be sufficient to blight the very fairest Eden; so indeed would any one of these three vital errors, of which the last is of course the most utterly destructive. A Millennium may be yet in store for man; we hope it, and believe it; a period of happiness and peace in the era of the Church's glories; but even then, evil will be lessened, not removed; even then that fatal necessity which attaches pain and suffering to error, will be in full and inevitable operation: even then GOD's justice will punish sinners. Nothing can be weaker, vainer, more diametrically opposed to all the teaching of experience, to all the evidence of reality, than that specious benevolence, that indiscriminate charity, which would merge right and wrong on a kind of general happiness principle, and, attributing its own weakness to the Almighty, would either have Him annihilate that freedom of choice on which He has thought fit to rear the moral world, or would have Him act with supreme indifference to his own great law of compensation, and make the evil-hearted happy, despite their selfishness and sin. But more on this theme anon, when we come to Beldagon Church.

Let us now, ere we proceed to that poem, pause to ask our readers, whether we have or have not convinced them that Ernest Jones is a true, nay, and even a great poet? Where, since the days of Pope and Dryden, will they find such grand sustained heroic verse? And Mr. Jones's poetry has an element wanting to all the poetry of the seventeenth century, viz. the element of earnestness and passion. But how stately is the march of these lines, like the ocean tide majestically rolling in, wave after wave, in never-failing time and order, though now and then the billows be crested with some superfluous foam! What a power of conception have we not witnessed! What a grandeur of expression! What real beauty! Was this a poem to treat with an air of patronage, let us ask; condescendingly patting the author on the back, like the conceited "Leader," and its fellows? We repeat, that it is the total absence of any approximation to Tennysonianism which makes us value Mr. Jones's poetry as poetry so highly. It is high time for a literary reaction against a mannerism, which however delightful, threatens to overflood

us with its morbid sweetness; and in this point of view Ernest Jones's muse may have a really important office to perform. Let small critics sneer to the utmost of their small ability, such genius as his must needs prove crushing to these wights; and the time may not be far distant when they will scarcely know how to express their sense of that genius too extravagantly; for mediocrity, being guided by fashion, not by instinct or true judgment, is ever in extremes of praise or blame. We shall now pass to a poem which has scarcely any thing political about it, because we wish to satisfy those who may yet be disposed to maintain, on the score of Ernest Jones's democracy, destructiveness, and demagoguery, that he can be no true poet.

This is a tale of Florence in the olden time, when, as the poet tells us, "Florence alone was bright;" to speak by the card, it is entitled, "The Painter of Florence: a domestic poem, being a story within a story." This last novelty of nomenclature the poem derives from the singular and somewhat inartistic length of its metrical introduction, which is English, while the story's self is Italian in its theme. The poet conceives himself, namely, to be paying a visit in a certain country-house, where he beholds a work of art, a beautiful picture, which he describes very glowingly, and which suggests to his imagination the tale of the Painter of Florence. The introduction, though spirited, must not detain us long; there we have a terse narrative of the ruin of the last scion of an ancient aristocratic line, mainly through the villany of his lawyer and agent, who prompts and plays upon his vices, and who finally, having "sucked the victim dry," turns him adrift, and takes possession of his fathers' halls. He is a busy, bustling, mean and cunning, vulgar and overbearing, representative of the moneyocracy, and is exceedingly well depicted, he, and his titled wife also, whom he marries for her title's sake. As a specimen of our author's powers in this peculiar line of biting satire, we shall extract the following passage: it is a little coarse, perhaps, but assuredly keen and graphic.

The Lady Malice is tall and thin;
Her skin is of a dusky tan,
With black hairs dotting her pointed chin;
She's like a long, lean, lanky man!
Her virtue's positively fierce;
Her sharp eyes every weakness pierce,
Sure some inherent vice to find
In every phase of human kind.
The simplest mood, the weakest mien,
She *speckles* with her venom'd spleen,
Construing to some thought obscene;
Shred by shred, and bit by bit,
With lewd delight dissecting it;
Till sin's worst school is found to be
Near her polluting purity.

. . . . .

Devilson's thick set, short, and red;
Nine-tenths of the man are his paunch and
    head;
His hair is tufty, dense, and dark;
His small eyes flash with a cold grey spark,
Whose fitful glimmer will oft reveal
When a flinty thought strikes on his heart
    of steel.
He's sensual lips and a bold hook-nose;
And he makes himself felt wherever he
    goes!

For the rest of this amiable portraiture we refer our readers to the original; we mean to Mr. Ernest Jones's poem,—not to the original whom he draws, though it is more than possible that such an one might not be sought for vainly within the circle of the reader's own acquaintance. Well, the poet is on a visit to this respectable country squire and his lady; (by the bye he does not seem over grateful to his hosts;) after dinner, Devilson, the new lord of the manor, falls asleep, and the poet's eye wanders to a picture on the wall. This is a magnificent work of art, pourtraying the return of a Florentine army in triumph after a great victory just achieved. The poet gazes, until the image of the bygone painter wakes a kindred ardour in his soul; till this "work of buried genius," as he calls it, conveys its tale of the past to his imagining; and this tale he then proceeds to tell. It commences with these fine lines:—

At Florence in the dark ages,
    When Florence alone was bright,
(She has left on her marble pages
    Her testament of light;)

At Florence in the dark ages,
    When Florence alone was free,
(She rose, in the pride of her sages,
    Like the sun on a troubled sea;)

While yet as an ark she drifted
    On the earth's barbarian flood,
And the wreck of the arts uplifted
    From the deluge of human blood;

Where many a feast of glory
    And deed of worth were done,—
From the links of her broken story
    I have saved to the world this one.

There is a peculiar wildness, freshness, and originality in these lines, which will scarcely fail to be appreciated; a fancy rich in its excess, an easy power that sports with verse and melody. Nor less original of its kind is what follows:—

Round Florence the tempests are clouding;
    The mountains a deluge have hurl'd;

For the tyrants of nations are crowding
    To blot that fair light from the world.

Like vultures that sweep from the passes
    To come to the feast of the dead,
In black, heavy, motionless masses
    Their mighty battalions are spread.

'Tis eve: and the soldiers of Florence
    To meet them are marching amain:
The foe stand like ocean awaiting
    The streamlet that glides o'er the plain.

Then the blood of the best and the bravest
    Had poured like the rain on the sod—
But the spirit of night stood between them,
    Proclaiming the truce of their God.

It touches the heart of the tyrant—
    It gives him the time to repent:—
The morn on the mountain has risen!
    The hour of salvation is spent!

The multitudes break into motion,
    The trumpets are stirring the flood:—
An islet surrounded by ocean,
    The ranks of the citizens stood.

But the vanguard is Valour and Glory;
    The phalanx is Freedom and Right;
The leaders are Honour and Duty:
    Are *they* soldiers to fail in the fight?

Then hail to thee! Florence the fearless!
    And hail to thee! Florence the fair!
Ere the mist from the mountain has faded,
    What a triumph of arms shall be there!

So Florence wins the day, and its senators decree a mighty prize to the painter who in one work of genius shall commemorate the return from the field of battle of Florence' victor sons. Many embark in the glorious competition, for which a three years' term is granted; amongst them, a student, "the Painter of Florence," whose name does not appear. He has long loved the daughter of an artisan, and has been loved again, but her father discourages his suit, esteeming the youth a dreamer; and so he appears indeed, for as yet he has accomplished nothing great, and even now, with such a prize before him, it is long ere he can commence to realize his ideal. The poet thus defends him:—

Men counted him a dreamer. Dreams
Are but the light of clearer skies,
Too dazzling for our naked eyes:
And, when we catch their flashing beams,
We turn aside, and call them, *dreams.*
O, trust me, every truth that yet
In greatness rose and sorrow set,

That time to ripening glory nursed,
Was called an idle dream at first.

And so he passed through want and ill,
And lived neglected and unknown:
Courage he lacked not, neither skill,
But that fixed impulse of the will,
That guides to fame, and guides alone.
And opportunity ne'er smiled,
Without which, genius' royal child,
Is but a king without a throne.

His feverish efforts to achieve the sighed-for work of
art are happily described: at last, after two years have
flown, he seems to pass the Rubicon, he has fairly
started on his high endeavour; but alack! meanwhile,
fever is eating his very life away. He begins to fear he
shall die young. Here occur these fine lines:—

'Twas on an eve of autumn pale
That first he felt his strength to fail.
The sun o'er Spain had shone its last;
The leaves around were falling fast;
The western clouds were turning grey;
And Earth and Heaven seem'd to say,
'Passing away! Passing away!'

However hope revives under the influence of love, and
meanwhile the picture grows beneath his airy brush:
its progress is finely shadowed forth. But the hour of
decision comes at last. On the fated morn the young
student is waiting the decree in his chamber, too weak
and ill to leave it, flushed with fever's pangs: there he
is visited by the maiden of his love and by her father.
From this point forward we must let the poet speak
for himself, merely premising that we scarcely know
a passage more graphic and exciting in the whole range
of narrative poetry; neither Byron nor Scott, we think,
has surpassed it:—reader! be not captious!

A gentle hand tapp'd on his chamber door,
And a soft voice call'd;—'tis the voice of
  Lenore!—
Spirit of light, before passing the grave,
Angel of life! art thou come to save?
She knew the hours were hard to bear;
That the heart will fail and the spirit break
When life and more than life's at stake—
And had won on her father to bring her
  there:
But *he* sat him down,
With a silent frown,
Half anger'd to deem he had been so weak.
The painter's face with a smile is bright
As he reads his hope in the maiden's eyes;
But *her* cheek turns pale as the lustre dies,
Till it hangs on his lip like the mournful
  light
Of a wreck that may sink ere the proud sunrise.

And his fancy was busy again within
To think how much better his work might
  have been,
With a light brought there, and a shade
  thrown here:
'Twas well that he had not the canvas
  near,
For the painters, then, were Despair and
  Fear.

But hark! a sound in the distance steals:
'Tis a shout—a shout in the distance peals:
It gathers—it deepens—it rolls this way—
'Lenora, haste to the casement—say!'
''Tis finished! but *who* has won the day?'

Near and more near
Is the loud acclaim;
You could almost hear
The victorious name:
'They come,—by the beat
Of their flooding feet;
Now, now, they are reaching the end of the
  street!'

The maiden's heart is fluttering wild—
And even the father arose from his seat
And stood by his child,—
But incredulous smiled,—
'There's a way to the left: they will turn to
  the square—
No! onward! right onward! they pause not
  there!
And the senators pass
Through the multitude's mass!
Scarce three doors off—they come! they
  come!'

The maiden has sunk from the window
  side.—
'Tis past a fear! 'tis past a doubt!
There's a stir within, there's a rush without,
They mount the stairs, the door flies
  wide—
O joy to the Lover, and joy to the Bride.
The eldest of the train advances;
In his hand the garland glances;
Gold—precious, glittering to the sight;
Pledge of hopes that are still more bright,
For love is wreathed in its leaves of light!

They call him. Is their voice unheard?
He rose not, as in duty bound;
He bowed not, as they gather'd round;
They placed the garland on his head:
He gave no thanks, he spoke no word,
But slowly sunk like a drooping flower
Beneath the weight of too full a shower—
The Painter of Florence was dead!

We need not subjoin the close of this sad story; nor the final burst of invective in which the author indulges at the expense of the picture-galleries of the great; the more unjust, since our noblemen display so liberal a spirit in exhibiting their treasures to the public gaze. But how much lyric energy and passion do we not find in this poem, glowing and rich with radiant colours, and exulting in rhythmical freedom and poetic power. We cannot pause to dilate upon its excellencies, though these are assuredly many, for our article has already extended itself to an alarming length. And, on this same account, we cannot afford to comment long upon "Beldagon Church," another poem in this same series, imbued with the most destructive and antichristian tendencies, in which the worship of nature is contrasted with the worship of God, to the supposed advantage of the former. Thus we are told that—

> The blossom-loving bee,
> Neglectful of her Maker
> Though 'tis Sunday-morn,
> Little Sabbath-breaker,
> Winds her humming horn.

Beldagon's cathedral fame is then described, with "stately pews in rival rows," "cushioned seats," "oaken screen," &c. But first, the poet leads us forth to admire the ritual of nature. Much of this gospel of rationalism is, as might be expected, dreamy, indistinct, and moonshiny, in the highest degree; but it is impossible not to recognise the grace and lightness of these lines:—

> Mistily, dreamily, steals a faint glimmer;
> Hill-tops grow lighter, tho' stars become
>   dimmer:
>   First, a streak of grey;
>   Then a line of green;
>   Then a sea of roses,
>   With golden isles between.
> All along the dawnlit prairies
> Stand the flowers, like tip-toe fairies
>   Waiting for the early dew:
>   Listening,
>   Glistening,
>   As the morning
> Walks their airy muster thro',
> All the new-born blossoms christening
> With a sacrament of dew.
> And from them, a flower with wings,
> Their angel that watch'd through the night,
> The beautiful butterfly springs
>   To the light.

This is poetry; but much which follows is forced and unnatural, with a poor and too transparent aim after "naiveté" and innocence; and almost sickening, in our estimation, is the "Io Pæan" sung to the rationalist's

deity of his own creation,—a deity—shall we dare to say it?—of very milk and water. Having pronounced a verdict of condemnation on these pretended raptures, we pass to the service of Beldagon Church, the delineation of which possesses at least some spirit. The ascent of the bishop to the pulpit is cleverly portrayed:—

> Then like the flutter of a full pit
>   When a favourite passage comes,
> As the bishop mounts the pulpit,
>   Sink the whispers, coughs, and hums:
> And here and there a scattered sinner,
>   Winking in the house of God,
>   Shows he
>   Knows the
>   Rosy,
>   Cosy,
>   Dosy,
>   Prosy,
> Bishop with a smile and nod.

Then comes an onslaught on the fatness of the clergy, commencing—

> The prelate bows his cushion'd knee,
> Oh, the prelate's fat to see!

And ending—

> From mitre tall to gold-laced hat,
> Fat's the place—and all are fat!

which we are inclined to pronounce a fair hit enough: and then follows from this "cosy, dosy, bishop," one of the most powerful rhymed sermons that it would be possible for the mind of man to conceive, contrasting indeed most favourably in its straightforward truthfulness and keen severity, with the fantastic and artificial raptures of the poet over "nature's ritual." Of course the intention is to make the bishop the prophet and advocate of slavery and woe: but his discourse establishes that self-evident fact from which we derive the need for a revelation,—the fact that this is a fallen world, a world subject to a curse. Setting aside a certain amount of exaggeration and of one-sided vindictiveness of purpose, and the total absence of the doctrine of earth's redemption by the Saviour of mankind (a vital deficiency this, of course)—still, setting these things for the moment on one side, or making allowance for them, the sermon of the Bishop of Beldagon remains unanswerable on deistical principles, ay, or on atheistical either. We cannot express our admiration too highly of this most powerful composition, the author of which has thought to condemn Christianity, while he has really sealed the condemnation of his own weak and morbid "natural religion," with his faith in a rose-water Providence, that would have made this earth a heaven were it not for the vices of nobles and of kings. Some part of this striking discourse we must at least cite, and we know not where to begin save with the beginning. Here then follows the opening of the Bishop of Beldagon's sermon:—

Sink and tremble, wretched sinners! The Almighty Lord has hurl'd

His curse for everlasting on a lost and guilty world:

Upon the ground beneath your feet, upon the sky above your head,

Upon the womb that brings you forth, upon the toil that gives you bread,

On all that lives and breathes and moves, in earth and air and wave,

On all that feels and dreams and thinks, on cradle, house, and grave,

For Adam murder'd innocence—and since the world became its hearse,

Throughout the living sphere extending breeds and spreads the dreadful curse.

—The seasons through Creation bear our globe continually

To show its shame to every star that frowns from the recoiling sky:

And savage comets come and gaze, and fly in horror from the sight,

To tell it through unfathomed distance to each undiscover'd light.

Sin, its ghastly wound inflicting, damns, us to eternal pain—

And from the heart of human nature, flows an ever-bleeding vein.

You may blame your institutions, blame your masters, rulers, kings:

This is idle: 'tis the curse eternal, festering as it clings.

Change them—sweep them to destruction, as the billow sweeps the shore!

Misery, pain, and death, the curse, the curse will rankle but the more.—

If it were not thus, in nature you would surely witness joy—

Gaze around you, and behold the never-ceasing curse destroy:

Flower and leaf and blade and blossom languish in a slow decay:

Fish on fish, and bird on bird, and beast on beast, unceasing prey—

Take the smallest drop of water—see, with microscopic view,

Thousand creatures ravin, slaughter, mangle, cripple, maim, pursue.

Breathe the air—where million beings in unending conflict dwell

Every tiny bosom raging with the raging Fires of hell!

And the curse eternal gives them weapons

kindred to their hearts,

Claw, and tusk, and venom'd fang, and web, and coil, and poisoned

Nature is one scene of murder, misery, malice, pain, and sin,

And earth and air and fire and water grudge the little peace you win;

Blight and mildew, hail and tempest, drought and flood your harvests spoil,

Disputing inch by inch the conquests of your heart-subduing toil.

Now, it is true that the exaggeration of all this is self-evident; but not less evident is its partial truth. Manifest it is, we affirm, manifest and indisputable, that a curse has fallen on the world of nature, as well as on the world of mind. If you will not admit this, only one of two alternatives remains: either you must contend that the Deity is indifferent to the happiness of his creatures, or, plainly, not beneficent,—or if you reject this supposition with horror, you can only take refuge in a yet darker as well as utterly irrational creed, the creed of atheism: you must deny God altogether; you must deny Design and Providence, you must ascribe all you behold to an inexorable chance, a blind necessity. Against this the instincts of the human heart rebel, which teach it that "something holy lives above the skies," the very organs of reverence, awe, and wonder demand a fitting object, and can find one only in the Godhead. Design, we affirm, whatever the Newmans and the Froudes may tell us, is self-evident throughout the world-mechanism of creation: all things proclaim, "There is a God!" But those facts which the chartist poet has placed before us remain indisputable: life itself, is maintained by death; evil is interwoven with all things which we behold. How is this? How can this be? One answer only is possible. Evil is the consequence of sin: and sin itself was the free choice of those creatures whom the Almighty had created supremely happy and supremely good, but capable of fall, because free agents. This is the *only* possible answer that imagination or reason could devise and it is the answer of Revelation; that Revelation which proves its Divine origin by its perfect solution of all enigmas of existence; that Revelation, which has been born witness to by the wisest, holiest, purest, greatest of mankind; by a series of prophets, all claiming supernatural powers, all evincing amazing genius, boundless courage, perfect self-devotion, meekness, purity, the very ideal of all moral virtues, and who, nevertheless, if not really gifted with that supernatural power which they professed to exercise—a power to which a Mahomet dared to lay no claim,—must have been the very vilest of impostors;—a Revelation borne witness to by the mightiest of all poets, by the gravest of all seers by the most stubborn and stiffnecked of all nations, a nation scattered over the face of all the globe, a standing record of Almighty vengeance;—borne witness to by saints and martyrs the meekest and the bravest; by Apostles, twelve poor and ignorant men, who by their preaching regenerated a world, who, exhibiting in their lives the highest pattern of morality laid them down at last for the truths which they had witnessed,—or, if you think it were reasonable to believe so, for the fictions they had coated;—a Revelation, finally proclaimed by Him, who was promised from the beginning, who was hoped for by all the patriarchs, who was heralded by all the prophets, who appeared at last in the light of day to declare Himself the Son of the Living God: *Such a Revelation* stands on a basis that never can be shaken; that may well disdain all the rebellious waves that dash against its rock, whether the puny frettings of a philosophic Newman, or the bolder dash of a Froude, or the angry foam of an Ernest Jones.

It is needless to enlarge upon this subject here. But we repeat, the Bishop of Beldagon's sermon is perfectly unanswerable: sin has entered into the world, that world which issued happy and glorious from its Maker's hands; and by sin has entered woe. Yet, though on the animal creation and on nature's self the curse has fallen, let it not for an instant be conceived that the life of the creatures is not happy on the whole. True it is that creation groaneth and travelleth; yet the mere gift of existence is a boon and a blessing. By God's mercy life itself remains a joy to *all* the creatures, and the moment of death or of destruction is comparatively a moment only. It is the inevitable tribute paid by *all* creatures and things to the reign of death and sin. Yet even the insects, of which our anti-christian poet speaks, are blithesome and happy; as far as they are concerned, as far as the animal world generally is concerned, pain remains the exception, not the rule. The amount of evil which exists in creation proves that sin, resulting from the free *will* of the creature, whether man or angel, has entered into the world, and has infected it, drawing down the just punishment of the Almighty: yet does beneficence remain the rule which governs nature's laws, so that it is abundantly manifest that the Almighty must have willed originally the happiness of all his creatures. And if so, what remains to justify the course of Providence? Even the great mystery of REDEMPTION; that Divine, awful, and ever-glorious sacrifice, that stupendous work of love, the contemplation of which must fill our mortal hearts with joy and wonder. This it is which heals the breach, which solders the rent, which reconciles the creature and Creator.

Rightly Ernest Jones proceeds to show, through the medium of his episcopal sermon, that in the world of mind as well as in the world of matter, evil has gained a lodgement; that man cannot rely upon his brother-man; that selfishness, and not love, has become the master-motive of society. But utterly do we repudiate, as Christian Churchmen, that conclusion, which he places on his bishops lips, that nothing can be done

for either rich or poor; that all must writhe for ever under the incurable curse; for this fictitious bishop simply ignores the blessings of Redemption!. . .

And let it not be thought that in thus saying we are indirectly promoting the progress of democracy; for it is not Mr. Ernest Jones, the demagogue, we have to fear, but rather Lord John Russell, the reforming prime minister. The common sense of the English nation will induce them to resist the onset of open and avowed democracy; they know well that there is no tyranny so absolute or so hateful as that of the one despotic majority; they know well that the great glory of our constitution has been, that it guarded against this tyranny, whilst it supplied a medium for the representation of every class; the working classes who have not the suffrage, making their wishes known by means of public meetings, petitions, and, above all, by the press; while the House of Commons represents (speaking broadly) the middle; and the House of Lords, the upper classes. The great principle which lies at the root of our British Constitution may be said to be the necessity for the division of power: it is right indeed, it is essential, that, in the long run, in the end, the common sense of the majority should rule; but then this majority must not be that of the moment, but that of years; it must not be a bare numerical majority, but that of the real knowledge, and wisdom, and science of the country which, after all, at the best, are liable to err: but what would be more terrible, let us ask, than the absolute reign of a single body, elected by the one majority, against whose decisions there could be no appeal?

We do not now purpose to argue this matter at any length at the fag end of our article; we are sure that the common sense of most Englishmen will revolt against the reign of such a majority as this, and will infinitely prefer our ancient government by Queen, Lords, and Commons, under which no sudden changes of importance can be effected, though the voice of the nation will always make itself heard in the end. We do not want an all-powerful, irresistible House of Commons; we are disposed to admit, indeed, that if any measure be sent up from that house repeatedly with vast and increasing majorites, the peers, generally speaking, will do well to yield; but we need a barrier against popular error and the mere love of novelty, and this is supplied by the existence of the two higher branches of the legislature. Now we believe that if the House of Commons directly represented the one majority of the nation, instead of the majority of the middle classes, as at present, it would be perfectly irresistible, and that the House of Lords would of necessity become a nullity. And therefore it is that we are so strongly opposed to any measure tending even in this direction. As it is, the commons are only too powerful; yet they do not directly represent the masses, and indirectly the masses are equally represented by the Peers; but the opposition of three hundred men to a body chosen by the one majority of the nation, whether under household or universal suffrage, would, we are persuaded, be weak, and almost nominal. Therefore does Lord John Russell's bill for a large increase in the suffrage appear so exceedingly dangerous to us. Any increase is to be dreaded, as tending to establish the supreme authority of the one tyrannical majority; in fact, the very existence of the constitution, with its fundamental principle of division of power, is assuredly here at stake.

Lord John Russell must know this; he has shown by his speeches in the house that he knows it: how can he then be instrumental to the ruin of his country?

But we may be told, the working classes will never rest satisfied without the suffrage, whatever be the consequence. We *do* not believe it: we do not think the majority would care one straw for the suffrage, were their social rights secured to them: the suffrage, we consider, should be within the reach of an honest and intelligent artisan who would make some sacrifices to secure it (and so it is at present); but it should be a privilege, and not the common right of all: and this last, a right, it cannot be without erecting the despotism of one tyrant majority, and whelming Queen, Lords, and Commons in one common ruin.

What would be the immediate effect of a large increase of the suffrage, such as Lord John Russell proposes? The return of a very democratic House of Commons, who would assuredly aspire to grasp all power—who would scarcely know how to refuse consistently that universal suffrage which would then be loudly clamoured for. And in any case, the days of the House of Lords would then, we fear, be numbered: it might linger for a few years as the shadow of its former self, until it gradually melted away; or if the thinking and more highly educated classes of this country were not disposed to submit without a struggle to the triumph of democracy, to the despotism of the one tyrant majority, then a civil war might be the issue. What then is most to be dreaded, in our opinion, is the *gradual extension of the suffrage,* whereby more and more of the governing power must be absorbed into a single branch of the legislature, rendering the others comparatively valueless; and if Lord John Russell's bill should prove half as comprehensive as we arc credibly informed it will be, it alone will suffice to destroy the equilibrium of our commonweal.

Some may suppose we are indulging in too melancholy anticipations, that our fears are, at all events, exceedingly exaggerated, but this is not the case; for the balance of the British Constitution it is essential that the House of Commons should not directly represent the majority of the population, or anything approximating to it; the danger is very near and very great, and it can scarcely be exaggerated. We apprehend no perils from open democracy, or from demagogism, least of all, from physical force chartism; but we *do* fear the gradual sapping of the very basis of our social state. In this point of view it seems to us expedient to give publicity to the sentiments and opinions of such thinkers as Mr. Ernest Jones, that men may know whither Lord John Russell is endeavouring constitutionally to conduct them. The barefaced monopoly of power by one majority England would not tolerate; but the gradual increase of the suffrage, however inevitably tending to that fatal goal, may be acceded to almost without a struggle. Lord John Russell will certainly not thank us for the compliment, but we must think him a far more dangerous enemy of the constitution, whether consciously or unconsciously, not only than Mr. Ernest Jones, the chartist laureate, but also than all the chartist orators throughout the country, and the whole of the scattered forces of democracy.

Notes

[1] The italics are throughout our own.

[2] The Cromwells and the Cobdens.

John B. Mitchell

SOURCE: "Aesthetic Problems of the Development of the Proletarian-Revolutionary Novel in 19th-Century Britain," in *Zeitschrift für Anglistik und Amerikanistik,* Vol. 11, No. 3, 1963, pp. 248-64.

[The following excerpt offers a Marxist analysis of the tension between aesthetic value and political purpose in Chartist fiction, with an extended discussion of Thomas Wheeler's Sunshine and Shadow.*]*

What strikes one when analysing working-class literature in Britain prior to the appearance of our first mature proletarian novel, *The Ragged Trousered Philanthropists,* in the 1900s, is the gap in aesthetic achievement between the lyrical poetry and the imaginative prose. The poetry of Ernest Jones, Massey, Linton, Robert Brough, Francis Adams, Jim Connell, William Morris, Tom Maguire, etc. preserves and continues the best in the revolutionary-romantic tradition and at times attains and even surpasses the achievements of contemporary bourgeois poets; the *novels* of Jones, Wheeler, Bramsbury and others, on the other hand, while making tremendously important historical contributions to the subject-matter of the novel, are, aesthetically, on an immeasurably lower level than the poetry (in the case of Jones written by the same man!) or the contemporary bourgeois novel.

I have both read and heard certain attempts at explaining this. Our Marxist critics often attribute the early rise to pre-eminence of the lyrical genres by the fact that lyrical poetry, by its nature, is *tactical,* able quickly and effectively to deal with the day-to-day questions as they arise, to enter directly into the struggle. While this is doubtlessly *one* reason for the dominance of the lyrical genres (though I think not the only one) it does not explain why the novel *failed* to develop earlier than the imperialist era. After all, by the end of the forties, when the best Chartist poetry appeared, the modern proletariat had already been in existence for decades and had gathered a rich and varied fund of experience, more than enough to provide both the basis and the need for the novel as a *strategic* literary genre. In conversation I have often been presented with the argument that in poetry the workers already had a long popular-democratic and revolutionary-romantic tradition to build on, that verse by its very nature is far nearer to the popular folk-culture and therefore does not need the relatively high level of literacy and formal cultural background needed both for the production and reception of novels. There is no doubt some truth in the first part of this argument, but even here one should be careful—after all there were the popular democratic novels of the utopian socialists at the end of the 18th century, and there was the great tradition of the 'bourgeois' novel (which Dr. Arnold Kettle has shown to be in many profound ways anti-bourgeois[1]) from Defoe to Dickens, which could then have provided a fruitful basis as it did in fact later for Robert Tressell. As for the second part of the above statement, Marx and Engels again and again pointed to the rich and varied cultural activities of the workers in their clubs, discussion groups and unious where the newest developments in culture and science were picked up with a fearlessness which put the bourgeoisie to shame. One last example. In discussion with colleagues in the English Institute in Berlin I have been told that the reason why Jones and his 19th-century successors did not write good novels was because they looked upon the novel form only as a convenient dress for their philosophical and political ideas. True! but it is really begging the question—which is *why* did they have this narrow formalistic relationship to the novel.

I propose that it was because of the still relative poverty of their grasp of the new working-class reality as a relatively permanent, historically 'right', humanly valid mode of human existence; that is, that intimate, positive aesthetic subject-object relationship between the worker as subject and existing working-class reality as object, which would have forced the appearance of true novels as the dialectical unity of a special kind of aesthetic content and the corresponding kind of aesthetic form, did not come into existence until the era of imperialism. (See the almost simultaneous 'break-

through' of the proletarian-revolutionary novel in the works of Gorki, Nexö, Tressell, etc.)

What do we mean by the aesthetic subject and object and the *relation* between the two? Hans Koch, in his *Marxism and Aesthetics* explains it thus:—

Koch follows Anton Burov[2] in emphasizing that since art is a relatively independent branch of the human consciousness it, like science, philosophy, etc., must have its own specific object-of-knowledge in reality. Koch, while agreeing that 'man' (as a concrete, all-sided totality) is the main aesthetic object-of-knowledge, takes a wider view, within this context, than Burov. He says that the whole of reality is the aesthetic object of art, not any certain group of phenomena. But at the same time he emphasizes that it is a certain *aspect* of the whole of reality, its phenomena seen from a special point of view. All processes, relationships, phenomena are the object of art, not as processes, etc. *as such,* but in their *Bezug auf die Menschen*[3], in their importance, meaning, value (or vice versa) for man, as a concrete, all-sided subject under concrete historical conditions. Basing himself on the thesis put forward by Hegel and developed by Marx (*Economic and Philosophical Manuscripts*) that every product of human labour, as well as being a use-value or an exchange-value, represents an externalisation or objectification of man's specific human quality (*Vergegenständlichung der menschlichen Wesenskräfte*[4]), an expression of the historical level of his human universality, Koch defines this last aspect of phenomena as the 'channel' through which the aesthetic relationship between man and his world functions. Nor should this be seen narrowly as applying only to the direct products of social man; as man in his historical development comes to press the whole of nature more and more universally into his service, so more and more sectors of reality come directly or indirectly to take on the stamp of man, to present him with an 'open book' of his own human powers and potentials, his universality. As an example Koch shows that in man's dawn the stars and other heavenly bodies did not seem beautiful to him and only became so when he entered into a conscious, positive relation with them—for instance, to find his way through deserts or to foretell the dates of the Nile floods. They became objects of aesthetic curiosity, therefore, when they began "to give practical and objective expression to the strength, power and ability of the human race"[5]. Thus sectors of reality which were at best neutral and often seemingly presenting an alien, independent, threatening power *against* man, came with time to be objects of aesthetic curiosity and appreciation.

From the foregoing it is clear that it is not enough for a phenomenon to exist *objectively* as a 'manifestation of man's essential human qualities': "But that there is an object there for the subject is not enough; there must also be a subject there for the object in order to transform the latter from a potential to an actual object of aesthetic appreciation. The object needs the subject, as the Sleeping Beauty needed the prince's kiss, in order to awake into reality."[6] Koch continues: the situation of man in class society, and above all in industrial capitalist society, means that huge sectors of natural and social reality remain only potential aesthetic objects for man. Alienation in its different forms of existence creates a distorting lense between man and large areas of reality making them appear neutral or turning them into something against man, and, what is important, not only against him but against him in the form of alien, uncontrollable, enemy forces.

Now the novel as a form of aesthetic reflection of man in society, with its peculiarly close, intimate, 'empirical', universal and (at least under the conditions of its birth) positive relationship between the subject (the writer and the reader) and the object (existing man in existing society), demands, I propose, much more than the lyrical genres, an extremely high degree of realisation on the part of the aesthetic subject of the *human validity,* the importance *'for* man' of the sector of human reality seen as aesthetic object—despite all contradictions and difficulties in which this object, seen on the 'short-term' social time-scale, may be caught up.

Thus, for the novel to arise in the first place man's attitude to himself must be one of *humanism.* There was no novel in the Middle Ages because the prevalent attitude to man was anti-humanist. It was only when, on the basis of the huge strides made in the sphere of material production, man began to doubt if he was indeed a worthless worm, hopelessly crushed by his burden of sin, began to doubt if the point of reference of true validity and worth indeed lay not in the realm of man but in the supernatural realms of the Catholic religion, when he began to explain, judge, evaluate man in terms of *man,* and not of God, when he began to recognize his own essential human qualities and universality for what they really were, only then could the "curiosity about men and women"[7], the interest in the 'howness' as well as the 'whatness' of human character and action, which is a pre-requisite of the novel, arise. Fox points out that Chaucer and Boccaccio, at the dawn of the Renaissance, showed first this most important feature of the novelist.

Thus, for a *popular* tradition in the novel to exist, the novelist must see the common people, to a lesser or greater degree as, even in their existing form, in the midst of their misery and degradation, humanly valid, in the last resort containing within themselves the only ultimate yardsticks of human value. In a word, modifying the above definition of humanism, the truly popular novelist must express a *popular Humanism.* This strategic belief in and self-confidence of the common

people is, to a varying degree, present in the novels of Defoe, Fielding and Dickens. It is the central core of what Arnold Kettle defines as the decisive element in Dickens's greatness—his "popular sensibility"[8]: "My faith in the people governing is, on the whole, infinitesimal; my faith in the People governed, is, on the whole, illimitable."[9] In our connection, as Kettle points out, the capital 'P' for the second 'people' is very significant. Kettle uses the word 'sensibility' rather than, say, 'philosophy' very consciously. The above statement of Dickens's is shown as the organised intellectual statement of a popular point of view which is not confined to his *ideas* (in fact it sometimes contradicts these ideas) but is the essential quality of his whole sensibility as a totality of his intellectual, emotional, moral and sensual perspectives and attitudes. And it is the sensibility that is decisive for an artist—"the important thing about an artist is not his opinions (on that level) but his *sensibility,* his all-round apprehension and comprehension of things."[10] The very nature of art itself bears out this statement; if we accept that art addresses itself to man as a totality of his intellectual, emotional, moral and sensual aspects, then we must accept that the process of creation also works along the same unified totality of 'channels'. Marx points out that man recognizes a phenomenon as a 'manifestation of man's essential human qualities' with his whole sensibility: "Thus man is affirmed in the objective world not only in the act of thinking, but with *all* his senses."[11]

Therefore it was not enough for the artist on the side of the workers to be 'for the people', to affirm their aims and aspirations at the conscious level of his views (though this was enough, I propose, to 'carry' the lyrical *romantic* genres); to be a true proletarian novelist, to be *driven* to write novels by an inexhaustible intellectual, emotional, moral and sensual curiosity about the actual, concrete, existing life of the working class, this reality had to be apprehended by the aesthetic subject as the chief social 'manifestation of man's essential human qualities' at the level of his *whole* sensibility, at the effortless level of 'second nature'. I propose that this kind of mature, intimate, *positive* aesthetic subject-object relationship between the worker as artist and existing, actual working-class reality, despite all its over-layers of degradation, only matured with the general maturing of the international revolutionary proletariat in the age of imperialism, that only then did a true, mature working-class sensibility, that is a proletarian Humanism *in our sense,* become relatively fully developed.

Dickens, as Kettle points out, did not represent a working-class sensibility or Humanism (using the term in our modified sense of working-class=humanity), but a *popular* sensibility. Dickens expresses the point of view of the London plebean masses—a conglomeration of small-traders, dwarf-bourgeoisie, hawkers, semi-proletarian elements, craftsmen, etc., i. e. a form of popular life which in comparison to the industrial proletariat already in existence in the north, represented an archaic society whose days were already numbered. Dickens, whose London novels live through their popular point of view, did not understand and partly feared the new People in the north (see *Hard Times*). The social basis for a fully valid tradition of the popular novel of the Dickensian type was finally destroyed with the collapse of the 'old' popular London way of life in the 1860s. The new stage in the popular tradition would have to be built on the strategic self-confidence of the revolutionary proletariat. We have already mentioned the names of certain English proletarian-revolutionary novelists in the 19th century. These writers were unable to pick up where Dickens had left off. This was first achieved by Tressell in the 1900s. *Objectively,* of course, the proletariat, with its rich history and experience, was already in the 19th century a potential aesthetic object of unparalleled richness and complexity. But the worker-writer as aesthetic subject was not, it would seem, yet ready to give this 'Sleeping Beauty' the Prince's kiss which would awaken it into life in the form of the novel. For the worker in both the great periods of proletarian literary activity in the 19th century (Chartism and the second half of the 1880s) the forces *alienating* him from a proper grasp of himself and the life of his class as, even in its existing form, aesthetically an object 'for man', were still stronger than his developing healthy grasp of its true human validity and importance. Certainly no other class had entered history under less favourable conditions for recognizing themselves as the chief social 'manifestation of man's essential human qualities'. Engels puts his finger on the crux of the matter: "In European countries, it took the working class years and years before they fully realized the fact that they formed a distinct and, under the existing social conditions, a permanent class of modern society"[12].

I would like now to examine a typical novel of the Chartist period and relate its central aesthetic weaknesses to certain concrete conditions of the time which hindered the development of a mature aesthetic subject-object relationship, a proletarian *Humanism* in our sense. With only slight modifications my remarks on this novel apply to all our proletarian-revolutionary novels prior to *The Ragged Trousered Philanthropists*.

The novel I want to deal with here is *Sunshine and Shadows* by the worker-writer Thomas Martin Wheeler, a leading Chartist militant, who in the years following 1848, when he wrote this book, was moving rapidly towards the left wing of the movement dominated by the Chartist leader and Wheeler's fellow-writer Ernest Jones. *Sunshine and Shadows* appeared in the Chartist newspaper *The Northern Star* from 1849 to 1850.

This is one of a group of works by Wheeler and Jones written after the cold douche of 1848 which represent the highest achievement by the Chartists in the field of the novel. As a result of the sobering effect of the defeat of 1848, which revealed the strength and relative 'permanence' of both capitalism and the proletariat, a new urge is noticeable to analyse more painstakingly the existing society in its own terms. The publication of *The Manifesto of the Communist Party,* showing the historical destiny of the working class as the continuers of humanity, was also an important inspiration for the sharp move in these years from romanticism to the *beginnings* of realism in the proletarian novel.

The story of *Sunshine and Shadows* is as follows: Arthur Morton and Walter North are school friends. Arthur is from a worker's family; Walter's father is a 'self-made man', a successful wine merchant. Walter has a sister, Julia, a rose among the philistine thorns. Arthur is apprenticed to a Liberal newspaper after he leaves school. At this period the world appears to him as a topsy-turvy mass of arbitrary injustice. Arthur is a rebel, but his revolt is vague. At the end of his apprenticeship he goes to London and is appalled at the luxury and misery which rub shoulders there. He cannot find a job anywhere. Meanwhile Walter has succeeded to his father's business. If Arthur's conscience has been awakened, Walter has smothered his. He has two ambitions—to marry into the aristocracy and to get into Parliament. He forces his sister Julia to marry old Sir Jasper Baldwin, the aristocratic governor of one of the Windward Islands, to further the first of these ends.

Starvation drives Arthur to Birmingham where he arrives at the height of the early Chartist agitation. Here he comes in contact with ideas that give concrete shape to his own vague discontent. He becomes a Chartist. In showing Arthur's motives here to be of the highest, Wheeler is (as throughout the book) polemicising against the calumny showered on the Chartist workers by the propagandists of the ruling class. Arthur is under the impression that the pure reasonableness of the Charter will sweep all before it.

As a result of internal bickering, the National Convention in London collapses and Birmingham now becomes the centre of the progressive core of the Convention. At a mass rally in the Bull Ring Arthur makes his first public political speech—which we are told was impassioned—and he is filled with joy at his ability to move the listeners. The police attack the Convention. The Chartists hit back and fire houses in the Bull Ring. Arthur disapproves but, inevitably, is arrested and charged with arson. He manages to escape and flees to America. On board ship he is deeply impressed by the beauty of the sea. During a storm Arthur's courage is contrasted to the abject terror of the rich passengers. Shipwreck. Arthur is picked up by the *Esmeralda* bound for the West Indies. On board he meets Julia on her way to her husband. They fall in love. Once in the West Indies, Arthur soon realizes that the freed slaves have only exchanged one kind of slavery for another. Julia languishes in the prescribed romantic manner in her luxurious house-prison. In a delirium she speaks of her love for Arthur and is overheard by Sir Jasper. During an absence of Sir Jasper's Arthur arrives to find her dying. A 'pathetic' but perfectly 'innocent' love scene follows. Arthur is thrown into jail by Sir Jasper—which gives Wheeler the chance to declare the class nature of the law. Julia dies and Sir Jasper suffers a Gradgrindian change of heart.

Meanwhile Walter North has, by devious devices, secured, in Clarence Fitzherbert, the aristocratic wife he had been aiming at and soon procures his seat in Parliament through shady dealings with the Anti-Corn Law League. Having gained his life ambitions Walter sinks into comfortable obscurity—but he fails to win happiness. Here Wheeler declares the ineffectuality of Parliament in the grip of party monopoly—it should be filled with revolutionary representatives of the people.

Sir Jasper releases Arthur and they become something like 'brothers in grief'. Arthur settles in America. He is disappointed; it is not the Promised Land but there still appears to be more hope for it than for England.

1842. Arthur is in England again, in the industrial north, which is in the grip of slump, misery and revolutionary ferment. The unrest boils over. The middle-class Anti-Corn Law League try to use the mass movement to frighten the landed aristocracy into conceding their demands. To this end they convince the workers round Manchester to start a general strike. In the midst of all this the Chartist leadership remains passive. The masses soon shake themselves free of middle-class control and turn the strike into a weapon for the winning of the Six Points. A thoroughly frightened middle class loose the full force of the state against the workers. The Chartist Convention meets too late and the movement is crushed.

Arthur is sent as an envoy from the northern leaders to London. There he meets the great negro Chartist leader Cuffay. In London he falls in love with a Chartist working girl called Mary Graham. She is beautiful, without false modesty, deeply political and intelligent, but she is more suited to the domestic fireside than to the public platform. Now follow two years of idyllic family life complete with cottage, lawn, geraniums and cultural evenings round the fireside. Calamity smashes the idyll. Slump and unemployment result in the death of their oldest child and a serious illness for Mary. Arthur is driven to desperation. He attacks a rich man in the street and robs him. This money,

which he told Mary he found, sets them up again a little, but his peace of mind, like that of Walter (the man he robbed, now Lord Maxwell), is lost for ever.

Winter 1847. Arthur is now much less romantic—a hardened working-class politician. Yet he still believes (like Wheeler) in the power of practical experiment and example. Thus he supports the utopian National Land Company. According to Wheeler the Company failed, not because the basic idea was wrong, but because of the imperfections of the people involved.

1847-1848. Mass upheaval. The Chartist leaders are again split and fail to act at the decisive moment. A witch hunt follows. Arthur is given the job of touring the north to gauge the temper of the people. He sees the failure of the land settlements but still believes them to be the yeast that will activate the surrounding mass of agricultural labourers. The Whigs use spies to provoke the Chartist remnants to secret plotting and then to denounce them. Their heroleader, Ernest Jones, is flung into jail. Arthur escapes by the skin of his teeth and flees abroad, where he lives on a see-saw of wild anticipation and black despair. Walter North on the other hand has a more even existence—unrelieved boredom. Arthur's wife and child keep up their spirits and are supported in England by the democratic grapevine.

Here, for the first time, we are dealing with the Chartist movement under its own name. The basic content of the novel is the actual history of Chartism from the first National Petition to the last. Its general themes are for the most part those already introduced by Ernest Jones (in his case indirectly):—

1. An evaluation of the whole of the Chartist experience with special reference to its mistakes and weaknesses.

2. A polemic against the slanderous picture of the Chartists given in bourgeois propaganda in general and the bourgeois novel in particular.

3. A polemic against the ideas of class collaboration which were then being peddled more and more by the ruling class.

4. The open championing of revolutionary struggle.

5. The problem of human happiness under capitalism.

When Wheeler wrote *Sunshine and Shadows* his idealist Owenite past still exercised a certain influence on his ideas. Yet because he was (unlike Jones) himself a worker who had *experienced* the fate of the workers and the whole rise and fall of the movement 'on his own back', he was able to make an original contribution to the development of the proletarian-revolutionary novel which, despite his ultimate aesthetic failure, must be taken into account.

In certain important points *Sunshine and Shadows* might be said to sketch out in rough the whole general shape which the thematic of the international proletarian-revolutionary novel was to take.

Like Jones, much of Wheeler's attention is given to a critique of the weaknesses of the Chartist movement which led to its defeat. But whereas Jones concentrated on the theoretical weaknesses and confusion of the Chartist workers and the resulting squabbles which paved the way for the success of agents-provocateur, Wheeler concentrates on the strategy and tactics of the *leadership,* the National Convention and the National Charter Association, which failed to give the revolutionary masses adequate leadership at the moments of crisis. Wheeler makes it clear that "Whatever the reasons for the ultimate defeat of Chartism, lack of fighting spirit among the masses was not one of them"[13]. Thus Wheeler is the first to bring in as a general theme the policy and activity of the working-class party.

But perhaps his greatest historical contribution was to create the broad prototype of the proletarian hero of the future. In contrast to Jones, where the main interest still lies with the bourgeois anti-hero, Wheeler makes the career of the worker-hero the backbone of his book. At the outset Arthur Morton is an ordinary class-conscious British worker with many of the typical illusions. From here we follow his intellectual and spiritual development in conjunction with his broadening social experience and his activity in the developing mass movement. In relating the human development of his hero in this way to the development of the organised mass political movement, Wheeler is the first real forerunner of the modern proletarian novel.

Arthur's character is to a large extent a polemic against the slanderous picture of the revolutionary worker-leader as a sub-human animal. Wheeler it was who first, in Arthur, gives a true picture of the working-class militant of the day. When Arthur makes his first public speech in the Bull Ring he is shown as being inspired by the highest emotions. As the incorruptible voice and teacher of the masses he is the forerunner of a whole series of proletarian propagandists in our literature of which Tressell's Owen is perhaps the outstanding example.

Another aspect of Wheeler's polemic is his attempt to show Arthur as a deeply *human,* many-sided personality. There is some attempt therefore to show Arthur not only in his directly political 'public' aspects, but also in his 'private', inner-life, in his love for a woman, his high sensitivity to beauty and the poetry of wild nature.

In his portrait of the working-class woman, too, Wheeler is a pioneer. His Mary Graham is a huge step forward from Jones who is at his weakest in his female characters. Jones's women stand outside everyday problems and struggles as something to be romantically worshipped whatever their class position may be. Wheeler gives his women class characteristics. Mary Graham is politically conscious to a high degree, intelligent and with a role (even if subordinate) to play alongside man in the struggle. She is an ancestor of the two Paulines in *The Revolution in Tanner's Lane,* of the woman hero in Morris's *Pilgrims of Hope* and many others. Above all, in her steadfastness, intelligence, realism and devotion to her family she already sketches in all the chief characteristics of Nora Owen in *The Ragged Trousered Philanthropists.*

These are the important historical contributions we owe to Thomas Martin Wheeler. But when all is said and done they are no more than contributions of undigested raw material. A further advance to the final conquering of the realistic novel was blocked by the insurmountable fact that these early writers were not yet really writing as novelists at all. The initial starting point for Wheeler as for Jones is that of the political publicist. His object of study is the Chartist movement, its mistakes, strengths and weaknesses *as a movement per se.* He starts from this point of view and invents his artistic framework, his characters and situations as *illustrations* of this. As Plechanov says—"If instead of depicting character the writer makes use of logical arguments, or his characters are invented only to drive home an argument, then he is not an artist but a pamphleteer."[14] This was to a greater or lesser extent true of all the proletarian-revolutionary novels in England before Tressell. Tressell's statement in his preface to *The Ragged Trousered Philanthropists* that his book "is not a treatise or essay, but a novel" the main object being "to write a readable story full of human interest and based on the happenings of everyday life" represents nothing less than an aesthetic revolution in the proletarian-revolutionary novel. This becomes clear if we compare it with what the Soviet scholar Dogel says about Wheeler: "As with the other Chartists Wheeler's views on the relationship between form and content in a work of art were unsound, and this fact reacted on the structure of his novel. In Wheeler's opinion any work of art consists of two elements existing independently of each other; the basis of the work is made up of 'actual facts', 'truth', while the 'realm of romance', the 'artistic fantasy', serves only to ornament these facts so as to make them interesting and attractive for the readers. The 'facts' contain the educative, didactic core of the book, its ideological-political content, whereas the 'fantasy' acts only as a frame, as an artistic form for the presentation of the ideas, the 'facts'."[15]

As in Jones the artistic form remains separate from the content because the content itself is not yet an aesthetic content!

Now because Jones, Wheeler and the others were still using art (at least in the novel) as 'sugar for the pill', it was only natural that they should turn to the kind of sugar which they thought would sell their message most easily, that is, the kind of fashionable techniques which were generally accepted as 'artistic'. Thus they tended to attach themselves to the fashionable love, mystery and adventure plot of the third-rate pulp literature of the day rather than to those elements in the great realist tradition which could have provided them with a fruitful foundation. Although Wheeler was freer of 'romantic' elements than Jones, we see the same tendency in the way he takes over certain techniques from the contemporary petty-bourgeois moralising novel. This is above all true of his 'philosophical' digressions, his 'Purple Passages' narrated in a grandiose 'poetic' prose. Thus Arthur's thoughts appear as 'noble' apostrophes beginning 'O thou Ocean' (or 'London', etc.). Because the basic material itself, as apprehended by Wheeler, does not contain the Beautiful it is *added on* in this way 'from the outside', in the form alone.

Under these circumstances Wheeler's characters (despite his attempt to give us Arthur 'in the round') are flat types, differentiated from each other only at the level of their political opinions and social-economic activity. We are told much about the 'what' of what they do, but almost nothing about the 'how'.

Thus there can be no question yet of the worker-writer producing a novel from a 'spontaneous', positive aesthetic *need*—the need to express the life of the workers as, despite all alienation and misery, a positive, valid *life,* as the only social 'manifestation of man's essential human qualities', and *from this point of view* to depict the capitalist class as Anti-Humanity hindering the free development of this way of life whose potentials *we already grasp in the concrete form of their beginnings in capitalist society.* Wheeler wishes to show that man's life as at present constituted is *totally* unnatural, that it must be wholly eradicated and a return made to a natural life based on the free cultivation of the land. To this end (or rather because of this poverty of his grasp of the true, positive nature of working class life) his picture of this life is one-sided, flat, and therefore abstract—a picture confined, after all, to its 'public', 'official' level—an unrelieved Hell-on-earth of misery, oppression, unemployment, starvation and death, relieved only by the desperate efforts of the workers to free themselves at the 'public', 'official' level. We get some idea of what they seek to free themselves *from,* but *what,* in human terms, they seek to *free* is totally absent. We do not experience their rich, manifold,

indestructible, creative *life,* illuminated from the inside.

The best socialist realists and popular writers, from Dickens, through Tressell, Gorki and Barbusse to Fadeyev, Bruno Apitz and the rest, have always been able to recognize under the misery, alienation and degradation of the present such 'moments of synthesis', where we glimpse in the concrete, *existing* features of popular or proletarian life and struggle in the broadest, most all-sided sense, the essential features the 'first buds' of the future life of free humanity. The greatness of a book like *The Young Guard* lies to no small degree in the way the author does not only show the kind of existence the young Soviet patriots are fighting *against* plus the fight at the highest most organised level, but, through revealing to us 'moments of synthesis' in the midst of the Fascist occupation, when the young people meet together, where the forces of oppression are for the moment pushed to the side-lines, when the lads and girls fleetingly live their own kind of lives on their own terms, we are made aware of the kind of life, in concrete human terms, that they are fighting *for.* In this way their struggle at the highest level gains tremendously in pathos, in emotional content; their heroism at this level is seen as the logical conclusion of their all-sided humanity.

Marx was able to recognize, in the life and activity of the proletariat, even in the Chartist period, the first buds of the future of humanity: "When communist *workmen* associate with one another, theory, propaganda, etc. is their first end. But at the same time, as a result of this association, they acquire a new need— the need for society—and what appears as a means becomes an end. You can observe this practical process in its most splendid results whenever you see French socialist workers together. Such things as smoking, drinking, eating, etc. are no longer means of contact or means that bring together. Company, association and conversation . . . are enough for them; the brotherhood of man is no mere phrase with them, but a fact of life."[16]

As a result of their failure to grasp this forward pointing beauty in its concrete, manifold, universal, everyday forms, the worker-heroes and the struggle itself, in these 19th-century novelists, tend to be flat, abstract, cut off from the real vitality of the workers and therefore lacking in sufficient emotional content.

It is a sign of the immaturity of a working-class Humanism in our sense in the Chartist era that they do not yet have a clear, continuous grasp of the class struggle as 'us' *versus* 'them', as Humanity *versus* Anti-Humanity. It was this immaturity which allowed Owenite utopian ideas of a higher humanity above the bounds of classes to hold their ground in the thinking of the workers for so long. The proletarian novel was not yet ready to do as the popular realist Dickens had done—to look degradation in the face and see Humanity there.[17] They still recognized, it would seem, certain points of 'general-human' reference outside the bounds of the working class, a supra-class morality in relation to which the worker-writer felt obliged to *defend* the proletariat to some 'general-human' public. Thus, much of Wheeler's time is taken up with a defence of the moral excellence of the workers against the slander of the propagandists of the ruling class. For this reason the element of self-criticism which these books certainly contain remains a *tactical* criticism of their methods and organisation, not a deep-going self-criticism of the worker as a Man.

In his moral defence of the workers, therefore Wheeler actually *suppresses* the problems of spiritual and mental degradation, which, although not the main part, is an important part of the truth about the masses under capitalism.

This assumption of a common bond of humanity, of oppressors and oppressed being equally crippled in their happiness by the cursed system, affected also the picture given of the ruling class and the general shape of the plot. Writing towards the end of his life Engels once said of the theory of the class struggle in his early *Condition of the Working Class*: "Thus great stress is laid on the dictum that Communism is not a mere party doctrine of the working class, but a theory compassing the emancipation of society at large, including the capitalist class, from its present narrow conditions. This is true enough in the abstract, but absolutely useless, and sometimes worse in practice."[18] This reflected the weakness of the early proletariat as a whole in their grasp of the true nature of their class as Humanity with a capital 'H'. Whereas Tressell, with his view of the bosses as Anti-Humanity 'didn't care a damn' whether the capitalists were happy or unhappy, but showed them primarily in their social-political and economic activity, the Chartist novelists tended, defensively, to concentrate on the moral-spiritual degradation of the bosses and their inability to find happiness in spite of their wealth. Thus we have again, as in the case of the workers, a one-sided, undynamic view of the ruling class, a view which could not really help the proletariat as it should to acquaint themselves with the really dangerous features of their enemy. We are even expected to feel a certain amount of pity for Walter North and Sir Jasper, miserable in the midst of their riches.

In the field of the plot this assumption of a common humanity, of a 'pan-human' morality and emotions leads naturally to the type of plot which involves members of the two enemy classes in *personal* relationships. In Wheeler's *Sunshine and Shadows* Arthur Morton, the worker, and Walter North, the future capitalist, start off as school friends where the quali-

ties of the one are shown as complementing the opposite qualities of the other. This kind of thing, which puts the members of the two classes in a *personal* relationship untypical of the *cash-nexus* relationship of reality, is Wheeler's way of saying that, where the narrowing and twisting pressures of capitalism are absent (here in the school), the differing human qualities which (according to Wheeler) are possessed by the middle class ('worldy influence', 'business habits') and by the workers ('strong sense', 'sturdy independence' and 'generous enthusiasm') come together to form a unity of complementary opposites, which guarantees real freedom to both sides. Later, when the former friends take their places in the 'wide world', as exploiter and exploited, this non-antagonistic contradiction turns into an antagonistic one and the happiness of both is ultimately ruined.

The almost universal appearance of the, in reality, highly untypical 'love-triangle' involving a worker, a man from the ruling class and a woman (from either class) in our pre-Tressell proletarian novel is also, I propose, conditioned by this defensive, moral approach. In the present case there is the Arthur—Julia—Sir Jasper theme plus the 'complication' of Walter's behaviour to his sister. By this means the actions and motives of the three principal characters are measured and contrasted against the same woman-yardstick. Up to Tressell, where, for the first time, man's relationship to his labour comes into its own as (alongside the 'love-relationship') the chief expression of the level of his essential human qualities, the English working-class novel (like the bourgeois novel) relied almost entirely on the 'love-relationship' to epitomize the human quality of their heroes. Thus the highly developed humanity of Arthur Morton is epitomized in his pure and poetic love for Julia. This is contrasted to the behaviour towards her of her brother and husband; the first uses her as a mere pawn to further his selfish ambitions, the second to satisfy his lust and his pride. She is the common measuring rod against which the morality of the ruling class and the working class are compared and contrasted.

How is this lack of a real aesthetic content, this lack of the inexhaustible curiosity about working men and women, which must be the basis of the true proletarian novel, this lack of a mature aesthetic subject-object relationship to be explained in the light of the actual state of development of the working class and society as a whole in the Chartist era?

Dona Torr defines the character of Chartism thus: "The important thing . . . is that Chartism coincided precisely with the point of transition between the prehistory and the history of the British working class."[19] Morton and Tate have pointed out that huge sections of the Chartist army were composed of desperate hand weavers: "They reflected in a most striking way the fact that the British working class was still a new class, still in the process of formation *and still often hoping for a reversal of history by which the handworker could regain his lost prosperity*[20] (italics mine; J. B. M.).

And indeed, this new proletariat, still in the process of formation, entered upon its career under conditions peculiarly inauspicious for the development of a proletarian Humanism in our modified sense. The life of the masses in the first two thirds of the 18th century could hardly be called enviable, yet the proletariat of the early 19th century often looked back to it with a nostalgic longing. The industrial revolution and the social revolution which accompanied it replaced the old People with the Proletariat, washed away the old life with its established traditions and familiar land-marks.

Objectively the life of the masses in the '30s and '40s of the 19th century was indeed more miserable than it had been before and, perhaps, has been since. There is no need here to go into the frightful conditions under which the new proletariat had to exist. They are well-known. The 1840s were a period when young industrial capitalism really seemed to be staggering on its feet under the weight of its glaring contradictions. Thus the material misery, as such and alone, was not the only cause of the spiritual misery and confusion of the masses at that time. Their material misery seemed part of a whole world gone crazy, stood on its head. Their fate seemed to be in the grip of an *inhuman power over which men had lost control.* One must remember in this connection that the classical defensive and offensive organisations of the proletariat were, throughout the period, at best fleeting and immature. The Hammonds say: "The men and women of Lancashire and Yorkshire felt of this new power that it was inhuman, that it disregarded all their instincts and sensibilities, that it brought into their lives an *inexorable force,* destroying and scattering their customs, their traditions, their freedom, their ties of family and home, their dignity and character as men and women"[21] (italics mine).

In this crazy world everything was turned into its opposite. The more wealth the people produced (and there had never been so much material wealth in the country before), the poorer they themselves became, the harder and longer they worked the more surely they were doomed to be thrown onto the streets by the inexplicable economic crashes which burst in on capitalist and worker alike with a diabolical regularity. Last but not least the vaunted freedom of contract had turned into the most complete and inescapable slavery of modern times. The proletariat had been stripped of all property except their labour power, and even this was only in the most formal sense their own. No longer had they even the semblance of freedom in the labour-process itself. For the first time in modern society, alienation had encompassed the actual process of production, man's central human life-activity. Human industry, which Marx defines as "the *open* book of *man's essential powers*"[22], the central field for the manifestation of man's essential human powers, was now a *shut* book to the producers themselves. Thus this great avenue for recognizing their human validity, for self-expression, and therefore for the old art was closed to them and had become an endless torture. Alienation now seemed universal, the workers were only just beginning to develop their own organised revolutionary activity as a defence against it and counter to it. Thus they were not yet able to see their own peculiar type of human power and universality externalised, 'thingified' in their great political-cultural achievements in union organisation, etc. This was only to occur universally and dramatically in the age of imperialism.

While thus the people had not yet had enough time to develop a new type of understanding of their own nature and worth, the attitude of the ruling class to them served to underline the feeling that they were a helot population out-side the bounds of the fully human community: "For the first time there existed a vast proletariat, with no property but its labour, and therefore in the eyes of its rulers bound by no ties to the society in which it lived except by the ties that discipline could create."[23]

This was epitomized in the new Poor Law, which summed up, in its ferocious denial of all social responsibility for the distressed, in its branding of the poor man as a criminal, the total repudiation by the ruling class of the People as Humanity.

As we have said, the proletariat was not yet really aware of its new type of revolutionary human validity. The science of historical materialism which laid bare the necessary but passing nature of capitalist industrialism and the historical perspectives of the proletariat in which the right of the workers to the title of Humanity was proved beyond all gainsay, only appeared at the very end of the period. Thus they still tended to think of human validity in the traditional terms of property. As Engels remarks, these early workers had an "inherent respect for the sacredness of property"[24]. In this way the fact that the bourgeoisie 'locked them out' from the 'human family' on this very basis certainly had a strong demoralizing effect. Thus the world as a whole, including the proletariat itself and all it stood for, was looked upon as an *alien, independent, threatening power,* something to be abolished lock, stock, and barrel, in all its aspects.

For the Chartist working class, with little understanding of the nature of capitalism and the essential nature of their own class, the whole of their world seemed to them one huge misunderstanding, a 'mistake' of history, something totally 'against man'. Furthermore, it was so illogical that sooner or later the patent common-sense and humanity of the Charter must be recognized by all and the whole silly system swept away. It was only temporary, a passing night-mare of which the proletariat, in all its ramifications, was just one part among many and should, like the rest, disappear without trace. Thus, although, in Chartism, the pre-1850 proletariat had a working-class Idea to set against the bourgeois Idea, it was a partly utopian Idea which misunderstood and underestimated the present and future role of the working class in history. In their hypothetical revolutionary solutions to the Great Mistake, their eyes were too often turned away from the proletariat as it actually was—the chief and central social 'manifestation of man's essential human qualities'.

Under these conditions of 'alienation from themselves' the 'curiosity about men and women', which Ralph Fox saw as the most important pre-supposition for the realistic novel, our complex, intimate, positive aesthetic subject-object relationship based on the recognition in the object of some aspect or aspects of man's power and universality, could not yet mature. A fully-fledged proletarian-revolutionary novel was therefore a historical impossibility in the age of Chartism.

Notes

1 *Essays on Socialist Realism and the British Cultural Tradition,* Arena Publications (no date); Kettle: *The Progressive Tradition in Bourgeois Culture,* London.

2 Anton Burov: *Das ästhetische Wesen der Kunst,* Berlin 1958.

3 Hans Koch: *Marxismus und Ästhetik,* Berlin 1961, p. 221, etc.

4 *ibid.,* p. 127, etc. (quoted from Marx).

5 *ibid.,* p. 111.

6 *ibid.,* p. 156. (Translations mine; J. B. M.)

7 Ralph Fox: *The Novel and the People,* London 1948, p. 53.

8 Arnold Kettle: "Dickens and the Popular Tradition," in *ZAA* 1961, No. 3.

9 *ibid.,* p. 237.

10 *ibid.,* p. 230.

11 Marx: *Economic and Philosophical Manuscripts of 1844,* Moscow 1961 (FLPH).

12 Engels: *The Condition of the Working Class in England,* FLPH, Moscow 1953 (Preface to the American Edition 1887).

13 Morton and Tate: *The British Labour Movement,* London 1956, p. 81.

14 Plechanov: *Art and Social Life,* London 1953, p. 183.

15 *Iz Istorii Demokraticheskoi Literaturi v Anglii,* Leningrad 1955, p. 185 (my translation; J. B. M.).

16 Karl Marx: *Economic and Political Manuscripts,* pp. 124-125.

17 *ZAA* 1961, No. 3, p. 244.

18 *Marx and Engels on Britain,* p. 22.

19 Dona Torr: *Tom Mann and his Times,* London 1956, p. 146.

20 *The British Labour Movement,* p. 82.

21 *The Town Labourer,* vol. 1, London 1949, p. 48.

22 Marx: *Economic and Political Manuscripts,* p. 109.

23 *The Town Labourer,* p. 68.

24 Engels: *Condition of the Working Class,* p. 248.

Martha Vicinus

SOURCE: "Chartist Poetry and Fiction: The Development of a Class-Based Literature," in *The Industrial Muse: A Study of Nineteenth Century British Working-Class Literature,* Croom Helm, London, 1974, pp. 94-139.

[*In the following excerpt from a book about nineteenth century British working-class literature, Vicinus provides a survey of Chartist literature, both poetry and fiction.*]

The Chartist movement occupies as significant a place in working-class literature as it does in the history of working people. In literature as in politics, it represented the most imposing attempt by working people to take control of their lives. The Chartists wanted to transform England into a representative democracy where the working-class voice would be heard. Their famous six points were aimed at making it possible for all Britons to participate in the political process. Only then would working people obtain universal suffrage, social justice, a taxation system that did not tax the poor to maintain the rich, and—most important—their dignity. The Chartist promise was so total that for a time it absorbed all other working-class activity; political, trade union, and cultural. From Brighton to Aberdeen, working men and women met weekly to seek the salvation of their class through their Chartist Association; Chartism became a way of life, a rich and varied experience that had a profound impact on its participants. Literature was a valued part of this way of life, and the foremost Chartist writers sought to create a class-based literature, written by and for the people. Their efforts influenced not only working men aspiring to become writers, but also the popular press and such middle-class writers as Charles Kingsley, Thomas Hughes and Dante Rossetti. Out of the political turmoil of Chartism came a new respect for people's literature.

Each wave of Chartist activity created particular demands, and produced distinct types of literature.[1] Over the years came an outpouring of speeches, essays, prison letters, dialogues, short stories, novels, songs, lyrical poems, epics, and later in the century, autobiographies. This variety grew out of many long-developing political and social movements. The language of class had developed in political struggles over the years 1790-1830, and with it a sharp and effective journalism.[2] The language of protest had developed from folk and religious sources, and found its literary outlet in broadsides. These two traditions joined in the propaganda of trade unionists and such groups as the Ten Hours Movement and the Anti-Poor Law agitation. Chartism alone attempted the development of a class literature, expressive of personal aspiration. Protest, politics and individual hope all came together.

Throughout the decade of 1838-48 the bulk of Chartist literature was exhortative and inspirational. . . . The concerns of this chapter are with those writers who had read deeply in the radical literary tradition of England and the Continent and wished to express through their own writings the 'impassioned truth' of Chartist politics. At the same time they hoped to fulfill the aesthetic precepts they had learned from the mainstream of English literature. They were deeply concerned with the relationship between politics and art—whether literature should describe conditions in need of change, or the future brotherhood of man, resulting from changed conditions; whether it should give readers a soothing escape from this life or a foretaste of a better life. Their goal was a new, class-based literature.

Chartist poets articulated the ideals of the movement. According to the times they urged political change or educational improvement. In their poetry they taught men about a just and moral world, while emphasizing the heinousness of existing conditions. When radical change seemed remote, however, writers stressed self-education as a means of ameliorating conditions for the entire working class. Intellectual autobiographies describing the growth of the poet's mind and his coming to terms with himself and society became common by the end of the Chartist period. But the political inheritance was never forgotten, and gave their poetry a wider social context and understanding. These poets will be discussed in part I.

The years 1848-53 were the richest period of working-class creativity until the dialect writers rose to prominence in the 1860s. Throughout England working men published each other's writing, started journals and took steps to strengthen class-oriented literature. The most important development of this period was the rise of fiction as a significant working-class artistic medium. The poets who composed serious verse had reached only a few of the best-educated Chartists; popular fiction, on the other hand, was more widely read by workers. The conclusion drawn by those interested in revitalizing political activity was to combine the idealism of poetry with the attractive plotting and characterization of fiction. The common man was made a hero, and his adventures were drawn from Chartist political and social events. Such fiction proved to be rare throughout the nineteenth century, and was not successfully attempted again until the very end of the century. Part II will discuss the strengths and weaknesses of this fiction of class struggle.

I. The Poetry of Impassioned Truth

The central task of Chartist poets, in contrast to Chartist propagandists and song writers, was to create a new poetic tradition which embodied their political ideals. The essentially private act of creative writing found its rationale in serving the political needs of the people. Indeed, the poet was most himself when he contributed to society poems that would educate, move and enlighten. As early as 1840 the editor of the *Chartist Circular* introduced a series entitled 'The Politics of Poets' with the proclamation 'Poets and their Poetry have, and will continue to exert an extensive influence on the destinies of Mankind.'[3] In working-class circles that pursued most ardently the goals of self- and class-improvement, poets were the acknowledged legislators of morality. It was the duty of every true Chartist writer to contribute to the great task of changing individuals, so they would change society.

These ideas had their roots in the previous generation of Romantic poets. Chartist writers eagerly imitated their subject matter and poetic style. Under the influence of Wordsworth and Keats, Nature was an unadulterated good, 'a poetry that never dies'; in turn the finest poem was like a work of Nature. The political poetry of Byron and Shelley, however, was most popular. Byron's fluid and colloquial style proved an excellent model for writing conversational verse; the mocking prose and verse dialogues between starving workers and the wealthy owners owe much to him. The exposure of hypocrisy and folly, a central theme in Byron, was transmuted by Chartists into descriptions of avarice and misused power. Byron's melodramatic verse and misunderstood heroes were less successfully imitated, often becoming bombastic posturing. Shelley's idealism and faith in human potential were fundamental tenets among all Chartists. He had been able to imbue such familiar, and well defined, abstractions as Liberty and Freedom with a mythic importance beyond specific battles for a free press or universal suffrage. But in the hands of less skilful writers the descriptions of such ideals too often became diffuse, static and even incomprehensible. Effective verse is not necessarily made up of references to the soul, Bright Liberty, tyrannous foes and hopeful tomorrows.

The single most important predecessor of Chartist poets was Ebenezer Elliott, the Corn-Law Rhymer (1781-1849), who paved the way for other 'poets of poverty'.[4] Elliott had been able to establish a very successful iron foundry in Sheffield and to retire to the country with £3,000, but throughout his life he wrote powerful indictments of the rich and their pernicious taxes on corn and other necessities. His descriptions and denunciations of poverty were popular among all classes, and so encouraged other working men to write about subjects closer to their personal experience than Nature. Moreover, Elliott always emphasized the concrete consequences of a particular evil, and not its place on a moral scale. The high price of corn meant forced emigration, overwork and child mortality, and not simply the transgressions of a callous government, as sometimes described by better-off Romantic poets. The virtues of concreteness, however, were offset by the accompanying emotional bombast. Elliott's fervid language and urgent appeals to God were appealing to those making their first attempts at verse. If reading Shelley encouraged personification and capitalizations, Elliott encouraged ranting and exclamation points

Elliott, in spite of his denunciation of Chartism after 1839, was admired as a living example of someone who wrote effective political poetry and who had portrayed sympathetically the sufferings of working people. Chartist poets were constantly reminded of their obligation to portray their own class in a favourable light, since many contemporary poets spoke of the 'unruly mob', or described the poor as naive fools. It was the duty of every working-class writer, as one critic in the *Northern Star* explained, 'never to miss an opportunity of doing honour to the nobility of [his] order.'[5] Ernest Jones took this advice one step further, arguing, 'It is necessary that democratic poets should, in their pages, *elevate* and not endanger the dignity of the democratic character.'[6] The weight of this obligation may explain the general lack of humour among the most ardent poets. They, like Elliott, refused to condone society's more foolish moments, which for them were immoral, unjust or hypocritical. Writing after the death of Chartism, but exemplifying many of its attitudes, Gerald Massey judged Thomas Hood with the lofty conclusion, 'Life is too real, too earnest, too solemn a thing, to be spent in producing or reading such light literature. . . . Earnestness is at the root of greatness and heroism.'[7] Only an earnest literature could educate and inspire.

Chartist poets were given the responsibility of fitting a new subject—working-class ideals—into the traditional forms of English poetry. Unlike . . . Chartist song writers, they were forging a new *written* working-class literature. As pioneers in creating a literature worthy of their people, they embraced the most respected styles of the time. They rarely used song metres or catchy rhymes; the sonnet, the epic and other complicated forms were preferred as more aesthetically important. Cooper wrote his epic, *The Purgatory of Suicides,* in the very difficult Spenserian stanza; it is a *tour de force* that earned him respect among the middle class and admiration among its few working-class readers. It is an extreme example of the problems all Chartist poets faced: how to write appealing and ennobling poetry that was intelligible to the working class. Some, like Cooper, settled for impressing their 'betters'. Most, however, addressed their verse to those educational Chartists anxious to master the riches of English literature. Despite their passionate political message, the difficulty of reading their poetry limited the audience of all Chartist poets. The division between oral and written literature—songs and poetry—was only partially bridged by writers and readers.

I have concentrated in this section on the four best-known writers: W. J. Linton, Ernest Jones, Gerald Massey and Thomas Cooper. Their poetry and writing mirror many of the strengths and difficulties of pioneering a written working-class literature. They were the most skilful in adapting a variety of poetic forms to their political subject matter; their imagery, metre and language could be effective and sophisticated. The four had very different political beliefs and wrote very different poetry, but for a time each was looked upon as an important poetic voice within the Chartist movement. Linton belonged to the radical tradition of the 1820s and early '30s, in which both the middle class and the working-class could co-exist; his political enemies were the aristocracy, the church and privilege. After he was disillusioned with Chartism, he became a republican and was active in supporting Mazzini.[8] Gerald Massey's politics were a diffuse form of revolutionary sentiment, unenlightened by any ideological comprehension. After his initial fervour died, he no longer wrote political poetry. Cooper's life was a series of conversions; although he briefly converted to Chartism and was an ardent leader, he was fundamentally most concerned with his own intellectual needs. Throughout his life he was an active proponent of self-help. Jones alone remained ideologically committed to Chartism. He was the only one of the four who was not self-educated, and he tried the hardest to write verse that was accessible to working-class readers. He used familiar metres, such as the ballad and rhymed couplets, and avoided recondite allusions and a literary tone.

The commitment to writing ennobling poetry went hand in hand with an earnest desire to master the literary and political antecedents of Chartism. The London engraver W. J. Linton (1812-97) wrote poetry for many years, first under his own name and then as 'Spartacus', which embodied his rather dated political beliefs and his wide reading in French and English. He published a weekly journal, *The National* (1839), in order to 'supply the working classes with political and other information not open to them with their limited means for purchase and time for study.'[9] He spent long hours copying out sections of Godwin's *Political Justice,* translating Condorcet, Voltaire and Robespierre, and preparing engravings for the cover. His series, 'Hymns to the Unenfranchised' are sophisticated and clear, albeit poetically stiff, descriptions of the oppression of the poor. The tenth hymn, showing the influence of Shelley and Elliott, is a good example of the strengths and weaknesses of early Chartist poetry:

> Truth is no more the anarch Custom's prey;
>   Man, the poor serf, by kings and priests
>   long hounded
> Into the den of Woe, now turns at bay:
>   The trampler is unhorsed, the hunter
>   wounded.
>
> We sought for peace—ye gave us toil and
>   war;
>   We begg'd for quiet bread—and stones
>   were given:—[Taxing us to build new
>   churches in a time of famine (Linton's
>   footnote).]
> Tyrants and priests! we will be scourged no
>   more:
>   The chains of loyalty and faith are riven.
>
> What bargain have your boasted victories
>   bought?
>   Church-rates and gyves, corn-laws and
>   desolation:
> Tyrants and priests! we need not *your*
>   support;—
>   The Nation will work out its own
>   salvation.
>
> We claim Man's equal rights; we will no
>   ruin

> Even unto the robbers:—Love, Truth-
>   gender'd,
> Dwelleth with Justice: we to all men doing
>   That we require shall unto us be
>   render'd.[10]

The form of this poem is far more complex than those works intended primarily for singing (though obviously not all songs have easy words—witness 'The Internationale'). The sharply broken lines, alternating masculine and feminine rhymes and intricate sentence structure force the reader to go slowly, savouring each phrase and considering its implications. Linton presents a vision of a better world that can be wrested from the existing unjust world through the concerted action of all truth-loving men. The static reified world of 'The Pit Boy' or 'The Miner's Doom' is the reverse of the world described here by Linton; social inequality and injustice are the result of human actions, and can be changed by human actions. The literary expression of man's ability to transform existing conditions and build a new society was Chartism's contribution to working-class literature.

Ernest Jones (1819-68) was particularly successful in embodying Chartist ideals and actions in his poetry. A barrister from an aristocratic family, Jones had already published poetry before joining the Chartist movement.[11] Although not of working-class background, he belongs in this discussion because of his importance as Chartism's finest poet and novelist; his influence among working men who wrote both within and without the movement was great. Jones did not enter the Chartist movement until the spring of 1846; Chartist poets at this stage wrote about not only 'Tyrants and priests', but also about the future brotherhood of man. Their readers understood their own oppression, and wanted descriptions of the new world that political change would bring. Jones was a strong advocate of O'Connor's Land Plan as a means of establishing a just social order. All of his verse supporting the Plan urged a united assault on current conditions, and the rapid establishment of the new society. A popular recitation piece among Chartists was 'The Factory Town', describing the hideousness of factory life and the joys of rural life under the Plan.

> Fear ye not your masters' power;
>   Men are strong when men unite;
> Fear ye not one stormy hour:
>   *Banded millions need not fight.*
>
> Then, how many a happy village
>   Shall be smiling o'er the plain,
> Amid the corn-field's pleasant tillage,
>   And the orchard's rich domain!
>
> While, the rotting roof and rafter,
>   Drops the factory, stone by stone,

> Echoing loud with childhood's laughter,
>   Where it rung with manhood's groan![12]

The Ten Hours Movement had published many doleful verses describing the factory system, but their poets had never been able to give much life or energy to their static portraits of suffering. Jones, on the other hand, explained what individual workers could do to bring about change and to make possible the paradise of rural resettlement.

Jones was highly aware of the importance of intangible feelings and emotions in galvanizing the oppressed. Descriptions of injustice and oppression could anger workers, but appeals to their idealism could focus that anger and channel it toward political action. He believed working men wanted social change both to right their own injustices and to establish a world in which all people could flourish. Early in 1848, before the Continental revolutions, he published 'The Funeral of the Year and Its Epitaph', a long description of corruption, suffering and death. The poem ends, however, on an optimistic note, with a consideration of the battles undertaken for freedom and justice. European working men who have fought these battles have learned to act as brothers, and have therefore moved closer toward realizing their goals:

> Pause, reader! pause; *that* side the shadow
>   lies,
> But turn on *this* as well thine equal eyes.
> This year has stirred the nations far and
>   wide,
> And woke in slavery's heart a manly pride;
> Hark to the clank of chains, as yet untorn,
> But not as erst in tame supineness worn.
> As break the rivers at the thaw-winds' call
> The icy bondage of their wintry thrall,
> And dash their waves in volumes vast
>   along,
> Sounding through many lands the self-same
>   song—
> So one great pulse in nations' hearts has
>   wrought.
> Beating harmonious to the self-same
>   thought.
> Old rivals now no longer look askance,
> But England holds the olive branch to
>   France.
> The Teuton walks the Rhine's contested
>   strand,
> Nor fears the Lurlei's swan-eclipsing hand;
> The Celt and Saxon meet no more as foes
> But twine the hardy shamrock round the
>   rose;
> And bigotry, oppression's bitterest rod,
> Sinks fast before the ennobling thought of
>   God.
> 'All men *are* brethren!' how the watchwords run!

> And now men *act* as such, then freedom's
>   won.
>
> Old year! old year! sleep peaceful in thy
>   grave.
> Thou camest to teach, to punish, and to
>   save.[13]

Although Jones has not described the conflict between '*that* side' and '*this*', he has explained metaphorically the psychological changes occurring among the seekers of freedom; the images drawn from nature make their victory seem inevitable. By pointing to the idealism among working people of many nationalities, he justifies the Chartist cause and its struggle for a more complete victory. The poem presupposes fundamental social change, and denies the legitimacy of the existing social and political order. The rendering of justice, emphasized by Linton, is no longer sufficient, and the old social order is to be swept away.

The theme of class conflict was carried on in the later years of Chartism by Gerald Massey (1828-1907). Massey's life is a remarkable example of politics and poetry yielding worldly success. The son of a canal boatman, his childhood was spent in unrelieved poverty, first as a silk factory operative and straw plaiter, and then as an errand boy in London. In 1849 he edited and wrote almost singlehandedly the Uxbridge *Spirit of Freedom*. His journalistic experience gave him valuable contacts, and he was soon publishing his verse in Chartist journals. In 1851 he published his first volume of verse, *Voices of Freedom and Lyrics of Love*, later issued as *Poems and Ballads* (1854). The middle-class literati saw the craggy well-built Massey as a prototype success story, made a bit more delicious by his righteous indignation at the sufferings of the less fortunate. Favourable reviews soon led Massey out of radical circles and into a career as a lecturer, specializing in mesmerism and phrenology.[14]

During his political phase Massey was unabashedly among the reddest of the red. He was strongly influenced by Julian Harney, who introduced him to the revolutionary movements of the Continent. He was even more enthusiastic than Jones about the brotherhood of man and the inevitable triumph of liberal democracies throughout Europe. In his political verse he emphasized ideals such as freedom and justice that would arouse men to political action. As the possibility of revolution faded, his poetry became more fervently optimistic:

> Fling out the red Banner! in mountain and
>   valley
>   Let Earth feel the tread of the free once
>   again;
> Now soldiers of Freedom, for love of God!
>   rally,

Old earth yearns to know that her children
   are men.
We are nerv'd by a million wrongs, burning,
   and bleeding;
   Bold thoughts leap to birth,—but the bold
      deeds must come.
And whenever Humanity's yearning and
   pleading,
   One battle for liberty, strike we heart-
      home!

Fling out the red Banner! its fiery front
   under
   Come gather ye, gather ye, champions of
      Right!
And roll round the world with the voice of
   God's thunder
   The wrongs we've to reckon—oppressors
      to smite!
They deem that we strike no more, like the
   old Hero-band,
   Martyrdom's own, battle-hearted and
      brave,
Blood of Christ! Brothers mine, it were
   sweet but to see ye stand,

. . . . .

Fling out the red Banner! the patriots
   perish.
   But where their bones whiten, the seed
      striketh root;
Their heart's-life ran red, the great harvest
   to cherish,
   Then gather ye, reapers, and garner the
      fruit.
Victory! victory! Tyrants are quaking!
   The Titan of Toil from the bloody thrall
      starts;
The slaves are awaking—the dawnlight is
   breaking—
   The footfall of Freedom, beats quick at
      our hearts![15]

'Our Symbol', or as it was called in later editions, 'The Song of the Red Republican', is far more inflated than anything Linton or Jones wrote. 'Millions of wrongs', but no one is specifically mentioned; the images of battle do not lead anywhere, except perhaps to a quickening of the reader's spirit. Yet the emotional impact is dissipated by the extravagant language. Moreover, the class struggle is reduced to 'soldiers of Freedom' and 'champions of Right', rather than specific, recognizable persons who have suffered injustice. Harney pointedly criticized Massey's political poems for 'a painful striving for effect by means of big words and monstrous fantasies', and for mentioning God more than a hundred times in an eighty-page volume.[16]

'The Song of the Red Republican' illustrates one of the main difficulties in writing political poetry: writers did not visualize clearly their message and its recipients. 'The footfall of Freedom' beating at the heart gives no clear image of power or change, but instead a peculiar sense of emptiness, as if Massey were not quite sure whom he was addressing, or if anyone were listening anymore. This confusion was accentuated by an unclear notion of the appropriate subject matter and style at a time when Chartism was dying. At one point Massey had declared, 'There is more poetry to be *lived* than to be written! There is no poetry like that of a noble life, wrought out amidst suffering and martyrdom.'[17] Yet Massey did not choose to write about noble suffering or 'the byways and nooks of the world.' Instead his political verse was either an idealistic exhortation such as 'Red Republican', or a description of the world after 'glory' had been achieved. Unable to dramatize the quiet lives he praised, Massey attempted to dramatize artificially his political ideals, making heavy use of the command form, personification and exclamation points.

Exhortatory literature loses its force very quickly; the harder Massey and others tried to be passionate and powerful, the duller they became. Ernest Jones had long warned novice authors, 'when the truths of a principle are once established in the minds of millions, unless a *new* argument is advanced against them, we cannot burthen our readers with the repetition of an oft told tale.'[18] 'Something more' was needed. The answer was poetry as a good in and of itself, offering delights that could not be found elsewhere. The style and framework of political verse were often kept, but the intentions had shifted. Harney, in recommending Tennyson, caught much of the new Chartist priority for literature: 'His poetry is a very world of wondrous beauty—purifying and ennobling beauty; and working men should be made acquainted with it that they may get beauty into their souls, and thence into their daily lives.'[19] To 'get beauty' would sustain a man through dark political times.

Here again Massey reflected the mood of the time. In 'The Chivalry of Labour Exhorted to the Worship of Beauty', he urged his readers to look beyond themselves to Nature:

Come out of the den of darkness and the
   city's toil of sin,
Put on your radiant Manhood, and the
   Angel's blessing win!
Where wealthier sunlight comes from
   Heaven, like welcome-smiles of God,
And Earth's blind yearnings leap to life in
   flowers, from out the sod:
Come worship Beauty in the forest-temple,
   dim and hush,
Where stands Magnificence dreaming! and

God burneth in the bush:
Or where the old hills worship with their
   silence for a psalm,
Or ocean's weary heart doth keep the
   sabbath of its calm
Come let us worship Beauty with the
   knightly faith of old.
O Chivalry of Labour toiling for the Age of
   Gold!

Come let us worship Beauty: she hath
   subtle power to start
Heroic work and deed out-flashing from the
   humblest heart:
Great feelings will gush unawares, and
   freshly as the first
Rich Rainbow that up startled Heaven in
   tearful splendour burst.
O blessed are her lineaments, and wondrous
   are her ways
To repicture God's worn likeness in the
   suffering human face!
Our bliss shall richly overbrim like sunset in
   the west,
And we shall dream immortal dreams and
   banquet with the Blest.
Then let us worship Beauty with the
   knightly faith of old.
O Chiralry of Labour toiling for the Age of
   Gold![20]

The substance of this poem is little more than a series of images based on that familiar Victorian cliché, man is closer to God in nature than in the city. The final couplet of each stanza, however, shows the grafting of Carlyle's work ethic on the Chartist idea of class pride. The poem readjusts politics to serve literature, instead of vice versa.

The shift away from a political poetry describing fundamental grievances and their redress was reflected in Massey's self-image. At first he appears to have hoped to revive the people through his violent language and fiery manner. He dedicated his 1851 volume to a fellow Chartist, William Cooper (no relation to Thomas), with a long introductory letter explaining why he had written such verse as 'The Song of the Red Republican', 'The Men of Forty-Eight', and 'The Red Banner':

I shall be accused of sowing class-hatred, and yet, my friend, I do not seek to fling fire-brands among the combustibles of society. I yearn to raise my brethren into loveable beings, and when I smite their hearts, I would rather they should gush with the healing waters of love than the fearful fires of hatred: but looking on the wrongs which are daily done in the land, will sometimes make the blood rush to the heart, and crimson to the brow. Who can see the masses ruthlessly

robbed of all the fruits of their industry, of all the sweet pleasures of life, and of that nobleness which should crown human nature as with a crown of glory, and not strive to arouse them to a sense of their degradation, and urge them to end the bitter bondage and the murderous martyrdom of Toil! Not he who feels concentrated and crushing upon himself the slavery of millions.[21]

In this passage we are back to the language of 1839 and the physical-force rhetoric of necessary violence in the name of essential change—and yet conditions had changed, making such a call an impossible hope for a handful, in comparison to the thousands of a previous decade.

Massey, like his predecessors, argued that his purpose in writing poetry was to instruct men in how they could love and understand one another better. But, given the 'murderous martyrdom of Toil', he is forced to write inflammatory verse, urging toilers to rise up against their oppressors. His readers, however, did not join him singing 'Fling out the red Banner!' and Massey himself changed. In the preface to the third edition of 1854, the dedication to William Cooper was dropped and Massey's poetic purpose shifted to a form of amelioration in line with such poems as 'The Chivalry of Labour Exhorted to the Worship of Beauty'. He now calls his political poetry 'memorials of my past', kept as 'some worn out garment because he had passed through the furnace in it.' Through a long quotation by 'the rebel', Massey places himself at one remove from an altered version of the above quotation:

'It is not', says he, 'that I seek to sow dissension between classes and class, or fling firebrands among the combustibles of society; for when I smite the hearts of my fellows, I would rather they should gush with the healing waters of love, than with the fearful fires of hatred. I yearn to raise them into loveable beings. I would kindle in the hearts of the masses a sense of the beauty and grandeur of the universe, call forth the lineaments of Divinity in their poor wan faces, give them glimpses of the grace and glory of Love and the marvellous significance of Life, and elevate the standard of Humanity for all. But strange wrongs are daily done in the land, bitter feelings are felt, and wild words will be spoken. It is not for myself that I have uncurtained some scenes of my life to the public gaze, but as an illustration of the lives of others, who suffer and toil on, "die, and make no sign;" and because one's own personal experience is of more value than that of others taken upon hearsay.'[22]

The function of poetry, as well as Massey's self-image, has changed radically here. It is not a call to action, but a means to elevate and ennoble the masses. 'Nature', 'Divinity', 'Love' and 'Humanity' have replaced 'slavery', 'human nature', 'degradation' and 'nobleness'. The working-class is no longer denied justice by a corrupt system, but is in need of personal enlightenment and improvement. By reading the elevating poetry of a fellow worker, each would feel an answering chord of nobility in his heart, and become sufficiently strengthened to see 'beauty and grandeur' in spite of his poverty. In turn, the poet would educate middle-class readers about the ways and thoughts of the mute workers who 'suffer and toil on'. Massey now sees the working-class poet as a pacifier of his class—the poor must be taught not to speak 'wild words' or have 'bitter feelings', but to know 'the standard of Humanity for all', regardless of class divisions. The radical demand for more education and opportunity has become a conservative force, reinforcing existing values rather than those of a developing class.

One of the major difficulties faced by political poets was to combine literary enthusiasm and political beliefs in a manner attractive to their less educated peers. At every stage of the movement leaders encouraged self-education, particularly through literature. As one Barnsley Chartist explained in his introductory remarks to an evening school club rules, 'An extensive Literary Education, may be classified amongst the highest of all earthly enjoyments; not only, in its beneficial effects on the Individual who possesses it, but, in its application conducive to the welfare of society at large.'[23] The political justification for reading and writing poetry was its power as spiritual leavening among the mass of people. In a review of a volume of poetry edited by members of the National Chartist Association, the *English Chartist Circular* said, 'We rejoice . . . because we regard "Singing for the Million" as something to glory in—something towards the great work of regenerating the now mentally debased— to cheer the physically oppressed,—and to stimulate men to noble deeds for Truth and Freedom's sake.'[24] Educational Chartists were convinced that nothing would be more effective in strengthening working-class unity over time than a thoroughly moral education. Literature, which could be made readily available to all, provided the foundation.

The first stage in the literary education of working men was resurrecting their own heritage. Linton's *The National* was only one of many journals that published excerpts from politically sympathetic artists. The Glasgow *Chartist Circular* (1839-41) ran a series called 'The Politics of Poetry', including the major contemporary poets, Scots poets from all periods and minor poets with working-class backgrounds. At the conclusion of an essay on Wordsworth and Elliott, the editor, William Thomson, declared, 'Let the people bathe deep in the light of the accumulated genius of many ages, and armed at all points "with heaven-born knowledge"—let them enter boldly on the conflict between

light and darkness, and tyrants alone have cause to fear the issue of the contest.'[25] He advocated Chartist schools (with a recommended one teacher for every 150 pupils) because he hated the literature he had been forced to read as a child. In thenew schools honest Burns and not the toadying Allan Ramsey would be taught. Throughout Julian Harney's editorship of the *Northern Star* (1845-50, 1852) long excerpts of radical English poetry were published; Milton, Thomson, Shelley and Byron were his favourites. In 1846 he published a series on American democrats and agrarianists, devoting much space to his friend and Chartist sympathizer, John Greenleaf Whittier. He encouraged readers to send in their own works, asking particularly for poems to commemorate the Hungarian and Italian patriots who had fled their native lands.

Educational Chartists also looked to the most famous writers of the day to provide a literature suitable for uplifting the working class. Ernest Jones rhetorically asked, 'Can Tennyson do no more than troll a courtly lay?' The 'cheap and nasty' products of serialized fiction, street broadsides and the music hall did not have sufficient literary merit, and for many Chartists they seemed to be specifically designed to drug the political consciousness of the reader.[26] The middle-class novels of industrialism, such as Mrs Trollope's *Michael Armstrong* (1839-40) and Mrs Gaskell's *Mary Barton* (1848), with their anti-union and anti-Chartist positions, were scarcely likely to win many readers among militant working men. Jones warned contemporary authors-the natural artistic leaders of society-of their duty to be relevant, 'We say to the great minds of the day, come among the people, write for the people, and your fame will live for ever. The people's instinct will give life to your philosophy, and the genius of the favoured few will hand down peace and plenty, knowledge and power, as an heirloom to posterity.'[27] Literature honestly written about the working class would bring both the writer and his audience— from all classes—a better understanding of society.

Chartist educators put most of their energy into teaching fellow workers how to write a literature worthy of their class. As Thomas Cooper explained in a letter addressed 'To the Young Men of the Working Classes', it was,

> a matter of the highest necessity, that you all join hands and head to create a literature of your own. Your own prose, your own poetry . . . would put you all more fully in possession of each other's thoughts and thus give you a higher respect for each other, and a clearer perception of what you can do when united.[28]

He went on to give practical advice on how to write poetry, suggesting that young men should read widely to form their own poetic taste, and to remember to 'use plain words', and avoid 'inflation of expression—over-swelling words—sound without sense—and exaggerated sentimentalism.'[29] It was advice Massey—and Cooper himself—would have done well to accept. The pedagogical as well as moral benefits of writing poetry were emphasized by John Burland a Chartist teacher from Barnsley. He found each part of poetry—the metrics, metaphors, word selection and logical construction—conducive to learning, and stated triumphantly, 'the person who assiduously endeavours to become a good poet, cannot do otherwise than become an elegant and accomplished scholar.'[30] The mastery of the forms of poetry encouraged both 'intellectual and moral progress' which in turn made men worthy of suffrage.

The best-known conjunction of literary education and Chartist principles was Thomas Cooper's Shakespearean Chartist Association, which flourished in Leicester in 1841 and 1842. Under Cooper's leadership classes were formed with such names as 'Major Cartwright Class', 'John Milton Class' and 'George Washington Class'.[31] He combined the teaching of poetry and politics by encouraging men to write political hymns and poems, which were published as a small six-penny volume. . . . Events chastened many Leicester Chartists, and by the end of the 1840s the poets had turned from passionate hymns to poems of self-development. William Jones in the introduction to his dream vision *The Spirit; or A Dream in the Woodlands* (1849) explained his change,

> . . . the earlier shapings of his subject were somewhat imbued with vindictiveness, couched in terms construable into personality; but sober reflection taught him to regard the enunciation of such feelings as calculated only to do mischief - whether resorted to by rich or poor. Besides, it is his firm conviction that social wrong, and the morally degrading causes which have pressed so long and so heavily upon working-men, especially in manufacturing districts, can only have permanent removal in proportion to the growth of te masses in Knowledge, Temperance and Self-Respect. If the subsequent thoughts, finding expression in rhyme, have a tendency to hasten such happy result, the end of their publication will be answered, and the writer have reason to rejoice that he embraced the opportunity to spread the principles of Progression and Peace amongst his fellow men.[32]

The working class is itself now blamed for the social wrongs pressing down upon it—a conclusion very close to Gerald Massey's, and a long way from Chartist ideas about social oppression.

'Thoughts finding expression in rhyme' is a good description of Chartist poetry after 1848; Thomas Cooper (1805-92) however, tried to combine his learning, personal beliefs and political hopes in his poetry.

As a youth he had devoted himself to mastering six languages, science, mathematics and a variety of other disciplines, almost without companionship or encouragement. For several years he ran a large school in Lincolnshire, but his learning offended the more narrow-minded parents. In time he took up journalism and later lecturing, the two careers he was to pursue for the rest of his life. At the age of fifty he reconverted—on the platform—to Christianity, and devoted the remainder of his long life to the Baptist ministry. For a brief period he led a large Chartist association in Leicester, providing not only classes, but also a coffee-house, newspapers and general guidance. Convicted in 1843 of sedition, he was imprisoned for two years. During this time he wrote *The Purgatory of Suicides*, an epic in Spenserian rhyme, describing all manner of classical, medieval and modern suicides. A monument to Cooper's learning, it is virtually unreadable. The political content is murky because of the long digressions and descriptions, but several Romans speak in favour of Chartist principles, and in one of the more dramatic sections, Judas, of all people, heaps invective upon Castlereagh.

While Cooper was in gaol he received an anonymous offer of tuition at Cambridge, with the stipulation that he forego politics. He turned down the offer, but his epic was living proof that he was as learned as any poet with a Cambridge degree. A mixture of pride, self-seeking and abnegation characterized many of Cooper's literary efforts. In his introduction to Book II he compares himself, with some modesty, to the greatest of previous poets:

> Lyre of my fatherland! anew, to wake
> thy solemn shell, I come,—with trembling
>   hand,—
> Feeling my rudeness doth harsh discord
>   make
> With strings great minstrels all divinely
>   spanned.
> How shall a thrall essay to join your
>   band,—
> Ye freeborn spirits whose bold music fired
> My freeborn sires to draw the glittering
>   brand
> For home and England,—or, in arms
>   attired,
> To awe their lion kings who to sole power
>   aspired?
>
> How shall a thrall, from humble labour
>   sprung,
> Successful, strike the lyre in scornful age,
> When full-voiced bards have each
>   neglected sung,
> And loftiest rhyme is deemed a worthless
>   page
> By crowds that bow in Mammon-

vassalage?
Gray Prudence saith the world will
    disregard
My harping rude,—or term it sacrilege
That captive leveller hath rashly dared
To touch the sacred function of the tuneful
    bard.

．．．．．

Poet of Paradise,—whose glory illumed
My path of youthful penury, till grew
The desert to a garden, and Life bloomed
With hope and joy,' midst suffering,—
    honour due
I cannot render thee; but reverence true
This heart shall give thee, till it reach the
    verge
Where human splendours lose their
    lustrous hue;
And, when, in death, mortal joys all
    merge—
Thy grand and gorgeous music, Milton, be
    my dirge!—[33]

Cooper aimed to create a working man's epic, but he was unable to carry his idea one step further, and argue for a new literary aesthetic. Although he takes pride in his background of 'humble labour', he was determined to write an epic worthy of past giants, and not of interest to the 'crowds that bow in Mammon-vassalage.' In later editions this line was toned down to 'And Taste doth browse on bestial pasturage', but the connotations of an unenlightened, materialistic general public remain. For all of his Chartist commitment, Cooper saw himself as an intellectual leader, apart from the masses.

In his autobiography (1872) Cooper explained at length his difficulties in finding a publisher, for the benefit of other poor men seeking to publish their poems. Despite his inordinate pride, he was indebted to the kindness of many influential men; Disraeli, Harrison Ainsworth, John Forster and Douglas Jerrold all read the manuscript and offered advice, often accompanied by letters of recommendation to prominent publishers. Within three months of his release from prison Cooper found a sympathetic radical publisher; the epic went through three editions between 1845 and 1853, and was reviewed quite widely.[34] As Douglas Jerrold explained, a Chartist poet had a better chance of being listened to than a conservative, 'inasmuch as there is to be expected from him newer developments than can be hoped for from one of an expiring creed.'[35] A more difficult issue, discussed at greater length in the next two chapters, was whether middle-class reviewers took the work seriously, or patronized it as an interesting example of working-class talent.

In spite of many stirring passages, the political intention of *The Purgatory of Suicides* was obscured by the deliberately self-advertising display of information. Reviewers of every persuasion criticized the work for what Jerrold called 'its perpetual display of learning and allusions to subjects that can only be familiar to persons more than commonly well read, and not to the class with which the author so specifically delights to connect himself.' Cooper was trapped by his painfully acquired learning and his middle-class aesthetics. In the 1877 edition of Cooper's collected poetry he apologized for the political passages in *The Purgatory of Suicides*, and like Massey, defended his fight 'for Human Freedom', which his 'Mind-history' records. He claimed his most lasting personal gain from writing the epic was as an outlet against bitterness in times of personal depression. He had to be content with distant admiration from both the middle-class and the working class.

It was often a hard and lonely battle for such autodidacts as Cooper, who spent many hours of their youth reading into the night, breaking away from the lure of politics and comradeship to return to yet another book, mathematics problem or half-completed poem. Although their efforts might be praised by sympathetic men such as Jerrold, too often they found no place in the swirling events surrounding the Chartist movement, and were sent back into their isolated world of books after a brief foray into leadership. It was only in a later generation that such men could find a role for themselves within the complexities of working-class society—and even then . . . they found many limitations, and changed their own high ideals about literature and art to suit their audience and its politics.

II. Chartist Fiction

Just as the better-educated Chartist had a taste for the dignities and forms of traditional poetry, so had he a distaste for the conservative social message of popular fiction. In 1841 William Thomson made a characteristic attack upon the publishers of serial fiction for encouraging a love of aristocratic romance among the poor. Whenever a hero appeared in humble life he was invariably found to be a long-lost son of an aristocrat whose innate nobility shone through in spite of his poor associates. Thomson called for 'a Radical Literary Reform', in which 'The virtues of the masses should be sought out and extolled; the iniquities of the *titled* honestly exposed and condemned. Every man should be praised or blamed as he merits, and false glory extinguished. All men are equal, distinction is artificial, and the vile press has spread the iniquity.'[36] His suggested solution proved too simple: 'the intelligent people' were to cease reading such works that 'wickedly trample on their rights, and unjustly elevate their oppressors.' But Chartist writers were not slow to recognize the need for their own literature to counteract the demeaning portrayal of working people and the adulation of the aristocracy. In addition to their poetry column, Chartist newspapers and periodicals ran sketches that 'sought out and extolled' the virtues of the working class. Particularly in the late 'forties fiction became more important for Chartists, and a number of writers tried their hand at sketches and novels.

Chartists used two basic forms of fiction: the moral fable and the popular novel. The fable appealed primarily to educational Chartists who sought a literature reflecting their best hopes and aspirations while condemning the social conditions that perpetrated so much suffering and lack of opportunity. Thomas Cooper is the best known exponent of this type of fiction, although many others wrote fables, including W.J. Linton and Ernest Jones. The more innovative form was the popular novel, particularly as written by G. W. M. Reynolds, a Chartist sympathizer and pioneer in combining romance and politics.[37] Writers placed in a class context such traditional ingredients as unrequited love, a hero of superior character and heart-stirring adventures. The latter came largely from the Chartist movement itself. Wheeler's *Sunshine and Shadow* (1849-50), published in the *Northern Star,* is the most narrowly political. Thomas Frost, who had written for Salisbury Square publishers, had several commissions from political magazines. Ernest Jones was probably the most outstanding writer in this group; his education and wealthy background enabled him to write about every level of society. *De Brassier: A Democratic Romance* (1851-2) and *Women's Wrongs* (1852) were his most widely admired political novels.

Chartists began writing novels based on popular fiction when the movement began to falter politically. They needed an alternative form of fiction to encourage potential members and to sustain the faithful. Their material was drawn from earlier Chartist agitation to remind readers of their rich political heritage, and to show the link between it and the less promising present. Readers could see the mistakes and strengths of the past and plan for more effective political work. Thomas Martin Wheeler in his introduction to *Sunshine and Shadow* pointed out the need to attract young people:

> . . . the opponents of our principles have been allowed to wield the power of imagination over the youth of our party, without any effort on our part to occupy this wide and fruitful plain. Would that some of the many talented minds acknowledging our tenets, would achieve that supremacy in the novel which Thomas Cooper has done in the epic.[38]

Wheeler, like Cooper, wanted a fiction that working men would recognize as an intellectual achievement by one of their own class. Ernest Jones settled more openly for an entertaining plot, declaring, 'I do not see why Truth should always be dressed in stern and repulsive garb. The more attractive you make her, the more easily she will progress.'[39]

All Chartist fiction was built upon stereotyped characterization and plotting. Authors consciously broke away from the character development and unified action found in the bourgeois novel in order to emphasize the political implications of a situation. Readers were expected to identify with the hero only as a typical honest-hearted working man who embodied their best characteristics. A great many events befall the hero in order to document as fully as possible the oppression of the working class. Characters frequently die not simply as a convenient way to end a story, but also to bring home the inevitable conclusion of oppression left unchanged. The courage of the hero combined with his many misfortunes focuses the anger of the reader against those in power. It is a literature designed to increase social tension rather than to provide an explanation for injustice. Because both the characters and the events are familiar to the reader, he is not waylaid by a consideration of motivations and alternatives. Psychological analysis gives way to a political analysis of why good people are trodden down by circumstances. This fiction first quickens the reader's existing anger, and then channels it toward a political outlet.

Both the moral fables and the popular fiction shared a vision of society as corrupt and in need of change; they are part of what William Empson has called 'the realistic pastoral', in which the focus upon human waste and social injustice yields in the reader a fuller conception of the possibilities of life.[40] While writing in a realistic mode, all Chartist novelists expressed a hope for a better future which is close to a pastoral world where conflicts can be reconciled and the simple, natural human sentiments can reign unchallenged. In judging the contrast between what is—human waste—with what should and could be—human fulfilment—an author will soften at least some elements of class conflict in order to present the means of changing the old into the new. If he does not do so, the difficulties of affecting change seem insurmountable, and the reader will not believe in the promise of fulfilment. Moreover, if the potential conflict appears too destructive, the reader may consider the price of change, even when it brings improvement for himself, to be too high. Sympathizers from all classes are needed to bring about a people's revolution. At the same time the hope of a new society involves a simplification of the complex—a process which concentrates and makes more forceful the wrongs suffered by the people, and thereby heightens the sense of class conflict. These two contradictory tendencies are reconciled in the hero. Whether passive (as in the moral fable) or active (as in the popular novel), he embodies certain ideals which placed him at odds with the existing society, and closer to the envisioned new society. He is linked to the people through his common shared humanity, but separate from them through his superior political idealism.

The hero, as the mouthpiece of the author, often carried a very heavy share of the moral burden. Authors started with their political ideas and then tried to build characters and actions around them; the results were necessarily mixed. At its worst, a piece became wooden propaganda, but the best narratives combined emotionally-charged action with effective analysis. Jones, in *De Brassier,* describes the motivations and satisfactions of a mob plundering a banker's home; at the same time he analyzes the moral dilemma faced by the hero in this situation. If he defends the banker he will lose all credibility with the men, but if he permits them to continue he knows the general public will turn against the cause of democracy. Jones does not evade the implications of political activity and does not flinch from portraying characteristics he sees as weaknesses of the people. The hero could also be a means of demonstrating the relationship between personal oppression and political change. Bitter poverty teaches Arthur, of *Sunshine and Shadow,* the necessity of working for the realization of concrete changes within his own lifetime. Unlike Chartist poetry, which often simply asserted a position, in fiction writers could portray characters and situations that brought to life complex political problems.

The moral fable was adapted from religious and folk traditions. During the early years of Chartism it was primarily a simple means of explaining everyday injustices suffered by working people. Traditional religious connotations gave the fable greater emotional and symbolic weight than its simple form might indicate. Since fables and illustrative anecdotes were frequently used in Chartist speeches, readers found an immediate relation between their reading and what they had heard at a political rally. Moreover, fables were built upon oral traditions; they clarified and focused knowledge that had been shared among working people in Chartist discussions and meetings. With this background the connection between the disasters sketched in a tale and political action was easily made. By sharpening the consciousness of oppression, fables encouraged greater political commitment.

W. J. Linton published a characteristic series called 'Records of the World's Justice', told by a 'Hardwareman', in *The National* (1839). Each sketch revolves around a particular case of the rich and powerful destroying the poor and honest. Realistic descriptions of working conditions and poverty are combined with allegorical characters and plots. The characters act out their parts (Honest Age, Corrupt Par-

son, Faithful Child, etc.) to formula, leading to a Chartist moral. The series served as a model for other writers, and was reprinted in the *English Chartist Circular* (1841-3) along with Linton's 'Hymns to the Unenfranchised'.

In 'The Pauper' Ashton, representing Honest Age, is unable to pay his church-rate of three shillings, and so the Law drives him from his home. He had been a day labourer of 'irreproachable' character, whose 'little store' of savings had been exhausted by illness and hard times. He lost two sons through impressment during the Napoleonic Wars; one daughter had been seduced by Mr Euston and had died on the streets. His remaining daughter is unable to earn enough by her needle to keep them in food and pay the church-rate. His house is seized to pay the rate and,

> The Honourable Mr. Euston is now a Viscount with a pension of £5,000 a year, his wife having been, with his consent, one of the king's mistresses. He has never done a real day's work in his life. His hardest work has been legislating— I mean picking the pockets of industrious folk and endeavouring to demoralize the people: the last I am sure is easy to him. Now I don't like to differ from the world, but this is what I call a pauper: I may be wrong, for they say a pauper is one who lives on *charity,* and the *noble* Viscount lives by robbery. I am a rough plain man—some say I am as stiff and hard-hearted as one of my own steel pokers—yet I do wish for a somewhat better distribution of property (to be made in a spirit of good-will, on the live-and-let-live system,) so as to prevent all kinds of pauperism, which must be very unpleasant (to say the least of it) even to a Viscount.[41]

While the reader might identify with Ashton, he is not expected to agree with his Job-like patience; rather, the hardwareman's ironic rhetoric implies the necessity of political action.

Later authors of this form added more direct conversations and action, but the basic formula remained unaltered. For example, Jones's 'The London Door-Step' (1848)[42] describes the death of an honourable woman picked up for vagrancy when she rested momentarily on the door step of a mansion in Grosvenor Square, where the man within earns £15,000, has two country homes and a government position. Her husband had left Leicester some weeks previous in search of work. Attempting to stop a policeman from beating a woman after the famous Kennington Common meeting, he was struck with a truncheon and died. His wife, unable to find him, sinks onto the door step under the burden of hunger, fear and exhaustion. The 'proud aristocrat' within sends his 'powdered lackey' to expel 'that drunken woman'. Jones anathamatizes him as 'A SOCIAL MURDERER' for his unwillingness to share 'a trifle with that wretched victim'. The language is more lurid than Linton's, but the convention of piling indignities upon the poor victim, and the political moral are unchanged.

With the decline of Chartism the political message of fables changed. Educational Chartists were probably influenced by the rise of the new purified press of the late 'forties and early 'fifties. Fiction, previously refused by the uplifting educational journals, became their mainstay, albeit greatly chastened. *Eliza Cook's Journal* (1849-54), *The Family Economist* (1848-60), *The Family Friend* (1849-1921) and other journals sponsored by religious groups all contained stories and novels that an ex-Chartist could use as a model for his own writings, rather than the more inflammatory works of Linton or Jones. These journals appealed to the better-educated working families who saw their interests as divergent from the poorer members of the working class. Their political fiction, therefore, conveyed a very different message—one of self-help, improvement and ameliorating conditions within society. Specific problems were to be solved by applying specific solutions, and the general ills of capitalism were ignored.

Thomas Cooper's *Wise Saws and Modern Instances* (1845) is an example of this kind of fiction. In his preface he defined the purpose of art quite modestly, declaring, 'Higher merit than naturalness, combined with truth is not claimed for any of the stories: they are, simply, such as any man may write who has the least power of pourtraying [sic] the images which human life, in some of its humblest, least disguised forms, has impressed upon his memory . . .'[43] 'Naturalness' meant an accurate portrayal of many plain folk, often going back to his early days in Gainsborough, but 'truth' demanded a morally uplifting conclusion to each sketch, and frequently disguised persons provided unexpected aid in times of distress. Cooper clearly intended his stories to be read by working people; many of them were published in the more respectable political monthlies of the late Chartist period. But he also, as with *The Purgatory of Suicides,* had his eye on sympathetic members of the middle class. While critical of conditions that had led to extreme poverty, his solution was largely dependent upon outside help from the financially secure.

The difficulties of combining realism and instruction can be seen in *Seth Thompson, the Stockinger,* written while Cooper was in jail. After years of semi-starvation in the slums of Leicester, Seth and his family are saved by the opportune arrival of a long-lost uncle:

> Seth blushed, as he took his dish of potatoes, and offered the stranger his fragment of a seat. And the stranger blushed, too, but refused the seat with a look of so much benevolence that

Seth's heart glowed to behold it; and his wife set down her porringer, and hushed the children that the stranger might deliver his errand with the greater ease . . .

> 'Are working people in Leicestershire usually so uncomfortably situated as you appear to be?' asked the stranger in a tone of deep commiseration which he appeared to be unable to control.

Seth Thompson and his wife looked uneasily at each other, and then fixed their gaze on the floor.

> 'Why, sir,' replied Seth, blushing more deeply than before, 'we married very betime, and our family, you see, has grown very fast; we hope things will mend a little with us when some o' the children are old enough to earn a little. We've only been badly off as yet, but you'd find a many not much better off, sir, I assure you, in Hinckley and elsewhere.'

The stranger paused again, and the working of his features manifested strong inward feeling.

> 'I see nothing but potatoes,' he resumed; 'I hope your meal is unusually poor to-day, and that you and your family generally have a little meat at dinner.'

> 'Meat, sir!' exclaimed Seth; 'we have not known what it is to set a bit of meat before our children more than three times since the first was born; we usually had a little for our Sunday dinner when we were first married, but we can't afford it now!'

> 'Great God!' cried the stranger, with a look that demonstrated his agony of grief and indignation, 'is this England,—the happy England, that I have heard the blacks in the West Indies talk of as a Paradise?'[44]

Seth is given £50 and a half-yearly remittance, with which he sets up a shop, employing stockingers at a fair rate. He regularly lends money to the man from whom he rents the stocking frames, until a business reversal sends him into bankruptcy, leaving Seth with the bills. Disillusioned with England, Seth and his family decide to join his uncle in the West Indies.

This story compares poorly with a similar incident described in Cooper's autobiography (1872). As a newly-arrived journalist he had attended a Chartist meeting in Leicester, and on the way home around eleven o'clock, he overheard the sound of stockingers at work:

'Do your stocking weavers often work so late as this?' I asked of some of the men who were leaving the meeting.

'No, not often: work's over scarce for that', they answered; 'but we're glad to work at any hour, when we can get work to do.'

'Then your hosiery trade is not good in Leicester?' I observed.

'Good! It's been good for nought this many a year,' said one of the men: 'We've a bit of a spurt now and then. But we soon go back again to starvation!'

'And what may be the average earnings of a stocking weaver?' I asked,—'I mean when a man is fully employed.'

'About four and sixpence,' was the reply.

That was the exact answer; but I had no right conception of its meaning. I remembered that my own earnings as a handicraft had been low, because I was not allowed to work for the best shops. And I knew that working men in full employ, in the towns of Lincolnshire, were understood to be paid tolerably well. I had never, till now, had any experience of the condition of a great part of the manufacturing population of England, and so my rejoiner was natural. The reply it evoked was the first utterance that revealed to me the real state of suffering in which thousands in England were living.

'Four and sixpence,' I said; 'well, six fours are twenty-four, and six sixpences are three shillings: that's seven-and-twenty shillings a week. The wages are not so bad when you are in work.'

'What are you talking about?' said they. 'You mean four and sixpence a day; but we mean four and sixpence a week.'

'Four and sixpence a week!' I exclaimed. 'You don't mean that men have to work in those stocking frames that I hear going now, a whole week for four and sixpence. How can they maintain their wives and children?'

'Ay, you may well ask that,' said one of them, sadly.[45]

Cooper has vividly recreated his personal shock, leaving the reader to draw his own conclusions. Unfortunately he was never able to dramatize the difficulties of working-class life as well as this in his fiction. Seth Thompson seems more remote than the anonymous stockingers of Cooper's autobiography. The ignorant reader is able to identify and learn with Cooper, but in *Seth Thompson* the feelings of the stockinger and his uncle remain artificial and stereotyped. Both utter the clichés of the time—the stranger echoes Oastler's attack on 'white slavery' in northern factories, and Seth accepts contemporary Malthusian arguments against premature marriage. The uncle asks all the questions in order to do something for his relative; Seth does not save himself, in direct contradiction to the basic tenets of Chartist education.

In 'The Autobiography of Timothy Twinckle', written for the *Northern Tribune* (1854-5), Cooper carried the doctrine of self-help within a just capitalist society one step further. In so doing he joined the many working men who had turned to trade unions, co-operative organizations and the Liberal Party following the decline of the Chartist movement. Young Timothy, after being wrongfully accused of theft by his master, is sent to 'a good plain school' by 'the son of my mother's old master, Squire Heartwell'. In due course he is apprenticed, applies himself 'assiduously' and becomes a 'freeman'. He saves money, is made manager of a business, and eventually becomes the owner. In old age he reflects,

> All I need say is—there is money to be made in old England without going to the gold-diggings. Economy—strict economy, in the outset—Industry and Perseverance—these are qualities which can scarcely fail to lead to Independence. Let the reader cultivate them, keeping his conscience clean of wrongdoing and oppressing his follows, and he may reach the vale of life with the sun shining clearly and lightly overhead—not withstanding that when he first set out to climb that hill the storm threatened to overwhelm him.[46]

Within a decade Cooper changed from seeing poverty as inevitable and emigration a solution to a full acceptance of self-help combined with help from above. However, he did not consider how one could accumulate capital from the labour of others without 'wronging and oppressing' them. The labour theory of value has been rejected for individual self-improvement. Moreover, Cooper assumes harmonious relationships between the classes. Without obligation the son of the squire helped the son of a former servant; the boy proves himself worthy of trust when he comes to treat his own workers justly. The tone of self-congratulation, so evident in the story, was frequently part of a respectable working man's writing at this time.

Cooper's short stories about working-class conditions emphasized the underlying similarity of all men, rich or poor, a position emphasized by Dickens and many lesser novelists of the mid-century. In 1851-2 he wrote a Chartist novel, which he implied in his autobiography was much better than Charles Kingsley's *Alton*

Locke. The manuscript has not survived; there is no way of knowing whether the political perspective was different from his short stories. The refusal inlater years to write a specifically political novel, despite theurgings of his friends, may have been because of his distaste for reluctant publishers, but it is undoubtedly symptomatic of his shift from political activity to educational work.

Others, more committed to the Chartist movement than Cooper, were not willing to concede a unity of interests, but they were forced to justify their cause in a way that had not been necessary earlier. Since they did not write for money or fame, they were not constrained by market conditions, but they could not veer too far from the familiar, lest they repel the average novel reader. Moreover, they wished to teach their readers about the strengths and weaknesses of the past, and to encourage the faltering to continue their political activities. They had to create attractive stories that could carry their political message realistically and forcefully.

Chartist novelists readily borrowed the conventions of popular fiction: the heroine was a passive victim; the villain was brought to justice by fortuitous events; the hero was manly, idealistic and honest; the aristocracy was selfish and cruel, but had its heartaches. Vague democratic principles rather than particular Chartist demands made up most speeches and actions. Emotionally charged situations carried the political burden; class conflict was justified through the villainy perpetrated by a careless and selfish member of the ruling class. Seduction of an innocent servant girl, the dismissal of a faithful retainer, or a more personal cruelty all pinpointed his perfidy, which was then declared to be typical of his class. A tortuous plot frequently led up to a confrontation between the hero and the villain; a fair damsel was the reward. Often enough the villain won her, but the forces of democracy, it was implied, would eventually triumph, and so the brave hero continued his political work despite a heavy heart.

Unable to control much of their situation, working people found emotional satisfaction in these conventions. They could identify more readily with a hero or heroine who was largely a victim of circumstances; such a character showed how misfortune was not a reflection of one's own personal worth. At the same time, melodrama often showed the joys of goodness rewarded through a *deus ex machina*. The appearance of Seth's rich uncle is emotionally, if not rationally, satisfying. And yet, Chartist novelists wrote out of a belief in the possibility of change. As Jones insisted,

> It is folly to say 'we can't help it,' 'we are the creatures of circumstances'—'we are what society makes us.' We *can* help it—we can *create circumstances*—we can make *society*—or whence the efforts to redress and reform—moral, social, political, religious?[47]

Charles Kingsley, author of Alton Locke.

The problem was how to graft a sense of political instrumentality upon a melodramatic plot. The less skilful sacrificed their political message to the exigencies of romance. The machinations of the upper-class villain gave opportunity to pillory those in power, but the emotional interest centres on the young lovers. The overall impression is of thwarted love, with political principles often reduced to a hatred of the upper-classes. The more sophisticated writers altered conventions in order to show men working together, creating circumstances. A disaster, such as the burning down of a factory, was used to show men organizing for a better tomorrow. The superior knowledge and good character of the hero occasionally enabled him to influence the course of events. The constraints of the plot, however, were most frequently broken by an authorial interruption calling for united political action on the part of the readers.

Thomas Frost's *The Secret* is an example of an adventure story that provided readers vicarious revenge against the ruling class. Frost (1820-89?), a Croydon printer turned journalist, had been active in the Chartist movement while earning his living writing serial novels, political essays and miscellaneous pieces. In 1850 he was hired by the *National Instructor* (1850) to write a tale that would appeal to its Chartist readers.[48] 'The secret' revolves around an incident that occurred twenty years before the novel opens. An embittered Vincent had exchanged his granddaughter for that of the aristocrat who had seduced his sister. Over the years he chuckles at the results. His 'granddaughter' Lizzie is seduced by her employer's son, and has an illegitimate child. In the meantime his true granddaughter has grown up with an unusually firm and charitable character, and happily marries a wealthy earl of like mind. All is then revealed to the Duke. He attempts to 'save' Lizzie by placing her with a family in the country to learn proper manners and speech. But she has fallen in love with Ernest Rodwell, an upright Chartist compositor, and in the face of the Duke's wrath, marries him. Her happiness thereby foils the artful Vincent and solves all for the Duke, who has found nurture stronger than nature. The only variation from the standard plot is Lizzie's marriage; a few seduced, but modest, women might find happiness with an understanding Chartist.

In a similarly melodramatic series, *Women's Wrongs,* Ernest Jones describes the plight of a poor working man's wife, a young milliner, a tradesman's daughter and a lady of title. He insisted he was painting 'life *as it is*—no poet's fancy, no romancer's dream . . . the romance of fiction cannot equal the romance of truth.'[49] 'The romance of truth' actually betrays a remarkable number of characteristics drawn from the popular novel—lovers are totally unable to reveal their affection and endure tortured lives; aristocratic society is decadent and depraved, but its finest heroes and heroines survive virtually untouched; innocent and faithful love is invariably distorted by society, and the penalty falls most cruelly upon women, etc. For all of the variety of classes represented, Jones does not describe women from the same class as the majority of the readers of *Notes to the People.* The question of how politically aware men treat their women is not posed. The reader can look upon the mistreatment of women in other classes with disgust, but can avoid considering too closely his own possible failings.

What strikes the reader most about both these works is the emphasis upon the violent and vengeful. In the first sketch of *Women's Wrongs* the labourer murders his former employer, and his wife is hanged for concealing him. The gory details, including burying the mutilated body, are spun out through several episodes. Social criticism remains oblique; the husband is fired because he is drunk and inefficient, and not for political reasons. The story points to how society's injustices warp men. Melodrama reaches the depths of bathos in 'The Young Milliner' episode. The medical student has deserted the pregnant milliner, and she dies in a charity hospital. Her body is then used during a medical lecture; the story ends as the student faints in moral anguish. Like Jones, Frost insures that all the enemies of the workers are portrayed at their most venal and gullible. Vincent leers and snickers over the

fate of Lizzie and the torments of the Duke. Like the woman in 'A London Door-Step', Lizzie is mistaken for a drunken prostitute and spends a hideously degrading night in jail. The ambitious sister of Lizzie's seducer marries a forger masquerading as an exiled French marquis; she ends her days the mistress of a local merchant.

Such stories as *Women's Wrongs* and *The Secret,* like so many popular novels, permit the reader to have his cake and eat it. The corruptness of the aristocracy is denounced at the same time long passages are devoted to dramatizing the delights of wealth. In *The Secret* much of Vincent's pleasure comes from seeing his grandchild ensconced amidst all the luxuries of the day. Jones describes with relish how Lady Honora's 'better impulses' are 'polluted' by her environment. She is depraved by attending balls that appear extraordinarily attractive:

> It was at that hour of the evening, in which the imagination, heated by a thousand voluptuous images, conjured up by the ball, loses itself in wild and ardent vision—before fatigue tames down its warmer impulses. There seemed something dreamily intoxicating in the air—the mingled atmosphere of scents and flowers, throbbing with the rapid pulse of music. A burning dew glistened on the purest, fairest brow—and while the gay brilliancy of the hot saloon stimulated and excited, the quiet, warm gloom of the half-seen country wooed to voluptuous and mysterious retirement.[50]

Her poor, spurned lover stands by, commenting bitterly about the 'band of moral assassins' at the ball. The reader is encouraged to enjoy the immoral scene while condemning it—and confirming his prejudices.

Women's Wrongs and *The Secret* share many characteristics with moral fables. In order to portray clear examples of good and evil both types mixed sordid details, the victimization of the innocent and the timely juxtaposition of characters. The irrational accusation of dishonesty against Timothy Twinckle is less obviously dramatic than the contemptuous treatment of Lizzie by her seducer, but the emotional intent is the same. Both the fable and popular fiction point to the unjust attitudes and behaviour of the powerful against the powerless. The melodrama and moralizing in all of these stories was designed to encourage anger and resistance in the reader. Cooper channels these feelings toward Timothy's wordly success as an adult; Frost toward Lizzie's eventual happiness with Ernest. Frost affirms the superiority of an upright mechanic in comparison with the Duke's hypocritical world, and thereby affirms the values of his own readers, and not that of the middle class or the aristocracy. Neither Jones nor Linton provide any solutions outside a continued political commitment. However, in their works the need for change is overwhelmingly clear. It only remains for the reader to take up the issues they have clarified in their fiction.

Two Chartist novels, both the work of leaders, are important because they sought to make Chartists aware of the complexity of radical political action. Ernest Jones, in *De Brassier: A Democratic Romance,* and Thomas Martin Wheeler, in *Sunshine and Shadow,* each wrote about the Chartist movement in fictional form while it was still alive. Wheeler (1811-62) had been a baker, gardener and school teacher, but from 1840 until the mid-'fifties he held a variety of posts in the Chartist Association. He served as secretary of the Chartist Land Company, and was a successful participant in the settlement at O'Connorsville. He had written verse in praise of the experiment, but had done no other writing before beginning his novel.[51] Ernest Jones had considerable experience in Chartist writing and speech making, in addition to the creative writing he had done from childhood. Both men were convinced that the events in which they themselves had participated would interest readers if described in the guise of fiction. Whatever disadvantages there might be in choosing such familiar and recent events were offset by the advantages of placing politics at the heart of their plots.

The Secret and *Women's Wrongs* encouragd class conflict through hatred of the ruling class. *De Brassier* and *Sunshine and Shadow* have their full share of selfish and oppressive aristocrats, but the focus is upon the people's own movement. Jones and Wheeler concentrate on examining the basis of a class-divided society, even to the detriment of the forward movement of the plot. This places the behaviour of individuals in a political and social context; hatred of the ruling class arises out of a class analysis. For example, both writers include scenes of crime. They do not excuse the criminals, but argue that great poverty and great wealth cannot exist together in a healthy state. Hatred and crime are the inevitable result of England's unhealthy condition. Until a just society exists, class solidarity is the workers' only protection against the economic, social and political power of the wealthy. This perspective differs sharply from the middle-class protest novels of the 1840s. Mrs Gaskell, Disraeli and Dickens all sought a solution to social problems through better understanding between the classes. In their works conflict is reduced to a failure of communication or to the weaknesses of individuals within each class. Unions, Chartism and any other form of organized class solidarity are treated with fear and distortion; indeed, these middle-class writers were unable to believe that the working class was capable of organizing itself for social betterment. Christian fellow feeling and gradual amelioration are their solutions to social problems. Jones and Wheeler, as champions of class conflict, followed a new course in their presentation of the social system

from the perspective of the politically aware working man.

The purpose of *De Brassier* was to examine 'why democracy has so often been foiled', or as Jones explained more explicitly in Part II, 'The object of "De Brassier" is to show the People how they have but too often been deceived and betrayed by their own presumed friends. Deceived and betrayed, not by an individual selling them to the government, but by the individual *selling them to himself*.'[52] Although he insisted that the novel contained no portrayals of Chartists, many of the characters and episodes appear to be modelled after well-known persons, and the opinions expressed by the two heroes, Edward and Latimer, are clearly those espoused by Jones. Readers may have mistaken the demagogic, self-seeking De Brassier for Feargus O'Connor. But rather than reading the novel as a *roman à clef,* it is more interesting as a tale of 'the dangers from within' the democratic movement. Jones shows every known weakness of the movement and gives every possible strength to the government and the forces of oppression. He saw the novel as a warning to his readers not to repeat either the errors of the past or the worst evils described in the novel.

The plot of *De Brassier* is exceptionally complicated, with many sub-plots designed to drive home particular political points. The action centres on the well-known aristocrat, Simon De Brassier, who tempestuously leads the people forward in massive marches, appeals to parliament and other activities similar to the Chartist movement of 1838-9. De Brassier successfully blackens the reputations of upright and committed leaders, such as Latimer, a middle-class sympathizer, and Edward, a mechanic. As social tensions come to a head, De Brassier temporizes, and the democratic cause loses the initiative; the government easily defeats a divided and dispirited people. The oppressive treatment of tenants and farm workers by De Brassier's older brother forms an important sub-plot. In this case, revenge is enacted by an embittered woman who has plotted against her seducer, De Brassier's brother, for over a decade. In another sub-plot Jones attacks the banking and factory interests, while adding a romantic touch. Latimer's beloved is the daughter of a selfish and avaricious self-made banker, Henry Dorville. Edward, in the meantime, pines after a woman who loves Simon De Brassier. Jones did not finish the novel; it ends with the successful destruction of the people's movement by the government, and the sentencing of every leader except De Brassier, who escapes into parliament, where he mismanages government funds with impunity.

The novel contrasts the lack of foresight of the people with the well-developed sense of cause and effect of the rich. Repeatedly the people are moved to act without considering the long-range implications of their actions, while the rich always look ahead. De Brassier invests in stock when the market falls as a result of his agitation, he sells at a great profit when his failures in leadership steady the market. Henry Dorville insures his factory for twice its value, hoping his workmen will burn it down and save him the cost of buying new equipment and making necessary repairs. He then retires to a safe seaside resort. Only avarice brings him back; it leads ultimately to his death, but Dorville's weakness is that of a self-made man. The aristocracy may fear the people on occasion, but it always has plenty of toadies and spies who keep it informed of the divisions and weaknesses within their movement. At one point the Cabinet meets to discuss quelling the people, after a luxurious dinner at Lord Weathercock's mansion. Sir Gaffer Grim speaks of 'anarchy and infidelity', and Weathercock mocks him for wearing a mask amongst the Cabinet members—'Call all things by their right names here—truth and enlightenment.' Jones gives the rich no honest motivations, but always credits them with hypocrisy, greed and a love of power. Moreover, they always know how to control those without power. Weathercock had formerly led a popular movement, and accurately assesses how to defeat the democrats:

> Believe me, my dear Grim,—temporise—procrastinate. Popular enthusiasm is at its height now. It never lasts long. Give them no pretext for an immediate outbreak— don't interfere with them—let them commit outrages, they have not done so yet—they will be sure to do so when non-interference and the presumption of self reliance intoxicate them a little more. There are still many of them whom the first act of violence will estrange—it will cause bickerings among themselves, personal antagonisms will ensue—some will be for standing still, merely because others are for going on, and *vice versa;* then the masses will be disgusted at their own leaders—numbers will go home; and then, at last, the time will have arrived to strike a blow. Then, and not till then, the leaders must be seized— and a blow struck, the blood of which shall not be wiped from the memory of the people for a hundred years.[53]

His advice, of course, yields complete success. Although Jones repeatedly speaks of the working class uniting to gain power, his presentation of the united upper classes appears overwhelming. Indeed, at times the only logical action seems to be the long maturing revenge against a single person such as Vincent and the seduced Maline commit. Jones gave the upper classes so much power in order to warn working people against underestimating their enemies. In the past fiery Chartist speech makers had told their followers that firmness of purpose and moral superiority would bring down the government. These simplicities angered Jones, who hoped through his novel to en-

courage a more analytic and considered political position among his readers.

While the rich appear totally selfish and their spies totally powerful, the workers compound their own powerlessness through a love of drama, style and blood. Jones, like Thomson a decade earlier, chastises the poor for their fascination with the aristocracy. Much of De Brassier's initial appeal comes from his dashing aristocratic manner and well-known connections. Latimer loses favour when he sacrifices the advantages of birth to the people's cause. The most common political mistake is following false leadership while denying the true. 'The fitful, selfish, and uncertain guidance of De Brassier' enchants them. Even when his thundering rhetoric on behalf of arrested men yields more severe sentences, the prisoners are proud of his speech and their own self-importance; they give no thought to the years away from home, but yield to the drama of the moment. Repeatedly the people see De Brassier's manner and not his message; in spite of patent lies and prevarications, as long as he appears noble, they forget the past and obey his rulings. Latimer and Edward, in contrast, must suffer mockery, accusations of spying, poverty and general disrepute for their efforts to aid the people. Speaking out of personal experience, Jones describes the reluctance of the people to support their own leaders, particularly when their advice is unpopular; the ordinary organizer or editor was expected to live by his wits while the people fought for a fair day's wage. Finally, Jones was particularly scathing about the petty divisions within the movement. Time and again in *De Brassier* divisions from within prevent the defeat of the oppressors.

In spite of all these weaknesses, Jones remains resolutely loyal to the people. They are deluded and misguided, but never depraved or dishonest. In the fury of just revenge they hold back from harming a woman, 'in angry generosity—one of these chivalric touches, nature's true romance, in which the sons of toil outvie the famed knighthood of the proudest aristocracy'. All possible sneers and attacks on the working class and its movement are examined and analysed without attempting to explain them away. In contrast to the middle-class novelists of the time, Jones never presented the working-class as children in need of instruction; whatever their faults, from ignorance or delusion, they were adults who must learn from their mistakes.

Thomas Martin Wheeler's *Sunshine and Shadow,* published in thirty-seven parts in the *Northern Star* (1849-50), is more narrowly concerned with the career of a single working man than *De Brassier*. Wheeler wrote his novel because 'Our novelists—even the most liberal—are unable to draw a democrat save in warpaint.' *Sunshine and Shadow* would 'prove that Chartism is not allied with base and vicious feelings, but that it is the offspring of high and generous inspirations—that it looks not to self but to mankind: that whilst working for the Present, it holds the future in its grasp, that it is founded upon justice and true to nature, and, therefore, must ultimately prevail.'[54]

Throughout the novel Wheeler emphasizes the high idealism that impels men to join the Chartist cause; the truly degraded are the unprincipled, who are guided solely by selfish desires.

The novel goes from the beginnings of Chartism until 1850. The difficulties of dealing with a subject all his readers knew are overcome by avoiding most of the major controversies and by leaving the hero's actual political activities vague. The plot revolves around Arthur Morton, a typical idealistic working man, who is drawn into the Chartist movement at an early age. He is first forced to flee England in 1839; in a storm he saves the sister of his boyhood friend, Walter North. A pure and holy love grows between him and Julia, married to the dastardly Sir Jasper, governor of a West Indies island. Soon after Julia's premature death, Arthur returns to England and once again throws himself into Chartism. He happily marries a young woman who ardently follows Chartist principles, but misfortune dogs him. After months of unemployment, Arthur succumbs to temptation, and robs a drunken merchant—his former school friend. 'His pure feelings of morality' have been 'broken and disturbed', but he is able to pay his bills and find work. Arthur bitterly returns once again to politics, determined to remove the evils besetting his own class 'with the iron weapons of reality' and 'the demonstrative power of practical experiment.' He becomes leader in the Land Plan, but once again government repression drives him into exile. The novel ends with his wife and daughter faithfully waiting his return, hopeful of the future.

The novel falls into two parts: in the first Arthur undergoes a series of romantic adventures in the manner of G. W. M. Reynolds, but in the second part his career becomes a paradigm of the idealistic working man beaten down by economic circumstances. Unlike Jones, Wheeler did not have any close knowledge of the upper classes, and he is at his weakest when attempting to dramatize their lives. Julia's forced marriage to Sir Jasper is the result of an unbelievable deception practiced by Sir Jasper and her brother. Walter dismisses all his servants one night, fills Sir Jasper with drink, and pushes him into Julia's bedroom. Once raped, she agrees that her only alternative is to marry the man. Wheeler appears to have contrived this brotherly sadism not so much out of hatred for the merchant class, as from his effort to keep Julia perfect. If she is beautiful and intelligent, she will not agree to marry Sir Jasper, so she must be tricked by an ambitious brother. Wheeler further titillates his audience with an extended discussion of the moral implications of Julia's love for Arthur.

> Let not the censorious or the prudish blame my heroine. Love in her was no crime, albeit she was the bride of another,—it was the result of feelings as pure as nature ever implanted in human breast; the treachery of her relatives, and the baseness of Sir Jasper, were the circumstances which caused it to verge upon crime—or rather, should we say, retributive justice. Let the saint and the hypocrite rail on—we write not for their perusal, we heed not their censure, we picture human nature as it is—veritable flesh and blood—glowing with warm and ardent feelings—feelings which are apt to overpower the judgment; but far better is it so than for us to fall into the Dead Sea waters of apathy, or wallow in the mire of cold and frigid selfishness.[55]

Several panting scenes later 'the pure and youthful pair' must part. This leads Wheeler into a long digression on society's cruelty to true lovers, hinting at the possibilities of love conquering all. But Julia chooses 'wealth and respect, but a blighted heart and an early grave', and 'the world's wisdom hallows her choice.' Perhaps, sighs Wheeler, her example may help to reform the world and change those customs which hallow a perverted marriage. As a final gesture toward his reader's vicarious sexual satisfaction, Julia is placed in quarters resembling a harem, where she pines away in spite of numerous black slaves catering to her every whim.

Fortunately Arthur is made of sterner stuff, and the novel returns to its political objectives. Jones's work is most interesting when he is dealing with the dilemmas of leadership; Wheeler is most interesting when he explores the problem of poverty and the respectable worker. Month after month of unemployment drives Arthur to the edge of insanity:

> Had he been alone in the world he could have battled with poverty, or if the struggle became too painful he could easily have withdrawn from the conflict, but his wife and children now bound him to life, he had their lives and welfare to protect, with the maddening knowledge that he was unable to perform it,—that he was a drag upon his wife's energies, a recipient of the in-finitessimal sum that is doled out to the poor sempstress, and to reflect upon it was to endanger the sanity of his intellect. Misery had set her mark upon him—the terrible struggles of his mind were visible in his features,—his former acquain-tance would not have recognized him, in the emaciated and haggard-eyed shadow that might occasionally be seen wandering through the streets of the metropolis, seeking bread but finding none; exploring, with ardent gaze, the very pave-ment of the streets in the vain hope of finding something . . . [56]

Wheeler is too honest to pretend that love strengthened under adversity. While Arthur and Mary do not cease to love each other, they no longer see the other as perfection embodied, nor do they find the same perfect congeniality in each other's company. Arthur torments himself watching Mary eke out a living he feels to be his duty to earn, and Mary must suffer from his moody bitterness. Absolute poverty reduces Arthur to 'apathetic dullness', dividing him from the rest of humanity, whose relative success only deepens the shadow of his own misery. Unlike the hand-loom weavers and stockingers of the North, Arthur is cut off from all companionship during his period of unemployment. Only after he is again at work does he have the energy to look about him and rejoin the Chartist movement. Wheeler's language is plain and harsh when he describes Arthur's descent into 'outcast humanity', with none of the falsely heightened tone he felt necessary for important occasions. It is a stark and moving account of a life many readers must have recognized.

After Arthur robs his old school friend, and feels he has desecrated the memory of Julia, Wheeler muses upon the effects of conscience on those 'driven by stern necessity' to thievery. While Arthur may suffer inwardly, he is not so overcome with remorse as to throw himself into the arms of bourgeois justice. The overwhelming guilt that seems to grip most Victorian heroes or heroines when they have transgressed society's laws, no matter what the circumstances, is seen as artificial and wrong by Wheeler. He does not excuse Arthur, but points to 'the laws of nature', which led him to take the only recourse open for survival. Attacking conventional morality, Wheeler explains,

> [B]ut better far to our ideas of religion and morality is the victim to one great and solitary crime, than the man of the world,—the respectable villain, whose whole life is a series of meanness and hypocrisy, unrelieved by magnanimity of any description,—true, he evades the law and the law's justice, but he is none the less a villain,—the gold that he accumulates may be encrusted with the gore of his starving victims,—the respectability of which he boasts may be based on the ruin and prostitution of hundreds,—the blighted hearts he has trampled upon may be thickly strewn about his path,—but he recks it not, the world smiles on him, he has no remnant of natural religion in his soul, and he knows no remorse; with demure and sanctified countenance he worships in the temple of his God, and boasts, with the Pharisee of old, 'that he is not a sinner like other men' . . . [57]

Throughout the novel Arthur consistently acts out of idealistic principles, whereas Walter North is utterly self-seeking. Arthur's wasted talents, idealism and leadership are but a single example of the price working people pay for society's injustices. The triumph of the democratic movement will bring a return to a natural state where man's natural impulses for goodness and happiness will flourish. Until then Arthur's life will be only a 'shadow' with a gleam of 'sunshine' in the distant future.

Sunshine and Shadow and *De Brassier* differ from the other stories discussed in this chapter in several ways. In these two novels Wheeler and Jones have kept political issues in the fore, and have not given easy solutions to the problems raised. Emigration, Heaven or an inheritance never occur; love is difficult and lovers do not live happily ever after. These authors attempted to recast the conservative plotting and characterization of the popular novel in order to create a new radical novel. Wheeler and Jones believed in the eventual triumph of revolutionary forces, but since change had not yet come and did not appear imminent, they left their novels open-ended. The only possible ending is revolution. Arthur's 'fate is still enveloped in darkness, what the mighty womb of time may bring forth we know not.' Edward and Latimer languish in jail. Unlike *The Secret* or Cooper's fables, there is no personal solution for these three heroes because their lives are entwined with the fate of Chartism.

Sunshine and Shadow and *De Brassier* raise the question of whether it is possible to write revolutionary fiction using a traditional form. The English bourgeois novel has been about a hero (or heroine) who tries and fails to surpass an objectively limited destiny; he becomes chastened and usually adjusts to his fate within a faulty society. In these two works the heroes attempt to change society rather than themselves. They are held back by conditions which the authors consider temporary—the ignorance and selfishness of men, or the power of their oppressors. Once these conditions change, society must necessarily change. But oppression and ignorance are so powerful in the novels that the reader is uncertain about the possibility of revolution. When the processes of change are shown, such as rioting and burning, they are fearsome and destructive of the people's cause. Melodramatic interventions, beyond the control of the heroes, only reinforce the hegemony of the ruling class. In both novels the possibility of a more perfect future is ever-present, but the process of class struggle takes its toll on the heroes. Since they must be left still believing in the cause, and unadjusted to a faulty society, the novels must be left unfinished. Had Chartism continued to develop culturally, it might have developed new fictional forms descriptive of working-class political life and future.

The thread of working-class fiction *by* working men remained slight throughout the century in England; sketches and poetry abound, but full length novels were more difficult and were susceptible to the latest fads. Wheeler and Jones were not able to free themselves entirely from the romantic clichés of the time, but they did establish a new standard of realism based not on the presuppositions of Mrs Gaskell, Disraeli or Dickens, but upon the realism of felt experience. Poverty and its numbing effects were often more powerfully described by Dickens, but Dickens did not give up his fairy-godfathers and happy endings, nor did he see the working man, united with men of his own class, as a source of social improvement. Jones dared to imagine the possibility of working men seizing power by insurrection, a position few other English writers took by 1850. His extremism was never imitated by contemporary working-class writers, with the possible exception of Gerald Massey, but he can be considered kin to William Morris and other late nineteenth-century socialists. Wheeler had more limited literary goals; he recognized the intrinsic interest of his own life and that of his fellow workers, and insisted that such a subject would interest his own class. In this, along with other Chartist poets and novelists, he looked forward to the dialect writers of the North, who flourished in the second half of the century.

Wheeler and Jones established the right of future working men to write a fiction of class solidarity. The importance of *struggle* as a part of literature was often forgotten by working-class writers, anxious to write about the idyllic moments of home life or to escape into poetic realms. The loss of struggle and conflict in their work was linked to the fate of the Chartist movement: co-operation among working men and the middle-class became the necessity of the 'fifties. The single-minded emphasis upon class struggle combined with the stereotypes of the popular novel had not been a wholly successful artistic venture. The safest course appeared to be that of the apolitical praisers of Nature, home and country. And so, with few exceptions, the working-class political novel ceased to be written or published.[58] . . . 'The Reform of Literature' demanded by Thomson involved more than a boycott, a few new novels, a discussion of needs—it demanded talent, time and political understanding. These qualities were seldom found together in the nineteenth-century working-class artist.

Notes

[1] The fullest discussion of Chartist literature to date is Y. V. Kovalev's introduction to his *An Anthology of Chartist Literature* (Moscow: Foreign Languages Publishing House, 1956). It has been translated twice: 'The Literature of Chartism', trans. J. C. Dombreck and Michael Beresford, *Victorian Studies*, II (1958), pp. 117-138; and 'Chartist Literature', *Our History*, 17 (Spring, 1960). John Miller discusses a few Chartist songs in 'Songs of the Labour Movement', *Our History*, 30 (Summer, 1963) and 'Songs of the British Radical and Labour Movement', *Marxism Today*, VII (1963), pp. 180-6. Kovalev's collection, in spite of a number of errors, is an important source of material which has unfortunately never been followed up by scholars. He has, however, emphasized the physical force and revolutionary elements of Chartism disproportionately.

[2] See Asa Briggs, 'The Language of "Class" in Early Nineteenth-Century England', *Essays in Labour History,* eds. Asa Briggs and John Saville (London: Macmillan, 1960), pp. 43-73; and Patricia Hollis, *The Pauper Press: A Study of Working Class Radicalism in the 1830s* (London: Oxford University Press, 1970). See also E. P. Thompson, *The Making of the English Working Class* (New York: Vintage, 1963), pp. 709-46. For a discussion of the efforts of the middle class to educate their 'inferiors' in a very different set of beliefs, see R. K. Webb, *The British Working Class Reader, 1790-1848* (London: Allen and Unwin, 1955), pp. 103-57.

[3] [William Thomson], 'The Politics of Poets', *The Chartist Circular,* 42 (11 July 1840), p. 170.

[4] Ebenezer Elliott was the most famous 'poet of the people' in the 1830s; there was extensive commentary on him and his poetry at the time in all the journals. See Simon Brown, *Ebenezer Elliott: The Corn Law Rhymer, A Bibliography and List of Letters* (Leicester: Victorian Studies Centre, 1971) for a complete listing of sources. See in particular Thomas Carlyle's review of his works in the *Edinburgh Review*, LX (1832), pp. 338-61; W. J. Fox's review in the *London Review*, I (1835), pp. 187-201; and Louis Etienne, 'Les poètes des pauvres en Angleterre; III Ebenezer Elliott', *Revue des deux mondes*, XXIII (1856), pp. 387-400. The standard biography is John Watkins, *Life, Poetry, and Letters of Ebenezer Elliott, the Corn-law Rhymer; with an abstract of his politics* (London: John Mortimer, 1850).

[5] 'William Thom, the Poet of Inverury', *Northern Star,* 14 September 1844.

[6] Ernest Jones, 'Literary Review: Ebenezer Jones', *The Labourer,* II (1847), p. 237. Italics in the original.

[7] 'Thomas Hood, Poet and Punster', *Hogg's Instructor,* n.s. IV (1855), p. 323. Quoted in Donald J. Gray, 'The Uses of Victorian Laughter', *Victorian Studies,* X (1966), p. 158.

[8] For a discussion of Linton's career, see F. B. Smith, *Radical Artisan: William James Linton 1812-97* (Manchester: University Press, 1973).

[9] W. J. Linton, *Memories* (London: Lawrence and Bullen, 1895), p. 75.

[10] *The National: A Library for the People,* I (1839), p. 289.

[11] Jones's life and political career are discussed in John Saville, *Ernest Jones: Chartist: Selections from the Writings and Speeches of Ernest Jones* (London: Lawrence and Wishart, 1952).

[12] *The Labourer,* I (1847), pp. 47-52. Italics in the original.

[13] *The Labourer,* III (1848), pp. 1-8. Italics in the original.

[14] The third edition of *Poems and Ballads* (New York: J. C. Derby [based on the 3rd London ed.], 1854) contains a biographical sketch by Samuel Smiles, reprinted from *Eliza Cook's Journal.* See also Buckner Trawick, 'The Works of Gerald Massey', unpub. diss. (Harvard University, 1942). For Massey's later career, see Trawick and also B. O. Flower, *Gerald Massey: Poet, Prophet and Mystic* (New York: Alliance Publishing Company, 1895). In the period of Victorian self-confidence of the 1860s, George Eliot could model her hero in *Felix Holt* (1866) after Massey, whereas the novelists of the 1840s saw Chartism as a threat to traditional values. The educational Chartists' plea for personal dignity was received sympathetically by Mrs Gaskell, Dickens, Disraeli and others, but the cry for freedom and power struck fear in their hearts. . . .

[15] 'Our Symbol', *Voices of Freedom and Lyrics of Love* (London: J. Watson, 1851), pp. 9-10. *Poems and Ballads,* pp. 181-2.

[16] 'Poetry for the People', *The Friend of the People,* II (3 May 1851), p. 196.

[17] 'Bandiera' [Gerald Massey], 'Poetry to be Lived', *The Red Republican,* I (6 July 1850), p. 19. Italics in the original.

[18] 'Literary Review', *The Labourer,* II (1847), p. 94. Italics in the original.

[19] 'Critic and Poet', 'Our May Garland', *Northern Star,* 8 May 1852. In the dialogue the poet is Gerald Massey; most of the arguments are excerpted from 'Poetry to be Lived'. Harney plays the role of the practical critic.

[20] *Poems and Ballads,* pp. 77-80.

[21] *Voices of Freedom and Lyrics of Love,* p.i. Also quoted in Harney's review, 'Poetry for the People', *The Friend of the People,* II (26 April 1851), p. 177.

[22] *Poems and Ballads,* pp. x-xi.

[23] *Rules of the Barnsley Franklin Club* (Barnsley: J. Elliott, 1845), n.p.

[24] *English Chartist Circular,* II (1842), p. 156.

[25] *The Chartist Circular,* 43 (18 July 1840), p. 182.

[26] For a discussion of popular fiction and its political and social implications, see Margaret Dalziel, *Popular Fiction 100 Years Ago* (London: Cohen and West, 1957); and Louis James, *Fiction for the Working Man, 1830-50* (London: Oxford University Press, 1963). See also Richard D. Altick, *The English Common Reader 1800-1900* (Chicago: University Press, 1957).

[27] 'Literary Review', *The Labourer,* I (1847), p. 96.

[28] *Cooper's Journal,* I (1850), p. 129.

[29] op. cit., pp. 129-32, 209-13.

[30] *Poems on Various Subjects* (Barnsley: J. Elliott, 1865), preface.

[31] Thomas Cooper, *Life* (London: Hodder and Stoughton, 1872), pp. 164-76. See also 'Poets of the People, III: Thomas Cooper', *Howitt's Journal,* III (1848), pp. 226, 242-7.

[32] *The Spirit; or a Dream in the Woodlands* (Leicester: Joseph Ayer, 1849), preface. See also the review of *The Spirit* in *The Leicestershire Movement: Voices from the Frame and the Factory, the Field and the Rail, etc.,* I (1850), pp. 78-9.

[33] *The Purgatory of Suicides, A Prison-Rhyme* (London: Jeremiah How, 1845), pp. 51, 56.

[34] Cooper, of course, thought he did not receive enough attention. But see Philarete Chasles, 'De la poesie chartiste en angleterre', *Revue des deux mondes,* XII (1845), pp. 326-339; [Charles Kingsley], 'Burns and His School', *North British Review,* XVI (1851-52), pp. 149-83 [authorship per Wellesley Index]; Douglas Jerrold, 'New Books', *Douglas Jerrold's Shilling Magazine,* III (1846), pp. 95-6.

[35] Douglas Jerrold, p. 95.

[36] 'Literary Reform', *The Chartist Circular,* 71 (30 January 1841), p. 299. Italics in the original.

[37] Very little work has been done on G. W. M. Reynolds. See 'Mischievous Literature', *The Bookseller* (July, 1868), pp. 445-9; J. V. Hunter, 'Reynolds: Sensational Novelist and Agitator,' *Book Handbook,* IV (1947), pp. 225-36; Dalziel, pp. 35-45; and James, passim.

[38] *Northern Star,* 31 March 1849.

[39] Preface, 'The History of the Democratic Movement, Compiled from the Journal of a Demagogue, the Confessions of a Democrat, and the Minutes of a Spy', *Notes to the People,* I (1851-52), p. 20.

[40] William Empson, *Some Versions of the Pastoral* (New York: New Directions, 1960), pp. 17-20.

[41] 'A Hardwareman', 'Records of the World's Justice: A Pauper', *The National,* I (1839), p. 26. Italics in the original.

[42] First published in *The Labourer,* III (1848), pp. 228-32. Reprinted in *Notes to the People,* I (1851-52), pp. 207-9.

[43] *Wise Saws and Modern Instances* (London: Jeremiah How, 1845), I. p. vii.

[44] *Wise Saws,* I, pp. 222-3.

[45] *Life,* pp. 138-9.

[46] *The Northern Tribune: A Periodical for the People,* I (1854), p. 199. Reprinted in *Old Fashioned Stories* (London: Hodder and Stoughton, 1874), pp. 354-65.

[47] Introduction to *Women's Wrongs,* Bk. IV, *Notes of the People,* II (1851-2), pp. 913-14. Italics in the original.

[48] Thomas Frost wrote two incomplete autobiographies, *Forty Years' Recollections, Literary and Political* (London: Sampson, Low, 1880), and *Reminiscences of a Country Journalist* (London: Ward and Downer, 1886). For a discussion of Frost's involvement with Salisbury Street fiction, see *Forty Years',* pp. 77-95, and *Reminiscences,* pp. 65-84. In later life Frost was the editor of a series of small weekly and daily newspapers. *The Secret* appears during the weeks of 25 May 1850 through 19 October 1850 in the *National Instructor.* As soon as it was finished he started another apolitical serial, which was never finished. He also published several sketches and short stories in the *National Instructor.*

[49] *Notes to the People,* II (1851-2), p. 515. Italics in the original. *Women's Wrongs* appeared regularly throughout vol. II; the fourth episode ('The Lady of Title') was not finished when the periodical died. The novel was later published separately as *Women's Wrongs: A Series of Tales* (London, 1855).

[50] op. cit., p. 939.

[51] A complete account of Wheeler's life is given by William Stevens, *A Memoir of Thomas Martin Wheeler* (London: John Bedford Leno, 1862). Wheeler's enthusiastic support of the Land Plan earned him a number of enemies within the Chartist movement. Wheeler ended his days as an insurance salesman, a job, according to Frost, that many political organizers took as a means of meeting working people and of avoiding reprisals from factory owners.

[52] *Notes to the People,* II (1851-2), p. 833. Italics in the original. *De Brassier* appeared regularly throughout vol. I, and was started again midway through vol. II. It was unfinished when the periodical died, and Jones appears never to have finished it. In the introduction to part II Jones disclaims representing 'particular individuals under the various characters he introduces in the work', and warns in characteristically florid style, that his readers must learn from the novel 'PREVENTION IS BETTER THAN CURE'.

[53] *De Brassier,* Ch. 18, *Notes to the People,* I (1851-2), p. 284.

[54] Ch. 37, *The Northern Star,* 5 January 1850.

[55] Ch. 12, op. cit., 23 June 1849.

[56] Ch. 30. op. cit., 27 October 1849.

[57] Ch. 33, op. cit., 1 December 1849.

[58] Nineteenth-century novels about class conflict from a working-class perspective are so few that a nearly complete list can be given here: W. E. Tirebuck, *Miss Grace of All Souls* (1895); H. J. Bramsbury, 'A Working Class Tragedy', published in *Justice* in 1889; John Law [Margaret Harkness], *A City Girl* (1887), *Out of Work* (1888) and *In Darkest London* (1890); and Robert Tressell [Robert Noonan], *Ragged Trousered Philanthropists* (completed 1911). See P. J. Keating, *The Working Classes in Victorian Fiction* (London: Routledge and Kegan Paul, 1971).

H. Gustav Klaus

SOURCE: "The Historical Bent of the Chartist Novel," in *The Literature of Labour: Two Hundred Years of Working-Class Writing,* The Harvester Press, 1985, pp. 46-61.

[*In the following excerpt, Klaus analyzes the use of the historical novel in Chartist fiction, and argues for its importance in the development of working-class literature.*]

The treatment of Chartism is symptomatic of the insularity that has overtaken so many academic disciplines: whereas the historians' fascination with the period manifests itself in dozens of publications every year, students of English have so far deemed it worthy of little more than the occasional footnote. It is not

Benjamin Disraeli, author of Sybil; or the Two Nations.

a question of parity, for Chartism's socio-historical significance clearly exceeds its standing in literary history. But if we agree with one definition of Chartism as 'a response of a *literate* and sophisticated working class, different in tone and temper from earlier protest movements',[1] then questions arise as to the scope, nature and artistic value of its literary output—questions, surely, to which students of English should be addressing themselves.

It would be presumptuous to attempt a comprehensive discussion of Chartist literature within the confines of a brief chapter, given its diversity and unwieldly profusion. Martha Vicinus lists 'speeches, essays, prison letters, dialogues, short stories, novels, songs, lyrical poems, epics, and, later in the century, autobiographies.'[2] To complete the tally, we should perhaps add politically committed literary criticism and the emergence of industrial reportage ('trades grievances').

In view of the multiplicity of genres, there is much to be said for concentrating at this stage on one particular area, that of the novel. But even here we immediately come up against a difficulty which is peculiar to Chartist literature as a whole, namely the virtual inaccessibility of the texts. Most Chartist fiction—indeed, most Chartist literature—was published in newspapers

and journals, and it was only the odd exceptional work which reached its readers in book form.[3] The serialisation of narrative and other works was of course not uncommon in the mid-nineteenth century, and many of the best-known novelists of the period availed themselves of the device (Dickens, Thackeray, Gaskell and others). However, when we examine the immediate context of such serial fiction, it is clear that most serial publications are at odds with the particular political and cultural ambience which radiates from the pages of the Chartist press. For a proper understanding of the Chartist conception of literature, it is vital at the outset to establish the nature of that journalistic context.

I

If there is one area which bears out Disraeli's apprehensive observation on the development of two separate 'nations' within one state, it is that of the press. The rise of a pauper press can be traced historically to the inability and unwillingness of the established periodicals to articulate any interests other than those of the ruling class. It was a state of affairs which continued fundamentally unchanged right up to the rise of Chartism as a mass movement at the end of the 1830s. Indeed, the war of 'the great unstamped' that had raged during the preceding two decades served merely to exacerbate the polarisation. When the struggle was over, effectively by 1836, it was clear that neither censorship nor the stamp tax could keep the poor men's newspapers down permanently. Individual papers may well have been killed off, but the journalism of the workers, artisans and radicals as a whole survived unscathed. And so it continued in the Chartist period: most Chartist periodicals had an extremely short life-span, but their impermanence was frequently overshadowed by the enthusiastic launching of yet another new publication.

The slogan, 'Knowledge is Power', which heralded the appearance of the *Poor Man's Guardian* (1831-5), was still redolent of enlightenment didacticism and hence not necessarily at odds with certain radical middle-class positions. In the Chartist press, however, an additional and decisive impulse is at work which is alien to bourgeois journalism, that is the emphasis on mobilisation and organisation. Ernest Jones, with whose work as a novelist we shall shortly concern ourselves, characterised this impulse, and thus the ideal conception of a Chartist organ, in the following terms:

> The very first, the most essential requisite of a movement is to have an organ to record its proceedings, to communicate through, with its several branches—to appeal through, to exhort through, to defend through, and to teach through. It is the fundamental bond of union, the ensign of progress, and the means of organisation.[4]

The function described here was fulfilled for many years by *The Northern Star* (1837-52). But besides this most durable of all the Chartist publications, the Chartist movement threw up a huge number of other papers and journals during its barely twenty-year history. All told there were nearly a hundred, but it is perhaps less their number than the fact that they were produced in centres throughout the regions which is most immediately striking. Wherever there was mass support for the six points of the Charter, efforts were made, using handbills, leaflets, tracts, newspapers or journals as the media of instruction to rally and mobilise the artisans and workers. The written and printed word carried many of the movement's great hopes for the progress and spread of reason. A proletarian public was thereby constituted which—for the first time in history—assumed national dimensions and expressed national aspirations, yet at the same time resisted unifying and centralising tendencies. The innumerable regional Chartist newspapers and magazines are therefore in no sense offshoots of a metropolitan-oriented paper—as tends to be the case of the ruling class's political press in the great provincial cities—but represent rather the outcome of self-discovery, solidarity and feelings of identity on a local level.

A further difference concerns disposition and status of literary texts in the newspapers of the period. It would be wrong to generalise and thereby gloss over the fine distinctions between one paper and another, but here again the two camps reveal clearly divergent tendencies. What is noticeable in the Chartist newspapers is that the literary columns, far from being consigned to a separate 'feuilleton' or arts section, enjoy equal prominence alongside the political, historical, temperance or whatever sections. Moreover, as often as not they have a close thematic or ideological affinity with the other columns. The literary texts published in the bourgeois press, on the other hand, are frequently found to bear little or no relation to the rest of the paper. Even when they are not actually hidden away among the political news, among the advertisements and—as industrialisation proceeds apace—the increasingly substantial economic section, they nonetheless constitute to an ever larger extent a foreign body in a whole that is directed by the principles of utilitarianism.

By contrast the Chartist press makes a constant programmatic point of emphasising the intimate relationship between literature and politics. Take, for instance, this statement from *The Labourer*:

> We, however, had one great goal before our eyes—the redemption of the Working classes from their thraldom—and to this object we have made the purpose of each article subservient . . . we have placed poetry and romance side by side with politics and history.

Arguing in a similar vein, the editor of *The Chartist Circular* adds that in selecting material strict criteria were applied:

> No silly romance—no coarse or immoral anecdote was to be admitted. In this generally fascinating walk of literature, all the biographical and historical sketches, all the narratives, stories, and occurrences written or selected for our periodical were to be such as would not only induce our youths to read, but have a tendency to impart to their minds a high moral tone—to inspire them with a noble love of liberty, and an honest detestation of every species of delusion and oppression.[5]

Ultimately, of course, the intermingling of literature and politics in Chartism is expressed most clearly in personal terms, in the fusion of poet/novelist and activist. The movement can no more bring forth the 'impartial' author or the author who writes about reality from a respectable distance than it can spawn 'specialists' or 'freelance Chartist writers'. In this it foreshadows a feature of the subsequent development of the working-class movement: just as all the most eminent Marxist theoreticians up to the beginning of the twentieth century put their principles into practice in the front ranks of the movement itself, so Chartism's most significant artistic contributions are made by authors who were active on its behalf as speakers, organisers and journalists. To take only a few examples from the field of fiction: Thomas Doubleday was editor of *The Northern Liberator* and one of the principal speakers at the 1839 mass rally in Newcastle; Thomas Cooper and Ernest Jones served two-year prison sentences for making inflammatory speeches; and Thomas Martin Wheeler was secretary of the National Land Company.

II

We have already detailed the many different genres which comprise the ensemble of Chartist literature. In so far as it is possible to draw any conclusions from an examination of a dozen of the more important periodicals,[6] the novel is very much a minority form, and particularly so during the first Chartist decade (1837-47). It is all the more instructive, them, to note the tendencies manifested in these early works. Serialisations such as *William Tell, or Switzerland Delivered; Calefi, an Authentic Tale of a Ferrarese Carbonaro; The Incendiary, a Tale of the German Peasant Wars;* or *Albert, or the Spirit of Freedom,* have a number of features in common. First they are set in foreign countries; second, they revolve around struggles for freedom; third, they are rooted in the past (even if their message points to the present); fourth, they are all translations. Just how rudimentary the Charists' own production of fiction was at that stage is confirmed by Wheeler's prefatory remark in his novel *Sunshine and Shadow*. Looking back at the literary record of the movement he notes:

> The fiction department of our literature has hitherto been neglected by the scribes of our body, and the opponents of our principles have been allowed to wield the power of imagination over the youth of our party, without any effort on our part to occupy this wide and fruitful plain.[7]

Wheeler perhaps overstates his case, but if what he has in mind is literary prose that focuses on the worker and renounces fanciful flights into the realms of the aristocracy, he is right. Jones's 1847 romances, for instance, continue to exhibit blatant concessions to the popular literary taste of melodrama, even if he is clearly concerned to portray the corruption and wickedness of those who seduce his working-class heroines as symptomatic of social conditions generally. But—and this is decisive—it is still the nobility and the military élite who are held to blame for such vices. The other principal enemy of the Chartists, the industrial bourgeoisie, does not figure at all in these romances. There was precious little innovation, either, in that early Chartist fiction which derived its themes from the freedom struggles of other peoples and other historical epochs. When *William Tell* was published in *The English Chartist Circular* in 1842, there were already at least four other versions of the story in circulation.[8] Works of this kind represented essentially an attempt to adapt the received form of the historical novel to more radical interpretations of the past.

Only two longer tales, both published anonymously and buried in obscurity for 140 years, stand out from the general run of early Chartist efforts: *Political Pilgrim's Progress* (1839) and *The Pioneers* (1842). *Political Pilgrim's Progress,* which has recently been attributed to Thomas Doubleday, first appeared in *The Northern Liberator.*[9] As its title indicates, it borrows a great deal from Bunyan, an astute move on the author's part, given the popularity which the original enjoyed among the literate artisans and workers. The visionary dream, the motif of the journey, the allegorical form, the use of personified abstractions—all these features reappear. Philosophically, however, *Political Pilgrim's Progress* marks a radical turn toward secular and contemporary political concerns. The obstacles and opponents that stand in Radical's way, as he moves from the City of Plunder to the City of Reform, are the oppressive powers and institutions of contemporary England as well as the intellectual and political adversaries to Chartism. Each and every confrontation which the protagonist has to win through, whether by argument or by struggle, is designed to raise the political awareness of the readers and, where necessary, to arm them in readiness for real struggles.

Similarly, *The Pioneers, or a Tale of the Radical Rising at Strathaven in 1820,* to give its full title, attempts to update and put to effective use a traditional form. It may well have been intended to become a large-scale project, but the Scottish *Chartist Circular,* in which it was serialised, ceased publication after the fourth instalment, and so it remains a fragment. *The Pioneers* distinguishes itself from the derivative historical novels mentioned earlier in two important respects.

For the first time, the struggle for freedom is no longer transposed to another country or an earlier epoch, but is located in the still-continuing historical present. The character of the novel therefore ceases to be metaphorical; it reflects the contemporary situation without resorting to complicated mediating devices. 'If we succeed', says one of the insurgents, 'it will not be a rebellion, it will be a revolution, and instead of punishment, we will receive the gratitude and thanks of a free and happy nation.'[10] As in *Political Pilgrim's Progress,* where Radical's companion, Moral Force, falls by the wayside, the reader can hardly fail to notice the warning that it may be necessary to prepare for armed struggle.

Secondly, the author is not afraid to deviate occasionally from Standard English when it comes to the dialogues, the use of Scottish dialect underscoring his solidarity with the people. In one scene where the fighters are requisitioning weapons, we find the following sentence: 'jist gae wa' and gie us thae guns, as we hae na' muckle time to palaver wi' ye'.'[11] Such unselfconscious use of the Scottish vernacular had of course been given considerable impetus by the breakthrough achieved earlier in Sir Walter Scott's novels, and it is noteworthy that there are no comparable passages in the prose of the English Chartists. In England even Elizabeth Gaskell, with regard to the use of working-class speech the most audacious of the social-problem novelists, felt obliged to defer to her readers' sensibilities by adding footnotes to, or translating into Standard English, the colloquial utterances of her working-class characters.[12]

It is true that *The Pioneers* (together with *Political Pilgrim's Progress,* though the character and thrust of the latter work is quite different) is something of an oasis in what is otherwise a fictional desert. Nonetheless, it does anticipate, and prepare the way, for developments later in the 1840s, when the Chartist novelists strove to consolidate its tentative advances. What were those developments and tendencies? First and foremost, continuing recourse to the historical novel as a generally appropriate genre; secondly, thematic concentration on events from the national past—or, more precisely, on the turbulent political history of the preceding fifty years; and thirdly, the taking up of local struggles and conflicts.

III

There are two particular novels which embody these tendencies at their most highly developed. They are generally regarded as the greatest achievements in the history of the Chartist novel—and, indeed, in contemporary socialist prose generally. Thomas Martin Wheeler's *Sunshine and Shadow, a Tale of the Nineteenth Century,* was published in 1849-50, and Ernest Jones's *De Brassier, A Democratic Romance, The History of a Democratic Movement, compiled from the journal of a demagogue, the confessions of a democrat, and the minutes of a spy,* appeared in 1851-2. The subtitles announce the choice of genre, and in fact the authors make no bones about it. In his foreword Jones declares, 'Fiction does no more than frame the historical picture', and Wheeler concludes his novel with the remark, 'Our object was to combine a History of Chartism, with the details of our story.'[13]

It is, then, all the more puzzling that the critics have made so little of the sense of history which both novels display. Martha Vicinus stresses the formal borrowings from the conventional melodramatic romances as one of their essential characteristics, whereas Jack Mitchell sees both works as examples of the political journalist gaining the upper hand over the novelist.[14] The presence of such elements, which militate against a realist narrative style, is undeniable, but they can only partially explain the strengths and weaknesses of the two novels.

The most immediately noticeable innovation in both novels is that they take Chartism itself as their subject matter. *De Brassier,* it is true, is written as a parable about the dangers that threaten 'every democratic movement' (the term Chartism is not used), but Wheeler, in accordance with his stated objective, actually mentions the movement by name. At this point a short summary of the two novels may help to make it clear that in neither case is Chartism treated peripherally.

De Brassier follows the progress of an impoverished nobleman to the leadership of a popular movement. After denouncing all his rivals and thereby eliminating them, he exploits the movement for his own private purposes and finally allows it to collapse in ruins. Some readers and critics have read the novel as a condemnatory attack on the Chartist leader, Feargus O'Connor, but the character study of a demagogue is only one aspect of the whole, and not a central one at that.[15] Jones is more concerned to represent the movement and its enemies in all their political, ideological and sociological complexity. He does this by means of extraordinarily complicated plots, constant changes of setting and a motley array of characters that need not detain us here. The novel is anyway most memorable for its individual vignettes: the description of an im-

pressive torchlight procession embracing thousands of workers and artisans, for instance, or the caricature of a Cabinet meeting (which was probably not too wide of the mark). And beyond that we are left with an overall impression that the author, for all that he criticises the desperado elements in the movement and, more generally, the corruptibility of the popular masses, never falters in his confidence in the ability of those selfsame masses to learn.

By comparison with the expansive, frequently melodramatic and bombastic scenic representations of Jones's novel, Wheeler's *Sunshine and Shadow* is a remarkably concise, sober and at times even lifeless work. The plot revolves entirely around the proletarian protagonist (and, in the early stages at least, his bourgeois counterpart), and follows his life with all its vicissitudes—one of the several levels of meaning of the 'sunshine and shadow' metaphor. But after a certain point Arthur Morton's life story is overtaken by developments in Chartist political history, and from then on the fate of both are seen to be inextricably interwoven. After making a rousing speech at the Birmingham Bull Ring, which leads to a riot (1839), the hero is forced to disappear into exile. It is not until 1842, when the next great wave of agitation is sweeping across the country, that he reappears in England. Given this interlocking construction, it is clear why Arthur—and not Edward, the colourless mechanic and ineffectual opponent of De Brassier—should have become the first 'broad prototype of the proletarian hero'.[16]

Both works end with the failure of the movement. Jones puts his finger on the smouldering internal disputes, the subjective factor, as the main cause; Wheeler, however, goes further and refers to 'the power of adverse circumstances'[17]—in other words, objective difficulties. There is yet another point of difference: Jones's (unfinished) novel breaks off at an earlier stage, whereas Wheeler brings his story almost up to the time of writing. Which leads us back once more to that aspect of the novels which has already been mentioned, the diminution of the gap between the time that is being narrated and the narrative time itself. In this case the process is pushed to the point where history appears to have actually caught up with the authors. Or to put it another way: the fact that the novel can now encompass Chartism—and in this context we should also mention *Alton Locke, Tailor and Poet* (1850) written by the Christian socialist, Charles Kingsley—is the surest indication that the movement is in decline.[18] For in order for it to be able to do so, certain conditions must obtain, particularly as far as the protagonists are concerned. The movement needs to be in all essentials 'reviewable', relatively complete and historically as close as possible. Only thus can it become the objective of aesthetic reflection—and it is important to stress 'aesthetic', because considerable differences can open up between the imaginative grasp of historical reality on the one hand and theoretical or political utterances about it on the other. While Jones—in the very periodical in which his novel was published—was still campaigning for the renewal of the Chartist movement, and while Wheeler was still championing the Land Plan at the time he was writing *Sunshine and Shadow* in O'Connorville, their novels convey the aesthetic recognition that the movement is finished, even if they do so without a trace of defeatism.[19]

What reasons prompted the Chartists to turn to the historical genre, what were their anticipations, what did they hope to achieve by their choice? The first thing to mention is that Chartism went hand in hand with a marked increase in historical consciousness. Ample evidence is provided by the movement's press, for there is hardly a journal that does not carry regular 'historical sketches'. But this concern with history, the interest in historical writings, and of course the predilection for the historical novel are not by any means peculiar to Chartism but common throughout the literate classes of the age. By the same token, there was nothing original in the fact that the Chartist novelists turned their attention to the nation's past and attempted to politicise the genre. The redoubtable Bulwer Lytton, highly esteemed by Wheeler as a practitioner of this particular form, had already trodden a similar path. He, too, viewed the terrain of history as a sounding board for the articulation of political propaganda, albeit in the interests of Disraeli's Tory democracy.

What sets the Chartists' understanding of history apart from most other contemporary conceptions is its operative principle. Characteristically, Jones's column in *Notes to the People* is entitled 'Lessons from History'. The writings of Bronterre O'Brien, the 'schoolmaster of Chartism', stress the role of the masses as the agents of history and introduce the concept of class as a historical category.[20] Historical consciousness thus comes to be regarded as a necessary precursor of class consciousness. In their novels Wheeler and Jones suggest as much when, faced with the problem of resolving the class conflict they have depicted, they adopt an uncompromising position. This is in stark contrast to the attitude of their middle-class contemporaries, the authors of the social-problem novels, who are more concerned to eliminate class conflict altogether, whether through a change of heart on the part of an individual or through pleas for mutual understanding.

The Chartist conception of history performs another function, too. It serves to keep in check the potentially overwhelming elements of melodrama and romance, as well as distancing the novel in terms of subject-matter from the elevated realms of the aristocracy.

Wheeler at least was fully aware of this: 'We might have made our tale more interesting, by drawing more largely from the regions of romance, but our task was to combine a History of Chartism, with the details of our story.'[21] Similarly, Jones's novel represents a marked advance in terms of realism on his earlier romances, *The Confessions of a King* and *The Romance of a People,* although the latter work, a 'historical tale, of the nineteenth century' to some extent presaged the new tendency.

The Chartists were right to contend that 'the voice of Romance must die before the words of History',[22] but the new direction they were taking imposed its own special burden on the novel. The novelist now ran the risk of descending to the level of a mere historiographer. And in fact there are long passages in Wheeler's work which are best described as narrative reporting rather than graphic representation. The author is constantly obliged to take himself in hand, as he does, for example, after a digression on the city of Birmingham: 'But we are not writing a political essay, and therefore must discontinue this theme.'[23] Moreover, his characters generally lack life because he insists on 'characterising' them directly, seldom allowing them to develop in the course of the action and almost never through dialogue.

Having escaped one dilemma, then, the socialist novel seemed to be moving towards yet another impasse. But even if one set of difficulties had replaced another, this is not to suggest that the novel was simply marking time. A number of advances had in fact been made without beat of drum. At the level of subject matter, for example, the goal of representing a worker in a positive light and making him the central figure in the story had been realised. When it is borne in mind that 'As recently as the 1830's it had often been doubted whether the middle classes were sufficiently interesting to have novels written about them',[24] then the fact that here was an even lower social class which had yet enforced its claim to be represented in literature is undoubtedly of major significance. Additionally, and of particular relevance to the aesthetics of literary production and reception, the leading Chartists recognised that the terrain of the novel could no longer be simply left in the hands of the upper classes; it was now the task of the working class 'to occupy this wide and fertile plain'.[25] And thirdly, the bourgeois entrepreneurs, in the shape of Walter North in *Sunshine and Shadow* and Dorville in *De Brassier,* were now clearly identified as the principal social adversaries of the working class, whereas in the romances the reader's outrage had always been directed against the nobility.

IV

It seems to me more fruitful to view the emergence and development of the nineteenth-century socialist novel as a history of such small steps forward (with of course the occasional reverse), rather than to get involved in the discussion as to why the Chartist novel did not advance beyond the rudimentary stage. If the assumption were to be proven that the nineteenth-century socialist novel cannot stand comparison with the socialist poetry of the same period, then we should indeed be confronted with a problem of general aesthetic relevance—and one, moreover, which could not be dismissed simply by pointing to the lack of creative talent among the working-class and socialist novelists. But the history of the genre is still too incomplete to warrant any such claim, and in any case the arguments which have so far been advanced, although correct in some respects, leave many questions unanswered. The most common contentions are:[26]

a. whereas the poem (hymn or song), a short form that is easy and quick to compose, can be made politically operative at any time and in any situation, the novel is by comparison an unwieldy medium;

b. poetry is rooted by tradition in popular culture, but the novel demands of author and reader alike a high level of education;

c. the Chartist poets (and their successors) were able to call for inspiration on the revolutionary example of the English Romantics (Shelley, Byron), whereas there was no such point of reference for the novelists;

d. the nineteenth-century socialist novelists too often regarded the novel as merely a vehicle for ideas.

Even the most recent and ambitious attempt to transcend such partial explanations and throw new light on the problem fails to lead us much further forward. Jack Mitchell, who regards everything that comes before Tressell's *The Ragged Trousered Philanthropists* as under-developed, argues that a proletariat that is still caught up in the process of developing and shaping itself will of necessity lack a coherent proletarian conception of man. Hence, he concludes, a highly developed socialist novel was a historical impossibility during the Chartist era. Referring to Wheeler and Jones, he writes:

the proletariat was not yet really aware of its new type of revolutionary human validity. . . . although, in Chartism, the pre-1850 proletariat had a working-class Idea to set against the bourgeois Idea, it was a partly utopian Idea which misunderstood and underestimated the present and future role of the working class in history.[27]

The trouble with this explanatory model is that it proceeds in almost hypostatising fashion from a proletar-

ian conception of man that has been fixed once and for all, whereas of course that conception, like the structure and social position of the working class itself, is subject to historical change. Apart from that the argument fails to tell us how it was that a quite different literary form of the period, the working-class autobiography, did in fact contain clearly delineated features of a proletarian conception of man. But the main weakness of Mitchell's case is that it is based on an over-estimation of Tressell, who seems to emerge like a giant out of nowhere.

My concern is not to gloss over the shortcomings of the Chartist novel, nor to belittle Tressell's achievement and talent. But given the present state of research, I believe that general aesthetic discussions should cede priority to the task of reconstructing the tradition itself. Without that knowledge, all attempts to clarify theoretical questions are bound to remain speculative. This is just one of several reasons for my asserting that the study of the Chartist novel, with all the artistic shortcomings referred to above, can be a meaningful and rewarding undertaking.

The Chartist novel merits critical attention because it occupies an early stage in that long if sporadic and uneven tradition which has seen working-class and socialist writers attempting to appropriate productively a literary form which, given its close ties with the rise and history of the middle class, turned out to be a major stumbling block. It is thus important not to approach the Chartist novels with false hopes. Generally speaking, 'working-class literature does not come on the scene with a triumphant succession of great artists.'[28] Hence the proposal to proceed from the small advances and successes and to take account of the reverses.

To concern oneself with the Chartist novel is to take stock of demands made of literature that are seldom encountered in modern literary theory, namely that it should be both operative and agitational. To put it crudely, the Chartists did not conceive of their works as art for art's sake, nor did they write in order to make money. Their best works are informed by the aim of contributing to the consolidation of the movement and driving a wedge into the hegemony of aristocratic and bourgeois culture. This they achieve by validating in aesthetic form the collective experiences of the working masses.

The period in which the Chartists were grappling with the problems of the novel form, the 1840s, is of special interest because it was then that the oppositional elements of proletarian culture began to acquire a literary dimension on an unprecedented, and even in later times rarely equalled, scale. With this development the ensemble of literary areas, practices and interests, was first properly constituted, which is still with us today, albeit in modified form. By this I mean the essentially different, if overlapping and contested areas of 'high-brow art', literature for mass-consumption—and, now, working-class and socialist literature.

Finally, a hint on method. The Chartist novel need not be studied in isolation; not only its aesthetic shortcomings, but also its promise and potential can best be worked out by undertaking an analysis that contrasts it with a novel written from a middle-class perspective that has a similar thematic orientation. The reverse also holds good: the works of Disraeli, Gaskell, Kingsley, Dickens and others should no longer be represented as the only examples of the early Victorian social-problem novel, but ought to be confronted with their Chartist opposite numbers.[29]

Notes

[1] J. F. C. Harrison and Dorothy Thompson, *Bibliography of the Chartist Movement* (Sussex, 1978), p.xi (my emphasis—HGK). I would like to acknowledge the help of Michael McColgan in preparing the English version of this chapter.

[2] Martha Vicinus, *The Industrial Muse: A Study of Nineteenth-Century British Working-Class Literature* (London, 1974), p. 94.

[3] Of the works discussed below only *Political Pilgrim's Progress* was reprinted in book form (Newcastle, 1839). Ernest Jones had his *Woman's Wrongs,* first serialised in *Notes to the People* (1851-2), republished as *Women's Wrongs. A Series of Tales* (London, 1855), and an altered version of his *The Romance of a People,* from *The Labourer* (1847-8), saw the light again as *The Maid of Warsaw, or the Tyrant Czar* (London, 1854).

[4] 'A People's Paper', *Notes to the People,* II (1852), p. 753.

[5] 'Preface', *The Labourer,* I (1847), no page numbers. This probably comes from the pen of Ernest Jones, the editor. 'Our Last Circular', *The Chartist Circular,* II, no. 146, 9 July 1842 (editor: William Thomson).

[6] I have consulted *The Northern Star, The Chartist Circular, The English Chartist Circular, Reynolds Political Instructor, The National, The Northern Liberator, The Labourer, Notes to the People, The Democratic Review, MacDoualls Chartist Journal and Trades Advocate, The Red Republican, The Friend of the People,* and *The Northern Tribune.* Details about these papers and journals in Harrison and Thompson, *op. cit.*

[7] Dedication to Feargus O'Connor prefacing ch. I, *The Northern Star,* 31 March 1849.

[8] Louis James, *Fiction for the Working Man* (Harmondsworth, 1974), p. 86.

[9] See Horst Rößer, 'Literatur und politische Agitation im Chartismus. Eine Studie zu Thomas Doubledays *Political Pilgrim's Progress*', *Englisch Amerikanische Studien,* III (1981), pp. 108-21. The work was serialised in *The Northern Liberator* from 19 January to 30 March 1839.

[10] *The Pioneers* was serialised in *The Chartist Circular,* II, from 21 May (no. 139) to 9 July 1842 (no. 146). The quotation is from 28 May 1842 (no. 140).

[11] *ibid.* 9 July 1842 (no. 146).

[12] See Elizabeth Gaskell, *Mary Barton. A Tale of Manchester Life* (London, 1848), esp. chs. I-X.

[13] 'Preface', *Notes to the People,* I (1851), p. 20; ch. XXXVII, *The Northern Star,* 5 January 1850 (my emphasis—HGK).

[14] Martha Vicinus, 'Chartist fiction and the development of a class-based literature', in H. Gustav Klaus, ed., *The Socialist Novel in Britain* (Brighton, 1982), pp. 9-10; Jack Mitchell, 'Aesthetic Problems of the Development of the Proletarian-Revolutionary Novel in Nineteenth-Century Britain', in David Craig ed., *Marxists on Literature* (Harmondsworth, 1975), p. 257.

[15] R. G. Gammage, *History of the Chartist Movement* (London, 1969 [1854]) pp. 361-6; Vicinus, 'Chartist fiction', pp. 19, 25. But see John Saville, *Ernest Jones: Chartist* (London, 1952), pp. 251-5 who categorically denies any such claim and argues in my view convincingly that 'by no stretch of imagination can O'Connor be identified with the character of Simon de Brassier' (p. 253). Peculiarly enough, if there are any parallels to be drawn between De Brassier and a real-life Chartist leader, then Jones himself comes nearest. Descending from an aristocratic family, he was initially a thoroughgoing conservative and joined the Chartist movement only after a financial disaster in 1845-6. cf. *Diary of Ernest Jones, 1839-47, Our History,* Pamphlet 21 (1961).

[16] Mitchell, *op. cit.* p. 256.

[17] Ch. XXXVII, *The Northern Star,* 5 January 1850.

[18] Kingsley started writing his novel at about the same time as Wheeler, early in 1849. Jones was then still in prison.

[19] cf. the opening lines of Jones's poem 'We Are Silent':

We are dead, and we are buried!
Revolution's soul is tame!
They are merry o'er our ashes,
And our tyrants rule the same!

The following verses 'But the Resurrection's coming/ As the Resurrection came', with their religious overtones, seem to affirm an unshakeable belief rather than actually refute the prevalent note of dejection. (*Notes to the People,* I, 1851, p. 92.)

[20] See, for instance, his *The Rise, Progress and Phases of Human Slavery,* serialised in *Reynolds Political Instructor,* I (1850), later reprinted in book form (London, 1885).

[21] Ch. XXXVII, *The Northern Star,* 5 January 1850.

[22] Ernest Jones, *The Romance of a People, The Labourer,* II (1847), p. 12. However, this work is still very much a blend of romance and older historical novel. Its theme is not English history, but scenes from the Polish freedom struggles.

[23] Ch. VIII, *The Northern Star,* 26 May 1849; see also ch. XXVII, 6 October 1849.

[24] Raymond Williams, 'Forms of English Fiction', in Francis Barker *et al.* eds., *1848: The Sociology of Literature* (Essex, 1978), p. 279.

[25] See note 7.

[26] The following arguments are summed up and criticised by Mitchell, *op. cit.* pp. 245-6.

[27] *ibid.* p. 265.

[28] Ashraf, *Englische Arbeiterliteratur,* p. 23 (my translation—HGK).

[29] Until some publisher undertakes to bring out these Chartist novels, there remains for study in class the problem of inaccessibility, though it is not really insurmountable. Most university libraries will have a copy of the 1968 reprint of Ernest Jones's *Notes to the People.* And it is always possible to order individual photostats from the British Museum Newspaper Library in Colindale, which has a file of *The Northern Star* (in the case of Wheeler's novel).

THE CHARTIST PRESS

Dorothy Thompson

SOURCE: "The Chartist Press," in *The Chartists,* Temple Smith, London, 1984, pp. 37-56.

[*In this excerpt, from a history of chartism, Thompson describes the development and characteristics of the Chartist press and explains its importance in creating a national movement.*]

Chartism came about because the people in the different manufacturing districts found themselves agreed on the need for a movement to protect their existing institutions and achievements, to resist the attacks being mounted on them by the newly-enfranchised employing class, and to press forward for more freedoms and a more equitable system of taxation, employment and citizenship than the society of the 1830s offered them. Other beliefs and other programmes were added to the central political demands of the Charter, and there were regional and occupational differences of emphasis. What was new and powerful about the movement, however, was its national character and the speed with which ideas and proposals for action were disseminated. This speed and this national dimension were achieved largely through the press.

The Chartist press was one of the foundations on which the movement was built, and one of the bridges with earlier movements. Of all the immediate precursors of Chartism, the 'war of the unstamped' was among the most significant and influential.[1] Not only were many of the leading journalists and platform orators veterans of the unstamped, but very many of the leading provincial radicals had first come to feel themselves part of a national movement through the part they had played in selling and distributing the papers. From the time of the Six Acts onwards, the Government's attempt to price newspapers out of the working people's reach by the imposition of a heavy stamp duty on each issue had been challenged by a number of radical journalists and publishers. Their main tactic was simply to publish and sell cheap periodicals without the necessary stamp, and to accept the inevitable punishment of fines or imprisonment.

The best and most influential of the unstamped journals was the London-based *Poor Man's Guardian* (1831-5). Its publisher, Henry Hetherington, a leader of the campaign, was a signatory of the People's Charter, and remained a radical and a Chartist until his death from cholera in 1849. The *Guardian*'s editor for most of its life was Bronterre O'Brien, at his best the ablest of all the radical journalists of this period. His main positive contribution to Chartism was made in its early years, when he ran *Bronterre's National Reformer* for the first quarter of 1837, edited the *Operative* from November 1838 to June 1839, and contributed regular columns to the early editions of the *Northern Star.* John Cleave, after Hetherington the most important of the metropolitan unstamped publishers, became the London agent for the *Northern Star* and published, among a great deal of other radical literature, the *English Chartist Circular* from 1841 to 1843.

William Carpenter, whose *Political Letters* in 1830 had been one of the first unstamped journals to earn its publisher a prison sentence, was editor of the *Charter* in 1839 and 1840, and the *Southern Star* in the first half of 1840. John Bell, editor of the *London Mercury* in 1837 and later associated with the Newcastle *Northern Liberator* in 1839 and 1840, had been associated as editor and publisher with the unstamped *New Political Register,* as well as having edited the radical, stamped, *True Sun.* William Benbow, a veteran of the National Union of the Working Classes in 1831 and 1832, and of almost all the radical agitations since the wars, had edited the *Tribune of the People* in 1832 and the *Agitator and Political Anatomist* in 1833, and continued to publish journals and pamphlets, including several editions of his *Grand National Holiday;* he was early in the Chartist movement, and was imprisoned for sedition in 1840. The inspector of prisons who interviewed him in 1841 noted:

> The name and character of this prisoner is familiar to all acquainted with agitation. The associate of Carlisle [*sic*] Hetherington and others, he is now 56 years of age and time seems to have abated nothing of his warmth in the cause of republicanism.[2]

J. B. Lorymer, who had edited several of the republican unstamped journals, was a founder member of the East London Democratic Association, and contributed to its journal the *London Democrat.* Richard Lee, printer and editor of the *Man* in 1834, was London correspondent of the *Northern Star* from 1839 to 1841 and the printer of the *English Chartist Circular.* In Yorkshire, Joshua Hobson, editor and publisher of the unstamped *Voice of the West Riding* (1833-5) and three times prosecuted, became the publisher and for a time the editor of the *Northern Star,* while his associate William Rider, who edited the *Voice* while Hobson was in prison, became a founder and leading member of the Leeds Working Men's Association and a delegate to the first Convention.

Continuity between the two movements can be seen in the persons of agents and distributors of the papers, as well as of journalists and publisher. Of the hundreds who sold the unstamped papers and served terms of imprisonment for doing so, many turned up as agents for the Chartist journals, and many more whose names have not survived may be assumed to have been among the earliest Chartists. The governor of Coldbath Fields prison, who had had charge of many of the vendors in the early thirties, recalled:

> Many of them were really good-tempered, and even facetious declaimers on popular rights, whose erratic ideas and mental dreaminess were of a very unusual stamp, and quite explained the visionary nature of their political creed. They delighted to call themselves 'working men', although they were unlike the general mass of working men. . . . A judicious alteration in the act regarding newspaper stamps deprived me of all my 'martyrs' and I have not the slightest notion how those men thereafter developed their political tendencies, but I surmise they swelled the cry for the 'People's Charter'.[3]

Best-known of the former vendors in later years was G. J. Harney, who had been imprisoned while still in his teens and went on to become editor of the *Northern Star* and one of the national leaders of Chartism throughout its existence. But other less well-known figures throughout the country bridge the gap between the two campaigns, people like Alice Mann in Leeds, Joshua Hobson of Ashton-under-Lyne, and Abel Heywood of Manchester, who had the Manchester agency for the *Northern Star* and acted for a time as Feargus O'Connor's business manager. In the West Riding James Ibbotson of Bradford, Titus Brooke of Dewsbury and Christopher Tinker of Huddersfield, all former prisoners of the Government, appeared as early agents for the *Star.* In Barnsley Joseph Lingard and his wife, who had been vendors of the unstamped journals, were agents for the Chartist papers, whilst four of the six agents listed as handling the *Star* in Birmingham in 1838 had been prosecuted for selling unstamped papers, including James Guest, who had first introduced the metropolitan journals to Birmingham when he began to sell *Carpenter's Political Letters* there in 1830.[4]

Among the immediate ancestors of the London Working Men's Association was the Association of Working Men to Procure a Cheap and Honest Press, formed early in 1836 with the help and encouragement of the American Dr Black, for the purpose of raising money and support for the imprisoned unstamped publishers. There was considerable overlap between this body and the LWMA formed later in the year. John Gast, the shipwright's leader, was a member of both, as were Robert Hartwell, Richard Moore and William Lovett.[5] Both in and out of Parliament, Feargus O'Connor was a prominent speaker on behalf of the unstamped, and of press freedom in general. He had been the chief supporter of the radical editors of the *True Sun,* imprisoned in 1834 under the law of libel for recommending the nonpayment of house and window tax in the campaign for a property tax, had spoken in their defence at public meetings, and presented in the House of Commons the petition against their imprisonment. The Marylebone Radical Association which he helped to found in 1835 had the freedom of the press as one of its founding aims, and the Univeral Suffrage Club which he started in association with Augustus Hardin Beaumont also included the fight against the stamp duty as one of its prime objects.[6]

The unstamped campaign was therefore part of the early political experience of a very large number of

Chartism's first leaders. Taking part in it had taught them certain important practical lessons. They had learnt how to write, publish and disseminate a tough, immediate radical propaganda, how to finance and organise a movement of resistance to authority, how to organise support for members and their families who were prosecuted and imprisoned. The campaign also brought home political convictions which were to form part of the consciousness of the Chartist years. After the Reform Bill, working-class radicals expressed feelings of betrayal towards those reformers among the middle classes who had used the rhetoric of liberty and equality, but who accepted the finality of the 1832 settlement. There were middle-class radicals in Parliament and outside, however, who continued to advocate an extension of the suffrage, and to accept a degree of cooperation on the question with working-class radicals. Some of these men were strongly opposed to the newspaper taxes, and mounted a campaign of petitions and meetings in support of their abolition. But as the campaign developed, a strong division emerged between this middle-class campaign and the law-breaking campaign of the unstamped. Even Cobbett, writing in friendship to Joshua Hobson in gaol, warned him of the folly of deliberately breaking the law and urged him not to do so again.[7] The parliamentary lobby against the taxes, and the educational and political-economic speakers outside the House, found the actions and the language of the radical unstamped sheets an embarrassment. On occasion they found it necessary to make public criticisms, and to dissociate themselves from such unwanted allies.[8] When the Newspaper Bill was brought in in 1836, and proposed to reduce the stamp duty to 1d, instead of to abolish it altogether, Thomas Wakley could find only one supporter for his motion for complete abolition. To the working-class and ultra-radical reformers this was betrayal on the lines of 1832. As the *Northern Star* later put it, the reduction 'made the rich man's paper cheaper, and the poor man's paper dearer'. An address issued by the Association of Working Men to Produce a Cheap and Honest Press declared:

> The stamp duty is to be reduced to a point which will permit newspapers to circulate freely among the middle classes, as if the press were actually free; while so much of the stamp duty is to be retained, and such an inquisitorial law is to be enacted in addition to all those now in force, as shall utterly prohibit the circulation of newspapers among the working classes.[9]

The radicals drew three conclusions from the experience—firstly the need to gain access to the law-making process, secondly the essentially property-defined nature of the social attitudes of the existing legislature, and thirdly the folly of relying on the support of allies and sympathisers among the higher classes. The Newspaper Act was another of the issues over which the

radicals quarrelled with Daniel O'Connell. In the earlier days of the campaign he had supported the complete repeal of the taxes, but in the event he supported the limited repeal of the 1836 Act. John Bell wrote:

> The productive classes of England have once more been betrayed by their leaders. Had Mr. O'Connell chosen, he could have forced the Whigs to repeal the whole of the taxes on political intelligence. It has suited Mr. O'Connell, however, to desert this mighty cause. His price is the Irish Corporations Bill . . .[10]

The 1836 Act, besides reducing the duty from 4d to 1d per copy (prepaid) on all newspapers, greatly increased the penalties for producing or possessing unstamped newspapers. In the two years before the Act, the unstamped publishers had become bolder, and had replaced the original small format of their journals by a full newspaper-sized broadsheet, and by an approach to the presentation of news which was more like that of a conventional stamped newspaper. In 1834 a judgement in court had declared that the *Poor Man's Guardian,* which had occasioned so many prosecutions and punishments, was not in fact a newspaper within the meaning of the Act. This decision, and the passing of the 1836 Act, left publishers with the alternatives of going back to small-sized cheap journals, carrying comment only, or of converting the large unstamped papers into legal newspapers, selling at a higher price. Hetherington decided to make his *Twopenny Dispatch* into a stamped journal, and in September 1836 it appeared as *The London Dispatch and People's Political and Social Reformer,* priced 3½d. Its publisher was apologetic about his submission, but justified it on the grounds of the new harsher penalties: 'Against a power like this, personal courage is useless . . . unless . . . some means can be devised either to print newspapers without types and presses, or render the premises . . . inaccessible to *armed force,* no unstamped paper can be attempted with success.'[11] Bronterre O'Brien used the other method. In January 1837 he produced a small paper, *Bronterre's National Reformer, In Government, Law, Property, Religion and Morals.* It consisted of four thin sheets, and sold for 1d, but contained no news. 'A hard case it is to be sure, for it is hard to write politics without glancing at the '*goings on*' around us, but the fault is of the liberal Whigs, not mine.'[12] The *Dispatch* needed to sell, Hetherington considered, 16,000 copies a week to pay its way. Bronterre need perhaps have sold far fewer, but his sale of 4,000 copies was not sufficient to sustain the journal, and it closed before the end of March.[13] The *Dispatch* was more successful, and lasted for three years; however, it never circulated outside London to any great extent, nor was it ever in any sense the journal of the Chartist movement. It was Radical in tone, supported universal suffrage and social and political equality, but was, like the LWMA itself, somehow too cautious and pompous in tone to become the journal of a movement as varied and popular as the early Chartist movement.

Before the foundation of the *Northern Star* in November 1837, Daniel Whittle Harvey's *True Sun* in London, and George Condy's *Manchester and Salford Advertiser* in the provinces were the newspapers most widely supported by radical working men. Few individual working people bought them, but in the alehouses and coffee-shops a selection of the most popular journals was available, and among serious-minded people the practice of joining together to subscribe to a weekly paper was clearly established well before the Chartist period, when it became very widespread. John Snowden recalled going as a young boy in the early thirties to the house of a 'good old radical' to read the *Leeds Mercury,* which cost 7½d a copy.[14] But like all the established journals, even the most liberal, the *Mercury* in the years after the reform agitation took an approach on certain critical issues which alienated its working-class readers. For a time the Yorkshire radicals moved their loyalties to the Tory *Leeds Intelligencer,* whose support for the factory movement under Richard Oastler was an important factor in the Tory—radical alliance which preceded Chartism in parts of the West Riding. The founding of the *Leeds Times,* under the more radical-liberal editorship of Robert Nicoll in 1837, was welcomed by the working-class radicals initially, until their loyalties were transferred to the *Star* later in the same year.

The *Manchester and Salford Advertiser* was unique among the commercial journals of the North of England in having as its editor a radical who not only supported the main planks of the working-class radical programme, but consistently urged the creation of independent working-class political organisations. George Condy, who shared with Thomas Ainge Devyr the unusual component of Irish Methodism in his ancestry, was an ultra-radical, factory reformer, strong opponent of the 1834 Poor Law, an advocate of universal suffrage and a founder-member of the Society for the Promotion of National Regeneration.

The *Advertiser* was the only stamped journal outside London to report the radical activity of the year 1834, and to record the widespread protests at the sentences on the Dorchester labourers. Its circulation was mainly in the radical strongholds of Lancashire, although its style made few concessions to a popular readership. The fact that its circulation dropped after the *Northern Star* started, and even more sharply after the end of 1839 when, after having initially welcomed Chartism without reserve, Condy declared it to have been betrayed by 'the pike and musket violence of the extremists', and offered the support of his journal to the Anti-Corn-Law League, suggests that it had been sustained between 1833 and 1837 by at least a section of

those who were to find the paper they really wanted in the *Northern Star.*

The unstamped journals had been in the main individual voices in the tradition of Cobbett. Among the Chartist journals this tradition was also maintained, and a series of mostly unstamped, usually locally-produced journals appeared. *Udgorn Cymru (The Trumpet of Wales)* was published in Merthyr Tydfil from the blacksmith's forge of David John, Unitarian minister and organiser of a Chartist school and Sunday school.[15] In Glasgow the *Chartist Circular* carried throughout its three years of life the measured, self-educating tone of its editor William Thomson. Its English near-contemporary, *The English Chartist Circular and Temperance Record for England and Wales,* edited by James Harris, had, in spite of a somewhat similar tone, a very different personality. It was made up far more of fairly long articles and disquisitions by reflecting Chartists from a variety of localities which varied from the verbosely uninformative addresses of poor John Watkins (whose own *London Chartist Monthly Magazine* appeared briefly in 1843)[16] to the interesting and sensitive biography of William Ellis which Thomas Cooper submitted in the aftermath of the Staffordshire riots. As the forties proceeded, more and more of these small, personal unstamped journals appeared. Peter Murray McDouall produced *McDouall's Chartist and Republican Journal* from Manchester in 1841, in whose columns he discussed political questions in a general manner, but in the context of current events. Thomas Cooper ran a whole series of small journals, starting with the *Midland Counties Illuminator* in 1841 which, for all the restriction of actual news, gives a good idea in its editorial and correspondence columns of the breadth of Chartist activities in the Leicester area in that year. The *Extinguisher* and the *Chartist Rushlight* appeared in 1841, *The Commonwealthsman or Chartist Advocate* in 1842.

It is clear that Cooper saw his work of organising and teaching his Chartist followers in the two years of his activity in Leicester as necessitating the use of regular printed material. In his letters some of the problems of the unstamped as against the stamped journals can be seen.[17] The stamp, as well as being a tax, was also the legal definition of a newspaper, and carried the privilege of free post. The *Northern Star,* for which Cooper was the local agent, was sent post-free, was despatched in large quantities and was invoiced by an efficient central office. The small unstamped papers which retailed at ½d or 1d a copy got no concessions from the post or railway, and could rarely have been worth the effort of handling them in terms of the profit they produced. Nevertheless, if they could be made to cover the cost of production, these small sheets enabled particular positions within the movement to be articulated, and the views or grievances of particular members to be aired. After his release from prison, Cooper found for a time that booklength work, lecturing and some occasional journalism in London filled his time. By 1849, however, he was again helping to edit a small journal, the *Plain Speaker,* which was followed in 1850 by *Cooper's Journal or Unfettered Thinker and Plain Speaker for Truth, Freedom and Progress*.

The last phase of Chartism saw a great proliferation of these small, personal journals. Harney edited the *Democratic Review* in 1849 and 1850, and the *Red Republican,* which started in June of the latter year, changing its name to the less controversial *Friend of the People* after a few months. Ernest Jones and Feargus O'Connor jointly edited the small monthly *Labourer* in 1847 and 1848, which closed with Jones's imprisonment. When he came out of gaol he started his weekly *Notes to the People,* which contains some of his best writing in prose and verse. In the introduction to the first volume, issued after six months, he complained that the paper had lost him money. Newsagents had refused to handle it or to display his bills. Where the bills had been displayed, the police, or on some occasions hostile radicals, had torn them down. But above all he complained that he had alienated his potential supporters.

> The readers of the 'Notes' may be expected to consist of political democrats, social democrats, trades' unionists and co-operators. A correspondent tells me, I have set to work just as though I intended systematically to destroy the circulation. Firstly, I estrange a large portion of the political reformers, by exposing and assailing demagoguism and pointing to the paramount importance of social measures. . . Secondly, by endeavouring to show that social reforms are unattainable to any great or permanent extent without previously securing political power, I am told that I alienate a second class of readers—those who look down with contempt on political agitation and think that the discussing of philosophical problems will batter down stone walls. Thirdly another body of readers are said to be driven away by my attempt to expose the injurious tendency the present cooperative movement has been assuming. . . . Fourthly a further section of readers are supposed to be estranged by the articles that seek to show the futility of any mere trades' union regenerating the social happiness and power of the working-classes.[18]

Nothing could illustrate more clearly the difference between the paper that is the voice of an individual and the paper that is the voice of a movement than this catalogue. By the early fifties the old Chartist journalists, including Jones, who did try, with his *People's Paper* from 1852 to 1858, to publish a national broadly-based weekly, had divided into small groups, publishing journals based on their own par-

ticular viewpoints, which had little sense of speaking for or to a movement. The tradition of popular radical journalism had been inherited by ex-Chartists like G. W. M. Reynolds and Edward Lloyd, for whom it was a commercial project. *Reynolds's Political Instructor,* issued weekly during the winter of 1849-50, while its editor was still very much committed to Chartism, survived for a further century as the radical weekly *Reynolds' News*.

As long as the newspaper stamp and advertisement duties existed, there was a place for the small non-newspaper, a vehicle for political opinions and controversy which could be produced well below the cost of a newspaper. Harney, who produced more than one such journal in the early 1850s, noted in the last volume of the *Northern Tribune,* which ended with the abolition of the stamp duty in 1855: 'The abolition of the 1d stamp on newspapers . . . will cause a revolution in journalistic literature, and in all periodical publications partaking of a political character. Indeed, for political periodicals there will be no place; they must become newspapers or nothing.'[19]

Small, unstamped journals and a mass of pamphlets and broadsides formed the basis of much of the political education and discussion in the Chartist movement. But the most important by far of all Chartist publications was the *Northern Star*. Most historians have suggested that O'Connor's leadership of Chartism derived from his ownership and control of the *Star*. Alone among Chartist journals it made a profit. It was taken in every part of Britain. Every kind of organisation, from the collection of funds to the organisation of rallies and lecture tours, was recorded in the *Star,* political issues of all kinds were thrashed out in its columns. News of the movement was printed in it, national and international news was printed and explained. The owner of such a vital part of the whole movement must have had an enormous advantage over any potential rivals for its leadership.

But this judgement, like so many, is an over-simplification. The *Star* was indeed a powerful force, but there was no intrinsic reason why it should have had a monopoly of Chartist support. At the time of its foundation several possible rivals were either in the field or soon to be launched. The *London Dispatch* might have exercised hegemony on behalf of the 'moderate' radicals in the movement, the *Manchester and Salford Advertiser* was already supporting the issues of trade union defence, hostility to the new Poor Law, support for the Canadian rebels and the demand for universal suffrage, which may have been said to have constituted the main issues on which radicals were exercised in the summer of 1837. The *Birmingham Journal* was under ultra-radical editorship, and was strongly in support of all the main radical demands; indeed it has often been considered as a Chartist newspaper in the early months of the movement. Had the majority of potential customers wanted a different kind of radical journal, a more moderate one, and one less committed to the particular views of Feargus O'Connor, there were such papers on offer. And since it is usually suggested that O'Connor started the paper with little or no contribution from his own pocket, it could also be said that any one else who wished to do so could have started a paper in opposition, or as an alternative to the *Star.* Other later attempts were made, notably the *Operative* and the *Southern Star,* both of which, incidentally, were welcomed and encouraged by O'Connor, but neither ever became financially viable.

The fact is that, so far from being used to impose his leadership on the movement, the *Northern Star* owed its success to the fact that it was Feargus O'Connor's paper. The immediate response and phenomenal early success of the paper showed that Feargus and his collaborators had judged the mood of provincial radicals correctly, in the timing, location and tone of the new paper. The continued and increasing success throughout 1838 and 1839 showed that O'Connor's method of running the paper satisfied a large readership.

Anyone who has read the *Star* knows that it is very far from being the kind of one-man paper that was traditional among radical journals. The paper had an editor who was a determined and opinionated radical, the Rev. William Hill, a Swedenborgian pastor from Hull who had formerly been a linen handloom weaver in Barnsley. Editorial control rested with Hill, and later with the other editors, Joshua Hobson from 1843 to 1845, and G. J. Harney from 1845 to 1850. O'Connor's role was as a major contributor—most weeks he wrote a front-page *Letter,* he occasionally wrote other columns, and he always ensured that his speeches were reported in full. But for the rest—the greater part of the paper—he allowed his editors and other staff considerable freedom. The *Northern Star* was run in accordance with O'Connor's idea of what a radical newspaper should be—and this was much more like a radical *Times* than like a reincarnation of Cobbett's *Political Register.* The paper succeeded because it was considered by its readers to be the paper of the Chartist movement, not simply the voice of Feargus O'Connor. This was a strength not only of the paper, but of the whole Chartist movement, and it was to a large degree O'Connor's contribution.

Chartism differed from earlier radical movements in scale more than in its programme. Its significance lay in its ability to hold together over a period of years a variety of impulses within a single programme, and to cover the whole of the British Isles in its appeal and its organisation. Corresponding societies were still illegal in Britain, and in any case the corresponding and

organising abilities and experience among the varied groups which made up the movement would never have been sufficient to have created a unified movement capable of mounting a sustained programme in the way that the Chartist movement did. The essential organising power was the *Star,* and the qualities which made it so were the abilities of its editorial directors and the overall policy of its owner.

The *Star* welcomed and reported all radical initiatives. Outright hostility was usually reserved for the Government and its supporters, the exponents of anti-radical policies or programmes, or occasionally for what were seen as divisive moves within the radical forces. It was this latter approach which has been held to show that the journal supported one faction only of the movement. Writers like Hovell used the term 'O'Connorite' as if it had been one faction among many contending for the loyalty of the ordinary supporters of the Charter, and suggested that the *Star* was used unfairly to assert the control of that group. But apart from the fact that the journals put out in direct opposition to what could be called 'O'Connorite' but should more properly be called 'mainstream' Chartism all failed to gain support and readership among the Chartists, a reading of the *Star* must dispel this picture. An enormous range of radical activity is reported. Socialism, Owenism, cooperation, Christian radicalism of many kinds, tradeunion activity, all appear regularly. Correspondence about the correct path for Chartists to take, criticism of the leadership—including on many occasions that of O'Connor himself—wrangles, accusations of bad faith or outright dishonesty, as well as thousands of reports of meetings, lectures, demonstrations and organisational matters of all kinds fill its columns. Most historians of the movement have abstracted their most telling criticisms of O'Connor from the columns of the *Star* itself, and certainly the information from which the biographies, political and personal, of the other leaders and activists of the movement are constructed derives almost entirely from the paper. It is a record of a movement which is remarkable for the fullness and variety it presents—compared with earlier and with subsequent radical journals.

The strength and novelty of the *star* lay in several things. Feargus was unquestionably the owner of the paper. He paid off the original shareholders as soon as he was able, and retained in his own hands the control and disposition of the profits. This was, of course, no new thing for radical publishers. Hetherington, Watson, Cleave, Carlile, all lived from their publishing ventures. Most of the earlier radicals had invested their profits in further publishing, often subsidising less popular or successful items with the profits from successful ones. O'Connor made a new departure in using the profits from the paper to subsidise the movement rather than further radical publishing. He appointed agents in the main provincial centres whose task was to report for the paper and to act as full-time organisers for the Chartist movement. Harney was paid £2 a week to do this in Sheffield in the early forties, George White in Birmingham, Edmund Stallwood in London, and a number of others at various times. In addition the profits from the sale of the paper enabled radical booksellers to rely on a regular income, and to themselves form a nucleus for the spreading of radical ideas and the sale of less profitable literature. Subventions from the *Star* profits went to help defray defence costs for Chartists on trial—including the very heavy costs of the Welsh trials—and to support the families of imprisoned Chartists. In 1848-50 payment from O'Connor relieved the London Chartists from the degrading punishment of oakum-picking. All these uses of the money helped, of course, to reinforce the power and prestige of the *Star*'s owner, and the patronage which he exercised within the movement. It also enabled a movement, which consisted in the main of people who would have been hard put to it to supply any kind of regular income, for ten years or more to sustain a reasonably stable leadership, and to offer at least some protection and care for those who suffered persecution and hardship for their part in it. The success of the *Northern Star* would have been impossible without the Chartist movement, but it is equally impossible to imagine Chartism without the *Star*.

The *Northern Star*, like the *London Dispatch*, felt it necessary to apologise to its readers in its first issue for its concession to the law in the form of payment of stamp duty. Clearly Feargus, just as much as Hetherington, expected his readers to come from among those who had supported the unstamped: 'Reader—Behold that little red spot, in the corner of my newspaper. That is the Stamp; the Whig *beauty* spot; your *plague* spot.' The issue of the remaining 1d duty was not forgotten, although it did not become a major part of the Chartist platform again until the end of the forties, when Harney joined in the lobbying which eventually led to its abolition in 1855. But once the *Star* got under way, it was able to make full use of the postal concessions, and soon took the lead in circulation among all the provincial weekly newspapers.

1837 was a good year to start a newspaper. New techniques of production were beginning, and the *Star* was able to gain the advantage over many of its rivals by the very fact that no provincial printer at the time had the resources to print a full-sized journal of the kind O'Connor proposed. Once the idea of the paper had been accepted by the northern radicals, the energy and enthusiasm which were O'Connor's chief characteristics would brook no obstacle. Machinery and type were bought in London and elsewhere, money was raised, some personally by O'Connor from the sale of property, more from loans and the sale of shares among radicals of some means—men like Lawrence Pitkethly and Peter Bussey helped to raise money in their localities, and Joseph Rayner Stephens sent £20 from Ashton. In November 1837 the first issue of three thousand was printed, and by the end of the year the paper was making a profit.[20]

The first editor was William Hill, a man who has left little impression of his personality for historians of Chartism to assess. Comments from contemporaries suggest a rather unsympathetic man, tough and ungenerous in many ways, as his replies to correspondents in the *Star* suggest, particularly some of his replies to aspiring poets. One writer describes him as humourless and verbose, and suggested that when a sharp and lively piece appeared in the editorial columns, it was generally assumed that it had been written by his wife. Yet under his editorship the *Star* was an excellent paper. The editorials are clear, well argued and hard-hitting, and there can be no doubt that in its most successful years the paper owed an enormous amount to Hill's guidance. There were other contributors who helped maintain the paper's standards. O'Brien brought a genuine journalistic talent to the work, and also the associations of the heroic age of the unstamped. Oastler wrote to Stephens urging him to 'tell O'Brien to put the *Poor Man's Guardian's* soul in the *Star*',[21] and in his regular letters in the early issues of the paper much of Bronterre's best writing can be found. Oastler too wrote long letters in the early issues of the paper, and the 'sermons' and other political speeches of Stephens were regularly reported.

The centre for the publication of the *Star* was the Leeds office of Joshua Hobson. Here the paper was set up, and the many pages of reports from Chartist leaders and correspondents throughout the country were sent. The tone was sharp, combative and provincial. The initial response came above all from the provincial centres. London was, as the delegates to the first Convention were to discover, out of step with the provinces in its political awareness. Writing from London in April 1838, O'Brien made the comment: 'Gentlemen—While you are rousing the sections in the north, we, in London, have fallen into a sort of Endymion's sleep, as though the combined juices of Mandrake, poppy and hemlock were our only potations . . .'[22] The provinces were ready for the *Star*, however, and it soon became the most widely-read journal of its time in Britain. It is difficult to make a numerical assessment of its readership. The practice of buying an individual copy of a newspaper hardly existed among the working people. Papers were read in coffee-shops, alehouses, reading-rooms. The correspondence of Thomas Cooper, when he was acting as agent for the *Star* and other papers, gives some indication of the way in which journals circulated. Single copies would be ordered, as when a correspondent ordered one copy of the *Star* and one of the *Noncon-*

formist 'for a newly-opened reading-room', but there is no way of computing how many readers would see each copy. George Robinson of Hinckley wrote:

> A party of friends met at my house last night and subscribed for the Star so be so kind as to send it without fail on Saturday . . . We think of meeting on a Sunday morning at some central spot between us and the villages and reading the Star and conversing together when weather is fair, otherwise at my house.[23]

This kind of joint subscription was very common, and most Chartist autobiographies and memoirs include an account of regular meetings to read the paper on Saturday afternoon or Sunday morning.

> As a schoolboy my Saturday forenoons were occupied in walking from Newton Heath to Abel Heywood's in Manchester and bringing back a copy of the *Northern Star* and a penny number of a tale about William Tell. In the afternoons I read aloud much of these for the edification of others, and I doubt not derived some good myself

one writer recalled more than half a century later.[24] Thomas Wood of Bingley recalled his early attempts at self-education in the West Riding weaving community:

> When near my sixteenth year I began to join in some fashion at a newspaper. A man lent me his newspaper when it was a week old for a penny, I giving him the paper back when I had had it a week. The paper was the *Northern Star,* edited by Fergus O'Connor a name at that time familiar as a household word throughout Yorkshire and Lancashire.[25]

Ben Brierly of Failsworth recalled that the *Star* was 'the only newspaper that appeared to circulate anywhere in that part of Lancashire.'[26] As a boy he read it weekly to his father and five others who subscribed to it jointly. From Dublin Peter Brophy took four hundred copies a week in 1842, and declared:

> The principles of the Charter are by means of the *Star* finding their way into the extremest towns in Ireland, and with all the opposition which our Association has met with and is likely to meet with from those that are interested in keeping up the delusion, we still progress . . .[27]

Clearly the paper's readership was much in excess of its circulation. Samuel Fielden recalled that in Todmorden in Lancashire in his father's time the people lined the street to await the arrival of the *Star* each week.[28] Such a weekly event must have developed its own significance, and the ritual of the arrival of the paper have been followed by the public reading and discussion of its contents. The 1,330 copies ordered weekly in Ashton-under-Lyne in February 1839 must have circulated among perhaps thousands of factory workers and provided the basis for many hundreds of readings and discussions.[29] In Rochdale, it was remembered that the *Star* had 'an enormous circulation, so much so that at last the mail coach was unable to carry them and a special conveyance drawn by four horses had to be employed to transport from town to town the heavy loads of this newspaper through Rochdale to Manchester'.[30]

It is possible from the returns of the newspaper stamps to get a rather more accurate idea of the number of copies that were printed of the *Star* than was possible for unstamped journals. Annual returns are given, and by averaging these it is possible to get some picture of the figures. In 1839, the year of the greatest numbers, the average weekly imprint was 36,000. The *Star* itself quoted 42,000 as the average for the period April to June of that year, so that the figure given by some contemporaries of 60,000 a week might just have been possible for one or two peak periods of excitement and interest. Such enormous numbers of newspapers caused distribution problems at all levels. Mail coaches to some provincial area were not accustomed to carrying large numbers of newspapers, and the postal authorities had to hire extra carts or wagons.[31] The small premises occupied by radical booksellers were often uncomfortably crowded. But the distribution system seems to have worked well. Sales never again reached the heights of those of 1839, but a very large printing continued to be distributed for another ten years.[32]

When it reached the agents, the paper was eagerly collected by coffee-house and beer-house keepers and local subscribers. Saturday evenings, Sundays and Mondays were the days on which it was read aloud to waiting groups by people like Gabriel Redfearn, blanket weaver of Littletown in the Spen valley, who would 'take up a position on the Bridge wall and read the paper to the loungers for hours at a stretch', in the summer, or in the winter read to a more select group around his fire.[33] The *letters* of Feargus, reports of speeches by all the leading figures, and probably the main leading articles could be communicated in this way. Feargus's letters were clearly intended to be read aloud, and to this extent the Cobbett tradition of direct communication with the readership was kept alive. The famous address which they often carried—to the fustian jackets, unshorn chins and blistered hands—was an oratorical device to extend the range of the printed word, and to limit any divisive effect which the use of print might have between the literate members of the community and the rest. The giving away of engravings of Chartist leaders and the use of blocks and cartoons in the paper had something of the same intention.

Nevertheless, each issue of the paper did contain matter that required closer attention. Donations and contributions to the National Rent collected to support Convention delegates in the early days, figures of returns of signatures to the national petitions, the names of committee members of the National Charter Association after its formation in 1840, the numbers of cards issued to branches, acknowledgement of the receipt of money for cards, and a host of important organisational details were published every week. The itineraries of travelling lecturers, location of large demonstrations, announcements of new publications, results of elections to the National Executive, all these required closer attention by the leaders and organisers in the localities. There were also parliamentary reports, foreign reports and other news items which required reading closely rather than mass declamation. The regular reports from the localities, of meetings, lectures, delegate meetings and discussions provided a record of the movement, and a chance for localities to see themselves in print and as part of a great number of similar groups. The paper appealed at some level to most of the active people in the movement. Its literary contents—and it published poems and reviews in every number—tended to appeal to the more serious readers, although there was an occasional comic or satirical poem and even more occasionally one in the form of a broadside ballad. As the forties continued, the quality of the staff employed on the paper became very high. Harney joined it in 1843, G. A. Fleming in 1844. In 1846 Ernest Jones became literary editor, by which time Harney had taken over the editorship. In 1844 it moved to London and changed its title to the *Northern Star and National Trades Journal,* and included, even more than hitherto, information and news about trade-union activity throughout the country. To some extent these later developments illustrate a process which was taking place in other aspects of the movement after 1842, the development of the structured and organised aspects of Chartism, and the pull away from the more popular, less self-conscious elements which had formed an important part of the movement and of the *Star*'s public in the early days. A sense that the journal was losing the attention of its provincial readership lay behind O'Connor's censure of Harney for his too great concentration on socialist news, home and foreign, in the late forties. He wrote to Harney, denying that he had advocated the exclusion of foreign news as such.

> . . . You . . . knew that in my directions about foreign news that I did not include either American, nor yet French, nor Irish, or Italian when of interest, but that I did refer to the fraternal news and conventions of nations. I had before given Mr. Jones and you instructions to court a good understanding with the French and American Democracy, and we have had less of American and French news than from any other quarter . . .[34]

In his own letter at this time, he urged his 'dear Friends' to

> . . . wean your minds from the consideration of foreign questions further than the effect they may have on ministerial action. Keep your minds steadily and steadfastly fixed upon 'Home sweet Home' . . . do not, I beg you, allow any question of the form of government to be mixed up in our defined principle of representation. Get the Charter, and your united will is omnipotent; no matter whether the Pope, the Devil, or the Pretender is on the throne.[35]

To the last, he objected to the concentration on sectarian interests, and tried to keep the paper on a level to interest the widest possible spectrum of radical working-class readership.

O'Connor always hoped that Chartism would support a daily paper. From August 1842 to February 1843 his ambition was realised, and he edited the London *Evening Star* as a Chartist daily. The paper, however, did not prosper, and lost several thousand pounds before it finally went out of business. No other attempt to found a daily was made, although O'Connor never totally abandoned the hope of doing so.

There were, as has been noted, a number of other Chartist journals in the movement's early years. None of these achieved the stability of the *Star*. Indeed, Francis Place, who kept a very close watch on the radical press, said that none of the Chartist papers with the exception of the *Northern Star* paid its expenses 'even at the time of the greatest excitement'.[36] Whether or not he was right about the *Northern Liberator* may be doubted. This was the longest-lived and liveliest of the other English Chartist newspapers. Founded originally by Augustus Hardin Beaumont, O'Connor's former colleague, it was bought in early 1838 by a local radical, Robert Blakey, a one-time mayor of Morpeth. Beaumont continued to edit it until his death in February 1838, when the direction was taken over by a talented team which included Thomas Ainge Devyr. Although a stamped journal, the *Liberator* did not make a bid for a national readership. It relied heavily on the *Star* for items about news from outside the north-east, and made use of the *Star* office in Leeds for any business transactions outside Newcastle. Its advertisement proclaimed:

> The Political Creed of the *Northern Liberator* may be thus abridged—
>
> FREEDOM OF THE PRESS
> UNIVERSAL SUFFRAGE.
>
> The *Northern Liberator* will urge the principles thus avowed by all the means that reason and

truth can supply, the only moral arms which are worthy of the people and its advocates.[37]

Nevertheless, Devyr and his colleagues were at the centre of the arming and conspiracy in Newcastle in the winter of 1839-40, and nothing in the paper's tone distinguishes it from that of the *Star*.[38] Its circulation in 1838 was said to be 4,000 copies a week, which probably increased in 1839. In 1840 it combined with the *Champion,* and continued as *Northern Liberator and Champion* until it closed finally in December of that year.

North of the border also several journals seem to have held their own in the early years of the movement. *The True Scotsman* edited by John Fraser was often coupled with the *Northern Star* as a place in which Chartist information should be recorded. Its editor was strongly opposed to violence and a supporter of temperance, but neither of these attitudes precluded an extremely militant tone on occasion. It continued to be published from the end of 1838 until the summer of 1843. The *Scottish Patriot,* published in Glasgow and edited by Robert Malcom, had a shorter life, lasting from mid-1839 until late 1841. It was the organ of the Glasgow trade unions as well as of the Chartist movement. In Dundee, the *Dundee Chronicle* was edited by R. J. Richardson in 1841 and John La Mont in 1842, and carried radical material including poetry. As in England, there were a number of smaller, short-lived journals putting over the views of sections of the movement in Scotland. In Wales, apart from *Udgorn Cymru* and its English-language companion the *Advocate and Merthyr Free Press,* Henry Vincent's *Western Vindicator,* published in Bath in 1839 and 1840, circulated widely and carried some articles in the Welsh language. After his release from prison, Vincent restarted the paper as the *National Vindicator and Liberator of the West and Wales,* editing it jointly with Robert Kemp Philp. In neither incarnation does the paper seem to have had a very large issue, but there is no doubt that in its early years it circulated widely in Wales and the West Country, where its editor was one of the most popular leaders. In London both the London Working Men's Association and the London Democratic Association had their papers—the *Charter* for the former, which ran from January 1839 to March 1840, and the *London Democrat,* journal of the LDA, edited by J. C. Coombe and G. J. Harney. In 1842 the supporters of the New Move put out the *National Association Gazette* edited by John Humffreys Parry, which ran for six months, but like the Association itself appeared to gain little popular support.

The thousands of copies of the *Star,* taken with the many smaller or shorter-lived journals, amounted to an enormous number of pages of print. If the great mass of pamphlet literature is added to this, it becomes clear that Chartism was in many places a movement of literate people. How far the printed word was a unifying force and how far it was a divisive one is a difficult question. Quite clearly the press provided a sense of national unity which the platform could not provide. It reached districts regularly which would have been inaccessible to speakers or organisers. But it also allowed oppositional views to be circulated—some of O'Brien's later publications, for example, like the *National Reformer* published in the Isle of Man between 1844 and 1847, were largely concerned with carrying on personal vendettas against other leaders. Pamphlets like those which John Watkins issued attacking O'Connor, or the series of hostile publications aimed at Ernest Jones in the later years of the movement, leave a strong sense of bitter and strident disagreement—a quality which many of the rank and file members found distasteful. When Ernest Jones started the *People's Paper* in 1852, Benjamin Wilson recorded:

> I wrote Mr Jones a letter asking him to keep personal quarrels out of the paper as they did no good. I received the following reply. . . . 'You may rest assured that as one of the objects of the paper is to lift the movement out of the grovelling depths of personal contention and ambition, so not one syllable of personality shall intrude itself into its columns.'[39]

The promise was not kept—indeed the fifties were to be the period of the most bitter quarrelling and recrimination among the old Chartists.

Notes

[1] Two very full accounts of the unstamped are to be found in P. Hollis *The Pauper Press* (1970) and Joel Wiener *The War of the Unstamped* (1969 Ithaca). Much of the information in the following paragraph is taken from these works.

[2] H.O. 20/10. For Benbow see I. J. Prothero, 'William Benbow and the concept of the "General Strike",' *Past and Present,* No. 63 (May 1971), and entry in *Dictionary of Labour Movement Biography,* John Saville and Joyce Bellamy (eds), Vol. 3.

[3] George Laval Chesterton, *Revelations of Prison Life* (2 vols, 1856), Vol. 1, pp. 195, 204.

[4] J. A. Epstein, 'Feargus O'Connor and the Northern Star', *International Review of Social History,* Vol. XXI, Part 1 (1976). A fuller discussion of some of the points in this section will be found in this article, and in my 'La Presse de la Classe Ouvrière Anglaise, 1836-1848' in Jacques Godechot (ed.), *La Presse Ouvrière 1819-1850* (Paris, 1966).

[5] D. J. Rowe, 'The London Working Men's Association and the People's Charter', *Past and Present,* No. 36 (April 1967).

6 J. A. Epstein, *The Lion of Freedom,* Chapter 1, for the pre-Chartist radical career of O'Connor.

7 Letter William Cobbett to Joshua Hobson (Tolsen Memorial Museum, Huddersfield).

8 J. Wiener, *War of the Unstamped,* p. 109. And see the press reports of the great Guildhall meeting called in March 1836 by the middle-class Association for the Abolition of the Stamp Duty on Newspapers.

9 Cited in J. Wiener, *op. cit.,* p. 271.

10 *New Weekly True Sun,* 19 March 1836.

11 *London Dispatch,* 17 December 1836.

12 *Bronterre's National Reformer,* Vol. 1, No. 1 (7 Jan. 1837).

13 *Ibid,* Vol. 1, No. 11 (18 March 1837).

14 *Halifax Courier,* 6 September 1884.

15 Angela V. John, 'The Chartist Endurance: Industrial South Wales, 1840-1868', *Morgannwg,* Vol. XV (1971).

16 For example, his 'Address to the Women of England' in Vol. 1, No. 13. The Ellis biography is in Vol. II, beginning at No. 143.

17 A valuable series of letters to Cooper is in T.S. 11/600, 601, 602.

18 *Notes to the People,* Introduction to Vol. 1, 1851.

19 The *Northern Tribune,* 19 May 1855. The paper was absorbed by the *Reasoner* in 1855.

20 For a full account see J. A. Epstein, 'Feargus O'Connor and the Northern Star', *International Review of Social History,* Vol. XXI, Part 1 (1976).

21 G. J. Holyoake, *Life of Joseph Rayner Stephens* (1881), p. 86.

22 *Northern Star,* 23 June 1838.

23 George Robinson to Thomas Cooper, T. S. 11/601 X/L05 744.

24 *Newcastle Weekly Chronicle,* 7 November 1896, letter from Thomas Hayes, Lower Crumpsall, Manchester.

25 Autobiography of Thomas Wood, engineer, of Bingley, reprinted in John Burnett (ed.), *Useful Toil* (1974), p. 308.

26 Ben Brierley, *Home Memories and Recollections of Life* (1886), p. 23.

27 Brophy to Cooper, 20 November 1841. T.S. 11/600.

28 Samuel Fielden, 'Autobiography' reprinted in Philip S. Foner (ed.), *The autobiographies of the Haymarket Martyrs* (New York, 1969).

29 *Northern Star,* 23 February 1839.

30 William Robertson, *The Social and Political History of Rochdale* (Rochdale n.d. [?1889]), p. 15.

31 W. J. O'Neill Daunt, *Eighty-five Years of Irish History 1800-1885* (1886), Vol. 1, p.268.

32 In the second half of 1839 the circulation of the *Star* averaged over 30,000; in 1840, 18,500; in 1841, 13,000; 1842, 12,500. After this sales fell more steeply, to 7,500 in 1844, 6,000 in 1846. The figures rose again to around 11,000 in 1847 and 12,000 in 1848. O'Connor claimed to have sold 21,000 copies of the issue of 15 April 1848. For 1849 the figures averaged 7,000 weekly, and for 1850, 5,000. For more detailed figures and for comparisons with other provincial weeklies, see Donald Read, *Press and People 1790-1850. Opinion in three English Cities* (1961), appendix.

33 Frank Peel, *Spen Valley Past and Present* (Heckmondwyke, 1893), p.319. Samuel Shaw, of Hyde, remembered his mother reading the *Star* aloud to his father and friends in the kitchen. Thomas Middleton, *History of Hyde* (Hyde, 1934) p. 122, and there are many more such accounts.

34 F. G. and R. M. Black (eds), *The Harney Papers* (Assen, 1969), p. 62.

35 *Northern Star,* 3 March 1839. Two weeks later, O'Connor was complaining that Harney 'looked upon the *Northern Star* as his property' and 'endeavoured to make it the organ of socialism and to merge the question of Chartism and the question of socialism'. For an interesting discussion of the divisive effects of republican and other ultra-radical ideas on the mass movement, see John Belchem, 'Republicanism, Popular Constitutionalism and the Radical Platform in early nineteenth century England', *Social History,* Vol. 6, No. 1.

36 British Museum, Add. MSS. 27, 820, f 25.

37 *Northern Star,* 21 Sept. 1839.

38 Thomas Ainge Devyr, *The Odd Book of the Nineteenth Century* (New York, 1882), Chapters XI, XII, XIII.

[39] Benjamin Wilson, *Struggles,* p. 19.

FURTHER READING

Aydelotte, William O. "The England of Marx and Mill as Reflected in Fiction." In *The Making of English History*, by Robert Livingston Schuyler and Herman Ausubel, pp. 511-21. New York: The Dryden Press, 1952.

Discusses the social criticism of early Victorian novelists in England, with some emphasis on the role of Charles Dickens.

Barker, Clive. "The Chartists, Theatre, Reform and Research." *Theatre Quarterly* 1, No. 4 (October-December 1971): 3-10.

Discusses Chartist involvement in community theater in Britain in the 1830s and urges further study.

Gammage, R. G. *History of the Chartist Movement.* London: Truslove and Hanson, 1894, 438 p.

Detailed early history of the Chartist movement from a participant.

Harrison, J. F. C., and Dorothy Thompson. *Bibliography of the Chartist Movement, 1837-1976.* Sussex: Harvester Press, 1978, 214 p.

Thorough bibliography of specifically Chartist writing and secondary studies.

Hobday, C. H. "The Chartists in Fiction." *Our Time* 7, No. 7 (April 1948): 72-173.

Discussion of Chartist fiction in the political and social context of the nineteenth century.

Hovell, Mark. *The Chartist Movement.* London: Longmans, Green and Co., 1918, 327 p.

Historical study of the Chartist movement.

James, Louis. *Fiction for the Working Man: 1830-1850.* London: Oxford University Press, 1963, 226 p.

A survey of literature written for urban, working-class readers in early Victorian England.

Kettle, Arnold. "The Early Victorian Social-Problem Novel." In *From Dickens to Hardy,* edited by Boris Ford, pp. 169-87. New York: Penguin, 1958.

A discussion of Chartist fiction, with analyses of several important Chartist novels.

Louvre, Alf. "Reading Bezer: Pun, Parody, and Radical Intervention in 19th Century Working Class Auto-biography." *Literature and History* 14, No. 1 (Spring 1988): 23-36.

Analysis of *The Autobiography of One of the Chartist Rebels of 1848,* by John James Bezer.

Peyrouton, N. C. "Dickens and the Chartists." *The Dickensian* 60 (part II), No. 343 (May 1964): 78-88.

Examines the relationship between Dickens and the Chartists, and compares their works.

Tillotson, Katherine. *Novels of the Eighteen-Forties.* Oxford: Clarendon Press, 1954, 319 p.

Provides an overview of novels of the decade, including detailed studies of four, including Gaskell's *Mary Barton.*

Towers, Dorothy. "The Chartist Poets." *Our Time* 7, No. 7 (April 1948): 68-169.

Discussion of Chartist poetry, comparing it to Romanticism.

Vicinus, Martha. "'To Live Free or Die': The Relationship Between Strategy and Style in Chartist Speeches, 1838-1839." *Style* 10, No. 4 (Fall 1976): 481-503.

Comparative analysis of early Chartist speeches and their importance in building the movement.

———. "Chartist Fiction and the Development of a Class-based Literature." In *The Socialist Novel in Britain: Towards the Recovery of a Tradition,* edited by H. Gustav Klaus, pp. 7-25. New York: St. Martin's Press, 1982.

An overview analysis of Chartist literature, examining the use of melodrama over realism in Chartist fiction.

West, Julius. *A History of the Chartist Movement.* Boston: Houghton Mifflin Co., 1920, 316 p.

Historical analysis of the development and collapse of the Chartist movement.

Italian Romanticism

INTRODUCTION

The history of Italy in the nineteenth century was one of struggle—for unity and for political autonomy as defined by the *Risorgimento* movement—and of victory, later realized in the democratic successes of 1861 and 1871. These tensions began after the collapse of the Napoleonic hegemony in Europe early in the century, as Austria once again exerted its control over the scattered states of the Italian peninsula. But Napoleon's regime had made the goal of future unification seem possible, and this goal of freedom was embraced by the artists and theorists of Romanticism, a movement that gathered force in the first decades of the nineteenth century and grew to dominance by mid-century. Among the movement's most eloquent proponents scholars number three writers generally considered to be at the forefront of the movement: Ugo Foscolo, Alessandro Manzoni, and Giacomo Leopardi. All of these writers, in their rejection of the slavish adherence to classical forms, in their emphasis on patriotism, Christianity, and humanity, and in their relentless search for truth, defined literature in Italy for more than half a century.

Scholars note that the first inklings of Romanticism in Italy come from the writings of the poet and dramatist Vittorio Alfieri late in the eighteenth century. Although a classicist in style and temperament, Alfieri, who wrote during the waning years of the *ancien regime*, was one of the first to acknowledge the stifling weight that tradition bore upon the Italian arts. Alfieri was followed by poet, novelist, and theorist Ugo Foscolo, a figure that some scholars rank as a pre-Romantic for rejecting the inherited trappings of neoclassicism in his epistolary novel *Ultime lettere di Jacopo Ortis* (1802) and in his poetry, including the verse of his *Dei Sepolcri* (1807). In both, scholars have observed that Foscolo retained classical forms and subjects, but provided a new, more personal focus.

Foscolo's poetry had anticipated the Romantic sensibility, though the period of Italian Romanticism did not officially begin, according to historians, until 1816 and the publication of Mme. de Staël's essay "De l'esprit des traductions" ("On the Method and Value of Translations") in the *Biblioteca Italiana*. In her article, de Staël urged Italians to free themselves of their obedience to traditionalism by translating the literary works of the north—the poetry of the French, Germans, and English. Her comments sparked immediate outrage in Italy, though several supporters of her position soon appeared. Among them, the poet Giovanni Berchet responded in his *Lettera semiseria di Grisostomo* of 1816. Crafted in a fictional idiom and arguing that modern poetry should appeal to the people, whether educated or not, the *Lettera* became a virtual manifesto of the newborn Romanticismo movement. In 1818 the Romantic literary journal *Il conciliatore* was formed and printed the thoughts of writers such as abbé Ludovico di Breme and Ermes Visconti. Di Breme gave his support to de Staël by advising Italian poets and novelists to modernize their writings, while Visconti defined the terms of Romanticism in his *Idee elementari sulla poesia Romantica* (1818). However, the periodical was dismantled by the Austrian government for its liberal political stance after little more than a year of publication, and some of its contributors, including Silvio Pellico, author of the patriotic drama *Francesca da Rimini* (1815), were later imprisoned. Pellico nevertheless remained an ardent Romantic, his autobiography *Le mie prigioni* (1832) describes the religious conversion he underwent while incarcerated and attests to the hardships he endured for his beliefs.

At this time perhaps the greatest figure in Italian Romanticism, Alessandro Manzoni—already a well-known poet and playwright—joined in the classico-Romantic debate. In the preface to his 1820 drama *Il Conte di Carmagnola,* Manzoni denounced the classical unities of time and place; three years later, in a widely circulated letter to the novelist Massimo D'Azeglio, he drafted what was to be his treatise on Romanticism. The work, which outlined what became the central precepts of Italian Romanticism, propelled Manzoni to the forefront of the movement. In it he called for modernity, innovation, and contemporary relevance in poetry. In addition, he declared the chief aim of Romantic poetry to be the quest for truth, and allied his project with historical progress, specifically, the unification of Italy. Manzoni set about achieving the latter in his first and only novel, *I promessi sposi* (*The Betrothed*), first published in 1827. The novel opposed the heroic ideals of classical literature, focusing instead on the lives of ordinary people—the Milanese under the domination of Spain in the seventeenth century. Its political commentary was obvious to Manzoni's contemporaries. Yet, in writing the novel, Manzoni undertook a task that no other writer in Italian before him had succeeded in completing: he created a work in the national language of Italy. At the time he began composing the novel—almost half a century before unification—Italy was composed of separate city-states, each with its own dialect, foreign to the others. Manzoni sought to overcome these barriers in the 1827 version of *I promessi sposi* by creating a new form of Italian, based on literary versions of the language, as well as Latin and French. Although it was a popular success, he thought this first edition stilted and artificial. So Manzoni devoted another decade and a half to the work, infusing it with the living, spoken language of Tuscany. The result is considered a masterpiece of historical fiction, surpassed in critical esteem in Italy only by Dante's *Divine Comedy*.

The Romantic ideals of Manzoni were further strengthened by the writings of Giacomo Leopardi. While not as well known as Manzoni during his lifetime, Leopardi is now considered among the greatest lyric poets of the era. His *Canti* (1831), more somber and melancholy than some of the verse of his predecessors, complements the theoretical writings of his journal *Zibaldone* (not published until 1898-1900). Both have provided twentieth-century scholars with greater insights into the nature of the Romantic project in Italy. Among the later Romantics, Ippolito Nievo, in his *Le confessioni di un italiano* (1867), continued Foscolo's trend toward heightened personalism, while Vincenzo Gioberti emphasized the political side of the movement. In his *Primato morale e civile degli italiani* (1843), Gioberti argued forcefully for Italian unity based upon the historical strength of Rome and the contemporary military power of Piedmont. Later, once political unification had become a reality, the composer Giuseppe Verdi celebrated the culmination of the *Risorgimento* in his opera *La Forza del destino* (1862).

REPRESENTATIVE WORKS

Vincenzo Bellini
Norma (opera) 1831

Giovanni Berchet
Lettera semiseria di Grisostomo (manifesto) 1816

Massimo D'Azeglio
Ettore Fieramosca (novel) 1833
Niccolò de' Lapi (novel) 1841

Gaetano Donizetti
Lucia di Lammermoor (opera) 1835
Don Pasquale (opera) 1843

Giacoma Durando
Della nazionalità italiana (manifesto) 1846

Ugo Foscolo
Ultime lettere di Jacopo Ortis [*Last Letters of Jacopo Ortis*] (novel) 1802
Dei Sepolcri (poetry) 1807

Vincenzo Gioberti
Primato morale e civile degli italiani (essay) 1843

Tommaseo Grossi
Marco Visconti (novel) 1834

Francesco Domenico Guerrazzi
Battaglia di Benevento (novel) 1827
Assedio di Firenze (novel) 1836

Giacomo Leopardi
Canti (poetry) 1831
Zibaldone (journal) 1898-1900

Alessandro Manzoni
Inni sacri (poetry) 1815-1822
Il Conte di Carmagnola (drama) 1820
I promessi sposi [*The Betrothed*] (novel) 1827, 1842

Giuseppe Mazzini
"Del romanzo in generale ed anche dei *Promessi sposi* di Alessandro Manzoni" (essay) 1828

Vincenzo Monti
"Per la liberzione d'Italia" (poetry) 1801

Giovan Battista Niccolini
Arnaldo da Brescia (drama) 1843

Ippolito Nievo
Le confessioni di un italiano (novel) 1867

Silvio Pellico
Francesca da Rimini (drama) 1815
Le mie prigioni (autobiography) 1832

Giuseppe Verdi
La Forza del destino (opera) 1862
Aida (opera) 1871

Ermes Visconti
Idee elementari sulla poesia Romantica (essay) 1818

ORIGINS AND OVERVIEWS

Kenneth McKenzie

SOURCE: "Romanticism in Italy," in *Publications of the Modern Language Association of America,* Vol. LV, No. 1, March, 1940, pp. 27-35.

[In the following essay, McKenzie recounts the origins and development of the Romantic movement in Italy.]

Italy, for obvious reasons, always kept closer than other countries to ancient classical literature. There the classic spirit was native, for the Italians were always conscious of being the heirs of the ancient Roman Empire; there Humanism and the Renaissance arose; there the counter-Reformation resisted the Protestant spirit of the northern countries; there Arcadian academies and pseudo-classicism flourished. But the Romantic attitude was present in many Italian writers from the Middle Ages on. Petrarch was romantic in his introspective melancholy, Ariosto was romantic in his love of picturesque adventure; yet both are classic in the perfection of their style as well as in their knowledge of antiquity. Thus the two tendencies existed side by side, frequently in the same man, although in theory Italy remained classicist until the end of the eighteenth century. The pre-romantic literature of France, England, and Germany was modified in Italy by the prevalent classical tradition, but it found there a fertile soil. As a literary movement, Romanticism in Italy is best considered as represented by a group of writers in the period which followed the collapse of Napoleon's empire.

By creating the Regno d'Italia in 1805, Napoleon had intended to make northern Italy a dependency of France; but in spite of himself he gave the Italians an object lesson which showed the possibility of national unity. When his empire came to an end in 1814, the former rulers returned to their possessions. The problem then was not only to achieve unity, but to end foreign domination. The nucleus from which grew the Italian nation was the small kingdom of Piedmont; but this fact was not recognized in the early years of the nineteenth century, and the movement toward unity and independence centered in Milan. There a reaction against the classicism which had flourished during the Napoleonic period was fused with the revolutionary political movement. Romanticism had its political aspect in other countries, but nowhere to the same degree as in Italy. It follows that Italian romanticism was practical, altruistic, and patriotic. With these circumstances in mind, some critics[1] have denied that the term *romantic* can properly be applied to this period of Italian literature.

The explosion of the spirit of revolt, as Farinelli expresses it, began in northern Europe; but the spiritual movement which arose in all nations is not to be judged by doctrinaire criticism. It is absurd, he says, to identify romanticism with Germanism, and classicism with Latinity. It is true that the Italian romanticists, like the French, believed that literary art has its practical use, while the Germans emphasized its inactive side; but this does not mean that either aspect is more authentic than the other. In fact, cosmopolitanism is one feature of the Romantic movement.[2] It became Italian in the sense that it undertook to liberate classicism from conventional academic restrictions, not to abolish it. The distinction between *classic* (or *classicist*) on the one hand and *romantic* on the other hand was never very clear in Italian literature, in spite of critical discussions. But the elements of development from ancient to medieval and modern were present in Italy as well as in France, where also the classic spirit was still powerful; whereas in Germany, England, and Spain literature had long shown traits which afterwards were called romantic, and classicism was foreign to the national character.

Some critics find the foundation of romanticism in eighteenth-century Italy, believing that the importance of foreign influences on Italian writers was on the whole superficial. De Sanctis in his *Storia della Letteratura Italiana* declares that the romantic school in Italy, while connected with German traditions and French methods, in essence remained Italian in its purposes and its forms. Certain it is that eighteenth-century Italy experienced an intellectual awakening which perpetuated itself in the following century. Gravina and Vico, with their interpretations of history, anticipated Herder, Hegel, and other Germans. Muratori published documents and studies which revived interest in the national history. Goldoni turned comedy from imitation of conventional models to realistic representation of the life of the people. Parini had in his satire a moral and educational motive; while he himself was satisfied with moderate social progress, he prefigured the Revolution. Alfieri was always an aristocrat and a classicist, yet no one contributed more than he to spreading the germs of revolt. All these men seem to have exercised less influence on literature than their importance as authors would lead us to expect; but in stimulating a spirit of independence their influence was immense. Thus the awakening of the Italian spirit, conditioned by the classic tradition, while it was helped, was not caused, by foreign influences.[3]

The leading Italian poets during the Napoleonic period were Vincenzo Monti and Ugo Foscolo. Monti was influenced by all types of literature, but attachment to antiquity formed the unity of his art. Foscolo began his career with the ultra-romantic *Ultime lettere di Jacopo Ortis* (1796-1802), in which he lamented both his personal misfortunes and the unhappy condition of Italy. This combination of motives gives the key to Italian romanticism. In his *Sepolcri* he was still interested in the condition of his country, but in his later poem *Le Grazie* he reverted to Greek mythology. After the romanticists had condemned the use of classical mythology, Monti wrote a "sermon" in defence of it. Monti and Foscolo, both classicists at heart, belong to the period of pre-romanticism.

The restoration of the former rulers in Italy after the fall of Napoleon disappointed the patriots who had hoped for a united country. Since the restored governments were reactionary, the promoters of a romantic revolt were under suspicion and were opposed by the classicists, who generally supported the existing political system. Thus romanticism inevitably came to be one aspect of the political Risorgimento. In purely literary matters the romanticists were not particularly unconventional. However, they studied the modern literature of their own and other countries, condemned imitation of the ancients, and aimed to put literature at the service of national education, an ideal scarcely known in previous ages. The two greatest Italian writers of the first half of the nineteenth century—Manzoni, who became the acknowledged leader of the romantic movement in so far as it was literary and educational, and Leopardi, who was at heart more romantic than Manzoni—kept aloof from the political polemics of the day; but their works nevertheless made an important contribution to the regeneration of the country.

It is usual to take as the beginning of the definite romantic movement in Italy the publication in 1816 of Mme de Staël's article exhorting the Italians to rouse themselves from their complacency and learn what was going on in other countries. But already in the previous year Manzoni had published his *Inni Sacri,* which De Sanctis has called "the first voices of the nineteenth century"; and in August, 1815, enormous enthusiasm had been aroused by the performance in Milan of Silvio Pellico's *Francesca da Rimini.* This tragedy, based on the best-known passage in Dante, is classical or at least Alfierian in form, with only four speaking characters and with observation of the rule of the unities; but its plot is medieval and national, and it is filled with romantic passion. It speedily became known all over Italy, although not printed until 1818. The passage that attracted particular attention was the monologue in which Paolo laments having fought in foreign wars when he should have reserved his sword for Italy; this speech was an anachronism in a play of the thirteenth century, but it seemed extraordinarily timely in the nineteenth, when in everyone's mind were the Italians in Napoleon's army who had laid down their lives in Germany and Russia. Pellico later wrote tragedies which in many ways departed from the classic rules, but none met the same success as *Francesca da Rimini.*

In 1816, under the patronage of the Austrian authorities in Milan, a periodical, *Biblioteca Italiana,* was established, which continued publication for many years. It soon became the organ of the classicists, since the Austrians used it for propaganda against the liberal movement. In the beginning, however, it was impartial and objective in its attitude, and not averse to introducing German ideas in northern Italy. The first number contained the famous article written by Mme de Staël especially for the *Biblioteca* and translated into Italian with the title "Sulla maniera e sulla utilità delle traduzioni." Her work was already well known; in 1807 she had published *Corinne ou l'Italie,* a story containing descriptions of Italian scenes. An Italian translation of *De l'Allemagne* appeared in 1814. The main point of the article in the *Biblioteca* was that Italians would do well to study foreign literature, in translation if necessary, not to imitate it but to broaden their outlook. Mme de Staël's article alarmed the classicists, who feared the corruption of their fixed ideals, and it angered nationalistically minded critics who chose to believe that she was belittling Italian genius. A furious debate arose; Mme de Staël was violently attacked and valiantly defended. In the same year (1816) there appeared a work which is spoken of as a manifesto of Romantic doctrines comparable to the "Préface de Cromwell" in France. This was the *Lettera semiseria de Grisostomo* by Giovanni Berchet. The author pretended to advise his son to write according to the dictates of his heart and the spirit of his country, abandoning the academic rules and standards of the prevailing classicism; as an example, he accompanied the letter with a translation of two ballads from the German of Bürger. Berchet knew English and German literature better than most of his Italian contemporaries, and the *Lettera semiseria,* as well as the patriotic ballads which he afterwards wrote in exile, contributed to the development of a national spirit by suggesting that Italians could do for their own country what other races were doing for theirs. As a matter of fact, a knowledge of foreign literatures was no new thing to the Milan of 1816, for that had begun half a century before. Thus both native and foreign elements combined to form the outlook of the intellectuals who were in revolt against the classicist restrictions on literary production and at the same time against the political impotence of Italy.

The houses of two Milanese aristocrats, Luigi Porro Lambertenghi and Federico Confalonieri, not themselves literary men, were centers where many forward-looking Italians and foreign visitors gathered to discuss questions of the day. So much dissatisfaction was felt with the growing conservatism of the *Biblioteca Italiana* that the project arose of establishing a journal to give voice to the ideas of the liberal group. After several abortive attempts, the semi-weekly *Conciliatore* was started in September, 1818. Silvio Pellico, Porro's secretary, had charge of seeing the journal through the press, and was the most regular contributor. His task was far from easy, for at the last moment the censor frequently required him to cut or rewrite articles, or to substitute new material. The various contributors differed among themselves in many matters, but were a unit in their devotion to the romantic movement in literature and in their determination to change the political situation. Although the romantic tendency of the articles published was confined to literary questions and perforce avoided politics, the connection between the two orders of ideas was clear to the Austrian authorities. Pellico was several times warned to be more careful, and finally in October, 1819, the attitude of the police became so threatening that it was decided to cease publication. The diffusion of the journal was slight; but its influence, both literary and political, was considerable. Finally, several of the *Conciliatore* group were arrested and condemned for high treason; others escaped from Italy and lived for years in exile. Pellico's *Le mie Prigioni,* written in 1832 after his release from prison, became one of the most famous books of the century. Patriotism continued to express itself in the theory and practice of romanticism until in 1859 Italy began in fact to free herself from foreign domination. During all this period, literature was employed in the service of the fatherland. But at the same time we may consider the ideas expressed in the *Conciliatore* from a purely literary point of view.

In the prospectus which Pietro Borsieri wrote for the first number the words *romantico, romanticismo* do not occur, but they appear in many of the later numbers. An article by the eminent economist Gian Domenico Romagnosi begins:

> Are you romantic?—No.—Are you classicist?—No.—What then?—I am *ilichiastico,* to say it in Greek; that is, adapted to the present age . . . Every age must find principles which obey only the laws of taste, reason and morality . . . We are always the children of the age and the place in which we live . . . To maintain among us the exclusive dominion of the classics is to wish a dead Italian poetry and a dead Italian language.[4]

A long article by Ermes Visconti, entitled "Idee elementari sulla poesia romantica," begins as follows:

> If the discussion for and against romanticism were in style only here in Milan, it would perhaps be well to let the style pass. But beyond the Alps the new literary system is discussed and will continue to be discussed, because it opposes many old errors and offers opportunity for many useful observations. True it is that its usefulness is diminished by the disagreement of various German writers as to the phrase *poesia romantica.* This phrase was invented to Germany to distinguish the proper characteristics of the art of modern poets from the qualities belonging exclusively to the ancient classics, so as to give due praise to the originality of the former in contrast to the pedantic partisans of those who merely copy antiquity.

In a "Dialogue on the dramatic unities of time and place," Visconti anticipates many of the arguments used later by Manzoni and Hugo; this was written and published in January, 1819—before the publication of

Manzoni's tragedies or of his celebrated letter on the unities. The discussion of romantic principles also appears in private letters of the time. Thus in 1819 Pellico wrote to his brother:

> From the way in which you speak of Romanticism you seem to think of it as a party into which I have been dragged. You are wrong. The word was not well chosen; but the doctrine is held by everyone who has clear-sighted intelligence. You know how Monti and Foscolo appreciated Shakespeare and Schiller before the word Romantic was used. Now perhaps they would call themselves Classicists. Time will clear away these uncertainties.

The connection of the literary movement with the political situation comes out clearly in a letter from Pellico to Porro: "At Turin, as in our cities in Lombardy, to say 'liberal' one says 'romantic'; no distinction is made. And 'classic' has become the synonym of reactionary, of spy."

From the period of which we have been speaking until after Rome had become the capital of united Italy, there lived in Milan a greater literary genius than any of the *Conciliatore* group, who sympathized with their purpose without sharing their activities. This was Alessandro Manzoni (1785-1873). In 1818 Manzoni began the historical studies on which were based his two tragedies, *Il Conte di Carmagnola* (1820) and *Adelchi* (1822), dealing with Italian history of the fifteenth and the eighth centuries respectively. These tragedies, like Alfieri's, are in blank verse, but, unlike them, employ many characters and do not observe the unities of time and place. They were adversely criticized in France by a certain Chauvet, whose name is now remembered only on account of the reply which Manzoni made to his criticism: this "Lettre à M.C. . . . sur l'unité de temps et de lieu dans la tragédie," together with Claude Fauriel's translation of the tragedies, was published in Paris in 1823. Victor Hugo can hardly have failed to see this publication; in any case, many of Manzoni's ideas reappear in the "Préface de Cromwell" (1827). It is true that some of these ideas were already more or less current both in France and in Italy; but it should be noted that Manzoni's thoroughly romantic tragedies antedate the French romantic drama. However, they did not lead to a development of a new dramatic form in Italy. On the other hand, Manzoni's great historical novel, *I Promessi Sposi* (1827), was followed by a host of imitations in the second quarter of the century, many of which are still read with interest. Later, fiction turned to realism but toward the close of the century in the novels of Fogazzaro it reverted to the moralizing romanticism of Manzoni.

If Berchet's *Lettera semiseria* may be called the militant manifesto of the Italian romanticists in their "Sturm und Drang" period—namely, from 1815 to the breaking up of the *Conciliatore* group by imprisonment and exile—a letter which Manzoni addressed in 1823 to Cesare d'Azeglio is to be regarded as the serene, carefully pondered statement of the principles of the school as understood and practised by the greatest Romantic writer of Italy.[5] Manzoni's central idea was that literature should be useful; in his famous phrase, "che la poesia, e la letteratura in genere, debba proporsi l'utile per iscopo, il vero per soggetto, e l'interessante per mezzo." This principle was to him more important than any consideration of school; when asked if romanticism would last, he replied that the name was already being forgotten, but that the influence of the movement would continue. The negative doctrines of the school were easy to define: to abandon imitation of the classics (they should be studied, as Mme de Staël had said of modern foreign literature, but not copied); to reject ancient mythology, which seemed to Manzoni idolatrous and contrary to Christianity; to base rules for writing not on arbitrary decisions, but on the human mind. The positive side of romantic doctrine was less easy to specify, and the romantic writers had been criticized for not agreeing among themselves. The basis of romanticism is individuality; yet all should agree, and according to Manzoni in general they do agree, in believing that literature must be useful, and must have as its source historical and moral truth. Just what is meant by "il vero" is, to be sure, open to discussion; but by excluding the false, the useless, the harmful, romanticism defines the truth. In Italy, Manzoni concludes, with an eye to the German models that were sometimes proposed, romanticism does not consist of a confused crowd of ghosts and witches, of search for the extravagant, of negation of common sense—such a romanticism Italians have good reason to reject and forget. In regard to the linguistic problem which had been debated with heat ever since the time of Dante, Manzoni rejected the arbitrary rules which tended to impede growth and make Italian a dead language: he based his style on the best contemporary usage, particularly that of Tuscany.

It should be evident from what precedes that the Italians were not ignorant of the methods of romantic writers in other countries, and that in adopting the principle of liberalism in art they restricted it with rules based on the conditions which confronted them in their own country at the moment. Manzoni did not advance the need for political revolution as a guiding principle in the literary movement; but nevertheless he aided the revolution, both by his insistence on strength of character and morality and by his picture, in *I Promessi Sposi,* of the abject condition of Lombardy under the Spanish dominion in the seventeenth century—a picture which drew attention, perhaps more pointedly than he intended, to the evils of the Austrian rule in his own day. The combined efforts of the romantic-minded Italians, whether or not they for-

mally espoused romanticism, finally made the political Risorgimento a reality. In this process the purely literary contribution of the generation of 1815 must not be overlooked, even though the contributions of the less gifted members of the group now have in many cases little intrinsic interest. This generation did in fact produce significant literary works: noble lyric poetry, keen critical discussions, important tragedies, and splendid historical fiction.

To sum up: In the eighteenth century Germany brought to a focus a movement which had long existed in different parts of Europe; the movement spread to Italy and France, where classicism was strongly entrenched, and there, as well as in England and Spain, it assumed forms peculiar to each country. It ran its course as a definite school, but its influence pervades all modern literature. The need for a renewal of vitality was characteristic of all countries, both those which were normally and fundamentally classic and those which were already romantic in a general sense. It is evident, then, that even though romanticism as a school originated in Germany, one of its important elements is its cosmopolitan and general European character. Manzoni's masterpiece is one of the great novels of world literature. The sublime poems of Leopardi, classical in their perfection of form, are filled with the spirit of romanticism; his "noia" is as significant in modern literature as the "sorrows" of Werther and the "ennui" of René. The critic Carducci observes that Manzoni was attracted more by the art of Goethe and Schiller than by that of men like Novalis, Tieck, and the Schlegels, and reduced to a clear expression of reality the nebulous spirit of German romanticism; while Leopardi romanticized the purity of the Greek attitude toward life and renewed the classic expression of the conflict of modern thought. Both these writers, by representing two different psychological states that were common to all Europe, became more universal than their immediate Italian predecessors. Both kept aloof from political agitation, yet their writings were transformed into battle-cries and Italy responded with the will to fight; with astonishment Europe saw this nation, which had been called the land of the dead, rise to throw off the shackles of foreign domination and affirm its independence. In 1902 the popular dramatist Rovetta produced a play dealing with the revolt against the Austrians in northern Italy in 1854; and the title of this play is appropriately *Romanticismo.*

Notes

[1] See a book with the provocative title *Il Romanticismo Italiano non esiste,* by Gina Martegiani (Firenze, 1908); and Guido Calgari, *Il Romanticismo in Germania e in Italia* (Milano, 1929).

[2] In the eighteenth century Baretti and Bertòla spread in Italy a knowledge of English and German literature.

The influence of Rousseau, of Richardson, Young, and Gray, and of the poems ascribed to Ossian was especially significant. But we have only to mention the names of Goethe, Mme de Staël, Stendhal, Musset, and Byron to show that the influence was far from being all in one direction.

[3] Natali maintains that even without foreign influences romanticism would have developed in Italy simultaneously with its appearance elsewhere.

[4] This recalls Stendhal's famous definition: "Le romantisme est l'art de présenter aux peuples les œuvres littéraires qui, dans l'état actuel de leurs habitudes et de leurs croyances, sont susceptibles de leur donner le plus de plaisir possible." The articles in the *Conciliatore* here cited, with a complete index of the 118 numbers of the journal, may be found in P. A. Menzio, *Dal "Conciliatore"* (Torino, 1921).

[5] The letter was not intended for publication. In 1846 it was printed without Manzoni's permission; later he was induced to revise it and in 1871 he published it with the title "Sul Romanticismo." It may be found, both in the original version with the title "Sopra i diversi sistemi di poesia" and in the revised version, with notes and bibliography, in *Scritti Postumi di Alessandro Manzoni a cura di* G. Sforza (Milano, 1900), vol. 1. For the relations of Manzoni to Fauriel, Stendhal, and Hugo, see R. Bray, *Chronologie du Romantisme* (Paris, 1932), Chap. v.

Harry Hearder

SOURCE: "Literature and the Opera," in *Italy in the Age of the Risorgimento, 1790-1870,* Longman, 1983, pp. 254-71.

[*In the following essay, Hearder surveys the major works of poetry, fiction, and drama produced by Italian artists in the period 1790-1870.*]

Italian nationalism in the nineteenth century was one aspect of the romantic movement. Yet to make such a generalization at once creates difficulties, since development of Italian literature in the period 1790-1870 involved the purifying and simplifying of an Italian national language, which can be seen as an essentially classical movement operating against the diversities of provincial dialects. The purification of the language can perhaps best be considered within the context of a study of the writing of Manzoni's masterpiece *I Promessi Sposi,* and will therefore be postponed until the novels of the period are surveyed. The creation of a genuinely national Italian literary language certainly owed more to creative writers than to grammarians or philologists. Yet the creative writers themselves were usually more concerned with politics than with lin-

guistics, and the broad generalization can be made that liberals and nationalists in the early nineteenth century were products of the romantic movement in literary as well as political terms, while conservatives still wrote in the classical tradition. In the last decade of the eighteenth century, however, Italian classical writers were still identified with the Enlightenment and were far from being reactionaries in a political sense.

Two journals were central to the politico-literary history of romanticism in Italy. *Il Conciliatore,* founded in September 1818 by Luigi Lambertenghi and Federico Confalonieri in Milan, was ostensibly a scientific-literary journal, but its romantic, liberal sentiments became increasingly obvious. It was suppressed by the Austrians in October 1819, but its influence in its short life had been considerable. . . . In the pages of the *Antologia* ideas and manners inherited from the Enlightenment met the newer ones of the Romantic movement. Especially after Niccolò Tommaseo took over the editorship of the journal in 1827 did it acquire a stronger spirit of romanticism, and with it of Italian nationalism.

The tension caused by the struggle between classicism and romanticism added greatly to the vitality of Italian literature during the period covered by this [essay]. As in the rest of Western Europe, the emergence of the Romantic movement led to remarkable achievements in the writing of lyric poetry. There is also a profusion of plays to be briefly surveyed, but Italian drama of the period has survived the test of time rather less well than has the poetry of Leopardi or Foscolo. As in Russia, France and Britain, the period marks the great age of the novel, although many works of the secondary Italian novelists have dated rather quickly: perhaps only Manzoni and Nievo have retained their freshness and brilliance into the late twentieth century.

The first poet who deserves consideration in a survey of this brevity is Giuseppe Parini. Born in 1729 near Como, into a poor family, Parini was trained for the priesthood in Milan. But he was a child of the Enlightenment, and although he never overtly rejected Christianity, his approach to religion was the abstract, sceptical one of his generation. His father died when he was still young, and he then knew acute poverty. His early life gave him a strength of character which enabled him to feel contempt for the purely pedagogic and academic aspects of the Enlightenment but also, later, to resist the fanaticism of the Jacobins. His integrity enabled him to span the two worlds of eighteenth-century classicism and revolutionary romanticism rather as Goethe did in Germany. Parini's major work, *Il Giorno,* belongs to an earlier period than that covered by this [essay], and to a civilized tradition of satire more typical of the eighteenth than of the nineteenth century. But by 1790 he had already recognized the need for change in Italy, although he was opposed to revolutionary or violent change. His judgements were always healthy, balanced ones. He rejected the more arid lapses of eighteenth-century classicism, but was determined to preserve its rationality, clarity and ability to compromise. When the French entered Milan in 1796 Parini was eager to receive them. He had no desire for Italy to be united, or even politically independent, but he welcomed the more generous of the ideas of 1789. He opposed the violent methods, rather than the principles, of the Jacobins. He died on 15 August 1799, when the Austrians had already re-entered Milan.

Besides *Il Giorno,* the *Odi* are usually considered to be his other major achievement, though they are not in fact a single work, but rather a collection of lyric poems composed between 1757 and 1795. The later of the *Odi* were written after the French Revolution—the *Dono* in 1790, *La Musica* in 1793, and in 1795 *A Silvia o sul vestire alla ghigliottina,* and *Alla Musa.* In particular, the *Messagio* and *Alla Musa* have a new sense of human tenderness which is beginning to break away from the formalism of Parini's own century, and from the artificial nature of some of his own earlier *Odi.* An episode often told of Parini can be perhaps repeated here, since it encapsulates the enlightenment and the humanity of the man. During the revolutionary period in Milan a noisy radical, or 'Jacobin' audience in the theatre were shouting 'Long live the Republic. Death to traitors.' An old gentleman stood up in one of the boxes and momentarily silenced the shouting by thundering 'Long live the Republic. Death to no one.' The old gentleman was Parini, and his courage was the measure of his independence of judgement and the surviving vitality of the world of the classical Enlightenment.

An equally courageous, though less balanced and more tormented, poet was Vittorio Alfieri. Born at Asti in Piedmont in January 1749, into a rich family of the nobility, Alfieri frantically desired success for himself as an individual. As a child he attempted suicide, and his autobiography suggests that for long periods of his life he was virtually deranged. His importance lay in the full extent to which he anticipated Italian romanticism and the cultural nationalism of the Risorgimento. . . . [He] must be considered later in this [essay] when Italian drama of the period is surveyed, but here his place as a precursor of the Romantic movement must be suggested.

Parini had still used the weapon of satire which the eighteenth century had brought to so fine an art. Alfieri, twenty years Parini's junior, stated his convictions with a brutal directness, thinking and writing at white heat. He was, in the words of De Sanctis, 'a gigantic and solitary figure, pointing a finger in accusation'.[1] Yet he had not started his formidable revolt against

society as a young man. Until he was twenty-six he lived the idle and dissipated life of an Italian nobleman, but with increasing dissatisfaction. He believed that in 1775 he experienced a 'conversion' in that he suddenly decided to concentrate on the writing of tragic drama, and so to provide Italy with a tradition which she had hitherto lacked. Yet his preparation for this task had been more thorough than he himself pretended. The deliberate training for a literary career came after his 'conversion' but, in his own feverish way, he already knew the world. He had travelled throughout Europe for some five years, getting involved in numerous love affairs, fighting duels and, again, attempting suicide. He developed a great contempt for the Europe of the *ancien regime,* considering the customs of Paris disgustingly false, and the Berlin of Frederick the Great a 'universal barracks'. The Vienna of Maria Theresa and the St Petersburg of Catherine the Great pleased him no better. As might have been expected, he was highly critical of the writings of Montesquieu and Voltaire. More surprisingly he reacted also against Rousseau, who was in so many respects a kindred spirit. Perhaps the strongest influences on him were Plutarch, Machiavelli, Cervantes and Shakespeare; for writers who were his own contemporaries he felt only antipathy.

Alfieri's main weakness was his lack of self-criticism, so that there is no steady development in the body of his work. His ideas, too, remained constant and unchanging. He felt great respect for the heroic individual—rather as Carlyle and Nietzsche were to do—and contempt for the universalism, philanthropy and even the humanitarianism of the Enlightenment. He believed that the individual must rebel with violence against the corrupt, formal and tyrannical world of eighteenth-century Europe. He had grown up, like most of the Piedmontese nobility, speaking and writing French: his Italian was not good. After his 'conversion' in 1775 he tried desperately to rectify this lack by reading the Italian classics, and in 1776 by moving to Florence, where the Italian accepted as the correct version of the national language was spoken.

From 1785 to 1792 he was living sometimes in Alsace, sometimes in Paris. In 1792 his house in Paris was sacked by the crowd. He moved again to Florence, where he stayed until his death in 1803. He had, like so many creative writers of Western Europe, welcomed the French Revolution but his experiences during the Jacobin period in Paris had embittered him, and in his last years he was even more lonely and depressed than he had been throughout the earlier part of his life. He is buried in Santa Croce, in Florence, the Westminster Abbey of Italy. His tomb was the work of Canova: that so turbulent a personality as Alfieri should have so serene and classical a tomb is perhaps the final incongruity.

In the history of Italian poetry there is also a contradiction in Alfieri in that he was determined never to write 'lyric' poetry in the strict sense of the term. He despised poetry which was simply a verbal accompaniment to music. Yet the rest of the world can recognize his *Rime* as genuine and sometimes great lyric poetry. It may well be that his concentration on tragic drama was a mistake.

If Alfieri was too obsessed with himself, Vincenzo Monti sold himself too completely to the external world. Monti was born in February 1754, in the Romagna. After studying medicine and law, with little conviction, at the University of Ferrara, he lived from 1778 until 1798 in Rome, working as a secretary for Luigi Braschi, a nephew of Pius VI. While Alfieri had fought his own private revolt against the universe, Monti was essentially a poet of the establishment—at first that of the Papacy, and then those of the Cisalpine Republic and the Italian Kingdom. But establishments rarely have at their disposal poets with the imagination and verbal dexterity of a Monti. Yet Monti's poetry, often of great beauty, is a façade, and the man behind it is never visible. Whether he had any basic convictions is open to doubt. In the pope's Rome he defended monarchy and Catholicism against the Terror in Paris; in Milan in 1797 he defended French and Cisalpine 'democracy'. In *Prometeo,* written in 1797, he paid his respects to Napoleon as the scourge of tyrants. By then his verse had turned against Catholicism and he had become concerned for the independence and freedom of Italy. In 1801, after Marengo, he wrote the short poem *Per la liberazione d'Italia,* which has a freshness and sincerity about it that at least puts his patriotism beyond doubt. Thereafter, however, he was essentially the official poet of the Napoleonic régime. Sadly, after 1815, he continued to be the Vicar of Bray, writing poems in honour of the Austrians. Yet his work remained fresh and vivid. In a sense Monti's achievement represented the triumph of art over honesty.

Italian Romanticism reached its fulfilment in Foscolo, and its peak in Leopardi. Foscolo and Leopardi were deeply sincere poets in a way that Monti could never have understood. Perhaps even Alfieri, tied up in his huge egoism, could not have understood the limpid honesty of these two great Romantic poets. But it would be a mistake to link Foscolo and Leopardi too closely together. Foscolo was more important in the history of the Risorgimento: Leopardi was more important in the history of humanity. Yet both of them used the Italian language to achieve a perfection which had not been achieved since the days of Dante and Petrarch.

Ugo Foscolo was born on the Greek island of Zakinthos or Zante in 1778, the son of an Italian doctor. Zante was at the time of Foscolo's birth under the sovereignty of the Republic of Venice. Foscolo was al-ways to claim a classical inheritance from Greece, and a romantic modern one from Venice. Perhaps because his father died when he was only ten, Ugo had a sense of purpose and moral responsibility at a very early age. When the French Revolution broke out, Ugo, young as he was, could sympathize with its aims. He had already read Alfieri, and his very first youthful rhymes were written in 1794. At 1797, when he was still only nineteen, he had a play, *Tieste,* performed in Venice, with great success. The romantic expression of sympathy for the French Revolution in these early writings of Foscolo obliged him to leave Venice. He returned very briefly when the *ancien régime* of the Doge fell, later in 1797, but had to depart once more when Napoleon sold Venice to the Austrians. This act of treachery on the part of Bonaparte was clearly a traumatic event for Foscolo, yet he was still prepared to fight for French-controlled Genoa in the campaign of 1799-1800. Meanwhile he had written the *Last Letters of Jacopo Ortis,* which was to be published in Milan in 1802, and will be considered later in the context of the Italian novel. But it is as a poet, not a novelist, that Foscolo holds so central a place in the history of Italian literature. A major work, the *Sepolcri,* was published in Brescia in 1807. During the Napoleonic period he lived a life of great political, military and literary activity. After the Restoration, in 1816, he settled in London, where his last years were ones of poverty and misery, although he was lionized by the Whig aristocracy. He died at Turnham Green in 1827, but in 1871 his remains were taken from London to Santa Croce.

Foscolo's genius was perhaps most perfectly expressed in his sonnets. The concept of poetry as 'the poet speaking to himself', which is still, in the late twentieth century, the more usually accepted one, was in Italy forcefully established by Foscolo. One of his best known sonnets is entitled, precisely, *"Di Se Stesso"* ("Of Himself"). While Alfieri had denied that his poetry had anything to do with music, Foscolo's control of the Italian language was such that he could not avoid writing verse of great verbal beauty. One example must suffice here, his sonnet *"To Evening,"* of which the first eight lines are:

> Forse perché della fatal quiete
> tu sei l'immago a me si cara vieni
> o sera! E quando ti corteggian liete
> le nubi estive e i zeffiri sereni,
>
> e quando dal nevoso aere inquiete
> tenebre e lunghe all'universo meni
> sempre scendi invocata, e le secrete
> vie del mio cor soavemente tieni.

To attempt to translate Foscolo or Leopardi seems almost blasphemous, but the attempt must be made.

These lines of Foscolo's *"Alla Sera"* might be rendered:

> Perhaps it is because you are the
> image of the fatal quiet of
> death that you are so dear
> to me, O evening. Whether you
> come with happy summer clouds and
> soft breezes, or from a snowy
> sky, bringing restless and long shadows
> to the world, you always
> come when you are sought
> and gently fill the secret paths of my heart.

One of the great patriotic Italian poets, Foscolo had a strong influence on Mazzini, who arrived in London after Foscolo's death and went to some length, successfully, to track down notes Foscolo had left on Dante. Another patriotic poet, not of the stature of Foscolo but worth more than many other poets of the Risorgimento, was Giovanni Berchet. Born in Milan in 1783, he played an important role in the early stages of the Romantic movement rather as a polemicist than a poet, and, in particular as a contributor to the *Conciliatore*. He attacked the provincialism of many of the classicists, and appealed for a popular, national literature, which would be a worthy part of a European literature. But writers should learn, he believed, to write in a simple and direct manner which would appeal to the mass of the people. Poetry had a social function to perform, a function which could not be achieved by esoteric or scholarly allusions. He himself employed no subtle or complex imagery, but as in *"Il Trovatore,"* one of his most popular poems, wrote with an almost childish sentiment. Berchet was exiled from Italy in 1821 and lived in London, Belgium and France before returning to play an active role in his home city during the *cinque giornate* of 1848. He was subsequently elected to the Piedmontese parliament and died in Turin in 1851.

Perhaps the greatest, if also the saddest, Italian poet of the nineteenth century was Giacomo Leopardi. Born in 1798 at Recanati, a little hill town near Ancona, in what was then the Papal States, Leopardi came from a family of the minor nobility. His father was an educated man and took pains to educate his eight children, of whom Giacomo was the eldest. In a sense, he was too successful. Giacomo remained glued to his father's well-stocked library. By the time he was sixteen he had written two tragedies and much poetry in Italian and short works in Latin. Whereas a sedentary scholar's life does little harm to most people, it was clearly dangerous to Giacomo, who became hunchbacked, suffered from very weak eyesight, and for much of his life was virtually an invalid.

His first successful poem, *"All'Italia,"* published in 1818, showed him to be at the age of twenty a part of the romantic patriotic movement, a movement which he was to go far beyond in later years:

> O patria mia, vedo le mura e gli archi
> E le colonne e i simulacri e l'erme
> Torri degli avi nostri,
> Ma la gloria non vedo . . .

> (O my fatherland, I see the walls
> and the arches and the columns and
> the crumbling towers of our ancestors,
> but the glory I do not see . . .)

The youthful Leopardi's approach to his country was thus one of regret for a lost past. The subsequent approach in his poetry to the human predicament was distilled from his own suffering. His extraordinary erudition—his knowledge of Latin, Greek, Hebrew, and the principal modern languages of Western Europe—never intruded into the purity of his poetry. Involuntarily he adopted Berchet's doctrine that poetry should be direct, never opaque, in its emotional appeal, but he employed imagery of an intensity beyond Berchet's wildest dreams. And, like Foscolo's, Leopardi's poetry created its own music, though perhaps less self-consciously than Foscolo's had done, because it was the product of a passive, repressed suffering, unlike that of Foscolo which had been active and aggressive. Leopardi was the victim of parents who loved him in a suffocating yet distant, a remote yet possessive, manner. They were determined that he should not leave home even when he was in his twenties, so that the Leopardi library became for Giacomo a prison, though a prison which nurtured a genius.

Finally in 1822 Giacomo's father agreed that he should leave Recanati and stay for a few months in Rome. But Leopardi's soul was by then restless and acutely pessimistic. He lived for periods in Milan, Bologna, Florence and Pisa. Perhaps, for the first time in his life, he found some peace and happiness in Pisa where, in 1828, he wrote *"A Silvia,"* a moving and remarkable poem of nostalgia. In 1827 he had worked briefly with the *Antologia* group of writers, and had quarrelled with Tommaseo, a man totally unworthy of the friendship of Leopardi.

In December 1828, in desperately ill health, he returned to Recanati. Only then, in contact with the bitter memories of his youth, and by some kind of desperate paradox, did he produce his truly great poetry. Three poems must be mentioned here: *"La quiete dopo la tempesta,"* and *"Il sabato del villaggio,"* both written in 1829, and the haunting and beautiful *"Canto notturno di un pastore errante nell'Asia"* in 1830, written seven years before his death.

"Il sabato del villaggio" miraculously conjures up peasant life in the little village before the holiday: the

preparations of Saturday evening before the Sunday festivities. Leopardi concludes the poem with a deep melancholy which is implied rather than stated:

> Questo di sette é il piu gradito giorno,
> pien di speme e di gioia:
> diman tristezza e noia
> recheran l'ore, ed al travaglio usato
> ciascun in suo pensier farà ritorno.
>
> Garzoncello scherzoso,
> cotesta età fiorita
> è come un giorno d'allegrezza pieno,
> giorno chiaro, sereno,
> che precorre alla festa di tua vita.
> Godi, fanciullo mio; state soave,
> stagion lieta è cotesta.
> altro dirti non vò; ma la tua festa
> ch'anco tardi a venir non ti sia grave.

> (This is the most welcome of seven days,
> full of hope and joy. Tomorrow the
> hours will bring sadness and boredom,
> and everyone in his mind will go back to
> his accustomed toil.
>   But for you, playful
> lad, this fresh age of yours is like
> a day full of happiness, a clear
> cloudless day which comes before the
> holiday of your life. Enjoy it, my
> child; it is a sweet state, a happy
> season. I will not tell you more; but
> do not mind if the waiting for your
> holiday is long).

The suggestion here that the expectation of joy is always greater than the joy itself is a poignant one, and the unspoken sadness of 'Altro dirti non vò' makes the poem one of Leopardi's most tragic statements. Yet this is only one which could be quoted from the rich store of Leopardi's powerful works. It was unlikely that another Italian poet in the nineteenth century would reach this degree of human understanding.

Between Leopardi and the culmination of Italian nationhood in 1870 there was perhaps only one other major poet who deserves attention here: Manzoni.

Alessandro Manzoni must be considered later as the most brilliant Italian novelist of the nineteenth century. As a poet his achievement was also far from negligible. He was born in 1785 in Milan. His mother, Giulia Beccaria, was Beccaria's daughter, so that Alessandro could hardly escape the inheritance of the Lombard Enlightenment. But his parents' marriage was legally ended in 1792, and his mother had settled in Paris with Carlo Imbonati, who is known to posterity mainly because famous writers—Stendhal and Manzoni himself—wrote so favourably of him. Alessandro's father was not over-concerned about the welfare of his son, who was taken care of, for some years, by an aunt. Manzoni's first poem, written at the age of sixteen in 1801, was *"Il Trionfo della Libertà,"* an exaltation of the French Revolution and its triumph over tyranny and superstition. Stylistically an imitation of Monti, it showed little promise. Its main importance was precisely that it secured the approval and gained the encouragement of Monti. When Imbonati, with whom Manzoni had developed a close understanding, died in 1805, Manzoni wrote *"In morte di Carlo Imbonati,"* published in Paris in 1806 and marking a very considerable development from his juvenile works. He lived in Paris for most of the period 1805 to 1810, marrying Henriette Blondel, the sixteen-year-old daughter of a Swiss Calvinist banker, in 1808. Within a few years both Henriette and Alessandro developed devoutly Catholic convictions, and in 1810 were married again according to Catholic rites. In that same year Manzoni returned to Milan, which remained his permanent residence—in spite of trips away from time to time—until his death in 1873.

In 1815 Manzoni had published the first four of his five *Inni Sacri;* no one had paid any attention to them. Yet, as De Sanctis was to point out, they constituted an important aspect of the romantic movement, in that they brought a return of a religious sensibility, and of medieval Christian preoccupations—with the Madonna and the saints—but in a modern form. Manzoni could not escape the rationality and secularism of the Enlightenment, nor could he escape the egalitarianism of the ideas of 1789, which he had already praised in his earlier youth. Throughout his life he was to believe—as Lammenais, but few other Catholics, were to believe—that there was no contradiction between the doctrines of Christ and the belief in the brotherhood of man. The fifth and last of the *Inni Sacri,* the *Passione,* was published in 1822, and was a more mature and profound work than the first four.

In 1821 he had written a patriotic poem, *"Marzo 1821,"* in which he had declared that the Ticino, the river marking the boundary between independent Piedmont and Austrian Lombardy, should 'no longer run between two alien shores'. In the optimism of the moment, he wrote: 'Let there never again be a place where there are barriers between Italy and Italy'. Although written in 1821 when he believed that the Piedmontese revolution would lead to the liberation of Lombardy, *"Marzo 1821"* was not published until 1848. His *"Cinque Maggio"* (May the 5th) was also written in 1821, that being the day of Napoleon's death. It is a strange poem, neither sympathetic nor hostile to Napoleon, but seeing him in the light of eternity and of Manzoni's profound religious convictions.

The first edition of *I Promessi Sposi* had appeared in 1827, and must be considered later in this chapter.

Manzoni's role in the Risorgimento was an ambiguous one. His devout Catholicism made it difficult for him to agree with the anti-clericalism of most of his nationalist contemporaries. But he believed that the pope should give up the temporal power; he refused all honours offered him by the Austrian government; during the *cinque giornate* of 1848 he encouraged his sons to fight on the barricades; in 1861 he accepted the rôle of a senator in the new Italian Parliament, thus ignoring Pius IX's instructions to Catholics to have nothing to do with the godless Kingdom of Italy. He lived on until 1873, dying at the age of eighty-nine.

There were, of course, a great number of lesser poets in nineteenth-century Italy, and a few of them acquired national fame. Luigi Mercantini, born in 1821 in the Papal States, was exiled after 1848 as a liberal. He returned in 1852, was a university professor at Bologna and Palermo, and died in 1872. One of his poems, *"La Spigolatrice di Sapri"* ('The Gleaner of Sapri'), had an immense popular success. Dealing with Pisacane's tragic expedition of 1857, it is written as though spoken by a Neapolitan girl, in simple language, although not in dialect. It is shamelessly sentimental, yet authentically catches the right note, with its chorus:

> Erano trecento, eran giovani e forti
> e sono morti!

> (They were three hundred, they were
> young and strong, and they are dead!)

> La disser ladri usciti dalle tane
> ma non portaron via nemmeno un pane.

> (They were said to be thieves escaped
> from prison but they did not take away
> even a loaf of bread.)

Even more famous than Mercantini was Goffredo Mameli, born in 1827, the son of a Genoese naval commander. Mameli wrote the *"Fratelli d'Italia,"* which became the Italian national anthem. He was killed, at the age of twenty-two, fighting with Garibaldi in the defence of the Roman Republic in 1849. That he may well have written more profound works is indicated by his long poem, *Un'idea.*

Apart from the poets who were to become popular in a patriotic sense, there was a subculture of dialect poetry, consisting mainly of lyrics of popular songs. In some cases the author is known, in many cases not. A long verse which was probably never sung in its entirety, but which was certainly intended to be sung rather than read or recited, was *"Su patriotus sardu a sos feudatarios"*. Written by the Sardinian Francesco Manno in 1794, it was popular during the peasants' revolt of 1796:

> Try to moderate your tyranny, you barons. . . .
> Be aware that there is a fire being lighted against
> you. Be aware that this is no game . . . that there
> is a storm brewing.

In the South there was a great proliferation of such verse of protest. In and after 1860 many songs were written in support of Garibaldi, but many, also, against him and in support of the Bourbons.[2]

In spite of the great heights reached by poetic expression during the romantic movement, it is still true that the literary form most typical of nineteenth-century Europe was the novel. It was in the nineteenth century that the novel was to settle into its classic form as a piece of direct prose narrative divided into chapters, written sometimes in the first person but more often in the third person. But the first influential novel published in nineteenth-century Italy, the *Last Letters of Jacopo Ortis* by Foscolo, took the form common in the eighteenth century of a sequence of letters which provide their own narrative. *Ortis* was published in Milan in 1802, during the life of Napoleon's Italian Republic. It was a central, if extreme, example of European romantic prose. Foscolo was influenced, as so many of the Romantics were, by Goethe's *Werther,* but *Ortis* is in no sense derivative. It is, in its extravagant way, a wonderful piece of writing. Jacopo, the fictitious letter-writer, has been deeply embittered by Napoleon's betrayal of Venice (this aspect of the book is clearly autobiographical), and having fallen deeply and hopelessly in love with a woman who cannot marry him, kills himself. In spite of its extravagance and melodrama, *Ortis* keeps the disbelief of the reader permanently suspended; it has an authenticity and a sincerity which many more restrained novels lack. Like Rousseau's *Rêveries d'un promeneur solitaire,* or Emily Brontë's *Wuthering Heights,* it is the work of a chaotic genius.

But it was with Manzoni that the novel reached its highest peak of achievement in nineteenth-century Italy, and it is perhaps at this point that something should be said of the final adoption of the Tuscan form of Italian as the written form of the national language. It could be said that the process by which the language of Florence became recognized as 'correct' Italian had started with Dante and was concluded by Manzoni's re-writing of *I Promessi Sposi* (*The Betrothed*).

Manzoni had strong views on the establishment of a national language. He believed that any attempt to create or evolve one by combining features of several different dialects was doomed to failure. The language spoken in one particular city had to be recognized as the national language, just as the language spoken in Paris—not, of course, the *patois,* but the language spoken by educated Parisians—had become recognized as correct French. The language, then, had to be an existing, organic one, but one capable of being adopted by writers who had hitherto written partly in dialect. The decision to choose one particular language would not be an arbitrary one, but would be suggested by historical factors. For Italy, because of the development of her literature, the national language could only be the language of Florence. These views were expressed in several writings, most of them of the years 1868-71, in other words long after the publication of *I Promessi Sposi.* But to write his great novel he had, of course, already had to select a language which would be popular and accepted on a national level.

The first edition of the novel was published over the years 1825 to 1827, in three parts. Manzoni then rewrote it in the correct Tuscan according to the linguistic doctrine he was beginning to evolve. He removed archaic expressions and dialect words which would not be understood in many parts of Italy. The revised edition was published between 1840 and 1842.

The scene of *I Promessi Sposi* was Lombardy under Spanish occupation in 1628-30. Manzoni was a modest man, and although he sometimes criticized Walter Scott, he admitted his debt to Scott and protested that he himself had simply written another of Scott's novels. Scott's reply—'Yes. But it is my best'—was certainly nearer the mark. Scott's novels rarely went beyond pleasing adventure stories, although their reputation throughout Europe in their day was immense. Manzoni's characters have an extra dimension of credibility—with the possible exception of Lucia, the heroine, who follows the stereotype of the virtuous and innocent maiden. The exploits of Manzoni's humble young hero and heroine are set against the broader picture of the horrors of the early seventeenth century—the Thirty Years War and the plague of 1630. The effectiveness of the novel lies in its lucid, vital narrative style, never rhetorical and only occasionally sentimental, his use of primary sources—mostly seventeenth-century memoirs—to get the feel of the period, and the richness of his canvas, as he himself put it in a letter to a friend, 'stuffed with peasants, nobles, monks, nuns, priests, magistrates, scholars, war, famine'.[3] There are many sequences and episodes in the book which are vividly memorable; two deserve mention here: the painful but convincing tale of the nun of Monza, and the brilliant account of the food riot and attack on the bakeries in Milan during the famine.

As an historical novelist [Massimo d'Azeglio] was of far smaller stature than Manzoni, but by no means a negligible figure. Azeglio published *Ettore Fieramosca* in 1833, and it had an immediate success. His second complete historical novel, *Niccolò de' Lapi,* was published in 1841. *Ettore Fieramosca* is set in the Franco-Spanish wars in Italy at the turn of the fifteenth century, the age of the Borgias. Cesare, indeed, is brought into the novel, rather unconvincingly. On the surface it appears to be a romantically patriotic work, as does *Niccolo de' Lapi,* which is concerned with the fight by the Florentine Republic for her survival in 1530. But Azeglio's other writings, and in particular his perceptive autobiography, *I miei ricordi,* first published in 1863, suggest that the somewhat naive element in his novels is due to his desire to appeal to nationalist sentiments in readers less sophisticated than himself. In Azeglio's novels the smiling face of the author can be seen shining through the mist of the melodrama. Occasionally in *Ettore Fieramosca* he apologizes for the violence and horrors he is describing: he knows that the reader, like the author, is tired of them, and he therefore moves to another matter. While these asides are rather endearing, they are reminiscent of an earlier literary style and cannot be said to contribute to a suspension of disbelief. In addition to his two finished novels, Azeglio left an unfinished one, *La Lega Lombarda,* which he was writing in 1843, and which he abandoned because of his growing interest in the political situation in the Papal States. Although only the first few chapters of *La Lega Lombarda* were written, they are enough to suggest that it would have been markedly superior to *Ettore Fieramosca,* and even more so to *Niccolò de' Lapi.* It is this fragment, in which the influence of Manzoni is clearly visible, which makes Azeglio worthy of mention in a brief survey of the Italian novel in the period.

Another novelist who played an important role in the political history of the Risorgimento . . . was Francesco Domenico Guerrazzi. Two of his novels had great success in his day—the *Battaglia di Benevento* published in 1827-8, and the *Assedio di Firenze,* published in 1836. Guerrazzi was strongly influenced by Byron, and has the extravagant, morbid and desperate features of romanticism carried to extremes. The *Assedio di Firenze,* however, is a powerful, if chaotic and frenetic, work. As with Azeglio, the author is always too near the surface of his creation, but Guerrazzi is far more sincere and serious than Azeglio. Although Guerrazzi was a Tuscan, his language was not the one to be recommended by Manzoni. *L'Assedio di Firenze* is full not only of archaic words and sentence constructions, but also of expressions from the dialect of Leghorn. It serves as a warning that it is not strictly accurate to say that 'Tuscan' became recognized as the correct Italian; it was the language of Florence, rather than Tuscan, which filled this rôle.

If the novels of d'Azeglio and Guerrazzi have dated rather rapidly, the single masterpiece of Ippolito Nievo, *Le confessioni di un italiano,* has acquired increasing respect with the passing of the decades. The psychological penetration of Nievo's novel is more to modern taste than anything written by Azeglio, Guerrazzi or, for that matter, Alfieri.

Ippolito Nievo was born in Padua in 1831. He fought with Garibaldi in Lombardy in 1859, and in Sicily in 1860. He was a Mazzinian, but by no means a simple Mazzinian. In a short work entitled *La rivoluzione nazionale* he argued that it would not be enough to unite Italy in a political sense: another kind of unification was needed, the unification of town and countryside, the unification of the literate population with the rural population. He wrote *The confessions of an Italian* between 1857 and 1858. The novel purports to be the autobiography of an old gentleman in his eighties who had lived from the last days of the ancient Republic of St Mark into the mid nineteenth century. Clearly parts of the novel are genuinely autobiographical, but what gives the novel some of its poignancy is the fact that Nievo himself died at the age of thirty. On 4 March 1861 Nievo set sail from the Italian mainland for Palermo. Neither Nievo nor the boat on which he was sailing were ever seen again.

That Nievo's novel has survived the ravages of time is partly due to his egocentric, complex, but in the end self-sacrificing, heroine, la Pisana, who is so much more interesting than Manzoni's Lucia. But it is also due to his subtle understanding of human reactions to events. The great sense of relief of the inhabitants of the castle of Fratta at the end of a siege results in everyone chattering at once:

> The state of mind of someone who has, or believes himself to have, escaped a mortal risk, is like that of someone who has received a favourable reply to a declaration of love. The same loquacity, the same willingness to give anything requested, the same lightheartedness. To put it in another way, all great joys are similar in their effects, while great sufferings have a very varied scale of manifestations. Human souls have a hundred senses for feeling misfortune, and only one for good fortune; and nature reveals not a little of the character of Guerrazzi, who has greater imagination for the miseries than for the precious things of life.[4]

Later in the novel Nievo contemplates the fact of death, and inserts a passage which is closer to Samuel Beckett's pessimism of the mid twentieth century than to anything written in Nievo's own lifetime:

> after the light the darkness,
> after the hope the oblivion,
> after everything nothing . . .[5]

It is, of course, impossible to say how Nievo would have developed had he lived. But it can surely be said that when he was drowned at the age of thirty, European literature lost a figure of profound significance.

The realist school of novelists had, in a sense, already started in France with Balzac, and was to continue with Flaubert and Zola. In Italy Giovanni Verga was to bring the realist novel and short story to their highest points of achievement. In 1865 he had left his native Sicily and in 1870 was living in Florence, which had been, for several years, the capital of Italy. This young man was to become, in several ways, the founder of modern Italian literature, but in 1870 his genius was still unrecognized, in spite of the publication of his first two novels.

In the nineteenth century, and especially in Italy, there is a strange paradox with regard to drama: much drama was written and performed, yet little of it was of real value. The Venetian dramatist Carlo Goldoni was still alive in 1790. He had written delightful plays of great subtlety and rich humour, but he belonged essentially to the earlier period. The only dramatist of any stature who clearly belongs to the Risorgimento is Vittorio Alfieri, the man who coined the very term 'risorgimento'.

In the course of twelve years—from 1775 to 1787—Alfieri wrote nineteen tragedies. The scene for most of them was the classical world of Greece or Rome. A few were concerned with more recent history—*Filippo, Maria Stuarda*—and one, *Saul,* with biblical history. That *Saul* was perhaps his greatest play suggests that Alfieri was closer in spirit to the Old Testament than to Greco-Roman civilization. If the spirit of the tragedies is romantic, the form is strictly classical. The three unities are observed, the scansion is regular, and the characters are very few in number. The plays are pared to the bone: no episode or scene takes place which is not essential to the single tragedy. Alfieri does not indulge in sub-plots or superfluous characters. In this sense his tragedies were closer to classical Greek drama than to anything written since. But if these were his strengths, his weaknesses were the two-dimensional nature of his characters, who lack any psychological subtlety, and the sheer monotony of his verse. Astringency in the writing of tragedy is not enough; somewhere in a great play there should be some real human beings. But the impact of his drama in its day was enormous, mainly because of its simple, direct political message: the heroes of his tragedies are almost always fighters for freedom against tyranny, and fighters who are doomed to become victims of the tragedy. Only when a slightly different flavour is added to this recipe—especially in *Saul* and *Mirra*—does Alfieri's art rise above its usual level.

Whatever might be said by way of negative criticism of Alfieri it has to be admitted that no drama which was written later during the Risorgimento had, or deserved, the same impact. A few dramatists, like the Tuscan Gian Battista Niccolini, were extravagantly praised in their day. Niccolini was given a huge tomb in Santa Croce, an absurdly extravagant recognition for his turgid plays, but none of Alfieri's successors had such an influence as Niccolini in popularizing the idea that tyranny must be fought in the cause of freedom.

If the prose and verse drama of the period has had a short life, one theatrical form—the opera—produced works which are still familiar to audiences all over the world. Opera was a comparatively recent art form, dating from the early seventeenth century, but it had been essentially an Italian invention, and if anyone can be called the 'inventor' of opera it must surely be Claudio Monteverdi, who had lived from 1567 to 1643. But it was in the nineteenth century that the opera reached its peak of popularity, and so far as Italy is concerned four composers deserve mention here: Donizetti, Rossini, Bellini and Verdi.

Gaetano Donizetti was born in 1797 in the lovely Lombard City of Bergamo. His father was a worker in the textile industry, but Gaetano's musical gifts gained him a place in the Philharmonic Lyceum at Bologna. His first success was with the opera *Anna Bolena* (Anne Boleyn), produced in Milan in 1830, and subsequently in Paris and London. In 1833 came *Lucrezia Borgia* in Milan, an opera based on Victor Hugo's work. *Lucia di Lammermoor,* based on Scott's novel, was first performed in 1835 in the San Carlo Theatre in Naples. Donizetti composed many operas at an incredible rate. If *Lucia* is his best known and most characteristic opera, *Don Pasquale,* composed in 1843, and first performed in Paris, was a light-hearted masterpiece. Donizetti's end was unhappy. He had probably suffered from syphilis for many years, and in 1848 had a complete mental breakdown, resulting in his being confined to an asylum near Paris. He and his music were typical products of the romantic age, but in Donizetti's case romanticism had no political overtones. He died in Bergamo in 1848, quite unaware of the nationalist storm which was brewing all around him. On his tomb in the church of Santa Maria Maggiore in Bergamo it is said of him that he was 'a fruitful discoverer of sacred and profane melodies'. The idea that he 'discovered' rather than 'composed' melodies is a pleasing one: the melodies, sacred or profane, must, of course, already exist in the ear of God; the individual composer, with the help of his muse, merely has to discover them. That Donizetti's voyage of discovery was a fruitful one can hardly be doubted.

An older contemporary of Donizetti, Gioacchino Rossini, lived twenty years longer and had a lifespan—1792-1868—which almost exactly corresponds with the period covered by this [essay].

Born in the little coastal town of Pesaro, in the Papal States, Rossini started his career, while still a boy, as an instrumentalist of some virtuosity. His first—and last—enthusiasms were for Mozart and Haydn. Like Donizetti's, Rossini's parents were humble people, and his childhood was an insecure one, but he, too, had gained a place at the Lyceum at Bologna. In 1810 Rossini left the Lyceum to go to Venice, where he had been commissioned to write a one-act opera. The result, the *Cambiale del Matrimonio,* was sufficiently successful to allow him to remain in Venice writing popular one-act operas. It was in Venice that Rossini wrote *Tancredi,* based on Voltaire's play, which spread his fame to all classes in the city. His next opera, *L'Italiana in Algeri,* is much better known today, yet he was still only twenty-one years old. In 1815 he moved to Naples, where he was given leave, in November, to go to Rome to write a single opera, which in the event turned out to be his most brilliant—*The Barber of Seville*. He wrote the score of *The Barber of Seville* in less than a fortnight. The use to which Rossini put Beaumarchais's play produced perhaps the most splendid comic opera of all time. Like Donizetti, Rossini continued to write operas at an amazing rate. That they could compose at such speed is indicative not only of their professionalism, but also of the popularity of opera as an entertainment in the nineteenth century, especially in Paris and Vienna, and more especially in Italy, where the great opera houses—La Scala in Milan, the San Carlo in Naples and the Fenice in Venice—were becoming more important than cathedrals in the spiritual life of the people.

The Barber in the long run was to prove to be Rossini's most successful opera. It was followed in 1816 by *Otello,* and in 1817 by *La Cenerentola* and *La Gazza Ladra (The Thieving Magpie),* the last two as original musically as the *Barber*. Praised by Beethoven and Schubert, Rossini was by the 1820s immensely popular throughout Europe. At one moment in 1823 twenty-three of his operas were being performed in different European cities. His culminating, and his most influential, work was *William Tell,* based on Schiller's play, and first performed in Paris in 1829. He felt, however, with some reason, that his popularity was on the wane, and for the last thirty-nine years of his life wrote no other opera.

If Rossini's impact on the world was greater than Bellini's, the latter composer could claim to have had a greater influence on younger composers, notably on Chopin. Vincenzo Bellini was born in Catania in 1801. His first successful opera was *Il Pirata,* which secured for him an international reputation. Performed for the first time in La Scala in 1827, it had a gentle simplicity combined with great technical skill which made it immediately appealing. His next opera of significance, *La Sonnambula,* was performed in Milan in 1831, not at La Scala, but at the Teatro Carcano. Far more important than these two operas was *Norma,* produced at La Scala in December 1831. Until that moment it had seemed unlikely that Bellini could produce an opera as powerful as *Norma*. Yet he followed

Giuseppe Verdi, conducting an orchestra.

it with one almost as powerful—*I Puritani,* first produced in Paris in 1835. Before the year was out Bellini was dead. He cannot be considered among the greatest of composers, but in his brief life of thirty-five years he had made a simple musical statement of very real value.

Most Italian poets, painters or sculptors came from the middle or upper classes. The most successful operatic composers came from humbler backgrounds. Giuseppe Verdi's father was an innkeeper, and in spirit a peasant. Verdi was born, in 1813, in the countryside of Parma. The early years of his career were ones of desperate struggle, but at the age of twenty-six he had his first opera performed at La Scala—*Oberto, Conte di San Bonifacio.* His life was then blighted by personal tragedy on an appalling scale: his wife and his two children died within two years. At that moment he could well have abandoned his career, but without enthusiasm continued to write music. In 1842 Verdi's *Nabucco* was produced at La Scala: it had an immense popular success. His next opera, *I Lombardi,* performed at La Scala in 1843, could be interpreted in a nationalist sense, and got him into trouble with the Austrian authorities. Donizetti, Rossini and Bellini had been apolitical. The same could certainly not be said

of Verdi. The people of Milan were quick to recognize the distinction. But Verdi was much more than a political propagandist. His *Macbeth,* produced in Florence in 1847, was to survive into an age which had long forgotten the Risorgimento.

In 1851 *Rigoletto* was produced in Venice. It was based on Victor Hugo's *Le Roi s'amuse,* and eventually secured Hugo's warm approval. Its permanent success since Verdi's death need hardly be stated here. *Il Trovatore* was first performed in Rome in 1853— a reminder that the Rome of the popes was not entirely dead between 1849 and 1870. In 1853 *La Traviata* was produced in Venice. Critics—especially in England—thought it was wickedly erotic. *Simon Boccanegra* was produced in Venice in 1857, and was not well received, although Verdi himself—rightly— always believed that it was one of his best works. In 1858 he hoped to produce *Un Ballo in Maschera* in Naples, but the Bourbon authorities prevented its production on the ridiculous grounds that the story involved the assassination of a monarch. Thus, almost by accident, Verdi became increasingly identified with the revolutionary movement, and a hero in the eyes of the liberals and nationalists. *Un Ballo in Maschera* was produced in Rome in 1859, with a changed plot to satisfy the censors. With the creation of the Kingdom of Italy Cavour persuaded Verdi to stand for parliament, which he did, much against his inclination. He was a deputy for five years, though not an active one. In 1862 the tragic opera, *La Forza del Destino,* was produced in the St Peterburg of Alexander II, who had just, by a stroke of the pen, emancipated millions of serfs. It could well be argued that *La Forza del Destino* was Verdi's most beautiful opera. His next opera, *Don Carlos,* produced in 1867, was uncharacteristic.

The true Verdi reached his culmination on Christmas Eve, 1871, with the production of *Aida* in Cairo. It was a daring and remarkable work, which confused and sometimes exasperated the critics when it was performed a few weeks later in Milan. But the critics have now been dead for some decades, and *Aida* is still very much alive.

Wagner believed that the combination of music and drama made opera the highest of the arts. The four Italian composers who have been considered here would all have been too wise to countenance such nonsense. Yet it is true that opera in nineteenth-century Italy was a vital part of national life, and a part of national life which cut across class divisions.

Notes

Obviously an enormous literature of editorial and critical work in many languages has been lavished on Italian poetry, drama and novel of the nineteenth century.

Here only a few hints can be given of the kind of material which is available. A starting-point must still be Francesco De Sanctis, whose *Storia della letteratura italiana,* edited by N. Gallo, is contained in a comparatively recent edition of the *Opere* of De Sanctis (Turin, 1958). More completely relevant to this chapter is the work of De Sanctis, *La letteratura italiana nel secolo XIX,* edited by Giorgio Candeloro and Carlo Muscetta under the titles of *Mazzini e la scuola democratica,* Turin, 1951, and *La scuola cattolico-liberale e il romanticismo a Napoli,* Turin, 1953.

An early study of Confalonieri was A. d'Ancona, *Federico Confalonieri,* Milan, 1898, and an enlightening study of three great eighteenth-century writers is Walter Binni, *Settecento maggiore: Goldoni, Parini, Alfieri,* Milan, 1978. For Monti there is Donata Chiomenti Vassalli, *Vincenzo Monti nel dramma dei suoi tempi,* Milan, 1968.

The national edition of the works of Ugo Foscolo deserves mention. Edited by a number of scholars, it was published in Florence in 14 volumes from 1932 to 1961. A fine biography of Leopardi in English is Iris Origo, *Leopardi. A biography,* London, 1935, and a collection of Leopardi's works has been edited by Walter Binni: *Tutte le opere di Giacomo Leopardi,* Florence, 2 vols, 1969.

For Manzoni there is a beautifully written work by Archibald Colquhoun, *Manzoni and his Times,* London, 1954. Relevant for Massimo d'Azeglio as a novelist is a work already mentioned for Chapter 8: Ronald Marshall, *Massimo d'Azeglio. An artist in politics, 1798-1866,* London, 1966. An early work on the novels of Guerrazzi [is] . . . mentioned in the notes to Chapter 3—Furio Lopez-Celly, *Francesco Domenico Guerrazzi nell'arte e nella vita,* Milan, 1918.

Writing on the opera has been, perhaps not surprisingly, rather less extensive than writing on literature. But musicology of the Italian nineteenth century is far from negligible. Herbert Weinstock has written on Donizetti and Rossini—*Donizetti and the world of opera in Italy, Paris and Vienna in the first half of the nineteenth century,* London, 1964, and *Rossini. A biography,* Oxford, 1968. In the same year Luigi Rognoni published a full biography, *Gioacchino Rossini,* Turin. For Bellini a good study is Francesco Pastura, *Vincenzo Bellini,* Turin, 1959, and an interesting recent work on Verdi is David R. Kimbell, *Verdi in the Age of Romanticism,* Cambridge, 1981.

¹ Francesco De Sanctis, *Storia della letteratura italiana,* Turin, 1951 edn, vol. II, p. 317.

² A fine selection of protest songs can be found in Giuseppe Vettori ed., *Canzoni italiane di protesta 1794/*

1974 dalla rivoluzione francese alla repressione cilena: Rome, 1976.

³ Quoted by Archibald Colquhoun, *op. cit.,* p. 170.

⁴ Ippolito Nievo, *Le confessioni di un italiano,* Milan, 1973, vol. 1, pp. 187-8.

⁵ *Ibid.,* vol. II, p. 450.

ITALIAN ROMANTIC THEORY

Francesco De Sanctis

SOURCE: "The New Literature," in *History of Italian Literature,* translated by Joan Redfern, 1931. Reprint, Basic Books, Inc., 1959, pp. 833-947.

[*In the following excerpt, De Sanctis describes the philosophical underpinnings of Italian Romanticism.*]

[At the opening of the nineteenth] century the Abate Monti was still in his zenith, with lesser planets revolving around him. Foscolo in his solitude was planning his *Grazie,* and Romagnosi was transmitting to the new generation the thought of the vanquished century. And precisely in 1815, amid the clamour of mighty events, there came to the light that little booklet called *Inni* which nobody bothered about. The eighteenth century was closed by Foscolo's *Odes;* the nineteenth was opened by Manzoni's *Hymns.* The first poems of the new century had names such as "Christmas," "The Passion," "The Resurrection," "Pentecost." Now the old literature, as we know, had never been wanting in its Christmases, Jesuses, and Marys, material for insipid canzoni and sonnets that have all fallen into oblivion. The simple and true religious feeling that had inspired the Church Fathers and Dante and Petrarch, and the artists, sculptors, and architects of ancient Italy, was lacking. That sacred material had been traversed by the seventeenth century and Arcadia, to vanish in the end before the mocking laugh of the eighteenth century. Now, at the opening of this nineteenth century, we have poetry making her concordat with the rest, and behold once more on the scene that old religious material, revived by a new inspiration.

What moves the poet in these *Inni* is no longer the mystery and sanctity of dogma. He does not receive the supernatural with devoutness, with the simplicity of a believer. His aim is, if we may use the expression, to naturalize the supernatural—to bring it down into the imagination. The supernatural is no longer a credo; it has been turned into an artistic motive. In reading these *Inni* we have somehow the impression that the young poet in writing them was faced by the sarcastic smile of Foscolo and Alfieri, and was afraid to present these old and used-up images except finely and artistically. He is not content to show them as holy, he wants them also to be beautiful. The Christian idea had returned above all as art, and in fact was the substance itself of the modern art that was known as "romantic." And the same road had been taken by criticism; from now onwards the expressions in use will be "classical," "romantic," "plastic," "sentimental," "infinite," and "finite." The classical in poetry had been challenged by the hymn, a form religious by its very nature, the poetry of the infinite and the supernatural. Yet Manzoni, in spite of his desire to be romantic, never ceases to be a classical writer. Climb as he will among the clouds of Sinai, he cannot hold out in those mists, and is forced each time to get back to earth; he is only able to receive what is clear, plastic, limited, and harmonious. His forms are descriptive, rhetorical, and literary, and at the same time are extremely effective because enlivened by invention and by new material. In reading Manzoni we are conscious of the new spirit holding its own against the invading religious ideas and refusing to be beaten—in fact conquering those religious ideas by absorbing them. We feel that it is looking for itself in them, and is finding itself in them.

The ideal basis of these *Inni* is fundamentally democratic. It is the idea of the century baptized and consecrated under the name of "the Christian idea," the equality of men who are all brothers in Christ, the rebuke of the oppressors and the glorification of the oppressed. It is the trinity, "liberty, equality, fraternity," evangelized; it is Christianity given back its idealism and penetrated by the modern spirit. The result is a serene and tranquil presentation, graphic in its visions, and simple and moving in its feelings, an ideal and reconciled world, in which the discords and pains of the earth are harmonized and appeased. We have the Lord, who in the midst of his sufferings thinks of the sons of Eve; we have Mary, to whose royal bosom the ordinary little woman brings her despised tears; we have the Holy Spirit, which descends like a healing breath amid the languid thoughts of the unfortunate; we have the kingdom of peace, which the world may mock at, but cannot take away. The poor and humble man, raising his eyes to Heaven—to "his own" Heaven—turns his laments to rejoicing, thinking of Him in whose image he is made.

In Manzoni's *Cinque Maggio* we have this same reconstruction of the heavenly world to the lyrical strains of peace and pardon, high above the angers and greeds of humanity. The things of humanity are seen from above, with the eye of the world beyond the grave. The *Cinque Maggio,* an epic composition in lyrical form, is extremely original. However great and mighty

the individual, he is nothing really but a vestige of the Creator, a "fateful" instrument of God. Earthly glory, even the truest of glory, in Heaven is but "silence and darkness." Beyond and above the noise of the earth is the peace of God. It is God who brings down and who raises up, who saddens and consoles. It is God who saves us from despair and leads us in the green pastures of hope. So here is the *deus ex machina* back on the scene—man and humanity as conceived in the Bible. History is shown as the inscrutable will of God. Why? We do not know. All we know is that God has willed it. We adore the mystery and bow to the decree. The less we understand events, the more we marvel, the more we are conscious of the Deity, the Incomprehensible. Even the history of yesterday becomes legendary. Napoleon is presented as a great miracle of God, a mighty vestige of the Creator. For what end? For what mission? We know not; it is the secret of God. He wills it. All that remains of history is the popular, the legendary, part, the part that strikes the imagination—battles, vicissitudes, miraculous conversions, great catastrophes, extraordinary events. What makes this poem an epic is not the greatness or morality of the ends, but the greatness and power of genius, the development of a force that partakes in its nature of the supernatural. There are nine strophes, each strophe so vast of perspective as to be almost a world in itself. The impression we get is of a pyramid. In each strophe Napoleon is shown us in a new aspect, but always colossal. The inspired eye of the poet, swift and penetrating, groups the years, fuses the events, devours space, gives us the illusion of the infinite. The proportions are enlarged by a work that is all perspective, with the utmost clearness and simplicity of expression. The images, the impressions, the sentiments, the forms, within those horizons become enlarged also, gaining in audacity of colouring and dimensions. We are shown, condensed, the life of the great man, in his deeds, in his inwardness, in his historical acts, in his influence on the men of his day, in his pensive solitude: an immense synthesis in which the events and the centuries seem hurried on and drawn forward by some higher power, in those *sdruccioli* lines, tripping on the heels of each other and barely controlled by the rhymes.

Such was the first movement of the nineteenth century—epico-lyrical. The poetic machinery had ceased to be classical and was now theological. But the machinery here is something more than colouring or embellishment; it is the content itself, brought back to life in the imagination—the content that is reconstructing in its own image the history of humanity and the heart of man. It is the lost Christ who has been found again in our own hearts; it is the miracle come back into history; it is the new blossoming of hope and prayer. The heart once more grows tender and accessible to gentle feelings; a breath of peace has descended on the discords and disillusions of the earth.

The thing that Foscolo had only glimpsed was painted now by Manzoni with youthful enthusiasm, a reflection of that religious enthusiasm which accompanied the exiled Pope on his return to Rome, which awakened in Alexander the ideal of a Christian federation, and which promised to tired men a new era of peace and repose. These were the illusions on which the new generation had been nourished. While the aged Foscolo was imagining a paradise of Graces, allegorizing modern things with ancient colours, Manzoni was reconstructing the Christian Paradise in accordance with the modern spirit. Mythology had gone, but classicism remained; the eighteenth century was rejected but its ideas remained. The frame was changed but the picture was the same picture. Take for instance the *Cinque Maggio*. The frame is an artistic illumination, a fine work of the imagination, which fails to arouse a single religious impression worth mentioning. But the picture is the history of a genius reconstructed by a genius. The thing of interest is not the frame but the picture.

With great rapidity the theological movement changed to a purely philosophical movement. God was the Absolute, the idea; Christ was the Idea in so far as it was realized; the Holy Spirit was the Word, the Idea reflected and become conscious: the Christian Trinity was made the basis of a philosophical trinity. The theological God was a formal, abstract God, without a content; God in His truth was the Holy Spirit, which recognized Itself in Nature. The three moments of its history were Logic, Nature, Spirit. And everything in this history was reasonable and inevitable. War, slavery, conquest, revolution, *coups d'état,* were the necessary phenomena of the spirit in its growth. The spirit had its laws just as Nature had its laws, and the history of the world was the history of the spirit, was a living logic, which could never be determined *a priori*. Religion, art, philosophy, law, were movements of the spirit in its unfolding. Nothing repeated itself; nothing died; everything changed and developed in a never-ceasing progress, which was the self-spiritualization of the idea, the increasingly clear consciousness of self, a greater reality.

In these ideas, codified by Hegel, we are conscious of Machiavelli, of Bruno, of Campanella, and especially of Vico. But it is a Vico *a priori*. The laws that he deduced from social facts are looked for *a priori,* in the very nature of the spirit. What we get is an appendix to the "new science"—its metaphysic under the name of "logic." Next we have real theogenies or philosophical epics appearing on the scene, with their ramifications: a philosophy of religions, a history of philosophy, a philosophy of art, a philosophy of law, a philosophy of history—all illumined by the greater planet, which is logic, or as Vico calls it, metaphysics. Science was entirely renewed in its content—not merely in the moral order but also in the physical order. There

was a philosophy of the spirit, but there was also a philosophy of Nature. Both in fact at bottom were the same philosophy; both were moments of the idea in its manifestation.

So instead of the old mysticism, founded on the inscrutable will of God and nourished by sentiment, there had come this pantheistic idealism. It was a system well adapted to the bourgeoisie, the cultured class, because on the one hand it rejected mysticism and partook of the lay and the scientific, and on the other hand it rejected materialism and condemned revolutions as plebeian and brutal. That conception of an irresistible progress based on the peaceful development of culture was thoroughly pleasing to the bourgeoisie. So instead of "revolution" we get "evolution," and instead of "liberty" we get "civilization" and "progress" and "culture." At last it seemed really possible to reconcile everything—authority and liberty, state and individual, religion and philosophy, past and future. Even ideas made peace with each other, like the rest. The official name given to this system was "Eclecticism." The Revolution had discarded its red robe and was learning to be Christian and moderate under the tricolour. As a last hope it was taking to constitutional forms, keeping at an equal distance the clericals with their mysticism, and the revolutionaries with their materialism. These ideas went the round of Europe and became the credo of the cultured classes. The Liberal party was constituted a centre between the clerical Right and the revolutionary Left, the parties known as "extreme." This ideal of the bourgeoisie was realized by Louis Philippe, and was consecrated by Eclecticism. After a long and painful gestation the world seemed at last to have come to birth. The problem was solved; the key to the riddle was found; God could rest. Reaction and revolution were no longer possible; peaceful and legitimate progress was assured. The bourgeoisie, under the name of the "Moderate Liberal Party," had the government in its hands, holding in check both the Left and the Right. It opposed the Jesuits and the Ultramontanes, but at the same time it honoured Christianity (which was now the idea reflected and become conscious, the spirit that recognizes itself). It rejected the supernatural, but at the same time it expounded it and respected it. It rejected the divine Christ, but it exalted the human Christ to the skies. And it spoke of religion with unction and of the ministers of God with reverence. Therefore without offending the prejudices of the masses it drew to its side the liberal Christians and the patriots. It censured the methods and the violence and the impatience of the Left, but accepted its ideas in the abstract, putting its faith in the slower but surer process of education and upbringing. In ways such as these the Revolution, under the guise of a reconciliation, became acceptable to the greater number, and took up its road again.

As the result of these ideas there arose a new literary criticism. In the eighteenth century, when everything was shouting for liberty, criticism had shouted with the rest. And to a certain extent it had won liberty. With the decline in prestige of rules and authority it had attained to a certain measure of independence, used by the best among the critics with good sense and also with good taste. The attention that had once been given to the machinery of literature was now turned on the productive force. The motive and the meaning of a work was now looked for not in the outer form of the composition, but in the qualities of the author. So art had its *"Cogito"* too; and it also had its formula—"The style is the man." But criticism was still an affair of impressions and observations rather than of judgments and principles. Now, with the rise of the new philosophy, in which the beautiful was given its place beside the good and the true, criticism acquired a scientific basis in logic; together with religion and law and history, it became a manifestation of the Idea. So now we get a philosophy of art, or in a word, aesthetics. The ideal course of humanity being established, art was given its place in the system like the rest; it was a manifestation of the idea, deriving its essence and character from the nature of the idea. The new criticism was primarily concerned with the idea; the formal qualities in a work became secondary. We have the pagan idea, the Oriental idea, the Christian or romantic idea, in philosophy, in the state, in art, in all the branches of social activity—a historical development *a priori,* in accordance with the laws or logic of the spirit. Every treatise on aesthetics or on anything else was preceded, as a matter of course, by a philosophy of the idea; the problem in art was to look for the idea and to judge the work in accordance with the idea. So once again we get the Christian-Platonic conception of art, which Dante formulated and Tasso revived; poetry once more was "the truth hidden under the veil of fables," or "the truth served in soft verses." With poetry once more the "veil of the idea" it follows that the mythical and allegorical forms returned into vogue. So the ideal conceptions became changed into ideal constructions, and the *Divine Comedy,* the subject of such number-less commentaries, had its counterpart in *Faust.*

A sort of philosophism became fashionable in literature, even with the best of the writers, even with Schiller. And not merely philosophy but history became a necessary preliminary to criticism. To seize the idea in its abstractness was not enough; it must be shown in its historical apparitions, its content. The customs, institutions, ideas, and tendencies of the century were minutely investigated. "The style is the man" gave way to a new motto: "Literature is the expression of society." The result was a double impulse, analytic and synthetic. The fact being once established that history was not an empirical and arbitrary succession of events, but on the contrary was a progressive and rational manifestation of the idea, or in a word, a living dialectic, the writers became attracted to synthesis. So now in literature we get real historical epics, in accordance with a preordained logic. The history of this world was rewritten, the road opened by Vico was traversed and retraversed by the metaphysical genius in every possible direction—in the different religions, in the arts, in the philosophies, in the laws, in the political institutions, in the whole of the moral, intellectual, and material life of peoples.

No one could resist the glamour of the Idea. This was the epic moment of all the sciences. On the other hand, these hasty syntheses, these often extremely risky solutions of problems of the utmost delicacy, were occasionally found to be contradicted by the known and proved facts of history and the sciences; the lacunae, the involuntary deceptions, the artificially induced interpretations, the throwing together of things that were utterly disparate, were obvious and glaring, were impossible to ignore. So side by side with this vast ideal construction there arose once more patient analysis. Vico's method was seen to be surer and safer, even if longer and more troublesome. So back came the work *a posteriori*—with patient and minute researches in the whole range of the knowable. The movement of erudition that had been cut short in Italy by the invasion of Cartesianism and the rise of the absolute systems of the eighteenth century started again with renewed vigour in the whole of Europe, but especially in Germany. There developed once more the historical sense and the habit of observation. Science grew wider; from the trunk of knowledge came new branches, more especially in Germany, and most of all in the natural sciences and in the teaching of philosophy. Galileos, Muratoris, and Vicos came back on the scene. The material of culture, which till now had been practically limited to the Graeco-Roman, became wider and deeper, and stretched its boundaries to include the Orient, the Middle Ages, and the Renaissance, and all with so great an activity in research and discovery that the whole of knowledge was renewed by it.

To sum up, there were two tendencies, face to face, the one ideal, the other historical. And they often met. The former proceeded by categories and constructions, the latter by observation and induction. The ideal school set great store by facts, proclaiming as it did that the true ideal was history, the idea realized. So it was not above and beyond history, in the regions of the absolute and unchangeable; on the contrary its metaphysics was at bottom nothing but an ideal in process of becoming, was history itself. Similarly, the historical school was anything but empirical and limited to the circle of facts, but had its preconceptions and conjectures like the other. Bold speculation and patient investigation moved forward together. And these two forces, at times parallel, at times in collision, set into action all the forces of the spirit. The century of luminaries was followed by the century of progress. The genius of the new century was the genius of Vico.

And side by side with Vico there arose to European fame both Bruno and Campanella. In these three great Italians the century recognized its fathers, its forerunners. The moral and intellectual lever, the Bible of the new century, was the *Scienza nuova* of Vico. It was seen to contain, in a condensed form, the three forces representative of the century: speculation, imagination, and erudition. Past and present made peace, each taking its own place in the fateful course of history—for what is the sense of fighting against Fate, getting angry with Fate? Dogmatism with its infallibility and scepticism with its irony gave up the field to criticism, or in other words to that superior view of the spirit that has gained self-consciousness and recognizes itself in the world and is not going to fight against itself.

The movement, of course, had its effect on literature also. Every work of literary criticism was ushered in with philosophy and history. A work of art was no longer regarded as an arbitrary and subjective product of the mind in its immutable rules and examples, but was a product, partly unconscious, of the spirit of the world at a given moment of its existence. A man of genius was the expression, condensed and sublimated, of the collective forces that constitute the individuality of a society or a century. Idea and content were given him together. The idea was around and about him, in the society that he had been born into, that had given him his education and upbringing. He drew his life from the common life of his day, except that the intelligent and emotional part of that life was more developed in the genius than in the ordinary man. His strength lay in being one in spirit with his day; and the result of this spiritual union between a writer and his material was the thing called "style." How should a writer be indifferent to his content when it was there and nowhere else that he must look for his inspiration and his rules? With this changed point of view came a change in criteria. The literature of the Renaissance was condemned as classical and conventional, and the use of mythology was ridiculed. Those rigid ideals, all of a piece, decorated with the name of "classical," were seen to be the ideal counterfeited, the idea in its empty abstraction—not the idea in its historical conditions, in the endless variety of its existence. Rhetoric and poetics declined; the empty forms of rhetoric and the mechanical and arbitrary rules of poetics were seen to be absurd. There returned to favour that old motto of Goldoni, "Paint from real life; avoid falsifying Nature." And side by side with this lively feeling for the real was the utmost solicitude for historical truth. The epic gave place to the romance, the tragedy to drama, and ballads, romances, fantasies, and hymns shone out brilliantly in new metres. Naturalness, simplicity, force, sentiment, and profundity were infinitely preferred to dignity or elegance, they were valued as the qualities nearest to the heart of the content. Dante, Shakespeare, Calderon, Ariosto—the writers considered the furthest removed from the classical—were the major planets. The Bible, Homer, and the primitive and spontaneous poets became the favourites. And often the rough chronicler was preferred to the elegant historian, and the songs of the people to serious poetry. What was valued now was the content in its native purity, not the content artificially altered in later times. History was pruned of its fantastic and poetic elements, of all that fictitious display which had arisen with the imitation of the classics. And poetry, by copying the spoken word and the popular forms, came nearer to prose.

René Wellek

SOURCE: "The Italian Critics," in *A History of Modern Criticism: 1750-1950; The Romantic Age,* Yale University Press, 1955, pp. 259-78.

[*In the following essay, Wellek evaluates the theoretical component of the Italian Romantic movement, especially in the critical thought of Ugo Foscolo and Giacomo Leopardi.*]

The Italian romantic movement is usually considered as beginning with the polemics stirred up by an article (1816) of Madame de Staël in which she urged the Italians to translate Shakespeare and recent English and German poetry rather than to remain content with classical mythology, which in the rest of Europe had been abandoned and forgotten.[1] Italian national vanity was deeply hurt; nevertheless, a group of younger people in Milan came to the defense of Madame de Staël. Lodovico di Breme condemned at length the low intellectual state of Italian literature at that time, drawing attention to the stir caused by the romantic-classical debate in France.[2] Giovanni Berchet (1783-1851), who later was to acquire fame as a poet, wrote the manifesto of the group, *Lettera semiseria di Grisostomo* (1816), which serves to introduce translations, in prose, of two of Bürger's ballads, "Der wilde Jäger" and "Lenore." Two German ballads, written as far back as 1773 under the stimulus of Percy's collection, were thus exhibited as specimens of the new "romantic" literature based on popular tradition. The introductory reflections, however, combine the Herderian view of poetry as universal and popular with a plea that literature be modern and useful. "Classical poetry is poetry of the dead, romantic poetry is poetry of the living."[3] Though Berchet recommends ballads based on Nordic superstitions of no relevance to the Italian situation, he can argue, however illogically, that "man cannot think of a distant man, in different circumstances from his, with the same interest as he thinks of himself and his neighbors. The tears of a poor peasant, the anguish of a cattle-driver, the profaned peace of a hermit cause pity"—yet we are scarcely moved by the misfortunes of the Atrides, Thyestes, and Priams of antiquity.[4] Classical themes are to be discarded, as are the rules of poetics, which have never yet made a true poet. The dramatic unities are a piece of absurd pedantry: the unity of time is a trick to make 36 hours equal 3. Berchet knew the *Dramatic Lectures* of A. W. Schlegel and Bouterwek's *History,* which he reviewed in 1818.[5] He is hardly a good critic, yet he is an important intermediary between Germany and Italy. He also was the first to formulate the issue clearly as one between conservatism and modernism, reaction and liberalism.

The romantic group then crystallized around the periodical *Il Conciliatore* (1818-19), in which Ludovico di Breme, Silvio Pellico (later to become the almost legendary martyr of the Italian *Risorgimento*), Ermes Visconti, and others discussed the question at great length. Though constant precautions against Austrian censorship (which very soon suppressed the sheet anyway) conceal political implications, we must always keep in mind that "modernity," "romanticism," meant for these Italians a renovation not only of literature but of Italian life in general, that the rebirth of literature was to them a preparation for the future independence and unity of Italy. From the point of view of literary theory they had nothing original to contribute. The most systematic statement in the *Conciliatore,* Ermes Visconti's *Idea elementaria sulla poesia romantica* (1818), is a reproduction of Schlegel's and Madame de Staël's distinctions between classicism, based on ancient mythology and manners, and romanticism, based on Christianity, chivalry, and modern discoveries. But the distinction is weakened by his admission of a neutral, mixed sort of poetry and by the astonishing declaration that there are no "essentially romantic or essentially classical styles."[6] The difference is all in the subject matter. Ancient religion and life are past and gone, and hence classical, while, for instance, America, discovered in modern times, is romantic. Visconti and the other Italian romantics especially attack the use of classical mythology in poetry, for they are tired of gods, Amors, nymphs, and satyrs inherited from 18th-century Arcadia. They recommend themes from Italian history, treated in a Christian spirit. The new poetry must be patriotic, Christian, and useful. This is the burden of Pellico's articles, which come to extremely relativistic conclusions as to the possibility of standards of criticism but escape complete skepticism by proclaiming the civic effect and utility of literature as its only measure.[7] Visconti, in a sprightly dialogue, attacked the unities of time and place with arguments drawn from Johnson and Schlegel: there is never complete illusion; Racine is badly handicapped by the observance of the rules, while Shakespeare, in his *Macbeth,* has the freedom to develop convincingly the psychology of his central figures. Characteristically, Visconti, in retelling *Macbeth,* leaves out the witches.[8] The argument in favor of the new dramatic system is one for psychological realism, truth to life and history.

This is also Manzoni's ideal. Alessandro Manzoni (1785-1873) was not a member of the *Conciliatore* group but was closely associated with it. Actually he became the one great Italian who expressly proclaimed himself a romanticist. Outside of Italy it is not generally realized what position of authority Manzoni eventually assumed in his nation. *I promessi sposi* in Italy is constantly—despite protests such as Croce's—placed beside the *Divine Comedy,* and the weight of Manzoni's austere moralism and poetic fame has given great prominence also to his views on literary criticism.

Manzoni began as a literary critic with a defense, in the *Preface,* of his tragedy *Il Conte di Carmagnola* (1820), which exactly fulfilled the demands of Visconti: it violated the unities and was based on Italian history. Manzoni quotes Schlegel and argues like Visconti against the unities of time and place and the inconveniences of the French system. He adds a general defense of the stage as an instrument of moral improvement. Manzoni, who by that time had been converted to a strict observance of Catholicism, was deeply impressed by the attacks on the stage made by Nicole, Bossuet, and Rousseau but hoped to refute them by his reform of the drama, which was to adhere very strictly to historical truth and by imaginative reconstruction was to supply the psychological truth implied in the historical events. To bolster his interpretation of the Carmagnola conspiracy Manzoni wrote an elaborate historical commentary and even divided his characters into "historical" and "invented."[9] The *Preface* elicited in France a defense of the unities by a little known writer, Victor Chauvet, to which Manzoni replied in a long piece, *Lettre à M. C———sur l'unité de temps et de lieu dans la tragédie* (1820). This is a very sober, dignified, well-reasoned statement of the case against the unities of time and space. In part Manzoni repeats the arguments known to Johnson and in part adopts Lessing's and Schlegel's argument that French tragedy, by adhering to the unities, violates the very principle of classicism, namely probability. The French sacrifice probability to the rules though the rules were supposedly made to preserve probability. Manzoni comes to a complete rejection of rules by asking, "If the great geniuses violate the rules, what reason is there to presume that they are based on nature and that they are good for anything?" Still, he insists strongly on the unity of action and on the purity of genre, rejecting tragi-comedy as "destroying the unity of impression necessary to the production of emotion and sympathy."[10]

The question of the unities is not, however, Manzoni's central concern. It is merely one instance of his interest in truth. The essence of poetry, he argues, is not invention of fact. All great works of art are based on events of history or on national traditions considered true in their time. Poetry is thus not in the events but only in the sentiments and discourses which the poet creates by entering sympathetically into their minds. Dramatic poetry aims at explaining what men have felt, willed, and suffered because of their actions. The poet is, we might draw the conclusion, a historian who, like Thucydides or Plutarch, invents the appropriate speeches and details for the events supplied by medieval chronicles.

Goethe, who reviewed the *Conte di Carmagnola* with high praise, knew that "for the poet no person is historical" and that all of Manzoni's characters should be and are ideal.[11] In a letter to Goethe Manzoni recognized that the division of characters into historical and ideal is a "mistake caused by his excessive adherence to the historical,"[12] and in the next tragedy, *Adelchi* (1822), the division disappeared. But Manzoni could not really have changed his attitude, since he added a long discourse on Langobard history, justifying every detail of the play.

In 1823 he wrote a letter to Marchese Cesare d'Azeglio, another statement in defense of romanticism, which again revolves around the concept of truth. Manzoni there distinguishes negative and positive sides of romanticism. On the negative side his distinction means the rejection of classical mythology (as false and idolatrous), of servile imitation, and of the rules and unities. On the positive side Manzoni admits that romanticism is a vague term, but it is so for an excellent reason. "In proposing that system of abolishing all the norms that are not truly general, permanent, and in every way reasonable, it makes their number much smaller and their selection much harder and slower."[13] Manzoni can think of only one common aim for the romanticists: poetry must propose truth as its object. Truth for Manzoni is, first of all, historical truth, the conquest by literature of a new theme, modern history, and then, though hardly distinguishable to his mind, the truth of Christianity, its ethics, its spirituality. Manzoni rejects as false the idea that romanticism has anything to do with witches, ghosts, and systematic disorder. Poetry was to him history, truthful history, and the novel, at which he was then working, *I promessi sposi* (1827) was to be a conscientious re-creation of the past, based on extensive research, in a Christian, Catholic spirit.

But soon after the novel had become the new Italian classic, Manzoni began to feel increasing scruples about the very possibility of a historical novel. *Del romanzo storico* (1845) is Manzoni's quiet, closely reasoned argument against the mixture of truth and fiction and thus against his own life work. He presents first the difficulties encountered by the reader who wants only historical truth. The very narrative form makes the demand impossible. But those who want fiction, a continuity of impression and total effect, cannot be satisfied either, because they can never abolish the distinction between the historical "consent" we give to a real figure such as Mary Queen of Scots or Bonnie Prince Charles or King Louis XI of France, and the other, "poetic consent" we give to probable events.[14] History and fiction are irreconcilable. The historical novel is a hybrid which must yield to the light of truth. To show that this is an inevitable process Manzoni seeks support in the history of the other comparable genres, the epic and tragedy. He believes that they were originally based on events considered and felt as true (like those of the Homeric epics or the Greek tragedies), but that late in the process of enlightenment they became increasingly involved in the conflict between fiction and reality and thus have become impossible in modern times. Manzoni's history of the epic and tragedy runs into great difficulties, however, since it is hardly convincing to think even of Homer's listeners as having been interested merely in truth in Manzoni's literal sense; and it is hardly possible to take the appeal to historical sources in medieval romances very seriously. How can Manzoni approve of Virgil, whom he greatly admires, without approving of the modern historical novel? But he makes good analyses of the difficulties of Tasso's *Gerusalemme liberata* and Voltaire's *Henriade* and everywhere finds support for his conclusion that a historical novel cannot be written, since it requires the author to supply the original and the portrait at the same time, both history and its fictional probable imitation.

One can dismiss Manzoni's troubles by means of Goethe's argument against his distinction between historical and fictional figures. All characters in a novel or play are ideal; the view that two kinds of consent are required is false. Even for a historical figure we need only poetic acceptance, the "willing suspension of disbelief," in Coleridge's phrase for illusion. At most, one could grant that Manzoni has proved that the historical novel cannot fulfill its professed task of recreating the past truthfully and that historical truth belongs in history and nowhere else. Manzoni clings to an interpretation of Aristotelian "verisimilitude" which, by definition, excludes history, and since he worships only "fact," he must end in rejecting even poetic truth and misunderstanding the very nature of art. Manzoni, quite honestly and logically, ceased to write fiction. But this abandonment of art in favor of truth should not be confused with the naturalism or realism of the 19th century which was then becoming vocal around him. Manzoni's faith in truth and historical fact is religious, as is obvious also from his late dialogue *Dell' invenzione* (1850), which propounds a theory, based on Rosmini's philosophy, that the artist does not create but merely finds the ideas existing eternally in the mind of God. Here Manzoni outlines a new apologetics of art which might have toned down his condemnation of fiction. But what is remembered to-day is Manzoni's honest grappling with the problem of a dual allegiance to history and fiction, which he could personally resolve only by repudiating art in favor of history. His preference was obvious in his early pronouncements on romantic tragedy, but the dilemma was then still concealed by his artistic instincts.

Thus it seems hardly surprising that a modern student could argue that there really was no Italian romanticism.[15] The group that called itself romantic had a concept of art which we could call rather realistic, moralistic, patriotic. Neither Manzoni nor the polemicists had a grasp of art as imagination, of the symbolic concept which we have seen expounded by the great romantic critics in Germany and England. But of course there are linkages and common sympathies: Schlegel was the propounder of the historical drama, as was Manzoni. Still, excessive attention to the professedly romantic group is misleading. Paradoxically, the two greatest Italian poets of the time, Ugo Foscolo and Giacomo Leopardi, who expressly attacked the theories of the romantic group, themselves best represent the turn in Italy toward doctrines which were the basis of European romanticism. [I thus completely disagree with the thesis of Borgese, *Storia della critica romantica in Italia,* which makes Italian romantic criticism merely a liberal neoclassicism.]

Ugo Foscolo (1778-1827), in the last year of his life, wrote an essay on the "New Dramatic School" attacking Manzoni's theories and his play *Il Conte di Carmagnola.* ["Della nuova scuola drammatica in Italia," *Opere edite e postume,* ed. Mayer and Orlandini, *4,* 293-338. The editor says that the article reprinted from the Italian MS was published in the first number of the *Foreign Quarterly Review,* 1826. But the article there on Manzoni has nothing to do with Foscolo's. I do not know the English review. The Italian text was first published in 1851.] The sharpness of the polemical tone is due to the old personal rivalry between the two men, to Foscolo's own disappointment with the stage and to the offense his Venetian patriotism took at the representation of the Doge and Senate in Manzoni's tragedy. Foscolo can argue in great detail that Manzoni is quite mistaken in his favorable view of the hero, the Count of Carmagnola, who was executed for treason by the Venetians, and he can show convincingly that Manzoni makes historical mistakes and commits anachronisms even in small verbal matters. The attack strikes more deeply when Foscolo argues against Manzoni's distinction of ideal and historical figures. "In any work of imagination everything depends on the incorporation and identification of reality and fiction." Illusion is achieved only when "truth and fiction, facing each other and in contact, not only lose their natural tendency of clashing but aid each other mutually to unite and fuse and to appear a single thing."[16] Foscolo holds

up Shakespeare's *Othello* as an example of the poet's power of emancipating himself from history. Italian romantic theory is suspect to him as an attack on the rights of imagination, as a turn toward the actual, the dreary reality which the poet should escape. German romanticism, which Foscolo knew only from Schlegel's *Lectures,* excites his distrust as mysticism and system-mongering. Foscolo even rejects all genre and school distinctions, saying that "every great production is an individual object which has different merits and distinct characteristics." He protests against the lumping together of different, supposedly classical schools of drama: the Greeks, the French, and the Italians (Alfieri). They seem to him all perfectly distinct. Even "each drama of the same poet, if he has genius, is more or less different from every other."[17]

The fine insights of this essay, its assertion of the power of imagination and the individuality of the work of art, are, however, the most brilliant flash of Foscolo's critical activity. The high level of the essay was never or very rarely reached before. Coming from it to an examination of the other critical writings, one must express a keen sense of disappointment. In part this is due simply to the external circumstances in which Foscolo's writing was produced. Much of his early criticism is in small prefaces or in formal orations at the University of Pavia which are full of fervid but bombastic academic oratory; much of the later writing, done in exile in England, sometimes preserved only in a wretched English translation, is heavily weighed down by a display of inert learning which Foscolo apparently felt to be demanded by the English periodicals or publishers for whom he was writing. His individuality is constantly cramped by his regard for the audience on which he felt dependent for his precarious living; he sometimes masks his personal remarks by attributing them to a "foreigner of great literary distinction."[18] He even supplied a rather lengthy description of the "Present State of Italian Literature," to John Hobhouse for publication under Hobhouse's name in *Historical Illustrations of the Fourth Canto of Childe Harold* (1818). [That Foscolo wrote this part of Hobhouse's book is proved conclusively by Vincent, *Byron, Hobhouse and Foscolo.*] Foscolo's many grandiose schemes for a history of Italian literature and for a *European Review* which would be devoted to "comparative criticism" and to tracing "the reciprocal influence of literature and manners,"[19] came to nothing, though fragments of his plans are realized in his *Essays on Petrarch* (1823)—his only book-form publication in English—in his editions, with long introductory dissertations, of the *Divine Comedy* and the *Decameron* (1825), and in scattered articles on Dante, Tasso, and the "narrative and romantic poets of Italy."[20]

But the fragmentariness and incompleteness, the heavy admixture of patriotic oratory and inert obsolete antiquarianism, are not the only causes of disappointment.

It is rather a certain lack of coherence and sharpness in the choice of ideas which make Foscolo an eclectic, a figure of transition who, however great his importance in the history of Italian criticism, will never acquire great stature in a European context. One could even make a case for Foscolo's criticism as a repertory of neoclassical commonplaces. He can talk about "instruction by delighting," about *Ut pictura poesis* as the "chief rule of poetry." He can define imagination in terms of 18th-century psychology as a power of visual recall.[21] But most frequently Foscolo wavers between two concepts of poetry: one of them emotionalist, deriving from Dubos and Diderot, the other Platonic, deriving from a reading of Plato himself and from the 18th-century tradition of idealizing aesthetics. In the self-portrait he wrote for Hobhouse, Foscolo claims "he would tear his heart from his bosom if he thought that a single pulsation was not the unconstrained and free movement of his soul."[22] The "flame of the heart" is his common phrase, and the purpose of poetry is defined as "making us strongly and fully feel our existence."[23] But this view exists side by side with Platonic idealism. The early Pavia lectures (1809) expound a curious concept of "eloquence" as the animating force behind all the arts and behind both prose and verse, which is identified with genius and inspiration in terms drawn from the polemics of Socrates against the sophistical rhetoricians.[24] Later Foscolo can also say that the poet does not imitate but selects, combines, and perfects the scattered beauties of the world; he abstracts and embellishes in order to create the ideal. The ideal is the "universal secret harmony, which man strives to find again in order to strengthen himself against the burdens and pains of his existence." Poetry thus satisfies our need to "veil the unpleasant reality of life with the dreams of imagination."[25] The poet is the man of feeling who expresses himself freely, and at the same time he is the creator of a world of ideals. He is also the total man who proceeds not by analysis but by synthesis. "The poets," he says in the *Essays on Petrarch*, "transform into living and eloquent images many ideas that lie dark and dumb in our mind, and it is by the magic presence of poetical images that we are suddenly and at once taught to feel, to imagine, to reason, and to meditate."[26]

Foscolo is saved from the consequences of mere emotionalism or Platonic idealism by his intense consciousness of the word, of the role of language and style in poetry. Many subtle comments on individual passages in Dante and Petrarch discuss the effect of single words. The detailed analyses of translations, either from Homer into Italian or Tasso into English, show Foscolo to be a true philologist, a "lover of words," whatever his technical shortcomings as an editor were. Foscolo knows the value of the study of revisions. "To develop the beauties of a poem the critic must go through the same reasonings and judg-

ments which ultimately determined the poet to write as he has done. But such a critic would be a poet." He adds, with a self-irony which could not have been apparent to the readers of an anonymous essay in the *Edinburgh Review,* "his ardent and impatient genius would never submit to the cold labor of criticism."[27] But Foscolo did submit and produced many textual and bibliographical investigations, learned and whimsical discussions of Catullus' *Hair of Berenice,* of the Greek *digamma,* of emendations in Dante, or of expurgations in various editions of the *Decameron.* Foscolo knew that "literature is joined to language" and that style is joined to "the intellectual faculty of every individual." Words have a long history which is a "confluence of minor and accessory meanings,"[28] of feelings and images, which differ with every language and which the poet knows and uses for his purposes.

Foscolo's chief importance, especially for Italy, lies in his attempt to see this conception of poetry as part of history, of a philosophy of human development, and thus as the basis of a scheme for Italian literary history and a program for his own time. Foscolo's concept of history is, no doubt, influenced by Vico, but more directly it derives from 18th-century primitivism in the mode of Rousseau and Herder. An early age of mythic, bardic, heroic poetry is imagined when all the kinds were mixed and the poet was a prophet and philosopher. Foscolo does not envisage this original poetry very clearly, though he reported, at length, on the ancient British druids and bards, drawing on a dissertation by William Owen.[29] Still, enough is known to Foscolo for him to justify the view that poetry was originally lyrical, lyrical-epic, and heroic and that it should become so again. Reviewing Monti's epic, *The Bard of the Black Forest,* he defends it with such historical arguments; his own *Grazie* he views as a mixture of the didactic, the lyric, and the epic. "Such perhaps was the first poetry." Such lyrical poetry is "the very summit of art." The ode celebrates gods and heroes and thus does not materially differ from ancient epic poetry.[30] Heroic and lyric are confused or identified, since the aim of poetry is the exaltation of our existence and the poet is a hero himself.

In his criticism Foscolo always makes the genre distinction between "romantic" and "heroic" poetry to the disadvantage of "romantic." Thus in his mind Tasso surpasses every other Italian poet except Dante. The burlesque tradition of Italian poetry, especially its last stage in Casti, is constantly disparaged, and even Ariosto, though greatly admired, is to Foscolo only the master of an inferior, less noble kind of poetry. Tasso is definitely separated from Ariosto by emphasis on the historical character of his theme, which to Foscolo is a history of the Crusades written as an example for Tasso's own time. The main point of many of Foscolo's acute observations on Wiffen's English translation of Tasso is in the charge that Wiffen ignores

Tasso's historical accuracy and makes him over into a poet of romance in the style of Spenser. Foscolo, for the sake of his lofty conception of the heroic, here runs counter to the evidence of the text and to the taste established since Hurd's plea for the Italians' "world of fine fabling."[31]

The historical scheme which follows from primitivism is that of the decay of imagination with the progress of civilization. Foscolo sees this process in antiquity. Homer and Pindar are the great ancients, while Virgil and Horace are artificial, derivative, and courtly. The process is seen repeated during the Middle Ages. There Dante is the exemplar of the free, heroic poet, while Petrarch and Boccaccio indicate the beginnings of decadence. Foscolo's conception of Dante is, in its detail, untenable, for he ascribes to him heretical ideas and sees him as a reformer of the Church not only in morals but also in ritual and dogma. Nevertheless, Foscolo, in his article on Dante and the long dissertation on the text, makes a real effort, remarkable for the time, to place Dante in his historical and intellectual context. He pays close attention to Dante's theology and political ideas, to his life and to the tradition of the text. The theories are frequently mistaken or based on insufficient information, but the comments are often sensitive and new: for instance, the discussion of the Francesca da Rimini episode makes much of the silence of her lover Paolo and interprets Dante's attitude toward the lovers persuasively and, on the whole, in agreement with most recent commentators.[32]

Foscolo also studied Petrarch very closely, not only the Italian poetry but also the Latin prose. He expounds his concept of courtly love and interprets his relation to Laura less sentimentally than was then the custom. But Petrarch is considered the representative of a new age of refinement which prepared the way for the later servitude of Italy. In an elaborate parallel between Dante and Petrarch Dante appears as the man of imagination and Petrarch the man of feeling. "Dante interests us for all mankind; while Petrarch is only interested in himself."[33] Dante is thus, as in Vico, the great primitive poet who serves as the foil to modern poetry, which has ceased to be so free, so original, and so individual. Molière and Pope are cited as examples of poetry which can trace shades of individuality for purposes of fine comedy; but comedy, in Foscolo's scheme can only seize "the exterior of character" which is determined by fashion and thus changes with every age, while genuine poetry, "whose business is with the human heart, is coeval and coextensive with human nature."[34] In general Foscolo complains that "when, in times of a more advanced civilization, the faculties of the critic and the poet tend to meet in the same minds, there arises a new poetry, less candid, less pure, more brilliant, mixed with metaphysics and a knowledge of the world. This is the poetry of Pope, Horace, Voltaire; mediocre minds prefer

it; and the highest imaginations despise it."[35] Foscolo must have realized that he himself belonged to this union of poet and critic, but he deplored it as a necessity of the time and tried to escape it.

If Italian decadence begins with Petrarch, Boccaccio will appear as an even greater corrupter. Foscolo, in spite of his erudite interest in the history of the text of the *Decameron,* professes to be shocked by its morals and disapproves of the influence of its style as a model of Italian prose. The humanistic 16th century seems to him an arid time, though he exempts Tasso and the much admired Machiavelli. The 17th century and the Arcadia appear to him periods of the deepest decadence. Baretti, though praised rather illogically for his general good influence, is judged very severely as a mere "ape" of Dr. Johnson.[36] Parini is to Foscolo the new Italian Virgil, and Alfieri seems to him greater than Corneille or Shakespeare. He is to him the model of the strong and free man, the poet of passion and power. Foscolo shared the high admiration of his contemporaries for Monti, but he disapproved of his shifting political allegiance and under cover of Hobhouse's name attacked him as a turncoat, drawing a parallel in Dryden.[37]

French literature is usually slighted in Foscolo's writings, though his admiration for Bayle, "a very great critic," stands out.[38] He wrote disparagingly of Rousseau and Madame de Staël, though his intellectual debt to both was very great.[39] He distrusted the Germans as mystics and scoffs at Goethe and Schlegel.[40] He admired only *Werther,* which was at least the technical model of his own *Jacopo Ortis.*

It is difficult to judge how much Foscolo knew of English literature. In England he conversed and wrote in French, but later he must have learned English well, since his reviews show appreciation of fine shades in English translations. But his comment on English literature is very limited. His admiration for Shakespeare is qualified by his neoclassical prejudices. He explains that seeing Shakespeare on the stage always increases his resistance, because in the theater he cannot follow the verbal beauties and sees only the action and business.[41] The reservation against Milton for lack of human interest is also conventional. Foscolo gives fervid praise to Gray's *Bard,* which seems to him both Pindaric and biblical in style.[42] He loved Sterne and translated the *Sentimental Journey.* His interest in his English contemporaries seems quite perfunctory: for example, he was shocked by the impiety of Byron's *Cain.*[43] There is a curious streak of the conventional and prudish in Foscolo's criticism which contradicts his own tumultuous erotic life and his exaltation of the strong and free man. But one must not forget that Foscolo had to struggle to keep his head above water in England and tried to make many adjustments to English respectability. He did not succeed, as witness the contemptuous comments in Sir Walter Scott's *Journal* or the quarrel with Hobhouse. [*The Journals* (Edinburgh, 1890), *I*, 14: "Talking of strangers, London held, some four or five years since, one of those animals who are lions at first but by transmutation of two seasons become in regular course boars. Ugo Foscolo by name, a haunter of Murray's shop and of literary parties. Ugly as a baboon, and intolerably conceited he spluttered, blustered and disputed without even knowing the principles upon which men of sense render a reason, and screamed all the while like a pig when they cut its throat." On the affair with Hobhouse see Vincent.] Nobody in England knew then that the exile hunted by bailiffs would become the symbol of the Italian *Risorgimento,* would be solemnly reburied in Florence's Santa Croce alongside Michelangelo, Machiavelli, Galileo, and Alfieri, and would be, even more recently, exalted and closely studied as one of the very greatest Italian poets. In the history of Italian criticism Foscolo will keep an important position as the first critic who broke with neoclassicism and introduced a historical scheme for the writing and criticism of Italian literature. But in a European context Foscolo is a latecomer, an eclectic somewhere in the transition from a preclassical Platonic idealism to a romantic view of history.

In critical ideas and temperament Leopardi seems to me much more original and striking. Giacomo Leopardi (1798-1837), a young man of eighteen and already a seasoned classical philologist, tried to intervene in the romanticism debate. He wrote a letter to the periodical which had published Madame de Staël's recommendations to translate Nordic literature, but the review refused to print it. Two years later in 1818, when the debate was again in full swing, Leopardi sent a long dissertation on romantic poetry to another review and was again rejected.[44] The first letter is a proud assertion of Italian patriotism. "If Europe does not know Parini, Alfieri, Monti, and Botta, the fault, it seems to me, is not Italy's."[45] Leopardi also argues against imitation, against any hope in the effect of translations, and, somewhat illogically, calls on Italians to read the Greeks and Romans and to ignore the Nordic writers. The later "Discourse of an Italian on Romantic Poetry," though diffuse and wordy, states the essence of the critical position he held for the remainder of his life. The romanticists (and Leopardi knew then only the Italians and Madame de Staël) are wrong because they do not understand that poetry is illusion, imaginative illusion which needs myth, ancient mythology, and the dream of the golden age. "See, then, manifest and palpable in us, and manifest and palpable to anyone, the overwhelming inclination toward the primitive; I mean in us ourselves, that is, in the men of this age, in those very ones whom the romantics try to persuade that the ancient and primitive manner of poetry does not do for them. Therefore, by the genius we all have from the memories of childhood,

one should judge how great is that [genius] we all have from unchanged and primitive nature, which is, neither more nor less, that nature which reveals itself and reigns in children; and the childish images and the fantasy we were speaking of are precisely the images and the fantasy of the ancients."[46] Poetry thus is rooted in our nostalgia for "nature," childhood, the youth of mankind. Our poets sing of nature and of the eternal and changeless matters and forms and things of beauty, in short, of the works of God; while the romanticists treat of civilization, of what is transitory and mutable—of the works of men.[47] Leopardi sees the contradiction between the recommendation of topicality, utility, and modernity in their manifestoes and the Nordic medievalism they want to introduce. But he did not see (and hardly could do so) that his own fervid Hellenism, with its identification of childhood, antiquity, and the age of poetry, was at the very center of much that elsewhere was called romanticism.

It cannot be denied that Leopardi's critical reflections are full of the doctrines and terms of neoclassicism. The several thousand pages of his commonplace books (*Zibaldone*) show an intense study of classical languages and authors, a technical, almost professional interest in classical scholarship. They are crowded with the names of German editors and commentators and many pages are taken up with quotations from Wolf and Müller on the Homeric question. Much of Leopardi's theorizing moves along well-worn grooves: imitation, delight as the end of poetry, style as the test of good art, and verisimilitude are the concepts that occur again and again. When Leopardi drew up the outline of an unwritten treatise, "On the Present Condition of Italian Literature," he filled it with recommendations to supply the various deficiencies of Italian literature in the different genres: he deplores the lack of an unaffected fluid harmonious prose, he wants to have Italian eloquence, a new comedy, a prose epic in the style of Fénelon's *Télémaque,* and so on.[48] It is hard to imagine anything more external and more "practical," even mechanical in its faith in corporate activity and the distinction of the kinds—even Leopardi's speculations on the relativity of beauty and taste hardly go beyond 18th-century skepticism.

Nor could one argue that Leopardi is sympathetically inclined to authors we would call romantic today. He admired *Werther* and *Corinne.*[49] Occasionally he has words of praise for Byron, though usually he considered him cold and affected, devoid of genuine feeling.[50] There is hardly a contemporary author whom Leopardi really admired. Foscolo and Manzoni come in only for very mild praise. [*Zibaldone, I,* 1425, speaks of "glimmer" of genius in Alfieri and Foscolo. Leopardi met Manzoni in 1827 and liked him as a person (*Lettere,* pp. 784, 826, 849), but his judgment of *I promessi sposi* is lukewarm (*Lettere,* pp. 783, 825, 849).] More and more, Leopardi thought of himself as alone in a period of decadence, and with the increase of his illness and isolation his bitterness found outlet in satires against modern progress and the century in general. Leopardi lived in the past, his own past, in ancient Italy, and in antiquity.

But if we go through the *Zibaldone,* we come across, among the welter of philological notes and reflections on the vanity of life and the need of illusion, a series of most remarkable pronouncements on literature which should change any superficial first impression of Leopardi's conventionality and neoclassical orthodoxy. Indeed, in these few pages, written mostly around 1827, Leopardi asserts more radically than anybody else in contemporary Europe the view that poetry is lyrical, "sentimental," and nothing else. Not only is the lyric called "the summit of poetry," "true and pure poetry in all its extension," "the eternal and universal kind because first in time,"[51] but the consequences of this view are very boldly drawn. Poetry, says Leopardi in a crucial entry, "consisted from the beginning in this kind alone, and its essence is always mainly in this kind, which almost becomes confused with it, and it is the most truly poetic [kind] of all poems, which are not poems except insofar as they are lyrical."[52] The lyric quality derives from sensibility or sentiment. But sentiment to Leopardi is not immediate emotion, as in the false simplicity of folk songs,[53] but rather reminiscence, memory, that recall of childhood and the past which made him a worshiper of antiquity. Mere excess of enthusiasm rather hinders poetry. His own poetry is conceived in a flash of inspiration lasting two minutes, but even the shortest poem takes two or three weeks to elaborate and revise. Yet without inspiration he could not have written, "Water could sooner flow from a tree trunk than a single verse from my brain."[54] Thus, Leopardi says, anticipating Poe, the "labors of poetry desire by their very nature to be short."[55]

Poetry, Leopardi argues, in flat contradiction to earlier pronouncements, is not and cannot be imitation. "The poet imagines: the imagination sees the world not as it is; it fabricates, invents." "The poet is a creator, an inventor," who writes "from his own intimate sentiment" because he has a "need to express the sentiments which he really experienced."[56] In these passages "imagination" and "sentiment" are identified, or at least juxtaposed. Yet often Leopardi draws a historical distinction between them: imagination belongs to antiquity and to childhood and is thus irrevocably past and gone, while sentiment which is reminiscent or even frankly called "the capacity of feeling pain" is the privilege and curse of the moderns.[57] The historical scheme implied is a simple one, Rousseauistic in implication, somewhat similar to Schiller's contrast between naive and sentimental. The ancients are nature; they lived in nature and created through imagination a beautiful world of illusion which made the darkness of

this world tolerable. "The works of genius," Leopardi reflects, "serve always as consolation, even when they depict the nothingness of things, even when they show us and make us feel the inevitable unhappiness of life, even when they express the most terrible despair."[58] Even the knowledge of the falsity of all beauty and greatness is itself beautiful and great. But with the progress of civilization and the spread of the enlightenment man has been thrown into an even deeper misery: the sources of imagination have dried up, the world of illusion has withered, and nothing is left for the poet but to express the feeling of sadness and despair. "The creative force of the imagination was exclusively the property of the ancients. Since then man has become permanently unhappy and what is worse has recognized the fact and thus caused and confirmed his unhappiness."[59]

Leopardi sees a confirmation of his historical scheme in his own personal history. He went through an early period of unconscious imaginative creation and then underwent a crisis in 1819 from which he learned to feel the misery of the world. "One can even say that, strictly speaking, only the ancients were poets and that today only the children and young men are, and that the moderns who have this name are nothing but philosophers. I, at least, became sentimental only when I lost imagination and became insensible to nature and dedicated to reason and truth, in short, a philosopher."[60] This self-condemnation to philosophy was not, however, final. It rather posed Leopardi's problem: can there be a poet in this modern age? Becoming a philosopher is obviously a denial of poetry. "The more poetry is philosophical, the less it is poetry."[61] Philosophy wants truth, poetry falsity and illusion. "Philosophy harms and destroys poetry. . . . There is an unsurmountable barrier, a sworn and mortal enmity between them, which cannot be abolished, reconciled or disguised."[62] If philosophy is hostile to poetry, so is science. Poetry has not improved since the time of Homer,[63] while science makes discoveries every day.

The process of fatal rationalization is illustrated also in the evolution of language. Original language is poetic, rich in connotations, metaphorical, vague, imprecise. Modern language tends toward the abstract, the technical term rather than the word. Leopardi thus constantly disparages the French language (and poetry) as mere prose and can exhort the poet to restore the original meanings of words, to preserve archaisms and to use poetic, indefinite, mysterious words.[64]

The emphasis on the lyric which we have met in Herder or Foscolo becomes much more startling in Leopardi when we see him draw the consequences and disparage the epic and the drama. This was far from the thought of Herder, who at most wanted to assimilate all genres into one. Leopardi makes similar attempts to deny the distinction between the lyrical and the epic. He calls the epic "a hymn in honor of heroes and peoples and armies: only a drawn-out hymn."[65] The epic "insofar as it conforms to nature and true poetry, that is, consists of short songs like the Homeric and Ossianic poems and of hymns, etc., rejoins the lyric."[66] Leopardi looks for support in Wolf's theory of the origin of Homer in songs, alludes even to Lachmann's transfer of Wolf's scheme to the *Nibelungenlied,* and notes down information on the lyrical meters of the oldest Roman epics.[67] But Leopardi speaks his mind more freely when he gives up such compromises and says that "an epic poem runs against the very nature of poetry. It demands a plan conceived and arranged in completely cold blood. What can a work which demands many years for its completion have to do with poetry? Poetry consists essentially in an impetus."[68]

The drama comes off even worse. It belongs even less to poetry than does the epic. "To pretend to have a passion, a character which he does not have (a necessity in the drama) is completely foreign to the poet: no less than the exact and patient observation of someone else's characters and passions. The more a man is a genius, the more he is a poet, so much the more has he sentiments of his own to expound, the more will he refuse to put on another personality, to speak in the person of another, to imitate."[69] Leopardi recognizes that "the novel, the story, etc. are much less alien to a man of genius than the drama, which is to him the most alien of all the genres of literature, because it requires the greatest closeness of imitation, the greatest transformation of the author into other individuals, the most complete renunciation and the most complete surrender of his own individuality, to which a man of genius clings more firmly than anybody else."[70] In a preface to an unfinished pastoral, *Telesilla* (1819), Leopardi had already rejected the "miserable trick of extremely intricate nodes and twists" of plot to keep the attention and curiosity of the spectators,[71] because plot was for him the lowest and least poetic of all the elements of poetry. Even Greek tragedy, which can hardly be condemned for sinning by excessive plot interest, seems to Leopardi material and external. The Greeks wanted strong effects, fierce, energetic sensations. Their favorite subjects were horrible and singular misfortunes, unique characters, unnatural passions; they were sensation hunters: something Byron and the romanticists liked and wanted. Neither does Aristophanes find grace in Leopardi's eyes: his comedies are full of unnatural fantastic inventions, allegorical figures, frogs, clouds, and birds.[72]

Given Leopardi's view of poetry, it is not surprising that finally there remained for him little to admire. There were the ancients, of course, Homer, Pindar, Anacreon, Virgil, Lucretius, and even Lucian, who remained the gods of his Parnassus. There was Dante, whose *Divine Comedy,* consistently enough, is called a "long lyric where the poet and his feelings are always in evidence."[73] There was Petrarch, who alone among the moderns has pathos and who obviously was the model of Leopardi's own early style. But he finally came to the conclusion that there are only very few poetic beauties in him to admire.[74] There was Tasso, for whose fate Leopardi had a personal tenderness, and there were a few fine things in Chiabrera and Testi. But Metastasio was the last singer of Italy, perhaps the only poet since Tasso. Parini did not have enough passion to be a poet, and even Alfieri was rather a philosopher (a reasoner in Leopardi's sense) than a poet.[75]

Leopardi's taste contracted more and more: his personal brand of poetry increasingly seemed to him the only genuine one. Such dogmatism is the right of every artist. After all, Leopardi was a poet first and foremost and a critic only intermittently. He had nothing of the tolerance, the curiosity for the creative world around him, which the great romantic critics had. In spite of his historical scheme of the decay of imagination, he is hardly imbued with a genuine historical spirit. Nevertheless the most original entries in *Zibaldone* must be singled out, for they represent the most complete reversal of the neoclassical hierarchy of genres. Drama and plot, which in Aristotle are the essence of poetry, are banned by Leopardi to its periphery. The lyric, which had been excluded by Bacon and Hobbes from poetry, and the expression of personal feeling, are the only poetry, the highest kind. The wheel has come to a full circle.

We must not forget that Leopardi's pronouncements remained in the privacy of his notebooks till the last decade of the 19th century and thus remained without influence in their time. The reconstruction of Italian criticism had to await the arrival of De Sanctis who loved and studied Leopardi, but drew his critical ideas from Hegel and the other Germans.

Notes

The pamphlets and articles of the "romanticism" debate are collected in *Discussioni e polemiche sul romanticismo (1816-1826),* ed. Egidio Bellorini, 2 vols. Bari, 1943. Berchet's contributions, however, must be seen in Giovanni Berchet, *Opere,* ed. Egidio Bellorini, Vol. 2 entitled *Scritti critici e letterari,* Bari, 1912.

Manzoni is quoted from *Opere varie,* ed. M. Barbi and F. Ghisalberti (Milan, 1943), Vol. 2.

Foscolo is quoted from *Opere edite e postume,* ed. E. Mayer and L. S. Orlandini, 11 vols. Florence, 1939. But the writings which are there retranslated into Italian are quoted from the English versions.

Leopardi is quoted from *Tutte le opere*, Classici Mondadori, ed. F. Flora, 5 vols. Florence, 1949: *Le poesie e le prose* (2 vols.); *Le lettere*; and *Zibaldone di pensieri* (2 vols.).

The only general study is Giuseppe A. Borgese, *Storia della critica romantica in Italia*, Naples, 1905; reprinted Florence, 1949.

On Manzoni see Joseph Francis De Simone, *Alessandro Manzoni: Esthetics and Literary Criticism*, New York, 1946—a diffuse description of his opinions. There are good comments in F. de Sanctis, "La Poetica di Manzoni" (1872), in *La letteratura italiana nel secolo XIX* (Bari, 1953), pp. 19-39; G. A. Levi, "Estetica Manzoniana," in *Giornale storico della letteratura italiana, 108* (1936), 25-270; and Ámado Alonso, *Ensayo sobre la novela histórica*, Buenos Aires, 1942.

On Foscolo, three books discuss the criticism: Eugenio Donadoni, *Ugo Foscolo, pensatore, critico, poeta*, 2d ed. Palermo, 1927; and Mario Fubini, *Ugo Foscolo*, Torino, 1928. Nicoletta Festa, *Foscolo Critico* (Florence, 1953) is the fullest and most enthusiastic discussion. See also Fubini's introduction to Foscolo's *Saggi letterari*, Torino, 1926; reprinted in *Romanticismo italiano* (Bari, 1953), pp. 106-60. F. Viglione, *Ugo Foscolo in Inghilterra* (Catania, 1910). E. R. Vincent, *Byron, Hobhouse and Foscolo* (Cambridge, 1949), and *Ugo Foscolo, an Italian in Regency England* (Cambridge, 1953) are largely biographical. Emilio Santini, "Poesia e lingua nelle lezioni pavesi del Foscolo," *Giornale storico della letteratura italiana, 110* (1937), 58-105, analyzes the early Platonism.

On Leopardi see a chapter in Karl Vossler, *Leopardi* (Munich, 1923) and two articles: E. Bertana, "La mente di Giacomo Leopardi in alcuni suoi Pensieri di bella letteratura italiana e di estetica," *Giornale storico della letteratura italiana, 41* (1903), 193-283; and M. Fubini, "L'estetica e la critica letteraria nei Pensieri di Giacomo Leopardi," *op. cit.*, 97 (1931), 241-81. Romualdo Giani, *L'estetica nei Pensieri di Giacomo Leopardi* (Torino, 1904, 2d ed. 1929) tries to construe a system of Leopardi's aesthetics.

[1] Madame de Staël, "Sulla maniera e l'utilità delle traduzioni," in *Biblioteca italiana* (1816), reprinted in *Discussioni e polemiche*, ed. Bellorini, I, 7-8: "Dovrebbero a mio avviso gl' italiani tradurre diligentemente assai delle recenti poesie inglesi e tedesche; onde mostrare qualche novità a' loro citadini, i quali per lo più stanno contenti all' antica mitologia, né pensano che quelle favole sono da un pezzo anticate, anzi il resto d'Europa le ha già abbandonate e dimentiche."

[2] Lodovico di Breme, "Intorno all' ingiustizia di alcuni giudizi letterari italiani," reprinted *ibid.*, I, 25-56, esp. 39.

[3] In Giovanni Berchet, *Opere,* ed. Bellorini, 2, 20: "Poesia de' morti, poesia de' vivi."

[4] *Ibid.*, p. 38: "L'uomo non può pensare all' uomo lontano e posto in circonstanze diverse dalle sue con quell' interesse medesimo, con cui egli pensa a se stesso ed a' vicini. Le lagrime del povero contadino, l'angoscia del mandriano, la pace dell' eremita profanata ci faranno pietá."

[5] *Ibid.*, pp. 73-100.

[6] In *Discussioni, I,* 436n.: "Non credo che sianvi stili essenzialmente romantici o essenzialmente classici."

[7] *Ibid.*, pp. 406-15.

[8] "Dialogo sulle unitá drammatiche di luogo e di tempo." *Ibid.*, 2, 29-45 (on *Macbeth*, p. 39).

[9] *Opere varie*, ed. Barbi and Ghisalberti, pp. 219-25: "Personaggi storici"; p. 236: "personaggi ideali."

[10] *Ibid.*, p. 363: "Si ce sont les grands génies qui violent les règles, quelle raison restera-t-il de présumer qu'elles sont fondées sur la nature, et qu'elles sont bonnes à quelque chose?" P. 332: "détruit l'unité d'impression nécessaire pour produire l'émotion et la sympathie."

[11] *Sämtliche Werke*, Jubiläumsausgabe, *37,* 166: "Für den Dichter ist keine Person historisch."

[12] Published by Goethe in Ger. trans., *ibid.* (January 23, 1821), pp. 182-4. Original in *Carteggio*, ed. G. Sforza and G. Gallavresi (Milan, 1912), *I,* 520: "un fallo tutto mio, e che ne fu cagione un attaccamento troppo scrupuloso alla esattezza storica."

[13] *Opere varie*, p. 615: "Proponendosi quel sistema d'escludere tutte le norme, che non siano veramente generali, perpetue, ragionevoli per ogni lato, viene a renderne più scarso il numero, o almeno più difficile e più lenta la scelta."

[14] *Ibid.*, p. 630. Manzoni alludes to the historical figures in Scott's *Monastery, Waverley*, and *Quentin Durward*.

[15] Gina Martegiani, *Il romanticismo italiano non esiste*, Florence, 1908.

[16] *Opere edite, 4,* 297: "In qualunque lavoro della immaginazione sta tutto nell' incorporare e identificare la realtà e la finzione"; p. 317: "L'illusione . . . non acquista potere magico irresistibile, se non allorchè la verità e la finzione ritrovandosi faccia a faccia e in contatto, non solo perdono la loro naturale tendenza a cozzare fra loro, ma s'ajutano

scambievolmente a riunirsi e confondersi e parere una cosa sola."

[17] *Ibid.*, p. 306: "Ma ciascuna produzione grande è un oggetto individuale che ha meriti diversi e caratteri distinti dalle altre"; p. 313: "Ciascun dramma dello stesso poeta, se ha genio, è più o meno diverso dall' altro."

[18] *Edinburgh Review, 29* (1818), p. 465n.

[19] *Opere edite, 4,* 7: "critique comparative," "l'influence réciproque de la littérature et des mœurs." A letter to John Murray, in 1817.

[20] The two Dante articles are in *Edinburgh Review, 29* (1818), 453-74, and *30* (1818), 317-51. "Narrative and Romantic Poems of the Italians," in *Quarterly Review, 21* (1819), 486-556. The review of Wiffen's *Tasso* is in the *Westminster Review, 6* (1826), 404-45. Other less important pieces are in the *New Monthly Magazine,* the *London Magazine,* the *European Review,* and the *Retrospective Review.* See the list in F. Viglione's *Ugo Foscolo in Inghilterra,* pp. 319-21.

[21] *Opere edite, 9,* 315: "La regola capitale della Poesia." *10,* 541.

[22] *Historical Illustrations of the Fourth Canto of Childe Harold* (London, 1818), p. 479.

[23] *Opere edite, 4,* 298: "La poesia tende a farci fortemente e pienamente sentire la nostra esistenza." Cf. *Essays on Petrarch* (London, 1821), p. 59.

[24] See Emilio Santini, "Poesia e lingua nelle lezioni pavesi del Foscolo," *Giornale storico della letteratura italiana, 110* (1937), 58-107.

[25] *Opere edite, 4,* 121: "Il poeta, il pittore e lo scultore non imitano copiando,—ma scelgono, combinano e immaginano perfette e riunite in un sola molte belle varietà che forse realmente esistono sparse e commiste a cose volgari." Cf. *4,* 122, 124: "Esiste nel mondo una universale secreta armonia, che l'uomo anela di ritrovare come necessaria à ristorare le fatiche e i dolori della sua esistenza"; p. 127: "Il genere umano ha bisogno di vestire de'sogni della immaginazione la nojosa realità della vita."

[26] *Essays on Petrarch,* p. 172. Cf. *Opere edite, 3,* 123.

[27] *Edinburgh Review, 29* (1818), 460.

[28] *Opere edite, 2,* 70: "La letteratura è annessa alla lingua"; p. 72: "La lingua è annessa allo stile, e lo stile alle facoltà intellettuali d'ogni individuo" p. 70: "conflato de' significati minimi ed accessorj."

[29] "Dissertazione storica intorno ai druidi e ai bardi britanni" (1812), *Opere edite, 2,* 347-80.

[30] On *Grazie* see *Opere edite, 9,* 208: "Tale fu forse la prima poesia." *9,* 211: "Il sommo dell' arte." *2,* 337: "La poesia lirica canta con entusiasmo le lodi de' numi e degli eroi."

[31] On Wiffen's *Tasso* in *Westminster Review.* See above, n. 20. Hurd's *Letters on Chivalry and Romance* (1762), No. 10: "If it were not for these *lies* of Gothic invention, I should scarcely be disposed to give the *Gierusalemme liberata* a second reading."

[32] *Opere edite, 3,* 370. ff.

[33] *Essays on Petrarch,* p. 185.

[34] *Edinburgh Review, 30* (1818), 345.

[35] *Lezioni di eloquenza,* p. 197, quoted in Donadoni's *Ugo Foscolo,* pp. 221-2: "Allorchè, in tempi d'una più avanzata civiltà, le facoltà del critico e del poeta vengono a combinarsi nei medisimi spiriti, nasce allora una novella poesia, meno franca, meno schietta, più brillante, mista di metafisica e di conoscenza del mondo. Essa è la poesia di Pope, d'Orazio, di Voltaire; le mediocri intelligenze la preferiscono; e le più elevate immaginazioni la disdegnano."

[36] *Opere edite, 10,* 464. Originally in *European Review, 4* (1824), 601-11.

[37] *Historical Illustrations,* p. 448.

[38] *Opere edite, 4,* 175. Also *3,* 275: "sommo critico."

[39] Cf. E. Bottasso, *Foscolo e Rousseau,* Torino, 1941.

[40] *Opere edite, 4,* 315, 305, 328.

[41] *Edinburgh Review, 29* (1818), 465n.

[42] *Opere edite, 1,* 519 (1808); on Milton, *Westminster Review, 6* (1826), 414.

[43] A letter to Lady Dacre, March, 1, 1822; *Opere edite, 8,* 60 f.; also *5,* 598 f.

[44] "Lettera ai sigg compilatori della Biblioteca Italiana in risposta a quella di Mad La Baronessa di Staël Holstein ai medesimi," dated July 18, 1816, in *Poesie e prose, 2,* 597 ff.; and "Discorso di un Italiano intorno alla poesia romantica," *ibid.,* pp. 467-549. Both were published first in 1906.

[45] *Ibid.,* p. 599: "Se Europa non conosce Parini, Alfieri, Monti, Botta, la colpa non parmi d'Italia."

[46] *Ibid.*, p. 481:

> Ecco dunque manifesta e palpabile in noi, e manifesta e palpabile a chicchessia la prepotente inclinazione al primitivo, dico in noi stessi, cioè negli uomini di questo tempo, in quei medesimi ai quali i romantici proccurano di persuadere che la maniera antica e primitiva di poesia non faccia per loro. Imperocchè dal genio che tutti abbiamo alle memorie della puerizia si deve stimare quanto sia quello che tutti abbiamo alla natura invariata e primitiva, la quale è nè più nè meno quella natura che si palesa e regna ne' putti, e le immagini fanciullesche e la fantasia che dicevamo, sono appunto le immagini e la fantasia degli antichi.

[47] *Ibid.*, p. 486: "I nostri cantano in genere più che possono la natura, e i romantici più che possono l'incivilimento, quelli le cose e le forme e le bellezze eterne e immutabili, e questi le transitorie e mutabili, quelli le opere di Dio, e questi le opere degli uomini."

[48] *Ibid., 1,* 694-7: "Della Condizione presente delle lettere italiane" (1819).

[49] *Zibaldone, 1,* 254, 86, 839; and 110, 113-6. Many passages are quoted from *Corinne* and commented upon.

[50] *Poesie e prose, 2,* 539-40, comments on some verses translated from Byron; *Zibaldone, 1,* 230, on *Corsair; 2,* 294n., 471, parallel with Monti; *2,* 681-2, Byron cold and monotonous.

[51] *Ibid., 1,* 243: "La lirica si può chiamare la cima il colmo la sommità della poesia." *Ibid., 2,* 1063: "vera e pura poesia in tutta la sua estensione." *Ibid.*, p. 1283: "genere, siccome primo di tempo, così eterno ed universale."

[52] *Ibid.*, p. 1284: "[La poesia] consistè da principio in questo genere solo, e la cui essenza sta sempre principalmente in esso genere, che quasi si confonde con lei, ed è il più veramente poetico di tutte le poesie, le quali non sono poesie se non in quanto son liriche."

[53] *Ibid., 1,* 29; on sentiment, *ibid., 2,* 1182; *Poesie e prose, 2,* 516-7.

[54] *Zibaldone, 1,* 505-6; *ibid., 2,* 1037-8; on his creative process, *Lettere,* pp. 477-8: "se l'inspirazione non mi nasce da sè, più facilmente uscirebbe acqua da un tronco, che un solo verso dal mio cervello."

[55] *Ibid., 2,* 1182: "I lavori di poesia vogliono per natura esser corti."

[56] *Ibid., 2,* 1183: "Il poeta immagina: l'immaginazione vede il mondo com non è . . . finge, inventa, non imita . . . creatore, inventore, non imitatore." *Ibid.*, p. 1182:

"Il poeta è spinto a poetare dall' intimo sentimento suo proprio . . . dal bisogno d'esprimere de' sentimenti ch'egli prova veramente."

[57] *Ibid.*, p. 14: "Una maggior capacità di dolore."

[58] *Ibid., 1,* 252-3: "Hanno questo di proprio le opere di genio, che quando anche rappresentino al vivo la nullità delle cose, quando anche dimostrino evidentemente e facciano sentire l'inevitabile infelicità della vita, quando anche esprimano le più terribili disperazioni . . . servono sempre di consolazione."

[59] *Ibid.*, p. 511: "La forza creatrice dell' animo appartenente alla immaginazione, è esclusivamente propria degli antichi. Dopo che l'uomo è divenuto stabilmente infelice, e, che peggio è, l'ha conosciuto, e così ha realizzata e confermata la sua infelicità."

[60] *Ibid.*, p. 163: "Così si può ben dire che in rigor di termini, poeti non erano se non gli antichi, e non sono ora se non i fanciulli, o giovanetti, e i moderni que hanno questo nome, non sono altro che filosofi. Ed io infatti no divenni sentimentale, se non quando perduta la fantasia divenni insensibile alla natura, e tutto dedito alla ragione e al vero, in somma filosofo."

[61] *Ibid.*, p. 828: "Ma la poesia, quanto è più filosofica, tanto meno è poesia."

[62] *Ibid.*, p. 829: "E quivi la filosofia nuoce e distrugge la poesia, e la poesia guasta e pregiudica la filosofia. Tra questa e quella esiste una barriera insormontabile, una nemicizia giurata e mortale, che non si può nè toglier di mezzo, e riconciliare, nè dissimulare."

[63] *Ibid.*, p. 87: "Tutto si è perfezionato da Omero in poi, ma non la poesia."

[64] *Poesie e prose, 1,* 157; *Zibaldone, 1,* 738, 1145, 1372, 1216-7.

[65] *Ibid., 2,* 1063: "Il poema epico . . . non è che un inno in onor degli eroi o delle nazioni o eserciti; solamente un inno prolungato."

[66] *Ibid.*, p. 1226: "L'epica, non solo per origine, ma totalmente, in quanto essa può esser conforme alla natura, e vera poesia, cioè consistente in brevi canti, come gli omerici, ossianici ec., ed in inni ec., rientra nella lirica."

[67] On Wolf, *ibid.*, pp. 1147 ff., 115-8; on *Nibelungen, ibid.*, pp. 1261 ff., from Niebuhr, in English translation; *ibid.*, p. 1268, on Roman metrics.

[68] *Ibid.*, p. 1181: "E infatti il poema epico è contro la natura della poesia: 1. domanda un piano concepito e ordinato con tutta freddezza; 2. che può aver a fare

colla poesia un lavoro che domanda più e più anni d'esecuzione? la poesia sta essenzialmente in un impeto."

[69] *Ibid.,* p. 1182:

Direi che la drammatica spetta alla poesia meno ancora che l'epica. . . . Il fingere di avere una passione, un carattere ch'ei non ha (cosa necessaria al drammatico) è cosa alienissima dal poeta; non meno che l'osservazione esatta e paziente de' caratteri e passioni altrui . . . Quanto più un uomo è di genio, quanto più è poeta, tanto più avrà de' sentimenti suoi proprii da esporre, tanto più sdegnerà di vestire un altro personaggio, di parlare in persona altrui, d'imitare.

[70] *Ibid.,* p. 1191: "Il romanzo, la novella ec. sono all' uomo di genio assai meno alieni che il dramma, il quale gli è il più alieno di tutti i generi di letteratura, perchè è quello che esige la maggior prossimità d'imitazione, la maggior trasformazione dell' autore in altri individui, la più intera rinunzia e il più intero spoglio della propria individualita, alla quale l'uomo di genio tiene più fortemente che alcun altro."

[71] *Poesie e prose, 1,* 424: "Quel miserabile mezzo dei nodi e viluppi intricatissimi in luogo della immagine continua viva ed efficace rappresentazione della natura e delle passioni umane."

[72] *Zibaldone, 2,* 473-6.

[73] *Ibid.,* p. 1230: "La *Divina Commedia* non è che una *lunga Lirica,* dov' è sempre in campo il poeta e i suoi propr, affetti."

[74] *Poesie e prose, 2,* 525, 518, etc.; *Lettere,* p. 712: "Io non trovo in lui se non pochissime, ma veramente pochissime bellezze poetiche" (1826).

[75] *Zibaldone, 1,* 499, 1425.

Grazia Avitabile

SOURCE: "Conclusion: Manzoni and Nicolini—1820-1823," in *The Controversy on Romanticism in Italy: First Phase, 1816-1823,* S. F. Vanni, 1959, pp. 135-48.

[*In the following essay, Avitabile summarizes the literary debate that raged between classicists and Romantics in Italy during the early nineteenth century.*]

By 1820 the classico-romantic controversy in Italy had receded and had almost achieved the status of belonging to the past and could, therefore, be viewed with historical perspective. Nicolini, in a lecture delivered at the University of Brescia in 1820, says:

Now that the passions have calmed down, now that we are enjoying a truce if not peace, now that the two camps have abandoned their arms if not actually shaken hands, the time is ripe to meditate calmly upon the dispute, to tell the story and to evaluate the result of the literary schism, to investigate its causes, to examine each point, distinguishing those dictated by prejudice from those based upon sound criticism.[1]

Nicolini insists that the dispute had not been useless or purely abstract, "those conflicts instead of deserving contempt left their unmistakable imprint upon taste, gave new impetus to studies . . ."[2]

Manzoni, in a letter to Cesare D'Azeglio dated 1823,[3] in speaking of romanticism uses the past tense as if referring to something that took place in the remote past. He appeals to his memory in reporting the more important "general rules" established by romanticists, although he admits that the effects of romanticism are still felt while he is writing. In fact he believes that many of the points made by romanticists are triumphing or about to triumph. Manzoni remarks that if a foreigner who had heard of the controversy were to ask at what stage is the question now,

one could bet one to a thousand that he would hear more or less the following answer: "Romanticism? It was discussed for a time but now no longer. The word itself is forgotten except that very occasionally one hears the epithet *romantic* used to characterize a strange proposition, a capricious mind, a lost cause . . ."[4]

If the foreigner were to insist in asking the meaning of romanticism, he would find that it commonly signifies "a medley of witches and ghosts, a systematic disorder, extravagant affectation, abjuration of common sense . . ." But romanticism, as it was understood by romanticists and by Manzoni himself,

not only has not fallen into decay, it lives, it prospers, it spreads day by day, and gradually it is invading all aesthetic theories. Its principles are very often repeated, applied, placed at the basis of literary criticism. In the writing of poetry one cannot help but note that the tendency is to attain the aims advocated by romanticism . . .[5]

Manzoni concludes: "Of the romantic battle all that has perished is the word. Nobody should wish to revive it, for the controversy would flare up again causing probable damage to the idea which is now living and growing in sufficient tranquillity."

The controversy seemed ended in the early twenties. Only a few articles appeared and most of them were reviews of Manzoni's tragedies. It may be noted that Giovanni Gherardini devoted a few chapters of his school textbook, *Elements of Poetry,*[6] to classic and romantic poetry. His position is unchanged from the one taken in his notes on Schlegel's *Course on Dramatic Literature*. But, despite his negative approach to romanticism and the fact that he considers it on the one hand as a "system" which offers nothing that is new[7] and on the other hand as a "doctrine" which is dangerous,[8] he admits that it is necessary for cultivated people to become acquainted with this pertinent question, which is heatedly debated in literary circles.[9] He does not distinguish between classic and classicist; thus he dismisses one of the main distinctions and basic points of Italian romanticists. He concludes by exhorting Italians to keep within their tradition and to realize that the poetic faculty is a talent which cannot be created but only guided by poetics.[10] Gherardini, in these chapters, adds nothing to the controversy but merely organizes the material for the purpose of instruction, and presents it with a classicist bias. Not until 1825-26 was there a new flare-up in the classico-romantic controversy in Italy, following the publication of Vincenzo Monti's *Sermon an Mythology*. The debate, however, was largely confined to the question of mythology.

The patriotic aspect of romanticism was temporarily in abeyance since most of the leaders had been imprisoned or had escaped abroad as exiles. The seeds had been sown, however, and in a few years they would bear the fruit of the Italian *Risorgimento*. It has been rightly observed that without romanticism the *Risorgimento* could not have happened.

In 1820 romanticism was actually gaining ground in the field of letters, as is shown in the writings of Nicolini and Manzoni, who, although sympathetic to romanticism, were serene and objective and whose essays provide a fitting conclusion to the first phase of the romantic controversy in Italy.

Nicolini reviews the dispute with extraordinary detachment for one who had taken part in it. He outlines the advantages and limitations of romanticism and is willing to acknowledge its excesses and the fanaticism that at times animated its supporters. He states that it is of no consequence "whether we take our pleasure in a classical or in a romantic manner as long as we enjoy ourselves."[11] He doubts whether the romantic system as developed in Germany or France could be accepted in its entirety in Italy, because of the peculiar character of Italians. Possibly he is so very conciliatory because he believes that the basic program of Italian romanticism is becoming accepted.

Nicolini states as an incontrovertible fact that in the Middle Ages there arose a new civilization; that historical circumstances and nationality have an influence on poetic genius; that poetry inspired by the national character and the contemporary scene is more sincere, vivid, and vigorous than the poetry which imitates other poetry or follows the rules of a school; and finally he states that every great work of whatever nation or age is unique and therefore different even in form from any other.[12] Nicolini believes that the above are fundamental truths, shown to be so by all great authors, acknowledged by the public, occasionally recognized even by critics. He affirms that these principles had never been organized into a system until recently, when some foreign critics defined as "classic" ancient poetry and modern poetry patterned on the ancient, and as "romantic" all the poetry written since the Middle Ages and inspired by the new civilization.[13]

In Italy, Nicolini explains, there was vehement opposition against romanticism despite the fact that the ideas associated with the term were not new. To Italians the movement seemed subversive, a threat to classic literature. To a large extent it was the character of Italians that caused literary disputes to become more violent than in any other nation, a character which is "irritable, imaginative, quick and frank."[14] Both parties, according to Nicolini, "jumped blindly into the fray, without sufficient knowledge or a definite aim," impelled by prejudice and fanaticism, "imputing to each other principles and claims which had never been advanced." On the one hand writers "damned and derided any theme, form, maxim, and even any sentence which showed the influence of antiquity"; on the other hand, other writers condemned as "scandalous and heretical any happy daring, any idea, sentiment or image drawn from foreign sources . . ." Charges and countercharges were made, with labels such as "mediocre talents" and "poor Italians" attributed respectively to classicists and romanticists. "The designations of romantic and classicist became pretexts for denunciation and persecution, the Italian Parnassus became a factory of excommunication."[15]

Having painted this vivid picture of the classico-romantic controversy, Nicolini comments that intolerance and fanatticism are the price paid for the establishment of any doctrine.[16] He believes that in spite of these disadvantages there are definite advantages, such as giving "greater force and solemnity" to the few truths expounded,[17] which he then enumerates and discusses.

One of the most controversial points, Nicolini points out, was the question of introducing and studying foreign literatures. Familiarity with foreign works, he asserts, is extremely useful for it increases tolerance, it shows that beauty has infinite aspects and ways of manifesting itself, that it is varied, uncodifiable, that it changes according to nations and historical times. This study leads to a more acute literary sense and to higher critical standards as well as to a broadening of literary horizons, so that the literature of all ages and of all countries becomes the property of all men.[18]

Ancient poetry is great and perfect in its own way, Nicolini continues, but should not be imitated as pedantically as the classicists claim. Classicists are superficial, they ignore the fact that classic poetry is the expression of a particular civilization, that modern poetry, in order to be equally successful, must be the expression of modern civilization. Balance, order, simplicity, symmetry, are the features of classical art. It does not follow that every work of art must possess the same attributes.[19] Form is inherent in the subject matter, is determined by it. Nicolini quotes from Schlegel in calling "mechanical" the form which is artificially imposed on the subject, and "organic" the form which results from the natural development of the subject.[20] He concludes that romantic form is "more complex rather than more irregular than the classic," and that classic form "is more simple rather than more regular than the romantic." Neither classicism nor romanticism is preferable, according to our author. "The former loves uniformity, the latter prefers variety; the one presents a picture of the whole, the other analyzes the several elements; in the one there is more idealism, serenity and art, in the other more truth, expressiveness and nature . . ." The two types should not be compared but judged in themselves and for themselves.[21]

More than any of the classicists, Nicolini is aware of the weaknesses of romanticism. The romanticists, he charges, were not aware that while they advocated freedom in literature, they denied this freedom to those who did not share their own point of view, that while they liberated poets from poetics and models, they compiled a new poetics and set up new models, and became slavish partisans of foreigners just as the classicists were of the ancients. Romanticists contradicted themselves in condemning the use of mythology in literature and yet condoning it for the visual arts.[22] Nicolini maintains that romanticists were too rigid in demanding the abolition of mythology, that they should have advocated limiting its use to what "is purely fantastic and popular."[23] He sees no reason for excluding the mythological heroes of antiquity and retaining those of the Round Table. In general, Nicolini asserts, romanticists were too systematic, too rigid in their views; they were too unilateral in their conception of literature, in considering it as the means to bring about moral progress; "they gave education as its purpose rather than pleasure, usefulness rather than beauty." Hence romanticists prescribed that the subject matter of poetry must be national and modern; they subordinated art to the intellectual needs of the public.[24]

Therefore, they judged poetry more by its intentions than by its effects. Poetry may be useful, he comments, but usefulness is not its primary function. Art is the result of inspiration, the product of "the imagination and the heart"; its aim is to give pleasure.[25] Producing delight, not the mark of originality or success in imitating, is essential in poetry as in every other work of art. "Originality is indeed the first glory of genius," Nicolini admits, but originality can be a negligible virtue just as imitation can produce an immortal poem.[26] Tolerance and freedom are essential in art. But Nicolini recognizes that certain limitations are imposed upon the artist by the particular customs and states which prevail in his own country. These limitations are not dictated by a poetics, but by the cultural and emotional "exigencies of the public."[27]

Manzoni, who had not taken an active part either in the controversy or in *Il Conciliatore,* is less severe than Nicolini towards romanticists. He thinks that romanticism represented a body of ideas which were understood in different ways by different people. It meant different things in different countries and also in different parts of Italy. But "in Milan, where the question was discussed at greater length and with greater intensity than elsewhere, the term . . . was used to represent a body of ideas more reasonable, more orderly, and more general than elsewhere."[28] He proceeds to outline the main points of romanticism and adds some personal considerations.

Manzoni distinguishes the "negative," that is the critical, from the "positive" aspect of romanticism, explaining very carefully why the negative is "by far the more precise, direct, and complete" of the two. Not only, he says, is human nature inclined to criticize and destroy, but romanticists intended to do away with all particular and contingent rules, and therefore they kept only the most "general, permanent, and reasonable" rules, which are hard to define. In addition, he feels that the discussion lasted too short a time to permit a full development of the positive aspects of romanticism, since the negative logically had to be advanced first. Manzoni notes also that the discussion became a controversy, and in any controversy it is tactically advantageous to attack the ideas of one's foe rather than to present one's own program. Romanticists enunciated only very general principles, so general that they offered to their adversaries many an opportunity to find fault with them. Nevertheless, the opponents of romanticism, in order to satirize it, were compelled to exaggerate and invent romantic principles which in fact had never been expounded or dreamed of by romanticists.[29]

Romanticism, according to Manzoni, "tended to exclude the use of mythology; the servile imitation of the classics; the rules based on particular facts and not on general principles, on the authority of rhetoricians and not on reason; it excluded especially the rule of the dramatic unities of time and place."[30]

There follows an objective and clear summary of the main arguments advanced for or against each of the above points. Manzoni underlines the bad faith of classicists in their assertion that romanticists advocated that the classics should no longer be studied. Romanticists "never dreamed of such a thing"; they were well aware that the study of great poets, especially classical, is a guide for the development of current poetic talent. Romanticists objected to arbitrary rules derived from the way of writing of the classics and to borrowing the point of view, the outlook on life, of the ancients.[31] Manzoni comments that romanticists would have done well to have asked for a definition of "rules," when told that they were essential because "adopted by all wise men" throughout the ages. They would have found that none could be given.[32]

In discussing mythology, Manzoni declares that to the already convincing arguments advanced against it by romanticists he himself would add the fact that mythology is "idolatrous" and contrary to Christian beliefs and principles.[33]

Manzoni concludes his presentation of the "negative" part of romanticism by commenting on the criticism made by classicists that the ideas advocated by romanticists were old and quite well known. He remarks that the question was not whether such ideas were new or old, but whether they were true or false, that the accusation of plagiarism advanced against romanticists was at odds with the accusation that they were excessively bold as innovators. Romanticists, Manzoni declares, studied the several principles enunciated by different authors in different ages and organized them into a coherent and suggestive system, which in itself is a great achievement.[34]

Manzoni also corrects the misconception that romanticists did not understand each other and did not agree among themselves. He states that on the contrary he is convinced that "few human systems have presented less dissent than the romantic." Romanticists were unanimous in believing "that poetry must have truth as object, as the sole source of noble and durable pleasure, since falsehood may divert the mind but cannot enrich it nor elevate it. . . ." They agreed that the means to render effective the object of poetry was to choose topics that could arouse interest in all classes of people, not in erudite circles alone.[35] Search for truth and its dissemination among the people is, for Manzoni, the essence, the positive aspect of Italian romanticism.

Manzoni discusses the "positive" aspect of romanticism as he sees it and in so doing presents his own point of view and the reasons for his sympathy for the

Giuseppe Verdi, composer.

movement, although he is well aware that not all the romanticists would agree entirely with him. He starts by admitting that the affirmation that "poetry must have truth for object" is very vague, that truth in art is not the equivalent of truth in the ordinary sense. He feels that the truth of art has never been successfully defined, that romanticism, "by specifying what is false, useless, pernicious," gives a more precise definition than "any other literary system" and points the way to further clarification. For Manzoni, the important element of romanticism is the search after truth, the striving against falsehoods and prejudices. In this search he sees a Christian tendency. Literary romanticism, he writes, "by advocating however vaguely all that is true, useful, good, reasonable, contributes verbally if in no other way to the same end as Christianity, or at least does not contradict it."[36]

This Christian tendency is what determines Manzoni's sympathy for romanticism. But he is fully aware that his Christian interpretation of the movement is personal, inasmuch as most romantic writers were not primarily concerned with Christianity.[37] Whether or not this religious interpretation is justified, Manzoni feels that the moral, social, and literary principles of romanticism deserve the recognition and support that they are gaining.

By 1823, when he wrote the letter on romanticism to the Marquis Cesare D'Azeglio, Manzoni had become known as a poet and a writer of tragedies, was admired in Italy, and had won the respect of Goethe. He was especially well known in France where he had been introduced into intellectual circles during his stay in Paris from 1805 to 1810 and had made a close and lasting friendship with Claude Fauriel, who looked after the publication of Manzoni's works in France. He had finished the first draft of his great novel *The Betrothed,* which was to be published within the next few years and was to give him widespread and lasting fame in Italy and abroad. It is not surprising, therefore, that Manzoni's letter to D'Azeglio should have acquired great authority in the field of Italian romanticism, overshadowing other writings on the subject. For the same reasons, and because of his writings opposing the unities of time and place in tragedy, Manzoni has been called by some critics the leader of the movement. It is noteworthy, however, that in spite of his sympathetic support of romanticism, he always kept aloof from the movement, and that his ideas, although clearly and systematically expressed, do little more than summarize the main points made by preceding writers. His personal position in accepting romanticism does add a new note to the theories expressed earlier, but keeps within the framework of a conception of literature subordinated to, and limited by, a moralistic purpose. This didacticism was one of the points accentuated by the *conciliatoristi.*

The fact that Manzoni accepted romanticism lent prestige and authority to the movement, especially in the early twenties when, many of the *conciliatoristi* having been imprisoned or having escaped into exile, the movement in Italy seemed to have lost momentum and leadership.

The vitality of romanticism as a modern spiritual movement emerges clearly from Manzoni's and Nicolini's remarks. In the romantic writings, they were able to distinguish what was unimportant and contingent—the exaggerations and rigidity associated with any theoretical formulation of new principles—from what was of true and lasting value—the advocation of the free expression of personality in deeds and writings.

Carlo Calcaterra, in the brilliant essay which precedes his edition of the manifestos, stated in 1951 that in the three manifestos the authors formulate theoretical principles in order to affirm the inner freedom of man and of the artist. This statement can be extended to all of the romantic writings. The romanticists opposed the aesthetic canon of neo-classicism, which was based on the belief that beauty is absolute and is manifested as such in the Parthenon or the Pantheon, in the poetry of Homer or Virgil, and later

of their imitators. The romantics opposed this doctrine by enlarging the field of aesthetics, by accepting other forms of expression in addition to the classical, by proclaiming Dante and Shakespeare as great as Homer and Virgil. Romanticism was not a denial of the classical tradition but a recognition of the creative spirit and originality of man in any and every form of expression.

This conception of art, which culminates on the one hand in the often vaguely formulated doctrines of the early Italian romantics, constitutes on the other hand the vital principle which animates literary criticism of later ages, for instance of Francesco De Sanctis. It constitutes the essential element of the poetry of Foscolo, Manzoni, and Leopardi in the first decades of the nineteenth century. It is at the basis of all of the following creative literature, be it the poetry of minor artists like Berchet or Mameli, or that of greater poets like Carducci and Pascoli, or the prose of Giovanni Verga.

As Carlo Calcaterra notes, the principle enunciated by the early romantics, that the human spirit is free and dynamic, led not only to a new literature but also to a new conception of life, which accepted the illogical, the irrational and the impossible, and made them logical, rational and possible. In Italy, it led to the *Risorgimento,* to the realization of what had seemed earlier an unattainable dream.

Notes

[1] Giuseppe Nicolini, "Del Fanatismo e della tolleranza. Saggio accademico," in *Disc. e pol.* . . . , vol. II, pp. 117-134; p. 118. This lecture was published for the first time in 1834.

[2] *Ibid.*

[3] Alessandro Manzoni, "Sul Romanticismo, lettera al Marchese Cesare D'Azeglio," dated Sept. 22, 1823, in *Tutte le opere,* ed. Giuseppe Lesca (Firenze, 1923). The letter was published by Manzoni in 1870.

[4] *Ibid.,* pp. 435-436.

[5] *Ibid.,* p. 436.

[6] Giovanni Gherardini, *Elementi di poesia ad uso delle scuole* (Milano, 1820); excerpts in *Disc. e pol.* . . . , vol. II, pp. 135-165.

[7] *Ibid.,* p. 143.

[8] *Ibid.,* p. 147.

[9] *Ibid.,* p. 135.

[10] *Ibid.,* p. 165.

[11] Nicolini, "Del Fanatismo . . . ," p. 133.

[12] *Ibid.,* p. 119.

[13] *Ibid.,* pp. 119-120.

[14] *Ibid.,* pp. 120-121.

[15] *Ibid.,* p. 121.

[16] *Ibid.,* p. 121.

[17] *Ibid.,* p. 122.

[18] *Ibid.,* pp. 123-124.

[19] *Ibid.,* pp. 124-125.

[20] *Ibid.,* p. 126.

[21] *Ibid.,* p. 127.

[22] *Ibid.,* pp. 128-130.

[23] *Ibid.,* p. 130.

[24] *Ibid.,* pp. 131-132.

[25] *Ibid.,* p. 132.

[26] *Ibid.,* p. 133.

[27] *Ibid.,* pp. 133-134.

[28] Manzoni, "Sul Romanticismo," p. 423.

[29] *Ibid.,* p. 432.

[30] *Ibid.,* pp. 423-424. In mentioning the "unities," Manzoni does not discuss the question but refers to his earlier publications: the already mentioned letter to M. Chauvet (see ch. VII, n. 63), and the preface to his own tragedy *Il Conte di Carmagnola,* published in 1820.

[31] Manzoni, "Sul Romanticismo," p. 426.

[32] *Ibid.,* p. 431.

[33] *Ibid.,* pp. 425-426.

[34] *Ibid.,* p. 432.

[35] *Ibid.,* p. 434.

[36] *Ibid.,* pp. 434-435.

[37] *Ibid.,* p. 434.

Franco Ferrucci

SOURCE: "Italian Romanticism: Myth vs. History," in *MLN,* Vol. 98, No. 1, January, 1983, pp. 111-17.

[*In the following essay Ferrucci compares the views of history and myth held by the major figures of the Italian Romantic period, including those of Ugo Foscolo, Giacomo Leopardi, Alessandro Manzoni, and others.*]

The modern notion of history was born in Italy, as elsewhere, between the late Enlightenment and the first wave of Romanticism. The effects of such a cultural revolution are visible in the three major Italian writers of the romantic period: Foscolo, Leopardi, and Manzoni.

Each of these writers has something different to say about history and what history is about. They are all witnessing the direction that history as a literary genre is taking: its transformation into a systematic study of the past, thus more of a science than a creative genre with moral purposes as it had been considered since ancient times and it was still viewed by Chateaubriand in those years.

In a page of his philosophical journal *Zibaldone* (I, 144) Leopardi acknowledges such transformation and writes:

> . . . il mondo umano è divenuto come il naturale, bisogna studiare gli avvenimenti come si studiano i fenomeni, e immaginare le forze motrici andando a tastoni come i fisici. Dal che si può vedere quanto sia scemata l'utilità della storia.

> . . . the world of mankind has become similar to the world of nature, it is necessary to study human events as scientific phenomena are studied, and to imagine their driving forces as the physicists do, groping and experimenting. From this fact one can see how weakened has become history's usefulness.

With his usual sharpness, Leopardi later observes that the very name *history* is a contradictory one. He recalls that Aristotle had given the label of history even to natural science; a label surviving today in the definition of "natural history". According to Leopardi, science is concerned with what does not change, like nature, history with what changes, like human events; the two terms are never put together unless they are misunderstood. There is here a pre-Darwinian idea of nature as immutable and a pre-scientific idea of history as being mainly a "narration". I shall focus on the latter, the former being beyond the scope of the present investigation. Let us pause in order to realize that the word "history" is in fact contradictory, and far more so than Leopardi suspected. History is both the tale and a study of the tale; the paradox is even clearer in Italian where the term *storia* is also used to signify a children's tale or even an invented presentation of reality (as in the French *histoire* or in the German *Geschichte*). I do not want to deal with the philosophical implication of such ambiguity; it is sufficient here to say that for Leopardi *storia* is a tale which is turning into a science, as a youth grows into an adult: acquiring knowledge and renouncing illusions.

There is another well known passage from *Zibaldone* that abundantly proves this point (25 novembre 1822,II, 21-22):

> La storia greca, romana ed ebrea contengono le reminiscenze delle idee acquistate da ciascuno nella prima fanciullezza. . . . Quindi lo interesse che ispirano le dette storie, e loro parti, e tutto ciò che loro appartiene; interesse unico nel suo genere, come fu osservato da Chateaubriand (*Gènie* etc.); interesse che non può mai esserci ispirato da verun' altra storia, sia anche più bella, varia, grande, e per se più importante delle sopraddette; sia anche più importante per noi, come le storie nazionali. Le suddette tre sono le più *interessanti* perché sono le più *note* . . . .

> Greek, Roman and Jewish history contain the memories of the ideas acquired by each man in early childhood. . . . Hence these histories and their parts and everything that belongs to them inspire an interest unique in its genre, as Chateaubriand observed (*Gènie* etc.); an interest that cannot be inspired in us by any other history, be it even more beautiful, varied, great and in itself more important than those mentioned above, or be it even more important for us, as are our national "histories". The three mentioned above are the most *interesting* because they are the best *known* . . . .

History and poetry seem to resemble each other; they both share the basic characteristic of being the *memory* of mankind, at both the collective and the individual level. Of course a modern historiographer would not deny that: but his attitude would be one of interpretation instead of trust. It is the same difference that separates today the notion of history from that of myth.

This is the point of conflict that we are trying to locate. It is a conflict that Leopardi inherits from the Italian 18th century more than from the romantic movement which he quickly dismissed and shunned. The Italian 18th century presents a twofold recreation of the mythical presence; as a decorative ornament of culture (also visible throughout the painting of the period) it was called mythology and this is the word we find in Leopardi, while the closest equivalent to the

word myth in Zibaldone is *storia*. Where did the merging of myth and history take place? Again in the 18th century, in the work of G. B. Vico, whose message was received in the same form by Foscolo and Leopardi. *La storia* is the memory of the past in the form of myth and poetry; it becomes a science in moments of scarce vitality, when everything becomes "reasonable" and "rational", i.e. without daring or passion. For Leopardi, as for Foscolo, history is a mythology (a fable) that attains a convincing level: the level of myth that only poets can reach. If this is true, it could also explain why in our post-romantic idiom *storia* means at the same time a truth and a lie.

One of the most famous passages in Foscolo is the page of his academic inauguration in Pavia where he addresses the Italian people and urges them to turn to their past. Here is what he says:

> O italiani, io vi esorto alle storie, perché niun popolo più di voi può mostrare nè più calamità da compiangere, nè più errori da evitare, nè più virtù che vi facciano rispettare, nè più grandi anime degne di essere liberate dalla oblivione da chiunque di noi sa che si deve amare e difendere ed onorare la terra che fu nutrice ai nostri padri ed a noi, e che darà pace e memoria alle nostre ceneri. Io vi esorto alle storie, perché angusta è l'arena degli oratori; e chi ormai può contendervi la poetica palma? Ma nelle storie tutta si spiega la nobiltà dello stile, tutti gli affetti della virtù, tutto l'incanto della poesia, tutti i precetti della sapienza, tutti i progressi e i benemeriti dell' italiano sapere.

> Italians, I exhort you to go back to the memories of history because there has never been a people who, more than you, can show more adversities to be deplored, more errors to be avoided, more virtues for which to be respected, more noble spirits, worthy of being freed from oblivion, by anyone (of us) who knows that the land that nourished us and our forefathers, the land that will give peace, and keep the memory of our ashes, has to be loved, honoured and defended. I urge you to go back to the memories of history because the rhetorical forum has narrowed; and who can now compete with you for the poetic laurel? But it is in history that all the nobility of the style, all the affects of virtue, all the enchantments of poetry, all the teachings of wisdom, all the progress, all the achievements of the Italian knowledge are so fully manifested.

It is the term *storie* which is the revealing one. Foscolo's exhortation to the Italians is to go back to *le storie* not to *la storia*: a historian would not use one word for the other. *Storia* as a science has no plural form; but *storia* as a tale has one indeed. *Le storie* are the events of the past conceived and presented as *legends* (etymologically: the things to be read) of a nation, the memorabilia which are not to be questioned or interpreted but simply re-enacted.

Vico's thought is acting on Foscolo even more directly than on Leopardi. Contemporary to the above quoted lines is the long poem *I Sepolcri,* his widely recognized masterpiece; here history plays a monumental role and it is presented not as an investigation but as an acceptance of the past. By definition a myth is to be either accepted or refused: if one tries to interpret it allegorically it is evident that the element of faith is no longer there. The figures of the great Italians evoked by Foscolo in *I Sepolcri* share the essence of mythical appearances: they exist beyond investigation, they simply *are,* like ancient monuments, or forces of nature. The fact that we are sure they have existed makes the myth possible since it makes it believable: which also explains why modern mythologies need a historical background in order to survive. They are dealing with a massive presence of history and attempt to transform it into a belief. The *nation* is one of these beliefs.

We are close to the identification of the split that occurs between Leopardi and Foscolo. They both think of history essentially as a mythological recreation of the past, as a collective poetry of mankind. They diverge on one fundamental issue: the mythological recreation is possible for Foscolo, not anymore for Leopardi. We are not coping with a minor divergence: the entire modern culture has been severed by this contrast. At the time of the *Sepolcri* and of the *Discorso Inaugurale,* Foscolo seems to have traced the territory of a new mythology: the history of the Italian people, supporting the rising myth of the nation. Something of that kind was happening all over Europe in the aftermath of the French Revolution and of the Napoleonic conquests. For the moment ancient Greece (often mentioned in *I Sepolcri*) provides the background, waiting to enter the scene as the protagonist of a new mythological rebirth: the one attempted by Foscolo in his last and unfinished poem *Le Grazie. Le Grazie,* just like the paintings of David and the sculptures of Canova, are inspired directly by hellenic mythology, they all share the fate of similar contemporary experiments in neo-classicism.

There is a word that appears both in Leopardi's and Foscolo's works which is the equivalent of what we call "myth": it is the term "illusions". To Foscolo illusions appear necessary, to Leopardi foolish; thus Leopardi will never accept the modern mythology of nationalism or any other effort to create a "progressive faith" that tries to explain the fate of mankind.

It would not be correct to assume that we are witnessing a case of contrast between a "sentimental" poet in the schillerian sense (Leopardi) and a "naive"

one (Foscolo): the distinction would rather be between a sentimental poet (still Leopardi) and a poet (like Foscolo) who tries very hard to be naive and to give new life to a myth by believing in it. Leopardi is contemplating a world in which ancient myths are dead and modern ones do not provide inspiration: the above quoted paragraph declaring the superiority of "Greek, Roman and Jewish history" over the national histories (here Leopardi uses the plural *storie*) might even be a direct answer to Foscolo's statement about the need to go back to the Italian *storie* in order to create a modern mythology, which is, a modern poetry. Leopardi accepts the role of the "sentimental" poet, the inspired philosopher who is conscious of living in a rational civilisation where myths are dead and history does not seem to make much sense. Both positions will have a future and each will open the road for generations to come.

Another writer, Manzoni, was coping in those same years with the dialectical relationship between myth and history. He does not attempt to recreate a classic (pagan) mythology nor to found a new mythology of the nation (although he writes a few patriotic poems): his mythology is a Christian one. Being a believer, Manzoni would not call the Christian faith "a myth", nonetheless his first major creative effort (the *Inni Sacri*) is the equivalent of Foscolo's return to the classic myth in *Le Grazie* (the two works belong to the same years). The events of the *Inni Sacri* (evoked by Manzoni) are all taken from the Gospels and are the mythological reservoir of the Christian tradition. It is very revealing that the last poem of the unfinished series, *La Pentecoste,* took so many years to complete. *La Pentecoste* deals with the spread of the Christian teaching and the birth of the Church as a social institution: we are here at the point of separation between Christianity as a myth (the New Testament) and the history of Christianity. Manzoni's mythological attempt enters a crisis when history appears.

Manzoni boldly accepts the challenge. After the *Inni Sacri* history is a pervasive presence in his work. Of the two tragedies *Adelchi* is rooted in the Middle Ages, *Il Conte di Carmagnola* in Renaissance Italy. They both present insoluble conflicts of Christian characters crushed by the violence that rules the world. In both cases Manzoni's conclusions seem to be that Christianity cannot prevail in this world: his heroes finally die willingly and without regrets. History is the territory that has to be crossed and finally abandoned when the promised land is near and myth is there to direct the pilgrims.

Manzoni's masterpiece, *I Promessi Sposi,* is a further step in this dialectical confrontation. In his novel Manzoni attempts no less than a reconciliation of myth and history. Staged in 17th century Lombardy, it presents the Church as the actual winner in the midst of worldly events, largely because of the incompetence of its opponents, but also because of the persistent appeal of its mythological foundation. If the Church can win over society, myth can overcome history. In order to achieve this result, Manzoni was obliged to perform a continuous, subtle manipulation of the historical material he had selected, presenting it in a biased light, or simply obliterating important aspects of it. The manipulation has been well documented and it is not my purpose to deal with this part of the problem. I want to stress that Manzoni is certainly, among the writers we have mentioned so far, the most "historically" minded; his curiosity for history is almost a professional one, his passion for archives and for the reconstruction of the sequence of past events is unknown to both Foscolo and Leopardi.

Paradoxically enough, the crisis between myth and history will occur again when Manzoni comes to the conclusion that it is not possible to overlook the claim of history to be a science; this leads to the dismissal of the historical novel in the *Discorso sul romanzo storico*. It is understandable why Manzoni presents the crisis in the form of an opposition between historical scruples and artistic impulses: he cannot admit that the basic contrast is between the historian's desire for truth and the believer's need for reassurance. If Manzoni condemns the historical novel it might be because he realizes, half consciously, that it would be difficult to create another great novel in which the Church would assume such a prominent role.

The historical novel will have a chance to survive in Italy through the substitution of the myth of patriotism for the myth of catholicism. In modern society nationalism is a more powerful drive than religion; it was particularly so in Italy and Germany, when in the course of the 19th century they both achieved geographical unity. In these two countries Romanticism and Nationalism are entangled in a way impossible elsewhere; although the aggressive connotation of nationalism will be absent from Italian culture until D'Annunzio.

I will rapidly explore the two major achievements in this direction. One is Nievo's long novel *Le Confessioni di un Italiano*. The idea is to conceive a historical narration as an autobiographical one: it is Rousseau added to Manzoni, the two writers most admired by Nievo. Following the long life of the protagonist we are brought to witness the birth of a nation, and in the osmosis, history finds a new justification. The myth belongs to the present not to the past; which accounts for the optimistic, almost jubilant mood of Nievo's narration. With Nievo we are led one step further in the relationship of myth and history. Once history is accepted as not being in contradiction with our hopes we observe a phenomenon that will grow vaster and vaster in modern civilisation, the sudden appearance of a *childhood* distinguished from the adult world of

historical events. The whole first (and most famous) section of Nievo's *Confessioni* is the memory of the protagonist as a child who, characteristically, lives among rural gentry immobilized and secluded from the movement of history, as is childhood itself. In decadent literature this separation will be seen as an irreducible opposition, generating regrets and nostalgia for a mythical individual past. Nievo is still sharing the romantic attitude toward the origins: they are the horizon of our fullfillment, a memory and a premonition at the same time.

The second great achievement is the *Storia della Letteratura Italiana* by the most famous Italian critic, Francesco De Sanctis. I do not hesitate to call this work one of the major historical novels of 19th century literature. The entire development of Italian culture throughout the centuries is seen as a growing living organism searching for its meaning and for its national identity. A great *Entwicklung* narration, the *Storia* by De Sanctis presents protagonists (the great authors of Italian literature) who have both a mythical and a historical status, like the heroes of ancient epic poetry. De Sanctis and Nievo have found a momentary equilibrium between myth and history, based on the patriotic enthusiasm of a young nation and on the credibility of what they narrate.

Born later in Italy than in other European countries Romanticism will last there as long as the search for national unity. In the latter part of the century a new phase of the dialectic relationship between myth and history will take place and will find new protagonists. The only myth left, the national one, will become more and more aggressive as if history were trying to suffocate it.

THE LANGUAGE OF ROMANTICISM

Sante Matteo

SOURCE: "The Centripetal Romantic: Symphonious Discourse in Polyphonous Italy," in *The Reasonable Romantic: Essays on Alessandro Manzoni,* edited by Sante Matteo and Larry H. Peer, Peter Lang, 1986, pp. 33-45

[*In the following essay, Matteo describes the fragmented condition of the Italian language at the time that Manzoni wrote his novel* I promessi sposi, *calling the work "the first truly Italian discourse" and "the foundation on which modern Italian literature and language have been built."*]

American students of Italian literature are often perplexed when they fail to find passages from Dante's

Divine Comedy or from Alessandro Manzoni's *I promessi sposi* (*The Betrothed*) in Italian literary anthologies, compilations of selected passages from what have been judged to be the great works of Italian literature. Dante and Manzoni, they have learned, are important writers in Italian literature. Why, therefore, are their works not included in Italian anthologies? Curiously enough, the omission of these two books from anthologies, far from being an indication that they are not highly regarded, is a sign of their exalted status.

Dante's poem and Manzoni's novel are seldom anthologized precisely because they are considered the two indisputable masterpieces of Italian literature. It would seem almost sacrilegious to select passages from them or to abridge them in any way. It is assumed that the Italian students for whom the anthologies are prepared are either already thoroughly familiar with the two books or will eventually read them in their entirety. The author of the *Divine Comedy* is considered the father of Italian literature and Italian language in general. Manzoni's *I promessi sposi* is considered the matrix of *modern* Italian literature and language. Manzoni's novel became a model for correct usage soon after its publication and continues to be the most frequently cited authority in Italian dictionaries of our own day.

Dante's importance is generally recognized even outside of Italy. The role that Manzoni has played in shaping Italian literature and Italian language, however, is not fully appreciated beyond the relatively narrow boundaries of Italian studies. It is often necessary, therefore, to inform American readers of the lofty position which *I promessi sposi* occupies in Italian literature. The real surprise for foreign readers (and for many Italian readers, for that matter) comes when they learn how the novel was written. For, *I promessi sposi,* the Italian novel par excellence, the model of correct Italian narrative prose, took almost two decades to write in its definitive version and had to be written with the aid of French-Italian and Latin-Italian dictionaries, and occasional consultations with the housemaid of the Manzoni household, who happened to be Tuscan. This was because Alessandro Manzoni, a writer from Milan, a city in Northern Italy, actually spoke French better than he spoke Italian!

How can that be? Was he perhaps a young, inexperienced writer who had grown up in France and was attempting his first writing in Italian? No, Manzoni was not just another provincial writer, nor an inexperienced amateur encountering the Italian language and Italian literature for the first time. When he sat down to try his hand at his first novel on April 12, 1821, he was a very accomplished and widely renowned artist of thirty-six.

He had been writing poetry for over twenty years, verses that had earned him an *international* reputation. His correspondents and admirers included, among many others, such literary figures as Goethe, Chateaubriand, and Lamartine. His very influential "Lettre à M. Chauvet sur l'unité de temps et de lieu dans la tragédie" (Letter to Mr. Chauvet on the Unity of Time and of Place in Tragedy), which argued against the classical Aristotelian unities of time and place as artificial, was written in 1820 and published in France in 1823. It contained many of the ideas later elaborated by Stendhal in his *Racine and Shakespeare,* 1825, and by Hugo in his *Préface de Cromwell,* 1827, considered important manifestoes of French Romanticism.[1]

Hence Manzoni was a widely known and respected artist and a leading figure not only in the Italian Romantic movement but in the larger context of European Romanticism. It is even more perplexing to realize that it was not, therefore, a young, uneducated, would-be novelist that had to resort to a French-Italian dictionary, but one of Italy's and Europe's leading literary figures. So, again the question: how was it possible that one of Italy's leading men of letters knew French better than Italian?

Manzoni, it should be pointed out, was by no means unique in this respect. As the noted Manzoni scholar and translator, Archibald Colquhoun, points out, echoing statements of all historians of the Italian language: "At the beginning of the nineteenth century the use of Italian as a current spoken language was almost regional to Tuscany; when used for verbal communication between inhabitants of the various parts of the peninsula, it was apt to sound as cumbrous and stilted as ecclesiastical latin" (214).

The vast majority of Italians simply did not speak Italian. They spoke their various and very diverse dialects: Sicilians spoke Sicilian; Neapolitans, Neapolitan; Venetians, Venetian; etc. Indeed, as a *spoken* language Italian hardly existed at all. The Tuscan dialects were the closest to it because literary Italian had originated in Tuscany, and more specifically in Florence, with the works of Dante, Petrarch, and Boccaccio in the thirteenth and fourteenth centuries. Yet even the spoken Tuscan dialects had subsequently evolved along different lines than the literary language and were restricted to limited boundaries, outside of which they could not be readily understood. In the first half of the Nineteenth Century, then, except for a somewhat artificial and limited *lingua franca* used by merchants and other travelers, the language we know as Italian existed almost exclusively as a *literary* language that could be used by only a few *litterati*.

Bruno Migliorini, the noted historian of the Italian language, points out that even by the time of Italian unification in 1861, the only Italians who received any sort of education were still limited to the aristocracy and to those who were preparing for the clergy. And even in these cases the language of instruction was usually Latin rather than Italian. Indeed, for many subjects, Latin remained the language of instruction in Italian universities until the end of the last century. The Italian that Manzoni and other writers of his generation knew was primarily the language of Italian poetry, a poetic idiom far removed from what people spoke. In Migliorini's words it was a "lingua letteraria tradizionale, troppo esclusivamente libresca e troppo poco popolare" (558) (a traditional *literary* language, too exclusively bookish and not in the least popular).

Not only was Italian not a spoken language, but even in its written form it lent itself more readily to poetry than to prose. Ironically, the culture that boasted a Boccaccio as the father of narrative prose fiction had lost the ability to narrate in a prose that was both realistic and artistic.[2]

After laboring on the novel for months, Manzoni put it aside and returned to poetry to finish his verse tragedy, *Adelchi*. He actually found verse much easier to write than prose since he had mastered Italian poetic language when he was still a boy. He was tempted to abandon the whole project of the novel and started working on yet another verse tragedy. He expressed his discouragement in a letter to his close friend and mentor, the French critic and historian, Claude Fauriel: "les difficultés qu'oppose la langue italienne à traiter ces sujets, elles sont réelles et grandes. . . . Je pense avec vous que bien écrire un roman en italien est une des choses les plus difficiles" (Caretti xi). (The difficulties posed by the Italian language when treating such matters are real and considerable. . . . I, like you, think that to write a good novel in Italian is a most difficult thing.)

However, reluctant to be defeated, a year after he had initially started the novel he picked it up again. He worked on it continuously and painstakingly for five years, using not only the French-Italian and Latin-Italian dictionaries already mentioned, but also a Milanese-Italian dictionary, because the words and expressions he needed would occur to him in those languages and not in so-called Italian.[3]

The novel was published in 1827 and received an immediate and clamorous success. Manzoni, however, was not satisfied with the language that he had labored so hard to create. He found it too artificial: "una . . . lingua . . . di laboratorio . . . un composto indigesto di frasi un po' lombarde, un po' toscane, un po' francesi, un po' anche latine" (Caretti xxi) (a laboratory language, an undigested mixture of phrases that were a bit Lombard, a bit Tuscan, a bit French, and even a bit Latin).

He quickly forbade further editions and set about revising the language of the novel again. He had decided that the Italian he wanted should not be drawn from books, especially not from poetry, but should be based on a currently spoken language. Otherwise it would be a "lingua morta" (dead language). Therefore, a living dialect had to be chosen and accepted by all Italians throughout the peninsula. The obvious choice, he concluded, had to be Florentine, the dialect closest to literary Italian because Italian literature had been born in Florence five centuries earlier when the masterpieces of the "tre corone Florentine" (the three florentine crowns: Dante, Petrarch, Boccaccio) had been written. As far as Manzoni was concerned, the choice had been made then. Now what he and other Italian writers had to do was to reacquaint themselves with the *living* language of Florence as it was currently spoken, use it in their writing, and thus diffuse it throughout the country. So, Manzoni actually headed for Florence in order to tuscanize the language of his novel, or in his famous metaphor, "a risciacquare i panni in Arno," to rinse his clothes in the Arno, the river that flows through Florence.[4]

The revision took him almost fifteen years and the definitive edition of the novel did not appear until 1840, almost two decades after he had started writing it. In fact, the novel was his last artistic literary creation. He continued to make minor revisions in its language practically until his death in 1873 at the age of 88. It could thus be said that Manzoni worked on this one novel for half a century.

It has been necessary to deal at some length with Manzoni's experience in writing his only novel not only because it is fascinating in itself, but because it is indicative of a serious obstacle facing any Italian novelists of the 19th century—the problem of language.

This was at least a twofold problem. First, most Italians, writers included, grew up speaking a dialect so different from Italian as to be practically a different language, unintelligible outside one's own region. This meant that in using the Italian language writers were essentially translating from their native dialects into what amounted to a foreign language. Secondly, the Italian into which they were translating was deficient. Having been transmitted only through literature, and primarily through a poetic tradition, it had become abstract in content, rigid in construction, and rhetorical in style.

Manzoni, even as a schoolboy, had not had much trouble writing about muses, lyres, mythological figures, or any other concepts that were readily available from Italy's long-established poetic idiom. However, he didn't want the protagonists of his novel to be pagan nymphs or mythological deities, but rather common people situated in a real epoch of Italian history: in the Lombardy of the 17th century under Spanish rule. He wanted to describe their poor environment in a realistic manner and to narrate events from everyday life.

He found that the words he needed to do this did not exist in the poetic Italian he knew. Many household items, for example had never been treated in poetry, and Manzoni knew the names for them only in dialect. In short, he simply found that the Italian language at his disposal consisted of an abstract, idealized vocabulary and a convoluted syntax which made it inadequate for the kind of prose narrative he wanted to write.

There were different ways in which to try to remedy the situation; but all were unsatisfactory to some extent. One alternative was simply to write in one's own dialect. After all, that's essentially what Dante and Boccaccio had done. But, in so doing, a writer would severely restrict the size of his audience. Moreover, most dialects only existed in spoken form and written codification would have been an enormous undertaking.

Another possibility would have been for each writer to create his own form of Italian, as Manzoni had first tried to do in his 1827 edition, basing it partly on the literary language, partly on his own dialect, partly on foreign languages, and on whatever else seemed to work. But this would have been extremely laborious, and would have resulted in books written in a multitude of individual languages.

A third option would have been for everyone to agree on the use of only one *living* dialect that could provide all the concrete words they needed, with Florentine as the obvious choice. Even in this case, however, writers had to express themselves in a language that was not their native tongue. Furthermore, there was the problem of diffusion, of making Florentine sufficiently known outside Florence so that people could read what was being written in it.

A glance across the Alps at the situation among French novelists of the same period offers an interesting contrast that will perhaps help us gauge the enormity of Manzoni's undertaking and appreciate more fully the scope of his accomplishment. Victor Hugo probably could not even have imagined working on the same novel for twenty years. According to A. J. George he subscribed to an "organic theory of creation" and didn't believe in revision at all:

> [U]n roman . . . naît, d'une façon en quelque sorte nécessaire, avec tous ses chapitres. . . . La greffe et la soudure prennent mal sur des oeuvres de cette nature, qui doivent jaillir d'un seul jet et rester telles quelles. Une fois la chose faite, ne vous ravisez pas, n'y retouchez plus. (in George 140-141)

> (A novel is born in a kind of necessary fashion, with all its chapters. Grafting and welding don't take well on works of this kind which have to shoot forth in a single spurt and remain as they're born. Once it's done, don't change your mind; don't make any changes.)

George informs us that Georges Sand had a similar attitude: "*Indiana* had been produced in a single outpouring, under the pressure of an emotion so powerful that she wrote almost automatically" (142). Stendhal's approach, though not nearly as mystical, indicated a similar facility in writing. In a letter to Balzac he claimed that "he had never considered the *art* of writing a novel. Making plans bored him. One night he wrote about twenty-five pages; on the next he reread the last four, then proceeded with his story" (George 149). As for Balzac, one need only consider his phenomenal prolificity to suspect that he didn't share Manzoni's trouble in finding the right words for what he wanted to say.

While such a radical difference in the writing experience between Manzoni and his French contemporaries was undoubtedly the result mostly of differences in personality and individual aesthetics, there is also the suspicion that another factor might well have been the accessibility of language itself. The language of the French authors was not only a literary language, but their *spoken* language as well. For them the act of writing came closer to being a matter of "speaking" their thoughts on paper. Any difficulties they may have experienced in writing were more likely to be of a stylistic or aesthetic nature rather than the result of the deficiency or inaccessibility of the language with which they were working.

Dialects in France were not nearly as divergent from the national language, nor as exclusive of it, as Italian dialects were. Standard French was known and used in the provinces for administrative, religious, educational, or other bureaucratic reasons, and had been so used for centuries. Italy, on the other hand, had been politically divided and linguistically fragmented for centuries. In most of her regions, duchies, principalities and other small states, the bureaucratic language was likely to be German, French, or Spanish, depending on which power was in control at the time.

Along with France's long political and geographic unity there had been other factors which had contributed to the linguistic unity of Italy's neighbors to the north but had had a limited impact in Italy: the Reformation, for example. Because reformers like Luther and Calvin had stressed that the Bible should be read by everyone, insisting that it be translated into the "vulgar tongues" and that the common people become literate enough to read it, national languages north of the Alps were more widely diffused among the masses. Catholic Italy, needless to say, didn't participate in such reforms to the same extent.

In France, furthermore, the Revolution and the Napoleonic Empire had greatly contributed to bring about a more propitious linguistic situation for novelists. As a bourgeois takeover, the French Revolution helped to shift the social focus of French culture. Art, literature, and language stopped being the property of the aristocracy and became more and more the property of "the people, that strange segment of the population which the revolution had thrust into prominence" (George 37). Under Napoleon, the highly centralized and widespread bureaucracy, the extensive military conscription in all regions of the country and consequent integration of more people into the mainstream of the national destiny, the emphasis on the education of the common man, all contributed to the diffusion of the French language to a greater segment of the population. As a result, during the period that followed, the period which goes under the label of "Romantic," the literary audience was substantially increased. In Marcel Cohen's words, "le texte est accessible à tous ceux qui parlent français" (253) (the text is accessible to all those who speak French).

In fact, most of the writing during the Romantic period was specifically addressed to this much wider audience. This was especially true of the novel. One reason for this was the social consciousness inherent in the Romantic movement, a legacy of the early ideals of the French Revolution. Another reason was that writers now had to make a living from their art by selling their books to a larger audience, for, as Cazamian points out, "the age of patrons now being decidedly over, literature as a career had to be self-supporting" (300). The result of all this was an even greater rapprochement between the written and the spoken language in France.

Though many of these social concerns and democratic impulses were felt in Italy around the same time—as were the effects of the Napoleonic reforms—conditions there didn't permit their implementation to the same degree as in France. Manzoni too, after all, wanted to write for the masses and not for a handful of the culturally privileged. That was one of the reasons that he had decided to write a novel in the first place, and why he had decided to write it with the common people as the protagonists. The problem was not only that there was no adequate language at his disposal, but there were no masses able to read his book even if he managed to find or create the language he needed. Italy had to wait for the Risorgimento to come to fruition, that is,

for national liberation and unification to take place in 1861, before it could set out on the road of achieving some sort of linguistic unity with the aid of universal education, centralized government bureaucracy, universal military conscription, national magazines and newspapers, etc.

When Stendhal, Balzac, and Hugo sat down to write their novels it wasn't likely to be nearly as frustrating an experience for them as it turned out to be for Manzoni. They had a fully expressive prose language to work with, a long, continuous and rich narrative tradition to draw from and react to, and a large audience that was both popular and educated who shared both their language and their literary tradition. Martin Turnell observes that in France the early part of the nineteenth century was "a period which was highly propitious for the great writer. . . . The writer could . . . apply the whole of his talent to his books; *he had no need to waste his energies trying to produce the conditions in which writing becomes possible* or resisting hostile tendencies" (14). (emphasis added)

The language at their disposal was sophisticated and flexible enough—containing a plurality of levels or registers—that they could manipulate it to produce very subtle, evocative effects. The French language was like a versatile musical instrument that they could use in original and innovative ways to create new sounds and new tunes. The simile is Stendhal's: "un roman est comme un archet, la caisse du violon qui rend les sons, c'est l'âme du lecteur" (in Turnell 6) (a novel is like a bow; and the chamber of the violin which sends out the sound is the mind of the reader).[5] Manzoni, on the other hand, had to build the instrument before he could start making his music with it; and then he had to devise a way to transmit the sound of that new instrument to the "caisse du violon, . . . l'âme du lecteur," i.e. to enable other Italians to understand his language. The fact that the language of the definitive version of the novel is, if anything, even more subtle and evocative than Stendhal's, is the result of his own herculean achievement in fashioning a new language and with it the conditions that made possible the emergence of a national, popular literary public.

An episode in *I promessi sposi,* accompanied by a revealing aside by the author, indicates the nature and the extent of the obstacles to linguistic and literary communication in Italy. The episode describes the attempts of Agnese and Renzo to communicate by letter. Because they belong to the lower classes and are therefore illiterate they have to rely on scribes, or professional letter writers. The author digresses to describe in humorous yet poignant detail how the illiterate peasant must go to the scribe and try to express his thoughts as best he can.

The letter writer understands a little, misunderstands a portion, and in putting it down on paper adds an expression here, takes one away there, in order to achieve the right effect, and ends up writing a letter very different from the one intended by the peasant. Then the letter is sent to the addressee, another illiterate peasant who also has to have recourse to a professional letter writer who in reading the letter interprets it according to his knowledge of language and rhetorical formulae, while the peasant bases his interpretation on his knowledge of the sender's personality and situation. The consequences of such a situation are that very little reliable communication can take place.

In talking about the difficulties of communication under such circumstances, the author makes it clear that he is also alluding to his own frustrations and to the conditions of Italian "letters" of his own time by an aside he makes in the middle of the episode, comparing the plight of the Italian writer to that of the scribe: "Con tutto ciò, al letterato suddetto non gli riesce sempre di dire tutto quel che vorrebbe; qualche volta gli accade di dire tutt'altro: accade anche a noi altri, che scriviamo per la stampa" (464). ("Moreover the literate friend may not always succeed in saying what he means. Sometimes he says something quite different. [We professional writers of books have been known to do the same]" [497].)

It's evident from this passage that for Manzoni the Italian language as it then existed could not be easily employed as a transparent vehicle for ideas and images, that, on the contrary, it was a problematic obstacle to the expression of those idea. His concern was not with the nature of language *per se;* his was a much more practical, and socially oriented preoccupation. He didn't wish to expound on the nature of the ineffable, on the inherent inadequacies or indeterminacy of writing or language in general, so much as to point out that certain conditions in Italy could be and should be changed so that such obstacles to communication as illiteracy might be overcome.

Manzoni was considered a leader in the Italian Romantic movement; and as such he certainly shared many of the ideals and concerns of European Romanticism. For instance, like Hugo, he wished to declare "guerre à la rhétorique" (war on rhetoric). He wanted to divorce literature and language from an artificial, restrictive tradition and bring them closer to the people, to what could be considered a spoken language. Yet his efforts actually consisted of avoiding or eliminating "local color" in his language, that quality which was avidly sought by the French and other Romantics. The trouble in Italy was too much "local color," with practically each locality speaking in a different dialect. Manzoni's desire was to centralize and unify the language. He wanted to bring about the conditions that would make communication possible among Italians of all regions.

Many of the French Romantics moved in an opposite direction. Since their language was already unified and centralized, and communication between regions was not as difficult as in Italy, they sought to bring *diversity* into their literary language rather than conformity, through the use of different types of language, or of different linguistic registers: dialects, slang, foreign words or expressions, technical jargon, argot, etc. Thus, Stendhal made extensive use of Italian words, phrases, even Italian syntax to better evoke the setting in *La Chartreuse de Parme*. Hugo resurrected many archaic, medieval words in *Notre Dame de Paris*. Georges Sand reproduced the dialect of her Berry region in her "romans champêtres" (country novels). Hugo and Balzac both made extensive use of *argot,* the slang of the urban masses and of the underworld.

France had been a unified nation for centuries, and most of the French people had acquired a strong sense of national identity. Politically, economically, and culturally it was a highly centralized country. Paris was the center of all; everything emanated from Paris: money, industry, fashions, literature, even language. Paris was not only the axis around which all French activity revolved; it also tended to impose prescriptive models or norms, on the whole of the French society. Under such highly centralized circumstances it was natural that the search for *new* meanings and for *new* ways of expression be *centrifugal* in nature. In such a centrally dominated situation a creative or original discourse could only be possible by branching out; by coming in contact with the *marginal* elements; by attempting to flee, in some way, from the center: whether it was to the past, to exotic lands, to the underworld, to the provincial countryside: wherever, as long as it was outside the dominant and thus potentially oppressive "norm."

Italy, by contrast, was highly decentralized and fragmented, and had so been for centuries. There was only a very vague sense of national unity based on geographic considerations, and very little sense of national identity. Its many small states were isolated and tended to be relatively non-communicant. There was no political axis around which Italianness could be defined, and no national model or "norm" to work with, and against. Under such circumstances the need to establish a national identity required a discourse that was *centripetal* in nature. An "Italian" discourse could take shape only by subduing or sacrificing the marginal elements; by reducing the differences, in an attempt to locate or establish a common center.

And it was precisely such an Italian discourse that Manzoni created with his novel, *I promessi sposi;* the first truly Italian discourse, the first that was meant to reach *all* Italians, in all regions and of all classes. With this one monumental work Manzoni not only provided Italy with a new national discourse, but also a new language to bear that discourse. Furthermore, with this new language he created the conditions for the birth of a new literary public, the first truly Italian reading public; and a new generation of writers, the first truly Italian writers. And all this almost singlehandedly! Yes, but what a hand! An iron hand in a velvet glove, as Carlo Dionisotti put it.[6]

Alessandro Manzoni didn't write any more novels or poetry after *I promessi sposi*. He didn't have to; Italians didn't require him to. Through his many, remaining years of artistic silence he continued to be revered as Italy's greatest writer. When he died in 1873 the entire nation mourned; and Italy *was* finally a free and unified nation. Giuseppe Verdi was moved to write his *Requiem,* one of his few non-operatic pieces, in honor of this man whom he considered not only Italy's greatest writer, but a great patriot. One novel, *I promessi sposi,* was enough; it is the foundation on which modern Italian literature and language have been built.

Works Cited

Bisi, Alceste. *L'Italie et le romantisme français*. Milan-Rome-Naples: Albrighi, Segati e C., 1914.

Caretti, Lanfranco. Introduction. *I promessi sposi*. By Alessandro Manzoni. Vol. 1: *Fermo e Lucia*. Vol. 2: Interlinear edition including the 1827 edition and the 1840 edition of *I promessi sposi*. Torino: Einaudi, 1971.

Cazamian, L. *A History of French Literature*. London: Oxford University Press, 1960.

Cohen, Marcel. *Histoire d'une langue: Le Français*. Paris: Les Editeurs Français Réunis, 1950.

Colquhoun, Archibald. *Manzoni and his Times*. London: J. M. Dent & Sons, Ltd., 1954.

Dionisotti, Carlo. *Geografia e storia della letteratura italiana*. Torino: Einaudi, 1967.

George, Albert Joseph. *The Development of French Romanticism*. Syracuse: Syracuse University Press, 1955.

Hall, Robert A. Jr. *The Italian Questione Della Lingua: An Interpretative Essay*. University of North Carolina Studies in Romance Languages and Literature, #11. Chapel Hill, N.C.: U. N. C. Press, 1942.

Holmes, Urban T., Jr. and Schutz, Alexander H. *A History of the French Language*. New York: Farrar & Rinehart, 1933.

Mancini, Albert N. "Note sulla poetica del romanzo italiano del Seicento." *MLN* 18.1 (1966): 33-54.

——. "Prosa e narrativa nelle poetiche romanzesche di metà Seicento, fra il Marini e il Morando." *Italica* 47 (1970): 387-417.

Manzoni, Alessandro. *The Betrothed*. Trans. Bruce Penman. New York: Penguin, 1972.

——. *I promessi sposi*. Vol. 2 of *Tutte le opere di Alessandro Manzoni*. Ed. Alberto Chiari and Fausto Ghisalberti. 7 vols. Milano: Mondadori, 1954.

Migliorini, Bruno. *Storia della lingua italiana*. Firenze: Sansoni, 1971.

Raya, Gino. *Il romanzo. Storia dei generi letterari italiani*. Milano: Vallardi, 1950.

Reynolds, Barbara. *The Linguistic Writings of Alessandro Manzoni: A Textual and Chronological Reconstruction*. Cambridge: W. Heiffer and Sons, Ltd., 1950.

Stendhal, (Beyle, Henri). *Le Rouge et le noir*. Paris: Garnier-Flammarion, 1964.

Turnell, Martin. *The Novel in France*. London: Hamish Hamilton, 1950.

Ullman, Stephen. *Style in the French Novel*. Cambridge: Cambridge University Press, 1957.

Notes

[1] Alceste Bisi in his *L'Italie et le romantisme français* noted Manzoni's considerable influence in France: "Les deux tragédies de Manzoni [*Adelchi, Il conte di Carmagnola*] précédées l'une d'une analyse de Goethe que Fauriel avait traduite de l'allemand, l'autre d'une analyse de Fauriel lui-même, furent ainsi mises, en France, à la portée des romantiques toujours en quête de nouveaux modèles, et particulièrement tendres à ceux qui portaient la marque de l'étranger. . . . La traduction de ces deux drames tout moderns 'les plus beaux,' dit Sainte-Beuve, 'qui aient été produits en Europe entre 1815 et 1830,' les mettant mieux à la portée du public français, fomenta les critiques passionnées des classiques" (185). (Manzoni's two tragedies [*Adelchi, The Count of Carmagnola*], one preceded by Goethe's analysis translated from the German by Fauriel, the other by Fauriel's own analysis, were thus put within reach of the Romantics in France who were always in search of new models, and were particularly receptive to those which bore a foreign stamp. . . . The translation of these two very modern plays, "the most beautiful," according to Sainte-Beuve, "that had been produced in Europe between 1815 and 1830," which put them within reach of the French public, served to stir up the impassioned criticism of the classics.) In response to the debate fueled

in part by his verse tragedies Manzoni wrote his famous letter to M. Chauvet: "Dans cette lettre, Manzoni, bien avant le célèbre 'Manifeste' de Victor Hugo, avec moins de bruit e plus de mesure, s'élève contre le despotisme des règles" (187). (In this letter, Manzoni, well before Victor Hugo's celebrated "Manifesto," with less noise and more measure, rises up against the despotism of the rules [of classical tragedy].) Unless otherwise indicated, translations from French and Italian are mine.

[2] The oft-encountered claim that *I promessi sposi* is the first Italian novel is, of course, not true. Both in Manzoni's time and in the two centuries preceding his, novels had been published in abundance in Italy, especially in the latter part of the eighteenth century, when in addition to novels by Italian writers, such as the prolific Pietro Chiari, there were many translations of French and English novels. However, these were not considered literary or artistic works. The intended reading public did not usually include that more refined segment of the population that read poetry or philosophical and scientific treatises. What needed to be done was to bridge the gap between these classes of readers and their respective literatures. Manzoni's novel was the first that succeeded in being literary and popular (and national) both in its content and in its language. For a more detailed account of how his novel constructs such a bridge between the literary elite and the popular see "Manzoni's 'Twenty-five Readers': The Other Betrothal in *I promessi sposi*" in this book. For a historical account of the novel in Italy see Gino Raya, *Il romanzo,* and the revealing studies of Albert Mancini on the Baroque novel in Italy.

[3] Later in his life Manzoni recalled with characteristic irony and humor the difficulties he had encountered in writing his novel: "E ci sarebbe da farvi più pietà ancora, se v'avessi a raccontare i travagli ne' quali so essersi trovato uno scrittore non toscano che, essendosi messo a comporre un lavoro mezzo storico e mezzo fantastico, e col fermo proposito di comporlo se ci riuscisse, in una lingua viva e vera, gli s'affacciavano alla mente, senza cercarle, espressioni proprie, calzanti, fatte apposta per i suoi concetti, ma erano del suo vernacolo, o d'una lingua straniera, o per avventura del latino, e naturalmente le scacciava come tentazioni; e di equivalenti, in quello che si chiama italiano, non ne vedeva, mentre le avrebbe dovute vedere, al pari di qualunque altro italiano, se ci fossero state" (in Caretti xxviii). (It would arouse even more pity in you if I were to tell you of the troubles encountered by a non-Tuscan writer who, having started to compose a work based partly on history and partly on fantasy with a firm resolution to compose it, if possible, in a true and living language, would with very little effort come up with correct and appropriate expressions made to order for his ideas; but they would be in his dialect, or in a foreign language, or even in Latin, and naturally

he chased them away as [evil] temptations; and he could not think of what the equivalent expressions would be in that which is called Italian; while he should have been able to find them, just like any other Italian, if they had existed.)

[4] For an account of the evolution of Manzoni's thoughts on language see Barbara Reynolds, *The Linguistic Writings of Alessandro Manzoni.* The monograph on *The Italian Questione Della Lingua* by Robert A. Hall, Jr. is also very useful in giving an account of the age-old problem of what the Italian language is to be and in situating Manzoni's contribution to the debate. See also Professor Hall's article in this book which updates his thinking on the so-called "soluzione manzoniana" (Manzonian solution) to the problem.

[5] Though I translate *âme,* whose primary meaning is "soul," as "mind" in this case, it could also be rendered as the "heart" of the reader. Furthermore, Stendhal is punning with a more technical meaning of the word *âme*: "the sound-post of a violin."

[6] "Ma nella prosa . . . mancavano le condizioni di una riforma: bisognava, come il Manzoni fece, ricominciare daccapo. I pochi lettori del Leopardi potevano, e in certa misura dovevano ritrovare il filo della tradizione. I molti lettori dei *Promessi sposi* erano guidati con mano ferrea guantata di un dole velluto su una via nuova, che era certo la via della nuova Italia, ma, e per ciò stesso, era diversa affatto dalla via vecchia" (98-99). (But in prose the conditions for reform were lacking. It was necessary to start from scratch, as Manzoni did. For the few readers of [the poet] Leopardi it was possible, to a certain degree mandatory, to remain tied to tradition. The many readers of *The Betrothed* were guided by an iron hand gloved in soft velvet onto a new path, which was certainly the path of the new Italy, but which, for this very reason, was completely different from the old path.)

Carolyn Springer

SOURCE: "The Risorgimento Debate: Mazzini and Gioberti," in *The Marble Wilderness: Ruins and Representation in Italian Romanticism, 1775-1850,* Cambridge University Press, 1987, pp. 136-57.

[In the following essay, Springer examines the importance of archaeological metaphors relating to the classical Roman past as part of the nationalist rhetoric of the democratic movement in Italy.]

If the primary strategy of Pio-Clementine and Restoration classicism was to create vast ceremonial spaces in which to display the spoils of recent excavations and proclaim the Pope's exclusive title to the complex legacy of Rome, [Guiseppe] Mazzini and other writers

Giuseppe Mazzini.

of the left dreamed of reclaiming the "marble wilderness" itself as a common ground for the democratic opposition.

In the works of Mazzini and other writers of the "scuola democratica,"[1] and in the works of other European writers sympathetic to the cause of Italian nationalism, the ruins of Rome are repeatedly invoked as a setting for revolutionary action—a transitional topos or "common place" in which to mobilize the scattered forces for Italian unity in preparation for the overthrow of the temporal power.

Recalling the archaeological experiment of the Roman Republic of 1798-9, writers such as Charles Didier—whose novel *Rome souterraine,* published in 1833, was much admired by Mazzini . . . —represent the ruins as the literal rallying point of the people and the site from which to move their assault on the Vatican. In Didier's fictionalized account of a *carbonaro* uprising, the church of San Lorenzo in Miranda, layered into the ruins of the Temple of Antoninus and Faustina at the edge of the Forum, is chosen as the rendezvous and base of operations of the *carbonari;* and it is to this site that the insurgents, having won an abandoned Vatican only to be routed from the Castel Sant'Angelo, retreat for the final siege in which

all but one of them will die, martyrs to the cause of a united Italy.

It is easy to understand why Mazzini, in a review of *Rome souterraine* published in the *Giovine Italia,*[3] applauded the metamorphosis of the ruins into barricades. By reclaiming the ruins as political symbols and deploying them in an "epic" narrative that promised wide popular appeal, Didier's text helped to counter an increasingly mannered "poetry of ruins" which throughout Europe had found in Rome its privileged setting.

Just as [Ugo] Foscolo in the *Sepolcri* had resisted the elegiac tendency of the English sepulchral tradition, both as political orator and literary critic Mazzini tirelessly campaigned against the shallow despair over Italy's fortunes made fashionable by Lamartine—declaring with Giusti to the alleged "terre des morts": "fin le vostre ruine / sono un'apoteosi."[4] It is characteristic of Mazzini's apocalyptically distended vision to move from the focus on the individual sculptural monument (increasingly delicate in Foscolo as he approached *Le grazie*) toward a wide-angle view of the entire monumental complex of Rome; but however that city is transfigured through Mazzini's myth of the "Terza Roma," as an ideal everywhere present in his writings it supplies a unifying image and *center* that had been lacking in Foscolo—. . . .

Where Mazzini, in the tradition of David and other artists of the French Revolution, exploits the full subversive potential of the classical landscape by reclaiming it as the stage for the austere trials of republican virtue—polemically overturning broken bas-reliefs, urns, and sarcophagi and aligning them as improvised barricades, introducing a new and severe visionary order into the picturesque disarray prized by the romantics—[Tommaseo] Gioberti is far less radical in his representation of Rome.

Although he too strategically exploits the archaeological metaphor, his emphasis is not on the actual elaboration of the site but on the hallucinatory display of the *artifact*—that fragile and priceless Italian *primato* lost through centuries of foreign domination.[5]

Where Mazzini develops the imagery of excavation—the search for civic and spiritual ideals long buried under the débris of the ancien régime, the patient shared work of *undermining* the remaining vestiges of that authority through the labyrinth of clandestine organization—Gioberti remains more consistently on the surface, denying the need to "break ground" at all, miraculously resurrecting an object of dubious authenticity from the depths of his own imagination.

In this [essay], devoted to the role of archaeology in the Risorgimento debate, I have chosen to focus on Mazzini and Gioberti because in the period leading up to the events of 1848 they represent the two rival forces most influential in shaping public opinion and enlisting widespread sympathy for the goal of a united Italy. Certainly some measure of their influence is due to the common strategy that I have pointed out here—an archaeological revival of the idea of Rome.

. . . . .

In his *Storia della politica estera italiana dal 1870 al 1896,* Federico Chabod has shown that the idea of Rome was not widely trusted by the left during the early years of the Risorgimento, precisely because of its imperial, papal, and Napoleonic associations.[6] It was largely due to the contribution of Gioberti and Mazzini that by mid-century the idea of Rome had gained sufficient popular appeal to displace its main rival iconography, that of the medieval communes (and signally of Florence), which had been used by writers as diverse as Cattaneo, Sismondi, and D'Azeglio implicitly to illustrate the advantage of a federalist system of government over those of a strongly centralized state.

That even then the question was not fully resolved is clear from Chabod's account of the continued debate during the 1860s on the choice of a capital city for the new Kingdom of Italy. Nonetheless, with the events of 1848-9—and especially Garibaldi's epic defense of the Roman Republic from the Janiculum—the image of Rome, with its rich landscape of *rovine esortatrici,* moved increasingly toward the foreground of nationalist discourse in Italy.

Italian archaeological inquiry was of course not limited to Rome during the first half of the nineteenth century. During the Napoleonic period, the success of such works as Vincenzo Cuoco's *Platone in Italia* (1804-6) and Micali's *L'Italia avanti il dominio dei Romani* (1810)[7] attests to a polemical revival of interest in pre-Roman civilizations, which like the cult of the medieval communes attempted to divert attention from the centralizing image of Rome by reconstructing the annals of previous civilizations assimilated by Rome during its conquest of the peninsula.

Where Cuoco's novel, in the tradition of Barthelemy's *Voyage du jeune Anarcharsis en Grèce,* was a freewheeling archaeologico-political fantasy whose only claim to historical authenticity was the purely formal conceit of the "found manuscript,"[8] Micali's study, despite the paucity of empirical evidence to support his theory, presented itself as a serious scientific treatise, complete with an erudite apparatus largely improvised to support his premise of a network of highly developed and differentiated autochthonous civilizations anterior to the Roman conquest.

That Micali himself did not fully anticipate or intend the politically subversive impact of his *Storia* as the century progressed does not alter its effective status as a prototypical narrative of resistance to Rome and an early attempt to rewrite the history of Italy from the perspective of the *vinti.* Although he notes Mazzini's distrust of this "letteratura pelasgica," and mentions Sismondi's concern that by fostering a retrospective resentment of Rome such rhetoric would lead to a devaluation of Italy's classical heritage and an alienation from its most precious moral and mythical resources, Trèves argues that the reaction to Rome was a salutary development, even a necessary condition of the nation's eventual reconciliation with and repossession of Rome: "Only by means of such historical inquiry into its own past could Italy come to understand the dialectical relationship between its classical and universalist heritage and its modern needs as a nation, between the two Romes of yesterday and the third, which it was necessary not to occupy but to create."[9]

Although the nationalistic revival of medieval vocabularies came relatively late to Italian architecture, notably with the work of Camillo Boito in the 1870s and the façade completions of the cathedrals of Florence and Milan,[10] the renewal of interest in the Middle Ages propagated by European romanticism did find expression in the archaeological reconstructions of episodes from Italian history attempted by the *romanzo storico* and history painting of the 1830s and 1840s.[11] Apart from purely sentimental approaches to the theme, such as Diodata Saluzzo's poem "Le rovine," a fantasy inspired by the view of a ruined medieval castle (which nonetheless was celebrated by Di Breme as the prototype of the modern romantic lyric),[12] there did evolve *a contrario,* out of the reactionary cult of the Middle Ages imposed by Restoration pedagogy to erase the memory of Jacobin classicism, that liberal and patriotic revaluation of the medieval communes . . . and whose genesis De Sanctis would recall in his 1866 funeral oration for Massimo D'Azeglio:

> In those days it was fashionable to study the Middle Ages. It was a reaction to the [dangerous example of] Greek and Roman history, to which [the authorities] attributed those revolutionary fantasies which had led us astray. To set us straight they prescribed the study of the medieval period, which represented the grandeur of the papacy and the principle of divine right; they devised a system, half mystical and half feudal, which they intended to be the catechism of the new generation . . .

> But no system . . . can arrest the forces of change. The idea of Italy was already alive in the minds of Italians, and it is the intellect that directs the process of history. D'Azeglio studied the Middle Ages in his own way and joined with other Italian writers. Together they forged a revolutionary image of medieval Italy . . . and it was this that

D'Azeglio represented in his paintings and novels.[13]

After a rapid summary of the episodes and protagonists favored by the new historical novel, De Sanctis concludes:

> This was the image of the Middle Ages forged by Massimo D'Azeglio. Recommended and encouraged by the authorities themselves, the study of medieval history turned against the Restoration and became one of the most effective components of our political regeneration. We searched not for . . . parchments, codices, institutions, and the claims to sovereignty of Popes and Emperors, but the traditions and charter of our own nationality . . . the image and proof of our own courage and grandeur as a people.

(285)

Though conscious of the limits of the medieval commune as a political ideal (for it was structurally more sympathetic to the federalist thesis), Mazzini himself applauded every effort to reconstruct "heroic" episodes from any period in Italian history that might serve as *exempla virtutis* to the present generation. In an essay of 1828, "Del romanzo in generale ed anche dei *Promessi sposi* di Alessandro Manzoni"—his first contribution to the ongoing debate on the validity of the historical novel as a genre—he not only defended its political and pedagogical utility but specifically recommended a medieval thematic:

> We exhort Italians to devote themselves ardently to this genre, and to take their subjects from medieval history, for those centuries, which the ruinous indifference of writers condemned so long to obscurity, are rich in edifying examples and sublime memories.[14]

Mazzini's endorsement of medieval themes in the novel concords with the preference for Hayez expressed in a later commentary on the "Pittura moderna in Italia." There Mazzini judges the most valuable contribution of the neoclassical school of Italian painting to have been the search for archaeological accuracy in the reconstruction of a milieu—a goal accordingly politicized by the medievalizing school of history painting headed by Francesco Hayez, who in his great crowded frescoes of historical events first gave concrete representation to the masses:

> By emphasizing the need for historical and architectural exactitude [the neoclassicists] prepared the way for the school which was to follow . . . [But the history painters] are the Precursors of the Nation's Art, just as the political martyrs are the Precursors of the Nation.[15]

Mazzini's aesthetic does not then exclude medieval themes; his approval of archaeological strategies of representation is conditional only on their progressive political function. Mazzini's primary concern is that the accurate reconstruction of a milieu be remembered as the means, and not the end, of the historical mode. He does not share with a Giacomo Durando that fanatical distrust of history that led the latter, in his 1846 manifesto *Della nazionalità italiana,* to reject every prior archaeological effort to forge a national consciousness as mere "idolatry of the antique"—accusing Dante, Machiavelli, Alfieri, Foscolo, et al., of fatally confusing politics and aesthetics:

> We have proposed to regenerate Italy as if it were a question of restoring a statue of Praxiteles, a text of Aristotle or of Cicero, without taking into consideration that what is "true and beautiful" in an aesthetic sense seldom varies, whereas what is "true and beautiful" in a social and political sense depends on the historical and geographical context. Art has become a tyrant among us . . . Art is destroying us.[16]

Yet Mazzini is fully aware of the dangers of encouraging any inquiry into the past that is not directed by and anchored in an immediate and creative concern for the future. In the spirit of Renaissance humanism as characterized by Thomas M. Greene,[17] Mazzini understands archaeology to be useful only insofar as it implies a "latent pressure on the present and future": the "will to form" that motivates his historical imagination is a dynamic and prospective force, alien to any retrospective or archaizing brand of classicism oriented toward the restoration of a static ideal.

Gioberti's *Primato,* with its promise of the literal restitution of the natural and inalienable title of "primogenito delle nazioni" to the Italian people, was certainly more deserving of Durando's skepticism than Mazzini's abstract and idealistic archaeology. In the following pages I will further question the function of archaeological imagery in the discourse of these two figures, and consider the measure in which it shapes their contrasting modes of representing the "Italian question" in the years leading up to 1848. I do not pretend to provide a more general presentation or critique of the political thought of either figure; as I mentioned earlier, my discussion of Gioberti will be deliberately limited to a single text, the *Primato morale e civile degli italiani* (1843), whereas most of my references to Mazzini will be culled from a series of essays which as part of his ongoing *critica militante* develop the imagery of archaeology in particularly striking ways.[18]

. . . . .

Any discussion of Gioberti's use of archaeology would have to begin by focusing on his "Esortazione ai colti giovani italiani," an explicit appeal to renew the study of classical antiquity in order to refresh the present generation's awareness of the dignity of its origins.

In this chapter of the *Primato* Gioberti deplores in general the neglect of archaeological inquiry in a region like Italy, naturally its privileged terrain:

> Italy and Greece are the two parts of Europe which contain the greatest relics of a past civilization, and rest on the ruins of an ancient world which was built and destroyed by the industry and barbarity of men. It is deplorable that there are so few Italians today desirous of studying their country's own ruins, and that this sort of inquiry, regarded as useless, is left to a handful of learned antiquarians.[19]

More specifically Gioberti recommends the revival of such study for its salutary effect on the young. The ritual contemplation of ruins represents in fact the climax of an austere pedagogical program that he proposes in order to remedy the corruption of Italy's present educational system. The "majesty of ruins" is a spectacle reserved for the highest grade of the initiate, who having honed their moral sensibilities through tireless mortification of the flesh ("let them harden their bodies to the hot sun, to the fatigue of running and other gymnastic exercises . . . let them eat frugally, sleep on a hard bed, and subject the body in every respect to the domination of the mind"), and trained their spiritual faculties through solitary communion with nature at its most "sublime" ("let them contemplate . . . divinity . . . in the cool shade, amid the rustling leaves of the forest, or . . . on the high and serene mountain passes"), will finally be prepared, in the contemplation of ruins, to accomplish that spiritual ascent enabling man to "climb against the current of years and centuries to the divine and mysterious source in which all originates."

But archaeology is more than a private spiritual exercise. To each nation as a whole, ruins represent an archive, a repository of information and concrete mode of access to its unwritten history. In a page that Mazzini could only have underscored, Gioberti develops this concept:

> Ruins are like the fossils of extinct nations and civilizations, and perpetuate the ages which have passed, representing their history in vivid and concrete form; indeed, the annals of more than one nation could be deduced from the description of its ruins. To write a history of Greece, Italy, or Spain based on the study of its ruins alone would be a challenging task, worthy of an eloquent philosopher.

From an awareness of history comes the power to shape the future; hence the creative and prospective nature of archaeology as a human science:

> Archaeology, no less than philology, far from being a sterile and moribund science, is a lively and exceedingly fertile discipline; for in addition to renewing the past, it serves to prepare the future of nations. Since the resurrection of a nation's monuments restores the very idea of its identity, it joins a nation's past with its future, and serves . . . to unite resurgent peoples, awakening and keeping their hopes alive . . .

In a passage that inevitably recalls the argument of the *Sepolcri* and the democratic view of ruins as a "common place" in which to mobilize a patriotic opposition, Gioberti declares:

> Therefore ruins often serve as the gathering-place of dispersed generations, and ensure the survival of cultures which have been suppressed and overthrown: scattered or crushed by force or by violence, even if they have been stripped of their name and language, these nations live on forever in the monuments of their ancestors.

Just as a single fallen column, in Gioberti's semiology of ruins, signifies survival rather than decay, the more complex image of a stratified monumental ruin site attests not to the violence of human history but to the overt presence of a providential plan: a "divine teleology of nations" that guarantees the preservation of one civilization through the temporary superimposition of another. This is the logic to be read in the apparently random movements of migrating tribes:

> . . . famous ruins serve to determine the patterns of migrating peoples and tribes . . . Thus it happens that several distinct civilizations converge on one site, and that one city rises on the ruins of another . . . Therefore I believe that monuments of all kinds are preserved not by chance but through a divine teleology of nations; and that a building which has survived the ravages of time and the violence of men is never a useless heap of bricks and stones.

It is the aura surrounding the monuments of the past that makes their study so valuable to the young, particularly in a period of moral and political upheaval:

> Ancient monuments are often more important than modern ones; especially when they are related to political history, and can renew the national consciousness of a people. Therefore educated young Italians would be wise not to ignore the ruins of their own country. Like the scholars who have patiently reconstructed ancient monuments, either lost or legendary, such as Achilles' shield, the tombs of Ozymandias and Porsena, the sarcophagi of Ephestius and Alexander, the labyrinth of Egypt, etc.; young Italian scholars, examining their own nation's history, should renew the most hallowed of its ancient traditions, *restoring not its fora, amphitheaters, and baths,*

but the unity, force, and grandeur of the ancient Italian nation. (Emphasis added)

Mazzini himself could have found little to quarrel with in this generic invocation of the archaeological metaphor in support of a patriotic discourse. Yet to distinguish his use of the metaphor from that of Gioberti, one need only consider the nature of those institutions in which Gioberti saw the "unity, force, and grandeur of the ancient Italian nation" to reside.

Although he implies the exclusion of Austria from a future confederation of Italian states,[20] Gioberti's proposal of a "return to origins" otherwise amounts to little more than an elaborate apology of the existing power structure in Italy. His famous theory of the two components of the Italian national character (elaborated in I, 179 ff.) provides an ingenious "genetic" explanation of the split between lay princes and papacy that revaluates that duality as the sole possible structuring principle of national unity:

> The unique character of Italians in matters of government results from the fusion of two components: one of which is natural, Pelasgic, Doric, Etruscan, Latin, and Roman, and derives from the racial stock and its primitive traditions; and the other supernatural, modern, Christian, Catholic, and Guelph, which results from beliefs and institutions which have taken root in Italy over the past fifteen centuries, and become second nature to the inhabitants of the Peninsula. These two elements, both distinctly Italian—though the first is civic and secular, the second religious and hieratic in nature—harmonize with each other; for inasmuch as they are logically simultaneous and chronologically successive, they complement each other, and correspond to the two great periods in our history before and after Christ, and to the two most powerful and admirable Italian institutions . . . that is, the Latin empire born from the Etruscan and Pelasgic civilization, and the civil dictatorship of the Pope in the Middle Ages . . . Both of these elements, native to Italy and Tuscan and Roman in origin, permeate every part of our political existence, through an elective aristocracy, the natural counselor and auxiliary of the princes . . . and a hieratic authority which presides over and unifies the individual governments, and is the governing principle of ecclesiastical society. Therefore popular governments are not appropriate to the institutions of the Peninsula . . .

Despite the apparent audacity of his proposal that the Pope be appointed head of a league of lay princes, the implications of Gioberti's neoguelph restoration are deeply conservative. The theme of the providential continuity between classical and Christian Rome, a bulwark of the Vatican's own apology of the temporal power, has merely been extended to the entire peninsula and made the basis of a triumphal characterization of a fixed national character, which provides a retrospective, pseudo-scientific sanction to the two forms of authority surviving in Italy but denies the emergence of that third force, the Popolo, which had recently found its spokesman in Mazzini.

The "Popolo" is only an abstraction, a chimera, argues Gioberti in implicit polemic with Mazzini. It can not be considered one of the raw materials of a national Risorgimento because it is an entity nowhere to be found in Italian political precedent. And Gioberti's own greatest strength, according to his pseudo-Machiavellian parenthesis of I, 118 ff. ("Scusa dell'autore se entra a discorrere di cose di Stato"), is his prudence in matters of politics:

> for I venture neither to fabricate new orders, nor to create the slightest new social entity; I have attempted only, with the greatest caution, to suggest the best possible arrangement among those elements which are already in existence.

In more explicit polemic with Mazzini, he warns in the "Esortazione agli esuli italiani" that nothing is more damaging to the cause of national unity than the exhortation to violence. The "intemperate doctrines" learned while in exile will never find widespread support in Italy; they can lead only to abortive revolutions and renewed governmental repression. Such setbacks are the more to be regretted because they derive from the imitation of foreigners (especially the French) and could be avoided by a realistic recognition of the Italian national temper: "because democratic, tumultuous, and licentious doctrines are contrary to our national character."

Elsewhere Gioberti is even more blunt in his rejection of a democratic alternative as both unworkable and undesirable in Italy:

> I believe the maxim to be extremely wise which says that everything possible should be done *for* the people, but nothing or very little *through* their participation; for the worst of all governments, and the one most contrary to the interests of all, is that of the people.

Not by imitating the error of the French—whose many heresies, political and religious, he condemns at length (I, 189 ff. and passim)—but by conforming to the precedents of their *own* history, will the Italians realize their unique and privileged destiny among nations. An impressive vocabulary is enlisted to support the ethnographic end of this argument: "Imitation is all the more repugnant to us, because our Pelasgic lineage is the ruling stock of the great Giapetic family of the Indogermanic branch . . ." (I, 187). But the defense of the *primato* concept returns inevitably to the archaeological metaphor, as he concludes:

Therefore, since the present is rooted in the past, the Italian statesman must have a broad and profound understanding of history, we might say of the *political archaeology of the nation* . . . (Emphasis added)

If Gioberti reserves his greatest scorn for the imitators of the "cosmopolitans" and "foreigners," seduced by every novelty, he warns too against the possible abuses of archaeology. The peculiar irony of what he calls the "ghibelline heresy" is its anachronistic attempt to return to pagan origins long since superseded and transvalued by the Church. Gioberti cites such figures as Cola di Rienzo, Arnaldo da Brescia, and Machiavelli himself as victims of a single "magnanimous error": a naïve enthusiasm for the study of classical antiquity that divorced them from Christian principles and led them to seek Italy's redemption in a literal restoration of its pagan past.

By ignoring the mediating tradition that had preserved ancient Rome and fulfilled its prefigured destiny, such men invited their own destruction; for they moved to sever the first component of the national character (Etruscan, Pelasgic, Roman, etc.) from the second which had preserved, nurtured, and perfected it. Gioberti's own polemic was not as anachronistic as it might first seem: Arnaldo da Brescia, here so heavily censured, was the hero of Giovanni Battista Niccolini's tragedy of the same year (1843).

Against the parable of such deluded antiquarians Gioberti envisions himself a successful Aesculapius— healing, restoring, re-membering the fragments of Italy's past by mustering every icon and emblem, however decrepit, in the service of a vast rhetorical synthesis. In his attempt to rally the broadest possible range of support among moderates and conservatives, he raises not only the sacred effigy of the Pope ("Doge and standard-bearer of the Italian confederation, paternal arbiter and peacemaker in Europe . . . spiritual father of the human race, heir and guardian of the grandeur of the Latin people," III, 262); but also the standard of the Piedmontese House of Savoy ("Della casa di Savoia e sue lodi," I, 132 ff.) and a host of lesser devices representing each of the surviving indigenous dynasties on Italian soil.

Throughout the *Primato* he is patiently solicitous of these private interests, assuring the princes that the unity of Italy will be accomplished "without wars, without revolutions, without offense to any rights, public or private" (II, 90); for it depends simply on the restoration of an established network of legitimate authorities.

"Certain utopians recommend the overthrow of the social order as a remedy for the current situation in Italy"; yet on the contrary, Gioberti claims, "the concepts of property and the inequality of fortunes are inseparable from all political life and from the laws of our own nature" (II, 215). The emphasis on *diritti* rather than *doveri* is obviously calculated; unlike Mazzini, Gioberti promises to salvage all and sacrifice nothing; and to reassure the new reigning house of Savoy he explains carefully:

> It is not a question of innovation, but simply of reviving an idea which is Italian, Catholic, and ancient in origin; and of implementing it peacefully, in the best interests of all, without offending . . . the rights of any individual.
>
> (I, 140)

Finally Gioberti argues that the reintegration of a fragmented Italy is only a prelude to the reintegration of Europe as a whole, divided against itself since the Protestant schism. In a passage reminiscent of Angelo Mai's oration he orients his public toward the far horizon of heterodoxy, praising the ongoing missionary work of the Church and promising a renewed Catholic crusade to the Orient as the ultimate goal and reward of an Italian *risorgimento*.

. . . . .

In his essentially encomiastic scheme and informing promise to preserve rather than subvert the present power structure of Italy, it is easy to discern the limits of Gioberti's archaeology. But it would be naïve to underestimate the extraordinary appeal of his *Primato* during the years immediately following its publication.[21] If his program for the union of Italy represents little more than a sanguine *description* of her composite features, we must nonetheless recognize the success of this very rhetorical strategy.

His approach to the question of Rome is a case in point. Though repeatedly throughout the *Primato* he returns to the image of Rome as eternal city, a phoenix continually reborn from its own ashes (I, 79), the fulcrum and cornerstone of Italian stability and (in yet another archaeological metaphor) the guardian of its Vestal fire (I, 78), it is only in the context of a panoramic review of Italian geography that he fully develops the crucial panegyric of Rome.

Gioberti's sketch of a "moral geography" of Italy (III, 159-93) is calculated to disarm regional resistance to Rome by framing the monumental image of Saint Peter's within a triumphal rhetorical tour of the entire peninsula that skillfully promotes the illusion of unity through the very description of diversity. Gioberti's stated premise is that "variety does not compromise the principle of unity . . . but on the contrary contributes to produce it." This applies particularly to a region like Italy, where a "genetic" predisposition to order naturally facilitates the harmonious integration of opposites:

. . . the Pelasgic race . . . is the one which is richest, most capable and best suited to unite all the ethnographic varieties and contradictions in a harmonious fashion, just as the ideal and apparent oppositions in the supreme Being are harmonized.

By virtue of its very diversity, Italy becomes in Gioberti's view not only a microcosm of Europe ("la sintesi e lo specchio di Europa") but an image of the Cosmos ("la più viva immagine del Cosmo"). By elevating Italy's geographic, ethnic, and political heterogeneity to a sign and precondition of its *primato* Gioberti disarms the opposition and smoothly paves his rhetorical path to Rome.

A practical advantage of his conciliatory mode is that on this rhetorical journey not even Florence need present an obstacle. Although he concedes that it is unusual to find two cities so close together, yet with such highly developed and distinct traditions, he is unwilling to admit any antagonism between them; even historically he characterizes their relationship as one of alternating hegemony and mutual regeneration rather than conflict.

In a favorite spatial metaphor that he frequently opposes to the circle (seen, like the geographical configuration of France, to imply all the dangers of excessive centralization), he describes Florence and Rome as the "two foci of the Italian ellipse" (179), logically sharing the function of directing the destinies of the peninsula. But their peaceful coexistence is ironically dependent on the surpassing prestige of Rome; if "Roma e Firenze fanno moralmente una sola metropoli," this is possible only because Rome so clearly prevails:

> as the sacred and cosmopolitan city, privileged seat of the Idea, guardian of doctrinal principles, archive of origins, throne of the priesthood, court of religion, and hence the city which inspires and directs all thought and action which proceed from the driving force of religion.
>
> (173)

Gioberti's formal "Elogio di Firenze" (175-7), complete with its tribute to the city's distant Etruscan origins, is then an impatient prelude to the acclamation of Rome (177-82). After a passing reproach to the "fiera e ingegnosa plebe romanesca," which through its archaic spirit of resistance to authority retarded the rise of the Church and with it the work of Italian unification (178), Gioberti admits:

> Yet in the case of Rome, all that is truly needed to excite and occupy the admiration of men is the hieratic, cosmopolitan, and monumental city. Whoever travels from Tuscany to Rome, passing through Umbria, already in the region of the upper

Tiber begins to sense the proximity of the sacred city . . .

And in his own version of the "entry into Rome" topos ("Ecco Roma!"), central to the genre of the travel narrative, he declares:

> If a learned German has compared Venice to an enormous ship anchored to the floor of the Adriatic, we may compare the seven-hilled city, which rises above the majestic silence of its *campagna,* to an immense pyramid rising in the midst of the desert.

This "desert" is neither the "vuota insalubre region" decried by Alfieri and a generation of Enlightenment intellectuals pressing for reform in the Papal States, nor the melancholy retreat favored by a certain romantic sensibility, but a sparkling visual setting for a monumental city that is the "privileged seat of the sublime." For Gioberti, in fact, Rome with its maze of ruins and monuments is a spectacular image of *order*:

> Rome . . . as a Christian and cosmopolitan city, resembles the monad of Leibniz; and its representative of the universe, whose various components it unites and expresses, not in the disorderly fashion of eclectic philosophy, but as harmoniously distinct, and governed by the principle of *creation*.

Incarnating this principle is of course the Pope,

> who fashioned the new city from the ruins of the ancient metropolis, and built one city on top of the other, just as God shaped our earth from the remains of an earlier globe, whose ruins are buried in the viscera of the mountains.

Noting that Gibbon himself praised the efforts of the popes to restore and preserve pagan monuments (and ignoring the parallel tradition of papal vandalism of ruins), Gioberti concludes:

> Therefore the ruins of pagan culture are scattered amidst the Christian monuments, and form a city of the dead which is intermingled with the city of the living, but subservient to it: for the principle of Christianity triumphs in Rome, and embracing all things in the power of its vast synthesis distributes and orders all things in their appropriate place.
>
> (179)

Gioberti clearly takes his distance from Gibbon, and from every other writer who had read in the Roman landscape the decadence of classical civilization (or indeed, of Italian civilization as a whole) when he envisions, even from the depths of the "città sotterranea e sepolcrale," the indistinct splendors of a "metropoli futura":

> A learned Englishman of the last century who chanced to hear, as he sat on the Capitoline, Christian psalms rising from the temple of Jupiter, began to reflect on the decline and fall of this long ruined empire, and resolved to reconstruct its history. It gives me greater pleasure to perceive in the solemnity of Christian Rome *a new order which is approaching,* and to announce its advent and greet its arrival. Hail, *oh Rome, city of memories, but even more of our hopes,* for you alone bear the seed of the unity of Italy and of the world . . . Located in the center of Italy, you are the common meeting-ground [*comune ritrovo*] of all her children; arriving from the north and south, from the mountains and the seacoasts, they come together in your womb: and there, speaking your language, they recognize their fellow countrymen, and blessed by the father, embrace as brothers. (Emphasis added)

. . . . .

The edifying parable, prophetic tone, and "comune ritrovo" theme inevitably recall Mazzini; but Mazzini's Third Rome would have risen on the ruins of the papacy. This is in fact the one reproach that qualifies his otherwise favorable review of Didier's *Rome souterraine* that I mentioned at the outset of this [essay].

Although Mazzini is grateful for Didier's solidarity with the Italian cause and congratulates the author for having created, in his character of Anselmo, a protagonist capable of representing that Popolo which he himself regarded as the sole possible source of Italy's redemption, Mazzini argues that the objective limit of Didier's political vision is his attachment to the persistent mirage of the papacy—by which Anselmo, in his maneuvers as double agent for the *carbonari* and *sanfedisti,* is fatally deceived.

Anselmo's continued fascination for the papacy is chiefly explained in the novel by the charismatic presence of the Cardinal de Pétralie—a Julien Sorel figure and "bâtard de la Sicile" grimly, ecstatically determined to rise from his humble origins to the office of pope—and like Julien a skillful *comédien,* secretly patterning his own meteoric career on a text (here, the biography of Sixtus V).[22] Nonetheless, Mazzini insists— a decade before Gioberti's *Primato* and the election of Pius IX—that the Pope will never play a role in the unification of Italy.

The neoguelph illusion from which Anselmo never manages to free himself thus represents for Mazzini the one reactionary tendency in Didier's novel. The ideological limits of Anselmo are those of *carbonarismo*

in general. As an ideal "type" of the emerging Popolo Anselmo is flawed, incomplete:

> For Anselmo, born of the people (like the *carbonaro* movement itself) has no faith in the people; though he glimpses the republican destiny of Italy, he looks to the papal tiara to provide a sanction for that destiny . . . : between the People and God, the sole terms of the future, this man of little faith introduces a third term which the century will discard.

(390)

Extending to the *carbonari* in general, for their lack of a coherent political program and willingness to compromise with the Church for the expulsion of Austria, a reproach that he repeatedly leveled against a nostalgic "poetry of ruins,"[23] Mazzini concludes that Anselmo,

> wandering among the sublime ruins of Rome, fell in love with the sun which was setting . . . He prostrated himself before that setting sun, and allured by the dream of restoring the ruins, was unable to distinguish the last ray cast by a dying institution from the first ray which shines from a third world still invisible.

(390-1)

If *carbonarismo* was historically unprepared to witness that "primo raggio" ("That first ray will come; but it will rise to illuminate a council, not a conclave . . ."), it nevertheless began the labyrinthine work of subverting the present power structure through its obscure maze of mines and countermines—the "catacombes politiques" traced by Didier in an effort to explain the unlikely collaboration of *carbonari* and *sanfedisti* in a novel pledged to historical verisimilitude:

> Italy, as we have said, is like ancient Egypt a land of mysteries and initiations. Its entire terrain is volcanic; thrones tremble there like the earth itself; when its surface is calm and carpeted with flowers that is perhaps the very moment when a mine will explode. In this vast subterranean network of mines and countermines which intersect in the darkness and undermine the foundations of the Italian dynasties, it often happens that one man's work aids another; but it is also common that, meeting underground as at the seige of Tortona, the miners stain the shadows with their blood.

(81)

One can not help recalling the extraordinary elaboration of this theme in Hugo's chapter, "Les mines et les mineurs," in *Les misérables* (1862). To cite just a brief portion of it here:

There are all sorts of excavations beneath the edifice of society . . . there is the religious mine, the philosophical mine, the political mine, the economic mine, the revolutionary mine. One man uses an idea to cleave the rock; another is armed with numbers, another with his anger, and they call to and answer each other from the catacombs. Utopias move in these subterranean channels and ramify in all directions; they meet at times and fraternize. Jean Jacques lends his pick to Diogenes, who lends him his lantern in turn; at times, though, they fight, and Calvin clutches Socinus by the hair. But nothing arrests or interrupts the tension of all their energies toward the object . . . Society hardly suspects this excavation, which leaves no traces on its surface and yet changes its entrails. So many subterranean levels, so many different works and varying extractions. What issues from all these profound trenches?—the future.[24]

Mazzini's own rhetoric is equally melodramatic. After congratulating Didier for his discovery of the "true" Italy ("l'Italia invisibile—l'Italia sotterranea"), he further strains the metaphor of a politico-religious "underground" by portraying the Popolo itself as a buried icon, a mystical artifact soon to be excavated and unveiled:

> The youth of Italy glimpsed their nation's own destiny, and drew near to see this destiny revealed. Incautious tyranny had prepared the moment by striking at the veils and symbols which swathed the sacred image of Italy's future, jealously guarded in Italy's subterranean depths. The new generation stripped off the last veil, and the *Word,* the secret of Italy appeared. It was the *People.*

(388)

It was because *carbonarismo* was unready for this revelation that Mazzini considers Didier's text a "historical" novel: a tribute and epitaph to the movement with a useful commemorative function, but itself an inadequate representation of the ongoing political struggle in Italy. This explains his later request to George Sand, in a letter of 1843, to write a novel that would glorify the Giovine Italia as Didier's *Rome souterraine* had the *carbonari,* by portraying "une Italie souterraine qui serait non l'épitaphe de la vieille et réactionnaire Italia . . . mais l'hymne du rajeunissement."[25]

If Mazzini judged Anselmo's attempted rapprochement between the *carbonari* and *sanfedisti* to be a particularly dangerous form of political collaboration, he did believe it necessary for the Giovine Italia to work closely with other sects both in Italy and throughout Europe. One of the unusual features of his program was in fact the requirement that all members of the Giovine Italia belong to other sects as well, in order to

direct the older organizations toward its new set of goals. This labyrinth of clandestine activity was complex and not easily penetrated; there were many cul-de-sacs and false leads, and much shifting terrain. But Mazzini's "catacombes politiques" were not the *Carceri* of Piranesi, full of blind staircases and deliberately skewed perspectives. The entire clandestine structure he helped to create was founded on the goal of communication ("On s'appelle et on se répond d'une catacombe à l'autre"); and his monumental city, the "Third Rome," would have shared none of Piranesi's sinister spatial humor.

Given the interest of Didier's *Rome souterraine* not only to Mazzini but to Garibaldi himself as a novelist, it may be helpful to examine the text very briefly here. On the whole the book reads like a revisionary topography of Rome; the table of contents, with its catalogue of monumental sites, would have looked familiar to any dilettante on a classical tour. But Didier's strategy is to exploit each of these settings as a contemporary frame for heroic action, as if by their historical and mythical associations monumental sites could indeed inspire "monumental" deeds (Foscolo's "egregie cose").

Since Didier's characters are constantly on the move, circulating throughout the city and outlying *campagna* in a continuing effort to communicate with and mobilize their fellow conspirators while avoiding detection themselves, the author is able (without abandoning all claim to verisimilitude) to range freely throughout the city of Rome, accompanying his characters like the crow in Pasolini's *Uccellacci e uccellini,* pursuing them tirelessly with edifying commentary on each Roman landmark that crosses their path. If this technique would be less successful today, Mazzini testifies to its popularity at the time ("Reviewers have long noted the many admirable qualities of Didier's novel . . . local color reproduced with marvellous accuracy, lively descriptions, erudition introduced without pedantry into the course of the action," p. 385). A tolerance for such intrusive archaeological narration had certainly been prepared in part by the diffusion of the *roman pédagogique,* at least since Barthélemy's *Anarcharsis.* In any case my point here is not to defend Didier's narrative technique but to suggest that his strategic focus on certain landmarks of the ancient city contributed to an Italian revision of the possibilities of Rome.

. . . . .

To retrace each character's complicated itineraries is not necessary here; but it may be useful to sketch the basic camps into which Didier's Rome is divided.

The locus of power is clearly represented by the Vatican (finally spared from destruction by the invading *carbonari* only through the intervention of Remo, the artist of the group: "Brûler les Loges de Raphael et la Transfiguration! . . . Brûler le Laocoön! Le Jugement dernier de Michel-Ange! Brûler l'Apollo du Belvedere! Sacrilège! Sacrilège! Sommes-nous donc des incendiaires? Que dirait l'Italie? Que dirait le monde?", 346-7); the Quirinal (seat of the Conclave and retreat of the Pope during the insurrection, 190 ff.), the Palazzo Madama (headquarters of the papal police, to whom Antonia, the jealous mistress of one of the insurgents, denounces the conspiracy, 157 ff.); and, ironically, the Piazza del Popolo (where Marius "le Trasteverin" is executed, like Arnaldo da Brescia before him, his scaffold erected at the base of the papal obelisk, 332).

The primary locus of the opposition, instead, is the Forum. Though forced to hide most of their men in the medieval tower of Astura, on the coast at a short distance from Rome, the *carbonari* base their military operations in the Forum itself. One early convocation in the Velabrum is foiled, as we have seen, by the jealous Antonia; but the conspirators escape through an underground passageway unknown to the police (165 ff.).

The Baths of Caracalla are the rendezvous of Anselmo and Marius the intransigent republican; here they debate political strategy while awaiting the decision of the Conclave. The Tomb of Bibulus (a plebeian aedile of the first century B.C.) is the scene of Marius's harangue to the Roman people following the election of the new pope; Didier supplies the entire Latin inscription to help us follow the impassioned epigraphy of this Rienzo reincarnate, who points to the words "Senatus Consulto Populique Iussu" as incontrovertible proof of the natural sovereignty of the Roman people (240).

To each of the principal characters is assigned a separate hill, commanding a distinct perspective of Rome, on which to confess his private life and political ideals. Marius chooses Monte Sacro (site of the popular revolt of 394 B.C. that resulted in the concession of the tribunes) as the site of his sunrise farewell to Anselmo (269 ff.). The Cardinal de Pétralie as a cleric prefers the right bank, and arranges to meet Anselmo on Monte Mario at sunset (118 ff.). Anselmo himself selects the overgrown gardens of the Villa Farnese on the Palatine, with its view of the Forum, as the site of his interview with the Cardinal (289).

But the action naturally climaxes in the Forum itself. Bombarded by papal cannon from the Palatine and surprised from the rear by the entry of enemy troops through their secret escape route, the *carbonari* besieged in the "maison du Forum" are swiftly massacred; but each dies crying "Vive l'Italie!" and the narrator, surveying the wreckage, concludes, "Jamais le Forum, ce vieux champ de bataille des Gracques,

des Barbares et des guerres civiles du moyen âge, jamais il n'avait vu une si épouvantable mêlée" (354).

Anselmo alone survives the attack and is left to find a hiding place till nightfall allows him to return safely home. Ironically, it is the Colosseum that affords greatest anonymity; though his meditations there are soon interrupted by the arrival of no less than the mother of Napoleon ("Si cette femme isolée n'était pas la Niobe des nations," the narrator remarks, echoing Byron's phrase, "c'était bien une Niobe comme elle, elle avait à pleurer, elle aussi, bien des enfants, bien des martyrs . . .").

But it is the sight of a procession of penitents in the arena below, praying for the Christian martyrs, that finally restores Anselmo's faith in the revolution, as he declares to the Capuchin monk who has come to console him on the death of his comrades: "Ce que les chrétiens étaient pour la Rome de Néron, nous le sommes, nous, pour la Rome du Vatican." The idyllic landscape of ruins ("le temps était splendide, les ruines toutes parfumées de fleurs sauvages . . ."), through the timely superimposition of a Christian spectacle, has been reclaimed by Didier's hero as a political symbol of an "avenir reparateur."

. . . . .

A good deal less skillfully Garibaldi, in his novel *Clelia* of 1870,[26] will exploit the same landscape as the setting for a fictionalized account of the Roman uprising of 1867, which had ended in disastrous defeat at the Villa Glori. As if to take up where Didier had left off, he stages the first assembly of his conspirators in the Colosseum itself—a revolutionary arena which, he proudly notes, bears no resemblance to the romantic moonlit ramble of foreign visitors to Rome ("It is customary for foreigners to visit the Colosseum by moonlight—but it should be seen on a black and stormy night—lit by lighting—rocked by thunder—and resounding with deep and unearthly echoes," II).

That such a public place, in the heart of the papal city, can afford safe rendezvous for three hundred conspirators, is due (the narrator explains) to the obscurantism of the clergy itself, which by fostering superstition and fear has created within its own walls an enclave for the opposition, a desert within the city abandoned at nightfall not only by the populace but by the priests themselves (13). Thus the single pair of papal guards who venture forth to investigate the gathering take flight at first sight of the conspirators, appropriately mistaking them for ghosts of the ancient Romans.

"It was a dark night—and huge black clouds were gathering over the holy city—blown by a violent scirocco wind . . ." The scene is set for the arrival of the Three Hundred, "wrapped in loose robes that looked like togas in the flickering light." Silently they file into the sole remaining loggia of the Colosseum: "No thrones, no tapestries adorned the enclosure.—(What use were ornaments to those who had pledged to die?)—The ruins were their walls, their rostrum and gallery" (12).

Their leader Attilio has only begun to address the conspirators when the ceremony is interrupted by a violent storm and the sudden apparition of a disheveled young woman, stumbling into the middle of the arena. "Povera Camilla!" exclaims the gallant Silvio, as she shrieks and faints in his arms: for he knows her to have been seduced and abandoned to a *manicomio* by a perfidious priest upon the murder of her illegitimate child . . . and it is her appearance that precipitates the bewildering whirl of events that will make up Garibaldi's novel.

I will not pursue the plot any further except to note that the political topography of the novel continues remarkably parallel to that of Didier. A second convocation in the catacombs beneath the Baths of Caracalla is, like the *carbonaro* reunion of the Velabrum, betrayed to the papal authorities by a spy, leaving the conspirators to disperse at great peril through the streets and ruins of Rome (100 ff.). Again a ruined medieval tower along the coastline serves as shelter for the fugitives (149), while the *campagna* as a whole is portrayed, along with the great marble wilderness of Rome, as the locus of political resistance, "un deserto . . . seminato di macerie" (95), officially belonging to the priests but effectively the asylum of beggars, bandits, and other victims of papal misgovernment.

That Garibaldi's sense of the political implications of archaeology naturally sought more concrete form of expression than the literary text is clear from his campaign during the 1870s to divert the Tiber from the city of Rome, opening a vast new field for excavation and eventually transforming the ancient river bed into an instructive "passeggiata archaeologica."[27]

This audacious proposal, while the cause of some embarrassment to the governing coalition of the Destra, wholly conformed to the heroic scale of the city envisioned by Mazzini—the Third Rome that he had invoked in a famous passage of 1859.[28]

"Venite meco," he began, leading the "giovani d'Italia" on an imaginary archaeological tour of the *campagna* north of Rome. "Seguitemi dove comincia la vasta campagna che fu, or sono tredici secoli, il convegno delle razze, perch'io vi ricordi dove batte il core d'Italia . . ."

Admonishing them that the ground beneath their feet is the "dust of nations," he invites them now to consider the view:

> The vast *campagna* is still and through its lonely wastes breathes a silence that fills the heart with sadness, as if one were wandering through a cemetery. But whoever, nourished by thoughts which have been steeled through hardship, stops in this solitary place in the evening, feels an indistinct murmur of life beneath his feet, which seems the sound of generations that await the command of a vigorous word to arise and repopulate those sites that seem created for a Council of Peoples . . .

With an increasingly hypnotic momentum he urges his listeners on, to a vantage point on the Via Cassia, "among extinguished volcanoes and Etruscan ruins," and gives this command:

> Stop here and gaze as far as you can toward the south and toward the Mediterranean. In the midst of these vast spaces you will glimpse, like a beacon in the ocean, an isolated point, a sign of distant grandeur. Kneel then and worship; for there beats the heart of Italy: there lies ROME in its eternal solemnity. And that eminent point is the Campidoglio of the Christian World. And a few steps away is the Campidoglio of the Pagan World. And those two fallen worlds await a third World, even more vast and sublime, which is being fashioned in the midst of its mighty ruins [*potenti rovine*]. And this is the Trinity of History whose Word is in Rome.

Rome's "potenti rovine" never gave birth to the ideal city of Mazzini. It is hard to guess what structures and spaces he might have invented to replace the broken thrones and altars of Europe. In Rome we can imagine a "Pantheon dell'Umanità" inspired by the visionary geometry of Boullée and Ledoux. Instead we have the Victor Emmanuel monument. Yet Mazzini's Third Rome remains, along with the neoguelph capital of Gioberti, one of the most influential nineteenth-century visions of the city, and illustrates the importance of archaeology to the nationalist rhetoric of the Risorgimento.

Notes

[1] In referring to "democratic" and "liberal" schools of Risorgimento thought, I am adopting the distinction first proposed by De Sanctis in his lectures of 1872-4, published as *La letteratura italiana nel secolo XIX*, II (Bari: Laterza, 1953).

[2] Charles Didier, *Rome souterraine* (Paris: Gosselin, 1841).

[3] "*Rome souterraine* par Charles Didier," originally published in vol. VI of *Giovine Italia*, reprinted in Mazzini's *Scritti editi ed inediti*, I (Imola: Galeati, 1906), pp. 385-92. This edition will be abbreviated henceforth as *S.E.I.*

[4] On Lamartine's "La terre des morts" and Giusti's rebuttal, see my Introduction.

[5] I should note here that this [essay's] discussion of Gioberti will be limited to his *Primato morale e civile degli italiani* (1843), rather than to his later political writings. For as Chabod argues in his *Storia della politica estera italiana dal 1870 al 1896,* I (Bari: Laterza, 1951), "quel che pesò sulla storia d'Italia fu, appunto, il *Primato*" (p. 199, note 2).

[6] Chabod, pp. 190-200.

[7] Vincenzo Cuoco, *Platone in Italia,* 2 vols. (Bari: Laterza, 1924), and Giuseppe Micali, *L'Italia avanti il dominio dei Romani* (Florence: Piatti, 1810).

[8] "The Greek manuscript whose translation I now present to you, oh reader, was discovered by my grandfather in the year 1774, as he dug the foundations for a country house he wished to build on the very site of ancient Eraclea," "Al lettore," I, p. 3.

[9] Piero Trèves, *L'idea di Roma e la cultura italiana del secolo XIX* (Milan: Ricciardi, 1962), pp. 30-1.

[10] See Carroll Meeks, "History of the Façades of the Cathedrals of Florence and Milan," in his *Italian Architecture 1750-1914* (New Haven: Yale University Press, 1966), pp. 220-37.

[11] On romantic history painting, see Fortunato Bellonzi, *La pittura di storia dell'Ottocento italiano* (Milan: Fabbri, 1967), and the exhibition catalogue *Romanticismo storico* (Florence: Centro Di, 1974).

[12] Both the poem and Di Breme's defense, "Intorno all'ingiustizia di alcuni giudizi letterari italiani," are reprinted in Carlo Calcaterra, ed., *I manifesti romantici del 1816* (Turin: U.T.E.T., 1968), pp. 81-124.

[13] De Sanctis, *Nuovi saggi critici* (Naples: Morano, 1888), p. 283.

[14] Mazzini, *S.E.I.,* I, pp. 34-5.

[15] *S.E.I.,* XXI, pp. 272 and 292.

[16] Giacomo Durando, *Della nazionalità italiana* (Lausanne: Bonamici, 1846), pp. 10-11.

[17] Thomas M. Greene, *The Light in Troy* (New Haven: Yale University Press, 1982), especially pp. 220-41.

[18] The bibliography on the Risorgimento is vast; for a general introduction, see Stuart Woolf, *A History of Italy 1700-1860: The Social Constraints of Political Change* (London: Methuen, 1979), which also appeared in an earlier Italian version in *Storia d'Italia,* III (Turin: Einaudi, 1973). Useful anthologies include Franco della Peruta, ed., *Scrittori politici dell'Ottocento* (Milan: Ricciardi, 1969) and the twin volumes edited by Vito Lo Curto, *Gli scrittori cattolici dalla Restaurazione all'Unità* (Bari: Laterza, 1976), and Giovanni Pirodda, *Mazzini e gli scrittori democratici* (Bari: Laterza, 1976). See also Ettore Passerin d'Entrèves, "Ideologie del Risorgimento," in *Storia della letteratura italiana,* ed. E. Cecchi and N. Sapegno VII, (Milan: Garzanti, 1969), pp. 201-413, which provides a particularly helpful bibliographical essay. The most recent major study of the Risorgimento in English is Clara M. Lovett's *The Democratic Movement in Italy, 1830-1976* (Cambridge: Harvard University Press, 1982).

[19] Vincenzo Gioberti, *Del primato morale e civile degli italiani,* 3 vols., ed. Gustavo Balsamo-Crivelli (Turin: U.T.E.T., 1932), I, pp. 205-6. All additional references will be identified as necessary in the text by page number.

[20] Gioberti avoids any explicit criticism of the Austrian presence in Italy in the *Primato,* but he dedicated the work to Silvio Pellico, the martyr of Austrian repression.

[21] The first 1500 copies of the *Primato* were rapidly followed by reprints and Vieusseux proposed a popular edition of 5000 copies. As Balbo wrote to Gioberti: "You are now a leader of a school." (Woolf, p. 343).

[22] The parallels between the two figures are probably not fortuitous; *Le rouge et le noir* was first published in 1830. On Stendhal's novel, see Peter Brooks, *Reading for the Plot: Design and Intention in Narrative* (New York: Alfred A. Knopf, 1984), pp. 62-89.

[23] See especially "Pensieri. Ai poeti del secolo XIX" (1832), *S.E.I.,* I, pp. 349-74; "Dell'arte in Italia, a proposito del *Marco Visconti,* romanzo di Tommaso Grossi" (1835), VIII, pp. 3-65; and "Byron e Goethe" (1840), XXI, pp. 187-241.

[24] Victor Hugo, *Les misérables* (Paris: Gallimard, 1951), pp. 757-8.

[25] George Sand, *Correspondance,* VI, ed. Georges Lubin (Paris: Garnier, 1969), p. 34: cited by Franco Venturi in "L'Italia fuori d'Italia," *Storia d'Italia,* III (Turin: Einaudi, 1973), p. 1362.

[26] Giuseppe Garibaldi, *Clelia: Il governo del monaco (Roma nel secolo XIX)* (Milan: Rechiedei, 1870).

[27] See Gabriele Morolli, "I progetti di Garibaldi per il Tevere," in the exhibition catalogue *Garibaldi: Arte e Storia,* I, pp. 94-112, and Alberto Caracciolo, *Roma capitale: Dal Risorgimento alla crisi dello Stato liberale* (Rome: Editori Riuniti, 1974), pp. 110-18.

[28] "Ai giovani d'Italia," *S.E.I.,* LXIV, pp. 155-215. Part of this passage is cited by Chabod, p. 196.

FURTHER READING

Avitabile, Grazia. *The Controversy on Romanticism in Italy: First Phase 1816-1823.* New York: S. F. Vanni, Publishers, 1959, 145 p.

> Endeavors "to present the basic ideas governing literary romanticism in Italy" by examining the theoretical writings of its adherents.

Barricelli, Jean-Pierre. "Romantic Writers and Music: The Case of Mazzini." *Studies in Romanticism* 14, No. 2 (Spring 1975): 95-117.

> Discusses music in relation to the philosophical theories of Giuseppe Mazzini, and as the romantic art *par excellence.*

Biasin, Gian-Paolo. "In the Primordial Origin of Evening." In *Italian Literary Icons,* pp. 18-47. Princeton, N.J.: Princeton University Press, 1985.

> Considers the new worldview expounded by the Italian Romantics in light of the theoretical work of Francesco Arcangeli and the poetry of Ugo Foscolo.

Brose, Margaret. "Leopardi's 'L'Infinito' and the Language of the Romantic Sublime." *Poetics Today* 4, No. 1 (1983): 47-71.

> Explores Giacomo Leopardi's aesthetic of the sublime and analyzes his poem "L'Infinito" (1819) as "a self-conscious demonstration of lyric transcendence."

Garnett, Richard. "The Revival," "The Regeneration," and "The Nineteenth Century—Middle Period." In *A History of Italian Literature,* pp. 327-93. New York: D. Appleton and Co., 1928.

> Chronological examination of the major figures in nineteenth-century Italian literature.

Kroeber, Karl. "The Reaper and the Sparrow: A Study of Romantic Style." *Comparative Literature* X, No. 3 (Summer 1958): 203-13

> Compares William Wordsworth's "The Solitary Reaper" with Leopardi's "Il passero solitario" in order to define the Romantic mode of representation.

————. *The Artifice of Reality: Poetic Style in Wordsworth, Foscolo, Keats, and Leopardi.* Madison: University of Wisconsin Press, 1964, 235 p.

> Traces developments in the Romantic theory of creativity through the work of four major figures of nineteenth-century English and Italian poetry.

Lovett, Clara M. *The Democratic Movement in Italy, 1830-1876.* Cambridge, Mass.: Harvard University Press, 1982, 285 p.

> A social, political, and cultural history of nineteenth-century Italy.

Silone, Ignazio. *The Living Thoughts of Mazzini.* London: Cassell and Co., 1939, 130 p.

> Critical analysis of Mazzini's political, literary, and theoretical writings.

Singh, G. *Leopardi and the Theory of Poetry.* Lexington: University of Kentucky Press, 1964, 365 p.

> Investigates Leopardi's literary theory and poetic style.

Springer, Carolyn. *The Marble Wilderness: Ruins and Representation in Italian Romanticism, 1775-1850.* Cambridge: Cambridge University Press, 1987, 198 p.

> Analyzes the importance of classical archaeology to the Italian Romantic imagination.

Vittorini, Domenico. "The Nineteenth-Century Novel." In *The Modern Italian Novel,* pp. 8-50. Philadelphia: University of Pennsylvania Press, 1930.

> Includes a discussion of Alessandro Manzoni's contribution to the historical novel and to the Romantic movement in Italy.

The Sentimental Novel

INTRODUCTION

The sentimental novel, also known as the domestic novel, deviated from the literary norms established by such authors as Herman Melville, Henry David Thoreau, and Mark Twain to focus on the intimate details of women's private lives during the nineteenth century. A form of literature which was most popular in early and mid-nineteenth century America, the sentimental novel is traditionally dismissed in literary histories, though works such as Susan Warner's *The Wide, Wide World* (1850), Harriet Beecher Stowe's *Uncle Tom's Cabin* (1852), and Maria Cummins' *The Lamplighter* (1854) were at one time among the most popular publications in American letters.

The sentimental novel has historical roots in Europe, particularly in Samuel Richardson's *Clarissa; or, The History of a Young Lady* (1747-48) and *Pamela; or, Virtue Rewarded* (1740), both of which tell of men seducing virtuous women. American authors in the early nineteenth century replicated and amplified this theme, though later domestic novels expanded the variety of conflicts and protagonists: the unique social, spiritual, political, and economic circumstances of nineteenth-century America conditioned the issues that confronted the female characters and the ways in which such issues were resolved. Sentimental novels appealed primarily to female and middle-class readers who, in colonial and Revolutionary America, were taught to read in order to teach their sons democratic ideals. This idea of influential republican motherhood evolved into the "cult of domesticity," in which women were the guardians of spirituality and virtue, and which is embodied in the domestic novels' morally pure protagonists—such as Little Eva, from *Uncle Tom's Cabin,* and Eliza Wharton, from *The Coquette* (1797).

Sentimental novels are traditionally contrasted with the writings of Melville, Thoreau, and Nathaniel Hawthorne, who exalted individuals who transgress against cultural conventions. The historical identification of the sentimental novel with the "feminization" of American, and especially Southern, culture reinforces the criticism that these works uncritically replicate conventional ideas and values. But the identification of women as protectors of the family links sentimental novelists with abolitionism, which often argued against slavery by noting its destructive impact upon families, and with other political movements such as prohibition. Consequently, some recent critics argue that domestic novels are less formulaic than initially perceived, and have interpreted them as expressions of proto-feminism and as attempts to celebrate the traditional role of women in society.

Despite the common criticism that sentimental fiction portrays an idealized account of domestic life, authors frequently insisted that their stories were grounded in reality, and feminist theorists such as Jane Tompkins and Cathy N. Davidson have challenged the idea that domestic novels are merely romantic and idealistic. Instead, these critics contend that the novels portray issues and characters that were relevant to nineteenth-century women—familial relations, issues of dependence and independence, and definitions of virtue and femininity. Although mundane and conventional behavior frequently dominates the private world represented in the domestic novel, the genre lends insight into both the cult of domesticity and the resistance to that ideal that emerged from the increased education of women under American republicanism.

REPRESENTATIVE WORKS

Louisa May Alcott
  Little Women 1869

Maria Cummins
  The Lamplighter 1854

Martha Finley
  Elsie Dinsmore 1867

Hannah Webster Foster
  The Coquette; or, The History of Eliza Wharton
    1797

Judith Sargent Murray
  Story of Margaretta 1798

Samuel Richardson
  Pamela; or, Virtue Rewarded 1740
  Clarissa; or, The History of a Young Lady. 7
    vols. 1747-48

Susanna Rowson
Charlotte Temple, a Tale of Truth 1794

E. D. E. N. Southworth
The Hidden Hand 1859

Harriet Beecher Stowe
Uncle Tom's Cabin 1852

Susan Warner [Elizabeth Wetherell]
The Wide, Wide World 1850

Augusta Evans Wilson
St. Elmo 1866

S. S. B. K. Wood
Amelia; or, The Influence of Virtue 1802

OVERVIEWS

Alexander Cowie

SOURCE: "The Vogue of the Domestic Novel: 1850-1870," in *South Atlantic Quarterly,* Vol. XLI, No. 4, October, 1942, pp. 416-24.

[*In the following essay, Cowie summarizes common plot elements of nineteenth-century sentimental novels, and argues that they prescribed conservative feminine values.*]

In 1842 William Gilmore Simms referred to Cooper's *Precaution* as "a very feeble work, . . . a second or third rate imitation of a very inferior school of writings, known as the social life novel." By the "social life novel," Simms meant a story in which the bulk of detail was made up of "the ordinary events of the household, or of the snug family circle." The action of such a story might reach its climax at a ball or a dinner party. To a man accustomed, as Simms was, to handling issues that determined the fate of states or nations, this sort of thing seemed paltry stuff, for it gave almost no play to the "imagination" or the "creative faculty." No wonder Cooper failed in *Precaution* and Scott in *St. Ronan's Well.* If such novels have to be written, let them be written by women.

Well, a few years after Simms wrote these words, women did bend themselves to producing the social or domestic novel with such zeal that they put a severe crimp in the sales of other varieties of fiction including Simms's specialty, the historical romance. Indeed, they all but pre-empted the field of fiction. The fifties and sixties saw the publication of scores of domestic novels by a variety of authors. Their sales were tremen-

dous. Maria Cummins's *Lamplighter* sold 40,000 copies within eight weeks. Two of Susan Warner's books, *The Wide, Wide World* and *Queechy,* sold an aggregate of 104,000 copies in three years. Mrs. Hentz's sales totaled 93,000 in three years. Mrs. Holmes's books reached a total of 2,000,000 sold copies. The demand for the books of Jane Augusta Evans Wilson may be partly judged by a notice printed in one edition of *St. Elmo:* "Special edition limited to 100,000 copies." Other writers of the school made almost comparable successes. The vogue of the form was perhaps greatest in the fifties and sixties; yet as late as 1872 the Boston Public Library "confessed . . . that the most popular authors of the day were Mary Holmes, Caroline Lee Hentz, and Mrs. Southworth." It is no accident that Joyce's *Ulysses,* set in 1904, reports Gerty MacDowell as having read *The Lamplighter.* Nor are people lacking in the present generation even among the intelligentsia who, if pressed, will blushingly admit that they have read and enjoyed *St. Elmo.*

The productions of this prolific race of novelists have generally been dismissed briefly by historians of literature as being subliterary, and therefore unworthy of critical attention. Granted that sales are no criterion of literary values, yet the vast popularity of these writers so affected the market for fiction and the standards of public taste that more serious artists were alarmed. In 1855 Hawthorne referred in exasperation to the authors as a "damned mob of scribbling women." Howells later had much ado to correct false artistic standards of taste they created. Some knowledge of the origin, aims, and vogue of such an influential school is essential to an understanding of the temper of the period and of the evolution of the novel.

The domestic novel had reciprocal relationships with various other forms of fiction. A precise definition is therefore difficult, but for the moment the domestic novel may be roughly defined, in its first phase at least, as an extended prose tale composed chiefly of commonplace household incidents and episodes loosely worked into a trite plot involving the fortunes of characters who exist less as individuals than as carriers of pious moral or religious sentiment. The thesis of such a book is that true happiness comes from submission to suffering. In its purest strain the domestic novel relied far more on religious sentiment than on romantic love, but as time went on the latter greatly increased its ratio and even an erotic element (for which the author acknowledged no responsibility) became dimly apparent between the lines. Other variations occur from author to author, but enough homogeneity obtains in the genre to give some validity to the following receipt to make a domestic novel.

First, take a young and not-too-pretty child about ten years old. Boys are possible, but girls are to be preferred, for the author and the increasing majority of

An illustration from Richardson's Pamela.

women readers will be more at home in the detail. Make sure that the child is, or is shortly to be, an orphan. If the mother is still living, put her to death very gradually in a scene of much sorrow and little physical suffering, uttering pious hopes and admonitions to the last. The father presumably died years ago under circumstances not well known. Now put the child under the care of a shrewish aunt, who resents being obliged to take care of her dead brother's brat. If it has been impossible to remove the father as suggested above, a reasonably good compromise will be to have him make a second marriage with a frivolous heartless society woman. In an emergency a cruel housekeeper will do. The child is now unhappy, undernourished, and underprivileged. She is exposed to the taunts of snobbish little rich girls. It is essential that she accidentally overhear unkind comments on her awkward clothes, rustic manners, bad behavior, or even her family honor. Slander may be used freely for spicing the plot. The child's behavior may in fact be actually bad in the beginning. She may "sass" her aunt. She may even shy a stone through a window.

But her worst sin is her "pride." Now introduce a young woman living not far away, who embodies all Christian virtues, especially humility. Let this lady kiss, pray over, and cry with the heroine at intervals of from three to four pages. The lady may or may not be blind; at any rate, she has had her sorrows and she is destined to die about two thirds of the way through the book of badly diagnosed tuberculosis. She will die at sunset—without a struggle. She is going home. Tears which have been flowing freely now practically inundate the book. The girl's only remaining friends are an eccentric (Barkis-like) teamster, and a wealthy (Cheeryble-like) merchant who now and then gives her a lollipop. In the meantime she has learned to subdue her pride and to submit graciously to the suffering which is the lot of all mortals in this shabby world. You may end your story here if you will, with the child on the verge of adolescence; but it is preferable to carry on a few years in order that the heroine may be menaced by a proud, handsome, moody, Rochester-like man aged about thirty who has traveled and sinned (very vaguely) in the Orient. He at first scarcely notices the meek little girl, but her bright spirit and vaguely-referred-to physical charms finally force him to admit to himself that he must have her. If it weren't for Queen Victoria he would try to seduce her, but as it is he is reduced to proposing marriage. To his astonishment she refuses. This sends him darkly off on more travels. The girl meanwhile has learned to support herself by teaching, acting as governess, or by writing, and she talks rather briskly about independence for women. Let her endure many trials and perform many pious acts. Monotony may be broken by a trip to Saratoga or by the introduction of some physical peril such as a carriage accident, an attack by a mad dog, or a fire. One day the moody man comes back, and finds her sitting in a cemetery. He proposes again and is accepted. Don't be alarmed at this: his pride has been humbled, too, and he is now reformed. He may even become a minister, but he has plenty of money. For her part, the heroine now drops all fantastic notions of female independence, for she realizes that a woman's greatest glory is wifely submission. The acid aunt either dies or experiences a change of heart toward the heroine. In the latter case she may be married off to the neighboring teamster (blacksmith will do). The wealthy merchant turns out to be the heroine's father: he wasn't really lost at sea! Everybody is now happy in a subdued, Christian sort of way.

This composite story is intended to give some idea of the domestic novel as it was practiced by Susan Warner, Maria Cummins, Jane Augusta Evans Wilson, Mrs. E. D. E. N. Southworth, Ann Sophia Stephens, Caroline Lee Hentz, Mrs. H. B. Goodwin, Marion Harland, E. P. Roe, and others from 1850 to 1872. Its descent in the family of fiction is complicated. It is obviously related to the novel of sensibility and as such it goes

back to *Pamela.* Miss Edgeworth was also an acknowledged ancestor of the type. But there are more
obvious relationships with four later British writers—
Bulwer, Dickens, Charlotte Brontë, and Mrs. Gaskell—
whose first published novels appeared respectively in
1829, 1837, 1847, and 1848. Bulwer provided a model
for drawing-room scenes and fascinating, wicked,
fashionable young men; Dickens, for pathetic little girls
and eccentric characters; Brontë, for the persecuted
governess; and Mrs. Gaskell, for idyllic village life.
From American novelists there was less that could be
borrowed handily. The sensitive, swooning heroine
lately released from the defunct Gothic romance and
the moribund historical romance could be drafted into
the service of the domestic novel, given a course of
intensive religious training, taught maneuvers of the
heart by Jane Eyre, and assigned to heavy emotional
duty on the domestic front. The kitchen realism which
Miss Sedgwick employed for the benefit of readers
beginning to tire of the details of military campaign
and Indian adventure could be easily imitated. Yet
models and inspirations outside the novel were perhaps quite as important: Mrs. Sigourney's tremendous
success in poems of religious sentiment, Fanny Fern's
domestic essays, Ik Marvel's dozing reveries, and the
variety of sentimental pieces whether essay, tale, or
poem, which filled the literary annuals and gift-books.
It is a fair guess that the domestic novel gradually
took over much of the public created by the gift-book
vogue, which, beginning in 1825 and carrying on to
the sixties, showed a marked decline shortly after 1850.
And when in 1853 Mrs. Stowe contributed Little Eva
to the gallery of sentimental heroines, there was no
stopping the lady novelists.

Obviously the domestic novel was not only a literary
phenomenon but a social one as well. Telescoped into
a few generalizations, the opinions it reflected and
promoted can be seen to have been of a distinctly
conservative nature. In effect, the domestic novel
functioned as a sort of benign moral police, whose
regulations were principally comprised under the heads
of religion and morality. The religion inculcated was
not heavily freighted with theological doctrines; it was
rather, as Gerty says in *The Lamplighter,* a "religion
of the heart" and as such was available to any one
ready to listen to the voice of God. Its chiefest enemies were Goethe, Emerson, and various other vendors of "transcendental sophistries" devised originally
in Germany. If the German vice was unorthodoxy, the
threat of the French was immorality. There was no
surer way of damning a character than by showing
him in the act of reading a French novel, particularly
one by Eugene Sue, whose *Mysteries of Paris* and *The
Wandering Jew* were promptly translated and published
in this country in the middle forties. The French,
moreover, were the prime exemplars of that fashionable life against which the domestic novelists protested—and sometimes protested too much. As for

formal education, the general tendency is to indorse a
simple type of curriculum in the local elementary
schools. Boarding schools are looked upon askance as
places where children are underfed and poorly instructed under the orders of a tyrannical, greedy head-
master. Colleges are tested for their religious tone:
Yale, for example, is preferred to Harvard and Columbia as the place where a lad can get "a granite foundation for . . . religion—everything solid and sound
there." It is conceded by another novelist, however,
that a Harvard commencement is an "intellectual banquet." Women's rights are smartly debated in practically every domestic novel. Keen feminist arguments
are met by the stock replies that women have intuition
but not reason, that they may lose feminine graces in
the pursuit of rights, and that men will deteriorate too
if the need for chivalry is removed. Such sex warfare
generally ends in an ignoble truce whereby the woman
barters all her advantages for a scrap of paper—a
marriage certificate. As for the heroine who takes to
writing as a career, she renounces that at the altar: a
bluestocking she must not be. Least of all should she
be a reformer. The lady novelists showed their conservatism in nothing so much as their universal detestation of reform movements. Charitable Christian deeds
performed by individuals were acceptable, but reform
movements were "radical." This attitude extended even
to the subject of slavery, which forms a staple of
conversation in many novels. It is argued, of course,
that to hold a human being in the condition of a chattel
is wrong, but nowhere is there much said for the
militant abolitionist. Moreover, the Southern cause is
well represented (especially since two of the principal
domestic novelists, Marion Harland and Jane Wilson,
were Southerners) and it is often argued that the position of a (contented) slave is considerably better than
that of "the miserable, half-starved seamstresses of
Boston and New York, who toil from dawn till dark,
with aching head and throbbing breast." In this debate, however, the novelist generally remains neutral.
Other political and economic problems are but lightly
touched. There are vague allusions to the beneficence
of "Republican institutions" and the dignity of labor,
but there is no systematic arraignment of the socioeconomic order even for those evils which closely
impinged upon domestic life—child labor, defective
factory conditions, and miscellaneous exploitation of
the poor classes—much less the growing political
corruption that was to flower rankly in the Gilded
Age. The domestic novelists handled no inflammable
social doctrine, for it was no part of their purpose to
create industrial unrest or to foment class hatred.

In most respects, then, the domestic novelists were
conservative socially. The pioneer spirit was not in
them, and they were not concerned with "progress."
Enough to be safe in the moment. Yet in one respect
they exhibited, perhaps unconsciously, a tendency
which has been ratified by later thinkers. This was

shown in their fundamental conception of the regeneration of a person given to evil courses. Instead of trying to stamp out evil violently as a sign of innate depravity, lodged in man ever since old Adam's first slip, they sought to lead the child to grace by kindly encouragement. The motive power was more often love or hope than fear. Satan's agency in sin was left out of consideration and causes were sought for nearer at hand, specifically in heredity and environment. Vicious surroundings accounted for undesirable traits which could be removed, but only gradually, by transplantation to a more favorable environment: "The plant that for years has been growing distorted, and dwelling in a barren spot, deprived of light and nourishment, withering in its leaves and blighted in its fruit, cannot at once recover from so cruel a blast. Transplanted to another soil, it must be directed in the right course, nourished with care and warmed with Heaven's light, ere it can recover from the shock occasioned by its early neglect, and find strength to expand its flowers and ripen its fruit." There was a perceptible swing from a theological to a scientific conception of the proper control of mental and moral states, for " 'there is mental as well as bodily sickness and a true physician should minister to both.' " In general the novels of this school show a tendency to rely on admonition rather than punishment as a means of discipline. There is less talk of the devil and more of angels, less forcing and more leading. To be sure such positive, optimistic doctrine was not wholly new in the 1850's, but it was of some significance in a social order only recently emerged from the depressing atmosphere of Calvinistic thought.

There can be no question of the tremendous vogue of the domestic sentimentalists or of their acceptable moral teaching. What can be said of the intrinsic merit of the books themselves? Very little. Obviously they are in no cases the product of first-rate writers. Yet some abilities must be looked for in novelists who were able to command the attention not only of the average intelligent reader but of the critics as well. If they had addressed themselves only to a semi-illiterate public, their sales would not have disturbed Hawthorne by the thought of potential readers lost; if their books had been totally devoid of literary merit, Howells would not have bothered to attack them. Evidently they were read by persons who were unaware of stooping to an unworthy variety of entertainment. Why? The simplest answer (beyond the religious content of the books) is that most of the domestic novelists exhibited a fairly good prose style: their books *looked* like literature. It was perhaps as easy for the untutored layman to confuse their work with genuine literature as to mistake the popular illustrations of Currier and Ives for great art. Almost every writer in the group wrote with great facility—perhaps a fatal facility—and some of them, notably Mrs. Wilson, had a gift for phrasing that would have done credit to more important books.

Nathaniel Hawthorne comments on the success of women writers and sentimental fiction:

America is now wholly given over to a d——d mob of scribbling women, and I should have no chance of success while the public taste is occupied with their trash—and should be ashamed of myself if I did succeed. What is the mystery of these innumerable editions of the Lamplighter, and other books neither better nor worse?——worse they could not be, and better they need not be, when they sell by the 100,000.

Letter to William D. Ticknor, January 19, 1855, in Letters of Hawthorne to William D. Ticknor, 1851-1864, *NCR/Microcard Editions, 1972.*

If an odious comparison may be admitted, it is likely that in sheer literary gifts Mrs. Wilson excelled her present-day successors, Faith Baldwin and Kathleen Norris.

For the rest, the plot is based on a framework of trite devices, such as mistaken identity and the long-lost relative, and set into motion by coincidence. The fuel is sentiment or emotion, which is used in such a rich mixture that overheating results. No great speed is attained, but there are many melodramatic crises. The characters are generally lacking in individuality except for an occasional minor person. There is much whimsy but little humor. The description of natural scenery is slight in amount, and the sense of place is almost negligible: in this respect the domestic novelists displayed little advance over the novelists of fifty years before. The principal structural defect is the almost universal practice of chopping the action up into short scenes of approximately equal length—a method which, though perhaps dictated in part by the exigencies of serial publication, is generally fatal to proportion. The story sprawls through several years—perhaps an average of six or seven. A chronological order is observed throughout to a point about two thirds or four fifths of the way through the book, when the author finally vouchsafes the explanation of whatever mysteries in the plot have been arbitrarily withheld. This explanation, which generally consists of the life story of one of the characters, is so long as to throw the whole book still more askew structurally. How much better results might be obtained by the condensation or complete omission of certain scenes and the selection of others for expansion, together with the judicious use of flash-backs, remained for Howells and James to demonstrate.

The domestic novel was a popular commodity in which originality was no great virtue. Even in its period it seemed somewhat old-fashioned. As time went on, the effects of excessive inbreeding finally foreshadowed its temporary extinction. Yet the species was amazingly tenacious, and its life span extended through the seventies and even beyond. Meantime there has appeared in the late 1860's the first publications of three men—Mark Twain, Howells, and James—destined in different ways to give American fiction more vitality and greater merit. Yet none of these men immediately preempted the field, and one of them, James, can scarcely be said to have had a popular vogue at all. Their immediate influence, like that of Whitman, was not widespread. The gravest threats to the domestic novel in the seventies and eighties were local-color fiction (often taking the form of the short story), the international or cosmopolitan novel (especially, in the popular field, the work of Francis Marion Crawford), and the historical romance, which was revived in the 1880's and 1890's. The development of the railroad contributed to the physical expansion of the country which brought the local-colorists into prominence; and the great increase in European travel in part prepared for the rise of "international" fiction. When "swaggering Americans were thronging Europe in great crowds," the novelist whose characters were followed to no point more remote than Saratoga began to seem a little provincial. As for the historical romance, its occasional recurrence is inevitable. At all events new costumes, gorgeous settings, and more "personalized" characters gave the historical romance a new vogue in the eighties. A little later, the panic of 1893 doubtless made romance even more welcome as a resource against incessant discussion of wages, strikes, monopolies, and economic depression. At all events the nineteenth-century domestic novel was by that time pretty well choked out by heavy competition except for the sporadic reappearances already noted.

M. G. Van Rensselaer decries the absence of "an indigenous school of fiction":

There is a very large demand with us for low-class fiction too—"low" in an artistic, not a moral, sense—but it is not of that I would speak. The thousand novels that supply it are indeed of native production: nothing could have more the flavor of the soil, nothing could be more genuinely local, more unlike English fiction of any grade whether high or low. But such books as these—Indian tales and Sunday-school stories, novels by Mrs. Holmes and Mrs. Southworth and Sylvanus Cobb and Miss Harland and E. P. Roe and Miss Warner and Miss Cummins and many others as unlike in kind, but as similar in artistic value,—such books as these are not properly literature in any true sense of the word. They no more form a national school of fiction than chromo-factories form a national school of art.

M. G. Van Rensselaer, in Lippincott's Magazine, *Vol. XXIII, No. 41, June, 1879.*

Mary Kelley

SOURCE: "The Sentimentalists: Promise and Betrayal in the Home," in *Signs: Journal of Women in Culture and Society,* Vol. 4, No. 3, Spring, 1979, pp. 434-46.

[*In the essay that follows, Kelley claims that authors of the domestic novel simultaneously glorified and protested women's domestic roles.*]

The sentimentalists, especially those who focused upon woman and her role in the family and society, have long been objects of neglect, dismissal, and scorn. Hawthorne's oft-repeated outburst that "America is now wholly given over to a d———d mob of scribbling women" was echoed a century later by Leslie Fiedler's ridicule of "the purely commercial purveyors of domestic sentiments."[1] Adopting a more fruitful perspective, other critics have chosen instead to concentrate upon the social and cultural values articulated by this popular and highly influential group of nineteenth-century writers of fiction. Generally the assessments have been strikingly dissimilar, even contradictory, as the interpretations of Alexander Cowie and Helen Waite Papashvily illustrate. Cowie painted the sentimentalists as ultraconservative, claiming that their fiction "functioned as a sort of benign moral police, whose regulations were principally comprised under the heads of religion and morality."[2] He contended that the image of woman in the fiction was that of a complacent, contented, protected lady; that the writers were undeviating in their banal support of the status quo: "Keen feminist arguments are met by the stock replies that women have intuition but not reason, that they may lose feminine graces in the pursuit of rights, and that men will deteriorate too if the need for chivalry is removed."[3] In direct contrast, Papashvily argued that the fiction betrayed an insidious distaste for the status quo and its male custodians, and that it "encouraged a pattern of feminine behavior so quietly ruthless, so subtly vicious that by comparison the ladies at Seneca appear angels of innocence."[4] In Papashvily's view, these writers believed that "female superiority had to be established and maintained",[5] their fiction, she insisted, constituted a virtual act of insurrection.

Such divergent perspectives as Cowie's and Papashvily's presented distorted assessments by defining the entire body of the literature in terms of certain specific aspects which they treated in isolation. By drawing upon nearly 200 volumes of novels, short stories, and essays written by the twelve women who were the major producers of this prose, as well as upon their personal papers which comprise several thousand letters, journals, and diaries, it is possible to offer an interpretation that not only encompasses the perspectives of Cowie, Papashvily, and others, but even goes beyond them.[6]

Moralists *non pareil,* the sentimentalists have been regarded as the foremost proponents of the nineteenth century's cult of domesticity. It is true that they subscribed to the traditional separation of spheres. As directed by God and in the interests of familial and societal order and stability, the wife was to defer to her husband as head of household.[7] The husband was responsible for conducting the affairs of society and for providing material support for the family. The wife's appointed function was to be the architect of the home—christened Eden. But to perceive the sentimentalists as simply sweet singers of domestic blissfulness, as songsters of the lives of idle, submissive, ornamental middle-class housewives is to ignore the strains in their fiction. In their effort to entertain, instruct, and share grievances with an audience that numbered in the hundreds of thousands, they imparted a contradictory message. They wrote of their domestic dream and revealed a deep discontent. In a hopeful vision of womanly glory, they promoted as a female archetype a strong, commanding, central figure in the home; a supportive and guiding redeemer for husband; a model and teacher of rectitude for children; and a reformer of and servant to an American society judged to be in dire need of regeneration. The emphasis always was on woman's selflessness and her service to the needs of others.

But the positive, forceful message rode and was partly generated by an undercurrent of dissatisfaction and despair. The determination to enhance woman's image and role represented a simultaneous attempt to protest the status of their female contemporaries and the moral condition of their country in the nineteenth century. Despite their assent and belief in woman's posture as one of deference to a male head-of-household, the glorification of woman as superior being was tantamount to a protest that she had to defer to an erring, inferior husband; the promotion of woman as strong and independent underlined her predicament as a dependent forced to rely upon an unreliable male; and the wonderment at woman's work implied a rejection of the characterization of woman's status as inferior. And in spite of their belief in the domestic as woman's properly restricted sphere, they were apprehensive that woman's position was dependent upon the stability of the family and fearful that, because of the burden of household duties and the demands of serving the needs of others, woman's autonomy was diminished and her individuality denied. Melodramatic and simplistic though the plots may be, wooden and stereotyped though the characters may appear, the protest in the novels and stories frequently preempted the prescription. In the prescription and the protest lay the promise and the betrayal of the nineteenth-century woman.

The sentimentalists did not write in a vacuum. Premature death and debilitating illness, financial fluctuations and domestic instability touched their own lives as children and as mature women. In a century of upheaval, movement, and turmoil, status was uncertain and social stability tenuous. America was economically and geographically expanding and changing and the agrarian and rural landscape was becoming industrial and urban. A nation dedicated to material progress invited the pursuit of the dollar, wild speculation, and rampant opportunism. The response of these writers was to express a nostalgia for an imagined past and a demand that society return to supposedly traditional, more communally oriented values. Their familial experience revealed to them the reality of the mutual dependence of human beings and they insisted that an increasingly pervasive individualism yield to an older ethic that gave precedence to the community—to the needs and desires of others. They deplored society's materialism and called for reimmersion in the spiritual. These goals, they believed, could only be achieved by women whom they promoted as superior, selfless, strong beings, and whom they heralded as society's moral guardians, reformers, and judges. The family, glorified as a source of virtue and as a sacred refuge from an increasingly competitive, fragmented, and transitory society, was regarded as the arena in which woman would fulfill her exemplary, anointed role.

The sentimentalists perceived a moral vacuum in a country that lacked a central authoritative force, and moved to fill it by dispensing prescription disguised as fantasy. As the daughters and wives of clergymen, legislators, journalists, educators, merchants, and jurists they came from families that provided a leading, prominent, active citizenry, accustomed to the tradition of overseeing its society's values and its nation's direction. As women they were restricted to the private domestic sphere, but as writers they in effect sought to comment upon and influence the very public life in which they had no part. They exercised the role without the title. In their unceasing efforts to proselytize their readers, they transformed the fiction into didactic essays, speaking directly to their readers in prefaces or intruding in the pages of their melodramas as author or omniscient narrator. Some even added footnotes. Uncertain of themselves as artists, they harbored no doubts that their art should have a moral purpose. All would have agreed with the view expressed by Augusta Evans Wilson in a letter to a friend: "Should not excelsior be the Watchword and motto of the true artist? Is not an artist a great reformer whose instructions are pictorial? Art should elevate, should refine, should sanctify the heart."[8] Echoing Wilson's credo, Mary J. Holmes wrote: "I mean always to write a good, pure, natural story, such as mothers are willing their daughters should read, and such as will do good instead of harm."[9] A model for society, Augusta Evans Wilson's heroine, Edna Earl, stood as the fictional counterpart of the sentimentalist writer: "The fondest hope of Edna's heart was to be useful in 'her day and generation'—to be an instrument of some good to her race. . . ."[10] As a writer, herself, she did not desire popularity " 'as an end, but as a means to an end—usefulness to my fellow creatures.' "[11]

Self-appointed critics of their society, the sentimentalists did not, however, stand alone in their demand that Americans adopt alternative values. Their attitudes were the secular equivalent to the righteous, reformist ethos of Protestantism. Their views reflected the convictions espoused by the Protestant ministry in various denominations. All twelve of the writers were committed Protestants. Most maintained close ties with ministers; three married members of the clergy. As writers, they regarded themselves as preachers of the fictional page. Catharine Maria Sedgwick, for example, earnestly professed to the clergyman William Ellery Channing that "neither pride nor humility should withhold us from the work to which we are clearly 'sent'."[12] Mary Virginia Terhune's heroine, Phemie Hart, perceives her purpose as a writer to parallel that of the minister: " 'If God had given me strength, it seemed to me that I should help the weak, if courage, I ought to cheer the desponding. If knowledge were mine, it should be shared with those who were ignorant.' "[13] Mirroring their clerical counterparts, the sentimentalists expressed the belief that their labors were totally dependent upon, and directed by, God's beneficence. In reply to Dorothea Dix's praise of *The Wide, Wide World,* Susan Warner rejected any credit for herself: "I do not deserve your commendations,—not in anywise. You say 'God bless me' for what I have done,—nay but I say 'Thank him for it,' and I wash my hands of all desert in the matter."[14] Maria Cummins ascribed all of her efforts to heaven; "If I have ever done anything worth doing, it has been through the motives and spirit" of God.[15] Harriet Beecher Stowe went so far as to exclaim that God, himself, had penned *Uncle Tom's Cabin.*

For the sentimentalists, piety involved more than an inner conviction. Love of God was expressed by love of others. To submit to the will of God did not imply passivity. Selflessness did not mean simple self-denial. One served God by actively serving others. Heroines and readers alike are told to obey God's command and defer their own needs and interests to those of others. Maria McIntosh's Augusta Moray is predictably admonished by an equally predictable figure, her minister, to " 'Get away from yourself—let your sympathies and work be no longer for yourself . . . but for the needy and sorrowing wherever you find them; and let your trust, your reliance be not on yourself, not on any human arm, but on God'."[16] " 'Learn above all things'," the headmistress of a female academy says sternly to Maria Cummins's Mabel Vaughan, " 'to beware of self-love, and cultivate to the utmost a universal charity'."[17] The heroines prove able students. E. D. E. N. Southworth's Catherine Kavanaugh "lived only for the good of others," having "grown to believe that there was no individual happiness for herself except in the service of others."[18] While the first, primary duty was to serve family, frequently anyone in need, or in need of reformation, became "family." The "ideal woman"—strong, active, and independent—is to serve family and community. The "fashionable woman" is a prominent object of derision and shame in the fiction not only because she symbolized the corrupting materialism of the age but because she lent credence to the notion that the middle-class woman was idle, narcissistic, and unproductive. The writers were adamant in their insistence that theirs was not a leisured class; theirs was not a philosophy of leisure.

Although the sentimentalists espoused the ministers' view that both man and woman were prone to the sin of selfishness, they chose to focus upon man's, and not woman's, transgressions. Man demonstrated his lack of piety by disregarding the needs of others. Novel after novel, story after story, repeated the melodramatic tale of man's obsessive quest for wealth and social position. They agreed, too, that human beings must strive for regeneration, but they stressed man's need of woman's aid to reform. Writing to her brother, Henry Ward Beecher, Harriet Beecher Stowe repeated the claim and the complaint that "it is the women who hold the faith in the world. The mothers and wives who suffer and must suffer to the end of time to bear the sins of the beloved in their own bodies."[19] These writers saw themselves as their brother's keeper, a term which was paradoxically more fitting for them than the clergy. Whereas ministers perceived themselves as responsible for the reformation of all human beings, regardless of sex, the sentimentalists called upon women to reform men whose sins most directly threatened the family.

Throughout the incredible events in the fiction, the bizarre and complicated plots, the heroine's superior character is apparent and her dominating presence felt. The pious, deferential chaste wife, while she could not be openly proclaimed the authoritative figure in the home, is directed to guide and influence her husband and becomes absolutely vital to his moral well-being. Harry Henderson in Harriet Beecher Stowe's *My Wife and I* describes his mother's power over his father as the "spiritual and invisible" power of the "soul over the body," a "'subtle and vital power which constantly gains control and holds every inch that it gains.'" However manipulative it may seem, the influence of Henderson's mother upon his father is, according to Stowe, stabilizing and uplifting. Gradually, and surely, she becomes his "leader and guide," and he in turn begins to exhibit "new and finer traits of tenderness and spirituality [that pervade] his character and his teachings." The father, himself, admits that his wife "'made me by her influence.'"[20]

Given the superiority of the female, it was logical for her to claim sole right to care for her children. Parton's "A Mother's Soliloquy" delineates the complete moral and physical dependence of the child upon the mother: "'I am the centre [of the child's] little world; its very life depends upon my faithful care.'" The language is saccharine, the tone maudlin, but the point is clear: "'It is my sweet duty to deck those dimpled limbs—to poise that tiny, trembling foot. Yet Stay,—my duty ends not here! A soul looks forth from those blue eyes—an undying spirit, that shall plume its wing for ceaseless flight guided by my erring hand.'"[21] The sentimentalists insisted that woman alone must train her children in virtue: "It is *her* hand which God appointed to trace the first character on man's unwritten mind," wrote Caroline Lee Hentz.[22] And Mary Virginia Terhune hoped her female readers could recognize the "grandeur of the work assigned to them." In fact, the writers claimed, as Terhune put it, that women were "the architects of the nation's fortunes, the sculptors, whose fair or foul handiwork is to outlast their age, to outlive Time, to remain through all Eternity."[23] Glorifying womanhood, the writers sought to impress on their female readers a domestic brand of noblesse oblige.

The wife and mother was appointed the architect of a home that was to embody perfection. "Home was her true sphere," wrote Caroline Howard Gilman, "there everything was managed with promptitude and decision."[24] While the supposedly responsible, reliable husband and father absented himself from the family on a daily basis in order to provide for its support and meet his obligations to the community, the wife and mother, as the family's vital, living center was so essential to the functioning of the home that its very existence could not be imagined without her. Likening the home to the church, Harriet Beecher Stowe stated that it was the "appointed sphere for woman, more holy than cloister, more saintly and pure than church and altar. . . . Priestess, wife, and mother, there she ministers daily in holy works of household peace."[25] The home was the only realm in which woman was supposed to reign. Anointed the moral guardian for all society, she was called upon to transform its values, and yet she was to achieve that goal within the confines of the home. As Catharine Maria Sedgwick suggested: "By an unobtrusive and unseen process, are the characters of men formed, at home, by the mother, the first teacher. There the moral nature is fixed." "I cannot believe that it was ever intended," Sedgwick stated categorically, "that women should lead armies, harangue in the halls of legislation, bustle up to ballot-boxes, or sit on judicial tribunals."[26] The boundaries of woman's realm could not be enlarged or her role extended, warned Augusta Evans Wilson, "without rendering the throne unsteady, and subverting God's law of order. Woman reigned by divine right only at home."[27] Glorified as a divinely appointed station for

woman, as a haven for man, and as a moral setting for the rearing of children, "home" was an Eden. Maria McIntosh dubbed it "the nursery of pure and high thoughts."[28] The source of virtue, the home was ipso facto the source of happiness. Mary Virginia Terhune rejoiced: "Home! wife! peace! Sweet synonyms that sum up the rapturous emotions of many a satisfied heart!"[29]

The shining image that the sentimentalists sought to promote, however, is eclipsed by the graven image they actually projected. The domestic dream proffered, it vanishes in due course. Prescription runs aground in the protest of the fiction. Of course, it was not the conscious intention of the sentimentalists to transmit to their readers a predominantly negative image of woman's role in the family and society. But their fiction is an apt illustration of D. H. Lawrence's remark on American literature in general: "Never trust the artist. Trust the tale."[30] As "artists" they intended to impress on their readers the example of superior heroines serving family and nation. They tried to project the Edenic image, the perfect home for their readers' worship and emulation. Nevertheless, the "tales" subverted their intentions. The novels and short stories coalesce into one long melodrama of heroines trying valiantly to meet the challenges of woman's role with partial success and little satisfaction. The glorified, heroic role envisioned for the wife is frequently seen as confining and stultifying. Social and economic disaster, sickness and death plague the performance of her roles. The achievement of Eden frequently eludes them and the ameliorative impact of their superior self-sacrificing nature is continually undermined by the impurity of those around them.

Although the writers did not hesitate to damn fashionable women obsessed with self-gratification who abandoned hearth and home as the focus of existence, most often, the villain was man. Impious, abusive of his privileged position as head of household, a trifler and despoiler of woman's sexual virtue, man was the threat to the domestic dream. At times, he is indifferent to the family's welfare, forgets or refuses to be a provider, neglects his children, and fails to abide by his wife's moral example. At other times, he is well-meaning but weak and irresponsible, incapable of performing his assigned role. That all men in the fiction are not evil incarnate tells us that the writers were not motivated by a vengeful hatred of men. The "ideal man" does make his infrequent appearance and his portrait amounts to a study in the feminization of the male. This male hero seeks above all to serve the needs of others, particularly of women. Nor did the sentimentalists think that every erring man was hopeless. In the most optimistic of instances, the morally flawed male is ultimately receptive to woman's moral direction. Led by the angels of mercy, man's self-concern gives way to concern for others, the harm done to others is rectified, the moral lesson imparted, and the novel or story concludes with the overwhelmed male bathing his mate in bathetic praise, and the woman, deluged in tears, consenting to continue as his mentor.

But man is not always redeemed in the fiction and there are not always happy endings. From the thicket of plots and subplots emerges the reprobate who is unresponsive to woman's ministrations, the unregenerated male whose corrupt values and destructive acts have a lasting impact. To such a man, money and social position are far more important than his intimates. Caroline Lee Hentz's *Rena: or, the Snowbird* accents man's quest for wealth and social position at all cost, including the seduction and betrayal of women, and the total neglect of familial obligations. Herbert Lindsay's finale is to commit suicide, but not before becoming Hentz's spokesman, in a lament that underlines the grievances women hold against men. "'I have chilled her by coldness, bruised her by harshness—yet she loves me still. Oh! woman, woman! great and marvelous is thy love! Ill-requited, wronged and suffering woman! surely there must be a heaven for thee, if not for transgressing man!'"[31] Herbert strikes the mournful note that reverberates through the sentimentalists' fiction.

By dwelling upon the immoral, at times, depraved, tyrannical male and his pillage of woman and the family, the sentimentalists revealed their dismal and dire prognosis of nineteenth-century society. The self-concerned, aggressive male in their fiction symbolizes the rampant, destructive individualism which they were convinced was preempting a higher commitment to community. Repudiating the prevalent notion that goods stood for greatness, the writers disdained materialism as the damnable worship of the golden calf. Not only did man's mania for money cloud his judgment, it corrupted his virtue. Materialistic, individualistic, immoral man appears again and again in their pages as the bellwether, the diseased product of a society obsessed with the money that bought privilege and power.

Man proves to be the leading villain in a play that was supposed to be an idyll of the home. Just as the chief beneficiaries of woman's reformation are man and the family, so the primary victims of man's immoral behavior are woman and the family. Instead of reformer, woman ends up the victim. The divinely ordained symbol of the home, on the one hand, woman also appears as thwarted, dissatisfied, and dejected, as physically and emotionally overburdened. In *Recollections of a Housekeeper,* Carolina Howard Gilman speaks of the "cares [that] eat away at her heart." Demands made upon her are unceasing as each "day presses on her with new toils, the night comes, and they are unfulfilled; she lies down in weariness, and rises with uncertainty." Gilman bemoans the fact that "many a woman breaks and sinks beneath the wear and tear of

the frame and the affections."[32] Maria McIntosh added her own note of distress for woman's plight: "Work—work—work, till heart and hand fail, till the cloud gather on her once sunny brow, and her cheeks grow pale, and friendly consumption come to give her rest from her labors in the grave, or the throbbing brain and over-anxious heart overpower the reason, and a lunatic asylum receive one more miserable inmate."[33] Citing an officers' report for the Retreat of the Insane in Hartford, Connecticut, McIntosh emphasized its claim that many young women sought refuge in "lunatic" hospitals, unable or unwilling to do battle any longer with their domestic circumstances. The primary architect of a home that was to embody peace, order, and perfection, woman was demoralized in her restricted sphere, denied the benefits of emotional and intellectual stimulation. In *Husbands and Homes,* Mary Virginia Terhune angrily charged that confinement and isolation "have racked and strained muscle and nerve, turned our daily bread into ashes, blunted our perceptions to all that was once beautiful to the sight, pleasant to the ear, stimulative to the intellect."[34]

The defects of man and the burdens of domesticity made it difficult if not impossible to create the idealized home and family. The sentimentalists had hoped to advance the nuclear family as the critical institution for the maintenance and reform of the social fabric, but as protestors they disclosed imperfections in its structure that precluded an adequate performance of its function. Death was its own final drama of the unrealized familial Eden. If the mother died, the husband might continue to provide material sustenance but was unsuited to discharge the responsibilities of his wife. His inadequate care promised wayward sons and daughters. Caroline Lee Hentz's Bryant Clinton is denied the "gentle, yet restraining influence which woman in her purity and excellence, ever asserts. . . ."[35] Encouraged to gamble by his father, Bryant goes into debt, robs a helpless widow, and is finally imprisoned. Because Augusta Temple's father instills the belief that physical appearance is more important than her conduct, he renders her "vain from adulation, and selfish from indulgence."[36]

When the father died, on the other hand, the mother was not prepared or encouraged to earn a livelihood for herself and her children. The widow and her children, isolated from both relatives and society, were left stranded in the home without adequate means of support. But it was the fate that awaited children when both parents died that signaled the final destruction of the nuclear family. No figure is either treated with greater emotion or sentimentality, or endures greater hardship and privation than the orphan who appears in the work of every writer. Maria Cummins's Gertrude Flint is the archetypal orphan. Cared for by a cruel old woman, Gertrude is totally neglected—"scantily clad, in garments of the poorest description . . . her complexion was sallow, and her whole appearance unhealthy." She is also denied affection: "No one loved her. . . . No one treated her kindly; no one tried to make her happy, or cared whether she were so."[37] Many, like Gertrude, are condemned to orphan asylums. In *Rose Clark,* Sara Parton describes the suffering resignation of orphans with their closely shaven heads, "lackluster eyes, stooping forms and pale faces . . . the hopeless, weary look on those subdued faces."[38]

The shift from prescription to protest and beyond in the fiction of the sentimentalists is accompanied by a critical and sometimes bitter disillusionment. This shift in tone symbolized a fall from innocence. In the interests of prescription and entertainment, the sentimentalists began with a blueprint of what family life in nineteenth-century America should be only to end by issuing what was a report on the condition of family life in nineteenth-century America. In the words of Mary Virginia Terhune, the writers became involved in "writing hard things and heavy to be borne by the young with whom hope is reality, and thoughts of love dearer than promise of life, wealth, and honor; but he who sketches from nature must, perforce, oftentimes fulfill the thankless task of iconoclast."[39] The writers attempted to project an ideal image of the home, the family, marriage, and domesticity, but the contrast between intention and realization is evident throughout. The fiction of the sentimentalists is, finally, expressive of a dark vision of nineteenth-century America, and not, as they wished, of the redemptive, idyllic, holy land.

Notes

This essay is derived from two different papers delivered at the Conference on the History of Women, sponsored by Women Historians of the Midwest, on October 25, 1975, in St. Paul, Minnesota and at the annual meeting of the Organization of American Historians, April 8, 1976, in St. Louis, Missouri. The papers and this essay are based upon a manuscript titled "The Crisis of Domesticity: Women Writing of Women in Nineteenth-Century America." Stow Persons's insights were extremely helpful at various stages. Good counsel was given as well by Susan Hartmann, Linda K. Kerber, Sharon O'Brien, and Barbara Miller Solomon. The preparation of this essay was supported in part by two faculty research awards from the Research Foundation of the City University of New York.

[1] Nathaniel Hawthorne to William D. Ticknor, January 1855, quoted in Caroline Ticknor, *Hawthorne and His Publisher* (Boston: Houghton Mifflin Co., 1913), pp. 141-42; Leslie Fiedler, *Love and Death in the American Novel* (New York: Criterion Books, 1960), p. 257.

[2] Alexander Cowie, "The Vogue of the Domestic Novel, 1850-1870," *South Atlantic Quarterly* 41 (October 1942): 420. Cowie's interpretation is echoed by other critics. Henry Nash Smith observed that "popular fiction was designed to soothe the sensibilities of its readers by fulfilling expectation and expressing only received ideas. . . . The best-selling novels of the 1850s thus express an ethos of conformity." John T. Frederick's evaluation of the best sellers of the 1850s ascribed the same type of didacticism to novels and short stories. In her analysis of literature by and about women published in the four decades before the Civil War, Barbara Welter claimed that the stereotype of the ideal woman included four attributes—piety, purity, submissiveness, and a dedication to domesticity. Welter argued that such literature supported a traditional view of women as inferior, passive supporters of men. See Herbert Ross Brown, *The Sentimental Novel in America, 1789-1860* (Durham, N.C.: Duke University Press, 1940); Henry Nash Smith, "The Scribbling Woman and the Cosmic Success Story," *Critical Inquiry* 1 (September 1974): 47-70; John T. Frederick, "Hawthorne's Scribbling Women," *New England Quarterly* 48 (June 1975): 231-40; Barbara Welter, "The Cult of True Womanhood: 1820-1860," *American Quarterly* 18 (Summer 1966): 151-74.

[3] Cowie, pp. 420-21.

[4] Helen Waite Papashvily, *All the Happy Endings: A Study of the Domestic Novel in America, the Women Who Wrote It, the Women Who Read It, in the Nineteenth Century* (New York: Harper & Bros., 1956), p. xvii. Dee Garrison's and Ann Douglas's views parallel Papashvily's. All agreed that the writers were bitterly hostile toward males and Garrison claimed that "common to all these bestsellers is a rejection of traditional authority, particularly in domestic life, in religious faith, and among class-ordered mankind." Douglas's article on Sara Parton argued that the writers urged women to remove themselves from the sphere of family and home. Papashvily, Garrison, and Douglas failed to note that the writers were not antagonistic to males per se, but to the individualistic and materialistic values of their time which men were thought to embody more than women. In her later book, Douglas more or less adopted the Cowie and Welter perspective. The heroine no longer wants liberation from the home and instead, as the ornamental middle-class housewife, has climbed atop her protected pedestal of leisure where she exhibits a "proto-consumer mentality." The latest study, Nina Baym's, presents a different perspective. Baym claimed that the fiction is generally and straightforwardly about the triumph of the feminine will: "Happily, our authors said, the world's hardships provide just the right situation for the development of individual character." For a woman, these authors maintained, children and husband "are not necessary for her identity" and "marriage cannot and should not

be the goal toward which women direct themselves." See Dee Garrison, "Immoral Fiction in the Late Victorian Library," *American Quarterly* 28 (Spring 1976): 71-89; Ann Douglas Wood, "The 'Scribbling Women' and Fanny Fern: Why Women Wrote," *American Quarterly* 23 (Spring 1971): 3-24; Ann Douglas, "The Literature of Impoverishment: The Women Local Colorists in America, 1865-1914," *Women's Studies: An Interdisciplinary Journal* 1 (1972): 3-45; Ann Douglas, *The Feminization of American Culture* (New York: Alfred A. Knopf, 1977); Nina Baym, *Woman's Fiction: A Guide to Novels by and about Women in America, 1820-1870* (Ithaca, N.Y.: Cornell University Press, 1978).

5 Papashvily, p. 95.

6 I am considering the novels, short stories, letters, diaries, and journals of the following sentimentalists—Maria Cummins, Caroline Howard Gilman, Caroline Lee Hentz, Mary J. Holmes, Maria McIntosh, Sara Parton, Catharine Maria Sedgwick, E. D. E. N. Southworth, Harriet Beecher Stowe, Mary Virginia Terhune, Susan Warner, and Augusta Evans Wilson.

7 As the sentimentalists clearly enunciated, the principle of a wife deferring to her husband was dictated by the tenets of Christianity. E. D. E. N. Southworth told her readers that the novelettes, "The Wife's Victory," and its sequel, "The Married Shrew," had been written "to illustrate that distinct principle of Christian ethics and social philosophy, indicated by the text of Scripture selected as [their] motto": "The husband is head of the wife, even as Christ is head of the Church; therefore, as the Church is subject to Christ, so let the wives be to their own husbands in everything" (Epn. 5: 23-24). E. D. E. N. Southworth, *The Wife's Victory and Other Nouvellettes* (Philadelphia: T. B. Peterson, 1854), p. 27.

8 Augusta Evans Wilson to Walter Clopton Harriss, 1856, quoted in William Perry Fidler, *Augusta Evans Wilson, 1835-1909* (University, Ala.: University of Alabama Press, 1951), p. 54.

9 Griswold, William M., comp., *Descriptive Lists of American International Romantic and British Novels,* Burt Franklin, Bibliography and Reference Series no. 135 (New York, 1968), pp. 63-64.

10 Augusta Evans Wilson, *St. Elmo* (New York: G. W. Carleton, 1866), p. 238.

11 Ibid., p. 457.

12 Catharine Maria Sedgwick to William Ellery Channing, August 24, 1837, Catharine Maria Sedgwick Papers, Massachusetts Historical Society, Boston, Mass.

13 Mary Virginia Terhune [Marion Harland], *Phemie's Temptation* (New York: Carleton, 1869), p. 178.

14 Susan Warner to Dorothea Dix, August 27, 1852, Miscellany, Houghton Library, Harvard University, Cambridge, Mass.

15 Maria Cummins to Annie Adams Fields, September 16, 1862, Miscellany, Houghton Library, Harvard University, Cambridge, Mass.

16 Maria McIntosh, *Two Pictures; Or What We Think of Ourselves, and What the World Thinks of Us* (New York: D. Appleton & Co., 1863), pp. 358-59.

17 Maria Cummins, *Mabel Vaughan* (Boston: John P. Jewett & Co., 1857), pp. 9-10.

18 E. D. E. N. Southworth, *The Curse of Clifton* (Philadelphia: T. B. Peterson & Bros. 1867/1853), p. 309. Throughout the remainder of this paper the original publication date of the novel or collection of short stories is noted following the virgule.

19 Harriet Beecher Stowe to Henry Ward Beecher, undated, Beecher Family Papers, Manuscript Division, Yale University Library, New Haven, Conn.

20 Harriet Beecher Stowe, *My Wife and I, or Harry Henderson's History* (Cambridge, Mass.: Houghton Mifflin & Co., 1896/1871), pp. 33-34.

21 Sara Parton [Fanny Fern], "A Mother's Soliloquy," *Fern Leaves from Fanny's Portfolio* (Auburn, N.Y.: Derby & Miller, 1853), p. 157.

22 Caroline Lee Hentz, "The Sex of the Soul," *The Banished Son; and Other Stories of the Heart* (Philadelphia: T. B. Peterson, 1856), p. 269.

23 Mary Virginia Terhune [Marion Harland], "A Christmas Talk with Mothers," *The Christmas Holly* (New York: Sheldon & Co., 1867), p. 54.

24 Caroline Howard Gilman, *Recollections of a Southern Matron* (New York: Harper & Bros., 1938), p. 24.

25 Harriet Beecher Stowe, *The Minister's Wooing* (Cambridge, Mass.: Houghton Mifflin & Co., 1896/1859), pp. 567-68.

26 Catharine Maria Sedgwick, *Means and Ends, or Self-Training* (Boston: Marsh, Capen, Lyon, & Webb, 1839), p. 210.

27 Augusta Evans Wilson, *St. Elmo* (New York: G. W. Carleton, 1866), p. 526.

[28] Maria McIntosh, *Woman in America: Her Work and Her Reward* (New York: D. Appleton & Co., 1850), p. 131.

[29] Mary Virginia Terhune [Marion Harland], "Nobody to Blame," *Husbands and Homes* (New York: Sheldon & Co., 1865), p. 47.

[30] D. H. Lawrence, *Studies in Classic American Literature* (Garden City, N.Y.: Doubleday Anchor Books, 1923), p. 13.

[31] Caroline Lee Hentz, *Rena: or, the Snowbird* (Philadelphia: A. Hart, Late Carey & Hart, 1852), p. 265.

[32] Caroline Howard Gilman [Mrs. Clarissa Packard], *Recollections of a Housekeeper* (New York: Harper & Bros., 1834), pp. 154-55.

[33] Maria McIntosh, *Woman in America: Her Work and Her Reward* (New York: D. Appleton & Co., 1850), pp. 136-37.

[34] Mary Virginia Terhune [Marion Harland], "Two Ways of Keeping a Wife," *Husbands and Homes* (New York: Sheldon & Co., 1865), p. 267.

[35] Caroline Lee Hentz, *Helen and Arthur; or, Miss Thusa's Spinning Wheel* (Philadelphia: T. B. Peterson & Bros., 1856/1853), p. 213.

[36] Caroline Lee Hentz, "Love after Marriage," *Love after Marriage; and Other Stories of the Heart* (Philadelphia: T. B. Peterson, 1857), p. 23.

[37] Maria Cummins, *The Lamplighter* (Chicago: Rand, McNally & Co., n.d./1854), pp. 5-6.

[38] Sara Parton [Fanny Fern], *Rose Clark* (New York: Mason Bros., 1856), p. 30.

[39] Mary Virginia Terhune [Marion Harland], *Ruby's Husband* (New York: Sheldon & Co., 1869), p. 355.

THE POLITICS OF DOMESTIC FICTION

Herbert Ross Brown

SOURCE: "The Sentimental Compromise," in *The Sentimental Novel in America, 1789-1860,* Duke University Press, 1940. Reprint, Pageant Books, Inc., 1959, pp. 358-70.

[*In the following chapter from his* The Sentimental Novel in America, 1789-1860, *Brown criticizes the sentimental novel for its idealism and consequent neglect of social and political issues.*]

The central experiment of the generation had been toward the reconciliation of unlikes—the humanitarian philosophy of enlightenment, perfectibility, democracy, beside the philosophy of acquisition, laissez-faire, gratuitous benevolence. Under this aegis people had played, very earnestly, many variants of a game which may be called Effects without Consequences. Religion without humility. Sensuality without smut. Laissez-faire without oppression. Benevolence without sacrifice. Little Latin and less tears. Salvation without pangs. Administration without statesmanship. Femininity without feminism. Food, and a cupboard undepleted. Bricks without straw. . . .

—E. D. Branch, *The Sentimental Years, 1836-1860.*

The generation which revealed itself in this abundant outpouring of sentimental novels was destined to witness stirring scenes in a great national drama. Historians have done full justice to the breath-taking events which were set in motion by the brash triumph of Andrew Jackson, and which came to an end in the *Sturm und Drang* of the Civil War. Few periods in history have been packed with elements so diverse and dynamic. The rise of the common man on the wings of the new democracy, the conquest of a continent, the voice of the West imperiously demanding to be heard in the councils of state, the widening breach between the planting and the commercial interest culminating in the victory of industrialism—these were but a few of the turbulent factors which added to the growing pains of an adolescent society. It was an era in which the sweep of powerful economic forces brought panics and prosperity and laid the foundations of vast private fortunes. Rapid technological advances carried in their wake unemployment, poverty, exploitation of labor, and widespread unrest. The generation learned to know the consequences of the "speed-up" in production methods and the effects of the "walk-out" and the strike. It was an age seething with movements and reforms: Millerism and Mormonism, Bloomerism and Transcendentalism, Temperance and Abolition. It was an epoch abounding in prodigies and paradoxes: anesthetics and animal magnetism, electric telegraphy and mesmerism, P. T. Barnum and Ralph Waldo Emerson, mass movements and individualism, Lowell factories and Brook Farm, *Godey's Lady's Book* and *Leaves of Grass,* the dime novel and *The Dial.* The national arena was thronged with a motley assembly: John Jacob Astor and Thoreau, "Fanny Fern" and Margaret Fuller, the Fox Sisters and Louis Agassiz, Professors Orson Fowler and Longfellow, Sam Houston and Henry Ward Beecher, Bronson Alcott and Horace Mann. Pervading everything was an exuberant optimism, as jaunty and as expansive as the frontier. The air was electric with hope and expectancy. Millerites eagerly awaited the Day of Judgment, and Perfectionists confidently scanned the horizon for a glimpse of the morning star of the Millennium. Few were the eyes discerning enough to descry the gathering storm clouds of the irrepressible conflict.

Least of all were the sentimental novelists fitted to enlighten their readers as to the real nature of their civilization. They winced before the realities of this raucous period in which were being fashioned the sinews of a new nation. Imbued with a lyric faith in the perfectibility of man, they regarded the America of their own day as a mere vestibule to Utopia. They preferred to dwell in a cozy cloudland of sentiment, secure in a haven of dreams. "Cares cannot come into this dreamland where I live. They sink with the dying street noise, and vanish with the embers of my fire." Thus Donald Grant Mitchell in his *Reveries of a Bachelor* sounded the graceful notes to which the sentimentalists beat their retreat. He touched the tender stops of the same popular theme of escape in *Dream Life*. With angry protests over the Fugitive Slave Law jangling in his ears, Mitchell retired to a farm in his Connecticut Xanadu where he fondled the fleecy cloud drifts of feeling that eternally floated upon "the great over-arching sky of thought." "I like to be rid of them all in this midsummer's day," he wrote of the feverish cares of the fifties. "I like to steep my soul in a sea of quiet, with nothing floating past me as I lie moored to my thought, but the perfume of flowers, and soaring birds, and shadows of clouds." In *Prue and I,* another cherished classic of the generation, George William Curtis savored the luxuries of a roseate world viewed through the spectacles of sentiment. The amiable Prue counted it as her chief blessing that her consort was not compelled to wear "the glasses of truth." The unfortunate Titbottom, whose spectacles were unrouged by sentiment, found them to be a sorry boon; they revealed too many sharp, unupholstered facts. "I longed to enjoy the luxury of ignorant feeling, to love without knowing," he confessed sadly, "to float like a leaf upon the eddies of life, drifted now to a sunny point, now to a solemn shade—now over glittering ripples, now over gleaming calms,—and not to determined ports, a trim vessel with an inexorable rudder." This mood so felicitously evoked by Mitchell and Curtis was in exquisite harmony with popular taste. *Prue and I* was saluted by some enthusiastic critics as the long overdue "great American novel." *Reveries of a Bachelor,* published in 1850, was pirated in fifty editions. More than a million copies were sold in authorized printings. Lulled into a comfortable complacency by soporifics such as these, society drifted pleasantly toward the edge of the whirlpool.

In *Letters and Leadership,* Mr. Van Wyck Brooks has written acutely of the failure of much of our literature to motivate the American scene and to impregnate it with meaning because that literature too often emanated from a national mind sealed against experience. His indictment applies with peculiar force to the writings of the sentimental novelists. They were escapists, artfully evading the experiences of their own day from which letters derive much of their strength. They fed the national complacency by shrouding the actualities of American life in the flattering mists of sentimental optimism. "Phrases take the place of deeds, sentiments those of facts, and grimaces those of benevolent looks," charged Fenimore Cooper in *The Sea Lions.* "How weak we are!" complained Caroline Chesebro' in *The Children of Light.* "We are so afraid of real things and earnest lives—so contented with shams and shows—so willing to put up with the intolerable cant of scribes, pharisees and hypocrites! This forever wishing, and never, by any mistake, doing!" Everywhere in popular fiction there was a tendency to idealize or to shy away from what Mitchell has disparagingly called the "definite, sharp business" of reality. In their aversion to stubborn facts, the sentimentalists resembled Jasper in *The Linwoods.* "He had an instinctive dislike of definitions, as they in Scriptures, who loved darkness, had to light," declared Miss Sedgwick. "He was fond of enveloping his meaning in shadowy analogies, which, like the moon, often led astray, with a beautiful but imperfect and illusive light." Bathed in the refulgent rays of sentiment, even the most barren aspects of the American landscape were thus gilded and transfigured; white democracy and black slavery, when seen through this fuzzy haze, appeared to be comfortably compatible.

At a time when things were in the saddle, and America was in the midst of a boastful materialism, the sentimentalists felt a need of enveloping the new industrial order in an aura of approval. Accepting without critical scrutiny the sanctions of the philosophy of acquisition, they dangled the tempting bait of material prosperity before the eyes of every reader. "Fortune almost literally knocks at every man's door, and the tide is sure to flow, and in many instances, reflow past the dwellings of all," Bickley promised in *The Aristocrat.* Drugged with the opiate of materialism, these writers succumbed without a struggle to the national acquisitiveness. Seldom have novelists been so thoroughly at the mercy of contemporaneity. The public table laden with lavish gifts is barred only to the vicious, boasted Miss Leslie in *Althea Vernon;* every industrious mechanic is on the certain road to plenty. "The prizes are open to all, and they fall with equal favour," corroborated Miss Sedgwick in *The Poor Rich Man and the Rich Poor Man.* "The poor family of this generation is the rich family of the next." Agreeable optimism was a popular ameliorative. "It is an almost invariable truth," proclaimed Lee in *The Contrast,* "that a man in this country, can obtain any place for which he is properly qualified." Aroused at "the mechanical philosophy" of materialism which enshrined greed as a virtue and stultified the aspirations of the human spirit, Emerson scouted the prevailing optimism of its jaunty apologists. "And all of us apologize when we ought not, and congratulate ourselves when we ought not," he lamented in his journal in 1839.

Unmindful of warnings such as this, the sentimental novelists persisted in their mission of putting their contemporaries on extremely pleasant terms with themselves. "In the laboring class, property is a sign of good morals," announced Catharine Sedgwick. "In this country nobody sinks into deep poverty, except by some vice, directly or indirectly." This same facile apologist further declared that "In all our widespread country there is very little necessary poverty. In New England *none* that is not the result of vice and disease." A footnote offered pleasant assurance that the same enviable conditions obtained in New York City, where only the sinful were poor. Timothy Shay Arthur found economics to be a benevolent, not a dismal, science, in which the laws of supply and demand benignly obeyed the dictates of a convenient morality. "If, in a particular branch of business, there should occur a surplus of labor," he observed cheerfully in *The Way to Prosper,* "those who are most skillful, and are at the same time, sober and industrious, will be those who will find employment; while the lazy, drunken, or bad workmen, will be driven off to other and less profitable callings." Over the swift rise of capitalistic industrialism was thrown the glamorous veil of individual freedom and initiative. "You will become exactly what you choose to make yourself. . . . Everything is possible, in any place where Providence has put you," asserted Susan Warner in *The Hills of the Shatemuc.* Mrs. Sarah Hale admitted that increased competitive pressures and new industrial techniques had resulted in some poverty, but found ample compensation in the independence and freedom of American laborers. These redeeming factors, she stated in *Northwood,* distinguish "the poorest of our free citizens from the peasantry of every other country in the world." In America of the fabulous forties every prospect pleased and only foreigners were vile. "We have no *low* in American society," remarked the author of *The Hypocrite.* The few ignorant and vicious exceptions were, for the most part, immigrants and these, he added complacently, were rapidly being reformed in our penitentiaries and state prisons.

The darker aspects of the new industrialism were either blithely ignored or bathed in the warm glow of optimism. Country lads seeking their fortunes found every mill town a veritable Paradise. "The factories appeared like an abode of enchantment," Judd wrote of his young hero in *Richard Edney,* "and the sight revived his heart, and gave him a pleasant impression of the city, as much as a splendid church, or a sunny park of trees, or fine gardens would have done." The operatives were represented as happy and content. Richard "envied the girls, some of whom he knew, who, through that troubled winter night, were tending their looms as in the warmth, beauty, and quietness of

a summer-day." Those who protested at the shameless exploitation of laborers were advised not to ponder too seriously over social maladjustments. "It is all very fair," Lee argued in *The Contrast.* "The rich pay their money to the poor, and in process of time, the poor, if they are industrious, grow rich." Miss Sedgwick expressed her indignation at the outcries sometimes heard against rich men. "Providence has bound the rich and poor by one chain," she had a capitalist declare in *The Poor Rich Man.* "Their interests are the same. If there were none of these hateful rich people," she asked, "who, think you, would build hospitals, and provide asylums for orphans, and for the deaf and dumb, and the blind?" The mercantile economy was endowed with the patriarchal ideals of the benevolent squirearchy which had dignified the life of an earlier generation. "The merchant of today is happier than was Columbus, or Drake, or Vespucius, or Raleigh, or Gilbert," averred Elizabeth Oakes Smith in *The Newsboy,* "for he holds in his good iron safe the wealth of a principality. . . . The chivalry of the olden time, the soul of a Bayard and a Raleigh, have been reproduced." He was, moreover, cited as the only true missionary of civilization. "He hears of famine, and oppression and suffering, and he waits no tardy movements of government, but a ship is freighted with the surplus products of an over-flowing soil, and away goes the American ship, wafted by the benedictions of thousands." If mercantile philanthropists seemed to show more zeal in dispatching succor to the remote places of the earth than to their needy neighbors at home, they merely afford one more instance of the failure of sentimental reformers to take themselves in hand before setting out to improve the world at large. Fashionable women who refused to pay a living wage to their seamstresses also eased their consciences by engaging in flattering humanitarian enterprises. "I sometimes think there is more kindness to the poor than there is justice," objected an underpaid worker in *Three Experiments in Living.* "The ladies are very good in getting up societies and fairs to help us; but they very often seem unwilling to pay us the full price of our labor. If they would *pay* us well, and *give* us less, it would be better for us." With sentimentalists, however, charity rarely began at home.

In their desire to represent human beings, not as they are, but as we should like to have them, the sentimental novelists almost invariably crowned their heroes' careers with worldly riches. The "success story" was immensely popular with a generation of readers who believed that every boy had an equal chance to become president. The saga of Benjamin Franklin strolling through Philadelphia with his rolls of bread under his arm, and the same Franklin, the idol of a brilliant circle at Versailles, was repeated in every household. Horace Courtenay, the ambitious hero of *The Cabin and the Parlor,* "had read of so many, who, like him, had started friendless boys, yet had finally won opulence and station, that he never, for a moment, doubted of success." Longfellow had provided a stirring motto for these aspiring youths whose lexicons contained no such word as *fail*. "I have written *Excelsior* on my banner," boasted Eugene in *Beulah,* "and I intend, like that noble youth, to press forward over every obstacle, mounting at every step, until I, too, stand on the highest pinnacle . . . I feel as if I should like to see Mr. Longfellow, to tell him how I thank him for having written it." Two avenues to riches were open to every boy, according to the author of the *New England Village Choir:* "The one was, to become a clerk of some wholesale or retail merchant in Boston, and the other, to pass through a college." Novelists usually were careful to clear the tracks and to give ambition the right of way. Benjamin Nelson in *The Weldron Family* found it was an easy leap from apprentice to partner: "Being an excellent book-keeper, and proving himself worthy of confidence by his strict integrity and unremitting attention to business, he had not been two years in the mercantile house in which he first engaged, ere he was taken into partnership by his employer." Typical of these success stories was Frederick Thomas's *Clinton Bradshaw* in which the hero advanced rapidly from law school to Congress without a serious setback in his career. The world seemed to be an easy oyster for fictional heroes to pry open. They invariably found pearls. Fenimore Cooper protested vainly at such sentimental mythmaking. "Success may be said to be certain," he wrote ironically in *Afloat and Ashore*. "I like the notion of beginning with nothing, it is so American!"

This sentimentalizing of reality is to be found at every point at which these novelists touched life. They wrote in a perpetual twilight of compromise and repression. Theirs was the captivating game of sporting decorously with indecency, of obscene thinking and strait-laced doing. Like Nora in Mrs. Hentz's *Robert Graham,* they laid the flattering unction to their souls that "It is not the *feeling* passion, but indulging it, that constitutes a sin." They betrayed a sniggering interest in sensuality without violating the merest punctilio of the moral proprieties. They were prudish Peeping Toms in a world of conventionally shaded windows; their lush modesty was nicely calculated to produce something between a smirk and a blush. "Well, there, as I live, was the prettiest *chambre à coucher* imaginable," exulted the author of *Blonde and Brunette* at the sight of a bridal suite. "The curtains were rich white silk damask looped with silver, the coverlet of white merino embroidered, the pillows and sheets trimmed with real Brussels." After reveling at length in other decorous details, Burdett revealed himself as a master in the tantalizing art of knowing just where to stop. There are those who are sensitive, he wrote solicitously, upon "approaching too near the awful secrets of wedlock." Edward Judson, known to a vast underworld of fiction readers as "Ned Buntline," delighted to conduct moral slumming excursions in his own novels. In *The Mysteries and Miseries of New York,* he introduced his hero to a bevy of prostitutes who were disporting themselves on "splendid ottomans." "You will find quite a variety," boasted the madame. "We have blondes and brunettes. The creole of the South; the lily of the Central States; and the snow-drop of the North." This and countless similar scenes served admirably to gratify prurient curiosity and to point an obvious moral. "Reader, we will not linger here in this garden of corruption," Judson wrote piously. "This is a book in which we have pledged ourselves not to write one line that we would not lay before a young sister's eye." There was probably no period in American history at which an ankle was so exciting, observed a recent historian of the era. The novelists made the most of it. "It is a confounded pretty foot," exclaimed a daring admirer in *Ruth Hall*. "I always put my coat on in the front entry, about the time she goes up stairs, to get a peep at it." Modesty without decency, love without sex, affection without passion—these were the prudish ingredients with which the sentimentalists worked. If any of them was ever tempted to call a spade a spade, he succeeded in resisting the impulse.

Much of the teaching in religious fiction was softened to an easy compliance with the universal desire for comfort and cheerfulness. In *Authorship,* John Neal scoffed at the widespread popularity of religious novels with their lessons heavily gilded with promises of durable material rewards. The church has "no god but gold," charged Samuel Judah in *The Buccaneers*. Fashionable sermons were as comfortably cushioned as the most expensive pews. A new minister in *Bubbleton Parish* was warned against preaching "practical sermons." "Our people generally prefer to have their pastor set forth the principles of the gospel in a forcible and attractive manner, instead of indulging in direct allusions, which are apt to irritate the feelings," advised a friendly parishioner. "It grieves them to see a minister disregard the apostolic method, and discuss in the pulpit irritating themes, such as can only mar the peace of a congregation, and disturb the unity of Christian sentiment." George William Curtis in *Potiphar Papers* described the readiness of the clergy to fill their sermons with the sonorous irrelevancies dear to the hearts of sentimentalists. "The cloth is very hard upon Cain, and completely routs the erring Kings of Judah," he noted. "The Spanish Inquisition, too, gets frightful knocks, and there is much eloquent exhortation to preach the gospel in the interior of Siam." Southern divines who were too honest to attempt to justify slavery by Scriptural authority took refuge in the safe doctrines of moderation and moral suasion. "I can but preach the gospel, teach the people the great law of love to God and man, and leave that to do the work gradually," concluded a pastor in *Honor*. "I say little about slavery, but much about justice and charity to all." To the underprivileged, the church urged the virtues of Christian resignation and the beauties of meek poverty. To wealthy communicants, she guaranteed salvation without pangs: "If you feel any wish to enter Heaven, just pave the way there by charity. It is the best road that I can point out to you, and has bridges in it, that will carry you over a multitude of sins." The Reverend Josiah Gilbert Holland found it difficult to believe that a good businessman could be "a very bad man." "Men who have exacted the last fraction of a cent with one hand, in the way of business," he submitted in his *Letters to the Joneses,* "have disbursed thousands of dollars with the other, in the way of charity." The sentimental pilgrim's progress to the Celestial City was made attractive by liberal stop-over privileges in Vanity Fair. There was abundant assurance, too, that even that pleasantly wicked city would, somehow or other, ultimately be washed clean with tears.

The most conspicuous failure of the sentimentalists was their inability to solve the irrepressible problem of slavery. Certainly they tried hard enough. All their cherished weapons: pleasant escape, artful dodging, cunning evasion, and comfortable compromise were brought to bear upon it without avail. Slavery stubbornly refused "to vanish like a dream" as Hawthorne had predicted it might if it were only unmolested. "But come, we will compromise—compromise cuts all the gordian knots now-a-days," urged an optimist in Miss Sedgwick's *Married or Single?* This was the sovereign specific in the pharmacopoeia of the sentimentalists, and they prescribed it confidently. For their facile faith in its powers there seemed to be ample warrant in the tactics of the nation's lawmakers. Had not repeated applications of this soothing emollient allayed the bothersome eruptions of this malady in 1787, 1820, 1833, and 1850? Surely, it might succeed once again. Slavery was an evil, to be sure, but one too subtly woven into the warp and woof of our existence to be handled rigorously. "It is a dark thread," admitted Caroline Lee Hentz in *Marcus Warland,* "but as it winds along, it gleams with bright and silvery lustre, and some of the most beautiful lights and shades of the texture are owing to the blending of these sable filaments." Were not slaves the best of domestic servants, their ebon faces shining in the glory of subserviency? Were they not happier singing spirituals by their cabin doors under the Southern moon than they would have been chanting cannibalistic war songs in darkest Africa? Had the annals of Christian benevolence anything to show more fair than the sight of a planter's wife tenderly nursing a sick old granny whose wool had grown white in her mistress's service? Were not planters carrying out God's own providence in acquainting the race of Ham with the consolations of the Gospel? What were a few short years in Louisiana rice fields to the priceless boon of eternal freedom in Beulah Land? Had not New Englanders quite enough to do to ameliorate the conditions of their own white slaves in the textile mills? Would Uncle Tom have been more comfortable in a miserable "company house" in Lawrence or Lowell than in his honeysuckle-embowered cabin in the genial Southland? Did millowners cheerfully pamper their aged operatives in their twilight years with inexhaustible fried chicken and endless holidays of sunny idleness? Slavery by any other name would be far from hideous. Was it not, after all, merely an evangelical course in compulsory manual training and Christianity, mercifully designed for a benighted race whose souls could be reclaimed by no other means? These were the questions being asked by sentimentalists on both sides of Mason and Dixon's line. Nor were the abolitionists more eager to put their own houses in order before they set out to reform those of their neighbors. In attacking the plantation system they closed their eyes to the factory system, and to the exploitative basis of their own raw industrialism in which they confused wage labor with free labor. As Parrington has observed, it was the familiar story of the kettle and the pot. Blinded by sectional economic interests, each side saw only half the truth. "They beheld the mote in a brother's eye, but considered not the beam that was in their own."

It would be uncritical to assume that the bombardment of Fort Sumter demolished the stronghold of the sentimentalists. Not unlike Major Anderson and his Union forces, they evacuated their position with colors flying and with drums beating. In the age of critical realism which followed the Civil War, they continued to recruit their readers from those who persisted in clinging to myths, who refused to recognize reality, and who sought in fiction an escape rather than a challenge. Lutestring enthusiasts are not peculiar to any age, although they found in the first generation of the American middle class a comfortable habitat. Worse than uncritical, moreover, would be the easy assumption that these sentimental novels never rang true, that they sprang from impulses which were wholly false, and that they failed to reflect the aspirations quietly cherished in thousands of hearts. The enlarged heart of sentimentality is a disease to which those who readily respond to the appeal of human nature are peculiarly susceptible. It is the excess of a virtue, the perversion of an ideal. No student of our national letters can escape the conviction that ours is an idealistic literature, fired with a passion for justice, liberty, and brotherhood. The failure of the sentimental compromise should teach our critics that theirs is the task of guiding the creative spirit to face squarely the realities of American life without losing its high ideals. Although an unwitting one, this is the most important lesson these faded favorites of an earlier generation have for us today.

Mary P. Ryan

SOURCE: "The Tears and Trials of Domesticity: Women's Fiction in the 1850s," in *The Empire of the Mother: American Writing about Domesticity, 1830-1860,* The Institute for Research in History and The Haworth Press, 1982, pp. 115-41.

[*In the following excerpt, Ryan contends that the cult of domesticity, with its emphasis on mothers as the protectors of morality, linked the sentimental novel to the abolitionist movement.*]

Most writers of the 1850s recorded only the routine discomforts of love and marriage. T.S. Arthur wrote in *Home Lights and Shadows,* "Oh, how dark the shadows at times, and how faint the sunshine" in the ordinary urban home.[1] In *Married Not Mated* Alice Carey wrote of the endurable but imperfect matches East and West. Grace Greenwood's light offering, *Greenwood Leaves,* recorded the bitter-sweet trials of domestic women:

It is one of my beliefs that every tolerably pretty maiden (present company excepted) who has arrived at the age of twenty and upwards, has known something like a disappointment of the heart.[2]

Greenwood's "heart histories" chronicled the commonplace anguish of her female acquaintances: unrequited love, deaths of grooms, marital misunderstandings, and, occasionally, a more exotic maladies, such as a groom's arrival at the altar to announce his marriage to the bride's sister.

Countless tears preceded the facile happy ending of a quiet domestic tableau. The most hackneyed and fre-quent causes of tears—lonely spinsterhood, unrequited heterosexual love, deviant sex roles, childhood nostalgia—fed off fundamental contradictions in the antebellum family system, especially its extreme gender asymmetry and the social isolation of the family. The cult of domesticity celebrated a logical and practical impossibility. It bred male and female into dichotomous roles and temperaments, then venerated their union and required their interdependence within an isolated home. The heterosexual tension was lodged at the very center of the domestic mode of social reproduction, and it cast a shadow over the empire of the mother. But it was the genius of this popular culture to inculcate domestic values and then provide, in the novel, an outlet for their expression and catharsis.

The torment of little heartaches and wholesale domestic disasters could not be disguised by a happy ending. They were, in fact, the substance and *raison d'être* of women's fiction in the 1850s. This literary genre did not aspire to some pristine aesthetic standard or to create an imaginary world of abstract beauty, symmetry, and order. Unlike the short family fiction of the 1830s and '40s, the domestic novel was more than an entertaining mode of instruction. The femininized novel of the 1850s was above all else a literary dramatization of the contradictions of the family and the gender system. It titillated readers with repeated images of the fears, annoyances, mundane anxieties, and cataclysmic possibilities of everyday domesticity.

All of this would have been benign enough were it not for the fact that the turgid logic of the cult of domesticity soon burst out of the confines of the novel and found its way into the turbulent center of American politics. Domesticity went on public trial in the 1850s as its tenets became intertwined with the issues of slavery and sectionalism. Popular fiction became a stormy courtroom where authors like Harriet Beecher Stowe argued the domestic merits of slavery, and Southern writers rose to defend the reputation of their families.

Thirty years earlier the discussion of slavery was primarily the prerogative of political and social elites. The intellectual agonies of men like Jefferson and documents like the Declaration of Independence had demolished the moral, political, and philosophical underpinnings for slavery. Yet these arguments were not circulated throughout the population by means of democratic associations or public podiums, much less novels. Several works of literature in the 1820s and '30s addressed themselves to the peculiar institution of the South. But most, like the rambling sketches of Southern life by John Pendleton Kennedy and Caroline Gilman and the stirring novels by Sarah Josepha Hale and Richard Hildreth, eschewed such staples of domestic fiction as romantic love, fragile femininity, and excessive maternal affection.[3] It was the abolitionist polemicists of the 1830s who first invested the question of slavery with domestic sentiments.

When American readers glanced upon the first page of the *Liberator* in the 1830s they found its title nearly eclipsed by the sketch on its masthead; a graphic portrayal of a slave family about to be wrenched apart on the auction block. The verbal as well as the pictorial imagery of the *Liberator* cultivated a personal, domestic response. The poetic salutation in the first issue of the *Liberator* read:

> Art thou a parent? Shall children be
> Rent from thy breast, like branches from the
>   tree
> And damned to servitude, in helplessness,
> On other shores, and thou ask no redress?[4]

The abolitionist movement ingeniously exploited the same family anxieties that fed reform associations and ladies' magazines in the 1830s.

Elizabeth Margaret Chandler utilized this ploy as early as 1829, when she issued her "Appeal to the Ladies of the United States":

> Mother, look down upon that infant slumbering by your side—have not his smiles become as it were a portion of your own existence? . . . Yet were it told to you that just when he was arisen into bold, glad boyhood, when his beautiful bright eyes began to kindle with awakening and early knowledge, when the deep feelings of his heart are beginning to gather themselves together— and reason and gratitude to mingle with his instinctive love—wert thou told then he should be torn from thee, and born away forever into hopeless, irremediable slavery—wouldst thou not rather that death should at once set his cold signet upon him, there where he sleeps in his innocent beauty in the cradle by thy side.[5]

Chandler created a sentimental device that became the mainstay of anti-slavery propaganda. She assumed that the American mother was bound to her child by the most exhaustive expenditure of affection, and that in the course of her gentle nurturing she would merge her own identity with his. When that child reached adolescence and set out on his own, the mother might well fear the breach of maternal ties just as her attentive care was bearing fruit. Chandler displaced this anxiety onto the slave child. This was the sentimental anti-slavery formula: the conversion of mundane apprehensions of domestic disruption into sympathy for the slave. Elizabeth Chandler, the anti-slavery analogue to Lydia Sigourney, wrote death-bed verse for the *Liberator's* Female Anti-Slavery column.

In the 1830s the potent combination of anti-slavery and domesticity caused widespread public consterna-

tion and exploded into anti-abolition riots and impassioned debates about women's proper sphere. In the wake of this controversy both abolitionism and domestic politics became relatively quiescent. It was not until the 1850s that the cult of domesticity became robust enough to sustain a new assault on the family life of the South.

In the two decades before the Civil War, as American editors and publishers unfurled the banners of motherhood and home, Harriet Beecher Stowe was acquiring the skills of domestic sentimentality. Her homiletic tales could be found in magazines from *Godey's* to the *Advocate of Moral Reform,* and were quite indistinguishable from the general run of ladies' magazine material. When her brother, Henry Ward, suggested that her literary abilities be used to forward the cause of the slave, Harriet Beecher Stowe was happy to oblige. The factual and didactic treatments of slavery compiled by the abolitionists of the 1830s, and especially Theodore and Angelina Grimké Weld's *Slavery as It Is,* supplied copious and powerful images of domestic disruption in the slave quarter which she speedily translated into a novel. When *Uncle Tom's Cabin* appeared in 1851 as a serial in the *National Era,* Stowe and the American public were ready, both having completed two decades of domestic education and experience.

Stowe pumped into *Uncle Tom's Cabin* a stream of evocative images drawn from the growing library of domesticity. She managed to weave all the themes of family literature—filial, parental, and conjugal anxieties—into one narrative. Stowe had polished the devices of domestic literature to perfection, painting dying children, anxious parents, and estranged lovers with a poignancy unrivaled in the literature of the period. The richness of detail and breadth of plot in the full-fledged novel allowed for the expression of cherished domestic values as well as innumerable domestic tensions. The anti-slavery novel provided a particularly convenient forum in which to portray familial disaster. In describing the villainous and alien institution to northern white readers, happy endings could be endlessly deferred; the suffering borne by black men and women could be described at length. The domestic disruptions of slave families were both dramatic enough and far enough removed from the experience of white middleclass Northerners to afford these readers an orgiastic domestic catharsis. No wonder, then, that *Uncle Tom's Cabin* became the most popular book of the nineteenth century, selling 300,000 copies in a year. Not even the pro-slavery forces were immune to Stowe's techniques; their novelistic rebuttals gingerly accepted her domestic premises.

By 1852 the American publishing industry had developed the marketing techniques and productive machinery to distribute Stowe's brew of domesticity and

135,000 SETS, 270,000 VOLUMES SOLD.

UNCLE TOM'S CABIN

FOR SALE HERE.

AN EDITION FOR THE MILLION, COMPLETE IN 1 Vol., PRICE 37 1-2 CENTS.
"   "   IN GERMAN, IN 1 Vol., PRICE 50 CENTS.
"   "   IN 2 Vols,. CLOTH, 6 PLATES, PRICE $1.50.
SUPERB ILLUSTRATED EDITION, IN 1 Vol., WITH 153 ENGRAVINGS,
PRICES FROM $2.50 TO $5.00.

The Greatest Book of the Age.

An advertisement for Stowe's Uncle Tom's Cabin.

anti-slavery sentiments throughout the land. Moreover, not even sectional animosity and the possibility of losing half their customers deterred American publishers from obliging the domestic tastes of their readers. Stowe's proven popularity outweighed omens of disunion, especially since her expressed purposes were conciliatory to North and South. Northern-based publishers, including Harpers and Ticknor and Fields, readily distributed pro-slavery novels of proven domestic worth by Southern women such as Caroline Lee Hentz and Maria McIntosh. These astute purveyors of public taste seemed confident that their sophisticated cultural system could absorb even the volatile issue of slavery.

Both the pro- and anti-slavery novels of the 1850s adopted the sentimental formula and the cult of domesticity wholesale. Each novel set out, first of all, to resolve the romantic difficulties of hero and heroine, and thus establish a home redolent with conjugal love. With white couples this was a simple matter, but infusing black characters with this sentimental notion often proved difficult, for pro- and anti-slavery writers alike. Both Stowe and the Southern apologist J. Thornton Randolph called on mulattoes to play the romantic lead among slaves. These authors also had some difficulty establishing sentimental filial ties among blacks. Again it was usually the mulatto mother who cherished the child in her arms. The mulattoes Charles and Cora of *The Cabin and the Parlor* represented the typical domestic tableau. "Oh! the bliss of that moment when the mother first feels another heart against her own. . . . The sight of Cora and his daughter was like sunshine on his [Charles'] soul."[6]

North and South were also in virtual agreement on their preferred child-rearing techniques. In fact, they often cooperated in rearing model children. The heroine of *The Planter's Northern Bride* was called upon to gently instill discipline in the indulged child of her Southern husband. Aunt Ophelia, Stowe's paradigm of New England virtue, played a similar role in the upbringing of southern children in *Uncle Tom's Cabin.* Pro- and anti-slavery authors also agreed on the angelic nature and redemptive power of such children.[7] The tearful death of little Eva was reenacted at the pathetic deathbed of a planter's son by the slavery apologist, Randolph. Thus, affectionate methods of child-rearing, like romantic love, were values held in common by both the advocates and the enemies of the slave system.

Finally both North and South pledged fictional allegiance to the power and passivity of the mother. The white heroine, North and South, was submissive, meek, and self-sacrificing, armed only with loving smiles and gentle persuasion. These weapons were sufficient, however, to direct husbands along the path to virtue and the correct attitude toward slavery. The coupling of moral power and feminine weakness served as a convenient method of castigating social evil without encouraging overt rebellion. Aunt Phillus, Mary Eastman's pro-slavery answer to Uncle Tom, managed to overpower her shiftless and drunken husband, while she herself was totally compliant before the slave system, submissive to master, mistress, and Christian God.[8] Stowe infused her heroines and, of course, Uncle Tom himself, with such feminine qualities. Eliza shuddered at George's defiance of his master, and discouraged his escape as well as any violent attack on the slave system. In the end, it was only the strength of her maternal instincts and the threat to her child that induced Eliza to brave the escape from slavery.[9]

All the novels of the 1850s upheld social peace and passivity, even while decrying the domestic monstrosities of both the slave system and industrial capitalism. Yet all the popular writers of the day, pro- and anti-slavery, had to expose the fragility of domestic ties and wrench families apart if they were to win the reader's empathy. By ascribing domestic infractions and failures to either North or South, novelists of the 1850s could not help but provoke or exacerbate sectional discord, and in the process transform the moral agency of women into a less benign and pacific influence.

In *Uncle Tom's Cabin* Harriet Beecher Stowe charted the progressive disintegration of Southern family life. In order to create a domestic plot out of the issue of slavery, Stowe had to instill strong family loyalties in the slave population. Thus, the planter's wife, Mrs. Shelby, was called upon to teach the principal slave characters, Uncle Tom, Chloe, George, and Eliza, "the duties of the family."[10] Yet this was a dubious service, for no sooner had she tied the domestic knot than her husband's economic straits induced him to sell Tom away from his wife Chloe. Tom then proceeded to the next scene of domestic disruption, the St. Claire household, where the corrupting effect of slavery upon the master's family was illustrated: he found a neurotic wife, weak husband, angelic but dying child, and the general disorder of a household operated by slaves. It was on this plantation that young Henrique St. Claire brutally whipped a slave companion, forcing his father to admit that "there is no doubt that our system is a difficult one to raise children under."[11] Even the sentimental *deus ex machina,* the deathbed wishes of the child Eva, could not prevent further domestic disintegration, and Tom proceeded to a third Southern household, the residence of Simon Legree. This was a burlesque of a home; its hearth was employed only to light Legree's cigars and heat his punch, not to warm the domestic circle. Herein was staged the most lurid episode of family disintegration, Legree's lecherous pursuit of both Emmeline, an innocent young girl newly torn from her mother, and Cassy, an embittered woman long deprived of her children. It was here also that Uncle Tom was finally rent from Chloe, by his death at Legree's hands. As Tom had been transported further South and deeper into domestic confusion, George and Eliza, on the other hand, had made their way North through a series of model domestic shelters.

The pro-slavery novels written in the wake of *Uncle Tom's Cabin* accepted Stowe's priorities and values, merely contending that Northern abolitionists were the cause of family disruption in the South, or that slavery provided more domestic security than did the industrial North. Caroline Hentz portrayed the Northern subversion of Southern domesticity in an incendiary guise. She pictured a Northern preacher ingratiating himself to a Southern family only to plot a slave insurrection. "We should like to ask him," she wrote, "if he has no home, no wife or child of his own, no household goods to defend, no domestic penetralia to keep sacred from intrusion."[12] Encouraging slaves to run away was another means by which Northerners reputedly disturbed the South's domestic peace. Hentz recorded the lament of one runaway:

> Sometimes it was the voice of Jim saying, "Crissey, Crissey, I told you neber to run away, you'll never see poor Jim no more!" Sometimes they were the voices of little children crying, "Mammy, mammy, arn't you neber coming agin."[13]

By such literary devices the blame for Southern domestic instability was shifted to the North.

Slavery apologists did not hesitate, moreover, to cast aspersions on the domestic life of the North. In *The Lofty and the Lowly,* Maria McIntosh described the family of the wealthy Northern merchant in which domestic values were sacrificed to the ambition of the father and the fashionable aspirations of the wife.[14] The plight of the Northern wage-earner provided even greater sentimental possibilities, and no one exploited them more thoroughly than did J. Thornton Randolph. In *The Cabin and the Parlor,* Horace, the fragile son of a deceased planter, ventured north to win his fortune in order to support his mother and sister. The naive Horace took a position as an office boy, finding to his dismay that his wages never rose even to a subsistence level. As Horace lay on his deathbed crying for his mother, Randolph admonished his Northern readers, "You make slaves of white children, poor orphans, and work them to death. You promise falsely."[15] Randolph also portrayed infanticide as a routine evil of the industrial North and inquired: "What must we think of that system which so brutalizes its victim that it destroys the natural instincts of the mother and makes her think more of a few shillings than of her child."[16] Finally, Randolph noted less spectacular and more prevalent Northern modes of breaking up families.

The operation of your social system does it continually by compelling families to separate in order that they can live, sending a son to California or the Quinea coast, a daughter West to teach school, or a father to India to die of cholera.[17]

In sum, apologists for slavery fictionally ascribed domestic instability to the North by means of familiar themes: sentimental deaths, brutality, and routine economic exigency.

Such images captured a mass reading audience and even stirred the domestic sensibilities of New England matrons like Lydia Maria Child, Lydia Sigourney and Catharine Sedgwick. Sigourney wrote in the fall of 1860, "my dear friend, I feel so sad-hearted about the clouds in our Southern horizon." Sigourney's sadness blended politics and domesticity. She traced her allegiance to the national union to childhood tales about the patriotism of Washington heard at her father's knee. She appealed to her friends to wield their feminine weapons, prayer and the gentle persuasion of brothers and husbands, to save the beloved Union. Catharine Sedgwick's consciousness of the slavery issue was also enveloped in domestic sentiments. Her interest was aroused by the masculine heroism and feminine values of John Brown, his "high and holy motives," "a beautiful example in this materialistic age."[18] John Brown's raid also sparked the domestic affections of Lydia Child, and rekindled her anti-slavery fervor. She was so touched by John Brown's heroism that she volunteered to be his personal nurse.

The reaction of these women to the slavery debates and sectional conflict of the 1850s illustrates the convergence of domesticity and politics. Sigourney, Sedgwick, and Child not only responded to politics as sensitive and maternal females, but with a strong sense of personal intimacy. In 1860 Lydia Child observed of the popular response to her anti-slavery writings: "More and more, I marvel at the interest people take in personalities. I take almost none in them, except where my affections are concerned."[19] Yet Child's own anti-slavery resurgence was intensely emotional. Her affections became attached to utter strangers like John Brown, just as masses of readers attached their emotions to fictional slave families. Moreover, images such as the dramatic gestures of John Brown, or the matronly grace of Harriet Beecher Stowe helped spread and intensify sectional feelings. When Calvin Stowe reportedly engaged in a polite conversation with the anti-slavery laggard, President Pierce, Lydia Child exclaimed, "If I were his wife, I'd sue for divorce and take it if I couldn't get it by petitioning."[20] This kind of political response not only identified the anti-slavery cause with the actions of a popular literary figure, but also translated politics into a domestic conflict. This melange of politics, popular literature, and family affairs illustrates the centrality of domesticity in the national system of values, and the curious and powerful way mass culture was injected into individual, immediate, "real," experience. Residents of isolated homes attached their personal loyalties and affixed their anxieties to the poignant domestic images and dramas that the American cultural network circulated throughout the nation.

Popular literature did not, however, put forward any viable social or political remedies for the domestic evils it catalogued with such morbid delight. Harriet Beecher Stowe was not an advocate of the immediate abolition of slavery, nor was J. Thornton Randolph plotting the overthrow of the capitalist system. The practical goal of the novelist was primarily to escort heroes and heroines toward a happy ending. The pro-slavery writer strove only to abate the sectional conflict that disturbed the peace of Southern families, and often designed an intersectional marriage alliance for this purpose. Occasionally the novel's resolution incorporated a broader population in the happy domestic finale. The double wedding that concluded McIntosh's *The Lofty and the Lowly* united the Southern hero to a Northern bride and a policy of benevolence toward his slave charges, while his Northern counterpart embraced a Southern wife and plans to build a utopian community for the employees of his factory. Yet such extensions of family responsibility were as rare in fiction as they were in fact in the 1850s. Customarily only the white families and a few trusted house slaves, largely mulattoes, emerged from these novels in full domestic ideality, as custodians of their own nuclear homes.[21]

Once again *Uncle Tom's Cabin* set the formula for this denouement of domesticity. The masculine exertions of George and the maternal loyalties of his wife propelled their escape from the slave system and won them their domestic reward: "A small neat tenement . . . the cheery fire blazes in the hearth; the tea-table covered with a snowy cloth stands prepared for the evening meal."[22] All this testified to Eliza's efficient home management, which enabled George to sit peacefully at his desk while his son was quietly at play. The hero of Stowe's second anti-slavery novel resided at book's end in a similar domestic refuge, a cozy farmhouse, where he reads to his son on a wintry evening. The ideal resolution of the tortuous plots of the slavery novels was simply the establishment of nuclear families, warm fortresses against the confusion and anonymity of the world outside. This resolution was reached, moreover, in the simple manner of a novel's plot, through the individual exertions of heroic characters without any intervening social policies or political decisions.

Writers who, by dint of gender, were steeped in domesticity, discouraged from intellectual exertion, and debarred from practical politics, often proved shoddy social theorists. The domestic argument constricted the oppression of slavery into the narrow vision of sentimental womanhood and contained neither a clear conception of freedom for the black man and woman nor a rational purpose for Civil War. The principle of human freedom stood on a shaky foundation of domestic priorities. *Uncle Tom's Cabin* subscribed to this definition of freedom:

> The right of a man to be a man and not a brute; the right to call the wife of his bosom his wife, to protect her from lawless violence; the right to protect and educate his child; the right to have a home of his own, a character of his own, unsubject to the will of another.[23]

Stowe rendered human rights nearly equivalent to the responsibilities of the model husband; freedom was submerged in domestic conformity. Moreover, this domestic construction of freedom left the female half of the population in the position of protected wife, rather like a child, and similar to the chattels of a benevolent master.

Didactic anti-slavery literature written by males often adopted this same interpretation of freedom. In his tract, "The Family Relation as Affected by Slavery," Charles K. Whipple, relying heavily on the writings of Frederick Law Olmstead and F. W. Higginson, selected slavery's degradation of the popular model of marriage as its greatest evil. This marriage is

> A community of interest not less than of affection. . . . It is the obvious duty as well as the right of a husband to provide for the defense, and security, and comfort, and happiness of his wife, before those of any other human being.[24]

Thus, for a female, the domestic rendition of freedom meant a protected, passive status, rather than control of her own existence. Black men fared no better than women of either race within this ethic. In Whipple's treatise the slave appeared primarily as a racial threat to the white family, a promiscuous example for pure women, a savage companion for angelic children.[25] The rights and dignity of black women and men were repeatedly obscured in the anti-slavery fiction of the 1850s, which abounded in portraits of sambo stereotypes dancing a jig, and favored mulattoes who assimilated the values and assumed the characteristics of white domestic heroes and heroines.

Moreover, the doctrine of domesticity sundered the more inclusive social organizations necessary to uphold human rights and to exercise human freedom. Whipple not only placed conjugal relations above the responsibilities to "any other human being," but also depreciated more extensive social ties. The last section of his tract, devoted to the "Bearing of Slavery on Society at Large," was very brief. Whipple simply stated:

> But is not this question already answered? We have seen the effect of slavery upon the family; and society at large is but an aggregate of families. Doth a fountain send forth at the same time sweet water and bitter?[26]

Whipple parroted the social theory that underlay the cult of domesticity. Individual family units could be relied upon to secure the common welfare and maintain social order. No intermediary institutions, no combination of critical citizens, no collective action by the oppressed, were necessary to ensure social justice.

These families, however, were prey to the values circulated by a centralized, profit-oriented publishing industry. This fountain of domestic values was spewing forth a bitter sectional brew by 1860. Even the gentle voice of Lydia Child rose to a shrill pitch in 1859. In a volume called *The Patriarchal Institution* Child's sentimental sympathy turned to sarcasm as she recommended the benefits of being a slave to her Northern reader: relief from domestic cares and expenses at the auction block, numerous opportunities for promiscuity, and the honor of having the master take your daughter as a mistress. The bitterness and personal immediacy of Child's tone were not likely to encourage sectional reconciliation.[27] It was in this atmosphere of outraged public opinion, with North pitted against South in angry defense of sacred domestic values, that the conflagration of Fort Sumter was ignited.

Surely the Civil War cannot be reduced to a by-product of domestic culture. But neither can it be fully understood without reference to the literary discourse which surrounded it and articulated and interpreted issues of slavery and sectionalism. When the United States came apart at its North-South seam in 1860, the national culture was still weakly woven together by the fragile threads of domestic ideology.

After three decades of sounding the alarm about the breach of family ties, writers and readers, North and South, had become accustomed to the language of domestic disruption and family tension. Domestic associations, symbols, and evocations had the ideological power to carry Americans toward Civil War. The most bitter trial of domesticity was conducted center stage, in the public sphere and on the battlefields of civil war.

Notes

1 Timothy Shay Arthur, *Homelights and Shadows* (New York, 1853), p. iii.

2 Grace Greenwood [Sara Clark], *Greenwood Leaves* (Boston, 1850), chap. 2.

3 Caroline Gilman, *Recollections of a Southern Matron* (New York, 1837), pp. 235-36; John Pendleton Kennedy, *Swallowbarn* (New York, 1851), pp. 461-90; Sarah Josepha Hale, *Northwood* (New York, 1852), pp. 121-22; William R. Taylor, *Cavalier and Yankee* (New York, 1961); Richard Hildreth, *The Slave* (New York, 1836), vol. 1, p. 6; vol. 2, p. 9.

4 *The Liberator,* 1, January 1, 1831, p. 1.

5 Ibid; *The Poetical Works of Elizabeth Margaret Chandler* (Philadelphia, 1837).

6 Thornton Randolph [Charles Jacobs Peterson], *The Cabin and the Parlor* (Philadelphia, 1852), pp. 124-25.

7 Caroline Lee Hentz, *The Planter's Northern Bride* (Philadelphia, 1851), pp. vii-viii; Stowe, *Uncle Tom's Cabin* (New York, Colliers Paperback Edition, 1962), pp. 294-308.

8 Hentz, *Planter's Northern Bride,* p. 206; Maria McIntosh, *The Lofty and the Lowly* (New York, 1852), pp. 5-6; Mary H. Eastman, *Aunt Phillus's Cabin* (Philadelphia, 1852), passim.

9 Stowe, *Uncle Tom,* pp. 69-73.

10 Ibid., p. 88.

11 Ibid., p. 325.

12 Hentz, *Planter's Northern Bride,* p. 457.

13 Ibid., p. 282.

14 McIntosh, *Lofty and Lowly,* chap. 1.

15 Peterson, *Cabin and Parlor,* p. 241.

16 Ibid., p. 171.

17 Ibid., p. 180.

18 Lydia Sigourney to Mary Patrick, November 24, 1860, Sigourney Papers [Massachusetts Historical Society (hereafter MHS)]; Catharine Sedgwick to Kate Minot, November 6, 1859, Sedgwick Papers MHS.

19 Lydia Child, fragment of letter, 1856, Loring Family Papers, [Schlesinger Library, Radcliffe College (hereafter SL)].

20 Child to Anna Loring, February 27, 1860, Loring Family Papers, SL.

[21] McIntosh, *Lofty and Lowly,* pp. 311-12; for a description of the wider networks among slaves, see Herbert Gutman, *The Black Family in Slavery and Freedom* (New York, 1976), especially chaps. 3, 4, 5.

[22] Stowe, *Uncle Tom,* pp. 490-91.

[23] Ibid., p. 44.

[24] Charles K. Whipple, *The Family Relationship as Affected by Slavery* (Cincinatti, 1858), p. 13.

[25] Ibid., pp. 14-15, 20.

[26] Ibid., p. 23.

[27] Lydia Maria Child, *The Patriarchal Institution* (New York, 1860), pp. 50-52.

Amy Schrager Lang

SOURCE: "Class and the Strategies of Sympathy," in *The Culture of Sentiment: Race, Gender, and Sentimentality in Nineteenth-Century America,* edited by Shirley Samuels, Oxford University Press, 1992, pp. 128-42.

[*In the essay that follows, Lang contends that the sentimental novel displaces class issues by reducing them to race and gender issues.*]

In 1851 the *North American Review* published a series of articles on political economy written by Francis Bowen, editor of the *Review* from 1843 until 1854 and, later, Alvord Professor of Natural Religion, Moral Philosophy, and Civil Polity at Harvard University. "There is a danger," Bowen wrote, "from which no civilized community is entirely free, lest the several classes of its society should nourish mutual jealousy and hatred, which may finally break out into open hostilities, under the mistaken opinion that their interests are opposite, and that one or more of them possess an undue advantage, which they are always ready to exercise by oppressing the others."[1] In the particular case of the United States, Bowen insisted, this mistaken opinion could only be held by those who failed to appreciate the "peculiar mobility" of American society. Today's pauper was, after all, tomorrow's merchant—"the man who labored for another last year," Abraham Lincoln declared, "this year labors for himself, and next year he will hire others to labor for him."[2]

This continuous displacement of master by man tended, in Bowen's view, to blur, if not altogether obliterate, the boundary between capital and labor. In fact, it was this very fluidity of boundaries that the term "class" was meant to capture; unlike "caste" or "rank," "class"

identified the groupings into which all societies naturally divided, the way stations en route from pauperism to wealth. Properly considered—that is, considered not historically but teleologically—class antagonism would thus necessarily dissolve in a perfect harmony of interests.

While not everyone agreed with Bowen's analysis of class in America, he was hardly alone in his attention to social taxonomy and the operation of class. Throughout the 1840s and 1850s, scholars, legislators, journalists, reformers, and writers of every political stripe ventured their opinions about the nature and ramifications of class in America. *Harper's Monthly* ran sketches of "The Factory Boy"; *Democratic Review* printed titles like "Poverty and Misery, versus Reform and Progress"; *Merchant's Magazine and Commercial Review, Southern Quarterly Review,* and *North American Review* devoted their pages to articles on "Abuses of Classification," "The Distribution of Wealth," and "The True Theory of Labor and Capital." Likewise, from the "Knights and Squires" of the *Pequod* to the fading aristocrats of the house of the seven gables, from the protagonists of domestic fiction, oppressed by the vicious poor and the dissolute rich alike, to Whitman's spectral "shape" rising from "[t]he ashes and the rags—its hands tight to the throats of kings," antebellum literature records the anxiety that accompanied the recognition and naming of class divisions in the United States in the years surrounding the European revolutions of 1848.

Not everyone, as I have suggested, shared Bowen's views. Nonetheless, while Europeans took to the streets, Americans increasingly promulgated and embraced images of harmony. Even as the extremes of wealth and poverty grew, as the women's rights movement gathered strength, and conflict over slavery intensified, the doctrine of the harmony of interests was expounded not only as economic theory but as spiritual principle. The consummate emblem of that harmony, bridging the economic and the spiritual, was the idealized middle-class home. If social mobility seemed to the likes of Bowen to assure a harmony of interests in the marketplace, the champions of domesticity saw in the stability of gender— that is, in the naturalizing and fixing of gender distinctions—the prospect of an even more perfect harmony. Like the vast, undifferentiated expanse of empire,[3] the narrow and highly ordered space of the middle-class home operated to contain the danger of class antagonism by providing an image of social harmony founded not on political principles or economic behavior but on the "natural" differentiation of the sexes. Nowhere is this image more clearly drawn than in domestic fiction, where the problem of class is neither resolved nor repressed but rather displaced, and where harmony—spiritual, familial, and social— is the highest good.

The displacement of class by gender is peculiarly apparent in a novel like Maria Cummins's 1854 bestseller *The Lamplighter,* a novel that conforms in every respect to our assumptions about domestic fiction. Cummins follows her young protagonist, Gerty Flint, from a childhood of poverty and abuse into middle-class comfort, piety, and marriage. An orphan of mysterious parentage, Gerty has been left, more or less accidentally, in the charge of her vicious landlady. Filled with a sense of the injustice of her lot, Gerty is befriended early in the story by a sympathetic local lamplighter who promises to "bring her something." Gerty, who needs everything, speculates about what the "something" might be: "Would it be something to eat? O, if it were only some shoes! But he wouldn't think of *that*."[4]

And indeed, he doesn't. The "something" turns out not to be shoes but a kitten, a gift which leaves Gerty in a quandary. In the slum in which Gerty lives, the narrator mildly observes, "there were a great many cats" and, appealing though Gerty finds them, she knows "that food and shelter were most grudgingly accorded to herself and would not certainly be extended to her pets."[5] Gerty understands all too well that pets are a luxury of the middle class; to the poor they are a burden, and so is the kitten to Gerty.

Nonetheless, the function of the gift is clear. The kitten elicits a maternal and self-sacrificing "tenderness" from the otherwise belligerent Gerty. It reveals her specifically feminine fitness to move out of her deprived and depraved surroundings. In fact, Gerty's affection for the kitten provokes the conflict with her slatternly and unfeeling guardian that leaves Gerty homeless—whereupon she is adopted by the lamplighter. The kitten, then, establishes Gerty's right to a home. Gerty joins the ranks of the worthy poor, where her schooling in self-control and the domestic arts commences immediately. Thus prepared, she rises eventually into the middle class.

In this brief episode, class is both superseded and made visible by gender. In lieu of the contingencies of history, Cummins offers the unchanging nature of women, incorporating maternal self-sacrifice, Christian forbearance, and innate gentility. No abstract or literary issue, the problem of class in *The Lamplighter* is a problem of material inequity; it is, literally, the problem of who does and who does not have shoes. But that problem is immediately tied to the matter of gender, which, on the one hand, serves as the lens through which substantial inequality becomes visible, and on the other hand, obscures its origin in class. The kitten and the shoes both imply and answer each other; to think about the kitten is to remember the shoes, but it is also to find a solution in kittens to the problems of bare feet.

The Lamplighter depends, in other words, on a strategy of displacement in which the language of class yields to the language of gender. The problem of poverty is not repressed but translated into a vocabulary that makes its redress inevitable: the distortions of poverty are answered by the naturalness of gender. Gerty stops breaking windows in retaliation for injuries done her, she exchanges rage for patience, the terms of her identity shift from poor to female, and she is awarded a home. Once gender is established as the source of social mobility and the guarantor of social harmony, the narrative focus shifts from social justice to individual reform, from deprivation to self-control.

Here, as elsewhere, what makes the erasure of class possible is not simply the fact that gender, like race, is deeply implicated in class status. Rather, gender and race are structurally able to substitute for class because the conjunction of attributes that define class position are rendered so intrinsic or else so transcendent that they pass either below or above history. As the contingency of social status is acknowledged, the potential for conflict becomes visible; conversely, that potential vanishes as the space between the attributes that are taken to constitute class and in which an explanation of their conjunction might be undertaken collapses. The doctrine of harmony, of which I would propose this is the literary analogue, subsumes difference into one harmonious whole by means of a kaleidoscopic substitution of terms, terms which compose the social vocabularies in which writers and critics alike govern and recover meaning.

For the most part, nineteenth-century public discourse about class has been elided in discussions of the social reality in which antebellum literature takes its place. Moreover, class itself—the experience of differentials of wealth, power, and prestige—has gone largely unaddressed as subject or structure in that literature. Instead, heightened critical interest in the constructed nature of race and gender has tended, paradoxically, to direct attention away from class, itself a wholly contingent category. Gender and race are imbued with the determinants of class which becomes, then, the silent term in the class-race-gender triad. Or, alternatively, the broadly economic terminology employed by many New Historicist critics in an effort to demonstrate the complicity of texts in the culture of their production has subordinated the problem of difference to the structural identity of the text with hegemonic culture. In both cases, the recognition and the erasure of class are virtually simultaneous; recent scholarship is, in this sense, oddly consonant with the literature it describes.

My intent in this [essay] is to demonstrate that vocabularies of class, race, and gender continually displace one another in mid-nineteenth-century sentimental fiction, and to investigate the impact of those displacements on the success of sentimental representation. *The Lamplighter* serves as a kind of normative model, intended to suggest the social and novelistic benefits of this pattern of displacement for the propagation of a doctrine of harmony. The two texts on which this chapter focuses—Harriet Beecher Stowe's *Uncle Tom's Cabin* (1852) and Rebecca Harding Davis's *Life in the Iron Mills* (1861)—diverge from this model not only in their structure but in their overt intent. In them, the commitment to social justice abandoned in *The Lamplighter* dramatically complicates the scheme I have described. In contrast to *The Lamplighter,* with its attention to the spiritual and social redemption of the individual, each of these texts treats the plight of a group of people—chattel slaves in one case and wage slaves in the other—for whom the prospect of mobility is closed, and each focuses on a protagonist whose gender identification is highly unstable.

In distinguishing her "primitive" method of storytelling from that of the novelist, one of the most popular sentimental writers of the mid-nineteenth century described herself as entering "unceremoniously and unannounced, into people's houses."[6] Just so do we enter Uncle Tom's cabin in chapter 4 of Harriet Beecher Stowe's famous antislavery narrative. We are invited inside not by the occupants of the cabin but by the narrator, who has already taken us on a tour of the plantation house. "Let us enter the dwelling," she suggests, and in we go. While Aunt Chloe tends to the baking, the eye of the narrator pans the cottage, noting its various domestic arrangements and arriving finally at "the hero of our story," Uncle Tom himself, whom we are offered in "daguerreotype."

> He was a large, broad-chested, powerfully-made man, of a full glossy black, and a face whose truly African features were characterized by an expression of grave and steady good sense, united with much kindliness and benevolence. There was something about his whole air self-respecting and dignified, yet united with a confiding and humble simplicity.[7]

The very fact that Tom is the subject of a portrait, albeit a photographic one, suggests, of course, that this is no "thing" but a man. Moreover, the identification of the portrait as a daguerreotype assures us of its fidelity not merely to the outward man but to the inner one—aspects of the self understood by sentimental culture to be inextricably connected. Like other features of Tom's representation, the daguerreotype operates to assure us of Tom's humanity.[8]

Equally striking, however, is the sureness of the artist's hand, her unhesitating ability to read Tom's character in his face. However exotic he may be—with his "truly African features"—Tom is no enigma. His blackness, the outward sign of his enslavement, is not opaque but, like a daguerreotype, a transparency through which his essential nature shines. Tom's condition as slave is, after all, only an accident of history; it neither obstructs our view of him nor does it, apparently, shape his character. He is as confidently drawn as any of the white planters, traders, mothers, or children in *Uncle Tom's Cabin.*

By contrast, when Rebecca Harding Davis introduces us to Hugh Wolfe, the working class "hero" of *Life in the Iron Mills,* the problem of literary representation and its adequacy arises immediately. The story of *Life in the Iron Mills* is a "simple" one. The hunchbacked Deborah, a picker in the cotton mills, is in love with her cousin Hugh Wolfe, a Welsh ironworker who does not reciprocate her feelings. Ignorant and inarticulate, Wolfe spends his idle moments at the foundry carving figures out of korl, a waste product of iron refining. One rainy night when she brings Wolfe his supper in the mill, Deborah witnesses a tour of inspection by the mill owner's son and several of his friends. Quite by accident, the visitors discover one of Wolfe's figures, "a woman, white, of giant proportions, crouching on the ground, her arms flung out in some wild gesture of warning."[9] One of the men—an aristocratic figure named Mitchell—comments on Wolfe's talent and on the impossibility of its development without money. Overhearing this, Deborah steals Mitchell's wallet containing a check for an enormous sum and gives it to Wolfe. Wolfe's first impulse is to return the wallet, but he is overcome by temptation. Arrested and sentenced to nineteen years in prison for the theft, Wolfe commits suicide. Deborah, after serving a much briefer prison term, is rescued by the Quakers and lives out her days in a neighboring community of Friends.

In sharp contrast to *Uncle Tom's Cabin,* when the narrator of *Life in the Iron Mills* sets out to introduce us to her protagonist, she is beset by difficulty. The narrator's view of the protagonist is obstructed, first, by a failure of vision itself. It is difficult, she observes, to see anything through the stifling smoke of the mills on a rainy day. But she is not only blinded by rain and smoke; her vision is impaired as well by the indistinctness of the object at which she is looking. Wolfe is one of "masses of men, with dull, besotted faces" (*IM,* 12), "myriads of . . . furnace-tenders" (*IM,* 14) any of whom might serve equally well as the object of her contemplation. In fact, the narrator herself does not know and thus cannot tell why she has chosen his story from all the others. The lives of the Wolfes are not individual but "like those of their class." Their "duplicates" are "swarming the streets to-day" (*IM,* 15). Davis has no trouble locating Wolfe in history—his own or the town's—or claiming him as a legitimate subject for her narrative. Rather, the problem is the portrait itself. While Uncle Tom can be

Harriet Beecher Stowe, 1853.

rendered with all the fidelity of the daguerreotype, Hugh Wolfe apparently cannot be drawn at all.

Both *Uncle Tom's Cabin* and *Life in the Iron Mills,* published just nine years later, sketch "life among the lowly." Each was written by a white, middle-class, Christian woman in an effort to arouse compassion for the victims of an unjust economic system to which neither had direct access. The comparison of these systems—chattel slavery and wage slavery—was, moreover, a staple of the slavery debate. Predictably, apologists for Southern slavery insisted that the plight of the wage slave was far worse than that of the chattel slave, who at the very least was clothed and fed. In lieu of the "false, antagonistic . . . relations" of the market, George Fitzhugh argued, slavery interposed the natural relations of the family. Abolitionists like Stowe likewise expounded the relationship between these forms of enslavement, contending that chattel slavery was only "the more bold and palpable infringement of human rights" (*UTC,* 231).

Stowe's famous indictment of chattel slavery stands, arguably, as the apotheosis of sentimental narrative. *Uncle Tom's Cabin* successfully normalizes the chattel slave—that is, it offers the grounds for the slaves' prospective membership in the middle class—thereby providing the theological, political and, most crucially, emotional basis for emancipation as well as the promise of "another and better day" of Christian brotherhood. Of course *Life in the Iron Mills* also invokes "the promise of the Dawn," but, unable even to represent its subject, it is unable to move beyond it into the golden future. The chattel slave not only can be daguerreotyped; he can be, as Uncle Tom is, transfigured. By attending to his story, we can move beyond history to the fulfillment of the kingdom of Christ in America. The wage slave, on the contrary, remains enmired almost to the point of invisibility in the mud of a present, sinful world. One is forced to ask why Davis's figure of the wage slave resists so thoroughly the sentimental treatment to which the chattel slave all too readily lends himself.

We can begin to answer that question by looking at the ways in which *Life in the Iron Mills* violates our expectations. Hugh Wolfe, "stooping all night over boiling cauldrons of metal, laired by day in dens of drunkenness and infamy" (*IM,* 12), is, by all rights, industry's victim, a martyr of the laboring classes—a Stephen Blackpool or perhaps a John Barton. We not only recognize his story, we anticipate the manner of its telling: the middle-class narrator who invites us to see "the romance" in the daily rounds of the Manchester mill hand or the American slave; the guide who, so to speak, familiarizes the lives of the lowly to the moral benefit of an all-comprehending reader and the social benefit of the oppressed. The tacit understanding is that the narrator's "lifelike" picture of how the other half lives, a picture both true and immediately apprehensible, will inspire our compassion as it did hers.

In *Life in the Iron Mills,* however, this sympathetic understanding is set aside from the outset. Accustomed to being invited into the story—"Let us enter the dwelling"—by a friendly narrator who resembles no one so much as ourselves, we are instead flatly shut out. "A cloudy day: do you know what that is in a town of iron-works?" (*IM,* 11). The question is not rhetorical but accusatory; clearly, we do *not* know what such a day in such a town is. "Dilettantes" in clean clothes who think "it an altogether serious thing to be alive" (*IM,* 12-13), we are repeatedly reminded by the narrator that we cannot possibly grasp the drunken jest, the horrible joke, that is the life of the ironworker. We are "another order of being" (*IM,* 27); between us and Wolfe lies "a great gulf never to be passed" (*IM,* 30). Egotists, Pantheists, Arminians all, we would rather busy ourselves "making straight paths for [our] feet on the hills" (*IM,* 14) than contemplate the "massed, vile, slimy lives" of people like the Wolfes.

Whereas the optimistic sentimental narrative ordinarily projects a sincere and highly impressionable reader from whose eyes the scales will fall upon being confronted with the truth, Davis's hostile narrator doubts even the willingness of her reader to come down into the "nightmare fog" where the mill workers live. This assault on the reader is, presumably, meant to dislodge us from our position of complacent indifference to the plight of the industrial worker. Self-regard, if nothing else, will lead us to disprove the narrator's charges against us by attending to her protagonist. But ultimately the story offers us no alternative position in which to locate ourselves. So blinded are we by middle-class privilege that we are, it would seem, incapable of useful intervention on behalf of the ironworker. And so brutalized is he by the conditions of industrial life that he too is unable to act. Chided into allying ourselves emotionally with the victims of industry, we nonetheless remain trapped in our own world.

No sooner, in fact, have we acknowledged both our reluctance and our ignorance and agreed to be instructed by the narrator, than we discover that she too is barred from the town. Standing at a window above the street, she can "scarcely see" the "crowd of drunken Irishmen" (*IM,* 11) idling away their time outside the grocery opposite. From the back window overlooking the river, her view is no better. But here the impediment is not the smoggy day but her own imagination, which associates the "dumb appeal upon the face of the negro-like river slavishly bearing its burden" with the "slow stream of human life creeping past" on the street. This "fancy" the narrator quickly dismisses as "an idle one." The river, figured as a chattel slave, is no "type" of the life of the wage slave, for its future "liberation" is assured: it flows eventually beyond the town into "odorous sunlight . . . air, fields and mountains." The "future of the Welsh puddler," by contrast, is "to be stowed away, after his grimy work is done, in a hole in the muddy graveyard" (*IM,* 13).

Brief—even casual—as it is, the association of chattel and wage slave in the figure of the river and the narrator's repudiation of that figure is instructive. What is most immediately striking, in this context, is its implication that the black, bowed though he is under the burden of slavery, is moving inexorably toward liberation—toward the sunshine. This is not, as I hope to show, just wishful thinking on Davis's part but consonant with a broader view of the nature of slavery among Northern whites. As important as the allusion to chattel slavery is, however, something less conspicuous but of equal importance happens in this passage: the association of the stream of life with the literal stream of the river is rejected as pathetic fallacy. Fancy, the artist's stock in trade, is shown, despite the narrator, to be not merely "idle" but actively misleading. In fact, the tendency of literary language throughout *Life in the Iron Mills* is to falsify.

The mills, for example, in which "crowds of half-clad men, looking like revengeful ghosts in the red light, hurried, throwing masses of glittering fire" (*IM,* 20), are early likened to a "street in Hell." And indeed, insofar as the mills are demonic places in which men are held in thrall to the "unsleeping engines" of industry, the comparison is evocative. Later in the story, however, one of the visitors to the ironworks reverts to this analogy, now casting it in the erudite language of the highly educated. "Your works look like Dante's Inferno," the aristocratic Mitchell comments to Kirby, the mill owner's son; "Yonder is Farinata himself in the burning tomb" (*IM,* 27). The allusion seems at first to have a salutory effect: it prompts Kirby to look "curiously around, as if seeing the faces of his hands for the first time." But if the point of the allusion is to intensify the real, to make us—or Kirby—feel more acutely the plight of the ironworkers, the reference to Dante fails, for Kirby replies, "They're bad enough, that's true" (*IM,* 27). This response, needless to say, misses the point—as does the association of the ironworker with the sinful Italian nobleman. But what, after all, is the point? The appropriation of the real to the literary is, as Davis's narrator presents it, precisely a way *not* to see. By first rewriting the mill worker as Farinata, and then by dismissing him as "bad" and thus deserving of such an inferno, the visitors render the hands invisible. The allusion solves the moral problem that might otherwise be posed by the condition of labor in the mills, and allows the visitors to turn their attention to what really matters, the hard facts of industry—"net profits," "coal facilities," "hands employed."

The repudiation, if not the unmasking, of the literary is perfectly in keeping with the dictates of sentimental storytelling of the kind *Uncle Tom's Cabin* represents, with its commitment to the artless, lifelike tale. In a letter to her editor just prior to the publication of the first installment of *Uncle Tom's Cabin,* Stowe outlined her intentions: "My vocation is simply that of a painter, and my object will be to hold up in the most lifelike and graphic manner possible Slavery." "There is," she continued, "no arguing with *pictures,* and everybody is impressed by them, whether they mean to be or not."[10] Stowe's account of her vocation strikes the keynote of sentimental fiction. "Unpretending" stories written to move and instruct the middle-class family cozily gathered around the hearth, these stories were not, their authors insisted, properly "literature"—that deathlike form with "stony eyes, fleshless joints, and ossified heart" fit only for the library shelf.[11]

This is not to say that the sentimentalist denied her invention. Despite her portrayal of herself as a painter who does not paint but only "holds up" the picture of slavery, Stowe explains in the preface to *The Key to Uncle Tom's Cabin* that "[i]n fictitious writing, it is possible to find refuge from the hard and the terrible, by inventing scenes and characters of a more pleasing nature."[12] *Uncle Tom's Cabin* may be "lifelike," but it is not a "work of fact." Quite the contrary, if her critics "call the fiction dreadful," she exclaims in an 1853 letter to the Earl of Shaftesbury, "what will they say of the fact, where I cannot deny, suppress, or color?"[13]

Stowe's two accounts of her role as artist are less contradictory than they at first appear. The lifelike tale told by the sentimental storyteller was no invention of a dissembling literary art. It was at once a story waiting to be told and a story everyone already knew—a kind of "found" art. And its claim to sincerity depended on its repudiation of the "literary." The novel, with its intricate plot and startling developments, substituted artifice for substance, erudition for feeling, author for subject. Sentimental writers embraced instead an ideal of self-effacing simplicity, of "naturalness." What allows Stowe simultaneously to claim artlessness and artistry, then, is a tacit agreement between the sentimental writer and reader that certain artifices will be accepted as "natural," and further that the "natural" will be understood to point toward the ideal.

In *Life in the Iron Mills,* however, the "simple" sentimental picture is rendered impossible by the inaccessibility of the mills to the middle-class narrator, "idly tapping on the window-pane" as if to draw our attention to the barrier that stands between her and the lives of those on the street below. But equally impossible is the self-consciously literary sketch of the kind Melville, for example, offers in "The Tartarus of Maids."[14] If the first possibility is foreclosed by the narrator's inability to "enter the dwelling" of the ironworker, the second is precluded by her inchoate recognition of the resemblance between economic and literary appropriation. She is no more willing to allegorize the mill worker than she is able to daguerreotype him.

In *Life in the Iron Mills* we are, in fact, in epistemological difficulty from the start. The narrator who demands that we "hide [our] disgust, take no heeds of [our] clean clothes, and come right down . . . into the thickest of the fog and mud and foul effluvia" (*IM,* 13) remains herself shut in the house. *If* we could "go into this mill," the narrator observes, we would surely discover there the "terrible tragedy" (*IM,* 23) of the mill worker, but this neither she nor we can do. The requirement that we enter the mill gives way to a far less strenuous request that we "hear this story." But of course we can only hear what the narrator can tell. And just as our narrator cannot enter the mills, so, she claims, she "can paint nothing" of the "reality of soul-starvation" that lurks behind the "besotted faces on the street" (*IM,* 23). Unable actually to enter or imaginatively to project herself into Wolfe's "dwelling," she can paint no "lifelike" picture.

Part of the problem is the ambiguity surrounding that "dwelling" itself. For Davis's mill workers, the central distinctions of middle-class culture are of no consequence. Home is no refuge, and labor is not productive but wasting. The cellar in which Wolfe lives is neither preferable to the mill where he spends most of his time nor, in a broad sense, any less its product than pig iron. Wolfe's "real" life—as worker and as artist—is led in the ironworks where, after laboring to transform ore into metal, he struggles in vain to transform industrial waste into art, to render the dregs of industry "beautiful and pure." But if Wolfe's home is "unnatural" by middle-class standards, so are all the other aspects of his life. For Wolfe, who labors at night and takes such rest as he can during the day, even time is inverted. And so too is gender: Wolfe's thin muscles, weak nerves, and "meek woman's face" belie his employment as an iron puddler and earn him the "sobriquet" Molly Wolfe.

Like Uncle Tom, then, Hugh Wolfe is a highly feminized figure—a figure, some have argued, for the female artist[15]—but the resemblance ends there. The feminization of Tom is part of a systematic attempt to invest slaves with piety, innocence, affection, and nobility of purpose—traits meant to assure white middle-class readers of the fundamental ethical and emotional identity of blacks and whites. Like Bowen's account of the false antagonism of labor and capital, *Uncle Tom's Cabin* presents the differing interests of slave and slaveholder as illusory, a chimera of history. Tom's feminine qualities are central to his role as harbinger of the social and spiritual millennium to come. By contrast, the feminization of Hugh Wolfe is utterly debilitating; rather than providing grounds for his future success, Wolfe's feminine qualities ensure his demise. They make him physically and emotionally unfit for the only life he is likely to know. Like the disconcerting strength of the korl woman, the weakness of the feminized Wolfe heightens rather than diminishes our sense of the unnaturalness of his life.

But whereas Davis continually draws our attention to the distortions of industrial life—from the comfortless cellar to Deborah's hunched back—the logic of *Uncle Tom's Cabin* directs us to see lives of the slaves as versions of our own. The slave quarters, for example, are as much the outgrowth of a particular system of economic exploitation as the tenements of the mill workers, but Tom's cabin is nonetheless presented to us not as a hovel but as a veritable bastion of domesticity. Only the easy intrusion of whites—slaveholders, traders, and narrators—into the cabin reminds us that, for the slave, there is no private life. In both *Uncle Tom's Cabin* and *Life in the Iron Mills,* then, the separate spheres of men and women, work and family, are compromised, but in one we witness the doomed but insistent efforts of the chattel slave to restore the boundary between these, while in the other, normalcy—

the social arrangements of the middle class—are beyond the imagination as well as the capacity of the characters. Unlike Chloe and Tom, neither Deborah nor Wolfe, for all their discontent, sees the middle class as imitable.

Having located her characters in a wholly alien world, it is not surprising that the narrator of *Life in the Iron Mills* can offer only the "fragments" of a story, the "outside outlines of a night" (*IM*, 23). By contrast, the narrator who so unceremoniously enters Uncle Tom's cabin is, so to speak, in full possession of her subject. Uncle Tom, after all, belongs quite literally to middle-class whites like herself—and her reader. This is not to suggest that Stowe did not mean to extend a full humanity to her slave characters; nevertheless, the central concern of *Uncle Tom's Cabin*—the transformation of a "thing" into a "man"—implies a plasticity that lends itself to Stowe's literary as well as her political purposes even as the form of representation she invokes—the daguerreotype—paradoxically hints at a deathlike fixing of its subject. The literal appropriation of the labor of slaves, in other words, facilitates their literary appropriation by the white artist.

Without rehearsing the arguments of the slavery debate, it is fair to say that, in that debate, the issue of slavery was as often as not subordinated to the question of the nature of blackness. For proponents of slavery, race served to naturalize the subordinate status of blacks. For others like Stowe who argued that racial difference was not sufficient to justify slavery, blackness nonetheless stood as a paradox. On the one hand, the black, dispossessed of himself, could be "owned," both actually and symbolically, by others. On the other hand, the black was taken to be profoundly unknowable, altogether unlike his white owner. Inscrutably black, essentially Other, and powerless to represent himself—legally or literarily—the American slave could, for these very reasons, be freely represented by the free white writer whose possession he was.

My point is not simply that, as Other, the slave was a blank screen on which the white writer could project any image she pleased. It is rather that blackness is widely understood in the mid-nineteenth century as a state of becoming. Even among the defenders of slavery, who insisted on the natural and therefore permanent "semi-civilization" of blacks, the question arose of what blacks would become over time, living among whites.[16] For romantic racialists like Stowe, the untapped potential of blacks was one of the most pressing arguments against slavery. Like the children (all of them girls) with whom he is continually associated, Uncle Tom is in the process of becoming—in Tom's case, becoming a Christian and ultimately a martyr, but in the case of other black characters, becoming independent, industrious, educated, prosperous, or pious. Like Alexander Kinmont, who claimed that blacks were destined to develop "a later but far nobler civilization" than that of whites, or William Ellery Channing, who saw in blacks "the germs of a meek, long-suffering, loving virtue,"[17] Stowe's narrative projects a rosy future in which the enslaved black emerges as free, Christian, and altogether respectable. Leaving aside Stowe's patronizing tone, that future is intimated from the outset by Uncle Tom's cabin, which—from its neat garden patch to the carpeted corner that serves as "drawing room" and the "brilliant scriptural prints" that decorate its walls—resembles nothing so much as a playhouse in which the life of middle-class adulthood is being rehearsed.

The prophetic mode of Stowe's narrative depends on the plasticity of its object, the black slave, and that plasticity, in turn, is a central feature of the developmental schemes used by whites to understand both the present and the future of the victims of chattel slavery. As yet unmade, the black could be molded to the artist's liking. In fact, he could be cast, as he is in *Uncle Tom's Cabin,* more or less in the image of his white creator. What is reflected here is not the sentimentalist's "ability to confuse the natural and the ideal"[18] so much as her willingness to reimagine the real as a type of the ideal. The success of *Uncle Tom's Cabin* depends on the narrator's capacity to project in fully realized form the man who lurks in the "thing" and, on the basis of this projection, to call for his emancipation. Insofar as it draws out the human potential, defined as the potential for middle-class respectability, in those whose full humanity is in doubt—the black or, more commonly, the poor and unruly orphan girl—sentimental narrative is oriented always toward the future[19] and, I would suggest, toward the home where differentials of class are most conspicuously inscribed.

Unlike the infinitely malleable Uncle Tom, however, Hugh Wolfe must be "hewed and hacked" out of the recalcitrant korl—the industrial waste that is both his sculptural medium and his matter—by a narrator who questions the capacity of literary language to make his story "a real thing" to her resisting reader. The object of the narrator's regard in *Life in the Iron Mills* is not the man *in posse* but the man the industrial world has already produced, the man with no future. Fixed in an interminable present, inarticulate, uneduated, born "in vice," "starved" in infancy, stained in body and soul, Wolfe is, so to speak, already completed—or rather, finished.

The irony is obvious, for Wolfe, unlike Uncle Tom, is free, white, and male. He is not legally bound to the mills; he is, as we say, master of his own destiny. As Doctor May, one of the visitors to the mill, complacently remarks, "you have it in you to be a great sculptor. . . . A man may make himself anything he chooses. . . . Make yourself what you will. It is your right" (*IM,* 37). A free agent by right, Wolfe is none-theless represented as entirely the product of his cir-cumstances, a figure not of human potential but of human waste.

But he is also, of course, a figure of the artist. The argument for Wolfe's humanity lies not in the man, dumb and brutelike, but in the korl woman, whose "wild, eager face, like that of a starving wolf's" (*IM,* 32) is, like the starving Hugh Wolfe, incomprehensible to the jeering Kirby and the complacent Doctor May. Nor can Wolfe explain it. Only the aristocratic Mitchell sees "the soul of the thing," but he sees it with an eye "bright and deep and cold as Arctic air," the eye of an "amused spectator at a play" (*IM,* 36). The korl sculp-ture, the tragedy of the furnace tender, the "rare mosaic" he examined that morning, and, we must assume, the peculiar institution of the South that he has come to the border state to "study"—these are to him as one. The narrator of *Life in the Iron Mills* must defend her subject not only against the Kirbys who would deny his soul and the genial Mays who would deny his plight but also, most crucially, against the tranquil gaze, the reified consciousness, of the Mitchells who see in Wolfe an "amusing study"—all of these, it must be added, versions of both narrator and reader.

Needless to say, the vehemence of the narrator, her inversion of the usual narrative stance, her insistence on the failure of narrative and her own inadequacy, are all calculated for effect. She does, after all, tell her story and more. As she herself admits, the "tiresome" story of Hugh Wolfe hides a "secret" that she "dare not put . . . into words," a "terrible dumb question" that is, paradoxically, "from the very extremity of its darkness, the most solemn prophecy . . . the world has known of the Hope to come" (*IM,* 14). The ques-tion—"Is this the End?"—is articulated only twice: once in the poetic epigraph that opens the story and again, at it close, by the korl woman.

Complicit though art may be in the system of capitalist exploitation, only art, it turns out, can speak the ter-rible question and reveal the prophecy. Wolfe is mute, but his sculpture is invested with the power of speech. The "pale, vague lips" of the korl woman "tremble" with the terrible question (*IM,* 64). Wolfe cannot be figured, much less transfigured, but the korl woman is touched by the "blessing hand" of the "Dawn" (*IM,* 65), just as Deborah, named after the Biblical proph-etess, is later touched by the Quaker woman.

Prophecy, both social and religious, fails in *Life in the Iron Mills* because in the end art has been made to substitute for life after all. That is to say, prophecy fails because the narrator has made us acutely aware not only of the distance between the artifice, the story

or the sculpture, and the Truth, the "reality" of Hugh Wolfe's "soul-starvation," but also of the inevitable tendency of art to appropriate the life of its subject, the mill hand, just as the mill owner appropriates his labor. Thus when we learn of Deborah's transforma-tion at the hands of the Quakers in a "homely pine house, on one of these hills" overlooking "broad, wooded slopes and clover-crimsoned meadows" (*IM,* 63), we realize that we are being asked to accept the pathetic fallacy of the river after all. Likewise when the narrator attempts, at the close of the story, to re-present the truth of Hugh Wolfe's futile life as a higher one, the transcendent truth of "the day that shall surely come," we resist; the narrator has, in effect, taught us too well. Fully persuaded that the ironworker lives and dies in the mills only to be replaced by his duplicate, that his aspirations will always be thwarted by the conditions of industrial life, we believe that he is America's future, that he will no more disappear than the wheels of industry grind to a halt; he prefigures not the millennium but, we suspect, the apocalypse.

Insofar as wage slavery is taken to be a necessary concomitant of industry, it is irremediable and, like the mills themselves, inescapable. But chattel slavery, by contrast, could be abolished, and that without endangering the nation. For Stowe's narrator, sla-very is not just a sin but an anachronism and an aberration. The remnant of an altogether un-Ameri-can seignorialism, it belongs to the feudal past, not to the democratic future. As George Harris's invocation of the American Revolution implies, slavery consti-tutes a falling away from the very ideals on which the nation was founded. Emancipation, in *Uncle Tom's Cabin,* does not threaten but guarantee the future of America; in fact, emancipation alone will avert the wrath of God and secure America for the millen-nium. Moreover, emancipation not only must but can be accomplished. Although the narrator goes to some lengths in *Uncle Tom's Cabin* to demonstrate the complicity of the North in Southern slavery, she understands the effects of emancipation as local and short-term. Once possessed of "property, reputation, and education" and all the advantages of "Christian republican society," the emancipated slaves can be returned to Africa to put into practice "the lessons they have learned in America" (*UTC,* 449).

If one were to credit their titles alone, to go from *Uncle Tom's Cabin* to *Life in the Iron Mills* is simply to go from home to work. At the imaginative center of Stowe's narrative is the family home: its affection-ate ties are the story's ideal, its disruption a sin, its absence the sign of an unredeemable evil. Uncle Tom's "real" life is led in his cabin, surrounded by his wife and children. An ideal site, the cabin thus can serve, at the end of the narrative, as a "memorial," pointing back to slavery, a death in life, and forward to eman-cipation, a life after death.

In establishing the emotional grounds for the identification of her middle-class reader with the slave, Stowe's narrator invests her black characters with the virtues they will, she assures us, come to have once free. In this sense, Uncle Tom fuses hope and destiny. Like their middle-class counterparts in antebellum America, the slaves in *Uncle Tom's Cabin* live "suspended between the facts of [their] present social condition and the promise of [their] future."[20] And just as the middle-class American was thus plagued with anxiety concerning his own social identity, so too was he plagued with anxiety over the "true" nature of the black. Arguably, in that anxiety we can read the demise of slavery. The sentimentalist's "monumental effort to reorganize culture from the woman's point of view"[21] is not, that is, without its class bias; in fact, the achievements of sentimentalism depend on its reorganization of culture from the point of view of the parlor, the "cultural podium" of the white middle-class woman.

The drive to impose the forms of the future on the present, so apparent in *Uncle Tom's Cabin,* is stymied in *Life in the Iron Mills,* where all forward movement is blocked by the combination of inadequate narrator, unwilling reader, and mute subject. As the English industrial novel suggests, even where home is a cellar with a pile of rotting straw for a bed, where "real" life is stooping over a cauldron of boiling metal all night, it is possible to project a future millennium in which masters and men, Christians all, unite. But it is possible only by an act of appropriation. With an irony that eludes its unselfconscious narrator, *Uncle Tom's Cabin* appropriates the black slave—an embodied object, a "thing" waiting to be claimed—in the interest of ending his appropriation by others. This irony is the stumbling block for the narrator of *Life in the Iron Mills.* Rejecting all modes of representation as forms of appropriation, refusing to pretend to know her subject just as she refuses to let her reader pretend to know what a cloudy day in an iron mill town is, she exposes the artless "scribbling women" and the erudite literary men—Stowe and Melville alike—in their truest character, as members of the possessing class.

Yet like them, she must find a way to tell her story. Freeing her eyes to see the promise of the dawn in the nearly impenetrable darkness of her story, she falls victim to the common fate of the reforming artist. Having refused to take possession of her human subject, she is, in the end, the uneasy possessor of the korl woman, the only remaining evidence of Wolfe's existence. *Uncle Tom's Cabin* ends with the inevitable transfiguration of Tom's homely dwelling into the symbolic site of liberation; *Life in the Iron Mills* ends, inevitably, as it began. Just as Hugh Wolfe is rendered invisible by the smoke of the mills at the beginning of the story, so at the end the visible, tangible figure of the korl woman, "a rough, ungainly thing," painful to look at, is kept hidden behind a curtain in the narrator's library.

The representational quandary posed by class is answered by recourse to gender as surely in *Life in the Iron Mills* as it is in *Uncle Tom's Cabin* (or, for that matter, in *The Lamplighter*), but the literary and political consequences for the story are altogether different. For Stowe, slavery is the testing ground of middle-class culture. The success of *Uncle Tom's Cabin* depends on the placement of the chattel slave in a developmental scheme which makes immanent his middle-class character and thus brings him, provisionally at least, into the world of the reader. The virtues of that world are measured, in turn, by its capacity to assimilate to itself both slave and slaveholder. The developmental scheme that governs the representation of slaves in *Uncle Tom's Cabin,* in other words, not only lends itself to the millennial hopes of the narrator, but also implies an absolute standard of value against which everyone and everything can be measured.

In Davis's grim account of industrial life, on the contrary, the shifting vocabularies of class and gender expose the limits of middle-class sentimental culture. At the end of *Life in the Iron Mills,* we are returned to the domestic world of the middle-class narrator which, unlike the satanic mills, "belongs to the open sunlight." But that world—a world in which vision is ostensibly restored—is one in which mill workers become once again invisible, a world from which darkness is banished, and in which epistemological problems are solved by faith. Having placed the wage slave out of sight of that world and beyond the ameliorative influence of genteel reform, Davis is left with only a morally equivocal art to mediate between the sunlit world of her middle-class reader and the gloom of the mills. Class cannot be dismissed as obscuring a deeper "human" reality, nor can it be dissolved into race or gender. Rather, class stands as irreducible to the end, and art—suspect from the first—emerges as the real subject of *Life in the Iron Mills.*

Notes

[1] Francis Bowen, "Philip's *Protection and Free Trade,"* *North American Review* 72 (1851): 415.

[2] Quoted in Wai-chee Dimock, *Empire for Liberty* (Princeton, N.J.: Princeton University Press, 1989), 18.

[3] I am thinking here of Wai-chee Dimock's argument in *Empire for Liberty* that the "expansionist social discourse of antebellum America" is characterized by the "spatialization of time" (15). This argument is, of course, a version of Myra Jehlen's thesis in *American Incarnation* (Cambridge, Mass.: Harvard University Press, 1986).

[4] Maria Cummins, *The Lamplighter* (Boston, 1854), 11.

[5] Ibid., 12.

[6] Fanny Fern, *Ruth Hall* (New Brunswick, N.J.: Rutgers University Press, 1986), 3.

[7] Harriet Beecher Stowe, *Uncle Tom's Cabin* (1852; New York: Harper & Row, 1958), 68. Hereafter cited in the text as *UTC*.

[8] The democratizing of portraiture—part, surely, of Stowe's point in choosing the daguerreotype as the form for Tom's representation—began with the publicizing of Daguerre's process in 1839. As other critics have suggested, the long exposure time required by daguerreotypy not only produced a deathlike rigidity in the features of the subject but made the dead the perfect subject. Nathaniel Hawthorne exploits this idea in the portraits of the Pyncheons in *The House of the Seven Gables*—as he does the notion that the daguerreotype exposes the truest, most hidden nature of its subject.

[9] Rebecca Harding Davis, *Life in the Iron Mills* (1861; Old Westbury, N. Y.: Feminist Press, 1972), 31. Hereafter cited in the text as *IM*.

[10] Quoted in Eric J. Sundquist, *New Essays on Uncle Tom's Cabin* (New York: Cambridge University Press, 1986), 9.

[11] Fanny Fern in *Rose Clark,* quoted in Nina Baym, *Woman's Fiction* (Ithaca, N.Y.: Cornell University Press, 1978), 33. Susan Warner insisted that her 1850 bestseller *The Wide, Wide World* was no "novel" but only a "story." Likewise, Fanny Fern refused to "dignify" *Ruth Hall* by calling it a novel.

[12] Harriet Beecher Stowe, *The Key to Uncle Tom's Cabin* (1853; New York: Arno Press, 1969), v.

[13] Ibid., vi.

[14] "The Tartarus of Maids" deploys erudite, "literary" language from the start: Melville's narrator passes through a "Dantean gateway" into a gorge called the "Devil's Dungeon," where the paper mill is located. As horrified as Davis's narrator by the exploitation he witnesses there, Melville's narrator has no difficulty in seeing or recounting what he sees—even when what he sees is his own complicity in the exploitative practices of the mill.

[15] See, for example, Maribel W. Molyneaux, "Sculpture in the Iron Mills: Rebecca Harding Davis's Korl Woman," *Women's Studies* 17 (1990): 157-77; Jean Pfaelzer, "Rebecca Harding Davis: Domesticity, Social Order, and the Industrial Novel," *International Journal of Women's Studies* 4 (May-June 1981): 234-44; Tillie Olsen, Biographical Interpretation, *Life in the Iron Mills* (Old Westbury, N.Y.: Feminist Press, 1972), 69-174.

[16] George Frederickson, *The Black Image in the White Mind: The Debate on Afro-American Character and Destiny, 1817-1914* (New York: Harper & Row, 1971), especially 51-58.

[17] Quoted in Frederickson, *Black Image,* 106-7.

[18] Karen Halttunen, *Confidence Men and Painted Women: A Study of Middle-Class Culture in America, 1830-1870* (New Haven, Conn.: Yale University Press, 1982), 83.

[19] As Elizabeth Ammons, Jane Tompkins, and others have argued, Uncle Tom is both infantilized *and* feminized. Likewise, as Jean Pfaelzer has suggested, Hugh Wolfe—whose "sobriquet" is "Molly Wolfe" and whose representative is the korl woman—is both a feminized character and a figure for the female artist: "Rebecca Harding Davis: Domesticity, Social Order, and the Industrial Novel," *International Journal of Women's Studies* 4 (1981): 234-44. In conjunction with my own, this line of argument suggests that one way to lend "plasticity" to the otherwise intractable mill worker was to associate him with women who, like chattel slaves, were understood by sentimental writers to be infinitely malleable subjects.

[20] Halttunen, *Confidence Men,* 192.

[21] Jane Tompkins, *Sensational Designs: The Cultural Work of American Fiction, 1790-1860* (New York: Oxford University Press, 1985), 124.

A LITERATURE OF RESISTANCE AND REPRESSION

Helen Waite Papashvily

SOURCE: "Foreword" to *All the Happy Endings: A Study of the Domestic Novel in America, the Women Who Wrote It, the Women Who Read It, in the Nineteenth Century,* Harper and Brothers, Publishers, 1956, pp. xiii-xvii.

[*In the following essay, Papashvily argues that the domestic novel constitutes a more subtle but equally powerful form of resistance to nineteenth-century patriarchy than the 1848 Seneca Falls convention.*]

On July 19, 1848, in Seneca Falls, New York, a Woman's Rights Convention, the first ever held, met and after two days of impassioned discussion issued to the press a Declaration of Sentiments beginning:

> The history of mankind is a history of repeated injuries and usurpations on the part of man toward woman, having in direct object the establishment of an absolute tyranny over her.

A detailed list of women's grievances followed. Man, the convention charged, had denied woman the franchise, a thorough education, and a chance at the more profitable occupations. He had taken her property and wages, taxed her without representation, made her morally an irresponsible being, usurped the prerogatives of Jehovah Himself over her conscience, and endeavored in every way that he could to destroy her confidence and lessen her self-respect. The assembly at Seneca Falls, determined to correct these injustices by every means possible, concluded on a threatening note:

> We shall employ agents, circulate tracts, petition state and national legislatures and endeavor to enlist the pulpit and press in our behalf . . .

Most men reading the accounts of the convention could congratulate themselves and each other on their good luck and good sense in possessing wives and daughters, sisters and mothers who never made such ridiculous accusations or impossible demands but stayed quietly at home content to reign like queens over pretty parlors.

Their dove-eyed darlings, all gentlemen no doubt felt confident, spent *their* leisure as ladies should. They embroidered and painted on velvet and copied verses into albums and pressed leaves and arranged bouquets according to the "language of flowers." At their rosewood pianos they sang and played fashionably pathetic refrains or, reclining on the sofa, they whiled away the time with a sweet novel by Mrs. E.D.E.N. Southworth or Augusta Evans Wilson or Mary J. Holmes or Martha Finley or Marion Harland or some other "scribbling woman."

If a curious husband or father glanced through one of these volumes he found a simple tale of home and family too full of sentiment, sacrifice, devotion and piety perhaps for masculine taste although most suitable and edifying for the female mind.

Throughout the nineteenth century this peculiar literary form, the domestic novel, flourished as never before or since. Hundreds of authors turned out thousands of titles that sold millions of copies. Scarcely a literate woman in the United States but read some of these novels—*The Wide, Wide World, Ishmael; or In the Depths, Tempest and Sunshine, Elsie Dinsmore, St. Elmo, Sunnybank*—to name but a few that in time acquired a kind of subclassic status.

Now these sentimental tales and their authors are almost, if not quite, forgotten by a new generation of readers; accorded only the briefest mention by literary historians, banished from library shelves. Yet such books possess greater value today, perhaps, than when they were written, for in them, as in all popular literature, are mirrored the fears and anxieties and frustrations, the plans and hopes and joys of those who read them so avidly. Their crumbling pages reveal the dream world of women—as it existed in the nineteenth century and lingered on to influence the twentieth.

The domestic or, according to its critics, the sentimental novel was in general what the terms imply—a tale of contemporary domestic life, ostensibly sentimental in tone and with few exceptions almost always written by women for women. This and a certain similarity in the binding style, "large, handsome duodecimo, cloth, gilt," would seem, at first glance, to be all many of the domestic novels had in common.

Some, in their gory sensationalism, rivaled the old ballad sheets and chap books while others, oozing sanctimonious piety, imitated tracts. Quite often, to avoid even the slightest taint of fiction, these novels bore as subtitles, "A True History," "Founded on Fact," "Drawn from Incidents in Real Life," or appeared disguised as diaries, memoirs, journals, collections of letters, autobiographies, or some similar form of eyewitness account by an innocent bystander.

A few of the authors wrote merely to amuse; more hoped to do that and at the same time plead a special cause or share their convictions on a variety of controversial subjects. Several of the domestic novelists had real talent, imagination and skill and one possessed true genius. Those who did not borrowed from their contemporaries and predecessors, thereby proving the feminine knack with leftovers as useful in the library as in the kitchen. A Richardson heroine, a Brontë hero, bits of pathos and drollery out of Dickens, a seasoning of supernatural horrors from Mrs. Radcliffe or Monk Lewis mixed well and liberally garnished with local color could be served up as original concoctions.

Yet, despite their varied form, basically the domestic novels were ever the same. The center of interest was the home although that edifice might range from one of Mrs. E.D.E.N. Southworth's noble English castles to the tastefully adorned wigwam of Malaeska in Mrs. Ann Stephens' book of the same name. The common woman was always glorified, her every thought, action, gesture, chance word fraught with esoteric meaning and far-reaching influence; her daily routine of cooking, washing, baking, nursing, scrubbing imbued with dramatic significance; her petty trials and small joys magnified to heroic proportions.

There were no historical figures, few excursions into the past or the future. Their own world and the immediate present occupied readers and writers exclusively.

The authors of the domestic novel shared curiously similar backgrounds. Almost all were women of upper-middle-class origin who began very early in life to write, frequently under pressure of sudden poverty. Several published while still in their teens (usually a temperance tale). A majority lived or visited in the South. Most important for many of these women, somewhere, sometime, someplace in her past some man—a father, a brother, a husband, a guardian—had proved unworthy of the trust and confidence she placed in him. This traumatic experience, never resolved, grew into a chronic grievance.

The small crimes of men—their propensity to make noise and dirt and war and trouble—the insensitivity, the violence, the lust inherent in the masculine character might sometimes be overlooked, but readers and writers and their unifying symbol, the heroines, could never forget how a man boasted and swaggered and threatened and promised and commanded—nor ever forgive that in the end he failed.

No man, fortunately for his peace of mind, ever discovered that the domestic novels were handbooks of another kind of feminine revolt—that these pretty tales reflected and encouraged a pattern of feminine behavior so quietly ruthless, so subtly vicious that by comparison the ladies at Seneca appear angels of innocence.

Even so astute an observer as Vernon K. Parrington could dismiss the sentimental novel as weak "cambric tea." Like the rest of his sex, he did not detect the faint bitter taste of poison in the cup nor recognize that these books were rather a witches' broth, a lethal draught brewed by women and used by women to destroy their common enemy, man.

It is not to be imagined that the ways and means of correcting a long list of feminine grievances were communicated on a conscious level. The link between reader and writer forged by every popular book is a mystic one. The writer may not know all he has said; the reader all he has heard; yet they understand each other perfectly.

Nineteenth-century women, if they were to achieve freedom in what seemed to them a hostile world, needed direction, inspiration, appreciation, reassurance, a sense of self-importance and of group unity, a plan of action.

The Seneca Falls Convention supplied this to a few women but uncounted hundreds and thousands more found *their* Declaration of Rights, *their* Statement of Intentions within the pages of the domestic novel.

Ann Douglas

SOURCE: "The Legacy of American Victorianism: The Meaning of Little Eva," in *The Feminization of American Culture,* Alfred A. Knopf, 1977, pp. 3-13.

[*In the essay that follows, Douglas asserts that the complex politics of sentimental novels emerges from a combination of American capitalism and Calvinism.*]

Today many Americans, intellectuals as well as less scholarly people, feel a particular fondness for the artifacts, the literature, the *mores* of our Victorian past.[1] I wrote [*The Feminization of American Culture,* in which this essay appears] because I am one of these people. As a child I read with formative intensity in a collection of Victorian sentimental fiction, a legacy from my grandmother's girlhood. Reading these stories, I first discovered the meaning of absorption: the pleasure and guilt of possessing a secret supply. I read through the "Elsie Dinsmore" books, the "Patty" books, and countless others; I followed the timid exploits of innumerable pale and pious heroines. But what I remember best, what was for me as for so many others, the archetypical and archetypically satisfying scene in this domestic genre, was the death of Little Eva in Harriet Beecher Stowe's novel, *Uncle Tom's Cabin.*

A pure and beautiful child in a wealthy southern family, Little Eva dies a lingering and sainted death of consumption. Her adoring Papa and a group of equally adoring slaves cluster in unspeakable grief around her bedside while she dispenses Christian wisdom and her own golden locks with profuse generosity. The poignancy of her closing scene is in no way diminished by the fact that a good third of the story is yet to come, and must proceed without her. Little Eva's significance has curiously little to do with the plot of the book in which she appears. For Little Eva gains her force not through what she does, not even through what she is, but through what she does and is to us, the readers.

Of course any character in any book is peculiarly available to her or his audience and dependent on it. A book can be produced by the millions, as this one was. Simply as a character in a story, Little Eva is a creature not only of her author's imagination but of her reader's fantasy; her life stems from our acceptance of her and our involvement with her. But Little Eva is one of us in more special ways. Her admirers have always been able to identify with her even while they worship, or weep, at her shrine. She does not demand the respect we accord a competitor. She is not extraordinarily gifted, or at least she is young enough so that her talents have not had the chance to take on formidable proportions. If she is lovely looking and has a great deal of money, Stowe makes it amply clear that these attributes are more a sign than a cause of her success. Little Eva's virtue lies partly in her femininity, surely a common enough commodity. And her greatest act is dying, something we all can and must do. Her death, moreover, is not particularly effective in any practical sense. During her last days, she urges her father to become a serious Christian and to free his slaves; he dies himself, however, before he has gotten around to doing either. Little Eva's death is not futile, but it is essentially decorative; and therein, perhaps, lay its charm for me and for others.

Stowe intended Little Eva's patient and protracted death as an exemplum of religious faith, but it does not operate exclusively as such. Little Eva is devout, precociously spiritual in a way that would have been as recognizable to an eighteenth-century theologian like Jonathan Edwards as to the typical mid-nineteenth-century reader. Yet her religious significance comes not only from her own extreme religiosity but also from the protective veneration it arouses in the other characters in the book, and presumably in her readers. Her religious identity, like her death, is confused with the response it evokes. It is important to note that Little Eva doesn't actually convert anyone. Her sainthood is there to precipitate our nostalgia and our narcissism. We are meant to bestow on her that fondness we reserve for the contemplation of our own softer emotions. If "camp" is art that is too excessive to be taken seriously, art that courts our "tenderness,"[2] then Little Eva suggests Christianity beginning to function as camp. Her only real demand on her readers is for self-indulgence.

Stowe's infantile heroine anticipates that exaltation of the average which is the trademark of mass culture. Vastly superior as she is to most of her figurative offspring, she is nonetheless the childish predecessor of Miss America, of "Teen Angel," of the ubiquitous, everyday, wonderful girl about whom thousands of popular songs and movies have been made. Like her descendants, she flatters the possibilities of her audience; she does not quicken their aspirations. In a sense, my introduction to Little Eva and to the Victorian scenes, objects, and sensibility of which she is suggestive was my introduction to consumerism. The pleasure Little Eva gave me provided historical and practical preparation for the equally indispensable and disquieting comforts of mass culture. Perhaps Victorian sentimentality appeals to us not because it is so remote but because it is so near. Its products have the heightened and endearing vigor that comes from being the first of a line, but their line continues, unbroken if debased, to our own day. We treat Victoriana today with the same ambiguity we reserve for the consumer

pleasures provided by our televisions, movie screens, and radios. Whatever our fondness for American Victorian culture, our critical evaluation of its most characteristic manifestations is often low. Terms like "camp" used to describe phenomena such as Little Eva socialize our ongoing, unexplored embarrassment. We Americans are, after all, the first society in history to locate and express many personal, "unique" feelings and responses through dime-a-dozen artifacts.

I will argue . . . for the intimate connection between critical aspects of Victorian culture and modern mass culture. Twentieth-century America is believed, if in pejorative senses, to be more "modern" than other modern cultures; nineteenth-century America was, in certain senses also usually considered pejorative, more Victorian than other countries to whom the term is applied. Even England, whose Queen was the source of the word "Victorian," was less entirely dominated by what we think of as the worst, the most sentimental, aspects of the Victorian spirit. It seems indicative, for example, that the Sunday School movement with its saccharine simplification of dogma found fewer obstacles and greater success in America than in England.[3] Putting it another way, I might say that Victorian culture in England represented a complex and intelligent collaboration of available resources unparalleled in America. My point can be clarified by glancing at Victorian literature in the two countries.

England's major writers—Charles Dickens, William Makepeace Thackeray, and George Eliot—dedicated their enormous talents to an exploration of Victorianism which, by the sheer fact of assuming its inescapability, complicated and enriched it. It was their treatment of their subject, not their subject, that distinguished them from other, less talented English writers. Even today they restore for us the context and possible seriousness of what are now more or less abandoned literary themes: feminine purity; the sanctity of the childish heart; above all, the meaning of religious conformity. In contrast, major American authors of the Victorian era like James Fenimore Cooper, Nathaniel Hawthorne, Henry David Thoreau, Herman Melville, and Walt Whitman turned their sights principally on values and scenes that operated as alternatives to cultural norms. Their subjects, as well as their styles, differed from those of many of their American contemporaries. They wrote dramas of the forest, the sea, the city. They sought to bring their readers into direct confrontation with the more brutal facts of America's explosive development. Thoreau, Cooper, Melville, and Whitman wrote principally about men, not girls and children, and they wrote about men engaged in economically and ecologically significant activities.[4] When they treated Victorian mores, with a few notable exceptions they either satirized them or lapsed into *pro forma* imitations of conventional models.[5] It was as if America's finest authors refused to redeem the virgin, the child, and the home from the isolation imposed precisely by their status as cult objects; they abandoned them to unreality. Here at mid-nineteenth century in America we see the beginnings of the split between elite and mass cultures so familiar today.

It is indicative of Victorian England's greater cultural cohesiveness that almost all the mid-nineteenth-century English authors we currently admire were admired by their contemporaries. In contrast, many of the American writers of the same period we now value were underrated and little read in their own time; those who, like Stowe, were highly esteemed are hardly studied today. Yet an examination of precisely what we dislike, at least theoretically, in the popular writers of the Victorian era—their debased religiosity, their sentimental peddling of Christian belief for its nostalgic value—is crucial for understanding American culture in the nineteenth century and in our own. The very ambiguity of our response is itself a motive for exploration.

Between 1820 and 1875,[6] in the midst of the transformation of the American economy into the most powerfully aggressive capitalist system in the world, American culture seemed bent on establishing a perpetual Mother's Day. As the secular activities of American life were demonstrating their utter supremacy, religion became the message of America's official and conventional cultural life. This religion was hardly the Calvinism of the founders of the Bay Colony or that of New England's great eighteenth-century divines. It was a far cry, moreover, from the faith which at least imaginatively still engaged serious authors like Melville and Hawthorne.

Under "Calvinism" we can place much of what rigorous theology Protestant Americans have ever officially accepted. Until roughly 1820, this theological tradition was a chief, perhaps the chief, vehicle of intellectual and cultural activity in American life. The Calvinist tradition culminated in the Edwardsean school:[7] most notably, Jonathan Edwards (1703-58) and his friends and followers, Samuel Hopkins (1721-1803), Joseph Bellamy (1719-90), and Nathaniel Emmons (1745-1840). The Edwardsean school has often been mythologized, but, whatever its very real faults, it undoubtedly constituted the most persuasive example of independent yet institutionalized thought to which our society has even temporarily given credence. Its members studied together; they trained, questioned, and defended one another. They exhibited with some consistency the intellectual rigor and imaginative precision difficult to achieve without collective effort, and certainly rare in more recent American annals.

For some time, roughly between 1740 and 1820, the rigor exhibited by the Edwardsean ministers seemed representative of the wider culture or at least welcomed by it. Edwardsean theology, however, outlived

its popular support. In the eighteenth and nineteenth centuries, as in the twentieth, the vast majority of American Christians identified themselves as members of one of the various Protestant groups.[8] Yet the differences between the Protestants of, say, 1800 and their descendants of 1875 and after are greater than the similarities. The everyday Protestant of 1800 subscribed to a rather complicated and rigidly defined body of dogma; attendance at a certain church had a markedly theological function. By 1875, American Protestants were much more likely to define their faith in terms of family morals, civic responsibility, and above all, in terms of the social function of churchgoing. Their actual creed was usually a liberal, even a sentimental one for which Edwards and his contemporaries would have felt scorn and horror. In an analogous way, Protestant churches over the same period shifted their emphasis from a primary concern with the doctrinal beliefs of their members to a preoccupation with numbers. In ecclesiastical and religious circles, attendance came to count for more than genuine adherence. Nothing could show better the late nineteenth-century Protestant Church's altered identity as an eager participant in the emerging consumer society than its obsession with popularity and its increasing disregard of intellectual issues.

The vitiation and near-disappearance of the Calvinist tradition have been sufficiently lamented, and perhaps insufficiently understood. The numerous historians and theologians of the last four decades who have recorded and mourned its loss themselves constitute an unofficial school which can loosely be termed "Neo-orthodox."[9] In analyzing Calvinism's decline, however, they have not examined all the evidence at their disposal. They have provided important studies of the effects of the democratic experiment in a new and unsettled land, effects all tending to a liberal creed in theology as in politics: immigration on a scale unparalleled in the modern world, huge labor resources facilitating rapid urbanization and industrialization, amalgamation of diverse cultural heritages often at the level of their lowest common denominator. Yet they have neglected what might be called the social history of Calvinist theology. They have given scant consideration to the changing nature of the ministry as a profession or to the men who entered its ranks during the critical decades between 1820 and 1875. And they have overlooked another group central to the rituals of that Victorian sentimentalism that did so much to gut Calvinist orthodoxy: Little Eva's most ardent admirers, the active middle-class Protestant women whose supposedly limited intelligences liberal piety was in part designed to flatter. As if in fear of contamination, historians have ignored the claims of what Harriet Beecher Stowe astutely called "Pink and White Tyranny":[10] the drive of nineteenth-century American women to gain power through the exploitation of their feminine identity as their society defined it.

These women did not hold offices or own businesses. They had little formal status in their culture, nor apparently did they seek it. They were not usually declared feminists or radical reformers. Increasingly exempt from the responsibilities of domestic industry, they were in a state of sociological transition. They comprised the bulk of educated churchgoers and the vast majority of the dependable reading public; in ever greater numbers, they edited magazines and wrote books for other women like themselves. They were becoming the prime consumers of American culture. As such they exerted an enormous influence on the chief male purveyors of that culture, the liberal, literate ministers and popular writers who were being read while Melville and Thoreau were ignored. These masculine groups, ministers and authors, occupied a precarious position in society. Writers had never received public support; ministers ceased to do so after 1833 when the "disestablishment" of the Protestant Church became officially complete in the United States. In very real ways, authors and clergymen were on the market; they could hardly afford to ignore their feminine customers and competitors.

What bound the minister and the lady together with the popular writer was their shared preoccupation with the lighter productions of the press; they wrote poetry, fiction, memoirs, sermons, and magazine pieces of every kind. What distinguished them from the writer, and made them uniquely central agents in the process of sentimentalization . . ., is the fact that their consuming interest in literature was relatively new. At the turn of the nineteenth century, the prominent Edwardsean minister, Nathaniel Emmons, returned a novel by Sir Walter Scott lent him by a friend with protestations of genuine horror. A scant fifty years later, serious ministers and orthodox professors of theology were making secular literature a concern and even an occupation. During the same period, women writers gradually flooded the market with their efforts. While a female author at the beginning of the nineteenth century was considered by definition an aberration from her sex, by its close she occupied an established if not a respected place. The Victorian lady and minister were joining, and changing, the literary scene.

Northeastern clergymen and middle-class literary women lacked power of any crudely tangible kind, and they were careful not to lay claim to it. Instead they wished to exert "influence," which they eulogized as a religious force.[11] They were asking for nothing more than offhand attention, and not even much of that: "influence" was to be discreetly omnipresent and omnipotent. This was the suasion of moral and psychic nurture, and it had a good deal less to do with the faith of the past and a good deal more to do with the advertising industry of the future than its proponents would have liked to believe. They exerted their "influence" chiefly through literature which was just in the process of becoming a mass medium. The press offered them the chance they were seeking to be unobtrusive and everywhere at the same time. They inevitably confused theology with religiosity, religiosity with literature, and literature with self-justification. They understandably attempted to stabilize and advertise in their work the values that cast their recessive position in the most favorable light. Even as they took full advantage of the new commercial possibilities technological revolutions in printing had made possible, they exercised an enormously conservative influence on their society.

On a thematic level, they specialized in the domestic and religious concerns considered appropriate for members of their profession or sex. But content was not the most important aspect of their work, nor of its conservative impulse. Ministerial and feminine authors were as involved with the method of consumption as with the article consumed. Despite their often prolific output, they were in a curious sense more interested in the business of reading than in that of writing. . . . Of course involvement and identification between authors and their readers was characteristically and broadly Victorian. Henry James could rebuke Anthony Trollope for his constant asides to the reader, for his casual admissions that he was making up a story to please an audience,[12] but Trollope was in the majority. To ask a Victorian author, American or British, not to address his readers was a bit like asking a modern-day telecaster to ignore his viewers. Literature then, like television now, was in the early phase of intense self-consciousness characteristic of a new mass medium: the transactions between cultural buyer and seller, producer and consumer shaped both the content and the form. The American groups I am discussing, however, showed an extraordinary degree, even by Victorian standards, of market-oriented alertness to their customers. They had a great deal in common with them.

The well-educated intellectual minister of the eighteenth century read omnivorously, but the dense argumentative tracts he tackled forced him to think, not to "read" in our modern sense; metaphorically speaking, he was producing, not consuming. His mid-nineteenth-century descendant was likely to show a love of fiction and poetry and a distaste for polemical theology; he preferred "light" to "heavy" reading. By the same token, numerous observers remarked on the fact that countless young Victorian women spent much of their middle-class girlhoods prostrate on chaise lounges with their heads buried in "worthless" novels. Their grandmothers, the critics insinuated, had spent their time studying the Bible and performing useful household chores. "Reading" in its new form was many things; among them it was an occupation for the unemployed, narcissistic self-education for those excluded from the harsh school of practical competition. Literary men of the cloth and middle-class women writers of the Victorian period knew from firsthand evidence that literature was functioning more and more as a form of leisure, a complicated mass dream-life in the busiest, most wide-awake society in the world. They could not be altogether ignorant that literature was revealing and supporting a special class, a class defined less by what its members produced than by what they consumed. When the minister and the lady put pen to paper, they had ever in their minds their reading counterparts; the small scale, the intimate scenes, the chatty tone of many of their works complement the presumably comfortable posture and domestic backdrop of their readers. They wrote not just to win adherents to their views, but to make converts to literature, to sustain and encourage the habit of reading itself.[13] Inevitably more serious writers like Melville attempted alternately to re-educate, defy, and ignore a public addicted to the absorption of sentimental fare.

To suggest that problems of professional class or sexual status played a part in the creation and character of nineteenth- and twentieth-century American culture is not, hopefully, to suggest a conspiracy view of history. The ministers and women I am considering were intent on claiming culture as their peculiar property, one conferring on them a special duty and prerogative. They were rightly insecure about their position in the broader society; they sought to gain indirect and compensatory control. Yet they were not insincere, ill-intentioned, or simple-minded. It must be remembered how these people saw themselves, and with what reason: they were Christians reinterpreting their faith as best they could in terms of the needs of their society. Their conscious motives were good—even praiseworthy; their effects were not altogether bad. Under the sanction of sentimentalism, lady and clergyman were able to cross the cruel lines laid down by sexual stereotyping in ways that were clearly historically important and undoubtedly personally fulfilling. She could become aggressive, even angry, in the name of various holy causes; he could become gentle, even nurturing, for the sake of moral overseeing, Whatever their ambiguities of motivation, both believed they had a genuine redemptive mission in their society: to propagate the potentially matriarchal virtues of nurture, generosity, and acceptance; to create the "culture of the feelings" that John Stuart Mill was to find during the same period in Wordsworth.[14] It is hardly altogether their fault that their efforts intensified sentimental rather than matriarchal values.

Moreover, whatever the errors of the sentimentalists, they paid for them. The losses sustained by the ministers and the women involved, as well as by the culture which was their arena, were enormous. The case of the ministers is clear-cut; they lost status and respect. The case of the women is equally painful, but more difficult to discuss, especially in the atmosphere of controversy that attends feminist argument today. I must add a personal note here. As I researched and wrote [The Feminization of American Culture] I experienced a confusion which perhaps other women scholars have felt in recent years. I expected to find my fathers and my mothers; instead I discovered my fathers and my sisters. The best of the men had access to solutions, and occasionally inspiring ones, which I appropriate only with the anxiety and effort that attend genuine aspiration. The problems of the women correspond to mine with a frightening accuracy that seems to set us outside the processes of history; the answers of even the finest of them were often mine, and sometimes largely unacceptable to me. I am tempted to account my response socialization, if not treachery. Siding with the enemy. But I think that is wrong.

I have a respect for so-called "toughness," not as a good in itself, not isolated and reified as it so often is in male-dominated cultures, but as the necessary preservative for all virtues, even those of gentleness and generosity. My respect is deeply ingrained; my commitment to feminism requires that I explore it, not that I abjure it. Much more important, it does no good to shirk the fact that nineteenth-century American society tried to damage women like Harriet Beecher Stowe—and succeeded. It is undeniable that the oppressed preserved, and were intended to preserve, crucial values threatened in the larger culture. But it is equally true that no one would protest oppression with fervor or justification if it did not in part accomplish its object: the curtailment of the possibilities of growth for significant portions of a given community. Nineteenth-century American women were oppressed, and damaged; inevitably, the influence they exerted in turn on their society was not altogether beneficial. The cruelest aspect of the process of oppression is the logic by which it forces its objects to be oppressive in turn, to do the dirty work of their society in several senses. Melville put the matter well: weakness, or even "depravity in the oppressed is no apology for the oppressor; but rather an additional stigma to him, as being, in a large degree, the effect and not the cause of oppression."[15] To view the victims of oppression simply as martyrs and heroes, however, undeniably heroic and martyred as they often were, is only to perpetuate the sentimental heresy I am attempting to study here.

I have been more interested in the effects than in the conscious motives of the women and ministers under consideration, for there is no better indication of their dilemma than the often wide and tragic divergence between the two. In the process of sentimentalization which they aided, many women and ministers espoused at least in theory to so-called passive virtues, admirable in themselves, and sorely needed in American life. They could not see to what alien uses their espousal might be put. Sentimentalism is a complex phenomenon. It asserts that the values a society's activity denies are precisely the ones it cherishes; it attempts to deal with the phenomenon of cultural bifurcation by the manipulation of nostalgia. Sentimentalism provides a way to protest a power to which one has already in part capitulated. It is a form of dragging one's heels. It always borders on dishonesty but it is a dishonesty for which there is no known substitute in a capitalist country. Many nineteenth-century Americans in the Northeast acted every day as if they believed that economic expansion, urbanization, and industrialization represented the greatest good. It is to their credit that they indirectly acknowledged that the pursuit of these "masculine" goals meant damaging, perhaps losing, another good, one they increasingly included under the "feminine" ideal. Yet the fact remains that their regret was calculated not to interfere with their actions. We remember that Little Eva's beautiful death, which Stowe presents as part of a protest against slavery, in no way hinders the working of that system. The minister and the lady were appointed by their society as the champions of sensibility. They were in the position of contestants in a fixed fight: they had agreed to put on a convincing show, and to lose. The fakery involved was finally crippling for all concerned.

The sentimentalization of theological and secular culture was an inevitable part of the self-evasion of a society both committed to laissez-faire industrial expansion and disturbed by its consequences. America, impelled by economic and social developments of international scope, abandoned its theological modes of thought at the same time its European counterparts abandoned theirs; it lacked, however, the means they possessed to create substitutes. American culture, younger and less formed than that of any European country, had not yet developed sufficiently rich and diversified secular traditions to serve as carriers for its ongoing intellectual life. The pressures for self-rationalization of the crudest kind were overpowering in a country propelled so rapidly toward industrial capitalism with so little cultural context to slow or complicate its course; sentimentalism provided the inevitable rationalization of the economic order.

In the modernization of American culture that began in the Victorian period, some basic law of dialectical motion was disrupted, unfulfilled, perhaps disproved. Calvinism was a great faith, with great limitations: it was repressive, authoritarian, dogmatic, patriarchal to an extreme. Its demise was inevitable, and in some real sense, welcome. Yet it deserved, and elsewhere and at other times found, great opponents. One could argue that the logical antagonist of Calvinism was a fully humanistic, historically minded romanticism. Exponents of such romanticism appeared in mid-nineteenth-century America—one thinks particularly of Margaret Fuller and Herman Melville—but they were

rare. In America, for economic and social reasons, Calvinism was largely defeated by an anti-intellectual sentimentalism purveyed by men and women whose victory did not achieve their finest goals; America lost its male-dominated theological tradition without gaining a comprehensive feminism or an adequately modernized religious sensibility. It is crucial that I be as clear here as I can. The tragedy of nineteenth-century northeastern society is not the demise of Calvinist patriarchal structures, but rather the failure of a viable, sexually diversified culture to replace them. "Feminization" inevitably guaranteed, not simply the loss of the finest values contained in Calvinism, but the continuation of male hegemony in different guises. The triumph of the "feminizing," sentimental forces that would generate mass culture redefined and perhaps limited the possibilities for change in American society. Sentimentalism, with its tendency to obfuscate the visible dynamics of development, heralded the cultural sprawl that has increasingly characterized post-Victorian life.

Notes

[1] On American Victorian culture, see Meade Minnegerode, *The Fabulous Forties 1840-1850* (New York, 1924), and E. Douglas Branch, *The Sentimental Years 1836-60* (New York and London, 1934). For important efforts to define "Victorianism" as an American phenomenon, see the essays in the special issue of *American Quarterly,* 27 (1975) entitled "Victorian Culture in America," particularly the lead article by Daniel Walker Howe, "American Victorianism as a Culture."

[2] See Susan Sontag, "Notes on 'Camp' "in *Against Interpretation and Other Essays* (New York, 1969), pp. 277-83.

[3] See Edwin Wilbur Rice, *The Sunday School Movement 1780-1917 and the American Sunday School Union 1817-1917* (Philadelphia, 1917), pp. 42 ff.

[4] Thoreau carefully told his readers in *Walden,* a rural narrative which is hardly a pastoral in any conventional sense, the monetary cost of his experiment in self-reliant solitude; and he never forgot the railroad whose cars thundered near his retreat. Cooper's Natty Bumppo, the hero of the Leatherstocking Tales, despite his religious adherence to conservation, is a hunter who kills more animals and Indians than he saves. Whether he likes it or not, Natty is the vanguard as well as the refugee of civilization, and his appearance in any forest prophesies its eventual demise. The great protagonist of Melville's *Moby Dick,* Ahab, whatever his spiritual quest, is a part of America's aggressive whaling industry, and as such, a proto-technocrat; if Natty's most intimate friend is his gun, Ahab's is his harpoon. The transcendental jingoism of Whitman's

early Manhattan persona is not designed to conceal the fact that he is celebrating the proliferating population, self-propagating machinery, and randomly abundant materialism of the most ruthlessly expanding and constricting city in the world.

[5] I am thinking here particularly of Hawthorne's treatment of the pure maiden figure: Priscilla in *The Blithedale Romance* (1852) and Hilda in *The Marble Faun* (1860).

[6] I hope the reasons I have chosen this period (1820-75) as the crucial one for the development of Victorian sentimentalism in the Northeast will become clear in the course of this book. Recent historical opinion has minimized the importance of the Civil War as a crucial dividing line for American culture. I will make just a few further points here. First, the period 1820-1875 includes the initial commercialization of culture, most notably the revolution in printing and the rise of nationally circulated magazines. Second, the most important work of the leading figures in the sentimentalization process . . . seems to appear and, more significantly, to receive its highest valuation during these years. Elizabeth Stuart Phelps, for example, who was born late in the period (1844), produces her most characteristic work, *The Gates Ajar,* in 1868; thereafter, she repeats herself and receives steadily less critical attention and praise until her death in 1911. Third, the period marks the time when the majority of Protestants in the Northeast changed from a strict to a "liberal" creed and when the Protestant Church forged its relationship with the newly commercialized culture: both changes are still in force today. . . .

[7] In discussing what I am calling Calvinism, the older Protestant tradition of the Northeast, I am focusing throughout this study on its eighteenth- rather than its seventeenth-century New England exponents not because the former were greater than the latter but because they were inevitably more directly influential on the nineteenth-century Protestant clergymen whose reformulation of Calvinist thought will be my chief concern. I use the term "Calvinism," despite its partial imprecision, because it was the word the ministerial and feminine groups I am studying most commonly employed to describe the older, sterner creed of their forebears.

[8] Martin Marty, in the "Foreword" to *Righteous Empire: The Protestant Experience in America* (New York, 1970), notes: "today seven out of ten citizens identify themselves as Protestants" (n.p.).

[9] For an excellent introduction to Neo-orthodoxy, see Sydney E. Ahlstrom, *A Religious History of the American People* (New Haven and London, 1972), pp. 932-48, and Martin E. Marty, *op. cit.,* pp. 233-43. For the most astute Neo-orthodox analysis of the American

religious tradition, see Francis Miller, Wilhelm Pauck, and H. Richard Niebuhr, *The Church Against the World* (Chicago, 1935), and H. Richard Niebuhr, *The Social Sources of Denominationalism* (New York, 1929). Scholars like Perry Miller, who might be seen as the head of "Neo-orthodox" historiography, did not necessarily share the religious beliefs of those they studied, or of the Neo-orthodox theologians (the Niebuhr brothers, Paul Tillich, and others) who began to write in the 1920s. But they are "Neo-orthodox" in the sense that they admire the Calvinist tradition and regret its passing.

[10] This is the title of a novel published by Stowe in 1871.

[11] My understanding of "influence" and how it functioned for the clerical and feminine groups under discussion was shaped by the work of Sigmund Freud and Heinz Kohut on narcissism as well as by the theories of a number of sociologists. I came to feel that, while Protestant ministers had been part of an elite group, they were increasingly joining middle-class women and becoming part of a special subculture. Such subculture groups, past and present, evince certain inherent patterns. Most simply, one might say that society forces members of a subculture at any moment of intersection with the larger culture into a constant, simplified, and often demeaning process of self-identification. The minister between 1820 and 1875 was beginning to experience the enforced self-simplification women had long known. In 1820 the statement "I am a minister" had a series of possible precise connotations, theological and political. By 1875, the statement meant roughly what it does today: it connotes vague churchbound efforts at "goodness." "I am a housewife," millions of American women have been explaining implicitly and explicitly for the last hundred and fifty years; yet, the term "housewife" is imprecise and obfuscating to an extreme. Surely there was (and is) as much difference between tending a childless urban apartment and running a fully populated farm household as there was between practicing law and selling merchandise. Yet just at the period when women were increasingly adopting a punitively generalized mode of self-description, men were labeling themselves in ever more specialized terms. The all-inclusive designation "lady" slowly gave way over the nineteenth century to the equally blank-check appellation "housewife." In contrast, the polite term "gentleman" had no real successor; it fragmented into a thousand parts, personal, political, and professional. Why have not men identified themselves by an equally adequate, or inadequate, catchall phrase such as "breadwinner"? Quite obviously, because society expresses its greater esteem for masculine occupations by honoring them with a highly differentiated nomenclature.

Naturally those belonging to a subculture will themselves be preoccupied with who they are, often in equally simplistic and distorted terms. They will struggle obsessively, repetitiously, and monotonously to deal with the burden of self-dislike implied and imposed by their society's apparently low evaluation of them. In a sense, they will be forced into some version of narcissism, by which I mean to suggest not only a psychological process but a sociological and even a political one. Narcissism is best defined not as exaggerated self-esteem but as a refusal to judge the self by alien, objective means, a willed inability to allow the world to play its customary role in the business of self-evaluation. Heinz Kohut has explained lucidly the causes for the development of narcissism: "Being threatened in the maintenance of a cohesive self because in early life . . . [the narcissist is] lacking in adequate confirming responses . . . from the environment, [he] turns to self-stimulation in order to retain [his] . . . precarious cohesion." The narcissist must always by definition be self-taught, because the world's lessons are inevitably unacceptable to his ego. He is committed not only to an underestimation of the force of facts, but, in Freud's words, to an "over-estimation of the power of wishes and mental processes. . . . a belief in the magical virtue of words and a method of dealing with the outer world—the art of magic." Narcissism can necessitate the replacement of society by the self, reality by literature. See Heinz Kohut, "Thoughts on Narcissism and Narcissistic Rage," a paper delivered as the A. A. Brill Lecture of the New York Psychoanalytic Society on November 30, 1971; Sigmund Freud, "On Narcissism: An Introduction" in *A General Selection from the Works of Sigmund Freud,* ed. John Rickman, M.D. (New York, 1957), p. 106. For a definition of minority groups, see Helen Mayer Hacker, "Women as a Minority Group," Bobbs-Merrill Reprint Series in the Social Sciences, 5-108. The ministry had constituted in the past what Suzanne Keller calls a "strategic elite"; see Suzanne Keller, *Beyond the Ruling Elite: Strategic Elites in Modern Society* (New York, 1963).

[12] See Henry James, "Anthony Trollope," in *The Future of the Novel: Essays on the Art of Fiction,* ed. Leon Edel (New York, 1956), pp. 247-8.

[13] There are many interesting studies of this aspect of the reading phenomenon. Works that particularly stimulated my thinking are the "Introduction" in *The Oven Birds: American Women on Womanhood 1820-1920,* ed. Gail Parker (New York, 1972), pp. 1-56; Roland Barthes, *The Pleasures of the Text,* trans. Richard Miller (New York, 1975); and Raymond Williams, "Base and Superstructure in Marxist Cultural Theory," *New Left Review* 82 (1973), especially 12-16.

[14] I am indebted for my understanding of the positive side of sentimentalism to the superb study by Elaine Showalter, *The Female Tradition in the English Novel:*

From Charlotte Brontë to Doris Lessing (Princeton, 1976). For the J. S. Mill reference, see *The Autobiography of John Stuart Mill* (New York, n.d.), pp. 103-17.

[15] Herman Melville, *White-Jacket, or the World in a Man-of-War* (New York, 1967), p. 141.

Cathy N. Davidson

SOURCE: "Flirting with Destiny: Ambivalence and Form in the Early American Sentimental Novel," in *Studies in American Fiction,* Vol. 10, No. 1, Spring, 1982, pp. 17-39.

[*In the following essay, Davidson argues that some domestic novels ironically subvert typical social constructions of femininity.*]

Even though the late eighteenth-century American public was "reading novels with increasingly greater frequency than it read other kinds of books," the growing popularity of fiction did not assure its respectability.[1] On the contrary, the rise of the novel in the United States elicited a general condemnation of the form.[2] Such prominent Americans as Timothy Dwight, Jonathan Edwards, Thomas Jefferson, Benjamin Rush, and Noah Webster all denounced the new genre, a genre that necessarily offended, by its very nature, those whose literary standards had been shaped by either a residual Colonial Puritanism or an emerging Yankee pragmatism.[3] Did novels promote the Kingdom of God? Could they further the wealth of man? On other grounds too fiction was deemed morally and social suspect. As Carl Van Doren has aptly observed:

> The dullest critics contended that novels were lies; the pious, that they served no virtuous purpose; the strenuous, that they softened sturdy minds; the utilitarian, that they crowded out more useful books; the realistic, that they painted adventure too romantic and love too vehement; the patriotic, that, dealing with European manners, they tended to confuse and dissatisfy republican youth. In the face of such censure American novelists came forward late and apologetically, armed for the most part with the plea that they told the truth, pointed to heaven, or devoutly believed in the new republic.[4]

In the face of such censure American novelists also came late to sustained considerations of craft and technique. "There was little time for [and little concern with] conscious artistry in the early novel."[5] Consequently, and as might be expected, America's pioneer novelists have been widely criticized for their aesthetic limitations. For example, Henri Petter begins his major work, *The Early American Novel,* by maintaining: "The three decades ending in 1820 are not considered a distinguished epoch either in the history of American writing or, more specifically, in the development of the American novel." Most of the early novels, Petter concludes in his first paragraph, exhibit a "widespread mediocrity" and justify the "complaints" that "turn up regularly" in the "book reviews" and "essays" of the time and even in the "prefaces" of the novels themselves.[6] However, despite the utilitarian, moralistic, and patriotic biases that hindered their course, a few early novelists still found ways to experiment with the conventional forms in which they were compelled to work and thereby circumvented, sometimes with surprising subtlety, the various criteria whereby they were condemned.

The form most commonly employed in late eighteenth-century America was the sentimental novel. These plots, centering on a possible seduction, were more acceptable than others borrowed from the burgeoning British novel for two reasons.[7] The social critics were placated by Richardsonian fables that advocated middle-class ideals regarding the necessity of and the necessary connection between virtuous maidenhood and holy matrimony. Moral critics were appeased by the way in which these same novels ostensibly fostered morality through pointed examples of virtue rewarded and vice punished. Writer and reader alike could take comfort in the salutary propriety of tales designed to promote both sanctity and connubial bliss. But demonstrating that the road to heaven and the road to family happiness were one and the same, early sentimental novelists too much simplified their moral cosmology. They saw "virtue" as merely chastity and "vice" as nothing more than virginity's loss.[8] Overtly, didactically, persistently, most of these writers proclaimed that female virginity had to be preserved at all cost and that its loss must necessarily lead to degradation and even death. They were, in short, morally simplistic, so much so that books that were sentimental to avoid being dismissed because they were "fictions" are now largely dismissed because they are "sentimental."

Nevertheless, some writers did manage to transcend the limitations commonly associated with the early American sentimental novel. Partially yielding to the pressures that Van Doren summarized these authors only appeared to write as convention required. Their books could be dedicated (literally) to the preservation of "female virtue" yet still exhibit a definite tension between the public morality apologetically espoused in the preface and the actions portrayed in the plot. Such a tension, in the better fiction, need not be surprising. The first American novelists insistently claimed that their works were founded on "truth" and "life." Yet the truths of life in the new republic, especially for women, the primary subjects of sentimental fiction, were often contradictory and confusing. Furthermore, since there was a wide disparity between accepted ideals regarding women and women's real status, those

writers who wished to explore the complexities of their society were partly at odds with a society that judged fiction tolerable only when it promulgated accepted moral dicta. That adversary relationship is a classic American phenomenon, and so is one predictable resolution of the impasse. Writers like William Hill Brown, Hannah Webster Foster, Isaac Mitchell, Judith Sargent Murray, Susanna Haswell Rowson, Rebecca Rush, and Tabitha Tenney perhaps at times subconsciously and certainly "covertly and by snatches" managed to present truths other than the expected ones. In the process—possibly because of the process—they also produced books that continue to merit the attention of both the cultural historian and the literary critic.[9]

This is not to say that the first American fictionalists are yet undiscovered Melvilles. The novels of the early national period deserve examination not because they are hitherto unappreciated literary masterpieces but because they mark the beginning of a tradition. Indeed, any attempt to explain either America's eighteenth-century sentimental fiction or its great nineteenth-century classics primarily in terms of their English parallels ignores the different ways in which the uncertain moral and social climate that succeeded the American Revolution set the first novels on the same course later—and more capably—followed by Hawthorne, Melville, James, and other major nineteenth-century authors.[10] In essence, the young American genre coped with repression by quickly passing into an adolescence accomplished in duplicity. If among these early authors there are no Melvilles, there are forerunners of his confidence men. To avoid moral censure, the writers of the early republic often hypocritically posed as plainspeaking advocates of simple virtue. To meet the unreasonable demand for truth in fiction, the first novelists sometimes lied.

Thus numerous early works such as *Fidelity Rewarded; or The History of Polly Granville* (1796), "founded on truth, and nature"; *Amelia; or, The Faithless Briton* (1798), based on "Recent Events"; and *Monima; or, the Beggar Girl* (1802), "chiefly founded on fact," masquerade as nonfiction novels or *romans a clef*.[11] As the first title clearly implies, the books are ostensibly histories with the names changed only to protect the principals. So established was the assertion of historical validity that William Hill Brown, in his second novel, *Ira and Isabella; or the Natural Children* (1807), burlesqued the usual title page by proclaiming that he was writing "A NOVEL, Founded in FICTION." In somewhat similar fashion, writers could also pragmatically pretend to advocate virtue while indulging in rumor-mongering of the basest sort. For example, William Hill Brown's first novel (and the first American novel), *The Power of Sympathy; or, The Triumph of Nature* (1789), purports "to expose the fatal Consequences, of SEDUCTION" and thereby "Promote the

Economy of Human Life" but also contains both footnotes and subplots detailing the various sexual transgressions—incest, adultery, cohabitation—of a few prominent late eighteenth-century Americans.[12] This book proved to be so scandalous and libelous (the claim to factuality was not always a fiction) that even the author cooperated in its "suppression." And still another version of authorial moral duplicity was suggested by the very structure of sentimental fiction. Writers regularly decried in their prefaces any topic that might, in other novels, sully virtue. They thereby condemned even while they composed voyeuristic tales that titillated, in imitation of one of the more dubious aspects of the Richardsonian tradition, with portraits of intended vice inching towards consummation.

In short, early American novelists resorted to a number of expedients, beginning with a predilection for sentimental plots, that served to diffuse the opprobrium under which they necessarily labored. Since most of them employed these devices in a conventional fashion, they continued to produce formula fiction—typical sentimental novels only slightly modified for the new American market. These authors, like James Butler or Martha Read or Helena Wells (to name but a few), are now largely forgotten and justifiably so. But a number of other writers went considerably beyond these ploys and exhibited a different order of duplicity in their attempts to acknowledge the limiting concerns of contemporary critics even as they expanded the action and the issues in their plots to engage more fully, aesthetically and intellectually, their readers' attention. It is this difficult balancing act— not always successfully executed—that characterizes the best early New World sentimental fiction and gives it its distinctive American tone. One example is Caroline Courtney, an obvious ancestress of Hawthorne's Hester Prynne. This protagonist in Samuel Relf's *Infidelity, or the Victims of Sentiment* (1797) obeys her parents and weds, much against her own wishes, the elderly Mr. Franks. For being a dutiful daughter she is punished by an unhappy marriage. Neglected by her cruel husband, the wife finds solace in the concern of a younger, more sympathetic man. That infatuation, apparently unconsummated, is still the "infidelity" of the title and brings death to both participants and disaster to their friends and families. Yet the epigraph to the novel reads "—'Tis not a sin to love," to which the reader can only reply that it was and it was not. Marriage is vindicated by the fatal consequences of its failure. The probably non-adulterous lovers are vindicated by their sinless love.

As a summary suggests, the sentimental writers who especially merit attention do so for the ways in which they could turn the sentimental on itself to question the very propositions they supposedly unquestionably extolled. So works such as Susanna Rowson's *Trials of the Human Heart* (1795)—in which the innocent Meriel marries Clement Rooksby at his mother's instigation and to save him from a disastrous affair but is rewarded by his abuse and philandering—or Relf's *Infidelity* portray unions that do not at all correspond to the pervasive sentimental ideal of tranquil, connubial domesticity, an ideal which is elsewhere espoused in even those novels themselves. These unhappy marriages, it should also be noted, are not originally merited by any consideration for which the wife can reasonably be blamed. Even more morally problematic is the tragic marriage between Mrs. Morley and the title character in S.S.B.K. Wood's *Dorval, or the Speculator* (1801). Unfortunately for Mrs. Morley, who was both a wealthy widow and a good woman, her husband turns out to be a fortune hunter, a bigamist, and a murderer. Virtue, the rock on which the sentimental novel was founded, goes quite unrewarded when a virtuous woman is wed to such a vicious man.

A different compromising of expected moral stances is sometimes seen in the supposed moral spokesmen themselves. Too often to be merely coincidental, the proponents of standard ideals are portrayed as almost self-parodies, characters too shallow and priggish to be taken seriously. Thus in *The Power of Sympathy* Worthy bases his frequent moral pronouncements on the wisdom gained in his "pilgrimage of two and twenty years" through this world of delusions.[13] Homilies are hardly validated when they are voiced by a callow youth.[14] In much the same fashion, Prudelia, in Susanna Rowson's *Mentoria; or the Young Lady's Friend* (1794) belies her Bunyanesque name and, despite her frequent sententia, proves to be merely a self-righteous busybody too concerned with uncovering the sins of her neighbors to cultivate any virtues of her own.

When conventional moral pronouncements are advanced by spokesmen such as Worthy and Prudelia the reader is encouraged to look beyond those pieties to discover deeper meanings and other truths. The form is also modified and its meaning altered when sentimental heroes are brought down from the heights of spiritual nobility and portrayed as believable characters. An example from *The Power of Sympathy* is germane. Harrington, the main male character in that novel, ignores Worthy's platitudinous advice and seeks refuge, instead, in suicide. That end is not a heroic vindication of high ideals. It is, considering the circumstances which prompt Harrington's death, understandably, fallibly, human. Or, conversely, moral issues are complicated when the "villain" of the piece is recast as more than just another advocate of illegitimate affairs. Belfield in Leonora Sansay's *Laura* (1809); Count Hubert in Isaac Mitchell's *The Asylum; or, Alonzo and Melissa* (1811); and, most obviously, Carwin in Charles Brockden Brown's *Wieland or The Transformation* (1798) are all examples of such humanized antagonists—the seducer who is himself seduced by delusions, misconceptions, and his own naive egotism. These characters suggest dangers other than, and embody the consequences of falls more subtle than, mere physical seduction.

Brown's Carwin is perhaps the most complex and certainly the most discussed villain in early American fiction.[15] But Montraville, in Susanna Rowson's *Charlotte. A Tale of Truth* (1794), provides an equally novel (and less analyzed) example of how effectively a few early authors could create rounded characters instead of merely those one-dimensional proponents of vice whose machinations generally spun the conventional sentimental plot.[16] Charlotte Temple elopes with this seducer partly because she has been misled by the dubious logic of Mademoiselle La Rue but primarily because she loves Montraville and fully expects that he will immediately marry her. That expectation is not unreasonable. He clearly loves her. The seducer in this first American bestseller sins primarily because he too sees himself as an honorable suitor anticipating wedlock. Charlotte, however, is no heiress, and marrying her would preclude the affluent life to which Montraville aspires. So he partly evades that first dilemma by procrastinating marriage. While he does so, he almost accidentally meets and then, conveniently, falls in love with a second woman who is virtuous, beautiful, kind, and even rich. Yet Charlotte, at this point, carries his child. Montraville's second moral quandary is therefore more pointed than was his first one. Should he remain with Charlotte, his pregnant mistress, or should he enter into a respectable and rewarding marriage?

Partly to exonerate Montraville, Rowson provides a second male character, Belcour, who tries to convince Montraville that he should affirm virtue by abandoning the now fallen Charlotte. That counsel is thoroughly conventional. Indeed, Belcour is a parallel and parody of the stock moral advisor. But this "moral" man does more than most in his efforts to see that "morality" prevails. Belcour even contrives to be found "sleeping" beside Charlotte, who really is asleep and quite unaware of the plot against her. The discovery of a betrayal that never took place finally brings Montraville to abandon Charlotte. The two former lovers are then further victimized by Belcour. This proponent of the sentimental credo that a "perfidious girl" such as the pregnant Miss Temple deserves whatever fate befalls her, employs that truism to justify keeping for himself the money provided by Montraville to take care of Charlotte.[17] So Montraville, the concerned seducer, is not the real villain in the novel, and a standard moral dictum is compromised by the way Belcour employs it to serve his vicious purpose.

Just as the seducer in some sentimental tales is humanized, so too is the woman he seduces. Instead of positing clear-cut moral choices between virtue and vice, a number of early novels present the heroine with more complicated and consequently more believable moral dilemmas. She must choose between respectability and love, for example, not between marriage and illicit sex.[18] Or she must decide between parents whom she loves and a lover whom her parents, often for no valid reason, oppose.[19] She must weigh the prospects of a restrictive domesticity against the freedom from stultifying convention that is promised by a passionate suitor.[20] Virtue is sometimes presented as no less demeaning than vice. Not infrequently, an intelligent young woman clearly foresees the protracted unhappiness that would be hers if she married the respectable male character whom society views as her proper mate. Moralists say that virtue should be rewarded. But is marriage to a stodgy moralist truly a reward for a sensitive heroine? In brief, in the best of these novels, the real issues of the plot do not always bear out the prefatory pieties and cannot be reduced to obvious lessons on how inevitably chastity is rewarded and seduction punished.

The apparent dichotomizing of male characters into "good" and "evil," the husband—actual or anticipated—and the seducer, is almost *pro forma* in some early American novels.[21] Contemporary critics may have been appeased by this didactic device, but the message of the novels often lies elsewhere. Written frequently by women, almost always for and about women, the best books of the time suggest questions about the slowly changing roles that were available to women—and to men—instead of positing absolute answers. What else can be made of fallen women who are more the victims of circumstance than the embodiments of sin and who scarcely deserve the punishments that are heaped upon them? Of seducers who are not villains? Of villains, like Belcour, who ascribe to the standard morality? Furthermore, the seducer, proud of his conquests but contemptuous of the women he seduces, often inversely mirrors the values of the moralist. The one, to prove his reputation, would despoil what the other, to prove his, would preserve. For each, the heroine is almost incidental. For the heroine, both are equally unappealing. She is caught in a double bind, and, in the best sentimental fiction, her predicament demonstrates that the postulated dichotomy of the clearly virtuous and the clearly vicious is itself a fiction.

Virtue (writ large) does not always save the heroine. Bombarded with pompous precepts on the one hand and assailed by promising temptations on the other, the perceptive female protagonist merits the reader's attention and sympathy. Prefatory statements to the contrary, hers is no easy choice. Chaste, she is rewarded by a limiting marriage, often to a limited man. Should she fall, her death is hardly triumphant proof that the social norms are just, that vice has been rightly punished. Anticipating the great romantic tradition, these protagonists seek to establish their own destinies.[22] Given the mores of late eighteenth-century

American society and the biological reality of pregnancy, they cannot succeed.

The ambivalence in the structure and resolution of the early American sentimental novel is not simply a fumbling towards moral and psychological subtlety. These works express a general uncertainty in the larger society of the time. During the last three decades of the eighteenth century numerous political and economic theorists proposed widely divergent courses that the new republic might follow. This period also saw a growing concern with questions about woman's role and woman's rights. Issues such as extending the franchise were discussed, and in New Jersey women were briefly allowed to vote.[23] The beginnings of the movement away from the agrarian "home" economy and towards a somewhat more urban economy in which wages were earned increasingly outside the home and mostly by men also brought into sharper focus questions about women's proper place. As recent historians have noted, Americans at this time extensively debated the political status of women, the importance of female education, the nature of marriage, the limits of sexual freedom, and the function of the family.[24] But what should be emphasized here is the way in which sentimental novels also reflect a pervasive concern with what later would be called the "woman question." Implicitly and explicitly, American novelists, like others in the new republic, advanced views that ranged from a conservative misogyny to an equalitarian liberalism and invoked social theorists as different as Rousseau and Wollstonecraft.

In *Emile* (1783), a book widely read in early America, Rousseau enunciated his belief in the innate inferiority of women and the consequent necessity for female subordination in all matters, domestic and social.[25] Before marriage, maidens were to be chaste, retiring, silent—rarely seen and never heard. After marriage, the good wife was to be ever attentive to her husband's needs and desires. Rousseau even maintained that education destroyed a woman's natural charm and equable disposition, thereby rendering her unfit to fulfill her chief function of happily bringing happiness to others. Two English writers who were widely read in America, the Reverend James Fordyce and Dr. John Gregory, had already popularized similar views. In *Sermons to Young Women* (1765), Fordyce maintained that a woman's most important function was to serve and please her man, while Dr. Gregory, in *The Father's Legacy to his Daughters* (1774), insisted that such traits as vitality and spirit were unfeminine, unfashionable, and unattractive. He argued that only a languishing, pallid passivity would attract a potential husband. There were American novelists who concurred with that viewpoint and advocated the ideal of the submissive helpmate. For example, Helena Wells, in *Constantia Neville; or, The West Indian* (1800), portrays a Mrs. Hayman who suffers patiently all the abuses heaped upon her by a cruel and loutish husband.[26] While engaged in such tasks as raising his illegitimate "offspring," she can still lecture the reader on the joys of being a good wife.

At the same time, however, another view of women was gaining an increasingly wide audience. Some spokesmen of the Revolution such as Thomas Paine argued that women should have greater political and social freedom. Daniel Defoe, who had modestly advocated women's rights as early as 1697, was exceptionally popular in America immediately after the War of Independence. Abigail Adams, in a number of letters to her husband, suggested (admittedly, with little success) that women be allowed some political voice in the new republic. More publicly, Judith Sargent Murray wrote several "Gleaner" essays in which she maintained that women had the same intelligence and abilities as men and therefore should have the same status.[27] This new equalitarian assessment also appears in the fiction of the time. Consistent with her theories, Murray allows her protagonist in "Story of Margaretta" (1798) to assess rationally the merits of an ominously named suitor, Sinisterus Courtland, and to decide that he is not suitable. Or Melissa Bloomfield, in Isaac Mitchell's sentimental protogothic novel, *The Asylum,* capably contends with threats from family, suitor, and the supernatural, while Deborah Sampson, in Herman Mann's *The Female Review: or, Memoirs of an American Young Lady* (1797), true to her last name, heroically opposes "tyranny" by disguising herself as a man and bravely defending her country during the Revolutionary War. Charles Brockden Brown also created a number of intelligent, capable fictional heroines and in *Alcuin; a dialogue* (1798) argued for women's education and greater political independence.

But the book that most significantly contributed to the equalitarian cause was surely Mary Wollstonecraft's *A Vindication of the Rights of Woman.* This work, printed in America in 1792 and reprinted in 1794, persuasively advocated the justice of sexual equality.[28] As the two printings indicate, *Vindication* was widely read in America. But a better indication of Wollstonecraft's impact in the United States is found in some of the negative tributes paid to her ideas.[29] Hannah Mather Crocker's *Observations on the Real Rights of Women* (1818) is, as its title implies, a counter-argument against Wollstonecraft. For Crocker, women's "real" rights are maintained by their continuing not to have any. Equally obvious, and humorously so, is a passage in S.S.B.K. Wood's *Amelia; or, The Influence of Virtue* (1802). In this novel Amelia, a standard and much put-upon sentimental heroine, "was not a disciple or pupil of Mary Woolstonecraft [sic]. . . . She was an old fashioned wife and she meant to obey her husband: she meant to do her duty in the strictest sense of the word. To perform it cheerfully would perhaps be painful, but . . . it would most assuredly be best."[30]

That quote from Mrs. Wood epitomizes the contradictions that underlie many eighteenth-century American novels. These fictions asserted that women were frail, could not act on their own or make a decision for themselves, and thus should enter into the permanent haven of marriage. Marriage, however, as even the fictional example of Amelia demonstrates, was not always a haven. In the late eighteenth century a married woman had no rights to money or property of her own but was herself almost a possession of her husband.[31] Thus, although characters such as Amelia or Mrs. Hayman submit to all that is required of them, given woman's legal status, they really have little other choice, and when these protagonists celebrate matrimony they almost always inadvertently admit to its limitations.[32]

Yet those who objected to matrimonial constraints did not reject marriage itself. The alternative, "spinsterhood," was generally conceded to be a woman's greatest defeat. In the mass culture of the time, particularly in the sentimental novel, the unmarried, middle-aged woman—the spinster—was portrayed as deserving derision and contempt.[33] Not surprisingly, proponents of women's rights did not recommend the single life. Even the "radical" Mary Wollstonecraft, in both her personal life and her public writings, insisted on marriage. She proposed, however, a union of equal partners instead of the prevailing concept of marriage which posited the bride's innocence, inexperience, and irrationality, and her consequent need for lawful love and careful guidance.

Of course, the helpless, young single woman (what the French would call the *jeune fille a marier*) was essential to the sentimental plot. Her limitations were regularly resolved positively by matrimony or proved negatively by seduction. But even this conventional view of woman's nature could be called into question by only a slight change of focus or timing. A heroine encountering a seducer well might demonstrate her need for a hero who will rescue her from the evils from which she cannot save herself. Yet if that good man is hard to find or arrives too late, there is an obvious lesson on the high cost of haplessness and a convincing demonstration that *she* should have been more capable. This second lesson, sometimes advanced in the plot, was also often argued in the preface. In fact, sentimental novelists prefatorially espoused the need for better female education, for moral awareness, for a certain capability almost as insistently as they advocated the innocent ideal of absolute chastity.

Just as Americans read such radicals as William Godwin, Mary Hays, Thomas Paine, and Mary Wollstonecraft, on the one hand, and conservatives such as William Beloe, James Fordyce, Elizabeth Hamilton, and Hannah More, on the other, so too was the sentimental novel pulled simultaneously in opposite directions.[34] One result is a polarized canon. Novels like *Amelia,* a conservative tract, can be contrasted to novels like Tabitha Tenney's *Female Quixotism: Exhibited in the Romantic Opinions and Extravagant Adventures of Dorcasina Sheldon* (1801), which thoroughly satirizes sentimental heroines such as Amelia. But the more intriguing result is the ambivalent vision of a number of novelists who could "neither believe" their own fables "nor rest content in their disbelief." With these authors, simple stereotypes of evil seducers and frail virgins give way to more intricate psychological and sociological investigations into human relationships, relationships that, in the eighteenth century as in the twentieth, must have been more complex than the moral lessons these first novelists were expected to exemplify.

It might be helpful to examine in some detail how these factors operate in a specific representative work, Hannah Webster Foster's *The Coquette; or, The History of Eliza Wharton* (1797). This first authentically American bestseller (written by a native-born American, first published in America, set in America, and concerned with American characters) is useful for several reasons.[35] To begin with, it employs a number of the processes whereby the trappings of the sentimental (stock figures, a fall, a moralistic ending) are subsumed into a story that does not simply prove the traditional moral. This same novel also demonstrates how real questions about woman's proper place could be advanced in the very form that supposedly provided socially conservative answers to those same questions. Far from being a paean to wedlock, *The Coquette* substantially justifies Eliza Wharton's originally jaundiced assessment of the happiness that would be hers if she allowed a moralizing clergyman suitor to "seduce [her] into matrimony."[36] Finally, partly transcending the conventions out of which it comes, *The Coquette* illustrates the art of the early American novel. And considering the moral, social, and critical climate in which these first novelists worked, the small ways in which they were artists should not be overlooked.

Part of Foster's art lies in the manner in which that art is hidden. *The Coquette* can be seen as little more than another minor variation on a basic theme. Eliza Wharton, the heroine, is courted by the respectable Reverend Boyer and the roguish Major Sanford. The former, at length, proposes matrimony; the latter, at equal length, does not. In hesitating between the two—hesitating, finally, too long for Boyer—Eliza acts contrary to the advice generously supplied by her concerned friends. Their concern was apparently justified. Eliza's infatuation with an obvious seducer eventually leads her into an illicit relationship. She becomes pregnant; she flees in the night to a lonely retreat; she bears an illegitimate baby; the child soon dies; so too does the mother, who, after her lonely death, is buried where "only the tears of strangers watered her grave" (p. 271). It would seem that the lesson apparent in this plot could scarcely be more clear.

A careful assessment of the novel, however, does not sustain this didactic summary. *The Coquette* is more than another demonstration of the fatal consequences of a "fate worse than death" and a consequent warning to female readers that they should avoid such lapses. From the first, the author counters the conventional interpretation that a superficial reading of her novel invites. Thus Eliza is not the frail, unthinking heroine who needs to be taken in hand by some strong, rational hero. Instead, she is portrayed as an unusually perceptive woman.[37] She can discuss politics intelligently with her friends. She can carefully assess private life too and, before her judgment is overcome by a personal disaster not of her own making, she is well aware of her own worth and the worth of those around her.

The novel, in fact, begins with Eliza's fortunate escape from an unsatisfactory marriage that she was about to enter only because she had not been guided by her own reason. The clergyman whom her family wished her to wed has just died. "No one," she writes in her first letter, "acquainted with the disparity of our tempers and dispositions, our views and designs, can suppose my heart much engaged in the alliance" (p. 133). But because "both nature and education had instilled into my mind an implicit obedience to the will and desires of my parents," she would have foregone "my fancy in this affair, determined that my reason should concur with theirs and on that to risk my future happiness" (p. 133). So the Reverend Haly's death thus proves to be, she observes, simply "a melancholy event that has lately extricated me from those shackles which parental authority had imposed on my mind" (p. 140). Prompted by that narrow escape, she plans to sample personal freedom before declining into a wife. She also determines to marry in the future only if reason and fancy, her mind and her heart, are both engaged.

Socially conservative readers well might find the seeds of Eliza's downfall in this daughter's belated declaration of independence and in her equalitarian concept of marriage. But again the book affirms Eliza's ideals. When she leaves her mother's home in which she was immured with her dying clergyman fiance she goes to visit her friends, the Richmans, whose marriage exemplifies the Wollstonecraft ideal of a partnership of equals. That relationship is Eliza's ideal too. Her "heart approved and applauded" (p. 181) this couple's happiness. Her tragedy is that she would enter into a similar union but encounters no equivalent of General Richman. What she is offered is the difficult choice between unsatisfactory alternatives, a common quandary in the better sentimental novels.

Eliza's continuing dilemma is early established through the conflicting claims of judgment and fancy, the judgment and fancy that she originally intended to reconcile before entering matrimony. She can esteem the Reverend Boyer's moral nature, admire Major Sanford's easy manners, but finds that they both lack the character of a General Richman. Neither really meets her requirements, and those requirements are not invalidated during the course of a novel. The Reverend Boyer, whom her friends particularly recommend, is in several senses a successor to the unsatisfactory Reverend Haly. When this second Reverend, whom Eliza encounters at the Richmans, immediately declares himself a suitor, she is not impressed by "his conversation, so similar to what I had often heard from a similar character" (p. 140). Somewhat later, she admits that she found his moral discourse, "for several hours together . . . rather sickening to my taste" and was "agreeably relieved" when Major Sanford intruded on the interview (p. 156). The Major might be a rake but at least he has some social polish. "What a pity," Eliza writes, with considerable justice, to one of her friends, "that the graces and virtues are not oftener united" (p. 148).

She hopes that a prospective husband would possess both the social graces that appeal to her fancy and the moral virtues that speak to her judgment. She expects that she must choose between the two. She is actually offered neither. Sanford's refinement and polish are merely the outward expressions of that gentleman's hypocritical misogyny. His letters to his one correspondent, Charles Deighton, are filled with stupid, shallow remarks about the stupidity and shallowness of women. He can be "severe upon the sex" because he has "found so many frail ones among them" (p. 234), as if he were a later day Diogenes searching for an honest woman. Furthermore, the frail deserve, he self-righteously claims, whatever punishments they might receive. Ascribing to the standard morality, he insists that should he decide to seduce Eliza and succeed in that enterprise, the fault would be entirely hers. "She knows my character and has no reason to wonder if I act consistently with it" (p. 176). Yet he has just implored her to "let the kind and lenient hand of friendship assist in directing my future steps" (p. 160). That pleading is hardly the open avowal of his character that he subsequently pretends he has made. He is just as hypocritically self-righteous with his wife, who certainly was not seduced, and conveniently blames her for her unhappiness when, after marriage, he still pursues Eliza. His wife, he claims, "wanted but very little solicitation to confer her self and fortune on so charming a fellow" as himself (p. 226). Such self-deluding justification continues until the end of the novel. It is only when he has lost everything—his wife, his mistress, his legitimate child, his illegitimate child, and the fortune for which he married—that he can, in uncharacteristic fashion, estimate his true worth.

He then sees that his sin was far blacker than his victim's, and in his last letter he draws "a deplorable yet a just, picture of" himself that is "totally the reverse of what I once appeared" (p. 269).

Foster's protagonist succumbs when she is apparently taken in by such a sham. Yet just as there is less to Sanford's character than immediately meets the eye, there is more to Eliza's fall. Certainly the seduction is not simply the consequence of his intriguingly dangerous charm working on a naive virgin's vanity. Once more Foster markedly departs from the basic sentimental plot even as she utilizes the essential element of that plot, the "seduction." Flighty, flirtatious girls were typically undone as much by their own foolishness as by the novel's villain. But as a free-spirited coquette, seemingly the perfect candidate for a seduction, Eliza was quite immune to Sanford's blandishments. She is seduced only after she has been cruelly disappointed by both Boyer and Sanford and has sunk into despondency; in brief, after she has given up coquetry. The act that brings the usual victim to her fall and suddenly requires her to see herself as fallen is mainly intended in *The Coquette* to affirm Eliza's sense that she is already defeated.

Foster alters the standard pattern in other ways too. For example, she reverses the usual relationship between sin and matrimony. In the novels of the time a seduction usually precluded a possibly desirable marriage. In *The Coquette,* however, the fact that an imperfect marriage does not occur sets the stage for the subsequent seduction. The author's plotting is here particularly effective, for Foster carefully structures the way in which her tragic comedy of errors develops to its necessary denouement and divides the process of Eliza's fall into three distinct parts, into, as it were, three parallel falls. The two earlier ones foreshadow and lead to the final disaster. The two later large steps on the road to ruin follow from the first, which is the miscarried marriage with the Reverend Boyer. Furthermore, that first failure is essentially similar to the victory with which the book begins, a reprieve from the undesired role of clergyman's wife. The escape which launched Eliza into life, later reenacted in a slightly different fashion, propels her towards disgrace and death.

When a second marriage does not occur, Eliza accepts the blame because she is stridently told that she is grievously at fault. But the fault is Boyer's, not his intended's. Seeing himself as duped by her "dissimulation" (p. 197) and an innocent victim caught in the "snares of the deluder" (p. 198), he is just as conveniently short-sighted about who should be blamed for what as even Sanford was. Indeed, Foster has this disappointed clergyman carry on very much as if he himself had just been seduced. Yet he is the one that "dissimulated" in their relationship. When Eliza did not

encourage his suit, they still agreed that he could "expatiate" on love, she writes, "provided he will let me take my own time for the consummation" (p. 184). But soon he will not be deterred because "she *pretended a promise from me* to wait her time" (p. 192, emphasis added). He would force the issue. While doing so, he finds her in conversation with Sanford and thereupon decides that *he* is completely betrayed. He denounces her; he allows her no opportunity to defend herself; she cannot even point out that she met with Sanford to tell him that she had decided to marry Boyer. So the supposed assignation with another does not prove her dishonesty. Quite the contrary. As Sanford notes in one of his letters, "she was entangled by a promise (not to marry this priest without my knowledge), which *her conscience* would not let her break" (p. 208, emphasis added).

Undone by that kept promise, Eliza is castigated as a villain when her "perfidy" is first discovered and is even more condemned in a hypocritically priggish letter that her "betrayed" lover soon sends her. In that missive Boyer first discusses the "innumerable instances of your impudence and misconduct which have fallen under my observation" (p. 198) and then assures her that his denunciations of her various failings derive not from a lover's "resentment" but from pure "benevolence" and his laudable desire that she should improve the state of her soul. In all he says he is only doing his "duty" as a clergyman (p. 200). He concludes in much that same vein with an arrogant insistence that she can address him later only if she concurs with his present assessment of his present action: "I wish not for an answer; my resolution is unalterably fixed. But should you hereafter be convinced of the justice of my conduct and become a convert to my advice, I shall be happy to hear it" (p. 200). In short, his moral virtues are as false and as self-serving as are Sanford's social graces.

Foster astutely demonstrates how her perceptive protagonist finally comes to believe that this pompous moralist was right. Eliza at first can well wonder "whether [she] had sustained a real loss in Mr. Boyer's departure?" (p. 207), but she soon retrospectively exaggerates the dubious merits of the Reverend Boyer as much as she has all along discounted the obvious faults of Major Sanford. Rejected by the one, abandoned by the other, she begins to realize her precarious position. Her "bloom is decreasing"; her "health is sensibly impaired" (p. 218). Her situation is the talk of the town. The prospect of becoming a spinster is not appealing. Eliza thinks of herself as humiliated, and by the standards of the time she is. She becomes depressed, loses her former confidence, and exists once again almost as a recluse in her mother's house. Her plight, as an unmarried woman, is brought vividly before her—and the reader's—eyes. She even stops writing letters which, in an epistolary novel, is a sure indication that something is wrong. But only from the point of view of one who fears spinsterhood does Boyer seem attractive. "His merit and worth now appear in the brightest colors" (p. 212), when earlier she was "strongly tempted . . . to laugh" at his solemn "sentiment and sobriety" (p. 184).

This dubious re-evaluation of Boyer brings about Eliza's second fall. She swallows her pride and writes to him, apologizing for her previous behavior. She abjectly asks if he will still have her. He will not. He has quickly recovered from his earlier infatuation and is preparing, he informs her, to marry another. The Reverend further patronizes his humbled former fiancee by cautioning her to pass the remainder of her days undeviating from the "paths of rectitude and innocence" (p. 216). Eliza is crushed. When she subsequently discovers that Sanford has married a rich heiress, she is even more defeated. So when Sanford, although married, addresses her again, she acquiesces not because of any ardent passion but out of loneliness and despair. She submits mostly because her pride has failed her and because she desires the disaster that she knows will be the consequence of her action.

"O my friend, I am undone" (p. 217), she writes on receiving Boyer's final letter. Significantly, she employs the phrase, "I am undone," which in a typical sentimental tale signals that the seduction has taken place. "His conduct," she continues, with an even more loaded word, assures her "ruin"; and later, in this same letter, she laments: "O that I had not written Mr. Boyer! By confessing my faults and by avowing my partiality to him, I have given him the power of triumphing in my distress; of returning to my tortured heart all the pangs of slighted love. And what have I now to console me?" (pp. 217-18). Three times Eliza voices the plaintive cry of the seduced woman that reverberates throughout any number of conventional sentimental tales. But Foster sounds that note in a different context. Her protagonist's seduction is psychologically realistic, artistically subtle. It is also, in effect, accomplished before it actually takes place. Defeated by circumstances in which she has not yet debased herself, Eliza will affirm that defeat in debasement. Lost already, she can find a bitter consolation only in her further fall.

That third and final fall, under these circumstances, does not prove, as Boyer with characteristic obtuseness concludes, that female virtue, "in the common acceptance of the term," is largely synonymous with female chastity (p. 193). It does not demonstrate, as Lucy Sumner, one of Eliza's correspondents, declaims in the obligatory moral which concludes the penultimate letter of the volume, "that virtue alone . . . can secure lasting felicity" (p. 270). Instead, there is a convincing study of the problems faced by an Eliza Wharton in a world of Boyers and Sanfords, in a world that is largely governed by the social thought of Boyers and Sanfords.

The novel that begins with happiness achieved through escape ends much the same way. When the Reverend Haly died, Eliza, spared from what would have been an unhappy union, could leave the narrow confines of her mother's house to discover the world. But what awaits her in the world is another marriage that does not take place, an affair that does. Considering these alternatives and the men who embody them, the last words of the novel, assuring the grieving mother that she must believe "your Eliza is happy," seem more than conventional consolation. Marriage has been conjoined, through the structure of the book, with spinsterhood and seduction as fates that one might well wish to avoid. And as *The Coquette* turns, in this strange fashion, full circle, the novelist as artist again calls into question the public stance taken by the author as moral historian.

Eliza Wharton sins and dies. Her death can convey the moral that the moral critics and readers of the time demanded. Yet the circumstances of that death seem designed to tease the more perceptive into thought. It is in precisely these interstices—the disjunctions between the conventional meanings and the covert ones— that the art of the American novel begins. For that reason alone these early sentimental novels merit more attention, and more credit, than they have generally received. Furthermore, if the very term "sentimental" almost assures neglect, one immediate consequence of that neglect is an uncertainty about the evolution of the American novel. That uncertainty is not resolved by moving the ostensible beginning of an American tradition back from James Fenimore Cooper and Washington Irving to Charles Brockden Brown. Instead, the real roots of American fiction are to be found exactly where one would expect them: in the first novels of the new republic, in sentimental tales that are sometimes surprisingly subtle, ironic, complex, almost—in a modern sense—unsentimental. As Walter P. Wenska, Jr., recently observed in his study of *The Coquette:* "The distance between seventeenth-century Boston and late-eighteenth-century New Haven is not great. Nor is it much farther to mid-nineteenth-century Concord or New York."[38] Neither is the journey retraced really that arduous, as scholars of literature can discover simply by reading some of these early novels, as they must discover if they wish to understand the origins of American fiction.

Notes

[1] Robert B. Winans, "The Growth of a Novel-Reading Public in Late-Eighteenth-Century America," *EAL,* 9 (1975), 272.

² For detailed assessments of the American critical attitude towards fiction, see G. Harrison Orians' "Censure of Fiction in American Romances and Magazines, 1789-1810," *PMLA,* 52 (1937), 195-214; Ormond E. Palmer, "Some Attitudes Toward Fiction in America to 1870, and a Bit Beyond," Diss. Univ. of Chicago, 1952; and William Charvat, *The Origins of American Critical Thought, 1810-1835* (Philadelphia: Univ. of Pennsylvania Press, 1936), especially pp. 7-26, 134-63.

³ Terence Martin, in *The Instructed Vision: Scottish Common Sense Philosophy and the Origins of American Fiction* (Bloomington: Indiana Univ. Press, 1961), has argued that Puritan ideas were revived by a burgeoning interest in Common Sense philosophy. This philosophy, especially taught in the late eighteenth and early nineteenth-century American academies, was also suspicious of the imagination. Thus "old [Puritan] arguments could be given a new force" and through these arguments "the imagination could be contained and controlled in a respectable, safe, and enlightened manner which would have important effects on the attempt to conceive and execute fiction" (p. 161). Martin also discusses (pp. 155-66) the ways in which the British and American critics of the time assessed novels from quite different perspectives.

⁴ *The American Novel, 1789-1939,* rev. ed. (New York: Macmillan, 1940), p. 4.

⁵ "Introduction," in *The Power of Sympathy and The Coquette,* ed. William S. Osborne (New Haven: College and University Press, 1970), p. 13.

⁶ Henri Petter, *The Early American Novel* (Columbus: Ohio State Univ. Press, 1971), p. 3.

⁷ Since we lack the sources necessary to do accurate "influence" studies, a comparative approach to the study of early American fiction is, as Henri Petter points out, "precariously conjectural more often than not" (p. x). However, a number of critics have provided illuminating insights into some of the ways in which eighteenth-century American novelists borrowed from their English counterparts. See Herbert Ross Brown, *The Sentimental Novel in America, 1789-1860* (Durham: Duke Univ. Press, 1940), pp. 28-51; Leslie A. Fiedler, *Love and Death in the American Novel* (New York: Criterion, 1960), pp. 23-104; and William Spengemann, *The Adventurous Muse: The Poetics of American Fiction, 1789-1900* (New Haven: Yale Univ. Press, 1977), especially pp. 68-118.

⁸ Mary Wollstonecraft, in *A Vindication of the Rights of Woman,* ed. Charles W. Hagelman, Jr. (1792; rpt. New York: W. W. Norton, 1967), early addressed herself to such a one-dimensional sounding of woman's virtues: "But, with respect to reputation, the attention is confined to a single virtue—chastity. If the honour of a woman, as it is absurdly called, be safe, she may neglect every social duty; nay, ruin her family by gaming and extravagance; yet still present a shameless front—for truly she is an honourable woman!" (p. 206).

⁹ In "Some Notes on Early American Fiction: Kelroy Was There," *SAF,* 5 (1977), 1-12, Harrison T. Meserole points out that few scholars have gone beyond Henri Petter's "compendious" survey of early American fiction to produce detailed studies of the novels themselves. Meserole also insists that "our most challenging task, in my judgment, is a reassessment of the early American novel" (p. 4). As he emphasizes, we have not yet distinguished those early novels that really merit neglect from those "undeservedly overlooked" (p. 5) works that do demand serious critical attention.

¹⁰ A recent study which defines the major differences between the nineteenth-century American and British fictional traditions is Ann Douglas's *The Feminization of American Culture* (New York: Knopf, 1978). Douglas notes the ways in which the major writers of Victorian England "dedicated their enormous talents to an exploration of Victorianism" while major nineteenth-century American writers "turned their sights principally on values and scenes that operated as alternatives to cultural norms" (p. 5). While accepting this crucial difference between serious American and British writers after 1820, one should note that the iconoclastic American tradition actually begins with the best early "sentimental" novelists whom Douglas overlooks in her study of the later sentimentalists.

¹¹ Quoted from the anonymous *Fidelity Rewarded* (Boston, 1796), p. 4; the anonymous *Amelia* (Boston, 1798), p. 2; and Martha Read's *Monima* (New York, 1802), p. v.

¹² *The Power of Sympathy* (1789), ed. William S. Kable (Columbus: Ohio State Univ. Press, 1969), p. 3. In his introduction, pp. xv-xxvi, Kable discusses the inauspicious publishing history of the "first American novel." See also Arthur W. Brayley, "The Real Author of 'The Power of Sympathy,'" *Bostonian,* 1, No. 3 (Dec., 1894), 224-33; Milton Ellis, "The Author of the First American Novel," *AL,* 4 (1932), 359-68; and Richard Walser, "More about the First American Novel," *AL,* 24 (1952), 352-57.

¹³ *The Power of Sympathy,* ed. William S. Kable, p. 10.

¹⁴ For an extended discussion of the ways in which even the first American novel deviates from what we now think of as the "sentimental formula," see Cathy N. Davidson, "*The Power of Sympathy* Reconsidered: William Hill Brown as Literary Craftsman," *EAL,* 10

(1975), 14-29. Leslie A. Fiedler, in *Love and Death in the American Novel,* points out how Mrs. Holmes, another moral spokesman in *The Power of Sympathy,* is also undercut. Fiedler maintains that "the book finally equivocates in a way not untypical of the later American novel" (p. 104).

[15] Because the fiction of Charles Brockden Brown has already been extensively assessed, references to his novels have been deliberately limited in order to emphasize the work of his less well-known predecessors and contemporaries. But a novel such as *Wieland* certainly fits within the framework of "unsentimental sentiment" explored in the present essay. See, especially, Larzer Ziff, "A Reading of *Wieland,*" *PMLA,* 77 (1962), 51-57, who argues that Brown transformed *Wieland* "from a sentimental romance into an antisentimental record of life" and thereby "perceived the theme and the manner of the American novel" a "half-century before the great literary movement in New England" (p. 57).

[16] By viewing Montraville as the typical seducer-villain and overlooking the problematic role played by Belcour, William Spengemann, in *The Adventurous Muse,* can dismiss *Charlotte Temple* as possibly "the most rigidly programmatic sentimental novel ever written" (p. 92). Nevertheless, Spengemann still concedes that "certain fictive energies seem to be at work, threatening to compromise the conservative values" of this novel (p. 90). See also, Wendy Martin, "Profile: Susanna Rowson, Early American Novelist," *Women's Studies,* 2, No. 1 (1974), 1-8.

[17] Susanna Rowson, *Charlotte Temple, A Tale of Truth,* ed. Clara M. and Rudolf Kirk (New Haven: College and University Press, 1964), p. 121.

[18] Thus, in the anonymous *Margaretta; or, the Intricacies of the Heart* (Philadelphia, 1807), the female protagonist prefers love to respectability and rejects dependable Captain Waller, who proposes matrimony, for the dashing Will de Burling, who plans to marry an heiress but will keep Margaretta as his mistress. As Margaretta then declares, "I think I was not destined by nature for an humble cottage" (p. 80). Later, after many trials and abductions, she finds that she must again choose between the good Waller and the handsome de Burling. Now herself possessed of both a title and a fortune, she once more bypasses respectability, this time for marriage to the penniless de Burling. Love and respectability are even more in conflict in those novels in which a mistreated wife is tempted by adultery, a sin more heinous to the sentimental tradition than seduction. In Helena Wells' *The Step-Mother; a Domestic Tale, from Real Life* (London, 1799), Caroline Williams insists that women must "think of *man* as a *lord* and *master,* from whose *will* there is no appeal" (II, p.

342, italics in the original). But unhappiness in marriage compromises this dicta and partially explains another wife's escape from a loveless marriage to an illicit love relationship.

[19] Perhaps as many as half of the sentimental novels written in America before 1820 employ the cruel parent motif. Good examples are the anonymous *The History of Constantius and Pulchera; or Constancy Rewarded* (Norwich, Conn., 1796); Mrs. Patterson's *The Unfortunate Lovers, and Cruel Parents* (n.p., 1797); and Margaret Botsford's *Adelaide* (Philadelphia, 1816), all of which pit harsh parents against young lovers. See Petter, *The Early American Novel,* pp. 188-209, for a fuller discussion of this theme; and Meserole, "Some Notes on Early American Fiction: Kelroy Was There," for an examination of Rebecca Rush's psychologically astute treatment of this same basic theme.

[20] Lucinda, an important subsidiary character in William Hill Brown's *Ira and Isabella,* postpones marriage in favor of a less settled life which includes numerous affairs. "Lively, affable, and simple" (p. 113), she consciously rejects the restraints of domesticity and yet is not punished for her choice. Similarly, the title character in Leonora Sansay's *Laura* (Philadelphia, 1809) rejects the respectable man her stepfather would have her marry in favor of Belfield, a medical student. Belfield has fits of debauchery but at least offers Laura a loving relationship characterized not only by physical but (even rarer) intellectual communion. Finally, Deborah Sampson, the heroine of *The Female Review; or, Memoirs of an American Young Lady* (Dedham, Mass., 1797), rejects both the conventions of domesticity *and* the passionate suitor when she repeatedly chooses not to wed in order to pursue her career as a Revolutionary soldier.

[21] The dichotomizing of good and evil male characters represents a significant thematic and structural departure from the pattern employed in *Pamela* and *Clarissa.* Thus Leslie A. Fielder, in *Love and Death in the American Novel,* notes that the American introduction of the virtuous hero stands "the Clarissa-archetype on its head" (p. 37) in that the main opposition is no longer between the capable "good" heroine and the "evil" man who assails her. Fiedler also suggests that this change takes place in the late nineteenth century. One must note, however, that the American pattern appears in even the first eighteenth-century sentimental fiction and when subtly employed allows for a characteristically American ambivalence and duplicity.

[22] In "*The Coquette* and the American Dream of Freedom," *EAL,* 12 (1977), 243-55, Walter P. Wenska, Jr. persuasively argues that *The Coquette* foreshadows the romantic tradition in American fiction.

[23] David Lee Clark, in *Brockden Brown and the Rights of Women* (Austin: Univ. of Texas Press, 1922), pp. 15-29, provides a concise and still reliable account of the post-Revolutionary debate regarding women's political status. For more contemporary assessments see Marguerite Fisher's "Eighteenth-Century Theorists of Women's Liberation" and Ralph Ketcham's "The Puritan Ethic in The Revolutionary Era: Abigail Adams and Thomas Jefferson," both in *"Remember the Ladies": New Perspectives on Women in American History,* ed. Carol V. R. George (Syracuse: Syracuse Univ. Press, 1975), pp. 39-47, 49-65.

[24] These same historians, it should be noted, question whether the nineteenth century actually marked an improvement in women's status or a retrogression from the heights attained at the end of the eighteenth century. It is not the purpose of this essay to enter into that complicated debate, the various sides of which are discussed by Nancy F. Cott in the "Conclusion" to her excellent study, *The Bonds of Womanhood: "Woman's Sphere" in New England, 1780-1835* (New Haven: Yale Univ. Press, 1977), pp. 197-206.

[25] Jean Jacques Rousseau, *Emilius and Sophia; or, A New System of Education,* trans. by "A Citizen of Geneva" (London, 1783). Those Americans who did not actually read Rousseau could have become familiar with his basic ideas through the even more popular writings of Hannah More, especially her *Essays for Young Ladies* (London, 1789).

[26] For an extended analysis of the "patient Griselda" motif in sentimental fiction, see Herbert Ross Brown's discussion in *The Sentimental Novel in America,* pp. 100-32.

[27] The cultural documents which advocated the cause of feminism in the eighteenth century are discussed in Mary Sumner Benson's *Women in Eighteenth-Century America* (New York: Columbia Univ. Press, 1935). A more recent study which covers the same ground is Barbara J. Berg's *The Remembered Gate: Origins of American Feminism* (New York: Oxford Univ. Press, 1978), pp. 11-29.

[28] Three recent essays perceptively discuss the American reaction to Wollstonecraft and "Wollstonecraftism." See R. M. Janes, "On the Reception of Mary Wollstonecraft's *A Vindication of the Rights of Woman,"* *Journal of the History of Ideas,* 39 (1978), 293-302; Patricia Jewell McAlexander, "The Creation of the American Eve: The Cultural Dialogue on the Nature and Role of Women in Late-Eighteenth-Century America," *EAL,* 9 (1975), 252-66; and Marcelle Thiebaux, "Mary Wollstonecraft in Federalist America: 1791-1802," in *The Evidence of the Imagination: Studies of Interactions between Life and Art in English Romantic Literature,* ed. Donald H. Reiman, et al. (New York: New York Univ. Press, 1978), pp. 195-245.

[29] For a fuller discussion of the negative reactions to Wollstonecraftism, see also Linda K. Kerber, "Daughters of Columbia: Educating Women for the Republic, 1787-1805," in *The Hofstadter Aegis: A Memorial,* ed. Eric L. McKitrick and Stanley M. Elkins (New York: Knopf, 1974), pp. 36-59.

[30] *Amelia; or, The Influence of Virtue* (Portsmouth, N.H., 1802), p. 103.

[31] Women's legal rights both before and after matrimony are discussed in Richard B. Morris, "Women's Rights in Early American Law," in *Studies in the History of American Law,* ed. Richard B. Morris (New York: Columbia Univ. Press, 1930), pp. 126-200; and, more recently, in Mary Beard, *Woman as Force in History* (New York: Collier, 1962), pp. 122-44.

[32] Gilbert Imlay, in *The Emigrants, & c. or The History of an Expatriated Family* (London, 1979), presents more directly the pitfalls of marriage. His novel includes numerous stories of emotionally, financially, and physically abused wives to underscore his message that "many misfortunes which daily happen in domestic life, and which too often precipitate women of the most virtuous inclinations into the gulf of ruin, proceed from the great difficulty there is in England [and America] of obtaining a divorce" (p. ix).

[33] We see one indication of the eighteenth-century disdain for the unmarried woman in the prefatory comments made by *Mrs.* Rowson, *Mrs.* Wood, and other writers, who insisted that their domestic roles were far more important than their careers (a word they would not have chosen). We also see typical portraits of the spinster in works like Mrs. Wells' *Constantia Neville* where the fifty-ish Miss Norcliffe is described as an almost hag-like "virago." But even though Miss Dorcasina Sheldon, in Tabitha Tenney's *Female Quixotism* (Boston, 1801), becomes increasingly foolish as she grows older, one other character, the sensible Mrs. Stanly, counters the prevailing view when she insists that it is "more respectable" to remain unmarried than to "marry barely for the sake of having a husband" or "merely to avoid the imputation of being an old maid" (II, 52).

[34] See Paul M. Spurlin, "Readership in the American Enlightenment," in *Literature and the History of Ideas,* ed. Charles G. S. Williams (Columbus: Ohio State Univ. Press, 1975), pp. 359-76; and also an important quantitative survey by David Lundberg and Henry F. May, "The Enlightened Reader in America," *AQ,* 28 (1976), 262-71 and appendix.

[35] The two bestsellers in America in the 1790s were Rowson's *Charlotte* (1794) and Foster's *The Coquette* (1797). Mrs. Rowson, however, was born in Portsmouth, England, where the first chapters of *Charlotte* take place.

36 *The Power of Sympathy and The Coquette,* ed. William S. Osborne, p. 184. Future references to this readily available paperback edition of *The Coquette* will be made parenthetically in the text.

37 *The Coquette,* which purports to be "A NOVEL; Founded on Fact" and is loosely based on the story of Elizabeth Whitman of Hartford, in this instance stays close to its source. Miss Whitman was a poet and something of an intellectual who moved in the best social circles but ended her life, as did Eliza Wharton, soon after bearing a still-born, illegitimate child. Some critics have also argued that Major Sanford is based on Pierrepont Edwards, a son of Jonathan Edwards. For hardly impartial discussions of this possibility, see Caroline W. H. Dall, *The Romance of the Association; or One Last Glimpse of Charlotte Temple and Eliza Wharton* (Cambridge: John Wilson and Son, 1875) and Charles K. Bolton, *The Elizabeth Whitman Mystery* (Peabody: Peabody Historical Society, 1912). A more factual account is Robert L. Shurter's "Mrs. Hannah Webster Foster and the Early American Novel," *AL,* 4 (1932), 306-08.

38 "*The Coquette* and the American Dream of Freedom," p. 253.

Orestes A. Brownson critiques the effects of sentimentalism:

The age in which we live is a sentimental age, and sentimentalism is the deadliest enemy to true piety, and to all real strength or worth of character. It enervates the soul, subverts the judgment, and lays the heart open to every temptation. The staple literature of our times, the staple reading of our youth of both sexes, is sentimental novels and love-tales, and the effect is manifest in the diseased state of the public mind, and in the growing effeminacy of character and depravation of morals. . . .

All books which seek the sources of their interest in the passion or sentiment of love are to be distrusted, and so indeed are all which, no matter in what degree, foster a sentimental tendency. The more delicate and refined the sentimentality, and the more apparently innocent and pure it may be, the more really dangerous it is. Works which are grossly sensual disgust all in whom corruption has not already commenced; but works which studiously avoid every indelicate expression or allusion, which seem to breathe an atmosphere of purity itself, excite no alarm, are read by the innocent and confiding, insinuate a fatal poison before it is suspected, and create a tone and temper of mind and heart which pave the way for corruption. . . .

Orestes A. Brownson, in Brownson's Quarterly Review, *January, 1847, reprinted in* The Works of Orestes A. Brownson, *Vol. XIX, Thorndike Nourse, 1885.*

Jane P. Tompkins

SOURCE: "The Other American Renaissance," in *The American Renaissance Reconsidered: Selected Papers from the English Institute, 1982-83,* edited by Walter Benn Michaels and Donald E. Pease, Johns Hopkins University Press, 1985, pp. 34-57.

[*In this essay, Tompkins defends the domestic novel against the common criticism that it portrays a narrow, trivial, and overly idealistic world. Only the footnoted material pertaining to the essay below has been reprinted in the "Notes" section.*]

The word *other* in my title refers to the fiction written during the period we know as the American Renaissance by writers whose names we do not know. The writer I am concerned with in particular is Susan Warner, who was born in the same year as Herman Melville and whose best-selling novel, *The Wide, Wide World,* was published in the same year as *Moby Dick.* But I am interested in Warner's novel not for the light it can shed on Melville;[1] I am interested in it because it represents an entire body of work that this century's critical tradition has largely ignored. According to that tradition, the "great" figures of the American Renaissance were a handful of men who refused to be taken in by the pieties of the age. These writers, according to Henry Nash Smith, were not afraid to "explore the dark underside of the psyche," or to tackle "ultimate social and intellectual issues"; and because they repudiated the culture's dominant system of values they were, in Perry Miller's words, "crushed by the juggernaut" of the popular sentimental novel.[2] The sentimental writers, on the other hand, are generally thought to have been out of touch with reality. What they produced, says Smith, was a literature of "reassurance," calculated to soothe the anxieties of an economically troubled age. To the "Common Man and Common Woman," fearful of challenge or change, they preached a "cosmic success story," which promised that the practice of virtue would lead to material success. Their subject matter—the tribulations of orphan girls—was innately trivial; their religious ideas were "little more than a blur of good intentions"; they "feared the probing of the inner life," and above all were committed to avoiding anything that might make the "undiscriminating mass" of their middle-brow readers "uncomfortable."[3]

My purpose today is to challenge that description of sentimental novels and to argue that their exclusion from the canon of American literature has been a mistake. My strategy will not be to compare what I have called the "other" American Renaissance to the dominant tradition (a dichotomy, ultimately, that is itself a misrepresentation) but to show what makes sentimental novels powerful and important in their own right. For once one has a grasp of the problems these writers were trying to solve, their solutions do not seem shallow or unrealistic; on the contrary, given the social circumstances within which they were obliged to work, their prescriptions for living seem at least as courageous as those put forward by the writers who said, "No, in thunder."

The Wide, Wide World, in 1851, caused an explosion in the literary marketplace that was absolutely unprecedented—nothing like it, in terms of sales, had ever been seen before. The next year, *Uncle Tom's Cabin* broke the records that Warner's novel had set. Two years later, Maria Cummins's *The Lamplighter*—the direct literary descendant of *The Wide, Wide World*—made another tremendous hit.[4] Yet Henry Nash Smith, who has devoted an entire book to studying the influence of popular fiction on classical American writing, dismisses the phenomenon, saying "it is impossible now to determine just what did happen to the market in the early 1850's."[5]

But it is not impossible to determine. The impact of sentimental novels is directly related to the cultural context that produced them. Once one begins to explore that context in even a preliminary way, the critical practice that assigns Hawthorne and Melville the role of heroes, the sentimental novelists the role of villains, and the public the role of their willing dupes, loses its credibility. The one great fact of American life during the period under consideration was the "terrific universality" of the revival.[6] Sentimental fiction was perhaps the most influential expression of the beliefs that animated the revival movement and shaped the character of American life in the years before the Civil War. Like their counterparts among the evangelical reformers, the sentimental novelists wrote to educate their readers in Christian perfection and to move the nation as a whole closer to the City of God. But in order to understand the appeal of their project one has to have some familiarity with the cultural discourse of the age for which they spoke.

The best place to begin is with some documents that, as far as I know, have never made their way into criticism of American Renaissance literature. These are the publications of the American Tract Society, the first organization in America to publish and distribute the printed word on a mass scale. Its literature is a testament both to the faith of antebellum Americans—to the shape of their dreams—and to what they experienced as everyday reality. It is only by attempting to see that reality from within the assumptions that founded it that one can arrive at a notion of what gave sentimental fiction its tremendous original force.

The Closet

The conception of reality on which the reform movement was based is nowhere more dramatically illus-

trated than in the activities of the New York City Tract Society, whose members, numbering in the thousands, attempted to help the city's poor by distributing a religious tract to every family in the city once a month.[7] The "Directions" that guided the Tract Visiters, printed on the back cover of the society's Annual Report, are as succinct a statement as one is likely to find of the politics of the reform movement. "Be much in prayer," the Directions said. "Endeavor to feel habitually and deeply that all your efforts will be in vain unless accompanied by the Holy Ghost. And this blessing you can expect only in answer to prayer. Pray, therefore, without ceasing. Go from your closet to your work and from your work return again to the closet."[8] If one can understand what made these Directions meaningful and effective for the people who carried them out, one is in a position to understand the power of sentimental fiction. For all sentimental novels take place, metaphorically and literally, within the "closet." Their heroines rarely get beyond the confines of a private space—the kitchen, the parlor, the upstairs chamber—but more important, most of what they do takes place inside the "closet" of the heart. For what the word *sentimental* really means in this context is that the arena of human action, as in the Tract Society Directions, has been defined not as the world but as the human soul. This fiction shares with the evangelical reform movement a theory of power that stipulates that all true action is not material but spiritual, that one obtains spiritual power through prayer, and that those who know how, in the privacy of their closets, to struggle for possession of their souls, will one day conquer the world through the power given them by God. This theory of power is one that made itself felt, not simply in the explicit assertions of religious propaganda, but as a principle of interpretation that gave form to experience itself, as the records the Tract Visiters left of their activities show.

The same beliefs that make the Directions to Tract Visiters intelligible structured what the Visiters actually saw as they went about their work. One Visiter, for example, records that a young woman who was dying of pulmonary consumption became concerned at the eleventh hour about the state of her soul and asked for spiritual help. "She was found by the Visiter," the report reads,

> supplied with a number of tracts, and kindly directed to the Saviour of sinners. . . . For some time clouds hung over her mind, but they were at length dispelled by the Sun of righteousness. . . . As she approached the hour which tries men's souls, her friends gathered around her; . . . and while they were engaged in a hymn her soul seemed to impart unnatural energy to her emaciated and dying body. To the astonishment of all, she said to her widowed mother, who bent anxiously over her. "Don't weep for me, I shall

soon be in the arms of my Saviour." She prayed fervently, and fell asleep in Jesus.[9]

Like all the fiction we label "sentimental" this narrative blots out the uglier details of life and cuts experience to fit a pattern of pious expectation. The anecdote tells nothing about the personality or background of the young woman, fails to represent even the barest facts of her disease or of her immediate surroundings. For these facts, it substitutes the panaceas of Christian piety—God's mercy on a miserable sinner, "falling asleep" in Jesus. Its plot follows a prescribed course from sin to salvation. But what is extraordinary about this anecdote is that it is not a work of fiction but a factual report. Though its facts do not correspond to what a twentieth-century observer would have recorded, had he or she been at the scene, they faithfully represent what the Tract Society member saw. Whereas a modern social worker would have described the woman's illness, its history and course of treatment, would have sketched in her socioeconomic background and that of her relatives and friends, the Tract Visiter sees only a spiritual predicament. Whereas the modern observer would have structured the events in a downward spiral, as the woman's condition deteriorated from serious to critical, and ended with her death, the report reverses that progression. Its movement is upward, from "thoughtfulness" to "conviction," to "great tranquility, joy, and triumph."[10]

The charge that has always been leveled against sentimental fiction in the twentieth century is that it is out of touch with reality, that it presents a picture of life so oversimplified and improbable, that only the most naive and self-deceiving reader could believe it. But the sense of the real which this criticism takes for granted is not the one that organized the perceptions of antebellum readers. Their assumptions were the same as those that structured the events of the report I have just quoted. For what I have been speaking about involves three distinct levels of apprehension: "reality itself" as it appears to people at a given time; what people will accept as an "accurate description" of reality; and novels and stories which, because they correspond to such descriptions, therefore seem true. The audience for whom the thoughtless young lady's conversion was a moving factual report found the tears and prayers of sentimental heroines equally compelling. This is so not because they did not know what good fiction was, or because their notions about human life were naive and superficial, but because the "order of things" to which both readers and fictions belonged was itself structured by narratives of this sort.

The report of the young woman's death is exactly analogous to the kind of exemplary narrative that had formed the consciousness of the nation in the early years of the nineteenth century. Such stories filled the religious publications distributed in unimaginably large quantities by organizations of the Evangelical United Front. The American Tract Society alone claims to have published thirty-seven million tracts at a time when the entire population of the country was only eleven million. The same kind of exemplary narratives was the staple of the McGuffey's readers on which virtually the entire nation had been schooled. They appeared in manuals of social behavior, and in instructional literature of every variety, filled the pages of popular magazines, and appeared even in the daily newspapers. As David Reynolds has recently demonstrated, the entire practice of pulpit oratory in this period shifted from an expository and abstract mode of explicating religious doctrine, to a mode in which sensational narratives carried the burden of theological precept.[11] These stories were always didactic in nature—illustrating the importance of a particular virtue—obedience, faith, sobriety—and they were usually sensational in content—the starving widow is saved at the last moment by a handsome stranger who turns out to be her son. But their sensationalism ultimately lies not so much in the dramatic nature of the events they describe as in the assumptions they make about the relation of human events to the spiritual realities that underlie them. One of their lessons is that all experience is sensational which has consequences for the saving or damning of a human soul. These religious assumptions, which organized the experience of most Americans in the antebellum era, are at work in the novels of writers like Stowe and Warner.

Thus, when critics dismiss sentimental fiction because it is out of touch with reality, they do so because the reality *they* perceive is organized according to a different set of conventions for constituting experience. For although the attack on sentimental fiction claims for itself freedom from the distorting effects of a naive religious perspective, the real naiveté is to think that *that* attack is launched from no perspective whatsoever, or that its perspective is disinterested and not culture-bound in the way that the sentimental novelists were. The popular fiction of the American Renaissance has been dismissed primarily because it follows from assumptions about the shape and meaning of existence that we no longer hold. But once one understands the coherence and force of those assumptions, the literature that helped to shape the world in their image no longer seems thoughtless or trivial. The conviction that human events are, ultimately and inevitably, shaped by secret prayer, produces a view of society in which orphan girls—like the heroine of Warner's novel—can hope to change the world.

Power

If the general charge against sentimental fiction has been that it is divorced from actual human experience, a more specific form of that charge is that these novels fail to deal with the brute facts of political and economic oppression, and therefore cut themselves off from the possibility of truly affecting the lives of their readers. Tremaine McDowell, writing in the *Literary History of the United States,* dismisses Mrs. Lydia Sigourney—who epitomizes the sentimental tradition for modern critics—by saying that although she "knew something of the humanitarian movements of the day, all . . . she did for Negroes, Indians, the poor, and the insane was to embalm them in her tears."[12] Such cutting remarks are never made about canonical authors of the period, though they, too, did nothing for "Negroes, Indians, the poor," and wrote about them considerably less than their female rivals. But what this sort of commentary reveals, beyond an automatic prejudice against sentimental writers, is its own failure to perceive that the great subject of sentimental fiction is preeminently a political issue. It is no exaggeration to say that domestic fiction is preoccupied, even obsessed, with the nature of power. Because they lived in a society that celebrated free enterprise and democratic government but were excluded from participating in either,[13] the two questions these female novelists never fail to ask are: what *is* power, and where is it located? Since they could neither own property, nor vote, nor speak in a public meeting if both sexes were present, women had to have a way of defining themselves that gave them power and status nevertheless, in their own eyes and in the eyes of the world. That is the problem sentimental fiction addresses.

In his characterization of American women, Tocqueville accurately described the solution to this problem as it appeared to an outsider. He noted that the interests of a "Puritanical" and "trading" nation lead Americans to require "much abnegation on the part of women, and a constant sacrifice of her pleasures to her duties." But, he continues, "I never observed that the women of America consider conjugal authority as a usurpation of their rights. . . . It appeared to me, on the contrary, that they attach a sort of pride to the voluntary surrender of their own will and make their boast to bend themselves to the yoke, not to shake it off."[14] The ethic of sentimental fiction was an ethic of submission. But the relation of these authors to their subservient condition and to the dominant beliefs about the nature and function of women was more complicated than Tocqueville supposed. The fact is that American women simply could not assume a stance of open rebellion against the conditions of their lives for they lacked the material means of escape or opposition. They had to stay put and submit. And so the domestic novelists made that necessity the basis on which to build a power structure of their own. Instead of rejecting the culture's value system outright, they appropriated it for their own use, subjecting the beliefs and customs that had molded them to a series of transformations that allowed them both to fulfill and transcend their appointed roles.

The process of transformation gets underway immediately in Warner's novel when the heroine, Ellen Montgomery, a child of ten, learns that her mother is about to leave on a long voyage for the sake of her health and that she will probably never see her mother again. The two have been weeping uncontrollably in one another's arms, when Mrs. Montgomery recollects herself and says: "Ellen! Ellen! listen to me . . . my child this is not right. Remember, my darling, who it is that brings this sorrow upon us,—though we *must* sorrow, we must not rebel."[15] Ellen's mother, who has been ordered to go on this voyage by her husband and her physician, accepts the features of her life as fixed and instructs her daughter to do the same. The message of this scene, and of most sentimental fiction, is "though we *must* sorrow, we must not rebel." This message can be understood in one of two ways. The most obvious is to read it as an example of how it worked to keep women down. This reading sees women as the dupes of a culture that taught them that disobedience to male authority was a "sin against heaven."[16] In this view, religion is nothing but an opiate for the oppressed and a myth that served the rulers of a "Puritanical" and "trading nation." In this view, the sentimental novelists, to use Ann Douglas's phrase, did "the dirty work" of their culture by teaching women how to become the agents of their own subjection.[17]

The problem with this reading is that it is too simplistic. First of all, it assumes that the ethic of submission was limited only to women. But as Lewis Saum has recently shown in his monumental study of the period, the need to submit to the dictates of divine providence was the most deeply held and pervasive belief of common people in this country before the Civil War.[18] Sentimental novelists spoke not only to women but to all who felt that the circumstances of their lives were beyond their power to control. Second, the women in these novels make submission "their boast" not because they enjoy it but because it gave them another ground on which to stand, a position that, while it fulfilled the social demands that were placed upon them, gave them a place from which to launch a counterstrategy against their worldly masters that would finally give them the upper hand. Submission, as it is presented throughout the novel, is never submission to the will of a husband or father, though that is what it appears to be on the surface; submission is first of all a self-willed act of conquest of one's own passions. Mrs. Montgomery tells Ellen that her tears of anger are "not right," that she must "command" and "compose" herself, because, she says, "You will hurt both yourself and me, my daughter, if you cannot."[19] Ellen will hurt herself by failing to submit because her submission is not capitulation to an external authority but the mastery of herself, and therefore, paradoxically, an assertion of autonomy. In its definition of power relations, the domestic novel operates here, and elsewhere, according to a principle of reversal whereby what is "least" in the world's eyes becomes "greatest" in its perspective. So "submission" becomes "self-conquest" and doing the will of one's husband or father brings an access of divine power. By conquering herself in the name of the highest possible authority, the dutiful woman merges her own authority with God's. When Mrs. Montgomery learns that her husband and doctor have ordered her to part from Ellen, she says to herself, "Not my will, but thine be done."[20] By making themselves into the vehicles of God's will, these female characters become nothing in themselves but all-powerful in relation to the world. Ceding themselves to the source of all power, they bypass worldly (male) authority and, as it were, cancel it out. The ability to "submit" in this way is presented, moreover, as the special prerogative of women, transmitted from mother to daughter. As the women in these novels teach one another how to "command" themselves, they bind themselves to one another and to God in a holy alliance against the men who control their material destinies. When Mr. Montgomery refuses his wife the money to buy Ellen a parting gift, it is no accident that she sells her own mother's ring to make the purchase; the ring symbolizes the tacit system of solidarity that exists among women in these books. Nor is it an accident that the gift Mrs. Montgomery gives her daughter is a Bible. The mother's Bible-gift, in sentimental literature, is invested with supernatural power because it testifies to the reality of the spiritual order where women hold dominion over everything by virtue of their submission on earth.[21]

The bypassing of worldly authority ultimately produces, in these novels, a feminist theology in which the godhead is re-fashioned into an image of maternal authority. When Mrs. Montgomery teaches Ellen what it means to trust in God, she asks her to describe her feelings toward herself, and tells her that "it is just so" that she wishes her to trust in God.[22] All that Ellen knows of God comes to her through the teaching and example of her mother, whose saintliness and love are images of his invisible perfection. The definition of the mother as the channel of God's grace, the medium through which he becomes known to mankind, locates the effective force of divinity in this world in women. Doing the will of God finally becomes identical with doing what one's mother wants. And if one is a woman, doing the will of God means obeying a divinity that comes to look more and more like oneself. Scene after scene in *The Wide, Wide World* ends with Ellen weeping in the arms of a kind mother-figure—a representative of God in human form. As Ellen matures, her spiritual counselors grow closer to her in age until finally she learns to control her passions on her own and becomes her own mother. Not coincidentally, the one completely happy, whole, and self-sufficient character in this book is an elderly woman who lives alone on a mountaintop and is, so to speak, a God unto herself. This is the condition toward which the novel's ethic of submission strives.

Warner's novel presents an image of people dominated by external authorities and forced to curb their own desires; but as they learn to transmute rebellious passion into humble conformity to others' wishes, their powerlessness becomes a source of strength. For the goal of sentimental fiction is to teach the reader how to live without power while waging a protracted struggle in which the strategies of the weak will finally inherit the earth.

Trifles

Although women were attempting to outflank men in the struggle for power by declaring that it was not the world that was important to conquer but one's own soul, they did in fact possess a territory of their own that was not purely spiritual. The territory I am referring to is the home, which provided women both with the means of immediate personal satisfaction and with the foundation of a religious faith. The emphasis on household tasks in these novels may seem to vindicate the charge that their subject matter is essentially trivial, but the charge of triviality is the effect of a critical perspective that regards household activity as unimportant. Women writers of the nineteenth century could not allow the one small corner of the universe they had been allotted to be defined as insignificant or peripheral and so they wrote about household routines in such a way that everything else appeared peripheral to them. The routines of the fireside acquire a sacramental power in the fiction of this period, and consequently, the faithful performance of household tasks is not merely a reflection or an expression of celestial love, but, as in this scene from Warner's novel, its point of origin and consummation.

> To make her mother's tea was Ellen's regular business. She treated it as a very grave affair, and loved it as one of the pleasantest in the course of the day. She used in the first place to make sure that the kettle really boiled; then she carefully poured some water into the tea-pot and rinsed it, both to make it clean and to make it hot; then she knew exactly how much tea to put in the tiny little tea-pot, which was just big enough to hold two cups of tea, and having poured a very little boiling water to it, she used to set it by the side of the fire while she made half a slice of toast. How careful Ellen was about that toast! The bread must not be cut too thick, nor too thin; the fire must, if possible, burn clear and bright, and she herself held the bread on a fork, just at the right distance from the coals to get it nicely browned without burning. When this was done to her satisfaction (and if the first piece failed she would take another), she filled up the little tea-pot from the boiling kettle, and proceeded to make a cup of tea. She knew, and was very careful to put in,

just the quantity of milk and sugar that her mother liked; and then she used to carry the tea and toast on a little tray to her mother's side, and very often held it there for her while she ate. All this Ellen did with the zeal that love gives, and though the same thing was to be gone over every night of the year, she was never wearied. It was a real pleasure; she had the greatest satisfaction in seeing that the little her mother could eat was prepared for her in the nicest possible manner; she knew her hands made it taste better; her mother often said so.[23]

The making of tea as it is described here is not a household task but a religious ceremony. It is also a strategy for survival. The dignity and potency of Ellen's life depend upon the sacredness she confers on small duties, and that is why the passage I have quoted focuses so obsessively and so reverentially on minute details. Ellen's preparation of her mother's tea has all the characteristics of a religious ritual. It is an activity that must be repeated ("the same thing was to be gone over every night of the year"), it must be repeated correctly ("Ellen knew exactly how much tea to put in the tiny little tea-pot," "the bread must not be cut too thick, nor too thin," "and if the first piece failed she would make another"), it must be repeated in the right spirit ("all this Ellen did with the zeal that love gives"), and it must be repeated by the right person (Ellen "knew her hands made it taste better; her mother often said so"). Ellen's hands make the tea and toast taste better because the ritual has worked, but it works not only because it has been performed correctly but because Ellen and her mother believe in it. The creation of moments of intimacy like this through the making of a cup of tea is what their lives depend on. What the ritual effects is the opening of the heart in an atmosphere of closeness, security, and love. The mutual tenderness, affection, and solicitude made visible in the performance of these homely acts are the values sacred to sentimental fiction and the reward it offers its readers for that other activity which must also be performed within the "closet"—the control of rebellious passion. While Ellen and her mother must submit to the will of God, expressed through the commands of husbands and doctors, they compensate for their servitude by celebrating daily their exclusive, mutually supportive love for one another.

The exigencies of a Puritanical and trading nation had put women in the home and barred the door; and so in order to survive, they had to imagine their prison as the site of bliss. In this respect, the taking of tea is no different from hoeing a bean patch on the shores of Walden Pond, or squeezing case aboard a whaling ship: they are parallel reactions against pain and bondage, and a means of salvation and grace. The spaces that American Renaissance writing marks out as the site of possible transcendence are not only the forest and the open sea. The hearth, in domestic fiction, is the site of a "movement inward," as far removed from the fetters of landlocked existence as the Pacific Ocean is from Coenties Slip.

The happiness that women engender in the home is not limited in its effects to women, although they alone are responsible for it. Like prayer, which must be carried on in solitude and secrecy in order to change the world, the happiness that women create in their domestic isolation finally reaches to the ends of the earth. The domestic ideology operates in this respect, as in every other, according to a logic of inversion. "Small acts, small kindnesses, small duties," writes the Reverend Peabody, "bring the happiness or misery . . . of a whole generation. Whatever of happiness is enjoyed . . . beyond the circle of domestic life, is little more than an offshoot from that central sun."[24] Not only happiness, but salvation itself is seen to depend upon the performance of homely tasks. "Common daily duties," says the Reverend Peabody, "become sacred and awful because of the momentous results that depend upon them. Performed or neglected, they are the witnesses that shall appear for or against us at the last day."[25] By investing the slightest acts with moral significance, disciples of the religion of domesticity make the destinies of the human race hang upon domestic routines. Ellen Montgomery treats the making of her mother's tea as "a very grave affair" because she knows that "momentous results" depend upon these trifles. The measuring out of life in coffeespoons, a modernist metaphor for insignificance and futility, is interpreted in sentimental discourse as a world-building activity. When it is done exactly right, and "with the zeal that love gives," it can save the world.

It may be inevitable at this point to object that such claims are merely the fantasies of a disenfranchised group, the line that society feeds members whom it wants to buy off with the illusion of strength while denying them any real power. But what is at stake in this discussion is precisely what constitutes "real" power. From a modern standpoint, the domestic ideal is self-defeating because it ignores the realities of political and economic life. But the world of nineteenth-century Americans was different. As Lewis Saum has written: "In popular thought of the pre-Civil War period, no theme was more pervasive or philosophically fundamental than the providential view. Simply put, that view held that, directly or indirectly, God controlled all things."[26] Given this context, the claims the domestic novel made for the power of Christian love and the sacred influence of women were not in the least exaggerated or illusory. The entire weight of Protestant Christianity and democratic nationalism stood behind them. The notion that women in the home exerted a moral force that shaped the destinies of the race had become central to this country's vision of itself as a redeemer nation. The ethic of submission and the celebration of domesticity, in an age dominated by the revival movement, were not losing strategies but a successful bid for status and sway. Even as thoroughgoingly cosmopolitan a man as Tocqueville became convinced of this as a result of his visit to the United States. "As for myself," he said,

> I do not hesitate to avow that, although the women of the United States are confined within a narrow circle of domestic life, and their situation is in some respects one of extreme dependence, I have nowhere seen women occupying a loftier position; and if I were asked, now that I am drawing to the close of this work, in which I have spoken of so many important things done by the Americans, to what the singular prosperity and growing strength of that people ought mainly to be attributed, I should reply—to the superiority of their women.[27]

Pain

The claims that sentimental fiction made for the importance of the spiritual life and for women's crucial role in the salvation of the race were not spurious or self-deceiving, because they were grounded in beliefs that had already organized the experience of most Americans. The sense of power and feelings of satisfaction that the religion of domesticity afforded were real, not just imagined, and they were bought and paid for at an almost incalculable price. The pain of learning to conquer her own passions is the central fact of the sentimental heroine's existence. For while a novel like *The Wide, Wide World* provides its readers with a design for living under drastically restricted conditions, at the same time it provides them with a catharsis of rage and grief that registers the cost of living according to that model. When Melville writes that Ahab "piled upon the white whale's hump the sum of all the general rage and hate felt by his whole race from Adam down, and then, as if his chest had been a mortar . . . burst his hot heart's shell upon it," he describes the venting of a rage that cannot be named as such in Warner's novel, but whose force is felt nevertheless in the deluge of the heroine's tears.[28] The force of those passions that must be curbed at all costs pushes to the surface again and again in her uncontrollable weeping. For although these novels are thought to have nothing to say about the human psyche, and to be unaware of "all the subtle demonisms of life and thought," in fact they focus exclusively on the emotions, and specifically on the psychological dynamics of living in a condition of servitude. The appeal of Warner's novel lay in the fact that it grappled directly with the emotional experience of its readership; it deals with the problem of powerlessness by showing how one copes with it hour by hour and minute by minute. For contrary to the longstanding consensus that sentimental novelists "couldn't face" the grim facts of their lives, their strength lay precisely in their dramatization of the heroine's suffering. It is a suffering that, the novelists resolutely insist,

their readers, too, must face or else remain unsaved. And they force their readers to face it by placing them inside the mind of someone whose life is a continual series of encounters with absolute authority. At times, the vulnerability of Warner's heroine, forced to live within the bounds authority prescribes and constantly under the pressure of a hostile supervision, becomes almost too painful to bear.

Warner's refusal to mitigate the narrow circumstances of her heroine's existence is particularly striking when one compares this novel to the opening of *Huckleberry Finn*. Both novels begin with a child who is at the mercy of a cruel parent, but the solutions they offer their protagonists are diametrically opposed. When Huck is trapped by his drunken father at the outset of Twain's novel, he concocts an elaborate ruse that allows him to escape. He kills a hog, scatters its blood around the cabin, drags a sack of meal across the threshold to imitate the imprint of a body, and disappears—hoping that his father and the townspeople will think he has been murdered, and of course, they do. This kind of artfully engineered escape, repeated several times throughout the story, is the structural principle of a novel that has for a long time been considered a benchmark of American literary realism. Twain himself, of course, is famous for his scoffing attacks on the escapism of sentimental and romantic fiction. But if one compares his handling of a child's relation to authority with Warner's, the events of *Huckleberry Finn* enact a dream of freedom and autonomy that goes beyond the bounds of the wildest romance. The scenario whereby the clever and deserving Huck repeatedly outwits his powerful adversaries acts out a kind of adolescent wish-fulfillment that Warner's novel never even glances at. When Ellen is sent by her father to live with a sadistic aunt in New England, when she is deeded by him a second time to an even more sinister set of relatives, there is absolutely nothing she can do. Ellen is never for a moment out of the power of her guardians and never will be, as long as she lives. Whereas the premise of Twain's novel is that, when faced by tyranny of any sort, you can simply run away, the problem that Warner's novel sets itself to solve is how to survive, given that you cannot.

In the light of this fact, it is particularly ironic that novels like Warner's should have come to be regarded as "escapist." Unlike their male counterparts, women writers of the nineteenth century could not walk out the door and become Mississippi riverboat captains, go off on whaling voyages, or build themselves cabins in the woods. Nevertheless, modern critics persist in believing that what sentimental novelists offered was an easy way out: a few trite formulas for the masses who were too cowardly to face the "blackness of darkness," too lazy to wrestle with moral dilemmas, too stupid to understand epistemological problems, and too hidebound to undertake "quarrels with God." But

Harriet Beecher Stowe.

"escape" is the one thing that sentimental novels never offer; on the contrary, they teach their readers that the only way to overcome tyranny is through the practice of a grueling and inexorable discipline. Ellen Montgomery says to her aunt early in the novel that if she were free to do what she wanted she would run away—and spends the rest of the novel learning to extirpate that impulse from her being. For not only can one not run away, in the world of sentimental fiction, one cannot protest the conditions under which one is forced to remain. Ahab's cosmic protest, "I'd strike the sun if it insulted me," epitomizes the self-assertive stance of the heroes of classical American fiction; sentimental heroines, forgoing such gestures, practice a heroism of self-renunciation. Theirs may be a quieter task but it is also more arduous, a taking apart and putting back together of the self that must be enacted over and over again, as the protagonist learns to quench the impulse to justify herself, and humbly asks the Lord for help in forgiving those who have wronged her. It is, as Ellen often says to her mentors, "hard."

In a sense, these novels resemble, more than anything else, training narratives: they are like documentaries, or made-for-TV movies that tell how Joe X, who grew up on the streets of Chicago, became a great

pitcher for the White Sox, or how Kathy Y overcame polio and skated her way to stardom. They involve laborious apprenticeships in which the protagonist, under the guidance of a mentor, undergoes repeated failures and humiliations in the course of mastering the principles of her vocation. As the novel progresses, the things that happen to Ellen Montgomery get worse and worse, and at the same time she is required to show an equanimity more unperturbed, and a humility more complete. Thus whereas at an early stage she must learn to repress violent outbursts of temper, later on even a faint expression of irritation crossing her face calls down the devastating rebukes of her mentors. As the first phase of her disciplinary education draws to its close, Ellen becomes her own spiritual taskmaster. Her mentors have succeeded in establishing God in Ellen's mind as an all-powerful internal "Friend" who watches everything she does. Now, when even a rebellious thought crosses Ellen's mind, she will abase herself before the authority she has internalized.

The last section of the novel puts Ellen's ability to accept whatever fate deals out to an even harsher series of tests. Her father dies and deeds her to some rich relatives in Scotland. She is cast on the wide world a second time, and this time there will be no mentors to guide her. Like all true Christians, Ellen must learn to rely on faith alone. The final chapters of *The Wide, Wide World* require of the heroine an extinction of her personality so complete that there is nothing of herself she can call her own. Ellen's Scottish relatives are spiritual tyrants. Whereas her Aunt Fortune has subjected her to constant household drudgery and frequently hurt her feelings, the Lindsays attempt to possess her soul. It is not enough that Ellen is a perfectly docile, charming, and virtuous child; she must be stripped of every vestige of her former identity. Ellen's uncle makes her call him "father" and she submits. He changes her name from Montgomery to Lindsay and she does not protest. He orders her to forget her nationality, forces her to drink wine, forbids her to speak of her former friends, refuses to let her talk of religion, and insists that she give up her sober ways and act "cheerful." To all of these demands Ellen submits, after much internal struggle, many tears and prayers, much consulting of her Bible and singing of hymns. "God will take care of me if I trust in Him," she says to herself, "it is none of my business." "God giveth grace to the humble, I will humble myself."[29]

Given the amount of pain that sentimental heroines endure, it is almost inconceivable that their stories should have been read as myths of "reassurance." The story of Ellen Montgomery's education is no more reassuring than the story of Job or *Pilgrim's Progress,* on which it was modeled, and its original readers apparently understood it in this way. A traveler to

England in the 1880s reported that the four books most frequently found in the homes of common people were the Bible, *Pilgrim's Progress, Uncle Tom's Cabin,* and *The Wide, Wide World.* Like the Job story and *Pilgrim's Progress, The Wide, Wide World* is a trial of faith; its emphasis falls not on last-minute redemption but on the toils and sorrows of the "way"—its protagonist, like theirs, is systematically stripped of every earthly support and then persecuted. Like these narratives, *The Wide, Wide World* teaches its readers, by example, how to live under such conditions, and like theirs, its lesson is that the only thing that really matters is faith in God and doing his will.

At the end-point of the disciplinary process, Ellen does not exist for herself at all any more, but only for others. Sanctified by the sacrifice of her own will, she becomes a mentor by example, teaching lessons in submissiveness through her humble bearing, downcast eyes, unruffled brow, and "peculiar grave look." She becomes a medium through which God's glory can show itself to men, a person who "supplied what was wanting everywhere; like the transparent glazing which painters use to spread over the dead color of their pictures; unknown, it was she gave life and harmony to the whole."[30] The ideal to which the novel educates its readers is the opposite of self-assertion; it is to become empty of self, an invisible transparency that nevertheless is miraculously responsible for the life in everything.

In an unfriendly review of Warner's book, Charles Kingsley quipped that it should have been called "The Narrow, Narrow World," and, of course, in a sense he was right. Although the frontispiece to the first illustrated edition shows a ship tossing on a stormy sea with the sun breaking through clouds in the background, all of the heroine's adventures take place in small enclosed spaces that are metaphors of the heart. The wideness of the world is to be measured not by geographical distances but by the fullness with which it manages to account for the experience of its readers. That experience, as I have argued, was shaped conclusively by the revival movement and by the social and economic conditions of American life in the antebellum years. For the sentimental writers, who were evangelical Christians, the world could be contracted to the dimensions of a closet without loss, because, according to their belief, it was in the closet that one received the power to save the world. When one has learned to master one's soul in private, one becomes "responsible," as Warner puts it, "for the life in everything." That theory of power is what made sentimental fiction a decisive social force, and it is formulated succinctly by the Reverend Dr. Patton, addressing the Fifteenth Annual Meeting of the Home Missionary Society, in words that recapitulate the world view I have attempted to summon up: "The history of the world," he said, "is the history of prayer. For this is the power that moves heaven. Yet it is the power which may be wielded by the humblest and obscurest saint. It will doubtless be found, in the great day, that many a popular and prominent man will be set aside; whilst the retired but pleading disciple, will be brought forth to great honor, as having alone in her closet, wrestled with the angel and prevailed."[31]

Notes

[1] That is how twentieth-century critics have usually treated this work. See, for example, Henry Nash Smith, "The Scribbling Women and the Cosmic Success Story," *Critical Inquiry* 1 (September 1974):47-49; John T. Frederick, "Hawthorne's 'Scribbling Women,'" *New England Quarterly* 48 (1975):321-40; Ramona T. Hull, "Scribbling Females and Serious Males: Hawthorne's Comments from Abroad on Some American Authors," *Nathaniel Hawthorne Journal* 5 (1975): 35-38.

[2] Smith, "The Scribbling Woman,"; Henry Nash Smith, *Democracy and the Novel* (New York: Oxford University Press, 1978), p. 12; Perry Miller, "The Romance and the Novel," *Nature's Nation* (Cambridge: Harvard University Press, Belknap Press, 1967), pp. 255-56.

[3] Smith, *Democracy and the Novel,* pp. 13-15.

[4] James D. Hart, *The Popular Book* (Berkeley and Los Angeles: University of California Press, 1950), pp. 93, 94, 111; Frank Luther Mott, *Golden Multitudes* (New York: MacMillan Co., 1947), pp. 122-25.

[5] Smith, *Democracy and the Novel,* p. 8.

[6] Perry Miller, *The Life of the Mind in America from the Revolution to the Civil War* (New York: Harcourt Brace & World, 1965).

[7] In March 1829, for example, a pamphlet entitled *Institution and Observance of the Sabbath* was distributed to 23,383 New York families. Charles Foster, *An Errand of Mercy: The Evangelical United Front, 1790-1837* (Chapel Hill: University of North Carolina Press, 1960), p. 187.

[8] New York City Tract Society, *Eleventh Annual Report* (New York, 1837), back cover.

[9] Ibid., pp. 51-52.

[10] Ibid.

[11] David Reynolds, "From Doctrine to Narrative: The Rise of Pulpit Story-Telling in America," *American Quarterly,* 32 (Winter 1980): 479-98.

[12] Tremaine McDowell, "Diversity and Innovation in New England," in *The Literary History of the United States,* ed. Robert E. Spiller et. al., 3d ed., rev. (New York: Macmillan Co., 1963), p. 289.

[13] In the first half of the nineteenth century, single women could own real property but married women could not. "Essentially," writes Lawrence Friedman in *A History of American Law* (New York: Simon & Schuster, 1973), "husband and wife were one flesh; but the man was the owner of that flesh" (p. 184). For a good discussion of the growing discrepancy, from the seventeenth century onward, between antipatriarchal theories of government and the reinforcement of patriarchal family structure, see Susan Miller Okin, "The Making of the Sentimental Family," *Philosophy and Public Affairs* 11 (Winter 1982):65-88.

[14] Alexis de Tocqueville, *Democracy in America,* 2 vols., trans. Henry Reive, rev. Francis Bowen, corrected and annotated Phillips Bradley (New York: Random House, Vintage Books, 1957), 2:223.

[15] Elizabeth Wetherell (Susan Warner), *The Wide, Wide World,* 2 vols. in 1 (1851; rpt. J. P. Lippincott & Co., 1886), 1:12.

[16] Rev. Orville Dewey, *A Discourse Preached in the City of Washington, on Sunday, June 27, 1852* (New York: Charles S. Francis & Co., 1852), p. 13. Dewey's sermon on obedience is characteristic of a general concern that a democratic government was breeding anarchy in the behavior of its citizens, and that obedience therefore must be the watchword of the day. In European society, Dewey argues, where the law of caste still reigns, there is a natural respect for order and authority. But "*here* and *now,*" he continues,

> all this is changed. . . . With no *appointed* superiors above us, we are liable enough to go to the opposite extreme; we are liable to forget that any body is to be obeyed—to forget even, that God is to be obeyed. . . . Only let every man, every youth, every child, think that he has the right to speak, act, do any where and every where, whatever any body else has the right to do; that he has as much right to his will as any body; and there is an end of society. That is to say let there be an end of obedience in the world, and there is an end of the world." (pp. 4-5).

Since, in Dewey's eyes, the home is the source of anarchy in the state, family discipline is the source of all good civil order, and therefore the goal of domestic education must be "a patient and perfect obedience" (p. 13).

> If the child is *never* permitted to disobey, it will soon cease to think of it as possible. And it should *never* be permitted! . . . Only when living under law—only when walking in obedience, is child or man, family or State, happy and truly prosperous. Selfish passion every where is anarchy, begetting injustice, and bringing forth destruction." (pp. 13-14)

Sentimental novels, along with advice books for young women, child-rearing manuals, and religious literature of all sorts, helped to inculcate the notion that obedience was a domestic as well as a civic virtue, especially in the case of women. Beginning in the 1830s, as Nancy Cott has shown, clergymen directed their sermons on the need for order in family and society especially at women, "vividly emphasizing the necessity for women to be subordinate to and dependent on their husbands" (Nancy F. Cott, *The Bonds of Womanhood: "Woman's Sphere" in New England, 1780-1835* [New Haven: Yale University Press, 1977], pp. 158-59).

[17] Ann Douglas, *The Feminization of American Culture* (New York: Alfred A. Knopf, 1977), p. 11.

[18] Lewis P. Saum, *The Popular Mood of Pre-Civil War America* (Westport, Conn.: Greenwood Press, 1980), chap. I, "Providence."

[19] Warner, *The Wide, Wide World,* 1:13.

[20] Ibid., 1:35.

[21] *Old Favorites from McGuffey's Readers* prints this poem, from the *Fourth Reader,* entitled "A Mother's Gift—The Bible" whose first stanza reads as follows:

> Remember, love, who gave thee this,
> When older days shall come,
> When she who had thine earliest kiss,
> Sleeps in her narrow home.
> Remember! 'twas a mother gave
> The gift to one she'd die to save!

The Bible is the symbol of the mother in sentimental literature, taking her place, after she is dead, serving as a reminder of her teachings, and as a token of her love. To forget what the Bible says is to forget one's mother:

> A parent's blessing on her son
> Goes with this holy thing;
> The love that would retain the one,
> Must to the other cling.

[22] Warner, *The Wide, Wide World,* 1:20.

[23] Ibid., 1:14.

[24] Rev. E. Peabody, "Importance of Trifles," in *The Little Republic, Original Articles by Various Hands,*

ed. Mrs. Eliza P. T. Smith (New York: Wiley & Putnam, 1848), p. 120. The "importance of trifles" theme is ubiquitous in nineteenth-century inspirational literature. It is directly related to the Christian rhetoric of inversion ("the last shall be first"), to the cultivation of the practical virtues of honesty, industry, frugality ("A stitch in time saves nine," "A penny saved is a penny earned"), and to the glorification of the mother's influence. In another essay in the same volume ("A Word to Mothers"), Timothy P. Smith writes "Let us not forget that the greatest results of the mind are produced by small, but continued, patient effort" (p. 210).

> As surely as a continued digging will wear away the mountain, so surely shall the persevering efforts of a Christian mother be crowned with success. . . . She is, through her children, casting pebbles into the bosom of society; but she cannot as easily watch the ripples made: no, they reach beyond the shore of mortal vision, and shall ripple on, in that sea that has neither shore nor bound, for weal or for woe, to them, and to the whole universal brother hood of man. (pp. 211-12)

[25] Peabody, "Importance of Trifles," in *The Little Republic,* pp. 124-25.

[26] Saum, *The Popular Mood,* p. 25.

[27] de Tocqueville, *Democracy in America,* 2:225.

[28] Herman Melville, *Moby-Dick or, The Whale,* edited with an Introduction and annotation by Charles Feidelson, Jr. (New York: Bobbs-Merrill, 1964), p. 247.

[29] Warner, *The Wide, Wide World,* 2:273.

[30] Ibid., 1:249.

[31] Rev. Dr. Patton, Address, American Home Missionary Society, *Fifteenth Report* (New York: William Osborn, 1842), p. 104.

Richard H. Brodhead

SOURCE: "Sparing the Rod: Discipline and Fiction in Antebellum America," in *Representations,* No. 21, Winter, 1988, pp. 67-96.

[In the following excerpt, Brodhead provides a psychological account of internalized moral discipline by a paradigmatic sentimental character. Only those footnotes pertaining to the following excerpt have been reprinted in the "Notes" section.]

Susan Warner's *The Wide, Wide World* (1851), which went on to become one of the four or five most widely read American novels of the whole nineteenth century, is often cited as the first of the new bestsellers. And it is Warner's book that offers the most impressive recognition of discipline through love as a culture-specific historical formation. *The Wide, Wide World* is a historical novel in a systematically restricted sense of the word. Throughout the book Warner poses the extradomestic world outside of her sphere, in a place unavailable to her literary knowing. Its initial harmony devastated by a lawsuit, neither the book's characters nor the book itself can get access to the transprivate world in which they could know what the suit's occasion was. Through the same strict observation of the limits of her sphere, Warner makes *history* in the usual sense unavailable to her knowing: what is going on in the world outside of certain family spaces is, in this book, a sealed book. But if she fails to locate her character's private lives in relation to any sort of generalized process of collective change, part of Warner's power as a writer is that she implicitly grasps the households she represents as historically different formations of the domestic sphere. Aunt Fortune, to whose grumpy care Warner's child heroine Ellen Montgomery is shipped off after the book's opening crisis, plays the role in *The Wide, Wide World* of fairy-tale's cruel stepmother. But Warner registers her milieu quite concretely—and registers it not in idiosyncratic or local-color detail only, but in such a way as to grasp its surface features' relation to its sociohistorical form. While this point is never commented on overtly, every feature of Aunt Fortune's household exemplifies the logic of the old-style household economy: Fortune is always busy, because this home is a place of work; her house is smelly and noisy, because this house is still a scene of production; her coverlets are of linsey-woolsey, because the necessities of life are still homemade in her world; she scorns Ellen's desire to go to school, because in her world knowledge means knowing how to do practically productive tasks; entertainment at her house takes the form of an apple-paring and pork-packing bee, because in her world entertainment is not disconnected from the household's economic productivity; and so on through a legion of comparable details. The other households in the book differ from Aunt Fortune's on every count. But they differ not just because they are the homes of other people, but because they embody different social formations of the home's place and work: the more genteel (and less productive) formation of a historically later phase, in the case of Alice and John Humphreys; the altogether leisured, pleasure-oriented formation of a Europeanized gentry class, in the case of the aristocratic Lindsays.

While this point too is never registered in any abstract form, Warner's picturing strikingly represents the discipline of love as inhering in a differentiated way in one of these social formations. In contrast to Aunt Fortune's, the household associated with Ellen's mother and Ellen's exemplary friend Alice is characterized by a raised threshold of decency and comfort. (Its furniture is tastefully ornamental, not only functional; Ellen's traumatic experiences at Aunt Fortune's suggest that she is used to indoor plumbing.) In it women are conspicuously exempted from productive functions. (Alice does the more delicate baking, but has a maid to do heavy housework; Ellen's mother, with the wearying exception of one shopping trip, does nothing at all.) Its forms of entertainment are mentally uplifting, and also unproductive and privatized. (Where Aunt Fortune has a bee, these women read.) And this household is also and indistinguishably two more things: it is affectionate, so much so that the cultivation of close relations might be said to *be its* productive activity; and it is pious, specifically in a way that makes its female heads feel called to the work of improving others' spiritual characters. (When Ellen first meets Alice, Alice at once picks up the task of revivalistically reforming Ellen's temper that her mother had left incomplete.) This reformatory lovingness is profoundly different from any disciplinary method seen elsewhere in the book. Aunt Fortune, untender and impious, is too busy to *care* about Ellen in Alice's and Mrs. Montgomery's way, let alone to care about her moral nurture; her discipline is confined to occasional bouts of highly arbitrary authoritarianism, backed up (in one instance) by blows.[36] The Lindsays, more genial but quite secular, try to make Ellen sleep late, drink wine, cut back on religious reading, and be more fun at parties: theirs is another discipline entirely, training for life in the very different gentry world. Moralizing lovingness is confined to scenes that have all the marks of the new middle-class feminine domesticity. Warner knows *that* discipline as *that* social formation's pastime and work; she knows *that* discipline as forming the *self that* world aims to reproduce.

Part of the distinction of *The Wide, Wide World* is that it specifies the cultural location of this *scheme* of acculturation so precisely. Another of its distinctions is that it plots the actual psychological transactions this scheme entails with unmatched precision and care. The novel begins, thus, by showing what it would mean, in human terms, to be encompassed with tenderness as this plan requires. Ellen Montgomery lives with her mother at the novel's opening, but this phrase does not begin to describe the form of their attachment. It would be more accurate to say that she lives *in* her mother, in the *Umwelt* her mother projects. Her mother is always with her, her mother is the whole world available to her (when her mother sleeps Ellen looks out the window, but the world outside the window is inaccessible to her; hired food preparers and even Ellen's father sometimes intrude on this domesticity, but when they withdraw "the mother and daughter were left, as they always loved to be, alone"; 1:43).

Enclosed within her mother's emotional presence, Ellen has been bred to a reciprocating strength of love that makes her feel each event first in terms of how it will bear on her mother's frame of mind. And this other-centeredness or (as we say) *considerateness* is what makes her responsive to the authority of her mother's codes. As she surrounds her child with her highly wrought emotionality, Mrs. Montgomery also fills the world so centered with moral prescription. She has a rule for everything, a rule in each case absolutely and equally obligatory: "Draw nigh to God" is her religious requirement for her daughter, but her rules of etiquette, even of fashion—one must never ask the names of strangers; girls' cloaks must be of medium-grade merino wool, and not green (1:26, 65, 56-57)—are put forward as binding in no less a degree. And as the beginning of the novel (a little pathetically) demonstrates, Ellen's love for this authority figure—her continual impulse to think of her mother before she thinks of herself, and the absolute imperative she feels under to maintain her mother's favorable emotional atmosphere—makes Ellen, in and of herself, want to do and be what her mother would require of her. While her mother pretends to nap in the first chapter, Ellen makes the tea and toast, not only makes them but makes them *just so,* with a ritualistic precision of observance. And she performs this labor and follows this tight prescription because the tea is for her mother, and she is driven by "the zeal that love gives" (1: 14). Crushed to hear that her mother (quite incomprehensibly) must abandon her and move with her father to Europe now that the lawsuit is lost, Ellen is required to suppress her grief in consideration of her mother's fragile state—"Try to compose yourself. I am afraid you will make me worse," the tyrannically delicate Mrs. Montgomery says. This injunction is hard for the aggrieved Ellen, but the stronger emotion of "love to her mother" has "power enough" to make her "exert all her self-command" (1:13).

What the opening of *The Wide, Wide World* really dramatizes is the primitive implantation of moral motivation, as discipline by intimacy specifies that practice. Made into a compulsive love seeker, Ellen shows how the child so determined becomes driven, by her heightened need to win and keep parental favor, not just to accept but really to *seek out* the authority of the parent's moral imperatives. What the rest of the novel then dramatizes is the ongoing career of authority seeking this primal scene initiates. Two facts, not one, constitute Ellen's initial world: the fact that the world is centered in the mother, and the fact that the mother is going to be lost. The news that inaugurates this narrative, the news that the lawsuit is lost and Ellen must be abandoned, carries a powerful sense of women's victimization by the nondomestic masculine economic world they are now dependent on but shut out from knowledge of. (When the separation scene finally arrives Ellen is viscerally wrenched from her mother by the disruptive stranger who is her father.) But in another sense the separation crisis that inaugurates this novel simply recognizes that oneness with the mother is what one cannot *not* lose—a fact that the child's new centrality to the mother's life in middle-class domesticity makes in new measure traumatic.

What the plot of this novel then shows is how an acculturation system like Ellen's makes this newly intensified grief of separation a psychic resource for the disciplining of the subject. In *The Wide, Wide World* to love one's mother is to wish to do things her way, but to love her and lose her is to have this wish heightened into full-fledged moral imperative. Loving and losing her mother commits Ellen to a career of seeking for substitutes for this lost beloved. But since the mark of others' substitutability for the mother is that they simultaneously give warm baths of affection and impose strict codes of obligation, this way of repairing an emotional breach drives Ellen deeper and deeper into the territory of psychological regulation. (The final beloved regulator, John Humphreys, does not even tell Ellen his final requirement of her, "but whatever it were, she was very sure she would do it!"; 2:333.) Coached by such surrogates, Ellen's achievement as the novel plots it is to move toward ever more perfect internalizations of parental authority—an achievement whose psychic payoff, as the book shows it, is to restore oneness with the mother now lost.[37] Conscience, at last grown strong enough to make her obey even the most outrageous of Aunt Fortune's commands, lets Ellen hear an inner voice that she knows as coming from "her mother's lips" (1:317). When she then undergoes the conversion her mother had covenanted her to, Ellen at once accepts the authority of her mother's religious system and recovers, through participation in that system, felt contact with the mother herself: after her conversion "there seemed to be a link of communion between her mother and her that was wanting before. The promise, written and believed in by the one, realized and rejoiced in by the other, was a dear something in common, though one had in the mean while removed to heaven, and the other was still a lingerer on the earth" (2:72).

Jane Tompkins, the strongest recent champion of Warner's novel, writes in a fine phrase that "a text depends upon its audience's beliefs not just in a gross general way, but intricately and precisely."[38] This is exactly the relation *The Wide, Wide World* has to the living-scenario adumbrated in the philosophy of disciplinary intimacy: proof that the world this novel knows and speaks is by no means only the (in her formulation apparently universal) mid-nineteenth-century American evangelicalism that Tompkins has nominated as its cultural context, but

the quite particular middle-class world (evangelical Protestantism was one of its constituents) that coalesced around this socializing strategy in the antebellum years. . . .

Notes

[36] Susan Warner, *The Wide, Wide World,* 2 vols. (1851; New York, 1856), 1:193. Numbers after subsequent quotations from the novel refer to pages in this text.

[37] My understanding of what might be called motivation-by-reunion has been helped by Nancy Schnog's unpublished essay "A History of Sentiment: Susan Warner's *The Wide, Wide World* in Psychosocial Perspective."

[38] Jane Tompkins, *Sensational Designs: The Cultural Work of American Fiction, 1790-1860* (New York, 1985), 156. The social undifferentiatedness of the context Tompkins proposes is evident throughout her otherwise useful chapter on Warner, "The Other American Renaissance": revivalism thus has "'terrific universality'" (149; the undisowned phrase is Perry Miller's); evangelical thought "pervaded people's perceptions" (156), informed "how people in the antebellum era thought" (158), and so on. . . .

Jane Tompkins discusses readers' responses to sentimental fiction:

The power of a sentimental novel to move its audience depends upon the audience's being in possession of the conceptual categories that constitute character and event. That storehouse of assumptions includes attitudes toward the family and toward social institutions; a definition of power and its relation to individual human feeling; notions of political and social equality; and above all, a set of religious beliefs that organizes and sustains the rest. Once in possession of the system of beliefs that undergirds the patterns of sentimental fiction, it is possible for modern readers to see how its tearful episodes and frequent violations of probability were invested with a structure of meanings that fixed these works, for nineteenth-century readers, not in the realm of fairy tale or escapist fantasy, but in the very bedrock of reality. I do not say that we can read sentimental fiction exactly as Stowe's audience did—that would be impossible—but that we can and should set aside the modernist prejudices which consign this fiction to oblivion, in order to see how and why it worked for its readers, in its time, with such unexampled effect.

Jane Tompkins, in Sensational Designs: The Cultural Work of American Fiction, 1790-1860, *Oxford University Press, 1985.*

THE RECEPTION OF SENTIMENTAL FICTION

Cathy N. Davidson

SOURCE: "Privileging the *Feme Covert:* The Sociology of Sentimental Fiction," in *Revolution and the Word: The Rise of the Novel in America,* Oxford University Press, 1986, pp. 110-150.

[*In the following chapter from* Revolution and the Word: The Rise of the Novel in America *(1986), Davidson discusses the popularity of sentimental novels and the social issues upon which they comment—including marriage, sexuality, childbearing, and domesticity.*]

> In the new Code of laws which I suppose it will be necessary for you to make I desire you would Remember the Ladies, and be more generous and favorable to them than your ancestors. Do not put such unlimited power into the hands of the Husbands. Remember all Men would be tyrants if they could. If perticuliar care and attention is not paid to the Ladies we are determined to foment a Rebellion, and will not hold ourselves bound by any Laws in which we have no voice, or Representation.

Abigail Adams to John Adams (March 31, 1776)

> As to your extraordinary Code of laws, I cannot but laugh. We have been told that our Struggle has loosened the bands of Government every where. That children and Apprentices were disobedient—that schools and Colledges were grown turbulent—that Indians slighted their Guardians and Negroes grew insolent to their masters. But your letter was the first Intimation that another Tribe more numerous and powerful than all the rest were grown discontented. . . . Depend upon it, We know better than to repeal our masculine systems.

John Adams to Abigail Adams (April 14, 1776)

The Sociology of the Female Reader

In centering his fictive universe on both seduction and female education, William Hill Brown dramatized one of the chief issues of his time and place—the status of women in the Republic. Seduction, of course, served as both metaphor and metonymy in summing up the society's contradictory views of women. The huge social interest vested in women's sexuality, which was fetishized into a necessary moral as well as a social and biological commodity, meant that women themselves had little voice in the matter. Female education was, then, in a number of the first sentimental novels, an education in the value of playing the proper sexual roles available to women who were thereby seduced

by the sentimental plot as well as in it. Wife or mistress, woman's function was to be socially possessed or dispossessed. Taken either way, she constituted mostly one more proof of male prerogatives and privilege. In other words, it is no surprise that *The Power of Sympathy* posits the very premise, the essential powerlessness of the female, that any real problematics of seduction might be expected to question.

Even on the level of narration, the first American novel confirms female victimization in that women are seduced in the novel not by their own uncontrollable desire but by the verbal chicanery of men. This masculine narrative superiority is part and parcel of the narrative method of *The Power of Sympathy.* Harrington can abandon his plan to "triumph over" Harriot, but he still dominates in all discourse between them. In the course of the novel, Harrington writes his friend Worthy twenty-six times; he writes Harriot only twice. Harrington's letters occupy almost half the entire narrative, Harriot's take up less than one tenth of the novel. Harrington's voice counts and is counted; it is *his* story he is telling, and that unequal distribution of story time tends to seduce the reader as well as the female protagonist whose tale has already been subsumed into Harrington's mastering narration. Who, after all, would want to identify with Harriot, who has no surplus of identity to lend to another?

The social and narrative problems that Hannah Webster Foster addresses are both similar to Brown's and a universe removed. While also concerned with the interrelationship between seduction and female education, Foster has significantly altered the plot structure of the sentimental novel by allowing her heroine some status and by relating the novel primarily from the female point of view. She thereby casts *The Coquette* as more a woman's story than a man's. Whereas Harrington relates his choice not to seduce Harriot but to marry her, Eliza Wharton must choose for herself between matrimony and coquetry, between one set of constraints and another. Still more to the point, by validating the capability of the finally fallen heroine, Foster affirms both the need to educate women and the uselessness of any such education in a society that has no place for educated women.

Eliza is a capable woman, yet she ultimately fails as miserably as any of the hapless victims in Brown's novel. I would suggest that this narrative bad end is not only crucial to *The Coquette* but is pointedly relevant to the whole debate on women's status carried on in diaries, letters, newspapers, magazines, and advice books of the time, and, of course, in the early sentimental novel as well. The horns of women's impossible dilemma can be summed up in two opposing questions: If a woman is inferior (susceptible to flattery, easily cajoled, prone to seduction), is she really educable, and, more to the point, does she in any way deserve a voice and a vote in the Republic? On the other hand, if some women are as capable as any man (Abigail Adams, Mercy Otis Warren, and other exemplary women), then why all the fuss about needing better schools, better education, and what is all this Wollstonecraftism about? It is an impasse that every woman's movement has had to face. If women are inferior, they can hardly expect to be treated as equals; if women are equal, then why the clamor for special privileges?

The Coquette, countering received ideas on women's circumscribed power and authority, was an important voice in the debate on women's role in the Republic. But unless the sociology of the early reader is kept in mind, the novel is deprived of its chief narrative thrust. The book gives us, essentially, a portrait of the life, loves, and death of a well-known woman of the new Republic sympathetically portrayed for this protagonist's unknown contemporaries. Elizabeth Whitman, Eliza Wharton's prototype, was much criticized and scorned in contemporaneous newspaper accounts. In the novel, however, she takes on a surprising dignity. And in the disjunctions between Eliza Wharton and "Elizabeth Whitman" (also a fiction in the sense that her scandalous life was thoroughly allegorized in dozens of sermons and editorials), we may catch some glimpses of an implied reader of early American fiction and read something of the dilemmas confronting her, too, in her society. Reading this reader, I would even maintain, is a necessary prerequisite to reading the novels she read.

The first step in that preliminary reading is to reconstruct the conditions under which she read.[1] We cannot simply reconstruct her, for she is no more a monolith than is "the female reader" today. However, her society tended to define her monolithically, as societies tend to define most members of low-prestige groups. Although the educated woman may well have enjoyed a more privileged life than her serving sister, by law vast differences in wealth, educational level, capability, class, or race were outweighed by one common feature. Both were "women," a social construct as much as a biological entity.

How was woman "written" in the society at large and how did the early novel both contribute to and countermand that social text? To answer the first part of this contextual question, I will necessarily conduct various forays into the history of emerging America. In answering the second part, I will chart the ways in which numerous sentimental novels entered into the public debates on women and incorporated different arguments on women's status into their very structures. Only then will I return to *The Coquette* to examine how cogently and capably Foster gave voice to the "hidden woman" and dramatized her demise both as a personal tragedy and a social failure. Just as *The*

Power of Sympathy can be seen as a countertext to the Bowdoin/Adams proclamations, so can *The Coquette,* as I shall subsequently argue, be seen as a counter text to the Elizabeth Whitman allegory of the fall of an intellectual woman.

Who were the implied readers of the early American sentimental novel? The novels themselves suggest a ready answer in that many of them are addressed, either prefatorially or in the text, to the "daughters of United Columbia," who are, implicitly or explicitly, young, white, of good New England stock, and for the most part unmarried. Their class, however, is rarely specified, and different novels give us female characters drawn from various social levels, ranging from the working poor to the relatively well-to-do. The very rich rarely appear in early novels except, occasionally, as seducer/villains or as wealthy women typically victimized by fortune hunters, which suggests that the wealthy were not paramount consumers of fiction. Similarly, although black women are sometimes included in subplots (typically to demonstrate the inhumanity of slavery), they are never the focus of sentimental intrigue nor is it likely that they read sentimental novels in any number. Finally, few of the novels focus significant attention on mature women, matrons. Sentiment seems to have been mostly a province of the young.

Young people constituted a ready audience. Because of the high mortality rate during the Revolutionary War and the population explosion in its aftermath, by the first decades of the nineteenth century, a full two-thirds of the white population of America was under the age of twenty-four.[2] Furthermore, because of the increasing attention to childhood education in the later part of the eighteenth century, young people, especially women, tended to be more literate than old people. The early American writer capitalized on this market of potential readers by featuring young people prominently in the plots of the majority of early American novels of all genres. In fact, the mean age of the hero and heroine in novels written in America before 1820 is under twenty-five, as was the national mean. Most of the plots of early American novels also center around issues of importance to young readers. In sentimental fiction, particularly, far more emphasis is placed on a young woman deciding whom to marry than on an older wife determining how best to raise her family.

An emphasis on marital decisions also reflects other demographic considerations. The average marriage age of the republican woman was between twenty-two and twenty-three years of age and her average life expectancy in 1800 was only forty-two years of age.[3] Since no college admitted women in America until 1837, when Oberlin first opened its doors to women, and since female secondary education was rare, a

Trini Alvarado, Susan Sarandon, Clair Danes, Kirsten Dunst, and Winona Ryder in a scene from the 1994 film version of Little Women.

significant portion of a woman's life (perhaps as much as one fifth) passed in what might be called a premarital state—beyond childhood but not yet, to use the eighteenth-century term, "settled."[4] While virtually all young women, even the wealthiest, were occupied either inside or outside the home in some kind of labor (sometimes remunerated, sometimes not), a woman's chief social goal during these years was to find a suitable husband, either independently or with the aid of her friends and family. Diaries of young women describe how part of virtually every day was spent visiting with one's friends and otherwise circulating, very much as do the characters in numerous sentimental novels.[5] Assessing one's male companions or studying men in company or sounding out one's acquaintances about a certain man's reputation are all recorded again and again and with good reason. Because of eighteenth-century laws of coverture, a woman had to be particularly careful in her choice of a mate, for, after marriage, she became, for all practical purposes, totally dependent upon her husband. Her rights would be "covered" by his, and it was his legal and social prerogative to define what those rights would be.

For the large available audience of unmarried young women, sentimental novels fulfilled the social function of testing some of the possibilities of romance and courtship—testing better conducted in the world of fiction than in the world of fact. Both Susanna Rowson and Hannah Foster demonstrated, for example, that a reformed rake did not make the best husband after all and that a womanizer was likely to also be a womanhater. But by portraying dashing roués, sentimental novelists still allowed women to vicariously participate in a range of relationships with diverse suitors and to imagine what the aftermath of marriage to different men might be like. Most of these novels, however, did portray, at least on one level of discourse, the dangers of unsuitable relationships and, as we have seen with *The Power of Sympathy,* graphically described the heavy portion of blame and suffering that would necessarily fall on the shoulders of the sexually transgressing woman.

The concomitant unstated premise of sentimental fiction is that the woman must take greater control of her life and must make shrewd judgments of the men who come into her life. Implicitly and explicitly, the novels acknowledge that married life can be bitterly unhappy and encourage women to circumvent disaster by weighing any prospective suitors in the balance of good sense—society's and her own. A novel such as Sukey Vickery's *Emily Hamilton,* to cite but one example, considers little more than questions of matrimony. Women who choose wisely are briefly described, catalogued, and ranged against a contrasting catalogue of women who do not. The most pathetic of the latter, a Mrs. Henderson who is brought to the verge of death by a violent, alcoholic, profligate, and emotionally abusive husband, was based on the sad life of one Mrs. Anderson, a neighbor of Vickery (who was herself an unmarried young woman when she penned her first and only novel).[6]

Mary Beth Norton has suggested that young women in early America, particularly those in the higher classes, may well have enjoyed more leisure during their premarital years than at any other time. The daughters of well-to-do families were often free of some of the household tasks that occupied their mothers such as overseeing the ever-fluctuating household help or raising children.[7] But these young women were by no means perpetually idle and looking about for a good read. On the contrary, one of the chief arguments against novel reading in the eighteenth century held that such idle employment kept young women from contributing to the family economy. Linda K. Kerber has noted, in this regard, that household manufacture occupied a large percentage of even upper- and middle-class women's time in both cities and the country until well into the middle of the nineteenth century and that unmarried daughters participated in virtually all aspects of household production, including working the loom and the spinning wheel.[8]

During their premarital years young women even of the middle classes often worked outside the home, especially as teachers, while those lower on the social scale could seek work as domestics or, increasingly, in the new factories or mills. Or young women might engage in various given-out industries and thereby earn a minimal income while working in the home (typically making straw bonnets or stitching boots or shoes).[9] Although officially "unsettled," women in their premarital years were very much a part of the domestic economy and even contributed to the beginnings of the industrial economy in early America.

Yet they still made time for novel reading, either as a respite from other work or often as an accompaniment to it. For example, young Julia Cowles of Connecticut squeezed in a full syllabus of novel reading *(The Unfortunate Lovers, Adventures of Innocence, The Boarding School, Sir Charles Grandison, Amelia, Memoirs of the Bloomsgrove Family)* amidst her round of household duties—washing, cleaning, quilting, spin-

ning, ironing, sewing: "Been so much engaged in read[ing] 'Grandison,'" she apologized to her diary, "that other things have been neglected, especially my journal." Or in Pennsylvania Molly Drinker read aloud from *The Mysteries of Udolpho* while her mother, Elizabeth, plied her needle—much the way Miss Granby reads aloud to Eliza Wharton and her mother in *The Coquette.* On another day, Mrs. Drinker herself read *The Haunted Priory* but then concluded her diary entry with a long list of the various household chores she had also accomplished "to shew that I have not spent the day reading."[10]

Women often met together to engage jointly in such tasks as sewing or quilting; while the others worked, one member of the group would read aloud—typically from a sentimental novel. Such group reading was often followed by discussions on topics ranging from national politics to local gossip. Not only was the novel thus made a part of the daily life of republican women, but the discourse of fiction was itself made contiguous with or incorporated into their discourse. In effect, then, just as a local scandal was easily fictionalized (a common source for sentimental novels), so, too, might the fiction be readily "scandalized" (that is, transformed by oral discourse and circulated as story). And through the grammar of these simple transformations, the news of the day—fictional, factual—could make its rounds.

Important social matters are reflected in sentimental plots, including the preoccupation with extramarital sex and the social and biological consequences of sexual trangressions. That preoccupation no doubt did not cause, as the critics of the early novel regularly asserted, a sharp rise in illegitimacy. But it is correlated with it. During the revolutionary and postrevolutionary era as many as 30 percent of all first births occurred less than nine months after marriage; the percentage of conceptions prior to or without benefit of matrimony was not equaled again until the present permissive era.[11] Many social authorities were alarmed by that new laxity, and the emerging novel provided them with a convenient scapegoat. I would suggest, however, that the novelist, as much as the professed moralist, simply perceived and addressed an issue of the time. The main difference was that the novelist's critique of illicit sexual behavior often had a feminist import and emphasized the unfortunate consequences of seduction for the individual woman, not the social mores (although these were in the novel, too) against which she had offended.

The sentimental novel also portrayed, frequently in graphic terms, the deaths of many characters in childbirth. Although, then as now, the overall life expectancy for women was higher than for men, every young woman facing marriage also faced the prospect of death in chidlbirth, which did increase woman's mortality rate above men's during prime childbearing years.[12] Julia Cowles was not too busy with her novels and her spinning to note that in 1802, in her small community of Farmington, Connecticut, four women between the ages of twenty and twenty-four had died, and she could not help but identify with them: "Shall I, who am now 17 years of age, live to see that time and leave, as 3 of them did, families? Ah! methinks I shall . . . be cut of[f] in the bloom of my life. . . . And time shall be no longer."[13] Cowles's diction and description come straight from the sentimental novels we retrospectively criticize for their lack of realism.

The lurid portrayal of death in childbirth allegorized what every early American woman already knew. Intercourse begot children and having to bear a child was a mixed blessing. In postrevolutionary America, birth control was still considered immoral, so even though earlier sanctions against premarital sex had waned to a certain extent, the biological realities of pregnancy, then as now, burdened only the newly "liberated" woman and not the long-liberated man, a fact virtually every sentimental novel emphasized (without ever mentioning birth control).[14] And, of course, death in childbirth could come to married and unmarried women alike.

Demographic studies indicate that the *average* number of children born to an American woman in 1800 was an extraordinary 7.04, a number which does not include pregnancies that ended in miscarriage or stillbirth.[15] A typical American woman could thus count on spending virtually all of her mature years bearing and raising children. Fertility was higher in America than in most European countries at the same time, and many a European visitor noted the remarkable change in New World women after marriage. As Alexis de Tocqueville observed, "in America the independence of women is irrecoverably lost in the bonds of marriage."[16] But it did not take de Tocqueville to tell them so. Norton has documented how some of these women described their own condition. One Molly Tilghman wrote of her sister, Henny, in 1788: "She is decidedly *gone* [pregnant] to my great grief, and to her own too." Or Abigail Adams employed another apt metaphor when she noted of a young woman in her family, "it is a sad slavery to have children as fast as she has."[17]

The high fertility rate of the postrevolutionary period is striking, but what is even more striking is the precipitous fall in the rate during the next century. The fertility rate declined by 23 percent before 1850, by 50 percent before 1900.[18] Since no new technologies for preventing births (such as the recent birth control pill) were developed during those years and since prophylactics were certainly known in late eighteenth-century America (and used widely in other countries, notably France), this striking decline in the birthrate reveals a massive change in American social attitudes even within a generation or two. Equally interesting is the fact that relatively few written documents survive to chart the changing social attitude except, perhaps, novels in which a small, intimate family of only three or four children more and more is posited as an ideal. It seems, then, that there was a dramatic shift from an abhorrence of contraception to a widespread but discreet and private reliance on methods of reducing family size. Carl N. Degler further argues that women were primarily responsible for this shift in attitude and that their increasingly asserted control over family size paved the way for greater reform movements at the end of the century. But whatever the causes and consequences, the unprecedented, rapid decline in fertility rates in the nineteenth century was one of the chief indices of women's changing role in family and society.[19]

Another index was the rising literacy and education levels of women. Nor does it seem merely coincidental that fertility rates fell almost 25 percent during the same period in which women's sign literacy rate (according to Kenneth A. Lockridge's data) more than doubled. Demographers chart a surprising correlation between the levels of education and fertility. More educated parents (the mother's education level being especially pertinent) tend to have fewer children.[20] The high correlation between increased female literacy and decreased fertility suggests that education brought with it a sense of control over one's body, over one's role in the reproductive process, and even some control over one's husband. I am not being entirely facetious, therefore, when I suggest that, with its double focus on improving female literacy and controlling sexuality, the sentimental novel may well have been the most effective means of birth control of the time.

By its emphasis on improved female education and its sensationalizing of the dangers of childbearing, the sentimental novel seems intimately linked—as mirror or catalyst or both—to larger social forces at work in the lives of women readers. But what was woman's status in the early years of the Republic, from 1789 to 1820? In almost all the sentimental novels, we see women dominated by larger social and economic forces, controlled by selfish parents, sadistic husbands, or strong-willed seducers. Viewing the typical sentimental novel as a reflection of the society, one must conclude that women were powerless and that the primary relationship between men and women entailed domination, exploitation, appropriation, and abandonment, on the one hand, and submission, appeasement, and other such defensive strategies on the other. Yet just how accurately did these novels reflect the lives of women readers and their relationships to the men in their lives?

As Perry Miller noted, the Revolution gave American legal thinkers a unique opportunity to invent new systems of law and new standards of justice.[21] For the most part, however, the new Republic modestly revised British principles and procedures and did so essentially to maintain the existing power structures of class, race, and gender in America. Marylynn Salmon has shown that most of the legal changes that occurred in America between 1775 and 1800, especially those bearing on women's rights, were "gradual, conservative, and frequently based upon English developments."[22] As American jurist St. George Tucker indicated in his 1803 annotations of *Blackstone's Commentaries,* a cornerstone of English law, American judicial practices preserved the inequities between men and women, particularly the idea that a married woman is a *feme covert* [sic], a hidden woman, whose rights are both absorbed by her husband and subject to her husband's will. Tucker also observed that American women were, de facto and de jure, victims of "taxation without representation; for they pay taxes without having the liberty of voting for representatives." As his very phrasing emphasizes, the Revolution freed America from an oppressive Colonial status, but it had not freed American women from their subservient status. As Tucker summed up the matter, "I fear that there is little reason for a compliment to our laws for their respect and favour to the female sex."[23]

Although the situation varied from state to state and sometimes from case to case, one can make a few generalizations about women's legal status in the new Republic. Before marriage, a young woman was typically considered the property of her father. Sometimes, as Kerber has pointed out, this concept of property could take grotesque forms. For example, in a Connecticut court case of *Samuel Mott* v. *Calvin Goddard* (September 1792), a father was able to sue his daughter's rapist for damages on the grounds that "the plaintiff's daughter and servant," by being made pregnant, had been rendered "unfit for service."[24] Kerber also notes that St. George Tucker was particularly offended by the terms of the proceedings whereby the rapist could be prosecuted only through the legal fiction that the victim's father's property had been irreparably damaged—a holdover from British law and a clear testimony to the woman's primary status as property not as person. In sentimental fiction, too, the unmarried young woman was, for all practical purposes, the property of her father. The common *Clarissa* theme of the avaricious parents who essentially sell their daughter into an economically advantageous marriage was not just an extravagant borrowing from earlier British fiction but was an apt metaphor for the legal status of the postrevolutionary American girl.

It was an apt metaphor for the legal status of republican wives as well. Marriage, for the women involved, was mostly a change in masters. The new bride, ad-mittedly, was to be protected by her husband, and she was protected, so far as the law was concerned, because her rights were subsumed in his. Yet as many legal historians have shown, a wife's status as *feme covert* effectively rendered her legally invisible. With some notable exceptions, the married woman typically lost her property upon marriage. She lost her legal right to make a will or to inherit property beyond the one-third widow's rights which, by common law, fell to her upon her husband's death. For the most part, in 1800, by law and by legal precedent, a married woman's signature had no weight on legal documents and she had no individual legal identity.[25]

As with many key historical issues, there is substantial debate over just how much coverture "actually" limited women's lives. The pioneering women's legal historian, Mary Beard, disputed nineteenth-century feminist reformers who described marriage, in Harriet Martineau's memorable phrase, as the "political nonexistence of women."[26] Beard argued that both the equity courts and common law gave married women far more legal rights than those allowed by Blackstone or codified into the statutes of the different states. Relatively speaking, Beard was right in stressing that equity and common law tended to extend to women some measure of power and control. But one can easily romanticize the degree of equality granted here, and recent studies of equity rulings by Salmon and Norma Basch suggest that Beard may well have been too optimistic in her estimates.[27] For the most part, the nineteenth-century reformers accurately perceived the injustices of coverture. In Basch's summation, "the law created an equation in which one plus one equaled one by erasing the female one." The married women's property acts passed in New York in the mid-nineteenth century (and the result of considerable reformist activity), not only improved women's prospects but provided the locus of further feminist protest by emphasizing that the traditional concept of coverture was a "source of crippling sexual discrimination." The antebellum feminists, Basch continues, were "neither naive nor misguided" in focusing their attack on coverture for that focus "was essential to an exploration of the conflict between motherhood and citizenship [and] the critical first stage in bridging the world of domesticity and the world of politics."[28]

Various commentators of the time emphasized women's legal powerlessness. One of the most eloquent assessments is that of Judge Hertell of New York, who in 1837 argued on behalf of a married woman's rights to retain her own property. Hertell noted that the current marriage laws gave a husband "uncontrolled, indefinite, irresponsible and arbitrary power" over every aspect of his wife's life and subjected her to an "abject state of surveillance to the will, commands, caprices, ill humours, angry passions, and mercenary, avaricious and selfish disposition, conduct and views of her husband." For Judge Hertell, a wife's situation, at least metaphorically and often literally, was comparable to slavery or imprisonment.[29] Cott, Norton, and Kerber have all found repeated statements in private papers of late eighteenth-century women about the privations of marriage; women such as Abigail Adams, diarist Eliza Southgate, Judith Sargent Murray, Susanna Rowson, Mercy Otis Warren, and others all noted that women suffered in life proportionate to the rights they surrendered by law.[30] Even Abigail Adams's request that her husband "Remember the Ladies" in the new Constitution was primarily addressed to the legal and social inequities of married women (rather than a more direct plea for political rights). "Do not put such unlimited power into the hands of the Husbands," she wrote, because "all Men would be tyrants if they could." She counseled her husband to "put it out of the power of the vicious and the Lawless to use us with cruelty and indignity with impunity."[31] Abigail Adams's prediction is starkly substantiated by a private complaint in verse by Grace Growden Galloway, the wife of politician Joseph Galloway:

> . . . I am Dead
> Dead to each pleasing thought each Joy of
>   Life
> Turn'd to that heavy lifeless lump a wife.[32]

The flat despair of that declaration of dependence and defeat anticipates writers such as Sylvia Plath or Ann Sexton, and emphasizes the debilitating potentialities inherent in the system of coverture.

Mrs. Galloway's private complaint remained private in her lifetime. It is now more acceptable for a woman to speak the woe that is marriage, especially her own, but it is now also more acceptable for a woman to remove herself from that same marriage. In the late eighteenth-century colonies, however, and also in the new Republic, divorce, for most women, was simply not an option. As a result of a British ruling, Colonial divorce bills were effectively rescinded in the decade preceding the Revolution. Pennsylvania and New York, for example, granted no divorces during the prerevolutionary era. Not until 1785 in Pennsylvania and 1787 in New York could any foundering marriage be officially dissolved. Maryland granted its first absolute divorce in 1790. There was, furthermore, a good deal of variation from state to state. In South Carolina, absolute divorces were not allowed until 1949 (although legal separations could be granted there by Courts of Chancery).[33] What was universal, however, was a declared, public, official abhorrence for divorce, and both social pressures and legal practice insisted on the sanctity of marriage. For example, until well into the next century, women were granted divorces only if they could prove extreme physical abuse and their own total innocence. Consequently, a "guilty" woman, whether confirmed adulteress or occasional shrew,

was often denied a court hearing. The impasse was early dramatized in Gilbert Imlay's sentimental novel, *The Emigrants* (1793), which was apparently written with some help from his lover, Mary Wollstonecraft, and is essentially a fictionalized tract in favor of divorce. As Imlay notes in his preface, "I have no doubt but the main misfortunes which daily happen in domestic life, and which too often precipitate women of the most virtuous inclinations into the gulf of ruin, proceed from the great difficulty there is . . . of obtaining a divorce."[34]

Women's restricted status within marriage (and the corresponding restrictions on divorce) presumed a patriarchal domestic order often breached during the Revolutionary War years when many American women were suddenly forced to survive without the economic assistance or legal protection of a husband. As numerous historians have demonstrated, the War ambiguously emphasized to women both their private capability and their public powerlessness. Thousands of women during the war suddenly became responsible for running a family business or for continuing the operations of a family farm. Those women, of course, were still also responsible for the array of household manufacture essential for survival in the rural market economy. Extant letters indicate that sometimes a conscientious husband might write home giving his wife advice on how to manage complex business or agricultural operations, but there was little he could actually do while he was away fighting and there was always the possibility of his death. Women managed, as they have managed during all wars, to keep the economy going, surreptitiously circumventing their lack of legal rights, often to their financial detriment. Many learned firsthand the shackles law placed upon them, as wives and also as widows. In most states, women could not legally inherit property or businesses. The assumption that they could not manage, at odds with the fact that they did, was rendered even more ridiculous when destitution at home followed the husband's death in the war. Only through extralegal maneuverings by widowed women and their male kin could the law's clear intent—property was to be controlled by men—sometimes be subverted.[35]

Having demonstrated their capability in the face of a national emergency, many women in the postwar years felt that they had fully earned those new rights and responsibilities which they had exercised, de facto, already. The new Constitution, however, did nothing to acknowledge women's contribution to the war effort. In only one state, New Jersey, and only briefly, were propertied women (black and white) granted the vote. That enfranchisement was unusual enough that newspapers as far away as Boston reported on women voting in local New Jersey elections.[36] Equal pay was not even an issue; it was assumed that women would earn less. Technically, a woman factory worker could not even collect her earnings without a man's signature (although this restriction may not have been widely enforced). Not until the end of the nineteenth century could a woman serve on a jury or, concomitantly, be tried by a jury at least partly of her peers. Married or single, she had virtually no rights within society and no visibility within the political operations of government, except as a symbol of that government—Columbia or Minerva or Liberty.

As one immediate consequence of the Revolution, the family and, more particularly, woman's role in the family became a matter of considerable social concern. There is almost a natural tendency, after any war, to seek within domesticity some release from what might be termed a postmartial letdown. The comfort and safety of hearth and home are welcomed, by women as well as men, after the dangers of battle, the chaos of war. There is something comforting in seeing that much of the old order survived. Consequently, Sally the Shopkeeper, like her latter-day daughter, Rosie the Riveter, soon found her new occupation gone and was obliged to return to her old one—tending house and husband and raising children to repeople the Republic.

Typically, too, after the War of Independence, some women were reluctant to relinquish the freedoms that they had gained while men were occupied elsewhere and otherwise. As a poem published in the *Massachusetts Magazine, or Monthly Museum* in 1794 proclaims:

> No ties shall perplex me, no fetters shall
>   bind,
> That innocent freedom that dwells in my
>   mind.
> At liberty's spring such draughts I've
>   imbib'd,
> That I hate all the doctrines of wedlock
>   prescrib'd.[37]

Or as another anonymous poem published the following year in the *Philadelphia Minerva* declares:

> Man boasts the noble cause
> Nor yields supine to laws
> Tyrants ordain;
> Let Woman have a share
> Nor yield to slavish fear,
> Her equal rights declare,
> And Well Maintain[38]

The diction has gone from post-Freneau to pre-Emerson, but the sentiments remain the same. A spirit of "woman's rights" was felt throughout postrevolutionary America, celebrated by some, derided by others.

Certain demographics of the time contributed to this strain of female independence. Studies of Massachusetts and Pennsylvania suggest that the number of unmarried and never-married women increased, as would be expected, in the postwar era. Many men had died in the war, leaving widows behind. Records show that a number of these widows (perhaps at least partly to circumvent legal problems arising from not being able to inherit their husband's land or business) quickly remarried, sometimes to relatives of the deceased husband, sometimes to men considerably younger than themselves, thus further depleting the pool of men available to a young woman reaching marriageable age.[39] But despite the surplus of unmarried women in the late eighteenth century, spinsterhood hardly embodied a respectable option in the society of the time. On the contrary, the spinster was an object of pervasive cultural ridicule. As we see in the plots of numerous sentimental novels, the specter of spinsterhood drove more than one sentimental heroine into the arms of a seducer. Eliza Wharton is merely one case in point, a case that I will subsequently consider in some detail. For the present, suffice to say that when, at the age of thirty-seven, she finally yielded to her seducer's blandishments, she knew exactly what she was doing, and so did many readers of the time who obviously sympathized with her plight.

The sentimental novel as a form mediated between (and fluctuated between) the hopes of a young woman who knew that her future would be largely determined by her marriage and her all-too-well-founded fears as to what her new status might entail—the legal liabilities of the *feme covert,* the threat of abandonment, the physical realities of repetitive pregnancy, and the danger of an early death during childbirth. Many republican women expressed deep reservations about marriage. "I keep my name still," Betsey Mayhew wrote to her good friend Pamela Dwight Sedgwick in 1782, "I think it is a good one and am determined not to change it without a prospect of some great advantage." Somewhat less hard headed but no less ambivalent was Sarah Hanschurst: "I often Run over in my mind, the many Disadvantages that Accrue to our Sex from an Alliance with the other," she wrote to her friend Sally Forbes, but "the thought of being Do[o]med to live alone I cant yet Reconcile . . . [T]he Appeallation of old Made . . . I don't believe one our Sex wou'd voluntarily Bare."[40] Or in the literature of the time, Mrs. Carter, in Charles Brockden Brown's *Alcuin,* can paraphrase Mary Wollstonecraft and insist that marriage is a vital institution "founded on free and mutual consent" and one that "cannot exist without friendship" or "without personal fidelity." For her, "as soon as the union ceases to be spontaneous it ceases to be just." Yet that idealistic portrait must be set against her own earlier description not of marriage as it should be but marriage as it too often was in America. The married woman "will be most applauded when she smiles with the most perseverance on her oppressor, and when, with the undistinguishing attachment of a dog, no caprice or cruelty shall be able to estrange her affection." Carter's final pronouncement on the role of women in marriage anticipates that of Judge Hertell: "Females are slaves."[41]

As any number of public and private documents attest, marriage was a crucial matter for women of the time. Just as they knew and differently adumbrated the central question in their lives, so, too, did the authors of the fictions they read, fictions that were primarily sentimental. That last literary adjective carries, in contemporary discourse, a heavy load of negative connotations and suggests self-indulgent fantasies bearing little relationship to real life. Yet the private and nonfictional commentaries of the time suggest a contiguity between the sociology of the early American family and the plots of the sentimental novel that is easily overlooked by the contemporary reader. Indeed, the seemingly melodramatic death with which so many of the sentimental novels end both fictionalizes and thematicizes the seriousness of the woman's questions raised in the plot. Given the political and legal realities of the time, the lack of birth control, the high fertility rate, and the substantial chances of death at an early age, many of the readers fared no better than did their most unfortunate fictional sisters.

The sentimental novel spoke far more directly to the fears and expectations of its original readers than our retrospective readings generally acknowledge. Conveniently divorcing the novel from the social milieu in which it was originally written and read, recent critics easily condemn as clichéd and overdone the plight of the assailed, sentimental heroine hovering momentously between what seems a mechanical fall (seduction), on the one hand, and an automatic salvation (marriage), on the other. Yet for her and her reader the choice was desperate. Moreover, if the right decision would not necessarily assure her happiness, the wrong one would guarantee suffering in abundance. So the contemporary critic literalizes and thereby trivializes what the contemporaneous reader took symbolically and thus seriously.

Style, too, has changed since the late eighteenth century, and the language of sentiment interposes itself between the modern reader and the eighteenth-century text. In our lean and antirhetorical time, the very excesses of the novel's sentimental "effusions" (a term derogatory in our vocabulary, not theirs) call the sentiments thereby expressed into question. Yet other discourse of the time employs much the same language as does the early American novel. Consider, for example, the courtship correspondence of John and Abigail Adams as represented by the following excerpt from a 1764 letter from John (signing himself Lysander) to Abigail (Diana):

You who have always softened and warmed my Heart, shall restore my Benevolence as well as my Health and Tranquility of mind. You shall polish and refine my sentiments of Life and manners, banish all the unsocial and ill-natured particles in my Composition, and form me to that happy Temper, that can reconcile a quick Discernment with a perfect Candour.[42]

Harrington himself could not have said it more sentimentally. As Jane Tompkins has recently reminded us, contemporary tastes and values applied indiscriminately to older literature may illuminate contemporary tastes and values but say little about the literature itself.[43]

Addressed to young female readers, the first novels performed vital functions within their society and did so more than parallel vehicles such as sermons or advice books. The most important of these functions in my view was the reappropriating of choice. "Seduction," at first glance, implies female powerlessness; nevertheless, by reading about a female character's good or bad decisions in sexual and marital matters, the early American woman could vicariously enact her own courtship and marriage fantasies. She could, at least in those fantasies, view her life as largely the consequence of her own choices and not merely as the product of the power of others in her life—the father's authority, the suitor's (honorable or dishonorable) guile, the husband's control. Thematicizing, then, the necessity of informed choice, these fictions championed the cause of female education that they typically proclaimed in their prefaces. Weighed in that balance, many of the novels of the time are not the frothy fictions that we commonly take them to be, but evince, instead, a solid social realism that also constitutes a critique (even if sometimes covert) of the patriarchal structure of that society. Thus, if many early novels end unhappily, it may be because they acknowledge the sad reality of marriage for many women. As Catherine Maria Sedgwick wryly notes in her story "Old Maids" (1835), it is best to conclude a story with the wedding if one wants to end on a happy day, for "it is not probable another will succeed it."[44]

Other forms of literature in the new Republic also specifically addressed the woman reader, most notably a wealth of advice literature often penned by clergymen. But this literature usually referred women more to the kitchen and the nursery than to the study or the library. Only in fiction would the average early woman reader encounter a version of her world existing for her sake, and, more important, only in the sentimental novel would her reading about this world be itself validated. As an added bonus, in not a few of these novels, women readers encountered women characters whose opinions mattered. Numerous sentimental novels, beginning with the first one, took time out from the main seduction plot to show women discussing politics, law, philosophy, and history—those same arenas of discourse from which the woman reader was often excluded. As Rachel M. Brownstein has recently observed, such reading, for women, serves crucial functions:

> Recognizing the problems and the conventions of a woman-centered novel, the reader feels part of a community and tradition of women who talk well about their lives and link them, by language, to larger subjects. Looking up from a novel about a girl's settling on a husband and a destiny so as to assert higher moral and aesthetic laws and her own alliance with them, the reader can feel the weight of her woman's life as serious, can see her own self as shapely and significant.[45]

A *feme covert,* a hidden woman, the early American reader had even greater motivation than the contemporary woman reader to find books that rendered her life, in fiction if not in fact, significant.

Sentimental Fiction as Social Commentary

Given a married woman's status as *feme covert,* many late eighteenth-century readers (particularly women readers) were, understandably, vitally concerned with marriage and strove to educate or otherwise prepare themselves to make a good choice in marriage. Questions of the importance and nature of the family and woman's role within the family were widely debated. As recent historians such as Degler, Kerber, and Norton, as well as Jay Fliegelman, Philip Greven, and Michael Zuckerman have pointed out, with considerable differences in emphasis or interpretation, there was in the eighteenth century at least a theoretical concern with reforming patriarchal structures. It has also been argued that some substantial changes did occur in the daily family life of Americans in the new Republic. Amorphous psychosociological shifts such as an emerging ideal of affectional marriage (rather than patriarchal authority and wifely subordination), a relaxing of parental control over one's offspring (especially in the matter of choosing marriage partners), an increased substitution of affection for authority in the dealings between parents and children, and a new emphasis on the mother's responsibility for imparting to her children both knowledge and principles of virtue have all been traced to the last part of the eighteenth century. All such changes, it has been further argued, became still more institutionalized in the next century through industrialization and the increasing gender specialization within the family. With the father cast as the primary wage earner and more and more employed away from the home, the mother, even if she also worked for wages, was deemed responsible for childrearing and household management.[46]

The extent and nature as well as the consequent implications of large changes in the family raise issues that simply do not admit definitive historical assessments. Did women, despite few advancements in political and legal rights, achieve a new domestic status that testified to an egalitarian impulse in the society as a whole, or was that new domestic status intended to tell a wife that she had none elsewhere and that her place was in the home? The very terms with which the question is posed invite a reading of the historian's personal predilections as much as of the historical record. Nor did the commentators of the time, unhindered or unhelped by any historical perspective, deal any more conclusively with the same question. Yet we can observe that the impetus of change was both proved and problemized by a wealth of advice literature that debated questions of domesticity, questions, not coincidentally, much debated in the early novel.

The sentimental novel, in particular, was generically suited to addressing, in detail, the range of ideological assessments of the family and the implications *for women* of different visions of what the family should be. Furthermore, since the sentimental novel focused almost exclusively on young women standing virtually on the doorstep of definitive marriage choices, it necessarily dramatized the grounds on which the final crucial step was taken. What qualities, in her, would promote a happy match? In him? How should she best be schooled to cultivate the former and to perceive the latter? Would a purely domestic course of training or formal schooling best foster her husband's future happiness? And hers as well? More specifically, and this was a major question of the day, did education enhance or impede a woman's chance of making a suitable match and, correspondingly, did education alter her expectations of what a good marriage should be? Was she to be the submissive helpmeet or the equal partner? Was she to be motivated mostly by duty or desire? What other questions should she be asking? To whom could she best turn for advice—suitors, friends, or parents? All such questions were extensively discussed in the didactic advice literature of the time, but they were worked out in far more detail and by example in the sentimental novels.

The didactic literature on the role of women tended to be divided into two highly polarized camps. The more prevalent of these, the conservative or traditional position, relied especially on the Biblical story of Eve's ordained subservient status to argue the justice of God and man's established ways with women. The opposing view, "equalitarian feminism" to use Cott's phrase, or the "group consciousness" movement, which took place between 1770 and 1800, admitted women's "shared weakness relative to men" but questioned "whether this weakness was natural or artificial, biological or cultural."[47] And if women's supposed "natural inferiority" were really imposed by custom and culture, then, the argument implicitly and often explicitly ran, it could largely be remedied through an equal or at least improved education. As we shall see, specific sentimental novels took up one or the other side of this debate, but at either pole, the need to portray with some recognizable validity the social conditions of the young women who might read a particular novel subtly altered its reading of her actual and ideal case.

Three writers—Jean-Jacques Rousseau, James Fordyce, and John Gregory—best represent the conservative or traditional view of the role of women. Although not American, they were each exceptionally popular in America. Both Rousseau's *Emile* and Gregory's *A Father's Legacy to His Daughters* (1774) were American best-sellers in 1775, and both, along with Fordyce's *Sermons to Young Women* (1765), were widely published and read in America in the postrevolutionary era.[48] In these three books, to summarize briefly, women were portrayed as naturally subservient within the family, and each author also argued that education made a woman less submissive and thus less appealing. In *Emile,* for example, the great French republican philosopher heaps contempt upon any woman who might believe that the new radicalism and egalitarianism somehow includes her. For Rousseau, any social contract between man and woman must be premised on her natural inferiority. Thus her necessary subordination in all matters, domestic and social.[49] Before marriage, maidens were to be chaste and retiring, rarely seen and seldom heard. After marriage, wives were to efface themselves in perpetual attendance on their husbands' needs and desires. Such service, moreover, should come naturally, and education, Rousseau argued, destroyed a woman's natural charm and equable disposition, thereby rendering her unfit to fulfill her chief function of happily bringing happiness to others. The Reverend James Fordyce and Dr. John Gregory popularized similar views. In *Sermons to Young Women,* Fordyce maintained that a woman's most important function was to serve and please her man, while Dr. Gregory asserted that such traits as vitality and spirit were unfeminine, unfashionable, and unattractive. He insisted that only a languishing, pallid passivity would attract a potential husband and repeatedly lays the blame for any domestic disharmony on woman's natural selfishness and vanities along with any unnatural and necessarily unrealistic education.

Books by Rousseau, Fordyce, Gregory, and other similar social theorists were widely read and discussed in postrevolutionary America; their ideas were paraphrased and promulgated in dozens of essays that appeared in newspapers and magazines. One representative sample of this social theory in the popular culture-advice column mode is "From a Mother to Her Daughter, Just on the Point of Marriage," from the *Boston Weekly Magazine* of 1804. The bride-to-be is counseled:

> You have a father, whose mild and beneficient exercise of authority must have taught you to wish, that your husband may possess all the prerogatives, which all laws, divine and human, have given him in the headship of his own house, and to remove far from you, every desire of degrading, much more of endeavoring to make him contemptible by any efforts to usurp his place yourself.

The young lady should have no problem; all her life has been a study in her subservient status. But even more conservative, or perhaps merely more explicit, is another piece, "Woman; An Apologue," from a different 1804 issue of the same paper:

> Women were created to be the companions of man, to please him, to solace him in his miseries, to console him in his sorrows, and not to partake with him the fatigue of war, of the sciences, and of government. Warlike women, learned women, and women who are politicians, equally abandon the circle which nature and institutions have traced round their sex; they convert themselves into men. . . . And, besides, where is the feeling and amiable woman who would exchange the ineffable happiness of being loved for the unsubstantial pleasure of fame?[50]

Fame, for a woman, is by definition (gender definition), unfeminine, infamous.

A few writers of sentimental novels championed this conservative view of woman's proper place and function. In Helena Wells's *Constantia Neville; or, The West Indian* (1800), for example, Mrs. Hayman patiently endures all the abuses heaped upon her by a cruel and loutish husband.[51] The more she suffers from the accepted status quo, the more she affirms it. Even while engaged in such tasks as raising her husband's illegitimate offspring (there are apparently several), Mrs. Hayman lectures the readers on the joys of being a dutiful wife. But when it comes to marital bliss there are singularly few objective correlatives in this novel. The protagonist can claim that she is content, but contemporary readers (in the unlikely event that the book might reach them—it was never reprinted) would doubtless reach a different verdict. Similarly, in S.S.B.K. Wood's *Amelia; or, The Influence of Virtue* (1802) the protagonist struggles to provide a "useful lesson" in submissive wifehood. Obeying the deathbed request of her adopted mother, Amelia marries Sir William Stanly only to learn that Sir William still loves another. Too sentimental a heroine to grant him a divorce, Amelia must accommodate herself to her husband's extended affair with the other woman. Through all, Amelia endures—virtuous, innocent, patient, perfect, and quite unappreciated. Like Mrs. Hayman, she even takes on the task of raising her husband's illegitimate child. As Wood assures us,

Amelia "was not a disciple or pupil of Mary Woolstonecraft [sic]. . . . She was an old fashioned wife and she meant to obey her husband: she meant to do her duty in the strictest sense of the word. To perform it cheerfully would perhaps be painful, but . . . it would most assuredly be best."[52]

This passage humorously epitomizes the contradictions that underlie the conservative sentimental novels. Both Mrs. Hayman and Amelia submit to all that is required of them. But given women's official status of the time, they really had little alternative. The fiction, in short, attempted to valorize a choice, where, according to that same fiction, there was none. The very form of the medium, too, worked against the message it was assigned to convey. Whereas a tract might extoll the virtues of submission in the face of all trials, a novel must *create* trials to which a dedicated heroine then virtuously submits. But those trials fully visualized give us not an inspiring icon of feminine virtue but a perturbing portrait of the young wife as perpetual victim. The tract can lecture in the abstract, but the conservative novel, portraying through concrete example, evokes (quite inappropriately for its own rhetorical purposes) the legal, social, and political status of the average female reader, and that reader is not apt to applaud the tortured image of her own condition. I would also suggest that fictions such as *Amelia* and *Constantia Neville* set forth the sad truths of many women's lives in the late eighteenth century more tellingly than did the overtly reformist novels. As heroines, Amelia and Mrs. Hayman are, ultimately, inescapably, failures—even if they do eventually receive some compensatory reward (i.e., heaven, authorial approval, etc.) They are failures because their stories deny any cult of ideal domesticity far more convincingly than their commentary affirms it. Indeed, and on an elementary level, the infidelities of the husbands suggest a breakdown of the family, a breakdown the wives are powerless to prevent. The heroines' suffering may be chaste, but it is also banal, even ignominious, and suggests that both wives would have done better if they (or their parents) had chosen more wisely. The novels end up inadvertently advocating the need for better female education and for greater female self-sufficiency, which is precisely what they set out to deny.

The sentimental plot simply would not serve the objectives which the conservative writers had drafted it to advance. Women, of course, could be portrayed as innately inferior to men; weak in body, mind, and spirit; needing guidance, counsel, a controlling hand. Marriage could be cast as the one proper refuge, after the father's home, from the dangers of the wide, wide world. Yet if the wife was protected by a caring husband, her wants essentially the same as his and his the same as hers, where then was woman's subservient status? Somehow her haven also had to be at least

in part or in potentiality her hell—or who was marriage for? That contradiction could neither be resolved nor glossed over but served instead to indict—to deconstruct—the very theory of domesticity that regularly led the conservative sentimental novel to this impasse. So Helena Wells, in *The Step-Mother; a Domestic Tale, from Real Life* (1799), for example, can urge her readers "to think of *man* as a *lord* and *master,* from whose *will* there is no appeal."[53] Thinking of not thinking; willed will-lessness; the appeal of the unappealing: The duplicity of the advice highlights the tyranny it would explain away, invokes the very appeal that it would deny, and since that appeal cannot be carried to a higher court (lord and master), God's ways to women are pointedly called into question. Simply put, this counsel for total defeat necessarily carries its own cry for radical revolution.

Interestingly enough, the most consistently conservative of the sentimental writers, S.S.B.K. Wood, seems to have practiced in her own life a more liberated philosophy than she promulgated in her fiction. There is, first, the obvious fact of her writing career. There is also the curious matter of Wood's tribute in the dedication to *Julia, and the Illuminated Baron* (1800) to "Constantia," who is none other than Judith Sargent Murray, the most vocal proponent of the equalitarian feminist position in early America.[54] That reference makes one wonder if the contradiction the modern reader discovers in Wood's portrayal of the submissive helpmeet is perhaps grounded partly in the ambivalence of the author and not just in the recalcitrance of the form.

Judith Sargent Murray, more than any other single American writer, represents the equalitarian position. Her *Gleaner* essays were published serially, republished in a collected edition that attracted nearly seven hundred subscribers, and were pirated (in whole or part) dozens of times in the 1790s.[55] Through their subject matter alone, these essays, dealing with such disparate topics as military strategy, the new Constitution, political philosophy, or legal reform attest to at least one woman's wide-ranging intelligence and her readiness to address cogently issues ostensibly beyond woman's ken. The most persistent topic of the *Gleaner* pieces, however, is closer to home but no less radical in its import and implications. Murray regularly advocated the need for better female education and argued the relationship between such education and greater independence. She also stressed the importance of female education for fulfilling the traditional role of wife and mother but noted, too, that "marriage should not be presented as a sumum bonum [sic]." For Murray, education would serve a woman in whatever state she happened to find herself. "The term *helpless widow,*" for example, "might be rendered as unfrequent and inapplicable as that of *helpless widower.*"[56] In one important essay, "On the Equality of the Sexes," Murray argued that if women lacked the same power of reason and judgment exhibited by men, it was only because they also lacked the proper training in those skills. Following Locke, she maintained that "we can only reason from what we know and if an opportunity for acquiring knowledge hath been denied us, the inferiority of our sex cannot fairly be deduced from thence."[57] Certain that education would bring advancement, Murray even predicted, "I expect to see our young women forming a new era in female history."[58]

Best known as an essayist, Murray was also an author of sentimental fiction. Most notable for my purposes is her novella, *Story of Margaretta* (1798), in which she reformulated the role of the sentimental heroine by revising that heroine's educational preparation for the role. In her essays, Murray had advocated that natural philosophy, astronomy, mathematics, geography, and history be taught along with such traditionally feminine subjects as painting, needlepoint, French, and piano playing. This is the curriculum set for the protagonist in *Story of Margaretta,* a work instructive, as Murray intended, in several different senses.

Margaretta Melworth begins her career as a sentimental heroine somewhat unthinking in her actions and apparently destined for disaster. Fortunately, however, she encounters a sagacious woman who teaches her that education is necessary for any woman who would answer sensibly the one question posed to almost all sentimental heroines: Whom shall I marry? This emphasis on education, often promised in the prefatory statements, is rarely so carefully executed as it is in Murray's plot. Because she gains some education, Margaretta escapes the standard sentimental role of the helpless victim of fate, fate typically taking the form of a designing man whose machinations the innocent heroine simply cannot decipher. Schooled to weigh the worth of various propositions and proposals, Margaretta has no problem disposing of those who are found wanting, especially an ominously named suitor (and would-be seducer), Sinisterus Courtland, who is, she later discovers, already married and the father of three children. With equal good judgment she chooses Edward Hamilton, and everything in the novel suggests that their union will be one of "mutual affection." That promised reward for female perspicacity is a powerful argument in favor of just such capability and also a not-so-covert suggestion that, in the schoolroom and the home, many women were being sadly short-changed.

Judith Sargent Murray was herself apparently inspired by the ideas and examples of other female philosophers, including Aphra Behn (1640-89), Mary Astell (1666-1731), Lady Mary Wortley Montagu (1689-1762), and, most specifically, Catharine Macaulay (1731-91), one of the finest historians and social philosophers of the late eighteenth century and the author

of the feminist *Letters on Education* (1790), a work advocating views on education similar to Murray's. Macaulay, incidentally, was widely known in the New World. As Dale Spender notes, she visited America in order to see and judge for herself the promise of the new country and she maintained an active correspondence with George Washington throughout the revolutionary period. Macaulay's inspiration can also be seen in the work of a number of other American feminists such as Abigail Adams, diarist Eliza Southgate, and the anonymous "Female Advocate," all of whom linked feminist reform with the promise implicit in the new republican form of government.[59]

For the earlier writers, however, and for Murray, too, feminist reform could best begin in the family. Women's greater domestic equality could then pave the way to larger forms of equality as well. As we see in *Story of Margaretta,* education allows for a rational choice of a good husband who believes in affection and not in wifely deference. Because Margaretta has proved herself to be both virtuous and wise, she *deserves* a larger role in the home and in society, and, conversely, because America is young and virtuous, it *needs* women like Margaretta. The implicit assumption here is that virtuous women will be rewarded; the governing term *virtue* has simply been redefined and the scope of the expected reward expanded to include not just a good marriage but greater legal and political power, too. In short, Murray does not share Mary Wollstonecraft's suspicion that oppressive systems are systematically and designedly so. She believes that the goodwill latent in the existing order might become the lever whereby that same order could be moved to be more just and fair.

If Wollstonecraft seems to have been the more perceptive of the two, Murray was still on firmer ground than were such advocates of social radicalism as Thomas Paine, Montesquieu, and Condorcet, all of whom expressed far less concern with women's continuing domestic subservience than with her coming political emancipation as part of a revolutionary reordering of society at large.[60] Somehow, these men seemed to assume, we could achieve the latter without altering the former. In contrast to that self-serving contradiction, we see a dilemma of the sentimental reformers, all of whom were going to alter the former without affecting the latter. The changes proposed by the reforming novelists turn out to be largely grounded in the old order, and what is advocated is a readjustment of the marriage contract rather than a second revolution led by "the Ladies."

Only a few novels significantly questioned received ideas as to woman's place. Fewer still disputed the sanctity of the sexual double standard, and even those did so with a measure of ambivalence. In James Butler's *Fortune's Foot-ball: or, The Adventures of Mercutio*

(1797), one woman character rails against the "tyrannical custom" which forbids women to make advances towards the men they might like. "How peculiarly hard that woman's situation, who possessing the most unadulterated passion . . . must, in obedience to an arbitrary custom, linger out her days in the most excruciating torture."[61] But after eight months of an illicit and apparently guilt-free relationship, the young woman dies at sea while her lover escapes to other adventures and liaisons. Conversely, but not altogether differently, Laura, in Leonora Sansay's 1809 novel of the same name, lives with Belfield without benefit of matrimony but then, after his death, her harrowing illness, and a bout of insanity, she meets a man with whom (so the novel portends) she might enjoy an egalitarian (and, this time, legal) match. And the double sexual standard is pointedly and overtly challenged by Gilbert Imlay, who argues in *The Emigrants* that men and women should be allowed the same sexual rights, including the right to divorce.[62] But Imlay does not envision female freedoms beyond sexual freedom, and his female characters are often Rousseauisticly passive helpmeets.

A few other novels also call into question the social program of the double standard. The title character of Sukey Vickery's *Emily Hamilton* observes "that the world has been too rigid, much too rigid, as respects the female sex," and at one point ironically argues that if we must accept the "assertion" (derived, she notes, from *Pamela*) that "reformed rakes make the best husbands" then "might it not be said with equal justice, that if a certain description of females were reformed, they would make the best wives?"[63] Or in the anonymous *Adventures of Jonathan Corncob, Loyal American Refugee* (1787) and in William Hill Brown's *Ira and Isabella,* minor women characters enjoy sexual freedom, but it is difficult to determine if these "loose women" serve as vehicles for or objects of an indiscriminate satire. For the most part, those who noted that the traditional double standard was unfair still had, when it came to sexual affairs, nothing else to put in its place.

No early American novelist went as far as Mary Wollstonecraft in reevaluating the political and sexual roles of women. Her *A Vindication of the Rights of Woman* (1792) was the single most important theoretical contribution to the egalitarian cause. Printed in America in 1792 and reprinted in 1794, the book persuasively advocated the justice of women's equality in matters social, political, and sexual.[64] Quantitative studies of the period indicate that Wollstonecraft's feminist tract was available from some 30 percent of the libraries in America (based on a controlled sample of libraries whose records still exist) during its first years in print, and the fact that it had its own American printing and reprinting similarly attests to its popularity.[65] Moreover, the *Vindication* appears in advertisements bound in the back of early American novels more often than any other philosophical tract (suggesting that publishers perceived that readers of novels might be predisposed to purchase this feminist book).

Like Montesquieu and Condorcet, Wollstonecraft argued that no society can call itself free unless it grants equality to both sexes. But more than either of the male social theorists, Mary Wollstonecraft focused on the usual workings of the matrimonial bond, on the biased nature of the social contract between the sexes, and on the freedoms women lost in order for men to be still more free. She did not reject marriage. On the contrary, she praised domestic union as humanity's highest state, but only if redefined as a partnership of equals, based on mutual affection and respect. Furthermore, unlike Murray and other American reformers, Wollstonecraft knew full well that marriage could not be restructured unless the society, too, was restructured. In the *Vindication,* she pointedly and systematically refutes the social vision promulgated by Rousseau, Fordyce, and Gregory, and she proposes an alternative organization in which men and women would have the same social and political privileges and would be allowed the same legal freedoms as well as freedom of movement, freedom of personal expression, and freedom of sexual expression.

Many Americans were intrigued by the promise implicit in Wollstonecraft's radicalism, but many others found her vision extremely threatening and labored to countermand it. For example, an article entitled "Rights to Woman" in the *New England Palladium* of 1802 portrayed a "Mary Wolstoncraft [*sic*] Godwin" sitting on a throne-like chair surrounded by a host of adoring women and a few quisling men. Arrogant, silly, and ugly, this parodic Wollstonecraft lectures her assembled audience on nature versus nurture and is especially convinced that, given the right physical conditioning, women can even be as strong as men. Her diatribe concludes when "the lady herself says, women are entitled to all the rights of men, and are capable of assuming the character of *manly women*."[66] This was a common refutation of Wollstonecraftism—it would make women manly, with bulging muscles and hair sprouting in inappropriate places, a metamorphosis to be avoided at all cost.

Wollstonecraft's ideas were all the more suspect when viewed in the lurid light that her life seemed to cast on her feminist philosophy. After she died of septicemia following the birth of her and William Godwin's daughter, a child conceived out of wedlock, Godwin published *Memoirs of the Author of "A Vindication of The Rights of Woman"* (1798). Intended to celebrate the strength and independence of Wollstonecraft's life and philosophy (which, Godwin insisted, changed much of his own thinking), the published memoirs, to say the least, fell far short of that objective. Not that the book failed to gain notice; it was translated almost immediately into French and German and was published in America in 1799 and again in 1804. Everywhere the reaction to the work was immediately and violently negative. Reviewers did not praise Wollstonecraft's unconventional thought but condemned her unconventional life. Her different affairs and her suicide attempts were read as a total refutation of her philosophy, so much so that Godwin attempted, in a second edition, to play down the damning evidence of Wollstonecraft's illicit relationships with other men. But it was too late. Once the *Memoirs* was published, Wollstonecraft was no longer a heroic "female Werter" [*sic*] (his term) or a challenging social thinker; she became, instead, an object lesson on the dangers of feminist ideas and ideals—as if a woman could not live in the world she advocated but had no problems in the one she opposed. Thus the *European Magazine* prophesied that the *Memoirs* would be read "with disgust by every female who has any pretensions to delicacy; with detestation by every one attached to the interests of religion and morality; and with indignation by any one who might feel any regard for the unhappy woman, whose frailties should have been buried in oblivion." Or the *Anti-Jacobin Review* not only railed against the impropriety of her life, but, in its index, listed under the heading "Prostitution" the cross reference, "See Mary Wollstone-craft." The *Memoirs* were thereby translated into a compelling argument for the status quo, and Wollstonecraftism (a word originally used to designate the equalitarian feminist movement) became a damning label for the loose feminine morals in which libertarian principles, ostensibly, necessarily ended.[67]

The life and death of Mary Wollstonecraft, thus interpreted, demonstrated how radical life imitated conservative art and thereby validated the social vision of the most reactionary of early American sentimental tales with their plots of aberrant female crime and consequent female punishment. Transformed from a feminist social theorist and philosopher into a fallen sentimental heroine, a woman who had loved badly and necessarily lost, Wollstonecraft, like many other female protagonists, provided merely another admonitory example of the downward path to sexual disgrace and dishonorable death. The parallels between this reading of her life and standard plots are obvious. Essentially, had she never asserted her own freedom, the whole tragedy could have been avoided. Here, especially, was a woman too capable for her own good, one who desperately required a father's, a husband's constraining hand. There are even the requisite hints of the happiness that might have been hers when, after a few preliminary and necessarily abortive affairs that drove her to attempted suicide, she meets the man she can truly love and finds him as ready to love her. But even here a fatal weakness undoes her.

She dies bearing the baby conceived out of wedlock, leaving him to mourn for some forty years his loss—and hers—before death claims him, too. Even better, a subsequent generation could read in the fate of Wollstonecraft's first daughter further proof of the mother's folly. In 1816, when Fanny Imlay, the illegitimate daughter of Wollstonecraft and Gilbert Imlay, discovered belatedly the sad facts of her own beginning, she took her life, leaving only a note to the world in which she described herself as "one whose birth was unfortunate," as sentimental an epilogue to a sentimental tale as anything a Mrs. Wood or a Mrs. Wells could ever conceive.

If even one of the most brilliant and independent women of the era could be so subject to the various ills that seduced female flesh was heir to—abandonment, temporary insanity, attempted suicide, death in childbirth, enduring infamy, and the suicide of an illegitimate daughter—how could the average American woman reader hope for a different outcome if she should venture the same perilous journey? Considering the referential powers attributed to texts in the late eighteenth century, it was tempting to "read" the *Memoirs* as the punishment meted out for the ideas promulgated in the *Vindication*. Justice had been done, and the very questions that Wollstonecraft was determined to pose had been, so far as her society was concerned, definitively answered. The *Memoirs* was further compromised by its timing, published during the violence of the French Revolution, which was viewed as a case study on the largest public level for all that was wrong with Wollstonecraftism or other such radical thinking, just as the author's life was viewed as her own refutation on a private and personal level. After 1799, virtually every portrait of Wollstonecraft in America was a negative one. To put oneself forward as a proponent of Wollstonecraftism was to advocate private licentiousness and public corruption. As America entered the nineteenth century, any new "rights" for women were simply the traditional ones reentrenched— a right to marriage, to children, to domesticity.

Writing in 1808, the Reverend Samuel Miller could heave a sigh of relief that the Wollstonecraftism of a few years earlier had thoroughly passed away. He, happily, even has to remind his readers what some of the unlikely tenets of that erstwhile radical feminism had actually been:

> Whatever opinion may be formed on this subject, I take for granted, we shall all agree, that Women ought not to be considered as destined to the same employments with Men; and, of course, that there is a species of education, and a sphere of action, which more particularly belong to them. There was a time indeed, when a very different doctrine had many advocates, and appeared to be growing popular:—viz. that in conducting education, and in selecting employments, all

distinctions of sex ought to be forgotten and confounded; and that females are as well fitted to fill the Academic Chair, to shine in the Senate, to adorn the Bench of Justice, and even to lead the train of War, as the more hardy sex. This delusion, however, is now generally discarded. It begins to be perceived, that the God of nature has raised everlasting barriers against such wild and mischievous speculations; and that to urge them, is to renounce reason, to contradict experience, to trample on the divine authority, and to degrade the usefulness, the honor, and the real enjoyments of the female sex.[68]

Perhaps because the novel as a genre was already associated with corruption and libertinism, after the publication of the *Memoirs* American sentimental writers were quick to deny that they might be guilty of borrowing from Wollstonecraft.[69] The contretemps over the *Memoirs* also effectively silenced many of the advocates of women's rights in America. Even though the Wollstonecraft scandal, grotesquely magnified by the Reign of Terror in France, did not necessarily *precipitate* a reactionary retrenchment, it certainly served as a potent sign of the dangers inherent in radical action and a symbol of the negative consequences, for women, of unconventional lifestyles.

It is not within the scope of this study to document and analyze what changes in the prescriptive literature occurred in the nineteenth century, but I wish to conclude, briefly, by suggesting that, over the course of the next generation, both the conservative side of the debate on the role of women and the reformist position gradually changed in tone and focus so that they were no longer dialectical opposites but rather simply different approaches to a similar view of woman as par excellence the republican mother.[70] A nineteenth-century rhetoric of "true womanhood" or a "cult of domesticity" extolled women as specially gifted for the crucial task of rearing children. As Ruth H. Bloch has observed, a new focus on motherhood effectively reversed an older Puritan emphasis on the paramount importance of the father in the intellectual, moral, and social molding of children.[71] And at least on the level of rhetoric, this hyperbolic language of republican motherhood also seemed to offer women new social status, as was argued in 1802 by the Reverend William Lyman:

> Mothers do, in a sense, hold the reigns of government and sway the ensigns of national prosperity and glory. Yea, they give direction to the moral sentiment of our rising hopes and contribute to form their moral state. To them therefore our eyes are turned in this demoralizing age, and of them we ask, that they would appreciate their worth and dignity, and exert all their influence to drive discord, infidelity, and licentiousness from our land.[72]

The question of political power—central to Wollstonecraftism and important to American reformers as well—was rendered irrelevant by this co-opting ideology that mothers were indirectly responsible for *everything* that was crucial in the society. In the words of one advocate of omnipotent motherhood, "compared with maternal influence, the combined authority of laws and armies and public sentiment are little things."[73]

With the cult of domesticity, there was also a shift in women's fiction. Earlier novels, as noted, had focused on women's life preparatory to marriage and posited a good marriage as virtue's reward. Portraying the lives of girls and unmarried young women, these novels necessarily described how such women proceeded within and around the restrictions placed upon them by their society, a plot structure that can be observed in progressive novels such as *The Coquette* and also more conservative books such as Wood's *Amelia* or *Julia.* To generalize, the plots of most sentimental novels of the early national period concentrate on a young woman's freedoms prior to wedlock, often epitomized (and tested) through the seduction plot or an equivalent subplot. But as Helen Waite Papashvily observes, after approximately 1818, the seduction plot virtually disappears from sentimental fiction, and, with the graphic exception of *The Scarlet Letter,* the "fallen woman" does not figure prominently in the design of nineteenth-century American fiction.[74] At the same time, the sentimental heroine grows up. Numerous nineteenth-century novels centered on older women working out their lives within their domestic sphere, whether as matron or "old maid."[75]

Writing in 1804 in the *Literary Magazine,* in an essay entitled "Female Learning," Charles Brockden Brown early identified the contradictions in the contemporary ideology of women, the presumed opposition between female intellect and domesticity. "A woman who hates reading," he countered, "is not necessarily a wise and prudent economist." But he also understood, with remarkable sensitivity, that polar categorizations of women—maternal paragon *or* learned woman, wife *or* author—necessarily diminished both the woman writer and the woman reader, who could always be condemned for being too much or not enough of one or the other. "Of that numerous class of females, who have cultivated their minds with science and literature, without publishing their labours, and who consequently are unknown to general inquirers; how many have preserved the balance immoveable between the opposite demands of the kitchen, the drawing room, the nursery, and the library? We may safely answer from our own experience, not one."[76] From the personal evidence Brown had at hand, women simply could not maintain rich intellectual lives while bearing the full burden of *perfect* domesticity. Despite the rhetoric, or perhaps because of it, during the first decades of the nineteenth century, a cult of "true womanhood" all but smothered the cry for female equality, a cry faintly but subversively heard in those sentimental novels such as *Charlotte Temple* and *The Coquette* that remained steady sellers into the last half of the nineteenth century and the dawnings of America's first full-fledged feminist movement.

Disjunctions in the Sentimental Structure

Just as women could ambivalently embrace the promise of marriage along with its promised restrictions and just as neither the reactionary nor the reformist novel could univocally assert its politics of marriage, so, too, do we regularly encounter in the very structure of the sentimental novel tensions and unresolved contradictions. There is often a glaring gap between the public morality officially espoused and the private behavior of the characters who voice or supposedly validate that morality. What is promised in the preface is not always proven in the plot. As earlier noted, much early sentimental fiction was forced into a difficult balancing act—not always successfully executed—between readerly demands (especially from the professional readers) for moralistic restraint and writerly demands for artistic license. But that wavering and uncertain balance can be read not just in the sociology of the production of these texts but in the texts themselves and even in the first readers of these texts. Indeed, I would suggest that these texts find one of their chief loci in the difference between the reader's private reservations about her own limited legal and social standing as opposed to her public acceptance of ostensibly unquestioned social values and established good order. Such private discourse mirrors a larger discourse between the reader and the sentimental novel in its different versions and between the novel in all its versions and the critics who saw it rightly as raising issues that they would have preferred to remain repressed.

Consider, for example, Samuel Relf's *Infidelity, or the Victims of Sentiment,* a novel to which I have previously referred as one of the few that survives with its original subscription list bound in the volume. Almost one half the book's original subscribers who can be identified by gender are women; two of the men who subscribed, James A. Neal and John Poor, were not only preceptor and principal, respectively, of young ladies' academies, but they advertised themselves as such in the subscription list itself (which, after all, is a *public* declaration of one's reading habits), suggesting that they approved of the "lesson" of the book for their charges. But what lesson did young women readers learn from Caroline Courntey, the heroine of the novel and an obvious ancestress of Hester Prynne? Like many a sentimental heroine, Caroline submits to her parents' judgment and weds, much against her own wishes, the elderly Mr. Franks. This dutiful daughter is thereby rewarded with an unhappy marriage. Neglected by her cruel husband, she finds solace in the concern of a younger, more sympathetic man. That infatuation, apparently unconsummated, is nevertheless the "infidelity" of the title and brings death to both participants and disaster to their friends and families. Yet the epigraph to the novel reads, "—'Tis not a sin to love." To which the reader can only reply that it was and it wasn't. Marriage is vindicated by the fatal consequences of its failure. The probably nonadulterous lovers are vindicated by their sinless love. "Persecuted innocence" (to use the novel's own diction) has been sacrificed in order that compromised propriety might be saved.[77]

Other characters took other ways to much the same sentimental impasse. Thus, the thoroughly virtuous Mrs. Morley in Wood's *Dorval* does not even flirt with the possibility of seduction. Unfortunately for that formerly wealthy former widow, her new husband turns out to be, in order, a fortune hunter, a bigamist, and a murderer. Feminine virtue, the rock on which the sentimental novel was founded, was, in this case, clearly no match for masculine vice. Or, in a somewhat different fashion, moral spokespersons could practice considerably less than they preached. The jejune and platitudinous Worthy in *The Power of Sympathy* is germane here, as is, in Susanna Rowson's *Mentoria; or the Young Lady's Friend* (1791), the equally inappropriately named Prudelia, whose ever-ready *sententia* serve mostly as a moral smoke screen behind which she busily pries into the possible sins of her neighbors instead of cultivating any virtues of her own.

The sentimental form was also modified and its meaning compounded when main characters were rendered novelistically, not morally; when they were brought down from the heights of spiritual grandeur to be portrayed as flawed and, consequently, as believable human beings. When Harrington, for example, ignores Worthy's long-winded advice and seeks refuge, instead, in suicide, his end is not a heroic vindication of high ideals but a recognition that his tragic dilemma lies beyond the reach and scope of any available code of conduct. The power of sympathy, in this text, runs head first into its own powerlessness in the face of overpowering incestuous desire. Conversely, moral issues are complicated when the villain of the piece is recast as more than just another advocate of illegitimate affairs. Belfield in Sansay's *Laura,* Count Hubert in Isaac Mitchell's *The Asylum; or, Alonzo and Melissa* (1811), and, most obviously, Carwin in Charles Brockden Brown's *Wieland, or the Transformation* (1798) are all examples of such humanized antagonists—the seducer who is himself seduced by delusions, misconceptions, and his own naive egotism. These characters suggest dangers other than and embody the consequences of falls more subtle than mere physical seduction.

Charles Brockden Brown's Carwin is perhaps the most complex and certainly the most discussed villain in early American fiction. But Montraville, in Rowson's *Charlotte Temple,* provides a less analyzed example of how problematic villains spin problematic plots.[78] Charlotte Temple, it will be remembered, elopes with this seducer partly because she has been misled by the dubious logic of Mademoiselle La Rue but primarily because she loves Montraville and fully expects that he will immediately marry her. The seducer in this best-seller sins primarily because he, too, sees himself as an honorable suitor anticipating wedlock. Charlotte, however, is no heiress, and marrying her would preclude the affluent life to which Montraville aspires. He partly evades that first dilemma by procrastinating marriage, which presently leads to his second dilemma when he chances to meet another woman who is virtuous, beautiful, kind, and even rich. Should he remain with Charlotte, his now pregnant mistress, or should he eschew vice, in favor of the virtue of a clearly rewarding marriage?

Partly to exonerate Montraville, Rowson provides a second male character, Belcour, who conventionally counsels that sin should not be sanctioned, that a mistress must be renounced. Belcour, a parallel and parody of the stock moral adviser, is determined to see "morality" prevail and even contrives to be found "sleeping" beside Charlotte, who really is asleep and quite unaware of the plot against her. The discovery of a "betrayal" that never took place persuades Montraville to abandon the young woman. The two former lovers are then further victimized by Belcour. As a proponent of the sentimental credo that a "perfidious girl" such as the pregnant Miss Temple deserves whatever fate befalls her, he keeps for himself the money provided by Montraville to take care of Charlotte.[79] So Montraville, the concerned seducer, is not the true villain of the piece, and a standard moral dictum is compromised by the way Belcour employs it to serve his vicious purpose.

Or perhaps Montraville is the real villain in that his villainy is so sanctioned by his society that it can pass as virtue. Rowson's larger point here well might be that a standard double standard of sexual conduct allows even a relatively decent young man to become, indirectly and second hand, a murderer. Montraville thus interpreted serves as a symptom of a much larger social phenomenon, just as Charlotte's fate also attests to the social context in which it is realized. She is a victim not so much of her wayward desires but of a shoddy education, of evil advisers (including one schoolteacher), of her legal and social inferiority. Many of the first commentators on the novel also read the book in this way—as a work of "truth" and "realism" in which Charlotte was rightly pitied and wrongly sentenced. Most notably, the assessment in the London *Critical Review* (1791) powerfully argued for both the truth of the work as a whole and the innocence of its title character. This review was tipped into early American and British editions of the book and was later reprinted opposite the preface in all eighteenth-century and many nineteenth-century American editions. As that review concludes:

> Charlotte dies a martyr to the inconstancy of her lover, and the treachery of his friend.—The situations are artless and affecting—the descriptions natural and pathetic; we should feel for Charlotte, if such a person ever existed, who, for one error, scarcely, perhaps, deserved so severe a punishment. If it is a fiction, poetic justice is not, we think, properly distributed.[80]

Rowson, I suspect, felt so, too. In a fiction grounded in sexual crime and feminine punishment, she problemizes the official justice ostensibly implicit in her conventional plot.

Other early novels also realigned what Herbert Ross Brown has called the "sentimental formula" ("a simple equation resting upon a belief in the spontaneous goodness and benevolence of man's original instincts").[81] For example, instead of positing clearcut moral choices between virtue, on the one hand, and vice, on the other, a number of early novels present heroines with more complicated and, consequently, more believable moral dilemmas. She must choose, say, between loveless respectability and unrespectable love, not simply between marriage and illicit sex. Thus, in the anonymous *Margaretta; or, the Intricacies of the Heart* (1807), the female protagonist prefers passion to propriety and rejects dependable Captain Waller, who proposes matrimony, for the dashing Will de Burling, who plans to marry an heiress but will keep Margaretta as his mistress. As Margaretta declares, "I think I was not destined by nature for an humble cottage."[82] Numerous abductions and other trials and tribulations later, she finds that she must again choose between the good Waller and the handsome de Burling. Now herself possessed of both a title and a fortune, she once more bypasses social respectability although settling this time for marriage but marriage to the penniless de Burling.

Or a husband could subvert the social authority implicit in his role by too much insisting on that role and authority. In Well's *The Step-Mother,* Caroline Williams, the put-upon heroine, repeatedly advocates that a woman do whatever her husband requires, but the reader sympathizes more with Mrs. Malcolm, an emotionally and perhaps physically abused wife, who escapes a loveless marriage to form an illicit love relationship with a young man of egalitarian views. Both women must balance the quite different questions of to obey or not to obey the husband, to resist or not to resist the tyrant. Or the parents' claims to control

Susanna Rowson.

the daughter could similarly be called into question by the very tyrannical overtones of their assertion. A protagonist must frequently choose between a father she loves and a lover her father, often for no valid reason, opposes. Almost half of the sentimental novels written in America before 1820 employ this cruel parent motif. One example is *The History of Constantius and Pulchera,* in which Pulchera's father forces her to break off her engagement to Constantius so that she can marry Le Monte whom she does not love and who, even worse, is French. Only after a mind-boggling series of misadventures on the high seas, in Europe, and in Canada are the true lovers reunited. All the calamities could have been avoided through a little parental reasonableness, but perhaps that is the point of the book. Or notice how *The Unfortunate Lovers, and Cruel Parents* (1797) advertises its plot in its title. And in both Charles Brockden Brown's *Clara Howard* (1801) and Margaret Botsford's *Adelaide* (1816), we see young men and women marry because of parental pressure, not from love, and suffer from that decision into the next generation.

The sentimental plot could also be complicated by posing, for the central heroine, the dubious charms of a restrictive domesticity, on the one hand, against the freedom from stultifying convention promised by a socially unsuitable but passionate suitor, on the other. In a few of these novels, virtue is presented as no less demeaning an alternative for an intelligent young woman than vice. Not infrequently, a capable heroine clearly foresees the protracted unhappiness that would be hers if she married the respectable male character whom society views as her proper mate. Just such a dilemma faces Deborah Sampson in *The Female Review,* which makes it easier for her to opt for transvestism and the army, a revolutionary choice for which she is not punished in the novel. Similarly, Martinette de Beauvais, in Charles Brockden Brown's *Ormond* (1799), disguises herself as "Martin" and enlists in freedom's cause, thereby acquiring an appropriate metaphoric platform from which to question the propriety of society in general and of woman's assigned roles in particular. These are extreme cases, but they reinforce choices made in other novels where a heroine sees the constrictions implicit in her proposed marriage. Moralists say that virtue should be rewarded. But is marriage to a stodgy moralist truly a reward for a sensitive, capable heroine? In the best of these novels, the issues raised by the plot often go considerably beyond the prefatory promise of safe social truth in fictional packaging.

Even the early sentimental novel cannot be reduced, then, to the simple formula that contemporary readers and critics commonly ascribe to it. The recipe was more complicated than we assume as, from the very beginning, one key ingredient was to experiment with the recipe. Instead of positing simple answers about the powers of pious procreation, many of the novels question the efficacy of the prevailing legal, political, and social values, even if the questioning is done by innuendo rather than by actual assertion of a contrary view. What else can we make of fallen women who are more the victims of circumstance than the embodiments of sin and who scarcely deserve the punishments that are heaped upon them? Of seducers who are not villains? Of villains, like Belcour, who ascribe to the standard morality? Furthermore, the seducer, proud of his conquests but contemptuous of the women he seduces, often inversely mirrors the values of the moralist. The one, to prove his reputation, would despoil what the other, to prove his, would preserve. For each, the heroine is almost incidental. For the heroine, both are equally unappealing. She is caught in a double bind, and, in the best sentimental novels, her predicament demonstrates that the postulated dichotomy of the clearly virtuous and the clearly vicious central to this fiction is itself a fiction.

Virtue (writ large) does not always save the heroine. Bombarded with pompous precepts, on the one hand, and assailed by promising temptations, on the other, the perceptive female protagonist merits the reader's attention and sympathy. Prefatory assurances to the contrary, hers is no easy choice. Chaste, she is rewarded by a limiting marriage, often to a limited man. Should she fall, her death is hardly triumphant proof that the social norms are just, that vice has been rightly punished. Anticipating the later Romantic tradition, these protagonists seek to establish their own destinies.[83] Given the mores of late eighteenth-century American society and the biological reality of pregnancy, they cannot succeed. But often we wish they could.

Reading The Coquette

William Godwin's 1798 publication of the *Memoirs* of Mary Wollstonecraft had the unexpected effect of immediately translating her life into an allegory of feminine crime and punishment, and American public opinion was quick to draw the reactionary moral. When a thirty-seven-year-old woman came to the Bell Tavern in Danvers (now Peabody), Massachusetts, to give birth to a stillborn child, and then followed that child to her own death on July 25, 1788, a similar fictionalizing was at once set in motion, as can be seen in even the first published account of the event which appeared in the *Salem Mercury* for July 29, 1788. Purportedly written by one Captain Goodhue, the landlord of the Bell Tavern, this first notice effectively balances asserted propriety (she was waiting for her husband) and suggested scandal (did she really have one?):

> Last Friday, a female stranger died at the Bell Tavern, in Danvers; and on Sunday her remains were decently interred. The circumstances relative to this woman are such as excite curiosity, and interest our feelings. She was brought to the Bell in a chaise . . . by a young man whom she had engaged for that purpose. . . . She remained at this inn till her death, in expectation of the arrival of her husband, whom she expected to come for her, and appeared anxious at his delay. She was averse to being interrogated concerning herself or connexions; and kept much retired to her chamber, employed in needlework, writing, etc. . . . Her conversation, her writings and her manners, bespoke the advantage of a respectable family and good education. Her person was agreeable; her deportment, amiable and engaging; and, though in a state of anxiety and suspense, she preserved a cheerfulness which seemed to be not the effect of insensibility, but of a firm and patient temper.[84]

Within days the account was picked up and reprinted by the *Massachusetts Centinel* and then in dozens of other newspapers throughout New England. It was the stuff of good rumor, of gossip, of sentimental novels.

What led to the Elizabeth Whitman mystery? Surely many another woman had borne a child out of wed-

lock and died of puerperal fever? But, as even the above report suggests, the essential appeal of this story was its contradictory nature. To start with, what was a nice woman like Elizabeth Whitman doing in a tavern like that and in that condition? Miss Whitman was the daughter of a highly respected minister, the Reverend Elnathan Whitman. On her mother's side, she was descended from the Stanley family that had governed Connecticut almost from its Colonial beginnings. She was also related to the Edwards family, to Aaron Burr, and to the poet John Trumbull. Two of her suitors had been Yale preceptors. She had corresponded regularly with Joel Barlow. Hartford's highest society knew and respected her for her wit, her intelligence, and her charm. Yet she died in a tavern, seduced and abandoned, a fate right out of the novels that vociferously warned against just that fate. Nor were the novels the only texts bearing on the matter of her demise. Once Whitman's identity was revealed, ministers, journalists, and free-lance moralists industriously made *meaning*—their meaning—of her otherwise incomprehensible life. In the redaction of an anonymous essayist in the *Boston Independent Chronicle* of September 11, 1788, for example, Elizabeth Whitman's life and death becomes, simply, "a good moral lecture to young ladies."[85]

Readers in the early Republic were well versed in the process whereby the complexities of a disordered life could be reduced to a simply ordered moral allegory. Virtually every condemned crook, con man, or other criminal recorded the outlines of his or her life before ascending to the gallows. Published in inexpensive chapbook form, republished in newspaper columns throughout America, these confessions straddled the line between truth and fiction as much as did the Elizabeth Whitman allegories that were reprinted all over New England. Most readers of *The Coquette* would have already known the outlines of Whitman's life either from the newspapers or from sermons of ministers who regularly mined gossip for material. These readers would also have known the lacunae in Whitman's story that have continued to intrigue biographers down to the present day. Although Whitman left a cache of poems and letters at her death, none refers to her lover by name—and the ironic pseudonym she used to refer to him, Fidelio, provides no clue to his identity either. Pierrepont Edwards, by the middle of the nineteenth century, was generally assumed to be the model for Major Peter Sanford, but other candidates for the honor have also been proposed: Aaron Burr, New York State Senator James Watson, Joel Barlow, and an unnamed French nobleman whose parents objected to his secret marriage to a Protestant minister's daughter from Connecticut. The secret marriage theme, incidentally, at one point had considerable currency. Caroline W. Dall (in 1875) and Charles Knowles Bolton (in 1912) both of them tried, a century after the events, to salvage the reputation of the lady by proposing a secret wedding.[86] In different ages, the historical record differently fabricates the story of Elizabeth Whitman—seduced woman or suffering wife, smirched or sacrificed or sanctified—mostly to confirm its story of itself. But Victorian hagiography or eighteenth-century moral tracts, the histories of Elizabeth Whitman all share the governing assumption that lost virginity signifies, for a woman, lost worth; that the sexual fall proves the social one, so much so that in this case the signifier and its significance are one and the same.

The earliest accounts of Whitman's decline and fall served the dual purpose of criticizing any intellectual pretensions that a woman might possess and of condemning the novel as a new form which fostered such pretensions. Whitman became, in effect, a case study, a woman first misled by her education into a taste for novels and then corrupted through indulging that unwholesome appetite. The first American novel argues, ironically, against novels by promulgating just this interpretation of this character's fate: "She was a great reader of novels and romances and having imbibed her ideas of *the characters of men,* from those fallacious sources, became vain and coquetish [*sic*], and rejected several offers of marriage, in expectation of receiving one more agreeable to her fanciful idea." It was the official view. In fact, William Hill Brown practically plagiarizes the verdict delivered in the *Massachusetts Centinel* on September 20, 1788: "She was *a great reader of romances,* and having formed her notions of happiness from that corrupt source, became vain and coquetish."[87] Thus was one of the most learned American women of her generation translated into a poor, pathetic victim of fiction whose dishonor and death could be partly redeemed only by serving to save others from a similar end.

To turn that well-known scandal and accepted story into one of the most reprinted early American novels, Hannah Webster Foster had to reread this protagonist and her plight, had to deconstruct the entrenched interpretation so that a novel one might be advanced. One of the more striking changes in Foster's different account is the deletion of the charge of an addiction to fiction. *The Power of Sympathy,* it will be recalled, did not even refer to itself as a novel on its title page, whereas in 1797, when *Charlotte Temple* was well on its way to becoming a steady seller, Ebenezer Larkin published a book that he hoped might be similarly successful under the title *The Coquette; or, The History of Eliza Wharton: A NOVEL.*[88] In the intervening decade, the novel had come of age in America and no longer needed the protective coloration provided by an occasional sermon against novel reading. In *The Coquette,* fiction is valorized. When Eliza is at her most rejected and depressed her friends and moral advisors send her novels to read. More pointedly, Eliza's se-

ducer, Major Sanford, numbers among his manifest faults a singular unfamiliarity with fiction, especially with the works of Richardson.[89]

Other alterations in the Whitman story were more subtle. Several historical characters, for example, underwent name changes while retaining the same initials, which suggests an intentional blurring of the division between fiction and fact and an invitation to the reader to enjoy that same blurring. Eliza Wharton both is and is not Elizabeth Whitman. Similarly, two of Whitman's historical suitors, the Reverend Joseph Howe (whom her parents originally chose for their daughter but who died before the marriage could take place) and the Reverend Joseph Buckminster (who subsequently sought her hand) are lightly fictionalized into the Reverends Haly and Boyer. Historical personages have also been advanced as the originals for the protagonist's women friends as well. But Peter Sanford (by initials or occupation) does not figure forth a historical personage but remains a literary one. A "second Lovelace," Elizabeth/Eliza's seducer becomes allegorized in Foster's novel very much as Whitman had been allegorized in the newspaper accounts. Conversely, the heroine gained in fiction the complexity of which she had been deprived in the early allegories of her life and death.

None of the early accounts of Whitman's life, for example, credit her with a rational weighing of a prospective husband's qualifications, despite the fact that her second suitor, the Reverend Buckminster, was well known in his day as a man subject to prolonged fits of depression and outbursts of uncontrolled temper. "She refused two as good offers of marriage as she deserved," avers the *Boston Independent Chronicle,* "because she aspired higher than to be a clergyman's wife; and having coquetted till past her prime, fell into criminal indulgences."[90] Foster, however, transforms this reductionist account. Elizabeth's anticlericalism and social climbing become Eliza's determination that her marriage must be an egalitarian match based on mutual affection. A clergyman's wife herself, Foster well knew just what that employment entailed (as is shown even more clearly in her second novel, *The Boarding School*), and, more to the point, her fictional Eliza, the daughter of a minister's wife, also knows the prerequisites for the position and knows, too, that she does not fit the bill. As she admits to her mother, "My disposition is not calculated for that sphere. There are duties arising from the station which I fear I should not be able to fulfill, cares and restraints to which I could not submit" (p. 162). Having narrowly escaped one loveless marriage—through the fortuitous death of the fiancé—imposed upon her by the "shackles" of "parental authority" (p. 140), she is determined to marry in the future only if reason and fancy, her mind and her heart, are both engaged.

Socially conservative readers may well have intimated the seeds of Eliza's downfall in this daughter's belated declaration of independence and her egalitarian concept of marriage. Foster, however, takes considerable pains to affirm her protagonist's ideals. When, early in the novel, she leaves her mother's home in which she was immured with her dying clergyman fiancé, she goes to visit her friends, the Richmans, whose marriage exemplifies the Wollstonecraftian ideal of a partnership of equals. That relationship is Eliza's ideal too. Her "heart approved and applauded" (p. 181) this couple's happiness. Her tragedy is not that she set her sights too high but that she encounters no equivalent of a General Richman. What she is offered, instead, is a difficult choice between unsatisfactory alternatives, a common quandary in early American sentimental novels, and a dilemma, no doubt, faced by many American young women.

The Coquette, then, is not simply an allegory of seduction. The generic shift from sermon to novel in the Whitman/Wharton narrative entails a concomitant transformation of focus and philosophy. Set within a specific context of limiting marriage laws and restrictive social mores, the novel is less a story of the wages of sin than a study of the wages of marriage. In the realistic world of this fictional account, virtue and virtuous women are not always rewarded. Sanford's lawfully wedded wife, for example, a woman shown to be intelligent, kind, honest, and attractive, fares almost as disastrously as Eliza. She is ruined financially by her marriage to Sanford, and her child, too, is stillborn. Furthermore, even Mrs. Richman, the epitome of republican motherhood in the novel, cannot be permanently happy within her familial sphere. "I grudge every moment that calls me from the pleasing scenes of domestic life" (p. 210), she writes, soon after the birth of her daughter—who soon afterwards dies, a realistic tempering of the proclaimed joys of domesticity.

By fictionalizing the lives of the women who surround Eliza, Foster provided her early readers with an opportunity to see, privileged in print, women very much like themselves. As the community of women within the novel exchange views and ideas on such crucial subjects as friendship, marriage, and economic security, their letters constitute a dialogical discourse in which the reader was also invited to participate if only vicariously. For its first audience particularly, *The Coquette* set forth a remarkably detailed assessment of the marital possibilities facing late eighteenth-century women of the middle- or upper-middle-classes. Crucial questions for just such women are asked and dramatized in the text. What were her choices? What kinds of behavior would promote or prevent certain matches? How do men view the whole matter of courtship and marriage? On that last score, the twelve letters that Sanford sends his friend, Charles Deighton,

provide a telling example of male discourse in contrast to female discourse, and Sanford effectively voices the self-justifying evasions, the hypocrisy, and the overt misogyny of the seducer. Similarly, the nine letters exchanged between the Reverend Boyer and his friend Selby attest to how much respectable men assume the subordinate status of women and thereby validate Eliza's apprehensions about the restricted life that would be hers if she were to marry Boyer and become a clergyman's wife.

The bulk of the novel is "woman-talk": women confiding, advising, chiding, warning, disagreeing, deceiving, and then confronting each other. A full two-thirds of the seventy-five letters that comprise *The Coquette* are written by women to women, and not always about the men in their lives. Eliza, especially, exhibits in her discourse the ideas and aspirations of a *feme sole*—the independent, unmarried woman. In contrast to that state is the status of Eliza's close friend and most regular correspondent, Lucy Freeman, who, in the course of the novel, marries to become Mrs. Sumner. As a married woman, she can no longer be so free as she formerly was with her time or attention. To quote Eliza: "Marriage is the tomb of friendship. It appears to me a very selfish state. Why do people in general, as soon as they are married, center all their cares, their concerns, and pleasures in their own families? Former acquaintances are neglected or forgotten; the tenderest ties between friends are weakened or dissolved; benevolence itself moves in a very limited sphere" (p. 150). "Women's sphere" is here aptly portrayed as "a very limited sphere"—a closed and enclosing concern for a husband's well-being—which gives us one of the earliest fictional critiques of the "cult of domesticity."

The Coquette, however, does not openly challenge the basic structure of patriarchal culture but, instead, exposes its fundamental injustices through the details and disasters of the plot. Consider, for example, how, after the Reverend Haly's death, Eliza's mother along with the young woman's female friends worry constantly about her marital prospects, for she does not have an inheritance of her own. They do not advise (much less prepare) her to earn a wage; they only urge her to obtain a husband who does. Yet her manifest talents—her beauty, her charm, her intelligence— constitute no negotiable capital in any matrimonial transaction. "Forgive my plainness," Eliza's friend, Lucy Freeman, writes of the Reverend Boyer. "His situation in life is, perhaps, as elevated as you have a right to claim" (p. 152). Neither does a fortune of one's own substantially alter one's case, as the example of Nancy Sanford amply attests. The wealthy woman, as much as the poor, is still dependent upon a husband's good sense and good will. All women are thus potential paupers and married women especially so. But without a husband to provide for her and lacking the skills to earn her own living, a woman's situation can be as desperate as was the historical Elizabeth Whitman's at the Bell Tavern. Dying, the abandoned woman left "2 ginneys, 1 crown, 2-4 pistoreens dollars," and a few other paltry possessions (six silver spoons, a few rings, a couple of dresses, handkerchiefs, ribbons, and caps; an "ink case with Sealing wax, wafers, etc."; and "Sundry Babe cloths").[91] That sad inventory, in actual and symbolic measure, movingly sums up the unmarried woman's social worth and her final estate.

Other features of the society are also summed up in the novel. As Eliza fully realizes, when a woman marries a man, she must marry not only into his class but into his occupation too. She anticipates being "completely miserable" (p. 153) as a minister's wife, and Sanford effectively reiterates those all-too-well-founded fears: "You are aware, I suppose, when you form a connection with that man, you must content yourself with a confinement to the tedious round of domestic duties, the pedantic conversation of scholars, and the invidious criticisms of the whole town" (p. 171). Boyer is a pompous, self-satisfied clergyman who attempts (the choice of words here is most appropriate) to "seduce [Eliza] into matrimony" (p. 184) by soberly expatiating on the advantages of being joined to such an admirable man as himself. "He is," Eliza writes, "very eloquent upon the subject; and his manners are so solemn that I am strongly tempted . . . to laugh" (p. 184). And so is the reader. But Major Sanford is hardly an alternative. Witty and charming as he may be, he is also a thoroughgoing misogynist, and a thoroughly dishonest one at that. His letters to Deighton are filled with stupid and shallow remarks about the stupidity and shallowness of women. He insists, for example, that he can be "severe upon the sex" because he has "found so many frail ones among them" (p. 234)—as if he were a latter-day Diogenes searching for an honest woman. He also insists that if he seduces Eliza, the fault will be entirely hers. "She knows my character and has no reason to wonder if I act consistently with it" (p. 176). Yet he has just implored her to "let the kind and lenient hand of friendship assist in directing my future steps" (p. 160), which is hardly the open avowal of his intentions that he subsequently and quite hypocritically pretends he has made.

What seemed to Eliza to be choices, alternative men and alternative lifestyles, do not constitute, then, a dialectic that will yield a final synthesis such as the egalitarian marriage of the Richmans. We have, instead, oppositions that cancel one another out to emphasize that the choices Boyer and Sanford embodied were not ultimately so different after all. For each, she was mostly a prize and a proof of his own prowess. In each case, more could be proved by discarding the prize than by claiming it. As will be remembered, Eliza does decide to marry the minister but "was entangled by a promise" (p. 208) to tell Sanford first. When

Boyer discovers his prospective bride in conversation with that rival, he storms from the scene. He will not hear Eliza's explanation, for his dashed hopes (he thinks) and offended vanity (we see) provide all the explanation he needs. Soon he is writing to renounce his love and to catalogue her various faults and failings and all from pure "benevolence." Sanford, delighted by his success in destroying Eliza's chances with Boyer, also soon leaves town. He goes away "on business" promising to return in a few months but, a year later, he is still gone and in that whole time he has not once written to the woman he claimed to love. Eliza, faced not with a freedom of choice but an absence of suitors, begins to realize that she has been played for a fool, a truth brought home even more forcefully when Boyer announces his engagement to a suitably appreciative, suitably proper woman and when Sanford finally returns, having acquired, while away, both a wife and that wife's fortune. Eliza naively sought to exercise her freedom only to learn that she had none.[92]

The course of that learning is crucial to the novel and must be examined in some detail, for the genesis of Eliza's fall lies at least as much in the virtues of Boyer as in the vices of Sanford. When that clergyman first goes off in his terminal huff, Eliza well can wonder "whether [she] had sustained a real loss in Mr. Boyer's departure?" (p. 207). But Sanford's subsequent departure along with the continuing absence of any other official suitors soon casts a different light on her first loss from which the second has followed. She must remain in the fishbowl of Hartford, scorned by those who knew all along that her flirtations—her decision to "sow all my wild oats" [very tame wild oats] (p. 186) before settling into the restricted role of the clergyman's wife—could only lead to disaster. Publicly humiliated by the way in which the town so obviously relishes and affirms her discomfiture, she is brought, partly through her failing spirits and partly through Mrs. Richman's counsel, to reevaluate the Reverend's dubious charms. Her letter to him is all humility and self-abnegation, but perhaps the most poignant detail in this pathetic missive is her hope that even if his "affections are entirely alienated or otherwise engaged," he still might consent to consider himself her friend. That last hope is as vain as all her others. Again Boyer writes to shower her with accusations before announcing his betrothal to "the virtuous, the amiable, the accomplished Maria Selby" and finally counseling Eliza to "adhere with undeviating exactness to the paths of rectitude and innocence" (p. 216).

"O my friend, I am undone" (p. 217), Eliza writes upon receiving Boyer's letter, using the precise word that in seduction novels typically signals a woman's fall. "His conduct," she continues with an even more loaded term, assures her "ruin." "By confessing my faults and by avowing my partiality to him, I have given him the power of triumphing in my distress; of returning to my tortured heart all the pangs of slighted love. And what have I now to console me?" (pp. 217-18). Three times Eliza voices the plaintive cry of the seduced woman. Soon thereafter, she falls more conventionally into the affair with Sanford and, concomitant with that fall, into physical infirmity, mental instability, and narrative invisibility. Increasingly, others must recount the story that was once her own but that in the very mode of its telling has been taken from her.

This negation of the female self—her freedoms, her possibilities—forms the basis of the sentimental plot, just as it informed the lives of a vast majority of the sentimental novel's readers. One effective method Foster employs to convey this demeaning of her central character is to have her literally render herself as she has been symbolically rendered by her society. At crucial junctures in the novel, Eliza *chooses* silence, but that narrative silence, a depotentizing in the novel as a whole, provides the subtext from which we can best read the protagonist's fall. How, Foster in effect asks, can a woman denied voice and will be seduced? Simply put, she has no say in the matter. Succumbing to Sanford merely confirms and symbolizes what rejection by Boyer has already proved. We have sex as an only half-sublimated suicide and as a decline into a figurative death (a horrific rendition of "the little death") that will soon slide into the real thing.

"How to write a novel about a person to whom nothing happens? A person to whom nothing but a love story is *supposed* to happen? A person inhabiting a world in which the only reality is frustration or endurance—or these plus an unbearably mystifying confusion?" These questions, rhetorical and very real, raised by Joanna Russ in her classic essay, "What Can a Heroine Do? Or Why Women Can't Write," perfectly epitomize the narrative problems Foster faces in rewriting Elizabeth Whitman's story.[93] The same general problem is inherent in the entire sentimental subgenre. How does one privilege the voice of a woman who, given the society in which the novel is written and read, enjoys neither voice nor privilege?

More specifically, how can the life and death of Elizabeth Whitman emphasize meanings other than those already overencoded in the society and overexpounded in innumerable sermons, newspaper accounts, and didactic essays of the time? Russ suggests that one form women have evolved for writing the essentially unwritable is, in her term, the "lyric mode"—that is, a fiction which organizes "discrete elements (images, events, scenes, passages, words, what-have-you) *around an unspoken thematic or emotional center.*" In circling around that unspoken, invisible center, the lyric novel necessarily repeats itself (which is also a quint-

essential feature of the epistolary form). That circling is the meaning; the novel is *about* this silent center because "there is no action possible to the central character and no series of events which will embody in clear, unequivocal, immediately graspable terms what the artist means" since the society precludes all the symbols and "myths of male culture" (like lighting out for the territories or signing on for a whaling voyage) that could serve to express—or to elude—the woman's situation for the woman reader. "There is nothing the female character can *do*—except exist, except think, except feel."[94] Eliza Wharton's long protracted fall and the silence that surrounds it constitutes the invisible center around which this sentimental novel turns.

The Coquette and other sentimental novels in the new Republic are ultimately about silence, subservience, stasis (the accepted attributes of women as traditionally defined) in contradistinction to conflicting impulses toward independence, action, and self-expression (the ideals of the new American nation). But what is the resolution of that central conflict? If the sentimental novel, as I am suggesting, entered fully into the current debates on the status of women, then what do we make of a novel such as *The Coquette* that jumbles all the terms? Mrs. Richman, like Judith Sargent Murray, argues that women must join men in articulating the political concerns of the nation—lest the emerging consensus be ludicrously one-sided—a position antithetical to that enunciated by writers from Rousseau to Chesterfield to Gregory. Yet Mrs. Richman advocates Eliza's marriage to Boyer. Is marriage to a Boyer the best that an intelligent, well-educated woman can do, particularly when the alternative, Major Sanford, is no alternative at all? "What a pity," Eliza confides to her friend Lucy, "that the graces and virtues are not oftener united! They must, however, meet in the man of my choice; and till I find such a one, I shall continue to subscribe my name Eliza Wharton" (p. 148). She does, of course, precisely that. As Eliza Wharton she departs initially from her mother's house and as Eliza Wharton still she departs finally and through death from the text of the novel, from the tragedy of her life, which hardly constitutes a vindication of the rights of women.

Eliza Wharton sins and dies. Her death can convey the conservative moral that many critics of the time demanded. Yet the circumstances of that death seem designed to tease the reader into thought. It is in precisely these interstices—the disjunctions between the conventional and the radical readings of the plot—that the early American sentimental novel flourishes. It is in the irresolution of Eliza Wharton's dilemma that the novel, as a genre, differentiates itself from the tract stories of Elizabeth Whitman in which the novel is grounded and which it ultimately transcends. Tracts readily prescribe how a young woman should lead her life and make her marriage. But in the fullness of *The*

Coquette, we see just how the governing equation that innocence and virtue are to be rewarded must break down in a society in which women have no power to procure their own rewards but depend, in marriages or affairs, on the luck of the draw. Thus the novel's surplus of socially unsanctioned significance calls the more conventionally grounded stories of Elizabeth Whitman into question. It is easy, of course, to avoid too much novel reading. It is also easy to avoid social climbing and an anticlerical cast of mind. But how does one escape the social parameters of female powerlessness and female constraint?

That rhetorical question is left pointedly unanswered in the novel by the juxtaposition of the independent Miss Wharton, *feme sole,* and Mrs. Wharton, the quintessential *feme covert,* who, as a virtuous widow, has been ironically deprived of her covering. If virtue is to be rewarded, then surely Mrs. Wharton's life should be rich, an example to both her daughter and the reader. Yet the mother is exactly what the daughter does not want to be, and the novel validates the daughter's judgment. Observing the older woman in conversation with Boyer, Eliza wryly recognizes that her mother would "make him a [better] wife than I" (p. 186). And Eliza is right. The mother is precisely the kind of woman whom Boyer should marry. Desiring little or nothing for herself, she is a cipher in search of an integer, an empty sign seeking for another's (a husband's) excess of significance to provide her own meaning. Quite characteristically, her endeavors to dispel her daughter's doubts about matrimony never address the substance of those doubts but slide into an extended encomium on the clergyman himself, his worth to the community, his friends, the rewards that will accrue from selfless devotion to such an unselfish man. For Mrs. Wharton, the worth of his wife, of any wife, is immaterial; her duties go without saying. As even that advice suggests, for this conventional woman, female being, by her own definition and her culture's definition, is nothingness.

As that advice also suggests, Mrs. Wharton's philosophy of wifehood considerably compromises her performance as a mother. The nullity at the core of the older woman's existence renders her utterly ineffectual as a moral guide, as a concerned advisor, and even as a sympathetic confidante of her daughter. Four times in the novel Eliza, on the verge of a mental breakdown, writes to a friend about how she must feign happiness so as not to perturb her poor mother. Her mother, in turn, confides to a friend that she suspects something might be bothering her daughter but she lacks the will to inquire what it might be. Instead, she stands silently by, a mute witness to her daughter's progressive physical and mental debilitation. Even more obvious, Eliza yields herself to Sanford virtually before her mother's eyes—first in her mother's garden and then, after the weather turns cold and

Eliza's health deteriorates, in her mother's parlor. It is a harrowing denouement: Eliza, physically emaciated and mentally deranged, allowing herself to be repeatedly "seduced" in her mother's house; Sanford triumphing over both women; Eliza presently dying; Mrs. Wharton wringing her hands, but living on as a continuing testimony to her daughter's tragic death and her own ineffectual life.

The full tragedy of the novel, however, is that ultimately there was no tragedy at all—only the banal predictability of a fall that was precisely what the most conservative proponents of the status quo labored to prevent. Or perhaps the tragedy is that it can readily be reduced to this formulation and is thus reduced even in the telling. Consider how Eliza's desire for freedom devolves into sexual acquiescence, accomplished with an appalling lack of desire. Eliza Wharton, vividly rendered in Foster's fiction, still cannot be separated from her story, which is necessarily conjoined with Elizabeth Whitman's different but finally unknowable story, so much so that the historical personage and the fictional person shared a common tombstone. It is as if the tragic and the trivial, the real character's puzzling death and the fictional character's problematic one, had all been interred together leaving the survivors—within the text and without—to puzzle out the meaning of it all.

The female mourners at the end of the novel articulate their sense of having lost through Eliza's death not only a friend and a relative, but also a part of themselves and their own desires. I would also suggest that many readers of the time, turning over a story they already knew and did not know at all, must have felt a similar shock of recognition, which might partly explain the great popularity of the novel. Writing a preface to the 1855 edition of *The Coquette,* Jane E. Locke referred to the extraordinary appeal of Foster's Eliza Wharton who had become, by that time, virtually a cult heroine in both her novelistic form and as dramatized in a popular 1802 play based on the novel, *The New England Coquette.*[95] Readers, according to Locke, read Eliza's story as their own and cherished her story, their story, the story of an "actual" American woman who had loved badly and lost. Here was a New England Clarissa who had lived in Hartford, who had attended the theater in Boston, who had died and was buried in Danvers—real places, places that one could visit. And the readers did, like pilgrims to a sacred shrine. Some nineteenth-century editions of *The Coquette* included engravings of the Bell Tavern in Danvers. Even after The Bell was torn down, its doorstep, upon which, according to legend, Whitman had written her initials as a signal to Fidelio, was removed to the Peabody Historical Society where, into the twentieth-century, lovers would come to look upon it and to touch it. Whitman's gravestone, in the Main Street Burial Ground and bearing essentially the same inscription reported in the novel, became a favorite trysting place for nineteenth-century sentimental lovers who during the century carried away portions of the gravestone to keep as talismans—like pieces of the One True Cross. By the twentieth century, the whole engraved name had been chipped away from the stone, its absence a tribute to Eliza's continuing cultural presence.

Mostly, however, Eliza/Elizabeth was honored by those who bought or borrowed *The Coquette* and read and reread it virtually into oblivion. Like such popular books as the *New England Primer* of which very few early copies remain today, less than a dozen copies of the first edition of this novel survive and equally few of the second edition of 1802. Yet editions of the book remained steadily in print until 1874. It enjoyed its greatest popularity between 1824 and 1828 when it was reissued eight times. And in 1866, it was still important enough to be added to the Peterson and Brothers "Dollar Series" of popular fiction—"The best, the largest, the handsomest, and the cheapest books in the world," according to the Peterson advertisements.[96] But most noteworthy for my purposes is the popularity of this text to late eighteenth-century readers. At a time when American novels were not plentiful (nor, for that matter, other books either), *The Coquette* occupied a special place. As Locke notes:

> It is not surprising that it thus took precedence in interest . . . of all American novels, at least throughout New England, and was found, in every cottage within its borders, beside the family Bible, and, though pitifully, yet almost as carefully treasured.[97]

Our retrospective reading, I have argued throughout this [essay], must somehow recover and make sense of that sense of treasuring lost.

Notes

[1] See Peter J. Rabinowitz, "Assertion and Assumption: Fictional Patterns and the External World," *PMLA*, 97 (May 1981), 408-19.

[2] J. Potter, "Growth of Population in the United States, 1700-1860," in David Glass and D. Eversley, eds., *Population in History* (London: Arnold, 1965), p. 271.

[3] Bernard Farber, *Guardians of Virtue: Salem Families in 1800* (New York: Basic Books, 1972), p. 41; and Robert V. Wells, "Family History and Demographic Transition," *Journal of Social History*, 9 (Fall 1975), 1-19.

[4] For a perceptive discussion of the changing American attitude toward adolescence, see James Axtell, *The School upon a Hill* (New Haven; Yale Univ. Press,

1974); and Joseph F. Kett, *Rites of Passage: Adolescence in America, 1790 to the Present* (New York: Basic Books, 1977), pp. 15-50.

[5] The Patty Rogers Diary, Manuscript Department, [American Antiquarian Society (herafter AAS)], records a constant and even exhausting round of social visiting as does the Elizabeth Bancroft Diary (also at AAS). The fluid social and courtship patterns of the early Republic are discussed in Ellen K. Rothman's study of 350 women's diaries, *Hands and Hearts: A History of Courtship in America* (New York: Basic Books, 1984).

[6] The story of Mrs. Anderson is told in Sukey Vickery's letter of July 19, 1799 to Adeline Hartwell, Sukey Vickery Papers, Manuscript Collection, AAS.

[7] Mary Beth Norton, *Liberty's Daughters: The Revolutionary Experience of American Women, 1750-1800* (Boston: Little, Brown, 1980), pp. 3-9.

[8] Linda K. Kerber, *Women of the Republic: Intellect and Ideology in Revolutionary America* (Chapel Hill: Univ. of North Carolina Press, 1980), p. 252; and Alice Kessler-Harris, *Women Have Always Worked* (Old Westbury, N.Y.: Feminist Press, 1980), pp. 6-35.

[9] Nancy F. Cott, *The Bonds of Womanhood: "Woman's Sphere" in New England, 1780-1835* (New Haven: Yale Univ. Press, 1977), pp. 39-41. James A. Henretta, in *The Evolution of American Society, 1700-1815: An Interdisciplinary Analysis* (Lexington, Mass.: D. C. Heath, 1973), notes that in 1776 in Philadelphia alone over four thousand women and children earned minimum wages by "putting out" their spinning for the local textile mills (p. 194). See also, Edith Abbot, *Women in Industry* (New York: D. Appleton, 1918), pp. 66-70, 262-316; and Rolla M. Tyron, *Household Manufactures in the United States, 1640-1860* (1917; repr. New York: Augustus M. Kelley, 1966), pp. 124-33.

[10] *The Diaries of Julia Cowles: A Connecticut Record, 1797-1803*, ed. Anna Roosevelt Cowles and Laura Hadley Moseley (New Haven: Yale Univ. Press, 1931), pp. 40-41; and the diary of Elizabeth Drinker, especially the entries for June 20, 1795 and February 29, 1796, Historical Society of Pennsylvania, Philadelphia.

[11] Arthur W. Calhoun, *A Social History of the American Family* (New York: Barnes & Noble, 1917), 51-64; Philip J. Greven, Jr., *Four Generations: Population, Land, and Family in Colonial Andover, Massachusetts* (Ithaca: Cornell Univ. Press, 1970), pp. 113-16; Henretta, *Evolution of American Society*, p. 133; Edward Shorter, "Illegitimacy, Sexual Revolution, and Social Change in Modern Europe," *Journal of Interdisciplinary History*, 2 (1971), 237-72; Daniel Scott Smith, "The Dating of the American Sexual Revolution: Evidence and Interpretation," in *The American*

Family in Social-Historical Perspective, ed. Michael Gordon (New York: St. Martin's Press, 1973), p. 323; and, especially, Daniel Scott Smith and Michael S. Hindus, "Premarital Pregnancy in America, 1640-1971: An Overview and Interpretation," *Journal of Interdisciplinary History,* 5 (1975), 537-70.

[12] Catherine M. Scholten, "'On the Importance of the Obstetrick Art': Changing Customs of Childbirth in America, 1760 to 1825," *William & Mary Quarterly,* 3rd ser., 34 (July 1977), 426-28; Daniel Scott Smith, *Population, Family, and Society in Hingham, Massachusetts, 1635-1880,* Ph.D. diss. Univ. of California, Berkeley, 1972, pp. 219-25; and Robert V. Wells, "Quaker Marriage Patterns in a Colonial Perspective, *William & Mary Quarterly,* 3rd ser., 29 (July 1972), 422.

[13] *The Diaries of Julia Cowles,* pp. 91-92, 94.

[14] Daniel Scott Smith, "Family Limitation, Sexual Control, and Domestic Feminism in Victorian America," in *Clio's Consciousness Raised,* ed. Lois Banner and Mary Hartman (New York: Harper & Row, 1974), pp. 119-36.

[15] Ansley J. Coale and Melvin Zelnick, *New Estimates of Fertility and Population in the United States* (Princeton: Princeton Univ. Press, 1963), pp. 35-36; Potter, "Growth of Population," pp. 644-47, 663, 679; Warren C. Sanderson, "Quantitative Aspects of Marriage Fertility and Family Limitation in Nineteenth-Century America: Another Application of the Coale Specifications," *Demography,* 16 (1979), 339-58; and Robert V. Wells, "Demographic Change and the Life Cycle of American Families," in Theodore K. Rabb and Robert I. Rotberg, eds., *The Family in History: Interdisciplinary Essays* (New York: Harper & Row, 1971), pp. 85-88.

[16] Alexis de Tocqueville, *Democracy in America,* 2 vols., ed., Phillips Bradley (New York: Vintage Books, 1945), 2:212.

[17] Molly Tilghman and Abigail Adams quoted in Norton, *Liberty's Daughters,* p. 75.

[18] Sanderson, "Quantitative Aspects," pp. 339-58.

[19] Carl N. Degler, *At Odds: Women and the Family in America from the Revolution to the Present* (New York: Oxford Univ. Press, 1980), p. 196; and Norman E. Himes, *Medical History of Contraception* (Baltimore: Williams & Wilkins, 1936); and Robert V. Wells, "Family Size and Fertility Control in Eighteenth-Century America: A Study of Quaker Families," *Population Studies,* 25 (1971), 75.

[20] Kenneth A. Lockridge, *Literacy in Colonial New England* (New York: Norton, 1974); and Maris A. Vinovskis, "Socioeconomic Determinants of Fertility," *Journal of Interdisciplinary History,* 6 (Winter 1976), 375-96; and Tamara K. Hareven and Maris A. Vinovskis, "Patterns of Childbearing in Late Nineteenth-Century America: The Determinants of Marital Fertility in Five Massachusetts Towns in 1880," in Tamara K. Hareven and Maris A. Vinovskis, eds., *Family and Population in Nineteenth Century America* (Princeton: Princeton Univ. Press, 1978), pp. 85-125; and Wells, "Family Size and Fertility Control," p. 76.

[21] Perry Miller, *The Life of the Mind in America* (New York: Harcourt, Brace & World, 1965), p. 128.

[22] Marylynn Salmon, "Life, Liberty, and Dower: The Legal Status of Women After the American Revolution," in *Women, War, and Revolution,* ed. Carol R. Berkin and Clara M. Lovett (New York: Holmes & Meier, 1980), p. 85.

[23] St. George Tucker quoted in Kerber, *Women of the Republic,* p. 137; Tucker, ed., *Blackstone's Commentaries: With Notes of Reference to the Constitution and Laws, of the Federal Government of the United States; and of the Commonwealth of Virginia,* 5 vols. (Philadelphia: Wm. Birch and Abraham Small, 1803), 2:445.

[24] Kerber, *Women of the Republic,* p. 140.

[25] For an intriguing discussion of how changing inheritance laws may have eventually contributed to redefining the married woman's status as an individual, see Kerber, ibid., pp. 140-55.

[26] Harriet Martineau is quoted in Joan Hoff Wilson, "The Illusion of Change: Women and the American Revolution," in Alfred F. Young, ed., *The American Revolution: Explorations in the History of American Radicalism* (Dekalb: Northern Illinois Univ. Press, 1976), p. 419.

[27] See Mary Beard, *Woman as Force in History* (New York: Macmillan, 1946). A similar view is supported by Richard B. Morris in *Studies in the History of Early American Law* (New York: Columbia Univ. Press, 1930); and Morris, ed., *Select Cases of the Mayor's Court of New York City* (Washington, D. C.: American Historical Assoc., 1935), pp. 21-25. For a revisionist view, see Norma Basch, *In the Eyes of the Law: Women, Marriage, and Property in Nineteenth-Century New York* (Ithaca: Cornell Univ. Press, 1982); Peggy Rabkin, "The Origins of Law Reform: The Social Significance of the Nineteenth-Century Codification Movement and Its Contribution to the Passage of the Early Married Woman's Property Acts," *Buffalo Law Review,* 24 (1974), 683-760; and Marylynn Salmon, "Life, Liberty, and Dower." See also Salmon's "Equality or Submersion? *Feme Covert* Status in Early Penn-

sylvania," in Carol Ruth Berkin and Mary Beth Norton, eds., *Women of America: A History* (Boston: Houghton Mifflin, 1979).

[28] Basch, *In the Eyes of the Law,* pp. 17, 232.

[29] Judge Hertell quoted in Cott, *Bonds of Womanhood,* p. 78.

[30] See especially, Norton's chapter, "As Independent as Circumstances Will Admit," which begins. "If any quality was antithetical to the colonial notion of femininity, it was autonomy" (*Liberty's Daughters,* p. 125).

[31] Abigail Adams in a letter to John Adams, March 31, 1776, repr. in Alice S. Rossi, ed., *The Feminist Papers: From Adams to de Beauvoir* (New York: Bantan Books, 1973), pp. 10-11.

[32] Grace Growden Galloway quoted in Norton, *Liberty's Daughters,* p. 45.

[33] Salmon, "Life, Liberty, and Dower," p. 97; Nancy F. Cott, "Divorce and the Changing Status of Women in Eighteenth-Century Massachusetts," *William & Mary Quarterly,* 3rd ser., 33 (October 1976), 586-614; Leonard Woods Labaree, ed. *Royal Instructions to British Colonial Governors, 1670-1776,* 2 vols. (New York: Appleton-Century, 1935), 1:155.

[34] Gilbert Imlay, *The Emigrants, & c., or The History of an Expatriated Family.* 3 vols. (London: A. Hamilton, 1793), 1:ix.

[35] Alice Morse Earle, *Colonial Dames and Good Wives* (1895; repr. New York: Frederick Ungar, 1962), pp. 247-53; Elizabeth F. Ellet, *The Women of the American Revolution* (New York: Scribner's, 1853-54), passim; Wendy Martin, "Women and the American Revolution," *Early American Literature,* 11 (1976-77), 322-35; and Norton, *Liberty's Daughters,* pp. 195-227.

[36] Sophie Drinker, "Votes for Women in Eighteenth-Century New Jersey," *New York Historical Society Proceedings,* 31 (1962), 80. See also the *Massachusetts Spy, or Worcester Gazette,* (November 1, 1797), under a "Rights of Women" headline: "At the late election in Elizabethtown, (N.J.) the Females asserted the privilege granted them by the laws of that state, and gave in their votes for members to represent them in the state legislature" (p. 3).

[37] "Lines, Written by a Lady, who was questioned respecting her inclination to marry," *Massachusetts Magazine, or Monthly Museum,* 6 (September 1794), 566.

[38] "Rights of Women, by a Lady," *Philadelphia Minerva,* October 17, 1795.

[39] Alexander Keyssar, "Widowhood in Eighteenth-Century Massachusetts: A Problem in the History of the Family," *Perspectives in American History,* 8 (1974), 83-119; Wells, "Family History," pp. 11-12; and Wells, "Quaker Marriage Patterns," pp. 433-34.

[40] Betsey Mayhew and Sarah Hanschurst quoted in Norton, *Liberty's Daughters,* p. 241. And for hundreds of comments about the advantages of remaining unmarried and the "Cult of Single Blessedness," see Lee Virginia Chambers-Schiller, *Liberty, A Better Husband: Single Women in America: The Generations of 1780-1840* (New Haven: Yale Univ. Press, 1984).

[41] Charles Brockden Brown, *Alcuin: A Dialogue,* ed. Lee R. Edwards (New York: Grossman, 1971), pp. 88; 24-25.

[42] Lyman H. Butterfield et al., eds., *Adams Family Correspondence,* 4 vols. (Cambridge: Harvard Univ. Press, 1963-73), 1:87.

[43] Jane Tompkins, *Sensational Designs: The Cultural Work of American Fiction, 1790-1860* (New York: Oxford Univ. Press, 1985).

[44] Catherine Maria Sedgwick, "Old Maids," in Susan Koppelman, ed., *Old Maids: Short Stories by Nineteenth-Century U.S. Women Writers* (New York: Pandora Press, 1984).

[45] Rachel M. Brownstein, *Becoming a Heroine: Reading About Women in Novels* (New York: Viking, 1982), p. 24.

[46] The historiography of changing family patterns is controversial and the picture tends to look different depending on what factors one includes. Class, regional, and racial factors all influence the interpretation in different ways. Degler, Kerber, and Norton, for example, all tend to see a changing family pattern with more options for women by the end of the eighteenth century, although Kerber, perhaps, views the situation less optimistically than the other historians. Lawrence Stone has charted a change in family structure in England during the eighteenth-century, especially an increase in affectional marriages and affectional modes of child-rearing. See his *The Family, Sex, and Marriage in England, 1500-1800* (New York: Harper & Row, 1977). A similar pattern is described in the U.S. by Jay Fliegelman, *Prodigals and Pilgrims: The American Revolution Against Patriarchal Authority, 1750-1800* (Cambridge: Cambridge Univ. Press, 1982); Daniel B. Smith, *Inside the Great House: Planter Family Life in Eighteenth-Century Chesapeake Society* (Ithaca: Cornell Univ. Press, 1980); and Ronald G. Walters, "The Family and Ante-Bellum Reform: An Interpretation," *Societas,* 3 (Summer 1973), 221-32. But Philip J. Greven, in *The Protestant Temperament: Patterns*

of Child-Rearing, Religious Experience, and the Self in Early America (New York: Knopf, 1978), argues for different methods of child-rearing occurring simultaneously rather than evolving. Michael Zuckerman, in "Penmanship Exercises for Saucy Sons: Some Thoughts on the Colonial Southern Family," *South Carolina History Review,* 84 (1983), 152-66, finds family patterns changing in the South by the end of the eighteenth century, while Jan Lewis, in *The Pursuit of Happiness: Family Values in Jefferson's Virginia* (New York: Cambridge Univ. Press, 1983), finds change occurring more gradually and much later. For a brief overview of the different arguments, see Thomas P. Slaughter, "Family Politics in Revolutionary America," *American Quarterly,* 36 (Fall 1984), 598-606. My own focus is not on how the family "actually" changed but how selected social commentators of the late eighteenth-century presented dialectical views of the family and woman's role in the family and society.

[47] Cott, *Bonds of Womanhood,* p. 202.

[48] David Lundberg and Henry F. May, "The Enlightened Reader in America," *American Quarterly,* 28 (Summer 1976), 262-71; app. Lundberg and May conclude that 40 percent of all the booksellers and libraries in their sample made *Emile* available to the American reading public. See also Paul M. Spurlin, *Rosseau in America, 1760-1809* (University: Univ. of Alabama Press, 1969).

[49] Jean-Jacques Rosseau, *Emilius and Sophia; or, A New System of Education,* trans. by "A Citizen of Geneva" (London: T. Becket and R. Baldwin, 1783).

[50] *Boston Weekly Magazine,* 2 (May 5, 1804), 110; 2 (March 24, 1804), 36.

[51] Helena Wells, *Constantia Neville; or, The West Indian* (London: C. Whittingham for T. Caddell, 1800).

[52] S.S.B.K. Wood, *Amelia; or, The Influence of Virtue. An Old Man's Story* (Portsmouth, N.H.: William Treadwell, 1802), p. 103.

[53] Helena Wells, *The Step-Mother; a Domestic Tale, from Real Life,* 2 vols. (London: T. N. Longman and O. Rees, 1799), 2:21-22.

[54] S.S.B.K. Wood, *Dorval, or the Speculator* (Portsmouth, N.H.: Nutting and Whitelock, 1801), p. 78; and her *Julia, and the Illuminated Baron* (Portsmouth, N.H.: Charles Peirce, 1800), pp. 81-82.

[55] When published serially in the *Massachusetts Magazine, or Monthly Museum* from 1792 to 1794, Murray's *Gleaner* essays were signed with a male pseudonym, "Mentor." Reprinted in three volumes in Boston in 1798, however, they were signed Constantia, and ear-

lier references suggest that, even before the collected edition, readers were aware that the Gleaner was a woman.

[56] Judith Sargent Murray, *The Gleaner: A Miscellaneous Production. In Three Volumes. By Constantia* (Boston: I. Thomas and E. T. Andrews, 1798), 1:167-68; 3:220.

[57] "On the Equality of the Sexes," *Massachusetts Magazine, or Monthly Museum,* 2 (March 1798), 132.

[58] Murray, *The Gleaner,* 3:189.

[59] For the British connection, see Dale Spender's indispensable, *Women of Ideas (And What Men Have Done to Them)* (London: Ark, 1982). For a discussion of the most prominent of the American feminists of the time, see Mary Sumner Benson, *Women in Eighteenth-Century America* (New York: Columbia Univ. Press, 1935); and Wilson, "The Illusion of Change," pp. 386-93, 426-31. The "Female Advocate" became a subject of some controversy in the magazines of the time owing to an anonymous pamphlet published in New Haven, Conn., in 1801 called, simply, *The Female Advocate.* This pamphlet especially emphasized the importance of a thorough female education and suggested, whimsically, that the doors of all institutions of higher learning be shut to men and opened to women for a period of time and then it be seen just which was the smarter sex. See also Eliza Southgate Bowne, *A Girls' Life Eighty Years Ago* (New York: Charles Scribner's Sons, 1887).

[60] See Charles Louis de Secondat, baron de Montesquieu, *The Spirit of Laws* (1748; repr. Berkeley: Univ. of California Press, 1977); and Marie Jean Antoine Nicolas Caritat, marquis de Condorcet, *Outline of an Historical View of the Progress of the Human Mind* (Philadelphia: Mathew Carey, 1796), esp. pp. 24-50. Condorcet's arguments on behalf of women are alluded to in Charles Brockden Brown's *Alcuin.* For a detailed discussion of Brown's feminist dialogue, see my essay, "The Matter and Manner of Charles Brockden Brown's *Alcuin,*" in *Critical Essays on Charles Brockden Brown,* ed. Bernard Rosenthal (Boston: G. K. Hall, 1981), pp. 71-86.

[61] James Butler, *Fortune's Foot-ball: or, The Adventures of Mercutio. Founded on Matters of Fact . . . ,* 2 vols. in 1 (Harrisburgh, Pa: John Wyeth, 1797), 1:145-46. (The title page indicates this novel was printed in 1797, although copyright was not secured until 1798.)

[62] Imlay, *The Emigrants,* pp. ii, 22-23, 66.

[63] Sukey Vickery, *Emily Hamilton, A Novel. Founded on Incidents in Real Life. By a Young Lady of Worces-*

ter County (Worcester, Mass: Isaiah Thomas, Jr., 1803), pp. 97-98, 108.

64 Three essays perceptively discuss the American reaction to Wollstonecraft and Wollstonecraftism. See R. M. Janes, "On the Reception of Mary Wollstonecraft's *A Vindication of the Rights of Woman." Journal of the History of Ideas,* 39 (April-June 1978), 293-302; Patricia Jewell McAlexander, "The Creation of the American Eve: The Cultural Dialogue on the Nature and Role of Women in Late-Eighteenth-Century America," *Early American Literature,* 9 (1975), 252-66; and Marcelle Thiebaux, "Mary Wollstonecraft in Federalist America: 1791-1802," in *The Evidence of the Imagination: Studies of Interactions Between Life and Art in English Romantic Literature,* ed. Donald H. Reiman et al. (New York: New York Univ. Press, 1978), pp. 195-245.

65 Lundberg and May, "Enlightened Reader," app.

66 *New England Palladium,* 19 (March 2, 1802), 1.

67 For a fuller discussion, see also Linda K. Kerber, "Daughters of Columbia: Educating Women for the Republic, 1787-1805," in *The Hofstadter Aegis: A Memorial,* ed. Eric L. McKitrick and Stanley M. Elkins (New York: Knopf, 1974), pp. 36-59. It must be emphasized that Godwin did not expect the *Memoirs* to in any way cast his deceased wife in a negative light. Utterly bereft at her death, Godwin moved his books and papers into her study and, until his own death forty years later, continued to work in Mary's room, among her belongings, beneath the magnificent portrait of her by John Opie. For an excellent discussion of the relationship between Godwin and Wollstonecraft and a sampling of early reviews of the *Memoirs* (including those quoted here), see Peter H. Marshall, *William Godwin* (New Haven: Yale Univ. Press, 1984), pp. 189-94.

68 Samuel Miller, "The Appropriate Duty and Ornament of the Female Sex," in *The Columbian Preacher; Or, A Collection of Original Sermons, from Preachers of Eminence in the United States. Embracing the Distinguishing Doctrines of Grace* (Catskill: Nathan Elliott, 1808), p. 253.

69 For an extended critique of Wollstonecraft's life and her ideas, see Benjamin Silliman, *Letters of Shahcoolen, A Hindu Philosopher, Residing in Philadelphia . . .* (Boston: Russell & Cutler, 1802), 29-32, 48. Two other novels denounced Wollstonecraft in the years immediately following the publication of the *Memoirs,* Wells's *Constantia Neville* and Wood's *Dorval.*

70 The complex and heated debate over the limits or possibilities of domesticity in the nineteenth century is outside the focus of the present study. For a survey of the basic positions, however, the reader should consult the "Conclusion" (pp. 197-206) of Nancy F. Cott's *Bonds of Womanhood.*

71 Ruth H. Block, "American Feminine Ideals in Transition: The Rise of the Moral Mother, 1785-1815," *Feminist Studies,* 4 (1978), 101-26. See also Mary Maples Dunn, "Saints and Sisters: Congregational and Quaker Women in the Early Colonial Period," in *Women in American Religion,* ed. Janet Wilson James (Philadelphia: Univ. of Pennsylvania Press, 1980), pp. 30-35; Linda K. Kerber, "Can a Woman Be an Individual? The Limits of Puritan Tradition in the Early Republic," *Texas Studies in Language and Literature,* 25 (Spring 1983), esp. 161-65; Anne L. Kuhn, *The Mother's Role in Childhood Education: New England Concepts, 1830-1860* (New Haven Yale Univ. Press, 1947); Gerald Moran and Maris Vinovskis, "The Puritan Family and Religion: A Critical Reappraisal," *William & Mary Quarterly,* 3rd ser., 39 (January 1982), 29-63; and Peter Gregg Slater, *Children in the New England Mind: In Death and In Life* (Hamden, Conn.: Shoe String Press [Archon Books], 1977), esp. chaps. 3, 4.

72 William Lyman, *A Virtuous Woman, the Bond of Domestic Union and the Source of Domestic Happiness* (New London, Conn.: S. Green, 1802), pp. 22-23.

73 *Parents' Magazine* (October 1840).

74 Helen Waite Papashivly, *All the Happy Endings* (New York: Harper, 1956), pp. 31-32.

75 There were, of course, exceptions to this rule, such as Cigarette, an adventurous young woman who finds her way through several complicated adventures. See Russel B. Nye, "The Novel as Dream and Weapon: Women's Popular Novels in the Nineteenth Century," *Historical Society of Michigan Chronicle,* 11 (4th qr. 1975), 2-18.

76 Charles Brockden Brown, "Female Learning," *Literary Magazine and American Register,* 1 (January 1804), 245.

77 Samuel Relf, *Infidelity, or the Victims of Sentiment* (Philadelphia: W. W. Woodward, 1797), title page; pp. 36-37.

78 By viewing Montraville as the stock seducer and overlooking the problematic role played by Belcour, William C. Spengemann, in *The Adventurous Muse: The Poetics of American Fiction, 1789-1900* (New Haven: Yale Univ. Press, 1977), can dismiss *Charlotte* as possibly "the most rigidly programmatic sentimental novel ever written" (p. 92). But he also concedes that "certain fictive energies seem to be at work, threat-

ening to compromise the conservative values" of this novel (p. 90).

[79] For an excellent assessment of Rowson's feminism and a discussion of her fictional strengths and weaknesses, see Patricia L. Parker's *Susanna Haswell Rowson* (Boston: Twayne, 1986). I am grateful to Professor Parker for making her manuscript available to me. See also, Eve Kornfeld, "Women in Post-Revolutionary American Culture: Susanna Haswell Rowson's American Career, 1792-1824," *Journal of American Culture,* 6 (Winter 1983), 56-62; Wendy Martin, "Profile: Susanna Rowson, Early American Novelist," *Women's Studies,* 2 (1974), 1-8; and Dorothy Weil, *In Defense of Women: Susanna Rowson* (University Park: Pennsylvania State Univ. Press, 1976), esp. pp. 31-64. The quotations are from the paperback edition of the novel "edited for modern readers" by Clara M. Kirk and Rudolf Kirk (New Haven: College & University Press, 1964), p. 121. Although this is the only readily available edition of the novel, it must be emphasized that it is neither a reprint of the original edition nor a scholarly modern edition of the work.

[80] *Critical Review* (London) for April 1791, repr. in Rowson's *Charlotte* (Philadelphia: Mathew Carey, 1794), n.p. For other sympathetic critical assessments, see the *Boston Weekly Magazine,* 1 (January 22, 1803), 53; and Samuel L. Knapp's "Memoir," in Rowson's posthumously published *Charlotte's Daughter: Or, The Three Orphans. A Sequel to Charlotte Temple . . .* (Boston: Richardson & Lord, 1828). pp. 3-20.

[81] Herbert Ross Brown, *The Sentimental Novel in America, 1789-1860* (Durham, N.C.: Duke Univ. Press, 1940), p. 176.

[82] *Margaretta; or, the Intricacies of the Heart* (Philadelphia: Samuel F. Bradford, 1807), p. 80. The anonymous author of this novel well may be alluding to Judith Sargent Murray's earlier "Story of Margaretta." Both on the level of plot and characterization there are definite similarities between the two works.

[83] See Leslie A. Fielder, *Love and Death in the American Novel,* rev. ed. (1960; rpt. New York: Dell, 1966), p. 93; and Walter P. Wenska, Jr., "*The Coquette* and the American Dream of Freedom," *Early American Literature,* 12 (1977-78), 243-55.

[84] The documents pertaining to Elizabeth Whitman's life and death (right down to an inventory of all she had with her at Bell Tavern when she died) have been included in Charles Knowles Bolton, *The Elizabeth Whitman Mystery* (Peabody, Mass.: Peabody Historical Society, 1912); Herbert Ross Brown, "Introduction" to *The Coquette* (New York: Facsimile Text Society, 1939), pp. v-xix; Caroline W. Dall, *The Romance of the Association: Or, One Last Glimpse of Charlotte Temple and Eliza\Wharton* (Cambridge, Mass.: Press of John Wilson, 1875); and Jane E. Locke, "Historical Preface, Including a Memoir of the Author" in *The Coquette* (Boston: Samuel Etheridge for E. Larkin, 1855), pp. 3-30. The article quoted from the *Salem Mercury* for July 29, 1788 is reprinted in Bolton, pp. 33-37.

[85] Anonymous essayist quoted in Bolton, *Elizabeth Whitman Mystery,* p. 59.

[86] Almost all discussions of *The Coquette* sooner or later raise the question of the real identity of Major Sanford. See Bolton, *Elizabeth Whitman Mystery,* pp. 109-32, for a summary of the early choices; and Alexander Cowie, *The Rise of the American Novel* (New York: American Book Company, 1948), p. 16; Dall, *Romance of the Association,* pp. 101-15; and James Woodress, *A Yankee's Odyssey: The Life of Joel Barlow* (New York: Lippincott, 1958), pp. 60-64.

[87] Quoted in Herbert Ross Brown's "Introduction" to *The Coquette,* p. xii.

[88] Despite its being generally acknowledged as the best of the early American sentimental novels, *The Coquette* has never been published in a modern edition using modern standards of textual accuracy. The only widely available edition of *The Coquette* is that edited by William S. Osborne with punctuation and spellings silently (and not always carefully) "edited for the modern reader." But because it is available in paperback, I have taken all my references from this edition (New Haven: College & University Press, 1970) and future references to this edition will be cited parenthetically within the text. Lillie Deming Loshe, *The Early American Novel, 1789-1830* (1907; repr. New York; Frederick Ungar, 1966), was one of the first critics to note that *The Coquette* "is superior to its predecessors in interest and especially in character-drawing" (p. 14).

[89] Sanford does, however, allude to Laurence Sterne in the letter in which he announces his triumph over Eliza—a fitting allusion considering Foster's comments about Sterne in *The Boarding School; or, Lessons of a Preceptress to her Pupils* (Boston: Isaiah Thomas and E. T. Andrews, 1798), warning her readers against the "licentious wit" that is "concealed under the artful blandishments of sympathetic sensibility" in Sterne's fiction (p. 205).

[90] Bolton, *Elizabeth Whitman Mystery,* pp. 39-41.

[91] Bolton, Ibid., pp. 59-60.

[92] I have elsewhere assessed at length the inadequacy of the choices presented to Eliza. See my article "Flirting with Destiny: Ambivalence and Form in the Early

American Sentimental Novel," *Studies in American Fiction,* 10 (Spring 1982), esp. 27-34.

[93] Joanna Russ, "What Can a Heroine Do? Or Why Women Can't Write," in *Images of Women in Fiction: Feminist Perspectives,* ed. Susan Koppelman Cornillon (Bowling Green, Ohio: Bowling Green University Popular Press, 1972), p. 13.

[94] Russ, ibid., pp. 12-13.

[95] Jane E. Locke, "Historical Preface," to her edition of *The Coquette,* pp. 3-30. The novel was dramatized by J. Horatio Nichols, *The New England Coquette: From the History of The Celebrated Eliza Wharton. A Tragic Drama, in Three Acts* (Salem: N. Coverly, 1802).

[96] Herbert Ross Brown, "Introduction," *The Coquette,* p. ix.

[97] Locke, "Historical Preface," p. 4.

FURTHER READING

Baym, Nina. "Susan Warner, Anna Warner, and Maria Cummins." In her *Woman's Fiction: A Guide to Novels by and about Women in America, 1820-1870,* pp. 140-74. Ithaca and London: Cornell University Press, 1978.

> Biographical and critical survey of the lives and works of Cummins and the Warner sisters.

Brown, Herbert Ross. *The Sentimental Novel in America 1789-1860.* New York: Pageant Books, 1959, 407 p.

> Provides a general history of the development of the sentimental novel from its British roots to the height of its popularity in America. The chapter "The Sentimental Compromise" is included in the above entry.

Cowie, Alexander. "Heart and Home: Domestic, Sentimental, Didactic Fiction." In his *The Rise of the American Novel,* pp. 9-21. New York: American Book Co., 1951.

> Explores the historical conditions that first yielded American sentimental fiction, and surveys the most important works of the period.

Fielder, Leslie A. "The Bourgeois Sentimental Novel and the Female Audience" In *Love and Death in the American Novel,* pp. 43-80. New York: Criterion Books, 1960.

> Examines the sentimental novel as a symptom of the American transformation of Puritanism into anti-intellectual bourgeois Christianity.

Fisher, Philip. "Making a Thing into a Man: The Sentimental Novel and Slavery." In his *Hard Facts: Setting and Form in the American Novel,* pp. 87-127. New York: Oxford University Press, 1985.

> Contends that sentimental novelists argued for abolitionism by defining individuals in the context of the family, which slavery threatens.

Freibert, Lucy M. and Barbara A. White, eds. *Hidden Hands: An Anthology of American Women Writers, 1790-1870.* New Brunswick, N.J.: Rutgers University Press, 1985, 409 p.

> Provides excerpts from several novels and pieces of literary criticism by and related to women authors of the late eighteenth and nineteenth centuries.

Hansen, Klaus P. "The Sentimental Novel and Its Feminist Critique." *Early American Literature* XXVI, No. 1 (1991): 39-54.

> Comments on several critical approaches, including those of Nina Baym and Cathy Davidson, and contends that while the female authors of sentimental novels apparently agreed with their social roles, the novels express an underlying resistance.

Harris, Susan K. *19th-Century American Women's Novels: Interpretative Strategies.* New York: Cambridge University Press, 1990, 236 p.

> Provides a critical history of nineteenth- and early twentieth-century writings by American women, focusing primarily on didactic novels.

Kelley, Mary. *Private Woman, Public Stage: Literary Domesticity in Nineteenth-Century America.* New York: Oxford University Press, 1984, 409 p.

> Resists the tendency to portray "literary domestics" as either one-dimensional conformists or subversives, and instead examines their published and unpublished works as revealing means of individual expression.

Petter, Henri. *The Early American Novel.* Columbus: Ohio State University Press, 1971, 500 p.

> Surveys the development of the American novel through 1820, with plot synopses.

Samuels, Shirley, ed. *The Culture of Sentiment: Race, Gender, and Sentimentality in Nineteenth-Century America.* New York: Oxford University Press, 1992, 349 p.

> Presents a number of articles by different authors to portray the development of the nation's identity through nineteenth-century sentimental literature.

Smith, Henry Nash. "The Scribbling Women and the Cosmic Success Story." *Critical Inquiry* I, No. 1 (September 1974): 47-70.

> Contrasts the alienation expressed by such authors as Hawthorne and Melville with the "ethos of conformity" typical of sentimental fiction.

Smith-Rosenberg, Carroll. "Domesticating 'Virtue'." In *Literature and the Body: Essays on Populations and*

Persons, edited by Elaine Scarry, pp. 160-84. Baltimore: Johns Hopkins University Press, 1988.

Contends that capitalist republicanism problematizes the relation between independence and feminine virtues in sentimental fiction.

Spengemann, William C. "The Poetics of Domesticity." In his *The Adventurous Muse: The Poetics of American Fiction, 1789-1900*, pp. 68-118. New Haven: Yale University Press, 1977.

Discusses the conflict between the English sentimental novel as it was appropriated by American authors, and the American sense of self-determination.

Tompkins, Jane. "The Other American Renaissance." In her *Sensational Designs: The Cultural Work of American Fiction 1790-1860*, pp. 147-85. New York: Oxford University Press, 1985.

Evaluates the reformist social and psychological projects of sentimental novels, focusing specifically on Susan Warner's *The Wide, Wide World*.

Victorian Fantasy Literature

INTRODUCTION

Fairy tales sparked a wave of controversy when they were first introduced into England in the early nineteenth century; they were not immediately welcomed as they had been in Germany and France. Fairy tales were considered to be strictly for children, and children's literature was expected to be didactic and moral—not entertaining. As the notions about children changed during the century, however, so did ideas about literature for children. Fairy tales gradually became more accepted, and eventually a branch of wholly entertaining children's literature began to flourish.

In the early 1800s, children were thought of as imperfectly formed adults, and most literature for them was educational, designed to instruct them in their responsibilities to family and church. The Romantic notion of a child became more popular in the second half of the century. This view encouraged imagination in children and promoted the ideas that children were innocently wise, and that in their naivete they possessed rationales and virtues that were lost to adults. Gradually, writers adhered to this concept of children and began to write stories to entertain. Early fairy tales still promoted Christianity and values of the church, concentrating on the spiritual development of the protagonist. Even so, objections to fantasy came primarily from church organizations, which attacked fairy tales as corrupters of childhood. Some literary critics also renounced fairy tales, equating "fantastic" with "unrealistic" and therefore unsuitable for rational English citizens.

Indeed, critics have shown that even as fantasy gained acceptance as literature for children, it was considered unacceptable for adults to enjoy the genre. It is for this reason, critics suggest, that with very few exceptions fairy tales were written for children, featuring children as heroes. In fact, critics point out that adults are generally absent from fairy tales in spite of numerous hidden sexual references found in most stories; the adults that do appear are tyrannical and cruel. In most fantasy literature, the child protagonist leaves the familiar world run by adults and embarks on a quest in a land of enchantment and magic, free from the laws of nature and facts of science. He typically benefits from a power or energy from nature or the earth, and usually is taught a moral lesson before leaving the fantasy realm and returning home, often forgetting about the adventure altogether.

Before the adventure is over, however, and sometimes before it begins, the hero receives guidance and instruction from a powerful or magical female, usually in the form of a grandmother or fairy grandmother. These female characters were the exception to the characteristically evil adults found elsewhere in the stories—though the women were still secondary figures, leaving the child in the foreground. Critics have pointed out that powerful female characters were commonly found in children's fairy tales before appearing regularly in adult literature. Nearly every fairy tale had such a figure, and critics often refer to works by women fantasy writers, such as Christina Rossetti's narrative poem *Goblin Market* (1862), as examples of early feminist writing. Critics suggest that because fairy tales were neither suitable for adults nor realistic, women who felt repressed in society and in their homes found in them an acceptable channel for strong female characters.

Male authors also used fairy tales to comment on social conditions in Victorian England. Critics have suggested that many popular authors used fairy tales to comment on the Industrial Revolution, to create ideal alternatives to unsatisfactory conditions of the real world, and to contrast Christianity with the materialism of English society. Critics have also argued that the most celebrated authors of fantasy—Charles Dickens, Charles Kingsley, Lewis Carroll, and George MacDonald—believed that humanity had become too mechanized and serious with the arrival of the Industrial Revolution. These authors wanted to restore enjoyment and recreation to, and inspire compassion for, the working class, and, critics suggest, offer an escape from reality by reversing the known and accepted rules of the real world. Carroll is generally credited with removing all the rules from his tales and writing the first amoral, and therefore totally fantastic fairy tale, *Alice's Adventures in Wonderland* (1865). In *Alice*, Carroll offered complete escape from the logical with no definite moral value attached. Some critics claim that Carroll's story is a parody of the critics of children's fantasy literature.

Critics generally agree that Carroll, Kingsley, and MacDonald were the premier fantasy writers of this era. All three were clergymen but each had a distinctly different approach to fairy tales. Critics cite Carroll's fantasies as being filled with sublimated sexual content, but praise his works for offering a complete escape from reality by reversing or altering laws of science to create worlds that are purely fantastic. Kingsley's works, most notably *The Water Babies* (1863), are, according to critics, filled with moral and allegorical themes regarding spiritual and physical cleansing, and often contain sexual overtones as well. MacDonald is generally noted by critics to offer an escape from reality based on a religious point of view, providing outstanding physical and notable psychological descriptions. Critics typically agree that MacDonald's ability to achieve the best balance between morality and imagination makes him the father of fantasy.

Victorian fantasy literature began as a way to combine education and entertainment for a child, but by the end of the century it had developed into a way to challenge a child's imagination and offer a reprieve from the everyday world of English life. In their quest to capture the world of childhood innocence as paradise, works by fairy tale authors led to the study of the imagination and of dream-worlds, which in turn prompted the study of psychology by such figures as Sigmund Freud and Carl Jung, and served as a precursor to twentieth-century science fiction.

REPRESENTATIVE WORKS

Charles Dickens
 A Christmas Carol (novel) 1843

C. L. Dodgson (Lewis Carroll)
 Alice's Adventure in Wonderland (novel) 1865
 Through the Looking-Glass (novel) 1871

Jean Ingelow
 Mopsa the Fairy (novel) 1869

Charles Kingsley
 The Water Babies: A Fairy Tale for a Land-Baby (novel) 1863

George MacDonald
 Phantastes (novel) 1858
 At the Back of the North Wind (novel) 1871
 The Princess and the Goblin (novel) 1872
 The Princess and Curdie (novel) 1883

Christina Rossetti
 Goblin Market (poetry) 1862

John Ruskin
 The King of the Golden River (novel) 1840

William Makepeace Thackery
 The Rose and the Ring (novel) 1855

OVERVIEWS

Michael C. Kotzin

SOURCE: "The Fairy Tale," in *Dickens and the Fairy Tale,* Bowling Green University Popular Press, 1972, pp. 7-31

[*In the essay below, Kotzin recounts the history of the Victorian fairy tale by examining its origins in folklore and German fairy tales and outlining the growth of fantasy as literature.*]

Fairy tales are perhaps more easily recognized than defined. Folklorists group them with other kinds of folktales, such as animal stories, jests, and fables. They are a type of narrative which has traditionally been told aloud by peoples throughout the world, and although some of the fairy tales in oral traditions have literary sources and many literary versions of the tales have been written, the popular, primitive origins of the fairy-tale genre are often thought of as having determined its character.

The tales get their name from their inclusion of "fairy," but that is a word with more than one meaning. Thomas Keightley speculated that the root of the word "fairy" was the Latin *fatum.* This led to the Latin verb *fatare* (to enchant) which in French became *faer,* from which was made the substantive *faerie,* "illusion, enchantment, the meaning of which was afterwards extended, particularly after it had been adopted into the English language." According to Keightley, then, the first meaning of "faerie" was illusion; the second the land of illusions; the third the inhabitants of that land; and the fourth an individual inhabitant.[1] J. R. R. Tolkien insists that the fairy tale gets its name from reference to the second of those meanings. He says: "Fairy-stories are not in normal English usage stories *about* fairies or elves, but stories about Fairy, that is *Faërie,* the realm or state in which fairies have their being."[2]

Particular qualities of the world of "Fairie" include the presence there of magical acts, the animation of non-living things, the transformation of one thing or person into another, and an unnaturally quick or unnaturally slow passage of time. Fairy tales are recognized by the recurrence in them of this subject matter, and by the recurrence of certain narrative patterns or combinations of them. The typical fairy tale has a central character, usually an isolated, virtuous young man or woman who is often a youngest child. This hero confronts a villain, such as a cruel stepmother or a supernatural figure such as a giant, ogre, or witch. He may receive help from a supernatural being, such as some sort of good fairy. He usually is victorious over his adversary, achieves comfort and happiness, and sometimes gets married.

Two other forms of narrative, myths and legends, share some of this content, but fairy tales frequently are distinguished from them, as they were by James Frazer. He defined myths as "mistaken explanations of phenomena, whether of human life or of external nature"; legends as "traditions, whether oral or written, which relate the fortunes of real people in the past, or which describe events, not necessarily human, that are said to have occurred at real places"; and he describes folktales as "narratives which, though they profess to describe actual occurrences, are in fact purely imaginary, having no other aim than the entertainment of the hearer and making no real claim on his credulity."[3] In other words, the subjects of myths are prehistorical, of legends historical, and of folktales ahistorical.

The lines dividing these categories are faint and overlapping, though, and fairy tales and legends are often particularly difficult to separate, especially in the English narrative tradition. The distinction between fairy tales and myths is easier. It can be made in various ways, one of which Frazer hints at: not only by content, but by function (myths, he says, explain; folktales entertain). A similar contrast of function was discovered by Bronislaw Malinowski among stories told on the Trobriand Islands. The mythology which Malinowski found on the Islands "expresses, enhances, and codifies belief; . . . safeguards and enforces morality; . . . vouches for the efficiency of ritual and contains practical rules for the guidance of man,"[4] and can be thought of as duplicating the function of Christian mythology in Victorian England. Similarly, the major function of folktales on the Islands, to provide amusement, was one of the major functions of fairy tales in Victorian England; but there was also another declared function: to have a moral effect. The first of these is perhaps the more "natural" function of fairy tales, but before amusement could be accepted as an official justification for allowing children to read fairy tales in England they had to be seen as fulfilling the second function too, and that did not happen until the nineteenth century. During the previous century the influence of didacticism and rationalism on the printing of children's books had helped bring fairy tales near extinction. But the few native fairy tales which had survived earlier hazards and a considerable supply of imported ones were given a new lease on life when, during the early Victorian period, certain Romantic ideas took hold. This history deserves to be told in some detail.

By the nineteenth century or sooner, most of the native fairy tales once available, and drawn upon by Shakespeare, Spenser, Peele, and Jonson, had become "scarce and fragmentary in England."[5] In 1822 Wilhelm Grimm speculated that "it is probable that the greater part of the stories known in Germany are indigenous in Great Britain also," but after citing a few of the types of stories found in both countries, he had to add that "little, however, has as yet been collected or communicated. This department of literature has been filled up by translations from the French." Grimm then summarized and discussed three "characteristic and genuine English stories" which had been printed by Benjamin Tabart earlier in the century: "Jack the Giant-killer," "Tom Thumb," and "Jack and the Beanstalk."[6] The truth, as discovered by later folklorists, appears to be that by that time there were few other "characteristic and genuine English stories" to collect—not much more than "Tom Tit Tot" (a kind of "Rumpelstiltskin"—AT 500) and "Dick Whittington and his Cat" (which can just barely be considered a fairy tale—AT 1651). Richard M. Dorson says: "The fact had become painfully evident, by the close of Victoria's reign, that the treasure trove of fairy tales unearthed for nearly every European country, in replica of the Grimms' discovery in Germany, would not be found in England. . . . Why had a blight struck Merry England? No one has yet produced a satisfactory answer."[7]

One theory is that French and German tales drove out the native ones,[8] but it seems to me that the most satisfactory answer to the problem was advanced by Edwin Sidney Hartland, who observed that whereas there are few English fairy tales, there is a considerable body of folktale material of the legend type, such as the Robin Hood tales. Hartland's theory was that Puritanism was responsible: the English Nonconformists of the sixteenth, seventeenth, and eighteenth centuries objected to the fantastic, obviously untrue stories and killed off much of the earlier native tradition;[9] the tales from France would then have been filling a vacuum. Whether or not that was the process, the result was that the imported tales became common. They were resisted for a long time by forces similar to the ones which perhaps had been responsible for a shortage of tales in the first place—by latter-day Puritans, the earnest Evangelicals, who objected to the frivolousness of the stories (despite the self-proclaimed moral intentions of some of them); by the newly-cultured, who objected to their primitiveness; and by the rationalists, who objected to their falseness. However, though the resistance temporarily prevented the tales from becoming accepted as children's literature, it could not prevent them from being translated and published, from appearing in chapbooks, and thence from entering the oral folk corpus.

Among the first fairy tales to be translated into English in the eighteenth century were those found in the *Thousand and One Nights,* also known as the *Arabian Nights Entertainment.* First collected in about 1550, the Arabic stories in that volume were translated into French by Antoine Galland in 1704, and from French to English by 1708 (and possibly as early as 1704[10]). In 1707 and 1716 there were separate translations of the courtly, literary *Les Contes des Fées* of Marie Catherine d'Aulnoy, which had appeared in France in about 1700, and in 1729 Robert Samber translated eight fairy tales which had been published in one volume in France in 1697 with the inscription *Contes de ma mère l'Oye.* Probably quite close to folk sources but beautifully polished by Charles Perrault or his son, the stories included "Sleeping Beauty," "Little Red-Riding Hood," "Bluebeard," "Puss-in-Boots," and "Cinderella," and in England became ascribed to "Mother Goose."[11]

All of these collections were reprinted during the eighteenth century, in part or in full, and so were translations of selections from other collections of fairy tales, including the forty-one volume *Le Cabinet des Fées* (1785-89), which held "Beauty and the Beast." The forces of enlightenment could not keep these stories out of the country. But they could keep them from entering whatever "recommended" lists there might have been for children. When John Newbery, the first publisher of children's books, entered the trade in the mid-'forties, he became known not for imaginative fairy tales, but for moral, instructive tales, which were to be the dominant acceptable children's fare for the rest of the century and the beginning of the next. When the fairy-type stories were printed by the official presses, they usually were made heavily didactic. And Newbery's followers were even more oppressively moral and insistently rational than he had been. He was interested in entertaining the child as well as educating him. (It was he, in fact, who attached the name of Mother Goose to nursery rhymes.) But those who next influenced children's reading had more limited goals. Mostly women, such as Anna Laetitia Barbauld and Sarah Trimmer, they advocated a predominantly didactic and factual literature for children and resisted irrational flights of imagination. In Mrs. Trimmer's aptly-named magazine, *The Guardian of Education* (1802-06), *Mother Bunch's Fairy Tales,* a collection of re-told d'Aulnoy stories which Newbery had found suitable enough to publish, was reviewed in this way: "Partial, as we confess ourselves to be, to most of the books of the old school, we cannot approve of those which are only fit to fill the head of children with confused notions of wonderful and supernatural events, brought about by the agency of imaginary beings. Mother Bunch's Tales are of this description." A review of the Mother Goose tales said: "Though we will remember the interest with which, in our childish days, when books of amusement for children were scarce, we read, or listened to the history of *'Little Red Riding Hood,'* and *'Blue Beard,'* &c. we do not wish to have such sensations awakened in the hearts of our grandchildren, by the same means; for the terrific images, which tales of this nature present to the imagination, usually make deep impressions, and injure the tender minds of children, by exciting unreasonable and groundless fear.

Neither do the generality of tales of this kind supply any moral instruction level to the infantine capacity."[12] An unidentified correspondent, who impressed Mrs. Trimmer as being "so good a judge of what children *ought* and *ought not* to read," shows the extreme of the state of affairs which prevailed at the beginning of the century. Referring to the most popular fairy tale in the world, she said that "Cinderella" "is perhaps one of the most exceptionable books that was ever written for children. . . . It paints some of the worst passions that can enter into the human breast, and of which little children should, if possible, be totally ignorant; such as envy, jealousy, a dislike to mothers-in-law and half-sisters, vanity, a love of dress, &c. &c."[13]

Some fairy tales, meanwhile, had survived in the *Arabian Nights,* which benefited from the Orientalism it stimulated, and which was imitated in English by the Rev. James Ridley's *Tales of the Genii.*[14] Some which came from France survived in another way. These stories were kept alive primarily thanks to chapbooks and the folk that the chapbooks brought them to. The chapbook, mostly a seventeenth, eighteenth, and early nineteenth-century phenomenon, was a cheap, illustrated form of popular entertainment which contained everything from riddles and jokes to Bible stories. An 1847 reviewer of fairy tales recalled "the days of their former popularity; when their fascinations were usually comprised within some half dozen greyish-white pages, displaying a curious combination of large and small type—the proportion varying according as a story of greater or less length had to be compressed within the same inexorable limits; and adorned with woodcuts, which, as some scribes would say, 'may be imagined better than described.'" In this format many sorts of stories with fairy-tale affinities—ones from the *Arabian Nights* and Perrault, chivalric romances reduced in length, native folktales—came to be associated. Though chapbooks were not printed specially for him, through them the English child as well as the folk could meet such figures as Aladdin, Bluebeard, St. George, Jack the Giant-Killer, and Tom Thumb.[15] The chapbook brought the imported, printed stories into the native, oral and sub-literary traditions. Lower-class and country-dwelling children heard the stories from their elders and, if they could, read them in chapbooks. Wealthier and urban children heard them from their lower-class and country nurses and, if they could, also read them in chapbooks. In these ways the stories were available to the Romantics who, applying their beliefs in the primacy of the child and the value of imagination, came to the defense of the tales and attacked the official children's reading.

In a letter to Coleridge dated October 23, 1802, Charles Lamb strongly attacked the anti-fairy tale educators, saying:

I am glad the snuff and Pi-pos's Books please. "Goody Two Shoes" is almost out of print. Mrs. Barbauld's stuff has banished all the old classics of the nursery; and the shopman at Newbery's hardly deigned to reach them off an old exploded corner of a shelf, when Mary asked for them. Mrs. B.'s and Mrs. Trimmer's nonsense lay in piles about. Knowledge insignificant and vapid as Mrs. B.'s books convey, it seems, must come to a child in the *shape of knowledge,* and his empty noddle must be turned with conceit of his own powers when he has learnt that a Horse is an animal, and Billy is better than a Horse, and such like; instead of that beautiful Interest in wild tales which made the child a man, while all the time he suspected himself to be no bigger than a child. Science has succeeded to Poetry no less in the little walks of children than with men. Is there no possibility of averting this sore evil? Think what you would have been now, if instead of being fed with Tales and old wives' fables in childhood, you had been crammed with geography and natural history?

Damn them!—I mean that cursed Barbauld Crew, those Blights and Blasts of all that is Human in man and child.[16]

Coleridge himself as a child had passionately read his father's copy of the *Arabian Nights,* and had read chapbook versions of "Jack the Giant-Killer," *The Seven Champions of Christendom,* and other stories. Later he had defended fairy tales for children, basing his judgment on his own experiences. On October 16, 1797, he wrote Thomas Poole how

from my early reading of fairy tales and genii, etc., etc., my mind had been habituated *to the Vast,* and I never regarded *my senses* in any way as the criteria of my belief. I regulated all my creeds by my conceptions, not by my *sight,* even at that age. Should children be permitted to read romances, and relations of giants and magicians and genii? I know all that has been said against it; but I have formed my faith in the affirmative. I know no other way of giving the mind a love of the Great and the Whole.[17]

Wordsworth also read and defended fairy tales. In *The Prelude* he remembered being "a Child not nine years old," and seeing "the shining streams / Of Fairy land, the Forests of Romance, (Book Five, ll. 474-77), and said that he "had a precious treasure at that time / A little, yellow canvas-cover'd Book, / A slender abstract of the Arabian Tales" (ll. 482-84). Earlier in the poem he criticized the current system of education by portraying a knowledgeable product of it (" . . . 'tis a Child, no Child, / But a dwarf Man" -ll. 294-95), and then said:

Meanwhile old Grandame Earth is grieved to find
The playthings, which her love design'd for him,

Unthought of: in their woodland beds the flowers
Weep, and the river sides are all forlorn.
(ll. 346-49)

. . . . .

Oh! give us once again the Wishing-Cap
Of Fortunatus, and the invisible Coat
Of Jack the Giant-killer, Robin Hood,
And Sabra in the forest with St. George!
The child, whose love is here, at least, doth reap
One precious gain, that he forgets himself.[18]
(ll. 364-69)

For Wordsworth, Nature is the best educator; next best, it would seem, or at least better than what was taught in the schools, are fairy tales.

Despite the Romantics (whose writings about the fairy tale frequently were private), children's reading continued to be "enlightened" early in the nineteenth century, and the fairy tale was threatened even in its underground form as folk and chapbook literature. But there were signs of change. The chapbook stories were given a new popular form as they began to be drawn upon for the plots of entertaining pantomimes put on in the theaters at Christmas time;[19] and a legitimate book publisher brought out a volume of fairy tales. He was Sir Richard Phillips who, in 1809, under the name of Benjamin Tabart, published some of the stories from Mother Goose, Countess d'Aulnoy, and the *Arabian Nights,* the three native tales cited by Grimm, and other legends and romances, under the title *Popular Fairy Tales; or, a Liliputian* [sic] *Library.* In a preface Phillips claimed that earlier English versions of the stories, presumably chapbook ones in particular, had been "obsolete in their style, . . . gross in their morals, and . . . vulgar in their details." His intention was "to elevate the language and sentiments to a level with the refined manners of the present age": to save the tales from the chapbooks. Though his intention of making the tales respectable in style and content was not based on didactic justification (on the contrary; he believed that he had produced "one of the most entertaining volumes in any language"[20]), didacticism still plays an obvious part in the versions of the stories he used. "Beauty and the Beast" is presented as an exemplum, and Jack of "Jack and the Beanstalk," his behavior explained by footnotes, is a good boy who is avenging his father's death and recovering stolen property. Still, this volume was a milestone.

But other publishers did not follow Phillips' lead. They did not yet publish semi-authentic fairy tales for the entertainment of children. When a second printing of the Tabart collection appeared in 1818, it evoked an important article from the pen of Francis Cohen, later

Francis Palgrave and the father of Francis Turner Palgrave, which describes the current situation. In the article Cohen claims that nursery stories have changed, that children's literature no longer is imaginative because fanciful stories are considered "too childish." The forces of enlightenment had done their job well. And what is more, Cohen maintains, the core of adult popular reading material has also changed: nurses no longer read fairy tales, so do not know them as well as they used to themselves, and are less able to tell them to children. "Scarcely any of the *chap books* which were formerly sold to the country people at fairs and markets have been able to maintain their ancient popularity; and we have almost witnessed the extinction of this branch of our national literature": Gothic romances are read instead of legends, newspapers instead of broadside ballads.[21]

Cohen, who regrets the disappearance of the old nursery stories, defends their value and spends most of his time noting the sharing by many peoples of similar stories. He, like Scott, is an example of the descendants of eighteenth-century antiquarians who accompanied or followed the brothers Grimm (to whom he refers with the highest praise) into the field of folklore. The German Grimms—themselves working in a tradition which had been strongly influenced by English forces, particularly by Ossian and by Percy, who had had a great effect on Herder—had more to do with the fate of the fairy tale in England than did any of their English Romantic contemporaries. Their most influential works were the *Kinder-und Hausmärchen,* that great collection of folktales recorded by them and published in Germany in 1812 and 1815; a scholarly study of the origins and diffusion of the tales attached in 1822 to an 1819 edition of them; and the *Deutsche Mythologie* (1835). The Grimms's method of collecting tales was in some ways duplicated by Thomas Crofton Croker for his *Fairy Legends and Traditions of the South of Ireland* (1825), though, as the title suggests and Richard M. Dorson points out, the content is "not *Märchen* or fictional fairy tales, but traditional stories about demonic beings."[22] Their kind of scholarly approach to tales was followed by Thomas Keightley in *The Fairy Mythology* (1828). And they were a specific influence on the third volume of Croker's work (1828), on an enlargement of Keightley's (1850), and on many other folklore studies from then on, such as Thomas Wright's *Essays on Subjects Connected with the Literature, Popular Superstitions, and History of England in the Middle Ages* (1846), and the studies of William John Thoms, coiner of the term "Folk-Lore" in the August 22, 1846, issue of the *Athenaeum* and founder in 1849 of *Notes and Queries.*

The Grimms were not only a major influence on folktale scholarship; they were also a major influence on the printing of fairy tales, for children as well as scholars.

Tabart's earlier collection had less of an effect than the *Kinder-und Hausmärchen* in bringing fairy tales to the child. As Cohen notes in his article, chapbooks were dying out; but the printing of fairy stories was soon to be made respectable. As he also notes, the folk were losing the tales; but children were gaining (or regaining) them.

In 1821, two years after Cohen's article appeared, Edgar Taylor published an article on "German Popular and Traditionary Literature" in which he said:

> There exists, at present, a very large and increasing class of readers, for whom the scattered fragments of olden time, as preserved in popular and traditionary tales, possess a powerful attraction. The taste for this species of literature has particularly manifested itself of late; the stories which had gone out of fashion during the prevalence of the prudery and artificial taste of the last century, began, at its close, to re-assert every where their ancient empire over the mind. Our literati had fancied themselves, and persuaded the world to think itself, too wise for such amusements—they considered themselves as come to man's estate, and determined, on a sudden, to put away childish things. The curious mementos of simple and primitive society, the precious glimmerings of historic light, which these invaluable relics have preserved, were rejected as beneath the dignity to which these philosophers aspired; and even children began to be fed with a stronger diet.

> A better taste, say the patrons of these blossoms of nature and fancy, is now springing up. Our scholars busy themselves in tracing out the genealogy and mythological connexions of Tom Thumb and Jack the Giant Killer; and surely if the grave and learned embark in these speculations, we are justified in expecting to be able to welcome the æra when our children shall be allowed once more to regale themselves with that mild food which will enliven their imaginations, and tempt them on through the thorny paths of education;—when the gay dreams of fairy innocence shall again hover around them, and scientific compendiums, lisping botanics, and leading-string mechanics, shall be postponed to the Delights of Valentine and Orson, the beautiful Magalona, or Fair Rosamond.[23]

In 1823, two years after he wrote this article, Taylor presented the first English translation of Grimm, called *German Popular Stories* and illustrated by George Cruikshank. In his preface Taylor indicated that folklore interests were among the reasons prompting him to publish the stories, but he also thought it important that the tales be made available to English children. Echoing his earlier statement, he said:

The popular tales of England have been too much neglected. They are nearly discarded from the libraries of childhood. Philosophy is made the companion of the nursery: we have lisping chemists and leading-string mathematicians: this is the age of reason, not of imagination; and the loveliest dreams of fairy innocence are considered as vain and frivolous. Much might be urged against this rigid and philosophic (or rather unphilosophic) exclusion of works of fancy and fiction. Our imagination is surely as susceptible of improvement by exercise, as our judgement or our memory; and so long as such fictions only are presented to the young mind as do not interfere with the important department of moral education, a beneficial effect must be produced by the pleasurable employment of a faculty in which so much of our happiness in every period of life consists.[24]

After Taylor's translation (and greatly because of it), ideas similar to those expressed earlier by the English Romantics began to be voiced more frequently. On January 16, 1823, Sir Walter Scott wrote Taylor a letter to thank him for his translation and to praise it. He said of the tales that "there is . . . a sort of wild fairy interest in them which makes me think them fully better adapted to awaken the imagination and soften the heart of childhood than the good-boy stories which have been in later years composed for them. . . . Our old wild fictions like our own simple music will have more effect in awakening the fancy & elevating the disposition than the colder and more elevated compositions of more clever authors & composers."[25] Several of the reviewers of Taylor's edition dealt with its antiquarian folklore qualities, but many also approached the collection as children's literature. A common reaction of a reviewer was that the tales reminded him of those he knew during his childhood, and that he felt it good that they were available to children again. Such was the position of the reviewer in *Gentleman's Magazine,* who recommended the book for children and adults, and of the one in *London Magazine,* who praised the stories as "delightful food for a child's imagination" and said: "It is the vice of parents now-a-days to load their children's minds with useful books. . . . Why should little children have grown-up minds?—Why should the dawning imagination be clouded and destroyed in its first trembling light? Is the imagination a thing given to be destroyed?—Oh no!"[26]

The response to Taylor's Grimm prompted a second volume in 1826, a time when Englishmen were being exposed to a related product of the German Romantic movement (some examples of which were in this second volume of Grimm), the *Kunstmärchen,* folk tales transformed into fantasy literature for adults. Johann August Musäus had been adapting folk tales for sophisticated adults as early as 1782, and Goethe used folklore motifs in his complex "Mährchen" of 1795. Then, with "Der blonde Eckbert" of 1797, Ludwig Tieck established the most common form the *Kunstmärchen* would take, in other stories of his and in works by Wackenroder, Novalis, Brentano, la Motte Fouqué, Chamisso, and E. T. A. Hoffmann. Musäus' collection of tales was translated by William Beckford and published as *Popular Tales of the Germans* in 1791. But England knew little about these writings until the appearance of Madame de Staël's *De l'Allemagne* of 1813, and even then, though la Motte Fouqué's *Undine* was translated in 1818, extensive translation awaited the stimulus of Taylor's translation of Grimm. It was followed by a flood.

Some of the most important translations of this time were: *Popular Tales of the Northern Nations* (1823—it included the first English translation of Tieck); Chamisso's *Peter Schlemihl* (1824); Thomas Roscoe's four volume translation *The German Novelists* (1826); and above all, Thomas Carlyle's four volume *German Romance: Specimens of its chief authors, with biographical and critical notes* (1827). Publication of such stories continued through the Victorian period, as their popularity increased, so that Tieck, for example, achieved his "banner year" in 1845, a year in which J. A. Froude, Julius Hare, and others translated a collection of his.[27]

By the 1830's, British writers were imitating the German tales, particularly in the magazines. *Peter Schlemihl* gave rise to "The Man Without a Shadow. Tale from the German" (*Pocket Magazine,* 1830) and to James Roscoe's "My After-Dinner Adventures with Peter Schlemihl" (*Blackwood's* and *Mirror of Literature,* 1839). Otmar's "Peter Claus" was imitated in "Dorf Juystein" (*Fraser's Magazine,* 1832). It had earlier been imitated by the American Washington Irving in "Rip Van Winkle" (1820), and Irving also imitated a Musäus story, in "The Legend of Sleepy Hollow" (1820). Two other American short story writers, who started out in the 'thirties, Edgar Allan Poe and Nathaniel Hawthorne, have been seen as if not influenced by, at least in the lines of, Hoffmann and Tieck.[28] In England the German Romantic fairy tale (especially Goethe's "Mährchen," which he had translated in 1825 and interpreted, as a "phantasmagory," in 1832) was one of the influences on Carlyle's *Sartor Resartus* in the 1830's and the Germans later inspired George MacDonald to write *Phantastes: A Faerie Romance for Men and Women* (1858).[29] But the major Victorian novelists were mostly to use fairy tales in more realistic ways, as we shall see.

During the same decade which saw the beginnings of extensive translation from and some imitations of German folktales, the English were putting native, French, and Arabian Nights tales to greater use as the bases of gay Christmas-time pantomimes. On December 26, 1825, according to the *Times* of that date, the child and his parents who sat through an ordinary play could then have seen *Harlequin and the Magic Rose; or, Beauty and the Beast* at Covent Garden, and at the Adelphi something called *The Three Golden Lamps; or, Harlequin and the Wizard Dwarf*. A decade later he could have seen *Whittington and his Cat* at Drury Lane, *Harlequin Jack and his Eleven Brothers* at the Victoria, and at the Adelphi both *The Elfin Queen* and *The Battle of the Fairies*. By the end of the 'thirties J. R. Planché had established himself as the master at this sort of thing, writing almost annually a clever extravaganza, full of horseplay, puns, and clever rhymes, and usually based on a story from Madam d'Aulnoy.

Finally, with fairy tales recognized as the subject of serious study by scholars, appreciated as the source of some popular adult literature, and enjoyed as holiday entertainment, in the late 1830's and the 1840's, the Romantic ideas about fairy tales were accorded a public acceptance, and the tales were widely praised as good children's literature, worth publishing. In two articles in 1842 and 1844 Elizabeth Eastlake pointed out that a recognition of the need for children's books had not necessarily resulted in appropriate books for children. She said that although children now had libraries, which their greatgrandmothers did not have, the books provided for them in those libraries are not necessarily better than the "fairy tales and marvellous histories" and "little tales of a moral tendency" which the ancestors had been able to obtain. Books today, she argued, do not separate entertainment and instruction, and fail to achieve either purpose. She reviewed those books which she considered bad, and she then listed examples of the kinds of books she considered good, including "Beauty and the Beast," "Jack and the Beanstalk," Grimm, and the *Arabian Nights* among those works which are good for entertainment.[30] The kinds of books she wanted were being published increasingly frequently even as she wrote. From that time on, English bookshelves were filled more and more with translations of foreign folktales, with new collections of the few native stories that could be found, which early reviewers of Taylor's Grimm had called for, and even with newly-composed fairy stories. The battle of the children's books continued, but fairy tales at last gained a recognition and availability they had lacked before.

The increased publication included new translations of Grimm in 1839, 1846, 1853, 1855, and frequently thereafter. There also were many reprintings, and a reviewer of one of the later editions of Edgar Taylor's translation of Grimm indicates the popularity the tales had reached by 1847. He says that Taylor's earlier claim that the tales were "out of fashion" is no longer true: "the more elegant guise in which our old friends present themselves, radiant in their gay bindings, and red and black title pages, would rather intimate that they are becoming very much the fashion."[31]

The new taste was encouraged by Robert Southey, who held an interest in folklore and included in *The doctor, &c.* (1837) as a chapter "for the nursery" a version of a popular tale, "The Story of the Three Bears."[32] The new fashion was also notably marked by translations of older collections of stories, such as the *Arabian Nights* in 1839-40 (by Edwin Lane) and Basile's *Pentamerone* of 1634-36 in 1848, and by the publication of anthologies which contained versions of stories from such standards as Mother Goose, Madame d'Aulnoy, and the Grimms, from other foreign sources, and from the native stock. These collections include Felix Summerly's (Henry Cole's) *Home Treasury*, 1841-49 (in one volume of which, *Beauty and the Beast*, the editor objected to other "modern English versions" which "are filled with moralizings on education, marriage, &c., futile attempts to grind everything as much as possible into dull logical probability. . . . I have thought it no sin . . . to attempt to re-write the legend more as a fairy tale than a lecture"); Ambrose Merton's (William John Thoms's) *The Old Story Books of England*, 1845, reprinted in 1846 as *Gammer Gurton's Pleasant Stories* and *Gammer Gurton's Famous Histories* (whose introductions said: "Their design is to cultivate the heart, to enrich the fancy, to stir up kindly feelings, to encourage a taste for the BEAUTIFUL, and to accomplish this by taking advantage of the youthful longing for amusement"); and Anthony Montalba's *Fairy Tales from All Nations*, 1849 (the preface of which declared that England had "cast off that pedantic folly" of condemning fairy tales "as merely idle things, or as pernicious occupations for faculties that should be always directed to serious and profitable concerns").[33] And there also was C. B. Burkhardt's *Fairy Tales and Legends of Many Nations*, 1849, J. R. Planché's translation of *Four and Twenty* [French] *Fairy Tales*, 1858, and Dinah Maria Mulock Craik's *The Fairy Book*, 1863.

Writers did not limit themselves to revising and reprinting old stories: they also began to write original ones which used fairytale motifs and patterns. Though such stories usually had moral implications, their authors also usually showed respect for their sources and acceptance of, even delight in, fantasy. The earliest was Catherine Sinclair's humorous "Uncle David's Nonsensical Story about Giants and Fairies" (in *Holiday House*, 1839). Then in 1841 John Ruskin wrote *The King of the Golden River*, more like a folktale and, as he said, "a fairly good imitation of Grimm and Dickens, mixed with a little true Alpine feeling of my own,"[34] which was not published until 1850. Another type of fairy tale was written by F. E. Paget in *The Hope of the Katzekopfs* (1844). This book begins as a burlesque of Court fairy tales which open with christenings and uninvited guests (e.g., AT 410), then becomes a serious version of the type, full of magic. But the full development of original fairy tales for children in England awaited another leader, and once again an influence came from abroad. This time it was the Danish Hans Christian Andersen, whose first collection of fairy stories appeared in 1835, and who was first translated into English in 1846. F. J. H. Darton says: "The fairytale had at last come into its own. The story of its struggle without the aid of originality like Andersen's had culminated in such versions as Tabart's and in the immediate success of *Grimm*. But now there was added the recognition that it was lawful, and even praiseworthy, to invent and release fantasy, and to circulate folk-lore itself."[35]

Among the many original children's fairy tales which followed until 1870, the year of Dickens' death, there was the rare *Alice Learmont* (1852) by Mrs. Craik, a sensitive, serious book which, like Ruskin's, seems especially close to the folk traditions. But more of the stories of the period followed Catherine Sinclair's in seeming to be presented for the entertainment of modern children (not as being true folktales), sometimes followed Paget's (and French ones) in adapting Court motifs, sometimes followed both in portraying visits to Fairyland—and often followed both, and Anderson's stories, in being freely fantastic. These stories included Thackeray's *The Rose and the Ring* (1854); Frances Browne's *Granny's Wonderful Chair and its Tales of Fairy Times* (1856); Harriet Parr's *Legends from Fairy Land* (1860) and its sequels; Charles Kingsley's *The Water Babies: A Fairy Tale for a Land Baby* (1863); Annie Keary's rather condescending *Little Wanderlin and other Fairy Tales* (1865); George MacDonald's several more serious works, with their debts to the Germans—"The Fairy Fleet: an English Mährchen" (1866), *Dealings with the Fairies* (1867, though parts of it appeared in 1864), and *At the Back of the North Wind* (serialized 1868-70); Jean Ingelow's *Mopsa the Fairy* (1869); and "Amelia and the Dwarfs" in Juliana Horatia Ewing's *The Brownies and other Tales* (1870).

Major "adult" authors were not only trying their hands at writing these children's stories, but also joined the ranks of their defenders. Thackeray, who showed his appreciation of fairy tales in two reviews, wrote the following in one of the brief interpolated essays in *Vanity Fair* (1847-48):

> Some time after this interview, it happened that Mr. Cuff, on a sunshiny afternoon, was in the neighbourhood of poor William Dobbin, who was lying under a tree in the play-ground, spelling over a favourite copy of the Arabian Nights which he had—apart from the rest of the school, who were persuing their various sports—quite lonely, and almost happy. If people would but leave children to themselves; if teachers would cease to bully them; if parents would not insist upon directing their thoughts, and dominating their

feelings—those feelings and thoughts which are a mystery to all (for how much do you and I know of each other, of our children, of our fathers, of our neighbour, and how far more beautiful and sacred are the thoughts of the poor lad or girl whom you govern likely to be, than those of the dull and world-corrupted person who rules him?)—if, I say, parents and masters would leave their children alone a little more,—small harm would accrue, although a less quantity of *as in præsenti* might be acquired (ch. 5).[36]

During the 1850's Dickens' journal *Household Words* presented articles which defended fairy tales more specifically and extensively than Thackeray's statement did, including ones by the poet and essayist R. H. Horne and the educator and literary scholar Henry Morley, who later was to publish several collections of original fairy tales.

Horne's article, "A Witch in the Nursery," objected to stories which contain excessive descriptions of death and violence, calling them immoral, but it defended as an alternative not directly didactic stories but others, ones such as Andersen's, which "indirectly" ("through the heart and the imagination") instill "the purest moral principles."[37] Morley's article, "The School of the Fairies," is a review of J. R. Planché's translation of Countess d'Aulnoy. It says that fairy tales have educational values: they teach children about different nationalities and they provide them with moral values such as sympathy for others. Morley says: "The mind has its own natural way of growing, as the body has, and at each stage of growth it asks for its own class of food. We injure minds or bodies by denying either. . . . Fairy tales . . . make the mind active, and indisposed for other work that does not give it enough exercise." He looks at d'Aulnoy's French tales, and sees what their traits are, and what values they can teach. And then he says that he

> would have them . . . set in their places among others, read in their turn with the legends gathered by the brothers Grimm, with choice tales from Musæus, and such more spiritual freaks of fancy as the fairy tales of Tieck and Goethe furnish; with the wild stories of Hoffmann; of course, with our own Red Riding Hood, and others of its class; with the Irish fairy legends; the story of King Arthur and his Round Table; with the Seven Champions of Christendom, and all the legends of the days of chivalry;—farther back still, with all the good fables ever written, up to Æsop, and up farther, to Pilpay; with the Arabian Nights; Greek and Roman legends; with choice gold of the fancy coined of old in Persia, China, Hindostan. The ways through which a happy child to guide, "in this delightful land of Faery,"

> Are so exceeding spacious and wide,
> And sprinkled with such sweet variety,

that we desire to claim for children right of way through all of them, with privilege to pick the flowers on all sides.[38]

In 1850 *The Prelude* was published, making public the ideas of the recently-deceased poet laureate. And at this time, while their ideas were being accepted, other Romantics were being cited. In 1853 the *Athenaeum*'s reviewer of a new translation of Grimm preceded a citation of Scott's 1823 letter to Edgar Taylor by saying:

We are also inclined to think, that a considerable *per contra* to any aspect of triviality is to be found in the superior moral tendency (as it appears to us) of these tales to that of *professedly* moral fictions. The former are less selfish and worldly-wise than the latter,—more truly good, and more spontaneous in their goodness. The one class aims at making us "respectable members of society,"—the other seeks to mould us into thoroughly kind, just, and considerate human beings.[39]

In 1860 the anonymous author of a *London Quarterly Review* article on "Children's Literature" quoted Coleridge on the fairy tale, agreed with him, and went on to say: "After all, it is a great point in education to awaken the curiosity, and feed the fancy, because we thus give a child a sense of the greatness of the universe in which he has come to live." Later, echoing Dickens' image in *Hard Times* of the children in M'Choakumchild's school being vessels waiting to be filled with facts, and anticipating "progressive" modern educators, he said:

On the whole, we may conclude that the great purpose of children's books is not so much to impart instruction, as to promote growth. We must not think of a child's mind as of a vessel, which it is for us to fill, but as a wonderfully organized instrument, which it is for us to develop and to set in motion. He will be well or ill educated, not according to the accuracy with which he retains the notions which have been impressed upon him from without, but according to the power which he puts forth from within, and to the activity and regularity with which the several feelers or *tentacula* of his nature lay hold on all that is to be seen and thought and known around him.

The writer suggests that the following question should be asked of good children's literature: "Above all, does it make the eye glisten and the cheek glow, and the limbs of the little one move with delight?" Of fairy tales he answers, yes.[40]

A mid-Victorian culmination in the acceptance of the fairy tale occurred in 1868, when the Edgar Taylor translation of Grimm was reprinted in one volume, complete with the Cruikshank illustrations, and with a new introduction by no less a figure than John Ruskin.

Ruskin, asserting that fairy tales are the best kind of literature for children, described the well-raised, well-educated child and said:

Children so trained have no need of moral fairy tales; but they will find in the apparently vain and fitful courses of any tradition of old time, honestly delivered to them, a teaching for which no other can be substituted, and of which the power cannot be measured; animating for them the material world with inextinguishable life, fortifying them against the glacial cold of selfish science, and preparing them submissively, and with no bitterness of astonishment, to behold, in later years, the mystery—divinely appointed to remain such to all human thought—of the fates that happen alike to the evil and the good.[41]

The cause for which the Romantics spoke came to have greater urgency as the conditions which provoked them to defend the fairy tale intensified during the Victorian period. Earnest, artless, middle-class Evangelicalism increased its influence; the educational theories of the Enlightenment were succeeded by those of its even less imaginative descendant. Utilitarianism; and the age of the city, industrialism, and science came fully into being. These conditions of England were objected to by Carlyle and by such followers and admirers of his as Ruskin and Kingsley. In discussing the fairy tale these men followed the Romantics by stressing its imaginative value in the new world. But they also reverted a bit to the position of the enemy: the educational values they pointed to in the tales, while not usually as simply and exclusively instructional as those the Enlightenment advocated, are more conventionally moral than those which had been defended by Wordsworth and Coleridge. With their statements in defense of the fairy tale (made more publicly than those of the Romantics had been), the Victorian men of letters probably contributed to its new status. In those statements and elsewhere, they reveal the synthesis of appreciation of the imagination and moral posture which characterizes the Victorian acceptance of the fairy tale.

Carlyle represents the two aspects of the position: he spoke for the powers of the imagination and helped bring the *Kunstmarchen* to England, and he was intensely moralistic. In his essay, Ruskin calls for the reading of authentic, fanciful fairy tales; but he also points to the moral values of such tales, and he used his own imaginative fairy tale to teach a moral lesson—how sympathy for a dog is rewarded, and how an "inheritance, which had been lost by cruelty, was regained by love."[42] Kingsley's fanciful *Water Babies*, in which there is playful defense of the existence of fairies and support of the fairy tale itself, is even more pointedly moral. To "little books" about "little people" the hero prefers "a jolly good fairy tale, about Jack the Giant-killer or Beauty and the Beast, which taught him something that he didn't know already" (ch. 8). From his experiences this hero learns about kindness, cleanliness, and self-sacrifice, among other things, and a "Moral" follows the "parable" to drive some of the lessons home for readers.[43] Even Thackeray, who could not write his fairy tale without making it in part a mock-fairy tale and who rejected the simple morality of virtue rewarded, imbued *The Rose and the Ring* with both delightful fantasy and the moral that "misfortune" is a useful and perhaps necessary condition for the molding of character.

Children's writers were even more inclined to reflect the view that fantasy is good for the child, and to conceive of moral purposes for their fantasies. Many followed the technique of Catherine Sinclair and made their fairy tales allegories. Hers is about Master No-book, the fairy Do-nothing who lives in Castle Needless, the fairy Teach-all, and so on. F. E. Paget's is about a child named "Eigenwilling," which he translates for us, and its ending resembles *Pilgrim's Progress*; his purpose in writing it was to see whether children's "hearts can be moved to noble and chivalrous feelings, and to shake off the hard, cold, calculating, worldly, selfish temper of the times, by being brought into more immediate contact with the ideal, the imaginary, and the romantic, than has been the fashion of late years."[44] Even in the stories which seem closest to folktales, such as *Alice Learmont* and some of the stories in *Granny's Wonderful Chair,* there usually is an unobtrusive moral thrust, one which, as Katharine M. Briggs says of Miss Browne's and some other stories, resembles the morality of many folktales, in which "generosity and a merry heart are the prime virtues."[45]

One should not think that all versions of fairy tales had only a tempered morality. There still were many original tales like Margaret Gatty's "The Fairy Godmother" (1851), not much of a fairy tale but heavily moral, and there still could be versions of traditional tales like the four presented by George Cruikshank in a Fairy Library (1853-54, 1864), stories insistently instructive, primarily in the virtues of temperance (in them giants and ogres are repeatedly overcome because they are drunk). The association of fairy tales with morality was so strong that a writer like Lewis Carroll, a man far from committed to didacticism, when writing about fairies ended up teaching a lesson (of the need to work before playing—"Bruno's Revenge," 1867). And George MacDonald, despite his flights of fantasy and his ability to usually keep the preacher in him under control, could burden *At the Back of the North Wind* with an ever-present didacticism. Still, the period saw, alongside of its morality, a real appreciation of fairy tales and of the kind of imagination which can create and respond to them.

The Victorian pater-familias, who was only recently persuaded of the Romantic claim that children were special and deserved special literature,[46] found that fairy tales filled the requirement best. Accepting their claimed morality and approving of their playfulness, he let them in to his child's nursery. He must have been reassured by their rather domestic nature (even the Grimms ascribe them to the nursery and the home), and their portrayal of love and marriage without sex. And he might have been attracted to them himself, for these reasons, for their sympathetic renderings of children, and for other reasons as well.

Beset by a changing world, the Victorian could find stability in the ordered, formulary structure of fairy tales. He could be called from his time and place to a soothing other world by the faintly blowing horns of Elfland. He could be taken from the corruptions of adulthood back to the innocence of childhood; from the ugly, competitive city to beautiful, sympathetic nature; from complex morality to the simple issue of good versus evil; from a difficult reality to a comforting world of imagination. The author of an 1855 article on "German Story-Books" says that he pleads "guilty to a very childlike love of story-books. . . . Although the days of our childhood are over and gone, we are by no means insensible to the charms of Cinderella." He admires the German appreciation of fairy tales, and goes on to say: "The *Volksmährchen* form the wonder-land, ever bright, and beautiful, and grand, into which the popular mind escapes from the dull and dusty paths of a toil-worn existence."[47] His speculation on the value of fairy tales for German peasants is suggestively appropriate for Victorian Englishmen, and the attraction was not only for the "popular mind."

The 1853 *Athenaeum* reviewer of Grimm, discussing this attraction of the tales, said:

> Another reason for the pleasure which imaginative men find in an occasional visit to infantine fairy-land, is probably to be found in the complete contrast which that land presents to the realities of life. . . . One of the great charms of a child's fairy tale is, in the utter absence of all reference to passion. . . . We hear, it is true, of love, and hate, and revenge; but in forms so different from those of the actual world, that our own feelings are untouched, and we are not tossed into the conflict of sympathy and antipathy. We behold all things as we beheld them in childhood— through the transparent medium of simple faith. Our intellect is not harassed, as we read, by being obliged to combat for or against any set of principles. We are no longer in the lists fighting for a dogma or a system. We have ceased for the nonce to be politicians, or sectarians, or casuists. The gates are shut upon the outer world,—shut even against ourselves, as we ordinarily appear. The fight of existence is excluded, and, for a little

space, disbelieved in. We only know that there is the earth all around us, and the conscious Heavens everywhere above us,—and noble, undiscovered regions in the distance, which we feel to be full of wonder, and magnificence, and mystery, and adventures without end.[48]

The youthful Tennyson, associating fairy tales with beauty, enchantment, stillness, and sleep, expressed their escapist attraction in such early poems of his as "Recollections of the Arabian Nights" (1830) and "The Sleeping Beauty" (1830). In a final enlargement of the latter poem ("The Day-Dream," 1842), he indicates another function for fairy tales. This version of the poem presents a daydreaming lover who imagines the fairy-tale prince achieving something which is denied to himself in his own waking life: the fulfillment of love (he says his beloved "sleeps a dreamless sleep to me; / A sleep by kisses undissolved"[49]). In other ways other Victorians, through identification of themselves with the heroes of fairy tales, could achieve a fulfillment of wishes, often of ones denied to them in their own lives. They could imagine themselves having their true worth recognized and attaining material wealth and happiness, with or without effort. And they could fulfill wishes they were less consciously aware of.

The author of the remarkable 1860 *London Quarterly Review* article on "Children's Literature" said: "Pictures and gay colors and romances do not give us literal truth, nor indeed truth in an objective sense at all; but they are true subjectively. They interpret our dreams and fancies to ourselves, and keep the imaginative power in healthy exercise, by employing it upon some object of external interest, when otherwise it would brood painfully and unhealthily upon itself."[50] Modern psychoanalysts have elaborated on some of these insights. Ernest Kris says that fairy tales enable children to work out their psychic fantasies vicariously, in a harmless way approved by society. As Kate Friedlaender puts it: "One reason, therefore, for the child's love of the fairy-tale is that he finds in it his own instinctual situation and meets again his own fantasies which explains the pleasure in reading or listening to fairy-stories [sic]; moreover, the fairy-tale's particular solutions for these conflicts appear to be a means for alleviating anxiety in the child."[51]

It is not only children who can find their psychic fantasies in fairy tales: adults can too, and that, psychoanalysts say, is because fairy tales seem to share a set of symbols with dreams, and therefore can function like them. C. G. Jung claims that "in myths and fairytales, as in dreams, the psyche tells its own story, and the interplay of the archetypes is revealed in its natural setting as 'formation, transformation / the eternal Mind's eternal recreation.'"[52] For Jung, in fairy tales as in dreams the archetypes are confronted in a concrete form and enable man to gain a particular

insight into the world and himself. Freud, who is more concerned than Jung with the fulfillment of wishes through particular symbols, says: "This symbolism is not peculiar to dreams, but is characteristic of unconscious ideation, in particular among the people, and is to be found in folklore, and in popular myths, legends, linguistic idioms, proverbial wisdom and current jokes, to a more complete extent than in dreams."[53] Without going in to the sometimes forced, sometimes contradictory interpretations that followers of these men have given specific tales, we can agree with them that fairy tales often seem dream-like and that they have a symbolic texture (which was also responded to by nineteenth-century solar mythologists, who interpreted the tales as describing the conflict between the sun and night);[54] and we can observe that the Victorians are notorious for having repressed certain basic urges, including ones which are acted out in fairy tales. These include the expression of violent impulses (the good as well as the evil in the tales have few inhibitions on this count) and of revolt against authority. Thus, while coming to him in the guise of innocent children's stories which he might have felt did not affect his feelings, fairy tales could on the one hand provide the troubled Victorian with an escape into a happy, ordered world, and on the other help him work out an urge for violent self-assertion against people he unknowingly felt aggressive towards, including his social betters.

And, finally, the fairy tale was not only moral entertainment, escape, and wish fulfillment. Psychoanalysts claim that the fairy tale is a symbolically realistic image of the urges of the psyche, and it in other ways too returned to the Victorian an image of himself. Its optimism was duplicated in an age in which fortunes were made and men flew up the ladder of success, and in which progress was speeded magically by "the fairy tales of science."[55] And it reflected reality in its darker parts, too. For fairy tales, before they reach their happy endings, have the nature not only of daydream but of nightmare too. In that age of anxiety, even when trying to escape, the Victorian might confront the nature of his own existence. There was no escape if, unlike the *Athenaeum* reviewer quoted above, one emotionally submitted himself to the tales. And no one submitted himself more thoroughly than Charles Dickens, for whom fairy tales were not just an occasional attraction, but a lifelong fascination.

Notes

[In the text, AT precedes type numbers, listed in Antti Aarne and Stith Thompson, *The Types of the Folktale* (Helsinki, 1961).]

[1] *The Fairy Mythology* (London, 1850), pp. 5-10. The *OED* entry for "fairy" is more or less similar. Katharine

M. Briggs defines the term as the "late, though general, name for the whole race. Originally Fay, from *Fatae,* the Fates. Faërie was first used for enchantment." *The Fairies in Tradition and Literature* (London, 1967), p. 217.

[2] "On Fairy Stories," *Tree and Leaf,* in *The Tolkien Reader* (New York, 1966), p. 9. As Tolkien points out (p. 4), the *OED* Supplement omits this meaning from its definitions of "fairy tale."

[3] *Apollodorus: The Library* (London, 1921), I, xxvii-xxix.

[4] "Myth in Primitive Psychology," *Magic, Science and Religion* (Garden City, N. Y., 1954), p. 101.

[5] Katharine M. Briggs, Introduction, *Folktales of England,* ed. Briggs and Ruth L. Tongue (London, 1965), pp. xxiii-xxvi. And see her "English Fairy Tales," *Internationaler Kongress der Volkserzählungsforscher in Kiel und Kopenhagen,* ed. Kurt Ranke (Berlin, 1961), pp. 38-43.

[6] Notes, *Grimm's Household Tales,* trans. and ed. Margaret Hunt (London, 1884), II, 501.

[7] Foreword, *Folktales of England,* ed. Briggs, p. vi.

[8] See Joseph Jacobs, *English Fairy Tales* (London, 1898), p. 229.

[9] *English Fairy and Other Folktales* (London, [1890]), pp. xii-xxi.

[10] See "Notes on Sales," *Times Literary Supplement,* April 10, 1930, 324. The periodical will hereafter be called *TLS.*

[11] On the controversy over authorship and for bibliographical information see: Andrew Lang, Introduction, *Perrault's Popular Tales,* ed. Lang (Oxford, 1888), pp. xxiv-xxxii; Percy Muir, *English Children's Books, 1600-1900* (London, 1954), pp. 45-51; Geoffrey Brereton, Introduction, *The Fairy Tales of Charles Perrault* (Harmondsworth, 1957), pp. xvii-xxii; and Marc Soriano, *Les Contes de Perrault* (Paris, 1968).

[12] *The Guardian of Education,* II (1803), 185-86.

[13] *Ibid,* 448.

[14] This popular collection of stories, frequently reprinted, was presented by Ridley in 1764 under the name of Sir Charles Morell, who supposedly heard them from their Eastern author, called Horam. Both the "Editor" and Horam claim moral purposes for the tales—but Horam ironically admits that the prince he made them up for actually became vicious. By 1808, the publishers made the claim of didacticism even stronger; they added a preface which identified Ridley as the author and praised his "manner of inculcating morality." *Tales of the Genii* (London, 1808), p. x.

On the book (and Dickens' connections with it) see Jane W. Stedman, "Good Spirits: Dickens's Childhood Reading," *Dickensian,* LXI (1965), 150-54.

[15] The quotation is from a review in the *British Quarterly Review,* VI (1847), 189.

The affinities of courtly romance and fairy tale are discussed by Erich Auerbach in ch. 6 of *Mimesis* (New York, 1957). They can be seen in such English romances as *Sir Gawain and the Green Knight* and the *Faerie Queene.* Edgar Osborne mentions the chapbook versions of romances as reposits of fairy-tale material in "Children's Books to 1800," *Junior Bookshelf,* IV (1939), 18-19. And see Florence V. Barry, *A Century of Children's Books* (London, 1922), pp. 14-16. On the chapbook see John Ashton, *Chapbooks of the Eighteenth Century* (London, 1882), and F. J. Harvey Darton, *Children's Books in England* (Cambridge, 1958), ch. 5. John Livingston Lowes said: "A book of surpassing interest could (and should) be written on the neglected influence of these enormously popular books of the folk." *The Road to Xanadu* (Boston, 1927), p. 461.

[16] *The Letters of Charles and Mary Lamb,* ed. E. V. Lucas (London, 1935), I, 326.

[17] *Letters of Samuel Taylor Coleridge,* ed. Ernest Hartley Coleridge (London, 1895), I, 16, And see 11-12, letter to Poole of October 9, 1797, and note on lecture of 1811; and Coleridge, *The Friend* (London, 1818), I, 252.

[18] *The Prelude,* ed. Ernest de Selincourt (London, 1926), p. 160, pp. 150-54 (text of 1805-06).

[19] See Allardyce Nicoll, *A History of Early Nineteenth Century Drama, 1800-1850* (Cambridge, 1955), pp. 152-54, and V. C. Clinton-Baddeley, *All Right on the Night* (London, 1954), ch. 8, "Traditions of the Pantomime," pp. 203-34.

[20] *Popular Fairy Tales* (London, 1818), pp. iii-iv.

[21] "Antiquities of Nursery Literature," *Quarterly Review,* XXI (1819), 91-92.

[22] Richard M. Dorson, *The British Folklorists: A History* (London, 1968), p. 45. The work is a source for much of my information on this subject. And see also Katharine M. Briggs, "The Influence of the Brothers Grimm in England," *Hessische Blätter Für Volkskunde,* LIV (1963), 511-24.

[23] "German Popular and Traditionary Literature," *New Monthly Magazine,* II (1821), 146-47.

[24] Preface to the Original Edition, *German Popular Stories* (London, 1869), p. xvi.

[25] *Letters,* VII, 312.

[26] *Gentleman's Magazine,* XCII, 2 (1822), 620-22; "Grimm's German Popular Stories," *London Magazine,* VII (1823), 91.

[27] Edwin H. Zeydel, *Ludwig Tieck and England: A Study in the Literary Relations of Germany and England During the Early Nineteenth Century* (Princeton, 1931), p. 71. On all of the translations see: Violet A. Stockley, *German Literature as Known in England, 1750-1830* (London, 1929); Bayard Quincy Morgan, *A Critical Bibliography of German Literature in English Translation, 1481-1927* (Stanford, 1938); and Max Batt, "The German Story in England About 1826," *Modern Philology,* V (1907), 167-76. And on the *Kunstmärchen* itself see Marianne Thalmann, *The Romantic Fairy Tale: Seeds of Surrealism,* trans. Mary B. Corcoran (Ann Arbor, 1964).

[28] See Henry A. Pochmann, *German Culture in America: Philosophical and Literary Influences, 1600-1900* (Madison, 1961); Palmer Cobb, *The Influence of E. T. A. Hoffmann on the Tales of Edgar Allan Poe* (Chapel Hill, 1908); Dorothy Scarborough, *The Supernatural in Modern English Fiction* (New York, 1917), pp. 56-59; and Eberhard Alsen, "Hawthorne: A Puritan Tieck," unpubl. diss. (Indiana, 1967). On its subject I benefitted from the use of Alsen's unpublished MS. "The 'German Tale' in the British Magazines, 1790-1840."

[29] Note to "The Tale by Goethe," *Fraser's Magazine,* VI (1832), 258. See G. B. Tennyson, *Sartor Called Resartus: The Genesis, Structure, and Style of Thomas Carlyle's First Major Work* (Princeton, 1965), esp. pp. 189-93; and Robert Lee Wolff, *The Golden Key: A Study of the Fiction of George MacDonald* (New Haven, 1961).

[30] "Books for Children," *Quarterly Review,* LXXI (1842), 55; "Children's Books," *Quarterly Review,* LXXIV (1844), 1-26.

[31] *British Quarterly Review,* VI (1847), 189.

[32] Folklorists now believe that this was not an original story. See Dorson, *The British Folklorists,* p. 95, and Briggs, *The Fairies,* p. 169, and especially her "The Three Bears," *International Congress for Folk-Narrative Research in Athens,* IV, ed. Georgios A. Megas (Athens, 1965), pp. 53-57.

[33] Cole, *Beauty and the Beast* (London, 1843), p. iv; Thoms, Note to Reader, *The Old Story Books of England* (Westminster, 1845), no p., and *Gammer Gurton's Pleasant Stories* and *Gammer Gurton's Famous Histories* (Westminster, 1846), no p.; Montalba, *Fairy Tales from All Nations* (London, 1849), no p.

[34] *Prœterita,* in *The Complete Works of John Ruskin,* ed. E. T. Cook and Alexander Wedderburn (London, 1903), XXXV, 304. The story revolves around Motif Q2, "kind and unkind," and resembles, e.g., AT 431.

[35] Darton, *Children's Books,* p. 247. See Elias Bredsdorff, *Danish Literature in English Translation, with a special Hans Christian Andersen Supplement: A Bibliography* (Copenhagen, 1950).

[36] *Vanity Fair,* ed. Geoffrey and Kathleen Tillotson (Boston, 1963). The reviews are: "Christmas Books—No. 2," *Morning Chronicle,* December 26, 1845, in *Thackeray's Contributions to the Morning Chronicle,* ed. Gordon N. Ray (Urbana, 1955), pp. 93-100 (on a new translation of Grimm); and "On Some Illustrated Children's Books," *Fraser's Magazine,* XXXIII (1846), 495-502 (greatly on Cole's and Thoms's collections).

[37] "A Witch in the Nursery," *Household Words,* September 20, 1851, 608. Hereafter I will abbreviate the title of the journal as *HW.*

[38] "The School of the Fairies," *HW,* June 30, 1855, 509-13. Morley had made similar points allegorically in "The Two Guides of the Child," *HW,* September 7, 1850, 560-61.

[39] *Athenaeum,* 1323 (1853), 284.

[40] "Children's Literature," *London Quarterly Review,* XIII (1860), 482, 486-87.

[41] Introduction, *German Popular Stories,* p. ix.

[42] *The King of the Golden River, Works,* I, 347.

[43] *The Water Babies* (London, 1882).

[44] *The Hope of the Katzekopfs* (London, 1846), pp. xvi-xvii.

[45] *The Fairies,* p. 186.

[46] See Peter Coveney, *The Image of Childhood* (Baltimore, 1967), which covers some of the same ground as I do, with different concerns.

[47] "German Story Books," *Chambers's Journal,* XXIV (1855), 316-17.

[48] *Athenaeum,* 284.

[49] "The Day-Dream," L'Envoi, ll. 50-51, *The Works of Tennyson,* ed. Hallam, Lord Tennyson (London, 1913), p. 108.

The same fairy tale (AT 410) provided the subject for escapist works in several media by the Pre-Raphaelite artist Edward Burne-Jones. See the reproduction of the series of tiles he did on it in 1862.

[50] "Children's Literature," 480. The final sentence echoes Wordsworth's claim that "the child, whose love is here, at least, doth reap/ One precious gain, that he forgets himself" (*Prelude,* ll. 368-69).

[51] Kris, *Psychoanalytic Explorations in Art* (New York, 1952), p. 42; Friedlaender, "Children's Books and Their Function in Latency and Prepuberty," *American Imago,* III (1942), 129.

[52] "The Phenomenology of the Spirit in Fairytales," *The Archetypes and the Collective Unconscious, The Collected Works,* trans. R. F. C. Hall (London, 1969), Vol. IX, part 1, 217.

[53] *The Interpretation of Dreams,* trans. and ed. James Strachey (New York, 1965), p. 386.

[54] Some specific interpretations can be compared. The Jungian Joseph Campbell considers the frog in "The Frog-King" (AT 440) to be "the representative of that unconscious deep . . . wherein are hoarded all of the rejected, unadmitted, unrecognized, unknown, or un-developed factors, laws and elements of existence." The Freudian Ernest Jones says: "The frog is in the unconscious a constant symbol of the male organ when viewed with disgust." Max Müller, leader of the solar-mythologist school, claimed that "frog was used as a name of the sun" and so the frog in the story really is the sun. Modern folklorist-anthropologists commonly reject these approaches. My point is not that the inter-pretations necessarily are valid, but that they represent an understandable type of response to the "flat," un-real, dream-like tales. One modern folklorist who agrees is Max Lüthi, who says: "It is indisputable that the *Märchen* plainly invites symbolic interpretation." He adds the necessary warning: "But in the interpretation of special traits opinions can differ, and arbitrary judg-ment easily slips in." "Aspects of the *Märchen* and the Legend," trans. Barbara Flynn, *Genre,* II (1969), 169. The quotations above are from Campbell, *The Hero With a Thousand Faces* (Cleveland, 1956), p. 52; Jones, "Psychoanalysis and Folklore," *Jubilee Congress of the Folklore Society: Papers and Transactions* (London, 1930), p. 233; and Müller, "Tales of the West Highlands" (1861), in *Chips from a German Workshop* (London, 1867), II, 247. The same three interpreta-tions are compared by Richard M. Dorson, in an ar-ticle in which he presents a standard folklorist critique of them. See "Theories of Myth and the Folklorist,"

Myth and Mythmaking, ed. Henry A. Murray (New York, 1960), pp. 76-89.

[55] Tennyson, "Locksley Hall" (1842), l. 12, *Works,* p. 98.

---

de Vries explains the word "Märchen":

[First] we must agree on the meaning of the word *"Märchen,"* which (like the Dutch *sprookje*) means simply "tale," thus corresponding to the French *conte populaire.* In Scandinavian it is called "adventure" (e.g., Danish *eventyr*) or, very colorlessly, "myth" (as in Swedish). These fuzzy designations (compare also the Russian *skazka* and the Finnish *tarina*) are in agreement with the contents of the famous book with which the Brothers Grimm stimulated fairy-tale research, the *Kinder- und Haus-märchen* ("Children's and Household Tales"), containing fables and pranks, even some legends, along with the fairy tales proper. Obviously, completely different products of the art of storytelling were here thrown into one pot. In the catalogue of types created by Antti Aarne and expanded by Stith Thompson, too, these forms exist peacefully side by side; but we are bound to make a distinction. Fable and prank are easily eliminated; the legend, too, does not belong here. What is left are the real fairy tales, separated by Aarne again into "magical tales" and "novella-like tales." The latter group shows many ties with the international literature of *novelle* which flowered in the late Middle Ages and drew mainly on the Orient for its subjects. This leaves as proper for our study the "magical fairy tales"—tales in which supernatural themes appear, such as personified beings (giants, dwarfs, fairies, Frau Holle), helpful animals (a horse gifted with human speech), transformations of enchanted humans into animals, and magical objects or actions.

Jan de Vries in Diogenes, *No. 22, Summer 1958.*

Patricia Miller

SOURCE: "The Importance of Being Earnest: The Fairy Tale in 19th-Century England," in *Children's Litera-ture Association Quarterly,* Vol. 7, No. 2, Summer, 1982, pp. 11-14.

[*In the following essay, Miller asserts that what dif-ferentiates Victorian fairy tales from European ones are the morality and earnestness of characters, par-ticularly those of Dickens and Ruskin.*]

Students of the history of children's literature are thoroughly familiar with the dispute surrounding the reputation of the fairy tale in England at the beginning of the 19th Century. On the one hand, moralists and religious leaders found it hard to believe that tales of giant beanstalks, seven-league boots, and men the size of one's thumb could provide ethical guidance for their young pupils. Similarly, educational reformers regarded fairy tales suspiciously because of their failure to teach anything specific. After all, weren't lessons in arithmetic, geography, and religion more valuable than having a good time?

In 1853, of course, Charles Dickens vigorously attacked these narrow and utilitarian views of fairy literature in his article, "Frauds on the Fairies," which asserted that in an age when men were rapidly becoming machines and slaves to reason, fairy tales were to be respected and permitted to do their important job of nurturing men's feelings and imagination. Dickens was also quick to point out, however, that in addition to providing imaginative stimulation to children, fairy tales could also *teach:*

> It would be hard to estimate the amount of gentleness and mercy that has made its way among us through these slight channels. Forbearance, courtesy, consideration for the poor and aged, kind treatment of animals, the love of nature, abhorrence of tyranny and brute force—many such good things have been nourished in the child's heart by this powerful aid.[1]

While Dickens' essay does much to defend fairy tales in general against the stern pietism of Puritan literature and the bleak didacticism of the Age of Reason, it does not address the unique qualities of the fairy tale in 19th-century England. How, for example, are the fairy tales of two eminent Victorians such as Dickens or John Ruskin different from those of Perrault or Grimm? What makes them distinctly Victorian?

One quality which helps to distinguish the Victorian fairy tale from its European counterparts is its unique quality of *earnestness.* The one thing that every scholar of 19th-century literature knows is that the Victorians were "earnest," but what is meant by this and why they were is difficult to say. We know that the Victorians regarded earnestness as a positive moral attribute, and that the absence of it—whether in an individual or in a society—was decidedly bad. Among modern critics, Walter Houghton has provided perhaps the most helpful definition of the term in *The Victorian Frame of Mind:*

> The [Victorian] prophets of earnestness were attacking a casual, easy-going, superficial, or frivolous attitude whether in intellectual or in moral life; and demanding that men should think and men should live with a high and serious purpose.[2]

Such purposefulness and revolt against moral indifference manifest themselves in much of the period's fiction and non-fiction for adults. For Thomas Carlyle in *Sartor Resartus,* earnestness is an assertion of Christian faith and a celebration of the virtues of hard work. For Tennyson in poems like "Ulysses," it is a quest for self-perfection and truth, an effort "to strive, to seek, to find, and not to yield." For novelists such as George Eliot and Dickens, earnestness is a scrupulous attention to matters of conscience and a desire for social responsibility in the face of an expanding industrialism. Finally, for Matthew Arnold, it is a belief in the transforming and sustaining power of love in a world which "hath really neither joy, nor love, nor light,/Nor certitude, nor peace, nor help for pain."[3]

But this value system of hard work, moral awareness, consideration for others, and love is present not only in the adult literature of the period, but also in the children's literature, particularly the fairy tale. In the Christmas books of Charles Dickens, published between 1843 and 1888, and in John Ruskin's fairy classic, *The King of the Golden River* (1857), one can find clear illustrations of the importance of being earnest. In fact, both works serve as paradigms of Victorian earnestness.

As Harry Stone acknowledges in *Dickens and the Invisible World,* Dickens' Christmas books are indebted to fairy tales: "The Christmas books draw their innermost energies from fairy tales: they exploit fairy-tale themes, fairy-tale happenings, and fairy-tale techniques. Indeed the Christmas books *are* fairy tales."[4] While *A Christmas Carol* has traditionally received the most attention, *The Cricket on the Hearth: A Fairy Tale of Home* (1843) deserves special attention because it epitomizes the earnest and purposeful temperament of the Victorians. The story focuses on the lives of seven main characters and a *genius loci,* a cricket whose chirp accentuates the qualities of earnestness that Dickens wants to underscore. John Peerybingle, a carrier, and Dot, his young bride, have an idyllic marriage with their baby until the appearance of a mysterious stranger, an old man, whom they take into their home. One evening John sees Dot talking privately with their visitor, who has removed his disguise and who is, in fact, a young man Dot's age. Peerybingle is horrified at what he believes is his wife's infidelity but says nothing at first. Later in the story it is revealed that the young man, Edward, *is* a friend of Dot's, but he has returned from the sea not to tear her away from her loving husband, but to enlist her aid in winning the affections of May Fielding, a beautiful young woman who is engaged to marry Gruff and Tackleton, a cruel and materialistic toy manufacturer.

Tackleton is also the employer of Caleb Plummer, an industrious and gentle-hearted man who lives in an old shack with his blind daughter, Bertha. Rather than revealing the sordidness and harshness of their life to Bertha, Caleb uses his imagination to convince her that

Charles Dickens in 1849.

they live in opulent surroundings and to make her "see" Tackleton as an eccentric benefactor, the Guardian Angel of their lives.

Throughout the tale, all of the characters, except for the villainous Tackleton, exhibit the many sides of earnestness. Particularly, John Peerybingle and Caleb Plummer demonstrate the moral value of hard work which is intrinsic to earnestness. In *Sartor Resartus* (1834) and *Past and Present* (1843), Thomas Carlyle encouraged his countrymen to "Produce! Produce! Were it but the pitifullest infinitesimal fraction of a Product, produce it, in God's name!"[5] For Carlyle and the other Victorian prophets of the age, work was not merely the performance of a task for money; instead, it was the way by which a man could measure his advance towards human perfection. Work was spiritually enriching and ennobling, and the best work was performed for the benefit of others. In *The Cricket On the Hearth,* John Peerybingle cheerfully works as a carrier to provide domestic comforts for his wife and child, while Caleb Plummer patiently accepts low wages

and intolerable working conditions to provide sustenance for his blind daughter, Bertha. In addition to the menial tasks that he performs for Tackleton, Plummer also has another vocation: to nurture Bertha's dreams of an elegant home and a happy life. In striving hard in many ways for "this one great sacred object,"[6] Plummer allows his work to perfect and purify him, to fulfill him in all that is best.

In their use of work to fulfill spiritual and emotional needs, both of these characters distinguish themselves from the Philistine Tackleton for whom work is an opportunity to take advantage of others and to please himself. It is ironic that Tackleton is a toy manufacturer, since his product suggests the spontaneity, sharing, and imagination of childhood, rather than the crass exploitation of others. Rather than sharing his fortune, Tackleton uses it to attract his young fiancée, May Fielding, for whom he has little love; she is merely another treasure to add to his hoard. While the home that he promises her will be full of material comforts, it will offer little emotional satisfaction, as his callous remark to John about domestic harmony reveals: "What is a home? Four walls and a ceiling!"[7]

Earnestness is also evident in the story through the characters' desires to preserve the centrality of love in their lives. Dot and John, Caleb and Bertha, May and Edward—all of these characters are motivated by a desire to be true to one another in spite of confusion and struggle. When John first discovers Dot speaking intimately with the stranger, he is heartbroken and angry. However, his love for her and his desire to see her as his heart has seen her—as a true and loving wife—banish his suspicions even before he discovers that she has been talking to Edward to help him woo May. When he tries to dwell upon her infidelity, he can only conjure up images of her goodness and constancy: "Rocking her little Baby in its cradle; singing to it softly; and resting her head upon [his] shoulder. . . . Although the shadow of the stranger fell at intervals . . . it never fell so darkly as at first."[8] Dot, in turn, knows her husband's suspicions but does not speak out to betray Edward; instead, she chooses to believe in John's love, and this reunites them at the end of the story.

In a similar way, Caleb Plummer earnestly centers his life in his love for his blind daughter. Through the power of his imagination

> the Blind Girl never knew that iron was rusting, wood rotting, paper peeling off; the very size, and shape, and true proportion of the dwelling, withering away. The Blind Girl never knew that ugly shapes of delft and earthenware were on the board; that sorrow and faint-heartedness were in the house; that Caleb's scanty hairs were turning greyer and greyer before her sightless face.[9]

When he confesses to her that he has lied to her about their life, he risks her hatred, but once again; he stresses that love has been his motivating factor:

> Your road in life was rough, my poor one . . . and I meant to make it smooth for you. I have altered objects, changed the characters of people, invented many things, that have never been, to make you happier. I have had concealments from you, put deceptions on you, God forgive me![10]

Like John the carrier, however, Bertha responds with love, not hatred when the truth is revealed, and she blesses her father for restoring her moral vision, the ability to "see" and to appreciate what is true:

> Dearest father . . . Everything is here—in you. The father that I loved so well; the father that I never loved enough, and never knew; the Benefactor whom I first began to reverence and love, because he had such sympathy for me; All are here in you. . . . The soul of all that was most dear to me is here—here, with the worn face, and the grey head! and I am NOT blind, father, any longer![11]

In all of these characters, then, and in their principal concerns, Dickens has provided a concise statement of the Victorian temperament, as he concludes the tale: "It was the most complete, unmitigated soul-fraught little piece of earnestness that you ever beheld in all your days."[12]

Like Dickens, John Ruskin also espouses the characteristic Victorian earnestness in *The King of the Golden River*. While the tale is patterned after a Grimm fairy tale, its themes are once again distinctly Victorian. The importance of hard work which is spiritually ennobling is stressed through the character of Gluck, the youngest of three brothers who lives in the Treasure Valley. Gluck patiently performs all of the unpleasant household chores that his two older brothers will not stoop to: "He was usually appointed to the honourable office of turnspit, when there was anything to roast. . . . At other times he used to clean the shoes, floors, and sometimes the plates, occasionally getting what was left on them by way of encouragement, and a wholesome quantity of dry blows, by way of education."[13] Gluck's hard work is accompanied by a Christian goodness of heart which prompts him to share what little he has with others. When, for example, the Southwest Wind visits his home one stormy evening, Gluck gives him his own small piece of mutton, even though he may go hungry himself and be punished for it: "'They promised me one slice today, sir,' he said; 'I can give you that, but not a bit more.'"[14]

Such hard work and altruism, however, are not characteristic of Gluck's two brothers, Hans and Schwartz, who exploit the Treasure Valley for their own wealth:

> They lived by farming in the Treasure Valley, and were very good farmers. They killed everything that did not pay for its eating. They shot the blackbirds, because they pecked the fruit; and killed the hedgehogs, lest they should suck the cows; they poisoned the crickets for eating the crumbs in the kitchen; and smothered the cicadas, which used to sing all summer in the lime trees. They worked their servants without any wages, till they would not work any more, and then quarrelled with them and turned them out of doors without paying them. . . . They generally contrived to keep their corn by them until it was very dear, and then sell it for twice its value; they had heaps of gold lying about on their floors, yet it was never known that they had given so much as a penny or a crust in charity; they never went to mass, grumbled perpetually at paying tithes; and were, in a word, of so cruel and grinding a temper, as to receive . . . the nickname of the "Black Brothers."[15]

In their exploitative view of work, in their materialism, and in their indifference to others, the Brothers are the antithesis of the earnestness which Gluck symbolizes. Their lack of earnestness is especially evident in their desire to possess all of the wealth of the Golden River for themselves. When Gluck tells them of the prophecy that promises wealth to the one who can climb to the top of the mountain and pour three drops of holy water into the river, the brothers set out greedily to claim their fortune. Each, however, is too corrupt to ever reach his goal. Neither asks for the requisite holy water honestly. Hans steals it, and Schwartz bribes a bad priest for it. Furthermore, each brother refuses to share his water—a simple act of charity—with the different characters they meet on the mountainside. Consequently, their quest ends in failure, and they are turned into black stones.

Gluck's trip up the mountainside contrasts sharply with his brothers' journeys in its earnestness of purpose. Unlike Hans and Schwartz, who plan to keep all of the gold in the river for themselves, Gluck sets out to gain his fortune so that he can share it with the inhabitants of the blighted valley. Unlike his brothers, he does not take the sanctity of his mission lightly. He asks a priest honestly for the holy water, and once he has received it, he does not hesitate to share it to the last drop with his companions on the mountainside—an old man, a child, and a dog. His kindness and sincerity are rewarded when he shakes three drops of dew into the stream, the river turns to gold, and the valley is restored to its original fertility and beauty:

> As Gluck gazed, fresh grass sprang beside the new streams and creeping plants grew, and climbed the moistening soil. Young flowers opened suddenly along the river sides, as stars leap out when twilight is deepening, and thickets of myrtle

and tendrils of vine, cast lengthening shadows over the valley as they grew. And thus the Treasure Valley became a garden again, and the inheritance which had been lost by cruelty, was regained by love.[16]

In addition to their moral thoughtfulness, their inquiring love of truth, and their devoted love of goodness, both *The Cricket on the Hearth* and *The King of the Golden River* share the Victorian concern for social responsibility which is a fundamental component of earnestness. In *The Cricket on the Hearth,* Dickens reveals the interrelatedness of human actions; no moral decision can affect only one person. Instead, moral choices reverberate throughout the fabric of society. Dot's decision to help Edward causes John pain and suffering until the truth is revealed; Tackleton's greed forces Caleb and Bertha into a life of degradation; Edward's return from sea saves May from a sterile marriage. In *The King of the Golden River* individual actions also echo throughout society. Hans' and Schwartz's callousness and materialism condemn the valley to blight and death. Gluck's simple acts of charity restore prosperity and wealth to the inhabitants of the Valley. In these two fairy tales of 19th-century England, then, earnestness is not merely a matter of self-perfection, but it is also the most desirable goal for an entire nation and an age.

Notes

[1] Charles Dickens, *Frauds on the Fairies,* in *A Peculiar Gift,* ed. Lance Salway (Kestrel Books: Harmonds works, 1976), p. 111.

[2] Walter Houghton, *The Victorian Frame of Mind, 1830-1870* (New Haven: Yale University Press, 1972), p. 222.

[3] Matthew Arnold, "Dover Beach" in *The Collected Prose and Poetry of Matthew Arnold,* ed. A. Dwight Culler (Boston: Houghton-Mifflin), p. 162.

[4] Harry Stone, *Dickens and the Invisible World* (Bloomington: Indiana University Press, 1979), p. 119.

[5] Thomas Carlyle, *Past and Present,* as quoted by Walter Houghton in *The Victorian Frame of Mind,* p. 253.

[6] Charles Dickens, *The Cricket on the Hearth: A Fairy Tale of Home* (London: Bradbury and Evans, 1846), p. 149.

[7] Dickens, p. 41.

[8] Dickens, p. 125.

[9] Dickens, p. 56.

[10] Dickens, p. 146.

[11] Dickens, p. 151.

[12] Dickens, p. 161.

[13] John Ruskin, *The King of the Golden River* (New York: Dover Publications, Inc., 1974), p. 16.

[14] Ruskin, p. 23.

[15] Ruskin, pp. 15-16.

[16] Ruskin, p. 67.

Roderick McGillis

SOURCE: "Fantasy as Adventure: Nineteenth Century Children's Fiction," in *Children's Literature Association Quarterly,* Vol. 8, No. 3, Fall, 1983, pp. 18-22.

[*In the essay below, McGillis examines the attitude displayed toward adventure in nineteenth-century fantasies, pointing in particular to the "deeply felt suspicion of fantasy adventure" common to many Victorian children's books.*]

I wish to extend Paul Zweig's comparison between the shaman and the storyteller to nineteenth century romance, especially in works for children.

In *The Adventurer,* Zweig suggests that in the nineteenth century, adventure, like the quest romance, became internalized; he also suggests that a "resemblance exists between the adventurer exploring the countries of the marvelous and the "absent" one: each finds his way to the "other" world and returns to tell the story."[1] The "absent one" is the shaman who, through illness or some other means, transports to a mysterious world of hidden realities. As Zweig argues:

> The shaman's vocation as an ecstatic traveler resembles that of the archaic adventurer. Both forge an immunity to the perils of the demonic world by mastering them. Both return from their journey bearing stories which sustain the humanity of those who are destined to exist within the circle of domestic realities. The story itself is a way of naming the unnameable, extending the net of language into the obscure seas which defy human foresight. Telling his tale of struggles and triumphs in the demon countries, the shaman pushes back the essential ignorance in which men live, by exposing a further reach of darkness to the clarity of words (pp. 90-91).

Although fear of the shaman—or what he represents—runs through much popular Victorian children's litera-

A scene from the 1933 film version of Alice's Adventures in Wonderland, *featuring Cary Grant as the Mock Turtle.*

ture, we can also recognize something of this character in the best works of the period. What makes George MacDonald's *At the Back of the North Wind* (1871) such a strong and effective book, and Lewis Carroll's *Alice's Adventures in Wonderland* (1865) such a troublesome and complex book, is their acceptance of what the shaman in his trance-like state stands for: the disruption of social reality, the overturning of easy certainties.

Most Victorian fantasies are uneasy with their notions of adventure, whether it be adventure in this world or in some "other" world. In Mrs. Ewing's *A Great Emergency* (1874), the narrator, nine-year-old Charlie, thinks that "to begin a life of adventure is to run away."[2] He and a friend hide on board a barge and float along a canal to London, where they intend to stow away on a ship bound for exotic shores. While on his "adventure," Charlie misses the great emergency of the title, which takes place back at his home; at the story's end he reflects: "in my vain, jealous

wild-goose chase after adventures I missed the chance of distinguishing myself in the only Great Emergency which has yet occurred in our family" (p. 148). As Gillian Avery remarks, "The story turns on this, that adventures are as likely to happen on one's own doorstep as over the other side of the fence," but more importantly she notes the "further moral," that the dullness of life is in fact "preferable to disaster."[3] In short, for Mrs. Ewing adventure is less than respectable. Charlie, an adult at the end of *A Great Emergency,* chides himself for being "still but too apt to dream!" (p. 147). Indeed, for a great number of Victorian writers for children, dreams are the stuff of childhood, acceptable if poorly moral, but to be set aside when one matures.

Attitudes to fantasy in the Victorian period may have been set by a work written before the turn of the nineteenth century, Coleridge's *Rime of the Ancient Mariner.*[4] Responding to Mrs. Barbauld's complaint that the poem lacked a moral, Coleridge asserted that it had too much moral. The pat "He prayeth best, who loveth best/All things both great and small" appeared, in retrospect, too moral to Coleridge, as if he realized that a story like the Mariner's was too rich, too haunting, too mysterious, to be captured in such aphoristic pointedness. Clearly, the wedding guest who listens to, who cannot choose but hear, the story perceives something other, something darker, which the moral conclusion the Mariner tags onto his story will not explain. The wedding guest departs a sadder and wiser man; he turns from the wedding feast, from the world of domestic relations and the celebration of the patterns of social reality. As listener to the story, he has been transported by the storyteller, the shamanistic Mariner who is periodically seized by a compulsion to retell the story of his own transport to a world where he struggled with demonic powers and confronted mysteries of the soul.

Coleridge's poem, then, exhibits two tendencies, both of which inform Victorian children's fantasies. First, there is the tendency to diminish adventure, to reduce it to moral statement, and in the process, devalue it. Once the adventure in a fantastic realm is over it is best to leave it behind, perhaps even to forget it, since it threatens to remove permanently those who experience it—like the mariner—from the duties and responsibilities of mature social activity. Second, there is the less-common (indeed, extremely rare) tendency to value the fantastic realm and those who return from it to speak of its mysteries as liberators from the inanimate cold world of duty and responsibility. The shaman's experience, which I am equating with a fictional character's or a reader's experience of fantasy, shakes those who hear it free of the lethargy of custom; it is subversive. From this perspective, Huck Finn participates in a shamanistic experience in lighting out, as he does, for the territories; he departs from the world of social contingencies to enter an "other" world. It is not difficult to understand why Twain's contemporaries were less than enthusiastic about the book.

Generally, Victorian children's books use the "other" world for both fantastic adventure and moral teaching, but they make clear their deeply felt suspicion of fantasy adventure. Examples are numerous. Jack, in Jean Ingelow's *Mopsa the Fairy* (1869), returns from Fairyland to sit on his father's knee and marvel "what a great thing a man was." Nothing so important exists in Fairyland and Jack is "glad he had come back."[5] Mrs. Molesworth's *The Cuckoo Clock* (1877) is perhaps clearer: the heroine, Griselda, dreams at the end of the book of the cuckoo for the last time. In the morning "her pillow was wet with tears" and Mrs. Molesworth writes, "Thus many stories end. She was happy, very happy, in the thought of her kind new friends; but there were tears for the one she felt she had said farewell to, even though he was only a cuckoo in a clock."[6]

The tone here is disquieting to a believer in fairyland, but even more disquieting is what Dinah Mulock has to say concerning belief in the wonders of fairyland in *The Little Lame Prince* (1874): "Now, I don't expect anybody to believe what I am going to relate, though a good many wise people have believed a good many sillier things. And as seeing's believing, and I never saw it, I cannot be expected implicitly to believe it myself, except in a sort of a way; and yet there is truth in it—for some people."[7]

A tension exists here; it is as if Mulock wanted to be sure that the child reader did not take this as too seriously real. Is the fairytale real or not? Only childhood knows fantasy. In *The Adventures of a Brownie*, Mulock makes it clear that the brownie exists only for the child:

> But, as Brownie was never seen, he was never suspected. And since he did no mischief—neither pinched the baby nor broke the toys, left no soap in the bath and no footmarks about the room—but was always a well-conducted Brownie in every way, he was allowed to inhabit the nursery (or supposed to do so, since, as nobody saw him, nobody could prevent him), until the children were grown up into men and women.

> After that he retired into his coal cellar, and for all I know he may live there still, and have gone through hundreds of adventures since; but as I never heard them, I can't tell them. Only I think if I could be a little child again, I should exceedingly like a Brownie to play with me. Should not you?[8]

For a writer like L. M. Montgomery—and for the most part Montgomery reflects the dominant nineteenth century attitudes—fantasy is wonderful in childhood, suggesting the child's independence of mind and his spirit of adventure. Anne of *Anne of Green Gables* (1908) and Davy Keith of *Anne of Avonlea* (1909) are refreshing counterparts to the many prim child characters in Victorian fiction, and Montgomery's attitude toward them differs markedly from, for example, Charlotte Yonge's attitude to Kate in *Countess Kate* (1862). In *Anne of Avonlea*, Anne confesses she likes Davy more than his better-behaved sister Dora because "Dora is too good."[9] If, however, the exuberance of the child and his or her indulgence in fantasy continues into adulthood, the adult, although he or she may be wonderfully kind and likeable, must remain at a remove from real life, arrested in development like poor Miss Lavender Lewis in *Anne of Avonlea*. When Miss Lavender finally does get married at a belated forty-five years of age, Montgomery writes: "Miss Lavender drove away from the old life of dreams and make-believes to a fuller life of realities in the busy world beyond" (p. 286).

What makes the first Anne book—*Anne of Green Gables*—so interesting is its attempt to depict Anne as an adventurer, one who, in Zweig's terms, disrupts the pattern of social experience, one whose individualism is irrepressible, one in flight from social norms and habitual responses. But the book finally fails in this valiant attempt; Anne cannot play the shaman's role since it is she, not the people of Avonlea, who needs healing, and this healing is profoundly integrative rather than subversive. Anne, and the Cuthberts, move closer to the community and its values. In a later book, *The Story Girl* (1911), Montgomery expresses with moving intensity the conflict between conformity and the pull to fantasy, in a passage that is a precise statement of the nineteenth century attitude I have been examining:

> There is such a place as fairyland—but only children can find the way to it. And they do not know that it is fairyland until they have grown so old that they forget the way. One bitter day, when they seek it and cannot find it, they realize what they have lost and that is the tragedy of life. One day the gates of Eden are shut behind them and the age of gold is over. Henceforth they must dwell in the common light of common day. Only a few, who remain children at heart, can ever find that fair, lost path again, and blessed are they above mortals. They, and only they can bring us tidings from that dear country where once we sojourned and from which we must evermore be exiles. The world calls them its singers and poets and artists and storytellers; but they are just people who have never forgotten the way to fairyland.[10]

Fantasy has a strong tendency toward subversion, or transgression.[11] It is *unheimlich*. At its best it shows us that our true home is elsewhere, not in the local communities in which we live day by day. Perhaps Lewis Carroll's *Alice's Adventures in Wonderland* furnishes us with the Victorian era's most compellingly ambivalent statement on fantasy. Alice's fantasy adventure is, of course, clearly a dream, her dream, and as such it is something Alice wakes from and leaves behind as she runs into tea. Alice leaves her sister by the tree pondering Alice's dream and imagining Alice as a grownup telling tales to young children. Alice's dream, in other words, won't leave her; instead her trip to the "other" world will turn Alice into a storyteller, a shaman, who makes the eyes of children "bright and eager with many a strange tale, perhaps even with the dream of Wonderland of long ago."[12] For these children there would not be the tedium of books "without pictures or conversations." Instead there will be Wonderland, the zany, the mad, the anarchic "other" world where above-ground certainties, social niceties, rules of decorum, and adult preoccupation with hierarchy, prestige, and justice are turned upside down. Here the rule is creative play, and

survival depends on how swiftly one can turn an axis into axes or adapt to a game in which all the objects are alive. Indeed, Alice's problem is her inability to accept an overturning of the rules she has come to accept as natural: "they don't seem to have any rules in particular," she complains during the croquet game.

Here we should detect an anomaly. Alice does not enter into the madcap activity of Wonderland; she rarely, if ever, sees the fun in the antics of those she meets. When the Cheshire cat tells her she must be mad "or you wouldn't have come here," Alice doesn't think "that proved it at all." She leaves the Mad Tea Party "in great disgust." She is glad when the Lobster Quadrille is over, and in the end she rejects the whole dream, scoffing that the Queen of Hearts and her court are "nothing but a pack of cards." Why would she remember with fondness a dream in which she was bossed, bullied, threatened, and belittled? All we know is that Alice runs off to tea thinking "what a wonderful dream it had been." Then Carroll shifts the point of view to Alice's sister, and as she contemplates Alice's dream, she domesticates it:

> So she sat on, with closed eyes, and half believed herself in Wonderland, though she knew she had but to open them again, and all would change to dull reality—the grass would be only rustling in the wind, and the pool rippling to the waving of the reeds—the rattling teacups would change to tinkling sheep bells, and the Queen's shrill cries to the voice of the shepherd boy—and the sneeze of the baby, the shriek of the Gryphon, and all the other queer noises, would change (she knew) to the confused clamor of the busy farmyard—while the lowing of the cattle in the distance would take the place of the Mock Turtle's heavy sobs (pp. 163-164).

The dream becomes a pastoral, just what Alice herself wanted in the first place when she saw through the tiny door the garden with its "bright flowers and cool fountains." But the pastoral feeling here is surely at variance with the disorder of the dream, its unsettling, nightmarish quality. Carroll refuses to decide whether the dream in all its subversive glory or the dream as filtered through a nostalgic recollection is what matters. Alice's sister only "half believes" herself in Wonderland; she knows she need only open her eyes to have all return to "dull reality." But Carroll's parenthetical remark that all would change (she knew) hints that for Carroll this dull reality might not be so dull. The tone here is elegaic, pastoral, and romantic (in a rather glib way), and it is difficult to accept that Carroll sees the rippling pool, waving reeds, tinkling sheep bells, lowing cattle, and all as dull. What has happened to the energetic play of the dream? In this, the first *Alice* book, Carroll's intense delight in adventure, his willingness to wander in wonderful seas because there is always a shore on the other side, is in the end tempered by his equally strong adherence to certitude and community. Alice will become a storyteller, and thus control the journey away from the familiar world; as adventurer she risked her life and sanity ("It's really dreadful . . . the way all the creatures argue. It's enough to drive one crazy," she says), but as storyteller she shall take on "the truest meaning of the shaman's role as healer" (Zweig, p. 93). But not if, as her sister projects, she tames the dream. By sliding into Alice's sister's point of view, Carroll leaves the question of the dream's subversive potential ambiguous.

Like so many nineteenth-century fantasists, Carroll might well be charged with reneging on his faith in the value of imagination. He might have something in common with those writers Anita Moss describes as having only a narrow, moralistic interest in fantasy. Speaking of Catherine Sinclair, F. E. Paget, Mark Lemon, Christina Rossetti, George MacDonald, and others, Moss writes,

> While all of these writers consciously espoused the value of the imagination and its function in the lives of children and their books, none of them sustained a commitment to the pleasures of fantasy and the imagination all the way through their stories. Sooner or later they all turned their fairytales into narrow lessons. In each story the child protagonist, often a lively and spirited child, is removed from the ordinary world to a fantastic world of terror, placed under the control of a tyrannical adult figure, and transformed into the pious and saintly children to which early Victorian audiences apparently responded. One notes in these stories a deep split in the creative purposes of the writers between their avowed attitudes toward fantasy, children, and the imagination and their actual practices, a bifurcation often manifested in the split structures of the stories themselves.[13]

Clearly, Carroll's *Alice* books escape such criticism through their sheer delight in invention, although the nuances I detect in the ending of *Alice's Adventures in Wonderland* are full-blown in *Sylvie and Bruno*. But George MacDonald is an altogether different case. Here is a writer whose commitment to imagination is fervent; for him, fantasy must inform reality at all times, not just in childhood and not merely at odd moments when we have time from the business of living to perk up our lives with a heady dose of moral fantasy. The book Moss cites as an example of MacDonald's "narrowly focused and unpleasant didacticism" (Moss, p. 132) is *The Lost Princess: A Double Story*. Now, only an insensitive reader would attempt to defend this book as completely successful, but it does offer a remarkably clear instance of MacDonald's belief in adventure. In Zweig's terms, MacDonald's sense of adventure may be closer to the non-adventure of *Robinson Crusoe,* since he places such emphasis on the domestic virtues of hard work and regularity, but MacDonald's insistence on constant movement, constant becoming, reminds us of the adventurer's compelling need to act and to contend.

The Lost Princess, first published as *The Wise Woman,*[14] concerns two young girls, one a princess and one a shepherd's daughter, one who is willful and given to tantrums, and one who is conceited and self-complacent, but both of whom are selfish and unpleasant. The girls are taken in hand by a mysterious wise woman, who lives in a strange house on a wild heath. One point in this relentlessly pointless book is that whether you live in a cottage or in a castle you are still susceptible to complacency, to a settled belief in the rightness of things as perceived by the mind habituated to the familiar. The Wise Woman's function is to break up the ice of fixed ideas and expectations, for she knows that without conflict, without the piquancy of fear, there will be no progression.

But MacDonald's is not a simple moralistic vision; he does not merely offer pat goals, although at times (and many times in this book) he does speak in moralistic aphorisms reminiscent of the he-prayeth-best-who-loveth-best variety. Like his Romantic precursors, MacDonald wishes to wake his readers from a sleep of reason, and his usual method is through polysemous and paradoxical language. For example, when he speaks of Agnes, the shepherd girl, MacDonald says that she "had very fair abilities, and, were she once but made humble, would be capable not only of doing a good deal in time but of beginning at once to grow to no end" (p. 52). Grow to no end? This colloquial utterance means that Agnes might grow into a much better child; in other words, it reads figuratively. But MacDonald also means quite literally that Agnes's growth will be endless, that no articulation of her final identity is possible, since existence means constant, indeed eternal, movement toward identity. The word "end" contains spatial and temporal significance; MacDonald refuses to posit a goal, a point in time or space to which we set our sights. Consequently, there can be no settling complacently in the thought that an end has been achieved.

What I referred to earlier as this "relentlessly pointless book" should be clearer now. MacDonald's books, his best books anyway, deliberately avoid closure. Here is the beginning of the book's final paragraph: "And that is all my double story. How double it is, if you care to know, you must find out. If you think it is not finished—I never knew a story that was." Stories, like life and like adventures, must not end. And MacDonald's challenge to the reader to find out just how double his story is ought to remind us of MacDonald's fierce belief in two worlds coterminus with each other; for MacDonald what we might call a fantasy world can, and for some adventurous spirits does, inform mundane reality.

We can see this interplay between fantasy and reality best in *At the Back of the North Wind,* a book that Colin Manlove argues has a similar bifurcation to the kind Moss describes:

> we must feel that the supernatural episodes are so divided from the natural as to suggest that the whole book is the result of two quite separate imaginative acts. In metaphysical terms, the two worlds do interpenetrate, inasmuch as we are shown that the sorrows of this life are divinely ordained for our supernatural good; and, since North Wind exists and operates within the "real" world, they are also to some extent physically linked. The latter world, however, never becomes transfigured, as North Wind is only occasionally present to Diamond . . . Perhaps some explanation for this lies in the fact that the "real" setting of this book is largely the city, London, and MacDonald was more able to find God (through his sub-vicars) immanent in country rather than town. . . . [15]

But such a "split" overlooks Diamond, who carries North Wind's spiritual influence to those who live "in the perfectly normal world of Victorian London" (Manlove, p. 80). As the narrator reminds the reader on several occasions, Diamond has been to the back of the north wind, to the "other" world, and the experience has made a poet of him, or in terms of this discussion, a shaman.[16] Diamond's shamanistic power is evident in the chapter titled, "The Drunken Cabman," which is structurally as well as thematically at the center of the book.

By this point, Diamond has been to the back of the north wind. His journey to this land of mysteries takes place during periods of illness; in short, Diamond's fever transports him the way the shaman's ecstasy transports him. Diamond's journey takes place in the first half of the book, and by the Drunken Cabman chapter he has already begun to assume a special, shamanistic status, exerting a positive influence on those he meets. At the beginning of the Drunken Cabman chapter Diamond hears a noise in the night; he rouses, realizes it is time that "somebody did something," puts on a few clothes, and goes to the drunken cabman's rooms, where he finds the cabman in a stupor, his wife sobbing, and their baby "wailing in the cradles." MacDonald refers to Diamond as "one of God's messengers," a psychopomp (or soul guide) in child's clothing. The dragon this messenger must face is Misery, and Diamond confronts it with songs, songs that put the cabman into a calming sleep. When he wakes, the cabman hears Diamond talking to the baby about the thirsty devil. Diamond's words are of little importance except as "chanting," as incantation. But

the effect on the cabman is reminiscent of the effect of the Ancient Mariner on the wedding guest. The cabman, MacDonald tells us, "could not withdraw his gaze from Diamond's white face and big eyes."[17] Rather than frightening the cabman, Diamond soothes him. The cabman, if not a sadder, is certainly a wiser man for the experience, and a transformation of his life begins.

The narrator is similarly drawn to Diamond: "It seemed to me, somehow, as if little Diamond possessed the secret of life, and was himself what he was so ready to think the lowest living thing—an angel of God with something special to say or do." The final chapters of the book recount the narrator's friendship for Diamond and his belief that Diamond has something precious to offer, but just what always remains slightly beyond understanding. What should be clear, however, is that in Diamond two worlds—fantasy and reality, dream and reality, the supernatural and the natural, the certain and the uncertain—are reconciled. Diamond subverts such categories, destroys our wrongheaded insistence on separating them, and consequently, removes the fear of the other world (some might call it Death in this instance) and inhibits us from the single vision of Nancy and Jim, who fear thunder and lightning. Diamond is an adventurer, not because he travels to the back of the north wind, but because of his intrepid faith in the rightness of things and his trust in the mystery of uncertainties. He never receives a definite answer as to whether North Wind is only a dream, yet dream or not she gives him strength and vision. Diamond, and all of MacDonald's heroes, are new kinds of adventurers, adventurers in imaginative and spiritual possibility. The monsters they face are Doubt, Misery, Fear, Death, and Self. They overcome by being, as MacDonald calls Diamond, "wise soldiers" prepared for conflict within and without, secure in the knowledge that to get to the back of the north wind is only the first stage on an endless journey.

Notes

[1] Paul Zweig, *The Adventurer: The Fate of Adventure in the Western World* (Princeton, N.Y., 1981; first published in 1974), p. 89.

[2] Mrs. Ewing, *A Great Emergency* (London, n.d.), p. 64. This is volume 11 of a complete edition of Mrs. Ewing's work published by the Society for Promoting Christian Knowledge.

[3] "Introduction," *A Great Emergency & A Very Ill-Tempered Family* (New York, 1969), p. 13.

[4] Stephen Prickett writes, "One way of seeing the roots of Victorian fantasy, as it were, in microcosm, is to look at the way in which the Victorians ap-

proached and attempted to interpret *The Ancient Mariner*" (*Victorian Fantasy,* Bloomington, 1979, p. 33.) Prickett's use of Coleridge's poem in the book differs from mine here.

[5] Jean Ingelow, *Mopsa the Fairy,* in *To the Land of Fair Delight* (London, 1960), p. 140.

[6] Mrs. Molesworth, *The Cuckoo Clock* (London, 1967), p. 165.

[7] Miss Mulock, *The Little Lame Prince* and *The Adventures of a Brownie* (New York, n.d.), p. 59.

[8] *Ibid.,* p. 245.

[9] L. M. Montgomery, *Anne of Avonlea* (New York, 1970), p. 88.

[10] *The Story Girl* (Ryerson, 1944), pp. 165-166.

[11] See Rosemary Jackson, *Fantasy: The Literature of Subversion* (London, 1981), especially pp. 63-72.

[12] Lewis Carroll, *The Annotated Alice* (Penguin, 1966), p. 164.

[13] Anita West Moss, "Crime and Punishment, or Development, in Fairy Tales," *Proceedings of the Seventh Annual Conference of the Children's Literature Association,* ed. Priscilla A. Ord (New York, 1982), p. 133.

[14] My text is *The Lost Princess: A Double Story* (London, 1965). The book first appeared in 1875 as *The Wise Woman: A Parable,* although it had previously appeared serially in *Good Things* (December 1874 through June 1875) under the title *A Double Story.* The book has also appeared with other titles: *Princess Rosamund: A Double Story* (1879) and *The Lost Princess; or The Wise Woman* (1895).

[15] *Modern Fantasy* (Cambridge, 1975), p. 81.

[16] During initiation rites the young man meets his anima. From a Jungian perspective, Diamond's experiences with the maternal North Wind are reminiscent of the shaman's training. Compare what happens in MacDonald's fantasy to this passage from Marie-Louise von Franz's "The Process of Individuation":

> One reported case tells of a young man who was being initiated by an older shaman and who was buried by him in a snow hole. He fell into a state of dreaminess and exhaustion. In this coma he suddenly saw a woman who emitted light. She instructed him in all he needed to know and later, as his protective spirit, helped him to practice his difficult profession by relating him to the powers of the beyond.

Man and His Symbols, ed. Carl G. Jung (New York, 1973), p. 186.

[17] My text is *At the Back of the North Wind* (New York, 1976). This is a facsimile of the first edition of 1871.

Jack Zipes

SOURCE: "Introduction" to *Victorian Fairy Tales: The Revolt of the Fairies and Elves,* edited by Jack Zipes, Methuen, 1987, pp. xiii-xxix.

[*In the following essay, Zipes highlights the changes in social conditions that led to a resurgence of fairy tales during the Victorian era and comments on the themes of change and social injustice that are found in many fairy stories.*]

In contrast to France and Germany, England did not experience the flowering of the literary fairy tale for children until the middle of the nineteenth century. This late flowering is somewhat puzzling, for Great Britain had been a fertile ground for folklore in the Middle Ages. Dazzling fairies, mischievous elves, frightening beasts, clumsy giants, daring thieves, clever peasants, cruel witches, stalwart knights, and damsels in distress had been the cultural staple of the peasants who told their tales at the hearth and in the fields throughout the British Isles. Extraordinary characters, miraculous events, superstitions, folk customs, and pagan rituals made their way quickly into the early vernacular English works by renowned authors such as Chaucer, Spenser, Swift, Marlowe, and Shakespeare; works which became part of the classical British literary tradition. However, the literary fairy tale failed to establish itself as an independent genre in the eighteenth century, when one might have expected it to bloom as it did in France. The fairies and elves seemed to have been banned from their homeland, as if a magic spell had been cast over Great Britain.

Yet it was not magic so much as the actual social enforcement of the Puritan cultural code which led to the suppression of the literary fairy tale in England. The domination of Calvinism after the Revolution of 1688 led to a stronger emphasis on preparing children and adults to be more concerned with moral character and conduct in this world rather than to prepare them for a life hereafter. Through virtuous behaviour and industry one would expect to be able to find the appropriate rewards in temporal society. Above all, Christian principles and the clear application of reason were supposed to provide the foundation for success and happiness in the family and at work. Rational judgment and distrust of the imagination were to be the guiding principles of the new enlightened guardians of Puritan culture and utilitarianism for the next two centuries. Despite the fact that the Puritans and later the utilitarians cannot be considered as monolithic entities, and despite the fact that they each often viewed the Enlightenment itself as a kind of utopian fantasy, they often assumed the same hostile position toward the fairy tale that bordered on the ridiculous. Here a parallel can be drawn to the situation described in E. T. A. Hoffmann's marvelous tale, *Little Zaches Named Zinnober,* where a fanatical prime minister representing the new laws of the Enlightenment, which are to be introduced into Prince Paphnutius' realm, argues that fairies are dangerous creatures and capable of all sorts of mischief. Consequently, the pompous prime minister declares:

> "Yes! I call them enemies of the enlightenment. They took advantage of the goodness of your blessed dead father and are to blame for the darkness that has overcome our dear state. They are conducting a dangerous business with wondrous things, and under the pretext of poetry, they are spreading uncanny poison that makes the people incapable of serving the enlightenment. Their customs offend the police in such a ghastly way that no civilized state should tolerate them in any way."

Obviously, England after 1688 was not entirely a police state, but the laws banning certain types of amusement in the theater, literature, and the arts had a far-reaching effect on the populace. In particular, the oral folk tales were not considered good subject matter for the cultivation of young souls, and thus the "civilized" appropriation of these tales which took place in France during the seventeenth and eighteenth centuries, undertaken by eminent writers such as Charles Perrault, Madame D'Aulnoy, Madame Le Prince de Beaumont, and many others, did not occur in England. On the contrary, the stories, poems, and novels written for children were mainly religious and instructional, and if literary fairy tales were written and published, they were transformed into didactic tales preaching hard work and pious behavior. Moreover, most of the fairy tales which circulated in printed form were chapbooks and pennybooks sold by peddlers to the lower classes. It was not considered proper to defend the fairies and elves—neither in literature for adults nor in literature for children.

The denigration of the fairy tale in England during the seventeenth and eighteenth centuries was in stark contrast to the cultivation of the tale in France and Germany, where it gradually came to express a new middle-class and aristocratic sensibility and flourished as an avant-garde form of art. In Great Britain the literary fairy tale was forced to go underground and was often woven into the plots of novels such as Richardson's *Pamela.* As an oral folk tale it could still dwell comfortably among the peasants, but the literary

institutionalization of the fairy-tale genre had to wait until the Romantic movement asserted the value of the imagination and fantasy at the end of the eighteenth century. Here it should be stressed that the English utilitarians of the late eighteenth century and the Romantics actually shared the same utopian zeal that emanated from the principles of the Enlightenment. However, they differed greatly as to how to realize those principles in the cultural life of English society. The Romantics sought to broaden the notions of the Enlightenment so that they would not become narrow and instrumentalized to serve vested class interests. In contrast, the utilitarians did indeed view the Romantics as "enemies of the Enlightenment" á la Hoffmann because they questioned the Protestant ethos and the prescriptions of order conceived by the utilitarians to establish the good society on earth. The questioning spirit of the Romantics enabled them to play a key role in fostering the rise of the literary fairy tale in Great Britain, for the symbolism of the tales gave them great freedom to experiment and express their doubts about the restricted view of the utilitarians and traditional religion. Robert Southey, Charles Lamb, Thomas Hood, Samuel Coleridge, and Hartley Coleridge all wrote interesting fairy tales along these lines, while Blake, Wordsworth, Keats, Byron, and Shelley helped to pave the way for the establishment of the genre and created a more receptive atmosphere for all forms of romance. In time, the return of the magic realm of the fairies and elves was viewed by the Romantics and many early Victorians as a necessary move to oppose the growing alienation in the public sphere due to industrialization and regimentation in the private sphere. Indeed, the Victorians became more aware of the subversive potential of the literary fairy tale to question the so-called productive forces of progress and the Enlightenment, for it was exactly at this point that the middle and upper classes consolidated their hold on the public sphere and determined the rules of rational discourse, government, and industry that guaranteed the promotion of their vested interests. Supported by the industrial revolution (1830-90), the rise of the middle classes meant an institutionalization of all forms of life and this in turn has had severe ramifications to the present day.

We tend to think of the industrial revolution mainly in economic and technological terms, but the impact of the industrial revolution was much more pervasive than this. It changed the very fabric of society in Great Britain, which became the world's first urban as well as industrial nation. Whereas the landed gentry and the rising middle classes benefited greatly from the innovations in commodities, techniques, and occupations that provided them with unprecedented comfort and cultural opportunities, such "progress" also brought its penalties with it. As Barry Supple has pointed out in *The Victorians:*

the impersonalization of factories, the imposition of a compelling and external discipline, the prolonged activity at the behest of machinery, the sheer problem of mass living in cities, the anonymity of the urban community, the obvious overcrowding in the badly built housing devoid of the countryside, the unchecked pollution—all these must have amounted to a marked deterioration in the circumstances, and therefore the standards of life for large numbers of people.

Such negative features of the industrial revolution did not go unnoticed by early Victorian writers and led to what is commonly called the "Condition of England Debate." In actuality, this was not a single debate but a series of controversies about the spiritual and material foundations of English life and it had a great effect on literary developments. For instance, as Catherine Gallagher has shown in her book *The Industrial Reformation of English Fiction 1832-1867,* disputes about the nature and possibility of human freedom, the sources of social cohesion, and the nature of representation were embraced by the novel and "unsettled fundamental assumptions of the novel form." Just as the novel developed a certain discourse and narrative strategies to respond to the Condition of England Debate, the literary fairy tale conceived its own unique aesthetic modes and themes to relate to this debate. Writers like Charles Dickens, Thomas Hood, Thomas Carlyle, John Ruskin, and William Thackeray were among the first to criticize the deleterious effects of the industrial revolution. Interestingly, they all employed the fairy tale at one point to question the injustice and inequalities engendered by the social upheaval in England. What is unique about the initial stage of the literary fairy-tale revival in England is that the *form itself* was part of the controversial subject matter of the larger Condition of England Debate. The shifting attitudes toward children, whose imaginations were gradually declared more innocent than sinful, allowed for greater use of works of fancy to educate and amuse them. Even so, despite changing attitudes, German, French, and Danish works of fantasy had first to pave the way for the resurgence of the literary fairy tale and the defense of the imagination in cultural products for children.

As we know, close to two centuries of British educators, writers, and publishers debated the merits of fairy tales and they were found—at least by the conservative camp, or what would be called the "moral majority" today—useless and dangerous for the moral education of young and old alike. Writers like Mrs Trimmer and Mrs Mortimer argued at the end of the eighteenth century that fairy tales made children depraved and turned them against the sacred institutions of society. Their arguments continued to be influential at the beginning of the nineteenth century, although in a somewhat modified form. For instance, one of the champions of the anti-fairy-tale school, Mrs Sherwood,

wrote the following in her book *The Governess, or The Little Female Academy* (1820):

> Instruction when conveyed through the medium of some beautiful story or pleasant tale, more easily insinuates itself into the youthful mind than any thing of a drier nature; yet the greatest care is necessary that the kind of instruction thus conveyed should be perfectly agreeable to the Christian dispensation. Fairy-tales therefore are in general an improper medium of instruction because it would be absurd in such tales to introduce Christian principles as motives of action. . . . On this account such tales should be very sparingly used, it being extremely difficult, if not impossible, from the reason I have specified, to render them really useful.

One way to oppose the rigid upholders of the Puritan law and order school was to import fairy tales from France, Germany, and Scandinavia and to translate them as exotic works of art. This mode of counter-attack by the defenders of fairy tales gained momentum at the beginning of the nineteenth century. In 1804 Benjamin Tabart began to publish a series of popular tales which eventually led to his book *Popular Fairy Tales* (1818) containing selections from *Mother Goose, The Arabian Nights, Robin Hood,* and Madame D'Aulnoy's tales. In 1818 Friedrich de la Motte Fouqué's *Undine* was published and gained acceptance because of its obvious Christian message about the pagan water nymph who leads a virtuous life once she gains a human soul. In 1823, John Harris, an enterprising publisher, who had already produced *Mother Bunch's Fairy Tales* in 1802, edited an important volume entitled *The Court of Oberon; or, The Temple of Fairies,* which contained tales from Perrault, D'Aulnoy, and *The Arabian Nights.* Coincidentally, this book appeared in the same year that the most important publication to stimulate an awakened interest in fairy tales for children *and* adults was issued, namely *German Popular Stories,* Edgar Taylor's translation of a selection from *Kinder- und Hausmärchen* by the brothers Grimm with illustrations by the gifted artist George Cruikshank. Taylor made an explicit reference to the debate concerning fairy tales in his introduction, in which he aligned himself with the "enemies of the Enlightenment":

> The popular tales of England have been too much neglected. They are nearly discarded from the libraries of childhood. Philosophy is made the companion of the nursery: we have lisping chemists and leading-string mathematicians; this is the age of reason, not of imagination; and the loveliest dreams of fairy innocence are considered as vain and frivolous. Much might be urged against this rigid and philosophic (or rather unphilosophic) exclusion of works of fancy and fiction. Our imagination is surely as susceptible of improvement by exercise, as our judgement or

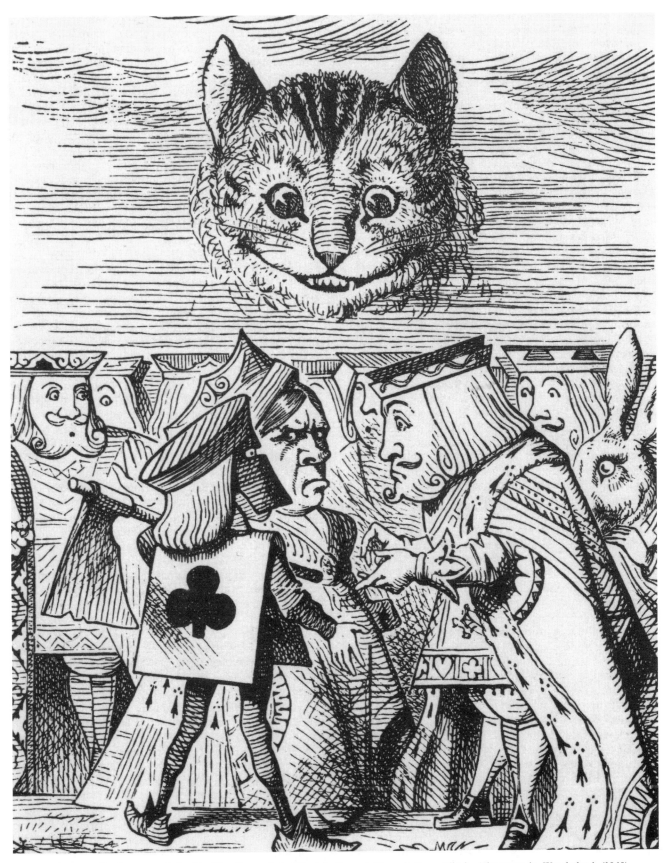

John Tenniel's depiction of the Cheshire Cat and the Queen's Croquet Ground. From Alice's Adventures in Wonderland *(1865).*

our memory; and so long as such fictions only are presented to the young mind as do not interfere with the important department of moral education, a beneficial effect must be produced by the pleasurable employment of a faculty in which so much of our happiness in every period of life consists.

The publication of *German Popular Stories* acted as a challenge to the anti-fairy-tale movement in Britain, and its favorable reception led to a second edition in 1826 and a new wave of translations. For instance, Thomas Carlyle published two volumes entitled *German Romances,* which included his translations of fairy tales by Musäus, Tieck, Chamisso, and Hoffmann in 1827. Also his unique book *Sartor Resartus* (1831) was based to a certain extent on Goethe's *Das Märchen.* Various English periodicals carried the translated tales of Otmar, Chamisso, Hoffmann, Tieck, Novalis, and Hauff in the 1830s, and new translations of the Grimm brothers' tales appeared in 1839, 1846, 1849, and 1855. In addition to the significant impact of the German tales, the arrival in 1846 of Hans Christian Andersen's *Wonderful Stories for Children,* translated by Mary Howitt, was a momentous occasion. His unusual tales, which combined fantasy with a moral impulse in line with traditional Christian standards, guaranteed the legitimacy of the literary fairy tale for middle-class audiences. From this point on, the fairy tale flowered in many different forms and colors and expanded its social discourse to cover such different topics as proper comportment for children, free will, social exploitation, political justice, and authoritarian government. The 1840s also saw the translation of the *Arabian Nights* (1840) by Edwin Lane; Felix Summerly's *Home Treasury* (1841-9), which included such works as *Little Red Riding Hood, Beauty and the Beast,* and *Jack and the Beanstalk;* Ambrose Merton's *The Old Story Books of England* (1845); and Anthony Montalba's *Fairy Tales of All Nations* (1849).

The gradual recognition and acceptance of the fairy tale by the middle classes, which had heretofore condemned the genre as frivolous and pernicious, did not mean that the Puritan outlook of the bourgeoisie had undergone a radical change, however. Indeed, to a certain extent, one can talk about a "cooption" of "the enemies of the Enlightenment." That is, middle-class writers, educators, publishers, and parents began to realize that the rigid, didactic training and literature used to rear their children was dulling their senses and creativity. Both children and adults needed more fanciful works to stimulate their imagination and keep them productive in the social and cultural spheres of British society. Emphasis was now placed on fairy-tale reading and storytelling as *recreation*—a period of time and a place in which the young could recuperate from instruction and training and re-create themselves,

so to speak, without the social pressure calculated to make every second morally and economically profitable. The stimulation of the imagination became just as important as the cultivation of reason for moral improvement. Although many tedious books of fairy tales with didactic lessons were published, such as Alfred Crowquill's *Crowquill's Fairy Book* (1840) and Mrs Alfred Gatty's *The Fairy Godmothers* (1851), various English writers began to explore the potential of the fairy tale as a form of literary communication that might convey both individual and social protest and personal conceptions of alternative, if not utopian, worlds. To write a fairy tale was considered by many writers a social symbolical act that could have implications for the education of children and the future of society.

In the period between 1840 and 1880 the general trend among the more prominent fairy-tale writers was to use the fairy-tale form in innovative ways to raise social consciousness about the disparities among the different social classes and the problems faced by the oppressed due to the industrial revolution. Numerous writers took a philanthropic view of the poor and underprivileged and sought to voice a concern about the cruel exploitation and deprivation of the young. It was almost as though the fairy tales were to instill a spirit of moral protest in the readers—and, as I mentioned, the Victorian writers always had two implied ideal readers in mind: the middle-class parent *and* child—so that they would take a noble and ethical stand against forces of intolerance and authoritarianism. For instance, John Ruskin's *King of the Golden River* (1841) . . . depicted two cruel brothers who almost destroy their younger brother Gluck because of their greed and dictatorial ways. Moreover, they threaten the laws of nature, reminding one of the cruel materialism of the industrial revolution. However, due to Gluck's innocence and compassion, he does not succumb to the brutality of his brothers and is eventually helped by the King of the Golden River to re-create an idyllic realm. Similarly, Francis Edward Paget wrote *The Hope of the Katzekopfs* in 1844 to decry the selfishness of a spoiled prince and convey a sense of self-discipline through the lessons taught by a fairy, an imp, and the old man Discipline. William Makepeace Thackeray composed *The Rose and the Ring* (1855), a delightful discourse on rightful and moral rule in which the humble Prince Giglio and Princess Rosalba regain their kingdoms from power-hungry and materialistic usurpers. Frances Browne also made a significant contribution to the fairy-tale genre with the publication of *Granny's Wonderful Chair* in 1856. Here the wonderful chair provides the framework for a group of connected tales told to the young girl Snowflower, whose virtuous and modest behavior parallels the conduct of the protagonists in the tales. Though poor and orphaned at the beginning of the book, Snowflower's diligence is rewarded at the end. The progression in

Granny's Wonderful Chair enables the reader to watch Snowflower learn and grow to be the "ideal" Victorian girl. Such is also the case in Charles Kingsley's *The Water Babies* (1863), except that here the model is a boy. To be exact it is Tom, a chimney sweep, who leaves his body behind him to become a water baby in the sea. There he (with others as well) undergoes various adventures and learns all about rewards and punishments for his behavior, especially from Mrs Bedonebyasyoudid. In the end he realizes that he must take the initiative in being good, for people always tend to reciprocate in kind.

Almost all the fairy tales of the 1840s and 1850s use allegorical forms to make a statement about Christian goodness in contrast to the greed and materialism that are apparently the most dangerous vices in English society. The moralistic tendency is most apparent in such works as Catherine Sinclair's "Uncle David's Nonsensical Story about Giants and Fairies" in *Holiday House* (1839), Clara de Chatelain's *The Silver Swan* (1847), Mark Lemon's *The Enchanted Doll* (1849) Alfred Crowquill's *The Giant Hands* (1856), and Mary and Elizabeth Kirby's *The Talking Bird* (1856). In each case the use of the fairy-tale form as a fanciful mode to delight readers is justified because of the seriousness of the subject matter. Consequently, the fairy tale at mid-century was a manifesto for itself and a social manifesto at the same time. The compulsion felt by writers to rationalize their preference for using the fairy tale to express their opinions about religion, education, and progress often undercut their aesthetic experiments. Nevertheless, even the boring allegorical fairy tales were an improvement on the stern, didactic tales of realism which English children had been obliged to read during the first part of the nineteenth century.

Underlying the efforts of the Victorian fairy-tale writers was also a psychological urge to recapture and retain childhood as a paradisiacal realm of innocence. This psychological drive was often mixed with a utopian belief that a more just society could be established on earth. U. C. Knoepflmacher makes the point in his essay "The Balancing of Child and Adult" (1983) that the Victorian writers' "regressive capacity can never bring about a total annihilation of the adult's self-awareness":

> Torn between the opposing demands of innocence and experience, the author who resorts to the wishful, magical thinking of the child nonetheless feels compelled, in varying degrees, to hold on to the grown-up's circumscribed notions about reality. In the better works of fantasy of the period, this dramatic tension between the adult and childhood selves becomes rich and elastic: conflict and harmony, friction and reconciliation, realism and wonder, are allowed to interpenetrate and coexist.

Knoepflmacher asserts that the regressive tendency balanced by self-awareness was a major feature of most Victorian fantasies. And, certainly, if we consider the three most important writers and defenders of fairy tales from 1840 to 1880, Charles Dickens, Lewis Carroll, and George MacDonald, it is apparent that their quest for a new fairy-tale form stemmed from a psychological rejection and rebellion against the "norms" of English society. If the industrial revolution had turned England upside down on the path toward progress, then these writers believed that English society had to be revolutionized once more to regain a sense of free play and human compassion. The remarkable achievement of Dickens, Carroll, and MacDonald lies in their artistic capacity to blend their regressive urges with progressive social concerns, without succumbing to overt didacticism.

In his essay "Frauds on Fairies" (1853) published in *Household Words,* Dickens took issue with George Cruikshank and any other writers who might seek to abuse the fairy tale by attaching explicit moral or ethical messages to it. Dickens argued:

> in an utilitarian age, of all other times, it is a matter of grave importance that fairy tales should be respected. Our English red tape is too magnificently red even to be employed in the tying up of such trifles, but everyone who has considered the subject knows full well that a nation without fancy, without some romance, never did, never can, never will, hold a great place under the sun.

Dickens himself tended to incorporate fairy-tale motifs and plots primarily in his novels and particularly in his *Christmas Books* (1843—5). It is almost as though he did not want to tarnish the childlike innocence of the tales that he read as a young boy—tales which incidentally filled him with hope during his difficult childhood—by replacing them with new ones. But Dickens did use the fairy tale to make political and social statements, as in *Prince Bull* (1855) and *The Thousand and One Humbugs* (1855), and his regressive longings for the innocent bliss of fairyland are made most evident in his essay *A Christmas Tree* (1850):

> Good for Christmas time is the ruddy color of the cloak, in which—the tree making a forest of itself for her to trip through, with her basket—Little Red Riding Hood comes to me one Christmas Eve, to give me information of the cruelty and treachery of that dissembling Wolf who ate her grandmother, without making any impression on his appetite, and then ate her, after making that ferocious joke about his teeth. She was my first love. I felt that if I could have married Little Red Riding-Hood, I should have known perfect bliss. But, it was not to be.

What was to be was Dickens' adult quest for fairy bliss in his novels, and it is not by chance that one of the last works he wrote toward the end of his life was "The Magic Fishbone" . . . , part of a collection of humorous stories for children entitled *Holiday Romance* (1868). Here Dickens parodied a helpless king as a salaried worker, who is accustomed to understanding everything with his reason. He becomes totally confused by the actions of his daughter Alicia, who receives a magic fishbone from a strange and brazen fairy named Grandmarina. Alicia does *not* use the fishbone when one would expect her to. Only when the king reveals to her that he can no longer provide for the family does Alicia make use of the magic fishbone. Suddenly Grandmarina arrives to bring about a comical ending in which the most preposterous changes occur. Nothing can be grasped through logic, and this is exactly Dickens' point: his droll tale—narrated from the viewpoint of a child—depends on the unusual deployment of fairy-tale motifs to question the conventional standards of society and to demonstrate that there is strength and soundness in the creativity of the young. The patriarchal figure of authority is at a loss to rule and provide, and the reversal of circumstances points to a need for change in social relations. The realm of genuine happiness that is glimpsed at the end of Dickens' fairy tale is a wish-fulfillment that he himself shared with many Victorians who were dissatisfied with social conditions in English society.

Like Dickens, Carroll fought tenaciously to keep the child alive in himself and in his fiction as a critic of the absurd rules and regulations of the adult Victorian world. In *Alice's Adventures in Wonderland* (1865) and *Through the Looking Glass* (1871) Carroll made one of the most radical statements on behalf of the fairy tale and the child's perspective by conceiving a fantastic plot without an ostensible moral purpose. The questioning spirit of the child is celebrated in the Alice books, and Carroll continually returned to the realm of fantasy in his remarkable fairy tale "Bruno's Revenge" (1867) . . . , which eventually served as the basis for his Sylvie and Bruno books (1889, 1893). The endeavor to reconcile the fairy world with the world of reality never meant compromising the imagination for Carroll. If anything, reason was to serve the imagination, to allow vital dreams of pleasure to take shape in a world that was threatening to turn those dreams into mere advertisements for better homes and better living, according to the plans of British industrial and urban leaders.

Carroll's deep-seated belief in the necessity of keeping alive the power of the imagination in children was shared by George MacDonald. In fact, after he had completed *Alice's Adventures in Wonderland* he sent the manuscript to the MacDonald family, who warmly encouraged him to have his fantastic narrative published. Though MacDonald himself was not as "radical" as Carroll in his own fairy tales, he was nonetheless just as pioneering in his endeavors to lend new shape and substance to the fairy-tale genre. In 1867 he published *Dealings with the Fairies,* which contained "The Light Princess," "The Giant's Heart," "The Shadows," "Cross Purposes," and "The Golden Key." Thereafter he continued to write fairy tales for children's magazines and included some in his novels. In fact, he wrote two compelling fairy-tale novels, *The Princess and the Goblin* (1872) and *The Princess and Curdie* (1883), which became classics in his own day. MacDonald stressed the aesthetic reversal of traditional fairy-tale schemes and motifs and social transformation in all his fairy tales. For instance, his most popular work, "The Light Princess," is a witty parody of *Sleeping Beauty* which stimulates serious reflection about social behavior and power through comical and unexpected changes in the traditional fairy-tale form and content. Here, a bumbling king and queen give birth to a daughter after many years of sterility, and because they insult one of the fairy godmothers their daughter is cursed with a lack of gravity. Thus, she can only fly around the court, and her hilarious behavior upsets the absurd conventions of the kingdom. But she is also potentially destructive, because she has no sense of balance and tends to seek to gratify her whims with little concern for other people. Only when she sees a humble prince about to die for her own pleasure does she develop human compassion and gain the gravity necessary for mature social interaction. MacDonald often turned the world upside-down and inside-out in his fairy tales, to demonstrate that society as it existed was based on false and artificial values. He purposely portrayed characters on quests to discover a divine spark within themselves, and self-discovery was always linked to a greater appreciation of other human beings and nature, as in the case of "The Day Boy and the Night Girl" (1882). . . . Domination is opposed by compassion. Magic is power used to attain self-awareness and sensitivity toward others. Fairy-tale writing itself becomes a means by which one can find the golden key for establishing harmony with the world—a utopian world, to be sure, that opens our eyes to the ossification of a society blind to its own faults and injustices.

The creation of fairy-tale worlds by British writers moved in two basic directions from 1860 until the turn of the century: conventionalism and utopianism. The majority of writers such as Dinah Mulock Craik (*The Fairy Book,* 1863), Annie Keary (*Little Wanderlin,* 1865), Tom Hood, (*Fairy Realm,* 1865, verse renditions of Perrault's prose tales), Harriet Parr (*Holme Lee's Fairy Tales,* 1868), Edward Knatchbull-Hugessen (*Moonshine,* 1871 and *Friends and Foes from Fairy Land,* 1886), Jean Ingelow (*The Little Wonder-Horn,* 1872), Mrs Molesworth (*The Tapestry Room,* 1879 and *Christmas-Tree Land,* 1884), Anne Isabella Ritchie

(*Five Old Friends and a Young Prince,* 1868 and *Bluebeard's Keys,* 1874), Christina Rossetti (*Speaking Likenesses,* 1874), Lucy Lane Clifford (*Anyhow Stories,* 1882), Harriet Childe Pemberton (*Fairy Tales for Every Day,* 1882), Andrew Lang (*The Princess Nobody,* 1884 and *The Gold of Fairnilee,* 1888), Herbert Inman (*The One-Eyed Griffin and Other Fairy Tales,* 1897), and Edith Nesbit (*The Book of Dragons,* 1900) conceived plots conventionally to reconcile themselves and their readers to the status quo of Victorian society. Their imaginative worlds could be called exercises in complicity with the traditional opponents of fairy tales, for there is rarely a hint of social criticism and subversion in their works. It is almost as if the wings of the fairies had been clipped, for the "little people" do not represent a real threat to the established Victorian norms. Magic and nonsense are not liberating forces. After a brief period of disturbance, the fairies, brownies, elves, or other extraordinary creatures generally enable the protagonists to integrate themselves into a prescribed social order. If the fairies create mischief that makes the protagonists and readers think critically about their situation, they ultimately do this in the name of sobriety. Perseverance, good sense, and diligence are championed as virtues that must be acquired through trials in magical realms to prove they will become mature "solid citizens."

Yet, even in the works of the conventional writers, there seems to be a longing to maintain a connection to the fairy realm. Some of them, like Ingelow, Molesworth, and Nesbit, even broke with convention at times. Respect was paid to those spirits of the imagination, the fairies, who reinvigorated British cultural life in the nineteenth century after years of banishment. Indeed, the return of the fairies became a permanent one, for writers of all kinds of persuasions discovered that they could be used to maintain a discourse about subjects germane to their heart. Unfortunately, by the end of the century such publishers as Raphael Tuck and Routledge could make standard commodities out of the fairy tales—mainly the classical European tales—and published thousands of toy books and picture books to earn grand profits from what used to be considered pernicious items for sons and daughters of the middle classes.

Fairy tales for profit and fairy tales of conventionality were disregarded by English writers of the utopian direction. Their tales reveal a profound belief in the power of the imagination as a potent force that can be used to question the value of existing social relations. There is also a moral impulse in this second direction. However, it does not lead to reconciliation with the status quo—rather, rebellion against convention and conformity. Fairy-tale protagonists are sent on quests which change them as the world around them also changes. The fairies and other magical creatures inspire and compel the protagonists to alter their lives

and pursue utopian dreams. In the works of MacDonald, Carroll, Mary De Morgan, Juliana Horatia Ewing, Oscar Wilde, Rudyard Kipling, Kenneth Grahame, Evelyn Sharp, and Laurence Housman the creation of fairy-tale worlds allows the writers to deal symbolically with social taboos and to suggest alternatives to common English practice, particularly in the spheres of child rearing and role-playing. In many instances the alternatives do not lead to a "happy end," or, if happiness is achieved, it is in stark contrast to the "happy" way of life in late Victorian and Edwardian England. In Humphrey Carpenter's critical study of the golden age of children's literature, *Secret Gardens* (1985), he makes the point that fantasy literature and fairy tales of the late nineteenth century stem from a deep dissatisfaction with the socio-political realities of England.

> While it was not overtly "realistic" and purported to have nothing to say about the "real" world, in this fantastic strain of writing may be found some profound observations about human character and contemporary society, and (strikingly often) about religion. It dealt largely with utopias, and posited the existence of Arcadian societies remote from the nature and concerns of the everyday world; yet in doing this it was commentary, often satirically and critically, on real life.

Clearly there are signs in the works of Carroll, MacDonald, Wilde, Ewing, De Morgan, Grahame, Sharp, Housman, Nesbit, and even Molesworth that they identified with the "enemies of the Enlightenment." In a period when first Christian socialism and later the Fabian movement had a widespread effect, these writers instilled a utopian spirit into the fairy-tale discourse that endowed the genre with a vigorous and unique quality of social criticism which was to be developed even further by later writers of faerie works such as A. A. Milne, J. R. R. Tolkien, C. S. Lewis, and T. H. White. This endowment in itself was the major accomplishment of the utopian fairy-tale writers. But there were other qualities and features that they contributed to the development of the literary fairy tale as genre which deserve our attention.

To begin with, there is a strong feminine, if not feminist, influence in the writing of *both* male and female writers. In contrast to the *Kunstmärchen* tradition in Germany and folklore in general, which were stamped by patriarchal concerns, British writers created strong women characters and placed great emphasis on the fusion of female and male qualities and equality between men and women. For instance, in most of MacDonald's tales, particularly "The Day Boy and the Night Girl" . . . , "Cross Purposes," and "Little Daylight," the male and female protagonists come to realize their mutual dependency. Their so-called masculine and feminine qualities are not genetically determined but are relative and assume their own particular value in given circumstances. What is often understood as masculine is feminine in MacDonald's tales. Gender has no specificity—rather, both male and female can develop courage, honesty, intelligence, compassion, etc. The most important goal in MacDonald's fairy tales lies beyond the limits set by society. The worth of an individual is indicated by his or her willingness to explore nature and to change according to the divine insights they gain. Magic is nothing else but the realization of the divine creative powers one possesses within oneself. Here MacDonald differed from many of the traditional Victorian writers by insisting on self-determination for women.

MacDonald was not alone in this conviction. Mary De Morgan, Juliana Horatia Ewing, Mary Louisa Molesworth, Evelyn Sharp, and Edith Nesbit all depicted female protagonists coming into their own and playing unusually strong roles in determining their own destinies. Princess Ursula's refusal to conform to the wishes of her ministers in De Morgan's "A Toy Princess" (1877) . . . celebrates the indomitable will of a young woman who is determined to run her life according to her needs rather than serve the royal court like a puppet. In Ewing's "The Ogre Courting" (1871) . . . Managing Molly, a clever peasant's daughter, maintains her independence while making a fool out of a brutal male oppressor. Mrs Molesworth's Princess Auréole in "Story of a King's Daughter" (1884) . . . uses another technique to tame the brute in man: she sets an example of compassion which eventually induces Prince Halbert to learn to feel for the sufferings of his fellow creatures. Princess Auréole uses her courage and imagination to get *her* way and *her* man in the end, just as Firefly in Sharp's "The Spell of the Magician's Daughter" (1902) . . . shows remarkable fortitude and creativity in disenchanting a country and captivating a young prince. Similarly the Princess in Nesbit's "The Last of the Dragons" (*c.* 1900) . . . acts in a very "unladylike" way by taking the initiative and defeating the last of the dragons with love.

In all of these tales—as well as in other works, such as Christina Rossetti's fascinating poem *The Goblin Market*—there is an intense quest for the female self. In contrast to such fairy tales as "Cinderella" (1868) by Anne Isabella Ritchie and "All my Doing" (1882) by Harriet Childe-Pemberton . . . ,are fascinating examples of female self-deprecation, the narratives by De Morgan, Ewing, Molesworth, Sharp, and Nesbit allow for women's voices and needs to be heard. The narrative strategies of these tales strongly suggest that utopia will not be just another men's world. What is significant about the "feminist" utopian tales is not so much the strength shown by the female protagonists, but the manner in which they expose oppression and hypocrisy. Here, the social critique is both implicit and explicit as it pertains to Victorian society. The new "feminine quality" in these tales is

part of the general re-utilization of the traditional fairy-tale motifs and topoi by utopian writers to express the need for a new type of government and society. All the formal aesthetic changes made in the tales are connected to an insistence that the substance of life be transformed, otherwise there will be alienation, petrification, and death. This is certainly the danger in De Morgan's "Toy Princess," and it is the reason why she also questioned and rejected arbitrary authority in such other tales as "The Necklace of Princess Fiormonde," "The Heart of Princess Joan," and "Three Clever Kings."

Male writers expressed their utopian inclinations in fairy tales by depicting English society as one which stifled and confined the creative energies of compassionate young protagonists. Both in his tales and his illustrations Laurence Housman portrayed Victorian society symbolically, as a rigid enclosure. In such tales as "The Rooted Lover" . . . , "The Bound Princess," "The White Doe," and "A Chinese Fairy-Tale," Housman's protagonists reject material gains to pursue love and beauty. The aesthetic composition of the fairy tale and the noble actions of his characters are contrasted to the vulgar materialism of late Victorian society. Such a view of British society was shared by Oscar Wilde, who developed his critique of greed and hypocrisy in his two collections of fairy tales, *The Happy Prince and Other Tales* (1888) and *The House of Pomegranates* (1891). In particular, "The Happy Prince" . . . is a sad commentary on how isolated the ruling class had become from the majority of English people by the end of the century. Like many utopian writers of this period, Wilde felt that social relations had become reified, and he disparaged the philanthropic movement of the upper classes as mere ornamental patchwork. If British society was to reform itself substantially, then not only had it to undergo a spiritual reformation, but class domination and the destructive effects of industrialization had also to be brought to an end.

To oppose class domination and the crass exploitation of the "little people" became the underlying bond of many utopian fairy-tale writers toward the end of the nineteenth century. The unique quality of the individual tales often depended on the non-conformist message and the "non-sensical" play with words, plots, and motifs. These made sense once the reader realized that the writers were endeavoring to subvert those so-called sensible standards which appeared to fulfill the needs of the people but actually deceived them. For example, a fairy tale such as Kenneth Grahame's "The Reluctant Dragon" (1898) . . . plays with the expectations of the readers and refuses to meet them because Grahame was more interested in fostering human compassion than in human deception. His tale reveals how the aggressive instincts of people can be manipulated and can lead to a false sense of chauvinism because of stereotyping—in this case, of knights and dragons. Kipling, too, in "The Potted Princess" (1893) . . . composed an interesting tale that experimented with audience expectations and deception. In the process it allows for the rise of a lowly prince and the transformation of a young boy into a tale teller. The theme of coming into one's own is closely tied to the rejection of the materialistic and artificial standards set by society.

The German Romantic writer Novalis, who had a great influence on MacDonald, once remarked, "Mensch werden ist eine Kunst"—to become a human being is an art. This remark could have been Kipling's motto for his tale, and it certainly could have been the unwritten slogan of the utopian fairy-tale writers by the end of the nineteenth century. The fairy tale itself exhibited possibilities for the young to transform themselves and society into those Arcadian dreams conceived in childhood that the writers did not want to leave behind them. The artwork of the fairy tale assumed a religious quality in its apparent denial of the material world.

It is not by chance that many of the late Victorian fairy-tale writers took a resolute stand against materialism. The industrial revolution had transformed an agrarian population into an urban one. Compelled to work and live according to a profit motive and competitive market conditions, people became accustomed to think instrumentally about gain and exploitation. Both in the middle and lower classes it became necessary to compete with and exploit others to achieve success and a modicum of comfort. Here, the Christian Church relied on philanthropy as a means to rationalize the material values of a society that had abandoned the essence of Christian humanism. This is why the Christian minister George MacDonald—and the same might be said of Lewis Carroll—distanced himself from the practices of the Anglican and Congregational Churches. Most of his works, particularly his two fairy-tale novels *The Princess and the Goblin* and *The Princess and Curdie,* decry the lust for money in all social classes and the abandonment of Christian values based on human compassion.

Toward the end of the nineteenth century there was a growing tendency among writers to support the ideas of Christian and Fabian socialism. This tendency also marked the rise of utopian literature which was connected to the fairy tale and indicated the writers' deep dissatisfaction with the way Great Britian had been drastically changed by the industrial revolution. William Morris' *News from Nowhere* (1891) and H. G. Wells' *The Time Machine* (1895) illustrate the criticism of those Victorian writers who feared that the machine age would destroy human creativity and integrity. Though Great Britain was at its height as Empire, there was also a strong sentiment among utopian writers that the Empire had sold its soul to attain power and was using its power to maintain a system of domination and exploitation.

It is interesting to note that many of the late Victorian fairy-tale writers held similar political views and worked in the same milieux in an effort to create a *different* English society. As is well known, MacDonald was a good friend of Ruskin and Carroll and shared many of the social convictions of Dickens and Morris, whom he also knew. Morris was very much influenced by Ruskin, and in turn his ideas attracted Mary De Morgan, Laurence Housman, and Walter Crane, who illustrated numerous fairy books. Kipling heard the tales of De Morgan as a child and was a great admirer of Juliana Horatia Ewing. Wilde studied with both Ruskin and Walter Pater and developed his own anarchical brand of socialism which he expressed in his essay "The Soul of Man under Socialism" (1889), written at the same time as his fairy tales. Crane illustrated *The Happy Prince and Other Tales* as well as *Christmas-Tree Land* by Mary Louisa Molesworth. Evelyn Sharp, Laurence Housman, and Kenneth Grahame belonged to the coterie of writers around *The Yellow Book* founded by John Lane, who wanted to establish a new aesthetics while at the same time retaining respect for traditional craftsmanship. Grahame was greatly influenced by Frederick James Furnivall, an active member of the Christian Socialist movement, who introduced him to the works of Ruskin and Morris. Sharp went on to become one of the leading members of the women's suffragette movement and a socialist. At times she had contact with Laurence Housman, who also declared himself a socialist pacifist and became active in the political and cultural struggles of the early twentieth century. Nesbit was one of the founders of the Fabian Society with her husband Hubert Bland, and she became close to George Bernard Shaw, H. G. Wells, and numerous other members of the Fabian movement.

The social and political views of the fairy-tale writers and the cultural climate of late Victorian society make it evident that they felt the future of Britain and the young was at stake in their literary production. Such investment in their work enables us to understand why the literary fairy tale finally became a viable genre in Britain. The revolt of the fairies in the early part of the nineteenth century and their reintegration into English literature occurred at a time when British society was undergoing momentous social and political changes. The Puritan ban on fairy-tale literature that had existed since the late seventeenth century was gradually lifted because the rational discourse of the Enlightenment did not allow sufficient means to voice doubts and protest about conditions in England during the industrial revolution. Though many of the new fairy tales were contradictory, they opened up possibilities for children and adults to formulate innovative views about socialization, religious training, authority, sex roles, and art. For many late Victorian authors, the writing of a fairy tale meant a process of creating an *other world,* from which vantage point they could survey conditions in the real world and compare them to their ideal projections. The personal impetus for writing fairy tales was simultaneously a social one for the Victorians. This social impetus has kept their tales alive and stimulating for us today, for the aesthetics of these fairy tales stems from an experimental spirit and social conscience that raises questions which twentieth-century reality has yet to answer. The "enemies of the Enlightenment" are still very much with us, and though they are often packaged as commodities and made to appear harmless, they will continue to touch a utopian chord in every reader who remains open to their call for change.

Colin N. Manlove

SOURCE: "Victorian and Modern Fantasy: Some Contrasts," in *The Celebration of the Fantastic: Selected Papers from the Tenth Anniversary International Conference on the Fantastic in the Arts,* edited by Donald E. Morse, Marshall B. Tymn, and Csilla Bertha, Greenwood Press, 1992, pp. 9-22.

[*In the following essay, Manlove investigates the differences between nineteenth- and twentieth-century fantasy, noting that Victorian authors questioned assumptions and relied on rules and logic more than present-day authors.*]

Although fantasy has developed out of all recognition from its origins, it may be of interest to retrace the journey. Rather too many accounts of fantasy, including mine, have emphasized its static quality, those elements that Poe shares with Pynchon, or MacDonald with Le Guin. But there are many differences too, and significant ones, which may be worth sketching, for fantasy has a history and is responsive to cultural or societal changes, a sort of random upthrust from the hidden creative magma. So what I want to look at are some of the *differences* between nineteenth- and twentieth-century fantasy.

Nineteenth-century fantasy sprang from two main sources: revived interest in the traditional fairy or folk tale and the German Romantic fairy tales of Novalis, Hoffmann, Tieck and de la Motte Fouqué, the latter mostly written around the period 1795-1820. Both these sources and its own nature made it "avant garde," at least in the sense that the Romantic use of the imagination in defiance of reason, sense-experience or even "realism" was considered dangerous and subversive in those days—particularly in relation to children, but also, as a legacy of the eighteenth century and the moral restraints of the nineteenth, in connection with the explosive effects it might have on the adult mind. When Novalis, writing from his own particular viewpoint of course, says that the true fairy tale is like nature, a chaos, without connection, a musically based fiction that strikes sparks of spiritual intuition as randomly as an Aeolian or wind-harp (III, 454 #986), the destructured form of the fairy tale that he is describing, and which is in different ways to be seen in his own *Heinrich von Ofterdingen,* in Hoffmann's *The Golden Pot* or *The Sandman,* in Carlyle's *Sartor Resartus,* MacDonald's *Phantastes,* Kingsley's *The Water-Babies,* or Carroll's *Alice,* is not different, so far as chaos or even "unconscious working" are concerned, from the present day postmodern fantasies of a Calvino, a Pynchon, or a García Márquez. And yet, how different, too! Novalis and Hoffmann are searching for a new key to beauty or truth, where those modern fantasies—if we may call them such—have often a more satiric aim, their destructuring of ordered forms and assumptions inviting us, like say, Swift in *Gulliver's Travels,* to make what sense we may out of disintegration. Novalis and Hoffmann invite us to see the chaotic truth behind the real; the postmodernists ask us to see reality as often meaningless chaos. It may not be insignificant that postmodern fantasy is often set in the city, whereas nineteenth-century fantasy often looks to nature. But the main point is that Victorian fantasy as it developed was arguably the most searching literature of its day, constantly questioning assumptions. It is in Victorian fantasy that one finds dramatized a resolution of the issues that arose from the impact of Darwin's theory of natural selection; in fantasy, also some of the most adventurous theological ideas are to be found (as in MacDonald or Kingsley); and in fantasy the structures of sense are questioned and transformed (as in Lear or Carroll). And all this from a genre that looks so constantly backward for its inspiration or starting point, to the old and the traditional: the recurrent fairy godmother, the magic wish, the evil stepmother, goblins, or wolf—old threats from older forests.

It is, curiously, in modern fantasy, at least of the moral or Christian type that is most widely known, that one finds a much greater degree of conservatism, a ritual enactment or recovery of old values, from the work of C. S. Lewis to Ursula Le Guin's Earthsea trilogy or Robert Silverberg's Valentine books. The work of Tolkien has in itself begotten a genre in which an elfish world, threatened by some dark force, is saved by some frail power for good in alliance with the forces of nature. This is true to the point where many people now see fantasy as synonymous with Tolkien. All such works—and one can include the likes of T. H. White's *The Once and Future King,* Stephen Donaldson's Thomas Covenant novels, or John Crowley's *Little, Big*—imply as response to this world the creation of another in which values under threat or extinct in this one may be seen to survive and even be victorious. In short, there is an air of nostalgia in much modern fantasy that is not generally to be found in that of the nineteenth century. If fantasy in the nineteenth century was in advance of the times, that of the twentieth has often lagged behind the times, looking to old medieval-type worlds and codes that no longer prevail. And perhaps the reason for this may not be far to seek, if we consider the loss of roots with nature in our world and the passing of old moral if not religious certainties.

So much by way of generalization. Let us now come to more particular features. Much nineteenth-century fantasy was written for children. This was partly because, by historical accident as Tolkien says, fairy tales had been relegated to the nursery, but also because the child's mind and imagination were felt to be much more free, and therefore more attuned to the magical, than that of the adult. One need not cite the constant Romantic outcries against the murdering influence of the adult intellect. This made it something of a paradox for adults to be inventing such stories, and there are awkward moments with grown-ups on their knees trying too hard to be children, but where the shared medium was the creative imagination, age need not come into it. Coleridge remarked how in his childhood reading of the *Arbian Nights* "my mind had been habituated *to the Vast* . . ." (I, 354 (no. 210); in an article for *Household Words* Dickens cursed the crew of contemporary moralists who warred against the fairy tale and the child's imagination (which he particularly defends in *Hard Times*); the *Quarterly Review* ran a major article in June and October 1844 extolling the child-like wonder of the fairy tale; Thackeray's *The Rose and the Ring* (1855) is a children's fireside pantomime; Kingsley prefaces *The Water-Babies* (1863) with the epigraph, "Come read me my riddle, each good little man; / If you cannot read it, no grown-up folk can"; George MacDonald says that he writes "for the childlike, whether of five, or fifty-five, or seventy-five" (317); the *Alice* books are narrated to a child. There are occasional more "adult" fantasies, such as Coleridge's *The Ancient Mariner,* William Morris's early romances (of 1858), and MacDonald's *Phantastes* (1858), which nevertheless appeals to the child-like understanding, or the comic fantasies of "F. Anstey." But if we compare this with the more "adult" orientation of many of the best known of modern fantasies—David Lindsay's *A Voyage to Arcturus* (1920), the fantasies of Charles Williams, of T. F. Powys, or E. R. Eddison, the planetary romances of C. S. Lewis, the Gormenghast books of Mervyn Peake, Tolkien's *The Lord of the Rings,* or T. H. White's *The Once and Future King*—the difference is obvious. Tolkien specifically denies that children have a particular taste for fairy tales.

Naturally in the Victorian period, with children in mind as audience, fantasy is frequently moral. From Mark Lemon in *The Enchanted Doll* (1849) or Mrs. Gatty in *The Fairy Godmothers* (1851) to the moralized stories of Mrs. Ewing or Mrs. Molesworth, the stress is there. The errant Prince Eigenwillig of F. E. Paget's *The Hope of the Katzekopfs* (1844) defeats the evil sprite Selbst (Self) when he learns to follow the principles of old man Discipline, *"Learn to live hardly; Deny yourself in things lawful; Love not comforts; Think of others first, and of yourself* last" (204). Many tales detail frightful punishments inflicted on refractory infants, from Struwwelpeter with his prodigious nails and hair or the digital amputations suffered by "Johnny Suck-a-Thumb," to the humans turned to monstrous forms of their sins in George MacDonald's *The Princess and Curdie.* Although morality is a marked feature of Victorian fantasy, there are several works of the period that turn away from it entirely, such as the *Alice* books, or Andrew Lang's *Prince Prigia* (1889) and *Prince Ricardo* (1893) or that invert it, such as Anstey's *Vice Versa* (1882), where a moralizing parent who complacently sends his son to boarding school is made to change places with him.

Actually the more distinctive feature of Victorian fantasy is not just its use of morality but its use of *rules.* Victorian fantasy is fascinated by rules, rules that govern not only behavior but the way a fantastic world exists. The *Alice* books are full of inverted or perverted logic, by which in a looking-glass world one must run to stay still or repair oneself with sticking plaster before one has been harmed. Rules are of the essence in fairy tales: "when you see this enchanted person you must touch him with this object"; "the princess will sleep for one hundred years until a prince comes to wake her"; "do not enter that room"; and this may explain the immense popularity of such tales in the nineteenth century. E. Nesbit's magic books are perhaps the culmination of logical fantasy: in her "Melisande" (1900), for example, we find the consequences of using a wish to have one's hair grow twice as fast every time it is cut. E. A. Abbott's *Flatland* (1884) is an exploration of a series of logically constructed worlds within the different numbers of dimensions in Flatland, Lineland, and Pointland. MacDonald's Anodos in *Phantastes* is surrounded by various implicit rules, which he violates. Often we see disobediece meet its punishment, usually after warnings from a fairy: because he did not heed the Fairy Serenissa's advice in Catherine Sinclair's "Uncle David's Nonsensical Story about Giants and Fairies" (1839),[1] the idle and greedy Master Nobook finds himself dangling from a meat-hook in Giant Snap-'em-up's larder; because he would not control his self-will, Eigenwillig in *The Hope of the Katzekopfs* becomes a human football. We can see disaster coming: we can see the choice made to transgress the limits. Now it would be false to say that no modern fantasy uses rules in a similar manner. The logic of the magic in Charles Williams's *Many Dimensions* (1931) or *The*

Place of the Lion (1931) is very fully developed, and the rules governing events in Diana Wynne Jones's *Archer's Goon* (1984) are extremely complex, even if there are some loose ends. But there are fewer of such fantasies than in the nineteenth century; which is perhaps hardly surprising given our more informal age. The contrast goes further. Nineteenth-century fantasy is governed by patterns and by logic: the twentieth-century variety, less overt in its organizing premises, tends rather to have behind it the form of myth. Here, instead of the form and standards being imposed on the narrative from above, they well up from beneath the story, part of the bubbling of the creative process, as C. S. Lewis would have put it (36). It can be said that where the nineteenth century used the fairy tale on a consciously moral or parodic level, modern fantasy is—perhaps curiously—more in touch with the unconscious roots of the form. Myths, whether Christian, pagan, Scandinavian, or other, are behind much modern fantasy, from C. S. Lewis's *The Lion, the Witch and the Wardrobe, Perelandra,* or *Till We Have Faces,* to Tolkien's *The Lord of the Rings,* Alan Garner's *The Owl Service* or T. H. White's *The Once and Future King.* One would expect twentieth-century fantasy to be more self-conscious than its earlier form, but in this respect that is not the case. This is not to deny that certain nineteenth-century fantasies, such as Browning's *Childe Roland,* William Morris's early romances, and MacDonald's *Phantastes,* are founded on unconscious creation, only that on the whole the structures that control and order nineteenth-century fantasy are usually of a more formal type than we find nowadays.

This emphasis on rules and conscious patterning in nineteenth-century fantasy plays dialectically against its surging and often chaotic variety. "A wonderful collection of things and events . . ." is how Novalis thought of what he called the fairy tale or "Märchen" in 1799 (III, 454 #986). And certainly such an account could be applied to many nineteenth-century fantasies, not just individually, but considered together. Nowadays we have a rough idea of what we understand by fantasy: we usually mean some post-Tolkienian sub-created world of idyllic nature in which elfish forces for good struggle against evil powers. We can speak now of classes of fantasy—of Christian fantasy as we find it in Lewis or Williams, of Celtic fantasy as we see it in Garner, Holdstock, or Marion Zimmer Bradley, of postmodernist fantasy as it appears in Calvino, Borges, Pynchon, or Salman Rushdie. Fantasy in the nineteenth century is a series of discrete creations having very little to do with one another. Each one can be regarded as experimental. Thackeray's "fireside pantomime" *The Rose and the Ring* is set in the absurd realm of Paflagonia; Kingsley's *The Water-Babies* describes the journey from stream to sea of a water-baby, and is pervaded by Kingsley's interests in marine biology, moral evolution, sanitation, and natural

theology; Carroll's *Alice* portrays a world of inverted sense in which flamingos serve as croquet mallets and Cheshire cats are shriveled to their grins. It is true that several fantasies of the nineteenth century use the techniques of the fairy tale as a starting point or a basis for parody; but the invented worlds the authors create remain clearly different from one another, much more than is the case with fantasy now, which is more aware of itself as a specific genre or mode.

This variety within nineteenth-century fantasy is seen within individual works as well. Many of them are made up of apparently discrete episodes. Anodos in MacDonald's *Phantastes* is nearly devoured by an ash tree; then he finds a white lady in a block of alabaster and sings to awaken her, has an evil shadow attach itself to him in the house of an ogress, enters a fairy palace by moonlight, reads a magic book about love on another planet, and so on. *Alice in Wonderland* on the surface follows Alice's wanderings through a series of different and apparently unrelated contexts, from the meeting with the Cheshire Cat to the Mad Hatter's Tea Party, the game of croquet, the lobster quadrille, and the trial of the tart-thief. A feature that goes with this is that many of the best-known nineteenth-century fantasies are without purpose or direction. It takes some time in *The Rose and the Ring* before Thackeray gets round to the issue of the necessary education of Prince Giglio, before which point we have had all sorts of absurd upsets with the magic rose and ring and been introduced to a gallery of different characters and interests. Kingsley only happens from time to time on his theme of the moral education of Tom, who simply travels where he will until he bumps into other water-babies in the sea. MacDonald's Anodos wanders through Fairyland for a long while without any aim or direction. His education may be being accomplished, but this is happening in an indirect way. Compare that with the quest stories of much modern fantasy, where the protagonist often has a direct goal or purpose from the outset: the destruction of evil magic in Charles Williams, the saving of a world in C. S. Lewis, the overthrow of a Dark Lord in Tolkien, the setting up of a Round Table in T. H. White, the hunting down of the evil released from the self in Ursula Le Guin, the search for Rocket 00000 in Pynchon's *Gravity's Rainbow.* The change to quest-type fantasy occurs quite markedly in the late romances of William Morris in the 1890s, as in the search for the Well at the World's end, which is quite strikingly different from the dream-like mode in which things happen in his earlier romances of the 1850s. And yet at the same time there is more sense of change and evolution in nineteenth-century fantasy, where we are constantly moved from one episode to another, leaving the characters in the last behind, while in modern fantasy we usually stay with the same central figures throughout.

Concomitant with this—perhaps caused by it, perhaps part of the nineteenth-century fascination for such things—is the sheer diversity of phenomena to be found in Victorian fantasy. Often it seems to be packed with as many different objects as possible, brought together as if by some conceit. In *Alice*:

> Tis the voice of the Lobster: I heard him declare
> You have baked me too brown, I must sugar my hair'
> As a duck with its eyelids, so he with his nose
> Trims his belt and his buttons, and turns out his toes.
>
> (139)

And in *The Water-Babies*

> in the water-forest he saw the water-monkeys and water-squirrels (they had all six legs, though . . .); and nimbly enough they ran among the branches. There were water-flowers here, too, in thousands; and Tom tried to pick them: but as soon as he touched them, they drew themselves in and turned into knots of jelly; and then Tom saw that they were all alive—bells, and stars, and wheels, and flowers, of all beautiful shapes and colours; and all alive and busy, just as Tom was. (97-8)

The mass of detail that surrounds the protagonist in much nineteenth-century fantasy is there not merely for ornament. Just as in the work of Dickens, a measure of commerce and exchange begins to take place between the human and the animate, or inanimate. Here Victorian fantasy seems to have much in common with a postmodern fantasy such as Pynchon's *Gravity's Rainbow,* but the impulse behind the one is an exuberant explosion of the self outwards, and of the other a movement inwards towards collapse and fragmentation.

Another motif in nineteenth-century fantasy is inversion or reversal. Clothes take on a reality superior to that of their wearers in Carlyle's *Sartor.* Tom in *The Water-Babies* must go backwards to go forwards to the Other-end-of-Nowhere. The progressively "older" men of the Sea, the Earth, and the Fire in MacDonald's "The Golden Key" grow steadily younger, until the last is a baby. *Alice Through the Looking-Glass* presents a world in which one must do the opposite of what one does in this world to survive or progress. Samuel Butler's inversion *Erewhon* (1872) gives us a world in which the sick are treated as criminals and the criminals as sick. F. Anstey's *Vice Versa* (1880) sends a tyrannous father to boarding school in place of his son. The emphasis is continually on upsetting presuppositions.

Nineteenth-century fantasy is pervaded by the use of metamorphosis. The student Anselmus in Hoffmann's *The Golden Pot* finds an elder-tree beneath which he is sitting transformed into a medium of crystalline sounds. In this medium he sees three twining serpents, which call to him and fill him with longing. This motif of change to the serpentine is also seen in the evil Geraldine of Coleridge's *Christabel,* and in Keats's *Lamia.* (Later the transformation involves often pigs, as in Morris's *Lindenborg Pool* or Lautréamont's *Maldoror* (1869), where the protagonist at one point inhabits a hog's body, or in *Alice,* in which the Duchess's baby turns into a pig, or in the anti-feminist *Pig-Faced Queen* (1874) by Edward Knatchbull-Hugessen.) Tom in Kingsley's *The Water-Babies* is changed from a boy chimney sweep to an eft "about 3.87902 inches long," in a stream; and after his theft of Mrs. Bedonebyasyoudid's sweets, he becomes covered all over with prickles. These changes for Kingsley express his idea that the soul makes the body, just as a snail makes its shell, and that evolution supposes a continual plasticity of bodily form. One could trace most nineteenth-century uses of metamorphosis to a sense of the contingency of the apparently actual and separate, which is quite different from Ovid's, or the traditional fairy tale's use of the idea, where it is either disguise, escape, or punishment, and is an extension of narrative purpose. George MacDonald's *Phantastes* starts with the basin in the room of the hero Anodos over-flowing and then turning into a stream, which runs over a carpet that turns to flower-covered grass, until his whole bedroom has melted into a forest glade in Fairyland. Lewis Carroll's Alice grows larger or smaller as she partakes of the magical liquid or cake, and the worlds she encounters are in part those of cards and chess-pieces brought to life. R. L. Stevenson's Jekyll, possessed by a sense of "the trembling immateriality, the mist-like transience, of this seemingly so solid body in which we walk attired" (109-110), transforms himself, with much sense of shuddering and shrinkage, to the evil Mr. Hyde. Oscar Wilde's Dorian Gray tries to cut himself off from change and ends in frightful metamorphosis and dissolution. H. G. Wells's Griffin makes his body invisible, and his Moreau, dedicated to ' "the study of the plasticity of human forms" ' (102), attempts to graft human qualities on to animals. Some transformations are of the "suppose" variety. Suppose a darning needle or an old lamppost felt and thought as we do. What would it be like to be them? Thus the urge behind several of Hans Andersen's stories (trans. 1846). Suppose we lived in a world of two dimensions only. How would life go on? How would it feel to be a triangle, a square, or a hexagon? So it is in E. A. Abbott's *Flatland.* In modern fantasy, where metamorphosis is much less frequently used, it is not often portrayed for its own sake, that is, as a means of getting one form to change into another to learn something or to make a point, as the hero of T. H. White's

The Once and Future King is taught the natures of animals by being temporarily turned into them, or Kafka's Gregor Samsa is transformed into a gigantic beetle for largely comic and satiric purposes. In postmodernist fantasy, where there may be shifts of self or perspective, this stems more from a sense of entropy, of the collapse of being to zero, than from an exuberant sense of its variety.[2] It can fairly be said that the nineteenth century delighted in the process of changeability itself. Twentieth-century fantasies that contain transformations usually show the consequence: they do not linger over the gradual alterations from one kind of being to another. Victorian fantasy, perhaps responding to the climate that produced Darwin, is remarkably full of a sense of the contingency of being. It was, after all, taken on one level, as a way of arguing for life beyond death: if we became men out of brutes, so we must become higher beings from the death of our human bodies, Tennyson on Hallam bids himself trust that "life is not as idle ore" and that "those we call the dead / Are breathers of an ampler day" ("In Memoriam," 118).

One might add to this element of changeability in nineteenth-century fantasy the fact that the "fictional microcosm," the world of the fantasy, is continually violated as it is not in all but postmodern varieties of fantasy today. An author will break off to moralize, to indulge in digressions or speculations, to talk directly to the audience, to question the fictive status of our own world, to interpolate alien stories, or to shift us abruptly from one world to another. Thus Thackeray in *The Rose and the Ring* states:

> The Fairy had provided King Giglio with a suit of armour, which was not only embroidered all over with jewels, and blinding to your eyes to look at, but was water-proof, gun-proof, and sword-proof; so that in the midst of the very hottest battles his Majesty rode about as calmly as if he had been a British Grenadier at Alma. Were I engaged in fighting for my country, *I* should like such a suit of armour as Prince Giglio wore; but, you know, he was a Prince of a fairy tale, and they always have those wonderful things. (113-14)

Or Lautréamont states in *Maldoror*, "I warn whoever is reading me to beware of forming a vague and all the more false idea of the beauties of literature I prune in my excessively swift proliferation of phrase . . ." (132). Or Kingsley voices, "Am I in earnest? Oh dear no! Don't you know that this is a fairy tale, and all fun and pretense; and that you are not to believe one word of it, even if it is true?" (76) Several of the main fantasies of the nineteenth century are framed as dreams, so that the status of their being is made open to question. MacDonald's *Phantastes* (1858) and *Lilith* (1895) have dream structures, and it is MacDonald's object to make us feel that such dreams may be more real than our realities. He follows Novalis in saying,

"Our life is no dream: but it should and will become one." The early romances of William Morris, such as *Lindenborg Pool, The Hollow Land,* or *The Story of the Unknown Church,* portray dream-like shifts of identity and transitions from world to world. The *Alice* books end with the prime inhabitants of Wonderland or Looking-Glass World being reduced to mere cards or chess pieces as Alice "wakes up." Many fantastic works are a mixture of narrative and speculation, Carlyle's *Sartor Resartus* and Kingsley's *The Water-Babies* for example. Such characteristics as already noted are not often to be found in twentieth-century fantasy apart from the postmodern variety. The object in Lewis, Eddison, Tolkien, White, or Peake is the creation of a consistent other world that our minds can enter. That world is not violated in any way. Tolkien, for example, specifically attacks the use of dream in fantasy, the suggestion that its world is contingent. This is one of the "reasons" why the morality or teaching in modern fantasy is much more implicit within the created fiction rather than stated overtly, as it is so often in Victorian fantasy.

But the fact is that in the nineteenth century the fantastic world is not portrayed as standing on its own, as it is more frequently now. C. S. Lewis wanted to create wholly *other* worlds, so he made his Mars, Venus, and Narnia. Tolkien's Middle-earth may have something to say to our world, but it is not reducible to an inverted image of it as might be said of MacDonald's *Phantastes* or Carroll's *Alice*. Modern fantasy frequently delights in the making of alternative worlds that we can treat as "realities" while we read. Their reference to our own world, where it exists, is oblique. Victorian fantasy rarely creates a fantastic world for its own sake, or on the same terms as those of Tolkien. Wonderland and Looking-Glass World are not places to look at: strictly they are not even places, but a series of positions and encounters to be experienced. Each of the creatures and people met is highly memorable and fantastic, but we are much less aware of a fantastic world existing on its own. The Fairy Land in MacDonald's *Phantastes* is also a series of encounters set in a medium that changes in parallel with the development of the protagonist. The Hollow Land in William Morris's story is a place of spiritual education more than a land in its own right. Abbott's *Flatland* is an Olympian portrayal of what life is generally like given the laws of that two-dimensional realm. But we do not fully enter it and ultimately consider it only as it reflects on the contingency and transient mores of our three-dimensional world. Many Victorian fantasies or fantastical works are actually portrayed as taking place within *our* world—Carlyle's *Sartor,* Dickens's *Christmas Carol,* Kingsley's *The Water-Babies,* MacDonald's *At the Back of the North Wind* (1871), Anstey's *Vice Versa* and *The Tinted Venus,* Kipling's *Puck of Pook's Hill,* E. Nesbit's (if we may take 1914 as the end point) magic books. Its close involvement with this world, whether as an inversion of it, an extension of it, or a commentary on it, lays nineteenth-century fantasy peculiarly open to the kind of theory of fantasy as hesitation between natural and supernatural readings that we find in Tzvetan Todorov (who finds such fantasy ends about 1890).

It is fair to say that nineteenth-century fantasy most often has its eye fixed on this world and that indeed such fantasy could be described as existing only when there is a gap between the two. In the sense of alienation that frequently characterizes twentieth-century literature, the fantastic might sometimes be said to exist rather where the self and the world are shown in *harmony,* that harmony now often being a possibility so remote as to seem fantastic. The fantastic events of Dickens's *A Christmas Carol* (1843) occur in a context where Scrooge has cut himself off from the world: he grinds down Bob Cratchit, refuses to recognize Christmas, and sits alone in his locked and empty house. In this situation he is forced to encounter the chained ghost of his former partner Jacob Marley and see his torments, and to meet the spirits of Christmas past, present and future, who show him his life as it has been, as it is now, and as it will become. The ghost and spirits break into Scrooge's locked house and self: the ghost clanks into his room late at night, the spirit of Christmas present holds high and uproarious revelry in his bedroom. The fantasy stops when Scrooge becomes integrated with the world and time. ' "I will live in the Past, the Present, and the Future. The Spirits of all Three shall stare within me. I will not shut out the lessons that they teach" ' (70). The fantastic here exists in a moral context, where there is refusal to be involved in life. We see it in others of Dickens's creations, from the self-enclosed Court of Chancery in *Bleak House* to the bizarre Miss Havisham in *Great Expectations,* who has stopped the clocks and hardened her heart against love. We see it too in Ruskin's *The King of the Golden River* (1851), where the wicked brothers have closed the door to visitors and refuse water to suppliants; in the isolations fantastically portrayed in Tennyson's "St. Simeon Stylites," "Tithonus," "The Lady of Shalott," "The Lotos Eaters," "Mariana," or "Ulysses" (though the separation is half-desired); in Stevenson's *Dr. Jekyll and Mr. Hyde* and Oscar Wilde's *The Picture of Dorian Gray,* where the characters have tried to dissociate themselves even from themselves while they indulge their evil sides.

But there are other forms of separation from the world than selfishness or self-enclosure. The fantasy of the *Alice* books exists by virtue of the continual comparisons we make between the worlds of nonsense Carroll has created and our world of seeming sense; and the same goes for the limericks of Edward Lear, who could (more harshly than Carroll) declare, "I begin to be vastly weary of hearing people talk nonsense—

unanswered not because they are unanswerable, but because they talk in pulpits" (302). Among other books that exist by virtue of their inversion of this world and its values are Carlyle's *Sartor Resartus* (1836), MacDonald's *Phantastes,* E. A. Abbott's *Flatland,* Samuel Butler's *Erewhon* (1872); or, in a different way, James Thomson's *The City of Dreadful Night* (1874), a Dantesque vision of modern urban life. Even Hardy's novels are fantasies in their use of coincidence: the failure of Tess's confessional letter, for instance, to reach Angel Clare before their marriage, and the subsequent blight on their relationship projects Hardy's view, expressed in his poetry also, that love unions are momentary, not lasting, and that there is always a divorce between the world and our wishes. Nineteenth-century fantasy often deals with the separation of self from true self, as in the many stories of shadows and of Doppelgängers, from Hoffmann and Chamisso to Gogol and Dostoevsky. Then, too, much Victorian fantasy is interested in death, that final separation between the self and the world. The theme of living death fascinates Tennyson; death, as Tolkien says, "is the theme that most inspired George MacDonald" (59), many of William Morris's early romances depict posthumous experiences, or experiences "out of life"; and there is a continuous spiritualist preoccupation in the work of Bulwer Lytton. It is in the nineteenth century also that we see the rise of the ghost or horror story, which usually portrays the breakdown of the controlled or rational self before the uncanny from beyond life, in Scott, Hogg, Poe, Dickens, Mrs. Gaskell, Le Fanu, and others.

In most nineteenth-century fantasies the protagonist is isolated. Tom is on his own in the stream and river in Kingsley's *The Water-Babies,* and he isolates himself by his wicked behavior when he meets the other water-babies; MacDonald's Anodos in *Phantastes* goes through Fairy Land alone; William Morris's Arnald in *The Hollow Land* is cut off from his former fellows; Alice is the only human in Wonderland or Looking-Glass World. By contrast, the hero in modern fantasy often operates within a group or fellowship, without which his efforts would be in vain—the groups of children in E. Nesbit's stories or C. S. Lewis's Narnia books, the four princes in E. R. Eddison's *The Worm Ouroboros* (1922), the company of the Ring in Tolkien's epic, the Round Table in T. H. White's *The Once and Future King,* and the group that surrounds the deposed ruler in Robert Silverberg's *Lord Valentine's Castle.*

There is often a certain "epic" character about modern fantasy that the nineteenth-century variety lacks. This may be due to the influence of the panoramic view of life in science fiction, starting perhaps with H. G. Wells's romances in the 1890s; equally it may be of a piece with the late nineteenth-century urge towards the writing of utopias, worlds either more advanced or more simple than our own (examples are Edward Bellamy's *Looking Backward* or William Morris's *News from Nowhere*). More generally it may be a product of twentieth-century internationalism, the growing sense of Planet Earth made up of a potential community of nations. Whichever it may be, much modern fantasy depicts situations in which the acts of individual characters determine the safety or otherwise of whole worlds. On Antony Durrant alone in Charles William's *The Place of the Lion* depends the protection of the earth from the magically released First Principles of creation, on Lewis's Ransom the continued innocence of the unfallen world of Perelandra, on Tolkien's Frodo the survival of Middle Earth, on Le Guin's Ged the continued vitality of Earthsea, and even Slothrup in Pynchon's *Gravity's Rainbow* is the focus of international interest.

One might almost say that modern fantasy is at least as much *ecological* as moral, involved with the protection of endangered environments as much as with the spiritual health of the protagonist. In no nineteenth-century fantasy is the concern with a threatened land or landscape as we see it in Lewis, Tolkien, or Le Guin. That note only begins to be sounded with William Morris's late work. The emphasis in nineteenth-century fantasy is much more individual. In *The Water-Babies* or *Phantastes* the whole concern is with what Tom and Anodos learn about themselves and with how they develop on their own in the midst of the worlds they encounter. Often such fantasies begin by isolating the protagonist from the rest of the world. From a chimney sweep Tom is made a water-baby in a stream. Anodos wakes in a world divorced from his own, in Fairy Land. Alice dreams her way into Wonderland. We should not perhaps underestimate here the Victorian fascination with the paradigm of spiritual development portrayed in what was one of their favorite books, Bunyan's *Pilgrim's Progress,* where the protagonist is severed from all his previous life to begin his journey through a strange spiritual obstacle course. Such worlds are as it were tailored to the ethical or other needs of the protagonist. But in much modern fantasy the fantastic world exists independently of the central figure, who lives to serve it rather than it him; quite often the hero is already a member of the strange world, whether a hobbit, a wizard, or a king, rather than being brought into it from outside. In this regard it can be observed that the evil most commonly attacked in nineteenth-century fantasy is that of greed or possessiveness, of seeking to draw things into the self—thus the inhospitable behavior of the brothers in Ruskin's *The King of the Golden River,* the sweets-stealing greed of Kingsley's Tom, the selfish desire of MacDonald's Anodos to possess the White Lady, the miserliness of Scrooge, the greed for youth and apparent innocence of Wilde's Dorian Gray. In modern fantasy the evil lies rather in the attempt to impose the self on others, in the more "epic" wish to

subdue worlds, in short, in lust for power, rather than in greed. Thus Charles Williams's Giles Tumulty in *Many Dimensions* (1931) wants the power given by a magic stone to rule the world; Tolkien's Sauron seeks complete control of Middle Earth; Peake's Steerpike plots to overthrow the ruling family of Gormenghast for his own purposes; Lewis's Orual in *Till We Have Faces* (1956) wishes no one but herself to have power over Psyche as his White Witch wants all Narnia to be under her heel.

There are doubtless other features differentiating nineteenth- and twentieth-century fantasy. One that comes to mind, for example, is that nineteenth-century fantasy has a leaning towards the feminine. The fairy tale with its usually female fairies, was one correlative for that Victorian adulation of the wise and maternal woman (as well as the fear of the dangerous and predatory female) that we see in much of their literature; today by contrast the accent seems to be much more on the heroic powers of the masculine—on Frodo, Ransom, Antony Durrant, Arthur, Titus, Ged, Lord Valentine—where previously "men" had often to be mothered into maturity in the faerian world, as in *The Rose and the Ring,* Morris's *The Hollow Land,* MacDonald's *Phantastes,* Kingsley's *The Water-Babies.* So much is this the case that a special branch of feminist fantasy has been developed, in part to counter this male domination of the genre.

If one were to attempt to isolate the most pervasive difference between nineteenth- and twentieth-century fantasy, it could be said to be the emphasis of much nineteenth-century fantasy on the local and the individual, even the supposedly inconsequential or eccentric—from children to nonsense, and from mad hatters to mad scientists. There is more of a sense of what Coleridge called "fancy" rather than "imagination," more stress on the invention of ordered details than their absorption into a larger thematic purpose as is the case more frequently now. But such an attempt to grasp the whole misses too many of the parts, too many of the peculiarities of the essentially varied mode of nineteenth-century fantasy—its adventurousness, its subversiveness, its love of metamorphosis. My main point in retracing the Victorian origins of modern fantasy has been to show that there are very real distinctions between the types of fantasy produced before and after about 1900, which is certainly one important factor to be taken into account when attempting to define the form. Within the genre the differences can be just as revealing as the similarities.

Notes

This essay was given as the 1989 International Association for the Fantastic in the Arts Distinguished Scholar Address

[1] In her *Holiday House* (1839), chapter ix.

[2] Lance Olsen describes it as "forms slipping into one another, epistemological unsteadiness," in his analysis of Carlos Fuentes' *Aura* (67).

Works Cited

Carroll, Lewis. *The Annotated Alice*. Ed. Martin Gardner. Harmondsworth: Penguin Books, 1970.

Coleridge, Samuel Taylor. *The Collected Letters of Samuel Taylor Coleridge*. Ed. E. L. Griggs, 4. vols. Oxford: the Clarendon Press, 1956.

Dickens, Charles. *A Christmas Carol*. In *Christmas Books*. London: Oxford University Press, 1954.

————. "Frauds on the Fairies." In *Household Words*, 8, no. 184 (1 October 1853).

Ducasse, Isadore comte de Lautréamont. *Maldoror*. Trans. Alexis Lykiard. London: Allison and Busby, 1970.

Kingsley, Charles. *The Water-Babies: A Fairy Tale for a Land-Baby*. London: Macmillan, 1863.

Lear, Edward. Letter to Chichester Fortescue, 15 March 1863. In Vivien Noakes, *Edward Lear: The Life of a Wanderer*. London: Collins, 1968.

Lewis, C. S. "Sometimes Fairy Stories May Say Best What's To Be Said." 1956. In *Of Other Worlds: Essays and Stories*. London: Geoffrey Bles, 1966.

McDonald, George. "The Fantastic Imagination." 1890. In *A Dish of Orts: Chiefly Papers on the Imagination, and on Shakespear*. London: Sampson Low, 1893.

Novalis. *Schriften*. Ed. Paul Kluckhohn and Richard Samuel. 3 vols. Stuttgart: Kolhammer, 1960-1968.

Olsen, Lance. *Ellipse of Uncertainty: An Introduction to Postmodernist Fantasy*. Westport, CT: Greenwood Press, 1987.

Paget, Charles. *The Hope of the Katzekopfs; or, the Sorrows of Selfishness. A Fairy Tale*. 2nd ed. London: Joseph Master, 1847.

Stevenson, Robert Lewis. *The Strange Case of Dr. Jekll and Mr. Hyde*. London: Longmans, Green and Co., 1886.

Titmarsh, Mr M. A. [William Makepeace Thackery]. *The Rose and the Ring: or, The History of Prince Giglio and Prince Bulbo, A Fireside Pantomime for Great and Small Children*. London: Smith, Elder and Co., 1855.

Tolkien, J. R. R. *Tree and Leaf*. London: Allen and Unwin, 1964.

Wells, H. G. *The Island of Doctor Moreau*. Harmondsworth: Penguin Books, 1946.

Prickett highlights what distinguishes Victorian fantasy from that of other eras:

[T]o see what is distinctively new about nineteenth-century fantasy we must look back at the period immediately preceding it. Out of a confluence of intermingled currents and eddies of thought we can, perhaps, select a number of streams which were to feed the reservoirs of Romanticism at the turn of the century. One is the idea of the 'Gothick'; another is a revival of religious mysticism and a renewed feeling for the numinous—the irrational and mysterious elements in religious experience; a third is the purely human revulsion against the squalid and degrading conditions of the early industrial revolution. In all three we can trace that curious ambivalence between 'imagination' and 'fantasy' that was to so haunt the Victorian consciousness, and turn it inwards towards the creation of dream-worlds.

Stephen Prickett, in Victorian Fantasy, *Indiana University Press, 1979.*

Karen Michalson

SOURCE: "Fantasy, Early Nineteenth-Century Reviewers, and Samuel Taylor Coleridge," in *Victorian Fantasy Literature: Literary Battles with Church and Empire*, The Edwin Mellen Press, 1990, pp. 1-19.

[In the following excerpt, Michalson illustrates the negative connotations Victorian critics associated with "fantastic" writing.]

> What, then, must be the effect of a confederated and indefatigable priesthood, who barely tolerate literature, and actually hate it, upon all those classes over whom literature has any influence![1]

Unhampered by the theories of reading and the philosophical/linguistic investigations into the nature of literary texts that we twentieth-century critics find so indispensable, the majority of readers in early nineteenth-century Britain had no problem defining fantasy.[2] For the purposes of this study, then, I do not intend to rely on any contemporary theoretically-oriented definition of fantasy but on the nineteenth-century's looser and perhaps intellectually less satisfactory understanding of fantasy literature as the stuff with magic and fairies and impossible occurrences in it. To say that a work or idea was "fantastic" was to dismiss it as unrealistic and therefore as unworthy of the time or consideration of a truly rational, scientific, progressive inheritor of the Enlightenment.[3] Fantasy belonged to the Renaissance with its quaint superstitions. Regrettably, it had lingered for the previous century among the less refined classes in chapbooks and imported fairy tales, and was now impertinently making a new appearance in the works of those suspect practitioners of the new school of poetry that took its impetus from (of all places) the Lake District. Most readers of taste didn't read it. Besides, the vast majority of the fairy tales which had been finding their way into nurseries and adult bookshelves over the last century were French, and to those upper class readers who had kept a wary eye on the Reign of Terror and the subsequent rise of Napoleon, anything French was probably bad. It was Madame d'Aulnoy's *Contes des fées,* translated into English in 1699 as *Tales of the Fairys,* whose immense popularity gave the fairy tale genre its name. In 1729 the first English translation of Charles Perrault's *Contes du temps passé* appeared in London as *Histories, or Tales of Past Times, By M. Perrault.* It was Madame Leprince de Beaumont who came to England in 1745 and included French fairy tales in her popular *Magasin des enfans, ou dialogues entre une sage Gouvernante et plusieurs de ses Élèves.* Beaumont's *Magasin* was first published in French in London in 1756 and then translated as *The Young Misses Magazine* in 1761.[4] As late as the 1860s English critics still routinely associated French literature with both fantasy and their own fears of an English revolution, as is apparent from contemporary reviews of the English sensation novels which enjoyed immense popularity during this decade.[5]

Because the word "fantasy" could be used to suggest backwardness and irrationality as well as to convey a sense of political unpopularity it became a useful pejorative in the hands of critics like Francis Jeffrey, editor of *The Edinburgh Review.* Early nineteenth century reviewers loved to engage in partisan politics, and their reactions to the literature of the day were often little more than excuses to launch attacks on Whig or Tory ideologies. Nice literary definitions were not their business, and they tended to use literary terms rather casually, relying on their commonly accepted sense. When the liberal Jeffrey wants to attack Wordsworth in 1808, after Wordsworth has become a Tory, he does so by trying to embarrass him in his new conservative stance by applying an eighteenth-century standard of verisimilitude to his work, adherence to this standard being a Tory trademark. Ever since the first edition of Johnson's *Dictionary* was published in 1755, and various grammars began to make their appearance throughout the second half of the eighteenth century, a sharp political division concerning the uses of literary and spoken language was recognized and adhered to by most conservative educated readers. It was believed by universal grammarians like James Harris and Lord Monboddo that there

was a one-to-one relationship between a word and the thing it describes, and that therefore the kind of language a person used directly revealed his mind, character, and morals. Abstract words were better than concrete, material words and particles were considered "the glory of grammatical art." To use abstractions and particles was to demonstrate that one's mind was not polluted with base, material passions but was elevated to the realms of pure reason. Abstractions were considered closer to the eternal truths and "facts" of existence. The baser language of the mercantile people, according to Johnson, was "in a great measure casual and mutable" and "therefore must be suffered to perish with other things unworthy of preservation." Most grammarians believed that peasants used too much fancy; they made up words to suit the expediency of the moment, words which varied from region to region. It was abstract references to universal truth and one-to-one correspondence with Reality which was supposed to infuse the language of the upper classes. This belief was still adhered to by early nineteenth-century conservatives, although their Whig counterparts became more willing to use the common, concrete language that Wordsworth's early Romantic poems made fashionable in more liberal circles. Not even the most liberal Whigs, however, went much beyond the language of early Wordsworthian nature Romanticism. The hard core fantasy poems of Shelley and Keats were not acceptable.[6]

Jeffrey's use of vague phrases like "real life" and "eternal and universal standard of truth" are clearly intended to stand in for rather complex Enlightenment aesthetic ideas. When he complains at length that Wordsworth's work is too "fantastic," he means, like most of his contemporaries, that it is too "unbelievable."[7] The word "fantastic" is used pejoratively three times:

> We allude now to the Wordsworths, and the Southeys, and Coleridges, and all that ambitious fraternity, that, with good intentions, and extraordinary talents, are labouring to bring back our poetry to the *fantasti*cal [my emphasis] oddity and puling childishness of Withers, Quarles, or Marvel. . . . Mr. Crabbe exhibits the common people of England pretty much as they are, and as they must appear to every one who will take the trouble of examining into their condition. . . . The gentlemen of the new school, on the other hand, scarcely ever condescend to take their subjects from any description of persons at all known to the common inhabitants of the world; but invent for themselves certain whimsical and unheard-of beings, to whom they impute some *fantasti*cal [my emphasis] combination of feelings, and then labour to excite our sympathy for them, either by placing them in incredible situations, or by some strained and exaggerated moralisation of a vague and tragical description. Mr. Crabbe, in short, shows us something which we have all

seen, or may see, in real life. . . . He delights us by the truth.[8]

Jeffrey takes it for granted that his readers will accept George Crabbe's realism as better than the invention of "whimsical and un-heard of beings"—as better than fantasy. What is truly odd about this review is that Jeffrey then includes a superfluous attack on Wordsworth's "Strange Fits of Passion Have I Known" as "fantastic." He writes of Wordsworth's poem:

> Now we leave it to any reader of common candour and discernment to say, whether these subtle representations of character and sentiment are drawn from that eternal and universal standard of truth and nature . . . or whether they are not formed, as we have ventured to allege, upon certain *fantastic* [my emphasis] and affected peculiarities in the mind or fancy of the author, into which it is most improbable that many of his readers will enter.[9]

The speaker in "Strange Fits of Passion Have I Known" is an ordinary rural inhabitant who remembers making evening visits to his lover's cottage, a fairly common occupation in the country, one would think. In fact, he's so ordinary and rational that he's actually troubled by what he calls his "*strange* [my emphasis] fits of passion," choosing to reveal his experiences "But in the Lover's ear alone." He attempts to distance himself from his superstitious association of the sinking moon with Lucy's death by referring to his evening visits as "sweet dreams" and he half denies that his superstitious fears are even products of his own mind by exclaiming "What fond and wayward thoughts will slide / Into a Lover's head!"[10] The speaker's apparent discomfort with his own thoughts when they tend toward mystical apprehensions makes it much easier to read him as a troubled rationalist than as a "whimsical and un-heard of being." Although Lucy herself is presented in this poem as a potentially mystical being, her status as such is only potential because we never get beyond the speaker's troubled perceptions, and it is precisely the speaker's trouble with his own perceptions which indicates that he privileges rationality. Such a speaker could give a reviewer like Jeffrey an excuse to praise the poem as "something which we have all seen, or may see, in real life" if he were inclined to do so. Yet if his goal is to attack Wordsworth's turncoat conservatism via a review of Crabbe's poems, it is both useful and convenient to dismiss Wordsworth's work as "fantastic" for it suggests all the aesthetic (and political) irrationality that Tories found distasteful. As a liberal, Jeffrey was hoping to call into question the purity of Wordsworth's newfound conservative stance.

Robert Southey's *Thalaba, The Destroyer: A Metrical Romance* was given similar treatment by the *Edinburgh Review* in an earlier article dated October 1802. The attack may well have been politically motivated; the reviewer applies a vague Enlightenment standard of "just imitations of nature" and by this time Southey's pantisocracy friends had long ago deplored his elitist tendencies. A few years earlier, Coleridge had been particularly aggrieved to learn that while Southey mouthed platitudes about an ideal, egalitarian society on the banks of the Susquehanna he insisted on wanting to bring servants along.[11] Yet unlike "Strange Fits of Passion Have I Known" *Thalaba* is indisputably a fantasy, and the reviewer has a field day deploring this fact. After a plot summary which serves as an excuse to mock Southey's use of magicians and magical items in his poem, the reviewer writes:

> From this little sketch of the story, our readers will easily perceive, that it consists altogether of the most wild and extravagant fictions, and openly sets nature and probability at defiance. In its action it is not an imitation of any thing; and excludes all rational criticism, as to the choice and succession of its incidents . . . The pleasure afforded by performances of this sort, is very much akin to that which may be derived from the exhibition of a harlequin farce, where, instead of just imitations of nature and human character, we are entertained with the transformation of cauliflowers and beer-barrels, the apparation of ghosts and devils, and all the other magic of the wooden sword. Those who can prefer this eternal sorcery to the just and modest representation of human actions and passions, will probably take more delight in walking among the holly griffins and yew sphinxes of the city gardener, than in ranging among the groves and lawns which have been laid out by a hand that feared to violate nature.[12]

Tory reviewers would occasionally savage pieces they found politically objectionable by referring to them in the language of fantasy. *The British Critic* ran a series of scathing reviews of Byron's *Don Juan* from August 1819 to December 1823. The anonymous reviewer of Cantos VI-VIII sums up Byron's literary career by complaining that at one time "the friends of literature and virtue mourned over the occasional perversion of Lord Byron's splendid talents" but now Byron's "spell and mystery" had become "as stale and palpable as most other pieces of solemn charlatanerie." He then sums up *Don Juan* by saying that Byron had "bestrode the broken knee'd hobby-horse of Radicalism," sinking "from the dignity of Milton's fallen angel, to the vulgar horned and tailed devil of a puppet-show."[13] Milton, of course, was one of the greatest fantasy writers who ever lived, yet he could get away with writing fantasy in part because he lived before the Age of Enlightenment when people were expected to be rational and in part because his works were heavily Protestant and easily lent themselves to domestication. For every politically threatening romantic who read Milton's Satan as a glorious rebellious anti-hero there were probably a dozen conservative Anglicans who attributed Satan's heroic qualities to his "fallen angel" status. It is therefore not surprising that the Anglican backed *British Critic* could attack Byron's literary and political radicalism with a demonic metaphor which is contrasted unfavorably to Milton's Satan. What is surprising is that the reviewer also uses a fantasy metaphor when he sarcastically refers to Byron's "spell and mystery," as a description of his literary career. His career is *then* accorded a special kind of "puppet-show" demonic status which is inferior to that of Milton's glorious creation, which, although unarguably fantastic, had the saving grace of being Christian in outlook. Byron's special status is surprising because one of the *British Critic*'s leading Whig opponents, the *Monthly Review,* accorded a similar status to Shelley's *Prometheus Unbound* when its anonymous reviewer felt that the drama had gone beyond the pale of acceptability. The *Monthly Review* was normally inclined to give the benefit of the doubt to radical poets, but like Byron, Shelley had crossed the line of "occasional perversion" into an aggressively anti-Christian stance that no radical who wished to maintain a toehold on respectability would endorse. His drama was troubling because it went beyond the pseudo-daring domesticated references to classical mythology embraced by fashionable readers by creating its own mythology and its own parallel world. In this sense, *Prometheus Unbound* was truly a fantasy, but like the improbable but not fantastic *Don Juan,* it was accorded outsider status. If Byron's sentiments were devilish but unworthy of Milton's Satan, Shelley's were unChristian but unworthy of respectable heathenism:

> There is an excess of fancy which rapidly degenerates into nonsense: if the *sublime* be closely allied to the *ridiculous,* the *fanciful* is twin-sister to the *foolish;* and really Mr. Shelley has worthily maintained the relationship. What, in the name of wonder on one side, and of common sense on the other, is the meaning of this metaphysical rhapsody about the unbinding of Prometheus? Greek plays, Mr. Shelley tells us in his preface, have been his study; and from them he has caught—what?—any thing but the tone and character of his story; which as little exhibits the distinct imaginations of the heathen mythology as it resembles the virtuous realities of the Christian faith. It is only *nonsense,* pure unmixed *nonsense. . . .* [14]

Fantasy was suspect in all political quarters, and anything fantastic occupied a status outside of the standard binary oppositions of Reality/Art, God/Devil-Heathen, Tory/Whig. Yet, as I said earlier, most reviewers were more worried about political ideologies than aesthetics, and their anti-fantasy stances were usually never more than casual side notes, convenient ways to prolong an attack against an already objectionable piece. The brunt of the objection to fantasy literature came not from literary reviewers but from adherents to various Christian sects both within and without the Anglican Church. That *Prometheus Unbound* as a fantasy was considered anti-Christian apart from Shelley's own avowed atheism can be surmised from this later portion of the above review:

> Where are the things, then, "not dreamt of in *our* philosophy?" The *'Prometheus Unbound'* is amply stored with such things. First, there is a *wicked supreme deity.*—Secondly, there is a Demogorgon, superior, in process of time, to that *supreme wickedness.* Thirdly, there are nymphs, naids, nereids, spirits of flood and fell, depth and height, the four elements, and fifty-four imaginary places of creation and residence.— Now, to what does all this tend? To nothing, positively to nothing. . . . [Shelley's] Manichean absurdities, his eternally indwelling notion of a good and evil principle fighting like furies on all occasions with their whole *posse comitatus* together, cross his clearer fancy, and lay the buildings of his better mind in glittering gorgeous ruins. . . . The benevolent opposition of Prometheus to the oppressive and atrocious rule of Jupiter forms the main object, as far as it can be understood, of this generally unintelligible work; though some of it can be understood too plainly; and the passage beginning, 'A woful sight,' at page 49, and ending, 'It hath become a curse,' must be most offensive, as it too evidently seems to have been intended to be, to every sect of Christians. [15]

The furious reactions of Christians of all stripes to fantasy literature in particular and novels in general had a profound impact on educational institutions and ultimately on the academic critical treatment of literary genres. . . .

Notes

[1] Robert Southey, *Quarterly Review,* 4 (1810): 506-507.

[2] On the other hand, in the past fifteen years there has not only been an upsurge of popular interest in fantasy literature, but a burgeoning of scholarly attempts at defining it. The most notable attempts at definition are Tzvetan Todorov, *The Fantastic: A Structural Approach to a Literary Genre,* trans. Richard Howard (Cleveland: The Press of Case Western Reserve University, 1973); Colin Manlove, *Modern Fantasy: Five Studies* (New York: Cambridge University, 1975); W.R. Irwin, *The Game of the Impossible: A Rhetoric of Fantasy* (Chicago: Univer-

sity of Illinois, 1976); Eric S. Rabkin, *The Fantastic in Literature* (Princeton: Princeton University, 1976); Christine Brooke-Rose, *A Rhetoric of the Unreal: Studies in Narrative and Structure, Especially of the Fantastic* (New York: Cambridge University, 1981); Kathryn Hume, *Fantasy and Mimesis: Responses to Reality in Western Literature* (New York: Methuen, 1984); and Lance Olsen, *Ellipses of Uncertainty: An Introduction to Postmodern Fantasy,* Contributions to the Study of Science Fiction and Fantasy, 26 (Westport, Connecticut: Greenwood, 1987).

[3] Thomas Hobbes had called imagination "decaying sense." Samuel Johnson defined the verb "to fancy" as "to believe without being able to prove" and the word "fantastick" as "irrational." See *Dr. Johnson's Critical Vocabulary: A Selection From His Dictionary,* ed. Richard L. Harp (New York: University Press of America, 1986) 83 and 84. The *OED* defines "fancy" as "an illusion of the senses, delusive imagination, hallucination" and "fantasy" as "the fact or habit of deluding onself by imaginary perceptions or reminiscences." See the compact edition, 1: 959 and 961. As one critic has recently written, there is a long tradition of fancy being defined as "an inferior version of experience that is at least once removed from reality." See Robert DeMaria, Jr., *Johnson's Dictionary and the Language of Learning* (Chapel Hill, North Carolina: University of North Carolina, 1986) 101.

[4] Many scholars have recounted the literary history of fairy tales in Great Britain. I have relied on Iona and Peter Opie, *The Classic Fairy Tales,* (New York: Oxford University Press, 1974) 17-31. Their account is handy, clear, and above all, concise.

[5] Most reviewers objected to the subject matter of sensation novels, which were full of bigamy, murder, incest, and adultery, and blamed the French for providing literary models for such plots. For many reviewers, the worst artistic crime of the French models was their tendency to falsify life and deviate from the standards of realism by showing vice triumphant. Mrs. Oliphant made it clear that a good part of her objection to such novels stemmed from what she perceived as an unrealistic portrayal of British middle class life. She objected to sensation novels in which an "intense appreciation of flesh and blood, this eagerness of physical sensation, is represented as the natural sentiment of English girls, and is offered to them . . . as the portrait of their own state of mind." She then praises Anthony Trollope's characters because "They live like the most of us. . . . They are like the honest English girls we know; and we cannot be sufficiently grateful to him for freeing us, so long as we are under his guidance, from that disgusting witch with her red or amber hair." See Mrs. Oliphant, "Novels," *Blackwoods Magazine* 102 (Sept. 1867): 265-80. Not only did

sensation novels border on the edges of fantasy by stretching the conventions of realism, presenting "disgusting witches" who committed adultery instead of "honest English girls" who presumably didn't, to many reviewers these novels suggested populist movements in their insistence on breaking down class barriers. In many sensation novels servants achieve high social status and masters lose their station. Worse than fictional class mingling was the reality that people from all walks of life were reading them. "Unhappily, the sensational novel is that one touch of anything but nature that makes the kitchen and the drawing-room kin." See "Our Novels. The Sensational School," *Temple Bar,* 29 (July 1870): 424. For a discussion of the sensation novel's threat to social distinctions see Winifred Hughes, *The Maniac in the Cellar: Sensation Novels of the 1860s* (Princeton, New Jersey: Princeton University, 1980) 42-46 and for a discussion of contemporary objections to these novels as French and unrealistic see R. C. Terry, *Victorian Popular Fiction, 1860-80* (Atlantic Highlands, New Jersey: Humanities Press, 1983) 58-63.

[6] Olivia Smith, *The Politics of Language 1791-1819* (Oxford: Clarendon, 1984) 1-34. I am indebted to Smith for the Johnson quotation as well.

[7] *OED,* Compact Edition, I, 961.

[8] Francis Jeffrey, rev. of Crabbe's *Poems, Edinburgh Review* 12 (April 1808): 133.

[9] Jeffrey 136.

[10] William Wordsworth, "Strange Fits of Passion Have I Known," *The Poetical Works of William Wordsworth,* ed. E. De Selincourt, 5 vols. (Oxford: Clarendon, 1944) 2: 29.

[11] Hunter Davies, *William Wordsworth: A Biography* (New York: Atheneum, 1980) 82.

[12] Rev. of *Thalaba, The Destroyer:* A Metrical Romance, *Edinburgh Review* 1 (Oct 1802): 75-76.

[13] From a review of *Don Juan VI-VIII* in *The British Critic* 20 (n.s.), (Aug 1823), qtd. in Theodore Redpath, ed., *The Young Romantics and Critical Opinion 1807-1824: Poetry of Byron, Shelley, and Keats as Seen By Their Contemporary Critics* (London: Harrap, 1973) 66-67.

[14] Review of *Prometheus Unbound, with other Poems, Monthly Review* 94 (Feb 1821), *Young Romantics and Critical Opinion* 357.

[15] Review of *Prometheus Unbound, Monthly Review, Young Romantics and Critical Opinion* 358.

MAJOR FIGURES

C. N. Manlove

SOURCE: "George MacDonald (1824-1905)," in *Modern Fantasy: Five Studies*, Cambridge University Press, 1975, pp. 55-98.

[*George MacDonald is considered by many to have been the greatest fantasy writer of the nineteenth century. In the following essay, Manlove argues that although MacDonald's scientific background and rigorous religious beliefs interfered with his ability to write a purely imaginative fantasy story free of intellectual explanations, MacDonald's stories still contain the feature of "myth," which MacDonald considered an important aspect of fairy tales. (Explanations for title abbreviations may be found at the end of the essay, preceding the Notes.)*]

'I wis we war a' deid!'

Phantastes (1858), *Dealings with the Fairies* (1867), *At the Back of the North Wind* (1871), *The Princess and the Goblin* (1872), *The Wise Woman* (1875), *The Princess and Curdie* (1883) and *Lilith* (1895) are the main fantasies or fairy-tales by George MacDonald. They are very unlike in form. The first and the last are written as dream-romances in which many of the adventures are random and apparently unconnected, and for most of the time the protagonists are 'adrift' in fairyland. The others, except for 'The Golden Key' in *Dealings with the Fairies*, follow much steadier and more obvious narrative paths, and explore the relations between fairyland and the 'real' world of everyday existence. *Phantastes, Lilith* and 'The Golden Key' would probably be termed 'adult', and the remainder 'juvenile' fantasies. Only a book would do justice to their variety; in this chapter we shall have to confine ourselves to large issues.

MacDonald was born and bred at Huntly in Aberdeenshire, and had a happy, if unhealthy, childhood.[1] At King's College, Aberdeen, from 1840 to 1845, he read Chemistry and Natural Philosophy, and graduated M.A. in April 1845. He was then attracted to the ministry, and after occasional family tutorships in London studied at Highbury College, a Congregational Theological Hall, from 1848 to 1850, whereupon he was offered a post (temporary at first) at Trinity Congregational Church, Arundel. In 1851 he married his cousin Louisa Powell, but the security on which this move was made was upset in 1853, when the disapproval of his parishioners at certain of his heterodox opinions—particularly his assertion that the heathen would enjoy a future state of probation—forced him finally to resign. He moved to Manchester, in the hope that it would prove a more fertile ground for liberal theology, but in fact the wave of dismissals of

freethinking clergy was by then national in scale; and, since MacDonald refused to compromise in the slightest degree, he did not secure a living. For most of the rest of his life he was self-employed and often poor, if his means were sometimes supplemented by friends such as Lady Byron.

His self-employment took the form mainly of lectures and bookwriting. The lectures started with Manchester Ladies College (1854), and were still going strong with a tour of America in 1872-3, during which he spoke on Burns more than forty times—each occasion, according to his son and biographer Greville, being a different lecture (MacDonald always spoke with passion and without notes). The last lecture course—48 lectures in 58 days—was in 1891. At first the subjects of his talks included chemistry and physics, but later, Christianity and English literature became the sole topics. He had a very poorly-paid professorship of English literature at Bedford College, London, from 1859 to 1867, but failed to secure the much better-paid Chair of Rhetoric at Edinburgh when it fell vacant in 1865.

His published work began in 1855 with his well-received poem *Within and Without,* and continued until 1897 with a further fifty-one titles, about half of which were novels (many of them 'three-deckers') of 'real' life; the remainder included adult and 'juvenile' fairy-tales, collections of short stories, other books for children, literary and critical essays, sermons and poems. MacDonald was concerned much more with proving himself as a poet than as a novelist, and wrote in the latter role largely to make money,[2] if at the same time to put over his Christian convictions in fictional guise. His novels, of which the best known—*David Elginbrod* (1863), *Alec Forbes of Howglen* (1865), *Robert Falconer* (1868) and *Malcolm* (1875)—are largely of Scottish life, sold well, especially in his later years. Yet as an author he never achieved major status; and moreover, despite the sales of his books, remained relatively poor.

Throughout his life, MacDonald suffered from a bronchial and asthmatic complaint which twice, after overwork and exposure, brought on haemoptysis and nearly killed him. He was never free of the ravages of eczema, which attacked him most fiercely in his last years. His life was punctuated by the deaths of near kin, including no less than four of his eleven children, among them Lilia Scott MacDonald, the beautiful, promising and especially beloved 'Christiana', in 1891, aged thirty-nine. However though they tried him sorely, none of these afflictions finally overthrew MacDonald's faith (see, for example, *GMDW,* pp. 475-6).

This last, and his happy marriage were the only unshakeable foundations MacDonald had in a life which was by any standards hard and frustrating. Much of

George MacDonald with his wife.

his misfortune MacDonald brought on himself, for he could have secured a living at any time had he been prepared to stifle the public expression of his unorthodoxy; and where this was not an issue, his rejection of all worldly motives filled the breach—while in America he was offered a pastorate on Fifth Avenue at a stipend of $20,000 per annum, but refused outright because he felt his motivation might be contaminated (*GMDW,* pp. 340, 459).

There was a strong mystic bent, consonant with his unworldliness, in MacDonald's character. On holiday in Switzerland in 1865, he spent all his time climbing mountains ('God's church towers') and inside steeples, and wrote to his wife, 'I am sure the only cure for you and me and all of us is getting up, up—into the divine air. I for my part choose the steeple-cure for my weariness. How will it be when I get amongst God's steeples?' (*GMDW,* pp. 348, 349).[3] Heights put him physically nearer God. He declared 'a passion for stairs', and saw life as a climb up a flight of them, 'Where death is one wide

landing to the rooms above' (ib. pp. 530, 485). Stairs occur symbolically in 'The Golden Key', *The Princess and the Goblin, Donal Grant* (1883) and *Lilith.*

All his life, MacDonald looked forward to his death and resurrection. Like Anodos in his *Phantastes,* he was convinced that a great good was coming to him. His letters of condolence ring with the certainty of future meetings. Just before the expected death of Lilia, he wrote to his wife,

> If it should please God to leave her, we shall all take care of her; if not, we shall find her soon at the farthest. The great creative love which has closed us in these heavy bodies will open the doors of our cages and let us fly free in his high liberty . . . Oh dear, what a mere inn of a place the world is! and thank God! we must widen and widen our thoughts and hearts. A great good is coming to us all—too big for this world to hold . . . (*GMDW,* p. 524; see also pp. 492, 528, 560)

None of this implied any disgust at life, nor any desire to opt out. MacDonald could never deplore a world created and sustained by his Father. But he did long for a closer meeting with him: he was as impatient as if life were God's garden-party and God were the last person to be met: 'I have all my life, I think, been attended (I would call it *haunted,* were it not that the word has the atmosphere about it of the undesired) by the feeling of a meeting at hand' (*GMDW,* p. 534). He had no fear of death, and hoped it would come to him sooner rather than later. On a voyage by yacht to Norway in 1869, he was very ill and had to stay battened under hatches in his bed while in Trondheim harbour; when the time came to move him and the hatch was opened, 'It was as if he looked out from his grave—the tall mast of the vessel rising from his cabin—that and the blue sky was all he saw—then he felt his Resurrection was come . . . It was his one spot of joy . . .' (*GMDW,* p. 396; see also p. 472). J. R. R. Tolkien is right when he says that 'Death is the theme that most inspired George MacDonald' (*Tree and Leaf* (1964), p. 59).

MacDonald was, however, often uneasy as a would-be mystic. Visionary intensity was bought at the price of narrowness; and narrowness begot in him unacknowledged tensions. He turned from his early studies in physics and chemistry absolutely, allowing science no place in the discovery of worthwhile knowledge; and in the same way he tended to reject the conscious sides of the human mind, the will and the intellect, for the unconscious imagination as the fount of true perception. Throughout his life he kept generally clear of intellectual debate, a practice in which he was assisted by his severance from the ministry and thus from established society and 'controversy, which I loathe' (*US 3,* p. 3): frockless he goes into 'The Wilderness' (so Greville entitles the chapter describing the immediate aftermath of Arundel), and there he hears few voices but his own. We are told almost nothing in Greville's biography of any meetings with scientists, philosophers or theologians of the day, and little of any literary acquaintance; where there is any, the bond is one of friendship rather than even friendly debate (as with Lewis Carroll and Ruskin), or else, in the case of the relations with Kingsley, Maurice, Emerson or Mark Twain, one of mutual admiration. MacDonald could never have had any relationship based in any degree on intellectual warfare, like that between Huxley and Kingsley. In fact, Greville tells us that in public his father fought shy of debate, and can offer as explanation only 'lest the apparent need to justify one's own opinion should outbid zeal for truth', which conveys little: if MacDonald were zealous, justifying his opinion would not come into it. Greville's quotation from Sir Henry Craik cuts nearer to the bone: this sees MacDonald as 'profuse in talk, often inspired by high imagination, but, I am inclined to think, rather uncertain about his own intellectual understanding as com-

pared with his fellows' (*GMDW,* p. 365). Greville, ever ready to justify his father, declares that this shows he was not sure how far *above* the others his mind was, whereas the point is MacDonald's inferiority complex.

In fact MacDonald illustrates some of the characteristic habits of Victorian clergy faced by Darwin—habits W. E. Houghton has described as 'evasion' and 'rigidity' (though there are more factors than Darwin behind MacDonald's possession of them). Rigidity is defined thus by Houghton, '[A] mark of the rigid mind is its adoption of extreme as well as narrow positions. If there is no effort to examine contrary theories, there is little likelihood of compromise or mediation.'[4] This may well partly explain the extremity of MacDonald's Christian Romanticism; and it may also account for what R. L. Wolff finds after examining all MacDonald's novels from 1868 onwards:

> The twenty-three novels here passed in review are all sermons, more or less. Yet we have not found in them a single new theological idea. By the time MacDonald wrote *Robert Falconer,* in 1868, he had already fully developed his conception of God, and of God's relationships to mankind, of heaven and hell, rewards and punishments . . . The critic of 1869, wishing to attack MacDonald as a theologian, had already before him all the essential texts available to the critic of 1897.[5]

The other face of this self-enclosure and intellectual uncertainty is a compensatory sense of personal election: here in particular MacDonald's Scottish and Calvinist background (however much he may have turned against the latter) stamp him unmistakably. In a letter to his father after he resigned from Arundel he wrote:

> I have no love for *any* sect of Christians as such . . . independent I mean to be, in the real sense of the word . . .
>
> . . . does not all history teach us that the forms in which truth has been taught, after being held heartily for a time, have by degrees come to be held merely traditionally and have died out and other forms arisen? which new forms have always been abused at first . . .
>
> . . . why be troubled because your son is not like other people? Perhaps it is *impossible* for him to be. Does not the spirit of God lead men and generations continually on to new truths? . . . you will not be sorry that your son cannot go with the many . . . If there is to be advance, it must begin with a few, and it is *possible* (I cannot say more, nor does modesty forbid my saying this) I may be one of the few. (*GMDW,* pp. 197-8)

Not for nothing does this sound like Bunyan's Christian: MacDonald was passionately fond of *Pilgrim's Progress*.[6] The world and his suppressed self might frame disturbing questions, but they would be pursuing a man running away with his fingers in his ears.

What we have in MacDonald is a rather nervous seer, a man who felt he ought to be a part of the world and controversy, but for reasons good and bad (and he knew them for both) did not want to be; a man who tried to do without a large part of himself and life so that his vision might remain pure. The trying is the trouble. Death may have been the most inspiring theme for MacDonald, but in more than a physical sense he found it hard to die.

MacDonald's 'faculty psychology'

For MacDonald the one road to God is out of the conscious self: 'our consciousness is to the extent of our being but as the flame of the volcano to the world-gulf whence it issues: in the gulf of our unknown being God works behind our consciousness' (*US 2*, p. 113). The self of the ego MacDonald sees as the source of evil; 'the one principle of hell', he declares, 'is—"I am my own" ' (*US 3*, p. 102). Yet this self is much less than one's true identity:

> man is dead if he know not the Power which is his cause, his deepest selfing self; the Presence which is not himself, and is nearer to him than himself; which is infinitely more himself, more his very being, than he is himself. The being of which we are conscious, is not our full self; the extent of our consciousness of our self is no measure of our self; our consciousness is infinitely less than we.[7]

To find his true self, a man must abandon his divisive consciousness and enter the unconscious tide of the universe: here the death-theme, as used for example in *Lilith,* is central; as Mr Raven tells Vane, ' "No-one who will not sleep can ever wake" ', and, ' "you will be dead, so long as you refuse to die" ' (pp. 58, 217).

What, then, of the role of the human will? MacDonald's mystic side inclines him to involuntarism: one goes to sleep, as in *Lilith,* and God takes over. Whatever a man tries to do against God's purposes is bound to fail because it is absurd, the attempt of the shadow of contingent being to defy the substance of its absolute existence; it is, to MacDonald 'a stream that cuts itself off from its source, and thinks to run on without it' or, 'the slavery of the creature who would cut his own stem from his root that he might call it his own and love it' (*US 3*, pp. 262, 91; see also 'Freedom', pp. 83-97). Lilith is told that her will is a mere ghost beside God's, ' "There is no slave but the creature that wills against its creator" ' (*Lilith*, p. 278). God is

both omnipresent—'There is no word to represent that which is not God, no word for the *where* without God in it; for it is not, could not be' (*US 3,* p. 252)—and inescapable: 'The instant a soul moves counter to the will of its prime cause, the universe is its prison; it dashes against the walls of it, and the sweetest of its uplifting and sustaining forces at once become its manacles and fetters' (*The Hope of the Gospel* (1892), p. 225).[8] Evil, from this point of view, is conceived as an eddy or backcurrent on the surface of a flood, itself borne forward by the greater flow in which it is set. Whether we will it or not (but MacDonald would say that our 'not willing' is but a truancy from our real will), we shall all go to heaven:

> He will have purity. It is not that the fire will burn us if we do not worship thus; but that the fire will burn us until we worship thus; yea, will go on burning within us after all that is foreign to it has yielded to its force, no longer with pain and consuming, but as the highest consciousness of life, the presence of God. (*US 1,* p. 31)

Thus evil has no final reality, 'What we call evil, is the only and best shape, which, for the person and his condition at the time, could be assumed by the best good', concludes Anodos in *Phantastes;* and in *Lilith,* at the other end of MacDonald's creative life, Vane says, 'I began to learn that . . . evil was only through good! selfishness but a parasite on the tree of life!' (p. 113).[9] In the novels, as has been remarked, sin tends to be treated as a fit of somnambulism.[10] And if evil goes, so too does hell: anti-Calvinist universalism is a frequent theme in MacDonald's work;[11] and Mara says in *Lilith* that the Great Shadow himself will eventually come to lie down and sleep in the house of Adam and Eve (pp. 301-2). With a position like this the orthodox notion of God's justice disappears.[12] MacDonald has been condemned as a 'benign determinist', and his universalist beliefs attacked as the products of a shallow optimism which refuses to take account of the nature of human free will;[13] but one can see how they follow from his mystic leanings.

A glance through MacDonald's theological writings however will show him frequently running clean counter to this view of him, where he stresses the importance and efficacy of human free will. Thus, 'the highest creation of God in man is his will'; '[man's] will must meet God's—a will *distinct* from God's, else were no *harmony* possible between them . . . God creates in the man the power to will His will'; 'if a man would be delivered from the evil in him, he must himself begin to cast it out'; 'We must, by a full act of the will, give ourselves altogether to righteousness'; '[God] gives us the will wherewith to will . . . but we ourselves must will the truth.'[14] MacDonald's argument is that one is only free when in God's service, that one's will only comes into being when in harmony with his, and that the choice of evil is an unreal one: thus 'Whoever will not do what God desires of him, is a slave whom God can compel to do it' (*US 3*, p. 86).[15] Clearly, one cannot have one's cake and eat it: if the choice of slavery to evil is no choice, then neither in another way is the choice of God; one is merely electing for the only course open, and it is a case of 'You may as well come quietly.'

What has happened here seems plain enough: aware that a mystical and involuntarist position is an inadequate view of man's relation to God, MacDonald has attempted to graft on to it a belief in free will which it will not take.

The 'mystic' MacDonald's attitude to the intellect, that other side of the conscious self, is similar to his view of the will. True understanding, he tells us, is unconscious, like the child's: to see properly, one must see not with the reasoning faculty but with the imagination, 'No wisdom of the wise can find out God . . . The simplicity of the whole natural relation is too deep for the philosopher . . . the child alone can understand God]' (*The Hope of the Gospel*, p. 163; see also p. 56). It is the cold self-distancing from the object which intellect involves that turns MacDonald against science:

> human science is but the backward undoing of the tapestry-web of God's science, works with its back to him, and is always leaving him—his intent, that is, his perfected work—behind it, always going farther and farther away from the point where his work culminates in revelation. (*US 3*, pp. 62-3)[16]

or again, 'To know a primrose is a higher thing than to know all the botany of it—just as to know Christ is an infinitely higher thing than to know all theology, all that is said about his person, or babbled about his work' (*US 2*, p. 236). What MacDonald is after here is mystic knowledge: for him, to know a thing aright is not to regard it from the distance of selfhood, but to become imaginatively identified with it, even to feel one's way into its being; he looks forward to the day when 'I trust, we shall be able to enter into [nature's] secrets from within them—by natural contact between our heart and theirs' (*US 2*, p. 237).

In part it is this mystic aim which is behind MacDonald's insistence on doing the truth rather than thinking about it, on obeying rather than waiting to be convinced: 'He who does that which he sees, shall understand; he who is set upon understanding rather than doing, shall go on stumbling and mistaking and speaking foolishness . . . It is he that runneth that shall read, and no other' (*US 2*, p. 119).[17] Hence the stress on work and duty: 'Work done is of more consequence for the future than the foresight of an

archangel' (ib. p. 56);[18] or again, 'With thy hands go and do thy duty, / And thy work will clear thine eyes.'[19]

Equally, however, behind these insistences lurk fears and doubts. Work, obedience, duty, anti-intellectualism—all have another side: as Houghton has shown they were methods resorted to by the Victorians to crush their intellectual and spiritual fright. MacDonald's personal involvement is given away not least by his obsession with these themes in his writings—there are few of his sermons where they do not appear in some form, especially the word 'obedience', to which he is almost pathologically addicted:[20] he is in part attacking the impertinence of his own intellect. Obedience now becomes not only a means to unconscious self-surrender, but of conscious suppression of self.

Not the least reason—apart from the fact that it is hard to jettison bits of oneself—for MacDonald's continued awareness of his intellect would have been that however much he might recommend the mystic knowing of a child it would for him as an adult (as Wordsworth's struggles testify) be an imperfectly or at best spasmodically realized ideal: he would continually be thrown out of mystic solution back on to himself and his uncertainties.

> Witness the dissatisfaction, yea desolation of my soul—wretched, alone, unfinished, without him! It cannot act from itself, save in God; acting from what seems itself without God, is no action at all, it is a mere yielding to impulse. All within is disorder and spasm. There is a cry behind me, and a voice before; instincts of betterment tell me I must rise above my present self—perhaps even above all my possible self: I see not how to obey, how to carry them out! I am shut up in a world of consciousness, an unknown *I* in an unknown world: surely this world of my unwilled, unchosen, compelled existence, cannot be shut out from him, cannot be unknown to him, cannot be impenetrable, impermeable, unpresent to him from whom I am! (*US 2*, pp. 77-8)

But perhaps an even simpler reason is that he never explains why God made men with intellects in the first place: if our intelligence is helpless to comprehend the simplest truths of nature, why then was it given to us? That he has no answer to the problem can only have added to MacDonald's uneasiness.

This uneasiness lies at the heart of his thinking on the creative imagination and its products, which, following his literary mentor Novalis, he terms 'fairy-tales'. He sees the fairy-tale in extreme Romantic terms, as a chaos, without connection, and yet at the same time insists that it should be governed by laws of self-consistency and moral responsibility.

Thus on the one side he views the workings of the creative imagination as wholly outside the control of the artist's conscious self:

> Lo, I must wait, unknowing
> What thought in me is growing,
> Until the thing to birth be brought!
>
> . . . . .
>
> I cannot say *I think*—
> I only stand upon the thought-well's brink:
> From darkness to the sun the water bubbles
>   up . . . [21]

Coleridge considered that, although begotten in the unconscious, such works did have in them the genetic strains of the organizing faculties, and hence an inherent unity; but since he sheerly divided will and intellect from the imagination, MacDonald sees them as totally patternless and chaotic. The same is true for him of the external world of nature: if the highest form of perception is via the imagination so defined and isolated, then nature is seen most truly when it is seen as a chaos devoid of any governing law. The triple equation of fairy-tale, imagination and nature is seen in the lengthy quotation from Novalis with which MacDonald prefaces *Phantastes*: Novalis sees his ideal of literature, 'Erzählungen ohne Zusammenhang, jedoch mit Association, wie Träume' ('stories without coherence, yet associational, like dreams'), as realized in the fairy-tale—

> Ein Mährchen ist wie ein Traumbild ohne Zusammenhang. Ein Ensemble wunderbarer Dinge und Begebenheiten, z.B. eine Musikalische Phantasie, die harmonischen Folgen einer Aeolsharfe, die Natur selbst.
>
> . . . hier tritt die Zeit der Anarchie, der Gesetzlosigkeit, Freiheit, der Naturstand der Natur, die Zeit vor der Welt ein.[22]

> (A fairy-tale is like a dream-picture without coherence, a collection of wonderful things and occurrences, e.g. a musical fantasy, the harmonic sequences of an Aeolian harp, nature itself.
>
> . . . this is where the time of anarchy comes in, of lawlessness, freedom, the natural condition of nature, the time before the world.)

Conversely, the ideal is imposed on reality: elsewhere he says, ' "Alles ist ein Mährchen." '[23]

For Novalis the images thrown out thus chaotically by the unconscious imagination have no deeper source than the human psyche, whether individual or collective. MacDonald, however, parts company here. He maintains the operations of the imagination are the workings of God in man: thus,

> If we . . . consider the so-called creative faculty in man, we shall find that in no *primary* sense is this faculty creative. Indeed, a man is rather *being thought* than *thinking*, when a new thought arises in his mind. (*ADO,* p. 4)[24]

'Unser Leben *ist* kein Traum—aber es soll und wird vielleicht einer werden' ('Our life is no dream, but it should and will perhaps become one'): MacDonald quotes this from Novalis[25] at the end of both *Phantastes* and *Lilith;* but to it he adds (at the end of the latter) an affirmation which puts his thought in another dimension—

> Man dreams and desires; God broods and wills and quickens.
>   When a man dreams his own dream, he is the sport of his dream; when
>   Another gives it him, that Other is able to fulfil it.

For MacDonald, the imagination, nature and the fairy-tale are, by being founded on God, founded on the *ne plus ultra* of meaning, law and coherent pattern: their chaotic appearance is not the final truth about them.[26] But because God's utterances are *ipso facto* beyond the human understanding, his creations must appear chaotic to all but the mystic or the child—and even they will not see very much, 'For in everything that God has made, there is layer upon layer of ascending significance.' In this way MacDonald can have it both ways—can be simultaneously 'chaotic' and responsible. Unfortunately in practice he was often to find this more than he could allow himself.

There then is one side of the picture—chaos, imagination and mystical meanings reign supreme. For the other, we can turn to the analogies MacDonald draws (in his essay on the fairy-tale, 'The Fantastic Imagination' (1893)) between the fairy-tale and music. He declares that the 'chaotic' fairy-tale is 'very like the sonata' (*ADO,* p. 318), because it works on the reader's emotions rather than his intellect, moving him though he does not understand finally what it means. 'A fairytale, a sonata, a gathering storm, a limitless night, seizes you and sweeps you away: do you begin at once to wrestle with it and ask whence its power over you, whither it is carrying you?' (*ADO,* p. 319). His thought on this subject becomes a trifle shaky, however, when a little later on in the same essay he goes on to liken the workings of the fairy-tale on the reader to the random play of the wind on that familiar Romantic instrument, the Aeolian harp (*ADO,* p. 321). On the one hand, structured music which holds the listener rapt from start to finish; on the other, haphazard twangings which make him twitch spasmodically, or what MacDonald calls the 'broken music' of fairy-tale that goes 'for a firefly that now flashes, now is dark, but may flash again' (ADO, pp. 322, 321).

Both these musical analogies imply that the reader responds involuntarily, that he is passive before the heart-pluckings of the fairy-tale. In fact MacDonald is by no means certain that he does. Thus it is that he sees his ideal reader as a child or a mother, because they do not ask questions: 'If any strain of my "broken music" make a child's eyes flash, or his mother's grow for a moment dim, my labour will not have been in vain' (ADO, p. 322).[27] But suppose the reader is a querulous academic?—'The best way,' answers MacDonald, 'is not to bring the forces of our intellect to bear upon it, but to be still and let it work on that part of us for whose sake it exists' (ADO, pp. 321-2). And if the reader finds himself unable to do even this? Presumably he has to silence himself,

> obedience alone places a man in the position in which he can see so as to judge that which is above him. In respect of great truths investigation goes for little, speculation for nothing; if a man would know them, he must obey them. Their nature is such that the only door into them is obedience. (ADO, p. 72)

In the end it seems that the reader's intellect is not to be stilled by the fairy-tale so much as suppressed voluntarily by himself. It can be seen, then, that MacDonald was fully aware of the persistence of intelligence in the reader. In fact it is with just such a reader that in his essay he has a debate. As we read this, and find the rather shrill MacDonald increasingly wavering between the definite and the indefinite in the fairy-tale, we begin to realize that the 'straw man' he uses may represent part of himself—that he, too, is partly the reader he tries to answer.

For instance, to his claim that the fairy-tale and music are identical in their workings, the 'straw man' asserts all too aptly, ' "But words are not music; words at least are meant and fitted to carry a precise meaning!" ' In reply, MacDonald says that words may convey meaning, but they can also be used to carry emotion, 'Have they only to describe, never to impress?' If this meant, 'Is it not possible for a word simultaneously to convey a meaning and provoke a feeling?', one might agree, but in fact MacDonald is at this point close to asserting that words can operate at a purely emotive or impressive level without any meaning, like music: 'That may be strong in colour which has no evident outline' (ADO, pp. 318, 319). Whether words can ever do this is surely very questionable: as Deryck Cooke says in his The Language of Music,[28] 'the difference [between literature and music] is that a word awakens both an emotional response and a comprehension of its meaning, whereas a note, having no

meaning, awakens only an emotional response' (p. 26).[29] Earlier MacDonald is much more conventional, when he can speak of the reader of fairy-tale using his intellect to draw meaning from it (ADO, pp. 316-17), or of words being used to move as well as to define, to have depth as well as length and breadth (ADO, pp. 318-19). Indeed he keeps to no one position throughout: here the fairy-tale operates like a sonata, there like the wind on an Aeolian harp; now it has meaning, now it is without one; here the sonata evokes the same feelings in its hearers, 'mind may approach mind, in the interpretation of a sonata, with the result of a more or less contenting consciousness of sympathy' (ADO, p. 318), and there, on the next page, no man feels the same as another, 'The law of each is in the mind of its composer; that law makes one man feel this way, another man feel that way. To one the sonata is a world of odour and beauty, to another of soothing only and sweetness.' If the whole essay is considered, it will be seen that in fact it falls into two parts: in the first MacDonald insists on the conformity of the fairy-tale to law, consistency and moral principles (up to p. 316), and in the second he speaks of its musicality and indefiniteness; the split expresses the division in his own creative purpose.

No doubt MacDonald might have objected to this critique that his thought was not meant to fit into any systematic scheme, 'We are far too anxious to be definite and to have finished, well-polished, sharp-edged systems . . . To no system would I subscribe' (GMDW, p. 155);[30] but one can justifiably retort that he has at least intended to give a systematic account of the workings of the imagination, and moreover, that the very provision by him of a theoretic background for the comprehension of works supposedly incomprehensible is a contradiction in terms.[31] To the larger inconsistencies of MacDonald's aesthetic thinking, then, we now turn.

How, for example, does the artist manage to view the world as a chaos without connection? Does such a vision come to him in a passive state, as it does to the Wordsworthian child, or does it require effort on the perceiver's part to see imaginatively, as it did for the adult Wordsworth and Coleridge? MacDonald may repeat Novalis' dictum, 'Die Welt ist ein Universaltropus des Geistes—Ein symbolisches Bild desselben' ('The world is a universal metaphor of the spirit—a symbolic picture of it'), as 'All that moves in the mind is symbolized in Nature . . . the world is a sensuous analysis of humanity',[32] but in fact for him such a mirror-relation does not precede, but follows the operation of the imagination which, working as a lamp, adjusts Nature until she is made to imitate mind,

> the world around [man] is an outward figuration of the condition of his mind . . . God has made the world that it should thus serve his creature . . .

The man has but to light the lamp within the form: his imagination is the light, it is not the form. Straightway the shining thought makes the form visible, and becomes itself visible through the form. (*ADO,* p. 5)[33]

The implied ease of neither the 'has but to' nor the 'Straightway' can remove the element of man selecting and ordering his experience, even if this process is unconscious. Clearly, the imagination operates by some sort of principles; moreover, they are human and not divine principles - it is 'the man' who does the lighting and focusing.

Nor is this all. As we saw above, MacDonald could revel in Novalis' 'Naturanarchie'[34] so long as this seeming chaos was really the expression of incomprehensible divine order and pattern—on the lines of St Paul's 'the natural man receiveth not the things of the Spirit of God: for they are foolishness unto him: neither can he know them, because they are spiritually discerned' (1 Cor. ii, 14). But when we find him distinguishing between imagination and fancy in terms of law versus lawlessness, we sense his reluctance to allow even an apparently chaotic art. The imagination is to be dutiful, responsible and deliberate,

> Licence is not what we claim when we assert the duty of the imagination to be that of following and finding out the work that God maketh. Her part is to understand God ere she attempts to utter man. Where is the room for being fanciful or riotous here? It is only the ill-bred, that is, the uncultivated imagination that will amuse itself where it ought to worship and work. (*ADO,* p. 12; cf. pp. 272-3, 279-80)

'Following and finding out' suggests a mode of conscious inquiry, especially when, as here, it is directed to a particular end (i.e. tracing God's image): where now are the surface truths of nature which no probing will reveal—'Nature . . . exists primarily for her face, her look, her appeals to the heart and the imagination, her simple service to human need, and not for the secrets to be discovered in her and turned to man's farther use' (*US 2,* pp. 235-6)? And where now the abolition of human responsibility that has been seen in MacDonald's thought so far? On that side the poet seemed a passive Aeolian harp, played on by God and nature; on this MacDonald can ask, 'Is not the *Poet,* the *Maker,* a less suitable name for him than the *Trouvère,* the *Finder?*' (*ADO,* p. 20).

Perhaps aware of some of these contradictions, MacDonald allows that imagination and fancy—for him the less responsible faculty—co-operate in artistic creation (though the latter is given an inferior role); but in so doing makes one more statement at variance with his view of art and nature as chaos,

beauty is the only stuff in which Truth can be clothed; and you may, if you will, call Imagination the tailor that cuts her garments to fit her, and Fancy his journeyman that puts the pieces of them together, or perhaps at most embroiders their button-holes. Obeying law, the maker works like his creator; not obeying law, he is such a fool as heaps a pile of stones and calls it a church. (*ADO,* p. 315)

Obeying law? The Romantic position he elsewhere adopted was founded on hatred of the definite, the systematic and the fixed: whence, therefore, this 'law'? 'Heaps a pile of stones and calls it a church'? But MacDonald has been adamant that the chaos of nature is chaos necessarily to us because nature is one of God's incomprehensible churches: surely his example should justify others? The asperity of the tone of these passages reveals his uncertainty.

What can MacDonald mean by 'law', when elsewhere he can maintain the essential disconnectedness of both nature and art, and man's inability to grasp the basic laws of his existence? In part he is referring to what we now call the 'inner consistency of reality',

> His [the artist's] world once invented, the highest law that comes next into play is, that there shall be harmony between the laws by which the new world has begun to exist; and in the process of his creation, the inventor must hold by those laws. The moment he forgets one of them, he makes the story, by its own postulates, incredible. To be able to live a moment in an imagined world, we must see the laws of its existence obeyed. Those broken, we fall out of it. (*ADO,* pp. 314-15)

All this makes perfect sense from H. G. Wells, but from a man who can also maintain that scientific and human laws of any kind have no ultimate validity, and that it is the business of art to found itself on just that degree of validity—namely, God—from such a man these statements make no sense at all. If nature is, to human eyes, a chaos, how can art, which imitates it, be anything but a chaotic swirl itself? 'Imagine,' says MacDonald, 'the gracious creatures of some childlike region of Fairyland talking either cockney or Gascon!' Yet such a yoking-together of heterogeneous ideas is the basis of much poetry, and, thinking of the comic juxtaposition of the mundane and the magical in E. Nesbit's work, can be utilized by tellers of fairy-tales also.

MacDonald's retreat into the human consciousness goes one step further when he asserts that moral laws cannot be invented in a work of art: physical laws can be invented, provided, as has been seen, they thereafter remain unbroken; but moral laws must be the same in art as they are in real life:

The laws of the spirit of man must hold, alike in this world and in any world he may invent. It were no offence to suppose a world in which everything repelled instead of attracted the things around it; it would be wicked to write a tale representing a man it called good as always doing bad things, or a man it called bad as always doing good things: the notion itself is absolutely lawless. In physical things a man may invent; in moral things he must obey—and take their laws with him into his invented world as well. (*ADO*, p. 316)[35]

Here one senses MacDonald ringing down a Victorian curtain on his own unorthodoxy.[36] The passage in itself is small, but it is symptomatic of the core of didacticism that is found in much of his work.

To sum up: the nearer MacDonald gets to his mystic and unconscious ideal, the more strongly he is pulled back by his conscious mind. We can now turn to see the effect of this tension on his fairy-tales; beginning with their 'unconscious' aspects.

The unconscious in MacDonald's fairy-tales

All of MacDonald's fairy-tales are set in landscapes which are symbols of mind, and are concerned with mental perception; and their Fairy Lands are invariably in the 'sub'-or 'super'-conscious.

Thus *Phantastes* is partly about its protagonist Anodos' efforts to lose his shadow of intellect and self-consciousness, which kills the mystery of Fairy Land for him; and when finally he has done so, he is fully unconscious—which explains why at the end, after his 'death', he becomes one with nature in the form of a flower or a cloud. The structure and texture of the whole story have a highly disconnected character which is meant—so much is shown by the quotations from Novalis at the beginning and at chapter-heads in the text—to imitate the nature of a dream. MacDonald, however, does not say that Anodos dreams his faërian experiences. It does seem that this is the case for much of the story, for Anodos finds himself in Fairy Land when he wakes one morning (suggesting that he is not awake): he is still in his room, but a stream is running through it from his overflowing basin, the furniture is covered with living ivy and clematis, the branches and leaves designed on the curtains are now part of a living tree and the walls have disappeared (*Phantastes*, pp. 9-11). Fairy Land has invaded his home, about which we hear no more until the end, after Anodos has 'died' with 'a pang and a terrible shudder' out of his cloud-being and back into this world, where 'I became once again conscious of a more limited, even a bodily and earthly life' (ib. p. 317). His sisters, however, in the first meeting we have with any other mortals, tell him that he has been away twenty-one days, and that on the morning of his disappearance they found the floor of his room flooded, while 'all that day, a wondrous and nearly impervious mist had hung about the castle and grounds' (ib. p. 320). Anodos, then, went to Fairy Land in cold fact. But that is partly MacDonald's point: he experienced reality as a dream; he went to Fairy Land, and yet Fairy Land is a vision; the central idea is the quotation from Novalis at the head of the last chapter, 'Unser Leben ist kein Traum, aber es soll und wird vielleicht einer werden.'

In *Lilith*, the central character Vane enters Fairy Land through a strange mirror-apparatus in the attic of his mansion. He refers to this garret as 'The brooding brain of the building', and asks, ' "If I know nothing of my own garret . . . what is there to secure me against my own brain?" ' (p. 17).[37] The symbol of the stair upwards as 'our own "secret stair" up to the wider vision' (*GMDW*, p. 482),[38] is clearly intended in this story, as it is in the two 'Curdie' books (*The Princess and the Goblin* and *The Princess and Curdie*), and at the end of 'The Golden Key'. Not only stairs and buildings, but doors, too, operate as symbolic entrances to the unconscious in *Lilith*. The Mr Raven Vane meets in Fairy Land tells him, ' "the more doors you go out of, the farther you get in!"'" and, ' "The universe is a riddle trying to get out, and you are holding your door hard against it" ' (pp. 13, 59). In this story again, Fairy Land is a realm found only in the subconscious; and the texture of the tale, despite the clear narrative, suggests a dream, in the way the images lunge at and fade from the eye. The end, however, is not like that of *Phantastes*: nobody appears to tell Vane that he was absent from his home for any length of time; and he is even left in doubt as to whether he has returned at all: 'Can it be that that last waking also was in the dream? that I am still in the chamber of death, asleep and dreaming, not yet ripe enough to wake?' (*Lilith*, p. 349).

There are other modes in which MacDonald's fairy-tales give primacy to the unconscious imagination. In the journey of the children Mossy and Tangle to the heavenly land 'whence the shadows fall', 'The Golden Key' describes the pilgrimage of the creative imagination to its source and sustainer. In *At the Back of the North Wind* the mystic lady of the North Wind visits the child-hero Diamond only when he is asleep and, as we shall see further, at random, as in a dream. The building imagery in the 'Curdie' books suggests the same theme. Certain ideas are recurrent. One of these is that seeing fairies or Fairy Land depends on seeing imaginatively. In *Lilith*, Mr Raven tells Vane that if he saw aright he would perceive Fairy Land existing bi-locally[39] with his real home, and vice versa. In that land he shows him a tree which, he informs the unbelieving Vane, ' "Stands on the hearth of your kitchen, and grows nearly straight up its chimney" '. He tells him that a rosebush is growing close by a lady playing the piano in the breakfast-room, and that some large heads of wild hyacinth ' "are inside the piano, among the strings of it, and give that peculiar sweetness to her playing" '; and later, ' "There! I smell Grieg's Wedding March in the quiver of those rose-petals!'" (pp. 25-7; cf. p. 210). Fairy Land is never far off in MacDonald's fantasies. In 'The Golden Key', Mossy can see its forested skirt from his aunt's house: 'It came close up to his great-aunt's garden, and, indeed, sent some straggling trees into it.'[40] The idea is always that you do not have to go anywhere to find Fairy Land: you simply have to see better what is before you, or as Mr Raven says, ' "Home is ever so far away in the palm of your hand, and how to get there it is of no use to tell you" ' (*Lilith*, p. 59). Thus North Wind comes to Diamond, and, in *The Princess and the Goblin,* Irene's strange 'grandmother' lives in the house of the princess. In the 'Curdie' books, the boy-miner Curdie has to see with the eyes of the child-like imagination before this mystic lady appears to him; and this theme of perception is symbolized by his hand which, after it has been purged in the lady's fire of roses, can through a handshake with another person tell Curdie what kind of beast-self the other man's soul is making him (unseen by unimaginative eyes) become.[41]

Granted this imaginative perception, what is thus seen will depend on the health of the soul's subconscious eye. In *The Princess and Curdie,* the old lady appears in the mines to Curdie and his father Peter as a beautiful woman, but tells them that their 'image' of her is quite different from the one the wicked see:

'For instance, if a thief were to come in here just now, he would think he saw the demon of the mine, all in green flames, come to protect her treasure, and would run like a hunted wild goat. I should be all the same, but his evil eyes would see me as I was not.'

When Curdie asks her why she does not appear as the old lady he saw her as the previous night, she replies, ' "Shapes are only dresses, Curdie, and dresses are only names. That which is inside is the same all the time." '[42] The mystic lady in *At the Back of the North Wind* says this also. Again, she appears to Diamond as a fair lady, but to a wicked nurse who ill-treats a baby, she appears as a wolf; the baby does not see the wolf-aspect, but the nurse does, ' "for that is what is growing to be her own shape inside of her" '.[43]

Perception in MacDonald's fairy-tales thus appears to border on the solipsistic. This is nowhere better seen than in comparing his use of the theory of spiritual (d)evolution with Kingsley's. With both, the theory implies that 'your soul makes your body, just as a snail makes his shell';[44] which is to say that if one lives a wicked life, one will take on a hierarchically low and ugly animal form after death, and that only gradually, through spiritual purification, will one as-

cend by a series of reincarnations through the ladder of creation to angelic status.[45] However, Kingsley was empiricist enough to believe that this law of spiritual (d)evolution could be scientifically demonstrated; and when his fictional humans die, they take on bodies of creatures—madrepore, crab, mylodon, ostrich, seabird or ape—which could be found in any zoology text-book; and if not so found (as in the case of water-babies, whose existence Kingsley spends much time trying to prove possible) ought to be. But where the bodies made by souls in Kingsley's work would thus most of them have received Darwin's seal of recognition, those in MacDonald's would have provoked querulous tones even from Pliny. The body of the dog Lina in *The Princess and Curdie* is an expression of the soul's wickedness when the creature was human, and is described as

[a] horrible mass of incongruities. She had a very short body, and very long legs made like an elephant's, so that in lying down she kneeled with both pairs. Her tail, which dragged on the floor behind her, was twice as long and quite as thick as her body. Her head was something between that of a polar bear and a snake. Her eyes were dark green, with a yellow light in them. Her under teeth came up like a fringe of icicles, only very white, outside of her upper lip. Her throat looked as if the hair had been plucked off. It showed a skin white and smooth.[46]

Forty-nine (the figure is MacDonald's) other 'devolved' creatures equally absurd in appearance feature in this book. The exemplars of spiritual evolution—for example, the air-fish and aëranths of 'The Golden Key'[47]—can be equally fanciful and extra-biological in their bodily representations of spirit. This carries the theory of soul making body a stage further than Kingsley: where he bows to the limiting reality of the natural order, MacDonald acknowledges only the freedom of the mind's creations. (Indeed, on practically every issue, even on those—such as their universalism, or their views of nature as chaos—which apparently unite them, Kingsley and MacDonald form a fascinating contrast, almost a Victorian *summa*.)

The oppositions in MacDonald's fantasy

There is little uniformity among the fairy-tales, and it is almost impossible to generalize about them. This can be seen from MacDonald's idea of 'chaos', which manifests itself in varying degrees and kinds. *Phantastes* is perhaps the most disconnected. There is no constant context: we are moved in its Fairy Land from comic flower-fairies who tease cats, to female statues that can be brought to life by song; from subterranean goblins or *Elementargeister* to a story of a loveless planet; from the Hoffmannesque tale of Cosmo the painter,[48] who has a hopeless love-affair via a magic mirror, to a submersible island cottage with four mystic exits; from a Spenserian account of knightly warfare with giants, to a Druidical religious sacrifice in a forest; and from a Poe-inspired fairy palace[49] to a self-begotten tower of pride. The story ends with an account of the hero's 'posthumous' metamorphoses into a flower and a cloud before he returns to the real world from which he set forth. In this respect the whole book appears to have been created in a series of dislocated imaginative bursts.

The Greek name, Anodos, of the hero, in its meaning of 'pathless' or 'having no way' is certainly apposite.[50] He starts with a longing to enter Fairy Land, but no particular reason for it. His little sister is reading him a fairy-tale and at the end Anodos says he would like to get there, but does not know how; and the next night, when he meets a fairy and gazes into her eyes, he is driven to look out of the window of his castle, and stands 'gazing on a whole heaven of stars, small and sparkling in the moonlight',

> Below lay a sea, still as death and hoary in the moon, sweeping into bays and around capes and islands, away, away, I knew not whither. Alas! it was no sea, but a low fog burnished by the moon. 'Surely there is such a sea somewhere!' said I to myself. A low sweet voice beside me replied—
>
> 'In Fairy Land, Anodos.' (*Phantastes*, pp. 7-8)

When at the end of the book Anodos tells us that 'I, who set out to find my Ideal, came back rejoicing that I had lost my Shadow' (321), a far more specific purpose than we have felt is implied.

Without real motive Anodos simply 'happens upon' many of his adventures. He follows a fairly constant eastward direction in Fairy Land,[51] though he neither says nor seems able to say why. At one point, after he has eaten strange nuts and fruits, 'I seemed to know better which direction to choose when any doubt arose' (54), but later he refers to 'my custom since I entered Fairy Land, of taking for a guide whatever I first found moving in any direction' (118-19), and speaks of 'Fairy Land, where one does very much as he pleases' (113). Many of his actions have no reason behind them. When in a dell he finds an alabaster statue of a woman, he removes the moss from it 'By an inexplicable, though by no means unusual kind of impulse' (58); and similarly 'uncaused' is the Orphean song he then utters to wake her up (60-4). Finding a bath in a fairy palace he later comes to, he is 'Led by an irresistible desire' (127) to plunge in; and in a hall of statues in the same palace, another Orphean urge drives him to sing (185-6). 'I must act and wander' (51), he says, and indeed there is something compulsive in many of his actions.[52] Some destinal force behind this is hinted: at one cottage he comes to, the wife tells him that ' "no one comes here but for some reason, either known to himself or to those who have

charge of him" ' (20); and at another, ' "I have heard, that, for those who enter Fairy Land, there is no way of going back. They must go on, and go through it. How, I do not in the least know" ' (90). However, this providential action is not made sufficiently evident in the story as a whole.

Nevertheless there are certain very real 'connective' elements in *Phantastes*. Quite early in the story, Anodos acquires some purpose in his adventures when he discovers the White Lady of the alabaster and falls in love with her. After he has wakened her, she flees from him, and much of the rest of the tale—the episode of the devouring Alder Maiden (whom he mistakes for her), the wakening of her statue in the fairy palace, his underground pursuit of her, the magic door of Sighs in the island cottage he visits (through which he sees her in the arms of another knight), his later self-denying squiredom to this knight, and his posthumous return to bless their union—is his search for her. Other parts of the narrative become linked when, early on, Anodos acquires his Shadow in the cottage of an ogress: as he says, 'Everything, henceforward, existed for me in its relation to my attendant' (99).[53] The Shadow withers faërian wonder (100-2), and, as his pride, shuts him in the Tower of Self (277-9).

The Shadow and White Lady themes are, moreover, linked: they are different aspects of possessiveness. The Shadow is the evil conscious self which seeks to have, and destroys in having, as Anodos breaks a little girl's harmonious crystal globe by laying hands on it (104-7); and his experience with his attendant teaches Anodos not to demand a return of his love for the White Lady. At the end, he announces,

> I knew now, that it is by loving, and not by being loved, that one can come nearest the soul of another; yea, that, where two love, it is the loving of each other, and not the being beloved by each other, that originates and perfects and assures their blessedness. I knew that love gives to him that loveth, power over any soul beloved, even if that soul know him not, bringing him inwardly close to that spirit; a power that cannot be but for good; for in proportion as selfishness intrudes, the love ceases, and the power which springs therefrom dies. Yet all love will, one day, meet with its return. All true love will, one day, behold its own image in the eyes of the beloved, and be humbly glad. This is possible in the realms of lofty Death. (316; cf. 287-8)

This rather unusual theme draws together many parts of the story into a scheme of definite meaning.

Thus, while *Phantastes* has many chaotic or connectionless features, it is clear that in many respects MacDonald tries to unify the story. One of the misfortunes of this is that once he lets his—and our—

organizing intellect into part of his tale, we begin to wonder why it has its disconnected form at all. More than this, since large parts of it are so made available to our understanding, we are encouraged to try to interpret the whole. And this is precisely what MacDonald says we cannot and should not try to do with the fairy-tale.

In sum, one would go so far as to say that the chaotic element of the story has so frightened MacDonald that he has been driven to impose meaning on it. He has done his own interpreting; he has wrung as much conceptual significance out of his tale as he can. It is almost as if he first imagined *Phantastes* and then applied his intellect to it—two acts by different areas of his mind. It is not surprising that the products of the two—image or motif, and significance—co-exist rather uneasily. The themes he has put into his story in fact start only half-way through the book, making the split even more marked.[54]

MacDonald's uncertainty in *Phantastes* is mirrored in the discordant modes of the style. One is 'purple' and highly emotive,

> a gush of joy sprang forth in my heart, and overflowed at my eyes. Through my tears, the whole landscape glimmered in such bewitching loveliness, that I felt as if I were entering Fairy Land for the first time, and some loving hand were waiting to cool my head, and a loving word to warm my heart. Roses, wild roses, everywhere! (112)

or again, when Anodos feels he may have lost his Shadow,

> as the hope arose within me, the sun came forth from a light fleecy cloud that swept across his face; and hill and dale, and the great river winding on through the still mysterious forest, flashed back his rays as with a silent shout of joy; all nature lived and glowed; the very earth grew warm beneath me; a magnificent dragon-fly went past me like an arrow from a bow, and a whole concert of birds burst into choral song. (125)[55]

Doubtless it was to this sort of thing that C. S. Lewis was referring when he spoke of the 'over-sweetness picked up from Novalis'.[56]

Interlaced with this emotive style there is a much more forensic and pompous one, which seems to be present to supply the kind of sober accuracy of sensation that the other lacks, but which in so doing becomes simply bleak. Thus, in his account of the lady in alabaster, Anodos tells us,

> What I did see appeared to me perfectly lovely; more near the face that had been born with me in my soul, than anything I had seen before in nature or art. The actual outlines of the rest of the form were so indistinct, that the more than semi-opacity of the alabaster seemed insufficient to account for the fact; and I conjectured that a light robe added its obscurity. (59)

The first part is a would-be musician of the emotions, and the second a police witness. Arriving in a hall in the fairy palace, Anodos observes that its roof

> was of a pale blue, spangled with constellations of silver stars, and supported by porphyry pillars of a paler red than ordinary.—In this house (I may remark in passing), silver seemed everywhere preferred to gold; and such was the purity of the air, that it showed nowhere signs of tarnishing. (126)

Here we have the Aberdeen chemistry graduate talking. Again, when Anodos is swimming in the mystic bath, the floor of which is (vaguely) paved with 'all kinds of refulgent stones, of every shape and hue', we are told, 'I rose to the surface, shook the water from my hair and swam as in a rainbow, amid the coruscations of the gems below seen through the agitation caused by my motion' (126, 127): first the poet's rainbow, then Newton's. In *Phantastes* objects are seen both as magic or mystic things, and merely as things: MacDonald seems unable to find balance or naturalness, and the reason is simply that he is in two minds over his material.

None of his other fairy-tales shows anything like the 'chaos' of *Phantastes*. *Lilith,* which is the most like it in form, is wholly organized by the theme of death and resurrection. It uses the four Dantean levels of allegory—the literal level in which Vane the protagonist enters Fairy Land and has a series of amazing adventures before returning to 'real' life; the moral or tropological level, by which Vane must die out of his old self into a new; the allegorical, insofar as this death and resurrection repeats Christ's redemptive act (seen here primarily in terms of humility); and the anagogical plane, whereby resurrection is the entry of mankind into Heaven—a level which, in keeping with MacDonald's universalism, includes the salvation of the Great Shadow, or Hell himself. There are elements in the story which fall short—one is thinking here particularly of the 'Little Ones' with all their nauseating precocity—but even these have an at least thematic relation (the development from childishness to child-likeness)[57] to the whole. It is true that Vane 'happens upon' Fairy Land in almost the same way as Anodos, but as soon as he gets there, Mr Raven appears and invites him to lie down and sleep in his hall of the dead—an invitation which, though Vane at first refuses it, he comes in the end to accept. Vane's activities are clearly governed and foreseen in a way that those of Anodos are not. Death in the story in part means the abandonment of the personal will: and on Vane's failure, until he finally submits, to achieve anything with the 'chaotic' self-will he asserts against Mr Raven, this fact is throughout a unifying ironic commentary.

At the Back of the North Wind,[58] which has a certain disconnectedness, is the story of a London cab-driver's son, Diamond, who becomes the friend of the mystic lady of the North Wind, and is taken by her on a number of adventures, including a visit to the country, which is in fact the fringes of heaven, at her 'back'. North Wind comes to Diamond as fitfully as the weather she is: sometimes it is the day following a previous visit, sometimes months elapse before she reappears, and Diamond has time almost to forget her existence. Nor are her visits governed by any single aim. When she first comes, he tries to follow her, but she abandons him suddenly for no apparent reason on the lawn of the house next door. Next time, she takes him flying with her over London, but when he sees a poor ragged girl being blown about in the lonely streets, and asks North Wind to help her, the lady refuses, and Diamond has her set him down so that he can do so. On the following visit, North Wind takes him out in a storm and leaves him in a cathedral while she goes on to sink a ship; and on the next, he travels with her to the North Pole, from where he goes to the country at her back. Thereafter she does not return to him till late in the book. In the interim, Diamond once has a dream about star angels; and the little girl he found in the streets, Nanny, who is now his friend, dreams that she has been taken into service by the man in the moon.

What we have in *At the Back of the North Wind* is virtually the structural imitation of the action of an Aeolian harp: just as the wind visits it at random, and as its music has no obvious pattern, so too with both the incidence and the nature of North Wind's appearances. It is this that gives the book its power, makes its texture so curiously realistic. This far its 'chaotic' quality lives up to MacDonald's theoretic statements about the fairy-tale.

Yet this chaos is a part more of structure than of meaning. We know where we are for most of the time—in the perfectly normal world of Victorian London. And as for the sections with North Wind, we know what she is and represents. Although she tells Diamond,

> 'I don't think I am just what you fancy me to be. I have to shape myself various ways to various people. But the heart of me is true. People call me

by dreadful names, and think they know all about me. But they don't. Sometimes they call me Bad Fortune, sometimes Evil Chance, sometimes Ruin; and they have another name for me which they think the most dreadful of all' (pp. 363-4)

she is denying not that she may be Fortune or Pain or Death, but that she is those things seen only in evil aspect. Knowing what she symbolizes, we know what is going on when Diamond meets her. Indeed, we are not very often 'at a loss' so far as our understanding of *At the Back of the North Wind* is concerned: the dreams of the star angels and of the man in the moon are not very clear in meaning, but have only a small part to play.

Further, the 'anarchic' structure of the book has certain limitations. While, in terms of the randomness of North Wind's visits, and the variety of Diamond's adventures with her, it is a virtue, we must feel that the supernatural episodes are so divided from the natural as to suggest that the whole book is the result of two quite separate imaginative acts. In metaphysical terms, the two worlds do interpenetrate, inasmuch as we are shown that the sorrows of this life are divinely ordained for our supernatural good; and, since North Wind exists and operates within the 'real' world, they are also to some extent physically linked. The latter world, however, never becomes transfigured, as North Wind is only occasionally present to Diamond (much of the book describes his normal life in London without much reference to her). Perhaps some explanation for this lies in the fact that the 'real' setting of this book is largely the city, London, and MacDonald was more able to find God (through his sub-vicars) immanent in country rather than town;[59] so great is the pressure of urban reality that Diamond all but forgets about North Wind when she is away, and thinks to the very end that she may have been an illusion. Whatever the reason, the two realms are split, and the book does not strike the reader as the result of a single creative act: into one side has gone the realistic, novel-writing MacDonald, and into the other the student of Faërie.

Most of MacDonald's other fairy-tales have a single story or causal sequence of motive and act that binds together all the episodes in them. *The Princess and the Goblin* (1872), is the tale of a princess, Irene, who lives in a castle on a mountain which is honeycombed with the (separated) mines of goblins and men. The goblins scheme to kidnap Irene and make her the wife of their prince, Harelip, or, alternatively, to flood the human mines; but in both aims, thanks to the help of the boy-miner Curdie and of Irene's mystical 'grand-mother', who lives at the top of the castle (and whose presence is known only to the princess) they are foiled. In the sequel to this book, *The Princess and Curdie* (1883), the rule of Irene's 'king-papa' is being sapped by wicked men, and he himself slowly murdered by

An illustration for MacDonald's The Light Princess.

poisonous drugs; Irene's grandmother sends Curdie, with a band of grotesque creatures as assistance, to the capital city of Gwyntystorm to save the kingdom. *The Wise Woman* (1875)[60] describes how a lady with magic powers takes two girls, one rich, one poor, but both wicked, from their corrupt family environments to her strange cottage on the heath, where she tries with mixed success to give them a moral education. 'The Golden Key', one of the short fairy-tales first published in *Dealings with the Fairies* (1867), is about two children who find a golden key at the end of a rainbow, and, with the help of yet another magical lady, set out to find the keyhole—which eventually they do, and pass through into the heavenly land, 'whence the shadows fall', for which they have been longing. Each of these tales is bound together under a single plot-motif which directs and informs almost every incident. In structural terms, therefore, there is no 'chaos'.

Nor, in the case of *The Princess and Curdie* and *The Wise Woman,* is there at the level of meaning either.

Both stories are heavily didactic, with frequent and ponderous authorial intrusions designed to force the significance of each episode on the reader. Of Curdie's state at the beginning of the former book, we are told that 'he was getting rather stupid—one of the chief signs of which was that he believed less and less in things he had never seen', and MacDonald gives us the theoretic background to this,

> There is this difference between the growth of some human beings and that of others: in the one case it is a continuous dying, in the other a continuous resurrection. One of the latter sort comes at length to know whether a thing is true the moment it comes before him; one of the former class grows more and more afraid of being taken in, so afraid of it that he takes himself in altogether . . .

and later, 'The child is not meant to die, but to be forever freshborn' (pp. 12, 12-13). From this ethical straitjacket the story rarely escapes; the symbolism of spinning-wheels, rose-fires, doves and buildings is more laboured, and the good-evil distinction much more rigidly enforced than in *The Princess and the Goblin.* Yet even *The Princess and Curdie* has areas which are not covered by any explicit or obvious meaning. *The Wise Woman,* however, is set wholly in a moral frame. Here the supernatural wise woman and her magic cottage are not interesting in and for themselves as Fairy Land is in *Phantastes:* the whole of the story is fixed on the spiritual tuition of two girls, one Rosamund, a bad-tempered princess, and the other Agnes, a spoilt country-girl, and the wise woman is purely the stimulus for their reform. Thus there is nothing very mysterious or supernatural at the centre of this story. Throughout there is an intrusive control on the part of the narrator which crushes all the independence out of the fictional world. Here is a typical passage from the book; it occurs when Agnes has finished cleaning out the cottage of the wise woman while she is away:

> By this time her old disposition had begun to rouse again. She had been doing her duty, and had in consequence begun again to think herself Somebody. However strange it may well seem, to do one's duty will make anyone conceited who only does it sometimes. Those who do it always would as soon think of being conceited of eating their dinner as of doing their duty. What honest boy would pride himself on not picking pockets? A thief who was trying to reform would. To be conceited of doing one's duty is then a sign of how little one does it, and how little one sees what a contemptible thing it is not to do it. Could any but a low creature be conceited of not being contemptible? Until our duty becomes to us common as breathing, we are poor creatures.[61]

The meaning of the entire story is made as obvious as this. We know the whys and wherefores of both the plot and the symbols of the story: manner and matter are alike without any dislocated or mysterious elements. This is the extreme of MacDonald's desertion of his theory of the imagination.

This is not to say that *any* abandonment of the theory necessarily produces inferior work: far from it. *The Princess and the Goblin,* 'The Golden Key' and one or two others of the shorter fairy-tales probably comprise the best of MacDonald's 'fairy' writing; he himself said of the first while it still had four months to run in serial form in *Good Words for the Young,* 'I know it is as good work of the kind as I can do, and I think will be the most complete thing I have done'.[62] In all of these stories there is no *structural* chaos—no breakdown of direction in the narrative, no jostling of disparate contexts. On the other hand, it is perhaps impossible to extract a connected meaning or 'allegory' from them: they are full of hints, but once one tries to capture these, the story either escapes or fades, like the radiant 'bird-butterfly' that, when caught by Vane in *Lilith,* loses its light and becomes 'a dead book with boards outspread' (pp. 62-3). We will take *The Princess and the Goblin* as illustration of this, since two writers have given it fairly detailed allegorical interpretation, and we can see how far their readings are borne out by the textual evidence (the narrative has already been briefly outlined above).

Readers have not been slow to point out the mental symbolism of the castle, with the old lady living at the top, Irene on the lower floors and the goblins tunnelling in the caverns beneath. G. K. Chesterton remarked, 'There is something not only imaginative but intimately true about the idea of the goblins being below the house and capable of besieging it from the cellars. When the evil things besieging us do appear, they do not appear outside but inside' (preface to *GMDW,* pp. 10-11). And C. S. Lewis, 'he [MacDonald] is quite as well aware as the moderns that the conscious self, the thing revealed by introspection, is a superficies. Hence the cellars and attics of the King's castle in *The Princess and the Goblins* [sic].'[63] Maud Bodkin seems to be recalling MacDonald's story in her *Archetypal Patterns in Poetry,*[64] where, speaking of the fountain-imagery of the subconscious in Coleridge's 'Kubla Khan', she mentions 'images of caverns and underground castle-vaults, goblin-tenanted, which I gathered from an absorbed reading of fairy-tales' (p. 114). All these are fairly vague and general accounts, and one feels that they rightly glance at some half-caught truth.

But when there is a greater degree of specificity, it is a different matter. R. L. Wolff declares that the goblins suggest

> the greedy, cunning side of our own human nature tunneling away in the secret subterranean

chambers of the subconscious and always threatening to take possession of the castle of our minds, unless we, like Curdie, remain on our guard against them, with the aid of our higher selves, which dwell like grandmother in the lofty towers of our personalities [65]

but seems to have forgotten that the hero, Curdie himself, spends much of his time 'tunneling away in the secret subterranean chambers of the subconscious'—the mines; more, that if one is considering the 'higher selves' as the purer, then one must draw the inevitable inference from the fact that the goblin mines run higher up in the mountain than those of Curdie and the human miners. 'Greedy' and 'cunning' hardly seem apt epithets for the goblins: they simply want to take the princess as hostage and marry her to the goblin prince Harelip so that ' "a peace, all to the advantage of the goblin kingdom, will be established for a generation at least" ' (p. 91). As for being cunning—even though MacDonald himself so terms them (5)—the story shows Curdie more so than they. Their plans are over-ponderous, with all the strengths and weaknesses of the bureaucratic mind; here they are in full pomposity,

> 'The information which the worthy Glump has given us . . . might have been of considerable import at the present moment, but for that other design already referred to, which naturally takes precedence. His Majesty, unwilling to proceed to extremities, and well aware that such measures sooner or later result in violent reactions, has excogitated a more fundamental and comprehensive measure, of which I need say no more.' (90)

Throughout the story, the goblins are given a comic treatment (for instance they can be routed if their opponents stamp on their feet) which prevents any too-ready extraction of serious moral lessons from the story. Wolff's account is weak in other respects. The goblins have no wish to take possession of the castle: they invade it with the intention of seizing the princess and leaving again. Again, on Irene's function in the story, a story whose title alone suggests that she is one of the important characters, Wolff is silent. 'With the aid of our higher selves'—for much of the story Curdie helps himself, and where he is helped by the grandmother, he for most of the time believes it is not she but lucky accident that has helped him. And the 'threatening to take possession of the castle of our minds' might stand up better if Curdie lived in the castle, which he of course does not.

Another Freudian account of this fairy-tale has similar weaknesses: that of Tony Tanner, 'Mountains and Depths—An Approach to Nineteenth-Century Dualism'. Tanner explores a Cartesian dualism between mind and body in Kingsley's *The Water-Babies* and MacDonald's story, in terms of a split between 'heights' and 'depths', the heights being the life of the spirit, and the depths that of the body and our earthy, realistic desires. Thus he sees the princess as being involved with both, since she lives half-way down a mountain while her father lives at the top and the goblins at the foot.[66] This partly distorts the story. The king's palace 'was built upon one of the mountains' (1), but this need not necessarily have been at the top, and it was built moreover on a different mountain from the one on which Irene lived. Again, the goblin mines must in places run higher up the mountain than Irene's castle or else they could never have flooded it (though it is true that they live below the surface where she does not).[67] But Tanner, having made his arbitrary distinction, is ready to apply the theory of 'id' versus 'ego' versus 'super-ego': the fact that the goblins, who used to live on the earth, have become uglier during their sojourn beneath it, shows

> The inflexible banishment of base urges by an imperious conscience—this description fits the story just as it fits the age in which it was written. But banishment is not extermination: the 'id' will out . . . And in the temporary absence of the king (the super-ego perhaps) the goblins lay two plots.

Let us consider this account in detail. First, the goblins were not banished: they went voluntarily underground after having had heavy taxes laid on them (3-4). 'Banishment is not extermination': is Tanner trying to say that the imperious conscience could only banish and not exterminate?—if so, one wonders what he makes of the almost total destruction of the goblins at the end of the story. 'The "id" will out': but the goblins do not in fact wish to come out, and are quite happy with their subterranean kingdom. The king is not temporarily absent: rather Irene is so from him, as she is being brought up in the country after her mother's death. Why should the king be any more the 'super-ego' than Irene's grandmother? And it is nowhere said that the goblins lay their plots because the king is away.

It is this sort of distortion that underlies all of Tanner's interpretation: of the second of the goblins' plots, he says, 'The palace of reasonable harmonious living (the image is employed in *Othello*) is threatened by a flood of murky underground water, the pressure of which has been building up since the goblins were banished underground—the schematic location of the hostile parties could hardly have clearer implications.' The image of 'The palace of reasonable harmonious living' may have been employed in *Othello* but one cannot see why that should make it apply here. The underground water is at no time said to be murky; we are told that when it burst into the open, the water was

'turbid', and that it 'glimmered fierce and foamy through the night' (304, 305); and even if the water had appeared 'murky' at that time, this would suggest no more than that its dirt was picked up during its flood, and not from its original stable condition in the mountain. In fact it might just as well be the baptismal and hygienic symbol that Tanner goes on to find it to be in *The Water-Babies*. Nor is it true that the pressure of this water (which comes from the natural reservoirs of the mountain (305)) has in any way altered from what it was before the goblins went down the mines; it is not its pressure, but goblin engineering, that turns it to a flood.

For the episode where the dirt Irene gathers in rescuing Curdie from the goblins in the mines is washed off her in a bath given her by her grandmother (233-5), Tanner has this explanation: 'The magic lady throughout the book represents a cleansing agency, a purifying power capable of eradicating all traces of any grimy involvements with the goblins.'[68] But it was not involvement with the goblins (or in terms of Tanner's allegory, submergence in base desires) that made the princess dirty; it was rescuing Curdie from mines which were as much his province as that of the goblins: that is, the princess got dirty through nobility and not sordidity.

Clearly Tanner's schematization will not do. Yet, as C. S. Lewis has said, 'no story can be devised by the wit of man which cannot be interpreted allegorically by the wit of some other man'.[69] No doubt one *could* strain past the difficulty of there being two spiritually different inhabitants of the 'id' or mines in MacDonald's story by saying, for example, that they represent the war of base with higher desires in natural man, a war that cannot finally be won by the latter without the help of supernatural grace from Christ (grandmother) mediated by the soul (Irene; though the name comes from the Greek meaning 'peace'). This sort of reading would, however, be artificial: the meaning would be tailored to, rather than begotten naturally by, the story. And here the correlative of Lewis' point must be insisted upon, 'We ought not to proceed to allegorize any work until we have plainly set out the reasons for regarding it as an allegory at all.'[70] The image of the castle and the mines which MacDonald has used in this story is very suggestive, but it does no more than suggest: and it cannot be earthed by any fixed interpretation without forfeiting the energy of the story—or, as MacDonald puts it, 'Caught in a hand which does not love its kind, [the fairy-tale] will turn into an insignificant, ugly thing, that can neither flash nor fly' (*ADO*, p. 321).[71] One of the sources of this power-in-suggestivity may be the fact that the image used is archetypal. But that the book does not invite the fixity of explication can readily be proved by contrasting it with its companion volume *The Princess and Curdie*, which, as we have seen, does so.

We can follow through the contrast between the allegorical and the symbolic in MacDonald's treatment of the incidental symbols within *The Princess and the Goblin* itself. One or two of them have an arranged significance (not that this is crudely done), but in the main they are left mysterious. Taken as a whole they perfectly endorse MacDonald's claim, 'A fairytale is not an allegory. There may be allegory in it, but it is not an allegory' (*ADO*, p. 317).[72]

Thus on the one hand the pigeons Irene's grandmother keeps could be symbols of the Holy Ghost; we are told that they fly back and forth ' "over the great sea" ' (115). Their eggs, on which the lady lives, might therefore represent the food of grace or even be eucharistic symbols. The significance of the ball of thread that she spins for the princess is clearer still. The thread is brought by the pigeons from the far-off land, and is made from ' "spider webs—of a particular kind" ' (ib.). During one of Irene's visits, the old lady tells her that there is a week's work left in the spinning of the thread before it will be ready (ib.): and before Irene leaves her, she puts the princess on trial to come back to her in a week's time as proof that she believes she is real (120). The thread, which is completed when Irene returns, thus signifies faith. This is further suggested when it is contrasted with the ordinary string which Curdie uses to guide himself back from his forays into the goblin mines: this string is on one occasion disturbed, and Curdie thereby falls into the hands of the goblins, but Irene's thread (which Curdie cannot feel) leads her straight to his rescue; and the chapters describing these incidents are called respectively 'Curdie's Clue' and 'Irene's Clue', thus emphasizing the contrast intended.

Other symbols are more obscure. The old lady has a moon-like lamp which can shine through the walls of the house and help to guide Irene back to her grandmother. But ' "it is not everybody can see it" '. What Irene sees is ' "not the light of it only—but the great round silvery lamp itself, hanging alone in the great open air high up" ' (150). If we call the lamp 'divine illumination', then it would seem that the source—God?—of this is also to be seen. If we call it the imagination (the old lady tells Irene that if the light were to go out, ' "you would fancy yourself lying in a bare garret, on a heap of old straw" ' (120), then it would fit both as a Romantic analogue (the lamp of creative perception) and as an illustration of MacDonald's idea that the creative unconscious has God working somewhere at its root. Yet not all the details support either reading. Why is it that the lamp is so well concealed that it is not seen more than five times in a hundred years?—there are surely more Christians and imaginative artists than that in such a length of time! (There is, incidentally, no hint of authorial pessimism in this book.)

As for the magic ointment with 'the sweetest odour . . . like that of roses and lilies' (117), with which the grandmother heals Irene's hand, or the fiery rose which cleans mud from a dress—these resist interpretation. In *The Princess and Curdie*, the flaming roses become, as the healing fire in which the sick king is laid (2nd ed. (1888), pp. 232-3), a symbol of sacrifice or of Christ's redemptive blood; but in the earlier book their meaning is more submerged (144ff.). Why, for instance, are they ' "too hot for [Irene] yet" ' (149)? Then there is the magic bath which her grandmother gives the princess, a 'large silver bath' of 'clear cool water', in which Irene 'saw no bottom, but the stars shining miles away, as it seemed, in a great blue gulf'; in it,

> When she opened her eyes, she saw nothing but a strange lovely blue over and beneath and all about her. The lady and the beautiful room had vanished from her sight, and she seemed utterly alone. But instead of being afraid, she felt more than happy—perfectly blissful. And from somewhere came the voice of the lady, singing a strange sweet song, of which she could distinguish every word; but of the sense she had only a feeling—no understanding. Nor could she remember a single line after it was gone . . .
>
> How long she lay in the water, she did not know. It seemed a long time—not from weariness, but from pleasure. (233, 234)

MacDonald is fond of symbols of baths: Mossy and Tangle in 'The Golden Key' have to immerse themselves in one belonging to the Old Man of the Sea, and Anodos in *Phantastes* frequently takes to the water, as for instance in the bath at the Fairy Palace, which beneath the surface appears like an ocean (pp. 126-8). These baths may in part be uterine symbols; but clearly there is much that is less comprehensible about them.[73] Perhaps the most puzzling symbol of all in *The Princess and the Goblin* is the fire-opal ring. The thread given to Irene by the lady is fastened at one end to this ring, which, when she is in danger, the princess is to take off and place under her pillow before following where the thread leads with her ring finger. The princess compares the stone in the ring to those in her grandmother's crown, and the old lady replies, ' "The stone in your ring is of the same sort—only not so good. It has only red, but mine have all colours, you see." ' When Irene asks what to say when her nurse Lootie asks her where she got the ring, her grandmother tells her, ' "*You* will ask *her* where you got it" ' (154), and in due course this strange prediction comes to pass:

> When the princess woke the next morning, her nurse was bending over her.
>
> 'How your ring does glow this morning, princess!—just like a fiery rose!' she said.

'Does it, Lootie?' returned Irene. 'Who gave me the ring, Lootie? I know I've had it a long time, but where did I get it? I don't remember.'

'I think it must have been your mother gave it you, princess; but really, for as long as you have worn it, I don't remember that ever I heard,' answered her nurse.

'I will ask my king-papa the next time he comes,' said Irene. (164)

This contradictory situation defies analysis, even if the likeness of the ring to 'a fiery rose' awakens thought. Her father, when questioned, tells Irene that the ring once belonged to her mother, and when the princess, who does not know that her mother is dead, asks why it is not her mother's now, the king replies, ' "Because she's gone where all those rings are made" ' (166).

If the symbolism in *The Princess and the Goblin* is only intermittently clear, that in 'The Golden Key' is almost wholly opaque. Both fairy-tales alike show clear, well-linked and structured plots with inner meanings which are by contrast disconnected (or impossible to allegorize) and randomly suggestive. The story in 'The Golden Key' of the search by Mossy and Tangle for the land 'whence the shadows fall' may be a broad containing allegory of the journey of the soul towards heaven, but the mysterious symbols and events and the mystic character of the journey itself hit us at a level beyond the powers of rationalization. As one strange image follows another: the golden key itself, the strange owl-headed fish with rainbow-wings that leads Mossy and Tangle to the old lady in the forest, the progressively 'older' men of the Sea, the Earth and the Fire, the last of whom is in fact a baby, the inexplicably different journeys of the two searchers— as we experience these, our critical and interpretative faculties are progressively silenced until we come involuntarily to follow MacDonald's prescription for reading a fairy-tale, 'The best way . . . is not to bring the forces of our intellect to bear upon it, but to be still and let it work on that part of us for whose sake it exists' (*ADO,* pp. 321-2).

Nevertheless it is now clear that in general MacDonald's theoretic statements about the chaos of fairy-tale are not absolutely realized in practice. He is not prepared to create works which are dislocated both in structure and in meaning, in form as well as content. If there is 'formal' chaos, as in *Phantastes,* he offers a clear organizational significance or interpretation of it; and vice versa. Always at the ready, too, is a willingness to drop both aspects of dislocation, as we see in *The Princess and Curdie* and in *The Wise Woman*. The reader, of course, is more likely to object to organized meaning, which imprisons response, than to ordered narrative, which does not, and this may explain why, say, *The Princess and the Goblin* is felt to be a better work of art than *Phantastes*; though this is perhaps also to be accounted for by the fact that the first seems to have been born of one consistent act of the imagination (the meaning incarnate in the story), where the latter appears made from two acts, the initial imaginative one and a subsequent intellectual one which is at war with the first. The ideal of the dream-like chaos of fairy-tale—one which, incidentally, its originator Novalis did not follow to the hilt in the frequently allegorical *Heinrich von Ofterdingen*—remained for MacDonald an ideal. He could not give what it asked of him: it pictured the world of fantasy as one in which anything could happen, a series of random events and images which would too readily expose its creator to the charge of irresponsibility, however much he might know that there was truth and order in the concealed heart of it; and that his conscious, 'intellectual' side could not bear.

Several critics, however—C. S. Lewis, followed by Auden and MacNeice—claim that all that we have noted so far in MacDonald's work does not affect what is for them the true character of his fantasies: their power as myths.[74] They believe that what is important is the bare sequence of events and images: anything beyond this—for them particularly the literary style, but also more generally whatever is personal about the work— is simply to be ignored for that which, as Lewis puts it,

> is in some ways more akin to music than to poetry—or at least to most poetry. It goes beyond the expression of things we have already felt. It arouses in us sensations we have never had before, never anticipated having, as though we had broken out of our normal mode of consciousness and 'possessed joys not promised to our birth'. It gets under our skin, hits us at a level deeper than our thoughts or even our passions, troubles oldest certainties till all questions are re-opened, and in general shocks us more fully awake than we are for most of our lives.

Clearly, predisposed as they are to ignore the persona of the author for a level below (or above) consciousness, these critics are in a sense MacDonald's ideal readers: they will not ask questions, will be untroubled by authorial uncertainties, and will be seized and carried away by the fairy-tale as MacDonald hoped. Thus Lewis can maintain that 'myth', of which he considers MacDonald to be the greatest modern creator, 'does not essentially exist in *words* at all', but purely as a sequence of events and images independent of form or articulation:

> In poetry the words are the body and the 'theme' or 'content' is the soul. But in myth the imagined events are the body and something inexpressible

is the soul: the words, or mime, or film, or pictorial series are not even clothes—they are not much more than a telephone. Of this I had evidence some years ago when I first heard the story of Kafka's *Castle* related in conversation and afterwards read the book for myself. The reading added nothing. I had already received the myth, which was all that mattered.[75]

It is however worth recalling that in his essay on the fantastic imagination MacDonald himself was concerned with the way *words* worked on the reader (if images and events came into it too, this was not to the exclusion of language). Again, he loved the peculiarly verbal medium of poetry and writing in it as well as fantasy. One should also consider that he revised his work continually; and Greville emphasizes his 'devotion to accuracy in form and polish' (*GMDW*, p. 539).[76]

The evidence of the fantasy, too, makes it hard to deny some part at least of the character of MacDonald's fairy-tales to the language in which they are written. One must doubt, for example, that where the language of a story is weak, the mythic power of that story will be unimpaired; or, to put it more generally, it is unlikely that where the author's imagination is not excited by his material his reader will, unless he is C. S. Lewis, entirely discount this. A look at a typical passage from *Phantastes* will show this more clearly: this is Anodos' description of the library he finds in the fairy palace, but the weakness is not attributable to Anodos—

> The library was a mighty hall, lighted from the roof, which was formed of something like glass, vaulted over in a single piece, and stained throughout with a great mysterious picture in gorgeous colouring. The walls were lined from floor to roof with books and books: most of them in ancient bindings, but some in strange new fashions which I had never seen, and which, were I to make the attempt, I could ill describe. All around the walls, in front of the books, ran galleries in rows, communicating by stairs. These galleries were built of all kinds of coloured stones; all sorts of marble and granite, with porphyry, jasper, lapis lazuli, agate, and various others, were ranged in wonderful melody of successive colours. Although the material, then, of which these galleries and stairs were built, rendered necessary a certain degree of massiveness in the construction, yet such was the size of the place, that they seemed to run along the walls like cords. Over some parts of the library, descended curtains of silk of various dyes, none of which I ever saw lifted while I was there; and I felt somehow that it would be presumptuous in me to venture to look within them. But the use of the other books seemed free; and day after day I came to the library, threw myself on one of the sumptuous

eastern carpets, which lay here and there on the floor, and read, and read, until weary. (pp. 130-1)

The roof was 'something like glass': in what way did it appear to differ? 'A great mysterious picture in gorgeous colouring' conveys little. What is meant by 'ancient bindings' or by the 'strange new fashions'?—ineffabilities such as 'were I to make the attempt, I could ill describe [them]' do not help. 'All kinds of . . . all sorts of': inspiration seems to have deserted MacDonald here. For the various stones there is no particularity, and they simply appear as a list from the Romantic geologist's handbook (this is a habit which bedevils poor-class fantasy); and at the end of it MacDonald gives up—'and various others'. 'Wonderful melody of successive colours' does not convey much (Huysmans is rather better at this sort of thing in *À Rebours*). 'Although the material, then' is a curious intrusion of the pompous building contractor, and the 'then' introduces the quite inappropriately argumentative; 'rendered necessary a certain degree of massiveness in the construction' continues this alien bureaucratic tang. Yet suddenly, we come upon a vivid touch: these heavy galleries ran along the walls 'like cords'; for an instant the whole place comes to life, and the colossal size of it is before us. Nebulosity, however, then returns: 'some parts', 'silk of various dyes', 'sumptuous eastern carpets'. MacDonald's imagination is so far subdued that he can produce the repetition of 'presumptuous' and 'sumptuous' two lines apart. It seems fair to say that the vagueness of the style here must remove power from the scene: if it does not excite MacDonald or Anodos very much, why should it affect us? This passage is, as we said, typical of *Phantastes:* there are occasional vivid touches in the book, like the hideous Ash and Alder trees, but the whole is poorly realized. When MacDonald said 'Let fairytale of mine go for a firefly that now flashes, now is dark, but may flash again' (*ADO*, p. 321), he was referring to the effect on his readers, but the remark could as well be applied to the effect of his material on his own imagination.[77]

Actually, in MacDonald's more successful fantasies—*The Princess and the Goblin* and 'The Golden Key', for instance—the material is felt and realized powerfully, because the linguistic medium is much less ornate and self-conscious:[78] it is designed to point beyond itself, in the way of the story of Cosmo that Anodos reads in the library of the fairy palace:

> It glowed and flashed the thoughts upon the soul with such a power that the medium disappeared from the consciousness, and it was occupied only with the things themselves. My representation of it must resemble a translation from a rich and powerful language, capable of embodying the thoughts of a splendidly developed people, into the meagre and half-articulate speech of a savage tribe. (*Phantastes*, pp. 145-6)[79]

The 'medium disappeared': ideally it should carry one so far and then drop away, like a rocket-stage. The account at the end of 'The Golden Key' when Mossy and Tangle are in the cave of the seven pillars of the rainbow, and find the lock for Mossy's golden key, illustrates this:

> It turned in the lock to the sounds of Aeolian music. A door opened upon slow hinges, and disclosed a winding stair within. The key vanished from his fingers. Tangle went up. Mossy followed. The door closed behind them. They climbed out of the earth; and, still climbing, rose above it. They were in the rainbow. Far abroad, over ocean and land, they could see through its transparent walls the earth beneath their feet. Stairs beside stairs wound up together, and beautiful beings of all ages climbed along with them.
>
> They knew that they were going up to the country whence the shadows fall.
>
> And by this time I think they must have got there.

The words, and the way they are used, are not intrusive. Understatement seems the aim. But then, that is the point: there is an art in concealment as much as in display. The simplicity of the language, and the straightforward and consistently direct manner in which the story is told, makes the whole far more moving and powerful than it would otherwise have been. If the tale had been written in the idiom of *Phantastes* it would have been shorn of its strength. Thus one cannot really use the bare 'pattern of events' as the sole basis of any mythopoeic nature MacDonald's fairy-tales may have: it is rather a pattern of events or images described in a certain manner. MacDonald's failures—and successes—as an artist in a linguistic medium are not to be other than wilfully ignored. The success of the myth cannot be viewed independently of the form of the work: the contradictions we have already seen in MacDonald must make themselves felt.

The higher consciousness

Even though the 'mythopoeic' critics are wrong to ignore the aspects of the fairy-tales that they do, there is one sense in which the picture we have assembled of MacDonald is lacking. We have been examining his fantasies largely from the point of view of how far they are open to, invite, or are given explanation, but those areas of them which have proved beyond comprehension have not been shown to be *necessarily* so— that is, mysterious because divine in origin. So far their obscurity could as well come from the depths of MacDonald's own mind as from the creative mind which, as he saw it, thinks us all. If the former is the case, their chaos will lack the justification MacDonald gave it and be suited to interpretation only in Freudian or Jungian terms; and the experiences of the charac-

ters will have no more than self-begotten reality. One is driven therefore to attempt an answer to the question: what proof have we that the obscurity of these fantasies stems not from a merely human unconscious mind, but from a divine source?

The problem is of course a very real one for MacDonald and for his characters, because of the stress on the mental basis of landscapes and perception, and the fact that all contact with the supernatural is via the unconscious or dreaming mind. Diamond frequently debates North Wind's reality with her, but ends 'more thoughtful than satisfied'.[80] The whole issue is put by Vane at the close of *Lilith:*

> In moments of doubt I cry,
>
> 'Could God Himself create such lovely things as I dreamed?'
>
> 'Whence then came thy dream?' answers Hope.
>
> 'Out of my dark self, into the light of my consciousness.'
>
> 'But whence first into thy dark self?' rejoins Hope.
>
> 'My brain was its mother, and the fever in my blood its father.'
>
> 'Say rather,' suggests Hope, 'thy brain was the violin whence it issued, and the fever in thy blood the bow that drew it forth.—But who made the violin? and who guided the bow across its strings? Say rather, again—who set the song birds each on its bough in the tree of life, and startled each in its order from its perch? Whence came the fantasia? and whence the life that danced thereto? Didst *thou* say, in the dark of thy own unconscious self, 'Let beauty be; let truth seem!' and straightway beauty was, and truth but seemed?'
>
> Man dreams and desires; God broods and wills and quickens.
>
> When a man dreams his own dream, he is the sport of his dream; when Another gives it him, that Other is able to fulfil it. (pp. 349-50)

Yet, at the last, it is still, 'I wait; asleep or awake, I wait.'

Let us consider an idea particularly developed by C. S. Lewis and at least latent in MacDonald's work. Certain images in life and art—not necessarily the same ones for everybody—can awaken extraordinarily powerful longings in the perceiver. Thus far Romantic *Sehnsucht* or 'spiritual yearning', as we see it in the quest of Novalis' Heinrich for the 'blue flower'. But Lewis goes further: the object of this longing, he says, can be identified as much as we like with things of a merely earthly category—say 'sublimated eroticism', 'beauty worship' or plain 'escapism'—but we know it is not these, but 'a desire for something that has never actually appeared in our experience'. 'Do what [we] will, then, we remain conscious of a desire which no natural happiness will satisfy'.[81] That longing is for heaven. 'The dialectic of Desire', Lewis claims, if 'faithfully followed, would retrieve all mistakes, head you off from all false paths, and force you not to propound, but to live through, a sort of ontological proof'.[82]

The next move is to say that such *Sehnsucht* is God talking to us directly. It is not only that we are calling for God, but that he is calling for us: or, as MacDonald puts it, 'the upstretched . . . meets the downstretched hand' (*ADO*, p. 72).[83] This mystic call is awakened by certain images, or patterns of images (for Lewis, story or myth is 'a net whereby to catch something else'[84]). But there is no pantheistic confusion: the images are wholly in God, but he is not wholly in them; hence the incarnational formula used by Charles Williams and Lewis, 'This also is Thou: neither is this Thou'.[85] Yet, this allowed, the experience of such images in life or in literature is one of a Real Presence. Or, to put it electrically, the image acts as a conductor between the two poles of longing to produce a linking spark. With such conductors, Lewis felt *Phantastes* to be filled, and indeed the book partly converted him, inasmuch as his imagination was 'baptise[d]' when he read it:[86] 'never had the wind of Joy blowing through any story been less separable from the story itself. Where the god and the *idolon* were most nearly one there was least danger of confounding them'.[87]

MacDonald himself speaks of *Sehnsucht* and relates it to a divine source,

> hints come to me from the realm unknown;
> Airs drift across the twilight border land,
> Odoured with life; and as from some far
>   strand
> Sea-murmured, whispers to my heart are
>   blown
> That fill me with a joy I cannot speak,
> Yea, from whose shadow words drop faint
>   and weak:
> Thee, God, I shadow in that region grand.[88]

Certain images in his experience seemed to him so especially designed to raise a longing for heaven that he believed they were particular manifestations of God. Jewels and flowers did this for him as well as stairs.[89] In a passage on the last, Greville sums up, in his 'halting words', a forty-year-old conversation with his father,

To him a symbol was far more than an arbitrary outward and visible sign of an abstract conception: its high virtue lay in a common *substance* with the idea presented. Perhaps this accounts for certain Roman Catholics claiming that he was never really outside the pale of the Church . . .

. . . He would allow that the algebraic symbol, which concerns only the three-dimensional, has no *substantial* relation to the unknown quantity; nor the 'tree where it falleth' to the man unredeemed, the comparison being false. But the rose, when it gives some glimmer of the freedom for which a man hungers, does so because of its *substantial* unity with the man, each in degree being a signature of God's immanence . . . [He] knows her for his sister the Rose, of spiritual substance one with himself. So may even a gem, giving from its heart reflections of heavenly glory, awaken like memory in ourselves and send our eyes upwards. So also may we find co-substance between the stairs of a cathedral-spire and our own 'secret stair' up to the wider vision. (*GMDW*, pp. 481-2)[90]

(It can be seen from this how much more mystical is MacDonald's approach to sacramentalism than that of Lewis).

One can thus say that MacDonald had a Christianized view of *Sehnsucht*. That he would not have intellectualized it as Lewis does leaves unaltered the probability that his fantasies are intended to work on the reader in the way that Lewis describes. The only theoretic obstacle to the success of the method is the reader's subjectivity (not everyone will respond to a given image of desire): and this MacDonald perhaps circumvents through his use of archetypal rather than 'algebraic' symbolism (as we saw, for example, in *The Princess and the Goblin*).

The images in MacDonald's fantasies may thus work sacramentally, and the reader may have a form of religious experience through them in a mode akin to Vane's reaction to the stones in the gate of heaven: 'I saw, not the intent alone, but the intender too; not the idea alone, but the imbodier present, the operant outsender' (*Lilith*, p. 347). However, at this point, in a work of literary criticism, one can do no more than shyly point to the possibilities. If one were to name the fantasy that most immediately suggests a sacramental working, it would be 'The Golden Key', which is itself the story of a journey to find the source of desire-provoking images. Some may feel it is more effectively present in the greater fluidity of verse, as in the song Diamond's mother reads to him[91] or the one Irene's grandmother sings while she spins in *The Princess and Curdie*.[92] MacDonald surrounds the latter poem with distracting cries of *O altitudo!*—

Oh, the sweet sounds of that spinning wheel! . . .
But for the voice that sang through it all, about
that I have no words to tell. It would make you
weep if I were able to tell you what it was like, it
was so beautiful and true and lovely;

yet even these self-conscious intrusions cannot bar
the effect of the poem itself—which the reader is now
left to contemplate,

> The stars are spinning their threads,
> And the clouds are the dust that flies,
> And the suns are weaving them up
> For the time when the sleepers shall rise.
>
> The ocean in music rolls,
> And gems are turning to eyes,
> And the trees are gathering souls
> For the day when the sleepers shall rise.
>
> The weepers are learning to smile.
> And laughter to glean the sighs;
> Burn and bury the care and guile,
> For the day when the sleepers shall rise.
>
> Oh, the dews and the moths and the daisy
> red,
> The larks and the glimmers and flows!
> The lilies and sparrows and daily bread,
> And the something that nobody knows!

To sum up: MacDonald is what one might call a would-
be 'exclusive' modern fantasist: he wants to have to
do with the world only as a house full of mystic
symbols, and with only the unconscious and imaginative side of the mind. But though he tries to shut out
the conscious selves of science and law, intellect and
will, they keep coming back to interrupt the proceedings.

His problem is also one of distance: though in terms
of location his fairylands may coincide with our world,
their disconnected nature and the unconscious state of
mind required to perceive them aright are conditions
of being so sheerly different from those taken to be
normal that, whether in grafting readily intelligible structure or meaning on to them, MacDonald is drawn to
make links with that normality.

We will find a different form of the problem of 'ex-
clusiveness' in fantasy when we come to consider
Tolkien [in a later chapter]; and of that of 'distance'—
with the fantastic world as a remote place rather than
a supranormal condition of being or perception—in the
work of Peake. It should however be pointed out that
it is, as was seen with Kingsley (and will be with
Lewis), apparently no easier to be 'near' or 'inclusive'
in fantasy: where mental and mimetic comprehensive-
ness is the aim, one side tends to devour the others.

Abbreviations

*ADO A Dish of Orts, Chiefly Papers on the Imagina-
tion, and on Shakespeare* (Sampson Low, 1893). All
the essays, save that on 'The Fantastic Imagination'
(pp. 313-22) were first published in *Orts* (1882)

DE David Elginbrod, 3 vols. (Hurst & Blackett, 1863)

GMDW Greville MacDonald, *George MacDonald and
his Wife* (Allen & Unwin, 1924)

Lilith Lilith, A Romance (Chatto & Windus, 1895)

*Phantastes Phantastes, A Faerie Romance for Men
and Women* (Smith, Elder, 1858)

RF Robert Falconer, 3 vols. (Hurst & Blackett, 1868)

US 1 Unspoken Sermons, (Strahan, 1867)

US 2 Unspoken Sermons, Second Series (Longmans,
Green, 1885)

US 3 Unspoken Sermons, Third Series (Longmans,
Green, 1889)

Notes

[1] See *GMDW* for the standard, if biased, biography; to
be supplemented by Greville MacDonald, *Reminiscences
of a Specialist* (Allen & Unwin, 1932), and Roderick
F. McGillis, 'The Fantastic Imagination: The Prose
Romances of George MacDonald', University of Reading PhD. thesis (1973), ch. i.

[2] G. M. Smith, the publisher of *Phantastes,* told
MacDonald that the popularity of the book was
unrepeatable, and that 'Nothing but fiction [by which
he meant novels of 'real life'] pays' (*GMDW,* p. 318).

[3] See also *GMDW,* pp. 349-51; *RF,* III, 6-7.

[4] Houghton, *The Victorian Frame of Mind* (Yale Univ.
Press, 1957), pp. 161-2; on 'dogmatism', 'rigidity'
and 'evasion', see chs. vi, vii and pp. 413-24.

[5] Robert Lee Wolff, *The Golden Key: A Study of the
Major Fiction of George MacDonald* (Yale Univ. Press,
1961), p. 305.

[6] See *GMDW,* pp. 470, 501-5, which describes how
the MacDonald family enacted and went on tour with
a dramatization by Mrs MacDonald of the second part
of Bunyan's work—MacDonald playing Greatheart—
'in the summers between 1879 and 1887 all over
England and even in Scotland' (p. 501). On the persistence of Calvinist habits of thought in MacDonald,
see e.g. his own admission in *US 3,* p. 145.

[7] *The Hope of the Gospel* (Ward, Lock, Bowden, 1892), p. 37.

[8] Cf. *The Diary of an Old Soul* (privately printed by Mr Hughes of Beaufort St, Chelsea, 1880), 20 January: 'Who thinks to thwart thy great laws' onward throng, / Is as a fly that creeps his foolish way / Athwart an engine's wheels in smooth resistless play.' Compare Kingsley (above, p. 41).

[9] Cf. *Alec Forbes of Howglen* (Hurst & Blackett, 1865), II, 242.

[10] Thomas Gunn Selby, 'George MacDonald and the Scottish School', *The Theology of Modern Fiction* (Kelly, 1896), p. 154.

[11] See particularly *RF*, I, ch. xii; and also *US 1*, pp. 48-9, 213-14.

[12] See e.g. 'Justice', *US 3*, pp. 109-62.

[13] Selby, 'George MacDonald and the Scottish School', p. 136. See also pp. 140-2, 154 ff.; and S. Law Wilson, 'The Theology of George MacDonald', *The Theology of Modern Literature* (Clark, 1899), pp. 288 ff. Wolff, *The Golden Key*, pp. 256-62, argues that MacDonald 'motherized' the universe because his own mother died when he was a child.

[14] *The Hope of the Gospel*, pp. 13, 14, 20, 38; *US 3*, pp. 80-1.

[15] See also, e.g., the analysis of Andrew Falconer in *RF*, III, 72-6, 222, 246, 252-4, 300-2.

[16] See also pp. 48, 63-9; and *ADO*, pp. 257-8.

[17] See also *US 3*, pp. 63, 150-2, 226; *Lilith*, pp. 210-11; *DE*, I, 52.

[18] See also, e.g., *US 3*, pp. 29, 70.

[19] 'A Book of Dreams', Part II, ii, *The Poetical Works of George MacDonald* (Chatto & Windus, 1893), I, 394. See also, e.g., *Alec Forbes*, I, 302-3: 'the door into life generally opens behind us, and a hand is put forth which draws us in backwards. The sole wisdom for man or boy who is haunted with the hovering of unseen wings, with the scent of unseen roses, and the subtle enticements of "melodies unheard", is *work*. If he follow any of those, they will vanish. But if he work, they will come unsought, and, while they come, he will believe that there is a fairy-land, where poets find their dreams, and prophets are laid hold of by their visions.'

[20] See, e.g., *US 2*, pp. 22, 75; *US 3*, pp. 43, 115, 152; *The Hope of the Gospel*, p. 18; *ADO*, pp. 72, 289.

[21] 'A Cry', *Poetical Works,* II, 214. See also *Adela Cathcart* (Hurst & Blackett, 1864), II, 59, 169-70; *DE*, III, 236; *RF*, II, 45-6.

[22] For the correct form and location, see Novalis, *Schriften*, ed. Paul Kluckhohn and Richard Samuel, 3 vols. (Kohlhammer, Stuttgart, 1960-8), III, 572 # 113, 454 # 986, 280 # 234, in that order. MacDonald used the edition of Ludwig Tieck and Fr. von Schlegel, Novalis, *Schriften* (Berlin, 1815), which conflated these variously-dated fragments by the addition of connectives, and incidentally made an error which neither MacDonald nor later publishers and editors of *Phantastes* perceived—it was first noticed by Wolff, *The Golden Key*, pp. 43-4—the writing of *zusammenhangend* for *unzusammenhangend* in the third use of the word in the conflated passage (not quoted here): see the 2nd ed. (Berlin, 1815), II, 233-4.

[23] Novalis, *Schriften*, ed. Kluckhohn and Samuel, III, 377 # 620. See also p. 449 # 940: 'Das Mährchen ist gleichsam der *Canon* der Poesie—alles poëtische muss mährchenhaft seyn. Der Dichter betet den Zufall an.' ('The fairy-tale is similarly the archetype of poetry—everything poetic must be fairy-tale-like. The poet worships chance.')

[24] See also *DE*, III, 194, where Harry says, ' "I never dream dreams; the dreams dream me" '; and *The Diary of an Old Soul*, 18 July, 'not that thou thinkest of, but thinkest me'.

[25] Novalis, *Schriften*, III, 281 # 237. See also *GMDW*, p. 518, and *The Portent* (Smith, Elder, 1864), p. 53.

[26] Cf. *US 1*, p. 67, which describes God speaking 'out of a region of realities which he knew could only be suggested—not represented—in the forms of intellect and speech'; and *ADO*, p. 215, which says of the man not in sympathy with God's ways, 'the confusion to him is *caused* by the order's being greater than he can comprehend'.

[27] Earlier in the essay, however, MacDonald declares that, 'For my part, I do not write for children, but for the child-like, whether of five, or fifty, or seventy-five' (317).

[28] Oxford University Press, 1959.

[29] See also, e.g., Graham Hough, *An Essay on Criticism* (Duckworth, 1966), pp. 130 ff. The symbolist resistance to analysis which he describes on p. 136 is of the class to which MacDonald belongs.

[30] On MacDonald's hatred of systems see also, e.g., *DE*, III, 201-2; *RF*, III, 134-8; *England's Antiphon* (Macmillan, 1874), pp. 278, 314-17; *US 3*, pp. 142-4, 257-8; *The Hope of the Gospel*, pp. 156-8, 183-4.

[31] Wilson, 'The Theology of George MacDonald', pp. 310-11, finds the same incongruity in MacDonald having set out, in his *Unspoken Sermons,* a systematic and dogmatic account of how to be undoctrinal: 'The book presents rather a singular inconsistency. It is extremely theological, though written by one who denounces theology in all the moods and tenses. It is a more or less formal expression of truth, though the product of one who is in revolt against all attempts at system-building. It is a dogmatic utterance from one who spends much of his breath in decrying dogma.'

[32] Novalis, *Schriften,* II, 600 # 349; MacDonald, *Orts,* p. 9. Cf. Novalis, 377 # 617, 'Was außer mir ist, ist gerade in mir, ist mein—und umgek[ehrt].' ('What is outside me is in fact inside me—is mine—and vice versa.') See also, e.g., II, 594 # 314; III, 301 # 338, 382 # 633.

[33] MacDonald does, however, add a footnote which attempts to minimize the conscious ordering implied in this: 'We would not be understood to say that the man works consciously even in this. Oftentimes, if not always, the vision arises in the mind, thought and form together.' Yet this still leaves the problem of why he expresses himself thus, if he may be misunderstood. On the background to the Romantic concept of creative perception, see M. H. Abrams, *The Mirror and the Lamp, Romantic Theory and the Critical Tradition* (Oxford Univ. Press, N.Y., 1953), ch. iii, sect. 3; ch. viii, sects. 3-5.

[34] Novalis, *Schriften,* III, 438 # 883; 'Im Mährchen ist ächte Naturanarchie.' ('The genuine anarchy of nature is in the fairy-tale.')

[35] Cf. *Lilith,* p. 51. This is paralleled by MacDonald's need to believe in a God whose notions of justice and goodness are the same as man's: a Father who is the apotheosis of human fatherhood (or perhaps more accurately, *motherhood,* since MacDonald stresses his mercy in what is arguably the cosmic projection of his search and longing for the mother he lost when young). Compare Kingsley, who also insists on the identity of God's moral principles and our own (see e.g. *CKL,* II, p. 105): this is surely a product of Victorian terror of the meaningless and impenetrable. See Wilson, 'The Theology of George MacDonald', pp. 294 ff. on this. Occasionally MacDonald can relax this rigidity: in *Adela Cathcart,* I, 181, Adela, with the support of the narrator, who is a persona of MacDonald, declares, "We must not judge the people in fairy tales by precisely the same conventionalities we have. They must be good after their own fashion."

[36] This is not to deny that part of MacDonald's difficulty here is also in trying to reconcile middle-of-the-road English, and extreme German Romantic theory—or, more specifically, Coleridge and Novalis.

[37] Cf. *Malcolm* (Henry S. King, 1875), II, 157, where 'The cellars are the metaphysics, the garrets the poetry of the house'; and the garrets are 'in harmony with the highest spiritual instincts'. The mental symbolism of buildings is pervasive in MacDonald's work.

[38] Cf. *England's Antiphon,* p. 256: 'the movements of man's life are in spirals: we go back whence we came, ever returning on our former traces, only upon a higher level, on the next upward coil of the spiral, so that it is a going back and a going forward ever and both at once.'

[39] This 'faculty of *bi-local existing*', common in MacDonald's fantasy, Greville ascribes to his father's reading of E. T. A. Hoffmann's *The Golden Pot [Der goldne Topf]*—see *GMDW,* p. 298. The demand for 'imaginative' perception in MacDonald's work is also shown by the way his characters can reach or communicate with the supernatural only in some state of unconsciousness. Perhaps the strangest example of this is 'The Carasoyn', where Colin can find the old fairy woman only when he has managed to lose himself (*Works of Fancy and Imagination* (Strahan, 1871), IX, 146-7, 198-9).

[40] *Dealings with the Fairies* (Strahan, 1867), p. 250. Cf. p. 209: 'No mortal, or fairy either, can tell where Fairy-land begins and where it ends.'

[41] *The Princess and Curdie* (2nd ed., Chatto & Windus, 1888), pp. 70-7, 80-4, 107, 149, 197, 202, 212.

[42] Ibid. p. 56.

[43] *At the Back of the North Wind* (Strahan, 1871), p. 37. See also pp. 363-4; and compare the chameleon behaviour of Anodos as an imaginative reader in *Phantastes,* pp. 132-3.

[44] *The Water-Babies* (Macmillan, 1863), p. 88; cf. MacDonald, *Donal Grant* (Kegan Paul, 1883), III, 9-11. Greville says that his father's understanding of 'ethical Evolution' antedated his knowledge of Darwin's *Descent of Man* and *Origin of Species* (*GMDW,* p. 217).

[45] Mr Raven in *Lilith* says, "Everyone, as you ought to know, has a beast-self—and a bird-self, and a stupid fish-self, ay, and a creeping serpent-self too—which it takes a deal of crushing to kill! In truth he has also a tree-self and a crystal-self, and I don't know how many selves more—all to get into harmony. You can tell what sort a man is by the creature that comes oftenest to the front" (p. 37). See also *Phantastes,* pp. 313-17, for the spiritual-evolutionary path followed by Anodos.

[46] *The Princess and Curdie*, p. 76. For other grotesques see, e.g., *The Princess and the Goblin* (Strahan, 1872), pp. 126-34; *Lilith*, pp. 64-5, 293-4.

[47] See *Dealings with the Fairies*, pp. 258-74, 283-4, 286-7; there are flying worms of light in *Lilith*, pp. 23, 60-3. For the possible origin of the airfish see *DE*, II, 35-6; when Hugh, tutoring Harry, speaks of men crawling about at the bottom of an ocean of air just as some fish crawl on the sea-floor, Harry asks, "Then the birds are the swimming fishes, are they not?"

[48] See Wolff, *The Golden Key*, pp. 78-9. For the German Romantic sources and analogues of MacDonald's work, both Wolff and McGillis, 'The Fantastic Imagination', should be consulted.

[49] See particularly 'The Masque of the Red Death'. There has been little account of what was surely the considerable influence of Poe—particularly in 'Ligeia', 'Eleonora', 'Berenice', and 'The Oval Portrait'—on MacDonald's imagination.

[50] The Greek ἄνοδος does however also contain the notion of an upwards direction; and, in one usage, that of the ascent of the soul to its origin (see Liddell and Scott, *Greek-English Lexicon*, 9th ed. (O.U.P., 1940), ἄνοδος, B, IV). There is a Sir Upward in *Lilith*.

[51] *Phantastes*, pp. 26, 40, 45, 78, 86, 287. He diverges only once (p. 11).

[52] Often this compulsiveness is sinful, and part of the moral theme of the book: when Anodos is led (by the farmer's son) to the prohibited ogress' cottage, 'An irresistible attraction caused me to enter'; and when he comes to the more forbidden closet-door within, 'Still the irresistible desire which had made me enter the building urged me: I must open that door, and see what was beyond it' (93, 94). That the same sort of unthinking impulse can be variously a good, a bad and an indifferent thing leads to confusion and difficulty in allowing their due weight to Anodos' failures.

[53] Up to this point Anodos receives little moral censure—another way in which this book defies patterning. Contrast *Lilith*, where Vane is under attack from the outset.

[54] In *Phantastes* we have a division analogous to that in many of MacDonald's novels: in the novels, for example *Alec Forbes of Howglen* or *Robert Falconer*, there is commonly a split between the side of MacDonald that likes to portray life in a mid-Victorian Scottish village realistically, for its own sake, and the side that wants to make people alter, develop spiritually; in *Phantastes* the division is rather more one between a mystic or obliquely symbolic mode of presentation and a didactic one.

[55] Cf. *RF*, II, 48-9, for a similar passage.

[56] Lewis, *George MacDonald: An Anthology* (Bles, 1946), p. 14.

[57] On this, see e.g. *DE*, I, 74; 'The Child in the Midst', *US 1*, pp. 1-26; McGillis, 'The Fantastic Imagination', ch. iii.

[58] First serialized in *Good Words for the Young* (Nov. 1868 to Oct. 1870), this book was apparently MacDonald's best-seller (*GMDW*, p. 361).

[59] See e.g. *RF*, III, 188-9; and 'A Manchester Poem', *Poetical Works*, I, 422-9.

[60] Also entitled *The Lost Princess, or The Wise Woman* in 1895.

[61] *The Wise Woman* (Strahan, 1875), pp. 107-8. Interestingly, C. S. Lewis admired this book (*George MacDonald*, p. 17).

[62] Letter of 25 Feb. 1871 from MacDonald to his wife (quoted in *GMDW*, p. 412). The serialization was from Nov. 1870 to June 1871; MacDonald was himself editor at the time—on which subject see *GMDW*, pp. 361-2, 411-12.

[63] Lewis, *George MacDonald*, pp. 19-20.

[64] Oxford University Press, 1934.

[65] *The Golden Key*, p. 166.

[66] Tony Tanner, 'Mountains and Depths—An Approach to Nineteenth-century Dualism', *Review of English Literature*, III, iv (Oct. 1962), 52.

[67] MacDonald does speak of the goblins as being subterranean (p. 4), but to square with the facts of the story this must be taken as 'beneath the earth' rather than 'in the depths'.

[68] 'Mountains and Depths', pp. 52-3, 53, 54.

[69] Lewis, *Of Other Worlds, Essays and Stories*, ed. W. Hooper (Bles, 1966), p. 57.

[70] Ibid. p. 58.

[71] Cf. Louis MacNeice, *Varieties of Parable* (Cambridge Univ. Press, 1965), p. 94, speaking of *Alice*: 'it would be a mistake . . . to try to pin down the allegory in any detail. And this would be even more of a mistake with George MacDonald.'

[72] Cf. MacDonald at *GMDW*, p. 297, on *Phantastes*; and *England's Antiphon*, p. 54: 'Allegory has her place,

and a lofty one, in literature; but when her plants cover the garden and run to seed, Allegory herself is ashamed of her children: the loveliest among them are despised for the general obtrusiveness of the family.'

73 MacDonald may owe something to the bath of Baptist total immersion in which Christiana and her children are washed in Interpreter's House in Part II of *Pilgrim's Progress.*

74 Lewis, *George MacDonald,* pp. 14-18; W. H. Auden, preface to Anne Fremantle, ed., *The Visionary Novels of George MacDonald* (N.Y., 1954); MacNeice, *Varieties of Parable,* pp. 94-101.

75 Lewis, *George MacDonald,* pp. 16-17, 15, 16. Auden, p.v., asserts that the kind of mythopoeic imagination MacDonald possessed has 'no necessary connection with the gift of verbal expression or the power to structure experience'. See also MacNeice, p. 95.

76 Cf. *GMDW,* pp. 218-19, 409; and 'On Polish', *ADO,* pp. 182-94.

77 See *Phantastes,* pp. 61, 133, 145-6; and *Lilith,* pp. 12, 60-1, for further attempts to excuse failures of realization; these would have more weight if the reader could *feel* the difficulty.

78 On this cf. 'On Polish', pp. 184-7.

79 Cf. pp. 131-3; and see *ADO,* p. 184, 'The most polished style will be that which most immediately and most truly flashes the meaning embodied in the utterance upon the mind of the listener or reader.'

80 *At the Back of the North Wind,* p. 376.

81 Lewis, 'The Weight of Glory', *They Asked For a Paper* (Bles, 1962), pp. 200, 201.

82 Lewis, *The Pilgrim's Regress, An Allegorical Apology for Christianity, Reason and Romanticism,* 3rd ed. (Bles, 1943), p. 10.

83 Cf. *The Diary of an Old Soul,* 1 May.

84 Lewis, 'On Stories', *Of Other Worlds,* p. 18.

85 See above, ch. 4, p. 111 and note 41.

86 Lewis, *George MacDonald,* p. 21; and *Surprised by Joy, The Shape of My Early Life* (Bles, 1955), pp. 168-71.

87 *Surprised by Joy,* p. 170.

88 *The Diary of an Old Soul,* 29 May. See also 3-7 April; *RF,* I, 243-4; *GMDW,* p. 339. Naturally,

MacDonald distinguishes between the image and its source (except where the image is of Christ himself): see *US 3,* pp. 50-2; *GMDW,* pp. 278-9; *The Diary of an Old Soul,* 25 Sept.; *Poetical Works,* I, pp. 8, 83-4, 138, 140, 276-7, 288-90, 333-5, 418.

89 See e.g. *GMDW,* p. 543; *Castle Warlock* (Sampson Low, 1882), III, 274-5; 'The Broken Swords', *Adela Cathcart,* II, 231-2 (passage used again in *ADO,* p. 234). But all things, if in varying degrees, were sacramental to MacDonald: speaking of the charm of the outside of a book, he says, 'It was a kind of sacrament—an outward and visible sign of an inward and spiritual grace; as indeed, what on God's earth is not?' (*The Portent,* p. 82). Cf. *US 3,* p. 31: 'the outermost husk of creation has correspondence with the deepest things of the Creator'; and, in the MS of the first draft of *Lilith,* approx. 3 pages from the end, describing heaven, "Now I know" said my father "why he gives precious stones to them that dwell on earth!—It is because they cannot always have the sun and rain of this country whence they went out to make them glad!"

90 Cf. *England's Antiphon,* pp. 186-9, 232; and the remarks on each man's true name or signature in *US 1,* pp. 105 ff.

91 *At the Back of the North Wind,* pp. 138-43.

92 2nd ed. (1888), pp. 66-7. As with the song about North Wind, MacDonald uses an Aeolian analogy prior to this: 'the lady began to sing . . . and the music of the wheel was like the music of an Aeolian harp blown upon by the wind that bloweth where it listeth' (p. 66).

George P. Landow

SOURCE: "And the World Became Strange: Realms of Literary Fantasy," in *The Aesthetics of Fantasy Literature and Art,* edited by Roger C. Schlobin, University of Notre Dame Press and The Harvester Press, 1982, pp. 105-42.

[*In the excerpt below, Landow, examining the major works of John Ruskin. George MacDonald. George Meredith, William Morris, and William Hope Hodgson, maintains that these authors did not write simple escapist fiction, but instead used fantasy to comment on serious issues.*]

In order to examine the characteristics of literary fantasy since 1850 in the most economical manner, I propose in the following pages to survey this Victorian and modern literary mode in terms of one work by each of five major authors—John Ruskin (1819-1900),

George MacDonald (1824-1905), George Meredith (1828-1909), William Morris (1834-1896), and William Hope Hodgson (1875-1918). These five works, each of which represents a particular form of fantastic fiction, will enable us to perceive the defining characteristics of this literary form while also permitting us to observe what the verbal and visual arts in this mode have in common.

John Ruskin's *The King of the Golden River* exemplifies the literary fairy tale, a form which, like the literary ballad, imitates the anonymous products of popular or folk tradition. Ruskin's tale, which he wrote in 1841, two years before he began *Modern Painters,* tells of Hans and Schwartz, two selfish, evil brothers whose greed costs them their Edenic Treasure Valley and then their lives, and of the third brother, Gluck, whose generosity and self-sacrifice restore the valley's fertility. One cold winter evening when Gluck is minding the house, a fairy visitor arrives and demands entrance:

> It was the most extraordinary looking little gentleman he had ever seen in his life. He had a very large nose, slightly brass-coloured, and expanding towards its termination into a development not unlike the lower extremity of a key bugle; his cheeks were very round, and very red, and might have warranted a supposition that he had been blowing a refractory fire for the last eight-and-forty hours; his eyes twinkled merrily through long silky eyelashes, his moustaches curled twice round like a corkscrew on each side of his mouth, and his hair, of a curious mixed pepper-and-salt colour, descended far over his shoulders. He was about four-feet-six in height, and wore a conical pointed cap of nearly the same altitude, decorated with a black feather some three feet long. His doublet was prolonged behind into something resembling a violent exaggeration of what is now termed a "swallow tail," but was much obscured by the swelling folds of an enormous black, glossy-looking cloak, which must have been very much too long in calm weather, as the wind, whistling around the old house, carried it clear out from the wearer's shoulders to about four times his own length.[3]

When the cruel, avaricious brothers return home, they expectedly order their strange visitor, who turns out to be South West Wind Esquire, to leave. At the stroke of midnight, the brothers are awakened by a tremendous crash to discover that their room is flooded. "They could see in the midst of it an enormous foam globe, spinning round, and bobbing up and down like a cork, on which, as on a most luxurious cushion, reclined the little old gentleman, cap and all. There was plenty of room for it now, for the roof was off" (1.323). The morning light reveals that their precious valley, whose riches they never shared, has been transformed into a desert of red sand, and so, not having

learned their lesson, they decamp for the nearest city where they set themselves up as cheating goldsmiths. Failing to prosper, they soon melt down all their hoarded gold until they have only Gluck's mug which an uncle had given the little boy. "The mug was a very odd mug to look at. The handle was formed of two wreaths of flowing golden hair, so finely spun that it looked more like silk than metal, and these wreaths descended into, and mixed with, a beard and whiskers of the same exquisite workmanship, which surrounded and decorated a very fierce little face, of the reddest gold imaginable, right in the front of the mug, with a pair of eyes in it which seemed to command its whole circumference" (1.326-27). Placing the mug in the melting pot, the brothers leave for the alehouse and instruct their younger brother to watch over the pot. While gazing out of a window at the desiccated remains of his beloved Treasure Valley, Gluck is astonished to hear the melted gold singing, and when on its orders he decants it, out jumps a golden dwarf a foot and a half high—the King of the Golden River, who had been enchanted by an evil spell. The grateful king thereupon rewards Gluck by telling him how to make his fortune: "'Whoever shall climb to the top of that mountain from which you see the Golden River issue, and shall cast into the stream at its source three drops of holy water, for him, and for him only, the river shall turn to gold. But no one failing in his first, can succeed in a second attempt; and if any one shall cast unholy water into the river, it will overwhelm him, and he will become a black stone'" (1.331). Predictably, the two brothers, who try to cheat each other, turn themselves into black stones, whereas Gluck, who gives his last holy water to an old man, a child, and a dog (all of whom turn out to be the dwarf king in magic guise), is rewarded again by the King of the Golden River with three drops of dew. When sprinkled on the source of the river, they transform the desert valley once again into an earthly paradise.

Although Ruskin uses the fairy tale to enforce the moral that selfishness is evil and destructive, its chief point is one central to his entire career as a critic of art and society—namely, as he put it in *Unto This Last* (1860), that "THERE IS NO WEALTH BUT LIFE. Life, including all its powers of love, of joy, and of admiration" (17.105). Nonetheless, his later statements about fantasy and imagination suggest that the understanding of these ideas is at most a secondary experience and not the primary one he intended. According to his lecture "Fairy Land" in *The Art of England* (1884), fantastic or fairy art is "the art which intends to address only childish imagination, and whose object is primarily to entertain with grace" (33.332). For him, such an aim is an extremely important one.

Ruskin has all too often been mistakenly thought to espouse a crude didacticism, in part because he advances so emphatically the notion that beginning artists should present visual truth. But, in fact, as he several times urges in *Modern Painters* and his other writings, the most valuable, most educational, most *moral* function of art is simply to be beautiful. He can take such an undidactic approach to the arts because his theories of beauty assume that beauty is a divinely intended pleasure the enjoyment of which is itself a moral and spiritual act. Similarly, when he writes of fairy literature and art for children, he opposes its vulgarization by didactic intent because he believes that exercising the young imagination is itself a most valuable purpose. Appropriately, Ruskin begins his lecture on fairy art by announcing that he will take on Dickens' Gradgrind, the archetypal utilitarian educator who wanted children to learn facts and suppress their imaginations. Like Dickens, Ruskin works within a moral and philosophical tradition which held that feeling and imagination play—and should play—crucial roles in moral decision; so that to develop the imagination is to develop a mature human mind. Ruskin therefore tells his audience that "it is quite an inexorable law of this poor human nature of ours, that in the development of its healthy infancy, it is put by Heaven under the absolute necessity of using its imagination as well as its lungs and its legs;—that it is forced to develop its power of invention, as a bird its feathers of flight" (33.329).

Although "Fairy Land" concerns itself largely with art and literature for children, his remarks decades before in *Modern Painters* make it abundantly clear that he conceives the fantastic imagination as one of the defining characteristics of humanity and its highest art. According to him, whereas the student artist and those of lesser imagination must concentrate upon topographical, realistic studies which store the mind with visual fact, the great artist, such as Turner, creates imaginative transformations of reality which most of his audience will receive as fantastic distortions—thus the need for criticism and for Ruskin to have begun *Modern Painters* in order to demonstrate to hostile critics that Turner's later visions of mist and fire were firmly based on reality. By creating such unusual and unexpected images of the world of matter and spirit, the great artist produces a work which enables us to perceive with his eyes and imagination. Each artist necessarily transforms the world according to the strengths and limitations of his own character, imagination, and age, and in the third volume of *Modern Painters* (1856), Ruskin endeavors to explain the various imaginative modes in which artists work. Purist art, for example, arises in the "unwillingness . . . to contemplate the various forms of definite evil which necessarily occur in . . . the world" (5.103-04). Artists, like Fra Angelico, "create for themselves an imaginary state, in which pain and imperfection either do not exist, or exist in some edgeless and enfeebled condition" (5.104). Turning to a lesser English example, he describes Thomas Stothard in terms strik-

ingly like those with which he was later to describe Kate Greenaway (Plate 7):

> It seems as if Stothard could not conceive wickedness, coarseness, or baseness; every one of his figures looks as if it had been copied from some creature who had never harboured an unkind thought, or permitted itself an ignoble action. With this intense love of mental purity is joined, in Stothard, a love of mere physical smoothness and softness, so that he lived in a universe of soft grass and stainless fountains, tender trees, and stones at which no foot could stumble. (5.105)

Although such art can provide us some brief respite from the pains of this life, it is, finds Ruskin, essentially childish and incomplete.

A potentially higher art appears in the grotesque, which takes three forms. The central mode of the grotesque arises from the fact that the human imagination "in its mocking or playful moods . . . is apt to jest, sometimes bitterly, with under-current of sternest pathos, sometimes waywardly, sometimes slightly and wickedly, with death and sin; hence an enormous mass of grotesque art, some most noble and useful, as Holbein's *Dance of Death,* and Albrecht Dürer's *Knight, Death and the Devil,* going down gradually through various conditions of less and less seriousness into an art whose only end is that of mere excitement, or to amuse by terror" (5.131). In addition to this darker form of the grotesque, which includes work ranging from traditional religious images of death and the devil to satire and horrific art, there is a comparatively rare form which arises "from an entirely healthful and open play of the imagination, as in Shakespeare's Ariel and Titania, and in Scott's White Lady" (5.131). This delicate fairy art is so seldom achieved because "the moment we begin to contemplate sinless beauty we are apt to get serious; and moral fairy tales, and such other innocent work, are hardly ever truly, that is to say, naturally, imaginative; but for the most part laborious inductions and compositions. The moment any real vitality enters them, they are nearly sure to become satirical, or slightly gloomy, and so connect themselves with the evil-enjoying branch" (5.131-32).

The third form of the grotesque, which served as the basis for Ruskin's conception of a high art suited to the Victorian age, is the "thoroughly noble one . . . which arises out of the use or fancy of tangible signs to set forth an otherwise less expressible truth; including nearly the whole range of symbolical and allegorical art and poetry" (5.132). Ruskin's valuable perception that fantastic art and literature form part of a continuum which includes sublime, symbolic, grotesque, and satirical works is particularly useful to anyone interested in this mode, because fantastic art does, in fact, share much with satire and symbol, caricature and sublime. After all, much of the delight of Caldecott's courting frog (Plate 4), Griset's fisherman (Plate 5), and Rackham's witches arises in the way they caricature normal humanity, and similarly, when we receive pleasure from this last artist's wonderfully humanized trees (Plate 9), it is precisely because they are so human; because, in other words, they share so much of the human that they enable us to see ourselves better because we see ourselves in such guise.

Such delightful, and often unsettling presentation of aspects of our everyday reality in strange form is also a common feature of literary fantasy and appears in works as different as *Alice in Wonderland* and *Peter Pan in Kensington Gardens*. But the literary fantasy's primary method is to transform not single elements in our world but that entire world itself, thus immersing us in another reality whose laws are different, often disconcerting, and occasionally terrifying. George MacDonald's *Phantastes* (1858), which will serve as our second major example, takes as its province the world of fairyland. Although MacDonald's fairyland, like that of Lord Dunsany's *The King of Elfland's Daughter,* borrows many features from the fairy tale, this far more complex fictional world is essentially a new creation through which its inventor can explore adult themes.

MacDonald opens his tale in our world, but by the second chapter he has transformed it into a very strange place indeed. The morning after his twenty-first birthday, when the orphan Anodos has come into his estates, he is greeted by a tiny fairy-figure able to vary her size at will, who announces that she is his grandmother and that she has come to inform him that he is about to make a voyage to Fairy Land. Anodos, who does not even believe in Fairy Land, is astonished to awaken the next morning to

> the sound of running water near me; and, looking out of bed, I saw that a large green marble basin, in which I was wont to wash, and which stood on a low pedestal of the same material in a corner of my room, was overflowing like a spring; and that a stream of clear water was running over the carpet, all the length of the room, finding its outlet I knew not where. And, stranger still, where this carpet, which I had myself designed to imitate a field of grass and daisies, bordered the course of the little stream, the grass-blades and daisies seemed to wave in a tiny breeze that followed the water's flow; while under the rivulet they bent and swayed with every motion of the changeful current, as if they were about to dissolve with it, and, forsaking their fixed form, become fluent as the waters.

My dressing-table was an old-fashioned piece of furniture of black oak, with drawers all down the front. These were elaborately carved in foliage, of which ivy formed the chief part. The nearer end of this table remained just as it had been, but on the further end a singular change had commenced. I happened to fix my eye on a little cluster of ivy-leaves. The first of these was evidently the work of the carver; the next looked curious; the third was unmistakably ivy; and just beyond it a tendril of clematis had twined itself about the gilt handle of one of the drawers. Hearing next a slight motion above me, I looked up, and saw that the branches and leaves designed upon the curtains of my bed were slightly in motion. Not knowing what change might follow next, I thought it high time to get up; and, springing from the bed, my bare feet alighted upon a cool green sward; and although I dressed in all haste, I found myself completing my toilet under the boughs of a great tree.[4]

This transformation of the main character's everyday reality into a far different one well exemplifies a central device of the literary fantasy.

Whereas the artist working with visual fantasy usually must place us immediately inside a fantastic kingdom, the creator of literary fantasy, who works with a narrative, sequential mode, has two choices. Like the artist he can open his work by immediately immersing us in his new world and such is the manner of proceeding adopted by William Morris in *The Water of the Wondrous Isles* and George Meredith in *The Shaving of Shagpat,* two works at which we shall soon look. The far more usual strategy is for the writer to employ some narrative device which displaces us from our everyday world into his created one. The most prosaic such device occurs in C. J. Cutliffe Hyne's *The Lost Continent* (1899), in which an adventurer discovers an ancient manuscript in a South American cave; when deciphered this manuscript turns out to contain the tale of Deucalion, the last survivor of Atlantis. A similar favorite device of this lost-world fiction so popular around 1900 is the discovery of a map which then leads the adventurous protagonists on a voyage of discovery which culminates in the fantastic world. In contrast, William Hope Hodgson's *The Night Land* (1912), William Morris' *The Dream of John Ball* (1888), and Lewis Carroll's *Alice* books (1865, 1871), use the device of the dream to move us into the fantastic realm, while the magic doorway or mirror, which appears in George MacDonald's *Lilith* (1895) and C. S. Lewis' Narnia books, is another effective means of transporting us to a fantastic world. Occasionally, as in *Through the Looking Glass,* an author may first employ a magical transformation and only later, at the story's end, reveal that the metamorphosis of reality actually occurred within a dream.

Since much of the fascination and delight which characterize the finest literary fantasies derive from their continual sharp contrast of fantastic and everyday existence, such devices of transformation are central to the form. Even Morris, who begins his narrative already within his imagined world, must find a means of displacing us from our usual conceptions of things, and so he employs a peculiar invented language and geography—a technique adopted by many subsequent authors—to insulate us from our world and its prosaic expectations. In the comparatively rare cases where the visual artist effects a transformation from our normal, prosaic world to his fantastic one within the picture itself he must similarly make use of formal devices. For example, in Rackham's *There's a whispering from tree to tree* (Plate 9) we perceive that the figures in the distance exist in a nonfantastic world, while the trees closest to the viewer become progressively more animated as they near the picture-plane. Rackham, in other words, has found a convincing means of showing how, as human beings withdraw from the forest, its hidden, fantastic life comes into being. To do so he has made use of devices of rational perspective to turn a potentially static image into a sequential, narrative one. Furthermore, by making the eye of the spectator effect this narrative or sequential progression, he has not only made him animate the picture himself but has also permitted him briefly to borrow the artist's vision and see, for a few moments, with his eyes.

Once we have entered the world of MacDonald's *Phantastes,* we soon discover that its laws, its principles of order, are completely different from those we know. As Anodos remarks, "it is no use trying to account for things in Fairy Land; and one who travels there soon learns to forget the very idea of doing so, and takes everything as it comes; like a child, who, being in a chronic condition of wonder, is surprised at nothing" (p. 33). In *Phantastes,* unlike more prosaic forms of fantastic fiction, such as that devoted to lost worlds, the principle of transformation continues to operate throughout the narrative, creating surprising incident and novel delight. Anodos finds a statue of a woman which springs to life; then he receives advice from an animated tree, finds a magic boat which takes him to a fairy palace, leaves it and finds himself in a wasteland, enters a cottage whose magic doors return him to his past, and so on. Such episodic narrative is entirely in keeping with the main drive of fantasy, which is to deny the primacy of our everyday laws of cause-and-effect.

Although *Phantastes* and similar works, such as David Lindsay's *A Voyage to Arcturus* (1920), deny the applicability of some of our basic facts of existence, these episodic plots are hardly random or chaotic, for as C. S. Lewis explains, "To construct plausible and moving 'other worlds,' you must draw on the only 'other world' we know, that of the spirit."[5] This fantastic world can take as many forms as the human spirit itself. For Lewis himself "the world of the spirit" is the world of Christian theology, and both his

Perelandra and Narnia series, like MacDonald's *Lilith,* are allegorical embodiments of the Christian truths of redemption and spiritual growth. David Lindsay, who finds such belief irrelevent to human needs, presents an entirely different set of embodied human (and alien) possibilities. For Morris, also a secular thinker, the world of the spirit takes the form of an ideal of sexual and social development. In *Phantastes,* which relates Anodos' discovery of the moral truth that one cannot find oneself until one loses sight of oneself and one's desires, the spirit is largely moral, though imbued with theological overtones.

Following the German art fairy tale or *Märchen,* MacDonald employs a dream or dreamlike structure, revealing that to him the world of the spirit must be seen in terms of human psychology, the human inner world. In fact, a great many Victorian and later fantasies employ such dream structure, for the movement into the subjective world of the mind is the first step into fantasy. Essentially, there are two ways to claim that the world of everyday reality, the world of the realistic novel, is inadequate to human needs: the first is to claim that a higher world of religious or political ideas and ideals is more important, more relevant; while the second is to claim that the inner worlds of the human mind, its subjective experiences, have primary value. Lewis and MacDonald embody the first view; Kafka and Lovecraft the second.

Novel and fantasy touch upon each other in this matter of the inner world, and if one envisages a spectrum of fictions with the realistic novels of Eliot and Trollope at one end and the fantasies of MacDonald and Lindsay at the other, the novel of psychological realism occupies a middle position—and shares qualities of both. Thus, *Jane Eyre,* which purports to convey both the objective experiences and inner world of its orphan protagonist, has as much in common with the creations of MacDonald as it does with those of Thackeray, Trollope, and Gaskell. Modernist and later fiction which employs stream-of-consciousness and episodic, discontinuous structure often seems far closer to *Phantastes* than to *Middlemarch* or *The Way We Live Now.*

Although it is one of the most imaginative of fantastic tales in its rich incident, unexpected transformations, and completely imagined landscapes, *Phantastes* ends by returning us to this world. MacDonald chooses to have Anodos leave Fairy Land in part because the now wiser hero must learn to apply the lessons learned there in this world. An even more important reason is that excessive dwelling in the inner world is dangerous and destructive: *Phantastes,* which opens with an epigraph from Shelly's "Alastor," demonstrates that an excessive yearning for the ideals created by our imaginations can destroy the self and others, particularly when the self has a Pygmalionlike vision and attempts to possess another human being as a means of fulfillment. In contrast, some of the greatest authors of later fantasy, including H. P. Lovecraft, Clark Ashton Smith, and Lord Dunsany, have chosen the road MacDonald rejected and written of dreamworlds more "real" than the waking world. Whereas Hodgson and Morris use the dream as a way of entering a supposedly existent future world, whether it be hundreds or millions of years distant in time, these others have employed the dream as a way into an entirely subjective realm to which the power of desire gives a higher reality—though one which is almost always destructive and cruel.

MacDonald's *Phantastes,* which combines the worlds of the fairy tale and the *Märchen,* exemplifies one chief form of literary fantasy. Another major form is the exotic tale set in the magical universe of the *Arabian Nights,* and this form has always held great appeal for illustrators. Like Shakespeare's *The Tempest* and *A Midsummer Night's Dream, The Arabian Nights, or the Book of a Thousand and One Nights* has provided a great source of inspiration for artists including John Dickson Batten; Edward Julius Detmold (Plate 6); Edmund Dulac; Arthur Boyd Houghton; Henry Justice Ford; Charles, Tom, and William Heath Robinson; and Sir John Tenniel. Artists and writers conceive of this exotic realm as sensual, lush with heavy perfumes, strange vegetation, and bright intense colors—a world of fierce justice and bizarre adventure in which lamps contain djinns or genies and great risks can bring great success. The visual side of this fascination with the exotic, which is one of the important currents of European and British romanticism, appears not only in fantastic illustration but also in scenes of life in the Middle East painted by so many nineteenth-century artists, including W. J. Muller, David Roberts, J. F. Lewis, William Holman Hunt, Joseph Farquharson, and Andrew Geddes.

George Meredith's first work of extended fiction, *The Shaving of Shagpat* (1855), offers us a glimpse at the literary use of the exotic fantasy at its most delightful. Like Dulac, who later imitated the conventions of Persian, Chinese, and Japanese art for his illustrations, Meredith uses the exotic style known to readers of *The Arabian Nights* to displace us into his fantastic imagined world: "Now, the story of Shibli Bagarag, and of the ball he followed, and of the subterranean kingdom he came to, and of the enchanted palace he entered, and of the sleeping king he shaved, and of the two princesses he released, and of the Afrite held in subjection by the arts of one and bottled by her, is it not known as 'twere written on the finger-nails of men and traced in their corner-robes?"[6] This tale of a brave and adventurous, if vain, barber begins as a spoof of the genre, because it has such an unusual hero and even more unusual villain, who at first seems little more than an obese pile of black hair—"indeed a

miracle of hairiness, black with hairs as he had been muzzled with it, and his head as it were a berry in a bush by reason of it. . . . Now would he close an eye, or move two fingers, but of other motion made he none, yet the people gazed at him with eagerness" (pp. 8-9). Meredith turns this apparent parody of the adventure tale into a straightforward exotic fantasy when he reveals that Shibli's future wife, the good sorceress Noorna, had unwittingly created this apparently comical monster, who possesses strong supernatural powers, when she placed in Shagpat's scalp the magical hair of the Genie Karaz, from whom she was fleeing. To save the world, which is increasingly coming under Shagpat's power of illusion, Shibli must pass repeated tests, obtain a magic sword, and destroy the source of evil magic.

Like the art and poetry of Beardsley (and like Wallace Stevens in "The Comedian as the Letter C"), Meredith employs the barber as a grotesque figure of the artist in a fallen world—a man who attempts to establish order and beauty which time and nature continually destroy. In Meredith this conception of the artist—for Shibli, like his creator, is a teller of tales—is treated only half-seriously. Meredith similarly handles and much qualifies traditional notions of adventure, heroism, and masculine strength. As the clear-sighted Noorna tells her father, the good Vizier Feshnavat, "there is all in this youth . . . that's desirable for the undertaking. . . . 'Tis clear that vanity will trip him, but honesty is a strong upholder; and he is one that hath the spirit of enterprise and the mask of dissimulation" (p. 95). In this most unpuritanic, un-English, un-Victorian world, dissimulation is a virtue, for Meredith has caught the tone of all great adventurers who descend from Odysseus to entertain us with cunning and resourcefulness. But despite the fact that Shibli is well aware of the dangers of vanity, he continually succumbs to it and is victorious only because Noorna scolds and rescues him until he is finally able to rescue her in turn. Like MacDonald's almost exactly contemporaneous *Phantastes, The Shaving of Shagpat* uses its fantastic events to present serious themes of human illusion, the dangers of pride, and the nature of true heroic action. In fact, its guiding ideas much resemble those of the usual nineteenth-century *Bildungsroman,* but unlike the realistic novel of growth and self-discovery, *Shagpat* does not dramatize major changes in the main character. We are warned against his immature vanity, we see its dangerous effects, and we see him conquer it, but as we close the covers of the book, we do not find Shibli, the barber turned monarch, essentially changed. We wonder what would happen to him without Noorna and hope she will never be far from his side.

As delightfully as Meredith enacts these serious themes, which incidentally also inspired his far different novels of high comedy, he most impresses us with his depiction of magical weapons and an underground world. Escaping the wiles of the evil sorceress Rabesqrat by means of a lily rooted in a living heart, Shibli enters the underground lands and begins a series of tests which gain him the magic sword he needs to destroy Shagpat. He strikes a magic door

> and discovered an opening into a strange dusky land, as it seemed a valley, on one side of which was a ragged copper sun setting low, large as a warrior's battered shield, giving deep red lights to a brook that fell, and over a flat stream a red reflection, and to the sides of the hills a dark red glow. The sky was a brown colour; the earth a deeper brown, like the skins of tawny lions. Trees with reddened stems stood about the valley, scattered and in groups, showing between their leaves the cheeks of melancholy fruits swarthily tinged, and toward the centre of the valley a shining palace was visible, supported by massive columns of marble reddened by that copper sun. (p. 177)

Entering the palace, Shibli survives a series of tests characteristic of the romance to gain the magic sword at last. The book closes after his triumphant battle against Shagpat, the Genie Karaz, and the evil sorceress Rabesqrat, who rely upon magical weapons and strange transformations. *The Shaving of Shagpat* is thus an important nineteenth-century precursor of the so-called "Sword-and-Sorcery" school of fantasy literature. This form, which was inspired largely by Lord Dunsany in his "The Fortress Unvanquishable, Save for Sacnoth" and similar writings, combined the ancient materials of *The Arabian Nights* with chivalric legend and dragonlore of the North. In the twentieth century this kind of fantasy became a mainstay of pulp magazines and, like space operas with science fiction, did much to lower the reputation of fantasy as a serious form. These elements have been developed far more successfully in recent decades by J. R. R. Tolkien and the Americans Ursula K. Le Guin and Anne McCaffrey.

Ruskin and MacDonald have guided us into the fantasy world of Fairy Land, and Meredith has shown us the universe of the exotic fantasy. An historically more important imaginative cosmos appears in the prose romances of William Morris. According to Lin Carter, the author of fantasy literature whose paperback editions of the masters of this mode have done so much to popularize it in America, Morris is the true creator of heroic fantasy:

> Oriental tales like *Vathek* and *The Shaving of Shagpat* are set—not in completely imaginary worlds of their authors' invention, as are the romances of William Morris—but in "literary" versions of the actual Middle East. . . . No one ever tried to write another *Vathek* or *Shagpat*,

and only a few books (such as the *Perelandra* trilogy of C. S. Lewis and David Lindsay's brilliant and astounding novel *A Voyage to Arcturus*) show to any extent the influence of *Lilith* and *Phantastes*. But the genre of heroic fantasy laid in an imaginary world descends from William Morris to Lord Dunsany and E. R. Eddison, and from thence to whole generations of writers such as James Branch Cabell, Fletcher Pratt (*The Blue Star*), Robert E. Howard, J. R. R. Tolkien, L. Sprague de Camp (*The Tritonian Ring* and *The Goblin Tower*), Fritz Leiber, Jack Vance, Jane Gaskell, [and] Lloyd Alexander. . . . From the world of the Wood and the world of the Well descend all the later worlds of fantastic fiction, Poictesme and Oz and Tormance, Barsoom and Narnia and Zothique, Gormenghast and Zimiamvia and Middle-Earth.[7]

Writers in the twentieth century have advanced farther down the road towards imagining alternate universes, for increasingly they have attempted, like de Camp, to people their worlds with new sentient creatures, societies, and entire congeries of legend, religion, and culture. Such movements of fantasy literature into the realm of speculative anthropology and theology make it clear that fantasy and romance create their imagined worlds as a means of exploring this one. It is important to emphasize once more the essential seriousness and potential humanistic contributions of such genres, since until recently their claims have been consistently scanted by academic critics and other advocates of "high" culture.

Similarly, students of Morris and Victorian culture have in general failed to see in his great prose romances anything more than escapist fiction. Although the obvious connections between his political beliefs and the propagandistic *A Dream of John Ball* (1888) and *News from Nowhere* (1891) have long been perceived, the equally important relation between these beliefs and the prose romances have not. One importance of the imagined world in *The Water of the Wondrous Isles* and similar writings is that it permits Morris to solve a basic problem confronting an author of political fiction—the problem of how to represent life in an ideal society which, by definition, does not exist under present conditions. The difficulty of dramatizing a positive political program is very great, and most successful political novels in fact take the form of satire or of a quasi-journalistic exposé of existing abuses. In contrast, Morris' romances take the more daring approach of creating the image of a better world for which man can strive. *A Dream of John Ball* is set in the fourteenth century and *News from Nowhere* takes place in the near future. In contrast, *The House of the Wolfings* (1888) and *The Roots of the Mountains* (1889) take place at that historical moment when Roman armies came into conflict with German tribal society, and although these works have major fantastic elements, their worlds are still largely historical reconstructions. Only with the great allegorical romances, *The Well at the World's End* (1896) and *The Water of the Wondrous Isles* (1897), does he bring to fruition his search for an ideal world in which to dramatize the problems of self and society which he had begun with his first prose fiction, *The Wood Beyond the World* (1894).

The Water of the Wondrous Isles, one of the finest as well as the most unusual of fantasies, well represents Morris' contribution to the genre. It is the tale of a young girl, Birdalone, who was kidnapped by a witch and raised in isolation. She escapes from her captor in the witch's magic Sending Boat and voyages to the Castle of the Quest by way of a series of fantastic islands. At the castle she falls in love with one of the knights, flees from him after she causes the death of another knight, and goes to live and work in a city. At last, she recognizes her duties to self, lover, and society, and she rescues her Arthur. As Barbara J. Bono, author of the most important study of Morris' fiction, points out:

> Birdalone's sojourn in and around the Water of the Wondrous Isles forms an extended allegory of sexual maturation. Her journey away from the Castle of the Quest to the City of the Five Crafts reverses this pattern as she gains experience of the world of societal relations. In her first journey across the lake she encounters many emblems of the destructive extremes of pure femaleness and pure maleness, beginning with the two offshore islets, Green Eyot and Rocky Eyot, and continued and developed in much more grotesque form in the isles of her later journey. If the witch's Isle of Increase Unsought is a Bower of Bliss of extreme female sensuality, the Isle of Nothing is the reductive expression of male sterility, while neither the lush beauty of the Isle of Queens nor the fierce stoniness of the Isle of Kings prevents these places from being essentially dead. . . . . After Birdalone's journey across the water she has both the nature-derived power and the experience of sexual awakening which will enable her to love.[8]

She must now learn the proper social context for her love, Bono adds, and the second half of the book is occupied with this social education, which "culminates in Birdalone and Arthur's decisions to leave their idyll of love to be reunited with their friends." Although Morris always presents nature as the source of his characters' strength, he emphasizes that such strength can only be developed and fulfilled within a community of other human beings.

Like Rossetti and Burne-Jones, Morris creates an ideal quasi-medieval fantasy world whose keynote is a spiritualized eroticism. Dante Gabriel Rossetti, who early came under the spell of chivalric romance and Dante's *Vita Nuova,* set the tone for many of his associates

when he placed his pensive, yearning lovers within medieval settings. In his early works Burne-Jones eagerly followed him into this fantasy world of passionate love and heroic rescues with *Clerk Saunders* (1861), *Iseult on the Ship* (1857), *The Knight's Farewell* (1858), and *Sir Galahad* (1858). Such Pre-Raphaelite visions of idealized romantic love in a medieval setting had an enormous influence on English Victorian fine and decorative arts. Painters as different as John William Waterhouse, J. R. Spencer Stanhope, John Melhuish Strudwick, and Walter Crane continued to paint in this mode for more than a half century after Rossetti began it, and its influence upon the decorative arts was as equally long-lived and interesting. The close association of this idealized medieval fantasy world and Pre-Raphaelite conceptions of ideal love had a particularly important effect on the decorative arts, for they gave a major impetus to the attempt by Morris and his associates to create a complete, aesthetically satisfying environment. They not only wanted to create well-designed implements and total settings for a full, humane existence, but they also wished to use them to transform their own living space into miniature fantasy worlds. The Victoria and Albert's *Saint George* Cabinet (1861), designed by Webb with scenes painted by Morris himself, and The *King René of Anjou's Honeymoon* Cabinet, designed by Seddon and decorated by Rossetti, Burne-Jones, Brown, and Prinsep for Morris, Marshall, Faulkner and Co., exemplify such use of Pre-Raphaelite themes to fantasize the implements of daily life.

Nonetheless, although Morris resembles other members of the Pre-Raphaelite movement when he makes romantic love in a quasi-medieval setting central to his prose romances, his characterization of Birdalone as a heroic, active, sensual young woman sounds an entirely new note. Both the early Pre-Raphaelite Brotherhood and the later aesthetic Pre-Raphaelitism, which evolved under Rossetti's direction and influence, depicted love from the male point of view. As a result, both earlier and later forms of Pre-Raphaelitism tend to present a particularly masculine conception of woman. Their peculiarly Victorian notion of female nature conceives of it dividing quite sharply into two diametrically opposed categories—the active Lilith figure who devours men, and the passive, pensive maiden who waits for a man to awaken or complete her partially formed nature. The active woman, of whom Victorian men seemed so fearful, appears as Rossetti's *Lady Lilith* and *Astarte Syriaca* and as Swinburne's Delores and his Venus in "Laus Veneris." This conception of the fatal, devouring woman, which so inspired illustrators such as Aubrey Beardsley and Alastair, plays a comparatively minor role in Pre-Raphaelite work. Far more important is the other more central conception of woman as a passive, contemplative creature awaiting the lover for awakening, salvation, or even creation. Many of the most important paintings of the early Brotherhood form a series on the theme of romantic love and its frequently tragic aftermath: Millais' *The Woodsman's Daughter* (1851), which is an illustration of Patmore's poem on the unrequited love of a young country girl for a squire's son, presents the first act of a drama which ends with the seduced girl's death, while his *Mariana* (1851) presents a young woman from Tennyson's poem awaiting her lover who does not arrive. The paintings by Hunt and Millais of *The Eve of St. Agnes* (1848, 1863) follow Keats's poem in depicting a successful close to a tale of romantic love, while Millais' *Lorenzo and Isabella* (1849) and Hunt's *Isabella and the Pot of Basil* (1867) illustrate another poem by this poet which ends tragically. Hunt's *The Pilgrim's Return* (1847) and his illustration to Tennyson's "The Ballad of Oriana" (1857) represent the lover mourning over his dead beloved, but the most famous example of the "dead woman" theme is, of course, Millais' *Ophelia* (1851), though Arthur Hughes and many other artists and sculptors attempted the same subject.

Whereas these early works in the Pre-Raphaelite hard-edge style present a precise historically locatable world in sharp outline and bright colors, Burne-Jones' paintings, which represent the high point of the aesthetic Pre-Raphaelitism that descends from Rossetti, set their figures in a sensual, penumbral world. A large proportion of Burne-Jones' major works concern themselves with embodying his fascination, almost obsession, with the relations of men and women. Taken together, these works comprise a sexual myth that had great appeal for the artist and his contemporaries. *St. George and the Dragon* (1868), *Cupid Delivering Psyche* (c.1871), and the *Perseus* series (1875-1888), like Rossetti's "The Wedding of St. George and the Princess Sabra" (1857), present various stages in the dominant male's rescue of the helpless maiden. Similarly, in *The Briar Rose* series (1870-1890) the heroic prince pierces the forbidding enchanted thicket in order to awaken this sleeping beauty, thus restoring her and her entire world to life. *King Cophetua and the Beggar Maid* (1880), which appropriately repeats the disposition of figures employed in his *Annunciation* (1876-1879), depicts a powerful male character essentially creating his beloved—a subject Burne-Jones rendered most elaborately in the *Pygmalion* series (1868-1870), a work which can stand as the type of his sexual myth. Here the young man literally creates his own ideal beloved and is blessed when Venus vivifies her—a Victorian dream come true! MacDonald's Anodos learns all too painfully that such attempts to discover, capture, and possess one's ideal in another person are a self-destructive form of aggression. The Pre-Raphaelites, on the other hand, tended to see this as the ideal form of romantic love—and as one attainable both in art and life. As is well known, members and associates of the Pre-Raphaelite circle married relatively uncultured and even illiterate young women whom they then sought to remake according to a desired image. Although Holman Hunt ultimately failed to be either Cophetua or Pygmalion to Annie Miller, Brown, Rossetti, and Morris married their young women.

Many of Burne-Jones' major depictions of this sexual fantasy derive from Morris' own *Earthly Paradise,* for which they began as illustrations, and it is certainly tempting to see Morris' radically different women of the late prose romances as his mature reaction against the results of attempting to embody such attitudes in real life. At any rate, Birdalone is a development of Pre-Raphaelite conceptions of idealized womanhood which move far beyond the all-too-Victorian world of erotic reverie created by his friends and associates. Although Birdalone shares the innocent beauty and grace, as well as the rich inner life of the Pre-Raphaelite heroine, she is a strong, active figure who not only shapes her own destiny but who also rescues her beloved and restores him to self, sanity, and civilization.

In contrast to Morris' progressive use of the fantasy, William Hope Hodgson, whose *The Night Land* (1912) exemplifies the darker or horrific form of this mode, uses it to embody reactionary social and sexual belief. His vision of a sunless earth millions of years in the future inhabited by Boschian monsters and fearsome spiritual and physical horror clearly is the product of that major cultural anxiety which John A. Lester, Jr. has analyzed in *Journey Through Despair, 1880-1914.*[9] Hodgson's vision of "the Last Redoubt—that great Pyramid of grey metal which held the last millions of this world from the power of the Slayers"[10] well expresses the attitudes of those many thinkers who feared that Western civilization was drawing to a close.

Hodgson relates his bizarre tale of the dark future in an archaic, almost Morrisian diction, which serves, like that of his predecessor, to displace the reader into his imaginative world. The unnamed teller of the tale is an English landowner of some unspecified but premodern age who grieves for his dead wife, Mirdath the Beautiful. He discovers that "at night in my sleep [I] waked into the future of this world, and [have] seen strange things and utter marvels. . . . In this last time of my visions, of which I would tell, it was not as if I *dreamed;* but, as it were, that I *waked* into the dark, in the future of this world. And the sun had died" (p. 34). The narrator, who preserves a memory of his earlier identity, discovers that he is a telepathically gifted youth trained to help preserve the great Redoubt. The burden of the tale, which follows the pattern of medieval romance, takes the form of the young man's perilous adventures in the Night Land to save a telepathic girl from the Lesser Refuge, a smaller redoubt of which all knowledge had been lost for thousands of years until the hero makes mental contact with it. The young woman, Naani, discovers herself to be the reincarnation of Mirdath, and so the two lovers are reunited after millions of years—but first they must make the journey to safety, crawling for days through total darkness, avoiding giants, ab-humans, enormous spiders, and a spiritual evil which is far more terrifying than these physical dangers. Hodgson's archaic and often repulsive ideas of the ideal relations between man and woman are appropriate to a work derived from chivalric romance, but his disturbing mixture of chivalric devotion and brutality—he obviously takes great pleasure in having the hero physically punish his beloved—adds a bizarre dimension to an already strange work. The weird love interludes which punctuate the return journey nonetheless do serve as effective counterpoints to the characters' horrific adventures, the imagination of which provides the main appeal of *The Night Land*.

Introducing us to this nightmarish future, the protagonist explains that the monstrously evil beings surrounding the Great Redoubt had their origin in the

> Days of the Darkening (which I might liken to a story which was believed doubtfully, much as we of this day believe the story of the Creation). A dim record there was of olden sciences (that are as yet far off in *our* future) which, disturbing the unmeasurable Outward Powers, had allow [sic] to pass the Barrier of Life some of these Monsters and Ab-human creatures. . . . And thus there had materialised, and in other cases developed, grotesque and horrible Creatures, which now beset the humans of this world. And where there was no power to take on material form, there had been allowed to certain dreadful Forces to have power to affect the life of the human spirit. . . . As that Eternal Night lengthened itself upon the world, the power of terror grew and strengthened. (pp. 44, 46)

Like the American H. P. Lovecraft, whose work also was often marred by repetition, stilted writing, and reactionary ideas, Hodgson's great gift was the ability to communicate this "power of terror." Both in *The Night Land* and *The Boats of the "Glen Carrig"* (1907), a tale of men shipwrecked on a monstrous island, he embodies all the fears that haunt men sleeping and waking—fears of dissolution, loss of identity, and helplessness in the presence of hideous evil.

Horror fiction takes two basic forms, the most popular of which is the horror or ghost story which reveals the presence of often unexpected terrors within a realistically conceived world. Edgar Allan Poe, Sheridan Le Fanu, Algernon Blackwood, Charles Dickens, Arthur Machen, and many authors of recent years have excelled in writing this sensational cousin to the realistic novel. Frequently, the narrator or main character is a skeptical, even unimaginative person who, by the tale's end, is either convinced of the existence of fantastic

horror breaking into his everyday world or punished for his skepticism by it. In contrast, the horrific fantasy—like the allegorical romances of Morris—takes place in either a fully created world or so emphasizes the hidden presence of such a world bordering on our own (or lying beneath it) that it subsumes the everyday world with which it began. Hodgson's books, Mervyn Peake's "Boy in Darkness," and Lovecraft's many tales exemplify such worlds of terrifying fantasy.

The evil which provides the horror in both forms of fiction—horror story and horrific fantasy—appears in a limited number of forms. First, there is the common use of Satanism and witchcraft, which obviously relies heavily on a Judaeo-Christian conception of evil that often receives a distinctly Manichean twist: the presence of Satanic evil in such overwhelming form makes the devil appear another deity of potency equal to God. Medieval grotesques, medieval and later representations of temptations and the Last Judgment, and the work of Bosch, Brueghel, and their imitators have provided powerful inspiration for artists and writers who work in this fantastic mode. In the period since 1850 it appears in illustration both in seriously horrific forms and in the more whimsical creations of Rackham's witches and Sime's "Devil with a Coal Scuttle." A second, closely-related source of evil, which present the continued existence of older, all-but-forgotten divinities and forces, derives from classical and Northern mythology and the darker side of fairy lore. Arthur Machen's "The Lost Brother" (from *The Three Imposters,* 1890) and Lovecraft's "The Dunwich Horror" exemplify the use in horrific fantasy of these dangerous, destructive, and often hideously cruel forces which remain outside the Judaeo-Christian scheme of things, while Sime's drawings for *The Fantasy of Life* (1901) represent their appearance in fantastic art.

The third source of horror, which occasionally combines with the previous two, derives from man's fear of formlessness, chaos, and devolution. Machen's "Novel of the White Powder" (1901), Lovecraft's "The Dunwich Horror," and the giant slugs and other creatures of *The Night Land* draw upon both our normal antipathy to slimy, decaying substances and our instinctive revulsion at the way death and dissolution reduce living form to shapelessness. As Barton L. St. Armand has pointed out in his study of Lovecraft, the American writer's use of such horrifying dissolution, which use embodies his existential nausea and fear of universal corruption, derives largely from the classical example of such an image—Poe's "The Facts in the Case of M. Valdemar."[11] At the conclusion of Poe's tale, Valdemar, who had been hypnotized at the point of death, is awakened from his trance and "his whole frame—within the space of a single minute, or even less, shrunk—crumbled—absolutely *rotted* away beneath my hands. Upon the bed, before the whole company, there lay a nearly liquid mass of loathsome—of detestable putrescence."[12] In Harry Clark's wonderfully grisly illustration of this passage, the onlookers recoil in horror at the disintegrating body, from which part of an arm has detached itself and from whose eyes and mouth blood and gore run.

Although Hodgson's *The Night Land* relies frequently on such horrific sensationalism, it is equally concerned with emphasizing the ability to endure this horror possessed "by that lonely and mighty hill of humanity, facing its end—so near the Eternal, and yet so far deferred in the minds and to the senses of those humans. And thus it hath been ever" (p. 46). Hodgson frequently attempts to show that his nightmarish cosmos has a serious general significance, that it is relevant to human experience throughout the ages. His remarks about evolution, science, and spirituality suggest that he took these points quite seriously and they are not, as is often the case in such stories, merely attempts to establish the credibility of a fictional world. The miraculous intervention of a good divinity in this Manichean world at points when the hero has otherwise no chance of survival further suggests that Hodgson believed that if man strove heroically to preserve love and humanity against the forces of evil, he might expect to be rewarded by supernatural aid which, while it might not bring him final victory, would allow him to battle on equal terms.

In fact, all the examples of fantasy at which we have looked turn out to be vehicles by which their authors dramatize ideas of high seriousness rather than mere escapist fictions. The essential seriousness of much fine fantastic literature in the nineteenth and early twentieth centuries appears nowhere more clearly than in works such as Charles Kingsley's *The Water-Babies* (1863) and George MacDonald's "The Golden Key" and *At the Back of the North Wind* (1871), which employ the great potential of fantasy as a literary mode to convey Christian ideas of the afterlife. *At the Back of the North Wind*, for instance, relates how a young boy has magical adventures in the company of the mysterious North Wind who we gradually come to realize is Death itself. In the nineteenth century, when diseases carried away many children before they reached their teens, sermons, tracts, and fiction often sought to console parents and prepare children for an early death by removing its terrors. Fantasy is far better suited than the tract or sermon to convey the essentially paradoxical notion that earthly life (which is but a preparation for a higher, fuller eternal life) is a form of death, while death (which at first seems so fearful) is the only means to true life. In the Gospels Christ tells His disciples that a seed can only bear fruit if it dies—if it loses its initial state and develops into another. The Christian lives with this paradox and must learn to redefine death, ultimately finding in it a new, higher, and essentially fantastic meaning. Since the

central principle of literary and visual fantasy is precisely such shifting of basic laws or meanings by which we experience the world, this artistic mode is well suited to embodying views which deny that everyday reality, the here and now, is either all-important or the only form of reality.

As the various works at which we have looked suggest, fantasy in fact comprises a second great tradition of English fiction. Even the Marxist critic Arnold Kettle, who despises the romance as the escapist fictions of a ruling class, recognizes that "all art is, in an important sense, an escape. . . . There is a sense in which the capacity to escape from his present experience . . . is man's greatest and distinguishing ability. . . . This fantastic quality of art, that it takes us out of the real world so that, as Shelley put it, it 'awakens and enlarges the mind itself by rendering it the receptacle of a thousand unapprehended combinations of thought,' this quality is not a trivial or accidental by-product but the very essence of the value of art. If art did in fact—as the ultra-naturalistic school tends to assume—merely paint a picture of what is, it would be a much less valuable form of human activity, for it would not alter men's consciousness but merely confirm it."[13] Kettle's important recognition of the essential value of escape or withdrawal from everyday life and its assumptions is developed independently by Morse Peckham into a compelling theory of the arts. According to his *Man's Rage for Chaos: Biology, Behavior, and the Arts,* the arts are "an adaptational mechanism" which acts as a "rehearsal for those real situations in which it is vital for our survival to endure cognitive tension, to refuse the comforts of validation . . . when such validation is inappropriate because too vital interests are at stake; art is the reinforcement of the capacity to endure disorientation so that a real and significant problem may emerge. Art is the exposure to the tensions and problems of a false world so that man may endure exposing himself to the tensions and problems of the real world."[14] Although neither Kettle nor Peckham concerns himself with fantastic literature and art, it seems probable that the strange worlds of such paintings and fictions have an equal if not greater capacity to return us to everyday life with our imaginations exercised and strengthened as do works of the realistic schools. Fantasy's essential abilities to entertain, instruct, and exercise the mind and spirit make it, in short, a major mode and one well worth serious, if delighted, attention.

Notes

[1] Richard Chase, *The American Novel and Its Tradition* (Garden City, N.Y.: Anchor/Doubleday, 1957), pp. 12-13.

[2] Eric S. Rabkin, *The Fantastic in Literature* (Princeton: Princeton University Press, 1976), p. 37.

[3] John Ruskin, *Works* (The Library Edition), eds. E. T. Cook and Alexander Wedderburn, 39 vols. (London: George Allen, 1903-1912), I, 316. Hereafter cited in the text by volume and page.

[4] George MacDonald, *Phantastes* (Grand Rapids, Mich.: Eerdmans, 1964), pp. 19-20. Hereafter cited in the text.

[5] C. S. Lewis, "On Stories," in *Of Other Worlds: Essays and Stories,* ed. Walter Hooper (New York: Harvest, 1975), p. 12.

[6] George Meredith, *The Shaving of Shagpat* (New York: Ballantine, 1970), p. 1. Hereafter cited in the text.

[7] Lin Carter, "About *The Well at the World's End* and William Morris," in *The Well at the World's End,* 2 vols. (New York: Ballantine, 1970), I, x-xi; II, [iii].

[8] Barbara J. Bono, "The Prose Fictions of William Morris: A Study in the Literary Aesthetic of a Victorian Social Reformer," *Victorian Poetry,* 13, no. 3-4 (1975), 52.

[9] John A. Lester, Jr., *Journey Through Despair, 1880-1914* (Princeton: Princeton University Press, 1968). See also Samuel Hynes, *The Edwardian Turn of Mind* (Princeton: Princeton University Press, 1968).

[10] William Hope Hodgson, *The Night Land* (Westport, Conn.: Hyperion, 1976), p. 34. Hereafter cited in the text.

[11] Barton L. St. Armand, *The Roots of Horror in the Fiction of H. P. Lovecraft* (Elizabethtown, N.Y.: Dragon Press, 1977), pp. 59-77.

[12] Edgar Allan Poe, *The Complete Tales and Poems* (New York: Modern Library, 1938), p. 103.

[13] Arnold Kettle, *An Introduction to the English Novel,* 2nd ed. (London: Hutchinson, 1967), I, 31.

[14] Morse Peckham, *Man's Rage for Chaos: Biology, Behavior, and the Arts* (New York: Schocken, 1967), p. 314.

Harry Stone

SOURCE: "The Christmas Books: 'Giving Nursery Tales a Higher Form'," in *Dickens and the Invisible World: Fairy Tales, Fantasy, and Novel-Making,* In-diana University Press, 1979. Reprint, Macmillan Press, Ltd., 1980, pp. 119-45.

[*Below, Stone examines Charles Dickens' use of supernatural events in his five Christmas books, and maintains that while the Christmas stories are unsatisfactory as literature, they played an important role in the development of fantasy elements in Dickens' later novels.*]

In the interval between the beginning of *Martin Chuzzlewit* and the completion of *Dombey and Son,* Dickens wrote five Christmas books: *A Christmas Carol* (1843), *The Chimes* (1844), *The Cricket on the Hearth* (1845), *The Battle of Life* (1846), and *The Haunted Man* (1848).[1] *The Haunted Man,* the last of the Christmas books, straddles the later limits of this interval. *The Haunted Man* was conceived and partly written in the interval, but not finished until *Dombey* was completed.[2] With the exception of *The Battle of Life,* which depends for its central mechanism on a straightforward analogy between life and an ancient battlefield, the Christmas books rely on fairy-tale machinery to gain their characteristic effects. But this puts the matter too restrictively. The Christmas books draw their innermost energies from fairy tales: they exploit fairy-tale themes, fairy-tale happenings, and fairy-tale techniques. Indeed the Christmas books *are* fairy tales. As Dickens himself put it, he was here taking old nursery tales and "giving them a higher form."[3]

The pattern that Dickens traces in each of his Christmas books—always excepting *The Battle of Life*—is the pattern that he followed with "Gabriel Grub" in *Pickwick.* The design could hardly be simpler or more direct. A protagonist who is mistaken or displays false values is forced, through a series of extraordinary events, to see his errors. This familiar, almost pedestrian given is interfused with fairy-tale elements, a commingling that shapes and transfigures every aspect of the design. Storybook signs set the mood, herald the onset of the action, and enforce the moral lessons. Magical happenings dominate the story. The crucial action takes place in a dream or vision presided over by supernatural creatures who control what goes on. The resolution occurs when the happenings of the vision—a magically telescoped survey of the protagonist's life, and a masquelike representation of the consequences of his false attitudes—force him to reassess his views. In the fashion of most fairy stories, the moral is strongly reiterated at the end.

This structure was of immense value to Dickens. It gave him a framework that provided an aesthetic justification for the legerdemain which in his earlier works, especially in his finales, had usually appeared, not as fairy-tale felicities, but as arbitrary fairy-tale wrenchings. He could now show misery and horror and yet do so in a context of joyful affirmation. He could depict evil flourishing to its ultimate flowering and still deny that flowering. He could introduce the most disparate scenes, events, and visions without losing the reader's confidence. He could manipulate time with no need to obey the ordinary laws of chronology. He could make his characters and events real when he wished them real, magical when he wished them magical. He could effect overnight conversions which could be justified aesthetically. He could teach by parable rather than exhortation. And he could deal with life in terms of a storybook logic that underscored both the real and the ideal.

These potentialities, fundamental ingredients in Dickens' mature narrative method (but there thoroughly assimilated to the dominant realism), are exploited with varying degrees of success in all the Christmas books. In *A Christmas Carol,* to take the first of the Christmas books, Dickens adapts fairy-tale effects and fairy-tale techniques with marvelous skill. All readers are aware of the ghosts and spirits that manipulate the story, but these supernatural beings are only the most obvious signs of a pervasive indebtedness to fairy stories. Dickens himself emphasized that indebtedness. He subtitled his novelette *A Ghost Story of Christmas,* and he followed this spectral overture with other magical associations, In the preface to the *Carol* he told potential readers that he had endeavored "in this ghostly little book, to raise the Ghost of an Idea." Then he went on: "May it haunt their houses pleasantly and no one wish to lay it!"[4] The chapter headings continue this emphasis. Four of the five headings reinforce supernatural expectations: "Marley's Ghost," "The First of the Three Spirits," "The Second of the Three Spirits," and "The Last of the Spirits." With such signposts at the outset, we can expect the journey itself to be full of wondrous events. We are not disappointed, though the opening begins disarmingly enough. It insists on the deadness of Marley and then drifts into a long, facetious reference to the ghost of Hamlet's father. The narrator's attitude is worldly and commonsensical, but Marley's deadness and the ghost of Hamlet's father set the scene for the wild events that are about to take place.

Scrooge sets the scene too. He has much of the archetypal miser in him, but he is more of an ordinary man than his immediate prototypes, prototypes such as Gabriel Grub, Arthur Gride, Ralph Nickleby, and Jonas Chuzzlewit. Yet at the same time Scrooge is compassed round with supernatural attributes that cunningly suffuse his fundamental realism. One soon sees how this process works. The freezing cold that pervades his inner being frosts all his external features and outward mannerisms (nipped and pointed nose, shrivelled cheek, stiffened gait, red eyes, blue lips, grating voice), and this glacial iciness chills all the world without. "He carried his own low temperature always about with him; he iced his office in the dog-

days; and didn't thaw it one degree at Christmas. . . . No warmth could warm, no wintry weather chill him."[5] In this respect Scrooge is a prototype of Mr. Dombey. That cold gentleman freezes and congeals his small universe with haughty frostiness.

The story proper of *A Christmas Carol* begins with the traditional "Once upon a time."[6] After this evocative opening Dickens quickly intensifies the storybook atmosphere. Scrooge lives in Marley's old chambers, and Marley died seven years ago on Christmas Eve, that is, seven years ago on the night the story opens. It is a foggy night. Nearby houses dwindle mysteriously into "mere phantoms"; ghostly forms loom dimly in the hazy mist.[7] Out of such details, out of cold, fog, and frost, and out of brief touches of contrasting warmth, Dickens builds an atmosphere dense with personification, animism, anthropomorphism, and the like. The inanimate world is alive and active; every structure, every object plays its percipient role in the unfolding drama. Buildings and gateways, bedposts and door knockers become sentient beings that conspire in a universal morality. Everything is connected by magical means to everything else. Scrooge's chambers are a case in point. The narrator tells us that they are in a lonely, isolated building that must have played hide-and-seek with other houses in its youth, run into a yard where it had no business to be, forgotten its way out again, and remained there ever since.[8] This lost, isolated, cutoff building, fit residence for a lost, isolated, cutoff man, has its own special weather and tutelary spirit. The fog and frost hang so heavy about the black old gateway of this building "that it seemed as if the Genius of the Weather sat in mournful meditation on the threshold."[9]

Given a universe so magical and responsive, we are hardly surprised when Scrooge momentarily sees Marley's face glowing faintly in his front-door knocker, its "ghostly spectacles turned up on its ghostly forehead."[10] When Scrooge sees an equally ghostly hearse on his staircase a few moments later, we know that he is in for a night of it. Thus we are fully prepared for Marley's ghost when it does appear, and we know how to interpret its every movement and accoutrement. Marley's ghost is a superb compound of social symbolism, wild imagination, realistic detail, and grisly humor. It moves in its own strange atmosphere, its hair and clothes stirring curiously, as though agitated by "the hot vapour from an oven"; it wears a bandage round its head, and when it removes this death cloth, its lower jaw drops down upon its breast.[11] Like Blake's city-pent Londoner, Marley's ghost drags and clanks its "mind-forg'd manacles," the chain it "forged in life" and girded on of its "own free will"; like the ghost of Hamlet's father, it is doomed to walk the night and wander restlessly abroad.[12] Scrooge is skeptical of this apparition, but he is no match for the ghost's supernatural power. Like the Ancient Mariner

Patrick Stewart performs a scene from Charles Dickens' A Christmas Carol *in 1994 at Christie's auction house.*

with the wedding guest, the ghost "hath his will." When Scrooge offers his last resistance, the ghost raises a frightful cry, shakes its chains appallingly, and takes the bandage from round its head. Scrooge falls on his knees and submits. Like the wedding guest, now Scrooge "cannot choose but hear." And as in the *Ancient Mariner,* where the wedding guest's struggle and reluctant submission help us suspend our disbelief, in *A Christmas Carol* Scrooge's struggle and submission help us to a like suspension. The ghost has accomplished its mission; the work of the three spirits, work that will culminate in Scrooge's redemption (and our enlightenment), can now begin.

The three spirits or ghosts (Dickens uses the terms interchangeably) are allegorical figures as well as supernatural agents. The Ghost of Christmas Past combines in his person and in his actions distance and closeness, childhood and age, forgetfulness and memory; in a similar fashion the Ghost of Christmas Present is a figure of ease, plenty, and joy—an embodiment of the meaning of Christmas; the Ghost of Christmas Yet to Come, on the other hand, a hooded and shrouded Death, bears implacable witness to the fatal course Scrooge has been pursuing. Each spirit, in other words, enacts a role and presides over scenes that befit its representation. But it is the scenes rather than the spirits that are all-important. The scenes embody Dickens' message in swift vignettes and unforgettable paradigms—Fezziwig's ball, the Cratchits' Christmas dinner, Scrooge's lonely grave. By means of the fairy-tale machinery Dickens can move instantaneously from magic-lantern picture to magic-lantern picture, juxtaposing, contrasting, commenting, and counterpointing, and he can do all this with absolute freedom and ease. He can evoke the crucial image, limn the archetypal scene, concentrate on the traumatic spot of time, with no need to sketch the valleys in between. Like Le Sage much earlier in *The Devil upon Two Sticks* (a boyhood favorite of Dickens), he can fly over the unsuspecting city, lift its imperturbable rooftops, and reveal swift tableaus of pathos and passion; like Joyce much later in the opening pages of *A Portrait of the Artist as a Young Man,* he can race through the years, linger here and there, and provide brief glimpses of the unregarded moments that move and shape us. The overall effect, however, is more like that of a richly colored Japanese screen. Amid swirling mists and dense clouds one glimpses prototypical scenes of serenity and turmoil, joy and nightmare horror.

Through Scrooge Dickens attempts to embody symbolic, social, psychological, and mythic truth. Scrooge is an outrageous miser and ogre, but he is also an emblem of more ordinary pathology: he is an epitome of all selfish and self-regarding men. In his latter aspect, he touches our lives. He allows us to see how self-interest—an impulse that motivates each one of us—can swell to monster proportions. He shows us how not to live, and then, at the end, he points us toward salvation. That lesson has social as well as symbolic ramifications. We are made to see that in grinding Bob Cratchit Scrooge grinds himself, that in letting Tiny Tim perish he perishes alive himself. All society is connected: individual actions are not self-contained and personal, they have social consequences; social evils are not limited and discrete, they taint the whole society. These ideas, of course, were not unique to Dickens. They were being preached by many Victorians, by two such different men—both friends of Dickens—as Douglas Jerrold and Thomas Carlyle, for example. But Dickens presents these ideas in a more seductive guise than any of his contemporaries. And he blends teaching with much else.

For one thing, he merges symbolic paradigms and social doctrines with psychological analysis. By means of a few swift childhood vignettes he gives us some notion of why Scrooge became what he is. The first spirit shows Scrooge an image of his early self: "a solitary child, neglected by his friends," and left alone in school at Christmas time.[13] This scene of loneliness and neglect is mitigated by a single relief: the boy's intense reading. The reading is not simply referred to, it comes to life, a bright pageant of color and warmth in his drab isolation. The exotic characters from that reading troop into the barren room and enact their familiar adventures. Scenes from *The Arabian Nights* flash before Scrooge, then images from *Valentine and Orson,* then vignettes from *The Arabian Nights* again, then episodes from *Robinson Crusoe*—all as of yore, all wonderfully thrilling and absorbing. Scrooge is beside himself with excitement. The long-forgotten memory of his lonely self and of his succoring reading softens him: he remembers what it was to be a child; he wishes that he had given something to the boy who sang a Christmas carol at his door the night before.[14] A moment later Scrooge is looking at a somewhat older image of his former self, again alone in a school, again left behind at Christmas time. But now his sister Fan enters and tells him that he can come home at last, that father is kinder now and will permit him to

return, that Scrooge is to be a man and "never to come back here" again.[15] These memories also soften Scrooge.

The memories, of course, are versions of Dickens' own experiences: the lonely boy "reading as if for life," and saved by that reading; the abandoned child, left in Chatham to finish the Christmas term, while the family goes off to London; the banished son (banished while Fanny remains free), exiled by his father to the blacking warehouse and then released by him at last. These wounding experiences, or rather the *Carol* version of them, help turn Scrooge (and here he is very different from the outward Dickens) into a lonely, isolated man intent on insulating himself from harm or hurt. In a subsequent vignette, a vignette between him and his fiancée, Scrooge chooses money over love. He is the victim of his earlier wound. He seeks through power and aggrandizement to gird himself against the vulnerability that had scarred his childhood. But in making himself invulnerable, he shuts out humanity as well. This happens to Scrooge because, paradoxically, in trying to triumph over his past, he has forgotten it; he has forgotten what it is to be a child, he has forgotten what it is to be lonely and friendless, to cry, laugh, imagine, yearn, and love. The first spirit, through memory, helps Scrooge recover his past, helps him recover the humanness (the responsiveness and fellow feeling) and the imagination (the reading and the visions) that were his birthright, that are every man's birthright.

All this, and much more, is done swiftly and economically with the aid of Dickens' fairy-tale format. The rapid shifts from scene to scene, the spirits' pointed questions and answers, the telescoping, blurring, and juxtaposition of time, the fusion of allegory, realism, psychology, and fancy—all are made possible, all are brought into order and believability, by Dickens' storybook atmosphere and storybook devices. *A Christmas Carol* has a greater unity of effect, a greater concentration of thematic purpose, a greater economy of means towards ends, and a greater sense of integration and cohesiveness than any previous work by Dickens.

A Christmas Carol is the finest of the Christmas books. This preeminence results from its consummate melding of the most archetypal losses, fears, and yearnings with the most lucid embodiment of such elements in characters and actions. No other Christmas book displays this perfect coming together of concept and vehicle. The result is a most powerful, almost mythic statement of widely held truths and aspirations. Scrooge represents every man who has hardened his heart, lost his ability to feel, separated himself from his fellow men, or sacrificed his life to ego, power, or accumulation. The symbolic force of Scrooge's conversion is allied to the relief we feel (since we are all Scrooges, in part) in knowing that we too can change and be reborn. This is why we are moved by the reborn Scrooge's childlike exultation in his prosaic physical surroundings, by his glee at still having time to give and share. We too can exult in "Golden sunlight; Heavenly sky; sweet fresh air; merry bells"; we too can cry, "Oh, glorious. Glorious!"; we too can give and share.[16] Scrooge assures us that we can advance from the prison of self to the paradise of community. The Carol's fairy-tale structure helps in that assurance. The structure evokes and objectifies the undefiled world of childhood and makes us feel that we, like Scrooge, can recapture it. Deep symbolic identifications such as these, identifications that stir us whether we are consciously aware of them or not, give A Christmas Carol its enduring grip on our culture. A Christmas Carol is a myth or fairy tale for our times, one that is still full of life and relevance. Its yearly resurrection in advertisement, cartoon, and television program, its reappearance in new versions (in Bergman's Wild Strawberries, to cite only one instance), testify to this.

Yet the vitality of A Christmas Carol raises other questions. Why is the Carol, which elaborates the central idea found in the Gabriel Grub story in Pickwick, so much better than its prototype? "Gabriel Grub" does not elicit the empathy of the Carol. This is so because Gabriel never ascends to universality; he is simply a mean man who is taught an idiosyncratic lesson. We see nothing of his childhood, of his development, of his future; we see nothing, in other words, of the shaping forces that would allow us to relate to his experiences. The story centers on his drunken vision; it scants his salvation and our enlightenment. Furthermore, "Gabriel Grub" lacks any rich social import. Unlike the Carol, there is virtually no interwining of plot with social criticism: no ideas about ignorance and want, no anatomy of materialism, no criticism of relations between employer and employee, no effective demonstration of how to live. Misanthropy is simply presented and then punished. I am not suggesting that a work of art must have a social message. I am simply affirming that part of the Carol's appeal comes from its powerful demonstration of how a man should live—live in society—if he is to save his soul, a kind of demonstration that is largely lacking in "Gabriel Grub."

By the same token, the supernatural machinery of "Gabriel Grub," despite successful local effects, is mechanical and abrupt. Unlike the Carol, where Marley's ghost is the culmination of many signs and actions, in "Gabriel Grub" the King of the Goblins appears with little preparation; again, unlike the Carol, where Marley's ghost is a prototype of Scrooge, and therefore deeply significant, in "Gabriel Grub" the King of the Goblins is simply an agency, a convenient manipulative device, a creature who has no relevance

to Gabriel's life and habits (other, perhaps, than being an emanation of Gabriel's habitual drunkenness). Even the Carol equivalents to the King of the Goblins, the three spirits, have an allegorical pertinence that the King of the Goblins lacks. In part these differences in the two stories are owing to differences in length, but more importantly they are owing to differences in conception and execution. Obviously the preeminence of the Carol, its elevation to culture fable, comes not from the basic ingredients—they can be found in "Gabriel Grub"—but from the perfect blending of well-wrought theme and well-wrought form. A Christmas Carol demonstrates how much more skilled Dickens had become in using fairy-tale conceptions to achieve that virtuoso blending, how adept he had become in using fairy-tale elements to integrate and convey his view of life.

A Christmas Carol is the best of the Christmas books, but it is not superior to the other Christmas books in all respects, and it is not always the most technically advanced. The second Christmas book, The Chimes, uses a more realistic, yet at the same time more imaginative, supernatural agency to guide the fairy-tale workings of the story—no convenient Carol ghosts here. In The Chimes the vibrations of the bells slowly take on magical qualities and superintend what takes place. The transformation of the bells into allegorical forces is done most elegantly. Dickens combines compelling exactitude and wonderful fancifulness. As in Chuzzlewit, the story opens with a personification of the wind, this time of a winter wind moaning and wailing through a London church at night. The wind sighs through aisle, vault, and altar, and it howls dismally in the steeple belfry where dwell the chimes that are the subject of the story. The personification of the wind is masterfully done—its airy presence is elaborately evocative and eerily powerful—but each figure and trope is rooted in a most meticulous realism.

The wind buffets and engulfs the church, and near the entrance to the church, in good weather and in foul, a poverty-stricken old ticket porter, Toby (or "Trotty") Veck, takes his stand. All day long he hears the bells chime, and all night too, for he lives hard by with his daughter, Meg. From his stand at the base of the tower, he often looks up at the bells as they chime, wonders how they are lodged, how cared for, and how rung. Trotty and the bells are much alike—the narrator draws a long analogy identifying the two.[17] Indeed over the years Trotty has grown to love the bells and to commune with them. He invests them with special powers; they are his friends, sometimes they talk to him.[18] Often the chimes seem to echo his thoughts, repeating and repeating some hope or fear in concise and cadenced measure.[19] All this is developed slowly and carefully so that realism, psychology, and fancifulness blend and reinforce one another.

As Dickens creates this aura, he also unfolds the story. The story takes place on the last day of the year. Trotty, at his chill post at the entrance to the church, is visited by his daughter, Meg, and her fiancé, Richard. Owing to their poverty, Meg and Richard have postponed their marriage for three years, but life is slipping past them, and now they want to marry on New Year's Day. As the old ticket porter and the young couple stand near the church door talking, they are confronted by three gentlemen who hold three commonplace attitudes toward the poor. Alderman Cute believes in putting the poor down; a red-faced gentleman recommends forcing them back to the "good old times"; and Mr. Filer treats them as lifeless columns of charts, averages, and statistics. Later in the afternoon Trotty meets a fourth gentleman, Sir Joseph Bowley, "The Poor Man's Friend and Father." This gentleman advocates a fourth attitude toward the poor. He requires that the poor be subservient and behave like dutiful children. The statements and actions of these four gentlemen, the newspaper reports Trotty has read concerning the crimes and atrocities of the poor, and his own grinding poverty cause him to feel that the poor are born bad, that they have no useful role to play in society, that they should not marry and multiply, and that they are better off dead.

That night at home, while Trotty is reading additional newspaper accounts of the depravities of the poor, the chimes ring out. They have been talking to Trotty all the day. Now they seem to call him, and they seem to echo his despair. The bells clang and clamor. They seem to say, "Haunt and hunt him, haunt and hunt him, Drag him to us, drag him to us!"[20] The bells clash and peal, louder and louder. Trotty feels pulled toward them. Partly as a result of that pull, partly because they seem so unusually loud, Trotty decides to see whether the bell-tower door is open. When he comes to the church he is astonished to find that the tower door is indeed open. He goes in to investigate and accidentally shuts the door, locking himself in. He begins to climb the tower, going round and round, up and up, encountering mysterious objects, hearing mysterious echoes. He finally feels a freshening and then a wind as he gropes toward the belfry. Now he is in the belfry. He can see the housetops and chimneys below him; he can see the tangled quarters in which he lives; he can see the dim lights in the distance, obscured and blurred by dark mists. He accidentally touches a bell rope, and then, as though "working out the spell upon him," he feels impelled to ascend the steep ladders toward the bells.[21] Finally, he reaches them. He can just faintly make out "their great shapes in the gloom . . . Shadowy, and dark, and dumb."[22] A heavy sense of loneliness and dread falls upon him as he climbs into this "airy nest of stone and metal."[23] His head spins. He calls out, "Halloa," hears the sound mournfully protracted by the echoes, and giddy and confused, sinks into a swoon.[24] At this point the second quarter of *The Chimes* ends.

It is only with the beginning of the third quarter—more than half way through the book—that the supernatural machinery of *The Chimes* takes over, a culmination that has been carefully prepared for by the slow accumulation of enchantment and by the events of the day. Trotty's swooning consciousness is now filled with dwarf creatures—phantoms, spirits, and elves—and with the jumbled thoughts and events of the last few hours. The tiny creatures cluster about him and also swarm through the surrounding city, attending all the actions and thoughts of the teeming multitudes who live nearby. Some of the phantoms are ugly, some handsome; some large, some small; some old, some young; some beat those they attend, some comfort them with music. They swarm about all the activities of life and death, filling the air and the habitations of men with restless and untiring motion. One becomes aware after a while that these tiny forms are creatures of the bells, and that they swarm through air and earth whenever the bells begin to chime. Trotty's "charmed footsteps" brought him to the belfry, but the airy elves proclaim their own identity. There is no mistaking that identity. Dickens personifies and allegorizes the vibrating bells with wonderful skill:

> As he gazed, the Chimes stopped. Instantaneous change! The whole swarm [of tiny creatures] fainted! their forms collapsed, their speed deserted them; they sought to fly, but in the act of falling died and melted into air. No fresh supply succeeded them. One straggler leaped down pretty briskly from the surface of the Great Bell, and alighted on his feet, but he was dead and gone before he could turn round. Some few of the late company who had gambolled in the tower, remained there, spinning over and over a little longer; but these became at every turn more faint, and few, and feeble, and soon went the way of the rest. The last of all was one small hunchback, who had got into an echoing corner, where he twirled and twirled, and floated by himself a long time; showing such perseverance, that at last he dwindled to a leg and even to a foot, before he finally retired; but he vanished in the end, and then the tower was silent.[25]

At this point Trotty dimly perceives in each bell a bearded figure of the bulk and stature of the bell, at once "a figure and the Bell itself."[26] Dickens develops these bell figures with rich and evocative symbolism. Mysterious and awful, they rest on nothing, their draped and hooded heads merged in the dim roof, their muffled hands upon their goblin mouths. They are hemmed about "in a very forest of hewn timber; from the entanglements, intricacies, and depths of which, as from among the boughs of a dead wood blighted for their phantom use, they kept their darksome and unwinking watch."²⁷ These figures are the goblins of the bells—the subtitle of *The Chimes* is *A Goblin Story of Some Bells that Rang an Old Year Out and a New Year In*. Once the bell goblins are delineated, the masque begins. As great blasts of air come moaning through the tower and then die away, the Great Bell, its voice low and deep, but sounding with the other bells as well, begins to speak.

Trotty has come to the nest of time; the voice of the bells is the voice of time. Time now takes Trotty and shows him what the future holds in store if the pernicious doctrines he has heard that day are allowed to generate their deadly spawn. As in *A Christmas Carol*, Trotty's enlightenment is effected by being swiftly conveyed through space and time and shown vignettes that embody these lessons—vignettes that depict the harrowing destruction of Meg, Richard, and the suffering hosts of the poor, vignettes that shadow forth the final fiery death of the society that mandates such wanton perishings.

The development of *The Chimes* up to the vignettes is spare and masterful. The conception of time as the didactic agency and its embodiment in the bells is much more functional and imaginative than the three spirits of *A Christmas Carol* and is much better integrated into the realistic texture of the story. But the vignettes themselves are often feverish and overdrawn, sometimes mawkish, sometimes touched with inflated rhetoric. As a consequence, the latter portions of *The Chimes* often dwindle into tractlike preaching and excess. This tendency is not surprising. Dickens regarded the Christmas books as vehicles for social teaching. He felt that at the Christmas season men's hearts were softened and receptive. At that time, by invoking the spirit of Christmas and utilizing the magic of fairy stories, by bringing his readers through such means closer to their childhood innocence and openness, he could steal into their hearts and move them to change. In *The Chimes* he hoped to strike "a great blow for the poor"—an end he had had in mind for several years.²⁸ This desire to strike heavily and decisively caused him to overdraw the last two quarters of the story. He literally abandoned himself to the writing. He was seized each day by "regular, ferocious excitement," and he blazed away "wrathful and red-hot" until deep in the afternoon.²⁹ The story, he confessed, "has great possession of me every moment in the day; and drags me where it will."³⁰ It often dragged him too far. *The Chimes,* despite many sections of memorable writing, lacks the mythlike universality of *A Christmas Carol.* It is too caught up in local wrongs and local satire to speak out engrossingly to later generations. It is a tract for the times, not a fable for posterity.

In his next Christmas book, *The Cricket on the Hearth: A Fairy Tale of Home*, Dickens is neither so urgent nor so insistent, but the work sinks under other dif-ficulties. *The Cricket* is compounded of hackneyed plot contrivances and sentimental tableaus: mysterious strangers, miserly old lechers, heart-of-oak laborers, coyly fluttering heroines, mistaken conclusions, transparent disguises, and unbelievable transformations. The story is a celebration of home—a fairy tale of home, as the subtitle has it—a celebration of trust, forbearing love, and simple domestic joys. For the most part these virtues (and the actions that convey them) are mechanically asserted and superficially manipulated; one rarely gets the feeling that Dickens' deepest energies are involved. It is not that he disbelieves in the virtues he is espousing, it is that the demonstration fails to fire his imagination. Yet there are exceptions to this generalization. The dog, Boxer, the toys created by Caleb Plummer, the antics of Tilly Slowboy—these and other touches flare into intermittent life.

There is also a more important imaginative conception that lives—and lives more steadily. This is the fairy-tale accompaniment, the magical song of the cricket. Yet this accompaniment exists primarily outside the main narrative. The magical chord sounds powerfully at the opening, reverberates strongly again when John Peerybingle sits through the night and contemplates murder, and then echoes briefly at the end. There are storybook elements elsewhere in the novelette, of course. I have already mentioned some of the folklore motifs and folklore characters that work lifelessly at the center of the story. There are occasional fairy-tale allusions and stylistic touches as well. Here, for example, is how the second section begins: "Caleb Plummer and his Blind Daughter lived all alone by themselves, as the Story-books say—and my blessing, with yours to back it I hope, on the Story-books, for saying anything in this workaday world!—Caleb Plummer and his Blind Daughter lived all alone by themselves, in a little cracked nutshell of a wooden house."³¹ This entrée forms a fitting opening for the strange storybook world the toymaker and his daughter live in and for the enchanted web of illusions the toymaker has spun round his blind child.

But the primary fairy-tale energy of the story is with the cricket, and to a lesser extent, with the kettle. These two commonplace adjuncts of hearth and home open the story; their music slowly fills the cottage fireside of John Peerybingle. In a long, intricate tour de force, Dickens brilliantly animates the humble kettle and lowly cricket, until their hum and chirp embody all the attributes of a happy home. That two-voiced sound, reassuring and irresistible, transformed into the essence of home, finally beams out into the world. Eventually "the kettle and the Cricket, at one and the same moment, and by some power of amalgamation best known to themselves, sent, each, his fireside song of comfort streaming into a ray of the candle that shone out through the window, and a long way down the lane. And this light, bursting on a certain person who, on the instant, approached towards it through the gloom, expressed the whole thing to him, literally in a twinkling, and cried, 'Welcome home, old fellow! Welcome home, my boy!'"[32] The cricket soon becomes the very embodiment of the Peerybingle household, a spirit whose chirp can incorporate and summon up all the succoring powers vested in that loving home. The cricket on the hearth of John Peerybingle's house—the narrator soon tells us this outright—is the "Genius of his Hearth and Home."[33] As the cricket chirps upon the hearth, its familiar song evokes memories, reveries, and dreams in those who hear its music. Transformed by such associations, the comforting song of the cricket gradually assumes a fairy shape, enters the room in that form as well, and mingles its beneficent powers with the thoughts and yearnings of those who dwell within its circling sound. By such means (only suggested here in barest outline) Dickens translates the chirping cricket into a supernatural power while yet retaining its ordinary reality.

The cricket is much less of an active agent than the three spirits of *A Christmas Carol* or the bells of *The Chimes*. The cricket never plucks John Peerybingle out of his home and transports him bodily through space and time. The chirp of the cricket (and the spirit that chirp represents) quiets, softens, and comforts. The fairy cricket that helps John Peerybingle survive his night of anguish and fury, and the saving visions that come to him under the influence of the cricket, are less the intrusions of a supernatural force than the symbolic representation (incarnated in the cricket and its spirit) of the saving power of memory and love—this power objectified in the specific scenes and actions that John Peerybingle remembers or projects as he muses under the influence of the cricket, that is, under the influence of hearth and home. In other words, the cricket (hearth and home) helps John Peerybingle save himself. On the one hand the cricket plays much less of an interventionary role than its earlier counterparts, on the other hand its role is more domesticated and psychological.

Dickens seems to have been discontented with the overt fairy-tale machinery of his Christmas books. The intrusive ghosts and spirits of the *Carol* had given way to the carefully generated bell goblins of *The Chimes*, which in turn had yielded to the more domesticated (and limited) crickets and kettles of *The Cricket on the Hearth*. In the next Christmas book, *The Battle of Life*, he dispensed with supernatural machinery altogether. *The Battle* is not only the least typical of the Christmas books but the least successful. Dickens came close to abandoning the work, and he was several times on the verge of breakdown. In part this was owing to overwork, to concurrently beginning a twenty-part novel, but more basically it was owing to the intractability of the material.

In many respects the *donnée* of *The Battle* deserved development in a full-length novel. *The Battle of Life* focuses on an attractive wastrel, Michael Warden, who is in love with an angelic woman, Marion Jeddler, a woman he is debarred from marrying. This theme of an appealing but unworthy man longing for a seraphic woman he cannot or should not have (Dickens returned to the theme in *A Tale of Two Cities*), requires, if it is to have any depth at all, careful development and analysis—a kind of anatomy all but ruled out in a brief Christmas book, especially a Christmas book shorn of its supernatural machinery. Without the storybook machinery to manipulate and foreshorten the theme, satisfactory elaboration was impossible. Dickens soon came to see this. "I have written nearly a third of [*The Battle of Life*]," he said. "It promises to be pretty; quite a new idea in the story, I hope; but to manage it without the supernatural agency now impossible of introduction, and yet to move it naturally within the required space, or with any shorter limit than a *Vicar of Wakefield*, I find to be a difficulty so perplexing . . . that I am fearful of wearing myself out if I go on."[34] Dickens, of course, did go on. The result is a savagely reduced work that sometimes reads like a scenario, sometimes like a breathless outline, and that lacks compelling life.

With *The Haunted Man*, the last of the Christmas books, Dickens turned back to his storybook format. In some respects he also turned back to the *Carol*. Like Scrooge, the protagonist of *The Haunted Man* must learn to live with his past if he is also to live in the present and the future. But the two works show marked differences in emphasis and technique. In *The Haunted Man* Dickens set out, in a much more self-conscious way than in the *Carol*, to unite psychological, social, and allegorical truth in a single realistic fairy-tale conception.

The Haunted Man tells the story of Mr. Redlaw, a learned and benevolent professor of chemistry who is appalled by the misery he sees about him. His own life has been filled with death, betrayal, and unfulfilled love, and he longs to blot out these memories that darken his daily existence. But his mind is confused and divided. Although he yearns to escape from painful memories, he broods over the past. One Christmas Eve as he sits before his fire haunted by sad recollections, that part of his mind which desires to suppress memory takes on corporeal being as a phantom mirror image of himself. The phantom presses its arguments powerfully and wins Redlaw to its point of view. Redlaw will forget, he will have surcease from feeling, but he will retain his learning and acuteness. But the gift, as so often in fairy stories, contains an additional feature: his forgetfulness will be transmitted to those he meets. Redlaw soon discovers that his gift is a curse. For in forgetting past sorrow and feeling, he has, like Scrooge, destroyed all that is softening and human in life. Despite his learning and benevolence, he has failed to grasp a simple, oft-repeated Romantic axiom (celebrated in such different works as Keats' "Ode on Melancholy" and Emerson's "Compensation") which states that suffering and joy, decay and beauty, loss and achievement are so intertwined that banishing one banishes the other. The unhappy multitudes whose misery he had hoped to relieve by his gift are not relieved. As he goes among them he produces discord; he destroys the knot of affection and forbearance that is the saving grace of their hard lives. Only two creatures take no infection from his approach. One, a street waif, remains unchanged because his bestial life has known no human feeling and so can know no loss. The other, Milly, the wife of one of Redlaw's servants, is love and goodness incarnate, and thus proof against his curse. His experiences teach him his error, and with the help of Milly, he redeems himself and removes the blight from those he has cursed.

The debt of *The Haunted Man* to fairy tales is pervasive. The full title of the story is *The Haunted Man and the Ghost's Bargain. A Fancy for Christmas-Time.* This spectral title is reinforced by the pictorial frontispiece and the pictorial title page that stand opposite one another and introduce the volume. The frontispiece (all illustrations were suggested and approved by Dickens) features Redlaw's ghostly alter ego whispering in his ear while devils, demons, and goblins contend with radiant angels. The title page depicts a bright angel and a dark, hooded phantom leading a child in different directions. These supernatural and allegorical associations are echoed in the title of the first chapter, "The Gift Bestowed." This title awakens additional fairy-tale associations, associations underlined by the other two chapter headings: "The Gift Diffused" and "The Gift Reversed." These storybook suggestions are further reinforced by the woodcut illustration that appears on the first page and that depicts, wreathed above giant shadows and looming forms, scenes from *The Arabian Nights, The Tales of the Genii,* and *Cinderella.* These graphic allusions mirror the text, for fairy tales and childhood storybooks, and in particular some of Dickens' favorite childhood storybooks, play a role in *The Haunted Man. The Arabian Nights, The Tales of the Genii, Jack the Giant Killer,* Dr. Watts' *Divine Songs,* and *The Children in the Wood* are all worked into the story. *The Children in the Wood,* as a matter of fact, is one of the tales that helps comfort and sustain the Tetterbys. It is also an index of their moral state. Like Scrooge, who is cold and flinty when he has forgotten such old companions as *The Arabian Nights, Valentine and Orson,* and *Robinson Crusoe,* and who is softened when he is made to remember them, the Tetterbys are harsh and hostile when they cannot respond to *The Children in the Wood,* loving and forbearing when they can.[35]

Many other allusions, graphic and literary, and many additional touches contribute to the magical atmosphere of *The Haunted Man,* but these features, important as they are, only serve to reinforce the more central fairytale resonances of the story, the witching chords of character and setting. Redlaw's home is a good example. It is an enchanted castle, a group of moldering medieval college buildings standing in the midst of the bustling city and wrapped in a gloomy atmosphere of murky shadows and muffled shapes. His home reminds one of a witch's castle. It was always "thundering with echoes when a distant voice was raised or a door was shut,—echoes, not confined to the many low passages and empty rooms, but rumbling and grumbling till they were stifled in the heavy air."[36] With descriptions such as this, and with scores of evocative suggestions and directive touches through all the early pages, Dickens intensifies his ghostly mood, until he creates an atmosphere in which the supernatural and the realistic mingle and then combine. Here, a few lines later, is Redlaw as he sits before the fire at the moment his Christmas Eve adventures begin:

> You should have seen him in his dwelling about twilight, in the dead winter time.

> When the wind was blowing, shrill and shrewd, with the going down of the blurred sun. When it was just so dark, as that the forms of things were indistinct and big—but not wholly lost. When sitters by the fire began to see wild faces and figures, mountains and abysses, ambuscades, and armies, in the coals.[37]

In this thickening twilight strange things happen. Shadows close in and gather like "mustering swarms of ghosts."[38] Then nurses turn into ogresses, rocking horses into monsters, hearth-tongs into straddling giants, and children, "half-scared and half-amused," into strangers to themselves.[39] The images and the associations these suggestions arouse are wonderfully appropriate, for they are compounded out of childhood fears and childhood fantasies—one thinks of Dickens listening to Mary Weller—but leavened now by adult insight and knowledge.

Redlaw partakes of this ambiance. He is another metamorphosis of a figure familiar in Dickens, the misanthropic witchlike sorcerer. Redlaw's witchlike appearance, his "hollow cheek . . . sunken brilliant eye . . . black attired figure . . . grizzled hair hanging, like tangled seaweed, about his face"; his witchlike traffic with phantoms and the secrets of nature (for he is a most learned chemist); and his witchlike ability to cast potent spells (he transmits as well as receives the gift)—all these mark him as the evil enchanter of fairy lore.[40] Yet like many of Dickens' witches and warlocks, like old Martin and Scrooge, for example, he is not entirely evil, he is a good human being in disguise or gone astray, he can be redeemed. And Milly, like her prototype, little Nell, in *The Old Curiosity Shop,* is the fairy princess, an embodiment of perfect goodness who will magically effect Redlaw's salvation. In *The Haunted Man* the Quilplike character who is evil incarnate (to continue the parallel with *The Old Curiosity Shop*) has undergone the greatest change. The beastlike incarnation of evil is now combined with the abandoned waif and becomes the beast-waif. Both the waif and the beast-waif are portentous characters whose origins go back to Dickens' own childhood, to his blacking-warehouse abandonment and street lounging, and both characters appear in his writings in countless permutations. In *A Christmas Carol* the chief embodiment of the waif, Tiny Tim, had appeared primarily in the image of Oliver, Smike, and little Nell, that is, as an innocent child condemned to unjust suffering. The more sinister personification of evil, the beast-waif, had emerged only in passing. This more malignant figure had been doubled in *A Christmas Carol,* but had entered the story only momentarily as the allegorical children Ignorance and Want, two demonstrations dragged into the fable as exhibits rather than actors. In *The Haunted Man* the very real beast-waif— "a baby savage, a young monster, a child who . . . would live and perish a mere beast"—has an active role in the story and becomes a central symbol not merely of nascent evil, but of society's guilt in producing evil.[41] Continuing the process begun in the other Christmas books, Dickens' recurrent fairy-tale figures— the excrescential or allegorical beast-waifs and ghosts, the more functional bell goblins and chirping crickets—are taking on an enlarged significance, and though retaining their fairy-tale origins, are becoming more closely linked with contemporary life, realistic psychology, and thematic motifs.

In *The Haunted Man* Dickens uses many additional devices commonly found in fairy stories. He uses portentous repetition, for instance, to enhance the tale's atmosphere of enchantment and to unify the work. The words of the phantom's gift-curse—"The gift that I have given, you shall give again, go where you will"—are repeated throughout the story and intensify this unity and enchantment. Redlaw soon discovers that "blowing in the wind, falling with the snow, drifting with the clouds, shining in the moonlight, and heavily looming in the darkness, were the Phantom's words, 'The gift that I have given, you shall give again, go where you will!'"[42] The repetition of the curse becomes, in storybook fashion, a magical refrain that gathers suspense until its climax and reversal when the curse-refrain is replaced by its opposite, a refrain that has been developed contrapuntally throughout the story: "Lord keep my memory green." But it is more than the fairy-tale curse, it is the imagery of Redlaw's loss associated with the curse—imagery connected with his new insensitivity to nature, time, and music—that is repeated. This repetition gradually swells into a leitmotif and sounds the knell of Redlaw's loss; the loss, in turn, through repetition and association, becomes incorporated into the curse. What Redlaw sees in nature, for example, in the blowing wind, the falling snow, the drifting clouds, the shining moonlight, is not an evocation of wildness and beauty, an experience full of associations that can quicken and comfort him, but mere physical fact. This is part of Redlaw's deprivation. He sees the curse in the blowing wind, the falling snow, and the other manifestations of nature, because the curse is an objectification of his inability to respond, an objectification of his longed-for inurement to feeling. Like Coleridge, Redlaw the analytical chemist can see, not feel, how beautiful the world is. Through such repetitions, linkings, and associations, Dickens gradually makes the curse embody Redlaw's grievous sin and loss.

There are other storybook elements in the curse. Each time the curse is transmitted, the recipient signifies his infection by a telltale action: "the wandering hand upon the forehead."[43] These and similar repetitions (which are frequently joined with one another) become increasingly magical and ritualistic, as in the following pattern of reiterations: "Three times, in their progress [Redlaw and the beast-waif] were side by side. Three times they stopped, being side by side. Three times the Chemist glanced down at [the beast-waif's] face, and shuddered as it forced upon him one reflection."[44] The dovetailing of such incantations and repetitions with their many analogues interconnects their meanings. For example, Dickens links the Redlaw—beast-waif walk and its three pauses (labeling them "first," "second," and "third") with images of memory, night, moonlight, and music—images he had been reiterating throughout the story by means of the poetic leitmotif associated with Redlaw's curse.[45] The leitmotif is coordinate with the curse, but it is more lyrical, connotative, and musical. It is another form of repetition and incantation—a linguistic extension of Dickens' fairy-tale recurrences—and it offers Dickens another means of sounding the keynote. Once this leitmotif and its many associations are established, Dickens is able, by means of the leitmotif (as well as by means of the curse), to call up Redlaw's loss with great economy and centripetal effect.

Paralleling and intermingling with the fairy-tale level of *The Haunted Man* is an allegorical level that underlines Dickens' message. Dickens was perfectly aware of the allegorical nature of what he had written. In the penultimate paragraph of *The Haunted Man* he has the narrator point to the possibility of such an interpretation: "Some people have said since, that [Redlaw] only thought what has been herein set down; others, that he read it in the fire, one winter night about the twilight time; others, that the Ghost was but the representation of his own gloomy thoughts, and Milly the embodiment of his better wisdom. *I* say nothing."

Dickens, through the narrator, was suggesting various modes of interpreting his story but very properly endorsing no single mode. Yet any reader who failed to make use of each of his suggestions would miss part of what he was saying.

The allegory of *The Haunted Man* is designed to enforce the message which the other levels develop—that good and evil are intertwined, that memories and feelings associate pain and joy, and that such associations can be dissolved only at the expense of that which makes one human. Redlaw, before he is given the gift, is man in his suffering but human condition; after the gift, he is man as a mere analytical chemist, man as an arid, dehumanized husk. The phantom is that portion of Redlaw's mind which longs for surcease from feeling and tempts him to an attitude toward himself and his fellows that will produce such surcease. The gift is the symbolic result of Redlaw's assent to these promptings of his mind; it is the effect on himself and others of acquiescing in such a philosophy. Milly stands for love, and the softening, saving influence of love. The beast-waif represents two things: first, human nature bereft of feeling and sympathy, that is, human nature completely dehumanized, human nature that displays the end result of Redlaw's foolish yearnings; and second, the evil and guilt of a society that produces creatures such as the beast-waif.

The allegory of character is intensified by the allegory of setting. The worn-out leftovers of Mr. Tetterby's defunct business are ever-present tokens of his ineffectual personality; the tortuous slum Redlaw visits mirrors the twisted lives he finds within. But the chief backdrop for the action—Redlaw's college chambers—is the most revealing of the settings. The fortress in which he lives is a fitting representation of his mind. And when his mind changes, sympathetic, almost magical transformations also occur in his frost-bound home. When he allows love to reenter his heart, his dungeon and heart reawaken alike: "Some blind groping of the morning made its way down into the forgotten crypt so cold and earthy . . . and stirred the dull deep sap in the lazy vegetation hanging to the walls, and quickened the slow principle of life within the little world of wonderful and delicate creation which existed there, with some faint knowledge that the sun was up."[46]

The allegory becomes most intense toward the end of the second chapter. Redlaw visits the slums with the beast-waif. During that visit he goes through all the experiences necessary to teach him the significance of his error. Upon his return he locks himself and the beast-waif into his lonely rooms and broods despairingly. After an interval, Milly knocks on Redlaw's door. "Pray, sir, let me in!" she cries.[47] Symbolically love is knocking at the locked chambers of Redlaw's

heart and asking to be let in. "No! not for the world!" is his ironic answer. The beast-waif, who has been fed and tended by Milly, cries out, "Let me go to her, will you?" (The evil that society has produced will respond to love, cries out for love.) Milly, not knowing Redlaw is the cause, tells him of the disasters his slum visit has brought. "Pray, sir, let me in," she repeats. Redlaw is horrified, contrite, anguished, but his heart is still frozen; he cannot really feel or remember, he is not yet ready to let love enter. "Pray, sir, let me in!" cries Milly, but Redlaw answers, "No! No! No!" and restrains the beast-waif "who was half-mad to pass him, and let her in." Redlaw prays to his phantom alter ego for relief, vows not to taint Milly with his curse, and, thus refusing to confront love, stands in an agony of guilt before the door he himself has locked. The phantom does not answer Redlaw's prayer. "The only reply still was, the boy struggling to get to her, while he held him back; and the cry, increasing in its energy . . . 'pray, pray, let me in!'"[48]

With these words the second chapter ends. Dickens' method is effective and sophisticated. It reminds one of Hawthorne's technique, of those portions of *The Scarlet Letter* or "Rappaccini's Daughter" in which the central allegory shades into subtle and varied suggestiveness. But that suggestiveness has other components than those so far discussed. For when Redlaw calls out to his fairy-tale phantom and hears Milly's allegorical plea, he is also acting out a psychological drama that has parallels in Dickens' life.

The third concurrent level of Redlaw's story—the psychological (and in this case the autobiographical)—appears in *The Haunted Man* from the beginning. Dickens makes it easy for the reader to regard the phantom as the representation of Redlaw's "gloomy thoughts." The phantom materializes only after many directive signs, which can be explained as natural or supernatural, have heralded its appearance. These manifestations come in conjunction with Redlaw's internal debating and self-absorption. Consequently, when the signs coalesce and then develop into the full-fledged phantom, the reader is ready to accept the apparition as another part of the storybook atmosphere, and as an appropriate representation of one portion of Redlaw's mind. Once the latter notion is established, the story becomes, like the story of murder-bent Jonas Chuzzlewit's two selves, a study of psychological strife. But here the technique is different from that used in *Chuzzlewit*. In *The Haunted Man* the conflict is depicted by utilizing the method Tennyson used in "The Two Voices"; Redlaw's divided mind is engaged in a dialogue with itself:

"If I could forget my sorrow and wrong, I would," the Ghost repeated. . . .

"Evil spirit of myself," returned the haunted man . . . "my life is darkened by that incessant whisper."

"It is an echo," said the Phantom.

"If it be an echo of my thoughts . . . why should I, therefore, be tormented? . . . Who would not forget their sorrows and their wrongs?"

"Who would not, truly, and be the happier and better for it?" said the Phantom. . . .

"Tempter," answered Redlaw . . . "I hear again an echo of my own mind."[49]

The Haunted Man was written under special stress. In the summer of 1848, while Dickens was planning to complete his long-postponed Christmas book, his sister Fanny lay dying wretchedly of consumption. Dickens visited her often during that summer. As he looked upon her gaunt body and grieved over her early decay, his mind kept turning to the days when he and she had been children together.[50] Fanny died on 2 September, and a month or so later Dickens sat down to finish *The Haunted Man*. *The Haunted Man* is a dirge to memory. It probes the deep dissatisfactions that had been stirred up and intensified by his sister's death. It also shadows forth an image of Dickens. Redlaw reminds us of Dickens. Like Redlaw, Dickens worked in his "inner chamber, part library and part laboratory"; like Redlaw, he was revered and famous; like Redlaw, he was a teacher upon whose words and works "a crowd of aspiring ears and eyes hung daily"; like Redlaw, he was surrounded by "a crowd of spectral shapes"; like Redlaw, he had the power "to uncombine" those phantoms and make them "give back their component parts"; like Redlaw, he would sit in his study "moving his thin mouth as if in speech, but silent as the dead."[51]

However, it is Redlaw's confrontation with his darker self that produces the most striking parallels. Through Redlaw and Redlaw's specter, Dickens summons up the shaping events of his own past:

"Look upon me!" said the Spectre. "I am he, neglected in my youth, and miserably poor, who strove and suffered, and still strove and suffered, until I hewed out knowledge from the mine where it was buried, and made rugged steps thereof, for my worn feet to rest and rise on."

"I *am* that man," returned the Chemist.

"No mother's self-denying love," pursued the Phantom, "no father's counsel, aided *me*. A stranger came into my father's place when I was but a child, and I was easily an alien from my mother's heart. My parents, at the best, were of that sort whose care soon ends, and whose duty is soon done; who cast their offspring loose, early, as birds do theirs; and, if they do well, claim the merit; and, if ill, the pity."

. . . . .

"I had a sister" [the Phantom went on]. . . . "Such glimpses of the light of home as I had ever known, had streamed from her. How young she was, how fair, how loving! I took her to the first poor roof that I was master of, and made it rich. She came into the darkness of my life, and made it bright."[52]

But this felicity does not last. Redlaw's most trusted friend betrays his sister and steals his fiancée. In the wake of this double catastrophe only one thing survives, or seems to survive—jilted sister cleaves to jilted brother.

"My sister" [continued the Phantom], "doubly dear, doubly devoted, doubly cheerful in my home, lived on to see me famous, and my old ambition so rewarded when its spring was broken, and then—"

"Then died," [Redlaw] interposed. "Died, gentle as ever, happy, and with no concern but for her brother."[53]

Redlaw cannot forget. He constantly chants his litany of woe. His words toll the knell of his (and Dickens') complaint: "Early unhappiness, a wound from a hand I loved and trusted, and a loss that nothing can replace." These old grievances haunt and torment Redlaw. "Thus," he continues, "I prey upon myself. Thus, memory is my curse; and, if I could forget my sorrow and my wrong, I would!"[54]

Yet it is not the autobiography or the message that makes *The Haunted Man* notable, it is the fairy-tale technique, or rather the refinement and integration of a constellation of fairy-tale techniques. These techniques help Dickens manipulate and interweave the various strands of his story—the social, allegorical, psychological, and fanciful—and make them part of a harmonious pattern.

The Haunted Man has other distinctions. It surpasses the earlier Christmas books in its self-conscious use of repetition, recurrence, and leitmotif. It also surpasses those works in its sophisticated fusion of realism, psychology, and allegory. All these elements are used in *The Haunted Man* to enforce the theme, and all are used to interrelate and unify. In this centripetal movement the fairy story dominates. It serves as subject matter, catalyst, and vehicle. The fairy tale enables Dickens to achieve his special goal. For the mood Dickens sets at the opening, the supernatural devices he uses to unify his plot and emphasize his message, and the fablelike quality he gives to what he is saying prepare the reader for the apocalyptic truth he is trying to convey—a truth in which simple realism, ordinary events, and humdrum detail are less important than a heightened, extrareal vision of life that quickens one's perception of the very reality it transcends.

Yet *The Haunted Man,* despite technical advances, powerful scenes, and memorable characters, fails and fades, especially in "The Gift Reversed." Milly, for one thing, is too angelic and too inanely self-congratulatory (a sort of Esther Summerson at her worst), and she is used, in the last chapter, as a mere agency for removing the curse. Furthermore, the last chapter is so clogged and tangled with melodramatic coincidences that it becomes huddled and implausible. Dickens digs up lost relations, rewards suffering fiancées, and rehabilitates suicidal derelicts. The earlier fusion of realism, psychology, and fantasy is sacrificed for the convenience of a neat winding up in the old wrenching storybook manner, and the violence done to everything but the fable reduces the effectiveness of the fable itself.

The preeminence of *A Christmas Carol* when compared to its counterparts can lead one to believe that the subsequent Christmas books represent a falling off, an effort by Dickens to repeat the *Carol* formula with imperfect success. But this is to neglect what Dickens attempted in his Christmas books and what he learned from them. After the *Carol* Dickens tried to locate the overt fairy-tale machinery in the more ordinary surroundings and experiences of life, in chimes, crickets, kettles, and divided minds. He attempted to emphasize the reality of these agencies, and he sought to distill his supernatural effects from that carefully nurtured reality—from vibrations, chirpings, and brooding questionings. He also began to reduce the overt fairy-tale machinery, to subject less of the story to its immediate control. The supernatural machinery, though carefully prepared for, enters *The Chimes* only at the middle. The artful storybook presences of *The Cricket,* subdued now in their supernatural attributes, emerge tactfully at the beginning and tactfully at the middle. In these later works, Dickens apparently wanted to retain the unified impact and fablelike quality of the *Carol* but to do so with an ever more dominant realism, or rather with a realism that would retain its ordinary truthfulness to life while revealing life's magic and interconnectedness. With *The Battle of Life,* he dispensed with the supernatural machinery altogether, but saddled himself with a *donnée* so novelistic, so needful of expansion and development, that without the aid of magical manipulation, he barely managed to sketch the story's high points, much less develop its psychological intricacies or numinous resonances. In *The Haunted Man* he went back to the *Carol* formula, but with increased attention to an array of more subtle fantasy devices—devices more amenable to a realistic context than phantoms and goblins, though he used these as well—devices that could help him compress, combine, and enlarge.

Yet the need to depend on phantoms and magical machinery was irksome and confining. Dickens felt trapped in the Christmas-book form. In his general preface (1852) to the Christmas books, he wrote: "The narrow space within which it was necessary to confine these Christmas Stories when they were originally published, rendered their construction a matter of some difficulty, and almost necessitated what is peculiar in their machinery. I never attempted great elaboration of detail in the working out of character within such limits, believing that it could not succeed. My purpose was, in a whimsical kind of masque which the good humour of the season justified, to awaken some loving and forbearing thoughts, never out of season in a Christian land."[55] In this statement three ideas emerge clearly: Dickens felt that the narrow space of the Christmas books confined and limited him; and he believed that the fairy story could be used to solve problems of construction and to convey truth in a special way. One would assume that the sequel to such postulates would be that Dickens would turn back to the novel, and that within that larger space he would use the fairy tale, much more self-consciously and elaborately now, to help him with structure and coherence and to provide him with additional means of conveying meaning. This, in fact, is what happened.

I do not mean to imply by this that Dickens abandoned the fairy tale as fairy tale. He subsequently wrote a number of veritable fairy stories—allegories, satires, burlesques, fables, and supernatural stories that were couched in fairy-tale guise. But these pieces were scattered and intermittent; most of them were offshoots of his topical journalism. They do not have the centrality and the importance of the Christmas books. The Christmas books are at the heart of Dickens' writing and experimenting in the mid-1840s. His later redactions of fairy stories testify to his continued devotion to the genre, but his deepest and most potent storybook energies—the energies that were coeval with his power to transcend and transform, the energies that had been slowly nurtured and crucially shaped by a thousand childhood forces, by the nightmare of the blacking warehouse, by the frustrations and achievements of the apprentice novels, and now by the equivocal lessons of the Christmas books—those energies were flowing elsewhere. They were flowing, of course, into his novels.

What the Christmas books added to Dickens' fairy-tale art and what they contributed to the later novels can be quickly sketched. The Christmas books helped Dickens overcome old difficulties, and they encouraged him to introduce new techniques. Through his

Christmas-book experimentation—though not exclusively by such means—Dickens learned how to make mood and atmosphere permeate every nuance of a story. He also evolved ways of making leitmotif, repetition, recurrence, and symbolism develop and integrate structure. In addition, the Christmas books helped him intensify and enrich his psychological analysis. The peculiar demands of the Christmas books encouraged him to convey states of mind through magically sympathetic objects and surroundings, to objectify internal divisions through doubles and alter egos, to depict psychological struggles through allegory and symbolism. Some of these techniques confirmed or amplified what Dickens had done earlier, others pushed him in new directions. In a similar way, his Christmas fairy tales showed him how to give the central realism of his story a consistent and thematic pattern of fancy and symbolism. What had heretofore been intermittent now became much more self-conscious, ordered, and regular. The Christmas novelettes also provided him with his first experience of completing a sizable fictional whole as a whole. They allowed him, five times over, to think and plan and write with an entirety in mind rather than a part. Dickens immediately recognized the importance of that overview. "When I see the effect of such a little *whole* as that," he wrote after finishing the *Carol,* "I have a strong sense of the immense effect I could produce with an entire book."[56]

In short, through the Christmas books and their fairy-tale potentialities, Dickens came to see more clearly how he could use fantasy to enhance character, scene, atmosphere, action, and meaning, and beyond that how he could use enchantment to bind the diverse elements of a fiction into a whole. One thing more. The Christmas books helped Dickens fuse the two dominant modes of his imagination. They helped him meld realism and fancy into rich thematic fullness. Through that new fullness, at once compellingly real and wildly fanciful, he could better convey the complexity and wonder of life.

One can see the experiments and lessons of the Christmas books reverberating in the subsequent novels. The bells and vibrations and clamor that pursue the despairing Trotty in *The Chimes* look forward to the bells and wheels and horses' feet that haunt the fleeing Carker in *Dombey.* The thematic weather that guides and unifies the *Carol* develops into the even more thematic weather that shapes and integrates *Bleak House.* The rudimentary analysis of Scrooge's childhood, its formative pressure on his adulthood, in *A Christmas Carol* turns into the more careful examination of Clennam's childhood and its consequences in *Little Dorrit.* The leitmotifs, repetitions, and incantations of *The Haunted Man* anticipate the analogous repetitions and recurrences of *A Tale of Two Cities.* The unity of mood, atmosphere, and theme that marks the *Carol* foreshadows the richer unity of tone and

ambiance that pervades *Great Expectations.* The dark double that objectifies Redlaw's alienation and self-division in *The Haunted Man* evolves into the two separate selves that epitomize the alienation and self-division of such different characters as Wemmick in *Great Expectations* and Jasper in *Edwin Drood.* In each instance—the instances could easily be multiplied—it is not simply the idea that is similar but the technique of conveying it; and in each instance the technique is rooted in Dickens' Christmas-book experimentation.

I am not suggesting that Dickens went to the Christmas books, deliberately extracted these storybook devices, and then applied them to his later novels as tested ways of solving certain literary problems. I am not even suggesting that he always identified these devices with his Christmas books or with fairy stories. Nor do I doubt that many additional factors—the theater, the works of other authors, the spirit of the age, to name only three—made their contributions to these special developments. I am simply emphasizing that the Christmas books played a pivotal role in these developments. First, they forced Dickens, over a period of years, to concentrate on fairy-tale modes, a concentration that was congenial to his lifelong imaginative bent. Second, they helped him, during a crucial pause in his novel writing, to solve difficult problems of construction, integration, and transcendence. When he came to face those same problems in his subsequent novels, it was only natural that he should utilize (whether consciously or not) the methods and devices that had served him well in the Christmas books.

Yet the Christmas books themselves were unsatisfactory. They were limiting and confining. They made elaborate analysis and intricate development virtually impossible. They were dependent upon machinery that did violence to reality. Dickens was not content to convey his vision of life through phantoms and goblins. He did not wish to confine his art to ghostly allegories and whimsical masques. He wanted to present life in its density, its solid reality, but at the same time convey its shimmering strangeness and wonder.

It is not surprising, therefore, that even as the idea for his last Christmas book worked slowly through his mind, he was embarking upon a new novel, *Dombey and Son,* a novel that would display a virtuoso fusion of reality and fantasy. *Dombey* was a departure. Unlike the earlier novels, it was rooted in the present. *Pickwick, Nickleby, Barnaby,* and all the other apprentice novels had been set in the historical past, or had been hazily located in the ambiguous purlieus of a largely vanished age. *Dombey* was of the moment; it was a book about "the way we live now." It dealt with businessmen and railroads, capital and labor, the concerns and problems of the day. Yet this new book, with its new subject matter, and its up-to-date milieu, was to have the old indebtedness to fairy stories—old now in the sense of continuity, not of method. Fairy tales would appear in *Dombey* in the old ways, but they would also appear in new configurations: as elaborations and refinements of Christmas-book techniques. These techniques would help give *Dombey* a richness and unity that his earlier novels had lacked. *Dombey* would be minutely realistic, deeply social, profoundly psychological—all in ways that went beyond what Dickens had done before; but it would also vibrate intensely with fantasy and wonder—also in ways that went beyond what he had done before. *Dombey,* like the Christmas books, would be a fairy tale for the times, but a fairy tale given a surpassingly "higher form."

Abbreviations

C The Chimes

CB Christmas Books

CC A Christmas Carol

CH The Cricket on the Hearth

CS Christmas Stories

F Forster's *Life*

HM The Haunted Man

NL Nonesuch *Letters*

Notes

[1] The dates given here refer to actual publication; the second and third books, though issued in December 1844 and December 1845 respectively, were dated the following year.

[2] F, 422-423, 466-467.

[3] F, 317.

[4] *CC,* 3.

[5] *CC,* i, 6.

[6] *CC,* i, 7.

[7] *CC,* i, 7.

[8] *CC,* i, 14.

[9] *CC,* i, 14.

[10] *CC,* i, 15.

[11] *CC,* i, 17-19.

[12] *CC,* i, 20.

[13] *CC,* ii, 30.

[14] *CC,* ii, 30-31.

[15] *CC,* ii, 32.

[16] *CC,* v, 83.

[17] *C,* i, 99.

[18] *C,* i, 99-100.

[19] *C,* i, 118.

[20] *C,* ii, 139.

[21] *C,* ii, 141.

[22] *C,* ii, 141.

[23] *C,* ii, 141.

[24] *C,* ii, 141.

[25] *C,* iii, 144.

[26] *C,* iii, 144.

[27] *C,* iii, 145.

[28] *NL,* I, 627.

[29] *NL.* I, 631.

[30] *NL,* I, 630.

[31] *CH,* ii, 220.

[32] *CH,* i 196.

[33] *CH,* i, 218.

[34] F, 426.

[35] *HM,* iii, 469.

[36] *HM,* i, 389.

[37] *HM,* i, 389.

[38] *HM,* i, 391.

[39] *HM,* i, 391.

[40] *HM,* i, 387-388.

[41] *HM,* i, 412.

[42] *HM,* ii, 442.

[43] *HM,* ii, 454.

[44] *HM,* ii, 446.

[45] *HM,* ii, 446-447.

[46] *HM,* iii, 465.

[47] *HM,* ii, 458.

[48] *HM,* ii, 458-459.

[49] *HM,* i, 409.

[50] *F,* 521.

[51] *HM,* i, 388.

[52] *HM,* i, 406-407.

[53] *HM,* i, 408.

[54] *HM,* i, 408.

[55] *CB,* xi. In the Preface (1868) to the Charles Dickens Edition of the Christmas books, Dickens amended the second sentence as follows: "I could not attempt great elaboration of detail, in the working out of character within such limits." In the next sentence he changed "My purpose" to "My chief purpose"—xi.

[56] *NL,* I, 549.

U. C. Knoepflmacher

SOURCE: "The Balancing of Child and Adult: An Approach to Victorian Fantasies for Children," in *Nineteenth-Century Fiction,* Vol. 37, No. 4, March, 1983, pp. 497-530.

[*In the essay below, Knoepflmacher proposes that the best authors of Victorian children's fantasy—especially Lewis Carroll and Rudyard Kipling—were able to successfully balance the friction between an adult's and a child's perception of events, and that this characteristic is what makes fantasy stories appealing to both audiences.*]

Much has been written on the socializing aspects of children's literature, on this or that classic's promotion of maturity and healthy growth. Yet children's books, especially works of fantasy, rely just as heavily on the artist's ability to tap a rich reservoir of regressive yearnings. Such works can be said to hover between the states of perception that William Blake had labeled innocence and experience. From the vantage point of experience, an adult imagination re-creates an earlier childhood self in order to steer it towards the reality principle. From the vantage point of innocence, however, that childhood agent may resist the imposition of adult values and stubbornly demand that its desire to linger in a realm of magic and wonder be satisfied. Like Blake's two "contrary states," these conflicting impulses thus remain locked into a dynamic that acknowledges the simultaneous yet opposing demands of growth and arrest.

It is no coincidence that the self-divided Victorians who found themselves "wandering between two worlds" in their Janus-like split between progress and nostalgia should have produced what has rightly been called "the Golden Age of children's books."[1] Earlier eras, if we are to believe Philippe Ariès and J. H. van den Berg, had little regard for the distinctions among children, adolescents, and young adults.[2] Gradually, however, as adulthood became more problematic, childhood became a state of its own. As early as 1839, Catherine Sinclair questioned the propriety of treating "young persons" as potential adults by exposing them to books that discouraged "all play of imagination" and that presented instead "a mere dry record of facts, unenlivened by . . . any excitement to the fancy."[3] In the next two decades major writers such as Dickens, Thackeray, and Ruskin, all of whom wrote at least one major fantasy for children, strongly agreed, with Ruskin even going so far as to dismiss those didactic tracts that had been so popular in England and America as nothing less than a violation of the child's "unquestioning innocence."[4]

By the last third of the nineteenth century, when fantasies for children flourished in England, authors went one step further by self-consciously admitting their own role as mediators between the states of childhood and maturity. Even before he implanted a version of himself as an aged bachelor-guide in the *Sylvie and Bruno* books (1889, 1893), the Lewis Carroll of *Through the Looking-Glass* (1871) could tell the dream-child in her "nest of gladness" that "we are but older children, dear."[5] And Alice herself is soon led to grasp what Carroll has come to understand, namely, that forward progress may be meaningless without a capacity for regress: to meet the Red Queen whose "adult" power she covets Alice must "try the plan" of walking backwards, "in the opposite direction," a strategy that "beautifully" succeeds for her as well as for her creator (ch. 2, p. 124). Similarly, on the very first page of his fine biography of Rudyard Kipling, Angus Wilson stresses Kipling's regressive respect for children and their imaginings, his ability to play with them—even in his sixties—"not, as so many adults do, in order to impose his own shapes, but to follow and to learn as well as to contribute."[6] Again, as Edith Nesbit,

Kipling's contemporary, remarked about her own creative powers of empathy: "There is only one way of understanding children; they cannot be understood by imagination, or observation, nor even by love. They can only be understood by memory. . . . I was a child once myself, and by some fortunate chance I remember exactly how I used to feel and think about things."[7]

Still, for the Victorians who wrote for children, this regressive capacity can never bring about a total annihilation of the adult's self-awareness. Their fictions, especially those which rely on some suspension of disbelief, inevitably incorporate that awareness through ironic distancing devices apparent to the adult, but not necessarily to the child, reader. Torn between the opposing demands of innocence and experience, the author who resorts to the wishful, magical thinking of the child nonetheless feels compelled, in varying degrees, to hold on to the grown-up's circumscribed notions about reality. In the better works of fantasy of the period, this dramatic tension between the outlooks of adult and childhood selves becomes rich and elastic: conflict and harmony, friction and reconciliation, realism and wonder, are allowed to interpenetrate and coexist. An author who, like Thackeray in *The Rose and the Ring,* addresses an older child may wish to undermine the improbabilities on which his fairy tale relies by playfully calling attention to the story's exaggerations and contradictions. And yet this seemingly "adult" implied author never promotes the skepticism that rules his cousin narrator in *Vanity Fair;* instead, to resolve the tensions on which his fantasy is built he resorts to the magical powers of a Fairy Blackstick who has herself become wary about the role of magic. Like this paradoxical deus ex machina who uses her spells to allow her nurslings to grow up in a world where they will no longer be aided by magic, Thackeray carefully steers between the realms of innocence and experience, subscribing to neither, and yet to both.

The division between the perspectives of the child and the grown-up not only led Victorian authors of children's fairy tales to devise fictional structures of considerable sophistication but also resulted in their simultaneous appeal to two distinct types of implied readers. The child addressed by many Victorian authors—the Effie Gray for whom Ruskin wrote *The King of the Golden River* as a young man of twenty-two, the Annie and Minnie Thackeray whom their father tried to divert during their stay in Rome, the Alice Liddell who insisted that Charles Lutwidge Dodgson "go on with my interminable fairy-tale" on the way to Godstow—formed a prime audience fit though few. This private child-auditor, who encouraged each storyteller to release childhood imaginings embedded within an adult logic, to reclaim the threatened child within, could eventually, upon the story's publication, be expanded into a larger, more impersonal audience of children. Yet the release and dissemination of the story also accentuated each teller's adult awareness of instability and change. Neither Effie Gray nor Alice Liddell were prepubescent girls any longer when the fables written for them were published; like Thackeray's daughters, they had become, or were in the way of becoming, grown-ups. What is more, the act of public transmission involved, by necessity, a consideration of an audience composed of parents, older family members, or governesses, an adult readership as related to the implied author's identity as a grown-up, socialized being as the child-auditor was related to the author's reawakened youthful self.

The acknowledgment of this second type of implied reader could manifest itself in a variety of ways, not only within each tale, but also through the superimposition of outward frames or bridges. In a suppressed epilogue to *The King of the Golden River* Ruskin felt compelled to allude to the "opinions of the old people of the valley" into which he had transported his regressive desire to erase adult rapacity and cruelty; his tone changes abruptly as he now speaks of the uncomprehending "haberdashers of the district" and refers, semi-ironically, to the "many and edifying comments from the mater" who is now said to have "related" to her children the fairy tale of his own invention.[8] Another kind of self-protectiveness informs the "prelude" to *The Rose and the Ring,* where Thackeray, as "M. A. Titmarsh," pays homage to the cooperative efforts of a fellow adult, his "friend, Miss Bunch, who was governess of a large family" living in the same "house inhabited by myself and my young charges"; it is this fellow occupant, "a lady of great fancy and droll imagination," who, according to Thackeray, supervised his drawings and helped him compose the "history" which both "recited to the little folks at night."[9] Adult transmission is equally prominent in both *Alice's Adventures in Wonderland* and *Through the Looking-Glass,* where the opening poems melancholically insist on distancing childhood reverie from adult realism and where Alice's older sister will be given the task of acting as the interpreter of the import of Alice's dreams.

Public utterance, then, reenforced a sense of self-division for the Victorian writers of fantasies for children and led them to address a double readership, the young child who (like Gluck, Giglio/Rosalba, Alice, or Mowgli) sets out on the road from innocence to experience and the adult who wants to travel back to, yet cannot remain arrested within, the pleasurable realm of magical thinking and wishfulness. If some, like Thackeray, brilliantly exploited the friction between these two perspectives, others more characteristically tried to effect a balance, often through the introduction of hybrid figures, childlike adults such as the Queen of Hearts or Nesbit's Jimmy, the Egyptologist in *The Story of the Amulet,* or miniaturized figures of adult power such as the King of the Golden River or the tiny animal guides, Molesworth's Cuckoo and Raven or Nesbit's Psammead and Phoenix. Some early moralists, still bound to those "many and edifying comments from the mater" which Ruskin slyly ridicules in his suppressed epilogue, found it difficult to master the division between child and adult. Yet even Margaret Gatty, the most influential of these maternal moralists, whose long-forgotten, brief parable "See-Saw" will be reproduced and analyzed below, was able to devise a mode that would be imitated, complicated, and refined by purer fantasists such as Carroll and Kipling, her admirers and successors. In the sections which follow, I shall accordingly treat "See-Saw" as a paradigm for these later elaborations.

I

"See-Saw" is one of the later tales that Margaret Scott Gatty incorporated into her immensely popular, five-volume *Parables from Nature,* which she published from 1855 until 1871, two years before her death. Unlike Lewis Carroll (whose work she highly esteemed and helped propagate) and unlike, too, her own daughter Juliana Horatia Gatty Ewing, who together with Jean Ingelow and Mary Louisa Molesworth deftly mined the veins of fantasy first tapped in *Alice's Adventures in Wonderland,* Mrs. Gatty belonged to an earlier, more utilitarian generation of writers who mixed fantasy with overt moralization and instruction. Though she would become renowned as a writer of juvenile literature and as the founder and editor, from 1866 onwards, of the popular *Aunt Judy's Magazine* for girls, Mrs. Gatty had begun her career with a biography of the Rev. Alexander John Scott, D.D., her gifted and permissive father, who as chaplain on board of the *Victory* was noted for having cradled the dying Lord Nelson at Trafalgar.

Margaret Gatty's true love remained natural history, especially marine studies. Upon publishing *The Fairy Godmothers* (1851), her first incursion into children's fantasy, she requested that her publisher repay her with monographs on zoophytes, sponges, and lithophytes.[10] Although her later writings for juveniles would help augment her clerical husband's meager salary and aid in the education of her nine surviving children, her continued absorption in seaside studies led her daughter Juliana, still a teenager at the time, to compose a parody of a poem by Kingsley in which she gently mocked the enraptured scientist. The writer who probably valued her single treatise on *The History of British Seaweeds* more than the twenty volumes for juvenile readers she also authored must, in her daughter's spoof, be wrested away from the rising tide by her hungry children clamoring for their meal. Imprudent and unladylike, she disregards the gurgling water in her boots as she observes a crab crawl over her foot and clasps a marine plant with "ungloved hands." Her engrossment is childlike, almost infantile: "O! is it weed or fish or floating hair? / A zoophyte so rare, / Or but a lump of hair, / My raptured eyeballs see? / Were ever pools so deep or day so fair—/ There's nothing like the sea!"[11] By way of contrast, the teenage daughter who satirizes this regressive behavior acts like a responsible adult: the girl is mother of the woman.

In most of her *Parables from Nature,* however, Mrs. Gatty could find an adult sanction and adult purpose for the childlike wonder she extracted from an animated Nature. She could be scientifically accurate, morally homiletic, and yet invest the ordinary with quasi-magical properties. Tales such as "The Law of the Wood," an ecological fable with possibly class-conscious social overtones, or "The Law of Authority and Obedience," a tale about cooperation within a beehive, are indeed "parables." Verifiable truths are made to yield the narrator's faith in moral design: "the instincts of nature confirm the reasoning conclusions of man."[12] Nature becomes anthropomorphized as in a fairy tale. But there is no need for excursions into wonderlands or for encounters with goblins, dwarfs, or fairies. Talking plants and animals, even a loquacious Day or Night or Fire, can instruct as well as delight.

"See-Saw" partakes of this mode yet also seems significantly different. Its protagonist is, in a sense, *un*natural—not a growing organic creature such as the young trees, insects, animals, and children who abound in the earlier parables but an inert stump of wood. And the children depicted in the story remain apart, oblivious to the tree stump's plight, never benefiting from the edification it, but not they, eventually receives. In their careless indifference, the children become outsiders, uneducatable and unattractive; yet in its self-pitying exaggerations, born of its hyperawareness of distance and change, the tree stump, too, though in the forefront, seems equally reprehensible. Indeed, as we shall see after a look at the tale itself (which I now reproduce), "See-Saw" can be read on one level as an allegory intended more for the adult reader than for the child listener.

SEE-SAW.[13]

"Turning to scorn with lips divine
The falsehood of extremes."—TENNYSON.

The felled oak in the corner of the timber-yard lay groaning under the plank, which a party of children had thrown across him to play see-saw upon.

Not that the plank was so heavy even with two or three little ones sitting on each end, nor that the oak was too weak to hold it up—though, of course, the pressure was pretty strong just at the centre, where the plank balanced. But it was such a use to be put to!

The other half of the tree had been cut into beautiful even planks, some time before, but this was the root end, and his time had not yet come, and he was getting impatient.

"Here we go up, up, up!" cried the children, as the plank rose into the sky on one side. "I shall catch the tree-tops—no! the church-steeple—no! the stars."

Or, "Here we go down, down, down!" cried the others. "Safe and snug on the ground—no! right through the world—no! out at the other side. Ah! steady there, stupid old stump!"

This was because the plank had swerved, not the tree.

And so the game went on; for the ups and downs came in turns, and the children shrieked with delight, and the poor tree groaned loudly all the time.

"And I am to sit here; and bear not only their weight but their blame, and be called stupid and be told to keep steady, when it is they who are giddy and can't be depended upon; and to be contented, while they do nothing but play pranks and enjoy themselves," said he; but said it to himself, for he did not know which to complain to—the children or the plank. As he groaned, however, he thought of the time when he was king of the little wood, where he had grown up from the acorn days of his babyhood, and it broke his heart to be so insignificant now.

"Why have they not cut me into planks like the rest?" continued he, angrily. "I might have led the see-saw myself then, as this fellow does, who leans so heavily on my back, without a thought that I am as good or better than himself. Why have they not given me the chance of enjoying myself like these others—up in the sky at one end, down on the ground at the other, full of energy and life? The whole timber-yard, but myself, has a chance. Position and honour, as well as pleasure, are for everybody except me. But I am to stick in a corner merely for others to steady themselves upon—unthought-of or despised, made a tool of—merely that.—Miserable me!"

Now this groaning was so dreadful, it woke the large garden snail in the grass hard by, whose custom it was to come out from his haunt under the timber-yard wall every morning at sunrise, and crawl round and round the felled oak, to see the world come to life, leaving a slimy track behind him on the bark wherever he moved. It was his constitutional stroll, and he had continued it all the season, pursuing his morning reflections without interruption, and taking his nap in the grass afterwards, as regularly as the days came round.

But napping through such lamentation was impossible, and accordingly he once more began to crawl up the side of the felled oak, his head turning now to one side, now to the other, his horns extended to the utmost, that, if possible, he might see what was the matter.

But he could not make out, though he kept all his eyes open, in the strict sense of the words: so by-and-bye he made the inquiry of his old friend the tree.

"What is the matter, do you ask?" groaned the oak more heavily than ever—"you who can change your position and act independently when you wish; you who are *not* left a useless log as I am, the scorn and sport of my own kith and kin? Yes, the very planks who balance themselves on my body, and mock me by their activity, have probably come from my own bosom, and once hung on me as branches, drinking in life from the life I gave. Oh miserable me! miserable, despised, useless!"

Now there may be plenty of animals to be found with more brilliant abilities and livelier imagination than the snail, but for gravity of demeanour and calmness of nerve who is his equal? and if a sound judgment be not behind such outward signs, there is no faith to be put in faces!

Accordingly, Sir Helix Hortensis—so let us call him—made no answer at first to the wailings of the oak. Three times he crawled round it, leaving three fresh traces of his transit, before he spoke, his horns turning hither and thither as those wonderful eyes at the end strove to take in the full state of the case. And his are not the eyes, you know, which waste their energies in scatter-brained staring. He keeps them cool in their cases till there is something to be looked at, and then turns them inside out to do their destined work.

And thus he looked, and he looked, and he looked, while the children went on shouting, and the plank went on see-sawing, and the tree went on groaning; and as he looked, he considered.

"Have you anything to say?" at last inquired the oak, who had had long experience of Sir Helix's wisdom.

"I have," answered the snail. "You don't know your own value, that's all."

"Ask the see-sawers my value!" exclaimed the prostrate tree, bitterly. "One up at the stars, another beyond the world! What am *I* doing meanwhile?"

"Holding them both up, which is more than they can do for themselves," muttered the snail, turning round to go back to the grass.

"But—but—stop a moment, dear Sir Helix; the see-sawers don't think that," argued the tree.

"They're all light-minded together, and don't think," sneered the snail. "Up in the sky one minute, down in the dust the next. Never you mind that. Everybody can't play at high jinks with comfort, luckily for the rest of the world. Sit fast, do your duty, and have faith. While they are going flightily up and down, your steady balance is the saving of both."

If major Victorian fantasies for children abound in color and motion, "See-Saw" almost exults in drabness and inertia. The parable's protagonist, the "stupid old stump" the children deride, is indeed "insignificant," having presumably been discarded because no "beautiful even planks" can be cut from its rough and knotty "root end." The plank that "leans so heavily" on its back can move up and down with the children. The tree stump, on the other hand, must remain fixed and immobile. And the narrative centered around it seems just as static, almost as if Mrs. Gatty wanted to extend the woodenness of her protagonist to the story itself.

In the parable's first half the stump's groans become so dominant that they not only drown out the children's exclamations but also displace a voice that might impart direction, or at least a new point of view, to what otherwise threatens to become monotonous. Yet at first Mrs. Gatty deliberately thwarts the reader's eagerness for a discernible authorial stance. We are forced to overhear a monologue. The stump speaks to itself because, we are told, it remains unsure as to whom "to complain to—the children or the plank." But there is no assurance that, even if it were to complain to either party, its words would be heard: both the children who speak in a closed chorus and the plank who remains mute throughout the story seem unlikely interlocutors. The narrator, too, appears to be immobilized, distanced from her own potential audience, whether of children or adults. How much does the narrator sympathize with the complaints of the stump? We cannot be sure. By calling the stump a "poor tree," the narrator seems to side with it and set herself in opposition to the "giddy" children who have dismissed it as "stupid." And yet the very prominence given to the trunk's wails becomes suspect. We increasingly are made to feel that the oak's self-pity is as exaggerated as the wishfulness of children who hope to catch stars and emerge at the world's "other side." A story that had promised, through its title, some balancing act now threatens to veer instead, as the Tennysonian epigraph suggests, into "the false-

hood of extremes." We are led to yearn for some traffic between those extremes. The children's innocence and the tree stump's experience remain excessively set apart. And that excess proves discomforting. If the tree stump is "getting impatient," so is the reader by the story's first half.

Not until the appearance of the snail, in the second half, does an expected mediator finally set the parable in motion. Hitherto, the plank on which the seesawers sit has been the only potential intermediary between the children and the superannuated stump who so nostalgically recalls "the acorn days of his babyhood." Unlike the stump, the plank can move with the children; it possesses—or so the stump assumes—"energy and life," a life, as we later discover, it in fact may owe to the mutilated speaker who tells us that this "kith and kin" once probably drank nourishment from its "own bosom." Associated with both the children and its parental trunk, the plank would thus be a likely mediator between youth and age, the verticality of hope and the horizontality of resignation. And yet this go between, in its total muteness, seems lifeless or at least asleep.

It thus devolves upon another sleeper, roused by the stump's groans, to assume the role the plank, like the narrator, has eschewed. It is the snail who fulfills our expectations by becoming an intermediary. Instinct with his own slow and deliberate motions, independent, he is not tied to the children's jerky impulsiveness. Indeed, this self-propelling creature, the narrator now volunteers, habitually crawls round the felled oak every morning "to see the world come to life." His appearance makes the story itself come alive. For he helps to animate not just the stump, by providing it with the interlocutor that had so far been missing, but also the aroused narrator, who, at last raised from her own torpor, seizes on "Sir Helix Hortensis" as an outlet for a more active and playful imagination. The tiny expositor frees the narrator, who had suppressed herself; her total endorsement of his point of view removes any previous misconception we might have had about her concurrence with the tree stump's paralyzing self-pity. If she has been too silent until now, that silence may have stemmed from a reflectiveness similar to the snail's own, for he too "at first" chooses to make "no answer" whatsoever "to the wailings of the oak."

The sober Sir Helix thus replaces the "prostrate tree" as a more appropriate representative of adult experience. More authoritative because of the wider purview that comes with his daily peregrinations, he can confirm, yet also soften, the stump's contempt for the "light-minded" children. For the snail is himself a more "light-minded" agent for Mrs. Gatty's intended emphasis. Though his "gravity" makes him a fit companion for the aged tree trunk, his very size and his mock-heroic demeanor also link him to the children who have defied the laws of gravity. If the children "go up, up, up" and "down, down, down," Sir Helix, too, is capable of contrary motions, "his head turning now to one side, now to the other." Though more judicious than they, he adopts their triplings. As they move up, they expect to "catch the tree-tops—no! the church-steeple—no! the stars"; as they move down, they wish to go "on the ground—no! right through the world—no! out at the other side." More solidly grounded, slower to speak, Sir Helix nonetheless also does things by threes: "Three times he crawled . . . , leaving three fresh traces of his transit." "And thus he looked, and he looked, and he looked." He speaks three times. His final message insists on a trinity of obligations ("Sit fast, do your duty, and have faith").

Although Mrs. Gatty endorses the snail's concluding homily, she also treats him with a levity not evident in the story's first half. Whereas the narrator stifled her own voice in recording the tree stump's lamentations, she now offers an extensive description of the garden snail before she chooses to reproduce his own sententious utterances. It is the eyes of the snail itself, "those wonderful eyes at the end" of his probing horns, that the reader, now at last overtly addressed as "you," is invited to behold. All of a sudden, Mrs. Gatty seems conscious of her double audience of children and adults. The child reader is clearly expected to relish her anthropomorphism: "his are not the eyes, you know, which waste their energies in scatter-brained staring." But if the child reader or child-auditor is regaled with such microscopic details, older readers, who might even be expected to know the Latin name for "garden snail," can cherish the mock-heroic touch in the author's dubbing of her miniknight: "Sir Helix Hortensis—so let us call him." Such readers might well appreciate other, more subtly embedded, mock-epic overtones: a horned creature who, like a snake, leaves a "slimy track" behind him, who moves "three times" before he delivers his first speech, seems a cousin of that other pseudo hero who thrice assayed to speak before haranguing the torpid and dejected fallen angels of *Paradise Lost*.

Sir Helix thus acts as a fulcrum between the seesawing imaginations of grown-up and child. His last words can be applied to his own role in the story. For it is his own "steady balance" between unreflecting childhood innocence and a paralyzing adult experience that Mrs. Gatty wants to tap in order to overcome the extremes she had represented by the children and the tree trunk. That those extremes seem to stem from a self-division within herself seems undeniable. Although the tree trunk is presented as a male figure, its allusion to the "kith and kin" that came from his "own bosom" and once drank "in life from the life I gave" suggests that its despondency may be akin to that of a mother-author who felt herself, in her old age, unduly re-

moved from children-auditors who had become unresponsive to her ministrating efforts at nurturance and instruction. A year before her death, Mrs. Gatty, who "had lost the power of writing with her own hand, and was gradually losing the power of speech," printed a poem, "Lines, 1872," about suffering and faith, which an admiring Lewis Carroll, who found them "so beautiful and touching," distributed among several of his little friends.[14] But "See-Saw" is more than a personal allegory. As both Lewis Carroll and Rudyard Kipling, that other admirer of Mrs. Gatty's work, would have understood, the story addresses the need to overcome the gap between the psychological extremes which it first isolates and then tries to recombine: the obsessive and self-conscious melancholy of an aging self approaching death and the unselfconsciousness of a childhood self that wishes to remain immune to the sobering aspects of growing up. The snail, who, as Mrs. Gatty would know, is also a hermaphroditic creature combining both male and female genders, manages to bridge the gap which in the first half of the story seemed to be so unsurmountable. As a childlike adult or an adult-seeming child, this creature anticipates similar mediators devised by later fantasists, Carroll's Humpty Dumpty and his White Knight, Kipling's White Seal and 'Stute Fish, Nesbit's Psammead and Phoenix. Though cruder certainly than the work of later fantasists, though still tilting excessively—despite its attempted balancing—towards the side of experience, Mrs. Gatty's parable nonetheless sets the stage for the more imaginative productions of her successors. Like Mrs. Gatty, Lewis Carroll and Rudyard Kipling tried to renovate and replenish an adult self-consciousness by turning to the wishful magical thinking of an earlier childhood phase. Unlike their predecessor, however, they creatively exploited the imbalance she tried to correct. A brief look at their work thus will permit us to assess the strides they took in handling the selfsame extremes presented so diagrammatically in "See-Saw."

II

When Lewis Carroll sent "Bruno's Revenge" as a contribution to Mrs. Gatty's *Aunt Judy's Magazine,* she welcomed it for being so "beautiful and fantastic and *childlike*"; his regressive talent, she felt, "is peculiarly your own, and as an Englishman you are almost unique in possessing it."[15] Nearly any portion of *Alice in Wonderland,* which Mrs. Gatty lavishly reviewed and promoted, and *Through the Looking-Glass,* which appeared two years before her death, is amenable to the same analysis to which "See-Saw" has been exposed. It is the later work, however, that most persistently dwells on the same "extremes" embodied in her parable.

The Alice of *Through the Looking-Glass,* however, is not at all like the unreflecting children in "See-Saw."

Alice, having tea with the March Hare and the Mad Hatter. Illustration by John Tenniel, from Alice's Adventures in Wonderland.

Quite to the contrary, this older child covets the "steady balance" that Sir Helix equated with a maturity opposed to "high jinks." If, in Wonderland, a younger Alice was forced to go "up and down" in uncontrolled fashion, in Looking-Glass-land she submits to the rules of an adult chess game. Her steady forward progress is towards the goal of queenhood: her crowning comes to signify adult powers she has already tried to adopt in her handling of the childish black kitten. Unlike Mrs. Gatty, however, Carroll is highly ambivalent towards the adult stage that Alice is so eager to embrace. Much more than Sir Helix, the "adult" figures Alice encounters are notable for their childishness and frailty. The miniscule Gnat who warns Alice about the wood where she will lose her name seems "to have sighed itself away" in its melancholy over the notion of a missing "miss" Alice. Yet Alice fearlessly penetrates the wood; though "a little timid about going into it," she makes "up her mind to go on: 'for I certainly won't go *back,*' she thought to herself, and this was the only way to the Eighth Square" (ch. 3, p. 135).

Alice's determination to proceed towards the Eighth Square in which she expects to come into possession of the powers associated with mature womanhood is repeatedly qualified by her encounters with her presumed superiors. Seeing the Lion and the Unicorn fight for the crown, Alice asks the White King, "Does—the one—that wins—get the crown?"

> "Dear me, no!" said the King. "What an idea!"

> "Would you—be good enough—" Alice panted out, after running a little further, "to stop a minute—just to get—one's breath again?"

> "I'm *good* enough," the King said, "only I'm not *strong* enough. You see, a minute goes by so fearfully quick. You might as well try to stop a Bandersnatch!" (ch. 7, p. 173)

Again and again, the crown of adult power becomes a questionable emblem. Beyond the forward progress to which Alice so readily submits lie dissolution and death. The King is as ineffectual as the silent Hatta, "only just out of prison," who silently weeps Gnat-like tears and tries to find some elementary solace by munching away and drinking tea. The Lion and the Unicorn prove to be as juvenile as that other pair of combatants, Tweedle-dee and Tweedle-dum. And Humpty Dumpty, despite his Carrollian mastery of language, cannot foresee the "heavy crash" that will mark the fall that Alice, but not he, is able to anticipate.

Carroll's reservations about Alice's egress from childhood are evident in Humpty Dumpty's earlier exchange with Alice:

> "Seven years and six months!" Humpty Dumpty repeated thoughtfully. "An uncomfortable sort of age. Now if you'd asked *my* advice, I'd have said 'Leave off at seven'—but it's too late now."
>
> "I never ask advice about growing," Alice said indignantly.
>
> "Too proud?" the other enquired.
>
> Alice felt even more indignant at this suggestion. "I mean," she said, "that one ca'n't help growing older."
>
> "*One* ca'n't, perhaps," said Humpty Dumpty; "but *two* can. With proper assistance, you might have left off at seven." (ch. 6, p. 162)

Convinced that they "had had quite enough of the subject of age," Alice is quick to change the subject by assuming control of the conversation: "if they really were to take turns in choosing subjects," she thinks, "it was *her* turn now." The seesawing reverts to her.

Neither Alice nor the child reader who may endorse her determination and hunger for grown-up power can entirely fathom the import of Humpty Dumpty's ominous remark. For this childlike adult speaks for a Carroll who had doubts about the stage of experience Alice still covets. Two might indeed have been able to prevent the girl from growing further—a Providence willing to cut short the child's earthly existence or a godlike artist who had already tried to detain Alice in the arrested, infantile world of Wonderland when she was still but seven. But in *Through the Looking-Glass,* published when the actual Alice Liddell had become a nineteen-year-old woman, Lewis Carroll yields to the inevitable, though not without struggle. As the about-to-be-shattered Humpty Dumpty comes to demonstrate, the realm of innocence cannot be maintained.

It is this adult self-consciousness that pierces through, again and again, the defusing humor of *Through the Looking-Glass.* Still, like the child readers whom Carroll encourages to identify with her resolve, the fictional Alice remains immune to Carroll's intimations of mortality. Shades of the prison house may begin to close upon the growing girl. But the determined child does not regard these omens, heavy as the frost with which the book opens, as oppressive "Fallings from us, vanishings." Only adult readers, from their own "place of thought"[16] in the realm of experience, can sense this counterbalancing presence. Like the White Knight who vainly tries to make Alice linger on the last square before the eighth by reciting his Wordsworthian "song," Carroll temporarily resigns himself to the inevitability of growth.

In chapter 8 of *Through the Looking-Glass* an omniscient narrator suddenly intrudes. Rather sentimentally, this narrator insists that in her later life a grown-up Alice will "most clearly" remember the love-offering which the White Knight is about to present just before she crosses the threshold that separates pawn from Queen, and girl from Woman:

> Years afterwards she could bring the whole scene back again, as if it had been only yesterday—the mild blue eyes and kindly smile of the Knight—the setting sun gleaming through his hair, and shining on his armour in a blaze of light that quite dazzled her—the horse quietly moving about, with the reins hanging loose on his neck, cropping the grass at her feet—and the black shadows of the forest behind—all this she took in like a picture, as, with one hand shading her eyes, she leant against a tree, watching the strange pair, and listening, in a half-dream, to the melancholy music of the song. (ch. 8, p. 187)

In its lyricism and its inordinate length, this sentence contains some of the same cadences—and same affect—produced at the end of *Alice's Adventures in Wonderland.* There, an older dreamer, Alice's sister, also "pictured" how a future Alice, "herself a grown woman," would remember "her own child-life, and the happy summer days" (ch. 12, p. 99).[17]

In *Through the Looking-Glass,* however, this anticipation of an adult's retrospection is ironically undercut. Its sentimentality seems suspect, for it belies Alice's responses, still in her fictional present, to the White Knight's overtures both before and after his song. As the Knight conducts Alice to the "end of the wood," he speaks of fusion and separation: he tells her how the mixed ingredients of one of his concoctions, a pudding, are "nicer" than each ingredient *"alone,"* only to note, "And here I must leave you." Convinced that she is saddened by the necessity of their parting, he offers his song as comfort. But the Knight is guilty of a misreading: he mistakes her look of puzzlement—for she is still "thinking of the pudding," as the narrator informs us—as an expression of sorrow (ch. 8, p.

186). The White Knight is thus guilty of projecting his own feelings on the unsorrowful child. A later Alice, now herself an adult, may be able to lyricize and pick up the note of "melancholy" that overwhelms him; but the child before him, impatient to move on, remains immune.

Like the Carroll who bemoans, in his dedicatory poem, that he and Alice Liddell, author and prime reader, "I and thou," have been thrust "half a life asunder," the White Knight tries to assuage his own separation anxieties and self-fragmentation through the "love-gift" of a story. But for all his sentimentality, the Carroll of the opening poem was more of a realist than the fantastical (and fantasizing) White Knight. Aware that "No thought of me shall find a place / In thy young life's hereafter—," Carroll remains content to detain his listener for the duration of his story: "Enough that now thou wilt not fail / To listen to my fairy-tale" (p. 103). At its best, the storyteller's art can, at a later time, reactivate the youthful imagination of an adult Alice Liddell. As Carroll's defensively parodic self-projection, however, the White Knight remains a solipsist, pitifully and comically divorced from his fictional interlocutor:

> "You are sad," the Knight said in an anxious tone: "let me sing you a song to comfort you."
>
> "Is it very long?" Alice asked, for she had heard a good deal of poetry that day.
>
> "It's long," said the Knight, "but it's very, *very* beautiful. Everybody that hears me sing it—either it brings the *tears* into their eyes, or else—"
>
> "Or else what?" said Alice, for the Knight had made a sudden pause.
>
> "Or else it doesn't, you know." (ch. 8, p. 186)

As an adult reader, Alice may falsify the past by choosing to remember the "melancholy music of the song" she is now forced to hear. Within the story, however, she is as little saddened by the Knight's recital of what is after all a comical rendering of unresponsiveness as the children in Gatty's "See-Saw" were by the adult tree stump's exaggerated lamentations. Indeed, the Knight, for all his self-forgetfulness, seems disappointed by her unemotional reception of his "love-gift." When Alice dutifully feels compelled to thank him and assure him that she "liked it very much," he replies rather "doubtfully": "I hope so, . . . but you didn't cry so much as I thought you would" (ch. 8, pp. 187, 190). She has, in fact, not cried at all. Carroll thus reintroduces his own, infinitely more complicated version of the selfsame gap that separated Gatty's aged tree trunk from the uncomprehending seesawers. Like the discarded tree stump, the elderly Knight who has reached the end of his road remains self-involved, swaddled in

a self-pity he cannot directly share with a child who firmly insists on her apartness.

The song the White Knight produces for Alice reenforces, in elliptical fashion, this emphasis on a psychic separation. Sung, significantly enough, to the tune of "I give thee all—I can no more," it stresses the incomprehension that isolates two speakers who, like Alice and the Knight himself, remain obsessively locked into their individual mental worlds. Carroll's decision to give the Knight an adaptation of the parody of "Resolution and Independence" he had previously published in 1856 as "Upon the Lonely Moor" was a careful and deliberate act of self-defense. It stemmed from his need to defuse the psychic division he also handled in his introductory poem and in "The Wasp in a Wig" episode he had originally intended to place between Alice's farewell to the Knight and her crowning as Queen.[18]

In Carroll's 1856 parody the speaker of the poem is a solipsistic "gentleman" who, in Wordsworthian fashion, appropriates the psyche of the rustic "boor" he encounters in a natural setting (p. 249) (just as, in the suppressed "Wasp in a Wig" episode, a genteel Alice was to encounter, and question, the boorish, lower-class wasp who grumbles about his "old bones").[19] In *Through the Looking-Glass,* however, this speaker has become a personation of a White Knight who is himself, like Humpty Dumpty or the White King (or the disappearing Gnat and dying Wasp), a personation of the book's implied author. In Tenniel's drawing it is unmistakably the White Knight himself who bodily seizes the aged, aged man. Yet the Knight's interlocutor may no longer be the counterpart of Wordsworth's old Leech-gatherer. Instead of being encountered on a moor, as in the original version, he now sits, like Humpty Dumpty, precariously perched on an elevation. The gate he sits on is, like the boundary Alice is about to traverse, a line of demarcation. His face remains curiously concealed in the drawing. His body is slumped backwards. The White Knight who grasps him may indeed be shaking him "from side to side," as Alice will later shake Red Queen into black kitten, dream into reality, child into adolescent. But the drawing remains ambiguous. The Knight may also be holding the gate-sitter to prevent him from tumbling backwards. Or, conversely, he may try to pull him over the gate. At any rate, the teetering figure is as unstable as the plank in Gatty's "See-Saw."

Who, then, *is* this aged, aged man of the second version? Seen from one perspective, he stands for an almost infantile regressiveness; seen from the other side of the line on which he, like Alice, is perched, he acts as a last memento mori for the girl who is so determined to push on into the realm of experience. Like Alice, the aged man is deferential to the interlocutor he addresses as "Your Honour"; still, though he acts as a willing pawn who subordinates himself to the White Knight's ruminations, he is also goal-oriented, repeatedly calling attention to his need for money. Like Alice again, he is obsessed with food—mutton pies, bread, buttered rolls; but in a fiction in which food and eating have consistently betokened death and strife (the bread-and-butter-fly who "would die" if bereft of weak tea and cream, the little oysters devoured by Walrus and Carpenter, the shattered shell of Humpty Dumpty, the plum cake that fails to prevent further dissolution) his obsession seems ominous.

The Knight begins his song, "I'll tell thee everything I can: / There's little to relate." And indeed as a "relation," a narrative, a story, the White Knight's Song exploits unrelatedness, discontinuity. Yet it is through this disjointedness that the Knight, and Carroll behind him, tries to relate adult to child, a divided author to his irreconcilable double readership. The song ends by mocking the same kind of sentimental remembrance with which an older Alice "could bring the whole scene back again"; it handles ironically those tears of nostalgia which the White Knight fails to induce:

> And now, if e'er by chance I put
>   My fingers into glue,
> Or madly squeeze a right-hand foot
>   Into a left-hand shoe,
> Or if I drop upon my toe
>   A very heavy weight,
> I weep, for it reminds me so
> Of that old man I used to know—
> Whose look was mild, whose speech was
>   slow,
> Whose hair was whiter than the snow,
>   . . . . .
>
> Who snorted like a buffalo—
> That summer evening long ago,
>   A-sitting on a gate.
>
> (ch. 8, pp. 189-90)

As in the pudding in which "mixing" impossibly isolated ingredients can still make a "difference," Carroll tries to decompound and blend what has been so irrefrangible. The "I" who was so apart from the "aged, aged man" appropriates him through the falsifications of nostalgia and memory; the Alice who was bored by the Knight's song will similarly remember his "mild blue eyes" in later days. In a world of nonrelation, the world to which Carroll would turn in his "Hunting of the Snark," the common experience of pain may lead us to "relate"—through fictions—what was otherwise unrelatable. Alice listens to the White Knight's song, "but no tears came into her eyes." In *Sylvie and Bruno*, the fairy-child will sob uncontrollably over the reality of death. In *Through the Looking Glass,* however, where Wordsworth's Leech-gatherer teeters on a gate, laughter can fend off thoughts that are too deep for

tears. The ironies that Carroll exploits in his comic masterpiece proved to be for him the only way to seesaw between the falsehood of extremes.

III

Rudyard Kipling opened his posthumously published *Something of Myself* (1937) with an epigraph he had been fond of quoting: "Give me the first six years of a child's life and you can have the rest."[20] Very early in his career as a writer, Kipling grasped the importance for his creativity of the special qualities of the privileged "child's life" on which he could draw. Whether written for adults or for a juvenile audience or for a joint readership, his best fables are profitably understood as attempts to recover the imaginative wholeness of the childhood psyche first threatened in the "House of Desolation" at Southsea (the emotional equivalent of Dickens's "blacking warehouse" trauma) and sorely tested again at the United Services College. The nurturance denied to Punch in the semiautobiographical "Baa Baa, Black Sheep" (1888) is extended to Mowgli when the foundling boy is given a surplus of mentors and parental surrogates in the animal and village worlds of *The Jungle Books* (1894, 1895). Yet the bitter adult ironies that undercut the happy ending of Punch's return to his mother are hardly expunged from *The Jungle Books*. For, as Angus Wilson well puts it, "Kipling . . . knew that to identify with children does not mean losing your adult identity."[21] Like Lewis Carroll and Margaret Gatty, Kipling never closed the gap that necessarily separated the two identities.

Still, more than Carroll and certainly more than the Mrs. Gatty whose *Parables from Nature* Kipling claimed to have at one time "imitated,"[22] he managed to maintain a highly fluid traffic, interchange, or "flirtation between the two worlds" of innocence and experience.[23] The ghost-child whom the adult narrator encounters at the end of "They" (1904) may well be a fictional incarnation of Kipling's own "best beloved" dead daughter Josephine; but this apparition is also, like Mowgli, Kim, and the little "Best Beloved" so affectionately addressed in the *Just So Stories* (1902), very much a resurrection of an ever-present child within. If Carroll, in the shape of the White Knight, must say good-bye to the growing Alice, Kipling joyously refused to part from this juvenile self. His ability to create flowing narrative modes that could be equally true to adult and child alike makes *The Jungle Books* and *Just So Stories* the truly imaginative achievements that they are.

Two stories (one from each work), "The White Seal" and "How the Whale Got His Throat," will have to suffice to illustrate this fluidity. Both stories are set in a world of water, the most fluid and primal of elements. Both revel in a kind of infantile freedom of movement that is reflected in the very liberties the narrator allows himself to take. Both are the initial unit in a narrative sequence that moves from simplicity and unrestraint to a more constricted and difficult order of relationships. As the first of the four interpolated animal tales which follow the three Mowgli stories in the first *Jungle Book,* "The White Seal" permits an escapism that is no longer possible in "Servants of the Queen," the fourth and last unit of the series. Kotick can lead his seal nation away from human predators in "The White Seal"; the animals in "Servants of the Queen" are yoked to humans in a hierarchical order of obligations. Even water has altered its symbolic meaning. The guarantor of freedom in the marine world of "The White Seal" now turns, in "Servants of the Queen," into an unceasing, mud-splattering rain-flood that presages the dissolution of civilization's attempts to bind man and beast into an alliance against primal chaos. A similar, though less acute, reversal in *Just So Stories* distances the opening "How the Whale Got His Throat" from the concluding "The Butterfly that Stamped," a story which, the narrator admits, is "quite different from the other stories."[24] The powerful Whale of the first story has turned into a puny, henpecked butterfly; the childlike Mariner has become "The Most Wise Sovereign Suleiman-bin-Daoud—Solomon the Son of David," a monarch who, like Victoria in "Servants of the Queen," tries to exert a dubious adult authority over a world of humans and beasts. The perspectives of innocence and experience are again reversed.

"The White Seal," however, not only counterbalances the sequence of stories it initiates but also acts as a ballast to the preceding sequence of Mowgli stories. "Tiger! Tiger!" has left the growing Mowgli on the threshold of maturity. He is triumphant, yet also a sadder and wiser man-cub. The killing of Shere Khan has turned out to be a hollow victory. For Mowgli now knows that his child-life among the wolves is over. His maturation as a manling, his very superiority to his animal brethren, now sets him apart from both jungle and village. He angrily refuses to lead the Free People who have degenerated into "lawlessness" and decides to "hunt alone."[25] The narrator concludes "Tiger! Tiger!" with a guarded concession that softens the impact of Mowgli's self-exile: "But he was not always alone, because, years afterward, he became a man and married." He then adds, as if in afterthought, "But that is a story for grown-ups" (p. 72).

Thus Mowgli is left wandering between two worlds. He is no longer the childish little frog of "Kaa's Hunting"; nor is he yet the mythical wood-god observed by an awed Englishman in the "adult" story of "In the Rukh" (1893), which Kipling had actually written before *The Jungle Books.* As his concluding song explains, he remains divided, an amphibian creature torn between two contrary states: "These two things fight together in me as the snakes fight / in the spring. The

water comes out of my eyes, yet / I laugh while it falls. Why? / I am two Mowglis" (p. 74). Like Carroll's "White Knight's Song," "Mowgli's Song" expresses the writer's own split emotions: it is both a lament and a cry of exultation. But, unlike Carroll, Kipling does not rest content with this expression of ambivalence. He follows "Tiger! Tiger!," the last Mowgli story of the first book, with "The White Seal," the beginning of a new sequence. The last words of Mowgli's song ("My heart is heavy with the things I do not understand") are followed by the reassuring lines of the "Seal Lullaby" that opens Kotick's story ("Oh! hush thee, my baby, the night is behind us, / And black are the waters that sparkled so green"). We have once more retrogressed into the security of a womblike world such as that of the cave in which Mother Wolf had first protected her adopted child.

The story of Kotick's election thus acts as a kind of looking-glass pendant to the previous account of Mowgli's own rise from precarious infancy to mastery. Like Mowgli, Kotick is unique, but the significance of his uniqueness is not as readily grasped by the creatures around him as Mowgli's was in his adopted jungle world. Whereas Raksha, the Wolf Mother, can immediately foretell that the bold brown baby who has pushed her cubs aside will develop into Shere Khan's killer, the simpler Mathka merely tells her husband, Sea Catch, that "our baby's going to be white!" (p. 77). The implications of this anomaly do not greatly disturb her or her mate. She is as placid and accepting as the young seals who blithely toddle into the slaughterhouse. The whiteness of her seal pup, however, sets him as much apart from the others as Mowgli's humanity had distinguished him from his wolf brothers. It is an emblematic token of his superiority, not just over seals "as stupid and unaccommodating as men" (p. 76) but also over the dull-witted Aleuts whose superstitious awe (so like Buldeo's in the Indian village) causes them to spare the pale mutant. In a way, however, the Aleuts are correct, for Kotick's extraordinariness does indeed make him seem unnatural. While Mowgli's conversion into the potential leader of the wolf pack is presented as the seemingly logical outgrowth of the combined teachings of Akela, Baloo, Bagheera, as well as of the development of his innately superior human intellect and instincts, Kotick's transformation into a kind of Moses who will lead the seal people into a promised land remains lodged in a quasi-evolutionary fairy tale. We are asked to believe that this shrewd observer possesses a near-human intelligence as well as superhuman strengths. Whereas all other seals seem infantile and slow and "need a long time to turn things over in their minds" (p. 92), Kotick alone acts as a responsible human adult would.

Having reached the threshold of manhood, Mowgli must choose self-exile from the inadequate social organizations of both jungle and village. Immersed as he is in a much simpler primal world, Kotick can use the experience gained during his own self-exile to induce a change in that childish seal world. He, too, has been "lonesome" as an adolescent. But he gathers information during this stage, exploring the North and South Pacific, questioning other marine mammals, until he at last finds the desired haven for his people. To win them over, he enlists the very "rage" that had confirmed Mowgli as a bitter outcast. Kotick's aggression is in the service of a social ideal. If the killing of Shere Khan remains above all an act of personal revenge that results in Mowgli's isolation from beasts and villagers alike, the epic defeat of "thousands" of rival seals by a bloodied Kotick, "red from head to tail," is undertaken for the benefit of the vanquished. Kotick thus adopts the role of leader rejected by Mowgli. He is, after all, a grown animal, not a growing human being. If Mowgli must hunt apart from man and wolf pack, Kotick conducts his "army" of ten thousand seals into the inland sea "where no man comes" (p. 92).

Both Kotick and Mowgli help dramatize Kipling's life-long yearning for a social organism that might offer on an adult level the same sense of wholeness he had enjoyed during his early Indian childhood. But Kotick's satisfaction of this yearning is cast as a wishful fable, a fantasy that younger readers may want to embrace but which older readers must recognize as being wrought by "fancy." In its narrative mode "The White Seal" differs sharply from the three Mowgli stories that precede it. Despite surface similarities—the continued reliance on talking animals, the common thematic emphasis on election, growth, and mastery—its texture is calculatedly antithetical.

If the anthropomorphism of the Mowgli stories is deftly concealed by a veneer of naturalism, it is blatantly exposed in "The White Seal." Before we hear Father Wolf speak in a human language, we are conditioned to observe his animal behavior: we see him wake up, scratch himself, yawn, and spread his paws. In "The White Seal," however, there is no such suspension of disbelief. Human talk and a human self-consciousness immediately set the tone. Realism is deliberately subverted. We must rely on a narrator who asks us to believe that the ensuing tale has been transmitted by "a very quaint little bird" (p. 75), Limmershin the Winter Wren, providentially blown onto the rigging of his Japan-bound steamship. And, instead of observing credible animal actions, we are made to overhear Matkah's slow-witted fighter-mate rebuking her in tones that are unmistakably parodic of human conversations: "Late as usual. Where *have* you been?" (p. 76). When Sea Catch proudly displays his wounds and "ribbons" to his spouse, she impatiently exclaims, "Oh, you men, you men!" (p. 77). Nor are the creatures whom Kotick will later encounter ever as realistically or lyrically presented as a Kaa or a Bagheera. Instead, like Tenniel

drawings or Disney caricatures (or like the cartoons which John Lockwood Kipling drew for his little son), they are persistently rendered as humans in animal attire. The walruses whom Kotick meets look at him "as you can fancy a club full of drowsy old gentlemen would look at a little boy" (p. 84). And the sea cows who go on "schlooping and grazing and chomping" as Kotick politely addresses them as "gentlemen," answer him "by bowing and waving their flippers like the Frog-Footman" in *Alice's Adventures in Wonderland* (p. 88). The literary cross-reference is clearly made with tongue-in-cheek by the playful narrator; we are dependent throughout on his intrusive point of view and cannot directly recover the perspectives of either his presumed informant ("Limmershin told me that") or of his presumed seal-hero ("'By the Great Combers of Magellan!' he said, beneath his moustache").

In "The White Seal" Kipling thus deliberately invokes the comic conventions of earlier Victorian children's classics: Limmershin resembles those other tiny animal guides found in Gatty, Carroll, or Molesworth; the Walrus is a cousin of the oyster-eater in *Through the Looking-Glass*. The introduction of this frame of reference may please the small child as well as the adult. But it also makes it more difficult for either implied reader to extend to Kotick the same empathy we are encouraged to feel when we observe Mowgli's acute growing pains and uncompleted identity. The adolescent Mowgli who at the end of "Tiger! Tiger!" cannot yet marry or "become a man" acts as the fulcrum that draws the sympathies of both the forward-looking child and the backward-looking adult. Kotick, however, cannot bring about such a fusion in perspectives. He may delay his mother's exhortations that he "marry and settle down" or his father's advice that "he grow up and be a big seal like your father" (pp. 87, 85), but when he finally does fight the recusant seal tribe, he is aided by that selfsame father and admiringly observed by both Matkah and the "seal that he was going to marry." The juvenile reader, especially if he is still a powerless "little boy" rather than a little girl, may find such prowess intensely gratifying: Kotick has after all now excelled his father's might and gained the admiration of his "cowered down" mother (p. 91). The adult reader, however, more attuned to the story's burlesque elements, is likelier to regard the extraordinary white seal as a mere agent for the narrator's own superior stance towards the marine world he so comically animates. When Kotick brands the speechless sea cows as "idiots" (p. 88) or when he contemptuously tells his immovable brethren, "I'm going to teach you now" (p. 91), he earns a far more elevated status than Mrs. Gatty's sententious garden snail. Kotick's ironic distance from the childish behavior of the subhuman sea creatures (and human Aleuts) he outwits and defeats and, what is more, his selfless concern for the survival of his species have the effect of making him seem a fellow grown-up to readers eager to regard their own competitiveness and aggression as serving some social superego. Child reader and adult reader alike may thus welcome this fable as a parable of nature that endorses instinct and socialization. But the pleasure each takes in its texture is achieved at quite different, possibly even antithetical, levels of identification.

A different blend of innocence and experience operates in "How the Whale Got His Throat" in a collection of stories addressed to an audience of even younger children. Here too the treatment is comical. And, once again, the emphasis falls on survival, adaptation, self-reliance. But the elements of implausibility, here as well as in the other *Just So Stories,* can be shared by child and grown-up. Whereas the adult reader of "The White Seal" is encouraged to maintain a detached superiority over the materials in the story, that reader now becomes the narrator's collaborator in a playful suspension of disbelief enacted in a game both can share with the small child-auditor. Like the other *Just So Stories,* "How the Whale Got His Throat" is what Roger Lancelyn Green calls an "unnatural history," a parable of anti-Nature.[26] For it sets out to dissolve the antithetical states of being of adult and child. And it does so by dissipating as well the fear of death experienced in Gatty's and Carroll's work, as well as in Kipling's own "White Seal."

If Kotick's cleverness permits him to lead his tribe away from the bloody slaughter of the Aleut killing-pens, it is the alliance of two puny creatures that will prevent the monstrous Whale from voraciously decimating all inhabitants of the sea. To protect itself from the Whale's hunger, the lonely "small 'Stute Fish" who speaks in "a small 'stute voice" leads the sea monster to consider a tastier morsel: "Noble and generous Cetacean, have you ever tasted Man?" (p. 3). Like the Bagheera who knew that the puny Mowgli could, as a human being, defeat the gluttonous Shere Khan, so does the 'Stute Fish anticipate the Whale's comeuppance. The shipwrecked Mariner, armed only with his suspenders and a jackknife, seems negligible as the Whale's opponent. Still, the 'Stute Fish warns the Whale that this creature is "a man-of-infinite-re-source-and-sagacity" (p. 4). Although the Whale fails to heed the warning, its repetition is not wasted on the reader. An alliance is formed, not just between 'Stute Fish and the Mariner but also between the narrator and his double readership. For if the child may empathize with the 'Stute Fish, both child and adult can identify with the "man-of-infinite-resource-and-sagacity" who, in Kipling's first illustration, is similarly dwarfed by the mighty whale.

Once "inside the Whale's warm, dark, inside cupboards," the Mariner behaves like an insouciant fetus: "he stumped and he jumped and he thumped and he bumped, and he pranced and he danced, and he banged and he clanged, and he hit and he bit, and he leaped and he creeped, and he prowled and he howled, and he hopped and he dropped, and he cried and he sighed, and he crawled and he bawled" (p. 5). But though deliciously childish, his behavior is calculated. He may be infantile (he has, after all, "his mummy's leave to paddle" in the ocean; p. 4), but he is not content with making the hiccoughing Whale gladly spew him back out again at his "natal-shore and the white-cliffs-of-Albion" (p. 5). The Mariner has yet to justify his election by the 'Stute Fish as one who, like Kotick and Mowgli, is capable of a higher form of mastery. Indeed, his infinite-resource-and-sagacity permits him to induce an evolutionary change that will hereafter save future victims from the Whale's appetite. For the Mariner is a tool-wielding creature, a man. His jack-knife, however, will not be used as the Indian dagger with which Mowgli slashes off Shere Khan's hide or the skinning tools with which the Aleuts rip off the furs of bludgeoned seals. It is not a weapon of aggression but a tool that enables him to perform a feat of prosthetic dentistry: the Mariner cuts up the raft "into a little square grating all running criss-cross," ties it "firm with his suspenders," and lodges it "good and tight into the Whale's throat" (p. 9). The death-inflicting gullet of the Whale is forever closed. 'Stute Fish and Mariner alike are safe.

The adult anxieties that make their way into the works of Mrs. Gatty and Carroll and that also infiltrate *The Jungle Book* stories are neatly defused in this comic parable. The reconciliation of extremes, not possible in "Tiger! Tiger!" and achieved only on separate levels in "The White Seal," is effected with seeming effortlessness through a regressive blending acceptable to both child and adult. The captions Kipling provided for his illustrations help further this harmonizing. The Whale, the first caption informs us, bears the name of Smiler. Though still mighty, the second caption notes, it was unable to revenge itself on the 'Stute Fish "till he got over his temper, and then they became good friends again."

Equilibrium is conveyed by Kipling's almost Blakean second drawing. The Whale, its mouth now firmly shut, cannot reach the little 'Stute Fish, safely concealed in a womblike sack "among the roots" that grow "in front of the Doors of the Equator." The drawing's composition balances the 'Stute Fish of Innocence with the Whale, who has been modified by Experience. The horizontal Equator is kept "in order" by two mythical guardians. These artificers guard the gates to an unknown higher reality, "kept shut, because a door ought always to be kept shut" (p. 10). Yet that higher reality is implied by the double consciousness of a Kipling eager to blend, as Blake had done, the two contrary states of perception into a third realm that might guarantee the inviolability of both child and adult.

IV

The intense consciousness of a double readership of child and adult that I have tried to trace in the work of Gatty, Carroll, and Kipling carries certain implications that I should very succinctly like to rehearse. These implications are both theoretical and historical. Recent critical theory has valuably insisted that the meaning of a text resides above all in the reader's experience of that text. That experience, all are agreed, is hardly uniform. And yet the ideal reader posited by critics such as Wayne Booth, Wolfgang Iser, and Stanley Fish inevitably remains an "informed" reader who, though capable of a sophisticated balancing of alternative meanings, nonetheless remains a single entity—an adult, in other words, far removed from those "immature readers" whom Booth dismisses for failing to achieve an ironic distance from Emma Woodhouse. Fantasies written for children, however, especially when as complex as the Alice or the Jungle books, do remind us that the innocent or immature reader's responses cannot be disregarded—that in fact such responses were courted and expected by authors similarly divided into mature and immature (or regressive) selves. Art theoreticians concerned with form and color in painting are highly interested in the creativity of the child. Literary theorists, on the other hand, as Felicity A. Hughes has pointed out, are notably uninterested in children's literature even though a child reader's perspective remains imbedded in the responses of every "informed" adult reader.[27]

This segregation has a historical origin. The double audience to whom Victorian fantasists appealed began to break down precisely when aesthetic theorists of the novel like George Moore and Henry James bemoaned the demands placed on the "serious" novelist by such a multileveled public. In 1885 Moore proclaimed: "Let us renounce the effort to reconcile these two irreconcilable things—art and young girls"; in 1899 James, somewhat more long-windedly, derogated the "literature, as it may be called for convenience, of children" for illustrating, as far as he was concerned, "the demoralisation, the vulgarisation of literature in general, the increasing familiarity of all such methods of communication, the making itself supremely felt, as it were, of the presence of the ladies and children—by whom I mean, in other words, the reader irreflective and uncritical."[28]

It seems time to reinstate that maligned "irreflective" reader, not only in our assessment of works expressly written for children but also of those mid-Victorian novelists whom James found similarly clumsy in their handling of their readership. For if, as I have tried to show, the Victorian fantasists who wrote for children inevitably incorporated an adult point of view into their fables of innocence, the reverse holds true for "adult" Victorian fiction, in which a regressive suspension of disbelief is persistently invoked to counter the disenchantments of experience. Mr. Pickwick's inviolable innocence offsets the "chicanery" and "imposture" of the adult world through which he wanders;[29] nourished by the old fairy tales told to her as a child by her nurse Bessie, Jane Eyre can find in Rochester a fellow believer in goblins and "men in green"; the "dreaming" narrator who stands on the stone bridge in the opening of The Mill on the Floss recognizes her former shape in the "little girl" who stands perilously poised at "the edge of the water."[30] Even in Middlemarch, that novel for grown-ups, as Virginia Woolf called it, Ladislaw and Dorothea become "like two children," with their hands clasped, as the angry lightning-storm hammers on the windowpanes. Childhood, invoked even in the most "adult" of Victorian fictions, remained a ballast that might insure author and reader against the dangers of succumbing to the "falsehood of extremes."

Notes

[1] Roger Lancelyn Green, *Mrs. Molesworth* (New York: Henry Z. Walck, 1964), p. 51.

[2] Ariès, *Centuries of Childhood: A Social History of Family Life,* trans. Robert Baldick (New York: Vintage Books, 1962), pp. 15-49, 365-415; Jan Hendrick van den Berg, *The Changing Nature of Man: Introduction to a Historical Psychology, Metabletica,* trans. H. F. Croes (New York: Norton, 1961), pp. 20-114. See, however, Lloyd deMause's reservations about Ariès's thesis ("The Evolution of Childhood," in *The History of Childhood,* ed. Lloyd deMause [New York: Harper, 1975], pp. 5-6), as well as the studies on nineteenth-century childhood by Priscilla Robertson ("Home As a Nest: Middle Class Childhood in Nineteenth-Century Europe," in *The History of Childhood,* pp. 407-31) and by David Grylls (*Guardians and Angels: Parents and Children in Nineteenth-Century Literature* [London and Boston: Faber, 1978]). Part One of Neil Postman's *The Disappearance of Childhood* (New York: Delacorte, 1982) contains a helpful overview (pp. 4-64).

[3] Introd., *Holiday House: A Book for the Young* (London: Simpkin, Marshall, 1839), quoted in Roger Lancelyn Green, *Tellers of Tales: Children's Books and Their Authors from 1800 to 1964,* rev. ed. (London: Edmund Ward, 1965), p. 18.

[4] "Fairy Stories" (1868), in *The Cestus of Aglaia and The Queen of the Air,* Vol. 19 of *The Works of John Ruskin,* ed. E. T. Cook and Alexander Wedderburn, Library ed., 39 vols. (London: G. Allen, 1903-12), p. 235. Ruskin's essay, first published as an introduction to the reprint of a collection of Grimm fairy tales titled *German Popular Stories,* trans. Edgar Taylor (London: J. C. Hotten, 1869), with illustrations after the original

designs by Cruikshank (1823, 1826), can also be found in *A Peculiar Gift: Nineteenth Century Writings on Books for Children,* ed. Lance Salway (Harmondsworth: Kestrel Books, 1976), pp. 127-32.

[5] *Alice in Wonderland: Authoritative Texts of "Alice's Adventures in Wonderland," "Through the Looking-Glass," "The Hunting of the Snark," Backgrounds, Essays in Criticism,* ed. Donald J. Gray (New York: Norton, 1971); further citations in my text are to this edition.

[6] *The Strange Ride of Rudyard Kipling: His Life and Works* (New York: Viking, 1978), p. 1.

[7] Quoted by Naomi Lewis in her introduction to *Fairy Stories,* by E. Nesbit [Bland], ed. Naomi Lewis (London: E. Benn, 1977), p. vii.

[8] *Early Prose Writings,* Vol. 1 of *The Works of John Ruskin,* p. 348.

[9] *The Christmas Books,* Vol. 16 of *Thackeray's Works,* 30 vols. (Boston: Estes and Lauriat, 1891), p. 197.

[10] Christabel Maxwell, *Mrs. Gatty and Mrs. Ewing* (London: Constable, 1949), p. 93.

[11] Quoted by Maxwell in *Mrs. Gatty and Mrs. Ewing,* p. 98.

[12] Margaret Gatty, "The Law of Authority and Obedience," *Parables from Nature* (London: G. Bell, 1910), p. 13.

[13] "See-Saw," *Parables from Nature,* pp. 315-17. The epigraph is taken from the concluding lines of Tennyson's "Of Old Sat Freedom on the Heights," a paean to the personification of Liberty as an aloof, "self-gathered," mighty, and grave "mother of majestic works."

[14] C. L. Dodgson to Caroline Erskine, 5 Dec. 1873, *The Letters of Lewis Carroll,* ed. Morton N. Cohen, 2 vols. (New York: Oxford Univ. Press, 1979), I, 200 n. 6; I, 200.

[15] *The Letters of Lewis Carroll,* I, 148 n. 1; Maxwell, *Mrs. Gatty and Mrs. Ewing,* pp. 149-50.

[16] "Ode: Intimations of Immortality from Recollections of Early Childhood," stanza ix, lines 144, 134, in *The Poetical Works of Wordsworth,* ed. Paul D. Sheats, Cambridge ed., rev. ed. (Boston: Houghton, 1982), p. 355.

[17] See also the conclusion of *Alice's Adventures Underground,* introd. Martin Gardner (New York: Dover, 1965), pp. 89-90.

[18] See *The Wasp in a Wig: A "Suppressed" Episode of "Through the Looking-Glass and What Alice Found There,"* ed. Edward Guiliano, introd. Martin Gardner (New York: Clarkson N. Potter, 1977).

[19] *The Wasp in a Wig,* p. 13; whereas Alice was hardly eager to have the White Knight recite poetry to her, she suggests to the Wasp that he cast his narrative in rhyme.

[20] *Something of Myself: For My Friends Known and Unknown* (London: Macmillan, 1937), p. 1.

[21] *The Strange Ride of Rudyard Kipling,* p. 229.

[22] *Something of Myself,* p. 33; the book was furnished to Kipling by the "three dear ladies" (Mrs. Winnard and the Misses Craik) whom he periodically visited while at the United Services College. He also held on during his lifetime to "a bound copy of *Aunt Judy's Magazine* of the early 'seventies," sent to him by his parents (p. 7). Roger Lancelyn Green, *Kipling and the Children* (London: Elek, 1965), rightly stresses the store of fantasy provided to Kipling the boy by earlier Victorian writers such as George MacDonald, Mary De Morgan, Jean Ingelow, and Lewis Carroll (who, in turn, came to admire Kipling's early poetry). But only J.M.S. Tompkins has seen fit to follow up Kipling's reference to Gatty's *Parables* by aligning it with some of the animal fables (*The Art of Rudyard Kipling* [London: Methuen, 1959]).

[23] Wilson, *The Strange Ride of Rudyard Kipling,* p. 229.

[24] *Just So Stories,* Vol. 20 of *The Writings in Prose and Verse of Rudyard Kipling,* 36 vols. (New York: Scribner's, 1897-1937), p. 259. Subsequent references to this edition are cited in the text.

[25] *The Jungle Books* (New York: New American Library, 1961), p. 71. This edition, which respects the original arrangement that Kipling later abrogated when he placed all Mowgli stories into a single Jungle Book, is cited hereafter in the text.

[26] *Kipling and the Children,* p. 181; Green might have recalled Gatty's work, however, before baldly stating that *Just So Stories* is a work with "no real literary ancestors" (p. 178).

[27] "Children's Literature: Theory and Practice," *ELH,* 45 (1978), 542-61.

[28] Quoted by Hughes in "Children's Literature: Theory and Practice," pp. 547, 546; the excerpts are from George Moore's *Literature at Nurse, or Circulating Morals,* ed. Pierre Coustillas (Hassocks, Sussex: Harvester Press, 1976), and from James's essay "The

Future of the Novel," in *The Future of the Novel: Essays on the Art of Fiction,* ed. Leon Edel (New York: Vintage Books, 1956).

[29] Harry Stone, *Dickens and the Invisible World: Fairy Tales, Fantasy, and Novel-Making* (Bloomington and London: Indiana Univ. Press, 1979), p. 72.

[30] *The Mill on the Floss,* ed. Gordon S. Haight (Boston: Houghton, 1961), p. 8.

Helson explores the charm of the character of Alice in Lewis Carroll's *Alice in Wonderland*:

The marvelously strange country of Alice's world can be experienced only through Alice's childlike tolerance and receptivity. Much of the charm of Alice lies in the fact that her efforts to be quite sensible and rational rebound queerly in the strange underground world, seeming utterly to defeat rationality. Yet at critical moments reason does bring Alice mastery of the situation.

Ravenna Helson in Children's Literature: The Great Excluded, *Vol. 3, 1974.*

Anita Moss

SOURCE: "Sacred and Secular Visions of Imagination and Reality in Nineteenth-Century British Fantasy for Children," in *Webs and Wardrobes: Humanist and Religious World Views in Children's Literature,* edited by Joseph O'Beirne Milner and Lucy Floyd Morcock Milner, University Press of America, 1987, pp. 66-78.

[*In the essay below, Moss contrasts the versions of fantasy offered by Lewis Carroll and George MacDonald. Moss describes MacDonald's fantasy land as one in which the child characters must rely on a divine power for guidance, while Carroll's child characters depend on and mature through their own intelligence.*]

Writing classic British children's fantasies in the 1860's and 1870's, George MacDonald and Lewis Carroll essentially established the traditions of modern fantasy. Though they were personal friends and admired one another's work, these two writers held profoundly different views of reality. MacDonald, strongly influenced by Romantic conceptions of childhood and imagination, saw the universe as an orderly and miraculous creation, the work of a loving God whose will would finally prevail. Carroll, despite his conscious expressions of faith, seemed in the *Alice* fantasies acutely aware of disorder and chaos, of an uncertain and ever-shifting reality. These contrasting

visions of reality provide the bases for two distinct traditions of fantasy which have found rich expression in the work of many other nineteenth- and twentieth-century fantasy writers. MacDonald established what has often been called "sacred" fantasy, a term which suggests that the imaginative quests and heroic efforts of human characters are performed in the service of a higher and divine order of reality. Lewis Carroll's fantasies, on the other hand, issue entirely from the imaginative faculties, the emotional fears and wishes of the child character. Carroll's *Alice* fantasies begin and end in the same place; they refer only to themselves and do not lead the reader into an awareness of divine reality. MacDonald's view of the imagination suggests that it is a mode of receiving divine revelation, while Carroll views it as a vehicle for the child's emotional survival and growth.

In many ways the fantastic works of George MacDonald assimilate ideas and techniques of emerging forms of fairytale and fantasy in nineteenth-century England. In the aftermath of the first expressions of Romanticism early in the century, some of the finest creative and critical minds increasingly turned to the imagination as a source of inspiration and sustenance in an age of anguished religious doubt and shifting values.[1] John Ruskin's literary fairy tale, *The King of the Golden River* (1851), combined an emphasis upon spiritual purity and social responsibility with a magical sense of nature and an idealized vision of childhood. In his famous fantasy, *The Water-Babies* (1863), Charles Kingsley attempted to reconcile the miracles of science with religious and social concerns. But George MacDonald explored these issues in the largest and most significant body of fantasy written in nineteenth-century England.

Several factors probably account for MacDonald's achievement. Born in Huntly in Aberdeenshire, Scotland, on December 10, 1824, MacDonald experienced in his childhood both the moral rigors of Calvinism and the picturesque landscape and the mysterious stories, legends, and ballads of the Celtic imagination.[2] A student of Romantic conceptions of nature, the imagination and the child, a Congregationalist minister who had to leave his pastorate for preaching what his congregation believed to be heretical German Romantic theology, an avid reader of German Romantic fairy tales, and an explorer of dreams, the unconscious, and psychic states such as mesmerism, MacDonald was uniquely prepared to weave these varied threads of conventions and ideas into a rich new tapestry. In so doing, he essentially established the conventions of modern British fantasy. In addition to his own Scottish background, MacDonald also had a clear understanding of the intellectual currents of his time. Like Kingsley, MacDonald was compelled in some way to compensate for anxieties resulting from religious doubt.

M. H. Abrams has explained that one of the major characteristics of Romantic writers is their penchant for attempting to make up for the loss of God, for a universe drained of supernatural meaning.

> In its central tradition Christian thought had posited three primary elements: God, nature, and the soul; with God, of course, utterly prepotent, as the creator and controller of the two others and as the end, the *telos,* of all natural process and human endeavor. The tendency in innovative Romantic thought (manifested in proportion as the thinker is or is not a Christian theist) is greatly to diminish, and at the extreme to eliminate the role of God, leaving as the prime agencies man and the world, mind and nature, the ego and the non-ego, the self and the not-self, spirit and the other, subject and object.[3]

Thus Wordsworth sought to unify the mind, the imagination, and nature. Poets such as Coleridge and Shelley manifest a marked interest in unconscious states of mind as a means of perception through which a higher reality is apprehended entirely and truly. And John Ruskin sees divine symbols not only in nature, but also in art. Nancy Mann has shown in her excellent dissertation that Victorian fantasy writers were occupied with similar concerns. While some of these writers, such as Lewis Carroll and William Morris were, either consciously or unconsciously, secularizers, Mann maintains that others such as Kingsley and MacDonald attempted to restore the "lost divine third term."[4] The revolution in ideas created by the Romantic movement, however, made it necessary for both Kingsley and MacDonald to embody the divine in significantly new ways. In *The Water-Babies,* then, Kingsley places his central character, Tom, in a totally secular and evil world and redeems him in the divine elements of nature. MacDonald's characters also begin their adventures in the context of the ordinary world. But they enter a fantasy world in which they encounter a divinely "other" presence, and then return to the ordinary world, where they may enact visionary truth in a social and ethical context. This characteristic pattern perhaps allows MacDonald to combine his visionary propensities with his Victorian (and Calvinist) need to keep his eye steadily upon duty in the social world.

Robert Lee Wolff, Richard Reis, C.N. Manlove, and Nancy Mann have all commented upon the "ordinariness" of MacDonald's intellect. Indeed he was not an original thinker, and he did not significantly modify ideas which came to him from theological writers of the past or those which came from the great seminal minds of the nineteenth century. For ideas on childhood, MacDonald drew heavily upon Wordsworth; he is indebted to Coleridge for conceptions of the imagination. The transcendentalism of Carlyle permeates MacDonald's works of fantasy, though in MacDonald this quality becomes a radical kind of immanence, rather than transcendence.

In matters of religious doctrine, MacDonald increasingly turned away from Calvinism (especially after the resignation of his only pulpit as a result of controversies over divine love and such questions as the damnation of the heathen and the place of animals in eternity). Having finally joined the Broad wing of the Established Church, MacDonald associated with religious liberals. He was influenced by the religious writers Jacob Boehme and William Law, who emphasized mystical experience, and by those who stressed tolerance and the importance of ethics, such as the Cambridge Platonists and F.D. Maurice.[5] MacDonald's theological notions began in childhood:

> I well remember feeling as a child that I did not care for God to love me if he did not love everybody: the kind of love I needed was the love that all men needed, the love that belonged to their nature as the children of the Father, a love he could not give me except he gave it to all men.[6]

Despite some private struggles with religious doubt resulting from the deaths of four of his eleven children, MacDonald's faith was never really in question. He believed unswervingly in a divine reality in which all dimensions of nature, including man, participate. Ultimately, through his fantasies, essays, and "unspoken sermons," MacDonald constructed a divine order of his own, using ideas from Pietism, Platonism, and Christian Socialism. In many respects the writing of fantasy became a way for MacDonald to embody his most deeply and profoundly felt convictions about the place of the divine spirit in the material world, and the relationship between adult and child, creature and creator, the imagination and spiritual growth. His ideas on the imagination are especially potent and have exerted a significant influence upon subsequent writers of fantasy. The imagination enables man to penetrate the divine essence and the productions of the pure imagination necessarily express the truths of that divine reality.[7]

In discussing the role of the imagination in his essay "The Imagination: Its Function and Its Culture," MacDonald explains that the imagination is "that faculty in man which is likest to the prime operation of the power of God."[8] Yet in MacDonald's view, man's imagination is only capable of revelation, not creation. Thoughts in man, he says, arise unconsciously. If the man is good, his perception of revelation will be the surest way to truth:

> We dare to claim for the true, childlike, humble imagination, such an inward oneness with the laws of the universe that it possesses in itself an insight into the very nature of things.[9]

Hence the miner boy, Curdie, and his father, Peter, in *The Princess and Curdie* (1883) see the Grandmother as a beautiful woman, "the whole creation . . . gathered in one centre of harmony and loveliness in the person of the ancient lady who stood before him in the summer of beauty and strength."[10] But the Mother of Light explains: "For instance, if a thief were to come in here just now, he would think he saw the demon of the mine, all in green flames" (p. 55). Thus the imagination, if the person is not good, can be a dangerous faculty which may lead one away from the truth. MacDonald explains:

> The imagination will work, if not for good, then for evil; if not for truth, then for falsehood; if not for life, then for death. The power that might have gone forth in conceiving the noblest forms of action, in realizing the lives of the true-hearted, the self-forgetting, will go forth in building airy castles of vain ambition. Seek not that your sons and daughters should not see visions, should not dream dreams; but that they should see true visions, that they should dream noble dreams.[11]

MacDonald demonstrates the dangerous possibilities of an impure imagination in several of his fantasies. Princess Rosamond in *The Wise Woman* (1875) imagines ravening wolves and other horrors which inhibit her progress and spiritual growth; Mr. Vane in *Lilith* (1895) imagines creatures of horror as he journeys through fairy land unless he is in the pure light of the moon. Invariably in the fantasies of MacDonald, a narcissistic imagination turned in on the self is at best self-centered and shallow, and at worst, diseased, perverse, and evil, a pattern prominent among Romantic writers. For MacDonald, the true end of the imagination and its activity is not excess but harmony: "A right imagination, being the reflex of the creation, will fall in with the divine order of things."[12]

In his essay "The Fantastic Imagination," originally published as a preface to a volume of his fairy tales, MacDonald reaffirms and amplifies his convictions on the nature of the imagination. A writer of fantasy may "invent a little world of his own, with its own laws; for there is that in him which delights in calling up new forms—which is the nearest perhaps he can come to creation."[13] In creating such an imaginary world, though, the writer of fantasy must create harmonious and consistent laws: "And in the process of his creation, the inventor must hold by those laws. The moment he forgets one of them, he makes the story, by its own postulates, incredible."[14]

The writer has no such freedom to invent in the moral world however: "In physical things a man may invent; in moral things he must obey—and take their laws with him into his invented world."[15] MacDonald also believes that the lessons acquired through imaginary

or visionary experience must be enacted or embodied concretely in the ordinary world. This conviction is expressed in many of his fantasies. In *Phantastes,* Anodos begins his experience in the ordinary world, and comes out renewed and ready to act upon his knowledge in the context of his moral and social life. The same pattern occurs in *At the Back of the North Wind* and *Lilith*.

MacDonald's solution to problems of faith is most persuasively expressed in those fantasies in which he can express intimations and suggestions of the divine without having to spell out its meaning. Again in "The Fantastic Imagination," MacDonald explains the symbolic nature of fairytales. He compares them to a sonata because they evoke "a suitable vagueness of emotion: a fairytale, a sonata, a gathering storm, a limitless might seizes you and sweeps you away . . . The greatest forces lie in the region of the uncomprehended."[16] The fairytale and fantasy provided forms, then, which enabled MacDonald to recreate manifestations of divine truth. Whatever doubts man may experience, MacDonald insists, the divine reality exists. And we can receive that truth by responding to it imaginatively rather than intellectually.

MacDonald's artistic success is greatest when he follows his own counsel and lets his unconscious imagination work without the interference of his conscious need to make morals explicit. When MacDonald the preacher works too hard and gets in the way of MacDonald the Romantic writer, the resulting fantasies often exhibit divided structures. For instance, the protagonists of *At the Back of the North Wind* and *Lilith* bounce back and forth between the ordinary world and the imaginary world. Likewise *The Wise Woman* (1875) manifests this split structure, a feature which C.N. Manlove has argued results from a divided vision of reality.

MacDonald, however resolutely he turned away from Calvinism, was not always entirely successful in unifying the Romantic and mystic dimensions of his thought with his unmistakably Victorian emphasis upon work, duty, and obedience. In some sermons, for example, MacDonald expresses the Romantic notion that knowledge results from the imaginative identification of subject with object: "To know a primrose is a higher thing than to know the botany of it."[17] And "I trust we shall be able to enter into its [nature's] secrets from within them—by natural contact between our heart and theirs."[18] If doubt interferes with such mystical identification, MacDonald advocates obedience and action: "He who does that which he sees, shall understand; he who is set upon understanding rather than doing, shall go on stumbling and mistaking and speaking foolishness."[19] MacDonald suggests, then, that in matters of faith, human beings had best suspend their rationalist analytical faculties in favor of the

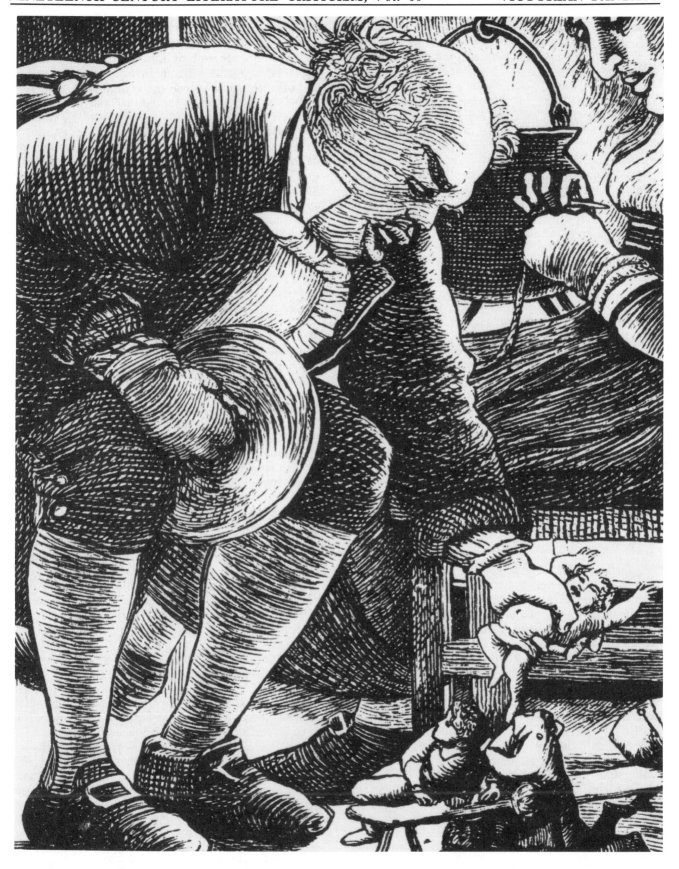

Arthur Hughes's rendition of "Giant Thunderthump," from George MacDonald's Dealings with the Fairies *(1869).*

imagination and the spirit. Yet his Calvinist upbringing undoubtedly causes him to insist that faith must also be accompanied by good works in the context of the social and ethical world.

Yet in his best works of fairy tale and fantasy, such works as *The Golden Key, The Princess and the Goblin,* and *The Princess and Curdie* in which MacDonald allows his own imagination to work freely, he achieves artistic unity through his skillful use of the quest romance form and through consistently used symbols. In these fantasies the child protagonists move through the fantasy world, where they are tested and where they acquire spiritual and moral truths which can then be enacted in the ordinary world.

The Romantic strain of fairy tale and fantasy which had slowly germinated in the early years of the nineteenth century evolved, then, to a rich culmination in the fantasies of George MacDonald. His use of such forms significantly modified images and ideas of childhood and imagination. MacDonald not only wrote fairy tales and fantasies, but actually created fully realized imaginary worlds of his own where characters apprehend divine truth and so attain higher and purer spiritual states of being.

Lewis Carroll also created an imaginary world of his own, controlled by its independent rules, and in doing so, his first two books for children, *The Adventures of Alice in Wonderland* (1865) and *Through the Looking Glass* (1871), broke free of the didactic tradition in unprecedented ways and changed the subsequent course of children's literature. They were, Harvey Darton has noted, "the spiritual volcano" of children's literature.

The facts about Charles Lutwidge Dodgson's (Lewis Carroll's) life are well-known. He enjoyed a relatively happy childhood in the rectory at Daresbury, where, despite the strongly religious atmosphere, he nevertheless learned at an early age to entertain the children with games, puzzles, drawings, puppets, plays, and stories. Later, Dodgson studied at Oxford, completing his Bachelor of Arts in 1855 and his Master of Arts in 1857. Although he took a deacon's orders in the Anglican Church, he spent most of his career in the secular role of lecturer in mathematics and logic at Christ's Church, Oxford. While Dodgson outwardly affirmed an orthodox faith, some writers have interpreted his fantasies as an indication of his deeply ambiguious views towards religious truth. The terrors and the chaos of the *Alice* fantasies suggest indeed that Lewis Carroll lacked the unswerving convictions in a divine order of reality which are manifested in MacDonald's best fantasy.[20] Carroll repeatedly relies on the humanistic and ordering processes of the mind and the imagination to maintain a precarious balance in the face of a terrifying and uncertain reality.

While the significance of Carroll's two *Alice* fantasies has been analyzed from almost every conceivable perspective, no account of nineteenth-century fantasy could be complete without investigating the role of Carroll's classic works in the evolution of the genre. And in a discussion of the secular and the sacred in children's literature, his work interestingly contrasts with MacDonald's. Intensely aware of the controversy between the didactic forces in children's literature and defenders of fairy tale, Carroll often mocks or parodies moral tales, instructional verse, and school lesson books. He thereby reveals fantasy and the imagination as means through which children may celebrate an unabashed and joyously free anarchy of their own. Unlike MacDonald's heroes and heroines who move through fantastic worlds to acquire moral virtue and spiritual vision, Carroll's character Alice confronts in her fantasy world some of her profoundest wishes and fears, conquers or rejects them, and so grows toward emotional maturity, rather than spiritual wisdom or purity. Carroll thus realizes an entirely new vision of childhood as a time when children use their imaginations and their intelligence, not in the service of redeeming a fallen creation, but as a way of protecting themselves from stifling adult authority and of acquiring more secure identities for themselves in the face of emotional terrors which threaten to annihilate identity and to impede initiative. At the same time that Carroll created his revolutionary "secular" image of childhood and the imagination in the *Alice* fantasies, he also helped to encourage the conventional and idealized myth of the Victorian child in articles, public addresses, and in his last fantasies *Sylvie and Bruno* (1890) and *Sylvie and Bruno Concluded* (1894). Thus, while Carroll consciously idealized a pastoral vision of childhood and its "golden summer afternoon," his *Alice* fantasies embodied the subterranean forces at work in the child's unconscious and thus revealed the minds and imaginations of children more vividly and complexly than any of his predecessors. He stresses the child's capacity to grow and to rely on his or her own capacities in order to make sense of the world.

Celebrating the uninhibited play of the child's intelligence and imagination, Carroll, unlike earlier writers of fairy tale and fantasy, sustained a commitment to both the pleasures and terrors of fantasy throughout the *Alice* books. Through parody and burlesque of the didactic tradition and through games, puzzles and language, Carroll deflates the adult world of authority and puts the child in control. He does not, as earlier writers of fantasy had done, whisk children off to fairy land only to place them under the dominion of powerful figures who provide all the answers, solve all the problems, and neutralize the child's spirit, initiative, and curiosity. Rather Carroll creates for them a fantasy world which renders the arbitrary authority and institutions of adults incoherent and ineffectual and which permits Alice to exercise her own judgments and to make her own decisions. Thoroughly familiar with the characteristic features of traditional fairy tales and other kinds of entertaining stories and amusements for children, Carroll mines this rich source in writing his *Alice* books, modifying such traditions to liberate children from the confining strictures of conventional moral tales, matter-of-fact educations, and arbitrary adult rules. In the two *Alice* books he does not impose upon his spirited child heroine the necessity to acquire conventional moral lessons and useful information. Rather, he imbues his early fantasies with all the more significance for children. Thus, he allows Alice to confront a threatening and sometimes terrifying psychological reality and dramatizes her aggressive assertion of identity in the face of it.

Alice's Adventure in Wonderland begins as Alice tumbles down the rabbit hole after the elusive White Rabbit. While intentionally pursuing the nervous creature, she clearly does not mean to plunge into a seemingly bottomless black hole. The fantasy begins, then, out of control, with a familiar but terrifying nightmare sensation—endlessly falling into darkness. As she falls, Alice consoles herself with language. She wonders about latitude and longitude, assuring herself that "Dinah'll miss me to-night, I should think."[21] Carroll thus shows that language, even the language of nonsense (because Alice does not know the meanings of the words that she utters) can help the child to conquer uncontrollable fears. (Indeed Carroll writes in the preface to *Sylvie and Bruno* that the most effective way to deal with "unholy thoughts" is through useful mental work.)[22] In the *Alice* books such mental work consists of riddles, puzzles, games, and nonsense. Carroll thus creates a new order of fantasy in which the minds and imaginations of children are engaged not only to provide them with amusement, but also with a means of warding off their terrors. This tendency is exemplified aptly in "The Mouse's Tale." The small, helpless creature confronts his fears of violent and arbitrary extinction in the form of a shaped verse with letters growing even smaller and trailing out almost altogether at the end of the "tale." By imposing his own comic shape and order, that of his "tail," upon his worst fears, the Mouse thus faces up to cunning old Fury, embodies him in a ludicrously humorous form, and through a language puzzle, conjures him into nothingness.[23]

Carroll's creation of Alice also marks a new and liberated vision of childhood, one which is all the more authentic because it depicts the emotions, hostilities, and necessary pretensions which real children experience in attempting to make sense of the adult world and in trying to accommodate themselves to the baffling demands of that world. The chaotic quality of the garden, for example, is a telling vision of a child's coming to terms with the fallibility of adults. From the perspective of children, adults, though apparently free to do as they please, may seem to inhabit an attractive and carefully controlled world. Once children reach the "garden" of adulthood, however, they find it full of the same chaotic and baffling anxieties, fears, frustrating constrictions and imperfections which trouble childhood. Carroll reverses the usual adult-child roles in his fantasies, but when Alice finds herself joining the adult game, she is just as muddled and confused as everyone else; as the Cheshire Cat observes, "We're all mad here."

In many ways Carroll suggests that we all remain confused children looking for the right rules in an ever-shifting and unmanageable reality. For Carroll, the imagination is "the necessary angel" which enables human beings to impose their own artificial constructs of order and meaning upon a reality which is essentially meaningless and disorderly. Alice thus achieves a kind of mastery in the fantasy world which she cannot achieve in the real world. She can acquire control over her own unwieldy fears and hostilities, shake the Red Queen into a helpless kitten, and thus face with more equanimity and self-assurance the domineering adults who scold her away from the warmth of the fire (a fitting emblem, perhaps, for adult pleasures and privileges). MacDonald takes children into a fantasy world and gives them spiritual nourishment in order that they may enact moral truth in ordinary reality. Carroll takes them into a fantasy world and gives them emotional sustenance and psychological confidence which they will need to survive in the wilderness of adult passions and desires. In the first, MacDonald implies that children must look beyond themselves for their ultimate resources. For Carroll, no omniscience resides in Wonderland for Alice to discover and depend upon. Alice's trust must be in her own human potential.

In MacDonald and Carroll, then, we find two distinctive modes of fantasy, each representing a different view of childhood, the imagination, and reality itself. In MacDonald's fantasies child characters appear as conventional emblems of innocence, like Little Diamond in *At the Back of the North Wind,* while Carroll explores the psychological and imaginative complexities of his little Alice. MacDonald sees the imagination as a rather passive faculty which enables the child to receive divine revelation, while Carroll's fantasies suggest that the imagination is a much stronger and more active force which works hard on chaotic experience to create what American poet Robert Frost has aptly called "a momentary stay against confusion."

Inevitably, subsequent fantasists have written in the shadow of these two original giants of fantastic invention. Their impact was immediate. One could discuss literally dozens of nineteenth-century fantasy writers who adapted these two traditions of fantasy for their own purposes. In the 1870's, Dinah Maria Mulock's *The Little Lame Prince* (1874) and Mrs. Molesworth's (Mary Louisa Stewart's) *The Tapestry Room* (1879) both reveal the influence of MacDonald and Carroll. In its vision of childhood, imagination, and character, *The Little Lame Prince* exhibits the sacred or visionary mode of fantasy and draws rather specifically upon MacDonald's classic work *At the Back of the North Wind* (1871), while Mrs. Molesworth's *The Tapestry Room* presents a humanistic vision of the child's fantastic world. A brief discussion of each of these successors may enrich the distinctions already explored between MacDonald and Carroll.

The Little Lame Prince is the story of Prince Dolor who, upon the occasion of his christening, is dropped by a careless nurse and made lame for life. A white-haired, but beautiful, fairy godmother (reminiscent of MacDonald's goddess-like grandmother figures who appear prominently in *The Princess and the Goblin* and *The Princess and Curdie*) comes to honor the child and to bring the sad news of the queen's death. Thereafter, she is the child's only friend and protector. When Prince Dolor's father, the King, dies of grief for his wife, the child's wicked uncle banishes the little lame prince to a remote tower and proclaims Prince Dolor, rightful king of the kingdom, dead.

Prince Dolor lives a tediously boring and unhappy life in the sealed tower with his ill-tempered nurse until his fairy godmother visits him and presents him with a magic traveling cloak. Thereafter the Little Lame Prince flies about on the cloud, seeing strange, disturbing sights, much as MacDonald's Little Diamond flies about with the North Wind. After viewing a bloody revolution following the death of his uncle, Prince Dolor returns to the tower to find that his nurse has deserted him. Five days later she returns with a legion of Prince Dolor's subjects who take him back to the palace and restore him to his throne. After ruling wisely and justly for many years, Prince Dolor turns his throne over to his nephew, bids his people farewell and departs on his magic traveling cloak, never to be seen again. Presumably he has entered a higher spiritual reality.

In her vision of childhood, Mulock follows MacDonald closely. Like MacDonald's Princess Irene of *The Princess and the Goblin* and Diamond of *At the Back of the North Wind,* Prince Dolor is a blessed child who effects a spiritual conversion in the iciest hearts. Prince Dolor is, moreover, an essentially passive and static character. His adventures are initiated for him by his fairy godmother. His imagination does not create; it merely allows him to receive revelation from the fairy godmother who is clearly the representative of a spiritual world of ideal value. She sounds in fact much like MacDonald's "Mother of Light":

> . . . the little lame Prince forgot his troubles in looking at her as her figure dilated, her eyes grew lustrous as stars, her very raiment brightened, and the whole room seemed filled with her beautiful and beneficent presence like light.[24]

Even in his adult years, Prince Dolor remains childlike, refusing to marry because "no wife in the world would have been found so perfect, so lovable, so tender to him in his weakness, as his beautiful old godmother" (p. 110). The prince is, in fact, passive to the point of being regressive, making up his mind to die because the world is so ugly. But the ultimate victory of the prince is assured from the beginning because he is so clearly aligned with both beneficent spiritual powers and the righteous human order.

Although Dinah Mulock's fantasy is derivative of MacDonald's fantasy in most respects, her writing lacks the literary power of MacDonald's best work. Mrs. Molesworth is a more original and more powerful writer than Mulock. Mrs. Molesworth's fantasy, *The Tapestry Room* (1879), contains features resembling the fantasies of both MacDonald and Carroll. However, like the *Alice* books, her fantasy reveals the imagination as a human, rather than divine, faculty, which enables children to create visions and to alleviate loneliness and boredom.

The Tapestry Room is set on a large estate in the French countryside where a lonely and bored little girl, Jeanne, plagues her old nurse, Marcelline, constantly for stories. She is much more like a real child than the idealized vision of children in the fantasies of MacDonald and Mulock. (One recalls, too, that Carroll's Alice embarks upon her fantasy to relieve boredom.) Unlike Alice who must venture into the fantastic world alone, Jeanne is accompanied by her cousin Hugh, who comes to live with Jeanne when his parents die. Hugh is given the tapestry room where he is quickly ushered into a strange fantasy land by Dudu the Raven and Houpet the Chicken. He visits the Forest of Rainbows and Frogland with Jeanne, and they experience a transcendent moment of vision. In ordinary reality Jeanne does not seem to remember this fantastic journey and, to the consternation of Hugh, appears to be content with mundane, childhood games, dolls' teaparties, and the like. One day, as the two children play a make-believe fairy game, they re-enter the world of fantasy. They are given luminous wings by Dudu the Raven and they enter a lovely chamber of white cats where a beautiful white lady spins stories for children. At the end of a fairy tale, the children are astonished (but the reader is not) to learn that the lovely white lady has been transformed into their old nurse Marcelline. Finally, in the last segment of *The Tapestry Room,* Dudu tells the children the adventurous history of their family and then unaccountably disappears.

In *The Tapestry Room,* the fantasy world is essentially the creation of the inventive imaginations of the children themselves. Magic and fantasy issue from an interweaving of ordinary reality and imaginative revery. Jeanne and Hugh endow the raven, the chicken, the guinea-pig, and the tortoise with magical power. The fantastic adventures of the two children are initiated, not by an external supernatural agent, but by Hugh's imaginative engagement with the mysterious tapestry, the portal into the fantastic world. The pictures on the tapestry in the moonlight lead the children to imagine both unspeakable terrors and visions of unutterable beauty. In the very center of the fantasy, at the height of their fantastic adventures in Frogland, Hugh and Jeanne listen to song of a dying swan and experience a transcendental, Wordsworthian "spot of time":

> The children listened breathlessly and in perfect silence at the wonderful notes which fell on their ears—notes which no words of mine could describe, for in themselves they were words, telling of suffering and sorrow, of beautiful things and sad things, of strange fantastic dreams, of sunshine and flowers and days of dreariness and solitude. Each and all came in their turn; but, at the last, all melted, all grew into one magnificent song of bliss and triumph . . . too pure and perfect to be imagined but in a dream. And as the last clear mellow notes fell on the children's ears, a sound of wings seemed to come with them, and gazing ever more intently towards the island, they saw rising upwards the pure white snow-like bird—upwards ever higher, till at last, with the sound of its own joyous song, it faded and melted into the opal radiance of the calm sky above.[25]

This central passage seems to hold the key to the essential meaning of *The Tapestry Room.* Beauty, spirit, enchanted vistas of heavenly firmament come from "the joyous song" of the swan, a traditional emblem of poetic creation and the workings of the imagination. When the song fades, so the enchantment fades. Transcendence comes through the child's imagination, permitting an "incredible glimpse," to borrow Eleanor Cameron's term, but only for a fleeting moment. Though the children try hard to sustain their vision, there was at last "no longer a trace of the swan's radiant flight . . . the children withdrew their eyes from the sky and looked at each other" (p. 98). Like Shelley's fading coal, the children's imaginative visions disappear and leave them with a sense of loss because the dream cannot be sustained. This pattern reminds us of the ending of *Through the Looking Glass* when Alice questions her own visions and asks, "Whose dream was it, kitty?" In the end, the children have moved away from their own visions, away from fairy tales into the harsh social, political histories of their families, and old Dudu the Raven, the emblem of the children's creative imaginations, has disappeared. The children sadly acknowledge, "I fear he will not come back . . . We shall have no more stories nor fairy adventures." The disappearance of Dudu suggests that the world of childhood imagination inevitably yields to the business of growing up.

In *The Tapestry Room,* then, Molesworth suggests that the world of fantasy exists only in the imaginations of children; Hugh, Jeanne, and Alice find themselves standing squarely in the gray pavement of ordinary reality, wondering whose dream it was. MacDonald and Mulock, in contrast, take their characters into a divine reality which is itself palpable and real. MacDonald's vision of this reality appears as an eternal possibility for the pure and the childlike. Hence in *The Golden Key* the most ancient and the wisest spiritual being is the Old Man of Fire, who appears as a tiny child, and Tangle and Mossy enter the column of rainbows, the bright vision which had initiated their quest. Little Diamond in *At the Back of the North Wind* is taken up into the wondrous country at the back of the north wind, while Mulock's Prince Dolor departs for the spiritual realm on his traveling cloak. In the fantasies of Carroll and Mrs. Molesworth, however, growth is towards emotional maturity, not towards spiritual purity. The characters and the reader are left wondering with the poet Keats, "Whither has fled the vision? Do I sleep or wake?"

Notes

[1] See C.N. Manlove, *Modern Fantasy.* Cambridge: Cambridge University Press, 1975, Nancy Mann, "George MacDonald and the Tradition of Victorian Fantasy". Diss. Stanford University, 1973, and Stephen Prickett, *Victorian Fantasy.* Bloomington: Indiana University Press, 1979 for comprehensive discussions of the relationships between shifting religious views and the emergence of fantasy in nineteenth-century Britain.

[2] Greville MacDonald. *George MacDonald and His Wife.* 1924; rpt. New York: Johnson, 1971, p. 20. The biographical facts concerning Charles Lutwidge Dodgson's life, his famous pseudonym "Lewis Carroll," his famous picnic with Alice Liddell and her sisters and the subsequent publication of *The Adventures of Alice in Wonderland* and *Through the Looking Glass* are so well known and have been so often recounted that I have not mentioned them in this text. However, the best biography on Lewis Carroll is still Derek Hudson. *Lewis Carroll.* London: Constable, 1954.

[3] M. H. Abrams. *Natural Supernaturalism: Tradition and Revolt in Romantic Literature.* New York: W.W. Norton, 1971, p. 91.

[4] Mann, p. 26.

[5] Mann, p. 56.

[6] George MacDonald. *Weighed and Wanting.* 1882, as quoted in Greville MacDonald, p. 85.

[7] In his chapter on MacDonald in *Modern Fantasy,* C.N. Manlove explores in some detail what he conceives to be a rather pervasive division in MacDonald's thought and literary art. According to Manlove, MacDonald avoided intellectual controversy because he was not skilled enough to handle debate. Behind MacDonald's affirmations Manlove sees fears and doubt: "MacDonald's personal involvement [in Victorian religious doubt] is given away not the least by his obsession with these themes in his writing—there are few of his sermons where they do not appear in some form, especially the word 'obedience,' to which he is almost pathologically addicted: he is in part attacking the impertinence of his own intellect. Obedience now becomes not only a means of his unconscious self-surrender, but of conscious suppression of self" (p. 63). Manlove documents rather carefully his argument that MacDonald experienced a conflict between his conscious role of zealous preacher and his identification with Christian Romanticism and mysticism. While there is some justice in Manlove's discussion, he seems to me somewhat unfair to MacDonald in failing to note that MacDonald's Romanticism can accommodate vagueness and even what seem to be contradictions and inconsistencies. His reluctance to enter into open debate surely is a manifestation also of his deep Romantic conviction that infinite truth cannot be pinned down concretely, rather than an issue of his limited intellectual capacities, as Manlove suggests. MacDonald's best fantasies embody spiritual truth which MacDonald believes cannot be apprehended by the intellect. Each fantasy is, in at least one sense, an apologetic for faith which MacDonald did see as threatened. He is least successful when he tries to make these lessons explicit. See Manlove, p. 55 ff.

[8] George MacDonald, "The Imagination: Its Function and Its Culture," *A Dish of Orts.* London: Edwin Dalton, 1908, p. 2.

[9] MacDonald, "The Imagination," p. 13.

[10] George MacDonald. *The Princess and Curdie.* Middlesex: Penguin Books, 1966, p. 49. Subsequent quotations from this text will be taken from this edition and page numbers indicated in the body of the text.

[11] "The Imagination: Its Function and Its Culture," p. 29.

[12] "The Imagination," p. 35.

[13] "The Fantastic Imagination," *A Dish of Orts,* p. 314.

[14] "The Fantastic Imagination," p. 314.

[15] "The Fantastic Imagination," p. 316.

[16] "The Fantastic Imagination," p. 319.

[17] George MacDonald. *Unspoken Sermons.* London: Longmans, Green, 1885, II, 236.

[18] *Unspoken Sermons,* II, 237.

[19] *Unspoken Sermons,* II, 119.

[20] For complete details concerning Lewis Carroll's life, his famous friendships with children, etc., see Derek Hudson. *Lewis Carroll.* London: Constable, 1954. All biographical information on Carroll in this article is taken from this source.

[21] Lewis Carroll, *Alice's Adventures in Wonderland,* in *The Complete Works of Lewis Carroll,* ed. Alexander Woollcott. London: Nonesuch Press, n.d., p. 20. Subsequent quotations will be taken from this edition; page numbers will be indicated in parentheses immediately following quoted passage.

[22] Lewis Carroll. *Sylvie and Bruno.* London: MacMillan, 1890, p. xv.

[23] For a detailed analysis of Carroll's use of nonsense language, see Elizabeth Sewell, *The Field of Nonsense.* London: Chatto and Windus, 1952.

[24] Dinah Mulock. *The Little Lame Prince.* 1874; rpt. Garden City: Doubleday, 1956, p. 36. Subsequent quotations will be taken from this edition; page numbers will be indicated in parentheses immediately following quoted passage.

[25] Mary Louisa Molesworth. *The Tapestry Room.* London: MacMillan and Company, 1879, pp. 97-98. Subsequent quotations will be taken from this edition; page numbers will be indicated in parentheses immediately following quoted passage.

WOMEN IN VICTORIAN FANTASY LITERATURE

Edith Lazaros Honig

SOURCE: "Magical Women: The Positive Force of Woman Power," in *Breaking the Angelic Image: Woman Power in Victorian Children's Fantasy,* Greenwood Press, 1988, pp. 111-32.

[*In the following essay, Honig explores the role of the magical female figure in Victorian children's fanta-sies, noting that it was in children's literature, rather than in adult fiction, that powerful, vibrant female characters were first portrayed.*]

In *The Uses of Enchantment: The Meaning and Importance of Fairy Tales,* Bruno Bettelheim tells us that the powerful witch, the magical woman who appears most prominently in classical fairy tales, can be good as well as evil. She can, like the witch in "Hansel and Gretel," be at first motherly and giving, but then her overwhelming power for evil asserts itself. It is this evil aspect of the witch that Bettelheim stresses. Bettelheim explains that the evil witch can be an important image for the developing child who can then view his or her own mother, when she seems harsh or punitive like the evil stepmother/witch of "Snow White," as a witch who has temporarily gained control of the good and loving mother's body. The child can hate the witch-mother without guilt and can be consoled by the assurance that the real mother will soon return.

Bettelheim's analysis has value for the study of child development, but it fails to expand upon the origins of witchcraft and the positive aspects of its power. Witchcraft was a Stone Age "religion" that linked women to nature.[1] Women who were believed to be witches were thought to "have power arising from a particular kind of knowledge, as in the case of 'wise women' who knew the curative powers of herbs and to whom people went for counsel and help."[2] Why then were witches associated with evil?

In *The Madwoman in the Attic,* Sandra Gilbert and Susan Gubar offer up their explanation. Drawing upon the same example of witchiness that Bettelheim uses, the evil stepmother of "Snow White," Gilbert and Gubar maintain that being a witch was the only option for a woman who wanted a life of "significant action." Such a life "for a woman is defined as a witch's life because it is so monstrous, so unnatural."[3] The wicked stepmother, in their words, is "a plotter, a plotmaker, a schemer, a witch, an artist, an impersonator, a woman of almost infinite creative energy, witty, wily, self-absorbed as all artists traditionally are."[4] In short, the witch becomes a metaphor for the writer.

While the adult fiction of the Victorian era, in common with that of the twentieth century, seldom contains portrayals of traditional magical witches, the witch-like figures outlined by Gilbert and Gubar abound. Any woman endowed with power, even power over herself, may be considered witch-like. After all, as Annis Pratt tells us in *Archetypal Patterns in Woman's Fiction,* "The accusation of 'witch' . . . springs from an intense societal fear of a powerful, untrammeled woman who . . . defies social norms."[5] So we can readily see Madame Walravens of Brontë's *Villette* as a witch. She has the egotism, energy, and demonic power that,

unsupplied with any socially acceptable channel, is the hallmark of the witch. She looks like a witch—three feet high, shapeless, with skinny hands that press the gold knob of a wandlike ivory staff. And Mrs. Reed, who is so harshly punitive in *Jane Fyre,* is clearly the evil stepmother witch type. Even Cathy Earnshaw, with her close ties to nature, is called a "ghostly female witch-child" when she returns to haunt her beloved Wuthering Heights.

It is abundantly clear from our discussions in previous chapters that Victorian women, especially mothers, were not accepted by society as figures of power and could not therefore be so presented in literature. The adult fiction of the era sometimes portrays girls with powerful personalities, but these generally grow into submissive adulthood; Jane Eyre and Maggie Tulliver are examples that come readily to mind. Apparently, upon the rare occasion that an author of adult fiction presents a woman as a figure of power, that author dares not strain the reader's credulity. The powerful woman is therefore presented as an unnatural aberration, a monster, a witch. She is not only an abnormal woman, but she is abnormal in a very negative way. The reader is not encouraged to sympathize with her (as critics Gilbert and Gubar clearly do), but to revile her. Madame Walravens and Mrs. Reed are witches, complete with all the negative connotations that adhere to the name "witch." Even Nina Auerbach, who in *Woman and the Demon* staunchly maintains that Victorian popular literature (as opposed to the mainstream, critically acclaimed literature) reflects the power of women, offers us negative portraits of demons and monsters—Bram Stoker's Lucy Westenra in *Dracula* and George du Maurier's Trilby in *Trilby*—to prove her point.

Just as children's fantasy takes a significant step away from its parent literature in its presentation of fiercely independent, powerful girls who show every promise of growing into independent, powerful women, Victorian children's fantasy also departs from adult fiction with the creation of the positive, powerful magical woman. Picking up on the positive aspects of both the original "wise women" witches who were close to nature and freely dispensed counsel and remedies, and of the witch that Gilbert and Gubar define—her creative energy, her talent for spinning stories—the figure of the magical woman is unique in her combination of almost godlike power with feminine grace, in a completely positive way. Auerbach seems to concur with this assessment, for in her only analysis of a magical woman from a children's fantasy, Old Irene of George MacDonald's *The Princess and the Goblin* and *The Princess and Curdie,* Auerbach states that this figure represents "the release of the victim [as a mythic Victorian female type] into the *full use of her power*" (italics mine).[6]

Gillian Avery notes in *Nineteenth Century Children: Heroes and Heroines in English Children's Stories 1780-1900,* that there is some ambiguity about the nature of the magical woman because she is supernatural. She may be mistaken for a witch, but that would be a misunderstanding of her true nature, for "in reality the character is one of love."[7] The magical woman of these fantasies is good and kind, but also wise and perceptive, a teller of tales, a giver of counsel who happens to be very beautiful and, significantly, quite maternal. Clearly, even children's fantasy, with all the extra leeway that writing for children rather than adults and the mode of fantasy itself provided, dared not portray mothers as figures of power. But it could and did transform the powerful mother into the more socially acceptable magical maternal power figure. This female figure was not so threatening because she was not literally a mother, nor was she presented as a real person. Society's carefully constructed image of women as subservient, inferior beings was not openly flouted because the magical woman could be readily dismissed as only magic, only nonsense, not real. Still, there is certainly an element of daring involved in the transformation of a powerful mother into a powerful, maternal magical woman, for while the magical woman retains the power of the witch, she has none of her negative aspects. So here for the first time in Victorian fiction we have women of power presented in a positive way.

Would a child reader perceive these powerful, almost majestic magical women as mothers? Would they have had psychological validity for the child in that role? I believe so, for the magical woman is invariably linked with the child in the fantasies. She is not even seen in the company of an adult. She is usually depicted teaching and nurturing the child. And let us not forget that the first power figure a child ever really encounters is his or her mother. She not only has given the child life, but assuming that the mother is the child's primary caretaker, she holds the power of life and death over the infant. To the young child, Mother is all-powerful, like a god. In fact, the child's early psychological perception of Mother is much closer to the portrayal of the magical woman than it would be to any more realistic portrayal of a mother. The older child reader would still retain enough of this early mother image to respond to the magical woman as a mother figure. Authors accentuated the maternal nature of the magical woman-child bond by not only depicting the two together, but by sometimes indicating that *only* a child could see or know the magical woman.

Exactly how and why is the magical woman presented? Where does she come from? How does she function as a source of power for good in the fantasies? Let us take a look at the development of the magical woman in some of our more enduring nineteenth-century English fantasies.

The classical evil witch figure does put in an appearance, but only in a handful of Victorian literary fairy tales—not in any of the longer fantasy novels. In two of these fairy tales, Tom Hood's *Petsetilla's Posy* (1870) and George MacDonald's *The Light Princess* (1867), the witch is almost an exact duplicate of the witch in "Sleeping Beauty." Hood's Aunt Sarah, an ugly and horrible sorceress, is insulted when King Bungo and Queen Belinda refuse to name their baby Sarah. She puts a curse on the child, decreeing that she shall marry a beggar. Similarly, the sour, spiteful, and wrinkled sister of the King in *The Light Princess* feels slighted because he has forgotten to invite her to his baby's christening. She therefore curses the baby princess with a lack of gravity. Both books are comical parodies of fairy tales, and neither witch figure is developed much. They seem to be there merely to fulfill a fairy tale's need for the obligatory witch.

MacDonald does give us a memorable and well-developed witch in the fascinating tale of *The Day Boy and the Night Girl* (1882). . . . The witch Watho seems to prefigure the many positive magical women that MacDonald creates in that she is a figure of magical power, a wise figure, a beauty, and a woman who is associated with the nurturing of children. In Watho, these good qualities have been subverted by her twisted cruelty. Therefore, she is a witch. MacDonald does, however, explain the source of her evil: She has a wolfish desire for knowledge just for the sake of knowledge. She wants to know everything no matter what the consequences. MacDonald says she "had a wolf in her mind."[8] Therefore, she is heartless enough to steal two infants and set up a bizarre scientific experiment in which she raises a boy to know only daylight and a girl to know only night and gauges the effects on their personalities.

This witch is a complex and powerful woman, almost admirable for these qualities. She cannot be accused of succumbing to feminine physical vanity, like Snow White's stepmother. Here is the sin of *hubris,* the placing of man's law over God's. Like Faust or Dr. Frankenstein, she is obsessed with the pursuit of knowledge for its own sake. Hers are not petty, "feminine" errors, but majestic flaws.

Yet, even her cruelty is tempered with some maternal love. If she did not have maternal longings, her experiment would never have taken the form of raising children. She nurtures them carefully and comes to love them. Still she is capable of cruelty to them. MacDonald explains the confusion of Watho's feelings: "In the hearts of witches, love and hate lie close together, and often tumble over each other"—a statement that rings true for all human beings, making

Watho a bit less monstrous (p. 452). Yet she is considered so powerful in her feminine form that her skin is impenetrable. Only when she turns herself into a wolf does she meet her demise, pierced by the arrow of Photogen, the day boy.

As a woman of great power who, though a witch, is not a completely negative, stereotypical, ugly old witch, Watho forms a bridge between two powerful women—the negative witch and the positive magical woman.

Another transitional magical woman is the fairy godmother. While fairies are slight, sexy, and pesky creatures, à la Tinkerbell, the few fairy godmothers we encounter in Victorian fantasy represent a primitive form of the positive magical woman. Certainly, fairy godmothers have power and they are positive female figures. There is however, an almost Disneyish cuteness about them, rather than the majesty projected by the magical women. Their power is all bound up in the welfare of the child, for that is the function of a fairy godmother—to watch over a child's well-being. The maternal element that is present in the make-up of the magical woman takes precedence here, whereas there is no suggestion of the godlike force and great wisdom of the magical woman.

Typical is the fairy godmother in *The Little Lame Prince* (1875) by Mrs. Craik. She is described as gray. "But there was nothing unpleasantly old about her, and her smile was as sweet and childlike as the Prince's own, which stole over his pale face the instant she came near enough to touch him."[9] This description immediately sets up the godmother's rapport with children, her maternal quality, but at the same time it is hardly a majestic description. Mrs. Craik acknowledges this, for in the story the godmother is so unprepossessing a figure that when she announces that she will be the child's godmother and look out for him, she is greeted with derisive laughter. Only when a man tries to strike her do her powers become apparent. She then defends herself in a very passive way—by melting out of range. Her powers are limited, too, for when the lame prince wishes he were someone else, she tells him, "'And you can't make yourself any different, nor can I do it either'" (p. 61). She proves to be an excellent maternal figure—devoted, full of fun, loving but not smothering. She sends a lark and a magpie out to keep an eye on the prince, while allowing him his independence.

With her magic, her maternity, her power, and her very positive image, the classical fairy godmother is a clear precursor of the magical woman. It remained for two of the finest children's authors of the Victorian era—Mrs. Mary Louisa Molesworth and George MacDonald—to add the requisite elements of majesty, godlike power, ties to nature, great wisdom, and artis-tic imagination that would make up the positive, powerful figure of the magical woman.

The fantasies of both Molesworth and MacDonald are filled with female figures, as indeed there seems to be an affinity between the fantastic and the female. Both Molesworth and MacDonald dared to create little girl heroines who were assertive and took charge of their lives, breaking the mold of the Angel in the House. Yet neither Molesworth nor MacDonald had ventured to create a mother of positive power. MacDonald's fantasies depict every other type of mother—from the idealized mother of *The Princess and Curdie* to the cruel mothers of *A Double Story* to the absent mothers of *The Day Boy and the Night Girl*, while Molesworth's very domestic stories consistently depict distant or absent mothers. MacDonald does give us a richly complex portrait of an independent single woman in Lillith of *The Cruel Painter*, but neither author dared to openly attack the stereotype of the submissive, domesticated, angelic mother—an image which their treatment of mother figures shows they did take issue with. The magical woman offered them a more socially sanctioned way to present a truly powerful mother figure, a woman who lives a life of "significant action" without being considered monstrous or witch-like.

The supernatural element in this figure paradoxically both adds to and detracts from our view of the power of woman. These women may be viewed as supremely powerful only because they are magical women, whereas real women are submissive and powerless. Yet, why have the authors chosen women to function in these books as godlike figures under whose guidance, as Gillian Avery puts it, "the protagonist gains mystic understanding"?[10] They could have chosen men. The choice of female figures, with their nurturing qualities, closeness to children in daily life, and their natural power over children, would, as noted earlier, be a psychologically valid one for the child reader. But it must also reveal something about the writer's image of mothers/women and even perhaps reveal something of the writer's own psychological needs. Robert Lee Wolff speculates in *The Golden Key* that MacDonald created the magical woman to fulfill his own needs for a powerful, positive mother figure. "It seems likely," writes Wolff, "that any special relationship to the magical woman was a psychic outgrowth of the death of his mother when he was eight years old."[11] Mrs. Molesworth was herself an almost magically high-powered woman—a mother of seven children, prolific author of over one hundred books, and head of her single-parent household, through years of life in army camps, and finally, legally, after separation from Major Molesworth. Although she hid behind the male pseudonym of Ennis Graham for years, the magical woman afforded her an opportunity to show the real power of women like herself.

Since Mrs. Molesworth's stories focus on the child in the nursery, Molesworth's fantastic figures, including her magical women, are not so well-developed as MacDonald's, but they do share certain characteristics. One very interesting Molesworth magical woman is the old lady in the Castle of Whiteness from *The Tapestry Room* (1879).

Rather than make the old lady a purely magical figure and limit her depiction to the fantastic episodes in the book, Molesworth weaves her into the domestic nursery scene in inventive fashion. The old lady turns into the children's quasi-magical nurse Marcelline. . . . Nurse Marcelline herself is old, yet beautiful, and tells enchanting stories that teach—all characteristics of the magical woman. The longest of these tales, told in its entirety, is "The Brown Bull of Norrowa," and it serves not only to foster the children's fantasy life and trust in the power of belief, but also to help them learn the value of patience and perseverance, as well as obedience and self-control (values that Molesworth stressed in *The Cuckoo Clock,* too). Marcelline's understanding of children is almost supernatural, for she seems to know Hugh's very thoughts, and Jeanne sometimes thinks that Marcelline comes from Fairyland. It is when the protagonists Jeanne and Hugh take a fantasy trip into the tapestry castle and meet the old lady that the magical nature of Marcelline is confirmed. The old lady literally spins the children a tale, and

> Strangely enough, as the story went on, it seemed more and more as if it were Marcelline's voice that was telling it, and at last Hugh looked up to see if it was still the white lady, whose knee his head was resting on. Jeanne too looked up at the same moment, and both children gave a little cry of surprise. The white lady had disappeared, and it was indeed Marcelline who was in her place.[12]

Not only is Marcelline there when they are ostensibly awakening from the dreamlike state of fantasy, but she knows what occurred while they were "gone." She asks them how they liked the story. And in answer to the children's bewildered queries, Marcelline admits her presence and direct involvement in their fantasy world by saying, "'I went to fetch you'" (p. 182).

The magical woman who is so dramatically transformed into Marcelline fits perfectly into the MacDonald mold. She is very kind and dreamy-looking—old and white-haired, yet beautiful. There is an irresistible, compelling force about her that attracts the children to her. Her wisdom is not only the wisdom of the mind, but the wisdom of the understanding heart. Molesworth tells us that her face "seemed to ask you questions, and yet to know more about you than you did yourself. It was impossible not to keep looking at her once you had begun" (p. 130). This sort of super-natural power is reminiscent of a witch's power, yet with none of the negative connotations connected with the witch. Unlike the fairy godmother or even the witch, the old lady is stern about keeping rules. She does not tolerate silliness or rudeness. This sternness adds authority to her depiction—the type of authority that MacDonald would develop further into the majestic, godlike presence of such magical females as the North Wind.

Like most of MacDonald's magical women, Molesworth's old lady is a creative artist, a story spinner. The symbolic association of the magical woman with spinning goes back at least to the witch in "Sleeping Beauty," but here it has been divested of its negative connotations. The old lady spins stories and sends them down to earth so she has the power to transmit her moral message, not only to the children she encounters directly, but to everyone. The fact that she must send the stories *down* suggests that she is up—in heaven, giving her a touch of magical majesty. Of course, sometimes the threads of her stories get twisted during their descent, and that is how stories get muddled.

Because her stories are told to children and teach children some valuable lessons, we can see the maternal side of the old lady. Molesworth reassures us on this point when she not only indicates that the children feel compelled to be with the old lady, but also actually turns this magical woman into their beloved nurse Marcelline. What better way to make the magical woman an intrinsic part of the children's lives? What better way to indicate that she is a sort of super-powered woman—artist and mother—much like Molesworth herself?

When the magical woman sets out directly to help children, we can readily see her roots both in the godmother figure of fairy tale tradition and in the witch as counsel-giver. Such a magical woman is Molesworth's Princess Forget-Me-Not from *The Children of the Castle* (1890). The Princess has the eternally youthful quality of the magical woman. And like other magical women, in sharp contrast to witches, she is lovely, with a clear voice, "beautiful, wonderful blue eyes, eyes like none she (Mavis) had ever seen," and she wears "soft silvery-blue garments floating round her." Her face is described as "sweet" but "grave."[13]

Though she is not described as old, she has appeared to generations of children—Hortensia when she was a little girl, Adam, his grandson Winifred, and finally the protagonist Mavis. It should perhaps be noted here that, like the other magical women we encounter in the works of both Molesworth and MacDonald, Princess Forget-Me-Not does not grow and develop in the course of the story, because she is already a perfect, magical being. But the child protagonists and the reader learn about different aspects of her character in the course of the story.

So Mavis learns, the more she gets to know the Princess, that although "her grave sad looks were like solemn music," her laugh was like "all the happy joyous things in the world had suddenly come together with warble and flutter of irrepressible glee" (p. 134). The touch of melancholy in her nature makes us take her much more seriously than the happy, bubbly godmother. It indicates the importance of her mission.

Princess Forget-Me-Not's mission is not to change the course of world events like some magical women do, but mother-like or godmother-like, to be an advocate for children. As an advocate with the power to make a difference, she is a woman of enviable strength. That children have called upon her for generations is proof of her efficacy. When Mavis has difficulties with her ill-behaved sister Ruby and her odious cousin Bertrand, Princess Forget-Me-Not explains to her the difference between right and wrong, the most central of all moral lessons, and she promises to shield the intended victims of Ruby's and Bertrand's cruel pranks. She also counsels Mavis (witch-like) on what course she should follow. With her supernatural understanding of human nature, she discerns that it will be easier to change Bertrand since he scarcely seems to know right from wrong, than it will be to persuade Ruby to follow the right when she has consciously chosen to swerve from it. Of course, being much more than human, Princess Forget-Me-Not succeeds in converting both of them, thereby solving the problems of Mavis.

As a female figure who serves as a child advocate, solving domestic problems with unusual discernment and skill, Princess Forget-Me-Not elevates the figure of the mother to a position of power. At the same time, she fits neatly into the scale of Molesworth's domestic drama.

In only one of Molesworth's fantasies do we find magical females who are natural forces, with all the attendant majesty thereof, rather than domestic figures. These are the four winds of *Four Winds Farm* (1887). Mrs. Molesworth may have felt that if one wind is good (the North Wind of MacDonald's *At the Back of the North Wind* [1871]), then surely four are better. The opposite of course is true: The law of diminishing returns prevails here. Still, even though the four winds sisters are derivative, as female figures of great power, majesty, and grace, and as females who are allied with nature, they are significant.

The North Wind and the East Wind are the stronger, icier winds who are somewhat contemptuous of their weaker sisters, the South and West Winds. Each one

is beautiful in an awesome, godlike way. The North Wind has snow wings that sparkle as she moves. She is described as being cold and stately, with a steel-blue veil covering her dusky head. The East Wind is less stately, but quicker—a gray-shrouded, nimble figure who seems to be everywhere at once. She too sparkles because of her bright eyes and the radiant red highlights in her otherwise grim robe. The shroudlike costume emphasizes the wind's power of life and death over mere mortals. Here are female figures elevated far beyond the pale powers of humans. They are godlike figures, stern and demanding. The East Wind pushes the hero Gratian about, making sure that he behaves as he should. Still, we see that in spite of being far removed from mortals, the winds are tied to the child hero, not unlike a supernaturally powerful mother. When Gratian runs for the doctor to help his sick mother, the North Wind's cold, powerful breath pushes him along.

The South and West Winds are portrayed as much gentler and less grave than their sisters. The West Wind has sweet laughter and the South Wind a "laughing rosy face." Glowing and lovely like their sisters, they too fulfill their natural duties—the West Wind is "Spirit of the Waves"—while maintaining a more tender motherly relationship with the hero. After all, gentle, tropical breezes can kiss, while icy blasts can only blow and bite. So the West Wind helps Gratian find a book he has lost and then kisses him with a kiss as soft as a butterfly's.

With these four magical female winds, Molesworth not only hearkens back to a time when women-witches were closely allied with nature, but for the first time in her work she depicts positive female figures in a role of almost godlike power. Although her magical women still fall short of MacDonald's standard, they make a strong statement about the tremendous capabilities of women and suggest that the proper sphere of women is limitless. They can rule the seas like the West Wind, the earth like the North Wind. They can control life and death like the East Wind. Though these messages are only implied, such implications are revolutionary ones for any Victorian writer to make, and took special courage coming from the pen of a vulnerable "female scribbler."

The magical women of George MacDonald follow a clear line of development that is wave-shaped, beginning to swell with the gentle and beautiful grandmother of *The Golden Key* (1867), cresting with the very powerful North Wind of *At the Back of the North Wind* (1871), and ebbing with the fading Old Irene of *The Princess and Curdie* (1883). During these sixteen active, writing years, MacDonald seems to have first grown in insight into the nature of power, the nature of women, and the nature of powerful women, and then grown more cynical, feeling the ineffectuality of all mortals—male and female—as much of his family was cut down by tuberculosis.

All of MacDonald's magical women, however, share certain characteristics. They are all maternal. Except for the North Wind, they are even called "grandmother," possibly a thinly veiled way of saying "mother." Or perhaps a grandmother is a maternal figure who has greater wisdom than a mother and a special rapport with the grandchildren whom she need not care for on a permanent basis and is therefore free to enjoy. In spite of being grandmothers, they are all beautiful, their outer beauty reflecting the purity of their inner beauty. For they are all good, though some are stern. They are all loving, wise, creative artists, and very powerful—females that are overwhelmingly positive—"mother-goddesses" as Robert Lee Wolff calls them.[14]

Wolff considers these magical women, these "mother-goddesses," an outlet for MacDonald's positive feelings about mothers. The juxtaposition of the words "mother" and "goddess" would seem to raise maternity itself to a godlike level, making the magical women into madonnas. But this reading ignores the very real power that these magical figures assert over natural forces, as well as children. So perhaps we should emphasize not maternity as divinity, but divinity as a feminine characteristic.

There is divinity in the aspect of MacDonald's first magical woman, Grandmother from *The Golden Key* (1867). Grandmother, for all her softness and compassion, rules over the fairies and the natural realm. Her power is evident in the description of her height and strength in contrast to the frail delicacy of a stereotypical Victorian beauty. The attractiveness of a weak, sickly woman is in her lack of power, her purely decorative value. Grandmother's beauty lies precisely in her power. And she is considered such a beauty that Tangle "had never seen anything so beautiful."[15] The rest of her physical description indicates her role as a ruler of nature. Her hair "had a tinge of dark green. She had not one ornament upon her, but she looked as if she had just put off quantities of diamonds and emeralds. . . . She was dressed in shining green" (p. 260). Like the magical women depicted by Molesworth, Grandmother has a shining charisma that signals her special, magical nature. The disparity between her great age and her youthful appearance also indicates her magical nature. MacDonald emphasizes here the value of age. The experience of a life well lived brings us not only wisdom, but beauty. So Grandmother does not tell Tangle she is beautiful in spite of her age. Rather, she attempts to prove to her that she *is* old by showing off her great beauty. This gives the child reader very good messages not only about old age, but about the nature of older women specifically. The promise of bright, independent, assertive young girls like Tangle need not wither into submissive adulthood, but instead can continue to grow and blossom into the beauty of a strong, powerful old lady.

Grandmother also teaches us how to handle that power. While all the animals, birds, fish, and plants obey her every wish, she is not imperious or conceited. She arbitrates with justice tempered with mercy. Nor is she stingy with her knowledge. She teaches Tangle the languages of all of nature.

As a grandmother to Tangle, she tempers her kindness with her wisdom. When she has taught Tangle all she needs to know and given her the security of her love, she pushes her out of the nest, fostering Tangle's growth and development rather than keeping her a baby.

The magical female figure of the North Wind from *At the Back of the North Wind* (1871), while sharing certain characteristics with Grandmother, is a much more complex creature. While Grandmother controls natural forces, the North Wind actually is a natural force—and one whose task is not always a pretty one.

Although a strong, cold wind can serve some good purposes—transporting sailboats, for example—the North Wind's tasks are generally more cruel ones—such as knocking people over. But, as MacDonald depicts her, the North Wind's ultimate mission is much more awful than this. She is the harbinger of death. It is she who takes people to the back of the North Wind to die.

Such a role of course endows her with tremendous—one might even say divine—power, though she seems to do the bidding of one even higher than she, rather than deciding by herself who shall live and who shall die. This personification of such awesome power in a female figure is unprecedented.

We can also see her power in her physical aspect. When Diamond first sees her he is entranced by her beauty:

> Leaning over him was the large beautiful pale face of a woman. Her dark eyes looked a little angry, for she had just begun to flash; but a quivering in her sweet upper lip made her look as if she were going to cry. What was most strange was that away from her head streamed out her black hair in every direction, so that the darkness in the hayloft looked as if it were made of her hair.[16]

Her size, her flash, and the hair that fills the hayloft all indicate awesome power, while the quivering lip gives her a touch of vulnerability to offset the brusqueness of her tone and the cruelty of her task. The North Wind's appearance, however, is not always the same.

MacDonald does something interesting here. The power of the wind's blast indicates her appearance. When she is a small breeze, she may be just a little animal; a little bigger, and she is a small girl. At her full height, she is a female of tremendous proportions.

But what of the cruelty of her task? Does MacDonald intend to link this female figure with the evil witch? Not really. Her small cruelties are strictly just retribution for sinners. She is good to the good, like the hero Diamond. It is her duty to knock over a drunken nurse, frightening her out of her wits and causing her to lose the position she does not deserve to hold. To accomplish this task, she assumes the guise of a wolf. But her true nature is not wolfish.

When she sinks ships filled with people, she admits, "'It is rather dreadful. But it is my work. I must do it!'" (p. 54). Killing is not cruel, for she only takes her victims to the back of the North Wind. In a larger, divine plan, drowning ships may be the shape that good takes. Robert Lee Wolff calls the North Wind "a divine, motherly messenger, with the wind's work to do."[17] Eric S. Rabkin goes a step further, saying that the North Wind's other name is Death and that in MacDonald's theology, "one dies into a better life of perfect communication, a fantastic reversal of human fears that . . . predicts the later poetry of T. S. Eliot. . . . he (MacDonald) takes the bold step of calling death the best thing in the world."[18] It is to be courted, not feared, for the back of the North Wind is a very peaceful place to be. It is only our limited understanding that keeps us from grasping the goodness of her nature. If all this seems rather metaphysical for a children's book, by the way, it is, and *At the Back of the North Wind,* in spite of some beautiful passages, is not entirely successful because of it.

It does, however, communicate some interesting things not only about women, but about mothers. The North Wind, for all her awesome power, reserves a special tenderness and care for the child Diamond, taking him by the hand and showing him her work. We know that she is more a mother than a friend to him, for her voice is like the voice of Diamond's own gentle mother. Even though Diamond's mother is stereotypically angelic and sweet (see chapter 1), and the North Wind is powerful, the two voices sound as one.

> Her voice was like the bass of a deep organ, without the groan in it; like the most delicate of violin tones without the wail in it; like the most glorious of trumpet-ejaculations without the defiance in it; like the sound of falling water without the clatter and clash in it: it was like all of them and neither of them—all of them without their faults, each of them without its peculiarity: after all, it was more like his *mother's voice* [italics mine] than anything else in the world. (p. 62)

Here is a mother at her most powerful in every positive sense of that word. This mother figure is awe-inspiring in her greatness, yet gentle. She elevates the level of mothers in a way that Diamond's own mother, with her unbelievable sweetness, fails to do. She shows us that power can speak in a feminine voice, and that it is not incompatible with motherly love.

So when this motherly figure takes Diamond himself to the back of the North Wind, the positive nature of the journey is confirmed. It is a land of flowers and rivers that flow with song, where people understand each other without speech and feel a sort of contentment that is better than mere happiness.

Never again would MacDonald create a magical woman who so completely dominated a book. Never again would MacDonald create a magical woman of such extraordinary power—power not only over a child, but over life and death.

In the next magical old lady MacDonald brings us, different fantastic functions are stressed. The primary magical purpose of Old Irene of *The Princess and the Goblin* (1872) seems twofold. She spins stories—a creative artist—and she initiates girls into the rites of sex—in a more direct manner than Grandmother of *The Golden Key,* who merely encourages Tangle to leave home with the boy Mossy.

The character of Old Irene, who is a very *positive* figure, clearly owes much to the tradition of the evil fairy/witch in "Sleeping Beauty." When the Princess Irene first encounters Old Irene, she is only eight years old, a bit young for any sexual initiation. But her second meeting with her magical great-great-grandmother parallels almost exactly Briar Rose's sixteenth birthday encounter with the bad fairy. Both girls are in a dreamlike state and ascend a long circular staircase almost against their will. Bruno Bettelheim, commenting on the Sleeping Beauty story, tells us that "such staircases typically stand for sexual experiences."[19] It is time for these girls to explore "the formerly inaccessible areas of existence, as represented by the hidden chamber where an old woman is spinning."[20] Both girls inquire about the spinning because the distaff, which in English has come to mean female, symbolizes the secrets of being a woman—according to Bettelheim, not so much intercourse as menstruation. This would explain why no male need participate in this initiation. It also explains of course Briar Rose's bleeding and the already wounded finger of Princess Irene which figures in the present scene too.

Here the two tales diverge. While Briar Rose pricks her finger in the fairy's chamber and then falls into a protective sleep which will preserve her from sexual encounters until she is old enough to handle them,

Irene spends the night with Old Irene and undergoes further sexual initiation. This is how Old Irene heals her wounded finger—" . . . she rubbed the ointment gently all over the hot swollen hand. Her touch was so pleasant and cool, that it seemed to drive away the pain and heat wherever it came."[21] The magical old lady then invites the Princess to sleep with her and even asks, with what certainly seems to be sexual coyness, "'You won't be afraid then to go to bed with such an old woman?'" (p. 121). The Princess is not afraid, so the old lady "drew her towards her," and, with increasing daring and intimacy, "kissed her on the forehead and the cheek and the mouth" (p. 122). When they get into bed together, the old lady undresses and asks, "'Shall I take you in my arms?'" (p. 123). The little Princess is nothing loath, so, clasped in each other's arms, they go to sleep. In the morning the girl's finger has healed—"the swelling had all gone down" (p. 124).

This overtly sexual encounter has some jarring undertones to it. The Princess's role, with the swelling finger that must be soothed with ointment and goes down in the morning after the night's sexual play, seems closer to that of the uninitiated male rather than the female. It is almost as if, being a man, MacDonald cannot help but view this experience from a male perspective. His own oedipal longings may be showing when he masculinizes Irene during her sexual scene with her grandmother. Let us not forget, however, that children of both sexes often have playful homosexual encounters during adolescence, with one partner taking a male role and the other a female one. It is a form of sexual initiation and practice. This scene between the two Irenes may be of the same nature.

So Old Irene, like the witches of old and like Grandmother of *The Golden Key,* spins tales and initiates girls into the mysteries of sex. But, like Grandmother, she is sweet and beautiful and has a real bond with children—clearly no witch. Old Irene's spinning can be viewed as not only a part of the process of sexual initiation. She spins threads of faith and love that bind young Irene to her and protect her from harm by the goblins of the title. Faith, love, and understanding are prerequisites for seeing Old Irene altogether. And the child princess is the only one who seems to be able to form that special bond between the young and the old.

Of course, like other magical women, great-great-grandmother does not always appear old and is always beautiful. When Princess Irene first meets her, she is a beautiful old lady with smooth, white skin and long, loose hair. But the hair is snow-white, and her very wise eyes indicate years of experience. The third time they meet, however, Old Irene has rich, golden hair that "seemed pouring down from her head, and vanishing in a golden mist ere it reached the floor. . . .

Her face was that of a woman of three-and-twenty" (p. 146). This time MacDonald has Old Irene openly criticize prejudice against the old: "It *is* so silly of people to fancy that old age means crookedness and witheredness and feebleness and sticks and spectacles and rheumatism and forgetfulness! . . . The right old age means strength and beauty and mirth and courage and clear eyes and strong painless limbs" (p. 158).

Note that this is a description of unusual strength for a Victorian woman of any age. Old Irene, for all her gentleness, is a strong and powerful female. "'I don't think you are ever afraid of anything!'" Princess Irene says to her admiringly (p. 159). And Old Irene answers, in her maternal way, that the only thing she is ever fearful about is the welfare of her children—not so much physically, as spiritually, but that she herself watches over—with the strength of a super-mom, a maternal figure of great magical power.

In the ensuing years between Old Irene's first appearance in *The Princess and the Goblin* (1872) and her farewell bow in the sequel *The Princess and Curdie* (1883), MacDonald would write a few more fantasies and create a few more magical women for them—most notably the Wise Woman of the horrifying *A Double Story* (1875) and the Old Woman of "The Carosoyn" (1882). His vision, however, was becoming increasingly bleak, his viewpoint turning essentially pessimistic. He still viewed women as figures of relative strength and power, so he still made them magically larger than life. But, as he began to write of the triumph of evil over good, the power of his good magical women became both harsher and yet somehow ineffectual. This can be most readily observed in the contrast between the Old Irene of *The Princess and the Goblin* and Old Irene as she appears eleven years later, in *The Princess and Curdie.*

Rather than remaining always vigorous and strong, this Old Irene reflects the moral state of the one who looks at her. When the miner boy Curdie comes to her to atone for having shot a pigeon, he has grown not evil, but very slack about trying to do good. The Old Irene that he meets for the first time is very old, "a small, withered creature . . . like a long-legged spider holding up its own web. . . . She sat crumpled together, a filmy thing that it seemed a puff would blow away, more like the body of a fly the big spider had sucked empty and left hanging in his web than anything else I can think of."[22] All her vitality has left her. She is barely there, just like Curdie's faith and goodness. But as Curdie speaks with her, becomes aware of his shortcomings, and vows to do better, his renewed moral strength is reflected in the renewed vigor of Old Irene who, before his very eyes, becomes the vigorous, full-bodied, silver-haired apparition who appeared to the Princess in the previous book. She is "as grand as she was old," but the complete compassion that was associated with Old Irene has been replaced by a severe mien. She seems saddened at the state that men are in and somewhat impatient with their shortcomings.

And no wonder, for the men who work in the mine are too common and corrupt to understand her. They have all heard of Old Irene, but consider her a witch, a figment of the imagination, or both. Perhaps, like the bulk of Victorian men, they cannot believe in a good woman of power. Either she does not exist or she must be a witch. Only Curdie and his family are both open-minded enough to believe in the possibility of Irene's existence and sensitive and refined enough to see her.

When Curdie and his father Peter meet Old Irene again, they have both grown so much in faith that not only do they stoutly believe in this magical woman, but they have defended her name to the other miners. Accordingly, reflecting their faith, Irene is a twenty-five-year-old beauty with golden hair and enough magical sparkle to light up a dusky mine shaft.

It is during this encounter that the great-great-grandmother teaches them some of her wisdom—that being poor is a privilege, for it makes you good; that appearances are deceiving and unimportant, that only a person's essence counts. With this as introduction, she then confirms that her appearance reflects the viewer:

> . . . it is one thing what you or your father may think about me, and quite another what a foolish or bad man may see in me. For instance, if a thief were to come in here just now, he could think he saw the demon of the mine, all in green flames. . . . I should be all the same, but his evil eyes would see me as I was not. (p. 56).

So naturally when Curdie, who has given himself in the old Princess's service, next sees her, Irene has grown younger and still more beautiful.

It is, however, this beautiful young creature who expounds the pessimistic world view of an embittered, old woman. She sees men going "'down the hill to the animals' country; . . . many men are actually, all their lives, going to be beasts'" (p. 71). She gives Curdie the power to tell if a man is really a beast just by a handshake, but how does she sensitize his hands to receive this power? By having him thrust them into fire and undergo unbearable pain. These harsh methods are not the ways of the Old Irene of *The Princess and the Goblin*.

The bleak outlook of Old Irene is echoed in the treatment Curdie receives from all the men he meets as he travels to the capital in the Princess's service. It is interesting to note that the only decent people he meets are female, and there is one good female to represent each age group—little Barbara, a child who plays with him; the baker's wife, who sells him the best bread and gives him water; and old Derba, Barbara's grandmother, who takes him in. As a woman who takes significant action, Derba too is considered a witch by her neighbors. But like others who have been called witches in fact and fiction through the ages, she "was only a wise woman" (p. 114).

As the story unfolds, the people of Gwyntystorm are mostly corrupt, and the entire court is involved in an evil plot to overthrow the king. After putting his characters through much hardship and struggle, MacDonald does allow Curdie and the royal family to win the day—with the help of Old Irene, who has assumed the guise of a maid.

But MacDonald does not stop there. In an appended chapter called, appropriately enough, "The End," the happy ending, which seemed forced on the pessimistic plot which preceded it, is twisted around. In two pages MacDonald presents his bleak, apocalyptic vision. After the rule of Curdie and Irene produces no heir, the people choose a new king whose greed for gold finally brings down the entire city "with a roaring crash. The cries of men and the shrieks of women went up with its dust, and then there was a great silence . . . the very name of Gwyntystorm has ceased from the lips of men." (p. 255).

And what of Old Irene who lived upstairs in the palace? Did she die with the city? Did she lose her magical power? Or was she just too disgusted with the state of mankind to care if they killed themselves off? Perhaps, responding to the state of the men around her, she finally withered into such a wisp that she was blown away with the wind. MacDonald does not tell us, but no matter how powerfully she has been presented, her absence at this crucial moment seems to belie her powers.

The changes in MacDonald's magical women match the growing pessimism in his outlook on the world, as it is expressed in his books in general. Robert Lee Wolff suggests that a series of deaths in MacDonald's family caused this change in his outlook. Wolff states, "We find few violent persons in the novels and fairy-tales written before the mid-1870s," then goes on to list the bleak characters and events in MacDonald's later books.[23] Within the context of *The Princess and Curdie,* Old Irene is still the strongest, most positive figure in the book. MacDonald therefore is still sending his readers very positive images of women and their capabilities. Perhaps he is indeed warning his readers that the tremendous, almost magical capabilities of women can fade away into waste and nothingness without the belief and support of both men and other women.

The magical women of MacDonald and Molesworth remain overwhelmingly? beautiful in their strength, awesome in their wisdom and power, and yet divinely motherly. This uniquely positive combination of two of the most harmful feminine stereotypes—witch and madonna—creates a new whole which shatters the Victorian myth of the helpless female, particularly the angelic, but ineffectual mother.

Fantasy? Magic? No matter. These are women. To the open mind and heart of the reader of fantasy, they live. And they would change the outlook of the children who came to know and love them. If adults were not, for the most part, reading about vibrant, achieving, powerful women, at least in fantasies children were. Authors of vision and courage were planting tiny seeds of rebellion, and if they received further nourishment, they might one day bear fruit.

Notes

[1] Elizabeth Goudge, *The White Witch* (London: Hodder & Stoughton, 1958), pp. 175-76.

[2] Mary Daly, *Beyond God the Father, Toward a Philosophy of Women's Liberation.* (Boston: Beacon Press, 1973), pp. 64-65.

[3] Sandra M. Gilbert and Susan Gubar, *The Madwoman in the Attic: The Woman Writer and the 19th Century Literary Imagination* (New Haven and London: Yale University Press, 1979), p. 42.

[4] Gilbert and Gubar, pp. 38-39.

[5] Annis Pratt, *Archetypal Patterns in Women's Fiction* (Bloomington: Indiana University Press, 1981), p. 122.

[6] Nina Auerbach, *Woman and the Demon: The Life of a Victorian Myth* (Cambridge: Harvard University Press, 1982), p. 39.

[7] Gillian Avery, *Nineteenth Century Children: Heroes and Heroines in English Children's Stories 1780-1000* (London: Hodder & Stoughton, 1965), p. 60.

[8] George MacDonald, *The Day Boy and the Night Girl* from Jonathan Cott, ed., *Beyond the Looking Glass: Extraordinary Works of Fairy Tale and Fantasy* (New York: Stonehill Publishing Co. & R. R. Bowker Co., 1973), p. 425. Subsequent page references are to this edition and will appear in the text.

[9] Dinah Maria Mulock Craik, *The Little Lame Prince* (New York: Grosset Dunlap Companion Library, 1965), p. 20. Subsequent page references are to this edition and will appear in the text.

[10] Avery, p. 60.

[11] Robert Lee Wolff, *The Golden Key: A Study of the Fiction of George MacDonald* (New Haven: Yale University Press, 1961), p. 14.

[12] Mary Louisa Molesworth, *The Tapestry Room* (London: Macmillan & Co., 1879), p. 181. Subsequent page references are to this edition and will appear in the text.

[13] Mary Louisa Molesworth, *The Children of the Castle* (New York: A. L. Burt Co. Publishers, 1890), p. 98. Subsequent page references are to this edition and will appear in the text.

[14] Wolff, p. 317.

[15] George MacDonald, "The Golden Key" from *Dealings With the Fairies* (London: Alexander Strahan, Publisher, 1867), p. 260. Subsequent page references are to this edition and will appear in the text.

[16] George MacDonald, *At the Back of the North Wind* (New York: A. L. Burt Co., Publishers, 1871), p. 10. Subsequent page references are to this edition and will appear in the text.

[17] Wolff, p. 155.

[18] Eric S. Rabkin, *The Fantastic in Literature* (Princeton: Princeton University Press, 1976), p. 105.

[19] Bruno Bettelheim, *The Uses of Enchantment: The Meaning and Importance of Fairy Tales* (New York: Alfred A. Knopf, 1976), p. 232.

[20] Bettelheim, p. 232.

[21] George MacDonald, *The Princess and the Goblin* (Philadelphia: J. B. Lippincott Co., 1907), p. 121. Subsequent page references are to this edition and will appear in the text.

[22] George MacDonald, *The Princess and Curdie* (Philadelphia: J. B. Lippincott Co., 1883), p. 23. Subsequent page references are to this edition and will appear in the text.

[23] Wolff, p. 383.

Zipes discusses the attraction folk and fairy tales present for readers:

Our lives are framed by folk and fairy tales, but in the frame-work we never fill in the meaning of the tales for ourselves. It remains illusive just as our own history remains illusive. From birth to death we hear and imbibe the lore of folk and fairy tales and sense that they can help us reach our destiny. They know and tell us that we want to become kings and queens, ontologically speaking to become masters of our own realms, in touch with the projects of our lives and the self-projections, to stand upright as makers of history. Folk and fairy tales illuminate the way. They anticipate the millennium. They ferret out deep-rooted wishes, needs, and wants and demonstrate how they all can be realized. In this regard folk and fairy tales present a challenge, for within the tales lies the hope of self-transformation and a better world.

Jack Zipes in Breaking the Magic Spell: Radical Theories of Folk and Fairy Tales, *Heinemann, 1979.*

Charlotte Spivak

SOURCE: "'The Hidden World Below': Victorian Women Fantasy Poets," in *The Poetic Fantastic: Studies in an Evolving Genre,* edited by Patrick D. Murphy and Vernon Hyles, Greenwood Press, 1989, pp. 53-64.

[*In the following essay, Spivak suggests that Victorian women writers turned to fantasy as a way to overcome the limitations society had placed on them, and highlights Christina Rossetti's* Goblin Market *(1862) as an example of feminist poetry.*]

The importance of fantastic poetry in the nineteenth century has been widely recognized. Coleridge comes to mind first, with "Kubla Khan" and "The Rime of the Ancient Mariner," but then so do Keats, Shelley, Tennyson, and even Browning. Among the minor host are Hood, Beddoes, Allingham, Dobell, and many others. What has been singularly neglected is the substantial body of fantastic verse written by women during this century. The one example known to most readers is Christina Rossetti's "Goblin Market," a tantalizing poem that has evoked myriad responses from critics. It has been read as an allegory of the origin of evil, a psychological study of a split personality, an exploration of conflict in the soul of an artist, and a lesbian tract.[1] Yet it has not been dealt with as fantasy, although the mere presence of the goblins would seem to invite such an approach. Because "Goblin Market" is not Rossetti's only fantastic poem and because she is not the only successful nineteenth-century woman

poet engaged in writing fantasy, I would like to explore her work in its historical and literary context.

Although Elizabeth Barret Browning lamented the lack of "grandmothers" to inspire the female poets of her time, two women deserving of the label are Felicia Hemans (1793-1835) and Laetitia Elizabeth Landon (1802-1838), known in her day as L. E. L. Both women sought to escape the severe limitations on experience available to their sex by turning to the imagination in writing poetry. Hemans focuses her imaginative powers on the exotic, the distant in time and space, in a series of poems relating exciting adventures in faraway places. Especially popular in the United States in her time, she is now the forgotten author of one remembered line, "The boy stood on the burning deck," and of one nostalgic lyric, "The Lost Chord."[2] In the early 1830s, however, the editions of her poetry outnumbered those of all other women poets then writing.

Landon, whose own life captured some of the glamour of Hemans' exotic verses, wrote a tribute to her rival poet, a touching lyric in which she taps the source of the fantastic imagination in her fellow poets.[3]

> Yet what is mind in women, but revealing
> In sweet clear light the hidden world below.[4]

The "hidden world below" may be read as simply the inner life, because women were denied active involvement in the outer world. Indeed, many nineteenth-century women poets did write simply and directly about their unfulfilled desires, their empty lives, their awareness of loss and deprivation. But the hidden world below is more than a store of repressed desires for unavailable activity. It is also that very world that produced the great poetic fantasies of the past. It is the world of the unconscious, with its fanciful images, its dream content, its mythic symbols, a world not affected by confinement or construction. The road to Xanadu also leads to the goblin market.

At once an example and a description of the fantastic imagination at work in a woman's inner world is revealed in the verses of Adelaide Proctor (1825—1864), a very popular poet who was a contemporary of Christina Rossetti. The speaker in the poem, "Pictures in the Fire," addresses a young child, apologizing for her lack of exciting experiences to tell, for she has had no adventures and taken no travels. Yet she can enthrall the child with the "strange sights" she sees by merely looking into the fire.

> There, last night, I saw a cavern,
>   Black as pitch; within it lay,
> Coiled in many folds, a dragon.
>   Glaring as if turned at bay.

And a knight in dismal armor
  On a winged eagle came,
To do battle with this dragon;
  And his crest was all of flame.

As I gazed, the dragon faded,
  And, instead, sat Pluto crowned
By a lake of burning fire;
  Spirits dark were crouching round.

(Proctor 89)

For Proctor nature can also inspire fantasy visions. As she recounts in her brief lyric, "In the wood," she meets a fairy at the foot of a tree.

Some magical words she uttered,
  I alone could understand,
For the sky grew bluer and brighter;
  While there rose on either hand
The cloudy walls of a palace
  That was built in Fairy-land.

(Proctor 122)

The poem ends with a straightforward explanation.

Shall I tell you what powerful fairy
  Built up this palace for me?
It was only a little white Violet
  I found at the root of a tree.

(Proctor 122—23)

The fireplace and a flower in the wood serve to awaken the poetic imagination with its images of dragons and fairy castles. The hidden world below can build its own palaces, perhaps not so stately as Xanadu but just as magical.

Another woman poet of this period whose name has been totally eclipsed by that of her father is Sara Coleridge (1802—1850), who wrote an elaborate fairy tale in the form of a narrative poem, "Phantasmion." This work features several well-drawn fantasy characters, including the fairy, Potentilla, protectress of the prince whose name gives the poem its title. Other fantasy figures are Oloola, the spirit of the storm, and Valhorga, the earth spirit. Episodic and romantic, interspersed with delightful lyrics, the poem has received little attention, partly because Sara devoted herself to editing her father's work, a task for which she achieved much more recognition. The fantasy ends with an appealing invitation:

Go, little book, and sing of love and beauty,
To tempt the worldling into fairy land;
Tell him that airy dreams are sacred duty,
Bring better wealth than aught his toils
  command.

(Miles 8:140)

Yet another contemporary woman poet, one whom Christina Rossetti regarded as a personal rival, is Jean Ingelow (1820—1897). When Ingelow's collection of poetry went into the eighth edition, Rossetti bitterly regretted her own lack of popular success. Ironically, Ingelow is at present remembered, if at all, for her charming fantasy novella, *Mopsa the Fairy,* which remains in print, unlike the poems.

Jean Ingelow's fantastic poetry treats the supernatural. One of her long poems, "Monitions of the Unseen," is an unusual blend of religious allegory, social commentary, and fantastic vision. Narrative in structure, the poem concerns a young curate who witnesses the death of a child near his church in an ancient city. The death, which occurs in a section of squalid poverty, moves him to pity and grief. He goes into the church to meditate, noticing at the gate an elderly beggar on the edge of death. Alone in the church, he feels depressed and laments his own failure: "Weed in the vineyard through the heat of the day, / And, overtasked, behold the weedy place / Grow ranker yet in spite of me" (421).

The realistic mode then shifts to the fantastic. The curate suddenly envisions in radiant light two ghostly figures, one of the dead child, now reborn, and one of the beggar before the gate, who has also died. After the apparition of the two angelic figures, the curate sees a host of evil birds, coming in the church in troops, stretching their evil necks, "and some were men-like, but their heads hung down" (424). He holds the child in his arms, protecting it from those fiendish presences: "He was afraid yet awful gladness reached / His soul" (426). After the apparitions leave the church and he is once more alone, he feels renewed in his religious mission. He will no longer question the value of his modest work, convinced now that even his small efforts help fulfill God's purposes.

The blatant didacticism of the poem is no doubt sufficient to ensure its enduring obscurity, but the way the supernatural element is handled is of interest for the fantasy critic. Ingelow chooses to transcend the social realism of the scenes involving the suffering child and the starving beggar by the creative transformation made possible through the fantastic impulse. The dramatic episode of the two ghostly presences and the monstrous birds makes the conversion of the young curate a dynamic experience in a way that no mere moralizing about the evils of poverty could do. The fantastic images speak with a directness from and to the hidden world below. Mere polemic would fail. The fiction of Dickens suggests an analogue. Probably his most popular and best remembered work is "The Christmas Carol," in which the conversion of Scrooge through his encounter with three spirits has made an indelible impression on readers.

Several of the Victorian woman poets turned to the fantasy of the supernatural, as did many male poets and novelists. Because of the new emphasis on rationalism that had begun in the eighteenth century, the supernatural world had been largely rejected and explained away, as a result of which, as Terry Castle puts it, the secular world became "metaphorically infused with a new mystical aura" (236). Along with the declining belief in an objective supernatural world, there developed a growing supernaturalism of the mind. One of the main currents in nineteenth-century literature is the desire to escape from the limitations of actuality and to forsake, at least imaginatively, the mundanity of the commonplace. Hence the popularity of the Gothic novel in this era, especially among women readers. At the same time, the growing dissociation from the corporeal reality of death gave way to a tendency to spectralize the dead. Philippe Aries notes that the repressive attitude toward physical death encouraged a spectralized mode of perception.[5]

Both horror and wonder poetry at this time manifest elements of the supernatural. It seems perhaps less suprising if one recalls the acceptance of occult experiences even among the educated. Elizabeth Barret Browning attended seances, as did Dante Gabriel Rossetti, especially after the death of his wife. On one occasion when Dante Gabriel was out walking with a friend, a chaffinch flew into his hand and nestled there. He was certain that it was the soul of his dead wife (Thomas 151).

Christina's poetry contains many elements of the supernatural. She wrote six poems specifically about ghosts. Not so well known as "Goblin Market," they are nonetheless fine lyrics with a deft touch for producing the "shiver" of perception in the reader. The earliest is "The Hour and the Ghost" in which the bride is lured away from the bridegroom by the ghost of her former lover. Cast as a dialogue among the three participants, it has a balladlike simplicity and narrative pace as it hurries toward the inevitable climax. In the ending the bride feels compelled to follow the former lover across the vast seas and into the cold, where they will "toss and howl and spin" (line 62).

In "A Chilly Night" the speaker, peering out of the window at midnight, perceives several ghosts outside, including the figure of her dead mother. No communication is possible, however, for the mother's blank eyes cannot see and the lonely daughter's voice cannot be heard. The description of the ghosts is evocative. They are shadowless, a detail that the earlier fantasist Dante Alighieri would appreciate—and as the night slowly wanes, so do they.

"The Ghost's Petition" concerns the perturbed spirit of a husband who cannot find rest because he contin-ues to sense his wife's lingering grief over his death. In this case there is communication, and he urges her to go on living and thereby permit him to rest in peace. The gender roles are reversed in "The Poor Ghost," in which it is the woman's ghost who returns to her lover. Her message to the living is much the same, as she begs him to cease mourning and leave her free to rest.

The situation in "At Home" is quite different. Here the ghostly visitor is not noticed at all by those still living in the house. There is pathos in the helpless invisibility of the solitary spirit who must remain outside what was once home. Such pathos also appears in "A Bird's Eye View," which draws on the folklore tradition of the raven's prophetic powers. Here two ominous ravens predict, with malicious delight, the sinking of the bridal ship, drowning the bride, all the crew, and "the silks and spices too" (74).

Christina Rossetti's fantastic imagination was by no means limited to ghosts and goblins. In several of her visionary poems she offers secondary world landscapes. One of her earliest poems, written at only sixteen, is called "Dead City." The dreamlike nature of the dead city evokes horror, for its many colorful splendors go unnoticed by its statue-cold inhabitants. The poem is cast as a journey from the blighted wood through total darkness to the goal, the dead city, which is ghostly white. The journey image occurs in several of Rossetti's longer visionary poems, such as "The Ballad of Boding." In this account of three barges, a "Love-ship," a "Worm-ship," and a third unnamed ship with a hard-working crew, the major fantasy element is the Monster that each of the ships encounters on its voyage. The Love-ship, with its pleasure seekers, founders in quicksand; the Worm-ship, with its power seekers, dashes on the rocks; the modest unnamed ship overcomes the Monster and arrives safely at port. The allegory is detailed but uncompromisingly clear, except for the Monster whose individual identity as a fantastic threat is imaginative and at times a bit comic.

Rossetti offers a very different kind of fantastic being in the short lyric called "Fata Morgana." Here a "blue-eyed phantom" runs ever before the weary poet, laughing and singing a "dreamy song," but always out of reach. The phantom may represent some elusive joy, but the poem does not explain. What makes it effective is the resonance of the fantasy image, which carries the weight of the poetic experience without recourse to allegory or explication.

Because "Goblin Market" is likely to be the most familiar of Rossetti's poems to a modern reader, I have left it to the last in order to establish it in the context of both her own fantasy poems and those of other women poets of that time. Part of that context is her own reading. We know that Christina was fond of

Gothic fiction, especially the novels of Radcliffe and Beckford's *Vathek*. She also admired Wilkie Collins's *The Moonstone*. Furthermore, she was widely read in myth and fantasy, such as Hone's compendium of lore, *The Everyday Book,* and *The Arabian Nights.* Along with her brothers and sisters, Christina was also an avid reader of Thomas Keightley's *Fairy Mythology,* a very popular work at the time. Keightley was a friend and a frequent visitor to the Rossetti household. *Fairy Mythology* includes tales of elves, fairies, trolls, and, most importantly for Christina's poem, of Norman "gobelins," who like to give sweets to children.[6] The frontispiece illustration of the book contains several mythical creatures, one of them a gnome with a parrot beak, which recalls Christina's parrot-voiced goblin. In her own water sketches for the poem one of the goblins appears as a parrot, coinciding with the description of the goblin merchants as having animal features:

> One had a cat's face,
> One whisked a tail,
> One tramped at a rat's pace,
> One crawled like a snail,
> One like a wombat prowled obtuse and
>   furry,
> One like a ratel tumbled hurry skurry.
>
> (71-76)

Accordingly, Dante Gabriel's sketch for the frontispiece of the first edition of his sister's poem displayed the head of a cat, a wombat, a rat, an owl, a cockatoo, and a sunfish (Thomas 158). In the context of her reading and her associations, it is not at all surprising that Christina in one of her long poems should reveal a tendency to mythologize about strange creatures who mingle with human beings and tempt them with otherwordly treats.

Christina warned against seeking a moral in "Goblin Market," an admonition that critics on the whole have been unable to accept. I tend to agree with Eleanor Walter Thomas, who writes that the poem is so perfect a work of art and so delightful a fancy that its critic feels that she should fall under condemnation with those who "murder to dissect and botanize where no trespassers should be admitted" (Thomas 155). The key word here is "fancy." Although critics will no doubt always find new meanings in Coleridge's albatross and Browning's dark tower, the power of the poems containing these images resides largely in the combination of total concreteness and infinite suggestiveness in these very images. The albatross and the tower speak directly to the reader in a way that their supposed meanings never can.

I would like to consider "Goblin Market" in terms of its mythic patterns and fantasy images. The underlying structure of the poem is the mythic journey of the hero. In this case the hero is female. As Joseph Campbell explains in his study of the monomyth, *The Hero with a Thousand Faces,* the journey begins with a call to adventure, which may be at first refused. There follows the crossing of the first threshold into a perilous, unknown realm. The hero then moves through the dangerous landcape, encountering a series of trials. This is the stage of the quest, which includes a literal or symbolic death, a descent to the underworld, and rebirth. In the final stage of the journey the hero returns with a precious "boon" with life-saving powers. The journey ends with the apotheosis of the hero.[7]

At the beginning of "Goblin Market," the sisters Laura and Lizzie receive the call to adventure as they crouch among the rushes at the brookside and hear the goblin merchants chanting to sell their wares. Lizzie puts her fingers in her ears, but Laura cannot resist listening to their cry. While Lizzie returns home, Laura stays on, offering a lock of her golden hair in payment for the goblin's fruit because she has no money. She consumes the luscious fruit voraciously, but when she goes home her sister upbraids her with warnings about the danger in her action. A friend of theirs has pined away and died as a result of eating the fruit. Over the next few days, Laura too begins to pine away, unable to do her share of the housework and weakening until on the point of death: "Laura dwindling / Seemed knocking at Death's door" (320—21). The threat of her sister's death inspires Lizzie to undertake the quest to save her. Lizzie's visit to the goblin merchants is a voyage to the underworld. She crosses the landscape of the wasteland—"the heath with clumps of furze"—at twilight, the dividing line that at once joins and divides darkness and light. Her quest is a physical and spiritual trial, as she heroically resists the blandishments of the goblins who insist that she stay and feast with them, but they respond by attacking her, clawing her with their nails, stamping on her feet, and pulling her hair:

> Tho' the goblins cuffed and caught her,
> Coaxed and fought her,
> Bullied and besought her,
> Scratched her, pinched her black as ink,
> Kicked and knocked her,
> Mauled and mocked her,
> Lizzie uttered not a word.
>
> (424—30)

Lizzie has "braved the glen" (473) and is able to return home with the juices of the fruit all over her face but not consumed. Laura eagerly tastes the juice as she hungrily kisses her sister, but it seems at first as if she will expire: "Sense failed in the moral strife" (513). Laura takes her journey to the underworld, losing consciousness. But in the morning she experiences resurrection, "Life out of death" (524). The ominous juices have in fact been their own antidote.

A scene from Christina Rossetti's Goblin Market, *drawn in 1865 by her brother Dante Gabriel Rossetti.*

In the final stanza of the poem the apotheosis occurs in the future. Many years afterward, when both girls have become wives and mothers, they remember their adventure when the sister stood in deadly peril "to win the fiery antidote" (559) to the fatal fruit. The sisters have shared the heroic quest. "Like two blossoms on one stem" (158), they have undertaken the heroic journey together.

What I wish to stress here is Christina's choice of the mythic fantasy structure for her poem. As Stephen Prickett notes, the poem "gains much of its power from its resistance to simple allegory" (106). Although its meanings abound as plentifully as the fruits in the goblin market, essentially the poem is a fantasy journey into a secondary world. Like many other nineteenth-century women poets, Rossetti thrived in the world of the imagination, to some extent in compensation for the limited experiences available to her in real life. In her case the extensive reading in myth and fairy tale inspired her to people "the hidden world below" with ghosts and goblins and to structure her narratives in otherworldly settings. Her imagination was visionary, and fantasy tended to erupt even in allegorical and religious verse.

Rossetti's fantasy poetry, like the verse of her predecessors Hemans and Landon and her contemporaries Proctor, Ingelow, and S. Coleridge, drew on the specifically hidden world of the nineteenth-century woman. Denied not merely activities but also the educational opportunities of men, these women turned both to books and to their own psyches for poetic imagery. Although the confessional and personal poems of these women, which drew on their domestic lives, have been recognized and generally condemned for their sentimentality and mundanity, their more inspired work, in the form of fantasy poetry, has been largely neglected. It deserves attention as the feminine vision it represents.

These women have thus suffered from a double bias, against women and against fantasy. It is revealing that a recent study by Anthony Harrison of Christina Rossetti in context neglects both her fellow female poets and her own fantasy poems. There is but one fleeting reference to Jean Ingelow as a rival poet, and the supernatural poems are not even cited in the index. It is also no coincidence that the women poets best remembered today are those who were closely associated with renowned male poets, with Browning and Rossetti as obvious examples. In Rossetti's case, there lingers a critical determination to identify her aesthetic with her brother's pre-Raphaelitism (Harrison 24).

All too often modern critics have distorted our understanding of women's fantasy poetry in the nineteenth century through their failure to rethink its inherent cultural values. For these women fantasy was not merely a subject but also a language. Unable to participate actively in the political and economic life of their time and unable to communicate directly with anyone about their hidden dreams and desires, they expressed their subjective experience of reality in the literary language of fantasy. When the experience of death transcended realistic descriptions of grief, they wrote poignantly of the ghost's return. When the impulse to heroism was blocked by the virtual imprisonment of their domestic lives, they could write of a journey to the land of goblins and of the heroic rescue of a beloved sister from their sinister magic. When they looked into the fire, they saw the dragons that their relentlessly protected daily lives could never permit. Their hidden world surfaced in the fantastic images of their visionary feminist poetry.

Notes

[1] These interpretations along with many others are cited and discussed in Charles, who concludes her book with the hope that in the future more attention will be paid to other works than "Goblin Market."

[2] Few readers would recognize the line as opening the poem "Casabianca."

[3] Leatitia Elizabeth Landon, who published her poems under "L. E. L.," encouraged the popular image of herself in London society as a kind of female Byron. Unfortunately her reputation suffered from her indiscreet relationships with two of her male editors. Surprising everyone by a sudden marriage to George MacLean, governor of an area in West Africa, she left with him for a three-year stay in Africa. A short time later she was found dead in her room with a prussic acid bottle nearby. Whether suicide, accident, or murder was never determined, but rumor had it that her husband had poisoned her.

[4] The poem "Felicia Hemans" is included in Vol. 8, pp. 109-11, of the Miles multi-volume anthology, which segregates the women poets into two separate volumes, 8 and 9. The fact of segregation tells us much about the attitude toward women writers at the time. The poem is also a subject of discussion in Rosenblum.

[5] Castle cites Philippe Aries whose work investigates the changing attitudes toward death through the centuries.

[6] Thomas cites other themes common to Rossetti and Keightley, such as the pining away of humans after their contact with elves and the danger in drinking fairy draughts.

[7] Campbell's concentration is entirely on the male hero, but the paradigm applies equally to the female. In Rossetti's poem the quest is shared by the two girls:

analogues for such sharing abound in heroic fantasy, as in *The Lord of the Rings* where Frodo and Sam share the quest to destroy the ring.

FURTHER READING

Criticism

Alderson, Brian. "Tracts, Rewards and Fairies: The Victorian Contribution to Children's Literature." In *Essays in the History of Publishing in the Celebration of the 250th Anniversary of the House of Longman 1724-1974,* edited by Asa Briggs, pp. 245-82. London: Longman Group Ltd., 1974.

　Chronicles the development of children's literature both as a genre and a business.

Apter, T. E. *Fantasy Literature: An Approach to Reality.* Bloomington: Indiana University Press, 1982, 161 p.

　Describes how psychoanalysis can be used to examine fantasy literature.

Auerbach, Nina and U. C. Knoepflmacher, eds. *Forbidden Journeys: Fairy Tales and Fantasies by Victorian Women Writers.* Chicago: The University of Chicago Press, 1992, 373 p.

　Surveys works by nineteenth-century women fantasy writers.

Briggs, K. M. "The Poets: Nineteenth Century and After." In *The Fairies in Tradition and Literature,* pp. 165-73. London: Routledge and Kegan Paul, 1967.

　Examines the consistency of fairy-tale themes despite changes in literary styles.

Carpenter, Humphrey. "Parson Lot Takes a Cold Bath: Charles Kingsley and *The Water Babies.*" In *Secret Gardens: A Study of the Golden Age of Children's Literature,* pp. 23-43. Boston, Mass.: Houghton Mifflin Company, 1985.

　Discusses the social themes of Kingsley's work and examines the personal events in Kingsley's life that contributed to the themes and characters of *The Water-Babies,* one of the first original English fairy tales.

Cott, Jonathan, ed. *Beyond the Looking Glass: Extraordinary Works of Fairy Tale and Fantasy.* New York: R. R. Bowker Co., 1973, 519 p.

　A collection of fantasy novels, stories, and poems with an introduction that explores characteristic themes of fairy tales.

de Vries, Jan. "The Problem of the Fairy Tale." *Diogenes,* No. 22 (Summer 1958): 1-15.

Traces the origin of the fairy tale genre across time and culture.

Gose, Elliot B., Jr. *Imagination Indulged: The Irrational in the Nineteenth-Century Novel.* Montreal: McGill-Queen's University Press, 1972, 182 p.

　Explores the interest in psychology of writers of imagination literature.

Helson, Ravenna. "The Psychological Origins of Fantasy for Children in Mid-Victorian England." *Children's Literature: The Great Excluded* 3 (1974): 66-76.

　Applies a Jungian psychological interpretation to major fantasy works of the nineteenth century.

Irwin, W. R. *The Game of the Impossible: A Rhetoric of Fantasy.* Urbana: University of Illinois Press, 1976, 215 p.

　Study of English and American fantasy since 1880.

Jackson, Rosemary. *Fantasy: The Literature of Subversion.* London: Methuen, 1981, 211 p.

　Argues that a wish for death is hidden in works written by prominent fantasy writers.

Manlove, C. N. *The Impulse of Fantasy Literature.* London: Macmillan Press Ltd., 1983, 174 p.

　The first chapter compares traditional fantasy with modern fantasy. Includes chapters examining the writings of E. Nesbit and George MacDonald.

Opie, Iona and Peter Opie. *The Classic Fairy Tales.* London: Oxford University Press, 1974, 255 p.

　Reprints classic fairy tales in their original format with historical and critical commentary on each.

Peppin, Brigid. *Fantasy: The Golden Age of Fantastic Illustration.* New York: Watson-Guptill Publications, 1975, 192 p.

　Highlights the growth in popularity and art of fantasy book illustrations in the late nineteenth and early twentieth century.

Prickett, Stephen. *Victorian Fantasy.* Bloomington: Indiana University Press, 1979, 257 p.

　Examines how changes in the perceived meaning of the term "fantasy" affected the literature of the nineteenth century.

Rabkin, Eric S. *The Fantastic in Literature.* Princeton: Princeton University Press, 1976, 234 p.

　Studies the effect of fantasy on art, literature and psychology.

Spivack, Charlotte. "The Perilous Realm: Phantasy as Literature." *The Centennial Review* XXV, No. 2 (Spring 1981): 133-49.

　Details some differences between the genre of fantasy literature and the fantastic elements of other literary genres.

Zipes, Jack. *Breaking the Magic Spell: Radical Theories of Folk and Fairy Tales*. London: Heinemann Educational Books Ltd., 1979, 201 p.

Surveys the social context of folklore and fairy tales.

Nineteenth-Century Literature Criticism

Topics Volume
Cumulative Indexes

Volumes 1-60

How to Use This Index

The main references

> Calvino, Italo
> 1923-1985.....CLC 5, 8, 11, 22, 33, 39,
>   73; SSC 3

list all author entries in the following Gale Literary Criticism series:

BLC = Black Literature Criticism
CLC = Contemporary Literary Criticism
CLR = Children's Literature Review
CMLC = Classical and Medieval Literature
        Criticism
DA = DISCovering Authors
DAB = DISCovering Authors: British
DAC = DISCovering Authors: Canadian
DAM = DISCovering Authors Modules
        DRAM: Dramatists module
        MST: Most-studied authors module
        MULT: Multicultural authors module
        NOV: Novelists module
        POET: Poets module
        POP: Popular/genre writers module

DC = Drama Criticism
HLC = Hispanic Literature Criticism
LC = Literature Criticism from 1400 to 1800
NCLC = Nineteenth-Century Literature Criticism
PC = Poetry Criticism
SSC = Short Story Criticism
TCLC = Twentieth-Century Literary Criticism
WLC = World Literature Criticism, 1500 to the
        Present

The cross-references

> See also CANR 23; CA 85-88;
>   obituary CA 116

list all author entries in the following Gale biographical and literary sources:

AAYA = Authors & Artists for Young Adults
AITN = Authors in the News
BEST = Bestsellers
BW = Black Writers
CA = Contemporary Authors
CAAS = Contemporary Authors
        Autobiography Series
CABS = Contemporary Authors
        Bibliographical Series
CANR = Contemporary Authors New
        Revision Series
CAP = Contemporary Authors Permanent
        Series
CDALB = Concise Dictionary of American
Literary Biography
CDBLB = Concise Dictionary of British
        Literary Biography

DLB = Dictionary of Literary Biography
DLBD = Dictionary of Literary Biography
        Documentary Series
DLBY = Dictionary of Literary Biography Yearbook
HW = Hispanic Writers
JRDA = Junior DISCovering Authors
MAICYA = Major Authors and Illustrators for
        Children and Young Adults
MTCW = Major 20th-Century Writers
NNAL = Native North American Literature
SAAS = Something about the Author Autobiography
        Series
SATA = Something about the Author
YABC = Yesterday's Authors of Books for Children

Literary Criticism Series
Cumulative Author Index

Abasiyanik, Sait Faik   1906-1954
See Sait Faik
See also CA 123

Abbey, Edward   1927-1989...... CLC 36, 59
See also CA 45-48; 128; CANR 2, 41

Abbott, Lee K(ittredge)   1947-...... CLC 48
See also CA 124; CANR 51; DLB 130

Abe, Kobo
1924-1993 .... CLC 8, 22, 53, 81;
DAM NOV
See also CA 65-68; 140; CANR 24; MTCW

Abelard, Peter   c. 1079-c. 1142 ... CMLC 11
See also DLB 115

Abell, Kjeld   1901-1961........... CLC 15
See also CA 111

Abish, Walter   1931-.............. CLC 22
See also CA 101; CANR 37; DLB 130

Abrahams, Peter (Henry)   1919- ..... CLC 4
See also BW 1; CA 57-60; CANR 26;
DLB 117; MTCW

Abrams, M(eyer) H(oward)   1912-... CLC 24
See also CA 57-60; CANR 13, 33; DLB 67

Abse, Dannie
1923- ... CLC 7, 29; DAB; DAM POET
See also CA 53-56; CAAS 1; CANR 4, 46;
DLB 27

Achebe, (Albert) Chinua(lumogu)
1930- ..... CLC 1, 3, 5, 7, 11, 26, 51, 75;
BLC; DA; DAB; DAC; DAM MST,
MULT, NOV; WLC
See also AAYA 15; BW 2; CA 1-4R;
CANR 6, 26, 47; CLR 20; DLB 117;
MAICYA; MTCW; SATA 40;
SATA-Brief 38

Acker, Kathy   1948- .... CLC 45
See also CA 117; 122; CANR 55

Ackroyd, Peter   1949-......... CLC 34, 52
See also CA 123; 127; CANR 51; DLB 155;
INT 127

Acorn, Milton   1923-........ CLC 15; DAC
See also CA 103; DLB 53; INT 103

Adamov, Arthur
1908-1970 .... CLC 4, 25; DAM DRAM
See also CA 17-18; 25-28R; CAP 2; MTCW

Adams, Alice (Boyd)
1926- .... CLC 6, 13, 46; SSC 24
See also CA 81-84; CANR 26, 53;
DLBY 86; INT CANR-26; MTCW

Adams, Andy   1859-1935.......... TCLC 56
See also YABC 1

Adams, Douglas (Noel)
1952- .... CLC 27, 60; DAM POP
See also AAYA 4; BEST 89:3; CA 106;
CANR 34; DLBY 83; JRDA

Adams, Francis   1862-1893....... NCLC 33

Adams, Henry (Brooks)
1838-1918 ..... TCLC 4, 52; DA; DAB;
DAC; DAM MST
See also CA 104; 133; DLB 12, 47

Adams, Richard (George)
1920- .... CLC 4, 5, 18; DAM NOV
See also AAYA 16; AITN 1, 2; CA 49-52;
CANR 3, 35; CLR 20; JRDA; MAICYA;
MTCW; SATA 7, 69

Adamson, Joy(-Friederike Victoria)
1910-1980 .... CLC 17
See also CA 69-72; 93-96; CANR 22;
MTCW; SATA 11; SATA-Obit 22

Adcock, Fleur   1934-............. CLC 41
See also CA 25-28R; CAAS 23; CANR 11,
34; DLB 40

Addams, Charles (Samuel)
1912-1988 .... CLC 30
See also CA 61-64; 126; CANR 12

Addison, Joseph   1672-1719 .... LC 18
See also CDBLB 1660-1789; DLB 101

Adler, Alfred (F.)   1870-1937 ...... TCLC 61
See also CA 119

Adler, C(arole) S(chwerdtfeger)
1932- .... CLC 35
See also AAYA 4; CA 89-92; CANR 19,
40; JRDA; MAICYA; SAAS 15;
SATA 26, 63

Adler, Renata   1938-............ CLC 8, 31
See also CA 49-52; CANR 5, 22, 52;
MTCW

Ady, Endre   1877-1919 .... TCLC 11
See also CA 107

Aeschylus
525B.C.-456B.C........ CMLC 11; DA;
DAB; DAC; DAM DRAM, MST
See also DLB 176

Afton, Effie
See Harper, Frances Ellen Watkins

Agapida, Fray Antonio
See Irving, Washington

Agee, James (Rufus)
1909-1955 .... TCLC 1, 19; DAM NOV
See also AITN 1; CA 108; 148;
CDALB 1941-1968; DLB 2, 26, 152

Aghill, Gordon
See Silverberg, Robert

Agnon, S(hmuel) Y(osef Halevi)
1888-1970 .... CLC 4, 8, 14
See also CA 17-18; 25-28R; CAP 2; MTCW

Agrippa von Nettesheim, Henry Cornelius
1486-1535 .... LC 27

Aherne, Owen
See Cassill, R(onald) V(erlin)

Ai   1947-................... CLC 4, 14, 69
See also CA 85-88; CAAS 13; DLB 120

Aickman, Robert (Fordyce)
1914-1981 .... CLC 57
See also CA 5-8R; CANR 3

Aiken, Conrad (Potter)
1889-1973 .... CLC 1, 3, 5, 10, 52;
DAM NOV, POET; SSC 9
See also CA 5-8R; 45-48; CANR 4;
CDALB 1929-1941; DLB 9, 45, 102;
MTCW; SATA 3, 30

Aiken, Joan (Delano)   1924-........ CLC 35
See also AAYA 1; CA 9-12R; CANR 4, 23,
34; CLR 1, 19; DLB 161; JRDA;
MAICYA; MTCW; SAAS 1; SATA 2,
30, 73

Ainsworth, William Harrison
1805-1882 .... NCLC 13
See also DLB 21; SATA 24

Aitmatov, Chingiz (Torekulovich)
1928-....................... CLC 71
See also CA 103; CANR 38; MTCW;
SATA 56

Akers, Floyd
See Baum, L(yman) Frank

Akhmadulina, Bella Akhatovna
1937-.......... CLC 53; DAM POET
See also CA 65-68

Akhmatova, Anna
1888-1966 .... CLC 11, 25, 64;
DAM POET; PC 2
See also CA 19-20; 25-28R; CANR 35;
CAP 1; MTCW

Aksakov, Sergei Timofeyvich
1791-1859 .... NCLC 2

Aksenov, Vassily
See Aksyonov, Vassily (Pavlovich)

Aksyonov, Vassily (Pavlovich)
1932-.................... CLC 22, 37
See also CA 53-56; CANR 12, 48

Akutagawa, Ryunosuke
1892-1927 .... TCLC 16
See also CA 117; 154

Alain   1868-1951 .... TCLC 41

Alain-Fournier................... TCLC 6
See also Fournier, Henri Alban
See also DLB 65

Alarcon, Pedro Antonio de
1833-1891 .... NCLC 1

Alas (y Urena), Leopoldo (Enrique Garcia)
1852-1901 .... TCLC 29
See also CA 113; 131; HW

Albee, Edward (Franklin III)
1928- ...... CLC 1, 2, 3, 5, 9, 11, 13, 25,
53, 86; DA; DAB; DAC; DAM DRAM,
MST; WLC
See also AITN 1; CA 5-8R; CABS 3;
CANR 8, 54; CDALB 1941-1968; DLB 7;
INT CANR-8; MTCW

Alberti, Rafael 1902- . . . . **CLC 7**
See also CA 85-88; DLB 108

Albert the Great 1200(?)-1280. . . . **CMLC 16**
See also DLB 115

Alcala-Galiano, Juan Valera y
See Valera y Alcala-Galiano, Juan

Alcott, Amos Bronson 1799-1888 . . **NCLC 1**
See also DLB 1

Alcott, Louisa May
1832-1888 . . . . . **NCLC 6, 58; DA; DAB;
DAC; DAM MST, NOV; WLC**
See also AAYA 20; CDALB 1865-1917;
CLR 1, 38; DLB 1, 42, 79; DLBD 14;
JRDA; MAICYA; YABC 1

Aldanov, M. A.
See Aldanov, Mark (Alexandrovich)

Aldanov, Mark (Alexandrovich)
1886(?)-1957 . . . . **TCLC 23**
See also CA 118

Aldington, Richard 1892-1962 . . . . . . **CLC 49**
See also CA 85-88; CANR 45; DLB 20, 36,
100, 149

Aldiss, Brian W(ilson)
1925- . . . . **CLC 5, 14, 40; DAM NOV**
See also CA 5-8R; CAAS 2; CANR 5, 28;
DLB 14; MTCW; SATA 34

Alegria, Claribel
1924- . . . . **CLC 75; DAM MULT**
See also CA 131; CAAS 15; DLB 145; HW

Alegria, Fernando 1918- . . . . **CLC 57**
See also CA 9-12R; CANR 5, 32; HW

Aleichem, Sholom . . . . **TCLC 1, 35**
See also Rabinovitch, Sholem

Aleixandre, Vicente
1898-1984 . . . . **CLC 9, 36; DAM POET;
PC 15**
See also CA 85-88; 114; CANR 26;
DLB 108; HW; MTCW

Alepoudelis, Odysseus
See Elytis, Odysseus

Aleshkovsky, Joseph 1929-
See Aleshkovsky, Yuz
See also CA 121; 128

Aleshkovsky, Yuz . . . . **CLC 44**
See also Aleshkovsky, Joseph

Alexander, Lloyd (Chudley) 1924- . . **CLC 35**
See also AAYA 1; CA 1-4R; CANR 1, 24,
38, 55; CLR 1, 5; DLB 52; JRDA;
MAICYA; MTCW; SAAS 19; SATA 3,
49, 81

Alexie, Sherman (Joseph, Jr.)
1966- . . . . **CLC 96; DAM MULT**
See also CA 138; DLB 175; NNAL

Alfau, Felipe 1902- . . . . **CLC 66**
See also CA 137

Alger, Horatio, Jr. 1832-1899 . . . . . **NCLC 8**
See also DLB 42; SATA 16

Algren, Nelson 1909-1981 . . . . **CLC 4, 10, 33**
See also CA 13-16R; 103; CANR 20;
CDALB 1941-1968; DLB 9; DLBY 81,
82; MTCW

Ali, Ahmed 1910- . . . . **CLC 69**
See also CA 25-28R; CANR 15, 34

Alighieri, Dante 1265-1321 . . . . **CMLC 3, 18**

Allan, John B.
See Westlake, Donald E(dwin)

Allen, Edward 1948- . . . . **CLC 59**

Allen, Paula Gunn
1939- . . . . **CLC 84; DAM MULT**
See also CA 112; 143; DLB 175; NNAL

Allen, Roland
See Ayckbourn, Alan

Allen, Sarah A.
See Hopkins, Pauline Elizabeth

Allen, Woody
1935- . . . . **CLC 16, 52; DAM POP**
See also AAYA 10; CA 33-36R; CANR 27,
38; DLB 44; MTCW

Allende, Isabel
1942- . . . . **CLC 39, 57, 97; DAM MULT,
NOV; HLC**
See also AAYA 18; CA 125; 130;
CANR 51; DLB 145; HW; INT 130;
MTCW

Alleyn, Ellen
See Rossetti, Christina (Georgina)

Allingham, Margery (Louise)
1904-1966 . . . . **CLC 19**
See also CA 5-8R; 25-28R; CANR 4;
DLB 77; MTCW

Allingham, William 1824-1889 . . . **NCLC 25**
See also DLB 35

Allison, Dorothy E. 1949- . . . . **CLC 78**
See also CA 140

Allston, Washington 1779-1843 . . . . **NCLC 2**
See also DLB 1

Almedingen, E. M. . . . . **CLC 12**
See also Almedingen, Martha Edith von
See also SATA 3

Almedingen, Martha Edith von 1898-1971
See Almedingen, E. M.
See also CA 1-4R; CANR 1

Almqvist, Carl Jonas Love
1793-1866 . . . . **NCLC 42**

Alonso, Damaso 1898-1990 . . . . **CLC 14**
See also CA 110; 131; 130; DLB 108; HW

Alov
See Gogol, Nikolai (Vasilyevich)

Alta 1942- . . . . **CLC 19**
See also CA 57-60

Alter, Robert B(ernard) 1935- . . . . . **CLC 34**
See also CA 49-52; CANR 1, 47

Alther, Lisa 1944- . . . . **CLC 7, 41**
See also CA 65-68; CANR 12, 30, 51;
MTCW

Altman, Robert 1925- . . . . **CLC 16**
See also CA 73-76; CANR 43

Alvarez, A(lfred) 1929- . . . . **CLC 5, 13**
See also CA 1-4R; CANR 3, 33; DLB 14,
40

Alvarez, Alejandro Rodriguez 1903-1965
See Casona, Alejandro
See also CA 131; 93-96; HW

Alvarez, Julia 1950- . . . . **CLC 93**
See also CA 147

Alvaro, Corrado 1896-1956 . . . . **TCLC 60**

Amado, Jorge
1912- . . . . **CLC 13, 40; DAM MULT,
NOV; HLC**
See also CA 77-80; CANR 35; DLB 113;
MTCW

Ambler, Eric 1909- . . . . **CLC 4, 6, 9**
See also CA 9-12R; CANR 7, 38; DLB 77;
MTCW

Amichai, Yehuda 1924- . . . . . . **CLC 9, 22, 57**
See also CA 85-88; CANR 46; MTCW

Amiel, Henri Frederic 1821-1881 . . **NCLC 4**

Amis, Kingsley (William)
1922-1995 . . . . . **CLC 1, 2, 3, 5, 8, 13, 40,
44; DA; DAB; DAC; DAM MST, NOV**
See also AITN 2; CA 9-12R; 150; CANR 8,
28, 54; CDBLB 1945-1960; DLB 15, 27,
100, 139; INT CANR-8; MTCW

Amis, Martin (Louis)
1949- . . . . **CLC 4, 9, 38, 62**
See also BEST 90:3; CA 65-68; CANR 8,
27, 54; DLB 14; INT CANR-27

Ammons, A(rchie) R(andolph)
1926- . . . . **CLC 2, 3, 5, 8, 9, 25, 57;
DAM POET; PC 16**
See also AITN 1; CA 9-12R; CANR 6, 36,
51; DLB 5, 165; MTCW

Amo, Tauraatua i
See Adams, Henry (Brooks)

Anand, Mulk Raj
1905- . . . . **CLC 23, 93; DAM NOV**
See also CA 65-68; CANR 32; MTCW

Anatol
See Schnitzler, Arthur

Anaximander
c. 610B.C.-c. 546B.C. . . . . **CMLC 22**

Anaya, Rudolfo A(lfonso)
1937- . . . . **CLC 23; DAM MULT, NOV;
HLC**
See also AAYA 20; CA 45-48; CAAS 4;
CANR 1, 32, 51; DLB 82; HW 1; MTCW

Andersen, Hans Christian
1805-1875 . . . . **NCLC 7; DA; DAB;
DAC; DAM MST, POP; SSC 6; WLC**
See also CLR 6; MAICYA; YABC 1

Anderson, C. Farley
See Mencken, H(enry) L(ouis); Nathan,
George Jean

Anderson, Jessica (Margaret) Queale
. . . . **CLC 37**
See also CA 9-12R; CANR 4

Anderson, Jon (Victor)
1940- . . . . **CLC 9; DAM POET**
See also CA 25-28R; CANR 20

Anderson, Lindsay (Gordon)
1923-1994 . . . . **CLC 20**
See also CA 125; 128; 146

Anderson, Maxwell
1888-1959 . . . . . . **TCLC 2; DAM DRAM**
See also CA 105; 152; DLB 7

Anderson, Poul (William) 1926- . . . . **CLC 15**
See also AAYA 5; CA 1-4R; CAAS 2;
CANR 2, 15, 34; DLB 8; INT CANR-15;
MTCW; SATA 90; SATA-Brief 39

Anderson, Robert (Woodruff)
1917- . . . . **CLC 23; DAM DRAM**
See also AITN 1; CA 21-24R; CANR 32;
DLB 7

Anderson, Sherwood
1876-1941 . . . . **TCLC 1, 10, 24; DA;**
DAB; DAC; DAM MST, NOV; SSC 1;
WLC
See also CA 104; 121; CDALB 1917-1929;
DLB 4, 9, 86; DLBD 1; MTCW

Andier, Pierre
See Desnos, Robert

Andouard
See Giraudoux, (Hippolyte) Jean

Andrade, Carlos Drummond de . . . . . . **CLC 18**
See also Drummond de Andrade, Carlos

Andrade, Mario de 1893-1945 . . . . . **TCLC 43**

Andreae, Johann V(alentin)
1586-1654 . . . . **LC 32**
See also DLB 164

Andreas-Salome, Lou 1861-1937 . . . **TCLC 56**
See also DLB 66

Andrewes, Lancelot 1555-1626 . . . . **LC 5**
See also DLB 151, 172

Andrews, Cicily Fairfield
See West, Rebecca

Andrews, Elton V.
See Pohl, Frederik

Andreyev, Leonid (Nikolaevich)
1871-1919 . . . . **TCLC 3**
See also CA 104

Andric, Ivo 1892-1975 . . . . **CLC 8**
See also CA 81-84; 57-60; CANR 43;
DLB 147; MTCW

Angelique, Pierre
See Bataille, Georges

Angell, Roger 1920- . . . . **CLC 26**
See also CA 57-60; CANR 13, 44; DLB 171

Angelou, Maya
1928- . . . . **CLC 12, 35, 64, 77; BLC; DA;**
DAB; DAC; DAM MST, MULT, POET,
POP
See also AAYA 7, 20; BW 2; CA 65-68;
CANR 19, 42; DLB 38; MTCW;
SATA 49

Annensky, Innokenty (Fyodorovich)
1856-1909 . . . . **TCLC 14**
See also CA 110; 155

Annunzio, Gabriele d'
See D'Annunzio, Gabriele

Anon, Charles Robert
See Pessoa, Fernando (Antonio Nogueira)

Anouilh, Jean (Marie Lucien Pierre)
1910-1987 . . . . . . **CLC 1, 3, 8, 13, 40, 50;**
DAM DRAM
See also CA 17-20R; 123; CANR 32;
MTCW

Anthony, Florence
See Ai

Anthony, John
See Ciardi, John (Anthony)

Anthony, Peter
See Shaffer, Anthony (Joshua); Shaffer,
Peter (Levin)

Anthony, Piers 1934- . . **CLC 35; DAM POP**
See also AAYA 11; CA 21-24R; CANR 28,
56; DLB 8; MTCW; SAAS 22; SATA 84

Antoine, Marc
See Proust, (Valentin-Louis-George-Eugene-)
Marcel

Antoninus, Brother
See Everson, William (Oliver)

Antonioni, Michelangelo 1912- . . . . . **CLC 20**
See also CA 73-76; CANR 45

Antschel, Paul 1920-1970
See Celan, Paul
See also CA 85-88; CANR 33; MTCW

Anwar, Chairil 1922-1949 . . . . **TCLC 22**
See also CA 121

Apollinaire, Guillaume
1880-1918 . . . . **TCLC 3, 8, 51;**
DAM POET; PC 7
See also Kostrowitzki, Wilhelm Apollinaris
de
See also CA 152

Appelfeld, Aharon 1932- . . . . **CLC 23, 47**
See also CA 112; 133

Apple, Max (Isaac) 1941- . . . . **CLC 9, 33**
See also CA 81-84; CANR 19, 54; DLB 130

Appleman, Philip (Dean) 1926- . . . . . **CLC 51**
See also CA 13-16R; CAAS 18; CANR 6,
29, 56

Appleton, Lawrence
See Lovecraft, H(oward) P(hillips)

Apteryx
See Eliot, T(homas) S(tearns)

Apuleius, (Lucius Madaurensis)
125(?)-175(?) . . . . **CMLC 1**

Aquin, Hubert 1929-1977 . . . . **CLC 15**
See also CA 105; DLB 53

Aragon, Louis
1897-1982 . . . . . **CLC 3, 22; DAM NOV,**
POET
See also CA 69-72; 108; CANR 28;
DLB 72; MTCW

Arany, Janos 1817-1882 . . . . **NCLC 34**

Arbuthnot, John 1667-1735 . . . . **LC 1**
See also DLB 101

Archer, Herbert Winslow
See Mencken, H(enry) L(ouis)

Archer, Jeffrey (Howard)
1940- . . . . **CLC 28; DAM POP**
See also AAYA 16; BEST 89:3; CA 77-80;
CANR 22, 52; INT CANR-22

Archer, Jules 1915- . . . . **CLC 12**
See also CA 9-12R; CANR 6; SAAS 5;
SATA 4, 85

Archer, Lee
See Ellison, Harlan (Jay)

Arden, John
1930- . . . . . **CLC 6, 13, 15; DAM DRAM**
See also CA 13-16R; CAAS 4; CANR 31;
DLB 13; MTCW

Arenas, Reinaldo
1943-1990 . . . . . . **CLC 41; DAM MULT;**
HLC
See also CA 124; 128; 133; DLB 145; HW

Arendt, Hannah 1906-1975 . . . . . **CLC 66, 98**
See also CA 17-20R; 61-64; CANR 26;
MTCW

Aretino, Pietro 1492-1556 . . . . **LC 12**

Arghezi, Tudor . . . . **CLC 80**
See also Theodorescu, Ion N.

Arguedas, Jose Maria
1911-1969 . . . . **CLC 10, 18**
See also CA 89-92; DLB 113; HW

Argueta, Manlio 1936- . . . . **CLC 31**
See also CA 131; DLB 145; HW

Ariosto, Ludovico 1474-1533 . . . . **LC 6**

Aristides
See Epstein, Joseph

Aristophanes
450B.C.-385B.C. . . . . **CMLC 4; DA;**
DAB; DAC; DAM DRAM, MST; DC 2
See also DLB 176

Arlt, Roberto (Godofredo Christophersen)
1900-1942 . . . . . **TCLC 29; DAM MULT;**
HLC
See also CA 123; 131; HW

Armah, Ayi Kwei
1939- . . . . **CLC 5, 33; BLC;**
DAM MULT, POET
See also BW 1; CA 61-64; CANR 21;
DLB 117; MTCW

Armatrading, Joan 1950- . . . . **CLC 17**
See also CA 114

Arnette, Robert
See Silverberg, Robert

Arnim, Achim von (Ludwig Joachim von
Arnim) 1781-1831 . . . . **NCLC 5**
See also DLB 90

Arnim, Bettina von 1785-1859 . . . . **NCLC 38**
See also DLB 90

Arnold, Matthew
1822-1888 . . . . . **NCLC 6, 29; DA; DAB;**
DAC; DAM MST, POET; PC 5; WLC
See also CDBLB 1832-1890; DLB 32, 57

Arnold, Thomas 1795-1842 . . . . . . **NCLC 18**
See also DLB 55

Arnow, Harriette (Louisa) Simpson
1908-1986 . . . . **CLC 2, 7, 18**
See also CA 9-12R; 118; CANR 14; DLB 6;
MTCW; SATA 42; SATA-Obit 47

Arp, Hans
See Arp, Jean

Arp, Jean 1887-1966 . . . . **CLC 5**
See also CA 81-84; 25-28R; CANR 42

Arrabal
See Arrabal, Fernando

Arrabal, Fernando 1932- . . . **CLC 2, 9, 18, 58**
See also CA 9-12R; CANR 15

Arrick, Fran . . . . **CLC 30**
See also Gaberman, Judie Angell

Artaud, Antonin (Marie Joseph)
1896-1948 . . . **TCLC 3, 36; DAM DRAM**
See also CA 104; 149

Arthur, Ruth M(abel) 1905-1979 . . . . **CLC 12**
See also CA 9-12R; 85-88; CANR 4;
SATA 7, 26

Artsybashev, Mikhail (Petrovich)
1878-1927 . . . . **TCLC 31**

Barthelme, Donald
    1931-1989 . . . . . . **CLC 1, 2, 3, 5, 6, 8, 13,**
            23, 46, 59; DAM NOV; SSC 2
    See also CA 21-24R; 129; CANR 20;
        DLB 2; DLBY 80, 89; MTCW; SATA 7;
        SATA-Obit 62

Barthelme, Frederick 1943- . . . . **CLC 36**
    See also CA 114; 122; DLBY 85; INT 122

Barthes, Roland (Gerard)
    1915-1980 . . . . **CLC 24, 83**
    See also CA 130; 97-100; MTCW

Barzun, Jacques (Martin) 1907- . . . . **CLC 51**
    See also CA 61-64; CANR 22

Bashevis, Isaac
    See Singer, Isaac Bashevis

Bashkirtseff, Marie 1859-1884 . . . **NCLC 27**

Basho
    See Matsuo Basho

Bass, Kingsley B., Jr.
    See Bullins, Ed

Bass, Rick 1958- . . . . **CLC 79**
    See also CA 126; CANR 53

Bassani, Giorgio 1916- . . . . **CLC 9**
    See also CA 65-68; CANR 33; DLB 128,
        177; MTCW

Bastos, Augusto (Antonio) Roa
    See Roa Bastos, Augusto (Antonio)

Bataille, Georges 1897-1962 . . . . **CLC 29**
    See also CA 101; 89-92

Bates, H(erbert) E(rnest)
    1905-1974 . . . . **CLC 46; DAB;**
                        DAM POP; SSC 10
    See also CA 93-96; 45-48; CANR 34;
        DLB 162; MTCW

Bauchart
    See Camus, Albert

Baudelaire, Charles
    1821-1867 . . . . **NCLC 6, 29, 55; DA;**
        DAB; DAC; DAM MST, POET; PC 1;
                        SSC 18; WLC

Baudrillard, Jean 1929- . . . . **CLC 60**

Baum, L(yman) Frank 1856-1919 . . . **TCLC 7**
    See also CA 108; 133; CLR 15; DLB 22;
        JRDA; MAICYA; MTCW; SATA 18

Baum, Louis F.
    See Baum, L(yman) Frank

Baumbach, Jonathan 1933- . . . . . . **CLC 6, 23**
    See also CA 13-16R; CAAS 5; CANR 12;
        DLBY 80; INT CANR-12; MTCW

Bausch, Richard (Carl) 1945- . . . . . . **CLC 51**
    See also CA 101; CAAS 14; CANR 43;
        DLB 130

Baxter, Charles
    1947- . . . . **CLC 45, 78; DAM POP**
    See also CA 57-60; CANR 40; DLB 130

Baxter, George Owen
    See Faust, Frederick (Schiller)

Baxter, James K(eir) 1926-1972 . . . . **CLC 14**
    See also CA 77-80

Baxter, John
    See Hunt, E(verette) Howard, (Jr.)

Bayer, Sylvia
    See Glassco, John

Baynton, Barbara 1857-1929 . . . . . . **TCLC 57**

Beagle, Peter S(oyer) 1939- . . . . **CLC 7**
    See also CA 9-12R; CANR 4, 51;
        DLBY 80; INT CANR-4; SATA 60

Bean, Normal
    See Burroughs, Edgar Rice

Beard, Charles A(ustin)
    1874-1948 . . . . **TCLC 15**
    See also CA 115; DLB 17; SATA 18

Beardsley, Aubrey 1872-1898 . . . . . **NCLC 6**

Beattie, Ann
    1947- . . . . **CLC 8, 13, 18, 40, 63;**
                    DAM NOV, POP; SSC 11
    See also BEST 90:2; CA 81-84; CANR 53;
        DLBY 82; MTCW

Beattie, James 1735-1803 . . . . **NCLC 25**
    See also DLB 109

Beauchamp, Kathleen Mansfield 1888-1923
    See Mansfield, Katherine
    See also CA 104; 134; DA; DAC;
        DAM MST

Beaumarchais, Pierre-Augustin Caron de
    1732-1799 . . . . **DC 4**
    See also DAM DRAM

Beaumont, Francis
    1584(?)-1616 . . . . **LC 33; DC 6**
    See also CDBLB Before 1660; DLB 58, 121

**Beauvoir, Simone (Lucie Ernestine Marie
    Bertrand) de**
    1908-1986 . . . . **CLC 1, 2, 4, 8, 14, 31, 44,**
        50, 71; DA; DAB; DAC; DAM MST,
                            NOV; WLC
    See also CA 9-12R; 118; CANR 28;
        DLB 72; DLBY 86; MTCW

Becker, Carl 1873-1945 . . . . **TCLC 63:**
    See also DLB 17

Becker, Jurek 1937- . . . . **CLC 7, 19**
    See also CA 85-88; DLB 75

Becker, Walter 1950- . . . . **CLC 26**

Beckett, Samuel (Barclay)
    1906-1989 . . . . . . **CLC 1, 2, 3, 4, 6, 9, 10,**
        11, 14, 18, 29, 57, 59, 83; DA; DAB;
        DAC; DAM DRAM, MST, NOV;
                        SSC 16; WLC
    See also CA 5-8R; 130; CANR 33;
        CDBLB 1945-1960; DLB 13, 15;
        DLBY 90; MTCW

Beckford, William 1760-1844 . . . . **NCLC 16**
    See also DLB 39

Beckman, Gunnel 1910- . . . . **CLC 26**
    See also CA 33-36R; CANR 15; CLR 25;
        MAICYA; SAAS 9; SATA 6

Becque, Henri 1837-1899 . . . . **NCLC 3**

Beddoes, Thomas Lovell
    1803-1849 . . . . **NCLC 3**
    See also DLB 96

Bede c. 673-735 . . . . **CMLC 20**
    See also DLB 146

Bedford, Donald F.
    See Fearing, Kenneth (Flexner)

Beecher, Catharine Esther
    1800-1878 . . . . **NCLC 30**
    See also DLB 1

Beecher, John 1904-1980 . . . . **CLC 6**
    See also AITN 1; CA 5-8R; 105; CANR 8

Beer, Johann 1655-1700 . . . . **LC 5**
    See also DLB 168

Beer, Patricia 1924- . . . . **CLC 58**
    See also CA 61-64; CANR 13, 46; DLB 40

Beerbohm, Max
    See Beerbohm, (Henry) Max(imilian)

Beerbohm, (Henry) Max(imilian)
    1872-1956 . . . . **TCLC 1, 24**
    See also CA 104; 154; DLB 34, 100

Beer-Hofmann, Richard
    1866-1945 . . . . **TCLC 60**
    See also DLB 81

Begiebing, Robert J(ohn) 1946- . . . . . **CLC 70**
    See also CA 122; CANR 40

Behan, Brendan
    1923-1964 . . . . **CLC 1, 8, 11, 15, 79;**
                                DAM DRAM
    See also CA 73-76; CANR 33;
        CDBLB 1945-1960; DLB 13; MTCW

Behn, Aphra
    1640(?)-1689 . . . . . . **LC 1, 30; DA; DAB;**
        DAC; DAM DRAM, MST, NOV,
                        POET; DC 4; PC 13; WLC
    See also DLB 39, 80, 131

Behrman, S(amuel) N(athaniel)
    1893-1973 . . . . **CLC 40**
    See also CA 13-16; 45-48; CAP 1; DLB 7,
        44

Belasco, David 1853-1931 . . . . **TCLC 3**
    See also CA 104; DLB 7

Belcheva, Elisaveta 1893- . . . . **CLC 10**
    See also Bagryana, Elisaveta

Beldone, Phil "Cheech"
    See Ellison, Harlan (Jay)

Beleno
    See Azuela, Mariano

Belinski, Vissarion Grigoryevich
    1811-1848 . . . . **NCLC 5**

Belitt, Ben 1911- . . . . **CLC 22**
    See also CA 13-16R; CAAS 4; CANR 7;
        DLB 5

Bell, Gertrude 1868-1926 . . . . **TCLC 67**
    See also DLB 174

Bell, James Madison
    1826-1902 . . . . **TCLC 43; BLC;**
                                DAM MULT
    See also BW 1; CA 122; 124; DLB 50

Bell, Madison Smartt 1957- . . . . **CLC 41**
    See also CA 111; CANR 28, 54

Bell, Marvin (Hartley)
    1937- . . . . **CLC 8, 31; DAM POET**
    See also CA 21-24R; CAAS 14; DLB 5;
        MTCW

Bell, W. L. D.
    See Mencken, H(enry) L(ouis)

Bellamy, Atwood C.
    See Mencken, H(enry) L(ouis)

Bellamy, Edward 1850-1898 . . . . . . **NCLC 4**
    See also DLB 12

Bellin, Edward J.
    See Kuttner, Henry

Belloc, (Joseph) Hilaire (Pierre Sebastien Rene Swanton)
  1870-1953 . . . **TCLC 7, 18; DAM POET**
  See also CA 106; 152; DLB 19, 100, 141, 174; YABC 1

Belloc, Joseph Peter Rene Hilaire
  See Belloc, (Joseph) Hilaire (Pierre Sebastien Rene Swanton)

Belloc, Joseph Pierre Hilaire
  See Belloc, (Joseph) Hilaire (Pierre Sebastien Rene Swanton)

Belloc, M. A.
  See Lowndes, Marie Adelaide (Belloc)

Bellow, Saul
  1915- . . . . . . **CLC 1, 2, 3, 6, 8, 10, 13, 15, 25, 33, 34, 63, 79; DA; DAB; DAC; DAM MST, NOV, POP; SSC 14; WLC**
  See also AITN 2; BEST 89:3; CA 5-8R; CABS 1; CANR 29, 53; CDALB 1941-1968; DLB 2, 28; DLBD 3; DLBY 82; MTCW

Belser, Reimond Karel Maria de   1929-
  See Ruyslinck, Ward
  See also CA 152

Bely, Andrey . . . . **TCLC 7; PC 11**
  See also Bugayev, Boris Nikolayevich

Benary, Margot
  See Benary-Isbert, Margot

Benary-Isbert, Margot   1889-1979 . . . **CLC 12**
  See also CA 5-8R; 89-92; CANR 4; CLR 12; MAICYA; SATA 2; SATA-Obit 21

Benavente (y Martinez), Jacinto
  1866-1954 . . . . . **TCLC 3; DAM DRAM, MULT**
  See also CA 106; 131; HW; MTCW

Benchley, Peter (Bradford)
  1940- . . . . . **CLC 4, 8; DAM NOV, POP**
  See also AAYA 14; AITN 2; CA 17-20R; CANR 12, 35; MTCW; SATA 3, 89

Benchley, Robert (Charles)
  1889-1945 . . . . **TCLC 1, 55**
  See also CA 105; 153; DLB 11

Benda, Julien   1867-1956 . . . . **TCLC 60**
  See also CA 120; 154

Benedict, Ruth   1887-1948 . . . . **TCLC 60**

Benedikt, Michael   1935- . . . . **CLC 4, 14**
  See also CA 13-16R; CANR 7; DLB 5

Benet, Juan   1927- . . . . **CLC 28**
  See also CA 143

Benet, Stephen Vincent
  1898-1943 . . . . . . **TCLC 7; DAM POET; SSC 10**
  See also CA 104; 152; DLB 4, 48, 102; YABC 1

Benet, William Rose
  1886-1950 . . . . . **TCLC 28; DAM POET**
  See also CA 118; 152; DLB 45

Benford, Gregory (Albert)   1941- . . . . **CLC 52**
  See also CA 69-72; CANR 12, 24, 49; DLBY 82

Bengtsson, Frans (Gunnar)
  1894-1954 . . . . **TCLC 48**

Benjamin, David
  See Slavitt, David R(ytman)

Benjamin, Lois
  See Gould, Lois

Benjamin, Walter   1892-1940 . . . . . . **TCLC 39**

Benn, Gottfried   1886-1956 . . . . **TCLC 3**
  See also CA 106; 153; DLB 56

Bennett, Alan
  1934- . . . **CLC 45, 77; DAB; DAM MST**
  See also CA 103; CANR 35, 55; MTCW

Bennett, (Enoch) Arnold
  1867-1931 . . . . **TCLC 5, 20**
  See also CA 106; 155; CDBLB 1890-1914; DLB 10, 34, 98, 135

Bennett, Elizabeth
  See Mitchell, Margaret (Munnerlyn)

Bennett, George Harold   1930-
  See Bennett, Hal
  See also BW 1; CA 97-100

Bennett, Hal . . . . **CLC 5**
  See also Bennett, George Harold
  See also DLB 33

Bennett, Jay   1912- . . . . **CLC 35**
  See also AAYA 10; CA 69-72; CANR 11, 42; JRDA; SAAS 4; SATA 41, 87; SATA-Brief 27

Bennett, Louise (Simone)
  1919- . . . . . **CLC 28; BLC; DAM MULT**
  See also BW 2; CA 151; DLB 117

Benson, E(dward) F(rederic)
  1867-1940 . . . . **TCLC 27**
  See also CA 114; DLB 135, 153

Benson, Jackson J.   1930- . . . . **CLC 34**
  See also CA 25-28R; DLB 111

Benson, Sally   1900-1972 . . . . **CLC 17**
  See also CA 19-20; 37-40R; CAP 1; SATA 1, 35; SATA-Obit 27

Benson, Stella   1892-1933 . . . . **TCLC 17**
  See also CA 117; 155; DLB 36, 162

Bentham, Jeremy   1748-1832 . . . . . **NCLC 38**
  See also DLB 107, 158

Bentley, E(dmund) C(lerihew)
  1875-1956 . . . . **TCLC 12**
  See also CA 108; DLB 70

Bentley, Eric (Russell)   1916- . . . . **CLC 24**
  See also CA 5-8R; CANR 6; INT CANR-6

Beranger, Pierre Jean de
  1780-1857 . . . . **NCLC 34**

Berdyaev, Nicolas
  See Berdyaev, Nikolai (Aleksandrovich)

Berdyaev, Nikolai (Aleksandrovich)
  1874-1948 . . . . **TCLC 67**
  See also CA 120

Berendt, John (Lawrence)   1939- . . . . **CLC 86**
  See also CA 146

Berger, Colonel
  See Malraux, (Georges-)Andre

Berger, John (Peter)   1926- . . . . . . **CLC 2, 19**
  See also CA 81-84; CANR 51; DLB 14

Berger, Melvin H.   1927- . . . . **CLC 12**
  See also CA 5-8R; CANR 4; CLR 32; SAAS 2; SATA 5, 88

Berger, Thomas (Louis)
  1924- . . . . **CLC 3, 5, 8, 11, 18, 38; DAM NOV**
  See also CA 1-4R; CANR 5, 28, 51; DLB 2; DLBY 80; INT CANR-28; MTCW

Bergman, (Ernst) Ingmar
  1918- . . . . **CLC 16, 72**
  See also CA 81-84; CANR 33

Bergson, Henri   1859-1941 . . . . **TCLC 32**

Bergstein, Eleanor   1938- . . . . **CLC 4**
  See also CA 53-56; CANR 5

Berkoff, Steven   1937- . . . . **CLC 56**
  See also CA 104

Bermant, Chaim (Icyk)   1929- . . . . . . **CLC 40**
  See also CA 57-60; CANR 6, 31, 57

Bern, Victoria
  See Fisher, M(ary) F(rances) K(ennedy)

Bernanos, (Paul Louis) Georges
  1888-1948 . . . . **TCLC 3**
  See also CA 104; 130; DLB 72

Bernard, April   1956- . . . . **CLC 59**
  See also CA 131

Berne, Victoria
  See Fisher, M(ary) F(rances) K(ennedy)

Bernhard, Thomas
  1931-1989 . . . . **CLC 3, 32, 61**
  See also CA 85-88; 127; CANR 32, 57; DLB 85, 124; MTCW

Berriault, Gina   1926- . . . . **CLC 54**
  See also CA 116; 129; DLB 130

Berrigan, Daniel   1921- . . . . **CLC 4**
  See also CA 33-36R; CAAS 1; CANR 11, 43; DLB 5

Berrigan, Edmund Joseph Michael, Jr.
  1934-1983
  See Berrigan, Ted
  See also CA 61-64; 110; CANR 14

Berrigan, Ted . . . . **CLC 37**
  See also Berrigan, Edmund Joseph Michael, Jr.
  See also DLB 5, 169

Berry, Charles Edward Anderson   1931-
  See Berry, Chuck
  See also CA 115

Berry, Chuck . . . . **CLC 17**
  See also Berry, Charles Edward Anderson

Berry, Jonas
  See Ashbery, John (Lawrence)

Berry, Wendell (Erdman)
  1934- . . . . **CLC 4, 6, 8, 27, 46; DAM POET**
  See also AITN 1; CA 73-76; CANR 50; DLB 5, 6

Berryman, John
  1914-1972 . . . . . . **CLC 1, 2, 3, 4, 6, 8, 10, 13, 25, 62; DAM POET**
  See also CA 13-16; CABS 2; CANR 35; CAP 1; CDALB 1941-1968; DLB 48; MTCW

Bertolucci, Bernardo   1940- . . . . **CLC 16**
  See also CA 106

Bertrand, Aloysius   1807-1841 . . . . **NCLC 31**

Bertran de Born   c. 1140-1215 . . . . . **CMLC 5**

Besant, Annie (Wood)   1847-1933 . . . **TCLC 9**
  See also CA 105

Bodker, Cecil   1927- .... **CLC 21**
See also CA 73-76; CANR 13, 44; CLR 23;
MAICYA; SATA 14

Boell, Heinrich (Theodor)
1917-1985 .... **CLC 2, 3, 6, 9, 11, 15, 27,**
32, 72; DA; DAB; DAC; DAM MST,
NOV; SSC 23; WLC
See also CA 21-24R; 116; CANR 24;
DLB 69; DLBY 85; MTCW

Boerne, Alfred
See Doeblin, Alfred

Boethius   480(?)-524(?) .... **CMLC 15**
See also DLB 115

Bogan, Louise
1897-1970 .... **CLC 4, 39, 46, 93;**
DAM POET; PC 12
See also CA 73-76; 25-28R; CANR 33;
DLB 45, 169; MTCW

Bogarde, Dirk .... **CLC 19**
See also Van Den Bogarde, Derek Jules
Gaspard Ulric Niven
See also DLB 14

Bogosian, Eric   1953- .... **CLC 45**
See also CA 138

Bograd, Larry   1953- .... **CLC 35**
See also CA 93-96; CANR 57; SAAS 21;
SATA 33, 89

Boiardo, Matteo Maria   1441-1494 .... **LC 6**

Boileau-Despreaux, Nicolas
1636-1711 .... **LC 3**

Bojer, Johan   1872-1959 .... **TCLC 64**

Boland, Eavan (Aisling)
1944- .... **CLC 40, 67; DAM POET**
See also CA 143; DLB 40

Bolt, Lee
See Faust, Frederick (Schiller)

Bolt, Robert (Oxton)
1924-1995 ...... **CLC 14; DAM DRAM**
See also CA 17-20R; 147; CANR 35;
DLB 13; MTCW

Bombet, Louis-Alexandre-Cesar
See Stendhal

Bomkauf
See Kaufman, Bob (Garnell)

Bonaventura .... **NCLC 35**
See also DLB 90

Bond, Edward
1934- ... **CLC 4, 6, 13, 23; DAM DRAM**
See also CA 25-28R; CANR 38; DLB 13;
MTCW

Bonham, Frank   1914-1989 .... **CLC 12**
See also AAYA 1; CA 9-12R; CANR 4, 36;
JRDA; MAICYA; SAAS 3; SATA 1, 49;
SATA-Obit 62

Bonnefoy, Yves
1923- ...... **CLC 9, 15, 58; DAM MST,**
POET
See also CA 85-88; CANR 33; MTCW

Bontemps, Arna(ud Wendell)
1902-1973 .... **CLC 1, 18; BLC;**
DAM MULT, NOV, POET
See also BW 1; CA 1-4R; 41-44R; CANR 4,
35; CLR 6; DLB 48, 51; JRDA;
MAICYA; MTCW; SATA 2, 44;
SATA-Obit 24

Booth, Martin   1944- .... **CLC 13**
See also CA 93-96; CAAS 2

Booth, Philip   1925- .... **CLC 23**
See also CA 5-8R; CANR 5; DLBY 82

Booth, Wayne C(layson)   1921- ..... **CLC 24**
See also CA 1-4R; CAAS 5; CANR 3, 43;
DLB 67

Borchert, Wolfgang   1921-1947 ..... **TCLC 5**
See also CA 104; DLB 69, 124

Borel, Petrus   1809-1859 .... **NCLC 41**

Borges, Jorge Luis
1899-1986 ... **CLC 1, 2, 3, 4, 6, 8, 9, 10,**
13, 19, 44, 48, 83; DA; DAB; DAC;
DAM MST, MULT; HLC; SSC 4; WLC
See also CA 19; CA 21-24R; CANR 19,
33; DLB 113; DLBY 86; HW; MTCW

Borowski, Tadeusz   1922-1951 ...... **TCLC 9**
See also CA 106; 154

Borrow, George (Henry)
1803-1881 .... **NCLC 9**
See also DLB 21, 55, 166

Bosman, Herman Charles
1905-1951 .... **TCLC 49**

Bosschere, Jean de   1878(?)-1953... **TCLC 19**
See also CA 115

Boswell, James
1740-1795 ...... **LC 4; DA; DAB; DAC;**
DAM MST; WLC
See also CDBLB 1660-1789; DLB 104, 142

Bottoms, David   1949- .... **CLC 53**
See also CA 105; CANR 22; DLB 120;
DLBY 83

Boucicault, Dion   1820-1890 ...... **NCLC 41**

Boucolon, Maryse   1937(?)-
See Conde, Maryse
See also CA 110; CANR 30, 53

Bourget, Paul (Charles Joseph)
1852-1935 .... **TCLC 12**
See also CA 107; DLB 123

Bourjaily, Vance (Nye)   1922- .... **CLC 8, 62**
See also CA 1-4R; CAAS 1; CANR 2;
DLB 2, 143

Bourne, Randolph S(illiman)
1886-1918 .... **TCLC 16**
See also CA 117; 155; DLB 63

Bova, Ben(jamin William)   1932- .... **CLC 45**
See also AAYA 16; CA 5-8R; CAAS 18;
CANR 11, 56; CLR 3; DLBY 81;
INT CANR-11; MAICYA; MTCW;
SATA 6, 68

Bowen, Elizabeth (Dorothea Cole)
1899-1973 ...... **CLC 1, 3, 6, 11, 15, 22;**
DAM NOV; SSC 3
See also CA 17-18; 41-44R; CANR 35;
CAP 2; CDBLB 1945-1960; DLB 15, 162;
MTCW

Bowering, George   1935- .... **CLC 15, 47**
See also CA 21-24R; CAAS 16; CANR 10;
DLB 53

Bowering, Marilyn R(uthe)   1949- ... **CLC 32**
See also CA 101; CANR 49

Bowers, Edgar   1924- .... **CLC 9**
See also CA 5-8R; CANR 24; DLB 5

Bowie, David .... **CLC 17**
See also Jones, David Robert

Bowles, Jane (Sydney)
1917-1973 .... **CLC 3, 68**
See also CA 19-20; 41-44R; CAP 2

Bowles, Paul (Frederick)
1910- .... **CLC 1, 2, 19, 53; SSC 3**
See also CA 1-4R; CAAS 1; CANR 1, 19,
50; DLB 5, 6; MTCW

Box, Edgar
See Vidal, Gore

Boyd, Nancy
See Millay, Edna St. Vincent

Boyd, William   1952- .... **CLC 28, 53, 70**
See also CA 114; 120; CANR 51

Boyle, Kay
1902-1992 ..... **CLC 1, 5, 19, 58; SSC 5**
See also CA 13-16R; 140; CAAS 1;
CANR 29; DLB 4, 9, 48, 86; DLBY 93;
MTCW

Boyle, Mark
See Kienzle, William X(avier)

Boyle, Patrick   1905-1982 .... **CLC 19**
See also CA 127

Boyle, T. C.   1948-
See Boyle, T(homas) Coraghessan

Boyle, T(homas) Coraghessan
1948- ..... **CLC 36, 55, 90; DAM POP;**
SSC 16
See also BEST 90:4; CA 120; CANR 44;
DLBY 86

Boz
See Dickens, Charles (John Huffam)

Brackenridge, Hugh Henry
1748-1816 .... **NCLC 7**
See also DLB 11, 37

Bradbury, Edward P.
See Moorcock, Michael (John)

Bradbury, Malcolm (Stanley)
1932- .... **CLC 32, 61; DAM NOV**
See also CA 1-4R; CANR 1, 33; DLB 14;
MTCW

Bradbury, Ray (Douglas)
1920- ..... **CLC 1, 3, 10, 15, 42, 98; DA;**
DAB; DAC; DAM MST, NOV, POP;
WLC
See also AAYA 15; AITN 1, 2; CA 1-4R;
CANR 2, 30; CDALB 1968-1988; DLB 2,
8; INT CANR-30; MTCW; SATA 11, 64

Bradford, Gamaliel   1863-1932..... **TCLC 36**
See also DLB 17

Bradley, David (Henry, Jr.)
1950- ..... **CLC 23; BLC; DAM MULT**
See also BW 1; CA 104; CANR 26; DLB 33

Bradley, John Ed(mund, Jr.)
1958- .... **CLC 55**
See also CA 139

Bradley, Marion Zimmer
1930- .... **CLC 30; DAM POP**
See also AAYA 9; CA 57-60; CAAS 10;
CANR 7, 31, 51; DLB 8; MTCW;
SATA 90

Bradstreet, Anne
1612(?)-1672 ...... **LC 4, 30; DA; DAC;**
DAM MST, POET; PC 10
See also CDALB 1640-1865; DLB 24

Brady, Joan   1939- .... **CLC 86**
See also CA 141

Bragg, Melvyn 1939- .... **CLC 10**
See also BEST 89:3; CA 57-60; CANR 10,
48; DLB 14

Braine, John (Gerard)
1922-1986 .... **CLC 1, 3, 41**
See also CA 1-4R; 120; CANR 1, 33;
CDBLB 1945-1960; DLB 15; DLBY 86;
MTCW

Brammer, William 1930(?)-1978 .... **CLC 31**
See also CA 77-80

Brancati, Vitaliano 1907-1954 ..... **TCLC 12**
See also CA 109

Brancato, Robin F(idler) 1936- ..... **CLC 35**
See also AAYA 9; CA 69-72; CANR 11,
45; CLR 32; JRDA; SAAS 9; SATA 23

Brand, Max
See Faust, Frederick (Schiller)

Brand, Millen 1906-1980 .... **CLC 7**
See also CA 21-24R; 97-100

Branden, Barbara .... **CLC 44**
See also CA 148

Brandes, Georg (Morris Cohen)
1842-1927 .... **TCLC 10**
See also CA 105

Brandys, Kazimierz 1916- .... **CLC 62**

Branley, Franklyn M(ansfield)
1915- .... **CLC 21**
See also CA 33-36R; CANR 14, 39;
CLR 13; MAICYA; SAAS 16; SATA 4,
68

Brathwaite, Edward Kamau
1930- .... **CLC 11; DAM POET**
See also BW 2; CA 25-28R; CANR 11, 26,
47; DLB 125

Brautigan, Richard (Gary)
1935-1984 .... **CLC 1, 3, 5, 9, 12, 34, 42;**
DAM NOV
See also CA 53-56; 113; CANR 34; DLB 2,
5; DLBY 80, 84; MTCW; SATA 56

Brave Bird, Mary 1953-
See Crow Dog, Mary (Ellen)
See also NNAL

Braverman, Kate 1950- .... **CLC 67**
See also CA 89-92

Brecht, Bertolt
1898-1956 ...... **TCLC 1, 6, 13, 35; DA;**
DAB; DAC; DAM DRAM, MST; DC 3;
WLC
See also CA 104; 133; DLB 56, 124; MTCW

Brecht, Eugen Berthold Friedrich
See Brecht, Bertolt

Bremer, Fredrika 1801-1865 ..... **NCLC 11**

Brennan, Christopher John
1870-1932 .... **TCLC 17**
See also CA 117

Brennan, Maeve 1917- .... **CLC 5**
See also CA 81-84

Brentano, Clemens (Maria)
1778-1842 .... **NCLC 1**
See also DLB 90

Brent of Bin Bin
See Franklin, (Stella Maraia Sarah) Miles

Brenton, Howard 1942- .... **CLC 31**
See also CA 69-72; CANR 33; DLB 13;
MTCW

Breslin, James 1930-
See Breslin, Jimmy
See also CA 73-76; CANR 31; DAM NOV;
MTCW

Breslin, Jimmy .... **CLC 4, 43**
See also Breslin, James
See also AITN 1

Bresson, Robert 1901- .... **CLC 16**
See also CA 110; CANR 49

Breton, Andre
1896-1966 ..... **CLC 2, 9, 15, 54; PC 15**
See also CA 19-20; 25-28R; CANR 40;
CAP 2; DLB 65; MTCW

Breytenbach, Breyten
1939(?)- ...... **CLC 23, 37; DAM POET**
See also CA 113; 129

Bridgers, Sue Ellen 1942- .... **CLC 26**
See also AAYA 8; CA 65-68; CANR 11,
36; CLR 18; DLB 52; JRDA; MAICYA;
SAAS 1; SATA 22, 90

Bridges, Robert (Seymour)
1844-1930 .... **TCLC 1; DAM POET**
See also CA 104; 152; CDBLB 1890-1914;
DLB 19, 98

Bridie, James .... **TCLC 3**
See also Mavor, Osborne Henry
See also DLB 10

Brin, David 1950- .... **CLC 34**
See also CA 102; CANR 24;
INT CANR-24; SATA 65

Brink, Andre (Philippus)
1935- .... **CLC 18, 36**
See also CA 104; CANR 39; INT 103;
MTCW

Brinsmead, H(esba) F(ay) 1922- .... **CLC 21**
See also CA 21-24R; CANR 10; MAICYA;
SAAS 5; SATA 18, 78

Brittain, Vera (Mary)
1893(?)-1970 .... **CLC 23**
See also CA 13-16; 25-28R; CAP 1; MTCW

Broch, Hermann 1886-1951 ...... **TCLC 20**
See also CA 117; DLB 85, 124

Brock, Rose
See Hansen, Joseph

Brodkey, Harold (Roy) 1930-1996 .. **CLC 56**
See also CA 111; 151; DLB 130

Brodsky, Iosif Alexandrovich 1940-1996
See Brodsky, Joseph
See also AITN 1; CA 41-44R; 151;
CANR 37; DAM POET; MTCW

Brodsky, Joseph
1940-1996 .. **CLC 4, 6, 13, 36, 100; PC 9**
See also Brodsky, Iosif Alexandrovich

Brodsky, Michael Mark 1948- ..... **CLC 19**
See also CA 102; CANR 18, 41

Bromell, Henry 1947- .... **CLC 5**
See also CA 53-56; CANR 9

Bromfield, Louis (Brucker)
1896-1956 .... **TCLC 11**
See also CA 107; 155; DLB 4, 9, 86

Broner, E(sther) M(asserman)
1930- .... **CLC 19**
See also CA 17-20R; CANR 8, 25; DLB 28

Bronk, William 1918- .... **CLC 10**
See also CA 89-92; CANR 23; DLB 165

Bronstein, Lev Davidovich
See Trotsky, Leon

Bronte, Anne 1820-1849 .... **NCLC 4**
See also DLB 21

Bronte, Charlotte
1816-1855 ..... **NCLC 3, 8, 33, 58; DA;**
DAB; DAC; DAM MST, NOV; WLC
See also AAYA 17; CDBLB 1832-1890;
DLB 21, 159

Bronte, Emily (Jane)
1818-1848 .... **NCLC 16, 35; DA; DAB;**
DAC; DAM MST, NOV, POET; PC 8;
WLC
See also AAYA 17; CDBLB 1832-1890;
DLB 21, 32

Brooke, Frances 1724-1789 .... **LC 6**
See also DLB 39, 99

Brooke, Henry 1703(?)-1783 .... **LC 1**
See also DLB 39

Brooke, Rupert (Chawner)
1887-1915 .... **TCLC 2, 7; DA; DAB;**
DAC; DAM MST, POET; WLC
See also CA 104; 132; CDBLB 1914-1945;
DLB 19; MTCW

Brooke-Haven, P.
See Wodehouse, P(elham) G(renville)

Brooke-Rose, Christine 1926- ...... **CLC 40**
See also CA 13-16R; DLB 14

Brookner, Anita
1928- .... **CLC 32, 34, 51; DAB;**
DAM POP
See also CA 114; 120; CANR 37, 56;
DLBY 87; MTCW

Brooks, Cleanth 1906-1994 ..... **CLC 24, 86**
See also CA 17-20R; 145; CANR 33, 35;
DLB 63; DLBY 94; INT CANR-35;
MTCW

Brooks, George
See Baum, L(yman) Frank

Brooks, Gwendolyn
1917- ...... **CLC 1, 2, 4, 5, 15, 49; BLC;**
DA; DAC; DAM MST, MULT, POET;
PC 7; WLC
See also AAYA 20; AITN 1; BW 2;
CA 1-4R; CANR 1, 27, 52;
CDALB 1941-1968; CLR 27; DLB 5, 76,
165; MTCW; SATA 6

Brooks, Mel .... **CLC 12**
See also Kaminsky, Melvin
See also AAYA 13; DLB 26

Brooks, Peter 1938- .... **CLC 34**
See also CA 45-48; CANR 1

Brooks, Van Wyck 1886-1963 ...... **CLC 29**
See also CA 1-4R; CANR 6; DLB 45, 63,
103

Brophy, Brigid (Antonia)
1929-1995 .... **CLC 6, 11, 29**
See also CA 5-8R; 149; CAAS 4; CANR 25,
53; DLB 14; MTCW

Brosman, Catharine Savage 1934- .... **CLC 9**
See also CA 61-64; CANR 21, 46

Brother Antoninus
See Everson, William (Oliver)

Broughton, T(homas) Alan 1936- ... **CLC 19**
See also CA 45-48; CANR 2, 23, 48

Broumas, Olga 1949- . . . . **CLC 10, 73**
See also CA 85-88; CANR 20

Brown, Alan 1951- . . . . **CLC 99**

Brown, Charles Brockden
1771-1810 . . . . **NCLC 22**
See also CDALB 1640-1865; DLB 37, 59,
73

Brown, Christy 1932-1981 . . . . **CLC 63**
See also CA 105; 104; DLB 14

Brown, Claude
1937- . . . . . **CLC 30; BLC; DAM MULT**
See also AAYA 7; BW 1; CA 73-76

Brown, Dee (Alexander)
1908- . . . . **CLC 18, 47; DAM POP**
See also CA 13-16R; CAAS 6; CANR 11,
45; DLBY 80; MTCW; SATA 5

Brown, George
See Wertmueller, Lina

Brown, George Douglas
1869-1902 . . . . **TCLC 28**

Brown, George Mackay
1921-1996 . . . . **CLC 5, 48, 100**
See also CA 21-24R; 151; CAAS 6;
CANR 12, 37; DLB 14, 27, 139; MTCW;
SATA 35

Brown, (William) Larry 1951- . . . . . . **CLC 73**
See also CA 130; 134; INT 133

Brown, Moses
See Barrett, William (Christopher)

Brown, Rita Mae
1944- . . . . . **CLC 18, 43, 79; DAM NOV,**
                                              POP
See also CA 45-48; CANR 2, 11, 35;
INT CANR-11; MTCW

Brown, Roderick (Langmere) Haig-
See Haig-Brown, Roderick (Langmere)

Brown, Rosellen 1939- . . . . **CLC 32**
See also CA 77-80; CAAS 10; CANR 14, 44

Brown, Sterling Allen
1901-1989 . . . . **CLC 1, 23, 59; BLC;**
                                     DAM MULT, POET
See also BW 1; CA 85-88; 127; CANR 26;
DLB 48, 51, 63; MTCW

Brown, Will
See Ainsworth, William Harrison

Brown, William Wells
1813-1884 . . . . **NCLC 2; BLC;**
                                        DAM MULT; DC 1
See also DLB 3, 50

Browne, (Clyde) Jackson 1948(?)- . . . **CLC 21**
See also CA 120

Browning, Elizabeth Barrett
1806-1861 . . . . . **NCLC 1, 16; DA; DAB;**
                          DAC; DAM MST, POET; PC 6; WLC
See also CDBLB 1832-1890; DLB 32

Browning, Robert
1812-1889 . . . . **NCLC 19; DA; DAB;**
                              DAC; DAM MST, POET; PC 2
See also CDBLB 1832-1890; DLB 32, 163;
YABC 1

Browning, Tod 1882-1962 . . . . **CLC 16**
See also CA 141; 117

Brownson, Orestes (Augustus)
1803-1876 . . . . **NCLC 50**

Bruccoli, Matthew J(oseph) 1931- . . **CLC 34**
See also CA 9-12R; CANR 7; DLB 103

Bruce, Lenny . . . . **CLC 21**
See also Schneider, Leonard Alfred

Bruin, John
See Brutus, Dennis

Brulard, Henri
See Stendhal

Brulls, Christian
See Simenon, Georges (Jacques Christian)

Brunner, John (Kilian Houston)
1934-1995 . . . . . . **CLC 8, 10; DAM POP**
See also CA 1-4R; 149; CAAS 8; CANR 2,
37; MTCW

Bruno, Giordano 1548-1600 . . . . **LC 27**

Brutus, Dennis
1924- . . . . . **CLC 43; BLC; DAM MULT,**
                                                      POET
See also BW 2; CA 49-52; CAAS 14;
CANR 2, 27, 42; DLB 117

Bryan, C(ourtlandt) D(ixon) B(arnes)
1936- . . . . **CLC 29**
See also CA 73-76; CANR 13;
INT CANR-13

Bryan, Michael
See Moore, Brian

Bryant, William Cullen
1794-1878 . . . . . **NCLC 6, 46; DA; DAB;**
                                   DAC; DAM MST, POET
See also CDALB 1640-1865; DLB 3, 43, 59

Bryusov, Valery Yakovlevich
1873-1924 . . . . **TCLC 10**
See also CA 107; 155

Buchan, John
1875-1940 . . . . **TCLC 41; DAB;**
                                               DAM POP
See also CA 108; 145; DLB 34, 70, 156;
YABC 2

Buchanan, George 1506-1582 . . . . **LC 4**

Buchheim, Lothar-Guenther 1918- . . . **CLC 6**
See also CA 85-88

Buchner, (Karl) Georg
1813-1837 . . . . **NCLC 26**

Buchwald, Art(hur) 1925- . . . . **CLC 33**
See also AITN 1; CA 5-8R; CANR 21;
MTCW; SATA 10

Buck, Pearl S(ydenstricker)
1892-1973 . . . . **CLC 7, 11, 18; DA; DAB;**
                                      DAC; DAM MST, NOV
See also AITN 1; CA 1-4R; 41-44R;
CANR 1, 34; DLB 9, 102; MTCW;
SATA 1, 25

Buckler, Ernest
1908-1984 . . **CLC 13; DAC; DAM MST**
See also CA 11-12; 114; CAP 1; DLB 68;
SATA 47

Buckley, Vincent (Thomas)
1925-1988 . . . . **CLC 57**
See also CA 101

Buckley, William F(rank), Jr.
1925- . . . . **CLC 7, 18, 37; DAM POP**
See also AITN 1; CA 1-4R; CANR 1, 24,
53; DLB 137; DLBY 80; INT CANR-24;
MTCW

Buechner, (Carl) Frederick
1926- . . . . . . **CLC 2, 4, 6, 9; DAM NOV**
See also CA 13-16R; CANR 11, 39;
DLBY 80; INT CANR-11; MTCW

Buell, John (Edward) 1927- . . . . **CLC 10**
See also CA 1-4R; DLB 53

Buero Vallejo, Antonio 1916- . . . **CLC 15, 46**
See also CA 106; CANR 24, 49; HW;
MTCW

Bufalino, Gesualdo 1920(?)- . . . . **CLC 74**

Bugayev, Boris Nikolayevich 1880-1934
See Bely, Andrey
See also CA 104

Bukowski, Charles
1920-1994 . . . . **CLC 2, 5, 9, 41, 82;**
                                        DAM NOV, POET
See also CA 17-20R; 144; CANR 40;
DLB 5, 130, 169; MTCW

Bulgakov, Mikhail (Afanas'evich)
1891-1940 . . . . **TCLC 2, 16;**
                                 DAM DRAM, NOV; SSC 18
See also CA 105; 152

Bulgya, Alexander Alexandrovich
1901-1956 . . . . **TCLC 53**
See also Fadeyev, Alexander
See also CA 117

Bullins, Ed
1935- . . . . **CLC 1, 5, 7; BLC;**
                               DAM DRAM, MULT; DC 6
See also BW 2; CA 49-52; CAAS 16;
CANR 24, 46; DLB 7, 38; MTCW

Bulwer-Lytton, Edward (George Earle Lytton)
1803-1873 . . . . **NCLC 1, 45**
See also DLB 21

Bunin, Ivan Alexeyevich
1870-1953 . . . . **TCLC 6; SSC 5**
See also CA 104

Bunting, Basil
1900-1985 . . . . **CLC 10, 39, 47;**
                                                DAM POET
See also CA 53-56; 115; CANR 7; DLB 20

Bunuel, Luis
1900-1983 . . . . **CLC 16, 80;**
                                         DAM MULT; HLC
See also CA 101; 110; CANR 32; HW

Bunyan, John
1628-1688 . . . . . . **LC 4; DA; DAB; DAC;**
                                   DAM MST; WLC
See also CDBLB 1660-1789; DLB 39

Burckhardt, Jacob (Christoph)
1818-1897 . . . . **NCLC 49**

Burford, Eleanor
See Hibbert, Eleanor Alice Burford

Burgess, Anthony
. **CLC 1, 2, 4, 5, 8, 10, 13, 15, 22, 40, 62,**
                                            81, 94; DAB
See also Wilson, John (Anthony) Burgess
See also AITN 1; CDBLB 1960 to Present;
DLB 14

Burke, Edmund
1729(?)-1797 . . . . . . **LC 7, 36; DA; DAB;**
                                 DAC; DAM MST; WLC
See also DLB 104

Campos, Alvaro de
See Pessoa, Fernando (Antonio Nogueira)

Camus, Albert
1913-1960 .... **CLC 1, 2, 4, 9, 11, 14, 32, 63, 69; DA; DAB; DAC; DAM DRAM, MST, NOV; DC 2; SSC 9; WLC**
See also CA 89-92; DLB 72; MTCW

Canby, Vincent 1924- .... **CLC 13**
See also CA 81-84

Cancale
See Desnos, Robert

Canetti, Elias
1905-1994 .... **CLC 3, 14, 25, 75, 86**
See also CA 21-24R; 146; CANR 23; DLB 85, 124; MTCW

Canin, Ethan 1960- .... **CLC 55**
See also CA 131; 135

Cannon, Curt
See Hunter, Evan

Cape, Judith
See Page, P(atricia) K(athleen)

Capek, Karel
1890-1938 ...... **TCLC 6, 37; DA; DAB; DAC; DAM DRAM, MST, NOV; DC 1; WLC**
See also CA 104; 140

Capote, Truman
1924-1984 ...... **CLC 1, 3, 8, 13, 19, 34, 38, 58; DA; DAB; DAC; DAM MST, NOV, POP; SSC 2; WLC**
See also CA 5-8R; 113; CANR 18; CDALB 1941-1968; DLB 2; DLBY 80, 84; MTCW; SATA 91

Capra, Frank 1897-1991 .... **CLC 16**
See also CA 61-64; 135

Caputo, Philip 1941- .... **CLC 32**
See also CA 73-76; CANR 40

Card, Orson Scott
1951- ...... **CLC 44, 47, 50; DAM POP**
See also AAYA 11; CA 102; CANR 27, 47; INT CANR-27; MTCW; SATA 83

Cardenal, Ernesto
1925- .... **CLC 31; DAM MULT, POET; HLC**
See also CA 49-52; CANR 2, 32; HW; MTCW

Cardozo, Benjamin N(athan)
1870-1938 .... **TCLC 65**
See also CA 117

Carducci, Giosue 1835-1907 ...... **TCLC 32**

Carew, Thomas 1595(?)-1640 .... **LC 13**
See also DLB 126

Carey, Ernestine Gilbreth 1908- .... **CLC 17**
See also CA 5-8R; SATA 2

Carey, Peter 1943- .... **CLC 40, 55, 96**
See also CA 123; 127; CANR 53; INT 127; MTCW

Carleton, William 1794-1869 ...... **NCLC 3**
See also DLB 159

Carlisle, Henry (Coffin) 1926- ...... **CLC 33**
See also CA 13-16R; CANR 15

Carlsen, Chris
See Holdstock, Robert P.

Carlson, Ron(ald F.) 1947- .... **CLC 54**
See also CA 105; CANR 27

Carlyle, Thomas
1795-1881 ...... **NCLC 22; DA; DAB; DAC; DAM MST**
See also CDBLB 1789-1832; DLB 55; 144

Carman, (William) Bliss
1861-1929 .... **TCLC 7; DAC**
See also CA 104; 152; DLB 92

Carnegie, Dale 1888-1955 .... **TCLC 53**

Carossa, Hans 1878-1956 .... **TCLC 48**
See also DLB 66

Carpenter, Don(ald Richard)
1931-1995 .... **CLC 41**
See also CA 45-48; 149; CANR 1

Carpentier (y Valmont), Alejo
1904-1980 .... **CLC 8, 11, 38; DAM MULT; HLC**
See also CA 65-68; 97-100; CANR 11; DLB 113; HW

Carr, Caleb 1955(?)- .... **CLC 86**
See also CA 147

Carr, Emily 1871-1945 .... **TCLC 32**
See also DLB 68

Carr, John Dickson 1906-1977 ...... **CLC 3**
See also CA 49-52; 69-72; CANR 3, 33; MTCW

Carr, Philippa
See Hibbert, Eleanor Alice Burford

Carr, Virginia Spencer 1929- .... **CLC 34**
See also CA 61-64; DLB 111

Carrere, Emmanuel 1957- .... **CLC 89**

Carrier, Roch
1937- ... **CLC 13, 78; DAC; DAM MST**
See also CA 130; DLB 53

Carroll, James P. 1943(?)- .... **CLC 38**
See also CA 81-84

Carroll, Jim 1951- .... **CLC 35**
See also AAYA 17; CA 45-48; CANR 42

Carroll, Lewis .... **NCLC 2, 53; WLC**
See also Dodgson, Charles Lutwidge
See also CDBLB 1832-1890; CLR 2, 18; DLB 18, 163; JRDA

Carroll, Paul Vincent 1900-1968 .... **CLC 10**
See also CA 9-12R; 25-28R; DLB 10

Carruth, Hayden
1921- ...... **CLC 4, 7, 10, 18, 84; PC 10**
See also CA 9-12R; CANR 4, 38; DLB 5, 165; INT CANR-4; MTCW; SATA 47

Carson, Rachel Louise
1907-1964 .... **CLC 71; DAM POP**
See also CA 77-80; CANR 35; MTCW; SATA 23

Carter, Angela (Olive)
1940-1992 ...... **CLC 5, 41, 76; SSC 13**
See also CA 53-56; 136; CANR 12, 36; DLB 14; MTCW; SATA 66; SATA-Obit 70

Carter, Nick
See Smith, Martin Cruz

Carver, Raymond
1938-1988 .... **CLC 22, 36, 53, 55; DAM NOV; SSC 8**
See also CA 33-36R; 126; CANR 17, 34; DLB 130; DLBY 84, 88; MTCW

Cary, Elizabeth, Lady Falkland
1585-1639 .... **LC 30**

Cary, (Arthur) Joyce (Lunel)
1888-1957 .... **TCLC 1, 29**
See also CA 104; CDBLB 1914-1945; DLB 15, 100

Casanova de Seingalt, Giovanni Jacopo
1725-1798 .... **LC 13**

Casares, Adolfo Bioy
See Bioy Casares, Adolfo

Casely-Hayford, J(oseph) E(phraim)
1866-1930 .... **TCLC 24; BLC; DAM MULT**
See also BW 2; CA 123; 152

Casey, John (Dudley) 1939- .... **CLC 59**
See also BEST 90:2; CA 69-72; CANR 23

Casey, Michael 1947- .... **CLC 2**
See also CA 65-68; DLB 5

Casey, Patrick
See Thurman, Wallace (Henry)

Casey, Warren (Peter) 1935-1988 ... **CLC 12**
See also CA 101; 127; INT 101

Casona, Alejandro .... **CLC 49**
See also Alvarez, Alejandro Rodriguez

Cassavetes, John 1929-1989 .... **CLC 20**
See also CA 85-88; 127

Cassian, Nina 1924- .... **PC 17**

Cassill, R(onald) V(erlin) 1919- ... **CLC 4, 23**
See also CA 9-12R; CAAS 1; CANR 7, 45; DLB 6

Cassirer, Ernst 1874-1945 .... **TCLC 61**

Cassity, (Allen) Turner 1929- .... **CLC 6, 42**
See also CA 17-20R; CAAS 8; CANR 11; DLB 105

Castaneda, Carlos 1931(?)- .... **CLC 12**
See also CA 25-28R; CANR 32; HW; MTCW

Castedo, Elena 1937- .... **CLC 65**
See also CA 132

Castedo-Ellerman, Elena
See Castedo, Elena

Castellanos, Rosario
1925-1974 ...... **CLC 66; DAM MULT; HLC**
See also CA 131; 53-56; DLB 113; HW

Castelvetro, Lodovico 1505-1571 ..... **LC 12**

Castiglione, Baldassare 1478-1529 ... **LC 12**

Castle, Robert
See Hamilton, Edmond

Castro, Guillen de 1569-1631 .... **LC 19**

Castro, Rosalia de
1837-1885 ...... **NCLC 3; DAM MULT**

Cather, Willa
See Cather, Willa Sibert

Cather, Willa Sibert
1873-1947 .... **TCLC 1, 11, 31; DA; DAB; DAC; DAM MST, NOV; SSC 2; WLC**
See also CA 104; 128; CDALB 1865-1917; DLB 9, 54, 78; DLBD 1; MTCW; SATA 30

Cato, Marcus Porcius
234B.C.-149B.C. .... **CMLC 21**

Catton, (Charles) Bruce
　　1899-1978 . . . . CLC 35
　　See also AITN 1; CA 5-8R; 81-84;
　　CANR 7; DLB 17; SATA 2;
　　SATA-Obit 24

Catullus　c. 84B.C.-c. 54B.C. . . . . . CMLC 18

Cauldwell, Frank
　　See King, Francis (Henry)

Caunitz, William J.　1933-1996 . . . . . CLC 34
　　See also BEST 89:3; CA 125; 130; 152;
　　INT 130

Causley, Charles (Stanley)　1917-. . . . . CLC 7
　　See also CA 9-12R; CANR 5, 35; CLR 30;
　　DLB 27; MTCW; SATA 3, 66

Caute, David　1936-. . . . CLC 29; DAM NOV
　　See also CA 1-4R; CAAS 4; CANR 1, 33;
　　DLB 14

Cavafy, C(onstantine) P(eter)
　　1863-1933 . . . . TCLC 2, 7; DAM POET
　　See also Kavafis, Konstantinos Petrou
　　See also CA 148

Cavallo, Evelyn
　　See Spark, Muriel (Sarah)

Cavanna, Betty . . . . CLC 12
　　See also Harrison, Elizabeth Cavanna
　　See also JRDA; MAICYA; SAAS 4;
　　SATA 1, 30

Cavendish, Margaret Lucas
　　1623-1673 . . . . LC 30
　　See also DLB 131

Caxton, William　1421(?)-1491(?). . . . . LC 17
　　See also DLB 170

Cayrol, Jean　1911-. . . . . CLC 11
　　See also CA 89-92; DLB 83

Cela, Camilo Jose
　　1916-. . . . . CLC 4, 13, 59; DAM MULT;
　　　　　　　　　　　　　　　　　　　　HLC
　　See also BEST 90:2; CA 21-24R; CAAS 10;
　　CANR 21, 32; DLBY 89; HW; MTCW

Celan, Paul . . . . . . CLC 10, 19, 53, 82; PC 10
　　See also Antschel, Paul
　　See also DLB 69

Celine, Louis-Ferdinand
　　. . . . . CLC 1, 3, 4, 7, 9, 15, 47
　　See also Destouches, Louis-Ferdinand
　　See also DLB 72

Cellini, Benvenuto　1500-1571 . . . . LC 7

Cendrars, Blaise . . . . CLC 18
　　See also Sauser-Hall, Frederic

Cernuda (y Bidon), Luis
　　1902-1963 . . . . CLC 54; DAM POET
　　See also CA 131; 89-92; DLB 134; HW

Cervantes (Saavedra), Miguel de
　　1547-1616 . . . . LC 6, 23; DA; DAB;
　　　　DAC; DAM MST, NOV; SSC 12; WLC

Cesaire, Aime (Fernand)
　　1913-. . . . . CLC 19, 32; BLC;
　　　　　　　　　　　　　　　　DAM MULT, POET
　　See also BW 2; CA 65-68; CANR 24, 43;
　　MTCW

Chabon, Michael　1963-. . . . . CLC 55
　　See also CA 139; CANR 57

Chabrol, Claude　1930-. . . . . CLC 16
　　See also CA 110

Challans, Mary　1905-1983
　　See Renault, Mary
　　See also CA 81-84; 111; SATA 23;
　　SATA-Obit 36

Challis, George
　　See Faust, Frederick (Schiller)

Chambers, Aidan　1934-. . . . . CLC 35
　　See also CA 25-28R; CANR 12, 31; JRDA;
　　MAICYA; SAAS 12; SATA 1, 69

Chambers, James　1948-
　　See Cliff, Jimmy
　　See also CA 124

Chambers, Jessie
　　See Lawrence, D(avid) H(erbert Richards)

Chambers, Robert W.　1865-1933. . . TCLC 41

Chandler, Raymond (Thornton)
　　1888-1959 . . . . TCLC 1, 7; SSC 23
　　See also CA 104; 129; CDALB 1929-1941;
　　DLBD 6; MTCW

Chang, Jung　1952-. . . . . CLC 71
　　See also CA 142

Channing, William Ellery
　　1780-1842 . . . . NCLC 17
　　See also DLB 1, 59

Chaplin, Charles Spencer
　　1889-1977 . . . . CLC 16
　　See also Chaplin, Charlie
　　See also CA 81-84; 73-76

Chaplin, Charlie
　　See Chaplin, Charles Spencer
　　See also DLB 44

Chapman, George
　　1559(?)-1634 . . . . . LC 22; DAM DRAM
　　See also DLB 62, 121

Chapman, Graham　1941-1989 . . . . . . CLC 21
　　See also Monty Python
　　See also CA 116; 129; CANR 35

Chapman, John Jay　1862-1933 . . . . . TCLC 7
　　See also CA 104

Chapman, Lee
　　See Bradley, Marion Zimmer

Chapman, Walker
　　See Silverberg, Robert

Chappell, Fred (Davis)　1936-. . . . CLC 40, 78
　　See also CA 5-8R; CAAS 4; CANR 8, 33;
　　DLB 6, 105

Char, Rene(-Emile)
　　1907-1988 . . . . CLC 9, 11, 14, 55;
　　　　　　　　　　　　　　　　　　　DAM POET
　　See also CA 13-16R; 124; CANR 32;
　　MTCW

Charby, Jay
　　See Ellison, Harlan (Jay)

Chardin, Pierre Teilhard de
　　See Teilhard de Chardin, (Marie Joseph)
　　Pierre

Charles I　1600-1649. . . . . LC 13

Charyn, Jerome　1937-. . . . . CLC 5, 8, 18
　　See also CA 5-8R; CAAS 1; CANR 7;
　　DLBY 83; MTCW

Chase, Mary (Coyle)　1907-1981 . . . . . . DC 1
　　See also CA 77-80; 105; SATA 17;
　　SATA-Obit 29

Chase, Mary Ellen　1887-1973. . . . . . CLC 2
　　See also CA 13-16; 41-44R; CAP 1;
　　SATA 10

Chase, Nicholas
　　See Hyde, Anthony

Chateaubriand, Francois Rene de
　　1768-1848 . . . . NCLC 3
　　See also DLB 119

Chatterje, Sarat Chandra　1876-1936(?)
　　See Chatterji, Saratchandra
　　See also CA 109

Chatterji, Bankim Chandra
　　1838-1894 . . . . NCLC 19

Chatterji, Saratchandra . . . . TCLC 13
　　See also Chatterje, Sarat Chandra

Chatterton, Thomas
　　1752-1770 . . . . LC 3; DAM POET
　　See also DLB 109

Chatwin, (Charles) Bruce
　　1940-1989 . . CLC 28, 57, 59; DAM POP
　　See also AAYA 4; BEST 90:1; CA 85-88;
　　127

Chaucer, Daniel
　　See Ford, Ford Madox

Chaucer, Geoffrey
　　1340(?)-1400 . . . . LC 17; DA; DAB;
　　　　　　　　　　　　DAC; DAM MST, POET
　　See also CDBLB Before 1660; DLB 146

Chaviaras, Strates　1935-
　　See Haviaras, Stratis
　　See also CA 105

Chayefsky, Paddy . . . . CLC 23
　　See also Chayefsky, Sidney
　　See also DLB 7, 44; DLBY 81

Chayefsky, Sidney　1923-1981
　　See Chayefsky, Paddy
　　See also CA 9-12R; 104; CANR 18;
　　DAM DRAM

Chedid, Andree　1920-. . . . . CLC 47
　　See also CA 145

Cheever, John
　　1912-1982 . . . . . . CLC 3, 7, 8, 11, 15, 25,
　　　　64; DA; DAB; DAC; DAM MST, NOV,
　　　　　　　　　　　　POP; SSC 1; WLC
　　See also CA 5-8R; 106; CABS 1; CANR 5,
　　27; CDALB 1941-1968; DLB 2, 102;
　　DLBY 80, 82; INT CANR-5; MTCW

Cheever, Susan　1943-. . . . . CLC 18, 48
　　See also CA 103; CANR 27, 51; DLBY 82;
　　INT CANR-27

Chekhonte, Antosha
　　See Chekhov, Anton (Pavlovich)

Chekhov, Anton (Pavlovich)
　　1860-1904 . . . . . TCLC 3, 10, 31, 55; DA;
　　　　DAB; DAC; DAM DRAM, MST; SSC 2;
　　　　　　　　　　　　　　　　　　　WLC
　　See also CA 104; 124; SATA 90

Chernyshevsky, Nikolay Gavrilovich
　　1828-1889 . . . . NCLC 1

Cherry, Carolyn Janice　1942-
　　See Cherryh, C. J.
　　See also CA 65-68; CANR 10

Cherryh, C. J. . . . . CLC 35
　　See also Cherry, Carolyn Janice
　　See also DLBY 80

Cook, Roy
See Silverberg, Robert

Cooke, Elizabeth 1948- . . . . **CLC 55**
See also CA 129

Cooke, John Esten 1830-1886. . . . . **NCLC 5**
See also DLB 3

Cooke, John Estes
See Baum, L(yman) Frank

Cooke, M. E.
See Creasey, John

Cooke, Margaret
See Creasey, John

Cook-Lynn, Elizabeth
1930- . . . . **CLC 93; DAM MULT**
See also CA 133; DLB 175; NNAL

Cooney, Ray . . . . **CLC 62**

Cooper, Douglas 1960- . . . . **CLC 86**

Cooper, Henry St. John
See Creasey, John

Cooper, J(oan) California
. . . . **CLC 56; DAM MULT**
See also AAYA 12; BW 1; CA 125;
CANR 55

Cooper, James Fenimore
1789-1851 . . . . **NCLC 1, 27, 54**
See also CDALB 1640-1865; DLB 3;
SATA 19

Coover, Robert (Lowell)
1932- . . . . **CLC 3, 7, 15, 32, 46, 87;**
DAM NOV; SSC 15
See also CA 45-48; CANR 3, 37; DLB 2;
DLBY 81; MTCW

Copeland, Stewart (Armstrong)
1952- . . . . **CLC 26**

Coppard, A(lfred) E(dgar)
1878-1957 . . . . **TCLC 5; SSC 21**
See also CA 114; DLB 162; YABC 1

Coppee, Francois 1842-1908 . . . . . . **TCLC 25**

Coppola, Francis Ford 1939- . . . . **CLC 16**
See also CA 77-80; CANR 40; DLB 44

Corbiere, Tristan 1845-1875 . . . . . **NCLC 43**

Corcoran, Barbara 1911- . . . . **CLC 17**
See also AAYA 14; CA 21-24R; CAAS 2;
CANR 11, 28, 48; DLB 52; JRDA;
SAAS 20; SATA 3, 77

Cordelier, Maurice
See Giraudoux, (Hippolyte) Jean

Corelli, Marie 1855-1924 . . . . **TCLC 51**
See also Mackay, Mary
See also DLB 34, 156

Corman, Cid. **CLC 9**
See also Corman, Sidney
See also CAAS 2; DLB 5

Corman, Sidney 1924-
See Corman, Cid
See also CA 85-88; CANR 44; DAM POET

Cormier, Robert (Edmund)
1925- . . . . **CLC 12, 30; DA; DAB; DAC;**
DAM MST, NOV
See also AAYA 3, 19; CA 1-4R; CANR 5,
23; CDALB 1968-1988; CLR 12; DLB 52;
INT CANR-23; JRDA; MAICYA;
MTCW; SATA 10, 45, 83

Corn, Alfred (DeWitt III) 1943- . . . . **CLC 33**
See also CA 104; CAAS 25; CANR 44;
DLB 120; DLBY 80

Corneille, Pierre
1606-1684 . . . . **LC 28; DAB; DAM MST**

Cornwell, David (John Moore)
1931- . . . . **CLC 9, 15; DAM POP**
See also le Carre, John
See also CA 5-8R; CANR 13, 33; MTCW

Corso, (Nunzio) Gregory 1930- . . . **CLC 1, 11**
See also CA 5-8R; CANR 41; DLB 5, 16;
MTCW

Cortazar, Julio
1914-1984 . . . . . . **CLC 2, 3, 5, 10, 13, 15,**
33, 34, 92; DAM MULT, NOV; HLC;
SSC 7
See also CA 21-24R; CANR 12, 32;
DLB 113; HW; MTCW

CORTES, HERNAN 1484-1547. . . . . **LC 31**

Corwin, Cecil
See Kornbluth, C(yril) M.

Cosic, Dobrica 1921- . . . . **CLC 14**
See also CA 122; 138

Costain, Thomas B(ertram)
1885-1965 . . . . **CLC 30**
See also CA 5-8R; 25-28R; DLB 9

Costantini, Humberto
1924(?)-1987 . . . . **CLC 49**
See also CA 131; 122; HW

Costello, Elvis 1955-. . . . . **CLC 21**

Cotter, Joseph Seamon Sr.
1861-1949 . . . . **TCLC 28; BLC;**
DAM MULT
See also BW 1; CA 124; DLB 50

Couch, Arthur Thomas Quiller
See Quiller-Couch, Arthur Thomas

Coulton, James
See Hansen, Joseph

Couperus, Louis (Marie Anne)
1863-1923 . . . . **TCLC 15**
See also CA 115

Coupland, Douglas
1961- . . . . **CLC 85; DAC; DAM POP**
See also CA 142; CANR 57

Court, Wesli
See Turco, Lewis (Putnam)

Courtenay, Bryce 1933-. . . . . **CLC 59**
See also CA 138

Courtney, Robert
See Ellison, Harlan (Jay)

Cousteau, Jacques-Yves 1910-. . . . . **CLC 30**
See also CA 65-68; CANR 15; MTCW;
SATA 38

Coward, Noel (Peirce)
1899-1973 . . . . **CLC 1, 9, 29, 51;**
DAM DRAM
See also AITN 1; CA 17-18; 41-44R;
CANR 35; CAP 2; CDBLB 1914-1945;
DLB 10; MTCW

Cowley, Malcolm 1898-1989 . . . . **CLC 39**
See also CA 5-8R; 128; CANR 3, 55;
DLB 4, 48; DLBY 81, 89; MTCW

Cowper, William
1731-1800 . . . . . . **NCLC 8; DAM POET**
See also DLB 104, 109

Cox, William Trevor
1928- . . . . **CLC 9, 14, 71; DAM NOV**
See also Trevor, William
See also CA 9-12R; CANR 4, 37, 55;
DLB 14; INT CANR-37; MTCW

Coyne, P. J.
See Masters, Hilary

Cozzens, James Gould
1903-1978 . . . . **CLC 1, 4, 11, 92**
See also CA 9-12R; 81-84; CANR 19;
CDALB 1941-1968; DLB 9; DLBD 2;
DLBY 84; MTCW

Crabbe, George 1754-1832. . . . . . . **NCLC 26**
See also DLB 93

Craddock, Charles Egbert
See Murfree, Mary Noailles

Craig, A. A.
See Anderson, Poul (William)

Craik, Dinah Maria (Mulock)
1826-1887 . . . . **NCLC 38**
See also DLB 35, 163; MAICYA; SATA 34

Cram, Ralph Adams 1863-1942. . . . **TCLC 45**

Crane, (Harold) Hart
1899-1932 . . . . **TCLC 2, 5; DA; DAB;**
DAC; DAM MST, POET; PC 3; WLC
See also CA 104; 127; CDALB 1917-1929;
DLB 4, 48; MTCW

Crane, R(onald) S(almon)
1886-1967 . . . . **CLC 27**
See also CA 85-88; DLB 63

Crane, Stephen (Townley)
1871-1900 . . . . **TCLC 11, 17, 32; DA;**
DAB; DAC; DAM MST, NOV, POET;
SSC 7; WLC
See also CA 109; 140; CDALB 1865-1917;
DLB 12, 54, 78; YABC 2

Crase, Douglas 1944-. . . . . **CLC 58**
See also CA 106

Crashaw, Richard 1612(?)-1649. . . . . **LC 24**
See also DLB 126

Craven, Margaret
1901-1980 . . . . **CLC 17; DAC**
See also CA 103

Crawford, F(rancis) Marion
1854-1909 . . . . **TCLC 10**
See also CA 107; DLB 71

Crawford, Isabella Valancy
1850-1887 . . . . **NCLC 12**
See also DLB 92

Crayon, Geoffrey
See Irving, Washington

Creasey, John 1908-1973. . . . . **CLC 11**
See also CA 5-8R; 41-44R; CANR 8;
DLB 77; MTCW

Crebillon, Claude Prosper Jolyot de (fils)
1707-1777 . . . . **LC 28**

Credo
See Creasey, John

Creeley, Robert (White)
1926- . . . . . **CLC 1, 2, 4, 8, 11, 15, 36, 78;**
DAM POET
See also CA 1-4R; CAAS 10; CANR 23, 43;
DLB 5, 16, 169; MTCW

Crews, Harry (Eugene)
    1935- .... CLC 6, 23, 49
    See also AITN 1; CA 25-28R; CANR 20,
    57; DLB 6, 143; MTCW

Crichton, (John) Michael
    1942- .... CLC 2, 6, 54, 90; DAM NOV,
                                            POP
    See also AAYA 10; AITN 2; CA 25-28R;
    CANR 13, 40, 54; DLBY 81;
    INT CANR-13; JRDA; MTCW; SATA 9,
    88

Crispin, Edmund .... CLC 22
    See also Montgomery, (Robert) Bruce
    See also DLB 87

Cristofer, Michael
    1945(?)- .... CLC 28; DAM DRAM
    See also CA 110; 152; DLB 7

Croce, Benedetto 1866-1952 ...... TCLC 37
    See also CA 120; 155

Crockett, David 1786-1836 .... NCLC 8
    See also DLB 3, 11

Crockett, Davy
    See Crockett, David

Crofts, Freeman Wills
    1879-1957 .... TCLC 55
    See also CA 115; DLB 77

Croker, John Wilson 1780-1857 .. NCLC 10
    See also DLB 110

Crommelynck, Fernand 1885-1970 .. CLC 75
    See also CA 89-92

Cronin, A(rchibald) J(oseph)
    1896-1981 .... CLC 32
    See also CA 1-4R; 102; CANR 5; SATA 47;
    SATA-Obit 25

Cross, Amanda
    See Heilbrun, Carolyn G(old)

Crothers, Rachel 1878(?)-1958..... TCLC 19
    See also CA 113; DLB 7

Croves, Hal
    See Traven, B.

Crow Dog, Mary (Ellen) (?)- .... CLC 93
    See also Brave Bird, Mary
    See also CA 154

Crowfield, Christopher
    See Stowe, Harriet (Elizabeth) Beecher

Crowley, Aleister................. TCLC 7
    See also Crowley, Edward Alexander

Crowley, Edward Alexander 1875-1947
    See Crowley, Aleister
    See also CA 104

Crowley, John 1942-............. CLC 57
    See also CA 61-64; CANR 43; DLBY 82;
    SATA 65

Crud
    See Crumb, R(obert)

Crumarums
    See Crumb, R(obert)

Crumb, R(obert) 1943-........... CLC 17
    See also CA 106

Crumbum
    See Crumb, R(obert)

Crumski
    See Crumb, R(obert)

Crum the Bum
    See Crumb, R(obert)

Crunk
    See Crumb, R(obert)

Crustt
    See Crumb, R(obert)

Cryer, Gretchen (Kiger) 1935-...... CLC 21
    See also CA 114; 123

Csath, Geza 1887-1919.......... TCLC 13
    See also CA 111

Cudlip, David 1933- .... CLC 34

Cullen, Countee
    1903-1946 ..... TCLC 4, 37; BLC; DA;
                DAC; DAM MST, MULT, POET
    See also BW 1; CA 108; 124;
    CDALB 1917-1929; DLB 4, 48, 51;
    MTCW; SATA 18

Cum, R.
    See Crumb, R(obert)

Cummings, Bruce F(rederick) 1889-1919
    See Barbellion, W. N. P.
    See also CA 123

Cummings, E(dward) E(stlin)
    1894-1962 ...... CLC 1, 3, 8, 12, 15, 68;
            DA; DAB; DAC; DAM MST, POET;
            PC 5; WLC 2
    See also CA 73-76; CANR 31;
    CDALB 1929-1941; DLB 4, 48; MTCW

Cunha, Euclides (Rodrigues Pimenta) da
    1866-1909 .... TCLC 24
    See also CA 123

Cunningham, E. V.
    See Fast, Howard (Melvin)

Cunningham, J(ames) V(incent)
    1911-1985 .... CLC 3, 31
    See also CA 1-4R; 115; CANR 1; DLB 5

Cunningham, Julia (Woolfolk)
    1916- .... CLC 12
    See also CA 9-12R; CANR 4, 19, 36;
    JRDA; MAICYA; SAAS 2; SATA 1, 26

Cunningham, Michael 1952- .... CLC 34
    See also CA 136

Cunninghame Graham, R(obert) B(ontine)
    1852-1936 .... TCLC 19
    See also Graham, R(obert) B(ontine)
    Cunninghame
    See also CA 119; DLB 98

Currie, Ellen 19(?)-.............. CLC 44

Curtin, Philip
    See Lowndes, Marie Adelaide (Belloc)

Curtis, Price
    See Ellison, Harlan (Jay)

Cutrate, Joe
    See Spiegelman, Art

Czaczkes, Shmuel Yosef
    See Agnon, S(hmuel) Y(osef Halevi)

Dabrowska, Maria (Szumska)
    1889-1965 .... CLC 15
    See also CA 106

Dabydeen, David 1955- .... CLC 34
    See also BW 1; CA 125; CANR 56

Dacey, Philip 1939- .... CLC 51
    See also CA 37-40R; CAAS 17; CANR 14,
    32; DLB 105

Dagerman, Stig (Halvard)
    1923-1954 .... TCLC 17
    See also CA 117; 155

Dahl, Roald
    1916-1990 ..... CLC 1, 6, 18, 79; DAB;
                DAC; DAM MST, NOV, POP
    See also AAYA 15; CA 1-4R; 133;
    CANR 6, 32, 37; CLR 1, 7, 41; DLB 139;
    JRDA; MAICYA; MTCW; SATA 1, 26,
    73; SATA-Obit 65

Dahlberg, Edward 1900-1977... CLC 1, 7, 14
    See also CA 9-12R; 69-72; CANR 31;
    DLB 48; MTCW

Dale, Colin...................... TCLC 18
    See also Lawrence, T(homas) E(dward)

Dale, George E.
    See Asimov, Isaac

Daly, Elizabeth 1878-1967........ CLC 52
    See also CA 23-24; 25-28R; CAP 2

Daly, Maureen 1921-............. CLC 17
    See also AAYA 5; CANR 37; JRDA;
    MAICYA; SAAS 1; SATA 2

Damas, Leon-Gontran 1912-1978 ... CLC 84
    See also BW 1; CA 125; 73-76

Dana, Richard Henry Sr.
    1787-1879 .... NCLC 53

Daniel, Samuel 1562(?)-1619........ LC 24
    See also DLB 62

Daniels, Brett
    See Adler, Renata

Dannay, Frederic
    1905-1982 .... CLC 11; DAM POP
    See also Queen, Ellery
    See also CA 1-4R; 107; CANR 1, 39;
    DLB 137; MTCW

D'Annunzio, Gabriele
    1863-1938 .... TCLC 6, 40
    See also CA 104; 155

Danois, N. le
    See Gourmont, Remy (-Marie-Charles) de

d'Antibes, Germain
    See Simenon, Georges (Jacques Christian)

Danticat, Edwidge 1969- .... CLC 94
    See also CA 152

Danvers, Dennis 1947-............ CLC 70

Danziger, Paula 1944- .... CLC 21
    See also AAYA 4; CA 112; 115; CANR 37;
    CLR 20; JRDA; MAICYA; SATA 36,
    63; SATA-Brief 30

Da Ponte, Lorenzo 1749-1838.... NCLC 50

Dario, Ruben
    1867-1916 ..... TCLC 4; DAM MULT;
                HLC; PC 15
    See also CA 131; HW; MTCW

Darley, George 1795-1846........ NCLC 2
    See also DLB 96

Darwin, Charles 1809-1882 ...... NCLC 57
    See also DLB 57, 166

Daryush, Elizabeth 1887-1977.... CLC 6, 19
    See also CA 49-52; CANR 3; DLB 20

Dashwood, Edmee Elizabeth Monica de la
    Pasture 1890-1943
    See Delafield, E. M.
    See also CA 119; 154

Daudet, (Louis Marie) Alphonse
1840-1897 .... NCLC 1
See also DLB 123

Daumal, Rene   1908-1944 .... TCLC 14
See also CA 114

Davenport, Guy (Mattison, Jr.)
1927- .... CLC 6, 14, 38; SSC 16
See also CA 33-36R; CANR 23; DLB 130

Davidson, Avram   1923-
See Queen, Ellery
See also CA 101; CANR 26; DLB 8

Davidson, Donald (Grady)
1893-1968 .... CLC 2, 13, 19
See also CA 5-8R; 25-28R; CANR 4;
DLB 45

Davidson, Hugh
See Hamilton, Edmond

Davidson, John   1857-1909 .... TCLC 24
See also CA 118; DLB 19

Davidson, Sara   1943- .... CLC 9
See also CA 81-84; CANR 44

Davie, Donald (Alfred)
1922-1995 .... CLC 5, 8, 10, 31
See also CA 1-4R; 149; CAAS 3; CANR 1,
44; DLB 27; MTCW

Davies, Ray(mond Douglas)   1944- .. CLC 21
See also CA 116; 146

Davies, Rhys   1903-1978 .... CLC 23
See also CA 9-12R; 81-84; CANR 4;
DLB 139

Davies, (William) Robertson
1913-1995 ..... CLC 2, 7, 13, 25, 42, 75,
91; DA; DAB; DAC; DAM MST, NOV,
POP; WLC
See also BEST 89:2; CA 33-36R; 150;
CANR 17, 42; DLB 68; INT CANR-17;
MTCW

Davies, W(illiam) H(enry)
1871-1940 .... TCLC 5
See also CA 104; DLB 19, 174

Davies, Walter C.
See Kornbluth, C(yril) M.

Davis, Angela (Yvonne)
1944- .... CLC 77; DAM MULT
See also BW 2; CA 57-60; CANR 10

Davis, B. Lynch
See Bioy Casares, Adolfo; Borges, Jorge
Luis

Davis, Gordon
See Hunt, E(verette) Howard, (Jr.)

Davis, Harold Lenoir   1896-1960 .... CLC 49
See also CA 89-92; DLB 9

Davis, Rebecca (Blaine) Harding
1831-1910 .... TCLC 6
See also CA 104; DLB 74

Davis, Richard Harding
1864-1916 .... TCLC 24
See also CA 114; DLB 12, 23, 78, 79;
DLBD 13

Davison, Frank Dalby   1893-1970 ... CLC 15
See also CA 116

Davison, Lawrence H.
See Lawrence, D(avid) H(erbert Richards)

Davison, Peter (Hubert)   1928- ..... CLC 28
See also CA 9-12R; CAAS 4; CANR 3, 43;
DLB 5

Davys, Mary   1674-1732 .... LC 1
See also DLB 39

Dawson, Fielding   1930- .... CLC 6
See also CA 85-88; DLB 130

Dawson, Peter
See Faust, Frederick (Schiller)

Day, Clarence (Shepard, Jr.)
1874-1935 .... TCLC 25
See also CA 108; DLB 11

Day, Thomas   1748-1789 .... LC 1
See also DLB 39; YABC 1

Day Lewis, C(ecil)
1904-1972 .... CLC 1, 6, 10;
DAM POET; PC 11
See also Blake, Nicholas
See also CA 13-16; 33-36R; CANR 34;
CAP 1; DLB 15, 20; MTCW

Dazai, Osamu .... TCLC 11
See also Tsushima, Shuji

de Andrade, Carlos Drummond
See Drummond de Andrade, Carlos

Deane, Norman
See Creasey, John

de Beauvoir, Simone (Lucie Ernestine Marie
Bertrand)
See Beauvoir, Simone (Lucie Ernestine
Marie Bertrand) de

de Brissac, Malcolm
See Dickinson, Peter (Malcolm)

de Chardin, Pierre Teilhard
See Teilhard de Chardin, (Marie Joseph)
Pierre

Dee, John   1527-1608 .... LC 20

Deer, Sandra   1940- .... CLC 45

De Ferrari, Gabriella   1941- .... CLC 65
See also CA 146

Defoe, Daniel
1660(?)-1731 .... LC 1; DA; DAB; DAC;
DAM MST, NOV; WLC
See also CDBLB 1660-1789; DLB 39, 95,
101; JRDA; MAICYA; SATA 22

de Gourmont, Remy(-Marie-Charles)
See Gourmont, Remy (-Marie-Charles) de

de Hartog, Jan   1914- .... CLC 19
See also CA 1-4R; CANR 1

de Hostos, E. M.
See Hostos (y Bonilla), Eugenio Maria de

de Hostos, Eugenio M.
See Hostos (y Bonilla), Eugenio Maria de

Deighton, Len .... CLC 4, 7, 22, 46
See also Deighton, Leonard Cyril
See also AAYA 6; BEST 89:2;
CDBLB 1960 to Present; DLB 87

Deighton, Leonard Cyril   1929-
See Deighton, Len
See also CA 9-12R; CANR 19, 33;
DAM NOV, POP; MTCW

Dekker, Thomas
1572(?)-1632 ..... LC 22; DAM DRAM
See also CDBLB Before 1660; DLB 62, 172

Delafield, E. M.   1890-1943 .... TCLC 61
See also Dashwood, Edmee Elizabeth
Monica de la Pasture
See also DLB 34

de la Mare, Walter (John)
1873-1956 .... TCLC 4, 53; DAB; DAC;
DAM MST, POET; SSC 14; WLC
See also CDBLB 1914-1945; CLR 23;
DLB 162; SATA 16

Delaney, Franey
See O'Hara, John (Henry)

Delaney, Shelagh
1939- .... CLC 29; DAM DRAM
See also CA 17-20R; CANR 30;
CDBLB 1960 to Present; DLB 13;
MTCW

Delany, Mary (Granville Pendarves)
1700-1788 .... LC 12

Delany, Samuel R(ay, Jr.)
1942- .... CLC 8, 14, 38; BLC;
DAM MULT
See also BW 2; CA 81-84; CANR 27, 43;
DLB 8, 33; MTCW

De La Ramee, (Marie) Louise   1839-1908
See Ouida
See also SATA 20

de la Roche, Mazo   1879-1961 ...... CLC 14
See also CA 85-88; CANR 30; DLB 68;
SATA 64

Delbanco, Nicholas (Franklin)
1942- .... CLC 6, 13
See also CA 17-20R; CAAS 2; CANR 29,
55; DLB 6

del Castillo, Michel   1933- .... CLC 38
See also CA 109

Deledda, Grazia (Cosima)
1875(?)-1936 .... TCLC 23
See also CA 123

Delibes, Miguel .... CLC 8, 18
See also Delibes Setien, Miguel

Delibes Setien, Miguel   1920-
See Delibes, Miguel
See also CA 45-48; CANR 1, 32; HW;
MTCW

DeLillo, Don
1936- ..... CLC 8, 10, 13, 27, 39, 54, 76;
DAM NOV, POP
See also BEST 89:1; CA 81-84; CANR 21;
DLB 6, 173; MTCW

de Lisser, H. G.
See De Lisser, H(erbert) G(eorge)
See also DLB 117

De Lisser, H(erbert) G(eorge)
1878-1944 .... TCLC 12
See also de Lisser, H. G.
See also BW 2; CA 109; 152

Deloria, Vine (Victor), Jr.
1933- .... CLC 21; DAM MULT
See also CA 53-56; CANR 5, 20, 48;
DLB 175; MTCW; NNAL; SATA 21

Del Vecchio, John M(ichael)
1947- .... CLC 29
See also CA 110; DLBD 9

de Man, Paul (Adolph Michel)
1919-1983 .... CLC 55
See also CA 128; 111; DLB 67; MTCW

De Marinis, Rick 1934- . . . . **CLC 54**
See also CA 57-60; CAAS 24; CANR 9, 25,
50

Dembry, R. Emmet
See Murfree, Mary Noailles

Demby, William
1922- . . . . . **CLC 53; BLC; DAM MULT**
See also BW 1; CA 81-84; DLB 33

de Menton, Francisco
See Chin, Frank (Chew, Jr.)

Demijohn, Thom
See Disch, Thomas M(ichael)

de Montherlant, Henry (Milon)
See Montherlant, Henry (Milon) de

Demosthenes 384B.C.-322B.C. . . . **CMLC 13**
See also DLB 176

de Natale, Francine
See Malzberg, Barry N(athaniel)

Denby, Edwin (Orr) 1903-1983 . . . . . **CLC 48**
See also CA 138; 110

Denis, Julio
See Cortazar, Julio

Denmark, Harrison
See Zelazny, Roger (Joseph)

Dennis, John 1658-1734 . . . . **LC 11**
See also DLB 101

Dennis, Nigel (Forbes) 1912-1989 . . . . **CLC 8**
See also CA 25-28R; 129; DLB 13, 15;
MTCW

De Palma, Brian (Russell) 1940- . . . . **CLC 20**
See also CA 109

De Quincey, Thomas 1785-1859 . . . **NCLC 4**
See also CDBLB 1789-1832; DLB 110; 144

Deren, Eleanora 1908(?)-1961
See Deren, Maya
See also CA 111

Deren, Maya . . . . **CLC 16**
See also Deren, Eleanora

Derleth, August (William)
1909-1971 . . . . **CLC 31**
See also CA 1-4R; 29-32R; CANR 4;
DLB 9; SATA 5

Der Nister 1884-1950 . . . . **TCLC 56**

de Routisie, Albert
See Aragon, Louis

Derrida, Jacques 1930- . . . . **CLC 24, 87**
See also CA 124; 127

Derry Down Derry
See Lear, Edward

Dersonnes, Jacques
See Simenon, Georges (Jacques Christian)

Desai, Anita
1937- . . . . **CLC 19, 37, 97; DAB;**
DAM NOV
See also CA 81-84; CANR 33, 53; MTCW;
SATA 63

de Saint-Luc, Jean
See Glassco, John

de Saint Roman, Arnaud
See Aragon, Louis

Descartes, Rene 1596-1650 . . . . . . **LC 20, 35**

De Sica, Vittorio 1901(?)-1974 . . . . . **CLC 20**
See also CA 117

Desnos, Robert 1900-1945 . . . . **TCLC 22**
See also CA 121; 151

Destouches, Louis-Ferdinand
1894-1961 . . . . **CLC 9, 15**
See also Celine, Louis-Ferdinand
See also CA 85-88; CANR 28; MTCW

de Tolignac, Gaston
See Griffith, D(avid Lewelyn) W(ark)

Deutsch, Babette 1895-1982 . . . . **CLC 18**
See also CA 1-4R; 108; CANR 4; DLB 45;
SATA 1; SATA-Obit 33

Devenant, William 1606-1649 . . . . . . **LC 13**

Devkota, Laxmiprasad
1909-1959 . . . . **TCLC 23**
See also CA 123

De Voto, Bernard (Augustine)
1897-1955 . . . . **TCLC 29**
See also CA 113; DLB 9

De Vries, Peter
1910-1993 . . . . **CLC 1, 2, 3, 7, 10, 28, 46;**
DAM NOV
See also CA 17-20R; 142; CANR 41;
DLB 6; DLBY 82; MTCW

Dexter, John
See Bradley, Marion Zimmer

Dexter, Martin
See Faust, Frederick (Schiller)

Dexter, Pete
1943- . . . . **CLC 34, 55; DAM POP**
See also BEST 89:2; CA 127; 131; INT 131;
MTCW

Diamano, Silmang
See Senghor, Leopold Sedar

Diamond, Neil 1941- . . . . **CLC 30**
See also CA 108

Diaz del Castillo, Bernal 1496-1584 . . **LC 31**

di Bassetto, Corno
See Shaw, George Bernard

Dick, Philip K(indred)
1928-1982 . . . . **CLC 10, 30, 72;**
DAM NOV, POP
See also CA 49-52; 106; CANR 2, 16;
DLB 8; MTCW

Dickens, Charles (John Huffam)
1812-1870 . . . . . . **NCLC 3, 8, 18, 26, 37,**
50; DA; DAB; DAC; DAM MST, NOV;
SSC 17; WLC
See also CDBLB 1832-1890; DLB 21, 55,
70, 159, 166; JRDA; MAICYA; SATA 15

Dickey, James (Lafayette)
1923-1997 . . . . **CLC 1, 2, 4, 7, 10, 15, 47;**
DAM NOV, POET, POP
See also AITN 1, 2; CA 9-12R; 156;
CABS 2; CANR 10, 48;
CDALB 1968-1988; DLB 5; DLBD 7;
DLBY 82, 93; INT CANR-10; MTCW

Dickey, William 1928-1994 . . . . . . **CLC 3, 28**
See also CA 9-12R; 145; CANR 24; DLB 5

Dickinson, Charles 1951- . . . . **CLC 49**
See also CA 128

Dickinson, Emily (Elizabeth)
1830-1886 . . . . **NCLC 21; DA; DAB;**
DAC; DAM MST, POET; PC 1; WLC
See also CDALB 1865-1917; DLB 1;
SATA 29

Dickinson, Peter (Malcolm)
1927- . . . . **CLC 12, 35**
See also AAYA 9; CA 41-44R; CANR 31;
CLR 29; DLB 87, 161; JRDA; MAICYA;
SATA 5, 62

Dickson, Carr
See Carr, John Dickson

Dickson, Carter
See Carr, John Dickson

Diderot, Denis 1713-1784 . . . . **LC 26**

Didion, Joan
1934- . . **CLC 1, 3, 8, 14, 32; DAM NOV**
See also AITN 1; CA 5-8R; CANR 14, 52;
CDALB 1968-1988; DLB 2, 173;
DLBY 81, 86; MTCW

Dietrich, Robert
See Hunt, E(verette) Howard, (Jr.)

Dillard, Annie
1945- . . . . **CLC 9, 60; DAM NOV**
See also AAYA 6; CA 49-52; CANR 3, 43;
DLBY 80; MTCW; SATA 10

Dillard, R(ichard) H(enry) W(ilde)
1937- . . . . **CLC 5**
See also CA 21-24R; CAAS 7; CANR 10;
DLB 5

Dillon, Eilis 1920-1994 . . . . **CLC 17**
See also CA 9-12R; 147; CAAS 3; CANR 4,
38; CLR 26; MAICYA; SATA 2, 74;
SATA-Obit 83

Dimont, Penelope
See Mortimer, Penelope (Ruth)

Dinesen, Isak . . . . **CLC 10, 29, 95; SSC 7**
See also Blixen, Karen (Christentze
Dinesen)

Ding Ling . . . . **CLC 68**
See also Chiang Pin-chin

Disch, Thomas M(ichael) 1940- . . . **CLC 7, 36**
See also AAYA 17; CA 21-24R; CAAS 4;
CANR 17, 36, 54; CLR 18; DLB 8;
MAICYA; MTCW; SAAS 15; SATA 92

Disch, Tom
See Disch, Thomas M(ichael)

d'Isly, Georges
See Simenon, Georges (Jacques Christian)

Disraeli, Benjamin 1804-1881 . . **NCLC 2, 39**
See also DLB 21, 55

Ditcum, Steve
See Crumb, R(obert)

Dixon, Paige
See Corcoran, Barbara

Dixon, Stephen 1936- . . . . . **CLC 52; SSC 16**
See also CA 89-92; CANR 17, 40, 54;
DLB 130

Dobell, Sydney Thompson
1824-1874 . . . . **NCLC 43**
See also DLB 32

Doblin, Alfred . . . . **TCLC 13**
See also Doeblin, Alfred

Dobrolyubov, Nikolai Alexandrovich
1836-1861 . . . . **NCLC 5**

Dobyns, Stephen 1941- . . . . **CLC 37**
See also CA 45-48; CANR 2, 18

Doctorow, E(dgar) L(aurence)
1931- ..... **CLC 6, 11, 15, 18, 37, 44, 65;**
DAM NOV, POP
See also AITN 2; BEST 89:3; CA 45-48;
CANR 2, 33, 51; CDALB 1968-1988;
DLB 2, 28, 173; DLBY 80; MTCW

Dodgson, Charles Lutwidge 1832-1898
See Carroll, Lewis
See also CLR 2; DA; DAB; DAC;
DAM MST, NOV, POET; MAICYA;
YABC 2

Dodson, Owen (Vincent)
1914-1983 .... **CLC 79; BLC;**
DAM MULT
See also BW 1; CA 65-68; 110; CANR 24;
DLB 76

Doeblin, Alfred 1878-1957 .... **TCLC 13**
See also Doblin, Alfred
See also CA 110; 141; DLB 66

Doerr, Harriet 1910- .... **CLC 34**
See also CA 117; 122; CANR 47; INT 122

Domecq, H(onorio) Bustos
See Bioy Casares, Adolfo; Borges, Jorge
Luis

Domini, Rey
See Lorde, Audre (Geraldine)

Dominique
See Proust, (Valentin-Louis-George-Eugene-)
Marcel

Don, A
See Stephen, Leslie

Donaldson, Stephen R.
1947- .... **CLC 46; DAM POP**
See also CA 89-92; CANR 13, 55;
INT CANR-13

Donleavy, J(ames) P(atrick)
1926- .... **CLC 1, 4, 6, 10, 45**
See also AITN 2; CA 9-12R; CANR 24, 49;
DLB 6, 173; INT CANR-24; MTCW

Donne, John
1572-1631 .... **LC 10, 24; DA; DAB;**
DAC; DAM MST, POET; PC 1
See also CDBLB Before 1660; DLB 121,
151

Donnell, David 1939(?)- .... **CLC 34**

Donoghue, P. S.
See Hunt, E(verette) Howard, (Jr.)

Donoso (Yanez), Jose
1924-1996 .... **CLC 4, 8, 11, 32, 99;**
DAM MULT; HLC
See also CA 81-84; 155; CANR 32;
DLB 113; HW; MTCW

Donovan, John 1928-1992 .... **CLC 35**
See also AAYA 20; CA 97-100; 137;
CLR 3; MAICYA; SATA 72;
SATA-Brief 29

Don Roberto
See Cunninghame Graham, R(obert)
B(ontine)

Doolittle, Hilda
1886-1961 ..... **CLC 3, 8, 14, 31, 34, 73;**
DA; DAC; DAM MST, POET; PC 5;
WLC
See also H. D.
See also CA 97-100; CANR 35; DLB 4, 45;
MTCW

Dorfman, Ariel
1942- .... **CLC 48, 77; DAM MULT;**
HLC
See also CA 124; 130; HW; INT 130

Dorn, Edward (Merton) 1929-... **CLC 10, 18**
See also CA 93-96; CANR 42; DLB 5;
INT 93-96

Dorsan, Luc
See Simenon, Georges (Jacques Christian)

Dorsange, Jean
See Simenon, Georges (Jacques Christian)

Dos Passos, John (Roderigo)
1896-1970 ...... **CLC 1, 4, 8, 11, 15, 25,**
34, 82; DA; DAB; DAC; DAM MST,
NOV; WLC
See also CA 1-4R; 29-32R; CANR 3;
CDALB 1929-1941; DLB 4, 9; DLBD 1;
MTCW

Dossage, Jean
See Simenon, Georges (Jacques Christian)

Dostoevsky, Fedor Mikhailovich
1821-1881 ...... **NCLC 2, 7, 21, 33, 43;**
DA; DAB; DAC; DAM MST, NOV;
SSC 2; WLC

Doughty, Charles M(ontagu)
1843-1926 .... **TCLC 27**
See also CA 115; DLB 19, 57, 174

Douglas, Ellen .... **CLC 73**
See also Haxton, Josephine Ayres;
Williamson, Ellen Douglas

Douglas, Gavin 1475(?)-1522 .... **LC 20**

Douglas, Keith 1920-1944 .... **TCLC 40**
See also DLB 27

Douglas, Leonard
See Bradbury, Ray (Douglas)

Douglas, Michael
See Crichton, (John) Michael

Douglas, Norman 1868-1952 ...... **TCLC 68**

Douglass, Frederick
1817(?)-1895 .... **NCLC 7, 55; BLC; DA;**
DAC; DAM MST, MULT; WLC
See also CDALB 1640-1865; DLB 1, 43, 50,
79; SATA 29

Dourado, (Waldomiro Freitas) Autran
1926- .... **CLC 23, 60**
See also CA 25-28R; CANR 34

Dourado, Waldomiro Autran
See Dourado, (Waldomiro Freitas) Autran

Dove, Rita (Frances)
1952- .... **CLC 50, 81; DAM MULT,**
POET; PC 6
See also BW 2; CA 109; CAAS 19;
CANR 27, 42; DLB 120

Dowell, Coleman 1925-1985 .... **CLC 60**
See also CA 25-28R; 117; CANR 10;
DLB 130

Dowson, Ernest (Christopher)
1867-1900 .... **TCLC 4**
See also CA 105; 150; DLB 19, 135

Doyle, A. Conan
See Doyle, Arthur Conan

Doyle, Arthur Conan
1859-1930 .... **TCLC 7; DA; DAB;**
DAC; DAM MST, NOV; SSC 12; WLC
See also AAYA 14; CA 104; 122;
CDBLB 1890-1914; DLB 18, 70, 156;
MTCW; SATA 24

Doyle, Conan
See Doyle, Arthur Conan

Doyle, John
See Graves, Robert (von Ranke)

Doyle, Roddy 1958(?)- .... **CLC 81**
See also AAYA 14; CA 143

Doyle, Sir A. Conan
See Doyle, Arthur Conan

Doyle, Sir Arthur Conan
See Doyle, Arthur Conan

Dr. A
See Asimov, Isaac; Silverstein, Alvin

Drabble, Margaret
1939- .... **CLC 2, 3, 5, 8, 10, 22, 53;**
DAB; DAC; DAM MST, NOV, POP
See also CA 13-16R; CANR 18, 35;
CDBLB 1960 to Present; DLB 14, 155;
MTCW; SATA 48

Drapier, M. B.
See Swift, Jonathan

Drayham, James
See Mencken, H(enry) L(ouis)

Drayton, Michael 1563-1631 .... **LC 8**

Dreadstone, Carl
See Campbell, (John) Ramsey

Dreiser, Theodore (Herman Albert)
1871-1945 .... **TCLC 10, 18, 35; DA;**
DAC; DAM MST, NOV; WLC
See also CA 106; 132; CDALB 1865-1917;
DLB 9, 12, 102, 137; DLBD 1; MTCW

Drexler, Rosalyn 1926- .... **CLC 2, 6**
See also CA 81-84

Dreyer, Carl Theodor 1889-1968.... **CLC 16**
See also CA 116

Drieu la Rochelle, Pierre(-Eugene)
1893-1945 .... **TCLC 21**
See also CA 117; DLB 72

Drinkwater, John 1882-1937 ...... **TCLC 57**
See also CA 109; 149; DLB 10, 19, 149

Drop Shot
See Cable, George Washington

Droste-Hulshoff, Annette Freiin von
1797-1848 .... **NCLC 3**
See also DLB 133

Drummond, Walter
See Silverberg, Robert

Drummond, William Henry
1854-1907 .... **TCLC 25**
See also DLB 92

Drummond de Andrade, Carlos
1902-1987 .... **CLC 18**
See also Andrade, Carlos Drummond de
See also CA 132; 123

Drury, Allen (Stuart) 1918- .... **CLC 37**
See also CA 57-60; CANR 18, 52;
INT CANR-18

Dryden, John
1631-1700 .... **LC 3, 21; DA; DAB;**
DAC; DAM DRAM, MST, POET;
DC 3; WLC
See also CDBLB 1660-1789; DLB 80, 101,
131

Duberman, Martin 1930- .... **CLC 8**
See also CA 1-4R; CANR 2

Dubie, Norman (Evans) 1945- ...... **CLC 36**
See also CA 69-72; CANR 12; DLB 120

Du Bois, W(illiam) E(dward) B(urghardt)
1868-1963 .... **CLC 1, 2, 13, 64, 96;**
BLC; DA; DAC; DAM MST, MULT,
NOV; WLC
See also BW 1; CA 85-88; CANR 34;
CDALB 1865-1917; DLB 47, 50, 91;
MTCW; SATA 42

Dubus, Andre
1936- .... **CLC 13, 36, 97; SSC 15**
See also CA 21-24R; CANR 17; DLB 130;
INT CANR-17

Duca Minimo
See D'Annunzio, Gabriele

Ducharme, Rejean 1941- .... **CLC 74**
See also DLB 60

Duclos, Charles Pinot 1704-1772 ..... **LC 1**

Dudek, Louis 1918- .... **CLC 11, 19**
See also CA 45-48; CAAS 14; CANR 1;
DLB 88

Duerrenmatt, Friedrich
1921-1990 ...... **CLC 1, 4, 8, 11, 15, 43;**
DAM DRAM
See also CA 17-20R; CANR 33; DLB 69,
124; MTCW

Duffy, Bruce (?)- .... **CLC 50**

Duffy, Maureen 1933- .... **CLC 37**
See also CA 25-28R; CANR 33; DLB 14;
MTCW

Dugan, Alan 1923- .... **CLC 2, 6**
See also CA 81-84; DLB 5

du Gard, Roger Martin
See Martin du Gard, Roger

Duhamel, Georges 1884-1966 .... **CLC 8**
See also CA 81-84; 25-28R; CANR 35;
DLB 65; MTCW

Dujardin, Edouard (Emile Louis)
1861-1949 .... **TCLC 13**
See also CA 109; DLB 123

Dumas, Alexandre (Davy de la Pailleterie)
1802-1870 .... **NCLC 11; DA; DAB;**
DAC; DAM MST, NOV; WLC
See also DLB 119; SATA 18

Dumas, Alexandre
1824-1895 .... **NCLC 9; DC 1**

Dumas, Claudine
See Malzberg, Barry N(athaniel)

Dumas, Henry L. 1934-1968 ..... **CLC 6, 62**
See also BW 1; CA 85-88; DLB 41

du Maurier, Daphne
1907-1989 .... **CLC 6, 11, 59; DAB;**
DAC; DAM MST, POP; SSC 18
See also CA 5-8R; 128; CANR 6, 55;
MTCW; SATA 27; SATA-Obit 60

Dunbar, Paul Laurence
1872-1906 ...... **TCLC 2, 12; BLC; DA;**
DAC; DAM MST, MULT, POET; PC 5;
SSC 8; WLC
See also BW 1; CA 104; 124;
CDALB 1865-1917; DLB 50, 54, 78;
SATA 34

Dunbar, William 1460(?)-1530(?) .... **LC 20**
See also DLB 132, 146

Duncan, Dora Angela
See Duncan, Isadora

Duncan, Isadora 1877(?)-1927..... **TCLC 68**
See also CA 118; 149

Duncan, Lois 1934- .... **CLC 26**
See also AAYA 4; CA 1-4R; CANR 2, 23,
36; CLR 29; JRDA; MAICYA; SAAS 2;
SATA 1, 36, 75

Duncan, Robert (Edward)
1919-1988 .... **CLC 1, 2, 4, 7, 15, 41, 55;**
DAM POET; PC 2
See also CA 9-12R; 124; CANR 28; DLB 5,
16; MTCW

Duncan, Sara Jeannette
1861-1922 .... **TCLC 60**
See also DLB 92

Dunlap, William 1766-1839 .... **NCLC 2**
See also DLB 30, 37, 59

Dunn, Douglas (Eaglesham)
1942- .... **CLC 6, 40**
See also CA 45-48; CANR 2, 33; DLB 40;
MTCW

Dunn, Katherine (Karen) 1945- ..... **CLC 71**
See also CA 33-36R

Dunn, Stephen 1939- .... **CLC 36**
See also CA 33-36R; CANR 12, 48, 53;
DLB 105

Dunne, Finley Peter 1867-1936.... **TCLC 28**
See also CA 108; DLB 11, 23

Dunne, John Gregory 1932- .... **CLC 28**
See also CA 25-28R; CANR 14, 50;
DLBY 80

Dunsany, Edward John Moreton Drax
Plunkett 1878-1957
See Dunsany, Lord
See also CA 104; 148; DLB 10

Dunsany, Lord................. TCLC 2, 59
See also Dunsany, Edward John Moreton
Drax Plunkett
See also DLB 77, 153, 156

du Perry, Jean
See Simenon, Georges (Jacques Christian)

Durang, Christopher (Ferdinand)
1949- .... **CLC 27, 38**
See also CA 105; CANR 50

Duras, Marguerite
1914-1996 ..... **CLC 3, 6, 11, 20, 34, 40,**
68, 100
See also CA 25-28R; 151; CANR 50;
DLB 83; MTCW

Durban, (Rosa) Pam 1947- .... **CLC 39**
See also CA 123

Durcan, Paul
1944- .... **CLC 43, 70; DAM POET**
See also CA 134

Durkheim, Emile 1858-1917 ...... **TCLC 55**

Durrell, Lawrence (George)
1912-1990 .... **CLC 1, 4, 6, 8, 13, 27, 41;**
DAM NOV
See also CA 9-12R; 132; CANR 40;
CDBLB 1945-1960; DLB 15, 27;
DLBY 90; MTCW

Durrenmatt, Friedrich
See Duerrenmatt, Friedrich

Dutt, Toru 1856-1877........... **NCLC 29**

Dwight, Timothy 1752-1817...... **NCLC 13**
See also DLB 37

Dworkin, Andrea 1946- .... **CLC 43**
See also CA 77-80; CAAS 21; CANR 16,
39; INT CANR-16; MTCW

Dwyer, Deanna
See Koontz, Dean R(ay)

Dwyer, K. R.
See Koontz, Dean R(ay)

Dylan, Bob 1941- ...... **CLC 3, 4, 6, 12, 77**
See also CA 41-44R; DLB 16

Eagleton, Terence (Francis) 1943-
See Eagleton, Terry
See also CA 57-60; CANR 7, 23; MTCW

Eagleton, Terry .... CLC 63
See also Eagleton, Terence (Francis)

Early, Jack
See Scoppettone, Sandra

East, Michael
See West, Morris L(anglo)

Eastaway, Edward
See Thomas, (Philip) Edward

Eastlake, William (Derry) 1917-..... **CLC 8**
See also CA 5-8R; CAAS 1; CANR 5;
DLB 6; INT CANR-5

Eastman, Charles A(lexander)
1858-1939 ..... **TCLC 55; DAM MULT**
See also DLB 175; NNAL; YABC 1

Eberhart, Richard (Ghormley)
1904- .. **CLC 3, 11, 19, 56; DAM POET**
See also CA 1-4R; CANR 2;
CDALB 1941-1968; DLB 48; MTCW

Eberstadt, Fernanda 1960-......... **CLC 39**
See also CA 136

Echegaray (y Eizaguirre), Jose (Maria Waldo)
1832-1916 .... **TCLC 4**
See also CA 104; CANR 32; HW; MTCW

Echeverria, (Jose) Esteban (Antonino)
1805-1851 .... **NCLC 18**

Echo
See Proust, (Valentin-Louis-George-Eugene-)
Marcel

Eckert, Allan W. 1931- .... **CLC 17**
See also AAYA 18; CA 13-16R; CANR 14,
45; INT CANR-14; SAAS 21; SATA 29,
91; SATA-Brief 27

Eckhart, Meister 1260(?)-1328(?) .. **CMLC 9**
See also DLB 115

Eckmar, F. R.
See de Hartog, Jan

Eco, Umberto
1932- ... **CLC 28, 60; DAM NOV, POP**
See also BEST 90:1; CA 77-80; CANR 12,
33, 55; MTCW

Eddison, E(ric) R(ucker)
1882-1945 . . . . **TCLC 15**
See also CA 109; 156

Edel, (Joseph) Leon 1907- . . . . . . **CLC 29, 34**
See also CA 1-4R; CANR 1, 22; DLB 103;
INT CANR-22

Eden, Emily 1797-1869 . . . . **NCLC 10**

Edgar, David
1948- . . . . **CLC 42; DAM DRAM**
See also CA 57-60; CANR 12; DLB 13;
MTCW

Edgerton, Clyde (Carlyle) 1944- . . . . **CLC 39**
See also AAYA 17; CA 118; 134; INT 134

Edgeworth, Maria 1768-1849. . . **NCLC 1, 51**
See also DLB 116, 159, 163; SATA 21

Edmonds, Paul
See Kuttner, Henry

Edmonds, Walter D(umaux) 1903- . . **CLC 35**
See also CA 5-8R; CANR 2; DLB 9;
MAICYA; SAAS 4; SATA 1, 27

Edmondson, Wallace
See Ellison, Harlan (Jay)

Edson, Russell . . . . **CLC 13**
See also CA 33-36R

Edwards, Bronwen Elizabeth
See Rose, Wendy

Edwards, G(erald) B(asil)
1899-1976 . . . . **CLC 25**
See also CA 110

Edwards, Gus 1939- . . . . **CLC 43**
See also CA 108; INT 108

Edwards, Jonathan
1703-1758 . . . . **LC 7; DA; DAC;**
DAM MST
See also DLB 24

Efron, Marina Ivanovna Tsvetaeva
See Tsvetaeva (Efron), Marina (Ivanovna)

Ehle, John (Marsden, Jr.) 1925- . . . . **CLC 27**
See also CA 9-12R

Ehrenbourg, Ilya (Grigoryevich)
See Ehrenburg, Ilya (Grigoryevich)

Ehrenburg, Ilya (Grigoryevich)
1891-1967 . . . . **CLC 18, 34, 62**
See also CA 102; 25-28R

Ehrenburg, Ilyo (Grigoryevich)
See Ehrenburg, Ilya (Grigoryevich)

Eich, Guenter 1907-1972 . . . . **CLC 15**
See also CA 111; 93-96; DLB 69, 124

Eichendorff, Joseph Freiherr von
1788-1857 . . . . **NCLC 8**
See also DLB 90

Eigner, Larry . . . . **CLC 9**
See also Eigner, Laurence (Joel)
See also CAAS 23; DLB 5

Eigner, Laurence (Joel) 1927-1996
See Eigner, Larry
See also CA 9-12R; 151; CANR 6

Einstein, Albert 1879-1955 . . . . **TCLC 65**
See also CA 121; 133; MTCW

Eiseley, Loren Corey 1907-1977 . . . . . **CLC 7**
See also AAYA 5; CA 1-4R; 73-76;
CANR 6

Eisenstadt, Jill 1963- . . . . **CLC 50**
See also CA 140

Eisenstein, Sergei (Mikhailovich)
1898-1948 . . . . **TCLC 57**
See also CA 114; 149

Eisner, Simon
See Kornbluth, C(yril) M.

Ekeloef, (Bengt) Gunnar
1907-1968 . . . . . . **CLC 27; DAM POET**
See also CA 123; 25-28R

Ekelof, (Bengt) Gunnar
See Ekeloef, (Bengt) Gunnar

Ekwensi, C. O. D.
See Ekwensi, Cyprian (Odiatu Duaka)

Ekwensi, Cyprian (Odiatu Duaka)
1921- . . . . . . **CLC 4; BLC; DAM MULT**
See also BW 2; CA 29-32R; CANR 18, 42;
DLB 117; MTCW; SATA 66

Elaine . . . . **TCLC 18**
See also Leverson, Ada

El Crummo
See Crumb, R(obert)

Elia
See Lamb, Charles

Eliade, Mircea 1907-1986 . . . . **CLC 19**
See also CA 65-68; 119; CANR 30; MTCW

Eliot, A. D.
See Jewett, (Theodora) Sarah Orne

Eliot, Alice
See Jewett, (Theodora) Sarah Orne

Eliot, Dan
See Silverberg, Robert

Eliot, George
1819-1880 . . . . . **NCLC 4, 13, 23, 41, 49;**
DA; DAB; DAC; DAM MST, NOV;
WLC
See also CDBLB 1832-1890; DLB 21, 35, 55

Eliot, John 1604-1690 . . . . **LC 5**
See also DLB 24

Eliot, T(homas) S(tearns)
1888-1965 . . . . . **CLC 1, 2, 3, 6, 9, 10, 13,**
15, 24, 34, 41, 55, 57; DA; DAB; DAC;
DAM DRAM, MST, POET; PC 5;
WLC 2
See also CA 5-8R; 25-28R; CANR 41;
CDALB 1929-1941; DLB 7, 10, 45, 63;
DLBY 88; MTCW

Elizabeth 1866-1941 . . . . **TCLC 41**

Elkin, Stanley L(awrence)
1930-1995 . . . . . . **CLC 4, 6, 9, 14, 27, 51,**
91; DAM NOV, POP; SSC 12
See also CA 9-12R; 148; CANR 8, 46;
DLB 2, 28; DLBY 80; INT CANR-8;
MTCW

Elledge, Scott . . . . **CLC 34**

Elliot, Don
See Silverberg, Robert

Elliott, Don
See Silverberg, Robert

Elliott, George P(aul) 1918-1980 . . . . . **CLC 2**
See also CA 1-4R; 97-100; CANR 2

Elliott, Janice 1931- . . . . **CLC 47**
See also CA 13-16R; CANR 8, 29; DLB 14

Elliott, Sumner Locke 1917-1991 . . . **CLC 38**
See also CA 5-8R; 134; CANR 2, 21

Elliott, William
See Bradbury, Ray (Douglas)

Ellis, A. E. . . . . **CLC 7**

Ellis, Alice Thomas . . . . **CLC 40**
See also Haycraft, Anna

Ellis, Bret Easton
1964- . . . . **CLC 39, 71; DAM POP**
See also AAYA 2; CA 118; 123; CANR 51;
INT 123

Ellis, (Henry) Havelock
1859-1939 . . . . **TCLC 14**
See also CA 109

Ellis, Landon
See Ellison, Harlan (Jay)

Ellis, Trey 1962- . . . . **CLC 55**
See also CA 146

Ellison, Harlan (Jay)
1934- . . . . . . **CLC 1, 13, 42; DAM POP;**
SSC 14
See also CA 5-8R; CANR 5, 46; DLB 8;
INT CANR-5; MTCW

Ellison, Ralph (Waldo)
1914-1994 . . . . **CLC 1, 3, 11, 54, 86;**
BLC; DA; DAB; DAC; DAM MST,
MULT, NOV; WLC
See also AAYA 19; BW 1; CA 9-12R; 145;
CANR 24, 53; CDALB 1941-1968;
DLB 2, 76; DLBY 94; MTCW

Ellmann, Lucy (Elizabeth) 1956- . . . . **CLC 61**
See also CA 128

Ellmann, Richard (David)
1918-1987 . . . . **CLC 50**
See also BEST 89:2; CA 1-4R; 122;
CANR 2, 28; DLB 103; DLBY 87;
MTCW

Elman, Richard 1934- . . . . **CLC 19**
See also CA 17-20R; CAAS 3; CANR 47

Elron
See Hubbard, L(afayette) Ron(ald)

Eluard, Paul . . . . **TCLC 7, 41**
See also Grindel, Eugene

Elyot, Sir Thomas 1490(?)-1546 . . . . . **LC 11**

Elytis, Odysseus
1911-1996 . . . . **CLC 15, 49, 100;**
DAM POET
See also CA 102; 151; MTCW

Emecheta, (Florence Onye) Buchi
1944- . . **CLC 14, 48; BLC; DAM MULT**
See also BW 2; CA 81-84; CANR 27;
DLB 117; MTCW; SATA 66

Emerson, Ralph Waldo
1803-1882 . . . . . **NCLC 1, 38; DA; DAB;**
DAC; DAM MST, POET; WLC
See also CDALB 1640-1865; DLB 1, 59, 73

Eminescu, Mihail 1850-1889 . . . . . **NCLC 33**

Empson, William
1906-1984 . . . . **CLC 3, 8, 19, 33, 34**
See also CA 17-20R; 112; CANR 31;
DLB 20; MTCW

Enchi Fumiko (Ueda) 1905-1986 . . . . **CLC 31**
See also CA 129; 121

Farren, Richard M.
　　See Betjeman, John

Fassbinder, Rainer Werner
　　1946-1982 . . . . **CLC 20**
　　See also CA 93-96; 106; CANR 31

Fast, Howard (Melvin)
　　1914- . . . . **CLC 23; DAM NOV**
　　See also AAYA 16; CA 1-4R; CAAS 18;
　　　CANR 1, 33, 54; DLB 9; INT CANR-33;
　　　SATA 7

Faulcon, Robert
　　See Holdstock, Robert P.

Faulkner, William (Cuthbert)
　　1897-1962 . . . . . **CLC 1, 3, 6, 8, 9, 11, 14,
　　　18, 28, 52, 68; DA; DAB; DAC;
　　　DAM MST, NOV; SSC 1; WLC**
　　See also AAYA 7; CA 81-84; CANR 33;
　　　CDALB 1929-1941; DLB 9, 11, 44, 102;
　　　DLBD 2; DLBY 86; MTCW

Fauset, Jessie Redmon
　　1884(?)-1961 . . . . **CLC 19, 54; BLC;
　　　DAM MULT**
　　See also BW 1; CA 109; DLB 51

Faust, Frederick (Schiller)
　　1892-1944(?) . . . . . **TCLC 49; DAM POP**
　　See also CA 108; 152

Faust, Irvin　1924- . . . . **CLC 8**
　　See also CA 33-36R; CANR 28; DLB 2, 28;
　　　DLBY 80

Fawkes, Guy
　　See Benchley, Robert (Charles)

Fearing, Kenneth (Flexner)
　　1902-1961 . . . . **CLC 51**
　　See also CA 93-96; DLB 9

Fecamps, Elise
　　See Creasey, John

Federman, Raymond　1928- . . . . . . **CLC 6, 47**
　　See also CA 17-20R; CAAS 8; CANR 10,
　　　43; DLBY 80

Federspiel, J(uerg) F.　1931- . . . . **CLC 42**
　　See also CA 146

Feiffer, Jules (Ralph)
　　1929- . . . . . . **CLC 2, 8, 64; DAM DRAM**
　　See also AAYA 3; CA 17-20R; CANR 30;
　　　DLB 7, 44; INT CANR-30; MTCW;
　　　SATA 8, 61

Feige, Hermann Albert Otto Maximilian
　　See Traven, B.

Feinberg, David B.　1956-1994 . . . . . . **CLC 59**
　　See also CA 135; 147

Feinstein, Elaine　1930- . . . . **CLC 36**
　　See also CA 69-72; CAAS 1; CANR 31;
　　　DLB 14, 40; MTCW

Feldman, Irving (Mordecai)　1928- . . . . **CLC 7**
　　See also CA 1-4R; CANR 1; DLB 169

Fellini, Federico　1920-1993 . . . . . **CLC 16, 85**
　　See also CA 65-68; 143; CANR 33

Felsen, Henry Gregor　1916- . . . . **CLC 17**
　　See also CA 1-4R; CANR 1; SAAS 2;
　　　SATA 1

Fenton, James Martin　1949- . . . . **CLC 32**
　　See also CA 102; DLB 40

Ferber, Edna　1887-1968 . . . . **CLC 18, 93**
　　See also AITN 1; CA 5-8R; 25-28R; DLB 9,
　　　28, 86; MTCW; SATA 7

Ferguson, Helen
　　See Kavan, Anna

Ferguson, Samuel　1810-1886 . . . . . **NCLC 33**
　　See also DLB 32

Fergusson, Robert　1750-1774 . . . . . . **LC 29**
　　See also DLB 109

Ferling, Lawrence
　　See Ferlinghetti, Lawrence (Monsanto)

Ferlinghetti, Lawrence (Monsanto)
　　1919(?)- . . . . **CLC 2, 6, 10, 27;
　　　DAM POET; PC 1**
　　See also CA 5-8R; CANR 3, 41;
　　　CDALB 1941-1968; DLB 5, 16; MTCW

Fernandez, Vicente Garcia Huidobro
　　See Huidobro Fernandez, Vicente Garcia

Ferrer, Gabriel (Francisco Victor) Miro
　　See Miro (Ferrer), Gabriel (Francisco
　　　Victor)

Ferrier, Susan (Edmonstone)
　　1782-1854 . . . . **NCLC 8**
　　See also DLB 116

Ferrigno, Robert　1948(?)- . . . . **CLC 65**
　　See also CA 140

Ferron, Jacques　1921-1985 . . . **CLC 94; DAC**
　　See also CA 117; 129; DLB 60

Feuchtwanger, Lion　1884-1958 . . . . . **TCLC 3**
　　See also CA 104; DLB 66

Feuillet, Octave　1821-1890 . . . . . . **NCLC 45**

Feydeau, Georges (Leon Jules Marie)
　　1862-1921 . . . . . **TCLC 22; DAM DRAM**
　　See also CA 113; 152

Ficino, Marsilio　1433-1499 . . . . **LC 12**

Fiedeler, Hans
　　See Doeblin, Alfred

Fiedler, Leslie A(aron)
　　1917- . . . . **CLC 4, 13, 24**
　　See also CA 9-12R; CANR 7; DLB 28, 67;
　　　MTCW

Field, Andrew　1938- . . . . **CLC 44**
　　See also CA 97-100; CANR 25

Field, Eugene　1850-1895 . . . . **NCLC 3**
　　See also DLB 23, 42, 140; DLBD 13;
　　　MAICYA; SATA 16

Field, Gans T.
　　See Wellman, Manly Wade

Field, Michael . . . . **TCLC 43**

Field, Peter
　　See Hobson, Laura Z(ametkin)

Fielding, Henry
　　1707-1754 . . . . . . **LC 1; DA; DAB; DAC;
　　　DAM DRAM, MST, NOV; WLC**
　　See also CDBLB 1660-1789; DLB 39, 84,
　　　101

Fielding, Sarah　1710-1768 . . . . **LC 1**
　　See also DLB 39

Fierstein, Harvey (Forbes)
　　1954- . . . . . **CLC 33; DAM DRAM, POP**
　　See also CA 123; 129

Figes, Eva　1932- . . . . **CLC 31**
　　See also CA 53-56; CANR 4, 44; DLB 14

Finch, Robert (Duer Claydon)
　　1900- . . . . **CLC 18**
　　See also CA 57-60; CANR 9, 24, 49;
　　　DLB 88

Findley, Timothy
　　1930- . . . . . . **CLC 27; DAC; DAM MST**
　　See also CA 25-28R; CANR 12, 42;
　　　DLB 53

Fink, William
　　See Mencken, H(enry) L(ouis)

Firbank, Louis　1942-
　　See Reed, Lou
　　See also CA 117

Firbank, (Arthur Annesley) Ronald
　　1886-1926 . . . . **TCLC 1**
　　See also CA 104; DLB 36

Fisher, M(ary) F(rances) K(ennedy)
　　1908-1992 . . . . **CLC 76, 87**
　　See also CA 77-80; 138; CANR 44

Fisher, Roy　1930- . . . . **CLC 25**
　　See also CA 81-84; CAAS 10; CANR 16;
　　　DLB 40

Fisher, Rudolph
　　1897-1934 . . . . **TCLC 11; BLC;
　　　DAM MULT; SSC 25**
　　See also BW 1; CA 107; 124; DLB 51, 102

Fisher, Vardis (Alvero)　1895-1968 . . . . **CLC 7**
　　See also CA 5-8R; 25-28R; DLB 9

Fiske, Tarleton
　　See Bloch, Robert (Albert)

Fitch, Clarke
　　See Sinclair, Upton (Beall)

Fitch, John IV
　　See Cormier, Robert (Edmund)

Fitzgerald, Captain Hugh
　　See Baum, L(yman) Frank

FitzGerald, Edward　1809-1883 . . . . **NCLC 9**
　　See also DLB 32

Fitzgerald, F(rancis) Scott (Key)
　　1896-1940 . . . . **TCLC 1, 6, 14, 28, 55;
　　　DA; DAB; DAC; DAM MST, NOV;
　　　SSC 6; WLC**
　　See also AITN 1; CA 110; 123;
　　　CDALB 1917-1929; DLB 4, 9, 86;
　　　DLBD 1; DLBY 81; MTCW

Fitzgerald, Penelope　1916- . . . **CLC 19, 51, 61**
　　See also CA 85-88; CAAS 10; CANR 56;
　　　DLB 14

Fitzgerald, Robert (Stuart)
　　1910-1985 . . . . **CLC 39**
　　See also CA 1-4R; 114; CANR 1; DLBY 80

FitzGerald, Robert D(avid)
　　1902-1987 . . . . **CLC 19**
　　See also CA 17-20R

Fitzgerald, Zelda (Sayre)
　　1900-1948 . . . . **TCLC 52**
　　See also CA 117; 126; DLBY 84

Flanagan, Thomas (James Bonner)
　　1923- . . . . **CLC 25, 52**
　　See also CA 108; CANR 55; DLBY 80;
　　　INT 108; MTCW

Flaubert, Gustave
　　1821-1880 . . . . **NCLC 2, 10, 19; DA;
　　　DAB; DAC; DAM MST, NOV; SSC 11;
　　　WLC**
　　See also DLB 119

Flecker, Herman Elroy
　　See Flecker, (Herman) James Elroy

Fredro, Aleksander 1793-1876...... **NCLC 8**

Freeling, Nicolas 1927- .... **CLC 38**
See also CA 49-52; CAAS 12; CANR 1, 17,
50; DLB 87

Freeman, Douglas Southall
1886-1953 .... **TCLC 11**
See also CA 109; DLB 17

Freeman, Judith 1946-............ **CLC 55**
See also CA 148

Freeman, Mary Eleanor Wilkins
1852-1930 .... **TCLC 9; SSC 1**
See also CA 106; DLB 12, 78

Freeman, R(ichard) Austin
1862-1943 .... **TCLC 21**
See also CA 113; DLB 70

French, Albert 1943- .... **CLC 86**

French, Marilyn
1929- .... **CLC 10, 18, 60;
DAM DRAM, NOV, POP**
See also CA 69-72; CANR 3, 31;
INT CANR-31; MTCW

French, Paul
See Asimov, Isaac

Freneau, Philip Morin 1752-1832.. **NCLC 1**
See also DLB 37, 43

Freud, Sigmund 1856-1939 .... **TCLC 52**
See also CA 115; 133; MTCW

Friedan, Betty (Naomi) 1921-...... **CLC 74**
See also CA 65-68; CANR 18, 45; MTCW

Friedlander, Saul 1932- .... **CLC 90**
See also CA 117; 130

Friedman, B(ernard) H(arper)
1926- .... **CLC 7**
See also CA 1-4R; CANR 3, 48

Friedman, Bruce Jay 1930-.... **CLC 3, 5, 56**
See also CA 9-12R; CANR 25, 52; DLB 2,
28; INT CANR-25

Friel, Brian 1929-.......... **CLC 5, 42, 59**
See also CA 21-24R; CANR 33; DLB 13;
MTCW

Friis-Baastad, Babbis Ellinor
1921-1970 .... **CLC 12**
See also CA 17-20R; 134; SATA 7

Frisch, Max (Rudolf)
1911-1991 ..... **CLC 3, 9, 14, 18, 32, 44;
DAM DRAM, NOV**
See also CA 85-88; 134; CANR 32;
DLB 69, 124; MTCW

Fromentin, Eugene (Samuel Auguste)
1820-1876 .... **NCLC 10**
See also DLB 123

Frost, Frederick
See Faust, Frederick (Schiller)

Frost, Robert (Lee)
1874-1963 .... **CLC 1, 3, 4, 9, 10, 13, 15,
26, 34, 44; DA; DAB; DAC; DAM MST,
POET; PC 1; WLC**
See also CA 89-92; CANR 33;
CDALB 1917-1929; DLB 54; DLBD 7;
MTCW; SATA 14

Froude, James Anthony
1818-1894 .... **NCLC 43**
See also DLB 18, 57, 144

Froy, Herald
See Waterhouse, Keith (Spencer)

Fry, Christopher
1907- ..... **CLC 2, 10, 14; DAM DRAM**
See also CA 17-20R; CAAS 23; CANR 9,
30; DLB 13; MTCW; SATA 66

Frye, (Herman) Northrop
1912-1991 .... **CLC 24, 70**
See also CA 5-8R; 133; CANR 8, 37;
DLB 67, 68; MTCW

Fuchs, Daniel 1909-1993 .... **CLC 8, 22**
See also CA 81-84; 142; CAAS 5;
CANR 40; DLB 9, 26, 28; DLBY 93

Fuchs, Daniel 1934-.............. **CLC 34**
See also CA 37-40R; CANR 14, 48

Fuentes, Carlos
1928- ...... **CLC 3, 8, 10, 13, 22, 41, 60;
DA; DAB; DAC; DAM MST, MULT,
NOV; HLC; SSC 24; WLC**
See also AAYA 4; AITN 2; CA 69-72;
CANR 10, 32; DLB 113; HW; MTCW

Fuentes, Gregorio Lopez y
See Lopez y Fuentes, Gregorio

Fugard, (Harold) Athol
1932- .... **CLC 5, 9, 14, 25, 40, 80;
DAM DRAM; DC 3**
See also AAYA 17; CA 85-88; CANR 32,
54; MTCW

Fugard, Sheila 1932- .... **CLC 48**
See also CA 125

Fuller, Charles (H., Jr.)
1939- .... **CLC 25; BLC; DAM DRAM,
MULT; DC 1**
See also BW 2; CA 108; 112; DLB 38;
INT 112; MTCW

Fuller, John (Leopold) 1937-....... **CLC 62**
See also CA 21-24R; CANR 9, 44; DLB 40

Fuller, Margaret .... **NCLC 5, 50**
See also Ossoli, Sarah Margaret (Fuller
marchesa d')

Fuller, Roy (Broadbent)
1912-1991 .... **CLC 4, 28**
See also CA 5-8R; 135; CAAS 10;
CANR 53; DLB 15, 20; SATA 87

Fulton, Alice 1952-............... **CLC 52**
See also CA 116; CANR 57

Furphy, Joseph 1843-1912........ **TCLC 25**

Fussell, Paul 1924-............... **CLC 74**
See also BEST 90:1; CA 17-20R; CANR 8,
21, 35; INT CANR-21; MTCW

Futabatei, Shimei 1864-1909...... **TCLC 44**

Futrelle, Jacques 1875-1912 ...... **TCLC 19**
See also CA 113; 155

Gaboriau, Emile 1835-1873 ...... **NCLC 14**

Gadda, Carlo Emilio 1893-1973 .... **CLC 11**
See also CA 89-92; DLB 177

Gaddis, William
1922- ..... **CLC 1, 3, 6, 8, 10, 19, 43, 86**
See also CA 17-20R; CANR 21, 48; DLB 2;
MTCW

Gage, Walter
See Inge, William (Motter)

Gaines, Ernest J(ames)
1933- .... **CLC 3, 11, 18, 86; BLC;
DAM MULT**
See also AAYA 18; AITN 1; BW 2;
CA 9-12R; CANR 6, 24, 42;
CDALB 1968-1988; DLB 2, 33, 152;
DLBY 80; MTCW; SATA 86

Gaitskill, Mary 1954-............. **CLC 69**
See also CA 128

Galdos, Benito Perez
See Perez Galdos, Benito

Gale, Zona
1874-1938 ...... **TCLC 7; DAM DRAM**
See also CA 105; 153; DLB 9, 78

Galeano, Eduardo (Hughes) 1940-... **CLC 72**
See also CA 29-32R; CANR 13, 32; HW

Galiano, Juan Valera y Alcala
See Valera y Alcala-Galiano, Juan

Gallagher, Tess
1943- .. **CLC 18, 63; DAM POET; PC 9**
See also CA 106; DLB 120

Gallant, Mavis
1922- .... **CLC 7, 18, 38; DAC;
DAM MST; SSC 5**
See also CA 69-72; CANR 29; DLB 53;
MTCW

Gallant, Roy A(rthur) 1924- .... **CLC 17**
See also CA 5-8R; CANR 4, 29, 54;
CLR 30; MAICYA; SATA 4, 68

Gallico, Paul (William) 1897-1976 ... **CLC 2**
See also AITN 1; CA 5-8R; 69-72;
CANR 23; DLB 9, 171; MAICYA;
SATA 13

Gallo, Max Louis 1932-........... **CLC 95**
See also CA 85-88

Gallois, Lucien
See Desnos, Robert

Gallup, Ralph
See Whitemore, Hugh (John)

Galsworthy, John
1867-1933 ...... **TCLC 1, 45; DA; DAB;
DAC; DAM DRAM, MST, NOV;
SSC 22; WLC 2**
See also CA 104; 141; CDBLB 1890-1914;
DLB 10, 34, 98, 162

Galt, John 1779-1839............ **NCLC 1**
See also DLB 99, 116, 159

Galvin, James 1951-.............. **CLC 38**
See also CA 108; CANR 26

Gamboa, Federico 1864-1939...... **TCLC 36**

Gandhi, M. K.
See Gandhi, Mohandas Karamchand

Gandhi, Mahatma
See Gandhi, Mohandas Karamchand

Gandhi, Mohandas Karamchand
1869-1948 ..... **TCLC 59; DAM MULT**
See also CA 121; 132; MTCW

Gann, Ernest Kellogg 1910-1991.... **CLC 23**
See also AITN 1; CA 1-4R; 136; CANR 1

Garcia, Cristina 1958- .... **CLC 76**
See also CA 141

Garcia Lorca, Federico
　　1898-1936 ... **TCLC 1, 7, 49; DA; DAB;**
　　　　DAC; DAM DRAM, MST, MULT,
　　　　POET; DC 2; HLC; PC 3; WLC
　　See also CA 104; 131; DLB 108; HW;
　　　　MTCW

Garcia Marquez, Gabriel (Jose)
　　1928- .... **CLC 2, 3, 8, 10, 15, 27, 47, 55,**
　　　　68; DA; DAB; DAC; DAM MST,
　　　　MULT, NOV, POP; HLC; SSC 8; WLC
　　See also AAYA 3; BEST 89:1, 90:4;
　　　　CA 33-36R; CANR 10, 28, 50; DLB 113;
　　　　HW; MTCW

Gard, Janice
　　See Latham, Jean Lee

Gard, Roger Martin du
　　See Martin du Gard, Roger

Gardam, Jane 1928- .... **CLC 43**
　　See also CA 49-52; CANR 2, 18, 33, 54;
　　　　CLR 12; DLB 14, 161; MAICYA;
　　　　MTCW; SAAS 9; SATA 39, 76;
　　　　SATA-Brief 28

Gardner, Herb(ert) 1934- .... **CLC 44**
　　See also CA 149

Gardner, John (Champlin), Jr.
　　1933-1982 ..... **CLC 2, 3, 5, 7, 8, 10, 18,**
　　　　28, 34; DAM NOV, POP; SSC 7
　　See also AITN 1; CA 65-68; 107;
　　　　CANR 33; DLB 2; DLBY 82; MTCW;
　　　　SATA 40; SATA-Obit 31

Gardner, John (Edmund)
　　1926- .... **CLC 30; DAM POP**
　　See also CA 103; CANR 15; MTCW

Gardner, Miriam
　　See Bradley, Marion Zimmer

Gardner, Noel
　　See Kuttner, Henry

Gardons, S. S.
　　See Snodgrass, W(illiam) D(e Witt)

Garfield, Leon 1921-1996 .... **CLC 12**
　　See also AAYA 8; CA 17-20R; 152;
　　　　CANR 38, 41; CLR 21; DLB 161; JRDA;
　　　　MAICYA; SATA 1, 32, 76;
　　　　SATA-Obit 90

Garland, (Hannibal) Hamlin
　　1860-1940 .... **TCLC 3; SSC 18**
　　See also CA 104; DLB 12, 71, 78

Garneau, (Hector de) Saint-Denys
　　1912-1943 .... **TCLC 13**
　　See also CA 111; DLB 88

Garner, Alan
　　1934- .... **CLC 17; DAB; DAM POP**
　　See also AAYA 18; CA 73-76; CANR 15;
　　　　CLR 20; DLB 161; MAICYA; MTCW;
　　　　SATA 18, 69

Garner, Hugh 1913-1979 .... **CLC 13**
　　See also CA 69-72; CANR 31; DLB 68

Garnett, David 1892-1981 .... **CLC 3**
　　See also CA 5-8R; 103; CANR 17; DLB 34

Garos, Stephanie
　　See Katz, Steve

Garrett, George (Palmer)
　　1929- .... **CLC 3, 11, 51**
　　See also CA 1-4R; CAAS 5; CANR 1, 42;
　　　　DLB 2, 5, 130, 152; DLBY 83

Garrick, David
　　1717-1779 .... **LC 15; DAM DRAM**
　　See also DLB 84

Garrigue, Jean 1914-1972 .... **CLC 2, 8**
　　See also CA 5-8R; 37-40R; CANR 20

Garrison, Frederick
　　See Sinclair, Upton (Beall)

Garth, Will
　　See Hamilton, Edmond; Kuttner, Henry

Garvey, Marcus (Moziah, Jr.)
　　1887-1940 .... **TCLC 41; BLC;**
　　　　DAM MULT
　　See also BW 1; CA 120; 124

Gary, Romain .... **CLC 25**
　　See also Kacew, Romain
　　See also DLB 83

Gascar, Pierre .... **CLC 11**
　　See also Fournier, Pierre

Gascoyne, David (Emery) 1916- .... **CLC 45**
　　See also CA 65-68; CANR 10, 28, 54;
　　　　DLB 20; MTCW

Gaskell, Elizabeth Cleghorn
　　1810-1865 .... **NCLC 5; DAB;**
　　　　DAM MST; SSC 25
　　See also CDBLB 1832-1890; DLB 21, 144,
　　　　159

Gass, William H(oward)
　　1924- ... **CLC 1, 2, 8, 11, 15, 39; SSC 12**
　　See also CA 17-20R; CANR 30; DLB 2;
　　　　MTCW

Gasset, Jose Ortega y
　　See Ortega y Gasset, Jose

Gates, Henry Louis, Jr.
　　1950- .... **CLC 65; DAM MULT**
　　See also BW 2; CA 109; CANR 25, 53;
　　　　DLB 67

Gautier, Theophile
　　1811-1872 .... **NCLC 1, 59;**
　　　　DAM POET; SSC 20
　　See also DLB 119

Gawsworth, John
　　See Bates, H(erbert) E(rnest)

Gay, Oliver
　　See Gogarty, Oliver St. John

Gaye, Marvin (Penze) 1939-1984 ... **CLC 26**
　　See also CA 112

Gebler, Carlo (Ernest) 1954- .... **CLC 39**
　　See also CA 119; 133

Gee, Maggie (Mary) 1948- .... **CLC 57**
　　See also CA 130

Gee, Maurice (Gough) 1931- .... **CLC 29**
　　See also CA 97-100; SATA 46

Gelbart, Larry (Simon) 1923- ... **CLC 21, 61**
　　See also CA 73-76; CANR 45

Gelber, Jack 1932- .... **CLC 1, 6, 14, 79**
　　See also CA 1-4R; CANR 2; DLB 7

Gellhorn, Martha (Ellis) 1908- .. **CLC 14, 60**
　　See also CA 77-80; CANR 44; DLBY 82

Genet, Jean
　　1910-1986 ...... **CLC 1, 2, 5, 10, 14, 44,**
　　　　46; DAM DRAM
　　See also CA 13-16R; CANR 18; DLB 72;
　　　　DLBY 86; MTCW

Gent, Peter 1942- .... **CLC 29**
　　See also AITN 1; CA 89-92; DLBY 82

Gentlewoman in New England, A
　　See Bradstreet, Anne

Gentlewoman in Those Parts, A
　　See Bradstreet, Anne

George, Jean Craighead 1919- ...... **CLC 35**
　　See also AAYA 8; CA 5-8R; CANR 25;
　　　　CLR 1; DLB 52; JRDA; MAICYA;
　　　　SATA 2, 68

George, Stefan (Anton)
　　1868-1933 .... **TCLC 2, 14**
　　See also CA 104

Georges, Georges Martin
　　See Simenon, Georges (Jacques Christian)

Gerhardi, William Alexander
　　See Gerhardie, William Alexander

Gerhardie, William Alexander
　　1895-1977 .... **CLC 5**
　　See also CA 25-28R; 73-76; CANR 18;
　　　　DLB 36

Gerstler, Amy 1956- .... **CLC 70**
　　See also CA 146

Gertler, T. .... **CLC 34**
　　See also CA 116; 121; INT 121

gfgg .... **CLC XvXzc**

Ghalib .... **NCLC 39**
　　See also Ghalib, Hsadullah Khan

Ghalib, Hsadullah Khan 1797-1869
　　See Ghalib
　　See also DAM POET

Ghelderode, Michel de
　　1898-1962 .... **CLC 6, 11; DAM DRAM**
　　See also CA 85-88; CANR 40

Ghiselin, Brewster 1903- .... **CLC 23**
　　See also CA 13-16R; CAAS 10; CANR 13

Ghose, Zulfikar 1935- .... **CLC 42**
　　See also CA 65-68

Ghosh, Amitav 1956- .... **CLC 44**
　　See also CA 147

Giacosa, Giuseppe 1847-1906 ...... **TCLC 7**
　　See also CA 104

Gibb, Lee
　　See Waterhouse, Keith (Spencer)

Gibbon, Lewis Grassic .... **TCLC 4**
　　See also Mitchell, James Leslie

Gibbons, Kaye
　　1960- .... **CLC 50, 88; DAM POP**
　　See also CA 151

Gibran, Kahlil
　　1883-1931 .... **TCLC 1, 9; DAM POET,**
　　　　POP; PC 9
　　See also CA 104; 150

Gibran, Khalil
　　See Gibran, Kahlil

Gibson, William
　　1914- .... **CLC 23; DA; DAB; DAC;**
　　　　DAM DRAM, MST
　　See also CA 9-12R; CANR 9, 42; DLB 7;
　　　　SATA 66

Gibson, William (Ford)
　　1948- .... **CLC 39, 63; DAM POP**
　　See also AAYA 12; CA 126; 133; CANR 52

Gide, Andre (Paul Guillaume)
1869-1951 .... **TCLC 5, 12, 36; DA; DAB; DAC; DAM MST, NOV; SSC 13; WLC**
See also CA 104; 124; DLB 65; MTCW

Gifford, Barry (Colby) 1946-....... **CLC 34**
See also CA 65-68; CANR 9, 30, 40

Gilbert, W(illiam) S(chwenck)
1836-1911 ..... **TCLC 3; DAM DRAM, POET**
See also CA 104; SATA 36

Gilbreth, Frank B., Jr. 1911-....... **CLC 17**
See also CA 9-12R; SATA 2

Gilchrist, Ellen
1935- .... **CLC 34, 48; DAM POP; SSC 14**
See also CA 113; 116; CANR 41; DLB 130; MTCW

Giles, Molly 1942-............... **CLC 39**
See also CA 126

Gill, Patrick
See Creasey, John

Gilliam, Terry (Vance) 1940-....... **CLC 21**
See also Monty Python
See also AAYA 19; CA 108; 113; CANR 35; INT 113

Gillian, Jerry
See Gilliam, Terry (Vance)

Gilliatt, Penelope (Ann Douglass)
1932-1993 .... **CLC 2, 10, 13, 53**
See also AITN 2; CA 13-16R; 141; CANR 49; DLB 14

Gilman, Charlotte (Anna) Perkins (Stetson)
1860-1935 .... **TCLC 9, 37; SSC 13**
See also CA 106; 150

Gilmour, David 1949-............ **CLC 35**
See also CA 138, 147

Gilpin, William 1724-1804....... **NCLC 30**

Gilray, J. D.
See Mencken, H(enry) L(ouis)

Gilroy, Frank D(aniel) 1925-....... **CLC 2**
See also CA 81-84; CANR 32; DLB 7

Gilstrap, John 1957(?)-............ **CLC 99**

Ginsberg, Allen
1926- ...... **CLC 1, 2, 3, 4, 6, 13, 36, 69; DA; DAB; DAC; DAM MST, POET; PC 4; WLC 3**
See also AITN 1; CA 1-4R; CANR 2, 41; CDALB 1941-1968; DLB 5, 16, 169; MTCW

Ginzburg, Natalia
1916-1991 .... **CLC 5, 11, 54, 70**
See also CA 85-88; 135; CANR 33; DLB 177; MTCW

Giono, Jean 1895-1970......... **CLC 4, 11**
See also CA 45-48; 29-32R; CANR 2, 35; DLB 72; MTCW

Giovanni, Nikki
1943- ...... **CLC 2, 4, 19, 64; BLC; DA; DAB; DAC; DAM MST, MULT, POET**
See also AITN 1; BW 2; CA 29-32R; CAAS 6; CANR 18, 41; CLR 6; DLB 5, 41; INT CANR-18; MAICYA; MTCW; SATA 24

Giovene, Andrea 1904-............ **CLC 7**
See also CA 85-88

Gippius, Zinaida (Nikolayevna) 1869-1945
See Hippius, Zinaida
See also CA 106

Giraudoux, (Hippolyte) Jean
1882-1944 .... **TCLC 2, 7; DAM DRAM**
See also CA 104; DLB 65

Gironella, Jose Maria 1917-....... **CLC 11**
See also CA 101

Gissing, George (Robert)
1857-1903 .... **TCLC 3, 24, 47**
See also CA 105; DLB 18, 135

Giurlani, Aldo
See Palazzeschi, Aldo

Gladkov, Fyodor (Vasilyevich)
1883-1958 .... **TCLC 27**

Glanville, Brian (Lester) 1931- ...... **CLC 6**
See also CA 5-8R; CAAS 9; CANR 3; DLB 15, 139; SATA 42

Glasgow, Ellen (Anderson Gholson)
1873(?)-1945 .... **TCLC 2, 7**
See also CA 104; DLB 9, 12

Glaspell, Susan 1882(?)-1948...... **TCLC 55**
See also CA 110; 154; DLB 7, 9, 78; YABC 2

Glassco, John 1909-1981 .... **CLC 9**
See also CA 13-16R; 102; CANR 15; DLB 68

Glasscock, Amnesia
See Steinbeck, John (Ernst)

Glasser, Ronald J. 1940(?)-........ **CLC 37**

Glassman, Joyce
See Johnson, Joyce

Glendinning, Victoria 1937-....... **CLC 50**
See also CA 120; 127; DLB 155

Glissant, Edouard
1928- **CLC 10, 68; DAM MULT**
See also CA 153

Gloag, Julian 1930- .... **CLC 40**
See also AITN 1; CA 65-68; CANR 10

Glowacki, Aleksander
See Prus, Boleslaw

Gluck, Louise (Elisabeth)
1943- .... **CLC 7, 22, 44, 81; DAM POET; PC 16**
See also CA 33-36R; CANR 40; DLB 5

Gobineau, Joseph Arthur (Comte) de
1816-1882 .... **NCLC 17**
See also DLB 123

Godard, Jean-Luc 1930-........... **CLC 20**
See also CA 93-96

Godden, (Margaret) Rumer 1907-... **CLC 53**
See also AAYA 6; CA 5-8R; CANR 4, 27, 36, 55; CLR 20; DLB 161; MAICYA; SAAS 12; SATA 3, 36

Godoy Alcayaga, Lucila 1889-1957
See Mistral, Gabriela
See also BW 2; CA 104; 131; DAM MULT; HW; MTCW

Godwin, Gail (Kathleen)
1937- .... **CLC 5, 8, 22, 31, 69; DAM POP**
See also CA 29-32R; CANR 15, 43; DLB 6; INT CANR-15; MTCW

Godwin, William 1756-1836...... **NCLC 14**
See also CDBLB 1789-1832; DLB 39, 104, 142, 158, 163

Goebbels, Josef
See Goebbels, (Paul) Joseph

Goebbels, (Paul) Joseph
1897-1945 .... **TCLC 68**
See also CA 115; 148

Goebbels, Joseph Paul
See Goebbels, (Paul) Joseph

Goethe, Johann Wolfgang von
1749-1832 .... **NCLC 4, 22, 34; DA; DAB; DAC; DAM DRAM, MST, POET; PC 5; WLC 3**
See also DLB 94

Gogarty, Oliver St. John
1878-1957 .... **TCLC 15**
See also CA 109; 150; DLB 15, 19

Gogol, Nikolai (Vasilyevich)
1809-1852 .... **NCLC 5, 15, 31; DA; DAB; DAC; DAM DRAM, MST; DC 1; SSC 4; WLC**

Goines, Donald
1937(?)-1974 .... **CLC 80; BLC; DAM MULT, POP**
See also AITN 1; BW 1; CA 124; 114; DLB 33

Gold, Herbert 1924-....... **CLC 4, 7, 14, 42**
See also CA 9-12R; CANR 17, 45; DLB 2; DLBY 81

Goldbarth, Albert 1948-........ **CLC 5, 38**
See also CA 53-56; CANR 6, 40; DLB 120

Goldberg, Anatol 1910-1982 .... **CLC 34**
See also CA 131; 117

Goldemberg, Isaac 1945-.......... **CLC 52**
See also CA 69-72; CAAS 12; CANR 11, 32; HW

Golding, William (Gerald)
1911-1993 .... **CLC 1, 2, 3, 8, 10, 17, 27, 58, 81; DA; DAB; DAC; DAM MST, NOV; WLC**
See also AAYA 5; CA 5-8R; 141; CANR 13, 33, 54; CDBLB 1945-1960; DLB 15, 100; MTCW

Goldman, Emma 1869-1940...... **TCLC 13**
See also CA 110; 150

Goldman, Francisco 1955-......... **CLC 76**

Goldman, William (W.) 1931-.... **CLC 1, 48**
See also CA 9-12R; CANR 29; DLB 44

Goldmann, Lucien 1913-1970 ...... **CLC 24**
See also CA 25-28; CAP 2

Goldoni, Carlo
1707-1793 .... **LC 4; DAM DRAM**

Goldsberry, Steven 1949-.......... **CLC 34**
See also CA 131

Goldsmith, Oliver
1728-1774 ...... **LC 2; DA; DAB; DAC; DAM DRAM, MST, NOV, POET; WLC**
See also CDBLB 1660-1789; DLB 39, 89, 104, 109, 142; SATA 26

Goldsmith, Peter
See Priestley, J(ohn) B(oynton)

Green, Julian (Hartridge)　1900-
See Green, Julien
See also CA 21-24R; CANR 33; DLB 4, 72;
MTCW

Green, Julien................ **CLC 3, 11, 77**
See also Green, Julian (Hartridge)

Green, Paul (Eliot)
1894-1981 ...... **CLC 25; DAM DRAM**
See also AITN 1; CA 5-8R; 103; CANR 3;
DLB 7, 9; DLBY 81

Greenberg, Ivan　1908-1973
See Rahv, Philip
See also CA 85-88

Greenberg, Joanne (Goldenberg)
1932-.................... **CLC 7, 30**
See also AAYA 12; CA 5-8R; CANR 14,
32; SATA 25

Greenberg, Richard　1959(?)-....... **CLC 57**
See also CA 138

Greene, Bette　1934-............. **CLC 30**
See also AAYA 7; CA 53-56; CANR 4;
CLR 2; JRDA; MAICYA; SAAS 16;
SATA 8

Greene, Gael.................... **CLC 8**
See also CA 13-16R; CANR 10

Greene, Graham
1904-1991 .... **CLC 1, 3, 6, 9, 14, 18, 27,
37, 70, 72; DA; DAB; DAC; DAM MST,
NOV; WLC**
See also AITN 2; CA 13-16R; 133;
CANR 35; CDBLB 1945-1960; DLB 13,
15, 77, 100, 162; DLBY 91; MTCW;
SATA 20

Greer, Richard
See Silverberg, Robert

Gregor, Arthur　1923-............. **CLC 9**
See also CA 25-28R; CAAS 10; CANR 11;
SATA 36

Gregor, Lee
See Pohl, Frederik

Gregory, Isabella Augusta (Persse)
1852-1932 .... **TCLC 1**
See also CA 104; DLB 10

Gregory, J. Dennis
See Williams, John A(lfred)

Grendon, Stephen
See Derleth, August (William)

Grenville, Kate　1950-............. **CLC 61**
See also CA 118; CANR 53

Grenville, Pelham
See Wodehouse, P(elham) G(renville)

Greve, Felix Paul (Berthold Friedrich)
1879-1948
See Grove, Frederick Philip
See also CA 104; 141; DAC; DAM MST

Grey, Zane
1872-1939 .... **TCLC 6; DAM POP**
See also CA 104; 132; DLB 9; MTCW

Grieg, (Johan) Nordahl (Brun)
1902-1943 .... **TCLC 10**
See also CA 107

Grieve, C(hristopher) M(urray)
1892-1978 .... **CLC 11, 19; DAM POET**
See also MacDiarmid, Hugh; Pteleon
See also CA 5-8R; 85-88; CANR 33;
MTCW

Griffin, Gerald　1803-1840 .... **NCLC 7**
See also DLB 159

Griffin, John Howard　1920-1980.... **CLC 68**
See also AITN 1; CA 1-4R; 101; CANR 2

Griffin, Peter　1942-................ **CLC 39**
See also CA 136

Griffith, D(avid Lewelyn) W(ark)
1875(?)-1948 .... **TCLC 68**
See also CA 119; 150

Griffith, Lawrence
See Griffith, D(avid Lewelyn) W(ark)

Griffiths, Trevor　1935-......... **CLC 13, 52**
See also CA 97-100; CANR 45; DLB 13

Grigson, Geoffrey (Edward Harvey)
1905-1985 .... **CLC 7, 39**
See also CA 25-28R; 118; CANR 20, 33;
DLB 27; MTCW

Grillparzer, Franz　1791-1872...... **NCLC 1**
See also DLB 133

Grimble, Reverend Charles James
See Eliot, T(homas) S(tearns)

Grimke, Charlotte L(ottie) Forten
1837(?)-1914
See Forten, Charlotte L.
See also BW 1; CA 117; 124; DAM MULT,
POET

Grimm, Jacob Ludwig Karl
1785-1863 .... **NCLC 3**
See also DLB 90; MAICYA; SATA 22

Grimm, Wilhelm Karl　1786-1859 .. **NCLC 3**
See also DLB 90; MAICYA; SATA 22

**Grimmelshausen, Johann Jakob Christoffel
von**　1621-1676 .... **LC 6**
See also DLB 168

Grindel, Eugene　1895-1952
See Eluard, Paul
See also CA 104

Grisham, John　1955- .. **CLC 84; DAM POP**
See also AAYA 14; CA 138; CANR 47

Grossman, David　1954-........... **CLC 67**
See also CA 138

Grossman, Vasily (Semenovich)
1905-1964 .... **CLC 41**
See also CA 124; 130; MTCW

Grove, Frederick Philip .... **TCLC 4**
See also Greve, Felix Paul (Berthold
Friedrich)
See also DLB 92

Grubb
See Crumb, R(obert)

Grumbach, Doris (Isaac)
1918- .... **CLC 13, 22, 64**
See also CA 5-8R; CAAS 2; CANR 9, 42;
INT CANR-9

Grundtvig, Nicolai Frederik Severin
1783-1872 .... **NCLC 1**

Grunge
See Crumb, R(obert)

Grunwald, Lisa　1959-............. **CLC 44**
See also CA 120

Guare, John
1938- .... **CLC 8, 14, 29, 67;
DAM DRAM**
See also CA 73-76; CANR 21; DLB 7;
MTCW

Gudjonsson, Halldor Kiljan　1902-
See Laxness, Halldor
See also CA 103

Guenter, Erich
See Eich, Guenter

Guest, Barbara　1920-............. **CLC 34**
See also CA 25-28R; CANR 11, 44; DLB 5

Guest, Judith (Ann)
1936- .... **CLC 8, 30; DAM NOV, POP**
See also AAYA 7; CA 77-80; CANR 15;
INT CANR-15; MTCW

Guevara, Che.............. **CLC 87; HLC**
See also Guevara (Serna), Ernesto

Guevara (Serna), Ernesto　1928-1967
See Guevara, Che
See also CA 127; 111; CANR 56;
DAM MULT; HW

Guild, Nicholas M.　1944-.......... **CLC 33**
See also CA 93-96

Guillemin, Jacques
See Sartre, Jean-Paul

Guillen, Jorge
1893-1984 ...... **CLC 11; DAM MULT,
POET**
See also CA 89-92; 112; DLB 108; HW

Guillen, Nicolas (Cristobal)
1902-1989 .... **CLC 48, 79; BLC;
DAM MST, MULT, POET; HLC**
See also BW 2; CA 116; 125; 129; HW

Guillevic, (Eugene)　1907-......... **CLC 33**
See also CA 93-96

Guillois
See Desnos, Robert

Guillois, Valentin
See Desnos, Robert

Guiney, Louise Imogen
1861-1920 .... **TCLC 41**
See also DLB 54

Guiraldes, Ricardo (Guillermo)
1886-1927 .... **TCLC 39**
See also CA 131; HW; MTCW

Gumilev, Nikolai Stephanovich
1886-1921 .... **TCLC 60**

Gunesekera, Romesh.............. **CLC 91**

Gunn, Bill .... **CLC 5**
See also Gunn, William Harrison
See also DLB 38

Gunn, Thom(son William)
1929- .... **CLC 3, 6, 18, 32, 81;
DAM POET**
See also CA 17-20R; CANR 9, 33;
CDBLB 1960 to Present; DLB 27;
INT CANR-33; MTCW

Gunn, William Harrison　1934(?)-1989
See Gunn, Bill
See also AITN 1; BW 1; CA 13-16R; 128;
CANR 12, 25

Gunnars, Kristjana　1948-.......... **CLC 69**
See also CA 113; DLB 60

Gurganus, Allan
1947- .... **CLC 70; DAM POP**
See also BEST 90:1; CA 135

Gurney, A(lbert) R(amsdell), Jr.
1930- .... **CLC 32, 50, 54; DAM DRAM**
See also CA 77-80; CANR 32

Harling, Robert 1951(?)- .... **CLC 53**
See also CA 147

Harmon, William (Ruth) 1938- ..... **CLC 38**
See also CA 33-36R; CANR 14, 32, 35;
SATA 65

Harper, F. E. W.
See Harper, Frances Ellen Watkins

Harper, Frances E. W.
See Harper, Frances Ellen Watkins

Harper, Frances E. Watkins
See Harper, Frances Ellen Watkins

Harper, Frances Ellen
See Harper, Frances Ellen Watkins

Harper, Frances Ellen Watkins
1825-1911 .... **TCLC 14; BLC;**
DAM MULT, POET
See also BW 1; CA 111; 125; DLB 50

Harper, Michael S(teven) 1938- .. **CLC 7, 22**
See also BW 1; CA 33-36R; CANR 24;
DLB 41

Harper, Mrs. F. E. W.
See Harper, Frances Ellen Watkins

Harris, Christie (Lucy) Irwin
1907- .... **CLC 12**
See also CA 5-8R; CANR 6; DLB 88;
JRDA; MAICYA; SAAS 10; SATA 6, 74

Harris, Frank 1856-1931 .... **TCLC 24**
See also CA 109; 150; DLB 156

Harris, George Washington
1814-1869 .... **NCLC 23**
See also DLB 3, 11

Harris, Joel Chandler
1848-1908 .... **TCLC 2; SSC 19**
See also CA 104; 137; DLB 11, 23, 42, 78,
91; MAICYA; YABC 1

Harris, John (Wyndham Parkes Lucas)
Beynon 1903-1969
See Wyndham, John
See also CA 102; 89-92

Harris, MacDonald .... **CLC 9**
See also Heiney, Donald (William)

Harris, Mark 1922- .... **CLC 19**
See also CA 5-8R; CAAS 3; CANR 2, 55;
DLB 2; DLBY 80

Harris, (Theodore) Wilson 1921-.... **CLC 25**
See also BW 2; CA 65-68; CAAS 16;
CANR 11, 27; DLB 117; MTCW

Harrison, Elizabeth Cavanna 1909-
See Cavanna, Betty
See also CA 9-12R; CANR 6, 27

Harrison, Harry (Max) 1925- ...... **CLC 42**
See also CA 1-4R; CANR 5, 21; DLB 8;
SATA 4

Harrison, James (Thomas)
1937- ...... **CLC 6, 14, 33, 66; SSC 19**
See also CA 13-16R; CANR 8, 51;
DLBY 82; INT CANR-8

Harrison, Jim
See Harrison, James (Thomas)

Harrison, Kathryn 1961- .... **CLC 70**
See also CA 144

Harrison, Tony 1937-............. **CLC 43**
See also CA 65-68; CANR 44; DLB 40;
MTCW

Harriss, Will(ard Irvin) 1922-...... **CLC 34**
See also CA 111

Harson, Sley
See Ellison, Harlan (Jay)

Hart, Ellis
See Ellison, Harlan (Jay)

Hart, Josephine
1942(?)- .... **CLC 70; DAM POP**
See also CA 138

Hart, Moss
1904-1961 ...... **CLC 66; DAM DRAM**
See also CA 109; 89-92; DLB 7

Harte, (Francis) Bret(t)
1836(?)-1902 .... **TCLC 1, 25; DA; DAC;**
DAM MST; SSC 8; WLC
See also CA 104; 140; CDALB 1865-1917;
DLB 12, 64, 74, 79; SATA 26

Hartley, L(eslie) P(oles)
1895-1972 .... **CLC 2, 22**
See also CA 45-48; 37-40R; CANR 33;
DLB 15, 139; MTCW

Hartman, Geoffrey H. 1929-....... **CLC 27**
See also CA 117; 125; DLB 67

Hartmann von Aue
c. 1160-c. 1205 .... **CMLC 15**
See also DLB 138

Hartmann von Aue 1170-1210.... **CMLC 15**

Haruf, Kent 1943- .... **CLC 34**
See also CA 149

Harwood, Ronald
1934- .... **CLC 32; DAM DRAM, MST**
See also CA 1-4R; CANR 4, 55; DLB 13

Hasek, Jaroslav (Matej Frantisek)
1883-1923 .... **TCLC 4**
See also CA 104; 129; MTCW

Hass, Robert
1941- .... **CLC 18, 39, 99; PC 16**
See also CA 111; CANR 30, 50; DLB 105

Hastings, Hudson
See Kuttner, Henry

Hastings, Selina. .... **CLC 44**

Hatteras, Amelia
See Mencken, H(enry) L(ouis)

Hatteras, Owen. .... **TCLC 18**
See also Mencken, H(enry) L(ouis); Nathan,
George Jean

Hauptmann, Gerhart (Johann Robert)
1862-1946 ...... **TCLC 4; DAM DRAM**
See also CA 104; 153; DLB 66, 118

Havel, Vaclav
1936- .... **CLC 25, 58, 65;**
DAM DRAM; DC 6
See also CA 104; CANR 36; MTCW

Haviaras, Stratis. .... **CLC 33**
See also Chaviaras, Strates

Hawes, Stephen 1475(?)-1523(?) ..... **LC 17**

Hawkes, John (Clendennin Burne, Jr.)
1925- ...... **CLC 1, 2, 3, 4, 7, 9, 14, 15,**
27, 49
See also CA 1-4R; CANR 2, 47; DLB 2, 7;
DLBY 80; MTCW

Hawking, S. W.
See Hawking, Stephen W(illiam)

Hawking, Stephen W(illiam)
1942- .... **CLC 63**
See also AAYA 13; BEST 89:1; CA 126;
129; CANR 48

Hawthorne, Julian 1846-1934 ..... **TCLC 25**

Hawthorne, Nathaniel
1804-1864 .... **NCLC 39; DA; DAB;**
DAC; DAM MST, NOV; SSC 3; WLC
See also AAYA 18; CDALB 1640-1865;
DLB 1, 74; YABC 2

Haxton, Josephine Ayres 1921-
See Douglas, Ellen
See also CA 115; CANR 41

Hayaseca y Eizaguirre, Jorge
See Echegaray (y Eizaguirre), Jose (Maria
Waldo)

Hayashi Fumiko 1904-1951....... **TCLC 27**

Haycraft, Anna
See Ellis, Alice Thomas
See also CA 122

Hayden, Robert E(arl)
1913-1980 ...... **CLC 5, 9, 14, 37; BLC;**
DA; DAC; DAM MST, MULT, POET;
PC 6
See also BW 1; CA 69-72; 97-100; CABS 2;
CANR 24; CDALB 1941-1968; DLB 5,
76; MTCW; SATA 19; SATA-Obit 26

Hayford, J(oseph) E(phraim) Casely
See Casely-Hayford, J(oseph) E(phraim)

Hayman, Ronald 1932-............ **CLC 44**
See also CA 25-28R; CANR 18, 50;
DLB 155

Haywood, Eliza (Fowler)
1693(?)-1756 .... **LC 1**

Hazlitt, William 1778-1830 ...... **NCLC 29**
See also DLB 110, 158

Hazzard, Shirley 1931- .... **CLC 18**
See also CA 9-12R; CANR 4; DLBY 82;
MTCW

Head, Bessie
1937-1986 .... **CLC 25, 67; BLC;**
DAM MULT
See also BW 2; CA 29-32R; 119; CANR 25;
DLB 117; MTCW

Headon, (Nicky) Topper 1956(?)- ... **CLC 30**

Heaney, Seamus (Justin)
1939- ...... **CLC 5, 7, 14, 25, 37, 74, 91;**
DAB; DAM POET
See also CA 85-88; CANR 25, 48;
CDBLB 1960 to Present; DLB 40;
DLBY 95; MTCW

Hearn, (Patricio) Lafcadio (Tessima Carlos)
1850-1904 .... **TCLC 9**
See also CA 105; DLB 12, 78

Hearne, Vicki 1946-.............. **CLC 56**
See also CA 139

Hearon, Shelby 1931-............. **CLC 63**
See also AITN 2; CA 25-28R; CANR 18,
48

Heat-Moon, William Least. .... **CLC 29**
See also Trogdon, William (Lewis)
See also AAYA 9

Hebbel, Friedrich
1813-1863 .... **NCLC 43; DAM DRAM**
See also DLB 129

Hibbert, Eleanor Alice Burford
1906-1993 . . . . **CLC 7; DAM POP**
See also BEST 90:4; CA 17-20R; 140;
CANR 9, 28; SATA 2; SATA-Obit 74

Hichens, Robert S.   1864-1950 . . . . . **TCLC 64**
See also DLB 153

Higgins, George V(incent)
1939- . . . . **CLC 4, 7, 10, 18**
See also CA 77-80; CAAS 5; CANR 17, 51;
DLB 2; DLBY 81; INT CANR-17;
MTCW

Higginson, Thomas Wentworth
1823-1911 . . . . **TCLC 36**
See also DLB 1, 64

Highet, Helen
See MacInnes, Helen (Clark)

Highsmith, (Mary) Patricia
1921-1995 . . . . **CLC 2, 4, 14, 42;
DAM NOV, POP**
See also CA 1-4R; 147; CANR 1, 20, 48;
MTCW

Highwater, Jamake (Mamake)
1942(?)- . . . . **CLC 12**
See also AAYA 7; CA 65-68; CAAS 7;
CANR 10, 34; CLR 17; DLB 52;
DLBY 85; JRDA; MAICYA; SATA 32,
69; SATA-Brief 30

Highway, Tomson
1951- . . . . . **CLC 92; DAC; DAM MULT**
See also CA 151; NNAL

Higuchi, Ichiyo   1872-1896 . . . . . . **NCLC 49**

Hijuelos, Oscar
1951- . . . . **CLC 65; DAM MULT, POP;
HLC**
See also BEST 90:1; CA 123; CANR 50;
DLB 145; HW

Hikmet, Nazim   1902(?)-1963 . . . . . . **CLC 40**
See also CA 141; 93-96

Hildegard von Bingen
1098-1179 . . . . **CMLC 20**
See also DLB 148

Hildesheimer, Wolfgang
1916-1991 . . . . **CLC 49**
See also CA 101; 135; DLB 69, 124

Hill, Geoffrey (William)
1932- . . . **CLC 5, 8, 18, 45; DAM POET**
See also CA 81-84; CANR 21;
CDBLB 1960 to Present; DLB 40;
MTCW

Hill, George Roy   1921- . . . . **CLC 26**
See also CA 110; 122

Hill, John
See Koontz, Dean R(ay)

Hill, Susan (Elizabeth)
1942- . . **CLC 4; DAB; DAM MST, NOV**
See also CA 33-36R; CANR 29; DLB 14,
139; MTCW

Hillerman, Tony
1925- . . . . **CLC 62; DAM POP**
See also AAYA 6; BEST 89:1; CA 29-32R;
CANR 21, 42; SATA 6

Hillesum, Etty   1914-1943 . . . . **TCLC 49**
See also CA 137

Hilliard, Noel (Harvey)   1929- . . . . . . **CLC 15**
See also CA 9-12R; CANR 7

Hillis, Rick   1956- . . . . **CLC 66**
See also CA 134

Hilton, James   1900-1954 . . . . **TCLC 21**
See also CA 108; DLB 34, 77; SATA 34

Himes, Chester (Bomar)
1909-1984 . . . . **CLC 2, 4, 7, 18, 58; BLC;
DAM MULT**
See also BW 2; CA 25-28R; 114; CANR 22;
DLB 2, 76, 143; MTCW

Hinde, Thomas . . . . **CLC 6, 11**
See also Chitty, Thomas Willes

Hindin, Nathan
See Bloch, Robert (Albert)

Hine, (William) Daryl   1936- . . . . **CLC 15**
See also CA 1-4R; CAAS 15; CANR 1, 20;
DLB 60

Hinkson, Katharine Tynan
See Tynan, Katharine

Hinton, S(usan) E(loise)
1950- . . . . **CLC 30; DA; DAB; DAC;
DAM MST, NOV**
See also AAYA 2; CA 81-84; CANR 32;
CLR 3, 23; JRDA; MAICYA; MTCW;
SATA 19, 58

Hippius, Zinaida . . . . **TCLC 9**
See also Gippius, Zinaida (Nikolayevna)

Hiraoka, Kimitake   1925-1970
See Mishima, Yukio
See also CA 97-100; 29-32R; DAM DRAM;
MTCW

Hirsch, E(ric) D(onald), Jr.   1928- . . . **CLC 79**
See also CA 25-28R; CANR 27, 51;
DLB 67; INT CANR-27; MTCW

Hirsch, Edward   1950- . . . . **CLC 31, 50**
See also CA 104; CANR 20, 42; DLB 120

Hitchcock, Alfred (Joseph)
1899-1980 . . . . **CLC 16**
See also CA 97-100; SATA 27;
SATA-Obit 24

Hitler, Adolf   1889-1945 . . . . **TCLC 53**
See also CA 117; 147

Hoagland, Edward   1932- . . . . **CLC 28**
See also CA 1-4R; CANR 2, 31, 57; DLB 6;
SATA 51

Hoban, Russell (Conwell)
1925- . . . . **CLC 7, 25; DAM NOV**
See also CA 5-8R; CANR 23, 37; CLR 3;
DLB 52; MAICYA; MTCW; SATA 1,
40, 78

Hobbes, Thomas   1588-1679 . . . . **LC 36**
See also DLB 151

Hobbs, Perry
See Blackmur, R(ichard) P(almer)

Hobson, Laura Z(ametkin)
1900-1986 . . . . **CLC 7, 25**
See also CA 17-20R; 118; CANR 55;
DLB 28; SATA 52

Hochhuth, Rolf
1931- . . . . . **CLC 4, 11, 18; DAM DRAM**
See also CA 5-8R; CANR 33; DLB 124;
MTCW

Hochman, Sandra   1936- . . . . **CLC 3, 8**
See also CA 5-8R; DLB 5

Hochwaelder, Fritz
1911-1986 . . . . . . **CLC 36; DAM DRAM**
See also CA 29-32R; 120; CANR 42;
MTCW

Hochwalder, Fritz
See Hochwaelder, Fritz

Hocking, Mary (Eunice)   1921- . . . . . **CLC 13**
See also CA 101; CANR 18, 40

Hodgins, Jack   1938- . . . . **CLC 23**
See also CA 93-96; DLB 60

Hodgson, William Hope
1877(?)-1918 . . . . **TCLC 13**
See also CA 111; DLB 70, 153, 156

Hoeg, Peter   1957- . . . . **CLC 95**
See also CA 151

Hoffman, Alice
1952- . . . . **CLC 51; DAM NOV**
See also CA 77-80; CANR 34; MTCW

Hoffman, Daniel (Gerard)
1923- . . . . **CLC 6, 13, 23**
See also CA 1-4R; CANR 4; DLB 5

Hoffman, Stanley   1944- . . . . **CLC 5**
See also CA 77-80

Hoffman, William M(oses)   1939- . . . **CLC 40**
See also CA 57-60; CANR 11

Hoffmann, E(rnst) T(heodor) A(madeus)
1776-1822 . . . . **NCLC 2; SSC 13**
See also DLB 90; SATA 27

Hofmann, Gert   1931- . . . . **CLC 54**
See also CA 128

Hofmannsthal, Hugo von
1874-1929 . . . . **TCLC 11; DAM DRAM;
DC 4**
See also CA 106; 153; DLB 81, 118

Hogan, Linda
1947- . . . . **CLC 73; DAM MULT**
See also CA 120; CANR 45; DLB 175;
NNAL

Hogarth, Charles
See Creasey, John

Hogarth, Emmett
See Polonsky, Abraham (Lincoln)

Hogg, James   1770-1835 . . . . **NCLC 4**
See also DLB 93, 116, 159

Holbach, Paul Henri Thiry Baron
1723-1789 . . . . **LC 14**

Holberg, Ludvig   1684-1754 . . . . **LC 6**

Holden, Ursula   1921- . . . . **CLC 18**
See also CA 101; CAAS 8; CANR 22

Holderlin, (Johann Christian) Friedrich
1770-1843 . . . . **NCLC 16; PC 4**

Holdstock, Robert
See Holdstock, Robert P.

Holdstock, Robert P.   1948- . . . . **CLC 39**
See also CA 131

Holland, Isabelle   1920- . . . . **CLC 21**
See also AAYA 11; CA 21-24R; CANR 10,
25, 47; JRDA; MAICYA; SATA 8, 70

Holland, Marcus
See Caldwell, (Janet Miriam) Taylor
(Holland)

Hollander, John   1929- . . . . . . **CLC 2, 5, 8, 14**
See also CA 1-4R; CANR 1, 52; DLB 5;
SATA 13

Hollander, Paul
See Silverberg, Robert

Holleran, Andrew 1943(?)-......... **CLC 38**
See also CA 144

Hollinghurst, Alan 1954-....... **CLC 55, 91**
See also CA 114

Hollis, Jim
See Summers, Hollis (Spurgeon, Jr.)

Holly, Buddy 1936-1959 .... **TCLC 65**

Holmes, John
See Souster, (Holmes) Raymond

Holmes, John Clellon 1926-1988.... **CLC 56**
See also CA 9-12R; 125; CANR 4; DLB 16

Holmes, Oliver Wendell
1809-1894 .... **NCLC 14**
See also CDALB 1640-1865; DLB 1;
SATA 34

Holmes, Raymond
See Souster, (Holmes) Raymond

Holt, Victoria
See Hibbert, Eleanor Alice Burford

Holub, Miroslav 1923-............. **CLC 4**
See also CA 21-24R; CANR 10

Homer
c. 8th cent. B.C.-..... **CMLC 1, 16; DA;**
DAB; DAC; DAM MST, POET
See also DLB 176

Honig, Edwin 1919- .... **CLC 33**
See also CA 5-8R; CAAS 8; CANR 4, 45;
DLB 5

Hood, Hugh (John Blagdon)
1928- .... **CLC 15, 28**
See also CA 49-52; CAAS 17; CANR 1, 33;
DLB 53

Hood, Thomas 1799-1845....... **NCLC 16**
See also DLB 96

Hooker, (Peter) Jeremy 1941-...... **CLC 43**
See also CA 77-80; CANR 22; DLB 40

hooks, bell .... **CLC 94**
See also Watkins, Gloria

Hope, A(lec) D(erwent) 1907- .... **CLC 3, 51**
See also CA 21-24R; CANR 33; MTCW

Hope, Brian
See Creasey, John

Hope, Christopher (David Tully)
1944- .... **CLC 52**
See also CA 106; CANR 47; SATA 62

Hopkins, Gerard Manley
1844-1889 .... **NCLC 17; DA; DAB;**
DAC; DAM MST, POET; PC 15; WLC
See also CDBLB 1890-1914; DLB 35, 57

Hopkins, John (Richard) 1931-...... **CLC 4**
See also CA 85-88

Hopkins, Pauline Elizabeth
1859-1930 .... **TCLC 28; BLC;**
DAM MULT
See also BW 2; CA 141; DLB 50

Hopkinson, Francis 1737-1791 ...... **LC 25**
See also DLB 31

Hopley-Woolrich, Cornell George 1903-1968
See Woolrich, Cornell
See also CA 13-14; CAP 1

Horatio
See Proust, (Valentin-Louis-George-Eugene-)
Marcel

Horgan, Paul (George Vincent O'Shaughnessy)
1903-1995 ...... **CLC 9, 53; DAM NOV**
See also CA 13-16R; 147; CANR 9, 35;
DLB 102; DLBY 85; INT CANR-9;
MTCW; SATA 13; SATA-Obit 84

Horn, Peter
See Kuttner, Henry

Hornem, Horace Esq.
See Byron, George Gordon (Noel)

Hornung, E(rnest) W(illiam)
1866-1921 .... **TCLC 59**
See also CA 108; DLB 70

Horovitz, Israel (Arthur)
1939- .... **CLC 56; DAM DRAM**
See also CA 33-36R; CANR 46; DLB 7

Horvath, Odon von
See Horvath, Oedoen von
See also DLB 85, 124

Horvath, Oedoen von 1901-1938... **TCLC 45**
See also Horvath, Odon von
See also CA 118

Horwitz, Julius 1920-1986........ **CLC 14**
See also CA 9-12R; 119; CANR 12

Hospital, Janette Turner 1942-..... **CLC 42**
See also CA 108; CANR 48

Hostos, E. M. de
See Hostos (y Bonilla), Eugenio Maria de

Hostos, Eugenio M. de
See Hostos (y Bonilla), Eugenio Maria de

Hostos, Eugenio Maria
See Hostos (y Bonilla), Eugenio Maria de

Hostos (y Bonilla), Eugenio Maria de
1839-1903 .... **TCLC 24**
See also CA 123; 131; HW

Houdini
See Lovecraft, H(oward) P(hillips)

Hougan, Carolyn 1943- .... **CLC 34**
See also CA 139

Household, Geoffrey (Edward West)
1900-1988 .... **CLC 11**
See also CA 77-80; 126; DLB 87; SATA 14;
SATA-Obit 59

Housman, A(lfred) E(dward)
1859-1936 ...... **TCLC 1, 10; DA; DAB;**
DAC; DAM MST, POET; PC 2
See also CA 104; 125; DLB 19; MTCW

Housman, Laurence 1865-1959..... **TCLC 7**
See also CA 106; 155; DLB 10; SATA 25

Howard, Elizabeth Jane 1923- ... **CLC 7, 29**
See also CA 5-8R; CANR 8

Howard, Maureen 1930- ..... **CLC 5, 14, 46**
See also CA 53-56; CANR 31; DLBY 83;
INT CANR-31; MTCW

Howard, Richard 1929- ...... **CLC 7, 10, 47**
See also AITN 1; CA 85-88; CANR 25;
DLB 5; INT CANR-25

Howard, Robert Ervin 1906-1936... **TCLC 8**
See also CA 105

Howard, Warren F.
See Pohl, Frederik

Howe, Fanny 1940- .... **CLC 47**
See also CA 117; SATA-Brief 52

Howe, Irving 1920-1993.......... **CLC 85**
See also CA 9-12R; 141; CANR 21, 50;
DLB 67; MTCW

Howe, Julia Ward 1819-1910 ..... **TCLC 21**
See also CA 117; DLB 1

Howe, Susan 1937-.............. **CLC 72**
See also DLB 120

Howe, Tina 1937-............... **CLC 48**
See also CA 109

Howell, James 1594(?)-1666 .... **LC 13**
See also DLB 151

Howells, W. D.
See Howells, William Dean

Howells, William D.
See Howells, William Dean

Howells, William Dean
1837-1920 .... **TCLC 7, 17, 41**
See also CA 104; 134; CDALB 1865-1917;
DLB 12, 64, 74, 79

Howes, Barbara 1914-1996 .... **CLC 15**
See also CA 9-12R; 151; CAAS 3;
CANR 53; SATA 5

Hrabal, Bohumil 1914-1997..... **CLC 13, 67**
See also CA 106; 156; CAAS 12; CANR 57

Hsun, Lu
See Lu Hsun

Hubbard, L(afayette) Ron(ald)
1911-1986 .... **CLC 43; DAM POP**
See also CA 77-80; 118; CANR 52

Huch, Ricarda (Octavia)
1864-1947 .... **TCLC 13**
See also CA 111; DLB 66

Huddle, David 1942- .... **CLC 49**
See also CA 57-60; CAAS 20; DLB 130

Hudson, Jeffrey
See Crichton, (John) Michael

Hudson, W(illiam) H(enry)
1841-1922 .... **TCLC 29**
See also CA 115; DLB 98, 153, 174;
SATA 35

Hueffer, Ford Madox
See Ford, Ford Madox

Hughart, Barry 1934-............. **CLC 39**
See also CA 137

Hughes, Colin
See Creasey, John

Hughes, David (John) 1930- .... **CLC 48**
See also CA 116; 129; DLB 14

Hughes, Edward James
See Hughes, Ted
See also DAM MST, POET

Hughes, (James) Langston
1902-1967 ..... **CLC 1, 5, 10, 15, 35, 44;**
BLC; DA; DAB; DAC; DAM DRAM,
MST, MULT, POET; DC 3; PC 1;
SSC 6; WLC
See also AAYA 12; BW 1; CA 1-4R;
25-28R; CANR 1, 34; CDALB 1929-1941;
CLR 17; DLB 4, 7, 48, 51, 86; JRDA;
MAICYA; MTCW; SATA 4, 33

Hughes, Richard (Arthur Warren)
1900-1976 ...... **CLC 1, 11; DAM NOV**
See also CA 5-8R; 65-68; CANR 4;
DLB 15, 161; MTCW; SATA 8;
SATA-Obit 25

Hughes, Ted
1930- .... **CLC 2, 4, 9, 14, 37; DAB;**
DAC; PC 7
See also Hughes, Edward James
See also CA 1-4R; CANR 1, 33; CLR 3;
DLB 40, 161; MAICYA; MTCW;
SATA 49; SATA-Brief 27

Hugo, Richard F(ranklin)
1923-1982 .... **CLC 6, 18, 32;**
DAM POET
See also CA 49-52; 108; CANR 3; DLB 5

Hugo, Victor (Marie)
1802-1885 .... **NCLC 3, 10, 21; DA;**
DAB; DAC; DAM DRAM, MST, NOV,
POET; PC 17; WLC
See also DLB 119; SATA 47

Huidobro, Vicente
See Huidobro Fernandez, Vicente Garcia

Huidobro Fernandez, Vicente Garcia
1893-1948 .... **TCLC 31**
See also CA 131; HW

Hulme, Keri 1947- .... **CLC 39**
See also CA 125; INT 125

Hulme, T(homas) E(rnest)
1883-1917 .... **TCLC 21**
See also CA 117; DLB 19

Hume, David 1711-1776............. **LC 7**
See also DLB 104

Humphrey, William 1924-......... **CLC 45**
See also CA 77-80; DLB 6

Humphreys, Emyr Owen 1919-..... **CLC 47**
See also CA 5-8R; CANR 3, 24; DLB 15

Humphreys, Josephine 1945-.... **CLC 34, 57**
See also CA 121; 127; INT 127

Huneker, James Gibbons
1857-1921 .... **TCLC 65**
See also DLB 71

Hungerford, Pixie
See Brinsmead, H(esba) F(ay)

Hunt, E(verette) Howard, (Jr.)
1918- .... **CLC 3**
See also AITN 1; CA 45-48; CANR 2, 47

Hunt, Kyle
See Creasey, John

Hunt, (James Henry) Leigh
1784-1859 ...... **NCLC 1; DAM POET**

Hunt, Marsha 1946-............. **CLC 70**
See also BW 2; CA 143

Hunt, Violet 1866-1942 .... **TCLC 53**
See also DLB 162

Hunter, E. Waldo
See Sturgeon, Theodore (Hamilton)

Hunter, Evan
1926- .... **CLC 11, 31; DAM POP**
See also CA 5-8R; CANR 5, 38; DLBY 82;
INT CANR-5; MTCW; SATA 25

Hunter, Kristin (Eggleston) 1931-... **CLC 35**
See also AITN 1; BW 1; CA 13-16R;
CANR 13; CLR 3; DLB 33;
INT CANR-13; MAICYA; SAAS 10;
SATA 12

Hunter, Mollie 1922-............. **CLC 21**
See also McIlwraith, Maureen Mollie
Hunter
See also AAYA 13; CANR 37; CLR 25;
DLB 161; JRDA; MAICYA; SAAS 7;
SATA 54

Hunter, Robert (?)-1734............. **LC 7**

Hurston, Zora Neale
1903-1960 .... **CLC 7, 30, 61; BLC; DA;**
DAC; DAM MST, MULT, NOV; SSC 4
See also AAYA 15; BW 1; CA 85-88;
DLB 51, 86; MTCW

Huston, John (Marcellus)
1906-1987 .... **CLC 20**
See also CA 73-76; 123; CANR 34; DLB 26

Hustvedt, Siri 1955-............. **CLC 76**
See also CA 137

Hutten, Ulrich von 1488-1523....... **LC 16**

Huxley, Aldous (Leonard)
1894-1963 ..... **CLC 1, 3, 4, 5, 8, 11, 18,**
35, 79; DA; DAB; DAC; DAM MST,
NOV; WLC
See also AAYA 11; CA 85-88; CANR 44;
CDBLB 1914-1945; DLB 36, 100, 162;
MTCW; SATA 63

Huysmans, Charles Marie Georges
1848-1907
See Huysmans, Joris-Karl
See also CA 104

Huysmans, Joris-Karl........... TCLC 7, 69
See also Huysmans, Charles Marie Georges
See also DLB 123

Hwang, David Henry
1957- .... **CLC 55; DAM DRAM; DC 4**
See also CA 127; 132; INT 132

Hyde, Anthony 1946-............. **CLC 42**
See also CA 136

Hyde, Margaret O(ldroyd) 1917- ... **CLC 21**
See also CA 1-4R; CANR 1, 36; CLR 23;
JRDA; MAICYA; SAAS 8; SATA 1, 42,
76

Hynes, James 1956(?)-............. **CLC 65**

Ian, Janis 1951- .... **CLC 21**
See also CA 105

Ibanez, Vicente Blasco
See Blasco Ibanez, Vicente

Ibarguengoitia, Jorge 1928-1983.... **CLC 37**
See also CA 124; 113; HW

Ibsen, Henrik (Johan)
1828-1906 ...... **TCLC 2, 8, 16, 37, 52;**
DA; DAB; DAC; DAM DRAM, MST;
DC 2; WLC
See also CA 104; 141

Ibuse Masuji 1898-1993.......... **CLC 22**
See also CA 127; 141

Ichikawa, Kon 1915-............. **CLC 20**
See also CA 121

Idle, Eric 1943-................. **CLC 21**
See also Monty Python
See also CA 116; CANR 35

Ignatow, David 1914-...... **CLC 4, 7, 14, 40**
See also CA 9-12R; CAAS 3; CANR 31, 57;
DLB 5

Ihimaera, Witi 1944- .... **CLC 46**
See also CA 77-80

Ilf, Ilya........................ TCLC 21
See also Fainzilberg, Ilya Arnoldovich

Illyes, Gyula 1902-1983............ **PC 16**
See also CA 114; 109

Immermann, Karl (Lebrecht)
1796-1840 .... **NCLC 4, 49**
See also DLB 133

Inclan, Ramon (Maria) del Valle
See Valle-Inclan, Ramon (Maria) del

Infante, G(uillermo) Cabrera
See Cabrera Infante, G(uillermo)

Ingalls, Rachel (Holmes) 1940-..... **CLC 42**
See also CA 123; 127

Ingamells, Rex 1913-1955 .... **TCLC 35**

Inge, William (Motter)
1913-1973 .. **CLC 1, 8, 19; DAM DRAM**
See also CA 9-12R; CDALB 1941-1968;
DLB 7; MTCW

Ingelow, Jean 1820-1897 .... **NCLC 39**
See also DLB 35, 163; SATA 33

Ingram, Willis J.
See Harris, Mark

Innaurato, Albert (F.) 1948(?)- .. **CLC 21, 60**
See also CA 115; 122; INT 122

Innes, Michael
See Stewart, J(ohn) I(nnes) M(ackintosh)

Ionesco, Eugene
1909-1994 .... **CLC 1, 4, 6, 9, 11, 15, 41,**
86; DA; DAB; DAC; DAM DRAM,
MST; WLC
See also CA 9-12R; 144; CANR 55;
MTCW; SATA 7; SATA-Obit 79

Iqbal, Muhammad 1873-1938 ..... **TCLC 28**

Ireland, Patrick
See O'Doherty, Brian

Iron, Ralph
See Schreiner, Olive (Emilie Albertina)

Irving, John (Winslow)
1942- ..... **CLC 13, 23, 38; DAM NOV,**
POP
See also AAYA 8; BEST 89:3; CA 25-28R;
CANR 28; DLB 6; DLBY 82; MTCW

Irving, Washington
1783-1859 ..... **NCLC 2, 19; DA; DAB;**
DAM MST; SSC 2; WLC
See also CDALB 1640-1865; DLB 3, 11, 30,
59, 73, 74; YABC 2

Irwin, P. K.
See Page, P(atricia) K(athleen)

Isaacs, Susan 1943- ... **CLC 32; DAM POP**
See also BEST 89:1; CA 89-92; CANR 20,
41; INT CANR-20; MTCW

Isherwood, Christopher (William Bradshaw)
1904-1986 .... **CLC 1, 9, 11, 14, 44;**
DAM DRAM, NOV
See also CA 13-16R; 117; CANR 35;
DLB 15; DLBY 86; MTCW

Ishiguro, Kazuo
1954- ...... **CLC 27, 56, 59; DAM NOV**
See also BEST 90:2; CA 120; CANR 49;
MTCW

Ishikawa, Hakuhin
See Ishikawa, Takuboku

Ishikawa, Takuboku
1886(?)-1912 .... **TCLC 15;**
DAM POET; PC 10
See also CA 113; 153

Iskander, Fazil 1929-............. **CLC 47**
See also CA 102

Isler, Alan (David) 1934-.......... **CLC 91**
See also CA 156

Ivan IV 1530-1584 .... **LC 17**

Ivanov, Vyacheslav Ivanovich
1866-1949 .... **TCLC 33**
See also CA 122

Ivask, Ivar Vidrik 1927-1992....... **CLC 14**
See also CA 37-40R; 139; CANR 24

Ives, Morgan
See Bradley, Marion Zimmer

J. R. S.
See Gogarty, Oliver St. John

Jabran, Kahlil
See Gibran, Kahlil

Jabran, Khalil
See Gibran, Kahlil

Jackson, Daniel
See Wingrove, David (John)

Jackson, Jesse 1908-1983 .... **CLC 12**
See also BW 1; CA 25-28R; 109; CANR 27;
CLR 28; MAICYA; SATA 2, 29;
SATA-Obit 48

Jackson, Laura (Riding) 1901-1991
See Riding, Laura
See also CA 65-68; 135; CANR 28; DLB 48

Jackson, Sam
See Trumbo, Dalton

Jackson, Sara
See Wingrove, David (John)

Jackson, Shirley
1919-1965 .... **CLC 11, 60, 87; DA;**
DAC; DAM MST; SSC 9; WLC
See also AAYA 9; CA 1-4R; 25-28R;
CANR 4, 52; CDALB 1941-1968; DLB 6;
SATA 2

Jacob, (Cyprien-)Max 1876-1944 ... **TCLC 6**
See also CA 104

Jacobs, Jim 1942-................ **CLC 12**
See also CA 97-100; INT 97-100

Jacobs, W(illiam) W(ymark)
1863-1943 .... **TCLC 22**
See also CA 121; DLB 135

Jacobsen, Jens Peter 1847-1885 .. **NCLC 34**

Jacobsen, Josephine 1908-......... **CLC 48**
See also CA 33-36R; CAAS 18; CANR 23,
48

Jacobson, Dan 1929- .... **CLC 4, 14**
See also CA 1-4R; CANR 2, 25; DLB 14;
MTCW

Jacqueline
See Carpentier (y Valmont), Alejo

Jagger, Mick 1944-.............. **CLC 17**

Jakes, John (William)
1932-...... **CLC 29; DAM NOV, POP**
See also BEST 89:4; CA 57-60; CANR 10,
43; DLBY 83; INT CANR-10; MTCW;
SATA 62

James, Andrew
See Kirkup, James

James, C(yril) L(ionel) R(obert)
1901-1989 .... **CLC 33**
See also BW 2; CA 117; 125; 128; DLB 125;
MTCW

James, Daniel (Lewis) 1911-1988
See Santiago, Danny
See also CA 125

James, Dynely
See Mayne, William (James Carter)

James, Henry Sr. 1811-1882..... **NCLC 53**

James, Henry
1843-1916 ...... **TCLC 2, 11, 24, 40, 47,**
64; DA; DAB; DAC; DAM MST, NOV;
SSC 8; WLC
See also CA 104; 132; CDALB 1865-1917;
DLB 12, 71, 74; DLBD 13; MTCW

James, M. R.
See James, Montague (Rhodes)
See also DLB 156

James, Montague (Rhodes)
1862-1936 .... **TCLC 6; SSC 16**
See also CA 104

James, P. D. .... **CLC 18, 46**
See also White, Phyllis Dorothy James
See also BEST 90:2; CDBLB 1960 to
Present; DLB 87

James, Philip
See Moorcock, Michael (John)

James, William 1842-1910..... **TCLC 15, 32**
See also CA 109

James I 1394-1437 .... **LC 20**

Jameson, Anna 1794-1860 .... **NCLC 43**
See also DLB 99, 166

Jami, Nur al-Din 'Abd al-Rahman
1414-1492 .... **LC 9**

Jandl, Ernst 1925- .... **CLC 34**

Janowitz, Tama
1957- .... **CLC 43; DAM POP**
See also CA 106; CANR 52

Japrisot, Sebastien 1931-.......... **CLC 90**

Jarrell, Randall
1914-1965 ...... **CLC 1, 2, 6, 9, 13, 49;**
DAM POET
See also CA 5-8R; 25-28R; CABS 2;
CANR 6, 34; CDALB 1941-1968; CLR 6;
DLB 48, 52; MAICYA; MTCW; SATA 7

Jarry, Alfred
1873-1907 .... **TCLC 2, 14;**
DAM DRAM; SSC 20
See also CA 104; 153

Jarvis, E. K.
See Bloch, Robert (Albert); Ellison, Harlan
(Jay); Silverberg, Robert

Jeake, Samuel, Jr.
See Aiken, Conrad (Potter)

Jean Paul 1763-1825 .... **NCLC 7**

Jefferies, (John) Richard
1848-1887 .... **NCLC 47**
See also DLB 98, 141; SATA 16

Jeffers, (John) Robinson
1887-1962 .... **CLC 2, 3, 11, 15, 54; DA;**
DAC; DAM MST, POET; PC 17; WLC
See also CA 85-88; CANR 35;
CDALB 1917-1929; DLB 45; MTCW

Jefferson, Janet
See Mencken, H(enry) L(ouis)

Jefferson, Thomas 1743-1826 .... **NCLC 11**
See also CDALB 1640-1865; DLB 31

Jeffrey, Francis 1773-1850....... **NCLC 33**
See also DLB 107

Jelakowitch, Ivan
See Heijermans, Herman

Jellicoe, (Patricia) Ann 1927-...... **CLC 27**
See also CA 85-88; DLB 13

Jen, Gish .... **CLC 70**
See also Jen, Lillian

Jen, Lillian 1956(?)-
See Jen, Gish
See also CA 135

Jenkins, (John) Robin 1912-....... **CLC 52**
See also CA 1-4R; CANR 1; DLB 14

Jennings, Elizabeth (Joan)
1926-..................... **CLC 5, 14**
See also CA 61-64; CAAS 5; CANR 8, 39;
DLB 27; MTCW; SATA 66

Jennings, Waylon 1937-.......... **CLC 21**

Jensen, Johannes V. 1873-1950.... **TCLC 41**

Jensen, Laura (Linnea) 1948- ...... **CLC 37**
See also CA 103

Jerome, Jerome K(lapka)
1859-1927 .... **TCLC 23**
See also CA 119; DLB 10, 34, 135

Jerrold, Douglas William
1803-1857 .... **NCLC 2**
See also DLB 158, 159

Jewett, (Theodora) Sarah Orne
1849-1909 .... **TCLC 1, 22; SSC 6**
See also CA 108; 127; DLB 12, 74;
SATA 15

Jewsbury, Geraldine (Endsor)
1812-1880 .... **NCLC 22**
See also DLB 21

Jhabvala, Ruth Prawer
1927- .... **CLC 4, 8, 29, 94; DAB;**
DAM NOV
See also CA 1-4R; CANR 2, 29, 51;
DLB 139; INT CANR-29; MTCW

Jibran, Kahlil
See Gibran, Kahlil

Jibran, Khalil
See Gibran, Kahlil

Jiles, Paulette 1943-........... **CLC 13, 58**
See also CA 101

Jimenez (Mantecon), Juan Ramon
1881-1958 ..... **TCLC 4; DAM MULT,**
POET; HLC; PC 7
See also CA 104; 131; DLB 134; HW;
MTCW

Jimenez, Ramon
See Jimenez (Mantecon), Juan Ramon

Jimenez Mantecon, Juan
See Jimenez (Mantecon), Juan Ramon

Joel, Billy .... **CLC 26**
See also Joel, William Martin

Joel, William Martin 1949-
See Joel, Billy
See also CA 108

John of the Cross, St. 1542-1591 .... **LC 18**

Johnson, B(ryan) S(tanley William)
1933-1973 .... **CLC 6, 9**
See also CA 9-12R; 53-56; CANR 9;
DLB 14, 40

Johnson, Benj. F. of Boo
See Riley, James Whitcomb

Johnson, Benjamin F. of Boo
See Riley, James Whitcomb

Johnson, Charles (Richard)
1948- .... **CLC 7, 51, 65; BLC;
DAM MULT**
See also BW 2; CA 116; CAAS 18;
CANR 42; DLB 33

Johnson, Denis 1949- .... **CLC 52**
See also CA 117; 121; DLB 120

Johnson, Diane 1934- .... **CLC 5, 13, 48**
See also CA 41-44R; CANR 17, 40;
DLBY 80; INT CANR-17; MTCW

Johnson, Eyvind (Olof Verner)
1900-1976 .... **CLC 14**
See also CA 73-76; 69-72; CANR 34

Johnson, J. R.
See James, C(yril) L(ionel) R(obert)

Johnson, James Weldon
1871-1938 .... **TCLC 3, 19; BLC;
DAM MULT, POET**
See also BW 1; CA 104; 125;
CDALB 1917-1929; CLR 32; DLB 51;
MTCW; SATA 31

Johnson, Joyce 1935- .... **CLC 58**
See also CA 125; 129

Johnson, Lionel (Pigot)
1867-1902 .... **TCLC 19**
See also CA 117; DLB 19

Johnson, Mel
See Malzberg, Barry N(athaniel)

Johnson, Pamela Hansford
1912-1981 .... **CLC 1, 7, 27**
See also CA 1-4R; 104; CANR 2, 28;
DLB 15; MTCW

Johnson, Robert 1911(?)-1938 ..... **TCLC 69**

Johnson, Samuel
1709-1784 ..... **LC 15; DA; DAB; DAC;
DAM MST; WLC**
See also CDBLB 1660-1789; DLB 39, 95,
104, 142

Johnson, Uwe
1934-1984 .... **CLC 5, 10, 15, 40**
See also CA 1-4R; 112; CANR 1, 39;
DLB 75; MTCW

Johnston, George (Benson) 1913- ... **CLC 51**
See also CA 1-4R; CANR 5, 20; DLB 88

Johnston, Jennifer 1930- .... **CLC 7**
See also CA 85-88; DLB 14

Jolley, (Monica) Elizabeth
1923- .... **CLC 46; SSC 19**
See also CA 127; CAAS 13

Jones, Arthur Llewellyn 1863-1947
See Machen, Arthur
See also CA 104

Jones, D(ouglas) G(ordon) 1929-.... **CLC 10**
See also CA 29-32R; CANR 13; DLB 53

Jones, David (Michael)
1895-1974 .... **CLC 2, 4, 7, 13, 42**
See also CA 9-12R; 53-56; CANR 28;
CDBLB 1945-1960; DLB 20, 100; MTCW

Jones, David Robert 1947-
See Bowie, David
See also CA 103

Jones, Diana Wynne 1934- .... **CLC 26**
See also AAYA 12; CA 49-52; CANR 4,
26, 56; CLR 23; DLB 161; JRDA;
MAICYA; SAAS 7; SATA 9, 70

Jones, Edward P. 1950- .... **CLC 76**
See also BW 2; CA 142

Jones, Gayl
1949- .... **CLC 6, 9; BLC; DAM MULT**
See also BW 2; CA 77-80; CANR 27;
DLB 33; MTCW

Jones, James 1921-1977.... **CLC 1, 3, 10, 39**
See also AITN 1, 2; CA 1-4R; 69-72;
CANR 6; DLB 2, 143; MTCW

Jones, John J.
See Lovecraft, H(oward) P(hillips)

Jones, LeRoi .... **CLC 1, 2, 3, 5, 10, 14**
See also Baraka, Amiri

Jones, Louis B. .... **CLC 65**
See also CA 141

Jones, Madison (Percy, Jr.) 1925- ... **CLC 4**
See also CA 13-16R; CAAS 11; CANR 7,
54; DLB 152

Jones, Mervyn 1922- .... **CLC 10, 52**
See also CA 45-48; CAAS 5; CANR 1;
MTCW

Jones, Mick 1956(?)- .... **CLC 30**

Jones, Nettie (Pearl) 1941- .... **CLC 34**
See also BW 2; CA 137; CAAS 20

Jones, Preston 1936-1979 .... **CLC 10**
See also CA 73-76; 89-92; DLB 7

Jones, Robert F(rancis) 1934-....... **CLC 7**
See also CA 49-52; CANR 2

Jones, Rod 1953- .... **CLC 50**
See also CA 128

Jones, Terence Graham Parry
1942- .... **CLC 21**
See also Jones, Terry; Monty Python
See also CA 112; 116; CANR 35; INT 116

Jones, Terry
See Jones, Terence Graham Parry
See also SATA 67; SATA-Brief 51

Jones, Thom 1945(?)- .... **CLC 81**

Jong, Erica
1942- .... **CLC 4, 6, 8, 18, 83;
DAM NOV, POP**
See also AITN 1; BEST 90:2; CA 73-76;
CANR 26, 52; DLB 2, 5, 28, 152;
INT CANR-26; MTCW

Jonson, Ben(jamin)
1572(?)-1637 ...... **LC 6, 33; DA; DAB;
DAC; DAM DRAM, MST, POET;
DC 4; PC 17; WLC**
See also CDBLB Before 1660; DLB 62, 121

Jordan, June
1936- ..... **CLC 5, 11, 23; DAM MULT,
POET**
See also AAYA 2; BW 2; CA 33-36R;
CANR 25; CLR 10; DLB 38; MAICYA;
MTCW; SATA 4

Jordan, Pat(rick M.) 1941- .... **CLC 37**
See also CA 33-36R

Jorgensen, Ivar
See Ellison, Harlan (Jay)

Jorgenson, Ivar
See Silverberg, Robert

Josephus, Flavius c. 37-100 ...... **CMLC 13**

Josipovici, Gabriel 1940- .... **CLC 6, 43**
See also CA 37-40R; CAAS 8; CANR 47;
DLB 14

Joubert, Joseph 1754-1824 .... **NCLC 9**

Jouve, Pierre Jean 1887-1976...... **CLC 47**
See also CA 65-68

Joyce, James (Augustine Aloysius)
1882-1941 .... **TCLC 3, 8, 16, 35, 52;
DA; DAB; DAC; DAM MST, NOV,
POET; SSC 3; WLC**
See also CA 104; 126; CDBLB 1914-1945;
DLB 10, 19, 36, 162; MTCW

Jozsef, Attila 1905-1937.......... **TCLC 22**
See also CA 116

Juana Ines de la Cruz 1651(?)-1695 ... **LC 5**

Judd, Cyril
See Kornbluth, C(yril) M.; Pohl, Frederik

Julian of Norwich 1342(?)-1416(?) .... **LC 6**
See also DLB 146

Juniper, Alex
See Hospital, Janette Turner

Junius
See Luxemburg, Rosa

Just, Ward (Swift) 1935- .... **CLC 4, 27**
See also CA 25-28R; CANR 32;
INT CANR-32

Justice, Donald (Rodney)
1925- .... **CLC 6, 19; DAM POET**
See also CA 5-8R; CANR 26, 54;
DLBY 83; INT CANR-26

Juvenal c. 55-c. 127 .... **CMLC 8**

Juvenis
See Bourne, Randolph S(illiman)

Kacew, Romain 1914-1980
See Gary, Romain
See also CA 108; 102

Kadare, Ismail 1936- .... **CLC 52**

Kadohata, Cynthia. .... **CLC 59**
See also CA 140

Kafka, Franz
1883-1924 .... **TCLC 2, 6, 13, 29, 47, 53;
DA; DAB; DAC; DAM MST, NOV;
SSC 5; WLC**
See also CA 105; 126; DLB 81; MTCW

Kahanovitsch, Pinkhes
See Der Nister

Kahn, Roger 1927- .... **CLC 30**
See also CA 25-28R; CANR 44; DLB 171;
SATA 37

Kain, Saul
See Sassoon, Siegfried (Lorraine)

Kaiser, Georg 1878-1945 .... **TCLC 9**
See also CA 106; DLB 124

Kaletski, Alexander 1946- .... **CLC 39**
See also CA 118; 143

Kalidasa fl. c. 400- .... **CMLC 9**

Kallman, Chester (Simon)
1921-1975 .... **CLC 2**
See also CA 45-48; 53-56; CANR 3

Kaminsky, Melvin 1926-
See Brooks, Mel
See also CA 65-68; CANR 16

Kaminsky, Stuart M(elvin) 1934- ... **CLC 59**
See also CA 73-76; CANR 29, 53

Kane, Francis
See Robbins, Harold

Kane, Paul
See Simon, Paul (Frederick)

Kane, Wilson
See Bloch, Robert (Albert)

Kanin, Garson 1912-............. **CLC 22**
See also AITN 1; CA 5-8R; CANR 7;
DLB 7

Kaniuk, Yoram 1930-............. **CLC 19**
See also CA 134

Kant, Immanuel 1724-1804 ...... **NCLC 27**
See also DLB 94

Kantor, MacKinlay 1904-1977 ...... **CLC 7**
See also CA 61-64; 73-76; DLB 9, 102

Kaplan, David Michael 1946- ...... **CLC 50**

Kaplan, James 1951- .... **CLC 59**
See also CA 135

Karageorge, Michael
See Anderson, Poul (William)

Karamzin, Nikolai Mikhailovich
1766-1826 .... **NCLC 3**
See also DLB 150

Karapanou, Margarita 1946-....... **CLC 13**
See also CA 101

Karinthy, Frigyes 1887-1938...... **TCLC 47**

Karl, Frederick R(obert) 1927- ..... **CLC 34**
See also CA 5-8R; CANR 3, 44

Kastel, Warren
See Silverberg, Robert

Kataev, Evgeny Petrovich 1903-1942
See Petrov, Evgeny
See also CA 120

Kataphusin
See Ruskin, John

Katz, Steve 1935-................ **CLC 47**
See also CA 25-28R; CAAS 14; CANR 12;
DLBY 83

Kauffman, Janet 1945-............ **CLC 42**
See also CA 117; CANR 43; DLBY 86

Kaufman, Bob (Garnell)
1925-1986 .... **CLC 49**
See also BW 1; CA 41-44R; 118; CANR 22;
DLB 16, 41

Kaufman, George S.
1889-1961 ...... **CLC 38; DAM DRAM**
See also CA 108; 93-96; DLB 7; INT 108

Kaufman, Sue .... **CLC 3, 8**
See also Barondess, Sue K(aufman)

Kavafis, Konstantinos Petrou 1863-1933
See Cavafy, C(onstantine) P(eter)
See also CA 104

Kavan, Anna 1901-1968...... **CLC 5, 13, 82**
See also CA 5-8R; CANR 6, 57; MTCW

Kavanagh, Dan
See Barnes, Julian (Patrick)

Kavanagh, Patrick (Joseph)
1904-1967 .... **CLC 22**
See also CA 123; 25-28R; DLB 15, 20;
MTCW

Kawabata, Yasunari
1899-1972 .... **CLC 2, 5, 9, 18;**
DAM MULT; SSC 17
See also CA 93-96; 33-36R

Kaye, M(ary) M(argaret) 1909-..... **CLC 28**
See also CA 89-92; CANR 24; MTCW;
SATA 62

Kaye, Mollie
See Kaye, M(ary) M(argaret)

Kaye-Smith, Sheila 1887-1956..... **TCLC 20**
See also CA 118; DLB 36

Kaymor, Patrice Maguilene
See Senghor, Leopold Sedar

Kazan, Elia 1909-........... **CLC 6, 16, 63**
See also CA 21-24R; CANR 32

Kazantzakis, Nikos
1883(?)-1957 .... **TCLC 2, 5, 33**
See also CA 105; 132; MTCW

Kazin, Alfred 1915- .... **CLC 34, 38**
See also CA 1-4R; CAAS 7; CANR 1, 45;
DLB 67

Keane, Mary Nesta (Skrine) 1904-1996
See Keane, Molly
See also CA 108; 114; 151

Keane, Molly.................... **CLC 31**
See also Keane, Mary Nesta (Skrine)
See also INT 114

Keates, Jonathan 19(?)-........... **CLC 34**

Keaton, Buster 1895-1966 .... **CLC 20**

Keats, John
1795-1821 .... **NCLC 8; DA; DAB;**
DAC; DAM MST, POET; PC 1; WLC
See also CDBLB 1789-1832; DLB 96, 110

Keene, Donald 1922- .... **CLC 34**
See also CA 1-4R; CANR 5

Keillor, Garrison .... **CLC 40**
See also Keillor, Gary (Edward)
See also AAYA 2; BEST 89:3; DLBY 87;
SATA 58

Keillor, Gary (Edward) 1942-
See Keillor, Garrison
See also CA 111; 117; CANR 36;
DAM POP; MTCW

Keith, Michael
See Hubbard, L(afayette) Ron(ald)

Keller, Gottfried 1819-1890....... **NCLC 2**
See also DLB 129

Kellerman, Jonathan
1949- .... **CLC 44; DAM POP**
See also BEST 90:1; CA 106; CANR 29, 51;
INT CANR-29

Kelley, William Melvin 1937-...... **CLC 22**
See also BW 1; CA 77-80; CANR 27;
DLB 33

Kellogg, Marjorie 1922-........... **CLC 2**
See also CA 81-84

Kellow, Kathleen
See Hibbert, Eleanor Alice Burford

Kelly, M(ilton) T(erry) 1947-....... **CLC 55**
See also CA 97-100; CAAS 22; CANR 19,
43

Kelman, James 1946-.......... **CLC 58, 86**
See also CA 148

Kemal, Yashar 1923- .... **CLC 14, 29**
See also CA 89-92; CANR 44

Kemble, Fanny 1809-1893 .... **NCLC 18**
See also DLB 32

Kemelman, Harry 1908-1996........ **CLC 2**
See also AITN 1; CA 9-12R; 155; CANR 6;
DLB 28

Kempe, Margery 1373(?)-1440(?) ..... **LC 6**
See also DLB 146

Kempis, Thomas a 1380-1471 .... **LC 11**

Kendall, Henry 1839-1882....... **NCLC 12**

Keneally, Thomas (Michael)
1935- ...... **CLC 5, 8, 10, 14, 19, 27, 43;**
DAM NOV
See also CA 85-88; CANR 10, 50; MTCW

Kennedy, Adrienne (Lita)
1931- ..... **CLC 66; BLC; DAM MULT;**
DC 5
See also BW 2; CA 103; CAAS 20; CABS 3;
CANR 26, 53; DLB 38

Kennedy, John Pendleton
1795-1870 .... **NCLC 2**
See also DLB 3

Kennedy, Joseph Charles 1929-
See Kennedy, X. J.
See also CA 1-4R; CANR 4, 30, 40;
SATA 14, 86

Kennedy, William
1928- ... **CLC 6, 28, 34, 53; DAM NOV**
See also AAYA 1; CA 85-88; CANR 14,
31; DLB 143; DLBY 85; INT CANR-31;
MTCW; SATA 57

Kennedy, X. J................... **CLC 8, 42**
See also Kennedy, Joseph Charles
See also CAAS 9; CLR 27; DLB 5;
SAAS 22

Kenny, Maurice (Francis)
1929- .... **CLC 87; DAM MULT**
See also CA 144; CAAS 22; DLB 175;
NNAL

Kent, Kelvin
See Kuttner, Henry

Kenton, Maxwell
See Southern, Terry

Kenyon, Robert O.
See Kuttner, Henry

Kerouac, Jack ..... **CLC 1, 2, 3, 5, 14, 29, 61**
See also Kerouac, Jean-Louis Lebris de
See also CDALB 1941-1968; DLB 2, 16;
DLBD 3; DLBY 95

Kerouac, Jean-Louis Lebris de 1922-1969
See Kerouac, Jack
See also AITN 1; CA 5-8R; 25-28R;
CANR 26, 54; DA; DAB; DAC;
DAM MST, NOV, POET, POP; MTCW;
WLC

Kerr, Jean 1923-............... **CLC 22**
See also CA 5-8R; CANR 7; INT CANR-7

Kerr, M. E. .... **CLC 12, 35**
See also Meaker, Marijane (Agnes)
See also AAYA 2; CLR 29; SAAS 1

Kerr, Robert .... **CLC 55**

Kerrigan, (Thomas) Anthony
1918-..................... **CLC 4, 6**
See also CA 49-52; CAAS 11; CANR 4

Kerry, Lois
See Duncan, Lois

Kesey, Ken (Elton)
1935-...... **CLC 1, 3, 6, 11, 46, 64; DA;**
DAB; DAC; DAM MST, NOV, POP;
WLC
See also CA 1-4R; CANR 22, 38;
CDALB 1968-1988; DLB 2, 16; MTCW;
SATA 66

Kesselring, Joseph (Otto)
1902-1967 ..... **CLC 45; DAM DRAM,**
MST
See also CA 150

Kessler, Jascha (Frederick) 1929-.... **CLC 4**
See also CA 17-20R; CANR 8, 48

Kettelkamp, Larry (Dale) 1933-.... **CLC 12**
See also CA 29-32R; CANR 16; SAAS 3;
SATA 2

Key, Ellen 1849-1926........... **TCLC 65**

Keyber, Conny
See Fielding, Henry

Keyes, Daniel
1927-............. **CLC 80; DA; DAC;**
DAM MST, NOV
See also CA 17-20R; CANR 10, 26, 54;
SATA 37

Keynes, John Maynard
1883-1946 .... **TCLC 64**
See also CA 114; DLBD 10

Khanshendel, Chiron
See Rose, Wendy

Khayyam, Omar
1048-1131 .... **CMLC 11; DAM POET;**
PC 8

Kherdian, David 1931-........... **CLC 6, 9**
See also CA 21-24R; CAAS 2; CANR 39;
CLR 24; JRDA; MAICYA; SATA 16, 74

Khlebnikov, Velimir .... **TCLC 20**
See also Khlebnikov, Viktor Vladimirovich

Khlebnikov, Viktor Vladimirovich 1885-1922
See Khlebnikov, Velimir
See also CA 117

Khodasevich, Vladislav (Felitsianovich)
1886-1939 .... **TCLC 15**
See also CA 115

Kielland, Alexander Lange
1849-1906 .... **TCLC 5**
See also CA 104

Kiely, Benedict 1919-......... **CLC 23, 43**
See also CA 1-4R; CANR 2; DLB 15

Kienzle, William X(avier)
1928-............. **CLC 25; DAM POP**
See also CA 93-96; CAAS 1; CANR 9, 31;
INT CANR-31; MTCW

Kierkegaard, Soren 1813-1855.... **NCLC 34**

Killens, John Oliver 1916-1987..... **CLC 10**
See also BW 2; CA 77-80; 123; CAAS 2;
CANR 26; DLB 33

Killigrew, Anne 1660-1685........... **LC 4**
See also DLB 131

Kim
See Simenon, Georges (Jacques Christian)

Kincaid, Jamaica
1949-............. **CLC 43, 68; BLC;**
DAM MULT, NOV
See also AAYA 13; BW 2; CA 125;
CANR 47; DLB 157

King, Francis (Henry)
1923-............. **CLC 8, 53; DAM NOV**
See also CA 1-4R; CANR 1, 33; DLB 15,
139; MTCW

King, Martin Luther, Jr.
1929-1968 .... **CLC 83; BLC; DA; DAB;**
DAC; DAM MST, MULT
See also BW 2; CA 25-28; CANR 27, 44;
CAP 2; MTCW; SATA 14

King, Stephen (Edwin)
1947-............. **CLC 12, 26, 37, 61;**
DAM NOV, POP; SSC 17
See also AAYA 1, 17; BEST 90:1;
CA 61-64; CANR 1, 30, 52; DLB 143;
DLBY 80; JRDA; MTCW; SATA 9, 55

King, Steve
See King, Stephen (Edwin)

King, Thomas
1943-..... **CLC 89; DAC; DAM MULT**
See also CA 144; DLB 175; NNAL

Kingman, Lee.................... CLC 17
See also Natti, (Mary) Lee
See also SAAS 3; SATA 1, 67

Kingsley, Charles 1819-1875..... **NCLC 35**
See also DLB 21, 32, 163; YABC 2

Kingsley, Sidney 1906-1995....... **CLC 44**
See also CA 85-88; 147; DLB 7

Kingsolver, Barbara
1955-......... **CLC 55, 81; DAM POP**
See also AAYA 15; CA 129; 134; INT 134

Kingston, Maxine (Ting Ting) Hong
1940-.... **CLC 12, 19, 58; DAM MULT,**
NOV
See also AAYA 8; CA 69-72; CANR 13,
38; DLB 173; DLBY 80; INT CANR-13;
MTCW; SATA 53

Kinnell, Galway
1927-.......... **CLC 1, 2, 3, 5, 13, 29**
See also CA 9-12R; CANR 10, 34; DLB 5;
DLBY 87; INT CANR-34; MTCW

Kinsella, Thomas 1928-......... **CLC 4, 19**
See also CA 17-20R; CANR 15; DLB 27;
MTCW

Kinsella, W(illiam) P(atrick)
1935-............. **CLC 27, 43; DAC;**
DAM NOV, POP
See also AAYA 7; CA 97-100; CAAS 7;
CANR 21, 35; INT CANR-21; MTCW

Kipling, (Joseph) Rudyard
1865-1936 ...... **TCLC 8, 17; DA; DAB;**
DAC; DAM MST, POET; PC 3; SSC 5;
WLC
See also CA 105; 120; CANR 33;
CDBLB 1890-1914; CLR 39; DLB 19, 34,
141, 156; MAICYA; MTCW; YABC 2

Kirkup, James 1918-............. **CLC 1**
See also CA 1-4R; CAAS 4; CANR 2;
DLB 27; SATA 12

Kirkwood, James 1930(?)-1989...... **CLC 9**
See also AITN 2; CA 1-4R; 128; CANR 6,
40

Kirshner, Sidney
See Kingsley, Sidney

Kis, Danilo 1935-1989 .... **CLC 57**
See also CA 109; 118; 129; MTCW

Kivi, Aleksis 1834-1872 .... **NCLC 30**

Kizer, Carolyn (Ashley)
1925-..... **CLC 15, 39, 80; DAM POET**
See also CA 65-68; CAAS 5; CANR 24;
DLB 5, 169

Klabund 1890-1928.............. **TCLC 44**
See also DLB 66

Klappert, Peter 1942-............. **CLC 57**
See also CA 33-36R; DLB 5

Klein, A(braham) M(oses)
1909-1972 .... **CLC 19; DAB; DAC;**
DAM MST
See also CA 101; 37-40R; DLB 68

Klein, Norma 1938-1989 .... **CLC 30**
See also AAYA 2; CA 41-44R; 128;
CANR 15, 37; CLR 2, 19;
INT CANR-15; JRDA; MAICYA;
SAAS 1; SATA 7, 57

Klein, T(heodore) E(ibon) D(onald)
1947-..................... **CLC 34**
See also CA 119; CANR 44

Kleist, Heinrich von
1777-1811 .... **NCLC 2, 37;**
DAM DRAM; SSC 22
See also DLB 90

Klima, Ivan 1931-..... **CLC 56; DAM NOV**
See also CA 25-28R; CANR 17, 50

Klimentov, Andrei Platonovich 1899-1951
See Platonov, Andrei
See also CA 108

Klinger, Friedrich Maximilian von
1752-1831 .... **NCLC 1**
See also DLB 94

Klopstock, Friedrich Gottlieb
1724-1803 .... **NCLC 11**
See also DLB 97

Knapp, Caroline 1959-............. **CLC 99**
See also CA 154

Knebel, Fletcher 1911-1993........ **CLC 14**
See also AITN 1; CA 1-4R; 140; CAAS 3;
CANR 1, 36; SATA 36; SATA-Obit 75

Knickerbocker, Diedrich
See Irving, Washington

Knight, Etheridge
1931-1991 .... **CLC 40; BLC;**
DAM POET; PC 14
See also BW 1; CA 21-24R; 133; CANR 23;
DLB 41

Knight, Sarah Kemble 1666-1727 ..... **LC 7**
See also DLB 24

Knister, Raymond 1899-1932...... **TCLC 56**
See also DLB 68

Kyprianos, Iossif
See Samarakis, Antonis

La Bruyere, Jean de 1645-1696...... **LC 17**

Lacan, Jacques (Marie Emile)
1901-1981.................... **CLC 75**
See also CA 121; 104

**Laclos, Pierre Ambroise Francois Choderlos
de** 1741-1803.............. **NCLC 4**

La Colere, Francois
See Aragon, Louis

Lacolere, Francois
See Aragon, Louis

La Deshabilleuse
See Simenon, Georges (Jacques Christian)

Lady Gregory
See Gregory, Isabella Augusta (Persse)

Lady of Quality, A
See Bagnold, Enid

**La Fayette, Marie (Madelaine Pioche de la
Vergne Comtes** 1634-1693....... **LC 2**

Lafayette, Rene
See Hubbard, L(afayette) Ron(ald)

Laforgue, Jules
1860-1887........ **NCLC 5, 53; PC 14;
SSC 20**

Lagerkvist, Paer (Fabian)
1891-1974.......... **CLC 7, 10, 13, 54;
DAM DRAM, NOV**
See also Lagerkvist, Par
See also CA 85-88; 49-52; MTCW

Lagerkvist, Par.................... **SSC 12**
See also Lagerkvist, Paer (Fabian)

Lagerloef, Selma (Ottiliana Lovisa)
1858-1940................ **TCLC 4, 36**
See also Lagerlof, Selma (Ottiliana Lovisa)
See also CA 108; SATA 15

Lagerlof, Selma (Ottiliana Lovisa)
See Lagerloef, Selma (Ottiliana Lovisa)
See also CLR 7; SATA 15

La Guma, (Justin) Alex(ander)
1925-1985........ **CLC 19; DAM NOV**
See also BW 1; CA 49-52; 118; CANR 25;
DLB 117; MTCW

Laidlaw, A. K.
See Grieve, C(hristopher) M(urray)

Lainez, Manuel Mujica
See Mujica Lainez, Manuel
See also HW

Laing, R(onald) D(avid)
1927-1989.................... **CLC 95**
See also CA 107; 129; CANR 34; MTCW

Lamartine, Alphonse (Marie Louis Prat) de
1790-1869..... **NCLC 11; DAM POET;
PC 16**

Lamb, Charles
1775-1834....... **NCLC 10; DA; DAB;
DAC; DAM MST; WLC**
See also CDBLB 1789-1832; DLB 93, 107,
163; SATA 17

Lamb, Lady Caroline 1785-1828.. **NCLC 38**
See also DLB 116

Lamming, George (William)
1927-............ **CLC 2, 4, 66; BLC;
DAM MULT**
See also BW 2; CA 85-88; CANR 26;
DLB 125; MTCW

L'Amour, Louis (Dearborn)
1908-1988.... **CLC 25, 55; DAM NOV,
POP**
See also AAYA 16; AITN 2; BEST 89:2;
CA 1-4R; 125; CANR 3, 25, 40;
DLBY 80; MTCW

Lampedusa, Giuseppe (Tomasi) di
1896-1957................. **TCLC 13**
See also Tomasi di Lampedusa, Giuseppe
See also DLB 177

Lampman, Archibald 1861-1899.. **NCLC 25**
See also DLB 92

Lancaster, Bruce 1896-1963........ **CLC 36**
See also CA 9-10; CAP 1; SATA 9

Lanchester, John.................. **CLC 99**

Landau, Mark Alexandrovich
See Aldanov, Mark (Alexandrovich)

Landau-Aldanov, Mark Alexandrovich
See Aldanov, Mark (Alexandrovich)

Landis, Jerry
See Simon, Paul (Frederick)

Landis, John 1950-.............. **CLC 26**
See also CA 112; 122

Landolfi, Tommaso 1908-1979... **CLC 11, 49**
See also CA 127; 117; DLB 177

Landon, Letitia Elizabeth
1802-1838................ **NCLC 15**
See also DLB 96

Landor, Walter Savage
1775-1864................ **NCLC 14**
See also DLB 93, 107

Landwirth, Heinz 1927-
See Lind, Jakov
See also CA 9-12R; CANR 7

Lane, Patrick
1939-............ **CLC 25; DAM POET**
See also CA 97-100; CANR 54; DLB 53;
INT 97-100

Lang, Andrew 1844-1912........ **TCLC 16**
See also CA 114; 137; DLB 98, 141;
MAICYA; SATA 16

Lang, Fritz 1890-1976............ **CLC 20**
See also CA 77-80; 69-72; CANR 30

Lange, John
See Crichton, (John) Michael

Langer, Elinor 1939-............. **CLC 34**
See also CA 121

Langland, William
1330(?)-1400(?)...... **LC 19; DA; DAB;
DAC; DAM MST, POET**
See also DLB 146

Langstaff, Launcelot
See Irving, Washington

Lanier, Sidney
1842-1881...... **NCLC 6; DAM POET**
See also DLB 64; DLBD 13; MAICYA;
SATA 18

Lanyer, Aemilia 1569-1645..... **LC 10, 30**
See also DLB 121

Lao Tzu....................... **CMLC 7**

Lapine, James (Elliot) 1949-....... **CLC 39**
See also CA 123; 130; CANR 54; INT 130

Larbaud, Valery (Nicolas)
1881-1957................. **TCLC 9**
See also CA 106; 152

Lardner, Ring
See Lardner, Ring(gold) W(ilmer)

Lardner, Ring W., Jr.
See Lardner, Ring(gold) W(ilmer)

Lardner, Ring(gold) W(ilmer)
1885-1933............... **TCLC 2, 14**
See also CA 104; 131; CDALB 1917-1929;
DLB 11, 25, 86; MTCW

Laredo, Betty
See Codrescu, Andrei

Larkin, Maia
See Wojciechowska, Maia (Teresa)

Larkin, Philip (Arthur)
1922-1985.... **CLC 3, 5, 8, 9, 13, 18, 33,
39, 64; DAB; DAM MST, POET**
See also CA 5-8R; 117; CANR 24;
CDBLB 1960 to Present; DLB 27;
MTCW

Larra (y Sanchez de Castro), Mariano Jose de
1809-1837................ **NCLC 17**

Larsen, Eric 1941-............... **CLC 55**
See also CA 132

Larsen, Nella
1891-1964............. **CLC 37; BLC;
DAM MULT**
See also BW 1; CA 125; DLB 51

Larson, Charles R(aymond) 1938-... **CLC 31**
See also CA 53-56; CANR 4

Larson, Jonathan 1961(?)-1996..... **CLC 99**

Las Casas, Bartolome de 1474-1566.. **LC 31**

Lasker-Schueler, Else 1869-1945.. **TCLC 57**
See also DLB 66, 124

Latham, Jean Lee 1902-........... **CLC 12**
See also AITN 1; CA 5-8R; CANR 7;
MAICYA; SATA 2, 68

Latham, Mavis
See Clark, Mavis Thorpe

Lathen, Emma.................... **CLC 2**
See also Hennissart, Martha; Latsis, Mary
J(ane)

Lathrop, Francis
See Leiber, Fritz (Reuter, Jr.)

Latsis, Mary J(ane)
See Lathen, Emma
See also CA 85-88

Lattimore, Richmond (Alexander)
1906-1984.................... **CLC 3**
See also CA 1-4R; 112; CANR 1

Laughlin, James 1914-............ **CLC 49**
See also CA 21-24R; CAAS 22; CANR 9,
47; DLB 48

Laurence, (Jean) Margaret (Wemyss)
1926-1987........ **CLC 3, 6, 13, 50, 62;
DAC; DAM MST; SSC 7**
See also CA 5-8R; 121; CANR 33; DLB 53;
MTCW; SATA-Obit 50

Laurent, Antoine 1952-........... **CLC 50**

Lauscher, Hermann
See Hesse, Hermann

Lemann, Nancy 1956-............ **CLC 39**
See also CA 118; 136

Lemonnier, (Antoine Louis) Camille
1844-1913 .... **TCLC 22**
See also CA 121

Lenau, Nikolaus 1802-1850...... **NCLC 16**

L'Engle, Madeleine (Camp Franklin)
1918- .... **CLC 12; DAM POP**
See also AAYA 1; AITN 2; CA 1-4R;
CANR 3, 21, 39; CLR 1, 14; DLB 52;
JRDA; MAICYA; MTCW; SAAS 15;
SATA 1, 27, 75

Lengyel, Jozsef 1896-1975......... **CLC 7**
See also CA 85-88; 57-60

Lenin 1870-1924
See Lenin, V. I.
See also CA 121

Lenin, V. I. .... **TCLC 67**
See also Lenin

Lennon, John (Ono)
1940-1980 .... **CLC 12, 35**
See also CA 102

Lennox, Charlotte Ramsay
1729(?)-1804 .... **NCLC 23**
See also DLB 39

Lentricchia, Frank (Jr.) 1940-...... **CLC 34**
See also CA 25-28R; CANR 19

Lenz, Siegfried 1926-............ **CLC 27**
See also CA 89-92; DLB 75

Leonard, Elmore (John, Jr.)
1925-..... **CLC 28, 34, 71; DAM POP**
See also AITN 1; BEST 89:1, 90:4;
CA 81-84; CANR 12, 28, 53; DLB 173;
INT CANR-28; MTCW

Leonard, Hugh.................... **CLC 19**
See also Byrne, John Keyes
See also DLB 13

Leonov, Leonid (Maximovich)
1899-1994 .... **CLC 92; DAM NOV**
See also CA 129; MTCW

Leopardi, (Conte) Giacomo
1798-1837 .... **NCLC 22**

Le Reveler
See Artaud, Antonin (Marie Joseph)

Lerman, Eleanor 1952-............ **CLC 9**
See also CA 85-88

Lerman, Rhoda 1936-............ **CLC 56**
See also CA 49-52

Lermontov, Mikhail Yuryevich
1814-1841 .... **NCLC 47**

Leroux, Gaston 1868-1927....... **TCLC 25**
See also CA 108; 136; SATA 65

Lesage, Alain-Rene 1668-1747...... **LC 28**

Leskov, Nikolai (Semyonovich)
1831-1895 .... **NCLC 25**

Lessing, Doris (May)
1919-..... **CLC 1, 2, 3, 6, 10, 15, 22, 40,
94; DA; DAB; DAC; DAM MST, NOV;
SSC 6**
See also CA 9-12R; CAAS 14; CANR 33,
54; CDBLB 1960 to Present; DLB 15,
139; DLBY 85; MTCW

Lessing, Gotthold Ephraim
1729-1781 .... **LC 8**
See also DLB 97

Lester, Richard 1932-............ **CLC 20**

Lever, Charles (James)
1806-1872 .... **NCLC 23**
See also DLB 21

Leverson, Ada 1865(?)-1936(?) .... **TCLC 18**
See also Elaine
See also CA 117; DLB 153

Levertov, Denise
1923- ...... **CLC 1, 2, 3, 5, 8, 15, 28, 66;
DAM POET; PC 11**
See also CA 1-4R; CAAS 19; CANR 3, 29,
50; DLB 5, 165; INT CANR-29; MTCW

Levi, Jonathan.................... **CLC 76**

Levi, Peter (Chad Tigar) 1931-..... **CLC 41**
See also CA 5-8R; CANR 34; DLB 40

Levi, Primo
1919-1987 .... **CLC 37, 50; SSC 12**
See also CA 13-16R; 122; CANR 12, 33;
DLB 177; MTCW

Levin, Ira 1929- ..... **CLC 3, 6; DAM POP**
See also CA 21-24R; CANR 17, 44;
MTCW; SATA 66

Levin, Meyer
1905-1981 .... **CLC 7; DAM POP**
See also AITN 1; CA 9-12R; 104;
CANR 15; DLB 9, 28; DLBY 81;
SATA 21; SATA-Obit 27

Levine, Norman 1924-............ **CLC 54**
See also CA 73-76; CAAS 23; CANR 14;
DLB 88

Levine, Philip
1928- .... **CLC 2, 4, 5, 9, 14, 33;
DAM POET**
See also CA 9-12R; CANR 9, 37, 52;
DLB 5

Levinson, Deirdre 1931-.......... **CLC 49**
See also CA 73-76

Levi-Strauss, Claude 1908- .... **CLC 38**
See also CA 1-4R; CANR 6, 32, 57; MTCW

Levitin, Sonia (Wolff) 1934- .... **CLC 17**
See also AAYA 13; CA 29-32R; CANR 14,
32; JRDA; MAICYA; SAAS 2; SATA 4,
68

Levon, O. U.
See Kesey, Ken (Elton)

Levy, Amy 1861-1889.......... **NCLC 59**
See also DLB 156

Lewes, George Henry
1817-1878 .... **NCLC 25**
See also DLB 55, 144

Lewis, Alun 1915-1944........... **TCLC 3**
See also CA 104; DLB 20, 162

Lewis, C. Day
See Day Lewis, C(ecil)

Lewis, C(live) S(taples)
1898-1963 ..... **CLC 1, 3, 6, 14, 27; DA;
DAB; DAC; DAM MST, NOV, POP;
WLC**
See also AAYA 3; CA 81-84; CANR 33;
CDBLB 1945-1960; CLR 3, 27; DLB 15,
100, 160; JRDA; MAICYA; MTCW;
SATA 13

Lewis, Janet 1899-............. **CLC 41**
See also Winters, Janet Lewis
See also CA 9-12R; CANR 29; CAP 1;
DLBY 87

Lewis, Matthew Gregory
1775-1818 .... **NCLC 11**
See also DLB 39, 158

Lewis, (Harry) Sinclair
1885-1951 ..... **TCLC 4, 13, 23, 39; DA;
DAB; DAC; DAM MST, NOV; WLC**
See also CA 104; 133; CDALB 1917-1929;
DLB 9, 102; DLBD 1; MTCW

Lewis, (Percy) Wyndham
1884(?)-1957 .... **TCLC 2, 9**
See also CA 104; DLB 15

Lewisohn, Ludwig 1883-1955...... **TCLC 19**
See also CA 107; DLB 4, 9, 28, 102

Leyner, Mark 1956-.............. **CLC 92**
See also CA 110; CANR 28, 53

Lezama Lima, Jose
1910-1976 .... **CLC 4, 10; DAM MULT**
See also CA 77-80; DLB 113; HW

L'Heureux, John (Clarke) 1934-.... **CLC 52**
See also CA 13-16R; CANR 23, 45

Liddell, C. H.
See Kuttner, Henry

Lie, Jonas (Lauritz Idemil)
1833-1908(?) .... **TCLC 5**
See also CA 115

Lieber, Joel 1937-1971............. **CLC 6**
See also CA 73-76; 29-32R

Lieber, Stanley Martin
See Lee, Stan

Lieberman, Laurence (James)
1935-..................... **CLC 4, 36**
See also CA 17-20R; CANR 8, 36

Lieksman, Anders
See Haavikko, Paavo Juhani

Li Fei-kan 1904-
See Pa Chin
See also CA 105

Lifton, Robert Jay 1926-.......... **CLC 67**
See also CA 17-20R; CANR 27;
INT CANR-27; SATA 66

Lightfoot, Gordon 1938-.......... **CLC 26**
See also CA 109

Lightman, Alan P. 1948- .... **CLC 81**
See also CA 141

Ligotti, Thomas (Robert)
1953-.............. **CLC 44; SSC 16**
See also CA 123; CANR 49

Li Ho 791-817.................... **PC 13**

Liliencron, (Friedrich Adolf Axel) Detlev von
1844-1909 .... **TCLC 18**
See also CA 117

Lilly, William 1602-1681.......... **LC 27**

Lima, Jose Lezama
See Lezama Lima, Jose

Lima Barreto, Afonso Henrique de
1881-1922 .... **TCLC 23**
See also CA 117

Limonov, Edward 1944-.......... **CLC 67**
See also CA 137

Lin, Frank
See Atherton, Gertrude (Franklin Horn)

Lincoln, Abraham 1809-1865..... **NCLC 18**

Lowry, (Clarence) Malcolm
1909-1957 . . . . **TCLC 6, 40**
See also CA 105; 131; CDBLB 1945-1960;
DLB 15; MTCW

Lowry, Mina Gertrude 1882-1966
See Loy, Mina
See also CA 113

Loxsmith, John
See Brunner, John (Kilian Houston)

Loy, Mina . . . . **CLC 28; DAM POET; PC 16**
See also Lowry, Mina Gertrude
See also DLB 4, 54

Loyson-Bridet
See Schwob, (Mayer Andre) Marcel

Lucas, Craig 1951- . . . . **CLC 64**
See also CA 137

Lucas, George 1944- . . . . **CLC 16**
See also AAYA 1; CA 77-80; CANR 30;
SATA 56

Lucas, Hans
See Godard, Jean-Luc

Lucas, Victoria
See Plath, Sylvia

Ludlam, Charles 1943-1987 . . . . . **CLC 46, 50**
See also CA 85-88; 122

Ludlum, Robert
1927- . . . **CLC 22, 43; DAM NOV, POP**
See also AAYA 10; BEST 89:1, 90:3;
CA 33-36R; CANR 25, 41; DLBY 82;
MTCW

Ludwig, Ken . . . . **CLC 60**

Ludwig, Otto 1813-1865 . . . . **NCLC 4**
See also DLB 129

Lugones, Leopoldo 1874-1938 . . . . . **TCLC 15**
See also CA 116; 131; HW

Lu Hsun 1881-1936 . . . . . . **TCLC 3; SSC 20**
See also Shu-Jen, Chou

Lukacs, George . . . . **CLC 24**
See also Lukacs, Gyorgy (Szegeny von)

Lukacs, Gyorgy (Szegeny von) 1885-1971
See Lukacs, George
See also CA 101; 29-32R

Luke, Peter (Ambrose Cyprian)
1919-1995 . . . . **CLC 38**
See also CA 81-84; 147; DLB 13

Lunar, Dennis
See Mungo, Raymond

Lurie, Alison 1926- . . . . **CLC 4, 5, 18, 39**
See also CA 1-4R; CANR 2, 17, 50; DLB 2;
MTCW; SATA 46

Lustig, Arnost 1926- . . . . **CLC 56**
See also AAYA 3; CA 69-72; CANR 47;
SATA 56

Luther, Martin 1483-1546 . . . . **LC 9, 37**

Luxemburg, Rosa 1870(?)-1919 . . . . **TCLC 63**
See also CA 118

Luzi, Mario 1914- . . . . **CLC 13**
See also CA 61-64; CANR 9; DLB 128

Lyly, John 1554(?)-1606 . . . . **DC 7**
See also DAM DRAM; DLB 62, 167

L'Ymagier
See Gourmont, Remy (-Marie-Charles) de

Lynch, B. Suarez
See Bioy Casares, Adolfo; Borges, Jorge
Luis

Lynch, David (K.) 1946- . . . . **CLC 66**
See also CA 124; 129

Lynch, James
See Andreyev, Leonid (Nikolaevich)

Lynch Davis, B.
See Bioy Casares, Adolfo; Borges, Jorge
Luis

Lyndsay, Sir David 1490-1555 . . . . . . **LC 20**

Lynn, Kenneth S(chuyler) 1923- . . . . **CLC 50**
See also CA 1-4R; CANR 3, 27

Lynx
See West, Rebecca

Lyons, Marcus
See Blish, James (Benjamin)

Lyre, Pinchbeck
See Sassoon, Siegfried (Lorraine)

Lytle, Andrew (Nelson) 1902-1995 . . **CLC 22**
See also CA 9-12R; 150; DLB 6; DLBY 95

Lyttelton, George 1709-1773 . . . . **LC 10**

Maas, Peter 1929- . . . . **CLC 29**
See also CA 93-96; INT 93-96

Macaulay, Rose 1881-1958 . . . . . **TCLC 7, 44**
See also CA 104; DLB 36

Macaulay, Thomas Babington
1800-1859 . . . . **NCLC 42**
See also CDBLB 1832-1890; DLB 32, 55

MacBeth, George (Mann)
1932-1992 . . . . **CLC 2, 5, 9**
See also CA 25-28R; 136; DLB 40; MTCW;
SATA 4; SATA-Obit 70

MacCaig, Norman (Alexander)
1910- . . . . . **CLC 36; DAB; DAM POET**
See also CA 9-12R; CANR 3, 34; DLB 27

MacCarthy, (Sir Charles Otto) Desmond
1877-1952 . . . . **TCLC 36**

MacDiarmid, Hugh
. . . . **CLC 2, 4, 11, 19, 63; PC 9**
See also Grieve, C(hristopher) M(urray)
See also CDBLB 1945-1960; DLB 20

MacDonald, Anson
See Heinlein, Robert A(nson)

Macdonald, Cynthia 1928- . . . . . . **CLC 13, 19**
See also CA 49-52; CANR 4, 44; DLB 105

MacDonald, George 1824-1905 . . . . . **TCLC 9**
See also CA 106; 137; DLB 18, 163;
MAICYA; SATA 33

Macdonald, John
See Millar, Kenneth

MacDonald, John D(ann)
1916-1986 . . . . **CLC 3, 27, 44;
DAM NOV, POP**
See also CA 1-4R; 121; CANR 1, 19;
DLB 8; DLBY 86; MTCW

Macdonald, John Ross
See Millar, Kenneth

Macdonald, Ross . . . . . **CLC 1, 2, 3, 14, 34, 41**
See also Millar, Kenneth
See also DLBD 6

MacDougal, John
See Blish, James (Benjamin)

MacEwen, Gwendolyn (Margaret)
1941-1987 . . . . **CLC 13, 55**
See also CA 9-12R; 124; CANR 7, 22;
DLB 53; SATA 50; SATA-Obit 55

Macha, Karel Hynek 1810-1846 . . **NCLC 46**

Machado (y Ruiz), Antonio
1875-1939 . . . . **TCLC 3**
See also CA 104; DLB 108

Machado de Assis, Joaquim Maria
1839-1908 . . . . . **TCLC 10; BLC; SSC 24**
See also CA 107; 153

Machen, Arthur . . . . **TCLC 4; SSC 20**
See also Jones, Arthur Llewellyn
See also DLB 36, 156

Machiavelli, Niccolo
1469-1527 . . . . **LC 8, 36; DA; DAB;
DAC; DAM MST**

MacInnes, Colin 1914-1976 . . . . . . **CLC 4, 23**
See also CA 69-72; 65-68; CANR 21;
DLB 14; MTCW

MacInnes, Helen (Clark)
1907-1985 . . . . . **CLC 27, 39; DAM POP**
See also CA 1-4R; 117; CANR 1, 28;
DLB 87; MTCW; SATA 22;
SATA-Obit 44

Mackay, Mary 1855-1924
See Corelli, Marie
See also CA 118

Mackenzie, Compton (Edward Montague)
1883-1972 . . . . **CLC 18**
See also CA 21-22; 37-40R; CAP 2;
DLB 34, 100

Mackenzie, Henry 1745-1831 . . . . **NCLC 41**
See also DLB 39

Mackintosh, Elizabeth 1896(?)-1952
See Tey, Josephine
See also CA 110

MacLaren, James
See Grieve, C(hristopher) M(urray)

Mac Laverty, Bernard 1942- . . . . **CLC 31**
See also CA 116; 118; CANR 43; INT 118

MacLean, Alistair (Stuart)
1922-1987 . . . . **CLC 3, 13, 50, 63;
DAM POP**
See also CA 57-60; 121; CANR 28; MTCW;
SATA 23; SATA-Obit 50

Maclean, Norman (Fitzroy)
1902-1990 . . . . **CLC 78; DAM POP;
SSC 13**
See also CA 102; 132; CANR 49

MacLeish, Archibald
1892-1982 . . . . **CLC 3, 8, 14, 68;
DAM POET**
See also CA 9-12R; 106; CANR 33; DLB 4,
7, 45; DLBY 82; MTCW

MacLennan, (John) Hugh
1907-1990 . . . . **CLC 2, 14, 92; DAC;
DAM MST**
See also CA 5-8R; 142; CANR 33; DLB 68;
MTCW

MacLeod, Alistair
1936- . . . . . . **CLC 56; DAC; DAM MST**
See also CA 123; DLB 60

MacNeice, (Frederick) Louis
        1907-1963 . . . . . . CLC 1, 4, 10, 53; DAB;
                                    DAM POET
    See also CA 85-88; DLB 10, 20; MTCW

MacNeill, Dand
    See Fraser, George MacDonald

Macpherson, James   1736-1796 . . . . . . LC 29
    See also DLB 109

Macpherson, (Jean) Jay   1931- . . . . . CLC 14
    See also CA 5-8R; DLB 53

MacShane, Frank   1927- . . . . CLC 39
    See also CA 9-12R; CANR 3, 33; DLB 111

Macumber, Mari
    See Sandoz, Mari(e Susette)

Madach, Imre   1823-1864 . . . . NCLC 19

Madden, (Jerry) David   1933- . . . . CLC 5, 15
    See also CA 1-4R; CAAS 3; CANR 4, 45;
        DLB 6; MTCW

Maddern, Al(an)
    See Ellison, Harlan (Jay)

Madhubuti, Haki R.
        1942- . . . . CLC 6, 73; BLC;
                                    DAM MULT, POET; PC 5
    See also Lee, Don L.
    See also BW 2; CA 73-76; CANR 24, 51;
        DLB 5, 41; DLBD 8

Maepenn, Hugh
    See Kuttner, Henry

Maepenn, K. H.
    See Kuttner, Henry

Maeterlinck, Maurice
        1862-1949 . . . . . . TCLC 3; DAM DRAM
    See also CA 104; 136; SATA 66

Maginn, William   1794-1842 . . . . . . NCLC 8
    See also DLB 110, 159

Mahapatra, Jayanta
        1928- . . . . CLC 33; DAM MULT
    See also CA 73-76; CAAS 9; CANR 15, 33

Mahfouz, Naguib (Abdel Aziz Al-Sabilgi)
        1911(?)-
    See Mahfuz, Najib
    See also BEST 89:2; CA 128; CANR 55;
        DAM NOV; MTCW

Mahfuz, Najib . . . . CLC 52, 55
    See also Mahfouz, Naguib (Abdel Aziz
        Al-Sabilgi)
    See also DLBY 88

Mahon, Derek   1941- . . . . CLC 27
    See also CA 113; 128; DLB 40

Mailer, Norman
        1923- . . . . . . CLC 1, 2, 3, 4, 5, 8, 11, 14,
                28, 39, 74; DA; DAB; DAC; DAM MST,
                                        NOV, POP
    See also AITN 2; CA 9-12R; CABS 1;
        CANR 28; CDALB 1968-1988; DLB 2,
        16, 28; DLBD 3; DLBY 80, 83; MTCW

Maillet, Antonine   1929- . . . . . . CLC 54; DAC
    See also CA 115; 120; CANR 46; DLB 60;
        INT 120

Mais, Roger   1905-1955 . . . . TCLC 8
    See also BW 1; CA 105; 124; DLB 125;
        MTCW

Maistre, Joseph de   1753-1821 . . . . NCLC 37

Maitland, Frederic   1850-1906 . . . . . TCLC 65

Maitland, Sara (Louise)   1950- . . . . . . CLC 49
    See also CA 69-72; CANR 13

Major, Clarence
        1936- . . . . CLC 3, 19, 48; BLC;
                                        DAM MULT
    See also BW 2; CA 21-24R; CAAS 6;
        CANR 13, 25, 53; DLB 33

Major, Kevin (Gerald)
        1949- . . . . CLC 26; DAC
    See also AAYA 16; CA 97-100; CANR 21,
        38; CLR 11; DLB 60; INT CANR-21;
        JRDA; MAICYA; SATA 32, 82

Maki, James
    See Ozu, Yasujiro

Malabaila, Damiano
    See Levi, Primo

Malamud, Bernard
        1914-1986 . . . . . . CLC 1, 2, 3, 5, 8, 9, 11,
                18, 27, 44, 78, 85; DA; DAB; DAC;
                DAM MST, NOV, POP; SSC 15; WLC
    See also AAYA 16; CA 5-8R; 118; CABS 1;
        CANR 28; CDALB 1941-1968; DLB 2,
        28, 152; DLBY 80, 86; MTCW

Malaparte, Curzio   1898-1957 . . . . . TCLC 52

Malcolm, Dan
    See Silverberg, Robert

Malcolm X . . . . CLC 82; BLC
    See also Little, Malcolm

Malherbe, Francois de   1555-1628 . . . . . LC 5

Mallarme, Stephane
        1842-1898 . . . . NCLC 4, 41;
                                    DAM POET; PC 4

Mallet-Joris, Francoise   1930- . . . . . . CLC 11
    See also CA 65-68; CANR 17; DLB 83

Malley, Ern
    See McAuley, James Phillip

Mallowan, Agatha Christie
    See Christie, Agatha (Mary Clarissa)

Maloff, Saul   1922- . . . . CLC 5
    See also CA 33-36R

Malone, Louis
    See MacNeice, (Frederick) Louis

Malone, Michael (Christopher)
        1942- . . . . CLC 43
    See also CA 77-80; CANR 14, 32, 57

Malory, (Sir) Thomas
        1410(?)-1471(?) . . . . . . LC 11; DA; DAB;
                                        DAC; DAM MST
    See also CDBLB Before 1660; DLB 146;
        SATA 59; SATA-Brief 33

Malouf, (George Joseph) David
        1934- . . . . CLC 28, 86
    See also CA 124; CANR 50

Malraux, (Georges-)Andre
        1901-1976 . . . . . . CLC 1, 4, 9, 13, 15, 57;
                                        DAM NOV
    See also CA 21-22; 69-72; CANR 34;
        CAP 2; DLB 72; MTCW

Malzberg, Barry N(athaniel)   1939- . . . CLC 7
    See also CA 61-64; CAAS 4; CANR 16;
        DLB 8

Mamet, David (Alan)
        1947- . . . . CLC 9, 15, 34, 46, 91;
                                    DAM DRAM; DC 4
    See also AAYA 3; CA 81-84; CABS 3;
        CANR 15, 41; DLB 7; MTCW

Mamoulian, Rouben (Zachary)
        1897-1987 . . . . CLC 16
    See also CA 25-28R; 124

Mandelstam, Osip (Emilievich)
        1891(?)-1938(?) . . . . . . TCLC 2, 6; PC 14
    See also CA 104; 150

Mander, (Mary) Jane   1877-1949 . . . TCLC 31

Mandeville, John   fl. 1350- . . . . CMLC 19
    See also DLB 146

Mandiargues, Andre Pieyre de . . . . CLC 41
    See also Pieyre de Mandiargues, Andre
    See also DLB 83

Mandrake, Ethel Belle
    See Thurman, Wallace (Henry)

Mangan, James Clarence
        1803-1849 . . . . NCLC 27

Maniere, J.-E.
    See Giraudoux, (Hippolyte) Jean

Manley, (Mary) Delariviere
        1672(?)-1724 . . . . LC 1
    See also DLB 39, 80

Mann, Abel
    See Creasey, John

Mann, Emily   1952- . . . . DC 7
    See also CA 130; CANR 55

Mann, (Luiz) Heinrich   1871-1950 . . . TCLC 9
    See also CA 106; DLB 66

Mann, (Paul) Thomas
        1875-1955 . . . . TCLC 2, 8, 14, 21, 35, 44,
                60; DA; DAB; DAC; DAM MST, NOV;
                                        SSC 5; WLC
    See also CA 104; 128; DLB 66; MTCW

Mannheim, Karl   1893-1947 . . . . . . TCLC 65

Manning, David
    See Faust, Frederick (Schiller)

Manning, Frederic   1887(?)-1935 . . . TCLC 25
    See also CA 124

Manning, Olivia   1915-1980 . . . . . . CLC 5, 19
    See also CA 5-8R; 101; CANR 29; MTCW

Mano, D. Keith   1942- . . . . CLC 2, 10
    See also CA 25-28R; CAAS 6; CANR 26,
        57; DLB 6

Mansfield, Katherine
        . . TCLC 2, 8, 39; DAB; SSC 9, 23; WLC
    See also Beauchamp, Kathleen Mansfield
    See also DLB 162

Manso, Peter   1940- . . . . CLC 39
    See also CA 29-32R; CANR 44

Mantecon, Juan Jimenez
    See Jimenez (Mantecon), Juan Ramon

Manton, Peter
    See Creasey, John

Man Without a Spleen, A
    See Chekhov, Anton (Pavlovich)

Manzoni, Alessandro   1785-1873 . . NCLC 29

Mapu, Abraham (ben Jekutiel)
        1808-1867 . . . . NCLC 18

Mara, Sally
    See Queneau, Raymond

Marat, Jean Paul　1743-1793 . . . .　**LC 10**

Marcel, Gabriel Honore
　　1889-1973 . . . .　**CLC 15**
　See also CA 102; 45-48; MTCW

Marchbanks, Samuel
　See Davies, (William) Robertson

Marchi, Giacomo
　See Bassani, Giorgio

Margulies, Donald . . . .　**CLC 76**

Marie de France　c. 12th cent. -. . . .　**CMLC 8**

Marie de l'Incarnation　1599-1672 . . . .　**LC 10**

Marier, Captain Victor
　See Griffith, D(avid Lewelyn) W(ark)

Mariner, Scott
　See Pohl, Frederik

Marinetti, Filippo Tommaso
　　1876-1944 . . . .　**TCLC 10**
　See also CA 107; DLB 114

Marivaux, Pierre Carlet de Chamblain de
　　1688-1763 . . . .　**LC 4; DC 7**

Markandaya, Kamala . . . .　**CLC 8, 38**
　See also Taylor, Kamala (Purnaiya)

Markfield, Wallace　1926- . . . .　**CLC 8**
　See also CA 69-72; CAAS 3; DLB 2, 28

Markham, Edwin　1852-1940 . . . . . .　**TCLC 47**
　See also DLB 54

Markham, Robert
　See Amis, Kingsley (William)

Marks, J
　See Highwater, Jamake (Mamake)

Marks-Highwater, J
　See Highwater, Jamake (Mamake)

Markson, David M(errill)　1927- . . . .　**CLC 67**
　See also CA 49-52; CANR 1

Marley, Bob . . . .　**CLC 17**
　See also Marley, Robert Nesta

Marley, Robert Nesta　1945-1981
　See Marley, Bob
　See also CA 107; 103

Marlowe, Christopher
　　1564-1593 . . . . . .　**LC 22; DA; DAB; DAC;**
　　　　　　　DAM DRAM, MST; DC 1; WLC
　See also CDBLB Before 1660; DLB 62

Marlowe, Stephen　1928-
　See Queen, Ellery
　See also CA 13-16R; CANR 6, 55

Marmontel, Jean-Francois
　　1723-1799 . . . .　**LC 2**

Marquand, John P(hillips)
　　1893-1960 . . . .　**CLC 2, 10**
　See also CA 85-88; DLB 9, 102

Marques, Rene
　　1919-1979 . . . . . .　**CLC 96; DAM MULT;**
　　　　　　　　　　　　　　　　　　　　　　　　HLC
　See also CA 97-100; 85-88; DLB 113; HW

Marquez, Gabriel (Jose) Garcia
　See Garcia Marquez, Gabriel (Jose)

Marquis, Don(ald Robert Perry)
　　1878-1937 . . . .　**TCLC 7**
　See also CA 104; DLB 11, 25

Marric, J. J.
　See Creasey, John

Marrow, Bernard
　See Moore, Brian

Marryat, Frederick　1792-1848 . . . .　**NCLC 3**
　See also DLB 21, 163

Marsden, James
　See Creasey, John

Marsh, (Edith) Ngaio
　　1899-1982 . . . . . .　**CLC 7, 53; DAM POP**
　See also CA 9-12R; CANR 6; DLB 77;
　MTCW

Marshall, Garry　1934- . . . .　**CLC 17**
　See also AAYA 3; CA 111; SATA 60

Marshall, Paule
　　1929- . . . .　**CLC 27, 72; BLC;**
　　　　　　　　　　　　　　DAM MULT; SSC 3
　See also BW 2; CA 77-80; CANR 25;
　DLB 157; MTCW

Marsten, Richard
　See Hunter, Evan

Marston, John
　　1576-1634 . . . . . .　**LC 33; DAM DRAM**
　See also DLB 58, 172

Martha, Henry
　See Harris, Mark

Martial　c. 40-c. 104 . . . .　**PC 10**

Martin, Ken
　See Hubbard, L(afayette) Ron(ald)

Martin, Richard
　See Creasey, John

Martin, Steve　1945- . . . .　**CLC 30**
　See also CA 97-100; CANR 30; MTCW

Martin, Valerie　1948- . . . .　**CLC 89**
　See also BEST 90:2; CA 85-88; CANR 49

Martin, Violet Florence
　　1862-1915 . . . .　**TCLC 51**

Martin, Webber
　See Silverberg, Robert

Martindale, Patrick Victor
　See White, Patrick (Victor Martindale)

Martin du Gard, Roger
　　1881-1958 . . . .　**TCLC 24**
　See also CA 118; DLB 65

Martineau, Harriet　1802-1876 . . . .　**NCLC 26**
　See also DLB 21, 55, 159, 163, 166;
　YABC 2

Martines, Julia
　See O'Faolain, Julia

Martinez, Jacinto Benavente y
　See Benavente (y Martinez), Jacinto

Martinez Ruiz, Jose　1873-1967
　See Azorin; Ruiz, Jose Martinez
　See also CA 93-96; HW

Martinez Sierra, Gregorio
　　1881-1947 . . . .　**TCLC 6**
　See also CA 115

Martinez Sierra, Maria (de la O'LeJarraga)
　　1874-1974 . . . .　**TCLC 6**
　See also CA 115

Martinsen, Martin
　See Follett, Ken(neth Martin)

Martinson, Harry (Edmund)
　　1904-1978 . . . .　**CLC 14**
　See also CA 77-80; CANR 34

Marut, Ret
　See Traven, B.

Marut, Robert
　See Traven, B.

Marvell, Andrew
　　1621-1678 . . . . . .　**LC 4; DA; DAB; DAC;**
　　　　　　　　DAM MST, POET; PC 10; WLC
　See also CDBLB 1660-1789; DLB 131

Marx, Karl (Heinrich)
　　1818-1883 . . . .　**NCLC 17**
　See also DLB 129

Masaoka Shiki . . . .　**TCLC 18**
　See also Masaoka Tsunenori

Masaoka Tsunenori　1867-1902
　See Masaoka Shiki
　See also CA 117

Masefield, John (Edward)
　　1878-1967 . . . .　**CLC 11, 47; DAM POET**
　See also CA 19-20; 25-28R; CANR 33;
　CAP 2; CDBLB 1890-1914; DLB 10, 19,
　153, 160; MTCW; SATA 19

Maso, Carole　19(?)- . . . .　**CLC 44**

Mason, Bobbie Ann
　　1940- . . . .　**CLC 28, 43, 82; SSC 4**
　See also AAYA 5; CA 53-56; CANR 11,
　31; DLB 173; DLBY 87; INT CANR-31;
　MTCW

Mason, Ernst
　See Pohl, Frederik

Mason, Lee W.
　See Malzberg, Barry N(athaniel)

Mason, Nick　1945- . . . .　**CLC 35**

Mason, Tally
　See Derleth, August (William)

Mass, William
　See Gibson, William

Masters, Edgar Lee
　　1868-1950 . . . . . .　**TCLC 2, 25; DA; DAC;**
　　　　　　　　　　　DAM MST, POET; PC 1
　See also CA 104; 133; CDALB 1865-1917;
　DLB 54; MTCW

Masters, Hilary　1928- . . . .　**CLC 48**
　See also CA 25-28R; CANR 13, 47

Mastrosimone, William　19(?)- . . . . . .　**CLC 36**

Mathe, Albert
　See Camus, Albert

Matheson, Richard Burton　1926- . . .　**CLC 37**
　See also CA 97-100; DLB 8, 44; INT 97-100

Mathews, Harry　1930- . . . .　**CLC 6, 52**
　See also CA 21-24R; CAAS 6; CANR 18,
　40

Mathews, John Joseph
　　1894-1979 . . . . . .　**CLC 84; DAM MULT**
　See also CA 19-20; 142; CANR 45; CAP 2;
　DLB 175; NNAL

Mathias, Roland (Glyn)　1915- . . . . . .　**CLC 45**
　See also CA 97-100; CANR 19, 41; DLB 27

Matsuo Basho　1644-1694 . . . .　**PC 3**
　See also DAM POET

Mattheson, Rodney
　See Creasey, John

Matthews, Greg　1949- . . . .　**CLC 45**
　See also CA 135

Matthews, William 1942-.......... **CLC 40**
See also CA 29-32R; CAAS 18; CANR 12, 57; DLB 5

Matthias, John (Edward) 1941-...... **CLC 9**
See also CA 33-36R; CANR 56

Matthiessen, Peter
1927- .... **CLC 5, 7, 11, 32, 64; DAM NOV**
See also AAYA 6; BEST 90:4; CA 9-12R; CANR 21, 50; DLB 6, 173; MTCW; SATA 27

Maturin, Charles Robert
1780(?)-1824 .... **NCLC 6**

Matute (Ausejo), Ana Maria
1925-...................... **CLC 11**
See also CA 89-92; MTCW

Maugham, W. S.
See Maugham, W(illiam) Somerset

Maugham, W(illiam) Somerset
1874-1965 ...... **CLC 1, 11, 15, 67, 93; DA; DAB; DAC; DAM DRAM, MST, NOV; SSC 8; WLC**
See also CA 5-8R; 25-28R; CANR 40; CDBLB 1914-1945; DLB 10, 36, 77, 100, 162; MTCW; SATA 54

Maugham, William Somerset
See Maugham, W(illiam) Somerset

Maupassant, (Henri Rene Albert) Guy de
1850-1893 ..... **NCLC 1, 42; DA; DAB; DAC; DAM MST; SSC 1; WLC**
See also DLB 123

Maupin, Armistead
1944-............ **CLC 95; DAM POP**
See also CA 125; 130; INT 130

Maurhut, Richard
See Traven, B.

Mauriac, Claude 1914-1996........ **CLC 9**
See also CA 89-92; 152; DLB 83

Mauriac, Francois (Charles)
1885-1970 ...... **CLC 4, 9, 56; SSC 24**
See also CA 25-28; CAP 2; DLB 65; MTCW

Mavor, Osborne Henry 1888-1951
See Bridie, James
See also CA 104

Maxwell, William (Keepers, Jr.)
1908-...................... **CLC 19**
See also CA 93-96; CANR 54; DLBY 80; INT 93-96

May, Elaine 1932-............... **CLC 16**
See also CA 124; 142; DLB 44

Mayakovski, Vladimir (Vladimirovich)
1893-1930 .... **TCLC 4, 18**
See also CA 104

Mayhew, Henry 1812-1887 ...... **NCLC 31**
See also DLB 18, 55

Mayle, Peter 1939(?)-............. **CLC 89**
See also CA 139

Maynard, Joyce 1953-............ **CLC 23**
See also CA 111; 129

Mayne, William (James Carter)
1928-...................... **CLC 12**
See also AAYA 20; CA 9-12R; CANR 37; CLR 25; JRDA; MAICYA; SAAS 11; SATA 6, 68

Mayo, Jim
See L'Amour, Louis (Dearborn)

Maysles, Albert 1926-............ **CLC 16**
See also CA 29-32R

Maysles, David 1932-............. **CLC 16**

Mazer, Norma Fox 1931- .... **CLC 26**
See also AAYA 5; CA 69-72; CANR 12, 32; CLR 23; JRDA; MAICYA; SAAS 1; SATA 24, 67

Mazzini, Guiseppe 1805-1872 .... **NCLC 34**

McAuley, James Phillip
1917-1976 .... **CLC 45**
See also CA 97-100

McBain, Ed
See Hunter, Evan

McBrien, William Augustine
1930-...................... **CLC 44**
See also CA 107

McCaffrey, Anne (Inez)
1926-...... **CLC 17; DAM NOV, POP**
See also AAYA 6; BEST 89:2; CA 25-28R; CANR 15, 35, 55; DLB 8; JRDA; MAICYA; MTCW; SAAS 11; SATA 8, 70

McCall, Nathan 1955(?)-.......... **CLC 86**
See also CA 146

McCann, Arthur
See Campbell, John W(ood, Jr.)

McCann, Edson
See Pohl, Frederik

McCarthy, Charles, Jr. 1933-
See McCarthy, Cormac
See also CANR 42; DAM POP

McCarthy, Cormac 1933-..... **CLC 4, 57, 59**
See also McCarthy, Charles, Jr.
See also DLB 6, 143

McCarthy, Mary (Therese)
1912-1989 ...... **CLC 1, 3, 5, 14, 24, 39, 59; SSC 24**
See also CA 5-8R; 129; CANR 16, 50; DLB 2; DLBY 81; INT CANR-16; MTCW

McCartney, (James) Paul
1942-.................... **CLC 12, 35**
See also CA 146

McCauley, Stephen (D.) 1955- ..... **CLC 50**
See also CA 141

McClure, Michael (Thomas)
1932-..................... **CLC 6, 10**
See also CA 21-24R; CANR 17, 46; DLB 16

McCorkle, Jill (Collins) 1958-...... **CLC 51**
See also CA 121; DLBY 87

McCourt, James 1941-............. **CLC 5**
See also CA 57-60

McCoy, Horace (Stanley)
1897-1955 .... **TCLC 28**
See also CA 108; 155; DLB 9

McCrae, John 1872-1918........ **TCLC 12**
See also CA 109; DLB 92

McCreigh, James
See Pohl, Frederik

McCullers, (Lula) Carson (Smith)
1917-1967 .... **CLC 1, 4, 10, 12, 48, 100; DA; DAB; DAC; DAM MST, NOV; SSC 24; WLC**
See also CA 5-8R; 25-28R; CABS 1, 3; CANR 18; CDALB 1941-1968; DLB 2, 7, 173; MTCW; SATA 27

McCulloch, John Tyler
See Burroughs, Edgar Rice

McCullough, Colleen
1938(?)-.... **CLC 27; DAM NOV, POP**
See also CA 81-84; CANR 17, 46; MTCW

McDermott, Alice 1953- .... **CLC 90**
See also CA 109; CANR 40

McElroy, Joseph 1930- .... **CLC 5, 47**
See also CA 17-20R

McEwan, Ian (Russell)
1948-......... **CLC 13, 66; DAM NOV**
See also BEST 90:4; CA 61-64; CANR 14, 41; DLB 14; MTCW

McFadden, David 1940-........... **CLC 48**
See also CA 104; DLB 60; INT 104

McFarland, Dennis 1950- .... **CLC 65**

McGahern, John
1934-........... **CLC 5, 9, 48; SSC 17**
See also CA 17-20R; CANR 29; DLB 14; MTCW

McGinley, Patrick (Anthony)
1937-...................... **CLC 41**
See also CA 120; 127; CANR 56; INT 127

McGinley, Phyllis 1905-1978 ...... **CLC 14**
See also CA 9-12R; 77-80; CANR 19; DLB 11, 48; SATA 2, 44; SATA-Obit 24

McGinniss, Joe 1942-............. **CLC 32**
See also AITN 2; BEST 89:2; CA 25-28R; CANR 26; INT CANR-26

McGivern, Maureen Daly
See Daly, Maureen

McGrath, Patrick 1950-........... **CLC 55**
See also CA 136

McGrath, Thomas (Matthew)
1916-1990 .... **CLC 28, 59; DAM POET**
See also CA 9-12R; 132; CANR 6, 33; MTCW; SATA 41; SATA-Obit 66

McGuane, Thomas (Francis III)
1939-............... **CLC 3, 7, 18, 45**
See also AITN 2; CA 49-52; CANR 5, 24, 49; DLB 2; DLBY 80; INT CANR-24; MTCW

McGuckian, Medbh
1950-........... **CLC 48; DAM POET**
See also CA 143; DLB 40

McHale, Tom 1942(?)-1982....... **CLC 3, 5**
See also AITN 1; CA 77-80; 106

McIlvanney, William 1936-........ **CLC 42**
See also CA 25-28R; DLB 14

McIlwraith, Maureen Mollie Hunter
See Hunter, Mollie
See also SATA 2

McInerney, Jay
1955-............ **CLC 34; DAM POP**
See also AAYA 18; CA 116; 123; CANR 45; INT 123

McIntyre, Vonda N(eel) 1948- ..... **CLC 18**
See also CA 81-84; CANR 17, 34; MTCW

McKay, Claude
.... **TCLC 7, 41; BLC; DAB; PC 2**
See also McKay, Festus Claudius
See also DLB 4, 45, 51, 117

McKay, Festus Claudius 1889-1948
See McKay, Claude
See also BW 1; CA 104; 124; DA; DAC;
DAM MST, MULT, NOV, POET;
MTCW; WLC

McKuen, Rod 1933-............ **CLC 1, 3**
See also AITN 1; CA 41-44R; CANR 40

McLoughlin, R. B.
See Mencken, H(enry) L(ouis)

McLuhan, (Herbert) Marshall
1911-1980 .... **CLC 37, 83**
See also CA 9-12R; 102; CANR 12, 34;
DLB 88; INT CANR-12; MTCW

McMillan, Terry (L.)
1951-...... **CLC 50, 61; DAM MULT,
NOV, POP**
See also BW 2; CA 140

McMurtry, Larry (Jeff)
1936-.......... **CLC 2, 3, 7, 11, 27, 44;
DAM NOV, POP**
See also AAYA 15; AITN 2; BEST 89:2;
CA 5-8R; CANR 19, 43;
CDALB 1968-1988; DLB 2, 143;
DLBY 80, 87; MTCW

McNally, T. M. 1961-............ **CLC 82**

McNally, Terrence
1939-... **CLC 4, 7, 41, 91; DAM DRAM**
See also CA 45-48; CANR 2, 56; DLB 7

McNamer, Deirdre 1950-......... **CLC 70**

McNeile, Herman Cyril 1888-1937
See Sapper
See also DLB 77

McNickle, (William) D'Arcy
1904-1977 ...... **CLC 89; DAM MULT**
See also CA 9-12R; 85-88; CANR 5, 45;
DLB 175; NNAL; SATA-Obit 22

McPhee, John (Angus) 1931-...... **CLC 36**
See also BEST 90:1; CA 65-68; CANR 20,
46; MTCW

McPherson, James Alan
1943-..................... **CLC 19, 77**
See also BW 1; CA 25-28R; CAAS 17;
CANR 24; DLB 38; MTCW

McPherson, William (Alexander)
1933-..................... **CLC 34**
See also CA 69-72; CANR 28;
INT CANR-28

Mead, Margaret 1901-1978........ **CLC 37**
See also AITN 1; CA 1-4R; 81-84;
CANR 4; MTCW; SATA-Obit 20

Meaker, Marijane (Agnes) 1927-
See Kerr, M. E.
See also CA 107; CANR 37; INT 107;
JRDA; MAICYA; MTCW; SATA 20, 61

Medoff, Mark (Howard)
1940-........ **CLC 6, 23; DAM DRAM**
See also AITN 1; CA 53-56; CANR 5;
DLB 7; INT CANR-5

Medvedev, P. N.
See Bakhtin, Mikhail Mikhailovich

Meged, Aharon
See Megged, Aharon

Meged, Aron
See Megged, Aharon

Megged, Aharon 1920-............ **CLC 9**
See also CA 49-52; CAAS 13; CANR 1

Mehta, Ved (Parkash) 1934-....... **CLC 37**
See also CA 1-4R; CANR 2, 23; MTCW

Melanter
See Blackmore, R(ichard) D(oddridge)

Melikow, Loris
See Hofmannsthal, Hugo von

Melmoth, Sebastian
See Wilde, Oscar (Fingal O'Flahertie Wills)

Meltzer, Milton 1915-............ **CLC 26**
See also AAYA 8; CA 13-16R; CANR 38;
CLR 13; DLB 61; JRDA; MAICYA;
SAAS 1; SATA 1, 50, 80

Melville, Herman
1819-1891 ..... **NCLC 3, 12, 29, 45, 49;
DA; DAB; DAC; DAM MST, NOV;
SSC 1, 17; WLC**
See also CDALB 1640-1865; DLB 3, 74;
SATA 59

Menander
c. 342B.C.-c. 292B.C........ **CMLC 9;
DAM DRAM; DC 3**
See also DLB 176

Mencken, H(enry) L(ouis)
1880-1956 .... **TCLC 13**
See also CA 105; 125; CDALB 1917-1929;
DLB 11, 29, 63, 137; MTCW

Mendelsohn, Jane 1965(?)-........ **CLC 99**
See also CA 154

Mercer, David
1928-1980 .... **CLC 5; DAM DRAM**
See also CA 9-12R; 102; CANR 23;
DLB 13; MTCW

Merchant, Paul
See Ellison, Harlan (Jay)

Meredith, George
1828-1909 ... **TCLC 17, 43; DAM POET**
See also CA 117; 153; CDBLB 1832-1890;
DLB 18, 35, 57, 159

Meredith, William (Morris)
1919-.. **CLC 4, 13, 22, 55; DAM POET**
See also CA 9-12R; CAAS 14; CANR 6, 40;
DLB 5

Merezhkovsky, Dmitry Sergeyevich
1865-1941 .... **TCLC 29**

Merimee, Prosper
1803-1870 .... **NCLC 6; SSC 7**
See also DLB 119

Merkin, Daphne 1954-............ **CLC 44**
See also CA 123

Merlin, Arthur
See Blish, James (Benjamin)

Merrill, James (Ingram)
1926-1995 .... **CLC 2, 3, 6, 8, 13, 18, 34,
91; DAM POET**
See also CA 13-16R; 147; CANR 10, 49;
DLB 5, 165; DLBY 85; INT CANR-10;
MTCW

Merriman, Alex
See Silverberg, Robert

Merritt, E. B.
See Waddington, Miriam

Merton, Thomas
1915-1968 .. **CLC 1, 3, 11, 34, 83; PC 10**
See also CA 5-8R; 25-28R; CANR 22, 53;
DLB 48; DLBY 81; MTCW

Merwin, W(illiam) S(tanley)
1927-...... **CLC 1, 2, 3, 5, 8, 13, 18, 45,
88; DAM POET**
See also CA 13-16R; CANR 15, 51; DLB 5,
169; INT CANR-15; MTCW

Metcalf, John 1938-............. **CLC 37**
See also CA 113; DLB 60

Metcalf, Suzanne
See Baum, L(yman) Frank

Mew, Charlotte (Mary)
1870-1928 .... **TCLC 8**
See also CA 105; DLB 19, 135

Mewshaw, Michael 1943-.......... **CLC 9**
See also CA 53-56; CANR 7, 47; DLBY 80

Meyer, June
See Jordan, June

Meyer, Lynn
See Slavitt, David R(ytman)

Meyer-Meyrink, Gustav 1868-1932
See Meyrink, Gustav
See also CA 117

Meyers, Jeffrey 1939-............ **CLC 39**
See also CA 73-76; CANR 54; DLB 111

Meynell, Alice (Christina Gertrude Thompson)
1847-1922 .... **TCLC 6**
See also CA 104; DLB 19, 98

Meyrink, Gustav .... **TCLC 21**
See also Meyer-Meyrink, Gustav
See also DLB 81

Michaels, Leonard
1933-............. **CLC 6, 25; SSC 16**
See also CA 61-64; CANR 21; DLB 130;
MTCW

Michaux, Henri 1899-1984 ...... **CLC 8, 19**
See also CA 85-88; 114

Michelangelo 1475-1564............ **LC 12**

Michelet, Jules 1798-1874 ...... **NCLC 31**

Michener, James A(lbert)
1907(?)-.......... **CLC 1, 5, 11, 29, 60;
DAM NOV, POP**
See also AITN 1; BEST 90:1; CA 5-8R;
CANR 21, 45; DLB 6; MTCW

Mickiewicz, Adam 1798-1855 ..... **NCLC 3**

Middleton, Christopher 1926-...... **CLC 13**
See also CA 13-16R; CANR 29, 54;
DLB 40

Middleton, Richard (Barham)
1882-1911 .... **TCLC 56**
See also DLB 156

Middleton, Stanley 1919-........ **CLC 7, 38**
See also CA 25-28R; CAAS 23; CANR 21,
46; DLB 14

Middleton, Thomas
1580-1627 .... **LC 33; DAM DRAM,
MST; DC 5**
See also DLB 58

Migueis, Jose Rodrigues 1901-..... **CLC 10**

Mikszath, Kalman 1847-1910 ..... **TCLC 31**

Miles, Jack .... **CLC 100**

Newbound, Bernard Slade 1930-
See Slade, Bernard
See also CA 81-84; CANR 49;
DAM DRAM

Newby, P(ercy) H(oward)
1918- .... **CLC 2, 13; DAM NOV**
See also CA 5-8R; CANR 32; DLB 15;
MTCW

Newlove, Donald 1928- .... **CLC 6**
See also CA 29-32R; CANR 25

Newlove, John (Herbert) 1938-.... **CLC 14**
See also CA 21-24R; CANR 9, 25

Newman, Charles 1938-......... **CLC 2, 8**
See also CA 21-24R

Newman, Edwin (Harold) 1919- .... **CLC 14**
See also AITN 1; CA 69-72; CANR 5

Newman, John Henry
1801-1890 .... **NCLC 38**
See also DLB 18, 32, 55

Newton, Suzanne 1936- .... **CLC 35**
See also CA 41-44R; CANR 14; JRDA;
SATA 5, 77

Nexo, Martin Andersen
1869-1954 .... **TCLC 43**

Nezval, Vitezslav 1900-1958 ..... **TCLC 44**
See also CA 123

Ng, Fae Myenne 1957(?)-.......... **CLC 81**
See also CA 146

Ngema, Mbongeni 1955- .... **CLC 57**
See also BW 2; CA 143

Ngugi, James T(hiong'o)........ **CLC 3, 7, 13**
See also Ngugi wa Thiong'o

Ngugi wa Thiong'o
1938- ..... **CLC 36; BLC; DAM MULT,**
NOV

See also Ngugi, James T(hiong'o)
See also BW 2; CA 81-84; CANR 27;
DLB 125; MTCW

Nichol, B(arrie) P(hillip)
1944-1988 .... **CLC 18**
See also CA 53-56; DLB 53; SATA 66

Nichols, John (Treadwell) 1940-.... **CLC 38**
See also CA 9-12R; CAAS 2; CANR 6;
DLBY 82

Nichols, Leigh
See Koontz, Dean R(ay)

Nichols, Peter (Richard)
1927- .... **CLC 5, 36, 65**
See also CA 104; CANR 33; DLB 13;
MTCW

Nicolas, F. R. E.
See Freeling, Nicolas

Niedecker, Lorine
1903-1970 .... **CLC 10, 42; DAM POET**
See also CA 25-28; CAP 2; DLB 48

Nietzsche, Friedrich (Wilhelm)
1844-1900 .... **TCLC 10, 18, 55**
See also CA 107; 121; DLB 129

Nievo, Ippolito 1831-1861 .... **NCLC 22**

Nightingale, Anne Redmon 1943-
See Redmon, Anne
See also CA 103

Nik. T. O.
See Annensky, Innokenty (Fyodorovich)

Nin, Anais
1903-1977 ..... **CLC 1, 4, 8, 11, 14, 60;**
DAM NOV, POP; SSC 10
See also AITN 2; CA 13-16R; 69-72;
CANR 22, 53; DLB 2, 4, 152; MTCW

Nishiwaki, Junzaburo 1894-1982 .... **PC 15**
See also CA 107

Nissenson, Hugh 1933-............ **CLC 4, 9**
See also CA 17-20R; CANR 27; DLB 28

Niven, Larry .... **CLC 8**
See also Niven, Laurence Van Cott
See also DLB 8

Niven, Laurence Van Cott 1938-
See Niven, Larry
See also CA 21-24R; CAAS 12; CANR 14,
44; DAM POP; MTCW

Nixon, Agnes Eckhardt 1927-...... **CLC 21**
See also CA 110

Nizan, Paul 1905-1940.......... **TCLC 40**
See also DLB 72

Nkosi, Lewis
1936- ..... **CLC 45; BLC; DAM MULT**
See also BW 1; CA 65-68; CANR 27;
DLB 157

Nodier, (Jean) Charles (Emmanuel)
1780-1844 .... **NCLC 19**
See also DLB 119

Nolan, Christopher 1965-......... **CLC 58**
See also CA 111

Noon, Jeff 1957-................. **CLC 91**
See also CA 148

Norden, Charles
See Durrell, Lawrence (George)

Nordhoff, Charles (Bernard)
1887-1947 .... **TCLC 23**
See also CA 108; DLB 9; SATA 23

Norfolk, Lawrence 1963-.......... **CLC 76**
See also CA 144

Norman, Marsha
1947- .... **CLC 28; DAM DRAM**
See also CA 105; CABS 3; CANR 41;
DLBY 84

Norris, Benjamin Franklin, Jr.
1870-1902 .... **TCLC 24**
See also Norris, Frank
See also CA 110

Norris, Frank
See Norris, Benjamin Franklin, Jr.
See also CDALB 1865-1917; DLB 12, 71

Norris, Leslie 1921- .... **CLC 14**
See also CA 11-12; CANR 14; CAP 1;
DLB 27

North, Andrew
See Norton, Andre

North, Anthony
See Koontz, Dean R(ay)

North, Captain George
See Stevenson, Robert Louis (Balfour)

North, Milou
See Erdrich, Louise

Northrup, B. A.
See Hubbard, L(afayette) Ron(ald)

North Staffs
See Hulme, T(homas) E(rnest)

Norton, Alice Mary
See Norton, Andre
See also MAICYA; SATA 1, 43

Norton, Andre 1912- .... **CLC 12**
See also Norton, Alice Mary
See also AAYA 14; CA 1-4R; CANR 2, 31;
DLB 8, 52; JRDA; MTCW; SATA 91

Norton, Caroline 1808-1877...... **NCLC 47**
See also DLB 21, 159

Norway, Nevil Shute 1899-1960
See Shute, Nevil
See also CA 102; 93-96

Norwid, Cyprian Kamil
1821-1883 .... **NCLC 17**

Nosille, Nabrah
See Ellison, Harlan (Jay)

Nossack, Hans Erich 1901-1978..... **CLC 6**
See also CA 93-96; 85-88; DLB 69

Nostradamus 1503-1566.......... **LC 27**

Nosu, Chuji
See Ozu, Yasujiro

Notenburg, Eleanora (Genrikhovna) von
See Guro, Elena

Nova, Craig 1945-.............. **CLC 7, 31**
See also CA 45-48; CANR 2, 53

Novak, Joseph
See Kosinski, Jerzy (Nikodem)

Novalis 1772-1801 .... **NCLC 13**
See also DLB 90

Nowlan, Alden (Albert)
1933-1983 .. **CLC 15; DAC; DAM MST**
See also CA 9-12R; CANR 5; DLB 53

Noyes, Alfred 1880-1958 .... **TCLC 7**
See also CA 104; DLB 20

Nunn, Kem 19(?)-............... **CLC 34**

Nye, Robert
1939- .... **CLC 13, 42; DAM NOV**
See also CA 33-36R; CANR 29; DLB 14;
MTCW; SATA 6

Nyro, Laura 1947- .... **CLC 17**

Oates, Joyce Carol
1938-...... **CLC 1, 2, 3, 6, 9, 11, 15, 19,**
33, 52; DA; DAB; DAC; DAM MST,
NOV, POP; SSC 6; WLC
See also AAYA 15; AITN 1; BEST 89:2;
CA 5-8R; CANR 25, 45;
CDALB 1968-1988; DLB 2, 5, 130;
DLBY 81; INT CANR-25; MTCW

O'Brien, Darcy 1939-............. **CLC 11**
See also CA 21-24R; CANR 8

O'Brien, E. G.
See Clarke, Arthur C(harles)

O'Brien, Edna
1936- .... **CLC 3, 5, 8, 13, 36, 65;**
DAM NOV; SSC 10
See also CA 1-4R; CANR 6, 41;
CDBLB 1960 to Present; DLB 14;
MTCW

O'Brien, Fitz-James 1828-1862... **NCLC 21**
See also DLB 74

O'Brien, Flann........ **CLC 1, 4, 5, 7, 10, 47**
See also O Nuallain, Brian

O'Brien, Richard 1942- .... **CLC 17**
See also CA 124

O'Brien, Tim
1946- .... **CLC 7, 19, 40; DAM POP**
See also AAYA 16; CA 85-88; CANR 40;
DLB 152; DLBD 9; DLBY 80

Obstfelder, Sigbjoern 1866-1900... **TCLC 23**
See also CA 123

O'Casey, Sean
1880-1964 ...... **CLC 1, 5, 9, 11, 15, 88;**
DAB; DAC; DAM DRAM, MST
See also CA 89-92; CDBLB 1914-1945;
DLB 10; MTCW

O'Cathasaigh, Sean
See O'Casey, Sean

Ochs, Phil 1940-1976............. **CLC 17**
See also CA 65-68

O'Connor, Edwin (Greene)
1918-1968 .... **CLC 14**
See also CA 93-96; 25-28R

O'Connor, (Mary) Flannery
1925-1964 .... **CLC 1, 2, 3, 6, 10, 13, 15,**
21, 66; DA; DAB; DAC; DAM MST,
NOV; SSC 1, 23; WLC
See also AAYA 7; CA 1-4R; CANR 3, 41;
CDALB 1941-1968; DLB 2, 152;
DLBD 12; DLBY 80; MTCW

O'Connor, Frank........... **CLC 23; SSC 5**
See also O'Donovan, Michael John
See also DLB 162

O'Dell, Scott 1898-1989........... **CLC 30**
See also AAYA 3; CA 61-64; 129;
CANR 12, 30; CLR 1, 16; DLB 52;
JRDA; MAICYA; SATA 12, 60

Odets, Clifford
1906-1963 .... **CLC 2, 28, 98;**
DAM DRAM; DC 6
See also CA 85-88; DLB 7, 26; MTCW

O'Doherty, Brian 1934-........... **CLC 76**
See also CA 105

O'Donnell, K. M.
See Malzberg, Barry N(athaniel)

O'Donnell, Lawrence
See Kuttner, Henry

O'Donovan, Michael John
1903-1966 .... **CLC 14**
See also O'Connor, Frank
See also CA 93-96

Oe, Kenzaburo
1935- ..... **CLC 10, 36, 86; DAM NOV;**
SSC 20
See also CA 97-100; CANR 36, 50;
DLBY 94; MTCW

O'Faolain, Julia 1932-....... **CLC 6, 19, 47**
See also CA 81-84; CAAS 2; CANR 12;
DLB 14; MTCW

O'Faolain, Sean
1900-1991 .... **CLC 1, 7, 14, 32, 70;**
SSC 13
See also CA 61-64; 134; CANR 12;
DLB 15, 162; MTCW

O'Flaherty, Liam
1896-1984 .... **CLC 5, 34; SSC 6**
See also CA 101; 113; CANR 35; DLB 36,
162; DLBY 84; MTCW

Ogilvy, Gavin
See Barrie, J(ames) M(atthew)

O'Grady, Standish (James)
1846-1928 .... **TCLC 5**
See also CA 104

O'Grady, Timothy 1951-.......... **CLC 59**
See also CA 138

O'Hara, Frank
1926-1966 .... **CLC 2, 5, 13, 78;**
DAM POET
See also CA 9-12R; 25-28R; CANR 33;
DLB 5, 16; MTCW

O'Hara, John (Henry)
1905-1970 ...... **CLC 1, 2, 3, 6, 11, 42;**
DAM NOV; SSC 15
See also CA 5-8R; 25-28R; CANR 31;
CDALB 1929-1941; DLB 9, 86; DLBD 2;
MTCW

O Hehir, Diana 1922-............ **CLC 41**
See also CA 93-96

Okigbo, Christopher (Ifenayichukwu)
1932-1967 .... **CLC 25, 84; BLC;**
DAM MULT, POET; PC 7
See also BW 1; CA 77-80; DLB 125;
MTCW

Okri, Ben 1959- .... **CLC 87**
See also BW 2; CA 130; 138; DLB 157;
INT 138

Olds, Sharon
1942- ..... **CLC 32, 39, 85; DAM POET**
See also CA 101; CANR 18, 41; DLB 120

Oldstyle, Jonathan
See Irving, Washington

Olesha, Yuri (Karlovich)
1899-1960 .... **CLC 8**
See also CA 85-88

Oliphant, Laurence
1829(?)-1888 .... **NCLC 47**
See also DLB 18, 166

Oliphant, Margaret (Oliphant Wilson)
1828-1897 .... **NCLC 11; SSC 25**
See also DLB 18, 159

Oliver, Mary 1935-........ **CLC 19, 34, 98**
See also CA 21-24R; CANR 9, 43; DLB 5

Olivier, Laurence (Kerr)
1907-1989 .... **CLC 20**
See also CA 111; 150; 129

Olsen, Tillie
1913- ..... **CLC 4, 13; DA; DAB; DAC;**
DAM MST; SSC 11
See also CA 1-4R; CANR 1, 43; DLB 28;
DLBY 80; MTCW

Olson, Charles (John)
1910-1970 ..... **CLC 1, 2, 5, 6, 9, 11, 29;**
DAM POET
See also CA 13-16; 25-28R; CABS 2;
CANR 35; CAP 1; DLB 5, 16; MTCW

Olson, Toby 1937- .... **CLC 28**
See also CA 65-68; CANR 9, 31

Olyesha, Yuri
See Olesha, Yuri (Karlovich)

Ondaatje, (Philip) Michael
1943- .... **CLC 14, 29, 51, 76; DAB;**
DAC; DAM MST
See also CA 77-80; CANR 42; DLB 60

Oneal, Elizabeth 1934-
See Oneal, Zibby
See also CA 106; CANR 28; MAICYA;
SATA 30, 82

Oneal, Zibby .... **CLC 30**
See also Oneal, Elizabeth
See also AAYA 5; CLR 13; JRDA

O'Neill, Eugene (Gladstone)
1888-1953 ...... **TCLC 1, 6, 27, 49; DA;**
DAB; DAC; DAM DRAM, MST; WLC
See also AITN 1; CA 110; 132;
CDALB 1929-1941; DLB 7; MTCW

Onetti, Juan Carlos
1909-1994 .... **CLC 7, 10; DAM MULT,**
NOV; SSC 23
See also CA 85-88; 145; CANR 32;
DLB 113; HW; MTCW

O Nuallain, Brian 1911-1966
See O'Brien, Flann
See also CA 21-22; 25-28R; CAP 2

Oppen, George 1908-1984 .... **CLC 7, 13, 34**
See also CA 13-16R; 113; CANR 8; DLB 5,
165

Oppenheim, E(dward) Phillips
1866-1946 .... **TCLC 45**
See also CA 111; DLB 70

Origen c. 185-c. 254............ **CMLC 19**

Orlovitz, Gil 1918-1973 .... **CLC 22**
See also CA 77-80; 45-48; DLB 2, 5

Orris
See Ingelow, Jean

Ortega y Gasset, Jose
1883-1955 ..... **TCLC 9; DAM MULT;**
HLC
See also CA 106; 130; HW; MTCW

Ortese, Anna Maria 1914-........ **CLC 89**
See also DLB 177

Ortiz, Simon J(oseph)
1941- .... **CLC 45; DAM MULT,**
POET; PC 17
See also CA 134; DLB 120, 175; NNAL

Orton, Joe .... **CLC 4, 13, 43; DC 3**
See also Orton, John Kingsley
See also CDBLB 1960 to Present; DLB 13

Orton, John Kingsley 1933-1967
See Orton, Joe
See also CA 85-88; CANR 35;
DAM DRAM; MTCW

Orwell, George
..... **TCLC 2, 6, 15, 31, 51; DAB; WLC**
See also Blair, Eric (Arthur)
See also CDBLB 1945-1960; DLB 15, 98

Osborne, David
See Silverberg, Robert

Osborne, George
See Silverberg, Robert

Osborne, John (James)
1929-1994 ..... **CLC 1, 2, 5, 11, 45; DA;**
DAB; DAC; DAM DRAM, MST; WLC
See also CA 13-16R; 147; CANR 21, 56;
CDBLB 1945-1960; DLB 13; MTCW

Osborne, Lawrence 1958- .... **CLC 50**

Oshima, Nagisa 1932- .... **CLC 20**
See also CA 116; 121

Paulin, Thomas Neilson   1949-
See Paulin, Tom
See also CA 123; 128

Paulin, Tom . . . . CLC 37
See also Paulin, Thomas Neilson
See also DLB 40

Paustovsky, Konstantin (Georgievich)
1892-1968 . . . . CLC 40
See also CA 93-96; 25-28R

Pavese, Cesare
1908-1950 . . . . . TCLC 3; PC 13; SSC 19
See also CA 104; DLB 128, 177

Pavic, Milorad   1929- . . . . CLC 60
See also CA 136

Payne, Alan
See Jakes, John (William)

Paz, Gil
See Lugones, Leopoldo

Paz, Octavio
1914- . . . . CLC 3, 4, 6, 10, 19, 51, 65;
DA; DAB; DAC; DAM MST, MULT,
POET; HLC; PC 1; WLC
See also CA 73-76; CANR 32; DLBY 90;
HW; MTCW

p'Bitek, Okot
1931-1982 . . . . CLC 96; BLC;
DAM MULT
See also BW 2; CA 124; 107; DLB 125;
MTCW

Peacock, Molly   1947- . . . . CLC 60
See also CA 103; CAAS 21; CANR 52;
DLB 120

Peacock, Thomas Love
1785-1866 . . . . NCLC 22
See also DLB 96, 116

Peake, Mervyn   1911-1968 . . . . . . CLC 7, 54
See also CA 5-8R; 25-28R; CANR 3;
DLB 15, 160; MTCW; SATA 23

Pearce, Philippa . . . . CLC 21
See also Christie, (Ann) Philippa
See also CLR 9; DLB 161; MAICYA;
SATA 1, 67

Pearl, Eric
See Elman, Richard

Pearson, T(homas) R(eid)   1956- . . . . CLC 39
See also CA 120; 130; INT 130

Peck, Dale   1967- . . . . CLC 81
See also CA 146

Peck, John   1941- . . . . CLC 3
See also CA 49-52; CANR 3

Peck, Richard (Wayne)   1934- . . . . . . CLC 21
See also AAYA 1; CA 85-88; CANR 19,
38; CLR 15; INT CANR-19; JRDA;
MAICYA; SAAS 2; SATA 18, 55

Peck, Robert Newton
1928- . . CLC 17; DA; DAC; DAM MST
See also AAYA 3; CA 81-84; CANR 31;
JRDA; MAICYA; SAAS 1; SATA 21, 62

Peckinpah, (David) Sam(uel)
1925-1984 . . . . CLC 20
See also CA 109; 114

Pedersen, Knut   1859-1952
See Hamsun, Knut
See also CA 104; 119; MTCW

Peeslake, Gaffer
See Durrell, Lawrence (George)

Peguy, Charles Pierre
1873-1914 . . . . TCLC 10
See also CA 107

Pena, Ramon del Valle y
See Valle-Inclan, Ramon (Maria) del

Pendennis, Arthur Esquir
See Thackeray, William Makepeace

Penn, William   1644-1718 . . . . LC 25
See also DLB 24

Pepys, Samuel
1633-1703 . . . . . LC 11; DA; DAB; DAC;
DAM MST; WLC
See also CDBLB 1660-1789; DLB 101

Percy, Walker
1916-1990 . . . . CLC 2, 3, 6, 8, 14, 18, 47,
65; DAM NOV, POP
See also CA 1-4R; 131; CANR 1, 23;
DLB 2; DLBY 80, 90; MTCW

Perec, Georges   1936-1982 . . . . CLC 56
See also CA 141; DLB 83

Pereda (y Sanchez de Porrua), Jose Maria de
1833-1906 . . . . TCLC 16
See also CA 117

Pereda y Porrua, Jose Maria de
See Pereda (y Sanchez de Porrua), Jose
Maria de

Peregoy, George Weems
See Mencken, H(enry) L(ouis)

Perelman, S(idney) J(oseph)
1904-1979 . . . . . . CLC 3, 5, 9, 15, 23, 44,
49; DAM DRAM
See also AITN 1, 2; CA 73-76; 89-92;
CANR 18; DLB 11, 44; MTCW

Peret, Benjamin   1899-1959 . . . . . . TCLC 20
See also CA 117

Peretz, Isaac Loeb   1851(?)-1915 . . . TCLC 16
See also CA 109

Peretz, Yitzkhok Leibush
See Peretz, Isaac Loeb

Perez Galdos, Benito   1843-1920 . . . TCLC 27
See also CA 125; 153; HW

Perrault, Charles   1628-1703 . . . . LC 2
See also MAICYA; SATA 25

Perry, Brighton
See Sherwood, Robert E(mmet)

Perse, St.-John . . . . CLC 4, 11, 46
See also Leger, (Marie-Rene Auguste) Alexis
Saint-Leger

Perutz, Leo   1882-1957 . . . . TCLC 60
See also DLB 81

Peseenz, Tulio F.
See Lopez y Fuentes, Gregorio

Pesetsky, Bette   1932- . . . . CLC 28
See also CA 133; DLB 130

Peshkov, Alexei Maximovich   1868-1936
See Gorky, Maxim
See also CA 105; 141; DA; DAC;
DAM DRAM, MST, NOV

Pessoa, Fernando (Antonio Nogueira)
1888-1935 . . . . TCLC 27; HLC
See also CA 125

Peterkin, Julia Mood   1880-1961. . . . CLC 31
See also CA 102; DLB 9

Peters, Joan K.   1945-. . . . . CLC 39

Peters, Robert L(ouis)   1924-. . . . . . . CLC 7
See also CA 13-16R; CAAS 8; DLB 105

Petofi, Sandor   1823-1849. . . . . . . NCLC 21

Petrakis, Harry Mark   1923-. . . . . . . CLC 3
See also CA 9-12R; CANR 4, 30

Petrarch
1304-1374 . . . . CMLC 20; DAM POET;
PC 8

Petrov, Evgeny . . . . TCLC 21
See also Kataev, Evgeny Petrovich

Petry, Ann (Lane)   1908- . . . . . . CLC 1, 7, 18
See also BW 1; CA 5-8R; CAAS 6;
CANR 4, 46; CLR 12; DLB 76; JRDA;
MAICYA; MTCW; SATA 5

Petursson, Halligrimur   1614-1674 . . . . LC 8

Philips, Katherine   1632-1664. . . . . . . LC 30
See also DLB 131

Philipson, Morris H.   1926-. . . . . . . CLC 53
See also CA 1-4R; CANR 4

Phillips, Caryl
1958- . . . . CLC 96; DAM MULT
See also BW 2; CA 141; DLB 157

Phillips, David Graham
1867-1911 . . . . TCLC 44
See also CA 108; DLB 9, 12

Phillips, Jack
See Sandburg, Carl (August)

Phillips, Jayne Anne
1952- . . . . CLC 15, 33; SSC 16
See also CA 101; CANR 24, 50; DLBY 80;
INT CANR-24; MTCW

Phillips, Richard
See Dick, Philip K(indred)

Phillips, Robert (Schaeffer)   1938-. . . CLC 28
See also CA 17-20R; CAAS 13; CANR 8;
DLB 105

Phillips, Ward
See Lovecraft, H(oward) P(hillips)

Piccolo, Lucio   1901-1969. . . . . CLC 13
See also CA 97-100; DLB 114

Pickthall, Marjorie L(owry) C(hristie)
1883-1922 . . . . TCLC 21
See also CA 107; DLB 92

Pico della Mirandola, Giovanni
1463-1494 . . . . LC 15

Piercy, Marge
1936- . . . . CLC 3, 6, 14, 18, 27, 62
See also CA 21-24R; CAAS 1; CANR 13,
43; DLB 120; MTCW

Piers, Robert
See Anthony, Piers

Pieyre de Mandiargues, Andre   1909-1991
See Mandiargues, Andre Pieyre de
See also CA 103; 136; CANR 22

Pilnyak, Boris . . . . TCLC 23
See also Vogau, Boris Andreyevich

Pincherle, Alberto
1907-1990 . . . . . CLC 11, 18; DAM NOV
See also Moravia, Alberto
See also CA 25-28R; 132; CANR 33;
MTCW

Pinckney, Darryl 1953- . . . . **CLC 76**
See also BW 2; CA 143

Pindar 518B.C.-446B.C. . . . . **CMLC 12**
See also DLB 176

Pineda, Cecile 1942- . . . . **CLC 39**
See also CA 118

Pinero, Arthur Wing
1855-1934 . . . . . **TCLC 32; DAM DRAM**
See also CA 110; 153; DLB 10

Pinero, Miguel (Antonio Gomez)
1946-1988 . . . . **CLC 4, 55**
See also CA 61-64; 125; CANR 29; HW

Pinget, Robert 1919- . . . . **CLC 7, 13, 37**
See also CA 85-88; DLB 83

Pink Floyd
See Barrett, (Roger) Syd; Gilmour, David;
Mason, Nick; Waters, Roger; Wright,
Rick

Pinkney, Edward 1802-1828 . . . . . **NCLC 31**

Pinkwater, Daniel Manus 1941- . . . . **CLC 35**
See also Pinkwater, Manus
See also AAYA 1; CA 29-32R; CANR 12,
38; CLR 4; JRDA; MAICYA; SAAS 3;
SATA 46, 76

Pinkwater, Manus
See Pinkwater, Daniel Manus
See also SATA 8

Pinsky, Robert
1940- . . **CLC 9, 19, 38, 94; DAM POET**
See also CA 29-32R; CAAS 4; DLBY 82

Pinta, Harold
See Pinter, Harold

Pinter, Harold
1930- . . . . . **CLC 1, 3, 6, 9, 11, 15, 27, 58,
73; DA; DAB; DAC; DAM DRAM,
MST; WLC**
See also CA 5-8R; CANR 33; CDBLB 1960
to Present; DLB 13; MTCW

Piozzi, Hester Lynch (Thrale)
1741-1821 . . . . **NCLC 57**
See also DLB 104, 142

Pirandello, Luigi
1867-1936 . . . . . . **TCLC 4, 29; DA; DAB;
DAC; DAM DRAM, MST; DC 5;
SSC 22; WLC**
See also CA 104; 153

Pirsig, Robert M(aynard)
1928- . . . . **CLC 4, 6, 73; DAM POP**
See also CA 53-56; CANR 42; MTCW;
SATA 39

Pisarev, Dmitry Ivanovich
1840-1868 . . . . **NCLC 25**

Pix, Mary (Griffith) 1666-1709 . . . . . . **LC 8**
See also DLB 80

Pixerecourt, Guilbert de
1773-1844 . . . . **NCLC 39**

Plaidy, Jean
See Hibbert, Eleanor Alice Burford

Planche, James Robinson
1796-1880 . . . . **NCLC 42**

Plant, Robert 1948- . . . . **CLC 12**

Plante, David (Robert)
1940- . . . . **CLC 7, 23, 38; DAM NOV**
See also CA 37-40R; CANR 12, 36;
DLBY 83; INT CANR-12; MTCW

Plath, Sylvia
1932-1963 . . . . . **CLC 1, 2, 3, 5, 9, 11, 14,
17, 50, 51, 62; DA; DAB; DAC;
DAM MST, POET; PC 1; WLC**
See also AAYA 13; CA 19-20; CANR 34;
CAP 2; CDALB 1941-1968; DLB 5, 6,
152; MTCW

Plato
428(?)B.C.-348(?)B.C. . . . . . **CMLC 8; DA;
DAB; DAC; DAM MST**
See also DLB 176

Platonov, Andrei . . . . **TCLC 14**
See also Klimentov, Andrei Platonovich

Platt, Kin 1911- . . . . **CLC 26**
See also AAYA 11; CA 17-20R; CANR 11;
JRDA; SAAS 17; SATA 21, 86

Plautus c. 251B.C.-184B.C. . . . . **DC 6**

Plick et Plock
See Simenon, Georges (Jacques Christian)

Plimpton, George (Ames) 1927- . . . . . **CLC 36**
See also AITN 1; CA 21-24R; CANR 32;
MTCW; SATA 10

Plomer, William Charles Franklin
1903-1973 . . . . **CLC 4, 8**
See also CA 21-22; CANR 34; CAP 2;
DLB 20, 162; MTCW; SATA 24

Plowman, Piers
See Kavanagh, Patrick (Joseph)

Plum, J.
See Wodehouse, P(elham) G(renville)

Plumly, Stanley (Ross) 1939- . . . . . . **CLC 33**
See also CA 108; 110; DLB 5; INT 110

Plumpe, Friedrich Wilhelm
1888-1931 . . . . **TCLC 53**
See also CA 112

Poe, Edgar Allan
1809-1849 . . . . **NCLC 1, 16, 55; DA;
DAB; DAC; DAM MST, POET; PC 1;
SSC 1, 22; WLC**
See also AAYA 14; CDALB 1640-1865;
DLB 3, 59, 73, 74; SATA 23

Poet of Titchfield Street, The
See Pound, Ezra (Weston Loomis)

Pohl, Frederik 1919- . . . . . **CLC 18; SSC 25**
See also CA 61-64; CAAS 1; CANR 11, 37;
DLB 8; INT CANR-11; MTCW;
SATA 24

Poirier, Louis 1910-
See Gracq, Julien
See also CA 122; 126

Poitier, Sidney 1927- . . . . **CLC 26**
See also BW 1; CA 117

Polanski, Roman 1933- . . . . **CLC 16**
See also CA 77-80

Poliakoff, Stephen 1952- . . . . **CLC 38**
See also CA 106; DLB 13

Police, The
See Copeland, Stewart (Armstrong);
Summers, Andrew James; Sumner,
Gordon Matthew

Polidori, John William
1795-1821 . . . . **NCLC 51**
See also DLB 116

Pollitt, Katha 1949- . . . . **CLC 28**
See also CA 120; 122; MTCW

Pollock, (Mary) Sharon
1936- . . . . **CLC 50; DAC; DAM DRAM,
MST**
See also CA 141; DLB 60

Polo, Marco 1254-1324 . . . . **CMLC 15**

Polonsky, Abraham (Lincoln)
1910- . . . . **CLC 92**
See also CA 104; DLB 26; INT 104

Polybius c. 200B.C.-c. 118B.C. . . . . **CMLC 17**
See also DLB 176

Pomerance, Bernard
1940- . . . . **CLC 13; DAM DRAM**
See also CA 101; CANR 49

Ponge, Francis (Jean Gaston Alfred)
1899-1988 . . . . . **CLC 6, 18; DAM POET**
See also CA 85-88; 126; CANR 40

Pontoppidan, Henrik 1857-1943 . . . **TCLC 29**

Poole, Josephine . . . . **CLC 17**
See also Helyar, Jane Penelope Josephine
See also SAAS 2; SATA 5

Popa, Vasko 1922-1991 . . . . **CLC 19**
See also CA 112; 148

Pope, Alexander
1688-1744 . . . . . . **LC 3; DA; DAB; DAC;
DAM MST, POET; WLC**
See also CDBLB 1660-1789; DLB 95, 101

Porter, Connie (Rose) 1959(?)- . . . . . **CLC 70**
See also BW 2; CA 142; SATA 81

Porter, Gene(va Grace) Stratton
1863(?)-1924 . . . . **TCLC 21**
See also CA 112

Porter, Katherine Anne
1890-1980 . . . . . . **CLC 1, 3, 7, 10, 13, 15,
27; DA; DAB; DAC; DAM MST, NOV;
SSC 4**
See also AITN 2; CA 1-4R; 101; CANR 1;
DLB 4, 9, 102; DLBD 12; DLBY 80;
MTCW; SATA 39; SATA-Obit 23

Porter, Peter (Neville Frederick)
1929- . . . . **CLC 5, 13, 33**
See also CA 85-88; DLB 40

Porter, William Sydney 1862-1910
See Henry, O.
See also CA 104; 131; CDALB 1865-1917;
DA; DAB; DAC; DAM MST; DLB 12,
78, 79; MTCW; YABC 2

Portillo (y Pacheco), Jose Lopez
See Lopez Portillo (y Pacheco), Jose

Post, Melville Davisson
1869-1930 . . . . **TCLC 39**
See also CA 110

Potok, Chaim
1929- . . . . **CLC 2, 7, 14, 26; DAM NOV**
See also AAYA 15; AITN 1, 2; CA 17-20R;
CANR 19, 35; DLB 28, 152;
INT CANR-19; MTCW; SATA 33

Potter, Beatrice
See Webb, (Martha) Beatrice (Potter)
See also MAICYA

Potter, Dennis (Christopher George)
1935-1994 . . . . **CLC 58, 86**
See also CA 107; 145; CANR 33; MTCW

Pound, Ezra (Weston Loomis)
      1885-1972 ...... **CLC 1, 2, 3, 4, 5, 7, 10,**
        13, 18, 34, 48, 50; DA; DAB; DAC;
        DAM MST, POET; PC 4; WLC
      See also CA 5-8R; 37-40R; CANR 40;
        CDALB 1917-1929; DLB 4, 45, 63;
        MTCW

Povod, Reinaldo   1959-1994 .... **CLC 44**
      See also CA 136; 146

Powell, Adam Clayton, Jr.
      1908-1972 .... **CLC 89; BLC;**
                              DAM MULT
      See also BW 1; CA 102; 33-36R

Powell, Anthony (Dymoke)
      1905- .... **CLC 1, 3, 7, 9, 10, 31**
      See also CA 1-4R; CANR 1, 32;
        CDBLB 1945-1960; DLB 15; MTCW

Powell, Dawn   1897-1965 .... **CLC 66**
      See also CA 5-8R

Powell, Padgett   1952-............ **CLC 34**
      See also CA 126

Power, Susan..................... **CLC 91**

Powers, J(ames) F(arl)
      1917- .... **CLC 1, 4, 8, 57; SSC 4**
      See also CA 1-4R; CANR 2; DLB 130;
        MTCW

Powers, John J(ames)   1945-
      See Powers, John R.
      See also CA 69-72

Powers, John R. .... **CLC 66**
      See also Powers, John J(ames)

Powers, Richard (S.)   1957- .... **CLC 93**
      See also CA 148

Pownall, David   1938-............. **CLC 10**
      See also CA 89-92; CAAS 18; CANR 49;
        DLB 14

Powys, John Cowper
      1872-1963 .... **CLC 7, 9, 15, 46**
      See also CA 85-88; DLB 15; MTCW

Powys, T(heodore) F(rancis)
      1875-1953 .... **TCLC 9**
      See also CA 106; DLB 36, 162

Prager, Emily   1952-.............. **CLC 56**

Pratt, E(dwin) J(ohn)
      1883(?)-1964 .... **CLC 19; DAC;**
                              DAM POET
      See also CA 141; 93-96; DLB 92

Premchand..................... **TCLC 21**
      See also Srivastava, Dhanpat Rai

Preussler, Otfried   1923-.......... **CLC 17**
      See also CA 77-80; SATA 24

Prevert, Jacques (Henri Marie)
      1900-1977 .... **CLC 15**
      See also CA 77-80; 69-72; CANR 29;
        MTCW; SATA-Obit 30

Prevost, Abbe (Antoine Francois)
      1697-1763 .... **LC 1**

Price, (Edward) Reynolds
      1933- .... **CLC 3, 6, 13, 43, 50, 63;**
                         DAM NOV; SSC 22
      See also CA 1-4R; CANR 1, 37, 57; DLB 2;
        INT CANR-37

Price, Richard   1949- .... **CLC 6, 12**
      See also CA 49-52; CANR 3; DLBY 81

Prichard, Katharine Susannah
      1883-1969 .... **CLC 46**
      See also CA 11-12; CANR 33; CAP 1;
        MTCW; SATA 66

Priestley, J(ohn) B(oynton)
      1894-1984 .... **CLC 2, 5, 9, 34;**
                            DAM DRAM, NOV
      See also CA 9-12R; 113; CANR 33;
        CDBLB 1914-1945; DLB 10, 34, 77, 100,
        139; DLBY 84; MTCW

Prince   1958(?)-................. **CLC 35**

Prince, F(rank) T(empleton)   1912-.. **CLC 22**
      See also CA 101; CANR 43; DLB 20

Prince Kropotkin
      See Kropotkin, Peter (Aleksieevich)

Prior, Matthew   1664-1721.......... **LC 4**
      See also DLB 95

Pritchard, William H(arrison)
      1932-...................... **CLC 34**
      See also CA 65-68; CANR 23; DLB 111

Pritchett, V(ictor) S(awdon)
      1900- .... **CLC 5, 13, 15, 41;**
                          DAM NOV; SSC 14
      See also CA 61-64; CANR 31; DLB 15,
        139; MTCW

Private 19022
      See Manning, Frederic

Probst, Mark   1925-.............. **CLC 59**
      See also CA 130

Prokosch, Frederic   1908-1989.... **CLC 4, 48**
      See also CA 73-76; 128; DLB 48

Prophet, The
      See Dreiser, Theodore (Herman Albert)

Prose, Francine   1947-............ **CLC 45**
      See also CA 109; 112; CANR 46

Proudhon
      See Cunha, Euclides (Rodrigues Pimenta) da

Proulx, E. Annie   1935- .... **CLC 81**

Proust, (Valentin-Louis-George-Eugene-)
      Marcel
      1871-1922 .... **TCLC 7, 13, 33; DA;**
                DAB; DAC; DAM MST, NOV; WLC
      See also CA 104; 120; DLB 65; MTCW

Prowler, Harley
      See Masters, Edgar Lee

Prus, Boleslaw   1845-1912 .... **TCLC 48**

Pryor, Richard (Franklin Lenox Thomas)
      1940-...................... **CLC 26**
      See also CA 122

Przybyszewski, Stanislaw
      1868-1927 .... **TCLC 36**
      See also DLB 66

Pteleon
      See Grieve, C(hristopher) M(urray)
      See also DAM POET

Puckett, Lute
      See Masters, Edgar Lee

Puig, Manuel
      1932-1990 .... **CLC 3, 5, 10, 28, 65;**
                         DAM MULT; HLC
      See also CA 45-48; CANR 2, 32; DLB 113;
        HW; MTCW

Purdy, Al(fred Wellington)
      1918-.......... **CLC 3, 6, 14, 50; DAC;**
                        DAM MST, POET
      See also CA 81-84; CAAS 17; CANR 42;
        DLB 88

Purdy, James (Amos)
      1923-............. **CLC 2, 4, 10, 28, 52**
      See also CA 33-36R; CAAS 1; CANR 19,
        51; DLB 2; INT CANR-19; MTCW

Pure, Simon
      See Swinnerton, Frank Arthur

Pushkin, Alexander (Sergeyevich)
      1799-1837 ..... **NCLC 3, 27; DA; DAB;**
                DAC; DAM DRAM, MST, POET;
                                PC 10; WLC
      See also SATA 61

P'u Sung-ling   1640-1715 .... **LC 3**

Putnam, Arthur Lee
      See Alger, Horatio, Jr.

Puzo, Mario
      1920- ..... **CLC 1, 2, 6, 36; DAM NOV,**
                                        POP
      See also CA 65-68; CANR 4, 42; DLB 6;
        MTCW

Pygge, Edward
      See Barnes, Julian (Patrick)

Pym, Barbara (Mary Crampton)
      1913-1980 .... **CLC 13, 19, 37**
      See also CA 13-14; 97-100; CANR 13, 34;
        CAP 1; DLB 14; DLBY 87; MTCW

Pynchon, Thomas (Ruggles, Jr.)
      1937- ..... **CLC 2, 3, 6, 9, 11, 18, 33, 62,**
        72; DA; DAB; DAC; DAM MST, NOV,
                         POP; SSC 14; WLC
      See also BEST 90:2; CA 17-20R; CANR 22,
        46; DLB 2, 173; MTCW

Pythagoras
      c. 570B.C.-c. 500B.C......... **CMLC 22**
      See also DLB 176

Qian Zhongshu
      See Ch'ien Chung-shu

Qroll
      See Dagerman, Stig (Halvard)

Quarrington, Paul (Lewis)   1953-.... **CLC 65**
      See also CA 129

Quasimodo, Salvatore   1901-1968 ... **CLC 10**
      See also CA 13-16; 25-28R; CAP 1;
        DLB 114; MTCW

Quay, Stephen   1947- .... **CLC 95**

Quay, The Brothers
      See Quay, Stephen; Quay, Timothy

Quay, Timothy   1947- .... **CLC 95**

Queen, Ellery.................. **CLC 3, 11**
      See also Dannay, Frederic; Davidson,
        Avram; Lee, Manfred B(ennington);
        Marlowe, Stephen; Sturgeon, Theodore
        (Hamilton); Vance, John Holbrook

Queen, Ellery, Jr.
      See Dannay, Frederic; Lee, Manfred
        B(ennington)

Queneau, Raymond
      1903-1976 .... **CLC 2, 5, 10, 42**
      See also CA 77-80; 69-72; CANR 32;
        DLB 72; MTCW

Quevedo, Francisco de   1580-1645.... **LC 23**

Quiller-Couch, Arthur Thomas
  1863-1944 .... TCLC 53
  See also CA 118; DLB 135, 153

Quin, Ann (Marie) 1936-1973 .... CLC 6
  See also CA 9-12R; 45-48; DLB 14

Quinn, Martin
  See Smith, Martin Cruz

Quinn, Peter 1947-.............. CLC 91

Quinn, Simon
  See Smith, Martin Cruz

Quiroga, Horacio (Sylvestre)
  1878-1937 ..... TCLC 20; DAM MULT;
                                      HLC
  See also CA 117; 131; HW; MTCW

Quoirez, Francoise 1935-.......... CLC 9
  See also Sagan, Francoise
  See also CA 49-52; CANR 6, 39; MTCW

Raabe, Wilhelm 1831-1910 ...... TCLC 45
  See also DLB 129

Rabe, David (William)
  1940- ...... CLC 4, 8, 33; DAM DRAM
  See also CA 85-88; CABS 3; DLB 7

Rabelais, Francois
  1483-1553 ...... LC 5; DA; DAB; DAC;
                                  DAM MST; WLC

Rabinovitch, Sholem 1859-1916
  See Aleichem, Sholom
  See also CA 104

Rachilde 1860-1953 .... TCLC 67
  See also DLB 123

Racine, Jean
  1639-1699 .... LC 28; DAB; DAM MST

Radcliffe, Ann (Ward)
  1764-1823 .... NCLC 6, 55
  See also DLB 39

Radiguet, Raymond 1903-1923 .... TCLC 29
  See also DLB 65

Radnoti, Miklos 1909-1944 .... TCLC 16
  See also CA 118

Rado, James 1939-.............. CLC 17
  See also CA 105

Radvanyi, Netty 1900-1983
  See Seghers, Anna
  See also CA 85-88; 110

Rae, Ben
  See Griffiths, Trevor

Raeburn, John (Hay) 1941-........ CLC 34
  See also CA 57-60

Ragni, Gerome 1942-1991 .... CLC 17
  See also CA 105; 134

Rahv, Philip 1908-1973 .... CLC 24
  See also Greenberg, Ivan
  See also DLB 137

Raine, Craig 1944-.............. CLC 32
  See also CA 108; CANR 29, 51; DLB 40

Raine, Kathleen (Jessie) 1908- ... CLC 7, 45
  See also CA 85-88; CANR 46; DLB 20;
  MTCW

Rainis, Janis 1865-1929 .... TCLC 29

Rakosi, Carl..................... CLC 47
  See also Rawley, Callman
  See also CAAS 5

Raleigh, Richard
  See Lovecraft, H(oward) P(hillips)

Raleigh, Sir Walter 1554(?)-1618 .... LC 31
  See also CDBLB Before 1660; DLB 172

Rallentando, H. P.
  See Sayers, Dorothy L(eigh)

Ramal, Walter
  See de la Mare, Walter (John)

Ramon, Juan
  See Jimenez (Mantecon), Juan Ramon

Ramos, Graciliano 1892-1953 ..... TCLC 32

Rampersad, Arnold 1941-......... CLC 44
  See also BW 2; CA 127; 133; DLB 111;
  INT 133

Rampling, Anne
  See Rice, Anne

Ramsay, Allan 1684(?)-1758 .... LC 29
  See also DLB 95

Ramuz, Charles-Ferdinand
  1878-1947 .... TCLC 33

Rand, Ayn
  1905-1982 ...... CLC 3, 30, 44, 79; DA;
                        DAC; DAM MST, NOV, POP; WLC
  See also AAYA 10; CA 13-16R; 105;
  CANR 27; MTCW

Randall, Dudley (Felker)
  1914- ...... CLC 1; BLC; DAM MULT
  See also BW 1; CA 25-28R; CANR 23;
  DLB 41

Randall, Robert
  See Silverberg, Robert

Ranger, Ken
  See Creasey, John

Ransom, John Crowe
  1888-1974 .... CLC 2, 4, 5, 11, 24;
                                      DAM POET
  See also CA 5-8R; 49-52; CANR 6, 34;
  DLB 45, 63; MTCW

Rao, Raja 1909- ... CLC 25, 56; DAM NOV
  See also CA 73-76; CANR 51; MTCW

Raphael, Frederic (Michael)
  1931-..................... CLC 2, 14
  See also CA 1-4R; CANR 1; DLB 14

Ratcliffe, James P.
  See Mencken, H(enry) L(ouis)

Rathbone, Julian 1935- .... CLC 41
  See also CA 101; CANR 34

Rattigan, Terence (Mervyn)
  1911-1977 .... CLC 7; DAM DRAM
  See also CA 85-88; 73-76;
  CDBLB 1945-1960; DLB 13; MTCW

Ratushinskaya, Irina 1954- .... CLC 54
  See also CA 129

Raven, Simon (Arthur Noel)
  1927-..................... CLC 14
  See also CA 81-84

Rawley, Callman 1903-
  See Rakosi, Carl
  See also CA 21-24R; CANR 12, 32

Rawlings, Marjorie Kinnan
  1896-1953 .... TCLC 4
  See also AAYA 20; CA 104; 137; DLB 9,
  22, 102; JRDA; MAICYA; YABC 1

Ray, Satyajit
  1921-1992 ... CLC 16, 76; DAM MULT
  See also CA 114; 137

Read, Herbert Edward 1893-1968.... CLC 4
  See also CA 85-88; 25-28R; DLB 20, 149

Read, Piers Paul 1941- ...... CLC 4, 10, 25
  See also CA 21-24R; CANR 38; DLB 14;
  SATA 21

Reade, Charles 1814-1884 .... NCLC 2
  See also DLB 21

Reade, Hamish
  See Gray, Simon (James Holliday)

Reading, Peter 1946- .... CLC 47
  See also CA 103; CANR 46; DLB 40

Reaney, James
  1926- ...... CLC 13; DAC; DAM MST
  See also CA 41-44R; CAAS 15; CANR 42;
  DLB 68; SATA 43

Rebreanu, Liviu 1885-1944 .... TCLC 28

Rechy, John (Francisco)
  1934- .... CLC 1, 7, 14, 18;
                                  DAM MULT; HLC
  See also CA 5-8R; CAAS 4; CANR 6, 32;
  DLB 122; DLBY 82; HW; INT CANR-6

Redcam, Tom 1870-1933 .... TCLC 25

Reddin, Keith.................... CLC 67

Redgrove, Peter (William)
  1932-..................... CLC 6, 41
  See also CA 1-4R; CANR 3, 39; DLB 40

Redmon, Anne.................... CLC 22
  See also Nightingale, Anne Redmon
  See also DLBY 86

Reed, Eliot
  See Ambler, Eric

Reed, Ishmael
  1938-........ CLC 2, 3, 5, 6, 13, 32, 60;
                                  BLC; DAM MULT
  See also BW 2; CA 21-24R; CANR 25, 48;
  DLB 2, 5, 33, 169; DLBD 8; MTCW

Reed, John (Silas) 1887-1920 ...... TCLC 9
  See also CA 106

Reed, Lou....................... CLC 21
  See also Firbank, Louis

Reeve, Clara 1729-1807 .... NCLC 19
  See also DLB 39

Reich, Wilhelm 1897-1957........ TCLC 57

Reid, Christopher (John) 1949-..... CLC 33
  See also CA 140; DLB 40

Reid, Desmond
  See Moorcock, Michael (John)

Reid Banks, Lynne 1929-
  See Banks, Lynne Reid
  See also CA 1-4R; CANR 6, 22, 38;
  CLR 24; JRDA; MAICYA; SATA 22, 75

Reilly, William K.
  See Creasey, John

Reiner, Max
  See Caldwell, (Janet Miriam) Taylor
  (Holland)

Reis, Ricardo
  See Pessoa, Fernando (Antonio Nogueira)

Remarque, Erich Maria
  1898-1970 .... CLC 21; DA; DAB; DAC;
                                  DAM MST, NOV
  See also CA 77-80; 29-32R; DLB 56;
  MTCW

Remizov, A.
See Remizov, Aleksei (Mikhailovich)

Remizov, A. M.
See Remizov, Aleksei (Mikhailovich)

Remizov, Aleksei (Mikhailovich)
1877-1957 . . . . **TCLC 27**
See also CA 125; 133

Renan, Joseph Ernest
1823-1892 . . . . **NCLC 26**

Renard, Jules 1864-1910 . . . . **TCLC 17**
See also CA 117

Renault, Mary . . . . **CLC 3, 11, 17**
See also Challans, Mary
See also DLBY 83

Rendell, Ruth (Barbara)
1930- . . . . **CLC 28, 48; DAM POP**
See also Vine, Barbara
See also CA 109; CANR 32, 52; DLB 87;
INT CANR-32; MTCW

Renoir, Jean 1894-1979 . . . . **CLC 20**
See also CA 129; 85-88

Resnais, Alain 1922- . . . . **CLC 16**

Reverdy, Pierre 1889-1960 . . . . **CLC 53**
See also CA 97-100; 89-92

Rexroth, Kenneth
1905-1982 . . . . . . **CLC 1, 2, 6, 11, 22, 49;**
DAM POET
See also CA 5-8R; 107; CANR 14, 34;
CDALB 1941-1968; DLB 16, 48, 165;
DLBY 82; INT CANR-14; MTCW

Reyes, Alfonso 1889-1959 . . . . **TCLC 33**
See also CA 131; HW

Reyes y Basoalto, Ricardo Eliecer Neftali
See Neruda, Pablo

Reymont, Wladyslaw (Stanislaw)
1868(?)-1925 . . . . **TCLC 5**
See also CA 104

Reynolds, Jonathan 1942- . . . . **CLC 6, 38**
See also CA 65-68; CANR 28

Reynolds, Joshua 1723-1792 . . . . **LC 15**
See also DLB 104

Reynolds, Michael Shane 1937- . . . . **CLC 44**
See also CA 65-68; CANR 9

Reznikoff, Charles 1894-1976 . . . . **CLC 9**
See also CA 33-36; 61-64; CAP 2; DLB 28,
45

Rezzori (d'Arezzo), Gregor von
1914- . . . . **CLC 25**
See also CA 122; 136

Rhine, Richard
See Silverstein, Alvin

Rhodes, Eugene Manlove
1869-1934 . . . . **TCLC 53**

R'hoone
See Balzac, Honore de

Rhys, Jean
1890(?)-1979 . . . . **CLC 2, 4, 6, 14, 19, 51;**
DAM NOV; SSC 21
See also CA 25-28R; 85-88; CANR 35;
CDBLB 1945-1960; DLB 36, 117, 162;
MTCW

Ribeiro, Darcy 1922-1997 . . . . **CLC 34**
See also CA 33-36R; 156

Ribeiro, Joao Ubaldo (Osorio Pimentel)
1941- . . . . **CLC 10, 67**
See also CA 81-84

Ribman, Ronald (Burt) 1932- . . . . **CLC 7**
See also CA 21-24R; CANR 46

Ricci, Nino 1959- . . . . **CLC 70**
See also CA 137

Rice, Anne 1941- . . . . . **CLC 41; DAM POP**
See also AAYA 9; BEST 89:2; CA 65-68;
CANR 12, 36, 53

Rice, Elmer (Leopold)
1892-1967 . . . . **CLC 7, 49; DAM DRAM**
See also CA 21-22; 25-28R; CAP 2; DLB 4,
7; MTCW

Rice, Tim(othy Miles Bindon)
1944- . . . . **CLC 21**
See also CA 103; CANR 46

Rich, Adrienne (Cecile)
1929- . . . . **CLC 3, 6, 7, 11, 18, 36, 73, 76;**
DAM POET; PC 5
See also CA 9-12R; CANR 20, 53; DLB 5,
67; MTCW

Rich, Barbara
See Graves, Robert (von Ranke)

Rich, Robert
See Trumbo, Dalton

Richard, Keith . . . . **CLC 17**
See also Richards, Keith

Richards, David Adams
1950- . . . . **CLC 59; DAC**
See also CA 93-96; DLB 53

Richards, I(vor) A(rmstrong)
1893-1979 . . . . **CLC 14, 24**
See also CA 41-44R; 89-92; CANR 34;
DLB 27

Richards, Keith 1943-
See Richard, Keith
See also CA 107

Richardson, Anne
See Roiphe, Anne (Richardson)

Richardson, Dorothy Miller
1873-1957 . . . . **TCLC 3**
See also CA 104; DLB 36

Richardson, Ethel Florence (Lindesay)
1870-1946
See Richardson, Henry Handel
See also CA 105

Richardson, Henry Handel . . . . **TCLC 4**
See also Richardson, Ethel Florence
(Lindesay)

Richardson, John
1796-1852 . . . . **NCLC 55; DAC**
See also DLB 99

Richardson, Samuel
1689-1761 . . . . . . **LC 1; DA; DAB; DAC;**
DAM MST, NOV; WLC
See also CDBLB 1660-1789; DLB 39

Richler, Mordecai
1931- . . . . **CLC 3, 5, 9, 13, 18, 46, 70;**
DAC; DAM MST, NOV
See also AITN 1; CA 65-68; CANR 31;
CLR 17; DLB 53; MAICYA; MTCW;
SATA 44; SATA-Brief 27

Richter, Conrad (Michael)
1890-1968 . . . . **CLC 30**
See also CA 5-8R; 25-28R; CANR 23;
DLB 9; MTCW; SATA 3

Ricostranza, Tom
See Ellis, Trey

Riddell, J. H. 1832-1906 . . . . **TCLC 40**

Riding, Laura . . . . **CLC 3, 7**
See also Jackson, Laura (Riding)

Riefenstahl, Berta Helene Amalia 1902-
See Riefenstahl, Leni
See also CA 108

Riefenstahl, Leni . . . . **CLC 16**
See also Riefenstahl, Berta Helene Amalia

Riffe, Ernest
See Bergman, (Ernst) Ingmar

Riggs, (Rolla) Lynn
1899-1954 . . . . . **TCLC 56; DAM MULT**
See also CA 144; DLB 175; NNAL

Riley, James Whitcomb
1849-1916 . . . . . . **TCLC 51; DAM POET**
See also CA 118; 137; MAICYA; SATA 17

Riley, Tex
See Creasey, John

Rilke, Rainer Maria
1875-1926 . . . . **TCLC 1, 6, 19;**
DAM POET; PC 2
See also CA 104; 132; DLB 81; MTCW

Rimbaud, (Jean Nicolas) Arthur
1854-1891 . . . . . **NCLC 4, 35; DA; DAB;**
DAC; DAM MST, POET; PC 3; WLC

Rinehart, Mary Roberts
1876-1958 . . . . **TCLC 52**
See also CA 108

Ringmaster, The
See Mencken, H(enry) L(ouis)

Ringwood, Gwen(dolyn Margaret) Pharis
1910-1984 . . . . **CLC 48**
See also CA 148; 112; DLB 88

Rio, Michel 19(?)- . . . . **CLC 43**

Ritsos, Giannes
See Ritsos, Yannis

Ritsos, Yannis 1909-1990 . . . . . **CLC 6, 13, 31**
See also CA 77-80; 133; CANR 39; MTCW

Ritter, Erika 1948(?)- . . . . **CLC 52**

Rivera, Jose Eustasio 1889-1928 . . . **TCLC 35**
See also HW

Rivers, Conrad Kent 1933-1968 . . . . . . **CLC 1**
See also BW 1; CA 85-88; DLB 41

Rivers, Elfrida
See Bradley, Marion Zimmer

Riverside, John
See Heinlein, Robert A(nson)

Rizal, Jose 1861-1896 . . . . **NCLC 27**

Roa Bastos, Augusto (Antonio)
1917- . . . . . **CLC 45; DAM MULT; HLC**
See also CA 131; DLB 113; HW

Robbe-Grillet, Alain
1922- . . . . . . **CLC 1, 2, 4, 6, 8, 10, 14, 43**
See also CA 9-12R; CANR 33; DLB 83;
MTCW

Robbins, Harold
1916- . . . . **CLC 5; DAM NOV**
See also CA 73-76; CANR 26, 54; MTCW

Robbins, Thomas Eugene   1936-
See Robbins, Tom
See also CA 81-84; CANR 29; DAM NOV,
POP; MTCW

Robbins, Tom. . . . . CLC 9, 32, 64
See also Robbins, Thomas Eugene
See also BEST 90:3; DLBY 80

Robbins, Trina   1938- . . . . CLC 21
See also CA 128

Roberts, Charles G(eorge) D(ouglas)
1860-1943 . . . . TCLC 8
See also CA 105; CLR 33; DLB 92;
SATA 88; SATA-Brief 29

Roberts, Elizabeth Madox
1886-1941 . . . . TCLC 68
See also CA 111; DLB 9, 54, 102;
SATA 33; SATA-Brief 27

Roberts, Kate   1891-1985 . . . . CLC 15
See also CA 107; 116

Roberts, Keith (John Kingston)
1935- . . . . CLC 14
See also CA 25-28R; CANR 46

Roberts, Kenneth (Lewis)
1885-1957 . . . . TCLC 23
See also CA 109; DLB 9

Roberts, Michele (B.)   1949- . . . . CLC 48
See also CA 115

Robertson, Ellis
See Ellison, Harlan (Jay); Silverberg, Robert

Robertson, Thomas William
1829-1871 . . . . NCLC 35; DAM DRAM

Robinson, Edwin Arlington
1869-1935 . . . . TCLC 5; DA; DAC;
DAM MST, POET; PC 1
See also CA 104; 133; CDALB 1865-1917;
DLB 54; MTCW

Robinson, Henry Crabb
1775-1867 . . . . NCLC 15
See also DLB 107

Robinson, Jill   1936- . . . . CLC 10
See also CA 102; INT 102

Robinson, Kim Stanley   1952- . . . . . . CLC 34
See also CA 126

Robinson, Lloyd
See Silverberg, Robert

Robinson, Marilynne   1944- . . . . CLC 25
See also CA 116

Robinson, Smokey. . . . . CLC 21
See also Robinson, William, Jr.

Robinson, William, Jr.   1940-
See Robinson, Smokey
See also CA 116

Robison, Mary   1949- . . . . CLC 42, 98
See also CA 113; 116; DLB 130; INT 116

Rod, Edouard   1857-1910 . . . . TCLC 52

Roddenberry, Eugene Wesley   1921-1991
See Roddenberry, Gene
See also CA 110; 135; CANR 37; SATA 45;
SATA-Obit 69

Roddenberry, Gene . . . . CLC 17
See also Roddenberry, Eugene Wesley
See also AAYA 5; SATA-Obit 69

Rodgers, Mary   1931- . . . . CLC 12
See also CA 49-52; CANR 8, 55; CLR 20;
INT CANR-8; JRDA; MAICYA;
SATA 8

Rodgers, W(illiam) R(obert)
1909-1969 . . . . CLC 7
See also CA 85-88; DLB 20

Rodman, Eric
See Silverberg, Robert

Rodman, Howard   1920(?)-1985 . . . . . CLC 65
See also CA 118

Rodman, Maia
See Wojciechowska, Maia (Teresa)

Rodriguez, Claudio   1934- . . . . CLC 10
See also DLB 134

Roelvaag, O(le) E(dvart)
1876-1931 . . . . TCLC 17
See also CA 117; DLB 9

Roethke, Theodore (Huebner)
1908-1963 . . . . . . CLC 1, 3, 8, 11, 19, 46;
DAM POET; PC 15
See also CA 81-84; CABS 2;
CDALB 1941-1968; DLB 5; MTCW

Rogers, Thomas Hunton   1927- . . . . . CLC 57
See also CA 89-92; INT 89-92

Rogers, Will(iam Penn Adair)
1879-1935 . . . . . . TCLC 8; DAM MULT
See also CA 105; 144; DLB 11; NNAL

Rogin, Gilbert   1929- . . . . CLC 18
See also CA 65-68; CANR 15

Rohan, Koda . . . . TCLC 22
See also Koda Shigeyuki

Rohmer, Eric. . . . . CLC 16
See also Scherer, Jean-Marie Maurice

Rohmer, Sax . . . . TCLC 28
See also Ward, Arthur Henry Sarsfield
See also DLB 70

Roiphe, Anne (Richardson)
1935- . . . . CLC 3, 9
See also CA 89-92; CANR 45; DLBY 80;
INT 89-92

Rojas, Fernando de   1465-1541 . . . . . . LC 23

Rolfe, Frederick (William Serafino Austin
Lewis Mary)   1860-1913. . . . . . TCLC 12
See also CA 107; DLB 34, 156

Rolland, Romain   1866-1944. . . . . . . TCLC 23
See also CA 118; DLB 65

Rolle, Richard   c. 1300-c. 1349 . . . CMLC 21
See also DLB 146

Rolvaag, O(le) E(dvart)
See Roelvaag, O(le) E(dvart)

Romain Arnaud, Saint
See Aragon, Louis

Romains, Jules   1885-1972 . . . . CLC 7
See also CA 85-88; CANR 34; DLB 65;
MTCW

Romero, Jose Ruben   1890-1952 . . . TCLC 14
See also CA 114; 131; HW

Ronsard, Pierre de
1524-1585 . . . . LC 6; PC 11

Rooke, Leon
1934- . . . . CLC 25, 34; DAM POP
See also CA 25-28R; CANR 23, 53

Roosevelt, Theodore   1858-1919. . . . TCLC 69
See also CA 115; DLB 47

Roper, William   1498-1578 . . . . LC 10

Roquelaure, A. N.
See Rice, Anne

Rosa, Joao Guimaraes   1908-1967 . . . CLC 23
See also CA 89-92; DLB 113

Rose, Wendy
1948- . . . . CLC 85; DAM MULT; PC 13
See also CA 53-56; CANR 5, 51; DLB 175;
NNAL; SATA 12

Rosen, Richard (Dean)   1949-. . . . . . . CLC 39
See also CA 77-80; INT CANR-30

Rosenberg, Isaac   1890-1918. . . . . . . TCLC 12
See also CA 107; DLB 20

Rosenblatt, Joe . . . . CLC 15
See also Rosenblatt, Joseph

Rosenblatt, Joseph   1933-
See Rosenblatt, Joe
See also CA 89-92; INT 89-92

Rosenfeld, Samuel   1896-1963
See Tzara, Tristan
See also CA 89-92

Rosenstock, Sami
See Tzara, Tristan

Rosenstock, Samuel
See Tzara, Tristan

Rosenthal, M(acha) L(ouis)
1917-1996 . . . . CLC 28
See also CA 1-4R; 152; CAAS 6; CANR 4,
51; DLB 5; SATA 59

Ross, Barnaby
See Dannay, Frederic

Ross, Bernard L.
See Follett, Ken(neth Martin)

Ross, J. H.
See Lawrence, T(homas) E(dward)

Ross, Martin
See Martin, Violet Florence
See also DLB 135

Ross, (James) Sinclair
1908- . . . . . . CLC 13; DAC; DAM MST;
SSC 24
See also CA 73-76; DLB 88

Rossetti, Christina (Georgina)
1830-1894 . . . . . NCLC 2, 50; DA; DAB;
DAC; DAM MST, POET; PC 7; WLC
See also DLB 35, 163; MAICYA; SATA 20

Rossetti, Dante Gabriel
1828-1882 . . . . NCLC 4; DA; DAB;
DAC; DAM MST, POET; WLC
See also CDBLB 1832-1890; DLB 35

Rossner, Judith (Perelman)
1935- . . . . CLC 6, 9, 29
See also AITN 2; BEST 90:3; CA 17-20R;
CANR 18, 51; DLB 6; INT CANR-18;
MTCW

Rostand, Edmond (Eugene Alexis)
1868-1918 . . . . . . TCLC 6, 37; DA; DAB;
DAC; DAM DRAM, MST
See also CA 104; 126; MTCW

Roth, Henry   1906-1995 . . . . CLC 2, 6, 11
See also CA 11-12; 149; CANR 38; CAP 1;
DLB 28; MTCW

Salinas, Luis Omar
1937- ..... **CLC 90; DAM MULT; HLC**
See also CA 131; DLB 82; HW

Salinas (y Serrano), Pedro
1891(?)-1951 .... **TCLC 17**
See also CA 117; DLB 134

Salinger, J(erome) D(avid)
1919- ...... **CLC 1, 3, 8, 12, 55, 56; DA;**
DAB; DAC; DAM MST, NOV, POP;
SSC 2; WLC
See also AAYA 2; CA 5-8R; CANR 39;
CDALB 1941-1968; CLR 18; DLB 2, 102,
173; MAICYA; MTCW; SATA 67

Salisbury, John
See Caute, David

Salter, James 1925- .... **CLC 7, 52, 59**
See also CA 73-76; DLB 130

Saltus, Edgar (Everton)
1855-1921 .... **TCLC 8**
See also CA 105

Saltykov, Mikhail Evgrafovich
1826-1889 .... **NCLC 16**

Samarakis, Antonis 1919- .... **CLC 5**
See also CA 25-28R; CAAS 16; CANR 36

Sanchez, Florencio 1875-1910 ..... **TCLC 37**
See also CA 153; HW

Sanchez, Luis Rafael 1936- .... **CLC 23**
See also CA 128; DLB 145; HW

Sanchez, Sonia
1934- ...... **CLC 5; BLC; DAM MULT;**
PC 9
See also BW 2; CA 33-36R; CANR 24, 49;
CLR 18; DLB 41; DLBD 8; MAICYA;
MTCW; SATA 22

Sand, George
1804-1876 .... **NCLC 2, 42, 57; DA;**
DAB; DAC; DAM MST, NOV; WLC
See also DLB 119

Sandburg, Carl (August)
1878-1967 .... **CLC 1, 4, 10, 15, 35; DA;**
DAB; DAC; DAM MST, POET; PC 2;
WLC
See also CA 5-8R; 25-28R; CANR 35;
CDALB 1865-1917; DLB 17, 54;
MAICYA; MTCW; SATA 8

Sandburg, Charles
See Sandburg, Carl (August)

Sandburg, Charles A.
See Sandburg, Carl (August)

Sanders, (James) Ed(ward) 1939- ... **CLC 53**
See also CA 13-16R; CAAS 21; CANR 13,
44; DLB 16

Sanders, Lawrence
1920- .... **CLC 41; DAM POP**
See also BEST 89:4; CA 81-84; CANR 33;
MTCW

Sanders, Noah
See Blount, Roy (Alton), Jr.

Sanders, Winston P.
See Anderson, Poul (William)

Sandoz, Mari(e Susette)
1896-1966 .... **CLC 28**
See also CA 1-4R; 25-28R; CANR 17;
DLB 9; MTCW; SATA 5

Saner, Reg(inald Anthony) 1931- .... **CLC 9**
See also CA 65-68

Sannazaro, Jacopo 1456(?)-1530 ..... **LC 8**

Sansom, William
1912-1976 ..... **CLC 2, 6; DAM NOV;**
SSC 21
See also CA 5-8R; 65-68; CANR 42;
DLB 139; MTCW

Santayana, George 1863-1952 ..... **TCLC 40**
See also CA 115; DLB 54, 71; DLBD 13

Santiago, Danny .... **CLC 33**
See also James, Daniel (Lewis)
See also DLB 122

Santmyer, Helen Hoover
1895-1986 .... **CLC 33**
See also CA 1-4R; 118; CANR 15, 33;
DLBY 84; MTCW

Santos, Bienvenido N(uqui)
1911-1996 ..... **CLC 22; DAM MULT**
See also CA 101; 151; CANR 19, 46

Sapper .... **TCLC 44**
See also McNeile, Herman Cyril

Sapphire 1950- .... **CLC 99**

Sappho
fl. 6th cent. B.C.- .... **CMLC 3;**
DAM POET; PC 5
See also DLB 176

Sarduy, Severo 1937-1993 .... **CLC 6, 97**
See also CA 89-92; 142; DLB 113; HW

Sargeson, Frank 1903-1982 .... **CLC 31**
See also CA 25-28R; 106; CANR 38

Sarmiento, Felix Ruben Garcia
See Dario, Ruben

Saroyan, William
1908-1981 ..... **CLC 1, 8, 10, 29, 34, 56;**
DA; DAB; DAC; DAM DRAM, MST,
NOV; SSC 21; WLC
See also CA 5-8R; 103; CANR 30; DLB 7,
9, 86; DLBY 81; MTCW; SATA 23;
SATA-Obit 24

Sarraute, Nathalie
1900- .... **CLC 1, 2, 4, 8, 10, 31, 80**
See also CA 9-12R; CANR 23; DLB 83;
MTCW

Sarton, (Eleanor) May
1912-1995 .... **CLC 4, 14, 49, 91;**
DAM POET
See also CA 1-4R; 149; CANR 1, 34, 55;
DLB 48; DLBY 81; INT CANR-34;
MTCW; SATA 36; SATA-Obit 86

Sartre, Jean-Paul
1905-1980 .... **CLC 1, 4, 7, 9, 13, 18, 24,**
44, 50, 52; DA; DAB; DAC;
DAM DRAM, MST, NOV; DC 3; WLC
See also CA 9-12R; 97-100; CANR 21;
DLB 72; MTCW

Sassoon, Siegfried (Lorraine)
1886-1967 .... **CLC 36; DAB;**
DAM MST, NOV, POET; PC 12
See also CA 104; 25-28R; CANR 36;
DLB 20; MTCW

Satterfield, Charles
See Pohl, Frederik

Saul, John (W. III)
1942- ...... **CLC 46; DAM NOV, POP**
See also AAYA 10; BEST 90:4; CA 81-84;
CANR 16, 40

Saunders, Caleb
See Heinlein, Robert A(nson)

Saura (Atares), Carlos 1932- .... **CLC 20**
See also CA 114; 131; HW

Sauser-Hall, Frederic 1887-1961 .... **CLC 18**
See also Cendrars, Blaise
See also CA 102; 93-96; CANR 36; MTCW

Saussure, Ferdinand de
1857-1913 .... **TCLC 49**

Savage, Catharine
See Brosman, Catharine Savage

Savage, Thomas 1915- .... **CLC 40**
See also CA 126; 132; CAAS 15; INT 132

Savan, Glenn 19(?)- .... **CLC 50**

Sayers, Dorothy L(eigh)
1893-1957 ..... **TCLC 2, 15; DAM POP**
See also CA 104; 119; CDBLB 1914-1945;
DLB 10, 36, 77, 100; MTCW

Sayers, Valerie 1952- .... **CLC 50**
See also CA 134

Sayles, John (Thomas)
1950- .... **CLC 7, 10, 14**
See also CA 57-60; CANR 41; DLB 44

Scammell, Michael 1935- .... **CLC 34**
See also CA 156

Scannell, Vernon 1922- .... **CLC 49**
See also CA 5-8R; CANR 8, 24, 57;
DLB 27; SATA 59

Scarlett, Susan
See Streatfeild, (Mary) Noel

Schaeffer, Susan Fromberg
1941- .... **CLC 6, 11, 22**
See also CA 49-52; CANR 18; DLB 28;
MTCW; SATA 22

Schary, Jill
See Robinson, Jill

Schell, Jonathan 1943- .... **CLC 35**
See also CA 73-76; CANR 12

Schelling, Friedrich Wilhelm Joseph von
1775-1854 .... **NCLC 30**
See also DLB 90

Schendel, Arthur van 1874-1946 ... **TCLC 56**

Scherer, Jean-Marie Maurice 1920-
See Rohmer, Eric
See also CA 110

Schevill, James (Erwin) 1920- .... **CLC 7**
See also CA 5-8R; CAAS 12

Schiller, Friedrich
1759-1805 .... **NCLC 39; DAM DRAM**
See also DLB 94

Schisgal, Murray (Joseph) 1926- ..... **CLC 6**
See also CA 21-24R; CANR 48

Schlee, Ann 1934- .... **CLC 35**
See also CA 101; CANR 29; SATA 44;
SATA-Brief 36

Schlegel, August Wilhelm von
1767-1845 .... **NCLC 15**
See also DLB 94

Schlegel, Friedrich 1772-1829 .... **NCLC 45**
See also DLB 90

Schlegel, Johann Elias (von)
1719(?)-1749 ....,............... **LC 5**

Schlesinger, Arthur M(eier), Jr.
1917- .... CLC 84
See also AITN 1; CA 1-4R; CANR 1, 28;
DLB 17; INT CANR-28; MTCW;
SATA 61

Schmidt, Arno (Otto) 1914-1979.... CLC 56
See also CA 128; 109; DLB 69

Schmitz, Aron Hector 1861-1928
See Svevo, Italo
See also CA 104; 122; MTCW

Schnackenberg, Gjertrud 1953-..... CLC 40
See also CA 116; DLB 120

Schneider, Leonard Alfred 1925-1966
See Bruce, Lenny
See also CA 89-92

Schnitzler, Arthur
1862-1931 .... TCLC 4; SSC 15
See also CA 104; DLB 81, 118

Schopenhauer, Arthur
1788-1860 .... NCLC 51
See also DLB 90

Schor, Sandra (M.) 1932(?)-1990 ... CLC 65
See also CA 132

Schorer, Mark 1908-1977 .... CLC 9
See also CA 5-8R; 73-76; CANR 7;
DLB 103

Schrader, Paul (Joseph) 1946-...... CLC 26
See also CA 37-40R; CANR 41; DLB 44

Schreiner, Olive (Emilie Albertina)
1855-1920 .... TCLC 9
See also CA 105; DLB 18, 156

Schulberg, Budd (Wilson)
1914- .... CLC 7, 48
See also CA 25-28R; CANR 19; DLB 6, 26,
28; DLBY 81

Schulz, Bruno
1892-1942 .... TCLC 5, 51; SSC 13
See also CA 115; 123

Schulz, Charles M(onroe) 1922- .... CLC 12
See also CA 9-12R; CANR 6;
INT CANR-6; SATA 10

Schumacher, E(rnst) F(riedrich)
1911-1977 .... CLC 80
See also CA 81-84; 73-76; CANR 34

Schuyler, James Marcus
1923-1991 ..... CLC 5, 23; DAM POET
See also CA 101; 134; DLB 5, 169; INT 101

Schwartz, Delmore (David)
1913-1966 ... CLC 2, 4, 10, 45, 87; PC 8
See also CA 17-18; 25-28R; CANR 35;
CAP 2; DLB 28, 48; MTCW

Schwartz, Ernst
See Ozu, Yasujiro

Schwartz, John Burnham 1965- .... CLC 59
See also CA 132

Schwartz, Lynne Sharon 1939-..... CLC 31
See also CA 103; CANR 44

Schwartz, Muriel A.
See Eliot, T(homas) S(tearns)

Schwarz-Bart, Andre 1928-....... CLC 2, 4
See also CA 89-92

Schwarz-Bart, Simone 1938-........ CLC 7
See also BW 2; CA 97-100

Schwob, (Mayer Andre) Marcel
1867-1905 .... TCLC 20
See also CA 117; DLB 123

Sciascia, Leonardo
1921-1989 .... CLC 8, 9, 41
See also CA 85-88; 130; CANR 35;
DLB 177; MTCW

Scoppettone, Sandra 1936-........ CLC 26
See also AAYA 11; CA 5-8R; CANR 41;
SATA 9, 92

Scorsese, Martin 1942- .... CLC 20, 89
See also CA 110; 114; CANR 46

Scotland, Jay
See Jakes, John (William)

Scott, Duncan Campbell
1862-1947 .... TCLC 6; DAC
See also CA 104; 153; DLB 92

Scott, Evelyn 1893-1963........... CLC 43
See also CA 104; 112; DLB 9, 48

Scott, F(rancis) R(eginald)
1899-1985 .... CLC 22
See also CA 101; 114; DLB 88; INT 101

Scott, Frank
See Scott, F(rancis) R(eginald)

Scott, Joanna 1960- .... CLC 50
See also CA 126; CANR 53

Scott, Paul (Mark) 1920-1978.... CLC 9, 60
See also CA 81-84; 77-80; CANR 33;
DLB 14; MTCW

Scott, Walter
1771-1832 .... NCLC 15; DA; DAB;
DAC; DAM MST, NOV, POET; PC 13;
WLC
See also CDBLB 1789-1832; DLB 93, 107,
116, 144, 159; YABC 2

Scribe, (Augustin) Eugene
1791-1861 .... NCLC 16; DAM DRAM;
DC 5

Scrum, R.
See Crumb, R(obert)

Scudery, Madeleine de 1607-1701..... LC 2

Scum
See Crumb, R(obert)

Scumbag, Little Bobby
See Crumb, R(obert)

Seabrook, John
See Hubbard, L(afayette) Ron(ald)

Sealy, I. Allan 1951- .... CLC 55

Search, Alexander
See Pessoa, Fernando (Antonio Nogueira)

Sebastian, Lee
See Silverberg, Robert

Sebastian Owl
See Thompson, Hunter S(tockton)

Sebestyen, Ouida 1924- .... CLC 30
See also AAYA 8; CA 107; CANR 40;
CLR 17; JRDA; MAICYA; SAAS 10;
SATA 39

Secundus, H. Scriblerus
See Fielding, Henry

Sedges, John
See Buck, Pearl S(ydenstricker)

Sedgwick, Catharine Maria
1789-1867 .... NCLC 19
See also DLB 1, 74

Seelye, John 1931-................ CLC 7

Seferiades, Giorgos Stylianou 1900-1971
See Seferis, George
See also CA 5-8R; 33-36R; CANR 5, 36;
MTCW

Seferis, George .... CLC 5, 11
See also Seferiades, Giorgos Stylianou

Segal, Erich (Wolf)
1937- .... CLC 3, 10; DAM POP
See also BEST 89:1; CA 25-28R; CANR 20,
36; DLBY 86; INT CANR-20; MTCW

Seger, Bob 1945-................ CLC 35

Seghers, Anna .... CLC 7
See also Radvanyi, Netty
See also DLB 69

Seidel, Frederick (Lewis) 1936-..... CLC 18
See also CA 13-16R; CANR 8; DLBY 84

Seifert, Jaroslav
1901-1986 .... CLC 34, 44, 93
See also CA 127; MTCW

Sei Shonagon c. 966-1017(?) ...... CMLC 6

Selby, Hubert, Jr.
1928- .... CLC 1, 2, 4, 8; SSC 20
See also CA 13-16R; CANR 33; DLB 2

Selzer, Richard 1928-............. CLC 74
See also CA 65-68; CANR 14

Sembene, Ousmane
See Ousmane, Sembene

Senancour, Etienne Pivert de
1770-1846 .... NCLC 16
See also DLB 119

Sender, Ramon (Jose)
1902-1982 .. CLC 8; DAM MULT; HLC
See also CA 5-8R; 105; CANR 8; HW;
MTCW

Seneca, Lucius Annaeus
4B.C.-65...... CMLC 6; DAM DRAM;
DC 5

Senghor, Leopold Sedar
1906- ..... CLC 54; BLC; DAM MULT,
POET
See also BW 2; CA 116; 125; CANR 47;
MTCW

Serling, (Edward) Rod(man)
1924-1975 .... CLC 30
See also AAYA 14; AITN 1; CA 65-68;
57-60; DLB 26

Serna, Ramon Gomez de la
See Gomez de la Serna, Ramon

Serpieres
See Guillevic, (Eugene)

Service, Robert
See Service, Robert W(illiam)
See also DAB; DLB 92

Service, Robert W(illiam)
1874(?)-1958 ...... TCLC 15; DA; DAC;
DAM MST, POET; WLC
See also Service, Robert
See also CA 115; 140; SATA 20

Seth, Vikram
1952- ...... **CLC 43, 90; DAM MULT**
See also CA 121; 127; CANR 50; DLB 120;
INT 127

Seton, Cynthia Propper
1926-1982 .... **CLC 27**
See also CA 5-8R; 108; CANR 7

Seton, Ernest (Evan) Thompson
1860-1946 .... **TCLC 31**
See also CA 109; DLB 92; DLBD 13;
JRDA; SATA 18

Seton-Thompson, Ernest
See Seton, Ernest (Evan) Thompson

Settle, Mary Lee 1918- .... **CLC 19, 61**
See also CA 89-92; CAAS 1; CANR 44;
DLB 6; INT 89-92

Seuphor, Michel
See Arp, Jean

Sevigne, Marie (de Rabutin-Chantal) Marquise
de 1626-1696 .... **LC 11**

Sexton, Anne (Harvey)
1928-1974 .... **CLC 2, 4, 6, 8, 10, 15, 53;**
DA; DAB; DAC; DAM MST, POET;
PC 2; WLC
See also CA 1-4R; 53-56; CABS 2;
CANR 3, 36; CDALB 1941-1968; DLB 5,
169; MTCW; SATA 10

Shaara, Michael (Joseph, Jr.)
1929-1988 .... **CLC 15; DAM POP**
See also AITN 1; CA 102; 125; CANR 52;
DLBY 83

Shackleton, C. C.
See Aldiss, Brian W(ilson)

Shacochis, Bob .... **CLC 39**
See also Shacochis, Robert G.

Shacochis, Robert G. 1951-
See Shacochis, Bob
See also CA 119; 124; INT 124

Shaffer, Anthony (Joshua)
1926- .... **CLC 19; DAM DRAM**
See also CA 110; 116; DLB 13

Shaffer, Peter (Levin)
1926- ...... **CLC 5, 14, 18, 37, 60; DAB;**
DAM DRAM, MST; DC 7
See also CA 25-28R; CANR 25, 47;
CDBLB 1960 to Present; DLB 13;
MTCW

Shakey, Bernard
See Young, Neil

Shalamov, Varlam (Tikhonovich)
1907(?)-1982 .... **CLC 18**
See also CA 129; 105

Shamlu, Ahmad 1925- .... **CLC 10**

Shammas, Anton 1951-........... **CLC 55**

Shange, Ntozake
1948- .... **CLC 8, 25, 38, 74; BLC;**
DAM DRAM, MULT; DC 3
See also AAYA 9; BW 2; CA 85-88;
CABS 3; CANR 27, 48; DLB 38; MTCW

Shanley, John Patrick 1950- .... **CLC 75**
See also CA 128; 133

Shapcott, Thomas W(illiam) 1935- .. **CLC 38**
See also CA 69-72; CANR 49

Shapiro, Jane................... **CLC 76**

Shapiro, Karl (Jay) 1913- .. **CLC 4, 8, 15, 53**
See also CA 1-4R; CAAS 6; CANR 1, 36;
DLB 48; MTCW

Sharp, William 1855-1905 .... **TCLC 39**
See also DLB 156

Sharpe, Thomas Ridley 1928-
See Sharpe, Tom
See also CA 114; 122; INT 122

Sharpe, Tom..................... **CLC 36**
See also Sharpe, Thomas Ridley
See also DLB 14

Shaw, Bernard................... **TCLC 45**
See also Shaw, George Bernard
See also BW 1

Shaw, G. Bernard
See Shaw, George Bernard

Shaw, George Bernard
1856-1950 ... **TCLC 3, 9, 21; DA; DAB;**
DAC; DAM DRAM, MST; WLC
See also Shaw, Bernard
See also CA 104; 128; CDBLB 1914-1945;
DLB 10, 57; MTCW

Shaw, Henry Wheeler
1818-1885 .... **NCLC 15**
See also DLB 11

Shaw, Irwin
1913-1984 .... **CLC 7, 23, 34;**
DAM DRAM, POP
See also AITN 1; CA 13-16R; 112;
CANR 21; CDALB 1941-1968; DLB 6,
102; DLBY 84; MTCW

Shaw, Robert 1927-1978 .... **CLC 5**
See also AITN 1; CA 1-4R; 81-84;
CANR 4; DLB 13, 14

Shaw, T. E.
See Lawrence, T(homas) E(dward)

Shawn, Wallace 1943- .... **CLC 41**
See also CA 112

Shea, Lisa 1953-................. **CLC 86**
See also CA 147

Sheed, Wilfrid (John Joseph)
1930- .... **CLC 2, 4, 10, 53**
See also CA 65-68; CANR 30; DLB 6;
MTCW

Sheldon, Alice Hastings Bradley
1915(?)-1987
See Tiptree, James, Jr.
See also CA 108; 122; CANR 34; INT 108;
MTCW

Sheldon, John
See Bloch, Robert (Albert)

Shelley, Mary Wollstonecraft (Godwin)
1797-1851 .... **NCLC 14, 59; DA; DAB;**
DAC; DAM MST, NOV; WLC
See also AAYA 20; CDBLB 1789-1832;
DLB 110, 116, 159; SATA 29

Shelley, Percy Bysshe
1792-1822 .... **NCLC 18; DA; DAB;**
DAC; DAM MST, POET; PC 14; WLC
See also CDBLB 1789-1832; DLB 96, 110,
158

Shepard, Jim 1956-.............. **CLC 36**
See also CA 137; SATA 90

Shepard, Lucius 1947- .... **CLC 34**
See also CA 128; 141

Shepard, Sam
1943- .... **CLC 4, 6, 17, 34, 41, 44;**
DAM DRAM; DC 5
See also AAYA 1; CA 69-72; CABS 3;
CANR 22; DLB 7; MTCW

Shepherd, Michael
See Ludlum, Robert

Sherburne, Zoa (Morin) 1912-...... **CLC 30**
See also AAYA 13; CA 1-4R; CANR 3, 37;
MAICYA; SAAS 18; SATA 3

Sheridan, Frances 1724-1766........ **LC 7**
See also DLB 39, 84

Sheridan, Richard Brinsley
1751-1816 .... **NCLC 5; DA; DAB;**
DAC; DAM DRAM, MST; DC 1; WLC
See also CDBLB 1660-1789; DLB 89

Sherman, Jonathan Marc........... **CLC 55**

Sherman, Martin 1941(?)-......... **CLC 19**
See also CA 116; 123

Sherwin, Judith Johnson 1936-... **CLC 7, 15**
See also CA 25-28R; CANR 34

Sherwood, Frances 1940-.......... **CLC 81**
See also CA 146

Sherwood, Robert E(mmet)
1896-1955 ...... **TCLC 3; DAM DRAM**
See also CA 104; 153; DLB 7, 26

Shestov, Lev 1866-1938 .... **TCLC 56**

Shevchenko, Taras 1814-1861 .... **NCLC 54**

Shiel, M(atthew) P(hipps)
1865-1947 .... **TCLC 8**
See also CA 106; DLB 153

Shields, Carol 1935-......... **CLC 91; DAC**
See also CA 81-84; CANR 51

Shields, David 1956-.............. **CLC 97**
See also CA 124; CANR 48

Shiga, Naoya 1883-1971... **CLC 33; SSC 23**
See also CA 101; 33-36R

Shilts, Randy 1951-1994 .... **CLC 85**
See also AAYA 19; CA 115; 127; 144;
CANR 45; INT 127

Shimazaki, Haruki 1872-1943
See Shimazaki Toson
See also CA 105; 134

Shimazaki Toson.................. **TCLC 5**
See also Shimazaki, Haruki

Sholokhov, Mikhail (Aleksandrovich)
1905-1984 .... **CLC 7, 15**
See also CA 101; 112; MTCW;
SATA-Obit 36

Shone, Patric
See Hanley, James

Shreve, Susan Richards 1939-...... **CLC 23**
See also CA 49-52; CAAS 5; CANR 5, 38;
MAICYA; SATA 46; SATA-Brief 41

Shue, Larry
1946-1985 ...... **CLC 52; DAM DRAM**
See also CA 145; 117

Shu-Jen, Chou 1881-1936
See Lu Hsun
See also CA 104

Shulman, Alix Kates 1932- ...... **CLC 2, 10**
See also CA 29-32R; CANR 43; SATA 7

Shuster, Joe 1914- .... **CLC 21**

Slaughter, Carolyn 1946-. . . . . CLC 56
See also CA 85-88

Slaughter, Frank G(ill) 1908- . . . . . . CLC 29
See also AITN 2; CA 5-8R; CANR 5;
INT CANR-5

Slavitt, David R(ytman) 1935-. . . . CLC 5, 14
See also CA 21-24R; CAAS 3; CANR 41;
DLB 5, 6

Slesinger, Tess 1905-1945 . . . . TCLC 10
See also CA 107; DLB 102

Slessor, Kenneth 1901-1971. . . . . . . CLC 14
See also CA 102; 89-92

Slowacki, Juliusz 1809-1849 . . . . . NCLC 15

Smart, Christopher
1722-1771 . . . LC 3; DAM POET; PC 13
See also DLB 109

Smart, Elizabeth 1913-1986. . . . . . . CLC 54
See also CA 81-84; 118; DLB 88

Smiley, Jane (Graves)
1949- . . . . CLC 53, 76; DAM POP
See also CA 104; CANR 30, 50;
INT CANR-30

Smith, A(rthur) J(ames) M(arshall)
1902-1980 . . . . CLC 15; DAC
See also CA 1-4R; 102; CANR 4; DLB 88

Smith, Adam 1723-1790. . . . . LC 36
See also DLB 104

Smith, Alexander 1829-1867 . . . . . NCLC 59
See also DLB 32, 55

Smith, Anna Deavere 1950-. . . . . . . CLC 86
See also CA 133

Smith, Betty (Wehner) 1896-1972. . . CLC 19
See also CA 5-8R; 33-36R; DLBY 82;
SATA 6

Smith, Charlotte (Turner)
1749-1806 . . . . NCLC 23
See also DLB 39, 109

Smith, Clark Ashton 1893-1961 . . . . CLC 43
See also CA 143

Smith, Dave. . . . . CLC 22, 42
See also Smith, David (Jeddie)
See also CAAS 7; DLB 5

Smith, David (Jeddie) 1942-
See Smith, Dave
See also CA 49-52; CANR 1; DAM POET

Smith, Florence Margaret 1902-1971
See Smith, Stevie
See also CA 17-18; 29-32R; CANR 35;
CAP 2; DAM POET; MTCW

Smith, Iain Crichton 1928- . . . . CLC 64
See also CA 21-24R; DLB 40, 139

Smith, John 1580(?)-1631 . . . . LC 9

Smith, Johnston
See Crane, Stephen (Townley)

Smith, Joseph, Jr. 1805-1844 . . . . NCLC 53

Smith, Lee 1944-. . . . . CLC 25, 73
See also CA 114; 119; CANR 46; DLB 143;
DLBY 83; INT 119

Smith, Martin
See Smith, Martin Cruz

Smith, Martin Cruz
1942- . . . . . CLC 25; DAM MULT, POP
See also BEST 89:4; CA 85-88; CANR 6,
23, 43; INT CANR-23; NNAL

Smith, Mary-Ann Tirone 1944-. . . . . CLC 39
See also CA 118; 136

Smith, Patti 1946- . . . . CLC 12
See also CA 93-96

Smith, Pauline (Urmson)
1882-1959 . . . . TCLC 25

Smith, Rosamond
See Oates, Joyce Carol

Smith, Sheila Kaye
See Kaye-Smith, Sheila

Smith, Stevie . . . . . . CLC 3, 8, 25, 44; PC 12
See also Smith, Florence Margaret
See also DLB 20

Smith, Wilbur (Addison) 1933-. . . . . CLC 33
See also CA 13-16R; CANR 7, 46; MTCW

Smith, William Jay 1918- . . . . CLC 6
See also CA 5-8R; CANR 44; DLB 5;
MAICYA; SAAS 22; SATA 2, 68

Smith, Woodrow Wilson
See Kuttner, Henry

Smolenskin, Peretz 1842-1885. . . . NCLC 30

Smollett, Tobias (George) 1721-1771 . . LC 2
See also CDBLB 1660-1789; DLB 39, 104

Snodgrass, W(illiam) D(e Witt)
1926- . . . . CLC 2, 6, 10, 18, 68;
DAM POET
See also CA 1-4R; CANR 6, 36; DLB 5;
MTCW

Snow, C(harles) P(ercy)
1905-1980 . . . . CLC 1, 4, 6, 9, 13, 19;
DAM NOV
See also CA 5-8R; 101; CANR 28;
CDBLB 1945-1960; DLB 15, 77; MTCW

Snow, Frances Compton
See Adams, Henry (Brooks)

Snyder, Gary (Sherman)
1930- . . CLC 1, 2, 5, 9, 32; DAM POET
See also CA 17-20R; CANR 30; DLB 5, 16,
165

Snyder, Zilpha Keatley 1927- . . . . . . CLC 17
See also AAYA 15; CA 9-12R; CANR 38;
CLR 31; JRDA; MAICYA; SAAS 2;
SATA 1, 28, 75

Soares, Bernardo
See Pessoa, Fernando (Antonio Nogueira)

Sobh, A.
See Shamlu, Ahmad

Sobol, Joshua. . . . . CLC 60

Soderberg, Hjalmar 1869-1941 . . . . TCLC 39

Sodergran, Edith (Irene)
See Soedergran, Edith (Irene)

Soedergran, Edith (Irene)
1892-1923 . . . . TCLC 31

Softly, Edgar
See Lovecraft, H(oward) P(hillips)

Softly, Edward
See Lovecraft, H(oward) P(hillips)

Sokolov, Raymond 1941-. . . . . CLC 7
See also CA 85-88

Solo, Jay
See Ellison, Harlan (Jay)

Sologub, Fyodor . . . . TCLC 9
See also Teternikov, Fyodor Kuzmich

Solomons, Ikey Esquir
See Thackeray, William Makepeace

Solomos, Dionysios 1798-1857 . . . NCLC 15

Solwoska, Mara
See French, Marilyn

Solzhenitsyn, Aleksandr I(sayevich)
1918- . . . . . . CLC 1, 2, 4, 7, 9, 10, 18, 26,
34, 78; DA; DAB; DAC; DAM MST,
NOV; WLC
See also AITN 1; CA 69-72; CANR 40;
MTCW

Somers, Jane
See Lessing, Doris (May)

Somerville, Edith 1858-1949 . . . . . . TCLC 51
See also DLB 135

Somerville & Ross
See Martin, Violet Florence; Somerville,
Edith

Sommer, Scott 1951- . . . . CLC 25
See also CA 106

Sondheim, Stephen (Joshua)
1930- . . . . . . CLC 30, 39; DAM DRAM
See also AAYA 11; CA 103; CANR 47

Sontag, Susan
1933- . . . . CLC 1, 2, 10, 13, 31;
DAM POP
See also CA 17-20R; CANR 25, 51; DLB 2,
67; MTCW

Sophocles
496(?)B.C.-406(?)B.C. . . . . CMLC 2; DA;
DAB; DAC; DAM DRAM, MST; DC 1
See also DLB 176

Sordello 1189-1269. . . . . CMLC 15

Sorel, Julia
See Drexler, Rosalyn

Sorrentino, Gilbert
1929- . . . . CLC 3, 7, 14, 22, 40
See also CA 77-80; CANR 14, 33; DLB 5,
173; DLBY 80; INT CANR-14

Soto, Gary
1952- . . . . CLC 32, 80; DAM MULT;
HLC
See also AAYA 10; CA 119; 125;
CANR 50; CLR 38; DLB 82; HW;
INT 125; JRDA; SATA 80

Soupault, Philippe 1897-1990 . . . . . . CLC 68
See also CA 116; 147; 131

Souster, (Holmes) Raymond
1921- . . . CLC 5, 14; DAC; DAM POET
See also CA 13-16R; CAAS 14; CANR 13,
29, 53; DLB 88; SATA 63

Southern, Terry 1924(?)-1995 . . . . CLC 7
See also CA 1-4R; 150; CANR 1, 55;
DLB 2

Southey, Robert 1774-1843 . . . . NCLC 8
See also DLB 93, 107, 142; SATA 54

Southworth, Emma Dorothy Eliza Nevitte
1819-1899 . . . . NCLC 26

Souza, Ernest
See Scott, Evelyn

Soyinka, Wole
1934- . . . . **CLC 3, 5, 14, 36, 44; BLC;**
DA; DAB; DAC; DAM DRAM, MST,
MULT; DC 2; WLC
See also BW 2; CA 13-16R; CANR 27, 39;
DLB 125; MTCW

Spackman, W(illiam) M(ode)
1905-1990 . . . . **CLC 46**
See also CA 81-84; 132

Spacks, Barry (Bernard) 1931- . . . . . **CLC 14**
See also CA 154; CANR 33; DLB 105

Spanidou, Irini 1946- . . . . **CLC 44**

Spark, Muriel (Sarah)
1918- . . . . . **CLC 2, 3, 5, 8, 13, 18, 40, 94;**
DAB; DAC; DAM MST, NOV; SSC 10
See also CA 5-8R; CANR 12, 36;
CDBLB 1945-1960; DLB 15, 139;
INT CANR-12; MTCW

Spaulding, Douglas
See Bradbury, Ray (Douglas)

Spaulding, Leonard
See Bradbury, Ray (Douglas)

Spence, J. A. D.
See Eliot, T(homas) S(tearns)

Spencer, Elizabeth 1921- . . . . **CLC 22**
See also CA 13-16R; CANR 32; DLB 6;
MTCW; SATA 14

Spencer, Leonard G.
See Silverberg, Robert

Spencer, Scott 1945- . . . . **CLC 30**
See also CA 113; CANR 51; DLBY 86

Spender, Stephen (Harold)
1909-1995 . . . . . . **CLC 1, 2, 5, 10, 41, 91;**
DAM POET
See also CA 9-12R; 149; CANR 31, 54;
CDBLB 1945-1960; DLB 20; MTCW

Spengler, Oswald (Arnold Gottfried)
1880-1936 . . . . **TCLC 25**
See also CA 118

Spenser, Edmund
1552(?)-1599 . . . . **LC 5; DA; DAB; DAC;**
DAM MST, POET; PC 8; WLC
See also CDBLB Before 1660; DLB 167

Spicer, Jack
1925-1965 . . . . **CLC 8, 18, 72;**
DAM POET
See also CA 85-88; DLB 5, 16

Spiegelman, Art 1948- . . . . **CLC 76**
See also AAYA 10; CA 125; CANR 41, 55

Spielberg, Peter 1929- . . . . **CLC 6**
See also CA 5-8R; CANR 4, 48; DLBY 81

Spielberg, Steven 1947- . . . . **CLC 20**
See also AAYA 8; CA 77-80; CANR 32;
SATA 32

Spillane, Frank Morrison 1918-
See Spillane, Mickey
See also CA 25-28R; CANR 28; MTCW;
SATA 66

Spillane, Mickey . . . . **CLC 3, 13**
See also Spillane, Frank Morrison

Spinoza, Benedictus de 1632-1677 . . . . **LC 9**

Spinrad, Norman (Richard) 1940- . . . **CLC 46**
See also CA 37-40R; CAAS 19; CANR 20;
DLB 8; INT CANR-20

Spitteler, Carl (Friedrich Georg)
1845-1924 . . . . **TCLC 12**
See also CA 109; DLB 129

Spivack, Kathleen (Romola Drucker)
1938- . . . . **CLC 6**
See also CA 49-52

Spoto, Donald 1941- . . . . **CLC 39**
See also CA 65-68; CANR 11, 57

Springsteen, Bruce (F.) 1949- . . . . . . **CLC 17**
See also CA 111

Spurling, Hilary 1940- . . . . **CLC 34**
See also CA 104; CANR 25, 52

Spyker, John Howland
See Elman, Richard

Squires, (James) Radcliffe
1917-1993 . . . . **CLC 51**
See also CA 1-4R; 140; CANR 6, 21

Srivastava, Dhanpat Rai 1880(?)-1936
See Premchand
See also CA 118

Stacy, Donald
See Pohl, Frederik

Stael, Germaine de
See Stael-Holstein, Anne Louise Germaine
Necker Baronn
See also DLB 119

Stael-Holstein, Anne Louise Germaine Necker
Baronn 1766-1817 . . . . **NCLC 3**
See also Stael, Germaine de

Stafford, Jean 1915-1979 . . . **CLC 4, 7, 19, 68**
See also CA 1-4R; 85-88; CANR 3; DLB 2,
173; MTCW; SATA-Obit 22

Stafford, William (Edgar)
1914-1993 . . . **CLC 4, 7, 29; DAM POET**
See also CA 5-8R; 142; CAAS 3; CANR 5,
22; DLB 5; INT CANR-22

Staines, Trevor
See Brunner, John (Kilian Houston)

Stairs, Gordon
See Austin, Mary (Hunter)

Stannard, Martin 1947- . . . . **CLC 44**
See also CA 142; DLB 155

Stanton, Maura 1946- . . . . **CLC 9**
See also CA 89-92; CANR 15; DLB 120

Stanton, Schuyler
See Baum, L(yman) Frank

Stapledon, (William) Olaf
1886-1950 . . . . **TCLC 22**
See also CA 111; DLB 15

Starbuck, George (Edwin)
1931-1996 . . . . **CLC 53; DAM POET**
See also CA 21-24R; 153; CANR 23

Stark, Richard
See Westlake, Donald E(dwin)

Staunton, Schuyler
See Baum, L(yman) Frank

Stead, Christina (Ellen)
1902-1983 . . . . **CLC 2, 5, 8, 32, 80**
See also CA 13-16R; 109; CANR 33, 40;
MTCW

Stead, William Thomas
1849-1912 . . . . **TCLC 48**

Steele, Richard 1672-1729 . . . . **LC 18**
See also CDBLB 1660-1789; DLB 84, 101

Steele, Timothy (Reid) 1948- . . . . **CLC 45**
See also CA 93-96; CANR 16, 50; DLB 120

Steffens, (Joseph) Lincoln
1866-1936 . . . . **TCLC 20**
See also CA 117

Stegner, Wallace (Earle)
1909-1993 . . . **CLC 9, 49, 81; DAM NOV**
See also AITN 1; BEST 90:3; CA 1-4R;
141; CAAS 9; CANR 1, 21, 46; DLB 9;
DLBY 93; MTCW

Stein, Gertrude
1874-1946 . . . . . . **TCLC 1, 6, 28, 48; DA;**
DAB; DAC; DAM MST, NOV, POET;
WLC
See also CA 104; 132; CDALB 1917-1929;
DLB 4, 54, 86; MTCW

Steinbeck, John (Ernst)
1902-1968 . . . . . . **CLC 1, 5, 9, 13, 21, 34,**
45, 75; DA; DAB; DAC; DAM DRAM,
MST, NOV; SSC 11; WLC
See also AAYA 12; CA 1-4R; 25-28R;
CANR 1, 35; CDALB 1929-1941; DLB 7,
9; DLBD 2; MTCW; SATA 9

Steinem, Gloria 1934- . . . . **CLC 63**
See also CA 53-56; CANR 28, 51; MTCW

Steiner, George
1929- . . . . **CLC 24; DAM NOV**
See also CA 73-76; CANR 31; DLB 67;
MTCW; SATA 62

Steiner, K. Leslie
See Delany, Samuel R(ay, Jr.)

Steiner, Rudolf 1861-1925 . . . . **TCLC 13**
See also CA 107

Stendhal
1783-1842 . . . . **NCLC 23, 46; DA; DAB;**
DAC; DAM MST, NOV; WLC
See also DLB 119

Stephen, Leslie 1832-1904 . . . . **TCLC 23**
See also CA 123; DLB 57, 144

Stephen, Sir Leslie
See Stephen, Leslie

Stephen, Virginia
See Woolf, (Adeline) Virginia

Stephens, James 1882(?)-1950 . . . . . . **TCLC 4**
See also CA 104; DLB 19, 153, 162

Stephens, Reed
See Donaldson, Stephen R.

Steptoe, Lydia
See Barnes, Djuna

Sterchi, Beat 1949- . . . . **CLC 65**

Sterling, Brett
See Bradbury, Ray (Douglas); Hamilton,
Edmond

Sterling, Bruce 1954- . . . . **CLC 72**
See also CA 119; CANR 44

Sterling, George 1869-1926 . . . . **TCLC 20**
See also CA 117; DLB 54

Stern, Gerald 1925- . . . . **CLC 40, 100**
See also CA 81-84; CANR 28; DLB 105

Stern, Richard (Gustave) 1928- . . . **CLC 4, 39**
See also CA 1-4R; CANR 1, 25, 52;
DLBY 87; INT CANR-25

Sternberg, Josef von 1894-1969 . . . . . **CLC 20**
See also CA 81-84

Sterne, Laurence
1713-1768 ...... **LC 2; DA; DAB; DAC; DAM MST, NOV; WLC**
See also CDBLB 1660-1789; DLB 39

Sternheim, (William Adolf) Carl
1878-1942 .... **TCLC 8**
See also CA 105; DLB 56, 118

Stevens, Mark 1951- .... **CLC 34**
See also CA 122

Stevens, Wallace
1879-1955 .... **TCLC 3, 12, 45; DA; DAB; DAC; DAM MST, POET; PC 6; WLC**
See also CA 104; 124; CDALB 1929-1941; DLB 54; MTCW

Stevenson, Anne (Katharine)
1933- .... **CLC 7, 33**
See also CA 17-20R; CAAS 9; CANR 9, 33; DLB 40; MTCW

Stevenson, Robert Louis (Balfour)
1850-1894 ..... **NCLC 5, 14; DA; DAB; DAC; DAM MST, NOV; SSC 11; WLC**
See also CDBLB 1890-1914; CLR 10, 11; DLB 18, 57, 141, 156, 174; DLBD 13; JRDA; MAICYA; YABC 2

Stewart, J(ohn) I(nnes) M(ackintosh)
1906-1994 .... **CLC 7, 14, 32**
See also CA 85-88; 147; CAAS 3; CANR 47; MTCW

Stewart, Mary (Florence Elinor)
1916- .... **CLC 7, 35; DAB**
See also CA 1-4R; CANR 1; SATA 12

Stewart, Mary Rainbow
See Stewart, Mary (Florence Elinor)

Stifle, June
See Campbell, Maria

Stifter, Adalbert 1805-1868 ...... **NCLC 41**
See also DLB 133

Still, James 1906- .... **CLC 49**
See also CA 65-68; CAAS 17; CANR 10, 26; DLB 9; SATA 29

Sting
See Sumner, Gordon Matthew

Stirling, Arthur
See Sinclair, Upton (Beall)

Stitt, Milan 1941- .... **CLC 29**
See also CA 69-72

Stockton, Francis Richard 1834-1902
See Stockton, Frank R.
See also CA 108; 137; MAICYA; SATA 44

Stockton, Frank R. .... **TCLC 47**
See also Stockton, Francis Richard
See also DLB 42, 74; DLBD 13; SATA-Brief 32

Stoddard, Charles
See Kuttner, Henry

Stoker, Abraham 1847-1912
See Stoker, Bram
See also CA 105; DA; DAC; DAM MST, NOV; SATA 29

Stoker, Bram
1847-1912 .... **TCLC 8; DAB; WLC**
See also Stoker, Abraham
See also CA 150; CDBLB 1890-1914; DLB 36, 70

Stolz, Mary (Slattery) 1920- .... **CLC 12**
See also AAYA 8; AITN 1; CA 5-8R; CANR 13, 41; JRDA; MAICYA; SAAS 3; SATA 10, 71

Stone, Irving
1903-1989 .... **CLC 7; DAM POP**
See also AITN 1; CA 1-4R; 129; CAAS 3; CANR 1, 23; INT CANR-23; MTCW; SATA 3; SATA-Obit 64

Stone, Oliver (William) 1946- ...... **CLC 73**
See also AAYA 15; CA 110; CANR 55

Stone, Robert (Anthony)
1937- .... **CLC 5, 23, 42**
See also CA 85-88; CANR 23; DLB 152; INT CANR-23; MTCW

Stone, Zachary
See Follett, Ken(neth Martin)

Stoppard, Tom
1937- ...... **CLC 1, 3, 4, 5, 8, 15, 29, 34, 63, 91; DA; DAB; DAC; DAM DRAM, MST; DC 6; WLC**
See also CA 81-84; CANR 39; CDBLB 1960 to Present; DLB 13; DLBY 85; MTCW

Storey, David (Malcolm)
1933- ..... **CLC 2, 4, 5, 8; DAM DRAM**
See also CA 81-84; CANR 36; DLB 13, 14; MTCW

Storm, Hyemeyohsts
1935- .... **CLC 3; DAM MULT**
See also CA 81-84; CANR 45; NNAL

Storm, (Hans) Theodor (Woldsen)
1817-1888 .... **NCLC 1**

Storni, Alfonsina
1892-1938 ..... **TCLC 5; DAM MULT; HLC**
See also CA 104; 131; HW

Stout, Rex (Todhunter) 1886-1975 ... **CLC 3**
See also AITN 2; CA 61-64

Stow, (Julian) Randolph 1935- .. **CLC 23, 48**
See also CA 13-16R; CANR 33; MTCW

Stowe, Harriet (Elizabeth) Beecher
1811-1896 ..... **NCLC 3, 50; DA; DAB; DAC; DAM MST, NOV; WLC**
See also CDALB 1865-1917; DLB 1, 12, 42, 74; JRDA; MAICYA; YABC 1

Strachey, (Giles) Lytton
1880-1932 .... **TCLC 12**
See also CA 110; DLB 149; DLBD 10

Strand, Mark
1934- .. **CLC 6, 18, 41, 71; DAM POET**
See also CA 21-24R; CANR 40; DLB 5; SATA 41

Straub, Peter (Francis)
1943- .... **CLC 28; DAM POP**
See also BEST 89:1; CA 85-88; CANR 28; DLBY 84; MTCW

Strauss, Botho 1944- .... **CLC 22**
See also DLB 124

Streatfeild, (Mary) Noel
1895(?)-1986 .... **CLC 21**
See also CA 81-84; 120; CANR 31; CLR 17; DLB 160; MAICYA; SATA 20; SATA-Obit 48

Stribling, T(homas) S(igismund)
1881-1965 .... **CLC 23**
See also CA 107; DLB 9

Strindberg, (Johan) August
1849-1912 ...... **TCLC 1, 8, 21, 47; DA; DAB; DAC; DAM DRAM, MST; WLC**
See also CA 104; 135

Stringer, Arthur 1874-1950 .... **TCLC 37**
See also DLB 92

Stringer, David
See Roberts, Keith (John Kingston)

Strugatskii, Arkadii (Natanovich)
1925-1991 .... **CLC 27**
See also CA 106; 135

Strugatskii, Boris (Natanovich)
1933- .... **CLC 27**
See also CA 106

Strummer, Joe 1953(?)- .... **CLC 30**

Stuart, Don A.
See Campbell, John W(ood, Jr.)

Stuart, Ian
See MacLean, Alistair (Stuart)

Stuart, Jesse (Hilton)
1906-1984 .... **CLC 1, 8, 11, 14, 34**
See also CA 5-8R; 112; CANR 31; DLB 9, 48, 102; DLBY 84; SATA 2; SATA-Obit 36

Sturgeon, Theodore (Hamilton)
1918-1985 .... **CLC 22, 39**
See also Queen, Ellery
See also CA 81-84; 116; CANR 32; DLB 8; DLBY 85; MTCW

Sturges, Preston 1898-1959 .... **TCLC 48**
See also CA 114; 149; DLB 26

Styron, William
1925- .... **CLC 1, 3, 5, 11, 15, 60; DAM NOV, POP; SSC 25**
See also BEST 90:4; CA 5-8R; CANR 6, 33; CDALB 1968-1988; DLB 2, 143; DLBY 80; INT CANR-6; MTCW

Suarez Lynch, B.
See Bioy Casares, Adolfo; Borges, Jorge Luis

Su Chien 1884-1918
See Su Man-shu
See also CA 123

Suckow, Ruth 1892-1960 .... **SSC 18**
See also CA 113; DLB 9, 102

Sudermann, Hermann 1857-1928 .. **TCLC 15**
See also CA 107; DLB 118

Sue, Eugene 1804-1857 .... **NCLC 1**
See also DLB 119

Sueskind, Patrick 1949- .... **CLC 44**
See also Suskind, Patrick

Sukenick, Ronald 1932- ..... **CLC 3, 4, 6, 48**
See also CA 25-28R; CAAS 8; CANR 32; DLB 173; DLBY 81

Suknaski, Andrew 1942- .... **CLC 19**
See also CA 101; DLB 53

Sullivan, Vernon
See Vian, Boris

Sully Prudhomme 1839-1907 ...... **TCLC 31**

Su Man-shu .... **TCLC 24**
See also Su Chien

Summerforest, Ivy B.
See Kirkup, James

Summers, Andrew James 1942-..... **CLC 26**

Summers, Andy
See Summers, Andrew James

Summers, Hollis (Spurgeon, Jr.)
1916- .... **CLC 10**
See also CA 5-8R; CANR 3; DLB 6

Summers, (Alphonsus Joseph-Mary Augustus)
Montague 1880-1948........ **TCLC 16**
See also CA 118

Sumner, Gordon Matthew 1951-.... **CLC 26**

Surtees, Robert Smith
1803-1864 .... **NCLC 14**
See also DLB 21

Susann, Jacqueline 1921-1974...... **CLC 3**
See also AITN 1; CA 65-68; 53-56; MTCW

Su Shih 1036-1101 .... **CMLC 15**

Suskind, Patrick
See Sueskind, Patrick
See also CA 145

Sutcliff, Rosemary
1920-1992 .... **CLC 26; DAB; DAC;**
DAM MST, POP
See also AAYA 10; CA 5-8R; 139;
CANR 37; CLR 1, 37; JRDA; MAICYA;
SATA 6, 44, 78; SATA-Obit 73

Sutro, Alfred 1863-1933.......... **TCLC 6**
See also CA 105; DLB 10

Sutton, Henry
See Slavitt, David R(ytman)

Svevo, Italo
1861-1928 .... **TCLC 2, 35; SSC 25**
See also Schmitz, Aron Hector

Swados, Elizabeth (A.) 1951-....... **CLC 12**
See also CA 97-100; CANR 49; INT 97-100

Swados, Harvey 1920-1972 .... **CLC 5**
See also CA 5-8R; 37-40R; CANR 6;
DLB 2

Swan, Gladys 1934- .... **CLC 69**
See also CA 101; CANR 17, 39

Swarthout, Glendon (Fred)
1918-1992 .... **CLC 35**
See also CA 1-4R; 139; CANR 1, 47;
SATA 26

Sweet, Sarah C.
See Jewett, (Theodora) Sarah Orne

Swenson, May
1919-1989 .... **CLC 4, 14, 61; DA; DAB;**
DAC; DAM MST, POET; PC 14
See also CA 5-8R; 130; CANR 36; DLB 5;
MTCW; SATA 15

Swift, Augustus
See Lovecraft, H(oward) P(hillips)

Swift, Graham (Colin) 1949-.... **CLC 41, 88**
See also CA 117; 122; CANR 46

Swift, Jonathan
1667-1745 ...... **LC 1; DA; DAB; DAC;**
DAM MST, NOV, POET; PC 9; WLC
See also CDBLB 1660-1789; DLB 39, 95,
101; SATA 19

Swinburne, Algernon Charles
1837-1909 ...... **TCLC 8, 36; DA; DAB;**
DAC; DAM MST, POET; WLC
See also CA 105; 140; CDBLB 1832-1890;
DLB 35, 57

Swinfen, Ann.................... **CLC 34**

Swinnerton, Frank Arthur
1884-1982 .... **CLC 31**
See also CA 108; DLB 34

Swithen, John
See King, Stephen (Edwin)

Sylvia
See Ashton-Warner, Sylvia (Constance)

Symmes, Robert Edward
See Duncan, Robert (Edward)

Symonds, John Addington
1840-1893 .... **NCLC 34**
See also DLB 57, 144

Symons, Arthur 1865-1945 .... **TCLC 11**
See also CA 107; DLB 19, 57, 149

Symons, Julian (Gustave)
1912-1994 .... **CLC 2, 14, 32**
See also CA 49-52; 147; CAAS 3; CANR 3,
33; DLB 87, 155; DLBY 92; MTCW

Synge, (Edmund) J(ohn) M(illington)
1871-1909 .... **TCLC 6, 37;**
DAM DRAM; DC 2
See also CA 104; 141; CDBLB 1890-1914;
DLB 10, 19

Syruc, J.
See Milosz, Czeslaw

Szirtes, George 1948-............. **CLC 46**
See also CA 109; CANR 27

Szymborska, Wislawa 1923- .... **CLC 99**
See also CA 154

T. O., Nik
See Annensky, Innokenty (Fyodorovich)

Tabori, George 1914-............. **CLC 19**
See also CA 49-52; CANR 4

Tagore, Rabindranath
1861-1941 .... **TCLC 3, 53;**
DAM DRAM, POET; PC 8
See also CA 104; 120; MTCW

Taine, Hippolyte Adolphe
1828-1893 .... **NCLC 15**

Talese, Gay 1932-................ **CLC 37**
See also AITN 1; CA 1-4R; CANR 9;
INT CANR-9; MTCW

Tallent, Elizabeth (Ann) 1954- ..... **CLC 45**
See also CA 117; DLB 130

Tally, Ted 1952-................ **CLC 42**
See also CA 120; 124; INT 124

Tamayo y Baus, Manuel
1829-1898 .... **NCLC 1**

Tammsaare, A(nton) H(ansen)
1878-1940 .... **TCLC 27**

Tan, Amy (Ruth)
1952- .... **CLC 59; DAM MULT, NOV,**
POP
See also AAYA 9; BEST 89:3; CA 136;
CANR 54; DLB 173; SATA 75

Tandem, Felix
See Spitteler, Carl (Friedrich Georg)

Tanizaki, Jun'ichiro
1886-1965 ...... **CLC 8, 14, 28; SSC 21**
See also CA 93-96; 25-28R

Tanner, William
See Amis, Kingsley (William)

Tao Lao
See Storni, Alfonsina

Tarassoff, Lev
See Troyat, Henri

Tarbell, Ida M(inerva)
1857-1944 .... **TCLC 40**
See also CA 122; DLB 47

Tarkington, (Newton) Booth
1869-1946 .... **TCLC 9**
See also CA 110; 143; DLB 9, 102;
SATA 17

Tarkovsky, Andrei (Arsenyevich)
1932-1986 .... **CLC 75**
See also CA 127

Tartt, Donna 1964(?)-............. **CLC 76**
See also CA 142

Tasso, Torquato 1544-1595 .... **LC 5**

Tate, (John Orley) Allen
1899-1979 .... **CLC 2, 4, 6, 9, 11, 14, 24**
See also CA 5-8R; 85-88; CANR 32;
DLB 4, 45, 63; MTCW

Tate, Ellalice
See Hibbert, Eleanor Alice Burford

Tate, James (Vincent) 1943- ... **CLC 2, 6, 25**
See also CA 21-24R; CANR 29, 57; DLB 5,
169

Tavel, Ronald 1940-............... **CLC 6**
See also CA 21-24R; CANR 33

Taylor, C(ecil) P(hilip) 1929-1981... **CLC 27**
See also CA 25-28R; 105; CANR 47

Taylor, Edward
1642(?)-1729 .... **LC 11; DA; DAB;**
DAC; DAM MST, POET
See also DLB 24

Taylor, Eleanor Ross 1920-......... **CLC 5**
See also CA 81-84

Taylor, Elizabeth 1912-1975 ... **CLC 2, 4, 29**
See also CA 13-16R; CANR 9; DLB 139;
MTCW; SATA 13

Taylor, Henry (Splawn) 1942-...... **CLC 44**
See also CA 33-36R; CAAS 7; CANR 31;
DLB 5

Taylor, Kamala (Purnaiya) 1924-
See Markandaya, Kamala
See also CA 77-80

Taylor, Mildred D................ **CLC 21**
See also AAYA 10; BW 1; CA 85-88;
CANR 25; CLR 9; DLB 52; JRDA;
MAICYA; SAAS 5; SATA 15, 70

Taylor, Peter (Hillsman)
1917-1994 ..... **CLC 1, 4, 18, 37, 44, 50,**
71; SSC 10
See also CA 13-16R; 147; CANR 9, 50;
DLBY 81, 94; INT CANR-9; MTCW

Taylor, Robert Lewis 1912-........ **CLC 14**
See also CA 1-4R; CANR 3; SATA 10

Tchekhov, Anton
See Chekhov, Anton (Pavlovich)

Teasdale, Sara 1884-1933......... **TCLC 4**
See also CA 104; DLB 45; SATA 32

Tegner, Esaias 1782-1846........ **NCLC 2**

Teilhard de Chardin, (Marie Joseph) Pierre
　　1881-1955 .... **TCLC 9**
　　See also CA 105

Temple, Ann
　　See Mortimer, Penelope (Ruth)

Tennant, Emma (Christina)
　　1937- .... **CLC 13, 52**
　　See also CA 65-68; CAAS 9; CANR 10, 38;
　　DLB 14

Tenneshaw, S. M.
　　See Silverberg, Robert

Tennyson, Alfred
　　1809-1892 .... **NCLC 30; DA; DAB;**
　　　　DAC; DAM MST, POET; PC 6; WLC
　　See also CDBLB 1832-1890; DLB 32

Teran, Lisa St. Aubin de .... **CLC 36**
　　See also St. Aubin de Teran, Lisa

Terence
　　195(?)B.C.-159B.C..... **CMLC 14; DC 7**

Teresa de Jesus, St. 1515-1582 ...... **LC 18**

Terkel, Louis 1912-
　　See Terkel, Studs
　　See also CA 57-60; CANR 18, 45; MTCW

Terkel, Studs .... **CLC 38**
　　See also Terkel, Louis
　　See also AITN 1

Terry, C. V.
　　See Slaughter, Frank G(ill)

Terry, Megan 1932- .... **CLC 19**
　　See also CA 77-80; CABS 3; CANR 43;
　　DLB 7

Tertz, Abram
　　See Sinyavsky, Andrei (Donatevich)

Tesich, Steve 1943(?)-1996...... **CLC 40, 69**
　　See also CA 105; 152; DLBY 83

Teternikov, Fyodor Kuzmich 1863-1927
　　See Sologub, Fyodor
　　See also CA 104

Tevis, Walter 1928-1984 .... **CLC 42**
　　See also CA 113

Tey, Josephine .... **TCLC 14**
　　See also Mackintosh, Elizabeth
　　See also DLB 77

Thackeray, William Makepeace
　　1811-1863 .... **NCLC 5, 14, 22, 43; DA;**
　　　　DAB; DAC; DAM MST, NOV; WLC
　　See also CDBLB 1832-1890; DLB 21, 55,
　　159, 163; SATA 23

Thakura, Ravindranatha
　　See Tagore, Rabindranath

Tharoor, Shashi 1956- .... **CLC 70**
　　See also CA 141

Thelwell, Michael Miles 1939- ..... **CLC 22**
　　See also BW 2; CA 101

Theobald, Lewis, Jr.
　　See Lovecraft, H(oward) P(hillips)

Theodorescu, Ion N. 1880-1967
　　See Arghezi, Tudor
　　See also CA 116

Theriault, Yves
　　1915-1983 .. **CLC 79; DAC; DAM MST**
　　See also CA 102; DLB 88

Theroux, Alexander (Louis)
　　1939- .... **CLC 2, 25**
　　See also CA 85-88; CANR 20

Theroux, Paul (Edward)
　　1941- .... **CLC 5, 8, 11, 15, 28, 46;**
　　　　DAM POP
　　See also BEST 89:4; CA 33-36R; CANR 20,
　　45; DLB 2; MTCW; SATA 44

Thesen, Sharon 1946- .... **CLC 56**

Thevenin, Denis
　　See Duhamel, Georges

Thibault, Jacques Anatole Francois
　　1844-1924
　　See France, Anatole
　　See also CA 106; 127; DAM NOV; MTCW

Thiele, Colin (Milton) 1920- .... **CLC 17**
　　See also CA 29-32R; CANR 12, 28, 53;
　　CLR 27; MAICYA; SAAS 2; SATA 14,
　　72

Thomas, Audrey (Callahan)
　　1935- .... **CLC 7, 13, 37; SSC 20**
　　See also AITN 2; CA 21-24R; CAAS 19;
　　CANR 36; DLB 60; MTCW

Thomas, D(onald) M(ichael)
　　1935- .... **CLC 13, 22, 31**
　　See also CA 61-64; CAAS 11; CANR 17,
　　45; CDBLB 1960 to Present; DLB 40;
　　INT CANR-17; MTCW

Thomas, Dylan (Marlais)
　　1914-1953 ... **TCLC 1, 8, 45; DA; DAB;**
　　　　DAC; DAM DRAM, MST, POET;
　　　　PC 2; SSC 3; WLC
　　See also CA 104; 120; CDBLB 1945-1960;
　　DLB 13, 20, 139; MTCW; SATA 60

Thomas, (Philip) Edward
　　1878-1917 ...... **TCLC 10; DAM POET**
　　See also CA 106; 153; DLB 19

Thomas, Joyce Carol 1938- .... **CLC 35**
　　See also AAYA 12; BW 2; CA 113; 116;
　　CANR 48; CLR 19; DLB 33; INT 116;
　　JRDA; MAICYA; MTCW; SAAS 7;
　　SATA 40, 78

Thomas, Lewis 1913-1993 .... **CLC 35**
　　See also CA 85-88; 143; CANR 38; MTCW

Thomas, Paul
　　See Mann, (Paul) Thomas

Thomas, Piri 1928- .... **CLC 17**
　　See also CA 73-76; HW

Thomas, R(onald) S(tuart)
　　1913- .... **CLC 6, 13, 48; DAB;**
　　　　DAM POET
　　See also CA 89-92; CAAS 4; CANR 30;
　　CDBLB 1960 to Present; DLB 27;
　　MTCW

Thomas, Ross (Elmore) 1926-1995 .. **CLC 39**
　　See also CA 33-36R; 150; CANR 22

Thompson, Francis Clegg
　　See Mencken, H(enry) L(ouis)

Thompson, Francis Joseph
　　1859-1907 .... **TCLC 4**
　　See also CA 104; CDBLB 1890-1914;
　　DLB 19

Thompson, Hunter S(tockton)
　　1939- .... **CLC 9, 17, 40; DAM POP**
　　See also BEST 89:1; CA 17-20R; CANR 23,
　　46; MTCW

Thompson, James Myers
　　See Thompson, Jim (Myers)

Thompson, Jim (Myers)
　　1906-1977(?) .... **CLC 69**
　　See also CA 140

Thompson, Judith .... **CLC 39**

Thomson, James
　　1700-1748 ..... **LC 16, 29; DAM POET**
　　See also DLB 95

Thomson, James
　　1834-1882 ..... **NCLC 18; DAM POET**
　　See also DLB 35

Thoreau, Henry David
　　1817-1862 ..... **NCLC 7, 21; DA; DAB;**
　　　　DAC; DAM MST; WLC
　　See also CDALB 1640-1865; DLB 1

Thornton, Hall
　　See Silverberg, Robert

Thucydides c. 455B.C.-399B.C.... **CMLC 17**
　　See also DLB 176

Thurber, James (Grover)
　　1894-1961 .... **CLC 5, 11, 25; DA; DAB;**
　　　　DAC; DAM DRAM, MST, NOV; SSC 1
　　See also CA 73-76; CANR 17, 39;
　　CDALB 1929-1941; DLB 4, 11, 22, 102;
　　MAICYA; MTCW; SATA 13

Thurman, Wallace (Henry)
　　1902-1934 .... **TCLC 6; BLC;**
　　　　DAM MULT
　　See also BW 1; CA 104; 124; DLB 51

Ticheburn, Cheviot
　　See Ainsworth, William Harrison

Tieck, (Johann) Ludwig
　　1773-1853 .... **NCLC 5, 46**
　　See also DLB 90

Tiger, Derry
　　See Ellison, Harlan (Jay)

Tilghman, Christopher 1948(?)-..... **CLC 65**

Tillinghast, Richard (Williford)
　　1940- .... **CLC 29**
　　See also CA 29-32R; CAAS 23; CANR 26,
　　51

Timrod, Henry 1828-1867 .... **NCLC 25**
　　See also DLB 3

Tindall, Gillian 1938-.............. **CLC 7**
　　See also CA 21-24R; CANR 11

Tiptree, James, Jr. .... **CLC 48, 50**
　　See also Sheldon, Alice Hastings Bradley
　　See also DLB 8

Titmarsh, Michael Angelo
　　See Thackeray, William Makepeace

Tocqueville, Alexis (Charles Henri Maurice
　　Clerel Comte) 1805-1859 ..... **NCLC 7**

Tolkien, J(ohn) R(onald) R(euel)
　　1892-1973 .... **CLC 1, 2, 3, 8, 12, 38;**
　　　　DA; DAB; DAC; DAM MST, NOV,
　　　　POP; WLC
　　See also AAYA 10; AITN 1; CA 17-18;
　　45-48; CANR 36; CAP 2;
　　CDBLB 1914-1945; DLB 15, 160; JRDA;
　　MAICYA; MTCW; SATA 2, 32;
　　SATA-Obit 24

Toller, Ernst 1893-1939 .... **TCLC 10**
　　See also CA 107; DLB 124

Tolson, M. B.
See Tolson, Melvin B(eaunorus)

Tolson, Melvin B(eaunorus)
1898(?)-1966 . . . . **CLC 36; BLC;**
DAM MULT, POET
See also BW 1; CA 124; 89-92; DLB 48, 76

Tolstoi, Aleksei Nikolaevich
See Tolstoy, Alexey Nikolaevich

Tolstoy, Alexey Nikolaevich
1882-1945 . . . . **TCLC 18**
See also CA 107

Tolstoy, Count Leo
See Tolstoy, Leo (Nikolaevich)

Tolstoy, Leo (Nikolaevich)
1828-1910 . . . . . . **TCLC 4, 11, 17, 28, 44;**
DA; DAB; DAC; DAM MST, NOV;
SSC 9; WLC
See also CA 104; 123; SATA 26

Tomasi di Lampedusa, Giuseppe 1896-1957
See Lampedusa, Giuseppe (Tomasi) di
See also CA 111

Tomlin, Lily . . . . **CLC 17**
See also Tomlin, Mary Jean

Tomlin, Mary Jean 1939(?)-
See Tomlin, Lily
See also CA 117

Tomlinson, (Alfred) Charles
1927- . . . . **CLC 2, 4, 6, 13, 45;**
DAM POET; PC 17
See also CA 5-8R; CANR 33; DLB 40

Tonson, Jacob
See Bennett, (Enoch) Arnold

Toole, John Kennedy
1937-1969 . . . . **CLC 19, 64**
See also CA 104; DLBY 81

Toomer, Jean
1894-1967 . . . . . . **CLC 1, 4, 13, 22; BLC;**
DAM MULT; PC 7; SSC 1
See also BW 1; CA 85-88;
CDALB 1917-1929; DLB 45, 51; MTCW

Torley, Luke
See Blish, James (Benjamin)

Tornimparte, Alessandra
See Ginzburg, Natalia

Torre, Raoul della
See Mencken, H(enry) L(ouis)

Torrey, E(dwin) Fuller 1937- . . . . **CLC 34**
See also CA 119

Torsvan, Ben Traven
See Traven, B.

Torsvan, Benno Traven
See Traven, B.

Torsvan, Berick Traven
See Traven, B.

Torsvan, Berwick Traven
See Traven, B.

Torsvan, Bruno Traven
See Traven, B.

Torsvan, Traven
See Traven, B.

Tournier, Michel (Edouard)
1924- . . . . **CLC 6, 23, 36, 95;**
See also CA 49-52; CANR 3, 36; DLB 83;
MTCW; SATA 23

Tournimparte, Alessandra
See Ginzburg, Natalia

Towers, Ivar
See Kornbluth, C(yril) M.

Towne, Robert (Burton) 1936(?)- . . . . **CLC 87**
See also CA 108; DLB 44

Townsend, Sue 1946- . . **CLC 61; DAB; DAC**
See also CA 119; 127; INT 127; MTCW;
SATA 55; SATA-Brief 48

Townshend, Peter (Dennis Blandford)
1945- . . . . **CLC 17, 42**
See also CA 107

Tozzi, Federigo 1883-1920 . . . . **TCLC 31**

Traill, Catharine Parr
1802-1899 . . . . **NCLC 31**
See also DLB 99

Trakl, Georg 1887-1914 . . . . **TCLC 5**
See also CA 104

Transtroemer, Tomas (Goesta)
1931- . . . . **CLC 52, 65; DAM POET**
See also CA 117; 129; CAAS 17

Transtromer, Tomas Gosta
See Transtroemer, Tomas (Goesta)

Traven, B. (?)-1969 . . . . **CLC 8, 11**
See also CA 19-20; 25-28R; CAP 2; DLB 9,
56; MTCW

Treitel, Jonathan 1959- . . . . **CLC 70**

Tremain, Rose 1943- . . . . **CLC 42**
See also CA 97-100; CANR 44; DLB 14

Tremblay, Michel
1942- . . . . . . **CLC 29; DAC; DAM MST**
See also CA 116; 128; DLB 60; MTCW

Trevanian . . . . **CLC 29**
See also Whitaker, Rod(ney)

Trevor, Glen
See Hilton, James

Trevor, William
1928- . . . . . **CLC 7, 9, 14, 25, 71; SSC 21**
See also Cox, William Trevor
See also DLB 14, 139

Trifonov, Yuri (Valentinovich)
1925-1981 . . . . **CLC 45**
See also CA 126; 103; MTCW

Trilling, Lionel 1905-1975 . . . . **CLC 9, 11, 24**
See also CA 9-12R; 61-64; CANR 10;
DLB 28, 63; INT CANR-10; MTCW

Trimball, W. H.
See Mencken, H(enry) L(ouis)

Tristan
See Gomez de la Serna, Ramon

Tristram
See Housman, A(lfred) E(dward)

Trogdon, William (Lewis) 1939-
See Heat-Moon, William Least
See also CA 115; 119; CANR 47; INT 119

Trollope, Anthony
1815-1882 . . . . . **NCLC 6, 33; DA; DAB;**
DAC; DAM MST, NOV; WLC
See also CDBLB 1832-1890; DLB 21, 57,
159; SATA 22

Trollope, Frances 1779-1863 . . . . . **NCLC 30**
See also DLB 21, 166

Trotsky, Leon 1879-1940 . . . . **TCLC 22**
See also CA 118

Trotter (Cockburn), Catharine
1679-1749 . . . . **LC 8**
See also DLB 84

Trout, Kilgore
See Farmer, Philip Jose

Trow, George W. S. 1943- . . . . **CLC 52**
See also CA 126

Troyat, Henri 1911- . . . . **CLC 23**
See also CA 45-48; CANR 2, 33; MTCW

Trudeau, G(arretson) B(eekman) 1948-
See Trudeau, Garry B.
See also CA 81-84; CANR 31; SATA 35

Trudeau, Garry B. . . . . **CLC 12**
See also Trudeau, G(arretson) B(eekman)
See also AAYA 10; AITN 2

Truffaut, Francois 1932-1984 . . . . . . **CLC 20**
See also CA 81-84; 113; CANR 34

Trumbo, Dalton 1905-1976 . . . . **CLC 19**
See also CA 21-24R; 69-72; CANR 10;
DLB 26

Trumbull, John 1750-1831 . . . . **NCLC 30**
See also DLB 31

Trundlett, Helen B.
See Eliot, T(homas) S(tearns)

Tryon, Thomas
1926-1991 . . . . . . **CLC 3, 11; DAM POP**
See also AITN 1; CA 29-32R; 135;
CANR 32; MTCW

Tryon, Tom
See Tryon, Thomas

Ts'ao Hsueh-ch'in 1715(?)-1763 . . . . **LC 1**

Tsushima, Shuji 1909-1948
See Dazai, Osamu
See also CA 107

Tsvetaeva (Efron), Marina (Ivanovna)
1892-1941 . . . . **TCLC 7, 35; PC 14**
See also CA 104; 128; MTCW

Tuck, Lily 1938- . . . . **CLC 70**
See also CA 139

Tu Fu 712-770 . . . . **PC 9**
See also DAM MULT

Tunis, John R(oberts) 1889-1975 . . . **CLC 12**
See also CA 61-64; DLB 22, 171; JRDA;
MAICYA; SATA 37; SATA-Brief 30

Tuohy, Frank . . . . **CLC 37**
See also Tuohy, John Francis
See also DLB 14, 139

Tuohy, John Francis 1925-
See Tuohy, Frank
See also CA 5-8R; CANR 3, 47

Turco, Lewis (Putnam) 1934- . . . **CLC 11, 63**
See also CA 13-16R; CAAS 22; CANR 24,
51; DLBY 84

Turgenev, Ivan
1818-1883 . . . . **NCLC 21; DA; DAB;**
DAC; DAM MST, NOV; DC 7; SSC 7;
WLC

Turgot, Anne-Robert-Jacques
1727-1781 . . . . **LC 26**

Turner, Frederick 1943- . . . . **CLC 48**
See also CA 73-76; CAAS 10; CANR 12,
30, 56; DLB 40

Tutu, Desmond M(pilo)
1931- . . . . . **CLC 80; BLC; DAM MULT**
See also BW 1; CA 125

Tutuola, Amos
1920- . . . . **CLC 5, 14, 29; BLC;**
DAM MULT
See also BW 2; CA 9-12R; CANR 27;
DLB 125; MTCW

Twain, Mark
. . . . . **TCLC 6, 12, 19, 36, 48, 59; SSC 6;**
WLC
See also Clemens, Samuel Langhorne
See also AAYA 20; DLB 11, 12, 23, 64, 74

Tyler, Anne
1941- . . . . **CLC 7, 11, 18, 28, 44, 59;**
DAM NOV, POP
See also AAYA 18; BEST 89:1; CA 9-12R;
CANR 11, 33, 53; DLB 6, 143; DLBY 82;
MTCW; SATA 7, 90

Tyler, Royall 1757-1826 . . . . **NCLC 3**
See also DLB 37

Tynan, Katharine 1861-1931 . . . . . . **TCLC 3**
See also CA 104; DLB 153

Tyutchev, Fyodor 1803-1873 . . . . . **NCLC 34**

Tzara, Tristan
1896-1963 . . . . **CLC 47; DAM POET**
See also Rosenfeld, Samuel; Rosenstock,
Sami; Rosenstock, Samuel
See also CA 153

Uhry, Alfred
1936- . . . . . **CLC 55; DAM DRAM, POP**
See also CA 127; 133; INT 133

Ulf, Haerved
See Strindberg, (Johan) August

Ulf, Harved
See Strindberg, (Johan) August

Ulibarri, Sabine R(eyes)
1919- . . . . **CLC 83; DAM MULT**
See also CA 131; DLB 82; HW

Unamuno (y Jugo), Miguel de
1864-1936 . . . **TCLC 2, 9; DAM MULT,**
NOV; HLC; SSC 11
See also CA 104; 131; DLB 108; HW;
MTCW

Undercliffe, Errol
See Campbell, (John) Ramsey

Underwood, Miles
See Glassco, John

Undset, Sigrid
1882-1949 . . . . **TCLC 3; DA; DAB;**
DAC; DAM MST, NOV; WLC
See also CA 104; 129; MTCW

Ungaretti, Giuseppe
1888-1970 . . . . **CLC 7, 11, 15**
See also CA 19-20; 25-28R; CAP 2;
DLB 114

Unger, Douglas 1952- . . . . **CLC 34**
See also CA 130

Unsworth, Barry (Forster) 1930- . . . . **CLC 76**
See also CA 25-28R; CANR 30, 54

Updike, John (Hoyer)
1932- . . . . . . **CLC 1, 2, 3, 5, 7, 9, 13, 15,**
23, 34, 43, 70; DA; DAB; DAC;
DAM MST, NOV, POET, POP;
SSC 13; WLC
See also CA 1-4R; CABS 1; CANR 4, 33,
51; CDALB 1968-1988; DLB 2, 5, 143;
DLBD 3; DLBY 80, 82; MTCW

Upshaw, Margaret Mitchell
See Mitchell, Margaret (Munnerlyn)

Upton, Mark
See Sanders, Lawrence

Urdang, Constance (Henriette)
1922- . . . . **CLC 47**
See also CA 21-24R; CANR 9, 24

Uriel, Henry
See Faust, Frederick (Schiller)

Uris, Leon (Marcus)
1924- . . . . **CLC 7, 32; DAM NOV, POP**
See also AITN 1, 2; BEST 89:2; CA 1-4R;
CANR 1, 40; MTCW; SATA 49

Urmuz
See Codrescu, Andrei

Urquhart, Jane 1949- . . . . **CLC 90; DAC**
See also CA 113; CANR 32

Ustinov, Peter (Alexander) 1921- . . . . **CLC 1**
See also AITN 1; CA 13-16R; CANR 25,
51; DLB 13

Vaculik, Ludvik 1926- . . . . **CLC 7**
See also CA 53-56

Valdez, Luis (Miguel)
1940- . . . . . **CLC 84; DAM MULT; HLC**
See also CA 101; CANR 32; DLB 122; HW

Valenzuela, Luisa
1938- . . . **CLC 31; DAM MULT; SSC 14**
See also CA 101; CANR 32; DLB 113; HW

Valera y Alcala-Galiano, Juan
1824-1905 . . . . **TCLC 10**
See also CA 106

Valery, (Ambroise) Paul (Toussaint Jules)
1871-1945 . . . . **TCLC 4, 15;**
DAM POET; PC 9
See also CA 104; 122; MTCW

Valle-Inclan, Ramon (Maria) del
1866-1936 . . . . . **TCLC 5; DAM MULT;**
HLC
See also CA 106; 153; DLB 134

Vallejo, Antonio Buero
See Buero Vallejo, Antonio

Vallejo, Cesar (Abraham)
1892-1938 . . . . **TCLC 3, 56;**
DAM MULT; HLC
See also CA 105; 153; HW

Vallette, Marguerite Eymery
See Rachilde

Valle Y Pena, Ramon del
See Valle-Inclan, Ramon (Maria) del

Van Ash, Cay 1918- . . . . **CLC 34**

Vanbrugh, Sir John
1664-1726 . . . . **LC 21; DAM DRAM**
See also DLB 80

Van Campen, Karl
See Campbell, John W(ood, Jr.)

Vance, Gerald
See Silverberg, Robert

Vance, Jack . . . . **CLC 35**
See also Vance, John Holbrook
See also DLB 8

Vance, John Holbrook 1916-
See Queen, Ellery; Vance, Jack
See also CA 29-32R; CANR 17; MTCW

Van Den Bogarde, Derek Jules Gaspard Ulric
Niven 1921-
See Bogarde, Dirk
See also CA 77-80

Vandenburgh, Jane . . . . **CLC 59**

Vanderhaeghe, Guy 1951- . . . . **CLC 41**
See also CA 113

van der Post, Laurens (Jan)
1906-1996 . . . . **CLC 5**
See also CA 5-8R; 155; CANR 35

van de Wetering, Janwillem 1931- . . **CLC 47**
See also CA 49-52; CANR 4

Van Dine, S. S. . . . . **TCLC 23**
See also Wright, Willard Huntington

Van Doren, Carl (Clinton)
1885-1950 . . . . **TCLC 18**
See also CA 111

Van Doren, Mark 1894-1972 . . . . . **CLC 6, 10**
See also CA 1-4R; 37-40R; CANR 3;
DLB 45; MTCW

Van Druten, John (William)
1901-1957 . . . . **TCLC 2**
See also CA 104; DLB 10

Van Duyn, Mona (Jane)
1921- . . . . **CLC 3, 7, 63; DAM POET**
See also CA 9-12R; CANR 7, 38; DLB 5

Van Dyne, Edith
See Baum, L(yman) Frank

van Itallie, Jean-Claude 1936- . . . . **CLC 3**
See also CA 45-48; CAAS 2; CANR 1, 48;
DLB 7

van Ostaijen, Paul 1896-1928 . . . . . **TCLC 33**

Van Peebles, Melvin
1932- . . . . **CLC 2, 20; DAM MULT**
See also BW 2; CA 85-88; CANR 27

Vansittart, Peter 1920- . . . . **CLC 42**
See also CA 1-4R; CANR 3, 49

Van Vechten, Carl 1880-1964 . . . . . . **CLC 33**
See also CA 89-92; DLB 4, 9, 51

Van Vogt, A(lfred) E(lton) 1912- . . . . . **CLC 1**
See also CA 21-24R; CANR 28; DLB 8;
SATA 14

Varda, Agnes 1928- . . . . **CLC 16**
See also CA 116; 122

Vargas Llosa, (Jorge) Mario (Pedro)
1936- . . . . **CLC 3, 6, 9, 10, 15, 31, 42, 85;**
DA; DAB; DAC; DAM MST, MULT,
NOV; HLC
See also CA 73-76; CANR 18, 32, 42;
DLB 145; HW; MTCW

Vasiliu, Gheorghe 1881-1957
See Bacovia, George
See also CA 123

Vassa, Gustavus
See Equiano, Olaudah

Vassilikos, Vassilis 1933- . . . . **CLC 4, 8**
See also CA 81-84

Waldman, Anne 1945- . . . . **CLC 7**
See also CA 37-40R; CAAS 17; CANR 34;
DLB 16

Waldo, E. Hunter
See Sturgeon, Theodore (Hamilton)

Waldo, Edward Hamilton
See Sturgeon, Theodore (Hamilton)

Walker, Alice (Malsenior)
1944- . . . . **CLC 5, 6, 9, 19, 27, 46, 58;**
BLC; DA; DAB; DAC; DAM MST,
MULT, NOV, POET, POP; SSC 5
See also AAYA 3; BEST 89:4; BW 2;
CA 37-40R; CANR 9, 27, 49;
CDALB 1968-1988; DLB 6, 33, 143;
INT CANR-27; MTCW; SATA 31

Walker, David Harry 1911-1992 . . . . **CLC 14**
See also CA 1-4R; 137; CANR 1; SATA 8;
SATA-Obit 71

Walker, Edward Joseph 1934-
See Walker, Ted
See also CA 21-24R; CANR 12, 28, 53

Walker, George F.
1947- . . . . **CLC 44, 61; DAB; DAC;**
DAM MST
See also CA 103; CANR 21, 43; DLB 60

Walker, Joseph A.
1935- . . . . **CLC 19; DAM DRAM, MST**
See also BW 1; CA 89-92; CANR 26;
DLB 38

Walker, Margaret (Abigail)
1915- . . . . **CLC 1, 6; BLC; DAM MULT**
See also BW 2; CA 73-76; CANR 26, 54;
DLB 76, 152; MTCW

Walker, Ted . . . . **CLC 13**
See also Walker, Edward Joseph
See also DLB 40

Wallace, David Foster 1962- . . . . **CLC 50**
See also CA 132

Wallace, Dexter
See Masters, Edgar Lee

Wallace, (Richard Horatio) Edgar
1875-1932 . . . . **TCLC 57**
See also CA 115; DLB 70

Wallace, Irving
1916-1990 . . . . . **CLC 7, 13; DAM NOV,**
POP
See also AITN 1; CA 1-4R; 132; CAAS 1;
CANR 1, 27; INT CANR-27; MTCW

Wallant, Edward Lewis
1926-1962 . . . . **CLC 5, 10**
See also CA 1-4R; CANR 22; DLB 2, 28,
143; MTCW

Walley, Byron
See Card, Orson Scott

Walpole, Horace 1717-1797 . . . . **LC 2**
See also DLB 39, 104

Walpole, Hugh (Seymour)
1884-1941 . . . . **TCLC 5**
See also CA 104; DLB 34

Walser, Martin 1927- . . . . **CLC 27**
See also CA 57-60; CANR 8, 46; DLB 75,
124

Walser, Robert
1878-1956 . . . . **TCLC 18; SSC 20**
See also CA 118; DLB 66

Walsh, Jill Paton . . . . **CLC 35**
See also Paton Walsh, Gillian
See also AAYA 11; CLR 2; DLB 161;
SAAS 3

Walter, Villiam Christian
See Andersen, Hans Christian

Wambaugh, Joseph (Aloysius, Jr.)
1937- . . . . **CLC 3, 18; DAM NOV, POP**
See also AITN 1; BEST 89:3; CA 33-36R;
CANR 42; DLB 6; DLBY 83; MTCW

Ward, Arthur Henry Sarsfield 1883-1959
See Rohmer, Sax
See also CA 108

Ward, Douglas Turner 1930- . . . . **CLC 19**
See also BW 1; CA 81-84; CANR 27;
DLB 7, 38

Ward, Mary Augusta
See Ward, Mrs. Humphry

Ward, Mrs. Humphry
1851-1920 . . . . **TCLC 55**
See also DLB 18

Ward, Peter
See Faust, Frederick (Schiller)

Warhol, Andy 1928(?)-1987 . . . . **CLC 20**
See also AAYA 12; BEST 89:4; CA 89-92;
121; CANR 34

Warner, Francis (Robert le Plastrier)
1937- . . . . **CLC 14**
See also CA 53-56; CANR 11

Warner, Marina 1946- . . . . **CLC 59**
See also CA 65-68; CANR 21, 55

Warner, Rex (Ernest) 1905-1986 . . . . **CLC 45**
See also CA 89-92; 119; DLB 15

Warner, Susan (Bogert)
1819-1885 . . . . **NCLC 31**
See also DLB 3, 42

Warner, Sylvia (Constance) Ashton
See Ashton-Warner, Sylvia (Constance)

Warner, Sylvia Townsend
1893-1978 . . . . **CLC 7, 19; SSC 23**
See also CA 61-64; 77-80; CANR 16;
DLB 34, 139; MTCW

Warren, Mercy Otis 1728-1814 . . . **NCLC 13**
See also DLB 31

Warren, Robert Penn
1905-1989 . . . . **CLC 1, 4, 6, 8, 10, 13, 18,**
39, 53, 59; DA; DAB; DAC; DAM MST,
NOV, POET; SSC 4; WLC
See also AITN 1; CA 13-16R; 129;
CANR 10, 47; CDALB 1968-1988;
DLB 2, 48, 152; DLBY 80, 89;
INT CANR-10; MTCW; SATA 46;
SATA-Obit 63

Warshofsky, Isaac
See Singer, Isaac Bashevis

Warton, Thomas
1728-1790 . . . . **LC 15; DAM POET**
See also DLB 104, 109

Waruk, Kona
See Harris, (Theodore) Wilson

Warung, Price 1855-1911 . . . . **TCLC 45**

Warwick, Jarvis
See Garner, Hugh

Washington, Alex
See Harris, Mark

Washington, Booker T(aliaferro)
1856-1915 . . . . **TCLC 10; BLC;**
DAM MULT
See also BW 1; CA 114; 125; SATA 28

Washington, George 1732-1799 . . . . . . **LC 25**
See also DLB 31

Wassermann, (Karl) Jakob
1873-1934 . . . . **TCLC 6**
See also CA 104; DLB 66

Wasserstein, Wendy
1950- . . . . **CLC 32, 59, 90;**
DAM DRAM; DC 4
See also CA 121; 129; CABS 3; CANR 53;
INT 129

Waterhouse, Keith (Spencer)
1929- . . . . **CLC 47**
See also CA 5-8R; CANR 38; DLB 13, 15;
MTCW

Waters, Frank (Joseph)
1902-1995 . . . . **CLC 88**
See also CA 5-8R; 149; CAAS 13; CANR 3,
18; DLBY 86

Waters, Roger 1944- . . . . **CLC 35**

Watkins, Frances Ellen
See Harper, Frances Ellen Watkins

Watkins, Gerrold
See Malzberg, Barry N(athaniel)

Watkins, Gloria 1955(?)-
See hooks, bell
See also BW 2; CA 143

Watkins, Paul 1964- . . . . **CLC 55**
See also CA 132

Watkins, Vernon Phillips
1906-1967 . . . . **CLC 43**
See also CA 9-10; 25-28R; CAP 1; DLB 20

Watson, Irving S.
See Mencken, H(enry) L(ouis)

Watson, John H.
See Farmer, Philip Jose

Watson, Richard F.
See Silverberg, Robert

Waugh, Auberon (Alexander) 1939- . . **CLC 7**
See also CA 45-48; CANR 6, 22; DLB 14

Waugh, Evelyn (Arthur St. John)
1903-1966 . . . . . . **CLC 1, 3, 8, 13, 19, 27,**
44; DA; DAB; DAC; DAM MST, NOV,
POP; WLC
See also CA 85-88; 25-28R; CANR 22;
CDBLB 1914-1945; DLB 15, 162; MTCW

Waugh, Harriet 1944- . . . . **CLC 6**
See also CA 85-88; CANR 22

Ways, C. R.
See Blount, Roy (Alton), Jr.

Waystaff, Simon
See Swift, Jonathan

Webb, (Martha) Beatrice (Potter)
1858-1943 . . . . **TCLC 22**
See also Potter, Beatrice
See also CA 117

Webb, Charles (Richard) 1939- . . . . . . **CLC 7**
See also CA 25-28R

Webb, James H(enry), Jr. 1946- . . . . **CLC 22**
See also CA 81-84

White, Edmund (Valentine III)
1940- . . . . **CLC 27; DAM POP**
See also AAYA 7; CA 45-48; CANR 3, 19, 36; MTCW

White, Patrick (Victor Martindale)
1912-1990 . . **CLC 3, 4, 5, 7, 9, 18, 65, 69**
See also CA 81-84; 132; CANR 43; MTCW

White, Phyllis Dorothy James 1920-
See James, P. D.
See also CA 21-24R; CANR 17, 43;
DAM POP; MTCW

White, T(erence) H(anbury)
1906-1964 . . . . **CLC 30**
See also CA 73-76; CANR 37; DLB 160;
JRDA; MAICYA; SATA 12

White, Terence de Vere
1912-1994 . . . . **CLC 49**
See also CA 49-52; 145; CANR 3

White, Walter F(rancis)
1893-1955 . . . . **TCLC 15**
See also White, Walter
See also BW 1; CA 115; 124; DLB 51

White, William Hale 1831-1913
See Rutherford, Mark
See also CA 121

Whitehead, E(dward) A(nthony)
1933- . . . . **CLC 5**
See also CA 65-68

Whitemore, Hugh (John) 1936- . . . . . **CLC 37**
See also CA 132; INT 132

Whitman, Sarah Helen (Power)
1803-1878 . . . . **NCLC 19**
See also DLB 1

Whitman, Walt(er)
1819-1892 . . . . . **NCLC 4, 31; DA; DAB;**
DAC; DAM MST, POET; PC 3; WLC
See also CDALB 1640-1865; DLB 3, 64;
SATA 20

Whitney, Phyllis A(yame)
1903- . . . . **CLC 42; DAM POP**
See also AITN 2; BEST 90:3; CA 1-4R;
CANR 3, 25, 38; JRDA; MAICYA;
SATA 1, 30

Whittemore, (Edward) Reed (Jr.)
1919- . . . . **CLC 4**
See also CA 9-12R; CAAS 8; CANR 4;
DLB 5

Whittier, John Greenleaf
1807-1892 . . . . **NCLC 8, 59**
See also DLB 1

Whittlebot, Hernia
See Coward, Noel (Peirce)

Wicker, Thomas Grey 1926-
See Wicker, Tom
See also CA 65-68; CANR 21, 46

Wicker, Tom . . . . **CLC 7**
See also Wicker, Thomas Grey

Wideman, John Edgar
1941- . . . . **CLC 5, 34, 36, 67; BLC;**
DAM MULT
See also BW 2; CA 85-88; CANR 14, 42;
DLB 33, 143

Wiebe, Rudy (Henry)
1934- . . . . **CLC 6, 11, 14; DAC;**
DAM MST
See also CA 37-40R; CANR 42; DLB 60

Wieland, Christoph Martin
1733-1813 . . . . **NCLC 17**
See also DLB 97

Wiene, Robert 1881-1938 . . . . **TCLC 56**

Wieners, John 1934- . . . . **CLC 7**
See also CA 13-16R; DLB 16

Wiesel, Elie(zer)
1928- . . . . . . **CLC 3, 5, 11, 37; DA; DAB;**
DAC; DAM MST, NOV
See also AAYA 7; AITN 1; CA 5-8R;
CAAS 4; CANR 8, 40; DLB 83;
DLBY 87; INT CANR-8; MTCW;
SATA 56

Wiggins, Marianne 1947- . . . . **CLC 57**
See also BEST 89:3; CA 130

Wight, James Alfred 1916-
See Herriot, James
See also CA 77-80; SATA 55;
SATA-Brief 44

Wilbur, Richard (Purdy)
1921- . . . **CLC 3, 6, 9, 14, 53; DA; DAB;**
DAC; DAM MST, POET
See also CA 1-4R; CABS 2; CANR 2, 29;
DLB 5, 169; INT CANR-29; MTCW;
SATA 9

Wild, Peter 1940- . . . . **CLC 14**
See also CA 37-40R; DLB 5

Wilde, Oscar (Fingal O'Flahertie Wills)
1854(?)-1900 . . . . **TCLC 1, 8, 23, 41; DA;**
DAB; DAC; DAM DRAM, MST, NOV;
SSC 11; WLC
See also CA 104; 119; CDBLB 1890-1914;
DLB 10, 19, 34, 57, 141, 156; SATA 24

Wilder, Billy . . . . **CLC 20**
See also Wilder, Samuel
See also DLB 26

Wilder, Samuel 1906-
See Wilder, Billy
See also CA 89-92

Wilder, Thornton (Niven)
1897-1975 . . . . . . **CLC 1, 5, 6, 10, 15, 35,**
82; DA; DAB; DAC; DAM DRAM,
MST, NOV; DC 1; WLC
See also AITN 2; CA 13-16R; 61-64;
CANR 40; DLB 4, 7, 9; MTCW

Wilding, Michael 1942- . . . . **CLC 73**
See also CA 104; CANR 24, 49

Wiley, Richard 1944- . . . . **CLC 44**
See also CA 121; 129

Wilhelm, Kate . . . . **CLC 7**
See also Wilhelm, Katie Gertrude
See also AAYA 20; CAAS 5; DLB 8;
INT CANR-17

Wilhelm, Katie Gertrude 1928-
See Wilhelm, Kate
See also CA 37-40R; CANR 17, 36; MTCW

Wilkins, Mary
See Freeman, Mary Eleanor Wilkins

Willard, Nancy 1936- . . . . **CLC 7, 37**
See also CA 89-92; CANR 10, 39; CLR 5;
DLB 5, 52; MAICYA; MTCW;
SATA 37, 71; SATA-Brief 30

Williams, C(harles) K(enneth)
1936- . . . . **CLC 33, 56; DAM POET**
See also CA 37-40R; CAAS 26; CANR 57;
DLB 5

Williams, Charles
See Collier, James L(incoln)

Williams, Charles (Walter Stansby)
1886-1945 . . . . **TCLC 1, 11**
See also CA 104; DLB 100, 153

Williams, (George) Emlyn
1905-1987 . . . . . . **CLC 15; DAM DRAM**
See also CA 104; 123; CANR 36; DLB 10,
77; MTCW

Williams, Hugo 1942- . . . . **CLC 42**
See also CA 17-20R; CANR 45; DLB 40

Williams, J. Walker
See Wodehouse, P(elham) G(renville)

Williams, John A(lfred)
1925- . . . **CLC 5, 13; BLC; DAM MULT**
See also BW 2; CA 53-56; CAAS 3;
CANR 6, 26, 51; DLB 2, 33;
INT CANR-6

Williams, Jonathan (Chamberlain)
1929- . . . . **CLC 13**
See also CA 9-12R; CAAS 12; CANR 8;
DLB 5

Williams, Joy 1944- . . . . **CLC 31**
See also CA 41-44R; CANR 22, 48

Williams, Norman 1952- . . . . **CLC 39**
See also CA 118

Williams, Sherley Anne
1944- . . . . . **CLC 89; BLC; DAM MULT,**
POET
See also BW 2; CA 73-76; CANR 25;
DLB 41; INT CANR-25; SATA 78

Williams, Shirley
See Williams, Sherley Anne

Williams, Tennessee
1911-1983 . . . . . **CLC 1, 2, 5, 7, 8, 11, 15,**
19, 30, 39, 45, 71; DA; DAB; DAC;
DAM DRAM, MST; DC 4; WLC
See also AITN 1, 2; CA 5-8R; 108;
CABS 3; CANR 31; CDALB 1941-1968;
DLB 7; DLBD 4; DLBY 83; MTCW

Williams, Thomas (Alonzo)
1926-1990 . . . . **CLC 14**
See also CA 1-4R; 132; CANR 2

Williams, William C.
See Williams, William Carlos

Williams, William Carlos
1883-1963 . . . . **CLC 1, 2, 5, 9, 13, 22, 42,**
67; DA; DAB; DAC; DAM MST, POET;
PC 7
See also CA 89-92; CANR 34;
CDALB 1917-1929; DLB 4, 16, 54, 86;
MTCW

Williamson, David (Keith) 1942- . . . . **CLC 56**
See also CA 103; CANR 41

Williamson, Ellen Douglas 1905-1984
See Douglas, Ellen
See also CA 17-20R; 114; CANR 39

Williamson, Jack . . . . **CLC 29**
See also Williamson, John Stewart
See also CAAS 8; DLB 8

Williamson, John Stewart 1908-
See Williamson, Jack
See also CA 17-20R; CANR 23

Willie, Frederick
See Lovecraft, H(oward) P(hillips)

Willingham, Calder (Baynard, Jr.)
1922-1995 .... CLC **5, 51**
See also CA 5-8R; 147; CANR 3; DLB 2,
44; MTCW

Willis, Charles
See Clarke, Arthur C(harles)

Willy
See Colette, (Sidonie-Gabrielle)

Willy, Colette
See Colette, (Sidonie-Gabrielle)

Wilson, A(ndrew) N(orman) 1950- .. CLC **33**
See also CA 112; 122; DLB 14, 155

Wilson, Angus (Frank Johnstone)
1913-1991 .. CLC **2, 3, 5, 25, 34; SSC 21**
See also CA 5-8R; 134; CANR 21; DLB 15,
139, 155; MTCW

Wilson, August
1945- .... CLC **39, 50, 63; BLC; DA;**
DAB; DAC; DAM DRAM, MST,
MULT; DC 2
See also AAYA 16; BW 2; CA 115; 122;
CANR 42, 54; MTCW

Wilson, Brian 1942- .... CLC **12**

Wilson, Colin 1931- .... CLC **3, 14**
See also CA 1-4R; CAAS 5; CANR 1, 22,
33; DLB 14; MTCW

Wilson, Dirk
See Pohl, Frederik

Wilson, Edmund
1895-1972 .... CLC **1, 2, 3, 8, 24**
See also CA 1-4R; 37-40R; CANR 1, 46;
DLB 63; MTCW

Wilson, Ethel Davis (Bryant)
1888(?)-1980 .... CLC **13; DAC;**
DAM POET
See also CA 102; DLB 68; MTCW

Wilson, John 1785-1854 .... NCLC **5**

Wilson, John (Anthony) Burgess 1917-1993
See Burgess, Anthony
See also CA 1-4R; 143; CANR 2, 46; DAC;
DAM NOV; MTCW

Wilson, Lanford
1937- ..... CLC **7, 14, 36; DAM DRAM**
See also CA 17-20R; CABS 3; CANR 45;
DLB 7

Wilson, Robert M. 1944- .... CLC **7, 9**
See also CA 49-52; CANR 2, 41; MTCW

Wilson, Robert McLiam 1964- ..... CLC **59**
See also CA 132

Wilson, Sloan 1920- .... CLC **32**
See also CA 1-4R; CANR 1, 44

Wilson, Snoo 1948- .... CLC **33**
See also CA 69-72

Wilson, William S(mith) 1932- ..... CLC **49**
See also CA 81-84

Winchilsea, Anne (Kingsmill) Finch Counte
1661-1720 .... LC **3**

Windham, Basil
See Wodehouse, P(elham) G(renville)

Wingrove, David (John) 1954- ...... CLC **68**
See also CA 133

Winters, Janet Lewis .... CLC **41**
See also Lewis, Janet
See also DLBY 87

Winters, (Arthur) Yvor
1900-1968 .... CLC **4, 8, 32**
See also CA 11-12; 25-28R; CAP 1;
DLB 48; MTCW

Winterson, Jeanette
1959- .... CLC **64; DAM POP**
See also CA 136

Winthrop, John 1588-1649 .... LC **31**
See also DLB 24, 30

Wiseman, Frederick 1930- .... CLC **20**

Wister, Owen 1860-1938 .... TCLC **21**
See also CA 108; DLB 9, 78; SATA 62

Witkacy
See Witkiewicz, Stanislaw Ignacy

Witkiewicz, Stanislaw Ignacy
1885-1939 .... TCLC **8**
See also CA 105

Wittgenstein, Ludwig (Josef Johann)
1889-1951 .... TCLC **59**
See also CA 113

Wittig, Monique 1935(?)- .... CLC **22**
See also CA 116; 135; DLB 83

Wittlin, Jozef 1896-1976 .... CLC **25**
See also CA 49-52; 65-68; CANR 3

Wodehouse, P(elham) G(renville)
1881-1975 ... CLC **1, 2, 5, 10, 22; DAB;**
DAC; DAM NOV; SSC 2
See also AITN 2; CA 45-48; 57-60;
CANR 3, 33; CDBLB 1914-1945;
DLB 34, 162; MTCW; SATA 22

Woiwode, L.
See Woiwode, Larry (Alfred)

Woiwode, Larry (Alfred) 1941- ... CLC **6, 10**
See also CA 73-76; CANR 16; DLB 6;
INT CANR-16

Wojciechowska, Maia (Teresa)
1927- .... CLC **26**
See also AAYA 8; CA 9-12R; CANR 4, 41;
CLR 1; JRDA; MAICYA; SAAS 1;
SATA 1, 28, 83

Wolf, Christa 1929- .... CLC **14, 29, 58**
See also CA 85-88; CANR 45; DLB 75;
MTCW

Wolfe, Gene (Rodman)
1931- .... CLC **25; DAM POP**
See also CA 57-60; CAAS 9; CANR 6, 32;
DLB 8

Wolfe, George C. 1954- .... CLC **49**
See also CA 149

Wolfe, Thomas (Clayton)
1900-1938 ..... TCLC **4, 13, 29, 61; DA;**
DAB; DAC; DAM MST, NOV; WLC
See also CA 104; 132; CDALB 1929-1941;
DLB 9, 102; DLBD 2; DLBY 85; MTCW

Wolfe, Thomas Kennerly, Jr. 1931-
See Wolfe, Tom
See also CA 13-16R; CANR 9, 33;
DAM POP; INT CANR-9; MTCW

Wolfe, Tom .... CLC **1, 2, 9, 15, 35, 51**
See also Wolfe, Thomas Kennerly, Jr.
See also AAYA 8; AITN 2; BEST 89:1;
DLB 152

Wolff, Geoffrey (Ansell) 1937- ..... CLC **41**
See also CA 29-32R; CANR 29, 43

Wolff, Sonia
See Levitin, Sonia (Wolff)

Wolff, Tobias (Jonathan Ansell)
1945- .... CLC **39, 64**
See also AAYA 16; BEST 90:2; CA 114;
117; CAAS 22; CANR 54; DLB 130;
INT 117

Wolfram von Eschenbach
c. 1170-c. 1220 .... CMLC **5**
See also DLB 138

Wolitzer, Hilma 1930- .... CLC **17**
See also CA 65-68; CANR 18, 40;
INT CANR-18; SATA 31

Wollstonecraft, Mary 1759-1797 ...... LC **5**
See also CDBLB 1789-1832; DLB 39, 104,
158

Wonder, Stevie .... CLC **12**
See also Morris, Steveland Judkins

Wong, Jade Snow 1922- .... CLC **17**
See also CA 109

Woodcott, Keith
See Brunner, John (Kilian Houston)

Woodruff, Robert W.
See Mencken, H(enry) L(ouis)

Woolf, (Adeline) Virginia
1882-1941 .... TCLC **1, 5, 20, 43, 56;**
DA; DAB; DAC; DAM MST, NOV;
SSC 7; WLC
See also CA 104; 130; CDBLB 1914-1945;
DLB 36, 100, 162; DLBD 10; MTCW

Woollcott, Alexander (Humphreys)
1887-1943 .... TCLC **5**
See also CA 105; DLB 29

Woolrich, Cornell 1903-1968 .... CLC **77**
See also Hopley-Woolrich, Cornell George

Wordsworth, Dorothy
1771-1855 .... NCLC **25**
See also DLB 107

Wordsworth, William
1770-1850 .... NCLC **12, 38; DA; DAB;**
DAC; DAM MST, POET; PC 4; WLC
See also CDBLB 1789-1832; DLB 93, 107

Wouk, Herman
1915- .. CLC **1, 9, 38; DAM NOV, POP**
See also CA 5-8R; CANR 6, 33; DLBY 82;
INT CANR-6; MTCW

Wright, Charles (Penzel, Jr.)
1935- .... CLC **6, 13, 28**
See also CA 29-32R; CAAS 7; CANR 23,
36; DLB 165; DLBY 82; MTCW

Wright, Charles Stevenson
1932- .... CLC **49; BLC 3;**
DAM MULT, POET
See also BW 1; CA 9-12R; CANR 26;
DLB 33

Wright, Jack R.
See Harris, Mark

Wright, James (Arlington)
1927-1980 .... CLC **3, 5, 10, 28;**
DAM POET
See also AITN 2; CA 49-52; 97-100;
CANR 4, 34; DLB 5, 169; MTCW

Wright, Judith (Arundell)
1915- .... CLC **11, 53; PC 14**
See also CA 13-16R; CANR 31; MTCW;
SATA 14

Wright, L(aurali) R.   1939-......... **CLC 44**
See also CA 138

Wright, Richard (Nathaniel)
1908-1960 .... **CLC 1, 3, 4, 9, 14, 21, 48,
74; BLC; DA; DAB; DAC; DAM MST,
MULT, NOV; SSC 2; WLC**
See also AAYA 5; BW 1; CA 108;
CDALB 1929-1941; DLB 76, 102;
DLBD 2; MTCW

Wright, Richard B(ruce)   1937- ...... **CLC 6**
See also CA 85-88; DLB 53

Wright, Rick   1945-.............. **CLC 35**

Wright, Rowland
See Wells, Carolyn

Wright, Stephen Caldwell   1946- .... **CLC 33**
See also BW 2

Wright, Willard Huntington   1888-1939
See Van Dine, S. S.
See also CA 115

Wright, William   1930-............ **CLC 44**
See also CA 53-56; CANR 7, 23

Wroth, LadyMary   1587-1653(?) ..... **LC 30**
See also DLB 121

Wu Ch'eng-en   1500(?)-1582(?)....... **LC 7**

Wu Ching-tzu   1701-1754 .... **LC 2**

Wurlitzer, Rudolph   1938(?)- ... **CLC 2, 4, 15**
See also CA 85-88; DLB 173

Wycherley, William
1641-1715 ..... **LC 8, 21; DAM DRAM**
See also CDBLB 1660-1789; DLB 80

Wylie, Elinor (Morton Hoyt)
1885-1928 .... **TCLC 8**
See also CA 105; DLB 9, 45

Wylie, Philip (Gordon)   1902-1971... **CLC 43**
See also CA 21-22; 33-36R; CAP 2; DLB 9

Wyndham, John................... **CLC 19**
See also Harris, John (Wyndham Parkes
Lucas) Beynon

Wyss, Johann David Von
1743-1818 .... **NCLC 10**
See also JRDA; MAICYA; SATA 29;
SATA-Brief 27

Xenophon
c. 430B.C.-c. 354B.C........ **CMLC 17**
See also DLB 176

Yakumo Koizumi
See Hearn, (Patricio) Lafcadio (Tessima
Carlos)

Yanez, Jose Donoso
See Donoso (Yanez), Jose

Yanovsky, Basile S.
See Yanovsky, V(assily) S(emenovich)

Yanovsky, V(assily) S(emenovich)
1906-1989 .... **CLC 2, 18**
See also CA 97-100; 129

Yates, Richard   1926-1992 ..... **CLC 7, 8, 23**
See also CA 5-8R; 139; CANR 10, 43;
DLB 2; DLBY 81, 92; INT CANR-10

Yeats, W. B.
See Yeats, William Butler

Yeats, William Butler
1865-1939 ..... **TCLC 1, 11, 18, 31; DA;
DAB; DAC; DAM DRAM, MST,
POET; WLC**
See also CA 104; 127; CANR 45;
CDBLB 1890-1914; DLB 10, 19, 98, 156;
MTCW

Yehoshua, A(braham) B.
1936- .... **CLC 13, 31**
See also CA 33-36R; CANR 43

Yep, Laurence Michael   1948-...... **CLC 35**
See also AAYA 5; CA 49-52; CANR 1, 46;
CLR 3, 17; DLB 52; JRDA; MAICYA;
SATA 7, 69

Yerby, Frank G(arvin)
1916-1991 .... **CLC 1, 7, 22; BLC;
DAM MULT**
See also BW 1; CA 9-12R; 136; CANR 16,
52; DLB 76; INT CANR-16; MTCW

Yesenin, Sergei Alexandrovich
See Esenin, Sergei (Alexandrovich)

Yevtushenko, Yevgeny (Alexandrovich)
1933- .... **CLC 1, 3, 13, 26, 51;
DAM POET**
See also CA 81-84; CANR 33, 54; MTCW

Yezierska, Anzia   1885(?)-1970 ..... **CLC 46**
See also CA 126; 89-92; DLB 28; MTCW

Yglesias, Helen   1915-........... **CLC 7, 22**
See also CA 37-40R; CAAS 20; CANR 15;
INT CANR-15; MTCW

Yokomitsu Riichi   1898-1947 ...... **TCLC 47**

Yonge, Charlotte (Mary)
1823-1901 .... **TCLC 48**
See also CA 109; DLB 18, 163; SATA 17

York, Jeremy
See Creasey, John

York, Simon
See Heinlein, Robert A(nson)

Yorke, Henry Vincent   1905-1974 ... **CLC 13**
See also Green, Henry
See also CA 85-88; 49-52

Yosano Akiko   1878-1942.. **TCLC 59; PC 11**

Yoshimoto, Banana............... **CLC 84**
See also Yoshimoto, Mahoko

Yoshimoto, Mahoko   1964-
See Yoshimoto, Banana
See also CA 144

Young, Al(bert James)
1939- ..... **CLC 19; BLC; DAM MULT**
See also BW 2; CA 29-32R; CANR 26;
DLB 33

Young, Andrew (John)   1885-1971.... **CLC 5**
See also CA 5-8R; CANR 7, 29

Young, Collier
See Bloch, Robert (Albert)

Young, Edward   1683-1765 .... **LC 3**
See also DLB 95

Young, Marguerite (Vivian)
1909-1995 .... **CLC 82**
See also CA 13-16; 150; CAP 1

Young, Neil   1945-............... **CLC 17**
See also CA 110

Young Bear, Ray A.
1950- .... **CLC 94; DAM MULT**
See also CA 146; DLB 175; NNAL

Yourcenar, Marguerite
1903-1987 .... **CLC 19, 38, 50, 87;
DAM NOV**
See also CA 69-72; CANR 23; DLB 72;
DLBY 88; MTCW

Yurick, Sol   1925-................. **CLC 6**
See also CA 13-16R; CANR 25

Zabolotskii, Nikolai Alekseevich
1903-1958 .... **TCLC 52**
See also CA 116

Zamiatin, Yevgenii
See Zamyatin, Evgeny Ivanovich

Zamora, Bernice (B. Ortiz)
1938- ..... **CLC 89; DAM MULT; HLC**
See also CA 151; DLB 82; HW

Zamyatin, Evgeny Ivanovich
1884-1937 .... **TCLC 8, 37**
See also CA 105

Zangwill, Israel   1864-1926........ **TCLC 16**
See also CA 109; DLB 10, 135

Zappa, Francis Vincent, Jr.   1940-1993
See Zappa, Frank
See also CA 108; 143; CANR 57

Zappa, Frank.................... **CLC 17**
See also Zappa, Francis Vincent, Jr.

Zaturenska, Marya   1902-1982.... **CLC 6, 11**
See also CA 13-16R; 105; CANR 22

Zeami   1363-1443.................. **DC 7**

Zelazny, Roger (Joseph)
1937-1995 .... **CLC 21**
See also AAYA 7; CA 21-24R; 148;
CANR 26; DLB 8; MTCW; SATA 57;
SATA-Brief 39

Zhdanov, Andrei A(lexandrovich)
1896-1948 .... **TCLC 18**
See also CA 117

Zhukovsky, Vasily   1783-1852 .... **NCLC 35**

Ziegenhagen, Eric .... **CLC 55**

Zimmer, Jill Schary
See Robinson, Jill

Zimmerman, Robert
See Dylan, Bob

Zindel, Paul
1936- ..... **CLC 6, 26; DA; DAB; DAC;
DAM DRAM, MST, NOV; DC 5**
See also AAYA 2; CA 73-76; CANR 31;
CLR 3; DLB 7, 52; JRDA; MAICYA;
MTCW; SATA 16, 58

Zinov'Ev, A. A.
See Zinoviev, Alexander (Aleksandrovich)

Zinoviev, Alexander (Aleksandrovich)
1922- .... **CLC 19**
See also CA 116; 133; CAAS 10

Zoilus
See Lovecraft, H(oward) P(hillips)

Zola, Emile (Edouard Charles Antoine)
1840-1902 ...... **TCLC 1, 6, 21, 41; DA;
DAB; DAC; DAM MST, NOV; WLC**
See also CA 104; 138; DLB 123

Zoline, Pamela   1941-............. **CLC 62**

Zorrilla y Moral, Jose   1817-1893.. **NCLC 6**

Zoshchenko, Mikhail (Mikhailovich)
1895-1958 .... **TCLC 15; SSC 15**
See also CA 115

Literary Criticism Series
Cumulative Topic Index

This index lists all topic entries in Gale's *Classical and Medieval Literature Criticism, Contemporary Literary Criticism, Literature Criticism from 1400 to 1800, Nineteenth-Century Literature Criticism,* and *Twentieth-Century Literary Criticism.*

Topic Index

Topic Index

Topic Index

NCLC Cumulative Nationality Index